DICTIONARY OF BANKING

DICTIONARY OF BANKING

A CONCISE ENCYCLOPAEDIA OF BANKING LAW AND PRACTICE

by

WILLIAM THOMSON

RANK INSPECTOR

GYAN

Published by

Gyan Publishing House
5, Ansari Road
Daryaganj, New Delhi-110002
Phone: 011-47034999, 9811692060
E-mail: books@gyanbooks.com

Distribution Network
gyanbooks.com
India, USA, Canada, UK, Australia, France

ISBN : 978-81-212-2317-1 (PB)
First Published, 1911

2nd Impression 2021

Printed at: Gyan Press, Delhi.

Dictionary of Banking
Author: William Thomson

DICTIONARY OF BANKING

A CONCISE ENCYCLOPÆDIA OF BANKING LAW AND PRACTICE

BY

WILLIAM THOMSON

BANK INSPECTOR

LONDON

SIR ISAAC PITMAN & SONS, LTD., 1 AMEN CORNER, E.C.

BATH AND NEW YORK

PREFACE

THE Dictionary of Banking has been compiled in order to provide, in one volume, the means of obtaining information, with the minimum of trouble, upon any subject connected with the business of banking.

Hitherto it has been a matter of continual difficulty with many bank officials to know exactly where to turn for information upon certain subjects; but it is hoped and believed that the present volume will meet this difficulty, and that it will enable anyone to find in its pages a ready and reliable reference whenever the occasion arises.

The following pages include, as far as possible, a reference to all the various terms and matters which come within the scope of a banker's ordinary duties, as well as to other matters which arise out of, or are associated with, the business of banking, such as bankruptcy, company regulations, partnerships, stamp duties, stock exchange, winding up, etc.

The book is furnished with many cross-references, and at the end of each leading subject, *e.g.*, ACCOUNTS, BANKRUPTCY, BILL OF EXCHANGE, CHEQUE, COMPANIES, INSURANCE, MORTGAGE, STAMP DUTIES, STOCK EXCHANGE, TITLE DEEDS, will be found a list of the principal articles connected with that subject, which should facilitate the discovery of any particular point.

The whole of the Bills of Exchange Act, 1882, is given, the sections being distributed under the appropriate headings. Under the title BILLS OF EXCHANGE ACT, 1882, references are supplied to the various articles in which the different sections have been placed.

Many sections from other Acts, which are useful and interesting to bankers, are also included under the proper headings. For example, if information is required respecting the registration of a charge given by a company, the actual words of the Companies (Consolidation) Act, 1908, on that subject are quoted under REGISTRATION OF MORTGAGES AND CHARGES; and respecting the registration of a mortgage of a ship, the provisions of the Merchant Shipping Act, 1894, are set forth under SHIP-MORTGAGE, etc., and so in many other cases, an endeavour having been made, wherever practicable and necessary, to quote the sections of the Acts relating to matters of importance.

There is probably no subject of greater interest to branch managers and senior clerks than that of securities for advances, and consequently all matters connected with the examination of title deeds and the investigation of titles have been treated in the Dictionary in accordance with their importance.

In addition to the article on TITLE DEEDS, dealing with the matter in a general way, there is an article on TITLE DEEDS—NOTES RE TITLE, wherein is set out a number of the principal points which it is thought will prove useful in indicating what a banker should attend to when examining a parcel of deeds of freehold, leasehold, or copyhold property. If further information should be required on any of the points raised, the subject can be referred to in its alphabetical order in the book. A few questions relating to the value of a property which is offered as security are added to that article, and additional hints as to valuations, particularly for the benefit of younger managers, may be found under ADVANCES, FARM STOCK, LICENSED PROPERTY, SHIP—VALUATION OF, VALUATION.

With regard to securities other than title deeds, articles such as the following may be referred to :—AMERICAN RAILROAD CERTIFICATES, BEARER BONDS BILL OF LADING, BILL OF SALE, BOND OF CREDIT, CERTIFICATE, DEBENTURE, DEBTS—ASSIGNMENT OF, DOCK WARRANT, GUARANTEE, INSCRIBED STOCK, LIFE POLICY, NEGOTIABLE INSTRUMENTS, SHARES, etc.

A list of many of the abbreviations which are used in bank offices is supplied under ABBREVIATIONS. The article BANKRUPT PERSON contains separate headings relating to a bankrupt drawer, partner, payee, surety, etc. ; and under STATUTE OF LIMITATIONS the various sub-headings show how the statute affects the different matters with which a banker is concerned, such as a bank note, a bill of exchange, the drawer of a cheque, a guarantee, memorandum of deposit, promissory note, etc. A series of articles is supplied dealing with the position upon a death, *e.g.*, DEATH OF ACCEPTOR, ADMINISTRATOR, DRAWER, GUARANTOR, JOINT CUSTOMER, PARTNER, SHAREHOLDER, TRUSTEE, etc.

Specimens of indorsements which are usually accepted, as well as examples of those which are not, as a rule, passed by a banker, are given in tabular form under INDORSEMENT.

The Report of the Gold Reserves Committee in 1909 is given under GOLD RESERVES ; and under UNIFICATION OF LAWS OF BILLS OF EXCHANGE the various rules recommended by the conference of the National Law Association at Budapest in 1908 and at London in 1910 are set forth for the consideration of those who are interested.

The results of law cases have been given, wherever necessary, and in many instances the words of the judges are quoted. References are added to the various cases, and the abbreviations in the quotation of reports are explained on page vii.

To facilitate reference being made to law reports other than those that are quoted in the text, the date of the decision has been given in every instance.

The following books amongst others have been consulted in the preparation of the present volume :—

GRANT'S LAW OF BANKING	
THE LAW OF BANKING	HEBER HART, LL.D. (LOND.)
THE LAW OF BANKING	SIR JOHN R. PAGET, BART, K.C.
THE PRACTICE OF BANKING (4 Vols.)	JOHN HUTCHISON
BANKING AND NEGOTIABLE INSTRUMENTS	FRANK TILLYARD, M.A.
PITMAN'S BILLS, CHEQUES, AND NOTES	
ENGLISH PRACTICAL BANKING	T. B. MOXON
THE COUNTRY BANKER	GEORGE RAE
LOMBARD STREET	WALTER BAGEHOT
PITMAN'S BUSINESS MAN'S GUIDE	J. A. SLATER, B.A., LL.B. (LOND.)
PRESENT-DAY BANKING	F. E. STEELE
BANKING AND CURRENCY	ERNEST SYKES, B.A.
MY BANKER AND I	J. G. KIDDY
THE COUNTRY BANKER'S HANDBOOK	,,
HISTORY, PRINCIPLES, AND PRACTICE OF BANKING	J. W. GILBART
MONEY MARKET PRIMER	GEORGE CLARE
THE ELEMENTS OF BANKING	H. D. MACLEOD, M.A.
HANDBOOK ON JOINT STOCK COMPANIES	F. GORE-BROWNE, M.A., K.C., and W. JORDAN
BANKING LAW	W. WALLACE, M.A. and A. MCNEIL
QUESTIONS ON BANKING PRACTICE	
JOURNAL OF THE INSTITUTE OF BANKERS	
BANKERS' MAGAZINE	
BANKING ALMANAC	

I have to express my deep indebtedness to the many friends who have been kind enough to supply most useful information and to read and correct the sheets as they have passed through the press, and I desire especially to acknowledge the valuable assistance which I have received from Mr. J. A. Slater of the Middle Temple, Barrister-at-Law, in checking the points referring to banking law.

W. THOMSON.

NEWCASTLE-ON-TYNE.
January, 1911.

ABBREVIATIONS USED IN THIS BOOK WHEN REFERRING TO LAW CASES

A.C. or App. Cas. } Appeal Cases, Law Reports.
B. & Ad., Barnewall & Adolphus.
B. & C., Barnewall & Cresswell.
Burr., Burrows.
Be., Beavan.
C.B., Common Bench.
C.B.N.S., ,, ,, New Series.
C.P.D., Common Pleas Division, Law Reports.
Ch., Chancery, Law Reports.
Ch.D., Chancery Division, Law Reports.
Cl. & Fin., Clark & Finelly.
Cox C.C., Cox's Criminal Cases.
E. & B., Ellis & Blackburne.
Eq., Equity Cases, Law Reports.
H.L.C., Clark's House of Lords' Reports.
I.C.L R. Ir.R.C.L. } Irish Common Law Reports.
I.R., Irish Reports.
J. & H., Johnson & Hemming.
K.B., King's Bench, Law Reports.
L.J., C.P., Law Journal, Common Pleas.
L.J., Ch., ,, ,, Chancery.
L.J., Q.B., ,, ,, Queen's Bench.
L.R., Ex., Law Reports, Exchequer.
L.R., Ch., ,, ,, Chancery.
L.R., Q.B., ,, ,, Queen's Bench.
L.T., Law Times Reports.
M. & S., Maule & Selwyn.
Macq. H.L.R., Macqueen's Appeal Cases (Scotch).
Mer., Merivale.
Q.B., Queen's Bench Cases.
Q.B.D., ,, ,, Division.
Sol.J., *Solicitors' Journal.*
T.L.R., *Times* Law Reports.
T.R., Terms Reports.
W.R., Weekly Reporter.

Dictionary of Banking

@, At.
A/C., Account.
A/C., Account Current.
A/D., After Date.
A/o., Account of.
A/S., After Sight.
Acce., Acceptance.
Agt., Agreement.
Assigt., Assignment.

B.B., Branch Bill.
B/C., Bills for Collection.
B.D., Bill Discounted.
B/E., Bill of Exchange.
B.L., Bill Lodged.
B/L., Bill of Lading.
Bs/L., Bills of Lading.
B.N., Bank Note.
B.O., Branch Office.
B/P., Bills Payable.
B.P.B., Bank Post Bill.
B/R., Bills Receivable.
B/S., Bill of Sale.

C., Copper.
C., Country.
C/-, Coupon.
C.A., Credit Account.
$C^{a}/_{c}$, C/A., Current Account.
C.B., Country Bill.
C/B., Cash Book.
C.C., Cash Credit.
C.C., Country Cheque.
C.C., Country Clearing.
C.D., Cum Dividend.
C.H., Clearing House.
C.N., Country Note.
C.O., Cash Order.
C. of B., Confirmation of Balance.
C.O.D., Cash on Delivery.
C.P., Charter Party.
Cf. (Lat. *confer*), Compare.
Chq., Cheque.
Ck., Cheque.
Cp., Compare.
Com., Commission.
Contra, Against.
Cr., Creditor, Credit.
Cum D., With Dividend.
Cur., Curt., Current.

D., a penny. D is the first letter in *denarius* (Latin).
D., Deeds.
D.A., Deposit Account.
D/A., Days after Acceptance.
D/B., Day Book.
D/D., Days after Date.
D.P.B., Deposit Pass Book.
D/R., Deposit Receipt.
Deb., Debenture.
Dft., Draft.
Dis., Disct., Discount.
Div., Dividend.
Dols., Dollars.
Dr., Debtor.
D/S., Days after Sight.

E.E., Errors Excepted.
e.g. (Lat., *exempli gratia*), For example.
E/I., Endorsement Irregular.
E. & O.E., Errors and Omissions Excepted.
et seq. (Lat., *et sequentes*), And the following.
Ex. Cp. or x/cp., Ex Coupon.
Ex D. or x/d., Ex Dividend.
Ex. Int., Ex Interest.
Exch., Exchange.
Exct., Exec., Executor.
Execx., Executrix.
Exor., Executor.

F., Franc.
F.A.S., Free Alongside Ship.
F.O.B., Free on Board.
F/P., Fire Policy.
F.p., Fully Paid.
Fi. Fa., Fieri Facias. (*q.v.*)
Fo., Fol., Folio.

G., Gold.
G., Guarantee.

H.M.C., His Majesty's Customs.
H.M.S., His Majesty's Service.
H.O., Head Office.

Ib., Ibid. (Lat., *ibidem*), In the same place.
Id. (Lat., *idem*), The same.
I/I., Indorsement Irregular.
Ins., Insurance.
Inst., Instant, Of the Present Month.
Int., Interest.

1—(1535)

Inv., Invoice.
Irr., Irredeemable.

J/A., Joint Account.
Jour., Journal.
Jr., Junr., Junior.

L/A., Letter of Authority.
L.C., London Cheque.
L/C., Letter of Credit.
£E., Pounds, Egyptian.
L.O., London Office.
L/P., Life Policy.
L.S. (Lat., *Locus sigilli*), Place of the Seal.
L.s.d. (Lat., *Librae, solidi, denarii*), Pounds, Shillings, Pence.
£T., Pounds, Turkish.
Led., Ledger.
Ltd., Limited.

M. (Lat., *Mille*), Thousand.
M., Metropolitan.
M/C., Marginal Credit.
M/D., Months after Date.
M/D., Memorandum of Deposit.
M.O., Money Order.
M/P., Memorandum of Partnership.
MS., Manuscript.
M/S., Months after Sight.
MSS., Manuscripts.

N.A., New Account.
N/A., No Advice, No Account.
N/A., Non-acceptance.
N.B. (Lat., *Nota bene*), Take notice.
N/E., No Effects.
N/F., No Funds.
N/N., Not to be Noted.
N/O., No Orders.
No., Number.
N.P., Notary Public.
N.P.F., Not Provided For.
N.S., New Style.
N/S., Not Sufficient.
N.S.F., Not Sufficient Funds.

°, Degree.
O.A., Old Account.
O/A., On Account.
O/D., On Demand.
O/D., Overdraft.
O.K., All correct.
O.N., Own Notes.
% (Lat., *Per centum*), By the Hundred.
O.O., Own Occupation.
o/oo (Lat., *Per mille*), By the Thousand.
O.R., Official Receiver.
O.S., Old Style.
O/s., o/sg., Outstanding.

P/A., Power of Attorney.
P.A. (Lat., *Per annum*), Yearly.
P.B., Pass Book.
P/C., Price Current.
P.C. (Lat., *Per centum*), By the Hundred.
P. & L., Profit and Loss.
P/N., Pro. Note., Promissory Note.
P.O., Postal Order.
P.O.O., Post Office Order.
P.P., Per Procuration.
P.S. (Lat., *Post scriptum*), Postscript.
Payt., Payment.
Per an. (Lat., *Per annum*), Yearly.
Per ct. (Lat., *Per centum*), By the Hundred.
Per pro., Per procuration.
Pm., Premium.
Pro, For.
Pro tem. (Lat., *Pro tempore*), For the time being.
Prox. (Lat., *Proximo*), Next.

Qr., Quarter.
Q.v. (Lat., *Quod vide*), Which see.
Qy., Query.

R., Rupee.
R/A., Refer to Acceptor.
R.A.P., Rupees, Annas, Pies.
R/D., Refer to Drawer.
R/E., Repayable to either.
Recpt., Receipt.
Reg., Regd., Registered.
Rev. a/c., Revenue Account.
Rs., Rupees.
Rx., Ten Rupees.

S., Silver.
$, Dollars.
S.B., Special Bargain.
S.B., Sub Branch.
S.B., Short Bill.
S.C., Safe Custody.
S.O., Sub Office.
S.P.A., Sundry Persons' Account.
S.P., Suprà Protest.
S.S., Special Settlement.
S.S., Steamship.
S/V., Surrender Value.
St., Stet (Lat., *Stet*), Let it stand.
Ster., Stg., Sterling.
Stk., Stock.
Sy. Crs., Sundry Creditors.
Sy. Drs., Sundry Debtors.

T., Town.
T/o., Turnover.

T.Q., Tel Quel (*q.v.*).
T.T., Telegraphic Transfer.
Tfr., Transfer.

U.V., Uncollected Vouchers.
Ult. (Lat., *Ultimo*), Of the Last Month.

V. (Lat., *versus*), Against.
Via, By the way of.
Viz. (Lat., *Videlicet*), Namely.

W.W., Warehouse Warrant.
Wt., Warrant.

X.C., Ex Coupon.
X.D., Ex Dividend.
X.In., Ex Interest.

ABOVE PAR. (*Par*, Latin, equal.) When the market price of bonds, stocks, or shares is above the nominal or face value, they are said to be above par.

Equivalent phrases to "above par" and "below par" are respectively "at a premium" and "at a discount." (See PAR.)

ABRASION OF COINS. The loss of weight which occurs in coins which are in circulation through their constant use. After a certain time many coins become so much worn as to be below the minimum weight allowed by law; but so long as the impressions are discernible upon coins, the general public do not concern themselves very much with their weight. Anyone who has a coin tendered which is below the standard weight may, by law, cut or deface it. (See COINAGE, LIGHT GOLD.)

ABSOLUTE TITLE. Land may be registered under the Land Transfer Acts with Absolute Title; that is, the Registry examines the proprietor's title and confers on him an absolute right to the property, guaranteed by the Government against all the world. (See LAND REGISTRY.)

ABSTRACT OF TITLE. The Abstract of Title is not a part of the title, but is a document prepared by the vendor's solicitor to enable the purchaser to see how his title is derived. The purchaser of freehold property has the right to require an abstract tracing the title for the last forty years, or longer if necessary, to obtain a satisfactory commencement. The commencing deed is called the "root of title" (*q.v.*). It may, however, be agreed between the vendor and the purchaser to accept a shorter title than forty years, and twenty years are often taken as sufficient.

Commencing with the "root," the abstract should give in strict order of date a brief summary of the material parts of all deeds and documents which are necessary to show how the purchaser's title is obtained. It should show by whom the deeds are signed and witnessed, the amounts for which they are stamped, particulars of registration (if the property is situated in Yorkshire or Middlesex), and information regarding the probates of wills, etc.

An abstract of title usually accompanies most parcels of deeds. When a banker receives a bundle of deeds for security, he can look at the abstract, when there is a recent one, and see at once the various links in the chain of title. The deeds which are noted in the abstract may all be held by the banker, but very often the abstract will be found to give particulars of many deeds and documents which are not in the banker's hands. In fact, the banker may, perhaps, hold only one deed, say the conveyance to his customer, John Brown, from John Jones. In that case there should be an acknowledgment of the right to the production of the deeds necessary to show the title of John Jones.

If the property is leasehold, the abstract should commence with the lease or underlease. (See LEASEHOLD.)

In the case of copyhold land which has been converted into freehold by enfranchisement, a purchaser "shall not have the right to call for the title to make the enfranchisement" (Conveyancing Act, 1881, Section 3, s.s. 2.) But though the lord's title cannot be inquired into, the purchaser should still require the forty years' copyhold title. (See TITLE DEEDS.)

ACCEPTANCE. This word is commonly used as meaning a bill of exchange, that is, the actual bill itself, but an acceptance is really the writing across the face of a bill by which the drawee agrees to the order of the drawer. The drawee is the person to whom a bill is addressed by the drawer, and who is required to pay on demand, or at a fixed or determinable future time, a sum certain in money to or to the order of a specified person, or to bearer. If the drawee agrees to the drawer's order he signifies his assent by accepting the bill. When the drawee has accepted a bill he is called the acceptor.

An acceptance is defined by Section 17 of the Bills of Exchange Act, 1882, as follows

"(1) The acceptance of a bill is the signification by the drawee of his assent to the order of the drawer.

"(2) An acceptance is invalid unless it complies with the following conditions, namely:

"(a) It must be written on the bill and be signed by the drawee. The mere signature of the drawee without additional words is sufficient.

"(b) It must not express that the drawee will perform his promise by any other means than the payment of money."

As a rule a drawee accepts a bill after it has been fully completed and signed by the drawer; but by Section 18, "A bill may be accepted:—

"(1) Before it has been signed by the drawer, or while otherwise incomplete:

"(2) When it is overdue, or after it has been dishonoured by a previous refusal to accept, or by non-payment:

"(3) When a bill payable after sight is dishonoured by non-acceptance, and the drawee subsequently accepts it, the holder, in the absence of any different agreement, is entitled to have the bill accepted as of the date of first presentment to the drawee for acceptance."

There are two kinds of acceptances:

(1) General acceptance. (See ACCEPTANCE, GENERAL.)

(2) Qualified acceptance. (See ACCEPTANCE, QUALIFIED.)

"A general acceptance assents without qualification to the order of the drawer. A qualified acceptance in express terms varies the effect of the bill as drawn." (Section 19, s.s. 2.)

An acceptance is usually upon the face of the bill, but the drawee's signature placed upon the back of it is regarded as sufficient. In such a case it is usual to make a reference on the front of the bill to the fact that the acceptance is on the back. A drawee may accept a bill by merely writing his name across it, without any further words, but it is customary for the word "accepted" to be used. When the bill is domiciled, the name of the bank where it is payable follows the word "accepted," and then the acceptor signs his name. The commonest form of acceptance (a general acceptance) is:—

"Accepted, payable at the X & Y Banking Coy., Ltd., London. John Brown."

If the bill is payable at so many days after sight, the drawee must add the date of sighting to his acceptance. (See SIGHTING A BILL.)

If there are several drawees named on a bill, each one of them must sign the acceptance, but an order addressed to two drawees in the alternative, or to two or more drawees in succession, is not a bill of exchange. (See DRAWEE.)

Section 17 states that the acceptance must be signed by the drawee, but anyone who holds a proper authority from the drawee to accept bills may accept on his behalf.

Where the drawee is a firm, the partner who accepts must do so in the name of the firm. If the drawee is Mrs. John Brown, she should accept as "Mary Brown, wife (or widow) of John Brown." Where the drawee is a limited company, the acceptance should, to be correct, contain the name of the company as well as the signatures of the authorised officials.

With regard to the rules as to presentment of a bill for acceptance, see PRESENTMENT FOR ACCEPTANCE.

When a bill is duly presented for acceptance and is not accepted within the customary time, the person presenting it must treat it as dishonoured by non-acceptance. (See DISHONOUR OF BILL OF EXCHANGE.)

Until a drawee has accepted the bill he is not liable thereon, but in Scotland where the drawee has funds available for its payment, the bill operates as an assignment of the amount of the bill in favour of the holder from the time when the bill is presented to the drawee. (See DRAWEE.)

An acceptor is at liberty to cancel his acceptance provided that the bill is still in his own hands, and that he has not led any one to believe that he would accept it.

The liability of an acceptor is defined by Section 54:

"The acceptor of a bill, by accepting it—

"(1) Engages that he will pay it according to the tenor of his acceptance:

"(2) Is precluded from denying to a holder in due course:

"(a) The existence of the drawer, the genuineness of his signature, and his capacity and authority to draw the bill;

"(b) In the case of a bill payable to drawer's order, the then capacity of the drawer to indorse, but not the genuineness or validity of his indorsement;

"(c) In the case of a bill payable to the order of a third person, the existence of the payee and his then capacity to indorse, but not the genuineness or validity of his indorsement."

As an acceptor is responsible for the genuineness of the drawer's signature, a drawee consequently incurs an unnecessary liability if he accepts a bill before it has been signed by the drawer. If a bill is drawn per procuration or on behalf of the drawer, the drawee ought to satisfy himself before accepting the bill, that the drawer has authorised the bill to be drawn in that way. He is not liable for signatures, such as the payee's or an indorser's, which do not, in the ordinary course of things, appear upon a bill until after it has been accepted.

No person is liable as acceptor of a bill who has not signed it as such: Provided that (1) where a person signs a bill in a trade or assumed name, he is liable thereon as if he had signed it in his own name; (2) the signature of the name of a firm is equivalent to the signature by the person so signing of the names of all persons liable as partners in that firm (Section 23). In the case of a non-trading partnership, an acceptance by a partner binds himself alone and not the firm.

If there are several acceptors on a bill they are jointly liable, not jointly and severally.

Where a bill is accepted payable at the acceptor's bankers, that is a sufficient authority for the banker to debit it to his customer's account; but, in practice, country bankers often require particulars of acceptances falling due to be given, and a written order from the customer to pay them, though London bankers pay without any advice. Such an order does not require to be stamped.

The death or bankruptcy of an acceptor revokes a banker's authority to pay an acceptance.

If a banker is a holder for value, he may debit an acceptance to the acceptor's account, even if the acceptor has sent instructions not to pay the bill.

Where a bill is accepted, say, by John Brown payable at the British Bank, Leeds, although no drawee's name is mentioned in the bill, it may be debited to his account. A bill may also be charged to the acceptor's account which is accepted simply John Brown, if there is an indication elsewhere on the bill that it is payable at the British Bank, Leeds.

Many country customers accept their bills payable either at the London office of their banker or at their banker's London agents. (See RETIRING A BILL.) Two or three days before a bill falls due, the acceptor requests his banker in writing (by filling up the banker's printed form, and giving particulars of the bill and any documents that are attached) to instruct the London office to pay his acceptance. The order should be signed in the same way as cheques are drawn, or as may be arranged. A banker is not obliged to pay a bill accepted payable with him or to retire an acceptance payable in London, except by instructions or by custom. In *Bank of England* v. *Vagliano Brothers* (1891, A.C. 107), it was held that "if a banker undertakes the duty of paying his customer's acceptances, the arrangement is the result of some special agreement, expressed or implied." When a banker receives an order to retire a bill, he has to consider whether or not the account of his customer will admit of the payment of the bill. If unable to accede to his customer's request he informs his customer accordingly, but if all is well he charges the amount of the bill to his customer's account and credits it to his London agents (or London office), requesting them to pay the bill when presented.

Where instructions are received to cancel an order which has been given to retire an acceptance in London, it is necessary to make quite certain that the advice has not already been acted upon by the London agents and that they have cancelled the advice, before re-crediting the amount to the customer's account.

An order signed by a customer to retire an acceptance (whether his own or another person's) does not require a penny stamp to be affixed.

A bill often contains an indication as to where it shall be payable, e.g., "payable in London," but if there is no such indication, the drawee accepts it payable in the place where he lives, unless he follows the recognised custom and makes it payable in London.

If a bill is accepted payable at, say, the British Bank, Ltd., and no town is mentioned, it should be presented at the British

Bank in the town where the drawee is described as living.

In Scotland, acceptors usually sign their names under the drawer's signature, but when they accept the bill payable at their bankers, the acceptance is generally across the bill. (See BILL OF EXCHANGE.)

ACCEPTANCE FOR HONOUR. The drawer of a bill and any indorser may insert in the bill the name of a person to whom a holder may resort in case of need, that is in case the bill is dishonoured by non-acceptance or non-payment; such a person is called the referee in case of need. If the drawee refuses to accept the bill, the holder may, after the bill is protested for non-acceptance, present it to the referee in case of need. When the referee accepts it, he becomes an acceptor for honour.

After protest for non-acceptance, any person may, with the consent of the holder, accept a bill suprà protest for the honour of any party thereon. Section 65 of the Bills of Exchange Act, 1882, provides as follows:

"(1) Where a bill of exchange has been protested for dishonour by non-acceptance, or protested for better security, and is not overdue, any person, not being a party already liable thereon, may, with the consent of the holder, intervene and accept the bill suprà protest, for the honour of any party liable thereon, or for the honour of the person for whose account the bill is drawn.

"(2) A bill may be accepted for honour for part only of the sum for which it is drawn.

"(3) An acceptance for honour suprà protest in order to be valid must—

"(*a*) be written on the bill, and indicate that it is an acceptance for honour:

"(*b*) be signed by the acceptor for honour.

"(4) Where an acceptance for honour does not expressly state for whose honour it is made, it is deemed to be an acceptance for the honour of the drawer.

"(5) Where a bill payable after sight is accepted for honour, its maturity is calculated from the date of the noting for non-acceptance, and not from the date of the acceptance for honour."

An acceptance for honour is written across the bill as, "Accepted for the honour of John Brown, Thomas Jones," or, "Accepted suprà protest, Thomas Jones," or "Accepted for the honour of John Brown with £ for notarial charges, Thomas Jones," or, "Accepted S.P. (i.e. suprà protest), Thomas Jones."

The liability of an acceptor for honour is dealt with in Section 66 as follows:—

"(1) The acceptor for honour of a bill by accepting it engages that he will, on due presentment, pay the bill according to the tenor of his acceptance, if it is not paid by the drawee, provided it has been duly presented for payment, and protested for non-payment, and that he receives notice of these facts.

"(2) The acceptor for honour is liable to the holder and to all parties to the bill subsequent to the party for whose honour he has accepted." (See ACCEPTANCE, BILL OF EXCHANGE.)

ACCEPTANCE, GENERAL. When a drawee writes his name across a bill agreeing to the order of the drawer, it is called an acceptance of the bill. The Bills of Exchange Act, 1882, Section 19, defines two kinds of acceptances:—

"(1) An acceptance is either (*a*) general or (*b*) qualified. (See ACCEPTANCE, QUALIFIED.)

"(2) A general acceptance assents without qualification to the order of the drawer.

"(*c*) . . . An acceptance to pay at a particular place is a general acceptance, unless it expressly states that the bill is to be paid there only and not elsewhere."

The following are specimens of general acceptances:

John Brown.
Accepted, John Brown.
Accepted, John Brown, 2, King Street, Leeds.
Accepted, payable at X & Y Bank, Ltd., Leeds, John Brown.
Sighted, June 16, John Brown, Leeds.
Accepted, payable at A & B Bank, Ltd., London, per pro. John Brown, W. Robinson.

A holder of a general acceptance may present it to the acceptor himself, but, if there is a place of payment mentioned on the bill, unless it is presented at that place, he will lose his recourse against all the other parties to the bill. (See ACCEPTANCE, BILL OF EXCHANGE.)

ACCEPTANCE LEDGER. The ledger in which are entered, under the customer's name, particulars of bills accepted by the bank on his behalf.

ACCEPTANCE OF CHEQUES. (See CERTIFICATION OF CHEQUES.)

ACCEPTANCE, QUALIFIED. An acceptance is either general (see ACCEPTANCE, GENERAL) or qualified. Section 19 of the Bills of Exchange Act, 1882, defines a qualified acceptance as follows :—

"(2) . . . A qualified acceptance in express terms varies the effect of the bill as drawn.

"In particular an acceptance is qualified which is—

"(*a*) conditional, that is to say, which makes payment by the acceptor dependent on the fulfilment of a condition therein stated :

"(*b*) partial, that is to say, an acceptance to pay part only of the amount for which the bill is drawn:

"(*c*) local, that is to say, an acceptance to pay only at a particular specified place :

"An acceptance to pay at a particular place is a general acceptance, unless it expressly states that the bill is to be paid there only and not elsewhere :

"(*d*) Qualified as to time :

"(*e*) The acceptance of some one or more of the drawees, but not of all."

The following are specimens of qualified acceptances :—

Conditional. "Accepted, payable on delivery of bills of lading. J. Brown."

Partial. Bill drawn for £100. "Accepted for £50 only. J. Brown."

Local. "Accepted, payable at the X & Y Bank, Ltd., Leeds, and there only. J. Brown." In order to charge the acceptor and other parties, the bill must be presented for payment at the place named.

As to time. Bill drawn at three months' date. "Accepted, payable at six months' date. J. Brown."

Not accepted by all the drawees. Bill drawn on W. Brown, J. Jones, and W. Robinson. "Accepted, payable at X & Y Bank, Ltd. W. Robinson." In this case W. Robinson is liable to pay the bill.

The duties of the holder, the drawer, or the indorser of a qualified acceptance are set forth in Section 44 as follows :—

"(1) The holder of a bill may refuse to take a qualified acceptance, and if he does not obtain an unqualified acceptance may treat the bill as dishonoured by non-acceptance.

"(2) Where a qualified acceptance is taken, and the drawer or an indorser has not expressly or impliedly authorised the holder to take a qualified acceptance, or does not subsequently assent thereto, such drawer or indorser is discharged from his liability on the bill.

"The provisions of this subsection do not apply to a partial acceptance, whereof due notice has been given. Where a foreign bill has been accepted as to part, it must be protested as to the balance.

"(3) When the drawer or indorser of a bill receives notice of a qualified acceptance, and does not within a reasonable time express his dissent to the holder he shall be deemed to have assented thereto."

ACCEPTANCE REGISTER. The book in which are kept full particulars of all bills accepted by the bank for customers.

ACCEPTILATION. A formal discharge or release from a debt.

ACCEPTOR. When the drawee of a bill (that is, the person to whom the bill is addressed) agrees to the order of the drawer, he shows his assent by signing his name across the bill, that is he accepts it, and when that is done he is called the acceptor. The acceptor is the person who is expected to pay the bill at maturity.

In applying the provisions of Part IV of the Bills of Exchange Act, 1882, dealing with Promissory Notes, the maker of a note is to be deemed to correspond with the acceptor of a bill. If there are several acceptors of a bill they can only be liable jointly, but in the case of a promissory note the makers may be liable jointly, or jointly and severally, according to the wording of the note.

An acceptor is not discharged through any failure of a holder to present the bill to him at maturity for payment. He is liable thereon for six years. If an acceptor becomes bankrupt, his acceptances should be withdrawn by any customer for whom they have been discounted, though legally the withdrawal cannot be enforced before the bills mature. (See ACCEPTANCE, BILL OF EXCHANGE.)

ACCEPTORS' LEDGER. A separate account is opened in this ledger for each acceptor of bills discounted by the bank, so that the banker may see at a glance to what extent the acceptances of any person or firm have been discounted. In considering whether a bill should be discounted it is, of course, very important to know the amount for which the acceptor is already liable.

ACCOMMODATION BILL. A bill to which a person, called an accommodation party, puts his name to oblige or accommodate another person without receiving any consideration for so doing. The position of such a party is in fact, that of a surety or guarantor. Bills of this type are commonly called "kites," or "windmills," or "windbills." A may accept a bill for the accommodation of B the drawer, who is in need of money. A receives no consideration and does not expect to be called upon to pay the bill when due. B raises the necessary funds by discounting the bill, expecting that, at maturity, he will be in a position to meet the bill himself. If, however, he fails to do so, a holder for value, even though he knew it was an accommodation bill when he took it, can sue the acceptor and prior indorsers. But until value has been given, no one is liable on such a bill. When a banker discounts an accommodation bill he becomes a holder for value.

The Bills of Exchange Act, 1882, Section 28, defines an accommodation bill and the liability of an accommodation party as follows :—

"(1) An accommodation party to a bill is a person who has signed a bill as drawer, acceptor, or indorser, without receiving value therefor, and for the purpose of lending his name to some other person.

"(2) An accommodation party is liable on the bill to a holder for value; and it is immaterial whether, when such holder took the bill, he knew such party to be an accommodation party or not."

By Section 46, s.s. 2, presentment for payment is dispensed with :—

"(c) As regards the drawer, where the drawee or acceptor is not bound, as between himself and the drawer, to accept or pay the bill, and the drawer has no reason to believe that the bill would be paid if presented.

"(d) As regards an indorser, where the bill was accepted or made for the accommodation of that indorser and he has no reason to expect that the bill would be paid if presented."

Notice of dishonour is dispensed with, by Section 50, s.s. 2 :—

"(c) (4) Where the drawee or acceptor is as between himself and the drawer under no obligation to accept or pay the bill;

"(d) As regards the indorser,

"(3) Where the bill was accepted or made for his accommodation."

But to preserve the holder's rights against any prior parties the bill should be presented for payment at maturity.

By Section 59, s.s. 3 :—"Where an accommodation bill is paid in due course by the party accommodated, the bill is discharged."

Where a banker discounted a bill for the drawer, a customer, and was informed, after the bill was dishonoured, that it was an accommodation bill, and the banker agreed, at the drawer's request, not to apply to the acceptor but to depend upon him (the drawer), and his account afterwards showed a credit balance larger than the amount of the bill, it was held in *Marsh* v. *Houlditch* (an unreported case tried in 1818, and cited in Chitty, "Bills of Exchange," 11th ed., p. 290), that the banker was bound to have applied the balance in payment of the bill and that the acceptor was discharged. In his judgment, Mr. Justice Abbott said, "The banking account of the drawer with the plaintiffs having at one time, after the bill was due, been in his favour to a larger amount than the bill, the plaintiffs (the bankers) were bound to apply the balance in discharge of that bill, and could not keep it as a security for a fluctuating balance which might ultimately become due to them." (See BILL OF EXCHANGE.)

ACCOMMODATION PARTY. The person who signs a bill as drawer, acceptor, or indorser, without receiving any value therefor, for the purpose of accommodating some other person. An accommodation party is liable to a holder for value. (See ACCOMMODATION BILL.)

ACCORD AND SATISFACTION. Where a cheque for a certain amount is sent in payment of a debt greater than that sum, and the recipient of the cheque agrees to retain it, there is said to be an "accord and satisfaction." In his judgment (in *Day* v. *McLea*, 1889, 22 Q.B.D. 610), Lord Justice Bowen said: "Accord and satisfaction imply an agreement to take the money in satisfaction of the claim in respect of which it is sent. If accord is a question of agreement, there must be either two minds agreeing or one of the two persons acting in such a way as to induce the other to think that the money is taken in satisfaction of the claim, and to cause him to act upon that view."

ACCOUNT. (STOCK EXCHANGE.)

ACCOUNT DAY. Where securities are bought or sold on the Stock Exchange they may be "for cash" or "for the account," the term "for the account" meaning the period between the last settlement and the next, which period ends in the "account day," or "pay day," or "settling day." (See STOCK EXCHANGE.)

"ACCOUNT PAYEE." Cheques are frequently crossed :—

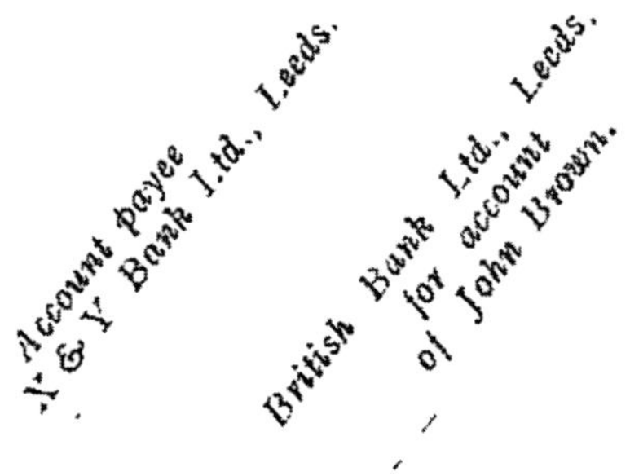

or with some variation of those forms.

The words are an indication to the collecting banker as to what is to be done with the proceeds of the cheque, but the banker on whom the cheque is drawn, so long as he pays it to the right banker, is not concerned with the words "account payee." In practice, a banker who receives such a cheque for collection, requires that it be placed to the credit of the account as indicated in the crossing. In *Bevan* v. *National Bank, Limited* (1907, 23 T.L.R. 65), Mr. Justice Channell said, "It was a direction to the receiving banker that the drawer desired to pay the particular cheque into the bank which kept the account of the payee. To disregard a direction of that kind, if the banker had information which might lead him to think that the account into which he was paying the cheque was not the payee's account, would be negligence."

It is not necessary for the collecting banker to place any note or indorsement upon the cheque that the amount has been placed to credit of the payee's account.

There is no provision in the Bills of Exchange Act, 1882, regarding the words "account payee" in connection with a crossing. Section 78 says that it shall not be lawful for any person, except as authorised by the Act, to add to the crossing. It is not understood, however, that such words are really an addition to the crossing. They may as a matter of convenience be placed close to a crossing, or even between the lines, but they would have the same effect wherever placed on the cheque, so long as the collecting banker could see them, and they may be placed with effect upon a cheque that is not crossed. (See CROSSED CHEQUE.)

ACCOUNTABLE RECEIPT. A receipt given for moneys or goods which have to be subsequently accounted for, such as a deposit receipt, a safe custody receipt. A fraudulent entry in a pass book has been held to be a forgery of an accountable receipt.

ACCOUNTS. Before a current account is opened for a stranger or a cheque book is given to him, a banker requires an introduction to be given by some reliable customer or person known to him.

The most convenient time to arrange matters regarding the conduct of the account is at the very beginning, e.g. in the case of a joint account, where either party is to sign, it is much easier to obtain the necessary authority when the account is opened than it is at a later date; and with regard to the accounts of companies, a copy of the resolution of the directors as to opening the account and signing cheques is likewise more readily given at the commencement.

Specimens of the signatures of all parties who are authorised to sign should be taken and preserved.

If the account is being transferred from another bank, it is useful to know the reason of the change.

When money is placed to the credit of an account, the banker becomes the debtor to the customer, and is under an obligation to honour all cheques (if in order) drawn upon the account by the customer to the extent of the funds in the account.

Where a customer has more than one account at the same branch, see SET OFF; and where he has accounts at different branches of the same bank, see BRANCHES.

As to accounts which contain money belonging to clients or others, see TRUSTEE.

In opening an account with a company the banker should make himself acquainted with its memorandum of association and articles of association. (See ADVANCES, AGENT, APPROPRIATION OF PAYMENTS, AUTHORITIES, BANKRUPT PERSON, CHURCHWARDENS, CLAYTON'S CASE, CLOSING AN ACCOUNT, COMPANIES, CURRENT ACCOUNT LEDGERS, CUSTOMER, DEAD ACCOUNT, DEATH OF CUSTOMER, DEPOSIT ACCOUNTS, EXECUTOR, GARNISHEE ORDER, HUSBAND AND WIFE ACCOUNT, IMPERSONAL ACCOUNTS, INFANTS, JOINT ACCOUNT, LOCAL AUTHORITIES, MANDATE, NURSING AN ACCOUNT, PARTNERSHIPS, PUBLIC ACCOUNT, SIGNATURE, SOCIETIES, STOCKBROKER'S LOANS, etc.)

ACCOUNTS OPENED AND CLOSED BOOK. This book, as its name implies, contains a complete list of all accounts which have been opened and of those which have been closed, the date of opening or closing being given in each case. A glance at this book, if it has been properly kept, will show whether accounts opened or accounts closed have been more numerous during any given period.

ACCRUED INTEREST. Interest to which a banker or a customer is entitled, but which is not actually received till a later date. At the end of a half-year, a banker, before ascertaining his profits, provides for the interest which has accrued up to date, and for which he is liable, on the outstanding deposit receipts ; he also takes into account the interest which has accrued upon investments or loans, and to which he is entitled, though the actual receipt of the dividends or interest will not take place till some date in the next half-year. (See ADJUSTMENT OF INTEREST ACCOUNT.)

A COMPTE. French, on account.

ACQUITTANCE. The document which releases a person from a debt or obligation.

ACT OF HONOUR. Where a bill has been dishonoured, and a person, not already a party to the bill, accepts or pays it for the honour of the drawer or an indorser, such acceptance or payment is called an act of honour.

ACTION. A civil proceeding in a court of law, commenced by writ, or in such other manner as may be prescribed by rules of court. Where a creditor has obtained judgment against a debtor, the court provides means of enforcing it. (See JUDGMENT CREDITOR.)

ACTIVE BONDS. Bonds upon which a fixed interest is payable from the date of issue. (See DEFERRED BONDS.)

ACTIVE CIRCULATION. The notes which are in circulation, that is notes which have been issued from a bank of issue and are in the hands of the public, as distinguished from those which, though printed and complete, are in the possession of the issuing bank.

ACTIVE PARTNER. A member of a partnership who takes an active part in the management of the business, as distinguished from a dormant or sleeping partner, who simply supplies capital and is not actively engaged in the actual work of the firm. A limited partner is somewhat similar to a sleeping partner. (See LIMITED PARTNERSHIP.)

ACTS OF BANKRUPTCY. When a debtor commits an act of bankruptcy, the Court may, on a bankruptcy petition being presented either by a creditor, or by the debtor, make a receiving order for the protection of the estate. The act must have been committed within three months before the presentation of the petition.

The various acts of bankruptcy are detailed in Section 4 of the Bankruptcy Act, 1883 :—

"(1) A debtor commits an act of bankruptcy in each of the following cases :—

"(*a*) If in England or elsewhere he makes a conveyance or assignment of his property to a trustee or trustees for the benefit of his creditors generally :

"(*b*) If in England or elsewhere he makes a fraudulent conveyance, gift, delivery, or transfer of his property, or of any part thereof :

"(*c*) If in England or elsewhere he makes any conveyance or transfer of his property or any part thereof, or creates any charge thereon which would under this or any other Act be void as a fraudulent preference if he were adjudged bankrupt.

"(*d*) If with intent to defeat or delay his creditors he does any of the following things, namely, departs out of England, or being out of England remains out of England, or departs from his dwelling-house, or otherwise absents himself, or begins to keep house:

"(e) A debtor commits an act of bankruptcy if execution against him has been levied by seizure of his goods under process in an action in any court, or in any civil proceeding in the High Court, and the goods have been either sold or held by the sheriff for twenty-one days.

Provided that, where an interpleader summons has been taken out in regard to the goods seized, the time elapsing between the date at which such summons is taken out and the date at which the sheriff is ordered to withdraw, or any interpleader issue ordered thereon is finally disposed of, shall not be taken into account in calculating such period of twenty-one days. (As amended by Section 1 of the Bankruptcy Act, 1890.)

"(f) If he files in the Court a declaration of his inability to pay his debts or presents a bankruptcy petition against himself:

"(g) If a creditor has obtained a final judgment against him for any amount, and execution thereon not having been stayed, has served on him in England, or, by leave of the Court, elsewhere, a bankruptcy notice under this Act, requiring him to pay the judgment debt in accordance with the terms of the judgment, or to secure or compound for it to the satisfaction of the creditor or the Court, and he does not, within seven days after service of the notice, in case the service is effected in England, and in case the service is effected elsewhere, then within the time limited in that behalf by the order giving leave to effect the service, either comply with the requirements of the notice, or satisfy the Court that he has a counter-claim set off or cross demand which equals or exceeds the amount of the judgment debt, and which he could not set up in the action in which the judgment was obtained:

"(h) If the debtor gives notice to any of his creditors that he has suspended, or that he is about to suspend, payment of his debts."

The phrase "begins to keep house" in sub-section (d) means to shut himself up in the house, or to refuse to see his creditors with the intention of delaying them.

An available act of bankruptcy means any act of bankruptcy available for a bankruptcy petition at the date of the presentation of the petition on which the receiving order is made (Section 168).

By an act of bankruptcy a bill which has been given in payment of a debt becomes immediately payable, and where any person liable upon a bill commits an act of bankruptcy a holder can present a petition upon his debt. (*Ex parte Raatz*, 1897, 2 Q.B. 80.)

When an act of bankruptcy has been committed by a customer, a banker must not pay any further cheques drawn upon his account.

A banker should exercise caution in deciding whether or not a customer has committed an act of bankruptcy, for there are circumstances which, at first sight, might lead him to conclude that such an act had been committed, but which may be found not to fulfil the legal requirements of an act of bankruptcy. For example, where a debtor called a meeting of his creditors and offered a composition, it was held not to be a sufficient notice of suspension; and a mere statement by the debtor that, in certain events, he will be obliged to suspend payment, is not sufficient. When a banker has any doubt on the matter he should take immediate steps to find out the exact position, and, in the meantime, should safeguard himself by not allowing any increase in an overdraft to take place.

In *Ponsford, Baker & Co.* v. *Union of London and Smith's Bank* (1906, 2 Ch. 444), Lord Justice Moulton said with reference to a man who has committed an act of bankruptcy: "Until commission of the act of bankruptcy he was, of course, the beneficial owner of whatever assets he possessed, but by the act of bankruptcy his title to be regarded as such beneficial owner is no longer absolute, but is contingent on no bankruptcy petition being presented within three months of the date of the act of bankruptcy which leads to a receiving order being made. If such receiving order be made, the whole of the assets vest in his trustee as from the date of the act of bankruptcy. He is, therefore, in the position that should such a contingency occur he is from the date of the act of bankruptcy something less than a mere trustee of his assets for the creditors in his bankruptcy. Until this state of suspense has been removed either by a receiving order or by lapse of time, he has no right to deal with those assets that were in his hands, and can give no title in them to any transferee with notice. Similarly with regard to the debts and other choses in action which form part of his estate, he cannot collect them or give a valid discharge for them, and any one making a payment to him with notice of the act of bankruptcy does so at his peril." (See BANKRUPTCY, RECEIVING ORDER.)

ACTUARY. An official in an insurance office skilled in the calculation of the values of life interests, and of the rates of premiums for life insurance, annuities, and other matters connected with the expectancy of life.

ADDING MACHINE. This machine is invaluable in offices where large quantities of cheques have to be listed and cast up. It has a keyboard which is used practically in the same way as a typewriter, and when the list is complete the correct total is immediately obtained by moving the lever at the side of the machine.

ADDRESSING MACHINE. Where envelopes require to be addressed to long lists of persons, as in the case of communications to shareholders every six months, machines may be obtained by which the work can be done much more rapidly than is possible by writing. Each address requires to be set up in type or cut on a stencil, according to the kind of machine in use. Of course after an interval of, say, six months, the plates of the machine will require numerous alterations in the names and addresses of the shareholders.

ADHESIVE STAMPS. By the Stamp Act, 1891 :—

"Section 7. Any stamp duties of an amount not exceeding two shillings and sixpence upon instruments which are permitted by law to be denoted by adhesive stamps not appropriated by any word or words on the face of them to any particular description of instrument, and any postage duties of the like amount, may be denoted by the same adhesive stamps."

"Section 9. (1) If any person—

"(*a*) Fraudulently removes or causes to be removed from any instrument any adhesive stamp, or affixes to any other instrument or uses for any postal purpose any adhesive stamp which has been so removed, with intent that the stamp may be used again; or

"(*b*) Sells or offers for sale, or utters, any adhesive stamp which has been so removed, or utters any instrument, having thereon any adhesive stamp which has to his knowledge been so removed as aforesaid;

he shall, in addition to any other fine or penalty to which he may be liable, incur a fine of fifty pounds.

"(2) The expression 'instrument' in this Section includes any post letter as defined by the Post Office Protection Act, 1884, and the cover of any post letter."

The stamp duty may be denoted by adhesive stamps in the following cases :—

Agreement, where the duty is sixpence only.

Bill of Exchange, Inland (on demand, at sight, on presentation, or within three days after date or sight).

Bill of Exchange, Foreign (on demand or not exceeding three days after date or sight a postage stamp; others require "appropriated" adhesive stamps).

Bill of Lading.

Certified copy from register of births, marriages, deaths, etc.

Charter Party.

Cheque.

Contract Note (appropriated stamp).

Dock Warrant.

Lease of any dwelling-house, or part thereof, for a term not exceeding a year at a rent not exceeding £10 per annum.

Lease of any furnished dwelling-house or apartments for a term less than a year.

Letter of renunciation.

Notarial Acts.

Policy of Insurance where the duty is one penny, other than sea or life insurance.

Proof of Debt in Bankruptcy (an appropriated stamp).

Protest of Bill of Exchange or Promissory Note.

Proxy, where the duty is one penny.

Receipts.

Voting paper, where the duty is one penny.

Warrant for goods. (See APPROPRIATED STAMPS, CANCELLATION OF STAMPS, STAMP DUTIES.)

ADJUDICATION OF BANKRUPTCY. Where a receiving order has been made against a debtor (see RECEIVING ORDER), though he is not at that date adjudged bankrupt, it means that, unless a composition or scheme of arrangement is accepted by the creditors, the court will, shortly, make an order adjudicating the debtor bankrupt.

Section 20 of the Bankruptcy Act, 1883, enacts :—

"(1) Where a receiving order is made against a debtor, then, if the creditors at the first meeting or any adjournment thereof by ordinary resolution resolve that the debtor be adjudged bankrupt, or pass no resolution, or if the creditors do not meet, or if a composition or scheme is not accepted or approved in pursuance of this Act within fourteen days after the conclusion of the examination of the debtor or such further time as the Court may allow, the Court shall adjudge the debtor bankrupt; and thereupon the property of the bankrupt shall become divisible among his creditors and shall vest in a trustee.

"(2) Notice of every order adjudging a debtor bankrupt, stating the name, address, and description of the bankrupt, the date of the adjudication, and the Court by which the adjudication is made, shall be gazetted and advertised in a local paper in the prescribed manner, and the date of the order shall for the purposes of this Act be the date of the adjudication."

The Court has power in certain cases to annul an adjudication. Section 35 provides :—

"(1) Where in the opinion of the Court a debtor ought not to have been adjudged bankrupt, or where it is proved to the satisfaction of the Court that the debts of the bankrupt are paid in full, the Court may, on the application of any person interested, by order, annul the adjudication."

The creditors may, if they think fit, at any time after a debtor is adjudicated a bankrupt, entertain a proposal for a composition in satisfaction of the debts due to them or for a scheme of arrangement of the bankrupt's affairs (Section 23).

Section 43 relates to the date when a bankruptcy is deemed to commence :—

"The bankruptcy of a debtor, whether the same takes place on the debtor's own petition or upon that of a creditor or creditors, shall be deemed to have relation back to, and to commence at, the time of the act of bankruptcy being committed on which a receiving order is made against him, or, if the bankrupt is proved to have committed more acts of bankruptcy than one, to have relation back to, and to commence at, the time of the first of the acts of bankruptcy proved to have been committed by the bankrupt within three months next preceding the date of the presentation of the bankruptcy petition; but no bankruptcy petition, receiving order, or adjudication shall be rendered invalid by reason of any act of bankruptcy anterior to the debt of the petitioning creditor." (See BANKRUPTCY.)

ADJUDICATION STAMPS. Where a doubt exists as to the stamp duty with which any instrument is chargeable, the opinion of the Board of Inland Revenue may be obtained as to the proper stamp. The instrument itself, and also a sufficient abstract thereof, must be lodged with the Controller of Stamps and Stores, Somerset House, and a separate abstract must be lodged with each deed. No document can be received for adjudication until it has been executed by all necessary parties. A security for advances without limit cannot be the subject of adjudication. Where it is claimed that collateral, auxiliary, additional, or substituted security duty only is payable, the principal or primary security must be produced before adjudication. In the case of a transfer of mortgage, the amount of interest in arrear (if any) at the date of transfer must be stated.

The regulations of the Stamp Act, 1891, with regard to these stamps are as follows :—

"Section 12. (1) Subject to such regulations as the Commissioners may think fit to make, the Commissioners may be required by any person to express their opinion with reference to any executed instrument upon the following questions :

(a) Whether it is chargeable with any duty ;

(b) With what amount of duty it is chargeable.

"(2) The Commissioners may require to be furnished with an abstract of the instrument, and also with such evidence as they may deem necessary, in order to show to their satisfaction whether all the facts and circumstances affecting the liability of the instrument to duty, or the amount of the duty chargeable thereon, are fully and truly set forth therein.

"(3) If the Commissioners are of opinion that the instrument is not chargeable with any duty, it may be stamped with a particular stamp denoting that it is not chargeable with any duty.

"(4) If the Commissioners are of opinion that the instrument is chargeable with duty, they shall assess the duty with which it is in their opinion chargeable, and when the instrument is stamped in accordance with the assessment it may be stamped with a particular stamp denoting that it is duly stamped.

(5) Every instrument stamped with the particular stamp denoting either that it is not chargeable with any duty, or is duly stamped, shall be admissible in evidence, and available for all purposes notwithstanding any objection relating to duty.

"(6) Provided as follows :—

(a) An instrument upon which the duty has been assessed by the Commissioners shall not, if it is unstamped or insufficiently stamped, be stamped otherwise than in accordance with the assessment ;

(b) Nothing in this Section shall extend to any instrument chargeable with *ad valorem* duty, and made as a security for money or stock without limit ; or shall authorise the stamping after the execution thereof of any instrument which by law cannot be stamped after execution ;

(c) A statutory declaration made for the purpose of this Section shall not be used against any person making the same in any proceeding whatever, except in an inquiry as to the duty with which the instrument to which it relates is chargeable ; and every person by whom any such declaration is made shall, on payment of the duty chargeable upon the instrument to which it relates, be relieved from any fine or disability to which he may be liable by reason of the omission to state truly in the instrument any fact or circumstance required by this Act to be stated therein."

By Section 13 any person who is dissatisfied with the assessment of the Commissioners may, within twenty-one days after the date of the assessment, and on payment of duty in conformity therewith, appeal to the High Court. If the assessment is confirmed, the court may make an order for payment to the Commissioners of the costs incurred by them in relation to the appeal.

By Section 74, s.s. 2 of the Finance (1909–10) Act, 1910, notwithstanding anything in Section 12 of the Stamp Act, 1891 (quoted above), the Commissioners may be required to express their opinion under that section on any conveyance or transfer operating as a voluntary disposition *inter vivos*, and no such conveyance or transfer shall be deemed to be duly stamped unless the Commissioners have expressed their opinion thereon in accordance with that Section. (See INCREMENT VALUE DUTY.)

ADJUSTMENT OF INTEREST ACCOUNT. An account which is made use of by bankers at each half-yearly balance to adjust certain items of interest. On the one side of the account are placed all amounts of interest which are due to the banker up to date, but which have not been received, such as interest due on investments; and on the other side, those sums which the banker has received and are strictly not yet due to be taken into profit, such as the amounts received from the discount of bills for the period from the last day of the half-year till the dates of maturity of the bills. On the same side the banker reserves the amount of interest which he is liable to pay upon his deposit receipts up to date.

ADMINISTRATION ORDER. An administration order is made by the county court against a debtor who is unable to pay an amount for which judgment has been obtained in a county court. An administration order is made only when the debtor's total indebtedness does not exceed £50.

Section 122 of the Bankruptcy Act, 1883, provides:—

"(1) Where a judgment has been obtained in a county court and the debtor is unable to pay the amount forthwith, and alleges that his whole indebtedness amounts to a sum not exceeding fifty pounds, inclusive of the debt for which the judgment is obtained, the county court may make an order providing for the administration of his estate, and for the payment of his debts by instalments or otherwise, and either in full or to such extent as to the county court under the circumstances of the case appears practicable, and subject to any conditions as to his future earnings or income which the court may think just.

"(2) The order shall not be invalid by reason only that the total amount of the debts is found at any time to exceed fifty pounds, but in such case the county court may, if it thinks fit, set aside the order.

"(3) Where, in the opinion of the county court in which the judgment is obtained, it would be inconvenient that that court should administer the estate, it shall cause a certificate of the judgment to be forwarded to the county court in the district of which the debtor or the majority of the creditors resides or reside, and thereupon the latter county court shall have all the powers which it would have under this Section, had the judgment been obtained in it."

With regard to the administration of a deceased insolvent's estate, see DEATH OF INSOLVENT DEBTOR. (See BANKRUPTCY.)

ADMINISTRATOR. Where a deceased person has left no will, the court appoints an administrator or administrators to wind up his estate. If the deceased has left a will, but does not name any one to act as executor, the court appoints an administrator granting him "letters of administration with the will annexed."

A banker does not allow any dealings with the account of a customer who has died intestate, or with any securities which may have been left in his hands by the deceased, until letters of administration have been granted. When letters have been exhibited, it is customary for the administrator to sign a cheque transferring any credit balance on the deceased's account to an account in his own name as administrator. If, however, the deceased's account is overdrawn, it will be paid off by the administrator, as may be arranged; the banker cannot transfer, from any account which the administrator may have opened, a sum to clear off the debt upon the deceased's account.

Upon the death of the sole or last surviving administrator, his executors, if any, do not undertake the duties; fresh letters of administration must be taken out. (See ADMINISTRATOR DE BONIS NON.)

An administrator winds up the deceased's affairs according to law, whilst an executor settles them according to the provisions of the will. In other respects, the remarks which apply to executors apply equally to administrators. (See EXECUTOR, LETTERS OF ADMINISTRATION.)

ADMINISTRATOR DE BONIS NON. A contraction for administrator *de bonis non administratis*, which means administrator of effects not administered. Where an administrator dies, or an executor dies without appointing an executor, and the duties connected with the administration have not been completed, the court will appoint another person, called an administrator *de bonis non* to complete the winding up of the estate.

ADMITTANCE.—The admittance of a copyholder is signified by the entry upon the court rolls when he is admitted by the lord of the manor as tenant of the copyhold land.

A copy admittance is given to the copyholder, which is his evidence of title to the property. (See COPYHOLD.)

The following is an example of an admittance :—

Manor of } The Court Leet and View of Frankpledge with the Court Baron and Customary Court of , Lord of the said Manor holden at within and for the said Manor on the day of , 19

Before , Steward.

Last admittance. 190 . To this Court came A. B. { eldest son and copyhold heir / devisee of the Will of C. D. } of C. D. deceased / deceased } (by E. F. his Attorney) and took of the Lord of the said Manor by the hands of his Steward.

£ s. d.
Rent
Fine ______

All that, etc.

of the apportioned yearly Copyhold Rent of . To hold the same to him his heirs and assigns for ever, according to the Custom of the Manor aforesaid. Paying the rents and performing the services of right due and accustomed and having paid the Lord for his Fine as in the margin and done his fealty is thereupon admitted tenant.

STEWARD.

AD REFERENDUM. Latin, to be further considered.

AD VALOREM. Latin, according to value. An *ad valorem* stamp duty is a duty calculated according to the value of the subject matter contained in a document. On a cheque for any amount, a bill payable on demand, or at sight, or on presentation, or not exceeding three days after date or sight, the stamp duty is one penny, but on bills and notes of any other kind the duty is an *ad valorem* one, calculated upon a certain scale according to the amount expressed in the document. A promissory note must always be stamped according to its amount, even though drawn on demand, at sight, etc.

The duty is also *ad valorem* upon many other documents—assignments of leases, conveyances, mortgages, transfers of stocks and shares, etc.

By the Stamp Act, 1891 :—

"Section 6. (1) Where an instrument is chargeable with *ad valorem* duty in respect of—

(*a*) any money in any foreign or colonial currency, or

(*b*) any stock or marketable security,

the duty shall be calculated on the value, on the day of the date of the instrument, of the money in British currency according to the current rate of exchange, or of the stock or security according to the average price thereof.

"(2) Where an instrument contains a statement of current rate of exchange, or average price, as the case may require, and is stamped in accordance with that statement, it is, so far as regards the subject matter of the statement, to be deemed duly stamped, unless or until it is shown that the statement is untrue, and that the instrument is in fact insufficiently stamped."

By the Finance Act, 1899 :—

"Section 12. (1) Where an instrument other than a bill of exchange or promissory note is charged with an *ad valorem* duty in respect of any money in any foreign or colonial currency, a rate of exchange for which is specified in the schedule to this Act, the stamp duty on that instrument shall, instead of being calculated as provided by Section six of the Stamp Act, 1891, be calculated according to the rate of exchange so specified.

"(2) The Commissioners may substitute, as respects any foreign or colonial currency mentioned in the Schedule to this Act, any rate of exchange for that specified in the Schedule, and may add to the Schedule a rate of exchange for any foreign or colonial currency not mentioned therein, and this Act shall be construed as if any rate of exchange for the time being substituted or added were contained in the said Schedule, and in the case of the substitution of a rate of exchange as if the rate for which the new rate is substituted were omitted from that Schedule.

"(3) Any substitution or addition so made by the Commissioners shall not take effect until it has been advertised in the *London Gazette* for two successive weeks."

"EQUIVALENTS IN STERLING OF FOREIGN CURRENCIES.

Gold dollar .	Five to one pound.
Silver dollar .	Ten to one pound.
Yen . . .	Ten to one pound.
Rouble . .	Ten to one pound.

Florins . . . Guilders . . . Gulden . . .	Twelve to one pound.
Rupee. . .	Fifteen to one pound.
Mark . . .	Twenty to one pound.
Franc . . . Lira . . .	Twenty-five to one pound."

ADVANCE NOTE. When a seaman signs his articles of agreement, he may receive an advance note for a month's wages. The note is drawn upon the owner of the vessel and is payable three days after the ship has sailed. They are subject to the same duty as Bills of Exchange.

ADVANCES. An advance is granted either by way of overdraft upon a current account, or by a loan upon a separate account, or, in some districts, upon a promissory note. The discounting of bills is practically the same as making an advance upon the security of the bills.

In considering an application for an advance, a branch manager is influenced by his own personal knowledge of the borrower, by the figures as shown by the certified balance sheet of the customer, and by the history of previous transactions and the various conclusions to be drawn from a careful study of the customer's account. Some of the questions which naturally arise in a banker's mind are: For how long is the advance required? If granted, is it likely to be repaid according to promise? For what purpose is the money required? What security is offered?

It may be impossible to entertain an application in the form in which it is first made by a customer. Francis E. Steele, in "Present-Day Banking," says: "Anybody can grant, or submit to his Head Office, a perfectly good proposal. Anybody can decline a transaction which is obviously impossible. Where the real skill of a bank manager proves itself is in getting a borrower so to modify an impracticable proposal that it will assume a shape in which it will be acceptable to himself and to his Head Office."

Securities such as second mortgages, reversions, building land, brick fields, shares with a liability attached, etc., are, as a rule, avoided by most bankers. "The most dangerous of all loans," wrote the late J. W. Gilbart, "are those which are made against unmarketable securities, such as mills, ironworks, coal mines, landed property, etc."

The securities most commonly favoured by bankers are first-class stocks and shares, deeds of readily realisable properties, good bearer bonds, guarantees by reliable sureties, and life policies to the extent of the surrender value.

With regard to unsecured advances, George Rae in "The Country Banker" puts the position in a most practical way. He supposes £1,000 to be advanced for three months without security and that the customer fails and pays 5*s.* in the pound. The profit on the transaction, taking all things into account, will not have much exceeded £5. "To secure this modest recompense or reward, you have risked £1,000 and actually lost £750. You will have to make 150 fresh advances of £1,000 each—that is to say, you will have to incur fresh uncovered risks to the amount of £150,000 to redeem your loss."

In granting a limit a banker should reserve to himself the right to cancel the limit, at any time, if he should deem it necessary. In *Rouse* v. *Bradford Banking Company*, (1894, A.C. 586), Lord Herschell said, at p. 595: "It is not necessary to consider what the rights of the bank were with regard to their debtors when they had agreed to an overdraft. The transaction is, of course, of the commonest. It may be that an overdraft does not prevent the bank who have agreed to give it from at any time giving notice that it is no longer to continue, and that they must be paid their money. This, I think, at least it does: if they have agreed to give an overdraft, they cannot refuse to honour cheques or drafts, within the limit of that overdraft, which have been drawn and put in circulation before any notice to the person to whom they have agreed to give the overdraft that the limit is to be withdrawn. That effect I think it has in point of law; whether it has more than that in point of law it is unnecessary to consider." The length of notice will depend upon what was arranged when the limit was granted; but a limit cannot be withdrawn before the expiration of the period for which it was sanctioned, unless the customer's position, or his security, has greatly changed for the worse.

Numerous small advances are, as a rule, more satisfactory than two or three loans for very large amounts.

Temporary accommodation is also much to be preferred to permanent loans.

In lending upon securities such as land, houses, shares, etc., it is customary to preserve a margin between the value of the security and the amount of the loan or overdraft. A house, for example, may have been recently built at a cost of £500, but a banker would not, as a rule, advance £500 upon it. In a few years the house, in all probability, may not be saleable at all at that figure, particularly at a forced sale. Shares, even though of first-class description, may easily, for various reasons, also fall in value. A prudent banker, therefore, in considering what value of securities he should have for an overdraft or loan, ever bears in mind the uncertainty of values and endeavours to protect himself by lending an amount less than the value of the security at the time the arrangement is made. The difference between the amount lent and the estimated value of the security is the "margin." The extent of the margin will differ according to the nature of the securities and the special circumstances of each case, but if a loan has been granted against shares with, say, a margin of 20 per cent., the banker will watch his securities, and, when they begin to fall and the margin to disappear, will require further securities to be given to restore the margin as agreed upon. The margin may be calculated either upon the value of the securities or upon the amount of the loan. The usual practice is to calculate it upon the value of the securities. The difference of the two methods is shown as follows :—

(1)

Value of securities	£10,000
Less 20 per cent. =	2,000
	£8,000 = Amount to be advanced.

(2)

Amount to be advanced	£8,000
Add 20 per cent.	1,600
	£9,600 = Value of securities required.

In each case the amount to be advanced is the same, £8,000, but in the former case the value of the securities will be £10,000, whereas in the latter case the value will be £9,600.

In cases where margins of a certain per cent. are required, the simple calculations are :—

If the margin is 25 per cent. deduct one-fourth from the value of the securities offered, e.g.—

	£2,000
Less one-fourth	500
	£1,500 = Amount to be advanced.

If a loan of £1,500 is applied for, the value of the security required to provide a 25 per cent. margin will be one-third of the £1,500 added to that amount, e.g.—

	£1,500
Add one-third .	500
	£2,000 = Security required.

If the margin is 20 per cent., on the same principle as above :—

Security offered .	£1,000
Less one-fifth .	200
	£800 = Amount to be advanced.
Loan required .	£800
Add one-fourth .	200
	£1,000 = Security required.

If the margin is 15 per cent. :—

Security offered .	£1,000
Less 15 per cent. .	150
	£850 = Amount to be advanced.
Loan required .	£850
Add [illegible]ths . .	150
(or roughly one-sixth) . . .	£1,000 = Security required.

If the margin is 10 per cent. :—

Security offered .	£1,000
Less one-tenth .	100
	£900 = Amount to be advanced.
Loan required .	£900
Add one-ninth .	100
	£1,000 = Security required.

When the amount of the loan required is known, the value of the securities necessary to obtain, say, a margin of 20 per cent. is arrived at by adding to the amount of the loan one-fourth of that loan, the reason being, of course, that when 20 per cent., or one-fifth, is deducted from the value of the securities, the difference (in this case supposed to be the loan) is in eightieths, and if twenty of those eightieths—that is, one-fourth—are added, the amount is restored to the original figure (in this case the value of the securities), e.g.—

	£100	= Security.
Deduct 20 per cent, or one-fifth	20	= Margin.
	£80	= Loan.
Add 20/80ths or one-fourth	20	= Margin
	£100	= Security.

ADVICE. When a banker issues a draft, he sends an advice, called a letter of advice, to the banker upon whom the draft has been drawn, giving him particulars of the amount, number, date, and payee, so that, when the instrument is presented for payment, the drawee banker may be able to satisfy himself that the draft is in order. In the absence of an advice, a banker would hesitate to pay a draft.

The word "advice" applies also to many other forms of intimation which a banker in the course of his business has to make to customers, other banks, and his own head office or London agents, such as advices of credits received, payments to be made, bills to be paid, etc.

ADVICE BOOK. The book in which particulars are entered of all drafts advised as having been drawn upon the bank.

"**ADVISE FATE.**" Where early notice is required as to the payment, or non-payment, of a cheque, the cheque is sent direct to the banker on whom it is drawn with a request to "advise fate." If a reply is required before return of post, a stamped telegram form should be enclosed for a reply by wire as soon as possible after the cheque is received.

If a wire is received asking if a certain cheque will be paid when presented, a banker should be careful to qualify an affirmative reply, otherwise he may find that, by the time the cheque is actually presented, the customer's account has altered so as not to admit of its payment, and yet he will, if he gave an unqualified reply, be liable to pay it.

AFFIDAVIT. A written declaration, given on oath, before some person who is entitled to administer an oath, as a solicitor who has been appointed a Commissioner for Oaths, a magistrate, consul, or notary public. The affidavit must give the person's name and address and be signed by him, and be attested by the person before whom it is sworn.

The fee of a Commissioner for Oaths for administering the oath is 1*s.* 6*d.*, with 1*s.* additional for each document attached to the affidavit. Such additional document is known as an "exhibit."

The word "affidavit" is Low Latin, and means "has pledged his faith." It was at one time usual for the document to commence thus: Affidavit N. M., etc.

By the Stamp Act, 1891, the duty is :—

	£	*s.*	*d.*
AFFIDAVIT and STATUTORY DECLARATION	0	2	6

Exemptions.

(1) Affidavit made for the immediate purpose of being filed, read, or used in any court, or before any judge, master, or officer of any court.

(2) Affidavit or declaration made upon a requisition of the commissioners of any public board of revenue, or any of the officers acting under them, or required by law.

(3) Affidavit or declaration which may be required at the Bank of England or the Bank of Ireland to prove the death of any proprietor of any stock transferable there, or to identify the person of any such proprietor, or to remove any other impediment to the transfer of any such stock.

(4) Affidavit or declaration relating to the loss, mutilation, or defacement of any bank note or bank post bill.

(5) Declaration required to be made pursuant to any Act relating to marriages in order to a marriage without licence.

(6) Declaration forming part of an application for a patent in conformity with the Patents, Designs, and Trade Marks Act, 1883.

AFFREIGHTMENT. A contract of affreightment is the agreement made by a shipowner to carry goods in consideration of a certain payment, called the freight.

When the contract is with respect to the use of the whole ship for the cargo, the terms are embodied in the CHARTER PARTY (*q.v.*), but if the contract is merely to convey certain goods, as part of the ship's cargo, the agreement is contained in the BILL OF LADING (*q.v.*).

AFTER HOURS. A transaction which occurs after the bank doors have been closed for business, is said to have taken place "after hours."

In country districts money may frequently be paid in after hours, and though it is not considered advisable to encourage the practice, a banker usually accommodates his customer by permitting it. If the books for the day have been closed, the customer dates the credit slip for the following day, and where cheques form part of the credit he is warned that they will not be sent forward for collection, or otherwise dealt with, until the next day. In such cases it is important that the paying-in slip be dated for the next day, otherwise the slip would be evidence that the money was paid in on the date shown on the slip. Where a customer requires the credit to be entered in his pass book when he hands over the money to the bank after hours, it should, of course, be entered as for the following day, so that the credit slip, the bank books and the pass book will all show the same date.

A banker, however, does not, as a rule, give cash for a cheque (unless it is the customer's own cheque) after hours. A drawer of a cheque has a right to stop payment of it and to give notice during business hours, and if a cheque is cashed after hours, the bank would be liable in the event of a notice to stop payment being received the following morning. (See BANK HOURS.)

AGE ADMITTED. (See LIFE POLICY.)

AGENCY. (See SUB-BRANCH.)

AGENDA. Literally, things to be done. The agenda are notes of various matters which are to be brought before the directors of a company, or before a meeting, for consideration. They are written upon a sheet of paper, or in the agenda books, and are used by the chairman in conducting the business of the meeting, a brief record being made opposite each entry as to how the matter is disposed of.

AGENT. An agent is a person who acts under authority from his principal, and the extent of his powers to bind his principal is limited to the terms of that authority. It is therefore necessary in dealing with an agent, in matters of any importance, to ascertain exactly what are his powers. If an agent is authorised to enter into a contract under seal, he must be appointed by deed. He may have authority to act only in some particular or special duty, as in the case of an agent empowered to purchase a house; or the authority may be of a much wider nature and constitute a person a general agent, as in the case of a manager of a branch bank, where he is authorised to take charge of the branch and conduct its business. The manager's actions will bind his principals within the scope of that business, and though there may be, as between the principals and the manager, a clear arrangement as to the limitation of the latter's authority, as regards a third party who has no knowledge of any such private arrangement, the principals will be bound by the manager's actions, even if he has disregarded that private arrangement.

Where a person's authority is unlimited, he is called an universal agent, and the principal is bound by whatever his agent does, so long as it is in accordance with the law of the land.

An agent has no power to delegate his authority to another person.

Where an agent in exercise of his authority, affixes his name to a bill of exchange, as drawer, acceptor, or indorser, he must be careful to sign in such a manner that no personal liability will attach to him. The addition of such words as "manager," "agent," "secretary" would not be sufficient to clear him from personal liability.

In *Leadbitter* v. *Farrow* (1816, 5 M. & S., at p. 349), Lord Ellenborough said: "Is it not an universal rule that a man who puts his name to a bill of exchange thereby makes himself personally liable, unless he states upon the face of the bill that he subscribes it for another, or by procuration of another, which are the words of exclusion? Unless he says plainly, 'I am the mere scribe,' he is liable."

The Bills of Exchange Act, 1882, Section 26, provides as follows:—

"(1) Where a person signs a bill as drawer, indorser, or acceptor, and adds words to his signature, indicating that he signs for or on behalf of a principal, or in a representative character, he is not personally liable thereon; but the mere addition to his signature of words describing him as an agent, or as filling a representative character, does not exempt him from personal liability.

"(2) In determining whether a signature on a bill is that of the principal or that of the agent by whose hand it is written, the construction most favourable to the validity of the instrument shall be adopted."

In signing for a company it is much better if an agent states definitely the capacity in which he signs, and prefixes the words per pro., e.g.,

per pro. T. Brown & Sons, Ltd.,
R. Jones, Secretary.
per pro. British Banking Co., Ltd.
T. Smith,
Manager.

But the form of signature, "T. Brown & Sons, Ltd., R. Jones, Secretary," without the prefix per pro., is very common.

With regard to a procuration signature, Section 25 enacts :—

"A signature by procuration operates as notice that the agent has but a limited authority to sign, and the principal is only bound by such signature if the agent in so signing was acting within the actual limits of his authority."

Where a signature is placed on a bill without the authority of the person whose signature it purports to be, the unauthorised signature is wholly inoperative. The supposed principal is not bound because it is not his signature; and the supposed agent is not bound on the bill because the signature pretends to be that of a principal. Apart from the bill, a person so signing would be liable for false representation of authority.

No person is liable as drawer, indorser, or acceptor of a bill who has not signed it as such, except where a person signs in a trade or assumed name, or in the name of a firm.

An agent may have authority, instead of signing per pro., to sign the actual name of his principal, or to impress the signature with a rubber stamp. Section 91 enacts :—

"(1) Where, by this Act, any instrument or writing is required to be signed by any person, it is not necessary that he should sign it with his own hand, but it is sufficient if his signature is written thereon by some other person by or under his authority.

"(2) In the case of a corporation, where, by this Act, any instrument or writing is required to be signed, it is sufficient if the instrument or writing be sealed with the corporate seal.

"But nothing in this Section shall be construed as requiring the bill or note of a corporation to be under seal."

An infant may act as an agent. An undischarged bankrupt may also act as agent.

It has been held in *Cookson* v. *Bank of England* (a case tried at the Guildhall in 1860, and approved by the Court of Common Pleas in Ireland in *Hare* v. *Copeland*, 1862, 13 J.C.L.R. 426), that, where an agent indorsed a cheque "per procuration Jackson & Co., A. Holmes, Agent," and he had no authority to indorse, the bank was protected.

An agent should not place to the credit of his own private account, cheques payable to his principal. Where the business requires this to be done, there should be a written authority from the principal.

Where cheques are to be signed by an agent, an authority or mandate should be given by the principal requesting the banker to honour such cheques, and if the agent is to have power to sign when the account is overdrawn, the authority should include that power. In the case of a limited company, a resolution should be passed by the directors as to the method in which cheques are to be signed, and a copy of the resolution, signed by the chairman, should be furnished to the banker.

On the death of the principal, any authority he has given to an agent to sign cheques is cancelled. The death of an agent does not prevent a banker paying a cheque signed by the agent on the account of his principal, and presented for payment after the agent's death.

The following case shows how necessary it is that an agent should, in order to avoid all risk, sign in such a manner that there may be no question that he does so merely as an agent :—

In *Chapman* v. *Smethurst* (1909, 1 K.B. 73), an action was brought on a promissory note :—"Six months after demand I promise to pay to Mrs. M. Chapman the sum of £300 for value received, together with 6 per cent. interest per annum. J. H. Smethurst's Laundry and Dye Works (Limited), J. H. Smethurst, Managing Director." The words "J. H. Smethurst's Laundry and Dye Works (Limited)" and "Managing Director" were placed on the note by means of a rubber stamp. Mr. Justice Channell held that the defendant was personally liable on the promissory note, because he had not added any words to show that he signed merely as the agent of the company. On appeal, however, it was held that the company could be sued on the note.

In *Landes* v. *Marcus & Davids* (1909, 25 T.L.R. 478), a cheque was signed by the defendants (directors of Marcus & Co., Limited), in favour of the plaintiff, in the following way: "B. Marcus, Director." "S. H. Davids, Director." The space for the secretary's signature was left blank. The name of the company was printed only at the top of the cheque. Although the directors added words to show their representative capacity, it was held that, in signing the cheques, they did not indicate that they did so on behalf of the company, and that they were personally liable on the cheque.

An agent cannot borrow money on behalf of his principal unless authorised to do so; and if a banker, with knowledge of the extent to which an agent may borrow, permits him to exceed his authority, the principal will not be liable. (See PER PROCURATION.)

AGENT DE CHANGE. A stockbroker on the Paris Exchange.

AGIO. The term used to express the difference in value between paper money and metallic money, or between one kind of metallic money and another. If an English sovereign is so much worn that it will not sell for its nominal value, the difference between its nominal value and what it sells for is called the agio.

AGREEMENT. By the Stamp Act, 1891, the regulations respecting the stamp duty on agreements are as follows:—

AGREEMENT or CONTRACT, accompanied with a deposit.
See MORTGAGE, etc., and Section 23 below, and Section 86 under MORTGAGE.

AGREEMENT for a lease or tack, or for any letting.
See LEASEHOLD, and Section 75.

AGREEMENT for sale of property.
See CONVEYANCE on SALE.

	£	s.	d.
AGREEMENT or CONTRACT made or entered into pursuant to the Highway Acts for or relating to the making, maintaining, or repairing of highways . . .	0	0	6
AGREEMENT or any MEMORANDUM of an AGREEMENT, made in England or Ireland under hand only, or made in Scotland without any clause of registration, and not otherwise specifically charged with any duty, whether the same be only evidence of a contract, or obligatory upon the parties from its being a written instrument	0	0	6

Exemptions.

(1) Agreement or memorandum the matter whereof is not of the value of £5.

(2) Agreement or memorandum for the hire of any labourer, artificer, manufacturer, or menial servant.

(3) Agreement, letter, or memorandum made for or relating to the sale of any goods, wares, or merchandise. [But by the Finance Act, 1907, Section 7, any agreement for or relating to the supply of goods on hire, whereby the goods in consideration of periodical payments will or may become the property of the person to whom they are supplied, shall be charged with stamp duty as an agreement, or, if under seal (or in Scotland with a clause of registration), as a deed, as the case requires.]

(4) Agreement or memorandum made between the master and mariners of any ship or vessel for wages on any voyage coastwise from port to port in the United Kingdom.

(5) Agreement entered into between a landlord and tenant pursuant to subsection six of Section

eight or sub-section two of Section twenty of the Land Law (Ireland) Act, 1881.

And see Sections 22 and 23, which are as follows :—

"22. The duty of sixpence upon an agreement may be denoted by an adhesive stamp, which is to be cancelled by the person by whom the agreement is first executed.

"23. (1) Every instrument under hand only (not being a promissory note or bill of exchange) given upon the occasion of the deposit of any share warrant or stock certificate to bearer, or foreign or colonial share certificate, or any security for money transferable by delivery, by way of security for any loan, shall be deemed to be an agreement, and shall be charged with duty accordingly.

"(2) Every instrument under hand only (not being a promissory note or bill of exchange) making redeemable or qualifying a duly stamped transfer, intended as a security, of any registered stock or marketable security, shall be deemed to be an agreement, and shall be charged with duty accordingly.

"(3) A release or discharge of any such instrument shall not be chargeable with any *ad valorem* duty."

An agreement under hand, chargeable with a duty of sixpence, if not stamped with an adhesive postage stamp (or stamps) at the time the document is signed, may be stamped with an impressed stamp within fourteen days from its date.

As to an agreement under seal, see BOND.

AGRICULTURAL BANK. (See CREDIT BANKS.)

AGRICULTURAL CREDIT SOCIETY. (See CREDIT BANKS.)

ALDGATE PUMP. A cheque with no effects has been likened to a draught on Aldgate Pump. The pun is on the word draught, meaning either an order on a bank or a draught of liquor. (Dr. Brewer's "Dictionary of Phrase and Fable.")

ALFONSO. (See FOREIGN MONEYS—SPAIN.)

ALLONGE. (Fr., *allongé*, lengthened.) An allonge is a slip of paper attached to a bill of exchange for the purpose of receiving indorsements, when the back of the bill itself has become completely covered by the indorsements of the various parties through whose hands the bill has passed and who have signed it. In order to prevent an allonge being removed from one bill and attached to another, it is the practice to write the first indorsement on the allonge over the junction of the two documents, so that it begins on the bill and ends on the allonge. In some countries a copy of the bill is used instead of an allonge. Section 32, s.s. 1 of the Bills of Exchange Act. 1882, provides that "an indorsement written on an allonge, or on a 'copy' of a bill issued or negotiated in a country where 'copies' are recognised, is deemed to be written on the bill itself."

An allonge does not require to be stamped, as it is merely a continuation of a bill which is stamped. (See BILL OF EXCHANGE.)

ALLOTMENT. An applicant for shares which are being issued by a company generally fills up a printed form of application supplied by the company, in which he requests that the shares he requires may be allotted to him. At the same time he either sends a cheque to the company for the deposit which is payable on application, or pays in the amount to the company's bankers. If his application is successful he will, in due course, receive a letter of allotment stating the number of shares which have been allotted to him, and requesting payment of the amount due per share upon allotment.

With regard to the allotment of share capital of a company, the Companies (Consolidation) Act, 1908, Section 85, provides as follows :—

"(1) No allotment shall be made of any share capital of a company offered to the public for subscription, unless the following conditions have been complied with, namely :—

(*a*) the amount (if any) fixed by the memorandum or articles and named in the prospectus as the minimum subscription upon which the directors may proceed to allotment ; or

(*b*) if no amount is so fixed and named, then the whole amount of the share capital so offered for subscription,

has been subscribed, and the sum payable on application for the amount so fixed and named, or for the whole amount offered for subscription, has been paid to and received by the company.

"(2) The amount so fixed and named and the whole amount aforesaid shall be reckoned exclusively of any amount payable otherwise than in cash, and is in this Act referred to as the minimum subscription.

(3) The amount payable on application on each share shall not be less than five per cent. of the nominal amount of the share.

(4) If the conditions aforesaid have not been complied with on the expiration of forty days after the first issue of the prospectus, all money received from applicants for shares shall be forthwith repaid to them without interest, and, if any such money is not so repaid within forty-eight days after the issue of the prospectus, the directors of the company shall be jointly and severally liable to repay that money with interest at the rate of five per centum per annum from the expiration of the forty-eighth day:

Provided that a director shall not be liable if he proves that the loss of the money was not due to any misconduct or negligence on his part.

(5) Any condition requiring or binding any applicant for shares to waive compliance with any requirement of this Section shall be void.

(6) This Section, except sub-section (3) thereof, shall not apply to any allotment of shares subsequent to the first allotment of shares offered to the public for subscription.

(7) In the case of the first allotment of share capital payable in cash of a company which does not issue any invitation to the public to subscribe for its shares, no allotment shall be made unless the minimum subscription (that is to say):—

(*a*) the amount (if any) fixed by the memorandum or articles and named in the statement in lieu of prospectus as the minimum subscription upon which the directors may proceed to allotment; or

(*b*) if no amount is so fixed and named, then the whole amount of the share capital other than that issued or agreed to be issued as fully or partly paid up otherwise than in cash,

has been subscribed and an amount not less than five per cent. of the nominal amount of each share payable in cash has been paid to and received by the company.

This subsection shall not apply to a private company or to a company which has allotted any shares or debentures before the first day of July nineteen hundred and eight."

When a company limited by shares makes any allotment, the company must, within one month thereafter, file with the registrar of companies a return of the allotments in accordance with Section 88 of the Act. (See COMPANIES, LETTER OF ALLOTMENT.)

ALLOTMENT LETTER. (See LETTER OF ALLOTMENT.)

ALLOTMENT NOTE. A note in an approved form signed by a seaman authorissing the owner of the ship to pay his wages (limited to one half) to a near relative or to a savings bank. The payment to a relative would not be made until a month subsequent to the date when he signed his articles of agreement, and to a savings bank it would not be made until three months subsequent to the date of the agreement.

ALLOTTEE. The person to whom shares in a company are allotted in response to an application for shares.

ALLOY. (From the French *à loi*, Latin *ad legem*, according to law.)

Gold and silver in the pure state are too soft to be used for coins, and therefore they are mixed with another metal, copper, called the alloy, in order to impart the requisite amount of hardness.

The light yellow colour of certain Australian sovereigns is due to the alloy being silver.

The standard fineness of gold coins is eleven-twelfths fine gold, one-twelfth alloy (copper), and of silver coins thirty-seven-fortieths fine silver and three-fortieths alloy (copper). Bronze coins are a mixed metal composed of copper, tin and zinc. (See COINAGE.)

ALTERATIONS. Where alterations are necessary in any of the books of a bank, they should be made carefully, the wrong entry being neatly ruled through, and the correct one written above or below it. Errors are not to be put right merely by the fresh figures being thickly written upon the top of the old ones. Some banks require that alterations in ledgers and other important books be made in red ink. If a ledger entry has been posted into a wrong account, it is customary, when rectifying the mistake, to quote the folio of the correct account.

Bankers do not, as a rule, issue a deposit receipt, or draft, showing any alteration in an important part. Where a mistake has been made in drawing such a document, it is considered desirable to have a fresh one written, rather than to issue one to the public showing evidences of carelessness or inaccuracy.

All material alterations in a bill must be initialled or signed by all the parties liable on the bill, and all alterations in a cheque must be confirmed by each drawer. It is not sufficient, in the case of a limited company's cheque, if a material alteration is initialled only by the secretary, unless, of course, the banker has authority to accept the signature of the secretary alone.

With regard to alterations in a bill of exchange Section 64 of the Bills of Exchange Act, 1882, enacts :—

"(1) Where a bill or acceptance is materially altered without the assent of all parties liable on the bill, the bill is avoided except as against a party who has himself made, authorised, or assented to the alteration, and subsequent indorsers :

"Provided that,

"Where a bill has been materially altered, but the alteration is not apparent, and the bill is in the hands of a holder in due course, such holder may avail himself of the bill as if it had not been altered, and may enforce payment of it according to its original tenor.

"(2) In particular the following alterations are material, namely, any alteration of the date, the sum payable, the time of payment, the place of payment, and, where a bill has been accepted generally, the addition of a place of payment without the acceptor's assent."

By Section 78 :—"A crossing authorised by this Act is a material part of the cheque ; it shall not be lawful for any person to obliterate or, except as authorised by this Act, to add to or alter the crossing."

The alterations authorised by the Bills of Exchange Act, 1882, are :—

Any holder may convert a blank indorsement into a special indorsement (Section 34, s.s. 4).

Where a cheque is uncrossed, the holder may cross it generally or specially.

Where crossed generally, the holder may cross it specially.

Where crossed generally or specially, the holder may add the words "not negotiable."

Where crossed specially, a banker to whom it is crossed may cross it specially to another banker for collection.

Where an uncrossed cheque, or a cheque crossed generally, is sent to a banker for collection, he may cross it specially to himself (Section 77).

Where a bill payable at a fixed period after date is issued undated, or an acceptance of a bill payable at a fixed period after sight is undated, any holder may insert the true date (Section 12).

A cheque which is payable to "bearer" may be altered by the payee to "order," but an alteration of a cheque from "order" to "bearer" must be initialled by all the drawers, and of a bill by all parties liable thereon. In *Aldous* v. *Cornwell* (1868, L.R. 3 Q.B. 573), where no time of payment was stated on a bill, it was held that the words "on demand" could be inserted.

In *Adelphi Bank* v. *Edwards* (1882, 26 Sol. J. 360), where the amount of a bill had been fraudulently altered by a holder, spaces having been left in drawing the bill, which enabled this to be done, Lord Justice Baggallay said : "It seems to me impossible to say that there was any duty on the part of the acceptor of the bill towards the party who might subsequently become the holder of the bill so to criticise, and so to examine the bill before he signed, as to put it out of the possibility of any additional words being afterwards inserted in it." This case was cited with approval in the well-known case of *Scholfield* v. *Earl of Londesborough* (1896, A.C. 514), which may be said to have settled the law as to alterations in bills of exchange.

In *Colonial Bank of Australasia* v. *Marshall* (1906, A.C. 559), a cheque was altered by a holder to a larger amount, blank spaces having been left. It was held that the mere fact of the drawer of a cheque leaving spaces which may be used by a fraudulent holder, is not of itself sufficient evidence of negligence on the part of the drawer to relieve the banker from liability. This decision is a very unfortunate one for bankers.

In bills and cheques where it is visible at

once that alterations have been made, a banker will, of course, take the greatest care to see that all material alterations are properly initialled. But from the above cases it is seen that a banker may find himself in possession of bills or cheques which have been fraudulently altered, and the alterations may not be discernible at all, owing to the drawer of the bill or cheque having left blank spaces when writing out the instruments. The banker may also find that, although the drawer drew the cheque carelessly and the acceptor accepted a bill drawn carelessly, he may not be able to prove in either case that the carelessness amounts to negligence in the eye of the law.

If a banker unfortunately "pays money belonging to the customer upon an order which is not genuine, he must suffer. To justify the payment he must show that the order is genuine, not in signature only, but in every respect" (*Hall* v. *Fuller*, 1826, 5 B. & C. 750).

Various protections have been devised in order to prevent, or to make difficult, the fraudulent alteration of a cheque. Words such as "under one hundred pounds" or "not exceeding one hundred pounds" are often written across, or stamped upon, a cheque; or the cheque may be perforated with those words.*

The body of a cheque may also be tinted, or printed over with words or a design to show more readily if an erasure takes place. Cheque paper is also specially prepared to prevent the use of chemicals being used to effect an alteration.

The following case illustrates the importance of seeing that any material alteration in a cheque is initialled by all the persons by whom the cheque is drawn.

In the *Kepitigalla Rubber Estates, Limited* v. *The National Bank of India, Limited* (1909, 2 K.B. 1010), the plaintiffs had given the defendants a written authority to honour cheques drawn by two directors and the secretary. A cheque for £150 was altered from "order" to "bearer" and initialled by the secretary, and the initials of one of the directors were forged by means of a rubber stamp. The other director signed the cheque, but did not initial the alteration. Mr. Justice Bray said: "With regard to the payment of the cheque for £150, where Mr. Lauder had not initialled the alteration from 'order' to 'bearer,' the accountants stated that it was usual for bankers to pay if two out of the three initialled the alteration. It seemed to me, however, that they would do this at their own risk; if Mr. Lauder never initialled or authorised the alteration the payment of the cheque by the bank would not be authorised."

Material alterations in a deed should be initialled by the parties signing the deed, and they should be specifically referred to in the attestation clause.

AMERICAN RAILROAD CERTIFICATES. These certificates partake of the nature of a registered holding and also of a bearer security. On the face is given the name of the registered holder of the shares and on the back is supplied a blank form of transfer, which, when signed by the registered holder, makes the certificate transferable by delivery like a bearer bond. The registered holder, however, is the person to whom the company sends the dividends, and the owner of the certificate (unless he gets registered himself) must apply to him for the dividend, producing the certificate to show that he is entitled to it. If, as is often the case, the registered holder is a well-known London firm, the application for the dividend may

*The following ingenious device to prevent alterations in the amount of a cheque is printed at the left-hand side of a certain form of cheque.

Not exceeding £10		No..... London, ...
,, ,, £30		
,, ,, £130		To X & Y Bank, Ltd.
,, ,, £230	220	
,, ,, £330		Pay............................or order
,, ,, £1,300		the Sum of Two hundred and Twenty Pounds
,, ,, £2,300		
,, ,, £3,300		£220—— J. BROWN.
,, ,, £10,000		

be easily made, but if the registered holder is not well known there may be considerable trouble in finding him. In some cases a commission is charged by the registered holder for receiving and paying over the dividend to the owner of the certificate.

These certificates differ from a bearer bond, in that a bearer bond is a "negotiable instrument," which a certificate of this description is not, and therefore they do not give to the owner any better title than the previous owner had. In practice, however, they pass from one person to another by mere delivery.

Trouble may arise to the unregistered owner owing to the death of the registered holder, or to the company requiring verification of the transferor's signature on the form of transfer. It is also possible for a charge to be registered on the company's books against the shares. To avoid trouble, a purchaser should have the shares registered in his own name.

When such certificates are purchased or taken as security, they should be indorsed by the registered holder, otherwise, in the event of his death, there would be considerable delay and expense in sending proof of death to America.

The following is the wording on a certificate of this nature :—

"This certifies that John Brown is the owner of ten paid shares of the Capital Stock of the Railway Company of one hundred dollars each, transferable only on the books of the company in person or by Attorney, and upon the surrender of this certificate.

"This certificate shall not become valid until countersigned by the transfer agent and also by the registrar of transfers."

On the back there appears the following :

"For value received have bargained, sold, assigned, and transferred, and by these presents do bargain, sell, assign, and transfer unto shares of the Capital Stock of the Railway Company mentioned in the within certificate, and do hereby constitute and appoint true and lawful Attorney, irrevocable, for and in name and stead, but to use to sell, assign, transfer, and set over all or any part of the said Stock, and for that purpose to make and execute all necessary acts of assignment and transfer, and one or more persons to substitute with like full power.

"Dated 19

"JOHN BROWN.

"Signed and acknowledged in presence of

"The witness must state his address and occupation. The Company reserves the right of requiring further identification of the transferor's signature.

"*Notice*.—The signature to this assignment must correspond with the name as written upon the face of the certificate, in every particular, without alteration or enlargement, or any change whatever." (See STOCK TRUST CERTIFICATE.)

AMORTISATION OR AMORTISEMENT. The redemption of loans or bonds by annual payments from a sinking fund. The sinking fund is built up for the purpose of redeeming annually such an amount of bonds as are due to be paid off, along with the interest on outstanding bonds.

An amortisation table is printed on certain bonds which are repayable in this manner, showing what amount is redeemable each year.

AMOUNT OF BILL OR CHEQUE. The amount must be "a sum certain in money." The amount is usually in words, in the body of a cheque, and, at the bottom left-hand corner, in figures. In bills the figures are usually at the top left-hand corner. The amount must be expressed in English money, and if it include a halfpenny, the halfpenny is disregarded.

The Bills of Exchange Act, 1882, does not specifically say that the amount must be stated in words, and it would therefore appear that a banker could not legally refuse payment of a cheque where the sum was expressed in figures only, instead of in words and figures. It is the practice, however, to return a cheque for completion when the amount is not in words. If the amount is in words only, it is customary to pay the cheque.

In drawing cheques, drafts, etc., the words of the amount should be written closely together, so as to prevent any possibility of an alteration, and the figures should be commenced close to the £, the space between the pounds and the shillings being filled with a line. Plain, large, and heavy figures help to prevent fraudulent alterations.

If a cheque is drawn as "Ten six shillings and eight pence," and the amount in figures clearly £10 6*s*. 8*d*., it is not usual to return the cheque merely because the word "pounds" has been omitted, if it is apparently only a clerical error.

As to a bill expressed in foreign money,

see FOREIGN BILL. (See ALTERATIONS, "AMOUNTS DIFFER.")

"AMOUNTS DIFFER." If the amount in words on a cheque or bill differs from the amount in figures, the cheque or bill is usually returned unpaid by the drawee banker, with the answer "amounts differ," or some similar words. Some bankers, however, pay the less amount.

In practice a banker rarely pays the amount in words if it is the larger amount, although by the Bills of Exchange Act, 1882, Section 9, s.s. 2, "where the sum payable is expressed in words and also in figures, and there is a discrepancy between the two, the sum denoted by the words is the amount payable." Most persons in dealing with cheques and bills look only at the figures and not at the words. Where a drawee accepts a bill on which the amount in figures is stated as £50, and he takes that as the amount of the bill when accepting it, not noticing that the words state the amount as "Five hundred pounds," no banker would be inclined to pay the amount in words, unless authorised by the acceptor to do so.

"AND REDUCED." Where the share capital of a company has been reduced, the words "and reduced" must be added to the name of the company, after the word "limited," until such date as the court may fix. (See REDUCTION OF SHARE CAPITAL.)

ANGLO A. A Stock Exchange name for Anglo-American Telegraph Company Deferred ordinary stock.

ANNA. (See FOREIGN MONEYS—INDIA.)

ANNUAL GENERAL MEETING. A general meeting of every company shall be held once at the least in every calendar year, and not more than fifteen months after the last preceding general meeting. (See Section 64 of the Companies (Consolidation) Act, 1908, under heading MEETINGS.)

Some companies have two general meetings each year. The usual business of a general meeting is receiving the report of the directors, considering the balance sheet, sanctioning a dividend, electing directors in place of those retiring by rotation, and appointing the auditors.

ANNUAL LIST OF MEMBERS OF COMPANY. By Section 21 of the Bank Charter Act, every banker in England and Wales must on the 1st day of January in each year, or within fifteen days thereafter, make a return to the Commissioners of Stamps and Taxes (now Inland Revenue) of his name, residence, and occupation, or in the case of a company or partnership, of the name, residence, and occupation of every member and also the name of the firm under which such banker or company carry on business. If a banker or company omits or refuses to make such return within the fifteen days mentioned, or shall wilfully make other than a true return, every one so offending shall forfeit the sum of £50.

By the same Section the Commissioners had to publish a copy of the return in certain newspapers, but, by Section 57 of 43 & 44 Vict. c. 20, it shall not be obligatory on the Commissioners to publish in any newspaper any return made to them by any banking company, which is duly registered under the provisions of 6 Geo. IV c. 42, 7 Geo. IV c. 46, 7 Geo. IV c. 67, and the Companies Acts or any of them.

The above return is not necessary if the provisions of the Companies (Consolidation) Act, 1908, with regard to the annual list of members are complied with, namely :—

Every company having a share capital shall once at least in every year send to the registrar of companies a list (called the "Annual Return") of all persons, who, on the fourteenth day after the first ordinary general meeting in the year, are members of the company, and of all persons who have ceased to be members since the date of the last return. The list must state the names, addresses, and occupations of all the past and present members therein mentioned, and the number of shares held by each of the existing members at the date of the return, specifying shares transferred since the date of the last return and the dates of registration of the transfers, and must contain a summary specifying various particulars regarding the shares. (For full details see Section 26, Companies (Consolidation) Act, 1908, under REGISTER OF MEMBERS OF COMPANY.) The list must be completed within seven days after the fourteenth day, above mentioned, and forwarded forthwith to the registrar.

The list for the registrar must be written upon special forms for the purpose, and be impressed with a five-shilling fee stamp. (See COMPANIES.)

ANNUAL RETURN. (See ANNUAL LIST OF MEMBERS OF COMPANY.)

ANNUITANT. A person who is in the receipt of an annuity.

ANNUITY. (From Latin *annus*, a year.) A sum of money paid yearly, or it may be by quarterly or half-yearly payments. A life annuity is payable only during a person's life-time; a perpetual annuity is payable in perpetuity. A deferred annuity is one which does not take effect till after a certain period, whereas an immediate annuity begins at once. A terminable annuity ceases at a certain fixed time.

An annuity may be created by will, or during the life-time of the donor. Annuities may be purchased from the Government or an insurance office. A person who has no one dependent upon him sometimes sinks his capital in the purchase of an annuity, which will produce a better income than if he lent or invested the money. An annual payment received from land is a rent, not an annuity.

Consols are really perpetual annuities, though it is customary to refer to Consols as stock, and to the half-yearly payments as dividends.

Table showing the value of an immediate life annuity of £1 according to the age and sex of the person upon whose life the annuity is to depend.

Age of the Person at the time of Purchase upon whose life the Annuity is to depend.	Males. Money to be paid down in One Sum at the time of Purchase.			Females. Money to be paid down in One Sum at the time of Purchase.		
	£	s.	d.	£	s.	d.
If 15 and under 16 . .	23	17	10	25	16	6
16 ,, 17 . .	23	13	6	25	12	7
17 ,, 18 . .	23	9	1	25	8	8
18 ,, 19 . .	23	4	9	25	4	8
19 ,, 20 . .	23	0	4	25	0	8
20 ,, 21 . .	22	15	10	24	16	6
21 ,, 22 . .	22	11	4	24	12	4
22 ,, 23 . .	22	6	9	24	8	1
23 ,, 24 . .	22	2	3	24	3	10
24 ,, 25 . .	21	17	7	23	19	5
25 ,, 26 . .	21	12	11	23	15	0
26 ,, 27 . .	21	8	3	23	10	6
27 ,, 28 . .	21	3	6	23	5	11
28 ,, 29 . .	20	18	9	23	1	3
29 ,, 30 . .	20	13	11	22	16	6
30 ,, 31 . .	20	9	1	22	11	8
31 ,, 32 . .	20	4	2	22	6	9
32 ,, 33 . .	19	19	2	22	1	9
33 ,, 34 . .	19	14	2	21	16	7
34 ,, 35 . .	19	9	2	21	11	5
35 ,, 36 . .	19	4	1	21	6	2
36 ,, 37 . .	18	18	11	21	0	9
37 ,, 38 . .	18	13	9	20	15	3
38 ,, 39 . .	18	8	6	20	9	7
39 ,, 40 . .	18	3	2	20	3	11
40 ,, 41 . .	17	17	10	19	18	0

The following is a form of an insurance company's annuity receipt:—

INSURANCE COMPANY.

Annuity Receipt No. Deposit £ Annuity £

Received from this day of 19 the sum of pounds, being the purchase money for an annuity of on the life of himself.

} Directors.

, Secretary.

By the Stamp Act, 1891:—

ANNUITY, conveyance in consideration of. (See CONVEYANCE ON SALE, and Section 56.)

purchase of. (See CONVEYANCE ON SALE, and Section 60.)

creation of, by way of security. (See MORTGAGE, etc., and Section 87.)

Instruments relating to, upon any other occasion. (See BOND, COVENANT, etc.)

ANSWERS. When a bill or cheque, for any reason, is returned unpaid, the answer given by the drawee banker, as the reason of its return, must not be at variance with the actual fact. The answer is usually written upon the bill or cheque. A banker might be held liable in damages if he returned a cheque marked "Refer to drawer" when the correct answer should have been "Postdated," or "Figures and words differ," or some similar answer.

It should be noted that a careless use of an abbreviated answer may render a banker liable. In an action on a returned bill which had been marked "N.A.," it was suggested that those letters meant "No assets" or "No account," as well as "No advice," which was the answer the banker intended to give.

In dishonouring a cheque presented across the counter, the reason for dishonouring it is not always written upon the cheque; a verbal answer is usually sufficient.

A banker is sometimes able to get a technical mistake in a cheque corrected by the drawer, and where this can be conveniently done it is much better than returning the cheque.

Where there are not sufficient funds to meet a cheque, and there is also a technical irregularity in it, when returning the cheque, the answer given often refers only to the irregularity and not to the want of funds.

particularly if it is expected that by the time the irregularity has been put right the banker will be in a position to pay it.

The words "Will pay on banker's confirmation" are occasionally added to an answer, when the sole reason for the return of the cheque is a technical one, such as "Indorsement irregular." If the drawer dies before the cheque arrives back, or the account changes so as not to admit of the cheque being debited, the banker is not liable, by reason of the words used, to pay the cheque. The words have reference only to the technical irregularity and not to the payment of the amount.

The following are some of the "answers" which are given on cheques and bills (the answer being generally written in ink on the left-hand top corner) :—

"Acceptor bankrupt."

"Acceptor dead." (See DEATH OF ACCEPTOR.)

"Account closed" (more often "No account").

"Amounts differ" (*q.v.*).

"Crossed to two bankers" (*q.v.*).

"Date incomplete."

"Drawer bankrupt."

"Drawer dead." (See DEATH OF DRAWER.)

"Effects not cleared" (*q.v.*).

"Incompletely signed" (or "Further signature required").

"Indorsement irregular."

"Indorsement required."

"Indorsement requires confirmation."

"Insufficient funds."

"Insufficiently stamped."

"Mutilated cheque" (*q.v.*).

"No account" (*q.v.*).

"No advice" (*q.v.*).

"No assets."

"No effects."

"No orders" (*q.v.*).

"Not provided for," "n.p.f." (*q.v.*).

"Not sufficient," "N.S." (*q.v.*) (also written "Not sufficient funds").

"Out of date." (See STALE CHEQUE.)

"Payment stopped" (*q.v.*).

"Postdated" (*q.v.*).

"Present again" (*q.v.*).

"Refer to acceptor." "R/A."

"Refer to drawer," "R/D." (*q.v.*).

"Re-present."

"Requires banker's crossing" (*q.v.*).

"Requires stamp of banker to whom crossed."

"Signature differs" (i.e., differs from the customer's usual hand or method of signing).

"Stale." (See STALE CHEQUE.)

"Words and figures differ." (See "AMOUNTS DIFFER.")

ANTE-DATED. Ante-dating is placing a date on a document prior to that on which it is actually signed.

A bill of exchange is not invalid by reason only that it is ante-dated (Section 13, s.s. 2, Bills of Exchange Act, 1882). The date of the stamp upon an ante-dated bill may therefore be subsequent to the date of the bill, and give the bill the appearance of not being in accordance with the Stamp Act, 1891, Section 37, s.s. 2 :—"No bill of exchange shall be stamped with an impressed stamp after the execution thereof."

APPLICATION FOR SHARES. A form of application for shares usually accompanies a prospectus offering to the public for subscription or purchase shares in a company.

When the form is filled up by an applicant, it is despatched, along with the sum payable on application, to the company or the company's bankers. If the application is successful, a letter of allotment (see ALLOTMENT) is sent to the applicant in due course.

The following is a specimen of an application form :—

THE BRITISH BAKING COMPANY, LIMITED.

Capital £ .

Divided into shares of £1 each.

Form of Application for Shares.

Payable on application ; on allotment ; one month after allotment ; and the balance as and when required, in calls of not more than per share, and at intervals of not less than months.

To the Directors of

The British Baking Company, Limited.

Gentlemen,—Having paid to your bankers the sum of £ , being a deposit of per share payable on application for shares in the above Company, I hereby request you to allot me that number of shares, and I agree to accept such shares, or any less number that may be allotted to me, upon the terms of the Company's Prospectus filed with the Registrar of Joint Stock Companies, and of the Memorandum and Articles of Association of the Company, and I authorise you to place my name upon the Register of Shareholders in respect of any shares so allotted to me.

Name (in full)

Address

Occupation or Description

Ordinary Signature

Date

Attached to the application form is usually

a form of receipt to be filled up by the banker when the money is paid :—

RECEIPT FOR PAYMENT ON APPLICATION.

Received the day of 19
of on account of the British Baking Company, Limited, the sum of £ being per share, payable on application, for shares of £1 each in the above-named Company.

For X and Y Bank, Ltd.

£

Stamp.

N.B.—This half, when receipted, must be preserved by the shareholder, to be exchanged in due course for the share certificate.

APPLICATION FORMS. A general term signifying any form which is filled up and signed by a customer when making an application to a banker, e.g., an application form for a deposit receipt or for a banker's draft.

APPLICATION PAYMENTS. Payments made by bankers, upon application, to wholesale houses in London, on behalf of country customers.

The practice is as follows: A country customer (generally a retail draper) hands to his banker a list of the payments which he wishes to be made to wholesale houses in London; the banker forwards to his London office, or London Agents, forms of cheques filled up with the various amounts, and drawn upon the London bank, to be sent to the wholesale creditor, or handed to him when applied for. Each cheque requires to be signed by the respective creditor as the drawer. These cheques must, like ordinary cheques, bear a penny stamp, and the Inland Revenue Authorities demand that the list supplied to the country banker must bear a penny stamp for each name on the list. Each separate payment, therefore, costs twopence for stamp duty.

APPOINTMENT. By the Stamp Act, 1891, the duty is :—

	£	s.	d.
APPOINTMENT of a new trustee, and APPOINTMENT in execution of a power of any property, or of any use, share, or interest in any property, by any instrument not being a will	0	10	0

And see Section 62, under heading CONVEYANCE.

APPRAISEMENT. The stamp duty upon an appraisement or valuation is given in the schedule to the Stamp Act, 1891, as follows :—

	£	s.	d.
APPRAISEMENT OR VALUATION of any property, or of any interest therein, or of the annual value thereof, or of any dilapidations, or of any repairs wanted, or of the materials and labour used or to be used in any building, or of any artificers' work whatsoever.			
Where the amount of the appraisement or valuation does not exceed £5	0	0	3
Exceeds £5 and does not exceed £10	0	0	6
,, £10 ,, ,, £20	0	1	0
,, £20 ,, ,, £30	0	1	6
,, £30 ,, ,, £40	0	2	0
,, £40 ,, ,, £50	0	2	6
,, £50 ,, ,, £100	0	5	0
,, £100 ,, ,, £200	0	10	0
,, £200 ,, ,, £500	0	15	0
,, £500	1	0	0

Exemptions.

(1) Appraisement or valuation made for, and for the information of, one party only, and not being in any manner obligatory as between parties either by agreement or operation of law.

(2) Appraisement or valuation made in pursuance of the order of any Court of Admiralty, or of any Court of Appeal, from a judgment of any Court of Admiralty.

(3) Appraisement or valuation of property of a deceased person made for the information of an executor or other person required to deliver in England or Ireland an affidavit, or to record in any commissary court in Scotland an inventory of the estate of such deceased person.

(4) Appraisement or valuation of any property made for the purpose of ascertaining the legacy or succession or account duty payable in respect thereof.

Section 24 of the same Act provides :—

"(1) Every appraiser, by whom an appraisement or valuation chargeable with stamp duty is made, shall, within fourteen days after the making thereof, write out the same, in words and figures showing the full amount thereof, upon duly stamped material, and if he neglects or omits so to do, or in any other manner discloses the amount of the appraisement or valuation, he shall incur a fine of fifty pounds.

"(2) Every person who receives from any appraiser, or pays for the making of, any such appraisement or valuation, shall, unless the same be written out and stamped as aforesaid, incur a fine of twenty pounds."

APPRAISER. A person who appraises or values property. The licence of an appraiser costs £2 per annum. (See APPRAISEMENT.)

APPRENTICE. In some banks all junior clerks, on entering the bank's service, are apprenticed either for a certain number of years or until they reach the age of twenty-one. An indenture of apprenticeship (stamp 2*s.* 6*d.*) is entered into, and the father or guardian is usually a party thereto. The apprentice agrees to serve faithfully, preserve secrets, and conduct himself in a proper manner; the father agrees to provide the apprentice with proper clothing, etc.; and the bank agrees to instruct the youth in the business of a banker.

APPROPRIATED STAMPS. Section 10 of the Stamp Act, 1891, enacts :—

"(1) A stamp which by any word or words on the face of it is appropriated to any particular description of instrument is not to be used, or, if used, is not to be available, for an instrument of any other description.

"(2) An instrument falling under the particular description to which any stamp is so appropriated as aforesaid is not to be deemed duly stamped, unless it is stamped with the stamp so appropriated."

Appropriated stamps are used for :—

Bankruptcy, proof of debt. The stamp is adhesive.

Brokers' contract notes. The stamp is adhesive.

Foreign bills—that is, bills and promissory notes drawn or made out of the United Kingdom except such as are payable on demand, at sight or on presentation, for which a postage stamp is used; or at not exceeding three days after date or sight, for which a postage or appropriated stamp may be used. See under BILL OF EXCHANGE. Foreign bill stamps are adhesive.

Inland bills and promissory notes drawn or made in the United Kingdom (except such as are payable on demand, at sight, or on presentation, or at not exceeding three days after date or sight, when a penny postage or impressed stamp may be used), and the appropriated stamps must be impressed.

APPROPRIATION OF PAYMENTS. If a customer pays in money for a particular purpose, the banker must apply it accordingly. For example, if an amount is paid in to meet a specified cheque or bill, it must be used for that purpose, but if the amount is paid in without any particular instructions being given, the banker may appropriate the money in reduction of the customer's indebtedness. According to the rule in Clayton's case, an amount paid to credit is held to be a payment of the earliest unpaid debit in the account, and it is the sum first paid in that is first drawn out. (See CLAYTON'S CASE.)

APPROVED ACCEPTANCE. A seller may agree to take an "approved acceptance" from a purchaser—that is, the acceptance must be one to which no reasonable objection can be raised.

APPURTENANCES. Things or rights which appertain or belong to a property and which pass along with the property.

ARBITRAGE. The purchase of securities on one stock exchange, or centre, and the immediate sale of the same securities on another stock exchange, or centre, where a higher price is ruling, in order to obtain the benefit of the difference in prices between the two markets. Arbitrage transactions take place in stocks and shares, in bills, and also in bullion.

ARBITRATION. A matter which is in dispute is often settled by means of arbitration—that is, the case is referred by the disputing parties to one or more persons, the arbitrators, who act as arbiters or judges, and upon whose decision the disputants agree to abide. The decision of an arbitrator is called the award. (See AWARD.)

By Section 119 of the Companies (Consolidation) Act, 1908 :—

"(1) A company may by writing under its common seal agree to refer and may refer to arbitration, in accordance with the Railway Companies Arbitration Act, 1859, any existing or future difference between itself and any other company or person.

"(2) Companies parties to the arbitration may delegate to the arbitrator power to settle any terms or to determine any matter capable of being lawfully settled or determined by the companies themselves, or by their directors or other managing body.

(3) All the provisions of the Railway Companies Arbitration Act, 1859, shall apply to arbitrations between companies and persons in pursuance of this Act; and in the construction of those provisions 'the companies' shall include companies under this Act." (See COMPANIES.)

ARBITRATION OF EXCHANGE. The operation by which a merchant pays a debt in one country by means of a bill payable in another. The price of bills payable in different centres is taken into account, and if it is found that it is cheaper to settle a debt in, say, Paris, by means of a bill upon, say, Amsterdam or Berlin, than by a bill upon Paris, the merchant takes advantage of that fact and makes payment accordingly.

Simple arbitration is where only one intermediate place is included in the transaction; where there are several places it is called compound arbitration.

ARRANGEMENT WITH CREDITORS. Where a person is unable to pay his debts he may (apart altogether from the Bankruptcy Acts) endeavour to make an arrangement with his creditors with respect to the money he owes to them. A debtor usually offers—

(1) To pay the creditors so much in the pound in full satisfaction of his debts to them (see COMPOSITION WITH CREDITORS); or

(2) To transfer his property to a trustee to be realised and the proceeds divided amongst the creditors. (See ASSIGNMENT FOR BENEFIT OF CREDITORS.)

If such an arrangement is made by deed or agreement, the deed of arrangement must be registered within seven days. (See DEED OF ARRANGEMENT.)

In the case of a proposed arrangement between a company and its creditors, the Companies (Consolidation) Act, 1908, Section 120, enacts:—

"(1) Where a compromise or arrangement is proposed between a company and its creditors or any class of them, or between the company and its members or any class of them, the court may, on the application in a summary way of the company or of any creditor or member of the company or, in the case of a company being wound up, of the liquidator, order a meeting of the creditors or class of creditors, or of the members of the company or class of members, as the case may be, to be summoned in such manner as the court directs.

"(2) If a majority in number representing three-fourths in value of the creditors or class of creditors, or members or class of members, as the case may be, present either in person or by proxy at the meeting, agree to any compromise or arrangement, the compromise or arrangement shall, if sanctioned by the court, be binding on all the creditors or the class of creditors, or on the members or class of members, as the case may be, and also on the company or, in the case of a company in the course of being wound up, on the liquidator and contributories of the company.

"(3) In this Section the expression 'company' means any company liable to be wound up under this Act."

ARRESTMENT. In Scotland, a legal process by which a banker is ordered not to part with funds belonging to a certain customer who is a debtor to the person on whose behalf the arrestment has taken place. The equivalent in England is attachment (*q.v.*).

ARTICLES OF ASSOCIATION. The articles of association are the regulations or bye-laws of a joint stock company by which its affairs are governed.

Subject to the provisions of the memorandum of association, a company can alter or add to the articles. (See Section 13, below.)

The memorandum forms the boundary to the directors' powers, but within that boundary the company can make its own rules and regulations, and these are contained in the articles of association.

Before dealing with a company a banker should be careful to make himself acquainted with the memorandum and articles of association of the company, and particularly as to the powers of the directors to borrow and to mortgage the company's property.

Every person dealing with a company is deemed to have notice of the contents of the memorandum and articles.

The following are the provisions contained in the Companies (Consolidation) Act, 1908 :—

Registration of Articles.

"10. (1) There may, in the case of a company limited by shares, and there shall in the case of a company limited by guarantee or unlimited, be registered with the memorandum articles of association signed by the subscribers to the memorandum and prescribing regulations for the company.

"(2) Articles of association may adopt all or any of the regulations contained in Table A. in the First Schedule to this Act.

(3) In the case of an unlimited company or a company limited by guarantee the articles, if the company has a share capital, must state the amount of share capital with which the company proposes to be registered.

(4) In the case of an unlimited company or a company limited by guarantee, if the company has not a share capital, the articles must state the number of members with which the company proposes to be registered, for the purpose of enabling the registrar to determine the fees payable on registration.

Application of Table A.

"11. In the case of a company limited by shares and registered after the commencement of this Act, if articles are not registered, or, if articles are registered, in so far as the articles do not exclude or modify the regulations in Table A. in the First Schedule to this Act, those regulations shall, so far as applicable, be the regulations of the company in the same manner and to the same extent as if they were contained in duly registered articles.

Form, Stamp, and Signature of Articles.

"12. Articles must—

(*a*) be printed ;

(*b*) be divided into paragraphs numbered consecutively ;

(*c*) bear the same stamp as if they were contained in a deed ; and

(*d*) be signed by each subscriber of the memorandum of association in the presence of at least one witness who must attest the signature, and that attestation shall be sufficient in Scotland as well as in England and Ireland.

Alteration of Articles by Special Resolution

"13. (1) Subject to the provisions of this Act and to the conditions contained in its memorandum, a company may by special resolution alter or add to its articles ; and any alteration or addition so made shall be as valid as if originally contained in the articles, and be subject in like manner to alteration by special resolution.

"(2) The power of altering articles under this section shall, in the case of an unlimited company formed and registered under the Joint Stock Companies Acts, extend to altering any regulations relating to the amount of capital or its distribution into shares, notwithstanding that those regulations are contained in the memorandum."

Table A., referred to in the above sections, contains regulations which may be adopted for a company's articles of association, but in many companies special articles are prepared. The regulations in Table A. relate to :—business, shares, lien, calls on shares, transfer and transmission of shares, forfeiture of shares, conversion of shares into stock, share warrants, alteration of capital, general meetings, proceedings at general meeting, votes of members, directors, powers and duties of directors, the seal, disqualifications of directors, rotation of directors, proceedings of directors, dividends and reserve, accounts, audit, notices.

The following sections set forth the general provisions of the Act with respect to the memorandum and articles :—

Effect of Memorandum and Articles.

"14. (1) The memorandum and articles shall, when registered, bind the company and the members thereof to the same extent as if they respectively had been signed and sealed by each member, and contained covenants on the part of each member, his heirs, executors, and administrators, to observe all the provisions of the memorandum and of the articles, subject to the provisions of this Act.

"(2) All money payable by any member to the company under the memorandum or articles shall be a debt due from him to the company, and in England and Ireland be of the nature of a specialty debt.

Registration of Memorandum and Articles.

"15. The memorandum and the articles (if any) shall be delivered to the registrar of companies for that part of the United Kingdom in which the registered office of the company is stated by the memorandum to be situate, and he shall retain and register them.

Effect of Registration.

"16. (1) On the registration of the memorandum of a company, the registrar shall certify under his hand that the company is incorporated, and in the case of a limited company that the company is limited.

"(2) From the date of incorporation mentioned in the certificate of incorporation, the subscribers of the memorandum together with such other persons as may from time to time become members of the company, shall be a body corporate by the name contained in the memorandum, capable forthwith of exercising all the functions of an incorporated company, and having perpetual succession and a common seal, with power to hold lands, but with such liability on the part of the members to contribute to the assets of the company in the event of its being wound up as is mentioned in this Act.

Conclusiveness of Certificate of Incorporation.

"17. (1) A certificate of incorporation given by the registrar in respect of any association shall be conclusive evidence that all the requirements of this Act in respect of registration and of matters precedent and incidental thereto have been complied with, and that the association is a company authorised to be registered and duly registered under this Act.

"(2) A statutory declaration by a solicitor of the High Court, and in Scotland by an enrolled law agent, engaged in the formation of the company, or by a person named in the articles as a director or secretary of the company, of compliance with all or any of the said requirements shall be produced to the registrar, and the registrar may accept such a declaration as sufficient evidence of compliance.

Copies of Memorandum and Articles to be given to Members.

"18. (1) Every company shall send to every member, at his request, and on payment of one shilling or such less sum as the company may prescribe, a copy of the memorandum and of the articles (if any).

"(2) If a company makes default in complying with the requirements of this Section, it shall be liable for each offence to a fine not exceeding one pound." (See COMPANIES, MEMORANDUM OF ASSOCIATION, TABLE A.)

"AS PER ADVICE." These words, when found upon a bill of exchange, imply that the drawer has drawn the bill in accordance with a letter of advice.

ASSETS. The goods, property, and resources of all kinds, of a company or an individual, which are available for the payment of the debts or liabilities. A banker's assets are his cash in hand or with his London agents or at the Bank of England, money at call and short notice, investments in Government and other securities, bills, advances to customers, premises, etc. (See BALANCE SHEET.)

ASSIGNMENT. To assign a right or a property is to transfer it, or make it over, to another person.

As to the stamp duty on an assignment by way of security, see MORTGAGE; and upon a sale or otherwise, see CONVEYANCE.

As to an assignment of a life policy, see LIFE POLICY.

ASSIGNMENT FOR BENEFIT OF CREDITORS. A person who is unable to pay his debts may legally call his creditors together and offer to transfer his property to a trustee, in order that it may be realised and the proceeds apportioned amongst the creditors, according to the amount of their claims, in full discharge of what he is owing to them.

The deed assigning the property to the trustee must be registered within seven days, otherwise it is void. (See DEED OF ARRANGEMENT.) Such a deed is binding only upon the creditors who assent to it.

An assignment of the debtor's property for the benefit of his creditors, is an arrangement quite apart from proceedings under the Bankruptcy Acts.

No further cheques must be paid upon

the account of a customer who has made an assignment.

Where a debtor assigns his property to a trustee for the benefit of his creditors it is an act of bankruptcy (see ACTS OF BANKRUPTCY), and a debtor may be adjudged a bankrupt upon a bankruptcy petition presented within three months from the date of an act of bankruptcy (see RECEIVING ORDER). When such a petition is presented and the debtor is made bankrupt, the deed of assignment becomes void. The trustee is therefore liable at any time within three months from the date of the deed of assignment, to be called upon, in the event of the debtor's bankruptcy, to hand over to the official receiver or trustee in bankruptcy, all funds and property of the debtor which have come into his possession since the date of the deed of assignment. Any balance in the hands of a banker should, therefore, not be paid to the trustee of a deed of assignment until the expiration of three months from the date thereof. (See BANKRUPTCY, COMPOSITION WITH CREDITORS.)

ASSIGNMENT OF DEBTS. (See DEBTS, ASSIGNMENT OF.)

ASSIGNMENT OF LIFE POLICY. (See LIFE POLICY.)

ASSOCIATION OF ENGLISH COUNTRY BANKERS. Every country bank in England and Wales is entitled to membership, and to one vote through its representative at any general meeting of the Association.

The annual subscription is :—

£2 for each bank having not more than fifteen branches.

£5 for each bank having more than fifteen but not more than fifty branches.

£10 10*s*. for each bank having more than fifty branches.

The affairs of the Association are managed by a president, vice-presidents, a general committee of not more than twenty-four members, and an executive council.

The Association appoints a secretary qualified to watch over, and report to the executive council on, all matters arising in Parliament or elsewhere affecting directly or indirectly the interests of the English country banks, or any section thereof.

If any questions arise affecting the special interests of issuing banks, or of non-issuing banks, or of private banks, or of joint stock banks, the members of the general committee representing such banks respectively are entitled to meet separately to discuss and to take action upon such questions, and have power to co-opt for such purpose representatives of any other banks having the same interests.

The annual general meeting of the Association is held in the month of May.

ASSOCIATIONS. (See SOCIETIES.)

ASSUMED NAME. Where a person trades in an assumed name, and signs cheques and bills in that name, it is customary for a banker to receive a written authority from him to honour cheques or bills when signed in the trade name. The authority is signed by the person in his real name and a specimen signature of the assumed name is given.

The Bills of Exchange Act, 1882, permits a bill to be signed in an assumed name. By Section 23 :—

"(1) Where a person signs a bill in a trade or assumed name, he is liable thereon as if he had signed it in his own name."

A purchaser of a business often assumes, for a time at any rate, the name of the person who built up the connection.

ASSURANCE. Originally the word "assurance" appears to have been applied only to life assurance, and the word "insurance" to fire insurance, but either word is now commonly used without regard to its original meaning. (See FIDELITY GUARANTEE, FIRE INSURANCE, LIFE POLICY, MARINE INSURANCE POLICY, POLICY OF INSURANCE, SINKING FUND ASSURANCE, SPECIE—TRANSMISSION OF.)

ATTACHMENT. Where a person has obtained a judgment for the recovery of money, he may, by application to the Court, obtain a garnishee order which, when served upon a banker, will attach any money in the banker's hands belonging to the person against whom judgment was given. (See GARNISHEE ORDER.)

ATTENDANCE BOOK. Most banks require every clerk to sign the attendance book on arrival at the office each morning, and to do so before a certain specified time, after which a line is usually ruled across the page, and all late arrivals must of necessity sign below it.

It is the duty of the chief clerk, or some other responsible official, to see that the book is duly signed day by day. In the case of absence on leave, or on annual holiday, or on account of illness, a note is made in the book to that effect.

The clerk who is always punctual is, as a rule, the one who may be depended upon to be up to time in the discharge of any duty which may be given to him to fulfil. Half an hour in the morning is more valuable than an hour at night, and he who turns up readily in the morning, because he wants to get on with his work, is worth more than the man who drags himself in at the last moment, merely because he knows he cannot with impunity delay his arrival any longer.

ATTESTATION. A formal witnessing of a signature.

In the case of a will, the testator's signature must be made, or acknowledged, by the testator in the presence of two or more witnesses present at the same time, each of whom must attest or "witness" the will. There is no special form of attestation necessary, but the following is a common attestation clause :—

"Signed by the said , the testator, in the presence of us, both present at the same time, who in his presence and at his request and in the presence of each other have hereunto set our names as witnesses.

"

"

The witnesses give their names, addresses and descriptions. A legacy to a witness or to the wife of a witness is void.

Where a signature is witnessed, as in the case of a transfer of shares, the form is usually :—

"Signed, sealed, and delivered by the above named in the presence of

"*Signature*
"*Address*
"*Occupation* ."

When a transfer is executed out of Great Britain the signature should be attested by H.M. Consul or Vice-Consul, a clergyman, magistrate, notary public, or other person holding a public appointment. When a witness is a female, she must state whether she is a spinster, wife or widow ; and if a wife she must give her husband's name, address and occupation.

Where any material alterations or interlineations have been made in a deed, they should be referred to in the attestation clause as having been made before execution of the document.

In a document under hand, a witness often signs simply as :—"Witness, John Brown," and gives his address and description.

In Scotland, as for example where a customer signs a banker's printed memorandum of deposit, a clause, called the "testing clause," in the following form is included before he signs :—

"In witness whereof these presents in so far as not printed written by *name of person who filled up the form*] and subscribed by me the said at upon the day of one thousand nine hundred and before these witnesses of [*description*] and of [*description*].

"*Witness*.
Witness."

The testing clause in a Scotch deed also states the number of pages on which it is written, and mentions any important alterations which have been made in the document.

Where a signature by "mark" is witnessed, the form is :—

his
John × Brown.
mark

Witness,
John Jones,
Warwick Road,
Carlisle, Builder.

In banks it is customary for two persons to witness a "mark."

In the case of a deed which is executed by a "mark," the words used are to the following effect :—

"Signed, sealed, and delivered by the above-named John Brown, he having signed by a mark in consequence of being unable to sign his name, in the presence of us, the deed having first been read over and explained to him when he appeared perfectly to understand the same."

In Scotland, when a person is unable to write, a deed must be executed for him by a notary public or a justice of the peace in the presence of two witnesses, as a deed cannot be executed by a mark.

ATTESTED COPY. A copy which is certified by a witness to be an exact copy of the original document. (See CERTIFIED COPY.)

The following is a specimen of the form of attestation at the foot of a copy of a document of several pages :—

"We have carefully examined this and the two foregoing sheets with the original document and attest it to be a true copy thereof. Dated this day of 19 .

} Clerks with Brown & Jones,
Solicitors, Carlisle."

For Stamp duty, see COPY.

ATTORNEY, LETTER AND POWER OF. (See POWER OF ATTORNEY.)

ATTORNEY, WARRANT OF. (See WARRANT OF ATTORNEY.)

ATTORNMENT. An attornment clause in a mortgage deed is where the mortgagor attorns or acknowledges himself the tenant of the mortgagee, at a rent usually of the same amount as the interest payable under the mortgage. By such a clause the relationship of landlord and tenant is created, and the mortgagee is thereby empowered to distrain for rent, and in that way enforce payment of the interest due on the debt. The rent must be a reasonable one, for if so excessive that it could never have been intended to be paid, it may be regarded by the Courts as an attempt to give the lender a preference in case of the debtor's bankruptcy. (See MORTGAGE.)

AUDITORS. The auditors of a company are appointed by the shareholders, and their particular function is to make an independent investigation of the company's affairs and to report to the shareholders.

The appointment, powers, and duties of auditors are set forth in the following sections of the Companies (Consolidation) Act, 1908 :—

Appointment and Remuneration of Auditors.

" 112. (1) Every company shall at each annual general meeting appoint an auditor or auditors to hold office until the next annual general meeting.

" (2) If an appointment of auditors is not made at an annual general meeting, the Board of Trade may, on the application of any member of the company, appoint an auditor of the company for the current year, and fix the remuneration to be paid to him by the company for his services.

(3) A director or officer of the company shall not be capable of being appointed auditor of the company.

" (4) A person, other than a retiring auditor, shall not be capable of being appointed auditor at an annual general meeting unless notice of an intention to nominate that person to the office of auditor has been given by a shareholder to the company not less than fourteen days before the annual general meeting, and the company shall send a copy of any such notice to the retiring auditor, and shall give notice thereof to the shareholders, either by advertisement or in any other mode allowed by the articles, not less than seven days before the annual general meeting :

Provided that if, after notice of the intention to nominate an auditor has been so given, an annual general meeting is called for a date fourteen days or less after the notice has been given, the notice, though not given within the time required by this provision, shall be deemed to have been properly given for the purposes thereof, and the notice to be sent or given by the company may, instead of being sent or given within the time required by this provision, be sent or given at the same time as the notice of the annual general meeting.

" (5) The first auditors of the company may be appointed by the directors before the statutory meeting, and if so appointed shall hold office until the first annual general meeting, unless previously removed by a resolution of the shareholders in general meeting, in which case the shareholders at that meeting may appoint auditors.

" (6) The directors may fill any casual vacancy in the office of auditor, but while any such vacancy continues the surviving or continuing auditor or auditors, if any, may act.

" (7) The remuneration of the auditors of a company shall be fixed by the company in general meeting, except that the remuneration of any auditors appointed before the statutory meeting, or to fill any casual vacancy, may be fixed by the directors.

Powers and Duties of Auditors.

" 113. (1) Every auditor of a company shall have a right of access at all times to the books and accounts and vouchers of the company, and shall be entitled to require from the directors and officers of the company such information and explanation as may be necessary for the performance of the duties of the auditors.

" (2) The auditors shall make a report to the shareholders on the accounts examined by them, and on every balance sheet laid before the company in general meeting during their tenure of office, and the report shall state—

(a) whether or not they have obtained all the information and explanations they have required ; and

(b) whether, in their opinion, the balance sheet referred to in the report is properly drawn up so as to exhibit a true and correct view of the state of the company's affairs according to the best of their information and the explanations given to them, and as shown by the books of the company.

" (3) The balance sheet shall be signed on behalf of the board by two of the directors of the company, or if there is only one director, by that director, and the auditors' report shall be attached to the balance sheet, or there shall be inserted at the foot of the balance sheet a reference to the report, and the report shall be read before the company in general meeting, and shall be open to inspection by any shareholder.

Any shareholder shall be entitled to be furnished with a copy of the balance sheet and auditors' report at a charge not exceeding sixpence for every hundred words.

" (4) If any copy of a balance sheet which has not been signed as required by this Section is issued, circulated, or published, or if any copy of a balance sheet is issued, circulated, or published without either having a copy of the auditors' report attached thereto or containing such reference to that report as is required by this Section, the company, and every director, manager, secretary, or other officer of the company who is knowingly a party to the default, shall on conviction be liable to a fine not exceeding fifty pounds.

" (5) In the case of a banking company registered after the fifteenth day of August eighteen hundred and seventy-nine—

(a) if the company has branch banks beyond the limits of Europe, it shall be sufficient if the auditor is allowed access to such copies of and extracts from the books and accounts of any such branch as have been transmitted to the head office of the company in the United Kingdom ; and

(b) the balance sheet must be signed by the secretary or manager (if any), and where there are more than three directors of the company by at least three of those directors, and where there are not more than three directors by all the directors.

Rights of Preference Shareholders, etc., as to Receipt and Inspection of Reports, etc.

" 114. (1) Holders of preference shares and debentures of a company shall have the same right to receive and inspect the balance sheets of the company and the reports of the auditors and other reports as is possessed by the holders of ordinary shares in the company.

" (2) This Section shall not apply to a private company, nor to a company registered before the first day of July nineteen hundred and eight."

By Section 81, the names and addresses of the auditors, if any, must appear on the prospectus of a company. (See BALANCE SHEET, COMPANIES.)

AUTHORISED CAPITAL. The capital of a company as authorised by its memorandum of association. It is called also the "nominal" and "registered" capital. (See CAPITAL.)

AUTHORITIES. The authorities which bankers may receive from customers are in connection with many different matters. In all cases they should be in writing, and, in many cases, bankers have their own printed forms, which they prefer to be used.

Authorities are given for a banker to pay, on certain dates, subscriptions to societies and clubs, premiums on policies, etc., also for the periodical transfer of an amount from the account of the customer giving the authority to the credit of an account with another bank or of another customer in the same bank. Such transfers are made in accordance with the instructions in the authority, whether weekly, monthly, quarterly, half-yearly, yearly, or on particular dates, or on particular occasions, as, for instance, where an authority is given to transfer a specified amount from a No. 1 account to a No. 2 account when the balance on the latter account is almost exhausted.

Bankers receive instructions to pay calls, to pay over certain sums in exchange for specified documents, and also to hand over documents in exchange for certain sums, and in each case the particular instructions contained in the authority must be carefully observed. A record is made in a diary of all special payments, and in some offices a note may also with advantage be kept in the bill case under the correct date. Where subscriptions and other periodical payments are numerous, it is customary to keep a special book for the purpose, and detail under each day everything which is due to be paid on that day. (See BANKER'S ORDER.)

Authorities are often given in connection with signing upon accounts. In each case particulars of the authority, and, if only for a fixed period, the date of its expiry, should be noted in the ledger against the account. It is an advantage if these authorities are signed in the presence of a bank official. (See JOINT ACCOUNT, MANDATE.)

There are also authorities to give up to a third party articles left for safe custody (see SAFE CUSTODY) and to give up deeds, certificates and other documents which are held as security for an overdraft or loan. When such authorities are acted upon, the person receiving the securities should, of course, give a receipt for them. Where a customer authorises a banker to lend his securities to a solicitor, an undertaking should be taken from the solicitor to return the securities. (See SOLICITOR'S UNDERTAKING.)

An authority in connection with one matter must not be taken to include another, e.g., an ordinary authority for signing upon an account does not empower the person in whose favour it is given to withdraw securities or arrange an overdraft limit.

For convenience of reference, it is a good plan to sort the authorities into alphabetical cases, or to enter particulars of them in books, duly indexed, each entry and authority being numbered.

AVAL. French. An indorsement upon a bill or promissory note by a person who signs as a surety. Section 56 of the Bills of Exchange Act, 1882, provides that where a person signs a bill otherwise than as drawer or acceptor, he thereby incurs the liabilities of an indorser to a holder in due course.

AVERAGE. The average bank rate is ascertained as follows :—

3 %	for 20 days	;	3 × 20 =	60
4 %	,, 60 ,,	;	4 × 60 =	240
2½ %	,, 10 ,,	;	2½ × 10 =	25
2 %	,, 12 ,,	;	2 × 12 =	24
	102	)		349

Average for that period = £3 8 5

The average balance of an account is ascertained in the same way :—

Balance £2,500	for 20 days	=	50,000
1,800	,, 62 ,,	=	111,600
450	,, 18 ,,	=	8,100
3,260	,, 81 ,,	=	264,060
	181	)	433,760

Average balance for half-year = £2,396

In this example it is supposed that the balance has varied only four times during the half-year.

AVERAGE (IN SHIPPING). The amount payable by the owner of a ship and by the owners of the cargo, in proportion to their individual interests, to make good any loss caused by throwing part of the cargo overboard or cutting away the masts or such like things, in order to prevent the loss of the ship and the rest of the cargo. (See GENERAL AVERAGE.)

AVERAGE ADJUSTER. A person who settles or adjusts the amount to be paid by the owner of the ship and the owners of the cargo, in connection with any intentional losses which have been made for the safety of the ship or the cargo. (See GENERAL AVERAGE.)

AVERAGE BOND. Where a ship has suffered an intentional loss of cargo in order to save the ship and the rest of the cargo, the master of the ship obtains from the consignees of the goods, before delivery is made, a bond under which they agree to pay their proportion of the general average as soon as the amount is ascertained. (See GENERAL AVERAGE.)

AVERAGE CLAUSE. The clause in a marine insurance policy which may provide that certain articles are free from average, unless general, or the ship be stranded, and that other articles are free from average under, say, three per cent., unless general, or the ship be stranded, sunk, burnt or on fire.

Under an average clause in a fire policy, in the event of a fire, the amount payable by the insurance company will be, if the property is only partially destroyed, and has not been insured up to the full value of the property, a proportioned amount of the damage, based upon the proportion which the amount insured bears to the full value of the property. Where a property, value £1,000, is insured for £500, and damage by fire occurs to the extent of £300, the amount which the company will pay will be £150—that is, half the loss, because the property was insured for only half its value.

AVERAGING (STOCK EXCHANGE). A "bull" speculator on the Stock Exchange buys more of a certain stock he holds, when the price has fallen, so as to make the average price of the whole purchase less than the price paid for the original purchase; and a "bear" speculator, when the price rises against him, sells more of the stock so as to average the price.

AWARD. The decision of an arbitrator upon any matter in dispute which has been referred to him by the disputants.

By the Revenue Act, 1906, the stamp duty upon an award in England or Ireland, and award or decreet arbitral in Scotland is ten shillings.

BACK BOND. BACK LETTER. In Scotland a back bond is a document which renders another bond null and void. Where an absolute disposition, or conveyance, of a property is taken by a banker as security, the deed is qualified by a back bond, or back letter, given by the banker to the debtor stating the conditions under which the debtor is entitled to request a reconveyance of the property from the banker. (See DISPOSITION ABSOLUTE.)

As to the stamp duty upon a back bond or back letter see MORTGAGE, and Section 86 of the Stamp Act, 1891, in that article. See also Section 23 under AGREEMENT.

BACKING A CHEQUE. Before a banker will give cash to a stranger for a cheque upon another bank, it must be indorsed by some reliable person known to the banker. This indorsing is called "backing the cheque." If the cheque should be dishonoured, the banker looks for repayment to the person who has "backed" it.

BACKWARDATION. Where a "bear" speculator on the Stock Exchange wishes to continue his account, instead of delivering on the settlement day the securities which he has sold, he arranges with his broker to postpone delivery. In such a case the broker must borrow the stock and pay for it at the "making up" price. If the demand for money by the "bulls" is greater than the demand for the stock in question by the "bears," the "bear" may receive interest (called contango) from the "bull" for the money lent to the "bull" on the borrowed stock, but if the demand for the stock is so great that there is a scarcity of it, the "bear" may have to pay a "backwardation" rate for the loan of the stock instead of the "bull" paying interest for the loan of the money. (See CONTANGO, STOCK EXCHANGE.)

BAGS. A Stock Exchange name for Buenos Ayres Great Southern Railway ordinary stock.

BAILEE. The person to whom goods are entrusted for a specific purpose by another person called the bailor. (See SAFE CUSTODY.)

BAILOR. The person who entrusts goods to another person (the bailee) for a specific purpose. (See SAFE CUSTODY.)

BALANCE BOOK. A book in which balances of accounts are entered in order to prove their accuracy with the balance as shown in the general ledger. For example, the balance book for the current account ledgers contains the names of all the accounts, and the balances, debit or credit, are entered therein weekly, or at such intervals as may be required, the final difference between the debit and credit columns agreeing with the balance of the current account totals account in the general ledger. Small branches prove the current accounts all together, but in large branches it is convenient, and saves much time, to balance each ledger separately. (See DAY BOOK.)

Some banks prove the current account ledgers by taking out the totals of the debit columns and the totals of the credit columns and agreeing each summation with the corresponding summation of totals in the general ledger.

The process of ascertaining if the final totals are correct is called striking a balance.

BALANCE OF ERRORS. An expression commonly used in banks to describe a "balance" which, at the time of obtaining it, was apparently correct, but which is subsequently found to be wrong, owing to an error for a similar amount on both sides of an account.

BALANCE SHEET. A balance sheet is a statement prepared so as to exhibit on the one hand the liabilities of a company, or person, and, on the other hand, the assets or property available to meet the liabilities.

A balance sheet must be so drawn up as to exhibit a truthful statement of the position. The position should not be represented as being better than it actually is, but the position may be better than is disclosed in the statement. Lord Justice Buckley has said: "The purpose of the balance sheet is primarily to show that the financial position of the company is at least as good as there stated, not to show that it is not and may not be better."

The balance sheet of a company must be signed on behalf of the board by two directors, or, if there is only one, by that director, and the auditors' report must be attached to the balance sheet or there must be a reference to it at the foot of the balance sheet, and the report must be read before the company in general meeting and shall be open to inspection by any shareholder. (See Section 113 of the Companies (Consolidation) Act, 1908, under AUDITORS.)

Section 26, s.s. 3 of that Act requires that the annual summary to be filed with the registrar of companies must (except where the company is a private company) include a statement, in the form of a balance sheet, audited by the company's auditors, containing a summary of its share capital, its liabilities, and its assets, and giving such particulars as will disclose the general nature of those liabilities and assets, and how the values of the fixed assets have been arrived at, but the balance sheet need not include a statement of profit and loss. (See REGISTER OF MEMBERS OF COMPANY.)

The articles of association of a company usually contain regulations regarding the balance sheet, but in companies which are governed by Table A. (see Section 11 under ARTICLES of ASSOCIATION) the following regulations apply:—

"106. Once at least in every year the directors shall lay before the company in general meeting a profit and loss account for the period since the preceding account or (in the case of the first account) since the incorporation of the company, made up to a date not more than six months before such meeting.

"107. A balance sheet shall be made out in every year and laid before the company in general meeting made up to a date not more than six months before such meeting. The balance sheet shall be accompanied by a report of the directors as to the state of the company's affairs, and the amount which they recommend to be paid by way of dividend, and the amount, if any, which they propose to carry to a reserve fund.

"108. A copy of the balance sheet and report shall, seven days previously to the meeting, be sent to the persons entitled to receive notices of general meetings in the manner in which notices are to be given hereunder."

Holders of preference shares and debentures have the same right to receive and inspect the balance sheets of the company as is possessed by the holders of the ordinary shares. (See Section 114 of the abovementioned Act, under AUDITORS.)

In the case of a banking company registered after August 15, 1879, the balance sheet must be signed by the secretary or manager, and where there are more than three directors of the company by at least three of those directors, and where there are not more than three directors by all the directors (Section 113, s.s. 5).

Every limited banking company must, on the first Monday in February and the first Tuesday in August in every year, make a statement of its capital, liabilities and assets in a prescribed form, and display a copy in its registered office and in every branch or place of business (Section 108). (See BANKING COMPANY.)

The auditors' certificate and report on a bank's balance sheet is usually in a form similar to the following:—

"We beg to report to the shareholders that we have examined the books and accounts of the X. & Y. Banking Company, Limited, at December 31, 19.., along with the securities representing the investments of the bank or held against loans, the bills discounted, and the cash balances at the head office and at several of the branch offices. We have obtained all the information and explanations which we have required, and, in our opinion, the foregoing balance sheet is properly drawn up so as to exhibit a true and correct view of the state of the bank's affairs, according to the best of our information and the explanations given to us, and as shown by the books of the company."

In considering a customer's balance sheet, a banker should scrutinise each individual item, and not be satisfied merely by ascertaining the difference between the total of the assets and the total of the liabilities. As to the liabilities, it may be taken for granted that the customer will have to meet all he has shown to the full extent, but there may be items on that side of the sheet which have been omitted or forgotten, and there may be also contingent liabilities, as, for example, in respect of any guarantees he may have given, which will not appear on his balance sheet. Such contingent liabilities should be revealed to the banker, as it is necessary that they be taken into account in obtaining a correct estimate of a person's position. If bills have been discounted for the customer, his liability for any which may be dishonoured should not be overlooked. The natural tendency is to minimise liabilities and to swell assets.

In considering the assets, the item "book debts" calls for inquiry. Is the money owing by reliable parties? Are the debtors few and the individual amounts large, or is the total spread over a large number of persons? If any portion is bad or doubtful the banker will not regard it as an asset. Has any provision been made for bad and doubtful debts? As to the value of the "stock," as shown in the balance sheet, it should be ascertained if it is taken at cost price or at the present market price. The nature of the stock must not be forgotten, because certain articles do not improve by keeping, or they may go out of fashion and have practically no value. A farm stock should be put down in a balance sheet at what it will sell at present, not at what the farmer anticipates it will produce two or three months ahead. It does not necessarily follow that all the sheep on a farm belong to the farmer who owns or rents the farm, nor that the stock in a shop always belongs to the shopkeeper. It is necessary to bear in mind that the value of the stock of a going concern is, as a rule, very different from that which prevails when the business comes to an end and the stock is sold by auction.

If the customer owns property it is desirable to ascertain the nature of the property and also whether the value in the balance sheet is a fair one. If there are any mortgages upon the property the amounts must, of course, be deducted, but as margins frequently disappear when the property is realised to repay the mortgagee, it is not wise, as a rule, to rely upon an asset of that description.

If the value of any shares is included, the present price should be ascertained, and a note made of any liability on the shares.

If the statement shows the existence of private loans, particulars should be furnished of the security which is held.

Each balance sheet must be separately studied in connection with the peculiarities of each trade, but, as a rule, the amount of book debts and stock as shown in a balance sheet requires a considerable allowance to be made in order to arrive at what may be regarded as the approximate sum which would be obtained if the debts were suddenly called in or the stock realised under the hammer. After allowing a liberal margin for that object, the banker should notice if the customer is in such a sound position that all his current liabilities could be cleared off, without requiring any amount which may be entered as the value of the premises in which his business is conducted. Machinery and similar assets should be regularly written down to provide for depreciation.

If the assets include an amount for goodwill, the banker will exclude it in making his estimate.

It should be ascertained whether or not interest upon capital has been deducted before arriving at the profits for the year.

A banker may have, in many cases, to help a customer in making out a balance sheet, and much may be done to assist in obtaining a statement from which nothing material has been omitted, and in which none of the assets are overstated. Such a balance sheet should be signed by the customer. Balance sheets should be preserved so that a new one may be compared with the previous ones.

The most satisfactory form of private balance sheet is one that is certified by an auditor or accountant.

A readiness on the part of a customer to supply particulars of his position begets confidence in a banker's mind. George Rae in "The Country Banker" says: "The solid man of business who, from pride or prejudice, hesitates to disclose the position of his business affairs to the confidential ears of his bankers, damnifies himself in two ways; on the one hand, he lessens the full measure of credit which he might obtain from them should he ever desire to borrow; on the other, he fails to furnish them with data whereon to speak of his position, with knowledge and decision, in reply to inquiries from without."

With respect to the balance sheet of a bank the usual items on the liabilities side are:—

Paid-up capital.
Reserve fund.
Deposits, current accounts, etc.
Acceptances, indorsements, etc.
Notes in circulation } Liabilities to the public.

On the assets side the items are :—

Cash in hand and at Bank of England.
Money at call and short notice.
Investments.
Bills discounted.
Current accounts and loans.
Acceptances and indorsements (as per centra).
Bank premises.

A banker endeavours to keep the assets in such a form that he may be able to provide for all demands which may be made upon him. One banker may consider it necessary, from the fluctuating nature of his deposits, to preserve a larger stock of cash in hand and money at call than another whose deposits are more stable. Money at call and short notice is called a banker's second line of defence. (See GOLD RESERVES.)

BALANCE TICKET. Where a certain number of shares has been sold and the certificate, which is sent by the seller's broker to the company's office for certification, is for a larger number than has been sold, a balance ticket is given to the broker for the remaining shares. When the new certificate for the unsold shares is ready, it can be obtained on delivery of the balance ticket. (See CERTIFIED TRANSFER.)

BANCO. A term applied to the standard money in which a bank, in some countries, kept its accounts, in order to distinguish it from the worn or depreciated currency of the country. Prior to 1873, the word was used in connection with the bank accounts at Hamburg.

BANIS. (See FOREIGN MONEYS—ROUMANIA.)

BANK. The word "bank" is said to be derived from the Italian word *banco*, a bench. The early bankers, the Jews in Lombardy, transacted their business at benches in the market-place. When a banker failed his *banco* was broken up by the people, whence our word bankrupt.

One of the earliest Italian banks, the Bank of Venice, was originated for the management of a public loan, or *monte*, as it was called. Macleod, in his "Elements of Banking," says :—"At that period the Germans were masters of a great part of Italy ; and the German word *banck* came to be used as well as its Italian equivalent *monte*, and was Italianised into *banco*, and the loans were called indifferently *monti* or *banchi*."

The principal business of a banker is to receive money from customers either on current account or on deposit account, and in the former case to pay cheques drawn by the customers. A banker also discounts bills and promissory notes, and makes advances either by way of a loan or of an overdraft. He undertakes the agency of other British banks and of foreign banks, effects purchases and sales of securities, issues circular notes and letters of credit, accepts bills for customers, undertakes the office of executor and trustee, and takes charge of securities and other valuables for customers. A banker often acts as treasurer for a local authority, and sometimes manages the issue of a loan for a foreign Government or for a corporation.

With reference to the use of the word "bank" Mr. Justice Eve has expressed an opinion in the recent case of *Saunders v. Carbonneau* (1910, unreported) that the "time has arrived when the legislature might well impose some restriction on the indiscriminate use of the term 'bank' by individuals and corporations whose business has no relation to banking, properly so-called."

The word "bank" is sometimes used in the singular and sometimes in the plural. It is customary to say, e.g., "the bank has a note issue," "the bank allows 2 per cent. interest," "the bank have considered your application," "the bank are willing to grant the loan." (See BANK OF DEPOSIT, BANK OF ENGLAND, BANK OF ISSUE, BANKING COMPANY, CHARTERED BANK, PRIVATE BANK.)

BANK BILL. A bill which is issued or accepted by a bank. The discount rates for bank bills are less than the rates for fine trade bills ; for example, when the rates for three months' bank bills are quoted at $2\frac{3}{16}$ to $2\frac{1}{4}$ per cent., trade bills may be quoted at, say, $2\frac{1}{2}$ to $2\frac{3}{4}$.

BANK BUILDINGS. (See BANK PREMISES.)

BANK CHARTER ACT, 1844 (7 & 8 VICT. c. 32). An Act to regulate the issue of bank notes and for giving to the Governor and Company of the Bank of England certain privileges for a limited period. The Act was passed on July 19, 1844, and still regulates the note issues in England. The main provisions of the Act are :—The Bank of England was to be divided into two departments, the issue department and the banking department. The directors were to transfer to the issue department securities to the extent of £14,000,000, of which the debt due by the public was to be a part, and also so much of the gold coin, gold and silver bullion as should not be required for the banking department, in exchange for bank notes. After the passing of the Act there were to be no new banks of issue in any part of the United Kingdom, and, if a banker ceased to issue his own notes, the Bank of England was empowered to increase its note issue against public securities by two-thirds of the amount of such issue withdrawn from circulation. A bank issuing notes on May 6, 1844, was allowed to continue to issue to an average amount as ascertained by the average amount of the bank's notes in circulation for twelve weeks preceding April 27. Issuing banks were to render accounts to the commissioners of Inland Revenue.

Previous to the passing of this Act bankers issued notes without restrictions, and it was anticipated that the restrictions imposed by the Act would have a beneficial effect in preventing the evils from which the country had suffered through an unrestricted issue. The working of the Act was soon tested. In 1847 a severe crisis occurred, but the Act did not fulfil what had been expected, and in order to save the situation the Government had to intervene and authorise the Bank to issue notes in excess of the amount as fixed by the Act. This is called the "Suspension of the Bank Act," and it was successful in restoring confidence. In November, 1857, another crisis occurred, and again the Government gave permission to the Bank to exceed its authorised issue, with the same result as on the previous occasion. In May, 1866, the Act was suspended for the third time, and, as before, the trouble soon passed away. In each case the "restrictive theory," as contained in the Act, entirely failed, and the free issue of notes, the "expansive theory," saved the country. H. D. Macleod says the expansive theory "was the only means of saving the Bank itself as well as every other bank from stopping payment. Thus we see the entire failure of Peel's expectations (that is, the restrictive theory in the Bank Charter Act). He took away the power of unlimited issues from the Bank, and imposed a rigorous numerical limit on its powers of issue, under the hope that he had prevented the recurrence of panics. But the panics recurred with precisely the same regularity as before; and therefore, in this sense, the Act has failed; and when monetary crises do occur, it is decisively proved that it is wholly incompetent to deal with them."

The Act regulating the issue of notes in Ireland is 8 & 9 Vict. c. 37, and the corresponding Act for Scotland is 8 & 9 Vict. c. 38. (See BANK NOTES, BANK OF ENGLAND, BANK OF ISSUE.)

BANK HOLIDAYS. The Act (34 Vict. c. 17) making provision for bank holidays, and respecting obligations to make payments and do other acts on such bank holidays, was passed on May 25, 1871. The Act is as follows:—

"Whereas it is expedient to make provision for rendering the day after Christmas Day, and also certain other days, bank holidays, and for enabling bank holidays to be appointed by royal proclamation:

"Be it enacted by the Queen's most excellent Majesty, by and with the advice and consent of the Lords Spiritual and Temporal, and Commons, in this present Parliament assembled, and by the authority of the same, as follows:

Bills due on Bank Holidays to be Payable on the Following Day.

"Section 1. After the passing of this Act the several days in the Schedule to this Act mentioned (and which days are in this Act hereinafter referred to as bank holidays) shall be kept as close holidays in all banks in England and Ireland and Scotland respectively, and all bills of exchange and promissory notes which are due and payable on any such bank holiday shall be payable, and in case of non-payment may be noted and protested, on the next following day, and not on such bank holiday; and any such noting or protest shall be as valid as if made on the day on which the bill or note was made due and payable; and for all the purposes of this Act the day next following a bank holiday shall mean the next following day on which a bill of exchange may be lawfully noted or protested.

Provision as to Notice of Dishonour and Presentation for Honour.

"2. When the day on which any notice of dishonour of an unpaid bill of exchange or promissory note should be given, or when the day on which a bill of exchange or promissory note should be presented or received for acceptance, or accepted or forwarded to any referee or referees, is a bank holiday, such notice of dishonour shall be given and such bill of exchange or promissory note shall be presented or forwarded on the day next following such bank holiday.

As to any Payments on Bank Holidays.

"3. No person shall be compellable to make any payment or to do any act upon such bank holidays which he would not be compellable to do or make on Christmas Day or Good Friday; and the obligation to make such payment and do such act shall apply to the day following such bank holiday; and the making of such payment and doing such act on such following day shall be equivalent to payment of the money or performance of the act on the holiday.

Appointment of Special Bank Holidays by Royal Proclamation.

"4. It shall be lawful for Her Majesty, from time to time, as to Her Majesty may seem fit, by proclamation in the manner in which solemn fasts or days of public thanksgiving may be appointed, to appoint a special day to be observed as a bank holiday, either throughout the United Kingdom or in any part thereof, or in any county, city, borough, or district therein, and any day so appointed shall be kept as a close holiday in all banks within the locality mentioned in such proclamation, and shall, as regards bills of exchange and promissory notes payable in such locality, be deemed to be a bank holiday for all purposes of this Act.

Day Appointed for Bank Holiday may be altered by Order in Council.

"5. It shall be lawful for Her Majesty in like manner, from time to time, when it is made to appear to Her Majesty in Council in any special case that in any year it is inexpedient that a day by this Act appointed for a bank holiday shall be a bank holiday, to declare that such day shall not in such year be a bank holiday, and to appoint such other day as to Her Majesty in council may seem fit to be a bank holiday instead of such day, and thereupon the day so appointed shall in such year be substituted for the day so appointed by this Act.

Exercise of Powers conferred by Sections 4 and 5 in Ireland by Lord-Lieutenant.

"6. The powers conferred by Sections 3 and 4 of this Act of Her Majesty may be exercised in Ireland, so far as relates to that part of the United Kingdom, by the Lord-Lieutenant of Ireland in Council.

Short Title.

"7. This Act may be cited for all purposes as 'The Bank Holidays Act, 1871.'

Schedule.

Bank Holidays in England and Ireland.

"Easter Monday.

The Monday in Whitsun week.

The first Monday in August.

The 26th day of December, if a week day."

(If the 26th December is a Sunday, Monday, 27th December, shall be a bank holiday. See Section 2 of the Act of 1875 given below.)

Bank Holidays in Scotland.

"New Year's Day.

Christmas Day.

If either of the above days falls on a Sunday the next following Monday shall be a bank holiday.

Good Friday.

The first Monday of May.

The first Monday of August."

By 3 Edw. 7 c. 1, Bank Holiday (Ireland) Act, 1903, St. Patrick's Day, March 17, when a week day shall be a bank holiday, but if March 17 is a Sunday, March 18 shall be a bank holiday.

Christmas Day and Good Friday, which are common law holidays in England and Ireland, are statutory holidays in Scotland.

The effect of bank holidays in connection with Days of Grace is dealt with in Section 14 of the Bills of Exchange Act, 1882 (see DAYS OF GRACE), and in connection with the reckoning of time under that Act it is dealt with in Section 92 (see BILLS OF EXCHANGE ACT, 1882).

HOLIDAYS EXTENSION ACT, 1875 (38 Vict. c. 13).

"Whereas it is expedient to amend 'The Bank Holidays Act, 1871' (in this Act referred to as the Holidays Act of 1871), and to extend certain of the holidays named therein to the customs, bonding warehouses, and docks, and to amend the Acts relating to holidays in the inland revenue offices in England and Ireland :—

"Be it therefore enacted, etc.

Days mentioned in Schedule to be Holidays.

"Section 1. From and after the passing of this Act, the several days and each and every of them in the Schedule to this Act mentioned, being holidays under the Holidays Act of 1871, shall be kept as public holidays in the customs, inland revenue offices, and bonding warehouses in England and Ireland respectively; and it shall be lawful for the directors or governing body (by whatever name known) of any dock or docks in England and Ireland respectively to cause the said days or any of them to be kept as holidays in such dock or docks, any restraining clause in any Act of Parliament notwithstanding: Provided that such directors or governing body shall give notice thereof by inserting an advertisement to that effect in some newspaper circulating in the locality of such dock or docks, and by affixing to the principal gates of the said dock or docks, or to some conspicuous place in the immediate neighbourhood, a notice to the same effect for at least a week immediately preceding any day which it is intended to observe as a holiday under this Act; and the anniversary of the coronation of Her Majesty and her successors, and the birthday of the Prince of Wales, shall no longer be kept as holidays in any inland revenue office in England or Ireland.

December 26 falling on Sunday.

"2. Whenever the 26th day of December shall fall on a Sunday, the Monday immediately next following, that is to say, the 27th day of December, shall be a holiday under this Act, and also under the Holidays Act of 1871.

Exercise of Powers by Lord-Lieutenant of Ireland.

"3. The powers conferred on Her Majesty by Sections 4 and 5 of the Holidays Act of 1871 may be exercised in Ireland, as far as relates to that part of the United Kingdom, by the Lord-Lieutenant in Council, and Section 6 of that Act is hereby repealed; and those powers of Her Majesty and of the Lord-Lieutenant in Council shall extend to holidays under this Act.

Short Title.

"4. This Act may be cited for all purposes as 'The Holidays Extension Act, 1875.'

Schedule.

"Easter Monday.
Monday in Whitsun week.
The first Monday in August.
The 26th of December (if a week day)."

(See TIME OF PAYMENT OF BILL.)

BANK HOLIDAYS ACT, 1871. (See BANK HOLIDAYS.)

BANK HOURS. The hours during which banks are open to do business with the public do not vary very much. The bankers in any one town generally agree to act together as to the hours when the doors will be opened and closed. From 9 or 10 a.m. till 3 or 4 p.m. are the hours which are usually considered sufficient, though in some market towns the banks continue open for an extra hour upon market days. In very small towns or in villages, the hours may be much shorter, and are regulated according to the amount of business to be done. Sub-branches are, in some cases, open only for two or three hours once a week, or as may be found necessary.

On the occasion of local holidays, bankers may agree to be open for only, say, an hour, or they may agree to close altogether, and in such cases due notice of the holiday must be exhibited in the bank for some time previously. When a banker closes upon a local holiday he must arrange for bills falling due to be attended to and also see if there is anything urgent in the remittances and correspondence.

Most banks have one half-day holiday in the week and close at either 12 or 1 o'clock. (See AFTER HOURS.)

BANK NOTE REGISTER. A book in which some bankers keep particulars of every Bank of England note which they receive, and of every one which is paid away. The name of the person from whom the note is received is recorded, and also the number date, place of issue, and amount. Each entry is numbered consecutively and the number is placed upon the corresponding note, so that by merely quoting that number, the note may at any time be turned up in the register and full particulars found. This running number is useful as a ready means of keeping a record of notes paid out across the counter and sent away by post. The date when a note is paid away may be marked against the entry made when it was received, or a separate book may be used for the purpose in which only the reference numbers need be copied, together with a note of the person to whom it was paid and the date.

BANK NOTES. Bank notes are promissory notes, issued by a bank and payable to bearer on demand, but unlike promissory notes they may be re-issued after payment. They are practically money and in the ordinary course of business are treated as cash.

The definition of a bank note by 17 & 18 Vict. c. 83, Section 11, is :—" All bills, drafts, or notes, other than notes of the Bank of England, which shall be issued by any banker, or the agent of any banker, for the payment of money to the bearer on demand; and all bills, drafts, or notes so issued which shall entitle or be intended to entitle the bearer or holder thereof, without indorsement, or without any further or other indorsement than may be thereon at the time of the issuing thereof, to the payment of any sum of money on demand, whether the same shall be so expressed or not, in whatever form and by whomsoever such bills, drafts, or notes shall be drawn or made, shall be deemed to be bank notes of the banker by whom or by whose agent the same shall be issued within the meaning of the 7 & 8 Vict. c. 32, and 8 & 9 Vict. cc. 37 & 38."

Notes may not be issued in England for a less sum than five pounds, but in Scotland and Ireland they may be issued for one pound and upwards. Notes for less than £5 were prohibited in England after April 5, 1829 (7 Geo. IV c. 6, Section 3).

The Chinese are said to have been the inventors of bank notes about the year 119 B.C.

The origin of bank notes in England is to be found in the receipts which goldsmiths gave for money left with them for safe keeping. At first they were special promises with regard to some particular money in their possession, but, afterwards, they became general promises to deliver a sum of money on demand.

Bank notes have relieved bankers and the public generally from many inconvenient transfers of large quantities of coins, which would otherwise have been necessary. Professor Jevons says: "I find that a Bank of England note weighs about 20¼ grains, whereas a single sovereign weighs about 123 grains, and the note may represent five, ten, fifty, a thousand or ten thousand such sovereigns with slight differences in printing."

A country bank which is authorised to issue its own notes, must take out a licence for each place where its notes are issued. (See LICENCE.) A country banker usually issues his own notes again and again until they become so soiled as to be unfit for further circulation, when he withdraws the worn ones and issues others in their place.

The duty upon bank notes, as imposed by the Stamp Act, 1891, is:—

BANK NOTE—	£	s.	d.
For money not exceeding £1	0	0	5
Exceeding £1 and not exceeding £2	0	0	10
,, £2 ,, £5	0	1	3
,, £5 ,, £10	0	1	9
,, £10 ,, £20	0	2	0
,, £20 ,, £30	0	3	0
,, £30 ,, £50	0	5	0
,, £50 ,, £100	0	8	6

And see Sections 29, 30 and 31 as follows:—

"29. For the purposes of this Act the expression 'banker' means any person carrying on the business of banking in the United Kingdom, and the expression 'Bank note' includes—

(a) Any bill of exchange or promissory note issued by any banker, other than the Bank of England, for the payment of money not exceeding one hundred pounds to the bearer on demand; and

(b) Any bill of exchange or promissory note so issued which entitles or is intended to entitle the bearer or holder thereof, without indorsement or without any further or other indorsement than may be thereon at the time of the issuing thereof, to the payment of money not exceeding one hundred pounds on demand, whether the same be so expressed or not and in whatever form and by whomsoever the bill or note is drawn or made.

"30. A bank note issued duly stamped, or issued unstamped by a banker duly licensed or otherwise authorised to issue unstamped bank notes, may be from time to time re-issued without being liable to any stamp duty by reason of the re-issuing.

"31. (1) If any banker, not being duly licensed or otherwise authorised to issue unstamped bank notes, issues, or permits to be issued, any bank note not being duly stamped, he shall incur a fine of fifty pounds.

"(2) If any person receives or takes in payment or as a security any bank note issued unstamped contrary to law, knowing the same to have been so issued, he shall incur a fine of twenty pounds."

By 9 Geo. IV c. 23, Section 7, bankers who are licensed to issue unstamped notes or bills shall pay:—

"As a composition for the duties which would otherwise have been payable for such promissory notes and bills of exchange issued or in circulation during such half-year, the sum of 3*s.* 6*d.* for every £100, and also for the fractional part of £100, of the said average amount or value of such notes and bills in circulation." (See BANK

CHARTER ACT, BANK OF ENGLAND NOTES, BANK OF ISSUE, COMPOSITION, COUNTRY BANK NOTES, FORGERY, HALF NOTES, INDORSEMENT ON BANK NOTE, LEGAL TENDER, LICENCE, NOTE REGISTER, NOTE RETURN, PAYMENT STOPPED (NOTES), POST, STATUTE OF LIMITATIONS, STOLEN BANK NOTES.)

BANK OF CIRCULATION. The same as BANK OF ISSUE (*q.v.*).

BANK OF DEPOSIT. A term applied to banks which receive deposits from their customers, but are not empowered to issue their own notes, to distinguish them from "banks of issue" which are authorised to issue their own notes.

BANK OF ENGLAND. In the year 1691, William Paterson, a native of Dumfriesshire, submitted to the Government a plan for the establishment of a national bank, and in the year 1694 the Bank of England, which has since become the greatest banking institution in the world, was incorporated by Act 5 & 6 William & Mary. The Act is entitled "An Act for granting to their Majesties several duties upon tonnage of ships and vessels, and upon beer, ale, and other liquors, for securing certain recompenses and advantages in the said Act mentioned, to such persons as shall voluntarily advance the sum of fifteen hundred thousand pounds towards carrying on the war with France." The Act authorised the raising of £1,200,000 by voluntary subscription, the subscribers to be incorporated under the style of "The Governor and Company of the Bank of England." The sum of £300,000 was also authorised to be raised by subscription and annuities granted to the subscribers. All the money was quickly subscribed, and a charter was granted on July 27, 1694, for eleven years, and it has since then been renewed from time to time.

Within three years the Bank was compelled to suspend payment.

In 1708, when the Bank Charter was renewed, a clause was inserted constituting the Bank of England the only joint stock bank in England. In 1718 subscriptions for Government loans were for the first time received at the Bank, and the Bank has been employed by the Government in similar transactions up to the present time.

In 1720 the Bank found itself in danger of being involved in the South Sea Company's ruin. In 1734 its business was transferred from the Grocers' Hall to a newly erected building in Threadneedle Street. The Bank commenced to issue Bank Post Bills in 1738 (see BANK POST BILL). A run upon the Bank took place in 1745, and in order to check it and to obtain time, it is related that the Directors arranged that employees of the Bank should present notes for payment and that the cashiers should pay those notes in sixpences. The employees who received the sixpences went out of the Bank, but slipped in by another door and paid in the money again. The Bank began to issue notes for £10 and £15 in 1759; previous to that year it would appear that the lowest amount of note issued was £20. In 1780 the Gordon Riots occurred, and for protection a company of Foot Guards did duty in the Bank, and ever since a company of Grenadier or Coldstream Guards have remained in the Bank during each night. In 1793, or practically one hundred years after the Bank was founded, notes for £5 were first issued. The capital of the Bank had by that time increased to £11,642,400. In 1797, owing to the effects of the unusual demand for specie, an Order in Council was issued "that it is indispensably necessary for the public service, that the Directors of the Bank of England should forbear issuing any cash in payment, until the sense of Parliament can be taken on the subject." . . .

Notes for £1 and £2 appeared for the first time in 1797. In the same year Peel's "Restriction Act" was passed. It is entitled "An Act for continuing for a limited time, the restriction contained in the minute of Council of the 26th of February, 1797, of payment of cash by the Bank."

In 1810, the Bullion Committee reported to the House of Commons upon the high price of bullion and the state of the circulating medium. In 1816, the Bank was authorised to increase its capital to £14,553,000, at which amount it still stands. In 1819 the Bank Restriction Act was further continued till 1820. On May 1, 1821, the Bank began to pay their notes in gold. In December, 1825, the Bank passed through a very severe time, and it appears that the credit of the Bank was saved by the finding of a box containing a quantity of one-pound notes. In 1826, notes under £5 were abolished; and the monopoly which the Bank had hitherto enjoyed was done away with except in London and within a radius of sixty-five miles thereof. In 1844, the Bank Charter Act was passed. It separated the Bank into two departments, the Issue

Department and the Banking Department. The Bank's note issue was limited to £14,000,000 against securities, part of which was the debt due from the public; for any notes issued in excess of that amount gold coins or gold or silver bullion must be deposited in the issue department. The net profit on any issue of notes against securities exceeding £14,000,000 is paid to the State. The Bank Act has been suspended on three occasions—in 1847, 1857 and 1866.

The Bank of England is the centre of the London money market, and to a very large extent, indeed, the heart of the money market of the world. Its advertised rate of discount, so well known as the "Bank Rate," is that upon which, in this country, all other discount rates, and the deposit rates allowed by banks, are more or less dependent.

The Bank keeps the national reserve of bullion, and as all other banks throughout the country keep an account with the Bank of England, either directly or indirectly (by keeping an account with a London agent, which agent keeps an account there), the Bank of England occupies the unique position of being the holder of the ultimate banking reserve. In a time of panic all banks fall back upon the Bank of England for supplies of gold.

The Bank carries on the ordinary business of banking, but in addition it has charge of the Government accounts and manages the National Debt, paying the dividends thereon. From the sums which are paid to the Bank for the management of the public debt, the Bank, by the Act of 1844, allows the State £180,000 per annum for the privileges which it enjoys. The remuneration for the management of the National Debt is fixed at an annual sum of £325 per £1,000,000 up to £500,000,000; £100 per £1,000,000 above £500,000,000, but the amount is not to be less than £160,000 per annum. The remuneration for the management of Exchequer Bonds and Bills is £100, and of Treasury Bills £200, for every £1,000,000 of such Bonds or Bills outstanding on the last day of the previous financial year (55 & 56 Vict. c. 48).

The Bank of England is, in the words of George Clare, "invested with a certain stateliness and dignity of standing, which place it *hors de concours*, and which restrain it from working, as other banks do, solely with a view to dividend-earning."

The following sections in the Bank Charter Act (7 & 8 Vict. c. 32) deal with the issue of notes by the Bank and with the privileges which it enjoys:—

"1. The issue of promissory notes of the Governor and Company of the Bank of England payable on demand shall be separated and thenceforth kept wholly distinct from the general banking business of the said Governor and Company; and the business of and relating to such issue shall be thenceforth conducted and carried on by the said Governor and Company in a separate department to be called 'The Issue Department of the Bank of England,' subject to the rules and regulations hereinafter contained; and it shall be lawful for the court of directors of the said Governor and Company, if they shall think fit, to appoint a committee or committees of directors for the conduct and management of such issue department of the Bank of England, and from time to time to remove the members, and define, alter, and regulate the constitution and powers of such committee, as they shall think fit, subject to any bye-laws, rules or regulations which may be made for that purpose: Provided nevertheless, that the said issue department shall always be kept separate and distinct from the banking department of the said Governor and Company.

"2. There shall be transferred, appropriated, and set apart by the said Governor and Company to the issue department of the Bank of England securities to the value of fourteen million pounds, whereof the debt due by the public to the said Governor and Company shall be and be deemed a part; and there shall also at the same time be transferred, appropriated, and set apart by the said Governor and Company to the said issue department so much of the gold coin and gold and silver bullion then held by the Bank of England as shall not be required by the banking department thereof; and thereupon there shall be delivered out of the said issue department into the said banking department of the Bank of England such an amount of Bank of England notes as, together with the Bank of England notes then in circulation, shall be equal to the aggregate amount of the securities, coin, and bullion so transferred to the said issue department of the Bank of England: and the whole amount of Bank of England notes then in circulation, including those delivered to the banking department of the Bank of

England as aforesaid, shall be deemed to be issued on the credit of such securities, coin, and bullion so appropriated and set apart to the said issue department; and from thenceforth it shall not be lawful for the said Governor and Company to increase the amount of securities for the time being in the said issue department, save as hereinafter is mentioned, but it shall be lawful for the said Governor and Company to diminish the amount of such securities, and again to increase the same to any sum not exceeding in the whole the sum of fourteen million pounds, and so from time to time as they shall see occasion; and from and after such transfer and appropriation to the said issue department as aforesaid it shall not be lawful for the said Governor and Company to issue Bank of England notes, either into the banking department of the Bank of England, or to any persons or person whatsoever, save in exchange for other Bank of England notes, or for gold coin or for gold or silver bullion received or purchased for the said issue department under the provisions of this Act, or in exchange for securities acquired and taken in the said issue department under the provisions herein contained: Provided always, that it shall be lawful for the said Governor and Company in their banking department to issue all such Bank of England notes as they shall at any time receive from the said issue department or otherwise, in the same manner in all respects as such issue would be lawful to any other person or persons.

"3. It shall not be lawful for the Bank of England to retain in the issue department of the said Bank at any one time an amount of silver bullion exceeding one-fourth part of the gold coin and bullion at such time held by the Bank of England in the issue department.

"4. All persons shall be entitled to demand from the issue department of the Bank of England, Bank of England notes in exchange for gold bullion, at the rate of £3 17*s.* 9*d.* per ounce of standard gold: Provided always, that the said Governor and Company shall in all cases be entitled to require such gold bullion to be melted and assayed by persons approved by the said Governor and Company at the expense of the parties tendering such gold bullion.

"5. Provided, always, that if any banker who on the 6th day of May, 1844, was issuing his own bank notes shall cease to issue his own bank notes, it shall be lawful for Her Majesty in Council at any time after the cessation of such issue, upon the application of the said Governor and Company, to authorise and empower the said Governor and Company to increase the amount of securities in the said issue department beyond the total sum or value of fourteen million pounds, and thereupon to issue additional Bank of England notes to an amount not exceeding such increased amount of securities specified in such Order in Council, and so from time to time: Provided always, that such increased amount of securities specified in such Order in Council, shall in no case exceed the proportion of two-thirds the amount of bank notes which the banker so ceasing to issue may have been authorised to issue under the provisions of this Act; and every such Order in Council shall be published in the next succeeding *London Gazette*.

"7. The said Governor and Company of the Bank of England shall be released and discharged from the payment of any stamp duty, or composition in respect of stamp duty, upon or in respect of their promissory notes payable to bearer on demand; and all such notes shall be and continue free and wholly exempt from all liability to any stamp duty whatsoever.

"9. In case, under the provisions hereinbefore contained, the securities held in the said issue department of the Bank of England shall at any time be increased beyond the total amount of fourteen million pounds, then and in each and every year in which the same shall happen, and so long as such increase shall continue, the said Governor and Company shall, in addition to the said annual sum of £180,000, make a further payment or allowance to the public, equal in amount to the net profit derived in the said issue department during the current year from such additional securities, after deducting the amount of the expenses occasioned by the additional issue during the same period, which expenses shall include the amount of any and every composition or payment to be made by the said Governor and Company to any banker in consideration of the discontinuance at any time hereafter of the issue of bank notes by such banker."

The position of the authorised issue of the Bank of England is as follows:—

Authorised by the Act of 1844 . . .	£14,000,000
Authorised by Order in Council:—	
1855. Dec. 7	475,000
1861. July 10	175,000
1866. Feb. 21	350,000

1881.	April 1	750,000
1887.	Sept. 15	450,000
1890.	Feb. 8	250,000
1894.	Jan. 29	350,000
1900.	Mar. 3	975,000
1902.	Aug. 11	400,000
1903.	Aug. 10	275,000
Total fixed issue		£18,450,000

(See BANK NOTES, BANK OF ISSUE, BANK RETURN.)

BANK OF ENGLAND NOTES. The Bank of England is a bank of issue, and may issue notes in England and Wales. The Bank is separated into two departments, the Issue Department and the Banking Department. It has the right to issue bank notes up to £14,000,000 against securities to that amount transferred to the issue department, and that amount may be increased by His Majesty in Council against further security to the extent of two-thirds of any banker's issue which has ceased. (See above figures.) Notes may also be issued by the issue department against gold and silver bullion or gold coins, but the silver bullion must not exceed one-fourth of the value of the gold coin and bullion. Bank of England notes are as good as cash, and are legal tender in England and Wales for any sum above £5, except by the Bank itself and its branches. All Bank of England notes are payable in gold at the head office, but at a branch only the notes are payable which were issued by that branch. Before giving cash for a note it is customary for the Bank to request the person presenting it, to write his name and address upon the back.

When notes are paid in to the Bank they are not reissued, but are cancelled and after five years are destroyed.

Bank of England notes may be signed by machinery instead of being written (16 & 17 Vict. c. 2, Section 1). The Bank has the sole right to issue notes within the City of London or within three miles thereof, and they are not subject to any stamp duty. They are issued for £5, £10, £20, £50, £100, £200, £500, and £1,000.

Where notes of the Bank of England, issued more than forty years ago, have not been presented for payment, the Bank of England is empowered by the Bank Act, 1892, to write off the amount, or any proportion of it, of such notes from the total amount issued by the issue department, and the Bank Charter Act, 1844, is to apply as if the amount so written off had not been issued, provided that—

"(a) A return of the amount of notes so written off shall be forthwith sent to the Treasury and laid by them before Parliament; and

"(b) This Section shall not affect the liability of the Bank to pay any note included in the amount so written off, and if it is presented for payment the amount shall either be paid out of the bank notes, gold coin, or bullion in the banking department; or, if it is exchanged for gold coin or bullion in the issue department, or for a note issued from the issue department, a corresponding amount of gold coin or bullion shall be transferred from the banking department and appropriated to the issue department."

Lord Mansfield (in *Miller* v. *Race*, 1758, 1 Burr. 452) said: "Bank notes are not goods, nor securities, nor documents for debts, nor are they so esteemed, but are treated as money, as cash, in the ordinary course and transaction of business by the general consent of mankind, which gives them the credit and currency of money, to all intents and purposes."

A material part of a Bank of England note, and of all bank notes, is the number. If a note is lost or stolen, the number often enables the loser who has kept a record of it to trace the note. The fact of notes being numbered and therefore traceable, no doubt often tends to prevent them being stolen, particularly if they are for the larger denominations.

The numbers also are necessary to the Bank in order that a correct register may be kept of all notes issued, and the date of issue, and that, when withdrawn from circulation, each note may be written off in the register as having been paid. (See BANK NOTES, BANK OF ENGLAND.)

BANK OF FRANCE. The most important financial institution in France. It was founded in 1800.

BANK OF ISSUE. A bank which issues its own notes payable to bearer on demand. The Bank of England is a bank of issue, and its issue is regulated by the Bank Charter Act, 1844 (see BANK OF ENGLAND and BANK OF ENGLAND NOTES). It can issue bank notes throughout England and Wales, and has the monopoly in London and within three miles thereof. The only other banks of issue are those which were lawfully issuing bank notes, on May 6, 1844.

The regulations regarding banks of issue

are contained in various acts of Parliament. All banks beyond sixty-five miles from London which were lawfully issuing their own notes on May 6, 1844, may continue to issue them, except those banks where the partners consisted at that date of not more than six persons and where the number of partners has since increased in number. Beyond three miles from London and within sixty-five miles, banks consisting of not more than six partners, who were lawfully issuing their own notes on May 6, 1844, may continue to issue them. There are thus three distinct areas defined in the Acts, (1) the City of London and within three miles thereof (counting from the Royal Exchange), where the Bank of England has the sole right to issue notes. (2) Beyond three and within sixty-five miles of London, where the Bank of England shares the right with banks of not more than six members, which were lawfully issuing notes on May 6, 1844. (3) Beyond sixty-five miles, where the Bank of England shares the right with the other banks which were lawfully issuing notes on May 6, 1844.

No person other than a banker who, on May 6, 1844, was lawfully issuing his own bank notes shall make or issue bank notes in any part of the United Kingdom.

If a country bank of issue opens an office in London, or, there being more than six partners, if it comes within sixty-five miles of London, it loses its right of issue. A bank which consisted of not more than six partners on May 6, 1844, will lose its right to issue notes after the number of partners therein shall exceed six in the whole, but two banks each consisting of not more than six partners may combine and unite their separate issues so long as the number of partners does not exceed six. A bank ceases to have the right of issue by bankruptcy, or by giving up business or by discontinuing its issue either by agreement with the Bank of England or otherwise. Where a private issuing bank is absorbed by a joint stock bank, its issue lapses, and if an amalgamation between two joint stock banks of issue results in the formation of a new bank, the issue of both the banks will lapse. The Bank of England has the right to increase its own issue against securities to the extent of two-thirds of all lapsed issues. The Bank of England has power under Sections 23 and 24 of the Bank Charter Act, 1844, to make payment of annual compositions to certain bankers on their giving up the privilege of issuing their own notes, but when such bankers cease to carry on business, it has been held that the compositions cease.

The amount of notes which may be issued by a bank of issue is fixed, and is the amount certified by the Commissioners of Stamps and Taxes as being the average amount of the bank notes of such bank as were in circulation during a period of twelve weeks preceding April 27, 1844.

If the monthly average circulation of bank notes of any banker shall at any time exceed the amount which the banker is authorised to issue, such banker shall in every such case forfeit a sum equal to the amount by which the average monthly circulation shall have exceeded the amount he was authorised to issue and to have in circulation.

A bank of issue registered as a limited company is not entitled to limited liability in respect of its notes, and the members thereof shall be liable in respect of its notes in the same manner as if it had been registered as an unlimited company. (See Section 251 of the Companies (Consolidation) Act, 1908, under BANKING COMPANY.)

The issue of bank notes in Ireland is regulated by 8 & 9 Vict. c. 37. The tender of a note or notes of the Bank of England is not a legal tender in Ireland, but nothing in the Act is to be construed as prohibiting the circulation in Ireland of the notes of the Bank of England. A banker in Ireland is prohibited from issuing notes in excess of the amount certified by the Commissioners (that is, the average amount of notes in circulation for one year previous to May 1, 1845), except against the monthly average amount of gold and silver coin held by such banker during the same period of four weeks.

As to the coin against which notes may be issued, there shall be included only the gold and silver coin held by such banker at the several head offices or principal places of issue in Ireland, such head offices or principal places not to exceed four in number, of which not more than two shall be situated in the same province ; and notes shall not be issued on any amount of silver coin exceeding the proportion of one-fourth part of the gold coin held by such banker. Bank notes issued in Ireland are to be "for payment of a sum in pounds sterling, without any fractional parts of a pound."

The issue of bank notes in Scotland is regulated by 8 & 9 Vict. c. 38, and the regulations are practically the same as for the banks in Ireland (see above), except that by Section 6 it shall not be lawful for any banker in Scotland to issue a greater amount of notes than the amount certified by the Commissioners and "the monthly average amount of gold and silver coin held by such banker at the head office or principal place of issue of such banker during the same period of four weeks."

In Scotland and Ireland bank notes may be for one pound and upwards, but in England the lowest amount is five pounds.

There are no notes legal tender in Scotland and none in Ireland, with the exception of Bank of Ireland notes in payment of part of the public revenue of Ireland. This exception is contained in 1 & 2 Geo. IV c. 72.

Principally through amalgamations, banks of issue are rapidly disappearing in England. The authorised issues at present are as follows :—

BANK OF ENGLAND.		
Issue authorised against securities .		£18,450,000
ENGLAND.		
Joint Stock Banks :—		
Bank of Whitehaven, Ltd.	£32,681	
Carlisle & Cumberland Banking Co., Ltd. . .	25,610	
Halifax Commercial Banking Co., Ltd. . . .	13,733	
Halifax Joint Stock Banking Co., Ltd. . . .	18,534	
Lincoln & Lindsey Banking Co., Ltd.	51,620	
Nottingham & Nottinghamshire Banking Co., Ltd..	29,477	
Sheffield & Hallamshire Bank, Ltd.	23,524	
Wilts & Dorset Banking Co., Ltd.	76,162	
		271,341
Private Banks :—		
Barnard & Co., Bedford .	34,218	
Beckett & Co., Leeds . .	130,757	
Beckett & Co., York & East Riding Bank. . . .	53,392	
Fox, Fowler & Co. . . .	6,528	
Gillett & Co., Banbury .	43,457	
Gillett & Co., Oxford . .	11,852	
Harris, Bulteel & Co., Naval Bank, Plymouth. . .	27,321	
Peacock, Willson & Co. .	51,615	
Simonds, J. & C., & Co. .	37,519	
Tubb & Co..	27,090	
		423,749
SCOTLAND :—		
Eight Joint Stock Banks		2,676,350
IRELAND :—		
Six Joint Stock Banks		6,354,494
Total		£28,175,934

To show how greatly the authorised issues of the English country banks have diminished, "in March, 1858, the fixed issues of the issuing private banks, 153 in number, amounted to £4,432,790, and those of the 63 issuing joint stock banks to £3,303,357" (Hutchison's "Practice of Banking," vol. II, p. 349). The authorised issue of the banks in Scotland in that year was £3,087,209, or only £410,000 more than at present, while that of the banks in Ireland remains the same as it was in 1858. (See BANK NOTES, LICENCE.)

BANK ORDER. The name given to the forms which are used in the Savings Bank department of the Halifax Joint Stock Banking Co., Limited, in connection with the Bank Order Scheme, which is being tried as an experiment.

Books containing definite numbers of printed Bank Order forms, of various denominations (different combinations of all or some of the following :—2*s.*, 2*s.* 6*d.*, 5*s.*, 10*s.*, 15*s.*, £1, £2, £3, £4, and £5 maximum) are supplied by the bank, on request, to persons opening an account in the Savings Bank department. The printed forms, of themselves, are simply an indication that depositors have available funds in the bank for not less than the amount printed on the face thereof.

The following is a specimen of a Bank Order form printed for £2 :—

No. 1348

This order must be presented for payment not later than December 31, 1913.

1d. Stamp.

To the HALIFAX JOINT STOCK BANKING CO., LTD.

Payable at the Head Office, Halifax, or any Branch.

SAVINGS BANK DEPARTMENT.

DEPOSITOR'S

£2 BANK ORDER. £2

TWO POUNDS.

On demand Pay Bearer the sum of Two Pounds.

Signature of Depositor } Account No. 99999.

The object of the Orders is to enable the depositors to withdraw money without production of the pass-book. The forms require no filling up whatever, but they must be signed by the depositor to whom they are supplied before payment will be made. A date is not required to be inserted. The forms can be used by the depositors in making payments to tradesmen, and interest is allowed by the bank on the amount represented by the Orders up to the month of their actual payment by the bank. In order to prevent any abuse of the printed Order forms, depositors are not supplied with them in excess of the amount of their deposits. In the event of the account being closed, all unused forms must be delivered up to the bank, and provision made for any Orders which are outstanding. The forms bear an impressed penny stamp. In order to prevent the Orders remaining out too long, a certain date is printed on the Orders, and they must be presented for payment before that date.

A pass-book specially adapted for the purposes of the system is provided, and the number of the account is placed on the Order forms by the bank.

BANK POST BILL. A Bank Post Bill may be described as a promissory note issued by the Bank of England (which is the only bank in this country that issues them) undertaking at, usually, seven days after sight to pay "this my sole bill" to a specified person or order. The following shows the form of one of these bills :—

No . London, February 1, 1910.
At seven days' sight I promise to pay this my sole Bill of Exchange to or order, fifty pounds sterling value received of .

Accepted February 1, 1910.
A. B.

For the Governor and Company of the Bank of England.

C. D.

Although practically a promissory note, it may also be described as a bill of exchange drawn and accepted by a bank. The acceptance may be on the bill when it is issued, but if it is to be sent into the country it may be unaccepted when issued.

When indorsed by the payee the bill is payable to bearer. They are issued for any amounts from £10 to £1,000.

Bank Post Bills of the Bank of England do not take days of grace.

Bank Post Bills were first issued in the year 1738. At that time highway robberies were very frequent, and it appears that these bills were originated on the suggestion of the Postmaster-General so that, being payable at seven days after sight, in case of the mails being robbed, the losers might have time to give notice of their loss and have payment of the bills stopped.

The following is a specimen of an Irish Bank Post Bill :—

Bank Post Bill
(under composition for stamp duty.) X. & Y. Bank of Ireland, Dublin , 1910.
Seven days after date pay to the order of the sum of sterling.
On account of the X. & Y. Bank of Ireland,
Manager.
To A. & B. Bank, Ltd., London.

Bank Post Bills of Irish banks may be drawn for £5 and upwards, payable at days after date or after sight, and they take the usual three days' grace.

BANK PREMISES. The premises of a banking company are frequently written down much below what may be regarded as their market value. In the case of the Bank of England its valuable property does not appear at all in the balance sheet.

Where the property is leasehold, the amount at which it stands in the books is reduced annually from profits by such an amount as will clear off the amount by the expiration of the lease. For example, if the outlay upon the land and buildings has been £2,000 and the term of the lease is fifty years, a sum of £40 should be set aside out of profits each year so that by the end of the term the balance at the debit of the premises account will be cleared off.

BANK PREMISES REDEMPTION FUND. The name of the account to which are credited, yearly or half-yearly, any sums which are set aside out of profits for the purpose of reducing, when necessary, the balance at the debit of bank premises account.

BANK RATE. The Bank Rate is the advertised minimum rate at which the Bank of England will discount approved bills of exchange (of not more than three months' currency) or grant short loans, but the rate which is actually charged to customers who keep their accounts with the Bank is the current market rate, which is, as a rule, a little lower than the Bank Rate. The Bank Rate is fixed by the Directors at their weekly meeting each Thursday, though alterations are sometimes made, when necessary, upon other days. The Rate is regulated according to the supply of money, on the one hand, and the demand for it, on the other. When the Bank reserve gets too low, the Directors raise the rate, but when the Directors find that they are in a position to increase their loans or discounts, the Rate is lowered. The reserve in the banking department is the most important cause of the rise or fall of the Bank Rate. A small reserve indicates a high Rate, and a large reserve a low Rate. The proportion of notes and gold to the deposits is on an average about forty-three per cent. A rise in the Bank Rate tends to attract gold to this country; a fall in the Rate encourages gold to go abroad. The Bank Rate is, therefore, of the utmost importance in protecting the national reserve of gold. The rates, whether for loans, discounts, or deposits, of all the other banks in the country are regulated, more or less, according to the Bank Rate.

The following table shows the changes in the Bank of England minimum rate of discount and the yearly average from 1821 :—

Date.		Per cent.	Yearly Average.		
			£	s.	d.
1821.	. . . . .	5	£5	0	0
1822.	June 22 . .	4 (Bills & Notes)	4	9	6
1823.	. . . . .	4	4	0	0
1824.	. . . . .	4	4	0	0
1825.	Dec. 13 . .	5	4	0	8
1826.	. . . . .	5	5	0	0
1827.	July 5 . .	4	4	10	2
1828.	. . . . .	4	4	0	0
1829.	. . . . .	4	4	0	0
1830.	. . . . .	4	4	0	0
1831.	. . . . .	4	4	0	0
1832.	. . . . .	4	4	0	0
1833.	. . . . .	4	4	0	0
1834.	. . . . .	4	4	0	0
1835.	. . . . .	4	4	0	0
1836.	July 21 . .	4½			
	Sept. 1 . .	5	4	7	9
1837.	. . . . .	5	5	0	0
1838.	Feb. 15 . .	4	4	2	6
1839.	May 16 . .	5			
	June 20 . .	5½			
	Aug. 1 . .	6	5	2	0
1840.	Jan. 23 . .	5	5	1	3
1841.	. . . . .	5	5	0	0
1842.	April 7 . .	4	4	5	4
1843.	. . . . .	4	4	0	0
1844.	Sept. 5 . .	2½ (Bills)			
		3 (Notes)	3	10	4
1845.	Mar. 13 . .	2½			
	Oct. 16 . .	3			
	Nov. 6 . .	3½	2	13	7
1846.	Aug. 27 . .	3	3	6	6
1847.	Jan. 14 . .	3½			
	,, 21 . .	4			
	April 8 . .	5			
	Aug. 2 . .	6			
	,, 5 . .	5½			
	Sept. 30 . .	6			
	Oct. 4 . .	6½			
	,, 25 . .	8 (Bank Charter Act suspended)			
	Nov. 22 . .	7			
	Dec. 2 . .	6			
	,, 23 . .	5	5	4	2
1848.	Jan. 27 . .	4			
	June 15 . .	3½			
	Nov. 22 . .	3	3	14	11
1849.	,, 22 . .	2½	2	19	0
1850.	Dec. 26 . .	3	2	10	1
1851.	. . . . .	3	3	0	0
1852.	Jan. 1 . .	2½			
	April 22 . .	2	2	3	0
1853.	Jan. 6 . .	2½			
	,, 20 . .	3			
	June 2 . .	3½			
	Sept. 1 . .	4			
	,, 15 . .	4½			
	,, 29 . .	5	3	13	11
1854.	May 11 . .	5½			
	Aug. 3 . .	5	5	2	3
1855.	April 5 . .	4½			
	May 3 . .	4			
	June 15 . .	3½			
	Sept. 6 . .	4			
	,, 13 . .	4½			
	,, 27 . .	5			
	Oct. 4 . .	5½			
	,, 18 . .	7	4	17	9
1856.	May 22 . .	6			
	,, 29 . .	5			
	June 26 . .	4½			
	Oct. 1 . .	5			
	,, 6 . .	7			
	Dec. 4 . .	6½			
	,, 18 . .	6	6	1	3
1857.	April 2 . .	6½			
	June 18 . .	6			
	July 16 . .	5½			
	Oct. 8 . .	6			
	,, 12 . .	7			
	,, 19 . .	8			
	Nov. 5 . .	9			
	,, 9 . .	10 (Bank Charter Act suspended Nov. 12)			
	Dec. 24 . .	8	6	12	11
1858.	Jan. 7 . .	6			
	,, 14 . .	5			
	,, 28 . .	4			
	Feb. 4 . .	3½			
	,, 11 . .	3			
	Dec. 9 . .	2½	3	4	7
1859.	April 28 . .	3½			
	May 5 . .	4½			
	June 2 . .	3½			
	,, 9 . .	3			
	July 14 . .	2½	2	14	8
1860.	Jan. 19 . .	3			
	,, 31 . .	4			
	Mar. 29 . .	4½			
	April 12 . .	5			
	May 10 . .	4½			
	,, 24 . .	4			
	Nov. 8 . .	4½			
	,, 13 . .	5			
	,, 15 . .	6			
	,, 29 . .	5			
	Dec. 31 . .	6	4	3	7
1861.	Jan. 7 . .	7			
	Feb. 14 . .	8			
	Mar. 21 . .	7			
	April 4 . .	6			
	,, 11 . .	5			
	May 16 . .	6			
	Aug. 1 . .	5			
	Aug. 15 . .	4½			
	,, 29 . .	4			
	Sept. 19 . .	3½			
	Nov. 7 . .	3	5	4	11
1862.	Jan. 9 . .	2½			

	Date.	Per cent.	Yearly Average. £ s. d.
1862.	May 22	3	
	July 10	2½	
	,, 24	2	
	Oct. 30	3	2 10 6
1863.	Jan. 15	4	
	,, 28	5	
	Feb. 19	4	
	April 23	3½	
	,, 30	3	
	May 16	3½	
	May 21	4	
	Nov. 2	5	
	,, 5	6	
	Dec. 2	7	
	,, 3	8	
	,, 24	7	4 8 2
1864.	Jan. 20	8	
	Feb. 11	7	
	,, 25	6	
	April 16	7	
	May 2	8	
	,, 5	9	
	,, 19	8	
	,, 26	7	
	June 16	6	
	July 25	7	
	Aug. 4	8	
	Sept. 8	9	
	Nov. 10	8	
	,, 24	7	
	Dec. 15	6	7 7 0
1865.	Jan. 12	5½	
	,, 26	5	
	Mar. 2	4½	
	,, 30	4	
	May 4	4½	
	,, 25	4	
	June 1	3½	
	,, 15	3	
	July 27	3½	
	Aug. 3	4	
	Sept. 28	4½	
	Oct. 2	5	
	,, 5	6	
	,, 7	7	
	Nov. 23	6	
	Dec. 28	7	4 15 6
1866.	Jan. 4	8	
	Feb. 22	7	
	Mar. 15	6	
	May 3	7	
	,, 8	8	
	,, 11	9	
	,, 12	10 (Bank Charter Act suspended)	
	Aug. 16	8	
	,, 23	7	
	,, 30	6	
	Sept. 6	5	
	,, 27	4½	
	Nov. 8	4	
	Dec. 20	3½	6 18 11
1867.	Feb. 7	3	
	May 30	2½	
	July 25	2	2 10 9
1868.	Nov. 19	2½	
	Dec. 3	3	2 1 11
1869.	April 1	4	
	May 6	4½	
	June 10	4	
	,, 24	3½	
1869.	July 15	3	
	Aug. 19	2½	
	Nov. 4	3	3 4 2
1870.	July 21	3½	
	,, 23	4	
	,, 28	5	
	Aug. 4	6	
	,, 11	5½	
	,, 18	4½	
	,, 25	4	
	Sept. 1	3½	
	,, 15	3	
	,, 29	2½	3 1 11
1871.	Mar. 2	3	
	April 13	2½	
	June 15	2¼	
	July 13	2	
	Sept. 21	3	
	,, 28	4	
	Oct. 7	5	
	Nov. 16	4	
	,, 30	3½	
	Dec. 14	3	2 17 8
1872.	April 4	3½	
	,, 11	4	
	May 9	5	
	,, 30	4	
	June 13	3½	
	,, 20	3	
	July 18	3½	
	Sept. 18	4	
	,, 26	4½	
	Oct. 3	5	
	,, 10	6	
	Nov. 9	7	
	,, 28	6	
	Dec. 12	5	4 1 11
1873.	Jan. 9	4½	
	,, 23	4	
	,, 30	3½	
	Mar. 26	4	
	May 7	4½	
	May 10	5	
	,, 17	6	
	June 4	7	
	,, 12	6	
	July 10	5	
	,, 17	4½	
	,, 24	4	
	,, 31	3½	
	Aug. 21	3	
	Sept. 25	4	
	,, 29	5	
	Oct. 14	6	
	,, 18	7	
	Nov. 1	8	
	,, 7	9	
	,, 20	8	
	,, 27	6	
	Dec. 4	5	
	,, 11	4½	4 15 10
1874.	Jan. 8	4	
	,, 15	3½	
	April 30	4	
	May 28	3½	
	June 4	3	
	,, 18	2½	
	July 30	3	
	Aug. 6	4	
	,, 20	3½	
	,, 27	3	
	Oct. 15	4	

	Date.	Per cent.	Yearly Average. £	s.	d.
1874.	Nov. 16	5			
	,, 30	6	3	13	10
1875.	Jan. 7	5			
	,, 14	4			
	,, 28	3			
	Feb. 18	3½			
	July 8	3			
	,, 29	2½			
	Aug. 12	2			
	Oct. 7	2½			
	,, 14	3½			
	,, 21	4			
	Nov. 18	3			
	Dec. 30	4	3	4	8
1876.	Jan. 6	5			
	,, 27	4			
	Mar. 23	3½			
	April 6	3			
	,, 20	2	2	12	2
1877.	May 3	3			
	July 5	2½			
	,, 12	2			
	Aug. 28	3			
	Oct. 4	4			
	,, 11	5			
	Nov. 29	4	2	18	0
1878.	Jan. 10	3			
	,, 31	2			
	Mar. 28	3			
	May 30	2½			
	June 27	3			
	July 4	3½			
	Aug. 1	4			
	,, 12	5			
	Oct. 14	6			
	Nov. 21	5	3	15	7
1879.	Jan. 16	4			
	,, 30	3			
	Mar 13	2½			
	April 10	2			
	Nov. 6	3	2	10	4
1880.	June 17	2½			
	Dec. 9	3	2	15	4
1881.	Jan. 13	3½			
	Feb. 17	3			
	April 28	2½			
	Aug. 18	3			
	,, 25	4			
	Oct. 6	5	3	10	0
1882.	Jan. 30	6			
	Feb. 23	5			
	Mar. 9	4			
	,, 23	3			
	Aug. 17	4			
	Sept. 14	5	4	2	8
1883.	Jan. 25	4			
	Feb. 15	3½			
	Mar. 1	3			
	May 10	4			
	Sept. 13	3½			
	,, 27	3	3	11	4
1884.	Feb. 7	3½			
	Mar. 13	3			
	April 3	2½			
	June 19	2			
	Oct. 9	3			
	,, 30	4			
	Nov. 6	5	2	19	1
1885.	Jan. 29	4			
	Mar. 19	3½			
	May 7	3			
	,, 14	2½			
1885.	May 28	2			
	Nov. 12	3			
	Dec. 17	4	2	17	7
1886.	Jan. 21	3			
	Feb. 18	2			
	May 6	3			
	June 10	2½			
	Aug. 26	3½			
	Oct. 21	4			
	Dec. 16	5	3	1	0
1887.	Feb. 3	4			
	Mar. 10	3½			
	,, 24	3			
	April 14	2½			
	,, 28	2			
	Aug. 4	3			
	Sept. 1	4	3	7	0
1888.	Jan. 12	3½			
	,, 19	3			
	Feb. 16	2½			
	Mar. 15	2			
	May 10	3			
	June 7	2½			
	Aug. 9	3			
	Sept. 13	4			
	Oct. 4	5	3	6	11
1889.	Jan. 10	4			
	,, 24	3½			
	,, 31	3			
	April 18	2½			
	Aug. 8	3			
	,, 29	4			
	Sept. 26	5			
	Dec. 30	6	3	10	11
1890.	Feb. 20	5			
	Mar. 6	4½			
	,, 13	4			
	April 10	3½			
	,, 17	3			
	June 26	4			
	July 31	5			
	Aug. 21	4			
	Sept. 25	5			
	Nov. 7	6			
	Dec. 4	5	4	10	5
1891.	Jan. 8	4			
	,, 22	3½			
	,, 29	3			
	April 16	3½			
	May 7	4			
	,, 14	5			
	June 4	4			
	,, 18	3			
	July 2	2½			
	Sept. 24	3			
	Oct. 29	4			
	Dec. 10	3½	3	5	2
1892.	Jan. 21	3			
	April 7	2½			
	,, 28	2			
	Oct. 20	3	2	10	6
1893.	Jan. 26	2½			
	May 4	3			
	May 11	3½			
	,, 18	4			
	June 8	3			
	,, 15	2½			
	Aug. 3	3			
	,, 10	4			
	,, 24	5			
	Sept. 14	4			
	,, 21	3½			

Year	Date	Per cent.	Yearly Average. £	s.	d.
1893.	Oct. 5	3	3	1	1
1894.	Feb. 1	2½			
	,, 22	2	2	2	3
1895.	. . .	2	2	0	0
1896.	Sept. 10	2½			
	,, 24	3			
	Oct. 22	4	2	9	8
1897.	Jan. 21	3½			
	Feb. 4	3			
	April 8	2½			
	May 13	2			
	Sept. 23	2½			
	Oct. 14	3	2	12	8
1898.	April 7	4			
	May 26	3½			
	June 2	3			
	,, 30	2½			
	Sept. 22	3			
	Oct. 13	4	3	4	11
1899.	Jan. 19	3½			
	Feb. 2	3			
	July 13	3½			
	Oct. 3	4½			
	,, 5	5			
	Nov. 30	6	3	15	1
1900.	Jan. 11	5			
	,, 18	4½			
	,, 25	4			
	May 24	3½			
	June 14	3			
	July 19	4	3	19	3
1901.	Jan. 3	5			
	Feb. 7	4½			
	,, 21	4			
	June 6	3½			
	,, 13	3			
	Oct. 31	4	3	14	4
1902.	Jan. 23	3½			
	Feb. 6	3			
	Oct. 2	4	3	6	7
1903.	May 21	3½			
	June 18	3			
	Sept. 3	4	3	15	0
1904.	April 14	3½			
	,, 21	3	3	6	1
1905.	Mar. 9	2½			
	Sept. 7	3			
	,, 28	4	3	0	1
1906.	April 5	3½			
	May 3	4			
	June 21	3½			
	Sept. 13	4			
	Oct. 11	5			
	,, 19	6	4	5	3
1907.	Jan. 17	5			
	April 11	4½			
	,, 25	4			
	Aug. 15	4½			
	Oct. 31	5½			
	Nov. 4	6			
	,, 7	7	4	18	5
1908.	Jan. 2	6			
	,, 16	5			
	,, 23	4			
	Mar. 5	3½			
	,, 19	3			
	May 28	2½	3	0	4
1909.	Jan. 14	3			
	April 1	2½			
	Oct. 7	3			
	,, 14	4			
	,, 21	5			
1909.	Dec. 9	4½	3	2	0
1910.	Jan. 6	4			
	,, 20	3½			
	Feb. 10	3			
	Mar. 17	4			
	June 2	3½			
	June 9	3			
	Sept. 29	4			
	Oct. 20	5			
	Dec. 1	4½			

BANK RATE BOOK. This book shows all the changes for a number of years past which have taken place in the Bank of England Rate, and whenever any alteration of the Rate occurs, a record of it, with the date of the change, is immediately entered. The average of the Bank Rate for the half-year and for the year are also entered in the book.

BANK RETURN. By the Bank Charter Act, 1844 (7 & 8 Vict. c. 32), Section 6, it is provided that the Bank of England issue a weekly return as to its financial position: "An account of the amount of Bank of England notes issued by the Issue Department of the Bank of England and of gold coin and of gold and silver bullion respectively, and of securities in the said Issue Department, and also an account of the capital stock, and the deposits, and of the money and securities belonging to the said Governor and Company in the Banking Department of the Bank of England, on some day in every week to be fixed by the Commissioners of Stamps and Taxes, shall be transmitted by the said Governor and Company weekly to the said Commissioners in the form prescribed in the schedule hereto annexed marked (A) and shall be published by the said Commissioners in the next succeeding *London Gazette*, in which the same may be conveniently inserted."

The Return is published on Thursdays, and is made up to the close of business on the previous day.

The weekly Return issued by the Bank of England on September 7, 1844 (that is, shortly after the Bank Charter Act was passed) is given for comparison with the weekly return of Wednesday, June 23, 1909.

ISSUE DEPARTMENT.

	September 7, 1844.	June 23, 1909.
Notes issued	£28,351,295	£57,706,245
Government Debt	£11,015,100	£11,015,100
Other securities	2,984,900	7,434,900
Gold coin and bullion	12,657,208	39,256,245
Silver bullion	1,694,087	
	£28,351,295	£57,706,245

BANKING DEPARTMENT.

	September 7, 1844.	June 23, 1909.
Proprietors' capital	£14,553,000	£14,553,000
Rest	3,564,729	3,107,086
Public deposits	3,630,809	13,409,696
Other deposits	8,644,348	44,890,022
Seven day and other Bills	1,030,354	47,660
	£31,423,240	£76,007,464
Government securities	£14,554,834	£15,368,812
Other securities	7,835,616	30,707,163
Notes	8,175,025	28,328,680
Gold and silver coin	857,765	1,602,809
	£31,423,240	£76,007,464

The Bank of England is divided into two parts, the Issue Department and the Banking Department. In the return for June 23, 1909, the Issue Department section shows on the one side the total amount of notes issued from that department, £57,706,245; and on the other side the manner in which they are secured, that is by the Government debt, £11,015,100 (the amount of the debt at the passing of the Bank Charter Act); other securities, £7,434,900; gold coin and bullion, £39,256,245. When the Bank Charter Act was passed the combined amount of the debt owing by the Government to the Bank and of other securities was £14,000,000, and as the amount is now £18,450,000, an increase of £4,450,000 has taken place, due to the Bank having taken advantage of the privilege granted to it under the Act of increasing its issue against securities to the extent of two thirds of the issues of country bankers which have lapsed. The Issue Department does not hold any silver bullion, although the Bank has power under the Act to issue notes against silver bullion to the extent of one-fourth of the gold. (See BANK OF ENGLAND.)

The first item in the Banking Department of the Return is the proprietors' capital, £14,553,000. The original capital of the Bank, when it was established in 1694, was £1,200,000, and it was increased from time to time until it reached the amount of £14,553,000 in 1816, at which figure it has continued ever since. The next item is the Rest or Reserve Fund, £3,107,086, which has been accumulated from profits and to which the profits are added from time to time. The dividends to the Bank proprietors are paid out of this account, but the amount of the Rest is never allowed to fall below £3,000,000.

Public deposits, £13,409,696, represent the moneys paid in to the Bank by the Government Departments, "including Exchequer, Savings Bank, Commissioners of National Debt and Dividend Accounts." In the March quarter the figures in this item increase very considerably owing to the income tax and other taxes which have been credited to the Government accounts.

Other deposits, £44,890,022, include the accounts of the ordinary customers of the Bank in London and at the branches of the Bank, and also the balances of the London clearing bankers and other London banks, and of many country banks. The Bank of England is thus the Bank upon which all other banks would rely in a time of pressure. In ordinary times when money is abundant and not in demand, the amount of other deposits increases, owing to bankers keeping larger balances in the bank, but when the demand for money becomes stronger the bankers' balances diminish and the amount of other deposits therefore decreases.

Seven day and other bills, £47,660, include Bank Post Bills (see BANK POST BILL). The other side of the Banking Department Return, the assets side, shows how the funds have been invested. The first item, Government securities, £15,368,812, are those (e.g., Consols, Treasury Bills, Exchequer Bonds) which are guaranteed by the British Government. The next item is "other securities," £30,707,163—that is, other than Government investments. It includes general investments, also bills which have been discounted for customers and bill brokers, and loans against securities.

The "Reserve" is formed of the next two items on the Return, notes unemployed, £28,328,680, and gold and silver coin, £1,602,809. The notes on hand are part of those shown by the Issue Department as notes issued to the Banking Department. According as gold comes into the country or leaves it, the amount of the Reserve will increase or decrease.

When the Bank Rate is raised it tends to prevent the outward flow of gold and encourages an inward flow. On the other hand, a reduction of the Bank Rate has an exactly opposite tendency.

BANK STOCK. The stock or capital of the Bank of England.

The Bank was established in 1694 with a capital of £1,200,000, and by the year 1816 it had been increased to £14,553,000, at which figure it still stands.

BANKER AND CUSTOMER. The ordinary relationship between a banker and a customer is that of debtor and creditor. When a customer pays in money to the credit of his account, the banker becomes the debtor and the customer the creditor, but when the banker makes a loan to a customer the position is reversed, as the customer is then the debtor and the banker the creditor. The money which a banker receives from a customer is at the free disposal of the banker; he may preserve it in his till, invest it in some security, or lend it out to another customer; but the customer retains the right to demand back a similar amount, or to draw cheques upon the banker up to that sum, the cheques being payable either to the customer himself or to some other person. The customer may also accept bills and arrange with the banker that they be charged to his account at maturity, or he may, in certain cases, make arrangements for the banker to accept bills on his behalf. In order to constitute a person a customer, Lord Davey said, in *Great Western Railway* v. *London and County Banking Co.* (1901, A.C. 414): "I think there must be some sort of account, either a deposit or a current account or some similar relation."

When money has lain dormant with a banker for six years, the Statute of Limitations no doubt applies, as in an ordinary case of debtor and creditor, but a banker never takes advantage of the statute, and is always ready to repay the money upon the demand of the customer or of his legal representatives. (See STATUTE OF LIMITATIONS, UNCLAIMED BALANCES.)

If a customer leaves with his banker a parcel of securities for safe custody, the banker's position is that of a bailee, and his liability depends, to a certain extent, upon whether he undertakes the duty gratuitously or for reward. The difference between a banker as a debtor to his customer and as a bailee may be illustrated as follows:—If John Brown pays in £20 to the credit of his account, the banker becomes Brown's debtor and is liable to repay to Brown £20 on demand, but until the demand is made the banker can do what he likes with the money, and the £20 which is ultimately repaid to Brown is not, of course, the same coins as were originally handed by Brown to the banker; but if Brown gives to the banker a sealed bag containing, say, coins to the value of £20 and leaves it for safe custody, the banker becomes a bailee and must take care of the bag, as entrusted to him, and return it, with the contents untouched, to the customer when required. (See SAFE CUSTODY.)

The position between banker and customer may also be that of mortgagee and mortgagor, as where a customer grants a mortgage, for a fixed amount, to the banker. In such a case the banker can charge simple interest only upon the loan account. (See INTEREST.)

A banker and his staff are bound to secrecy regarding the business and accounts of the customers, but a banker may, in certain cases, be compelled to give evidence in a court of law, and he may also be required to give a copy of entries in the books of the bank. (See BANKERS' BOOKS EVIDENCE ACT, 1879.)

As to a banker's position when he is requested by another banker to supply an opinion as to the status or sufficiency of a customer, see BANKER'S OPINION.

A bank which is empowered by its memorandum of association may act in the capacity of sole executor under a will, or as trustee under a will or settlement, or as custodian trustee. (See CUSTODIAN TRUSTEE.)

Further information respecting the various matters and positions by which a banker is brought into more or less direct contact with his customers will be found under the respective headings, and in particular the following articles may be referred to:—ACCOUNTS, ADVANCES, BANKRUPT PERSON, COLLECTING BANKER, COMPANIES, DEATH OF CUSTOMER, DEPOSIT RECEIPT, PARTNERSHIPS, PAYING BANKER, PROMISSORY NOTE, SECURITY, STOCKBROKING TRANSACTIONS.

BANKERS' BOOKS EVIDENCE ACT 1879 (42 VICT. c. 11). This Act was passed on May 23, 1879. Its principal object is to enable bankers to be freed from the inconvenience of having to produce books which are in use in their business.

"Section 3. Subject to the provisions of this Act, a copy of any entry in a banker's book shall in all legal proceedings be received as *primâ-facie* evidence of such entry, and of the matters, transactions, and accounts therein recorded.

"4. A copy of an entry in a banker's book shall not be received in evidence under this Act unless it be first proved that the book was at the time of the making of the entry one of the ordinary books of the bank, and that the entry was made in the usual and ordinary course of business, and that the book is in the custody or control of the bank.

"Such proof may be given by a partner or officer of the bank, and may be given orally or by an affidavit sworn before any Commissioner or person authorised to take affidavits.

"5. A copy of an entry in a banker's book shall not be received in evidence under this Act unless it be further proved that the copy has been examined with the original entry and is correct.

"Such proof shall be given by some person who has examined the copy with the original entry, and may be given either orally or by an affidavit sworn before any Commissioner or person authorised to take affidavits.

"6. A banker or officer of a bank shall not, in any legal proceeding to which the bank is not a party, be compellable to produce any banker's books, the contents of which can be proved under this Act, or to appear as a witness to prove the matters, transactions, and accounts therein recorded, unless by order of a judge made for special cause.

"7. On the application of any party to a legal proceeding, a Court or judge may order that such party be at liberty to inspect and take copies of any entries in a banker's book for any of the purposes of such proceedings. An order under this Section may be made either with or without summoning the bank or any other party, and shall be served on the bank three clear days before the same is to be obeyed, unless the Court or judge otherwise directs.

"8. The costs of any application to a Court or judge under or for the purposes of this Act, and the costs of anything done or to be done under an order of a Court or judge made under or for the purposes of this Act, shall be in the discretion of the Court or judge, who may order the same or any part thereof to be paid to any party by the bank, where the same have been occasioned by any default or delay on the part of the bank. Any such order against a bank may be enforced as if the bank was a party to the proceeding.

"9. In this Act the expressions 'bank' and 'banker' mean any person, persons, partnership, or company carrying on the business of bankers and having duly made a return to the Commissioners of Inland Revenue, and also any savings bank certified under the Acts relating to savings banks, and also any Post Office Savings Bank.

". . . Expressions in this Act relating to 'bankers' books' include ledgers, day books, cash books, account books, and all other books used in the ordinary business of the bank.

"11. Sunday, Christmas Day, Good Friday, and any bank holiday shall be excluded from the computation of time under this Act."

By the Revenue Act, 1882, Section 11, the expressions "bank" and "bankers" in the Bankers' Books Evidence Act, 1879, shall include any company carrying on the business of bankers, to which the provisions of the Companies Acts apply and who have duly furnished to the Registrar of Joint Stock Companies the specified list and summary with a list of the places where their business is carried on.

BANKERS' CLEARING HOUSE. (See CLEARING HOUSE.)

BANKERS' LEDGER. The ledger in which are kept the accounts with other banks. The details of all transactions between a bank, including the branches, and its correspondent, are so entered that when the other bank sends a copy of the account in its ledger, the individual items may be readily compared and ticked off.

There will generally be, in most of the bank accounts, a number of items outstanding; as, for instance, where a draft has been drawn and credited in the account of the bank on which it is drawn, the item will not appear in the drawee bank's statement, and will therefore not be ticked off, until the drawee bank has actually paid the draft and debited the amount in account.

BANKER'S MORTGAGE. A mortgage which is given to a banker as a continuing security to cover any sum which shall for the time being constitute the balance due to the banker from the borrower. In a banker's mortgage there is usually a covenant that his right to sell the property shall arise immediately on default, after demand, or after, say, one month following demand. (See LEGAL MORTGAGE.)

BANKER'S OPINION. When a banker gives an opinion, in answer to a confidential inquiry, regarding the financial position of a customer, he should exercise the greatest care, for if he says too little he may injure his customer in the mind of the person on whose behalf the inquiry is made, and if he says too much he may mislead the inquirer.

A mere verbal opinion does not render a banker liable to an action for damages. In order to create liability for a wilfully inaccurate or misleading opinion, the representation must be in writing and be signed by the person making it, and it is the actual person who signs it who is liable. If a bank manager gives a false opinion in writing, he is personally responsible and not the banking company of which he is an official.

Where a bank manager had given a banker's opinion and an action was brought for damages for misrepresentation (*Parsons v. Barclay & Co. and another*, 1910, 103 L.T. 196), Mr. Justice Ridley, in addressing the jury, said: " I have to tell you that it will not do for you to find it was an inaccurate description of the state of things with regard to Messrs. G., it must be inaccurate to the knowledge of the person who made it. Though with some qualification that would be a true statement, I think I will just give the definition which is usually accepted as the one which is to guide a jury in such cases. ' In order that the statement should be fraudulent,' which is necessary to prove in this case if the plaintiff is to recover, ' it must be made knowing it not to be true, or without belief that it is true, or it must have been made recklessly or carelessly as to whether it was true or false.' "

Judgment was given for the plaintiff. The defendant appealed, and the Court of Appeal reversed the judgment. The Master of the Rolls said: " He wished emphatically to repudiate the suggestion that, when a banker was asked for a reference of this kind, it was any part of his duty to make inquiries outside as to the solvency or otherwise of the person asked about, or to do anything more than answer the question put to him honestly from what he knew from the books and accounts before him. To hold otherwise would be a very dangerous thing to do, and would put an end to a very wholesome and useful practice and long established custom which was now largely followed by bankers." Lord Justice Farwell said: " I thought everyone knew that these inquiries between bankers were well understood, were familiar, and that nobody supposed that one bank could ask another to go and hunt about and make inquiries. If inquiries are to be made, let the inquiring bank make them. What he asks from the bank from whom he makes the inquiry is, knowledge to be found in their books as to the state of the man or the account about whom he is inquiring; and it is done, not from any question of duty or any consideration, except that mutual courtesy and hope of a *quid pro quo*, to which Lord Bramwell refers."

By Section 6 of 9 Geo. IV c. 14 (called Lord Tenterden's Act):—

" No action shall be brought whereby to charge any person upon or by reason of any representation or assurance made or given concerning or relating to the character, conduct, credit, ability, trade or dealings of any other person, to the intent or purpose that such other person may obtain credit, money, or goods upon, unless such representation or assurance be made in writing, signed by the party to be charged therewith."

As bankers' opinions are usually given with care and caution, it follows that the bankers to whom they are addressed should accept them in a similar spirit of caution.

Details of a customer's account should not, of course, be communicated to any one unless by the request of the customer.

BANKER'S ORDER. A written order given by a customer to a banker to make a payment or series of payments on his behalf. It is commonly used to give authority to a banker to pay subscriptions to clubs and societies year by year, insurance premiums, etc. The following is a specimen form:—

BANKER'S ORDER.

January 2, 1910.

To the British Banking Co., Ltd., Leeds.

Please to pay to the X. & Y. Bank, Ltd., London, the sum of £2 2*s*., my subscription to the A.B. Club for the year 1910, and a like sum on January 1 in each succeeding year until otherwise ordered.

Signed, JOHN BROWN.

N.B.—This form to be signed by the member and forwarded by him to his own banker.

A book, like a diary, should be kept and details given under each date of the subscriptions or other periodical payments which are due to be paid upon such date.

Orders may be given by shareholders to pay all dividends upon their shares in the bank to the credit of their account in the bank, or to another bank. The following is a specimen of a form used for such a purpose :—

To the X. & Y. Bank, Ltd., London.

The Bank is hereby authorised and requested to pay to A. & B. Bank, Ltd., Bristol [or to the credit of my account at your Bristol Branch], until this authority is revoked in writing, all dividends and bonuses now or hereafter payable on all shares in the Bank standing in the name of the undersigned.

Dated this tenth day of June, 1910.

(Usual signature) J. BROWN.

Name in full—John Brown,

Address—2, Lorne Crescent, Bristol.

N.B.—This order must be signed by all the parties in whose names the shares are registered and their addresses added.

STAMP DUTY.—By a minute of the Board of Inland Revenue, May, 1904, the Board desired " to mention that they have some reason to think that orders to bankers for the payment of sums of money at stated periods (e.g., club subscriptions, and instalments of the price of articles purchased on the hire system) are frequently not stamped. The omission of the stamp is doubtless due to a misapprehension as to the provisions of the law ; but it is clear that such orders fall within the definition in Section 32 (*b*) of the Stamp Act, and should in all cases bear stamps." (See under BILL OF EXCHANGE.) The various debits to a customer's account, which arise out of the order, do not require to be stamped.

An order to a banker to pay over a certain sum of money against delivery of specified securities is also chargeable with the stamp duty of one penny. (See STOCKBROKING TRANSACTIONS.)

BANKER'S PAYMENT. A payment made by one banker to another. In settlement of a local clearing, a draft may be issued for the balance which is due, or the money may be paid over through the London office of the one bank to the London office of the other. Where cheques are remitted direct from bank A to bank B, for payment over through London, bank B requests its London office or agents (bank C) to pay the amount to bank D (the London office or agents of A) for the credit of bank A.

BANKERS' RECEIPTS. Receipts given by bankers, on behalf of a company, for payments made on application for shares or for payments of calls. (See APPLICATION FOR SHARES.) Receipts on account of applications for shares must be preserved in order to be exchanged in due course for the share certificates. They do not form a security for an advance.

Receipts upon a duly stamped letter of allotment are exempt from stamp duty. (See RECEIPT, Exemption 11.)

BANKING COMPANY. The Sections of the Companies (Consolidation) Act, 1908, which particularly refer to banking companies are as follow :—

Section 1, s.s. 1 :—

" No company, association, or partnership consisting of more than ten persons shall be formed for the purpose of carrying on the business of banking, unless it is registered as a company under this Act, or is formed in pursuance of some other Act of Parliament, or of letters patent."

A statement is to be made by a limited banking company in accordance with Section 108, which is as follows :—

" (1) Every company being a limited banking company or an insurance company or a deposit, provident, or benefit society shall, before it commences business, and also on the first Monday in February and the first Tuesday in August in every year during which it carries on business, make a statement in the form marked C in the first schedule to this Act, or as near thereto as circumstances will admit.

" (2) A copy of the statement shall be put up in a conspicuous place in the registered office of the company, and in every branch office or place where the business of the company is carried on.

" (3) Every member and every creditor of the company shall be entitled to a copy of the statement, on payment of a sum not exceeding sixpence.

" (4) If default is made in compliance with this Section, the company shall be liable to a fine not exceeding five pounds for every day during which the default continues ; and every director and manager of the company who knowingly and wilfully authorises or permits the default shall be liable to the like penalty.

"(5) For the purposes of this Act a company that carries on the business of insurance in common with any other business or businesses shall be deemed to be an insurance company.

"(6) This Section shall not apply to any life assurance company nor any other assurance company to which the provisions of the Life Assurance Companies Acts, 1870 to 1872, as to the annual statements to be made by such a company, apply with or without modifications, if the company complies with those provisions.

FORM C.

"*Form of Statement to be published by Banking and Insurance Companies, and Deposit, Provident, or Benefit Societies.*

"* The share capital of the company is , divided into shares of each.

"The number of shares issued is

Calls to the amount of pounds per share have been made, under which the sum of pounds has been received

"The liabilities of the company on the first day of January (*or* July) were—

"Debts owing to sundry persons by the company.

"On judgment, £

"On specialty, £

"On notes or bills, £

"On simple contracts, £

"On estimated liabilities, £

"The assets of the company on that day were—

"Government securities [*stating them*]

"Bills of exchange and promissory notes, £

"Cash at the bankers, £

"Other securities, £ ."

By Section 109 it is provided that the Board of Trade may appoint one or mor competent inspectors to investigate th affairs of any company, and to repor thereon in such manner as the Board direct: in the case of a banking company having a share capital, on the application of members holding not less than one-third of the shares issued. (See INVESTIGATION OF COMPANY'S AFFAIRS.)

* If the company has no share capital the portion of the statement relating to capital and shares must be omitted.

By Section 113, s.s. 5:—

"In the case of a banking company registered after August 15, 1879:—

"(*a*) If the company has branch banks beyond the limits of Europe, it shall be sufficient if the auditor is allowed access to such copies of and extracts from the books and accounts of any such branch as have been transmitted to the head office of the company in the United Kingdom; and

"(*b*) The balance sheet must be signed by the secretary or manager (if any), and where there are more than three directors of the company by at least three of those directors, and where there are not more than three directors by all the directors."

The following two sections are to be read as part of Part VII of the Companies (Consolidation) Act.

"*Liability of Bank of Issue Unlimited in Respect of Notes.*

"251. (1) A bank of issue registered under this Act as a limited company shall not be entitled to limited liability in respect of its notes; and the members thereof shall be liable in respect of its notes in the same manner as if it had been registered as unlimited; but if, in the event of the company being wound up, the general assets are insufficient to satisfy the claims of both the note-holders and the general creditors, then the members, after satisfying the remaining demands of the note-holders, shall be liable to contribute towards payment of the debts of the general creditors a sum equal to the amount received by the note-holders out of the general assets.

"(2) For the purposes of this Section the expression 'the general assets' means the funds available for payment of the general creditor as well as the note-holder.

"(3) Any bank of issue registered under this Act as a limited company may state on its notes that the limited liability does not extend to its notes, and that the members of the company are liable in respect of its notes in the same manner as if it had been registered as an unlimited company."

On Registration of Banking Company with Limited Liability, Notice to be given to Customers.

"256. (1) Where a banking company which was in existence on the seventh day of August eighteen hundred and sixty-two proposes to register as a limited company, it shall, at least thirty days before so registering, give notice of its intention so to register to every person who has a banking account with the company, either by delivery of the notice to him, or by posting it to him at, or delivering it at, his last known address.

(2) If the company omits to give the notice required by this Section, then as between the company and the person for the time being interested in the account in respect of which the notice ought to have been given, and so far as respects the account down to the time at which notice is given, but not further or otherwise, the certificate of registration with limited liability shall have no operation."

Section 286, s.s. 1, repealed various Acts, provided that the repeal shall not affect :—

"(*d*) The continuance in force of the enactments set out in the second part of the sixth schedule to this Act, being the enactments continued in force by Section two hundred and five of the Companies Act, 1862."

The enactments referred to in that Section are :—

"An Act to regulate Joint Stock Banks in England (7 & 8 Vict. c. 113), Section 47.

Existing Companies to have the Powers of Suing and being Sued.

"Every company of more than six persons established on the sixth day of May one thousand eight hundred and forty-four, for the purpose of carrying on the trade or business of bankers within the distance of sixty-five miles from London, and not within the provisions of the Act passed in the session of the seventh and eighth years of Queen Victoria, chapter one hundred and thirteen, intituled 'An Act to regulate Joint Stock Banks in England,' shall have the same powers and privileges of suing and being sued in the name of any one of the public officers of such co-partnership as the nominal plaintiff, petitioner, or defendant on behalf of such co-partnership ; and all judgments, decrees, and orders made and obtained in any such suit may be enforced in like manner as is provided with respect to such companies carrying on the said trade or business at any place in England exceeding the distance of sixty-five miles from London under the provisions of the Country Bankers Act, 1826, provided that such first-mentioned company shall make out and deliver from time to time to the Commissioners of Inland Revenue the several accounts or returns required by the last-mentioned Act, and all the provisions of the last-recited Act as to such accounts or returns shall be taken to apply to the accounts or returns so made out and delivered by such first-mentioned companies as if they had been originally included in the provisions of the last-recited Act.

"The Joint Stock Banking Companies Act, 1857, Part of Section 12.

Power to form Banking Partnerships of Ten Persons.

"Notwithstanding anything contained in any Act passed in the session holden in the seventh and eighth years of Queen Victoria, chapter one hundred and thirteen, and intituled 'An Act to regulate Joint Stock Banks in England,' or in any other Act, it shall be lawful for any number of persons, not exceeding ten, to carry on in partnership the business of banking, in the same manner and upon the same conditions in all respects as any company of not more than six persons could before the passing of the Joint Stock Banking Companies Act, 1857, have carried on such business." (See Companies.)

BANKRUPT PERSON. A person who has been adjudicated a bankrupt by the Court of Bankruptcy. In the early days of banking, when a banker failed, his bench, or banco, at which he did business, was broken by the people, whence the word bankrupt. (It. *banco*, a bench. Lat. *ruptus*, broken.)

When a banker receives notice that a customer has committed an act of bankruptcy, or that a receiving order has been made, he must not pay any further cheques upon the account (not even if they have been specially provided for), and he should return them marked "Refer to drawer." (See Acts of Bankruptcy.) On the making of a receiving order an official receiver is thereby constituted receiver of the property of the debtor (see RECEIVING ORDER), and any funds which a banker may hold belonging to the debtor must be handed over, when required, to the official receiver or trustee in bankruptcy.

Any personal earnings of a bankrupt during his bankruptcy may be used by him for the support of himself and family, but, if he earns more than is reasonably necessary for such a purpose, the surplus belongs to the trustee, if he claims it. Such money includes wages earned by the personal labours of the bankrupt, but it does not include money earned by carrying on a trade or business.

Any property acquired by a bankrupt prior to his discharge is liable to be claimed by his trustee. In "The Laws of England," by the Earl of Halsbury, it is stated that "until the trustee intervenes, all transactions by a bankrupt after his adjudication with any person dealing with him *bonâ fide* and for value in respect of his after acquired property other than real estate, with or without knowledge of the bankruptcy, are valid; the trustee, when he intervenes, is bound by such transactions, and by the rights of third persons so acquired."

A banker cannot, as a rule, recognise which is "after acquired property" and which is not, and therefore he should not open an account with an undischarged bankrupt, nor should he cash a cheque to a payee or indorser who is known to be an undischarged bankrupt, otherwise he may come into conflict with the claims of the trustee and be obliged to account to him for moneys paid to the bankrupt or by the bankrupt's order.

Caution is necessary if the wife of an undischarged bankrupt wishes to open an account in order to carry on the business, unless the trustee has consented thereto.

With respect to a bankrupt obtaining credit, Section 31 of the Bankruptcy Act, 1883, provides :—

"Where an undischarged bankrupt who has been adjudged bankrupt under this Act obtains credit to the extent of twenty pounds or upwards from any person without informing such person that he is an undischarged bankrupt, he shall be guilty of a misdemeanor, and may be dealt with and punished as if he had been guilty of a misdemeanor under the Debtors Act, 1869, and the provisions of that Act shall apply to proceedings under this Section."

By Section 32 of the same Act :—

DISQUALIFICATIONS OF BANKRUPT.

"(1) Where a debtor is adjudged bankrupt he shall, subject to the provisions of this Act, be disqualified for—

(*a*) Sitting or voting in the House of Lords, or on any committee thereof, or being elected as a peer of Scotland or Ireland to sit and vote in the House of Lords;

(*b*) Being elected to, or sitting or voting in, the House of Commons, or on any committee thereof;

(*c*) Being appointed or acting as a justice of the peace;

(*d*) Being elected to or holding or exercising the office of mayor, alderman, or councillor;

(*e*) Being elected to or holding or exercising the office of guardian of the poor, overseer of the poor, member of a sanitary authority, or member of a school board, highway board, burial board, or select vestry.

"(2) The disqualifications to which a bankrupt is subject under this section shall be removed and cease if and when—

(*a*) the adjudication of bankruptcy against him is annulled; or

(*b*) he obtains from the Court his discharge with a certificate to the effect that his bankruptcy was caused by misfortune without any misconduct on his part.

The Court may grant or withhold such certificate as it thinks fit, but any refusal of such certificate shall be subject to appeal.

"(3) The disqualifications imposed by this Section shall extend to all parts of the United Kingdom.' (See BANKRUPTCY.)

BANKRUPT ACCEPTOR.—Where the acceptor of a bill which is not yet due becomes bankrupt, the banker cannot compel the person for whom he discounted the bill to take it up.

BANKRUPT AGENT.—Bankruptcy does not

prevent a person acting as agent, including the signing of cheques, if so authorised.

BANKRUPT DRAWEE.—Presentment of the bill may be made to him or to his trustee (Section 41, s.s. (*d*), Bills of Exchange Act).

BANKRUPT DRAWER.—No further cheques should be paid upon his account, with the exception of any cheque which the banker may have previously marked for payment at the drawer's request, or for the banker's own convenience in connection with the local clearing. (See MARKED CHEQUE.)

In the case of a bill, where both the drawer and the acceptor are bankrupt, the banker may claim for the full amount of the bill against both estates. But if a dividend has been declared on one of the estates before the banker sends in his proof of debt on the other estate, he can only claim for the balance after crediting the dividend. If there is any balance standing to credit of the customer it can be retained against the bill.

Where notice of dishonour requires to be given, it may be given either to the drawer himself or to his trustee.

BANKRUPT INDORSER.—A notice of dishonour may be given to the indorser himself or to his trustee. As to payments to a bankrupt indorser, see BANKRUPT PERSON.

INFANT.—An infant cannot be made bankrupt.

BANKRUPT, JOINT ACCOUNT, JOINT DEPOSITOR.—On the bankruptcy of one of joint customers, the other, or others, may draw any balance standing to credit. Where a loan has been made to two persons jointly, upon the bankruptcy of one, the other becomes liable for the full debt.

BANKRUPT, MARRIED WOMAN.—If she carries on a business entirely separate from her husband, she is, as regards her own property, subject to the bankruptcy laws.

BANKRUPT — PARTNERSHIP — PARTNER.—See Section 40 of the Bankruptcy Act, 1883, under PROOF OF DEBTS.

A partnership is dissolved by the bankruptcy of a partner. (See Section 33 of the Partnership Act, 1890, under PARTNERSHIPS.) The remaining partners may withdraw any balance standing at credit of the firm's account.

If a partner deposits his own personal securities for the firm's account, the banker may claim upon the bankrupt firm's estate for the full amount of the debt.

Where a partner has become bankrupt, he is no longer able by his acts to bind the firm ; but if another partner has, since the bankruptcy, represented himself as being still a partner with the bankrupt, he will be liable. (See PARTNERSHIPS.)

When a firm is bankrupt, the individual partners are also bankrupt, and no further operations on any of the accounts may take place.

BANKRUPT PAYEE.—The drawer of a cheque need not stop payment of it merely because the payee has become bankrupt ; but see BANKRUPT PERSON (above) with respect to a cheque when presented for payment by a bankrupt.

BANKRUPT, SAFE CUSTODY.—Any articles left for safe custody should not be given up to a bankrupt. When a receiving order is made the bankrupt's property vests in the official receiver.

BANKRUPT, SECURITIES.—See rules regarding securities under PROOF OF DEBTS.

Bankruptcy does not affect a banker's rights to any securities belonging to the bankrupt, over which the banker has merely an equitable charge.

Where securities have been given for the bankrupt's account by some one other than the debtor himself, the proceeds of such securities should be placed to a separate account until all the dividends have been received from the debtor's estate, unless the depositor thereof (or the guarantor, as the case may be) pays off the whole of the debt and claims himself upon the estate. The advantage of a collateral security, taken in the usual form, is that, if it is not sufficient to clear off the whole debt, the banker may claim for the full debt upon the bankrupt's estate, and then fall back upon the amount realised from that security, and thus in many cases obtain full repayment of the debt. (See GUARANTEE.)

BANKRUPT SURETY.—When a guarantor for an account becomes bankrupt the debtor's account should be stopped until fresh arrangements are made. If new security is not forthcoming and the debtor is unable to repay, the banker makes a claim upon the surety's estate.

VOLUNTARY CONVEYANCES AND TRANSFERS.—If bankruptcy occurs within two years after the date of a voluntary transfer, the transfer is void, and the trustee can claim the property. If bankruptcy occurs within ten years, the transfer is also void, unless it can be proved that the bankrupt was solvent, at the time of making the transfer, without the aid of the property comprised in the conveyance. (See BANKRUPTCY.)

BANKRUPTCY. When a person is unable to pay his debts, his property is, in certain circumstances, taken possession of by the official receiver or trustee in bankruptcy, who realises it and distributes the proceeds amongst the creditors. Such a proceeding is called bankruptcy, and the debtor is known as the bankrupt.

The law of bankruptcy in England is contained in the Bankruptcy Acts of 1883 46 & 47 Vict. c. 52) and 1890 (53 & 54 Vict. c. 71).

Where a debtor has committed an act of bankruptcy (see ACTS OF BANKRUPTCY), a creditor, or creditors, whose debt or debts amount to not less than £50, may petition the Court which has bankruptcy jurisdiction over the debtor, to make a receiving order (see RECEIVING ORDER), with the object of having the debtor's estate administered under the bankruptcy law for the benefit of the creditors. A bankruptcy petition may also be presented by the debtor himself. A debtor is not adjudged a bankrupt immediately upon the making of a receiving order, but a general meeting of creditors (see MEETING OF CREDITORS) is held shortly after the order is made, to consider whether a composition or scheme of arrangement shall be entertained or whether he shall be adjudged bankrupt.

After a receiving order is made, the debtor must make out and submit to the official receiver (that is, the official of the Court who takes control of the debtor's estate) a statement of his affairs. (See Section 16 of the 1883 Act, under RECEIVING ORDER. See also OFFICIAL RECEIVER.)

As soon as convenient after the expiration of the time for the submission of a debtor's statement of affairs, the Court shall hold a public sitting for the examination of the debtor, but the Court shall not declare that his examination is concluded until after the day appointed for the first meeting of creditors. (See PUBLIC EXAMINATION OF DEBTOR.)

If a debtor intends to make a proposal to his creditors for a composition in satisfaction of his debts, or a proposal for a scheme of arrangement of his affairs, he must, within four days of submitting his statement of affairs, or within such time as the official receiver may fix, lodge his proposal with the official receiver, embodying the terms of the composition or scheme and setting out particulars of any sureties or securities proposed. (See COMPOSITIONS.)

If the debtor's proposal is accepted by the creditors, the receiving order is discharged. If a trustee is not appointed, the official receiver acts as trustee for the purpose of receiving and distributing the composition, or for the purpose of carrying out the terms of the scheme. A creditor under a composition or scheme must lodge his proof of debt with the trustee.

If the composition or scheme is not accepted within fourteen days after the conclusion of the debtor's examination, or such time as is allowed by the Court, or if the creditors resolve that the debtor be adjudged bankrupt, or if they do not pass any resolution, the Court shall adjudge the debtor bankrupt (see ADJUDICATION OF BANKRUPTCY), and thereupon his property shall vest in a trustee (see TRUSTEE IN BANKRUPTCY), and be divisible amongst his creditors.

The bankruptcy of a debtor, whether it takes place on his own petition or that of a creditor, dates back to the time of the act of bankruptcy being committed on which the receiving order was made against him. (Section 43 of the Bankruptcy Act, 1883. See under ADJUDICATION OF BANKRUPTCY.)

The creditors may appoint a committee of inspection to superintend the administration of the bankrupt's property by the trustee. (See COMMITTEE OF INSPECTION.)

A trustee may be authorised by the Board of Trade to open a local banking account. (See Section 74 and rule 340 under TRUSTEE IN BANKRUPTCY.)

Where the committee of inspection approve, the trustee of a bankrupt's estate may pledge any deeds belonging to the estate, if the money is required for payment of the bankrupt's debts.

A creditor's claim against a bankrupt's estate must be made on oath and upon the prescribed form called the proof of debt. (See PROOF OF DEBTS.)

A bankrupt may, at any time after being adjudged bankrupt, apply to the Court for an order of discharge, and the Court shall appoint a day for hearing the application. (See DISCHARGE OF BANKRUPT.)

If a debtor gives a creditor a preference over other creditors, and he is adjudged a bankrupt on a petition presented within three months thereafter, the preference shall be deemed fraudulent and void as against the trustee. (See FRAUDULENT PREFERENCE.)

Any settlement of property shall, if the settlor becomes bankrupt within two years after the date of the settlement, be void against the trustee, or if he becomes bankrupt at any time within ten years after that date, be also void against the trustee, unless it is proved that the settlor was able to pay all his debts at the time he made the settlement, without the aid of the property comprised therein. (See SETTLEMENTS—SETTLOR BANKRUPT.)

Section 49 of the Bankruptcy Act, 1883, with respect to *bonâ fide* transactions without notice, provides as follows :—

"Subject to the foregoing provisions of this Act with respect to the effect of bankruptcy on an execution or attachment, and with respect to the avoidance of certain settlements and preferences, nothing in this Act shall invalidate, in the case of a bankruptcy—

(*a*) Any payment by the bankrupt to any of his creditors,

(*b*) Any payment or delivery to the bankrupt,

(*c*) Any conveyance or assignment by the bankrupt for valuable consideration,

(*d*) Any contract, dealing, or transaction by or with the bankrupt for valuable consideration,

Provided that both the following conditions are complied with, namely—

"(1) The payment, delivery, conveyance, assignment, contract, dealing, or transaction, as the case may be, takes place before the date of the receiving order ; and

"(2) The person (other than the debtor) to, by, or with whom the payment, delivery, conveyance, assignment, contract, dealing, or transaction was made, executed, or entered into, has not at the time of the payment, delivery, conveyance, assignment, contract, dealing, or transaction, notice of any available act of bankruptcy committed by the bankrupt before that time."

It is the duty of the trustee to declare and distribute dividends amongst the creditors who have proved their debts. (See DIVIDENDS—IN BANKRUPTCY.)

If a debtor's estate is not likely to exceed £300 in value, it may be administered in a simpler manner than in the case of an ordinary bankruptcy. (See SUMMARY ADMINISTRATION.)

Where a judgment has been obtained in a county court and the debtor is unable to pay, and his total indebtedness does not exceed £50, the county court may make an administration order. (See ADMINISTRATION ORDER.)

A debtor who is unable to pay his creditors is not always dealt with under the Bankruptcy Acts. He may call his creditors together and offer a composition, that is, to pay each creditor only so much in the pound (see COMPOSITION WITH CREDITORS), or he may offer to assign his property to a trustee, in order that it may be realised and the proceeds divided amongst the creditors. (See ASSIGNMENT FOR BENEFIT OF CREDITORS.) When an arrangement is made in either of those ways and is embodied in a deed or agreement, the deed of arrangement or agreement must be registered within seven days. (See DEED OF ARRANGEMENT.)

Property which is acquired by an undischarged bankrupt may be claimed by his trustee. (See BANKRUPT PERSON.)

The estate of a deceased debtor may be administered by the Court, according to the law of bankruptcy. (See DEATH OF INSOLVENT DEBTOR.)

An advertisement in the *London Gazette* of a receiving order or an adjudication order is conclusive evidence of the order having been made. (See GAZETTED.)

Stamp Duty.

By Section 144 of the Bankruptcy Act, 1883 :—"Every deed, conveyance, assignment, surrender, admission, or other assurance relating solely to freehold, leasehold, copyhold, or customary property, or to any mortgage, charge, or other incumbrance on, or any estate, right, or interest in any real or personal property which is part of the estate of any bankrupt, and which, after the execution of the deed, conveyance, assignment, surrender, admission, or other assurance, either at law or in equity, is or remains the estate of the bankrupt or of the trustee under the bankruptcy, and every power of attorney, proxy paper, writ, order, certificate, affidavit, bond, or other instrument or writing relating solely to the property of any bankrupt, or to any proceeding under any bankruptcy, shall be exempt from stamp duty, except in respect of fees under this Act."

By Section 16 of the Finance Act, 1895, the above Section " shall apply to the estates of companies wound up by order of the Court under the Companies Winding-up Act, 1890, and to such winding-up, in like manner as if the company were a bankrupt and the winding-up were a bankruptcy." (See ACTS OF BANKRUPTCY, ADJUDICATION OF BANKRUPTCY, ADMINISTRATION ORDER, AFTER ACQUIRED PROPERTY (under heading BANKRUPT PERSON), ASSIGNMENT FOR BENEFIT OF CREDITORS, BANKRUPT PERSON, COMMITTEE OF INSPECTION, COMPOSITION WITH CREDITORS, COMPOSITIONS (BANKRUPTCY ACT), DEATH OF INSOLVENT DEBTOR, DEED OF ARRANGEMENT, DISCHARGE OF BANKRUPT, DISQUALIFICATIONS OF BANKRUPT (under heading BANKRUPT PERSON), DIVIDENDS (IN BANKRUPTCY), FRAUDULENT PREFERENCE, INSOLVENCY, MEETING OF CREDITORS, OFFICIAL RECEIVER, PREFERENTIAL PAYMENTS, PROOF OF DEBTS, PUBLIC EXAMINATION OF DEBTOR, RECEIVING ORDER, REGISTRARS (IN BANKRUPTCY), SETTLEMENTS—SETTLOR BANKRUPT, SUMMARY ADMINISTRATION, TRUSTEE IN BANKRUPTCY.)

BANKRUPTCY PETITION. (See RECEIVING ORDER.)

BAR GOLD. Much of the Bank of England's stock of gold is not in the form of coins, but of bars, which, from an exporter's point of view, are often preferable, one reason being that the quantity lost by friction in transit is less in the case of bars than of coin. The Bank is bound to pay in sovereigns any amount of its notes that may be tendered, but if a bullion merchant prefers to take bars, the Bank raises no objection and usually charges the mint price of gold, i.e., £3 17*s.* 10½*d.* per oz.; should, however, the demand become sufficiently keen, the Bank may raise the price of bars (*not* raise the price of sovereigns, that it cannot do) to £3 17*s.* 11*d.* per oz., but it would not be worth while to increase it above this figure, for then an exporter would find it cheaper for his purpose to get sovereigns to be sent abroad, to fill the place of which the Bank would be reduced to having some of its bars minted.

Any one has the right to take bar gold to the Mint, provided that the value is not less than £20,000, and have it coined at the rate of £3 17*s.* 10½*d.* per oz. of standard gold, free of all expense of coining, but as a certain period must elapse before the bullion is turned into coins, during which time the owner of the gold would lose interest upon it, it is the practice to sell gold bullion to the Bank of England. The price at which the Bank of England must buy all gold that is offered to it is £3 17*s.* 9*d.* per oz. By the Bank Charter Act, 1844, Section 4, "all persons shall be entitled to demand from the issue department of the Bank of England, Bank of England notes in exchange for gold bullion at the rate of £3 17*s.* 9*d.* per oz. of standard gold: Provided always, that the said Governor and Company shall in all cases be entitled to require such gold bullion to be melted and assayed by persons approved by the said Governor and Company at the expense of the parties tendering such gold bullion." The notes can, of course, be at once exchanged for sovereigns. The difference of 1½*d.* per oz. between the buying and the selling prices forms the Bank's profit, or rather its remuneration for the trouble of getting the bullion minted if required, and for the loss of interest upon the bullion before it is turned into coins.

Bar gold is a kind of international currency travelling about from one nation to another in settlement of exchange balances without ever being minted into any country's coinage. (See MINT PRICE.)

BAR OF DOWER. That which bars or prevents a widow from obtaining dower. (See DOWER.)

BARGAIN AND SALE. This is a contract in English law, whereby property, either real or personal, is transferred from one person to another for a valuable consideration. The word "assignment" is, however, usually used for the transfer of personal property; consequently, bargain and sale may be described as a contract whereby real estate, that is, lands or tenements, whether in possession or in remainder, are conveyed from one person to another for a consideration. (See CUSTOMARY PROPERTY.)

BASE COINS. A banker is justified in breaking or destroying any base coins which come into his hands. Section 26 of 24 & 25 Vict. c. 99 enacts: "Where any coin shall be tendered as the Queen's current gold or silver coin to any person who shall suspect the same to be diminished otherwise than by reasonable wearing, or to be counterfeit, it shall be lawful for such person to cut, break, bend, or deface such coin, and if any coin so cut, broken, bent or defaced shall appear to be diminished otherwise than by reasonable wearing, or to be counterfeit, the person tendering the same shall bear the loss thereof, but if the same shall be of due weight, and shall appear to be lawful coin, the person cutting, breaking, bending, or defacing the same is hereby required to receive the same at the rate it was coined for; and if any dispute shall arise whether the coin so cut, broken, bent or defaced be diminished in manner aforesaid, or counterfeit, it shall be heard and finally determined in a summary manner by any justice of the peace, who is hereby empowered to examine upon oath as well the parties as any other person, in order to the decision of such dispute ; and the Tellers at the Receipt of Her Majesty's Exchequer, and their deputies and clerks, and the Receivers-General of every branch of Her Majesty's Revenue, are hereby required to cut, break, or deface, or cause to be cut, broken, or defaced every piece of counterfeit or unlawfully diminished gold or silver coin which shall be tendered to them in payment of any part of Her Majesty's Revenue."

Base silver coins are very frequently met with, and in some cases they are rather difficult at first sight to distinguish from genuine ones. Various tests are applied to a suspected "silver" coin. If it is a base one it will be easily cut, or bent, or broken, and its general appearance to the eye of an expert will call attention to its real nature. On close examination it will usually be found that the raised letters or figures are not so sharply defined as on a real coin. An examination of the milling will reveal a roughness and irregularity, which is often particularly noticeable at a spot on the edge representing the place where the metal was poured into the mould. Its weight and size may be tested with a good coin, and also its sound when thrown upon the counter. The sound by itself, however, is not sufficient, as a good coin which is cracked will not give the true ring. If caustic marks the coin black it reveals its baseness, but that test may be defeated if the surface is a thin coat of silver. A pocket lens is useful in the examination of a doubtful coin as it makes the roughness of a counterfeit coin more noticeable. Those officers who are much in contact with silver profess to be able to tell a false from a genuine coin by the touch, the false one having a "greasy" kind of feeling. "A coin or other object made of silver may be known by the following marks : (1) A fine pure white lustre, where newly rubbed or scraped ; (2) a blackish tint where the surface has long been exposed to the air ; (3) a moderate specific gravity ; (4) a good metallic ring when thrown down ; (5) considerable hardness ; (6) strong nitric acid dissolves silver, and the solution turns black if exposed to light" (Jevons).

"We can usually ascertain whether a coin consists of gold or not, by looking for three characteristic marks : (1) the brilliant yellow colour ; (2) the high specific gravity ; (3) the metallic ring of the coin when thrown down, which will prove the absence of lead or platinum in the interior of the coin. Gold is insoluble in all the simple acids and does not corrode or become tarnished in any way. Strong nitric acid will rapidly attack any coloured counterfeit metal, but will not touch standard gold, or will, at the most, feebly dissolve the copper and silver alloyed with it" (Jevons).

Where a customer receives money in payment of a cheque and takes it away without making any comment upon it, he cannot, legally, return to the banker and say that it contained a base coin. (See COINAGE.)

BAWBEE. The name of a coin, equal in value to the present halfpenny, which was at one time current in Scotland. It was issued in the reign of James V of Scotland.

The word is still frequently used in Scotland when speaking of a halfpenny.

BEAR AND BULL. Names given to speculators on a stock exchange. A bear is one who anticipates a fall in a certain security, and who sells stock which he does not possess, hoping to buy back afterwards at a lower price, the difference constituting his profit.

A bull, on the other hand, expects a stock to rise in price, and so he buys in, not with the intention of paying for it but with the object of selling out before the settling day at an advanced figure. (See BACKWARDATION, CONTANGO, STOCK EXCHANGE.)

BEARER (CHEQUE OR BILL). "Bearer," in the Bills of Exchange Act, 1882, means the person in possession of a bill or note which is payable to bearer (Section 2).

"A bill is payable to bearer which is expressed to be so payable, or on which the only or last indorsement is an indorsement in blank" (Section 8, s.s. 3).

"Where the payee is a fictitious or non-existing person the bill may be treated as payable to bearer" (Section 7, s.s. 3). A bill in these sections includes a cheque.

A bill (or cheque) payable to bearer does not require to be indorsed ; and a person cannot be sued upon it, so long as it is not indorsed by him. If, however, he indorses it, he may be sued thereon by any subsequent holder.

If a cheque drawn payable to bearer is indorsed "Pay J. Brown or order," it does not require John Brown's signature or any indorsement, as it is on the face of it a bearer cheque. Any indorsements on a bearer cheque need not be examined.

In practice, a bearer cheque may be altered by the payee from bearer to order, by simply striking out the printed word bearer, or by striking it out and writing the word order. Such an alteration does not require to be initialled.

An order cheque, however, can be altered on the face into a bearer cheque only by the drawer, who must initial the alteration; if there are more drawers than one, each must initial.

When an order cheque is indorsed in blank, that is, is not made payable to any one else by the payee or indorser, it becomes a cheque payable to bearer. Any holder may convert the blank indorsement into a special indorsement, and the cheque (or bill) would again become payable to order.

A cheque or bill payable to a fictitious or non-existing person is payable to bearer. In the case of *Bank of England* v. *Vagliano Brothers* (1891, A.C. 107), it was held that a fictitious or non-existing person included a real person who never had nor was intended to have any right to the bills. Lord Herschell said: "I have arrived at the conclusion that whenever the name inserted as that of the payee is so inserted by way of pretence merely, without any intention that payment shall only be made in conformity therewith, the payee is a fictitious person within the meaning of the statute, whether the name be that of an existing person or of one who has no existence."

A banker incurs no liability in paying, to the person presenting, an uncrossed cheque made payable to bearer by the drawer, even if the person who presents such cheque has stolen it. But in an exceptional case, such as where a cheque is payable to the "British Bank, Ltd., or bearer," a banker would require to be exceedingly careful in making inquiries before paying such a cheque to a stranger, for although it is payable to the bearer the banker knows that it is not the custom for a bank to send a cheque by a stranger to be cashed.

Where a person takes a cheque payable to bearer, it is advisable for him to get the transferor to indorse it and so make him a party to the cheque, as without the indorsement the transferor could not be sued upon the cheque.

A cheque payable to "Wages or order," "Cash or order," "House or order" or to any such impersonal word, is now usually treated as being payable to "order" and requiring the indorsement of the drawer. Such cheques should, when indorsed, be paid only to the drawer, or his representative who is known to be authorised to cash "wages," etc., cheques. Some bankers consider that a cheque payable in that manner is, by virtue of s.s. 3 of Section 7, quoted above, payable to "bearer," but the words "fictitious or non-existing person" can hardly be taken to include such words as "wages," "cash," etc.

In Scotland, it is customary to request the person receiving cash for a bearer cheque to indorse it. (See BILL OF EXCHANGE, CHEQUE.)

BEARER BONDS. A bearer bond, that is a bond which is payable to the bearer, in contradistinction to a bond which is registered in the name of the holder, passes by mere delivery the full benefits conferred by the bond, so long as the transferee takes it in good faith and for value and without notice of any defect in the transferor's title. If it should ultimately appear that the transferor had stolen the bond, or had otherwise a defective title, the transferee's right to retain the bond would not be affected. A bearer bond belongs to the class of documents called negotiable instruments. (See NEGOTIABLE INSTRUMENTS.) Formerly, only bearer bonds which were issued in foreign countries and treated in this country by merchants as negotiable, were regarded by the Courts as negotiable instruments, but, within recent years, debentures to bearer of an English company have been recognised by the Courts as negotiable instruments.

In *Edelstein* v. *Schuler* (1902, 2 K.B. 144), Bigham, J., said: "In my opinion the time has passed when the negotiability of bearer bonds, whether Government bonds or trading bonds, foreign or English, can be called in question in our Courts."

Attached to the bond, or in a separate sheet, is a series of coupons, each one being dated, if the interest is payable half-yearly, for a different half-year, and forming the warrant, upon production of which, the holder will be paid the interest represented by that coupon. Some coupons are not dated, being payable according to advertisement. A coupon sheet should not be detached from the bond. Securities to bearer, without the current coupon, are not a good delivery on the Stock Exchange. The possessor of bearer bonds should never write his name upon them, as it might cause them to form a bad delivery.

Bankers are frequently requested by customers to take charge of their bearer bonds and to collect the coupons as they fall due, and, in the case of bonds payable by periodical drawings, to watch the published lists of numbers which are drawn. All bearer bonds held by a banker, whether for safe custody or security, should be entered in a register immediately upon receipt, and it is preferable that all bearer securities held in any office should be entered in a separate book, or at any rate in a special section of the ordinary safe custody or securities register, so that any one can ascertain at once what bearer securities are held in that office. The number of each bond or bearer security should be entered in the register, and, when any of them are given up to the customers, a proper receipt should be taken, either in the book or on a separate slip, setting forth the actual numbers and descriptions of the bonds. Bearer securities being, like cash, transferable by delivery, it is necessary that a banker should take the greatest care of them, and in many banks all bearer securities are kept continuously under the control of two persons. Coupons should be entered up in a diary on the due dates, so that they may be cut off and sent for collection in good time and not be overlooked.

Certain bonds are drawn as being payable to the bearer, or "when registered, to the registered holder." In such cases the name of the registered holder is entered in a place provided on the back of the bond.

Where bearer bonds are given as security, a banker usually takes a memorandum or agreement showing the purpose for which they are lodged. No deed of transfer is necessary, as they pass to the holder by simple delivery, and even if the bonds form part of a trust and the banker had no notice of the trust when he took them as security, his title will not be affected. (See NEGOTIABLE INSTRUMENTS.) An advance should not, of course, be made against coupons without the bond.

When bonds are left for safe custody in joint names, particularly when the parties are trustees, the banker should be most careful not to part with the bonds unless upon the signatures of all the parties. It has been held that trustees may give authority to one of their number to cut off coupons from bonds deposited for safe custody as they fall due. In such a case it is the banker's duty to see that nothing more is removed than the coupons which are falling due. (See SAFE CUSTODY.)

As to Stamp Duties, see MARKETABLE SECURITY. (See AMERICAN RAILROAD CERTIFICATES, RUSSIAN BONDS.)

BEARER BONDS REGISTER. A record of all bearer securities, whether lodged for safe custody or for security, is, in some banks, kept in a separate "Bearer Bonds Register."

The same information is shown as in the SECURITIES BOOK (*q.v.*) and the SAFE CUSTODY REGISTER (*q.v.*), but in addition the number upon the face of each bond must be carefully recorded.

BEARER SCRIP. This is a document issued by a government or a company, upon a new issue of capital, until such time as all instalments have been paid and the definitive bond is ready. The bearer scrip, like the bearer bond which is eventually received, is treated as a negotiable instrument, that is a holder for value, without notice of any defect in the transferor's title, obtains a good title thereto. (See BEARER BONDS.)

BEDFORD LEVEL CORPORATION. Bedford Level is the name given to a tract of low-lying country comprising some 95,000 acres within the counties of Northampton, Norfolk, Suffolk, Lincoln, Cambridge and Huntingdon. A registry of deeds was established for the Bedford Level in 1663. By 15 Car. II c. 17, Section 8, it is provided that no lease, grant or conveyance of or charge out of or upon the said 95,000 acres or any part thereof, except leases for seven years or under in possession, shall be of force, but from the time it shall be entered upon the register.

By an Act passed in 1862 it was enacted that the registration of documents shall only apply to "Adventurers Land" situate within the limits of that part of the Bedford Level which is known as the South Level.

Although priority is secured by the registration of a conveyance or charge, it has been held that the omission to register does not invalidate the document as between the parties themselves so as to prevent an action upon its covenants.

The registration office of the Bedford Level Corporation is at Ely. When a deed is registered, a record is placed thereon by the Registrar. (See LAND REGISTRY—

MIDDLESEX DEEDS, YORKSHIRE REGISTRY OF DEEDS.)

BELOW PAR. When the market price of bonds, stocks, or shares is less than their nominal or face value they are said to be at a discount, or below par. (See PAR.)

BENEFICIAL OWNER. In a conveyance for valuable consideration, other than a mortgage, where the vendor conveys as "beneficial owner" those words have the meaning (Section 7 of the Conveyancing Act, 1881) that he impliedly covenants that he has full power to convey the property expressed to be conveyed, that the property shall be quietly entered upon and enjoyed by the person to whom the conveyance is made, that the property is freed and discharged from all incumbrances and claims other than those subject to which the conveyance is expressly made, and that he will execute any further deeds for further or more perfectly assuring the property to the person to whom the conveyance is made.

If the property is leasehold the "beneficial owner" also impliedly covenants that it is a good, valid and effectual lease, and that all rents and covenants have been paid and observed.

In the case of a conveyance of freehold property by way of mortgage, the "beneficial owner" implies that he has power to convey, that, if default is made in payment of the money intended to be secured, it shall be lawful for the mortgagee to enter into and hold the property, that the property is freed from all incumbrances other than those to which the mortgage is expressly made subject, and that he will execute any further necessary deed.

In a mortgage of leasehold property, that he will pay all rents and observe all covenants so long as any money remains unpaid. (See TITLE DEEDS.)

BENEFICIARY. A person who benefits under a will is called a beneficiary. He may receive either "real" property (see REALTY), in which case he is a devisee, or he may receive "personal" property (see PERSONALTY), when he is named a legatee.

BEQUEST. A gift or legacy of personal property by a will.

BERTHAS. A Stock Exchange name for London, Brighton, and South Coast Railway deferred ordinary stock.

BERWICKS. A Stock Exchange name for North Eastern Railway stock.

BILL AS SECURITY. Where a bill of exchange has been deposited or pledged as security for an advance, the holder of the bill is "deemed to be a holder for value to the extent of the sum for which he has a lien" (Section 27, s.s. 3, Bills of Exchange Act, 1882). Where the holder, e.g. a banker, sues upon the bill at maturity and recovers the amount of it, if the sum recovered is greater than the debt owing by the person who deposited the bill, he must pay over the difference to that person. If the depositor's title to the bill was in order, the banker can recover the whole amount of the bill, but if the depositor's title was defective the banker can recover the amount of the bill to the extent of his lien, provided he had no notice of the depositor's defective title when he took the bill.

When a bill is lodged as security, it should be indorsed by the person depositing it, and a memorandum of deposit should be signed by the depositor to make it clear that the bill is pledged as security. When a banker holds a bill as security, he must present it for payment at maturity, and if it is dishonoured, he must give due notice of the dishonour.

BILL BROKER. Bill brokers are merchants whose special business it is to buy and to sell bills. They buy them from traders and sell many of them to bankers, their profit being obtained from a difference in the rates, the bankers buying from the brokers at one-eighth or one-sixteenth per cent. per annum below the market rate. A country banker, although he discounts bills for his customers, does not obtain such a supply of first-class bills as he can procure from the brokers, and it is to his advantage to buy bills in this way, because he can purchase just when he pleases and what he pleases. If he anticipates requiring a certain sum of money at a certain date, he may purchase bills from the brokers which will mature at the time he requires the funds, and, in addition, in dealing with brokers and discount houses of high standing, he obtains their guarantee that the bills will be met at maturity. When bill brokers re-discount bills with bankers, instead of indorsing each bill they usually give a guarantee to cover all the bills. An exchange broker is a dealer in foreign bills.

Like all other merchants who deal in highly-priced commodities, bill brokers require a large amount of funds wherewith to trade; this is formed by their own capital (often great), loans from bankers repayable at call or at short notice, and, in many cases, deposits received from the public. A number of the most important bill broking concerns are limited companies. There are several methods in which bankers may lend money to bill brokers (when a banker buys bills, that is re-discounts the bills a broker has discounted, the transaction is not a loan but a purchase); he may lend an amount for a long fixed period, say thirty days, on the security of the deposit of a batch of bills, or for a short fixed period, say a week, or "from day to day," or "over night." The rate of interest charged is invariable during the period fixed, but, as a rule, the longer the period the higher the rate. The rate on "money over night," however, depends more than the others on the immediate necessities of the brokers, who have to meet requirements to-day but expect to be in funds to-morrow; this "money over night" rate is sometimes relatively high, because brokers are willing to pay a little more rather than have to borrow from the Bank of England, where their loan would have to be for a fixed period, say three to ten days, while the brokers might not want the money for so long.

BILL DIARY. In order that bills may not be overlooked, they are entered under their due dates in a diary. The entries in the diary are usually checked at intervals with the bill register to make sure that all bills have been included; the diary is also balanced periodically with the same book.

The diary may be divided into columns for different classes of bills, or, if numerous, a separate diary may be kept for each class.

BILL IN A SET. Foreign bills are usually drawn in several parts, and, for safety, the parts may be transmitted by separate mails. Where a bill is drawn in that way it is said to be drawn in a set, and the various parts constitute one bill.

The rules regarding a bill drawn in a set are dealt with in Section 71 of the Bills of Exchange Act, 1882, which is as follows:—

"(1) Where a bill is drawn in a set, each part of the set being numbered, and containing a reference to the other parts, the whole of the parts constitute one bill.

"(2) Where the holder of a set indorses two or more parts to different persons, he is liable on every such part, and every indorser subsequent to him is liable on the part he has himself indorsed as if the said parts were separate bills.

"(3) Where two or more parts of a set are negotiated to different holders in due course, the holder whose title first accrues is as between such holders deemed the true owner of the bill; but nothing in this subsection shall affect the rights of a person who in due course accepts or pays the part first presented to him.

"(4) The acceptancce may be written on any part, and it must be written on one part only. If the drawee accepts more than one part, and such accepted parts get into the hands of different holders in due course, he is liable on every such part as if it were a separate bill.

"(5) When the acceptor of a bill drawn in a set pays it without requiring the part bearing his acceptance to be delivered up to him, and that part at maturity is outstanding in the hands of a holder in due course, he is liable to the holder thereof.

"(6) Subject to the preceding rules, where any one part of a bill drawn in a set is discharged by payment or otherwise, the whole bill is discharged."

Where a bill is drawn in two parts, to save time one may be sent at once to the drawee for acceptance. The other part may be negotiated and contain a reference that the accepted part is in the possesson of a certain firm, as "First and in need with Messrs. Blank & Co., London."

A bill of lading is usually issued in a set, and each one is signed by some person authorised to sign the same on behalf of the shipowner, but he is liable only for one of them. As soon as one has been presented and the goods delivered, the others are void. But if the drawee of a bill of exchange accepts more parts than one, he is not discharged by paying one of them, but is liable on every such part. (See BILL OF LADING.)

The following is a specimen of a bill drawn in a set of three, though sets of three are not so often seen as formerly:—

(*First part.*) Leeds, February 10, 1910.
£100.

Sixty days after sight pay this first of exchange (second and third of the same tenor and date unpaid) to the order of John Brown, the sum of one hundred pounds, value received, which place to account as advised.

JOHN JONES.

To Wm. Robinson, Esq.,
New York.

The *second part* is exactly the same as the first part, except that the words in the parentheses become (first and third of the same tenor and date unpaid).

The *third part* is in all respects the same as the first and second parts, except that the words in the parentheses are (first and second of the same tenor and date unpaid).

Only one part of a set requires to be stamped. Upon proof of the loss or destruction of a duly stamped bill forming one of a set, any other bill of the set which has not been issued or in any manner negotiated apart from the lost or destroyed bill may, although unstamped, be admitted in evidence to prove the contents of the lost or destroyed bill (Section 39 of the Stamp Act, 1891). (See BILL OF EXCHANGE, FOREIGN BILL.)

BILL LEDGER. The same as Discount Ledger (*q.v.*).

BILL OF EXCHANGE. A bill of exchange is defined by the Bills of Exchange Act, 1882, Section 3, as follows :—

"(1) A bill of exchange is an unconditional order in writing, addressed by one person to another, signed by the person giving it, requiring the person to whom it is addressed to pay on demand or at a fixed or determinable future time a sum certain in money to or to the order of a specified person, or to bearer.

"(2) An instrument which does not comply with these conditions, or which orders any act to be done in addition to the payment of money, is not a bill of exchange.

"(3) An order to pay out of a particular fund is not unconditional within the meaning of this Section ; but an unqualified order to pay, coupled with (*a*) an indication of a particular fund out of which the drawee is to re-imburse himself or a particular account to be debited with the amount, or (*b*) a statement of the transaction which gives rise to the bill, is unconditional.

"(4) A bill is not invalid by reason—
 (*a*) That it is not dated ;
 (*b*) That it does not specify the value given, or that any value has been given therefor ;
 (*c*) That it does not specify the place where it is drawn or the place where it is payable."

With regard to the sum payable, Section 9 provides that :—

"(1) The sum payable by a bill is a sum certain within the meaning of this Act, although it is required to be paid—
 (*a*) With interest.
 (*b*) By stated instalments.
 (*c*) By stated instalments, with a provision that upon default in payment of any instalment the whole shall become due.
 (*d*) According to an indicated rate of exchange or according to a rate of exchange to be ascertained as directed by the bill.

"(2) Where the sum payable is expressed in words and also in figures, and there is a discrepancy between the two, the sum denoted by the words is the amount payable."

A bill may be written, printed, or type-written.

There is no particular form prescribed by the Act, but bills are nearly always drawn in the same way. The following are specimens of the ordinary forms of bills of exchange :—

Leeds, June 10, 1910.

£100

Stamp 1*s*.

Three months after date pay to {me or to my order / John Brown or order / bearer} the sum of one hundred pounds for value received.

JOHN JONES.

To Thomas Smith, Esq.,
24, River Street,
London.

Leeds, June 10, 1910.

£100

Stamp 1*d*.

On demand pay to John Brown or order the sum of one hundred pounds for value received.

JOHN JONES.

To Wm. Robinson, Esq.,
London.

The first record of the use of bills of exchange in England is stated to be in a statute of 3 Rich. II c. 3, in 1379. The original use of bills in this country appears to have been for the settlement of debts between merchants in England and those in another country. For example, where Brown in England owed money to Dumont in, say, France, he would draw a bill upon Hugo in that country, who happened to owe him money, requesting Hugo to pay the money to Dumont. In this way Brown paid his debt to Dumont without the necessity of sending gold from England to France.

It is said that bills were in common use in Venice as early as the thirteenth century. and that they were first used by the Florentines in the twelfth century. Inland bills were made legal in England in 1697.

The persons whose names appear upon a bill of exchange are the drawer, the drawee (who by accepting the bill becomes the acceptor), the payee (who may also be the drawer), and the indorser. These persons are called the parties to the bill. In addition there may also be the name of the drawee banker at whose office the acceptor makes the bill payable, but he is not one of "the parties" to the bill.

The parties who are closely related, as the drawer and the acceptor, an indorser and the indorser immediately preceding him, are the "immediate parties." The parties who are not closely related, as the drawer and an indorsee, are the "remote parties."

A bill may be an inland bill (that is, one both drawn and payable within the British Islands, or drawn within the British Islands upon some person resident therein), or a foreign bill (that is, one drawn otherwise than as an inland bill).

The holder of a bill of exchange may hold it till it is due and present it for payment himself; or he may negotiate the bill, that is, transfer it to another person; or he may leave it with his banker with a request that the bill be collected at maturity and the proceeds credited to his account; or he may take it to his banker, or to a bill broker, and after indorsing it have it discounted. By discounting a bill he receives at once the amount of the bill (which may not be payable by the acceptor for some months to come), less the amount charged for discounting it. The banker debits the amount of the bill to his bills discounted account and credits it, less the discount, to his customer's current account, the discount passing to the credit of discount account, the balance of which account is periodically transferred to profit and loss account.

A bill drawn payable on a contingency, such as at a certain period after the arrival of a ship, is not valid.

It is very desirable that bills and cheques should be written in ink and not be type-written, as instruments which are type-written are too easily altered.

In Pitman's "Bills, Cheques and Notes," eight excellent pieces of advice are given with respect to bills of exchange. The hints are principally for traders, though some of them are specially applicable to bankers, but all of them should form part of a banker's creed with regard to those instruments. They are given as "practical hints which may serve as warnings":—

1. Never draw or accept an accommodation bill, unless you are prepared to meet it whenever called upon.
2. When a bill has been drawn by you, endeavour to secure its acceptance before negotiating it.
3. Unless you are to be personally liable upon the bill, take care that any signature you place upon it, whether as drawer, acceptor, or indorser, shows clearly that you are signing in a representative capacity.
4. Never indorse a bill without receiving value for it.
5. Never discount a bill for a stranger. Be sure that you know the person from whom you receive a bill and take care that he indorses it.
6. Examine the bill carefully.
7. If you are the holder, present the bill for acceptance, if it has not been accepted, and for payment at the proper time. If either acceptance or payment is refused, give notice at once to every indorser and to the drawer, so as to hold each and all liable for payment.
8. Upon payment of a bill take care that you get the document into your own possession.

With respect to the proposed rules regarding the unification of the laws existing in different countries relating to bills of exchange, see UNIFICATION OF LAWS OF BILLS OF EXCHANGE.

By the Stamp Act, 1891, the duty is:—
BILL OF EXCHANGE—

	£	s.	d.
Payable on demand or at sight or on presentation . . .	0	0	1

And see Sections 32, 34, and 38, Stamp Act, 1891, given below.

This was extended by the Finance Act,

1899, Section 10, s.s. 2, to read as if the words "or within three days after date or sight" were contained therein after the word "presentation"; and this section has now been extended by Section 10 of the Revenue Act, 1909, which enacts as follows:—"The provisions in Sections 34 and 38 of the Stamp Act, 1891, which relate to bills of exchange payable on demand, or at sight, or on presentation, shall apply also to bills of exchange expressed to be payable at a period not exceeding three days after date or sight, which are chargeable with the duty of one penny under s.s. 2 of Section 10 of the Finance Act, 1899."

BILL OF EXCHANGE of any other kind whatsoever (*except a Bank Note*) and PROMISSORY NOTE of any kind whatsoever (*except a Bank Note*)—drawn, or expressed to be payable, or actually paid, or indorsed, or in any manner negotiated in the United Kingdom.

	£	s.	d.
Where the amount or value of the money for which the bill or note is drawn or made does not exceed £5	0	0	1
Exceeds £5 and does not exceed £10	0	0	2
" £10 " £25	0	0	3
" £25 " £50	0	0	6
" £50 " £75	0	0	9
" £75 " £100	0	1	0
" £100— for every £100, and also for any fractional part of £100, of such amount or value	0	1	0

Exemptions.

(1) Bill or note issued by the Bank of England or the Bank of Ireland.

(2) Draft or order drawn by any banker in the United Kingdom upon any other banker in the United Kingdom, not payable to bearer or to order, and used solely for the purpose of settling or clearing any account between such bankers.

(3) Letter written by a banker in the United Kingdom to any other banker in the United Kingdom, directing the payment of any sum of money, the same not being payable to bearer or to order, and such letter not being sent or delivered to the person to whom payment is to be made or to any person on his behalf.

(4) Letter of credit granted in the United Kingdom, authorising drafts to be drawn out of the United Kingdom payable in the United Kingdom.

(5) Draft or order drawn by the Paymaster-General on behalf of the Court of Chancery in England or by the Accountant - General of the Supreme Court of Judicature in Ireland.

(6) Warrant or order for the payment of any annuity granted by the National Debt Commissioners, or for the payment of any dividend or interest on any share in the Government or Parliamentary stocks or funds.

(7) Bill drawn by any person under the authority of the Admiralty, upon and payable by the Accountant-General of the Navy.

(8) Bill drawn (according to a form prescribed by Her Majesty's orders by any person duly authorised to draw the same) upon and payable out of any public account for any pay or allowance of the army or auxiliary forces or for any other expenditure connected therewith.

(9) Draft or order drawn upon any banker in the United Kingdom by an officer of a public department of the State for the payment of money out of a public account.

(10) Bill drawn in the United Kingdom for the sole purpose of remitting money to be placed to any account of public revenue.

[It has been held that this applies only to money which is already public money.]

(11) Coupon or warrant for interest attached to and issued with any security, or with an agreement or memorandum for the renewal or extension of time for payment of a security.

By the Finance Act, 1894, Section 40, a coupon or warrant for interest on a marketable security, being one of a set of coupons whether issued with the security or subsequently issued in a sheet, is exempt.

A coupon attached to a scrip certificate is not exempt. See also the exemptions in the article CHEQUE.

By the Finance Act, 1899, Section 10, the duty on Bills of Exchange drawn and expressed to be payable out of the United Kingdom, when actually paid or indorsed or in any manner negotiated in the United Kingdom, shall, where the amount of the money for which the bill is drawn exceeds fifty pounds, be reduced so as to be :—

Where the amount exceeds £50 and does not exceed £100, 6*d*.

Where the amount exceeds £100, 6*d*. for every £100, and also for any fractional part of £100 of that amount.

(Where the amount does not exceed £50, the duty is as in the Schedule above.)

For the purpose of stamp duty, a bill or promissory note which purports to be drawn or made out of the United Kingdom is treated as a foreign bill. The Isle of Man and the Channel Islands are out of the United Kingdom, and a bill drawn there and negotiated in the United Kingdom is therefore a foreign bill, so far as stamp duty is concerned. But under the Bills of Exchange Act, 1882 (Section 4) a bill drawn and payable within the British Islands (which include the Isle of Man and the Channel Islands) is an inland bill.

On inland bills payable on demand, or at sight, or on presentation, or not exceeding three days after sight or date, and on cheques, the penny stamp may be either impressed or adhesive. In the case of inland bills payable otherwise, the stamp must be impressed. An adhesive stamp must be properly cancelled by the person signing the bill. (See Section 38 below.)

On foreign bills, the duties are to be denoted by adhesive foreign bill stamps. If a bill drawn abroad is impressed with an English stamp it is not sufficient ; it must have the correct adhesive stamp affixed. If the bill is payable on demand, or not exceeding three days after date or sight, an ordinary penny postage stamp may be used. Any person into whose hands any such bill comes before it is stamped, must affix the proper stamp before dealing with the bill in any way. (See Section 35, below.)

Where the bill is drawn in foreign money, the amount, for the purposes of stamping, is calculated according to the rate of exchange current on the date of the bill, unless the rate is stated in the bill.

Interest upon a bill or note is not taken into account in calculating the amount of stamp duty. The duty is payable only upon the amount of the bill or note.

As to the duties upon promissory notes, see PROMISSORY NOTE.

The following sections are from the Stamp Act, 1891 (54 & 55 Vict. c. 39) :—

"32. For the purposes of this Act the expression 'bill of exchange' includes draft, order, cheque, and letter of credit, and any document or writing (except a bank note) entitling or purporting to entitle any person, whether named therein or not, to payment by any other person of, or to draw upon any other person for, any sum of money ; and the expression 'bill of exchange payable on demand' includes—

(*a*) An order for the payment of any sum of money by a bill of exchange or promissory note, or for the delivery of any bill of exchange or promissory note in satisfaction of any sum of money, or for the payment of any sum of money out of any particular fund which may or may not be available, or upon any condition or contingency which may or may not be performed or happen ; and

(*b*) An order for the payment of any sum of money weekly, monthly, or at any other stated periods, and also an order for the payment by any person at any time after the date thereof of any sum of money, and sent or delivered by the person making the same to the person by whom the payment is to be made, and not to the person to whom the payment is to be made, or to any person on his behalf.

"33. (1) For the purposes of this Act the expression 'promissory note' includes any document or writing (except a bank note) containing a promise to pay any sum of money.

"(2) A note promising the payment of any sum of money out of any particular fund which may or may not be available, or upon any condition or contingency which may or may not be performed or happen, is to be deemed a promissory note for that sum of money.

"34. (1) The fixed duty of one penny on a bill of exchange payable on demand or at sight or on presentation may be denoted by an adhesive stamp, which, where the bill is drawn in the United Kingdom, is to be cancelled by the person by whom the bill is signed before he delivers it out of his hands, custody, or power.

"(2) The *ad valorem* duties upon bills of exchange and promissory notes drawn or made out of the United Kingdom are to be denoted by adhesive stamps.

"35. (1) Every person into whose hands any bill of exchange or promissory note drawn or made out of the United Kingdom, comes in the United Kingdom before it is stamped shall, before he presents for payment, or indorses, transfers, or in any manner negotiates, or pays the bill or note, affix thereto a proper adhesive stamp or proper adhesive stamps of sufficient amount, and cancel every stamp so affixed thereto.

"(2) Provided as follows:

(*a*) If at the time when any such bill or note comes into the hands of any *bonâ fide* holder there is affixed thereto an adhesive stamp effectually cancelled, the stamp shall, so far as relates to the holder, be deemed to be duly cancelled, although it may not appear to have been affixed or cancelled by the proper person;

(*b*) If at the time when any such bill or note comes into the hands of any *bonâ fide* holder there is affixed thereto an adhesive stamp not duly cancelled, it shall be competent for the holder to cancel the stamp as if he were the person by whom it was affixed, and upon his so doing the bill or note shall be deemed duly stamped, and as valid and available as if the stamp had been cancelled by the person by whom it was affixed.

"(3) But neither of the foregoing provisos is to relieve any person from any fine or penalty incurred by him for not cancelling an adhesive stamp.

"36. A bill of exchange or promissory note which purports to be drawn or made out of the United Kingdom is, for the purpose of determining the mode in which the stamp duty thereon is to be denoted, to be deemed to have been so drawn or made, although it may in fact have been drawn or made within the United Kingdom.

"37. (1) Where a bill of exchange or promissory note has been written on material bearing an impressed stamp of sufficient amount but of improper denomination, it may be stamped with the proper stamp on payment of the duty, and a penalty of forty shillings if the bill or note be not then payable according to its tenor, or of ten pounds if the same be so payable.

"(2) Except as aforesaid, no bill of exchange or promissory note shall be stamped with an impressed stamp after the execution thereof.

"38. (1) Every person who issues, indorses, transfers, negotiates, presents for payment, or pays any bill of exchange or promissory note liable to duty and not being duly stamped shall incur a fine of ten pounds, and the person who takes or receives from any other person any such bill or note either in payment or as a security, or by purchase or otherwise, shall not be entitled to recover thereon, or to make the same available for any purpose whatever.

"(2) Provided that if any bill of exchange payable on demand or at sight or on presentation, is presented for payment unstamped, the person to whom it is presented may affix thereto an adhesive stamp of one penny, and cancel the same, as if he had been the drawer of the bill, and may thereupon pay the sum in the bill mentioned, and charge the duty in account against the person by whom the bill was drawn, or deduct the duty from the said sum, and the bill is, so far as respects the duty, to be deemed valid and available.

"(3) But the foregoing proviso is not to relieve any person from any fine or penalty incurred by him in relation to such bill.

"39. When a bill of exchange is drawn in a set according to the custom of merchants, and one of the set is duly stamped, the other or others of the set shall, unless issued or in some manner negotiated apart from the stamped bill, be exempt from duty; and upon proof of the loss or destruction of a duly stamped bill forming one of a set, any other bill of the set which has not been issued or in any manner negotiated apart from the lost or destroyed bill may, although unstamped, be admitted in evidence to prove the contents of the lost or destroyed bill."

If a receipt is placed upon a bill it requires a penny stamp, but the name of a banker (whether accompanied by words of receipt or not) written in the ordinary course of his business as a banker upon a bill of exchange or promissory note duly stamped, is exempt. (See RECEIPT.)

A foreign bill which is both drawn and payable abroad, does not require to be stamped in this country if received by a banker merely for acceptance and return; but if indorsed or negotiated in this country it must be stamped. See the following circular which was issued by the Board of Inland Revenue in May, 1907 :—

"The Board of Inland Revenue, having reason to believe that some misapprehension exists on the subject, desire to call attention to the fact that bills of exchange, although both drawn and expressed to be payable out of the United Kingdom, are nevertheless chargeable with stamp duty if 'actually paid, or indorsed, or in any manner negotiated in the United Kingdom.' (See BILL OF EXCHANGE, etc., in the first Schedule to the Stamp Act, 1891. See also Finance Act, 1899, Section 10.)

"The duty chargeable on a bill of this nature, if payable at a period exceeding three days after date or sight, is governed by the following scale :—

"When the amount or value of the money for which the Bill is drawn does not exceed £5 . . . . 1*d*.
Exceeds £5 and does not exceed £10 . 2*d*.
,, £10 ,, ,, £25 . 3*d*.
,, £25 ,, ,, £100 . 6*d*.
and where the amount exceeds £100, 6*d*. for every £100, and also for any fractional part of £100 of that amount.

"The Board further desire to call attention to Section 38 (1) of the Act of 1891 which imposes a fine of £10 upon every person who issues, indorses, transfers, negotiates, presents for payment, or pays any bill of exchange liable to duty and not duly stamped."

(See BILLS OF EXCHANGE ACT, 1882 (where a reference is given to the articles which include the various sections of the Act); ACCEPTANCE; ACCEPTANCE, GENERAL; ACCEPTANCE, QUALIFIED; ACCEPTANCE FOR HONOUR; ACCEPTOR, ACCOMMODATION BILL, AGENT, ALLONGE, ALTERATIONS, AMOUNT OF BILL OR CHEQUE, ANSWERS, ANTE DATED, BEARER, BILLS FOR COLLECTION, BILL IN A SET, CANCELLATION OF BILL OF EXCHANGE, CHEQUE, CONSIDERATION FOR BILL OF EXCHANGE, DATE, DAYS OF GRACE, DELIVERY OF BILL, DISHONOUR OF BILL OF EXCHANGE, DOCUMENTARY BILL, DRAFT AFTER DATE, DRAWEE, DRAWER, FOREIGN BILL, FORGERY, HOLDER FOR VALUE, HOLDER IN DUE COURSE, HOLDER OF BILL OF EXCHANGE, INCHOATE INSTRUMENT, INDORSEMENT, INDORSER, INLAND BILL, LOST BILL OF EXCHANGE, NEGOTIATION OF BILL OF EXCHANGE, NOTING, ORDER, OVERDUE BILL, PART PAYMENT, PARTIES TO BILL OF EXCHANGE, PAYEE, PAYING BANKER, PAYMENT BY, PAYMENT FOR HONOUR, PAYMENT OF BILL, POST DATED, PRESENTMENT FOR ACCEPTANCE, PRESENTMENT FOR PAYMENT, PROMISSORY NOTE, PROTEST, REFEREE IN CASE OF NEED, RETIRING A BILL, SUPRÀ PROTEST, TIME OF PAYMENT OF BILL, TRANSFEROR BY DELIVERY, UNIFICATION OF LAWS OF BILLS OF EXCHANGE.)

BILL OF LADING. A receipt for goods, upon shipment, signed by some person authorised to sign the same on behalf of the shipowner. The document states that the goods have been shipped in good order, and quotes the rate at which the freight is to be paid by the consignees. A note is usually made upon a bill of lading that the weight, quantity and quality of the cargo is unknown. The shipowner undertakes to deliver the goods at their destination in the same condition as they were when he received them.

Bills of Lading are usually drawn in sets of three, each one stamped, and in addition there are two copies, unstamped. Of these "copies" one is given to the master and the other is retained by the loading brokers. The "copies" are of no value. One of the three stamped bills of lading is sent by the shipper to the consignee by one mail, and another is sent to him by another route, if possible, or by the following mail, and the third is retained by the shipper as evidence in support of a claim for insurance, in the event of the ship being lost, that the goods were in that ship. On the arrival of the ship at its destination the consignee may, by handing the bill of lading to the master of the ship and paying all claims for freight and other charges, obtain possession of the goods. If the consignee wishes to transfer the goods to some other person, he can, by simply indorsing the bill of lading and delivering it to that person, constitute him the absolute owner of the goods. If such a transfer is made by the consignee in good faith and for value, the consignor's right to stop the goods in transit is cancelled; but as a bill of lading is not a negotiable instrument, it follows that if the person who transfers it has no title or a defective title to the goods, the person to whom it is transferred obtains no better title than the transferor had.

During the time a cargo is at sea, the bill of lading is the symbol of the cargo, and "the indorsement and delivery of the bill of lading operate as a symbolical delivery of the cargo."

If the consignee's name is not inserted in the bill of lading, the ownership of the goods remains in the consignor.

When the goods received on board are in good order and no adverse remarks, such as "boxes broken," etc., are made upon the bill of lading, it is called a clean bill of lading.

As already stated, the master of the ship delivers the goods to the person who presents the bill of lading, but if it should happen that two different purchasers have each received one of the bills of lading, the master is not liable if he delivers the goods to the purchaser who comes first with a bill of lading, provided, of course, he acts in good faith and has no notice of the conflicting claims. It will be noticed in the specimen, given below, of a bill of lading, that the master or purser affirms to (two or three, as the case may be) bills of lading, "one of which bills being accomplished, the others to stand void." It is therefore necessary, in order to have a complete security, that all the bills of lading should be held.

In addition to holding all the bills of lading, a "stop order" upon the goods may be lodged by the person about to make an advance upon them.

With regard to the three parts of a bill of lading Earl Cairns said (in *Glyn & Co.* v. *The East and West India Dock Co.*, 1882, 7 A.C. 591): "All that any person who advances money upon a bill of lading will have to do, if he sees, as he will see on the face of the bill of lading, that it has been signed in more parts than one, will be to require that all the parts are brought in—that is to say, that all the title-deeds are brought in. I know that that is the practice with regard to other title-deeds, and it strikes me with some surprise that any one would advance money upon a bill of lading without taking that course of requiring the delivery up of all the parts. If the person advancing the money does not choose to do that, another course which he may take is, to be vigilant and on the alert, and to take care that he is on the spot at the first arrival of the ship in the dock. If those who advance money on bills of lading do not adopt one or other of those courses, it appears to me that if they suffer, they suffer in consequence of their own act."

A banker who advances against wool (for example) which has been imported from abroad, may adopt the following course:—he may take up the bills of lading and instruct the shippers to send the wool by rail to his order. He may then direct the railway company to deliver it to the combers, on his behalf, who will ascertain and advise the banker as to the various qualities and quantities "tops" "middles," "bottoms," etc., so that he may see what it will realise at present quotations. When the customer sells the wool, the banker then orders it to be delivered in accordance with the customer's instructions against payment of the purchase price.

By Section 19, s.s. 3, Sale of Goods Act, 1893:—"Where the seller of goods draws on the buyer for the price, and transmits the bill of exchange and the bill of lading to the buyer together to secure acceptance or payment of the bill of exchange, the buyer is bound to return the bill of lading if he does not honour the bill of exchange, and if he wrongfully retains the bill of lading, the property in the goods does not pass to him."

Instead of sending bills of lading direct

to the consignee, the consignor may draw a bill of exchange upon the consignee for the value of the goods despatched and attach the bills of lading to the bill. Those documents may then be sent by the consignor's bankers to their correspondents in the town where the consignee lives, with a request to present the bill to the consignee for acceptance ; and instructions are often given that the bills of lading may be handed to the consignee upon his accepting the bill. The consignee can then obtain the goods, sell them and be in a position to meet his acceptance at maturity.

Frequently the consignor draws a bill upon the consignee and discounts it at his bankers, pledging the indorsed bills of lading as security, and the banker has to send forward the bill to his correspondents to obtain the drawee's acceptance (see DOCUMENTARY BILL) ; or the consignor may, under instructions, draw upon the consignee's banker, the bills of lading being attached to the bill of exchange.

When bills of lading are given as security, a memorandum of deposit, or note of hypothecation, is taken, which provides that, in default of payment, the banker may sell the goods represented by the bills. The document is usually stamped with a fixed duty of sixpence. In some cases, where an advance has been made upon bills of lading, the bills are handed to the borrower upon his signing a trust receipt. (See TRUST RECEIPT.)

Where a bill of lading is taken as security containing such a clause as "all conditions of every character as per Charter Party" (see below), the lender should ascertain what are the conditions in the Charter Party, as that document may reserve to the owners of the vessel the right of lien upon the cargo for payment of freight, demurrage and other charges.

A bill of lading pledged as security should be indorsed either in blank or to the banker. It has been held by the House of Lords that where a bill of lading is indorsed and pledged by way of security, that a banker indorsee is not subject to the same liabilities in respect of the goods as a person to whom a bill of lading is indorsed upon a sale of the goods (*Burdick* v. *Sewell*, 1884, 10 A.C. 74). But if the banker claims the goods in order to realise his security, he is then liable for the freight, warehouse charges, and all charges payable in accordance with the terms of the bill of lading.

Where a transfer of a bill of lading takes place, upon a sale of the goods, Section 1 of the Bills of Lading Act, 1855, enacts :—

"Every consignee of goods named in a bill of lading, and every indorsee of a bill of lading to whom the property in the goods therein mentioned shall pass, upon or by reason of such consignment or indorsement, shall have transferred to and vested in him all rights of suit, and be subject to the same liabilities in respect of such goods as if the contract contained in the bill of lading had been made with himself."

Where a banker, by instructions of a customer, accepts a bill drawn by a client of that customer against bills of lading, the banker will not be liable if the bills of lading should afterwards prove to be forgeries.

Bills of lading vary somewhat in form, but the general effect is the same. The following is a specimen of a simple form, though some bills of lading are much more elaborate :—

SHIPPED, in good order and well conditioned, by ....
.........., whose responsibility ceases on the present being signed, in and upon the good..........SHIP OR VESSEL, called the
....
whereof ....is master for this present Voyage, now lying in the Harbour of..........................
and bound for.......................
....
....
....
being marked and numbered as in the Margin, and to be delivered in like good order and well conditioned at the aforesaid Port of
....

(The Act of God, Perils of the Sea, Fire, Barratry of the Master and Crew, Enemies, Pirates and Robbers, Arrests and Restraints of Princes, Rulers and People, and other Accidents of Navigation excepted. Strandings and Collisions, and all losses and damages caused thereby, also excepted, even when occasioned by negligence, default, or error in judgment of the Pilot, Master, Mariners, or other Servant of the Shipowners, but nothing herein contained shall exempt the Shipowners from liability to pay for damage to cargo occasioned by bad stowage, by improper or insufficient dunnage or ventilation, or by improper opening of Valves, Sluices and Ports, or by causes other than those above excepted, and all the above exceptions are conditional on the Vessel being Seaworthy when she sails on the Voyage, but any latent defects in the Hull and Machinery shall not be considered unseaworthiness, provided the same do not result from want of due diligence of the Owners or any of them, or of the Ship's Husband or Manager), unto...................................
....

or to....................Assigns.—Freight to be paid by CONSIGNEES at the rate of ....Shillings and.............. Pence Sterling, per Ton of 20 Cwt. delivered, on the whole being delivered.............. ....and all Conditions of every character, as per Charter Party dated at............................ With average accustomed—IN WITNESS whereof, the Master or Purser of the said Ship hath affirmed to...............Bills of Lading, all of this Tenor and date, one of which bills being accomplished, the others to stand void.

Weight unknown.

Dated at........................19

....

Along with the bill of lading there should be the insurance policy (see MARINE INSURANCE POLICY), and the detailed description of the goods in the policy should agree with that in the bill of lading.

A "Port Bill of Lading" is one which is signed by the authorised person after the goods have been received by that person at the port of shipment.

A "Through Bill of Lading" is one which provides (or ought to provide) for the continuous responsibility of several railway companies and shipping companies from one place to another.

A "Custody Bill of Lading" is a new form created by the Bill of Lading Conference Committee in connection with the cotton trade, as announced in a circular dated January 6, 1909. "This Bill of Lading may be issued after proper delivery of the cotton, but before arrival of the vessel in port." Within three weeks from its date a master's (or agent's) receipt is to be furnished proving the actual shipment of the cotton. A custody bill of lading is to be clearly marked as such, to distinguish it from a "Port Bill of Lading." It can be issued only by shipowners or loading agents who have signed a letter of agreement with the Conference Committee. (Journal of Institute of Bankers, February, 1909.)

In view of recent cotton frauds in America, the following resolution has been agreed to (July, 1910) by certain bankers in London and Liverpool: "That the banks comprised in this committee agree that in the case of drafts drawn upon the banks against bills of lading for cotton negotiated through Exchange buyers in America, the banks will decline, from October 31 [since extended to December 31] onwards, to accept against bills of lading relating to such drafts unless the genuineness of the bills of lading, both as to signature and as to possession of the cotton by the carrier up to the time of issue, be guaranteed by such Exchange buyers to the satisfaction of the banks concerned."

The stamp duty (Stamp Act), 1891, is:—

	£	s.	d.
BILL OF LADING of or for any goods, merchandise, or effects to be exported or carried coastwise	0	0	6

And see Section 40, as follows:—

"(1) A bill of lading is not to be stamped after the execution thereof.

"(2) Every person who makes or executes any bill of lading not duly stamped shall incur a fine of fifty pounds."

(See CHARTER PARTY.)

BILL OF SALE. An assignment of personal chattels as security for a debt. Personal chattels include goods, furniture, and other articles capable of complete transfer by delivery. Trade machinery is deemed to be personal chattels. (See definition, as given in Bills of Sale Act, 1878, of "personal chattels" under CHATTELS.) Bills of sale are very rarely taken by bankers as security.

The registration of a bill of sale by a debtor should act as a danger signal to a banker.

Section 4 of the Bills of Sale Act, 1878, interprets the meaning of bill of sale as follows:—

"The expression 'bill of sale' shall include bills of sale, assignments, transfers, declarations of trust without transfer, inventories of goods with receipt thereto attached, or receipts for purchase moneys of goods, and other assurances of personal chattels, and also powers of attorney, authorities, or licences to take possession of personal chattels as security for any debt, and also any agreement, whether intended or not to be followed by the execution of any other instrument, by which a right in equity to any personal chattels, or to any charge or security thereon, shall be conferred, but shall not include the following documents; that is to say, assignments for the benefit of the creditors of the person making or giving the same, marriage settlements, transfers, or assignments of any ship or vessel, or any share thereof, transfers of goods in the ordinary course of business of any trade or calling, bills of sale of goods in foreign parts or at sea, bills of lading, India warrants, warehouse-keepers' certificates, warrants or orders for the delivery of goods, or any other documents used in the ordinary course of business as proof of the possession or control of goods, or authorising or purporting to authorise, either by indorsement or by delivery, the possessor of such document to transfer or receive goods thereby represented."

The Bills of Sale Act does not apply to any debentures issued by any mortgage, loan or other incorporated company, and secured upon the capital stock or goods, chattels, and effects of such company (Section 17 of Bills of Sale Act (1878) Amendment Act, 1882).

A bill of sale must be in accordance with the form given in the Schedule to the Bills of Sale Act (1878) Amendment Act, 1882 :—

FORM OF BILL OF SALE.

"This Indenture made the day of , between A. B. of of the one part and C. D. of of the other part, witnesseth that in consideration of the sum of £ now paid to A. B. by C. D., the receipt of which the said A. B. hereby acknowledges [or whatever else the consideration may be], he the said A. B. doth hereby assign unto C. D., his executors, administrators, and assigns, all and singular the several chattels and things specifically described in the Schedule hereto annexed by way of security for the payment of the sum of £ , and interest thereon at the rate of per cent. per annum [or whatever else may be the rate]. And the said A. B. doth further agree and declare that he will duly pay to the said C. D. the principal sum aforesaid, together with the interest then due, by equal payments of £ on the day of [or whatever else may be the stipulated times or time of payment]. And the said A. B. doth also agree with the said C. D. that he will [here insert terms as to insurance, payment of rent, or otherwise, which the parties may agree to for the maintenance or defeasance of the security].

Provided always, that the chattels hereby assigned shall not be liable to seizure or to be taken possession of by the said C. D. for any cause other than those specified in Section 7 of the Bills of Sale Act (1878) Amendment Act, 1882.

In witness whereof the said A. B. hath hereunto set his hand and seal the day and year first above written.

A. B. (L. S.)

Signed and sealed by the said
A. B. in the presence of me,
E. F.

[Add witness's name, address, and description.]"

The schedule must specifically describe the chattels which are assigned. It has been held, in the case of a bill of sale void because it was not drawn in accordance with the legal form, that the covenant in the bill to pay principal and interest was also void.

A bill of sale given in consideration of any sum under £30 shall be void (Section 12 of the above Act).

From the above form of bill of sale it will be seen that the amount which it is to secure must be a specified sum, and not, for example, a fluctuating balance.

A bill of sale must be registered within seven clear days after its execution ; and requires re-registration once at least every five years.

An assignment of a registered bill of sale does not require registration. Any person is entitled to search the register on payment of a fee of one shilling.

The grantee of a bill of sale may seize the chattels thereby assigned if the grantor makes default in payment of the sums secured by the instrument, or becomes bankrupt, or suffers any of the goods to be distrained for rent, rates, or taxes, or fraudulently removes any of the goods, or fails, without reasonable excuse, to produce to the grantee his last receipts for rent, rates and taxes, or if execution has been levied against the grantor's goods under any judgment at law (Section 7, Bills of Sale Amendment Act, 1882).

If two bills of sale are given upon the same property, priority is decided according to the order of the date of their registration.

A bill of sale is void if the grantor becomes bankrupt within two years after the date, or at any time within ten years unless the claimants can prove that the grantor was solvent at the time he gave the bill of sale. (See SETTLEMENTS—SETTLOR BANKRUPT.)

As to the stamp duty, the Stamp Act, 1891, says :—

BILL OF SALE—

Absolute. See CONVEYANCE ON SALE.

By way of security. See MORTGAGE, etc.

And see Section 41, as follows :—

"A bill of sale is not to be registered under any Act for the time being in force relating to the registration of bills of sale unless the original, duly stamped, is produced to the proper officer."

BILL OF SALE, SHIP. A registered ship, or a share therein, is transferred to a purchaser by a bill of sale. (See SHIP—MORTGAGE, etc.)

BILL REGISTER. The register contains a complete list of all bills which have been discounted. The following particulars are usually entered: Date when discounted and for whom, the drawer's and acceptor's names and place where domiciled, the date and amount of the bill, its currency and the date on which it is due. A column is also provided to show when the bill was remitted, and another to give the rate and amount of discount charged. Each entry in the register is usually numbered consecutively and the number written upon the bill. From the total of the bills so entered is deducted every night the amount of the bills which have matured during the day and the difference is the present amount under discount by the bank.

BILLON. Debased coin, due to the large proportion of copper alloy.

BILLS DISCOUNTED ACCOUNT. Bills of exchange which are discounted by a banker are debited to this account and credited to the customer's account, less the discount, the discount being passed into discount account. In some banks it is customary for branches to remit all bills to the head office, but if they are left at the branch they remain in bills discounted account until near maturity, when they are remitted for collection to the bank at which they are accepted payable.

BILLS DISCOUNTED BOOK. A list of all bills discounted is kept in this book and full particulars of each bill are given, e.g. date when discounted and for whom, the drawer's and acceptor's names, where and when payable, the amount, the currency, and the amount of discount received. In some banks the book is called the bill register. (See BILL REGISTER.)

BILLS FOR COLLECTION. Bills left for collection (or "short bills," as they are sometimes called, a term which originated in the custom of entering the bills in the customer's account in a column "short" of the cash column) are bills which a customer leaves with his banker to be collected at maturity and of which the proceeds are to be credited to his account. Such bills may be entered to the credit of an account kept for bills received for collection and to the debit of a contra account, so that a proper record may be preserved.

Where bills are paid to credit of an account and are neither discounted nor drawn against, the bills remain the property of the customer. If the account becomes overdrawn, the banker has a lien upon them to that extent. If the bills are discounted, they become the absolute property of the banker.

Bills left for collection, even if indorsed to the banker, do not form part of his assets, and if the banker becomes bankrupt the owner may, subject to any lien of the banker, recover the bills.

When bills sent by correspondents for collection are accompanied by instructions, such as, "Deliver documents against payment," "Incur no expense," "If unpaid do not protest," the instructions must be carefully attended to. Bankers usually keep a separate bill book in which particulars of bills for collection are entered. (See BILLS FOR COLLECTION BOOK.)

When a bill is sent out for collection, many bankers place the word "received" upon the back of the bill as a safeguard against the loss of the bill. A receipt by a banker upon a bill is exempt from stamp duty, but a receipt upon a bill by any other person is subject to the duty of one penny (see RECEIPT). (See BILL OF EXCHANGE.)

BILLS FOR COLLECTION BOOK. Bills which are left with a banker for collection (as distinguished from those which are discounted) are entered in this book, and all essential particulars of each bill should be given, e.g. date received and from whom, the drawer's and acceptor's names, where payable, the currency, the amount, when due, and when remitted.

BILLS OF EXCHANGE ACT, 1882 (45 & 46 VICT. c. 61). An Act to codify the law relating to bills of exchange, cheques, and promissory notes (August 18, 1882).

"Be it enacted by the Queen's most Excellent Majesty, by and with the advice and consent of the Lords Spiritual and Temporal, and Commons, in this present Parliament assembled, and by the authority of the same, as follows :—

PART I

PRELIMINARY

"1. This Act may be cited as the Bills of Exchange Act, 1882.

"2. In this Act, unless the context otherwise requires—

'Acceptance' means an acceptance completed by delivery or notification.

'Action' includes counterclaim and set off.

'Banker' includes a body of persons whether incorporated or not who carry on the business of banking.

'Bankrupt' includes any person whose estate is vested in a trustee or assignee under the law for the time being in force relating to bankruptcy.

'Bearer' means the person in possession of a bill or note which is payable to bearer.

'Bill' means bill of exchange, and 'note' means promissory note.

'Delivery' means transfer of possession, actual or constructive, from one person to another.

'Holder' means the payee or indorsee of a bill or note who is in possession of it, or the bearer thereof.

'Indorsement' means an indorsement completed by delivery.

'Issue' means the first delivery of a bill or note, complete in form to a person who takes it as a holder.

'Person' includes a body of persons whether incorporated or not.

'Value' means valuable consideration.

'Written' includes printed, and 'writing' includes print."

The following sections have a special reference to the Act itself :—

"92. Where, by this Act, the time limited for doing any act or thing is less than three days, in reckoning time, non-business days are excluded.

'Non-business days' for the purposes of this Act mean—

(*a*) Sunday, Good Friday, Christmas Day ;

(*b*) A bank holiday under the Bank Holidays Act, 1871, or Acts amending it ;

(*c*) A day appointed by Royal proclamation as a public fast or thanksgiving day.

Any other day is a business day.

"97. (1) The rules in bankruptcy relating to bills of exchange, promissory notes, and cheques, shall continue to apply thereto notwithstanding anything in this Act contained.

"(2) The rules of common law, including the law merchant, save in so far as they are inconsistent with the express provisions of this Act, shall continue to apply to bills of exchange, promissory notes, and cheques.

"(3) Nothing in this Act or in any repeal effected thereby shall affect :—

"(*a*) Any law or enactment for the time being in force relating to the revenue. [As amended by the Statute Law Revision Act, 1898.]

"(*b*) The provisions of the Companies Act, 1862, or Acts amending it, or any Act relating to joint stock banks or companies ;

"(*c*) The provisions of any Act relating to or confirming the privileges of the Bank of England or the Bank of Ireland respectively :

"(*d*) The validity of any usage relating to dividend warrants, or the indorsements thereof.

"98. Nothing in this Act or in any repeal effected thereby shall extend or restrict, or in any way alter or affect the law and practice in Scotland in regard to summary diligence.

"99. Where any Act or document refers to any enactment repealed by this Act, the Act or document shall be construed, and shall operate, as if it referred to the corresponding provisions of this Act.

"100. In any judicial proceeding in Scotland, any fact relating to a bill of exchange, bank cheque, or promissory note, which is relevant to any question of liability thereon, may be proved by parol evidence: Provided that this enactment shall not in any way affect the existing law and practice whereby the party who is, according to the tenor of any bill of exchange, bank cheque, or promissory note, debtor to the holder in the amount thereof, may be required, as a condition of obtaining a sist of diligence, or suspension of a charge, or threatened charge, to make such consignation, or to find such caution as the Court or judge before whom the cause is depending may require.

This Section shall not apply to any case where the bill of exchange, bank cheque, or promissory note has undergone the sexennial prescription."

All the other Sections of the Act will be found under the articles to which they refer. The following is a list of the sections and the articles to which reference may be made :—

PART I

PRELIMINARY

Section.			
1.	Short title		See above.
2.	Interpretation of terms		,, above.

PART II

BILLS OF EXCHANGE

Form and Interpretation

3.	Bill of exchange defined		See BILL OF EXCHANGE.
4.	Inland and foreign bills		,, INLAND BILL.
5.	Effect where different parties to bill are the same person		,, DRAWER. ,, DRAWEE.
6.	Address to drawee		,, DRAWEE.
7.	Certainty required as to payee		,, PAYEE.
8.	What bills are negotiable	s.s. 1, 2	,, NEGOTIATION OF BILL OF EXCHANGE.
		s.s. 3	,, BEARER.
		s.s. 4, 5	,, ORDER.
9.	Sum payable	s.s. 1, 2	,, BILL OF EXCHANGE.
		s.s. 3	,, INTEREST.
10.	Bill payable on demand		,, TIME OF PAYMENT OF BILL.
11.	Bill payable at a future time		,, do.
12.	Omission of date in bill payable after date		,, DATE.
13.	Ante-dating and post-dating		,, do.
14.	Computation of time of payment		,, TIME OF PAYMENT OF BILL.
15.	Case of need		,, REFEREE IN CASE OF NEED.
16.	Optional stipulations by drawer or indorser		,, DRAWER.
17.	Definition and requisites of acceptance		,, ACCEPTANCE.
18.	Time for acceptance		,, do.
19.	General and qualified acceptances		,, ACCEPTANCE, GENERAL. ,, ,, QUALIFIED.
20.	Inchoate Instruments		,, INCHOATE INSTRUMENT.
21.	Delivery		,, DELIVERY OF BILL.

Capacity and Authority of Parties

22.	Capacity of parties		See PARTIES TO BILL OF EXCHANGE.
23.	Signature essential to liability		,, do.
24.	Forged or unauthorised signature		,, FORGERY.
25.	Procuration signatures		,, AGENT.
26.	Person signing as agent or in representative capacity		,, do.

The Consideration for a Bill

27.	Value and holder for value	s.s. 1	See CONSIDERATION FOR BILL OF EXCHANGE.
		s.s. 2, 3	,, HOLDER FOR VALUE.
28.	Accommodation bill or party		,, ACCOMMODATION BILL.
29.	Holder in due course		,, HOLDER IN DUE COURSE.
30.	Presumption of value and good faith		,, do.

Negotiation of Bills

Section.		
31.	Negotiation of bill	See NEGOTIATION OF BILL OF EXCHANGE.
32.	Requisites of a valid indorsement	,, INDORSEMENT.
33.	Conditional indorsement	,, do.
34.	Indorsement in blank and special indorsement	,, do.
35.	Restrictive indorsement	,, do.
36.	Negotiation of overdue or dishonoured bill	,, NEGOTIATION OF BILL OF EXCHANGE.
37.	Negotiation of bill to party already liable thereon	,, do.
38.	Rights of the holder	,, HOLDER IN DUE COURSE.

General Duties of the Holder

39.	When presentment for acceptance is necessary	See PRESENTMENT FOR ACCEPTANCE.
40.	Time for presenting bill payable after sight	,, do.
41.	Rules as to presentment for acceptance, and excuses for non-presentment	,, do.
42.	Non-acceptance	,, DISHONOUR OF BILL OF EXCHANGE.
43.	Dishonour by non-acceptance and its consequences	,, do.
44.	Duties as to qualified acceptances	,, ACCEPTANCE, QUALIFIED.
45.	Rules as to presentment for payment	,, PRESENTMENT FOR PAYMENT.
46.	Excuses for delay or non-presentment for payment	,, do.
47.	Dishonour by non-payment	,, DISHONOUR OF BILL OF EXCHANGE.
48.	Notice of dishonour and effect of non-notice	,, do.
49.	Rules as to notice of dishonour	,, do.
50.	Excuses for non-notice and delay	,, do.
51.	Noting or protest of bill	,, PROTEST.
52.	Duties of holder as regards drawee or acceptor	,, PRESENTMENT FOR PAYMENT.

Liabilities of Parties

53.	Funds in hands of drawee	See DRAWEE.
54.	Liability of acceptor	,, ACCEPTANCE.
55.	Liability of drawer or indorser { s.s. 1	,, DRAWER.
	{ s.s. 2	,, INDORSER.
56.	Stranger signing bill liable as indorser	,, do.
57.	Measure of damages against parties to dishonoured bill	,, DISHONOUR OF BILL OF EXCHANGE.
58.	Transferor by delivery and transferee	,, TRANSFEROR BY DELIVERY.

Discharge of Bill

59.	Payment in due course	,, PAYMENT OF BILL.
60.	Banker paying demand draft whereon indorsement is forged	,, do.
61.	Acceptor, the holder at maturity	,, do.
62.	Express waiver or renunciation	,, do.
63.	Cancellation	,, CANCELLATION OF BILL OF EXCHANGE.
64.	Alteration of bill	,, ALTERATIONS.

Acceptance and Payment for Honour

65.	Acceptance for honour suprà protest	See ACCEPTANCE FOR HONOUR.
66.	Liability of acceptor for honour	,, do.
67.	Presentment to acceptor for honour	,, PRESENTMENT FOR PAYMENT.
68.	Payment for honour suprà protest	,, PAYMENT FOR HONOUR.

Lost Instruments

Section.		
69.	Holder's right to duplicate of lost bill	See LOST BILL OF EXCHANGE.
70.	Action on lost bill	,, do.

Bill in a Set

71.	Rules as to sets	See BILL IN A SET.

Conflict of Laws

72.	Rules where laws conflict	See FOREIGN BILL.

PART III

CHEQUES ON A BANKER

73.	Cheque defined	See CHEQUE.
74.	Presentment of cheque for payment	,, PRESENTMENT FOR PAYMENT.
75.	Revocation of banker's authority	,, PAYMENT OF CHEQUE.

Crossed Cheques

76.	General and special crossings defined	See CROSSED CHEQUE.
77.	Crossing by drawer or after issue	,, do.
78.	Crossing a material part of cheque	,, do.
79.	Duties of banker as to crossed cheques	,, do.
80.	Protection to banker and drawer where cheque is crossed	,, do.
81.	Effect of "not negotiable" crossing on holder	,, do.
82.	Protection to collecting banker	,, do.

PART IV

PROMISSORY NOTES

83.	Promissory note defined	See PROMISSORY NOTE.
84.	Delivery necessary	,, do.
85.	Joint and several notes	,, do.
86.	Note payable on demand	,, PRESENTMENT FOR PAYMENT.
87.	Presentment of note for payment	,, do.
88.	Liability of maker	,, PROMISSORY NOTE.
89.	Application of Part II to notes	,, do.

PART V

SUPPLEMENTARY

90.	Good faith	See GOOD FAITH.
91.	Signature by agent	,, AGENT.
92.	Computation of time	,, TIME OF PAYMENT OF BILL.
93.	When noting equivalent to protest	,, PROTEST.
94.	Protest when notary not accessible	,, do.
95.	Dividend warrants may be crossed	,, CROSSED CHEQUE.
96.	(Repealed by Statute Law Revision Act, 1898. 61 & 62 Vict. c. 22.)	
97.	Savings	,, above.
98.	Saving of summary diligence in Scotland	,, above.
99.	Construction with other Acts, etc.	,, above.
100.	Parol evidence allowed in certain judicial proceedings in Scotland	,, above.
	Schedule I. Form of Protest	,, PROTEST.

BILLS OF EXCHANGE (CROSSED CHEQUES) ACT, 1906 (6 EDW. VII c. 17). An Act to amend Section 82 of the Bills of Exchange Act, 1882 (August 4, 1906).

"Be it enacted by the King's most Excellent Majesty, by and with the advice and consent of the Lords Spiritual and Temporal, and Commons, in this present Parliament assembled, and by the authority of the same, as follows :—

"1. A banker receives payment of a crossed cheque for a customer within the meaning of Section 82 of the Bills of Exchange Act, 1882, notwithstanding that he credits his customer's account with the amount of the cheque before receiving payment thereof.

"2. This Act may be cited as the Bills of Exchange (crossed cheques) Act, 1906, and this Act and the Bills of Exchange Act, 1882, may be cited together as the Bills of Exchange Acts, 1882 and 1906."

The effect of this Act is to place a banker who credits the account of his customer with a cheque before he has collected it, in the same position as though he first of all collected the cheque and then placed the proceeds thereof to his customer's account. (See Section 82 of the Bills of Exchange Act, 1882, under CROSSED CHEQUE.)

BILLS REMITTED BOOK. This book contains particulars of all bills despatched to a banker's correspondents for collection ; where the bills are very numerous, separate books may be kept, if necessary, for bills remitted to London, to branches, to head office, or to country correspondents.

BIMETALLISM. Bimetallism is the system of coinage where there are two standards of value, gold and silver. In Britain, the system has been monometallic since 1816 ; that is, gold is the sole standard of value. In India, silver is the standard.

Much controversy has taken place with regard to the respective merits of monometallism and bimetallism, and various fruitless conferences have been held with the view of establishing silver as an international standard of value, as well as gold. If bimetallism were established, it would mean that both gold and silver would be legal tender to any amount (silver at present being merely token money and legal tender only to the extent of £2), that both these metals would require to be coined free of cost by the Mint, and that they would circulate at a ratio to each other as fixed by the Government.

Whatever may be the merits of a bimetallic system, it would appear doubtful, from a practical point of view, whether the present monometallic system, whatever may be its faults, which has hitherto served the country well, should be departed from in order to adopt a system of double standards which, apparently, has not hitherto proved a success in any country where it has been adopted.

The countries forming the Latin Monetary Union (*q.v.*) are bimetallic.

BLACK FRIDAY. May 11, 1866, on which day the firm of bill-brokers, Overend Gurney & Co., failed. There was a monetary panic in London, and to a large extent throughout the country.

BLANK CHEQUE. A cheque which is signed by the drawer without any amount being filled in. When such a cheque is issued, it is usually with the intention that the payee or some other authorised person should fill in an amount as sanctioned by the drawer. A blank cheque is an unsatisfactory document to give to anyone, as it might easily fall into the hands of some person who would make a wrong use of it.

BLANK INDORSEMENT. Where an indorsement on a bill of exchange specifies no indorsee, it is an indorsement in blank. A bill so indorsed becomes payable to bearer. The same term applies to the indorsement of cheques. (See INDORSEMENT.)

BLANK TRANSFER. A blank transfer of stock or shares is a transfer where the name of the transferee has not been filled in, or which is undated. It is sometimes used when shares are given as security for a debt, the intention being that if default is made in payment, the lender may fill in his own name, as transferee, or insert the date, and send the instrument forward for registration. If a blank transfer is to be held unstamped, it should not be dated, otherwise it cannot, after thirty days from execution, be stamped except under a penalty.

A blank transfer, however, in those companies where the transfer must be under seal, is not a very satisfactory security. In the case of *Powell* v. *London and Provincial Bank* (1893, 2 Ch. 555), a stock certificate and a blank transfer were given to the bank as security. The bank subsequently inserted its own name in the transfer and executed it, and was duly registered by the company. Lord Justice Lindley said : ". . . in order to acquire the legal title to stock or shares in companies governed by the Companies Clauses Consolidation Act, 1845, you must have a deed executed by the transferor, and you must have that transfer registered. Until you have got *both* you have not got the legal title in the transferee. Now what took place here was this: Mr. Edwards gave to the bank a transfer sealed by him, and, so far as form goes, probably delivered by him to the bank, but with blanks. It was not in a complete form. It was never in that form in which such an instrument, however much wax there might be at the bottom, could amount to a deed by the transferor. We all know that both at common law and under these statutes if you execute a transfer in blank, that instrument with the blanks is not a deed. Then what happened is this. That document so executed by Edwards in blank was filled up afterwards by the bank, probably as was intended, and the bank itself was put in as the transferee and the bank got itself registered. . . . What was the effect of what had been done? It was not that the bank got a good title. The registration of the stock in the bank, unless preceded by a valid deed transferring the stock from the owner of it, does not give the transferee a good title at all. We have not to consider the effect of documents executed in blank as agreements enforceable in equity. We have nothing to do with that, but we are considering the legal title of the bank. The bank had no legal title at all." In that case the stock certificate proved to be part of a trust estate, and the bank, although it had no notice of the trust, had its title postponed to the prior equitable title of the persons interested under the trust.

In the case of those companies where debentures and shares are transferable by an instrument under hand (a deed under seal not being required), a blank transfer does form a satisfactory security, and the transferee's name can subsequently be filled in. In the event of the transferor's death, however, before the blanks are filled up, the banker's authority to do so is cancelled.

The reason why a blank transfer under seal cannot legally have any blanks subsequently filled in by a banker is that a document under seal is a deed and takes effect from its delivery. To enable a blank transfer under seal to be effectually completed, the blanks should be filled in in the presence of the transferor, or by his authority under seal, or the deed should be re-delivered by him. (See CERTIFICATE, TRANSFER OF SHARES.)

BOARD OF GUARDIANS. (See GUARDIANS OF THE POOR.)

BODY CORPORATE. A number of persons which, by law, are formed into a corporation, and which continues as a distinct body irrespective of any changes which may take place amongst the members. (See CORPORATION.)

BONÂ FIDE. Latin, in good faith. The opposite to *bonâ fide* is *malâ fide*, in bad faith.

The Bills of Exchange Act, 1882, states that a thing is deemed to be done in good faith, within the meaning of the Act, where it is in fact done honestly, whether it is done negligently or not.

BOND. A bond is a document under seal whereby a person binds himself to pay a certain sum or to fulfil a certain contract.

For example, if Brown owes Jones £100, Brown may sign a bond for £200; that is, he binds himself for twice the actual amount intended to be secured, so as to cover principal, interest and all charges. The £200 is called the penalty, and the instrument usually continues: "Now the condition of the above written bond is such that if the above bounden Brown, his heirs, executors, or administrators shall pay unto the said Jones the sum of £100 by the instalments following . etc. . Then the above written bond shall be void, otherwise the same shall remain in full force."

The duties imposed by the Stamp Act, 1891, are as follows:—

BOND for securing the payment or repayment of money or the transfer or retransfer of stock.

See MORTGAGE, ETC., AND MARKETABLE SECURITY.

BOND in relation to any annuity upon the original creation and sale thereof.

See CONVEYANCE ON SALE.

BOND, COVENANT, OR INSTRUMENT of any kind whatsoever.

(1) Being the only or principal or primary security for any annuity (*except upon the original creation thereof by way of sale or security, and except a superannuation annuity*), or for any sum or sums of money at stated periods, not being interest for any principal sum secured by a duly stamped instrument, nor

rent reserved by a lease or tack.

£ s. d.

For a definite and certain period, so that the total amount to be ultimately payable can be ascertained. — The same *ad valorem* duty as a bond or covenant for such total amount.

(The Inland Revenue do not, in practice, charge duty on more than twenty times the annual sum.)

For the term of life or any other indefinite period.

For every £5, and also for any fractional part of £5, of the annuity or sum periodically payable. . 0 2 6

(2) Being a collateral or auxiliary or additional or substituted security for any of the above mentioned purposes where the principal or primary instrument is duly stamped.

Where the total amount to be ultimately payable can be ascertained . . . — The same *ad valorem* duty as a bond or covenant of the same kind for such total amount.

In any other case :

For every £5, and also for any fractional part of £5, of the annuity or sum periodically payable. . 0 0 6

(3) Being a grant or contract for payment of a superannuation annuity, that is to say, a deferred life annuity granted or secured to any person in consideration of annual premiums payable until he attains a specified age and so as to commence on his attaining that age.

For every £5 and also for any fractional part of £5 of the annuity . . . 0 0 6

Bond given pursuant to the directions of any Act, or of the Commissioners or the Commissioners. of Customs, or any of their officers, for or in respect of any of the duties of excise or customs, or for preventing frauds or evasions thereof, or for any other matter or thing relating thereto.

£ s. d.

Where the penalty of the bond does not exceed £150. — The same *ad valorem* duty as a bond for the amount of the penalty.

In any other case . . . 0 5 0

Exemption.

Bond given as aforesaid upon, or in relation to, the receiving or obtaining, or for entitling any person to receive or obtain, any drawback of any duty of excise or customs, for or in respect of any goods, wares, or merchandise exported or shipped to be exported from the United Kingdom to any parts beyond the seas, or upon or in relation to the obtaining of any debenture or certificate for entitling any person to receive any such drawback as aforesaid.

And see Section 42 as follows :—

"If any person required by any Act for the time being in force or by the Commissioners, or any of their officers, to give or enter into any bond for or in respect of any duty of excise, or for preventing any fraud or evasion in relation to any such duty, or for any matter or thing relating thereto, includes in one and the same bond any goods or things belonging to more persons than one, not being partners or joint tenants, or tenants in common, he shall for every offence incur a fine of fifty pounds."

£ s. d.

Bond on obtaining letters of administration in England or Ireland, or a confirmation of testament in Scotland 0 5 0

Exemptions.

(1) Bond given by the widow, child, father, mother, brother or sister, of any common seaman, marine or soldier, dying in the service of Her Majesty.

(2) Bond given by any person where the estate to be administered does not exceed £100 in value.

	£ s. d.
BOND of any kind whatsoever not specifically charged with any duty:	
Where the amount limited to be recoverable does not exceed £300	The same *ad valorem* duty as a bond for the amount limited.
In any other case . . .	0 10 0
BOND, accompanied with a deposit of title deeds, for making a mortgage, wadset, or other security on any estate or property therein comprised. See MORTGAGE, etc., and Section 86.	
BOND, DECLARATION, or other DEED or WRITING for making redeemable any disposition, assignation, or tack, apparently absolute, but intended only as a security. See MORTGAGE, etc., and Sections 23 under AGREEMENT and 86 under MORTGAGE.	

BOND TO BEARER. (See MARKETABLE SECURITY.)

BOND AND DISPOSITION IN SECURITY. In Scotland, the usual method of obtaining a security over heritable (or real) property is by way of a deed, called a bond and disposition in security. The deed is a combination of a personal bond by the debtor and a conveyance of property by the debtor (or by a third party) in favour of the banker lending the money. The advance, however, must be made at once and in one amount. The bond must be registered in the Register of Sasines and priority is obtained according to the date of registration.

Though the personal obligation in the bond can be enforced for repayment of whatever debt is due by the debtor to the banker, any surplus there may be on realisation of the property, cannot be held for any other debt than that specified in the deed. (See CONSIGNATION RECEIPT.)

BOND OF CAUTION. In Scotland, an obligation by one person as surety for another. (See BOND OF CREDIT.)

BOND OF CREDIT. In Scotland, a bond of credit, or "cash credit bond," is a personal security for a "cash credit." A cash credit is a term peculiar to Scotland, but it is practically the same as an overdraft on a current account in England. The debtor signs the bond, as well as the sureties, and they all acknowledge to have obtained the credit. To secure a cash credit to John Brown the document would begin: "We, John Brown and John Jones, having obtained a credit of one hundred pounds sterling with the Scots Bank on cash account in name of me, the said John Brown, do therefore hereby bind and oblige ourselves, our heirs, executors, and successors whatever, all conjunctly and severally to pay," etc. (See BOND OF CREDIT AND DISPOSITION IN SECURITY.)

BOND OF CREDIT AND DISPOSITION IN SECURITY. In Scotland, a "bond and disposition in security" creates a security over heritable property for a loan which is made at once and in one sum; but a "bond of credit and disposition" is a deed which enables heritable (real) property to be made available for a cash credit (that is, an overdraft on a working account, on which the full advance need not be taken in one amount). By law, however, the security is available only to the amount specified in the bond and three years' interest at 5 per cent. The deed is a combination of a "bond of credit" and a disposition or conveyance of property to the creditor. The bond must be registered in the Register of Sasines. (See BOND OF CREDIT, BOND AND DISPOSITION IN SECURITY.)

BONS. A name given to documents, such as French Treasury Bonds, upon which is printed the word "*bon*" in conjunction with the amount of the bond, e.g. "*Bon pour cent francs*," good for one hundred francs.

BONUS. The profits of an assurance company, which are distributed periodically to the policyholders, are called bonuses. Part of these "profits" arises from the unused portion of the "loading," as it is called; that is, the amount included in the premium rates specially to pay expenses. (See LIFE POLICY.)

The word is also applied to an extraordinary division of the profits of a company, in addition to the ordinary dividend.

BOOK DEBTS. The item "book debts," which appears upon the balance sheet of a trader or a trading concern, represents the amount owing for goods, etc., sold, as shown by the books. In considering such an item, it is necessary to ascertain whether the debts are owing merely by two or three individuals or firms, or are well spread over many debtors, and also to ascertain what proportion of the amount may be considered as good and likely to be paid, and what may be regarded as bad and what as doubtful.

BOOK VALUE. The value of a property

as it appears in the books of a company. According to circumstances, a book value may be either more or less than the actual market value.

BOOKS. The books in use are not the same in all banks. The rulings and method of keeping them vary, and in some cases a book which is used for a certain purpose in one bank may, under the same name, be used for a different purpose in another bank. All the books of a bank, however, from the humblest to the most important, are required to be neatly and accurately kept, and each member of the staff is expected to take a pride in so keeping any books for which he is responsible that, in the event of the books being at any time produced in Court, they will not afford an opportunity to any one for adverse criticism. Figures in ledgers, etc., should be called over day by day and all calculations be duly checked.

The following is a list of a number of the principal books in use (in some cases the same book appears under different names) though they will not all be found in any one bank :—

Acceptance Register.
Acceptance Ledger.
Acceptors' Ledger.
Accounts Opened and Closed Book.
Advice Book.
Attendance Book.
Balance Book.
Bank Note Register.
Bank Rate Book.
Bankers' Ledger.
Bearer Bonds Register.
Bill Diary.
Bill Ledger.
Bill Register.
Bills Discounted Book.
Bills for Collection Book.
Bills Remitted Book.
Branches Ledger.
Cash Balance Book.
Cash Book.
Check Ledger.
Cheque Book Register.
Circular Notes Book.
Clearing Book.
Coin Balance Book.
Common Seal Book.
Counter Cash Book.
Coupon Book.
Current Account Ledger.
Current Account Register.
Day Book.
Deposit Ledger.
Deposit Register.
Diaries.
Discount Cash Book.
Discount Day Book.
Discount Ledger.
Discount Register.
Dividend Register.
Draft Book.
Exchange Book.
General Ledger.
Investment Ledger.
Journal.
Key Register.
Letter Books.
Letters Despatched Register.
Letters of Credit.
Letters Received Register.
Loans Ledger.
Loans Register.
London Agent's Ledger.
Minute Book.
Money Book.
Money Lent and Lodged Book.
Note Register (for own issue).
Opinion Book.
Overdue Bills Book.
Pass Book Register.
Postage Book.
Probate Register.
Record of Cheques Book.
Remittance Book.
Returned Bills.
Safe Custody Register.
Securities Book.
Securities Journal.
Securities Ledger.
Shareholders' Ledger.
Shareholders' Register.
Short Bills Ledger.
Signature Book.
Staff Register.
Stock Exchange Transactions.
Teller's Cash Book.
Till Book.
Title Deeds Book.
Transfer Register.
Walks Book.
Waste Book.

BOROUGH ENGLISH. A peculiar custom in connection with real property in certain old cities and boroughs, by which the property descends to the youngest son instead of to the eldest.

BORROWED NOTE. A name sometimes given to the agreement which is signed by a borrower when bearer bonds or registered securities are given by him as cover for a loan. The agreement gives the banker authority to sell the securities in the event of the loan not being repaid at the specified time, or of the stipulated margin on the securities not being maintained.

BORROWING ON CONSOLS. This refers to a method adopted by the Bank of England for making an increase in its "Bank Rate" effective in preventing an undue drain of gold from its reserve. A large constituent of the item "Other Deposits" in the Bank Return is formed by the balances of the other London banks. In ordinary times, therefore, when the amount of "Other Deposits" is high, it implies that the money market (the London banks and bill brokers) has a considerable sum of floating money at its disposal, which, seeking for any profitable investment rather than lying idle in the hands of the Bank, competes for the bills that are offered for discount and so prevents the market rate of discount from closely following the Bank Rate. But the only certain way to counteract the outflow of gold from the country is to increase the value of money at home, which proceeding acts in two ways ; it renders the export of gold unprofitable, because it is so dear to buy, and it turns the foreign exchanges in favour of this country by encouraging bankers abroad to purchase London paper for the sake of the high rate of discount which they can get. The Bank of England, therefore, in order to get rid of this floating capital, which interferes with the effect of the Bank Rate, employ the somewhat drastic expedient of borrowing it themselves by selling consols for "money" and buying them back for the "account." The purchasers, whoever they may be, draw cheques on their accounts, soon absorbing the floating fund referred to and having the immediate effect of lessening the bankers' balances contained in the "Other Deposits."

Deprived of this means of competition

with the Bank of England, the money market has no alternative but speedily to raise its rate, and the desired result is obtained. (See BANK RATE, BANK RETURN.)

BORROWING POWERS. When a company wishes to borrow, a banker should, by careful reference to the memorandum and articles of association of the company, ascertain what powers to borrow, if any, are given therein, and what are the limitations of those powers. If a company has power to borrow, there may be a limit beyond which the directors cannot go, and a banker must make certain that any proposed advance will not, with any loans already obtained by the company, exceed the specified limit. It may be that the directors are unable to borrow except by resolution of the company, or they may be able to borrow but not have any power to mortgage the company's property. Directors must not act *ultra vires*—that is, beyond their powers. In dealing with a company it is of the first importance to see, as Lord Halsbury said (in *County of Gloucester Bank* v. *Rudry Merthyr Steam and House Coal Colliery Co.*, 1895, 1 Ch. 629), "that the acts which the company is purporting to do are acts within the general authority of the company, and if those public documents, which every one has a right to refer to, disclose an infirmity in their action, they take the consequences of dealing with a joint stock company which has apparently exceeded its authority."

Where nothing is said in the memorandum and articles as to borrowing, a right to borrow is presumed in the case of a trading company for the purposes of its ordinary business. The above remarks apply whether the company desires to borrow by way of overdraft (either unsecured or secured by a mortgage of its property), or by debentures, or by discounting bills. (See COMPANIES, COMPANY LIMITED BY SHARES.)

BOTTOMRY BOND. A document by which the master or captain of a ship charges or hypothecates the ship as security for the repayment of a loan. The circumstances under which such an instrument could be created are where the ship is in a foreign port and certain repairs are absolutely necessary in order to enable the ship to continue its voyage, and the captain has no other means of raising the money required to effect the repairs, and is unable to communicate with the owners. The money borrowed upon a bottomry bond is repayable only in the event of the ship reaching its destination. A lender must exercise the greatest care, as a captain has no authority to bind the ship-owner, except in case of necessity. (See RESPONDENTIA.)

BOUGHT NOTE. The contract note which is given by a stockbroker to his client, supplying particulars of a purchase which has been effected for him. (See CONTRACT NOTE.)

BOURSE. The name of the principal place in each country (or large town doing an active foreign trade) where the balance of trade between that country and others is settled by the mutual interchange of bills, and where merchants resort to buy and sell merchandise; they are international clearing-houses.

At a Bourse an exporter of goods to another country sells his draft, so getting payment for the goods exported; and it is there also that an importer goes to buy a draft (the same that the above exporter sells) which he remits to the foreign seller, so making payment for the goods imported.

In this country the foreign bill business is focussed at the Royal Exchange, London.

On the continent, stock exchange business is also conducted at the Bourses.

BRANCHES. For some purposes the branches of a bank are treated as though they were separate banks, e.g. one branch is not obliged to pay a cheque drawn upon another branch, and one branch may, in giving notice of dishonour, treat the other branch, in the matter of time, as a separate institution. On the other hand, branches are regarded as parts of one body in certain cases, e.g. a credit balance at one branch may be used to reduce an overdrawn account of the same customer at another branch; and where a customer has two accounts, one in credit at one branch and one overdrawn at another branch, and he presents a cheque at the branch with the credit balance, the banker is entitled, in considering whether he should pay the cheque, to regard the two accounts as one account, but if there has been an agreement, or the practice in the past has been to treat the two accounts as quite distinct, the banker could not, without due notice, suddenly change his method of dealing.

For most purposes the head office and branches are regarded as one body. It has been held that notice to the head office of an act of bankruptcy is equivalent to notice to the branches, allowing for reasonable time to communicate the notice to the branches.

A draft drawn by one branch upon another, or upon the head office, is not a cheque so far as the bank is concerned, and therefore protection against a forged indorsement is not obtained by Section 60 of the Bills of Exchange Act. It has been held, however (*Capital and Counties' Bank* v. *Gordon*, 1903, A.C. 240), that the bank is protected by Section 19 of the Stamp Act, 1853. (See DRAFT.)

Where a crossed cheque drawn on one branch is paid to credit of a customer's account at another branch of the same bank, the branches in such a case may be regarded either as one bank (in which case protection against a forged indorsement is obtained by Section 60 of the Bills of Exchange Act) or as practically two different banks, payment being made by one to the other (in which case the payment fulfils the requirements of Section 79).

A copy of the statement as prescribed by Section 108 of the Companies (Consolidation) Act, 1908, must be exhibited in a conspicuous place in every branch. (See under BANKING COMPANY.)

A customer may pay in at any branch to his credit at the branch where he keeps his account. He may also, as a rule, arrange to have his cheques cashed at other branches. In such a case the branch where his account is kept advises the branch where they are to be cashed to pay them up to a certain limited amount in any one day, or as may be desired, and furnishes at the same time a specimen of the drawer's signature. (See STANDING CREDITS.)

BRANCHES LEDGER. This book is kept at the head office and contains an account for each branch of the bank, into which accounts are posted all the transactions between the branches and the head office. The transactions may be entered up with a certain amount of detail, or daily totals only may be shown. Each branch keeps an account in the general ledger with the head office, posted either in detail or by daily totals, and this account should agree with the account for the branch at head office in the branches ledger. If the head office balance at the branch is debit, the balance shown in the ledger at head office will be credit. In order to ascertain accurately the profit made by each branch it is necessary for the head office to allow interest on the balance standing to a branch's credit, or, on the other hand, to charge interest on the amount which head office may have lent to a branch.

When a balance sheet of the bank is prepared, the branches ledger balance is set off against the balances at the branches.

BRASSAGE. A charge which was made at one time by the Mint, to cover the expense of coining, when any one took gold bullion to be coined. The charge was abolished in 1666. Sovereigns can now be obtained for bullion free of cost. (See SEIGNIORAGE.)

BREAKING UP VALUE. The value of a property merely as old material.

BRIGHTON A. A Stock Exchange name for London, Brighton and South Coast Railway deferred ordinary stock.

BROKEN ACCOUNT. An account is said to be "broken" when operations upon it are stopped, and all subsequent transactions are passed through a new account. This takes place, for example, upon the death of a surety, when a banker wishes to preserve his recourse against the estate of the deceased. Unless the debtor's account is broken, all payments to credit go to release the surety, and all debits form a fresh unsecured advance. (See "CLAYTON'S CASE.")

BROKERAGE. The charge of so much per cent. or per share made by a broker for carrying out the instructions of a client to buy or sell stocks or shares. (See STOCK-BROKER.)

BROKERS. Persons who buy and sell goods, bills, stocks and shares, etc., on behalf of other persons. (See BILL BROKER, STOCK-BROKER.)

BRONZE COINS. Bronze coins are issued by the Mint for a penny, half-penny and farthing. Copper coins (which were first issued in 1672) were replaced by bronze in 1860. They are still commonly called copper coins.

The composition of bronze is ninety-five parts of copper, four parts of tin, and one part of zinc.

Bronze coins are legal tender only to the extent of one shilling.

Slot gas meters have had a remarkable effect in withdrawing pennies from circulation, and producing quite a famine of "copper" in some districts until the meters are collected, when a sudden superabundance of copper is obtained. (See COINAGE.)

BRUM OR BRUMS. A Stock Exchange name for London and North-Western Railway Stock.

BUCKET SHOP. A slang term which is applied to an "outside" stockbroker's office, where the business is of a gambling nature. An outside broker is one who is not a member of the Stock Exchange.

BUILDING LAND. Building land is, as a rule, one of the most unsatisfactory securities which can be offered to a banker. At the time the security is taken there may, perhaps, be a large demand for building land in the neighbourhood, but there is no guarantee that the demand will continue. In a very short time it may cease altogether, and, for various reasons, some other district be favoured for street extensions. If the property comes into the banker's hands, he may fail to find anyone to purchase it at anything like its original cost, and the longer it is held the less its value may become. The surrounding houses or works which have appeared since the security was taken, may be objectionable, and no one will be inclined to build upon the land, and it may become practically worthless.

In considering the value of building land it should be noted whether any of the adjoining property owners have established any rights of light that would interfere with any buildings which might be contemplated for erection on the land.

BUILDING LEASE. The following exhibits the general form of a building lease :—

This Indenture made the day of 1910 Between hereinafter called the said lessor of the first part and hereinafter called the lessee of the second part Witnesseth that in consideration of the rent hereinafter reserved and of the covenants and agreements hereinafter contained and by or on the part of the lessee to be paid and performed He the said lessor, etc.

Doth by this deed appoint and demise unto the lessee

All that piece or parcel of ground, etc.

Together with easements and appurtenances to the said piece of ground belonging.

To have and to hold the said piece of ground unto the lessee from the 1st day of March, 1910, for the term of 99 years.

Yielding and paying therefor yearly and every year during the term hereby limited the yearly rent of pounds free from all taxes, save only the landlord's income tax.

And the lessee covenants

That the lessee will duly pay the said yearly rent, and all taxes.

And also that the lessee will within months from the date hereof erect dwelling houses upon the said ground to the reasonable satisfaction of the said lessor,

And also keep in good and substantial order and repair the said dwelling houses.

And in such good and substantial order and repair will on the expiration of the determination of the term hereby limited peaceably yield and deliver the same premises to the lessor.

And the lessee will insure the said dwelling houses.

Provided always and it is hereby agreed and declared that in case the said yearly rent of or any half-yearly payment shall be in arrear for the space of days, or in case the lessee or his sub-lessees shall not faithfully keep all the agreements and covenants in these presents contained, it shall be lawful for the lessor to re-enter upon the said ground and dwelling houses and the lessee and sub-lessees to expel and remove.

And the lessor covenants with the lessee that the lessee paying the yearly rent and observing the covenants and agreements shall peaceably hold and enjoy the said premises during the time hereby limited.

A building lease is usually granted for 99 years. In cases where the period is 999 years, it is practically equal to a freehold. (See LEASEHOLD.)

BUILDING SOCIETY. All societies formed under the Building Societies Acts, 1874 to 1894, must obtain a certificate of incorporation from the Registrar of Friendly Societies.

These incorporated societies are to be distinguished from an unincorporated society formed under the Act of 1836, and which has not since obtained a certificate of incorporation under the 1874 to 1894 Acts.

A terminating society means a society which by its rules is to terminate at a fixed date, or when a result specified in its rules is attained ; a permanent society means a society which has not by its rules any such fixed date or specified result at which it shall terminate.

With respect to incorporated societies, the Building Societies Act, 1874 (37 & 38 Vict. c. 42) provides as follows :—

"Section 15. With respect to the

borrowing of money by societies under this Act, the following provisions shall have effect:

"(1) Any society under this Act may receive deposits or loans, at interest, within the limits in this Section provided, from the members or other persons, or from corporate bodies, joint stock companies, or from any terminating building society, to be applied to the purposes of the society:

"(2) In a permanent society the total amount so received on deposit or loan and not repaid by the society shall not at any time exceed two-thirds of the amount for the time being secured to the society by mortgages from its members.

"(3) In a terminating society the total amount so received and not repaid may either be a sum not exceeding such two-thirds as aforesaid, or a sum not exceeding twelve months' subscriptions on the shares for the time being in force:

"(4) Any deposits with or loans to a society under this Act, made before the commencement of this Act in accordance with its certified rules, are hereby declared to be valid and binding on the society, but no further deposits or loans shall be received by such society, except within the limits provided by this section:

"(5) Every deposit book or acknowledgment or security of any kind given for a deposit or loan by a society shall have printed or written therein or thereon the whole of the fourteenth and fifteenth Sections of the present Act."

An overdraft to a building society is a loan within the meaning of the above Section.

"Section 14. The liability of any member of any society under this Act in respect of any share upon which no advance has been made shall be limited to the amount actually paid or in arrear on such share, and in respect of any share upon which an advance has been made shall be limited to the amount payable thereon under any mortgage or other security or under the rules of the society."

Part of Section 43 is as follows:—

"If any society under this Act receives loans or deposits in excess of the limits prescribed by this Act, the directors or committee of management of such society receiving such loans or deposits on its behalf shall be personally liable for the amount so received in excess."

In *Chapleo and Wife* v. *Brunswick Permanent Building Society and Others* (1881, 6 Q.B.D. 696), Bagallay, L. J., in the course of his judgment, said:—"Persons who deal with corporations and societies that owe their constitution to or have their powers defined or limited by Acts of Parliament, or are regulated by deeds of settlement or rules, deriving their effect more or less from Acts of Parliament, are bound to know or to ascertain for themselves the nature of the constitution, and the extent of the powers of the corporation or society with which they deal. The plaintiffs and every one else who have dealings with a building society are bound to know that such a society has no power of borrowing, except such as is conferred upon it by its rules, and if in dealing with such a society they neglect or fail to ascertain whether it has the power of borrowing, or whether any limited power it may have has been exceeded, they must take the consequences of their carelessness."

A society registered under the Act of 1836 and not incorporated under the Act of 1874 has no power of borrowing unless authorised by its rules. Section 1 of the 1894 Act provides that the rules of every society under the Building Societies Acts established or substituting a new set of rules for the existing rules after the passing of this Act shall set forth whether the society intends to borrow money, and, if so, within what limits, not exceeding those prescribed by the Building Societies Acts. The 1894 Act (Section 28) repealed a somewhat similar provision in the 1874 Act, Section 16, paragraph 2, which enacted that the rules should set forth whether the society intends to avail itself of the borrowing powers contained in this Act, and, if so, within what limits, not exceeding the limits prescribed by this Act. Therefore, where an advance is required by a building society, its rules should be carefully perused to ascertain (1) if the society has power to borrow, and to what extent; (2) if it has power to mortgage or pledge. If the society has such powers, it is necessary to see that such powers are not exceeded.

All cheques should be signed in accordance with the rules of the society.

Cheques drawn by, or on behalf of, a registered Friendly Society are exempt from stamp duty. The Friendly Societies Act, 1906, Section 33, provides that stamp duty shall not be chargeable upon a "draft or order or receipt given by or to a registered society or branch in respect of money payable by virtue of its rules or of this Act."

By Section 41 of the Building Societies Act, 1874 :—

"No rules of any society under this Act, nor any copy thereof, nor any power, warrant, or letter of attorney, granted or to be granted by any person as trustee for the society for the transfer of any share in the public funds standing in his name, nor any receipts given for any dividend in any public stock or fund, or interest of Exchequer bills, nor any receipt, nor any entry in any book of receipt, for money deposited in the funds of the society, nor for any money received by any member, his executors or administrators, assigns, or attorneys, from the funds of the society, nor any transfer of any share, nor any bond or other security to be given to or on account of the society, or by any officer thereof, nor any order on any officer for payment of money to any member, nor any appointment of any agent, nor any certificate or other instrument for the revocation of any such appointment, nor any other instrument or document whatever required or authorised to be given, issued, signed, made, or produced in pursuance of this Act, or of the rules of the society, shall be subject or liable to or charged with any stamp duty or duties whatsoever, provided that the exemption shall not extend to any mortgage."

An advance to a building society should, preferably, be made upon a separate loan account and not upon the ordinary current account, so that the danger of making advances in excess of the society's powers to borrow may be avoided.

When a mortgage to a building society is repaid, the society has power to indorse a receipt for the money upon the mortgage deed. The effect of such a receipt is to "vacate the mortgage," that is, it operates as a re-conveyance to the mortgagor. This statutory receipt is exempt from stamp duty. (See STATUTORY RECEIPT.)

With respect to unincorporated societies, by Section 89 of the Stamp Act, 1891, the exemption from stamp duty conferred by the Building Societies Act, 1836, 6 & 7 Will. IV c. 32, for the regulation of benefit building societies, shall not extend to any mortgage made after July 31, 1868, except a mortgage by a member of a benefit building society for securing the repayment to the society of money not exceeding £500.

BULL AND BEAR. Names given to the two kinds of speculators on a stock exchange.

A Bull is one who anticipates a rise in a certain stock ; he therefore buys in, not intending to pay for the purchase but hoping to sell out later at a profit.

A Bear, on the other hand, expects a certain security to fall in price, so he sells stock which he does not possess, with the object of buying in before settling day at a lower figure, in which case the difference would be his profit. (See BACKWARDATION, CONTANGO, STOCK EXCHANGE.)

BULLION. Gold and silver in bars or in the mass. The word is also used when speaking of large quantities of gold and silver coins, especially when regarded by weight.

Bullion is said to have been originally the name of the office or mint where the metal was stamped into coins.

By the Bank Charter Act, 1844, Section 4, "all persons shall be entitled to demand from the Issue Department of the Bank of England, Bank of England notes in exchange for gold bullion, at the rate of £3 17*s*. 9*d*. per ounce of standard gold : provided always that the said Governor and Company shall in all cases be entitled to require such gold bullion to be melted and assayed by persons approved by the said Governor and Company at the expense of the parties tendering such gold bullion." The bank notes can be immediately exchanged for sovereigns at the rate of £3 17*s*. 10½*d*. per ounce. The difference of 1½*d*. per ounce between gold bullion and gold coins represents the expenses and loss of interest upon the bullion before it is turned into coins.

Under the Coinage Act of 1870, anyone has the right to take bar gold, if of sufficient fineness, to the Mint and have it coined, free of expense, at the rate of £3 17*s*. 10½*d*. per ounce of standard gold, provided that the value is not less than £20,000, but the owner of the gold bullion has to wait for payment until it is coined. Anyone requiring coins for gold bullion would take it to the Bank of England, where, as stated above, notes at the rate of £3 17*s*. 9*d*. per ounce will be given at once.

BULLION POINTS. The same as "Specie Points" (*q.v.*).

BUYING IN. A Stock Exchange term. Where securities have not been delivered by a seller to a purchaser at the appointed time, they may be "bought in" by an official of the Stock Exchange. In the case of registered securities if not delivered within ten days they may be bought in against the seller on the eleventh day after the Ticket-day, or on any subsequent day, and the loss occasioned by such buying-in must be borne by the seller. (See SELLING OUT, STOCK EXCHANGE.)

CALENDAR. From the following tables the day of the week for any date from 1900 till 1950 can easily be ascertained. The one table contains ordinary years, the other table leap years.

If, for instance, it is required to know what day of the week March 13, 1900, was, find the year 1900 in the year column, then look to the left to find the month of March, and at the bottom of the column containing that month will be found the day of the week, Tuesday, in a line with the 13th on the right.

Jan. Oct.	May	Aug.	Feb. Mar. Nov.	June	Sept Dec.	April July	1905 1933 1911 1939 1922 1950
April July	Jan. Oct.	May	Aug.	Feb. Mar. Nov.	June	Sept. Dec.	1900 1923 1906 1934 1917 1945
Sept. Dec.	April July	Jan. Oct.	May	Aug.	Feb. Mar. Nov.	June	1901 1929 1907 1935 1918 1946
June	Sept. Dec.	April July	Jan. Oct.	May	Aug.	Feb. Mar. Nov.	1902 1930 1913 1941 1919 1947
Feb. Mar. Nov.	June	Sept. Dec.	April July	Jan. Oct.	May	Aug.	1903 1931 1914 1942 1925
Aug.	Feb. Mar. Nov.	June	Sept. Dec.	April July	Jan. Oct.	May	1909 1937 1915 1943 1926
May	Aug.	Feb. Mar. Nov.	June	Sept. Dec.	April July	Jan. Oct.	1910 1938 1921 1949 1927
Sun.	M.	Tu.	W.	Th.	F.	Sat.	1 8 15 22 29
M.	Tu.	W.	Th.	F.	Sat.	Sun.	2 9 16 23 30
Tu.	W.	Th.	F.	Sat.	Sun.	M.	3 10 17 24 31
W.	Th.	F.	Sat.	Sun.	M.	Tu.	4 11 18 25
Th.	F.	Sat.	Sun.	M.	Tu.	W.	5 12 19 26
F.	Sat.	Sun.	M.	Tu.	W.	Th.	6 13 20 27
Sat.	Sun.	M.	Tu.	W.	Th.	F	7 14 21 28

LEAP YEARS

Jan. April July	Oct.	May	Feb. Aug.	Mar. Nov.	June	Sept. Dec.	1928
Sept. Dec.	Jan. April July	Oct.	May	Feb. Aug.	Mar. Nov.	June	1912 1940
June	Sept. Dec.	Jan. April July	Oct.	May	Feb. Aug.	Mar. Nov.	1924

LEAP YEARS—*continued*

Mar. Nov.	June	Sept. Dec.	Jan. April July	Oct.	May	Feb. Aug.	1908 1936
Feb. Aug.	Mar. Nov.	June	Sept. Dec.	Jan. April July	Oct.	May	1920 1948
May	Feb. Aug.	Mar. Nov.	June	Sept. Dec.	Jan. April July	Oct.	1904 1932
Oct.	May	Feb. Aug.	Mar. Nov.	June	Sept. Dec.	Jan. April July	1916 1944
Sun.	M.	Tu.	W.	Th.	F.	Sat.	1 8 15 22 29
M.	Tu.	W	Th.	F.	Sat.	Sun.	2 9 16 23 30
Tu.	W.	Th.	F.	Sat.	Sun.	M.	3 10 17 24 31
W.	Th.	F.	Sat.	Sun.	M.	Tu.	4 11 18 25
Th.	F.	Sat.	Sun.	M.	Tu.	W.	5 12 19 26
F.	Sat.	Sun.	M.	Tu.	W.	Th.	6 13 20 27
Sat.	Sun.	M.	Tu.	W.	Th.	F.	7 14 21 28

CALEYS. A Stock Exchange name for Caledonian Railway ordinary stock.

CALL. A Stock Exchange term meaning the right to buy a specified security at a certain price within an arranged period. (See OPTIONS, STOCK EXCHANGE.)

CALL MONEY. (See MONEY AT CALL AND SHORT NOTICE.)

CALLED BOND. When a bond has been "called in" for payment on a certain date, it ceases to carry interest from that date.

CALLING OVER. "Calling over" is an essential part of the work of a bank office. The day books should be called over daily with the current account ledgers and other books into which the items have passed, each entry, as it is called out, being ticked with ink, in both books. In order that the calling over may be as effectual as possible, it is usually carried out, when practicable, by clerks other than those concerned in writing up the day books or posting the ledgers.

CALLS. Shares may be either fully paid or only partly paid. If the latter, the holders are liable, when called upon by the company, to pay up the amounts or "calls" as they are made. Calls should be made in accordance with the company's articles of association or the agreement when the shares were first issued. A limited company may, by special resolution, declare that any portion of its uncalled capital shall not be called up except in the event of the company being wound up. (See RESERVE LIABILITY.)

Some of the clauses of Table A with respect to calls (see Section 11 of the Companies (Consolidation) Act, 1908, under ARTICLES OF ASSOCIATION) are as follows :—

"12. The directors may from time to time

make calls upon the members in respect of any moneys unpaid on their shares, provided that no call shall exceed one-fourth of the nominal amount of the share, or be payable at less than one month from the last call; and each member shall (subject to receiving at least fourteen days' notice specifying the time or times of payment) pay to the company at the time or times so specified the amount called on his shares.

13. The joint holders of a share shall be jointly and severally liable to pay all calls in respect thereof.

"16. The directors may make arrangements on the issue of shares for a difference between the holders in the amount of calls to be paid and in the times of payment.

"17. The directors may, if they think fit, receive from any member willing to advance the same all or any part of the moneys uncalled and unpaid upon any shares held by him; and upon all or any of the moneys so advanced may (until the same would, but for such advance, become presently payable) pay interest at such rate (not exceeding, without the sanction of the company in general meeting, six per cent.) as may be agreed upon between the member paying the sum in advance and the directors."

There is usually a clause in the articles, that, in the event of non-payment of a call by a member, his shares will be liable to forfeiture.

A company can sue a member for payment of a call at any time within twenty years. (See CAPITAL, COMPANIES, SHARE CAPITAL.)

CAMBIST. A person who deals in foreign moneys, notes and bills of exchange. One who is skilled in the value of foreign moneys and the operations of exchange.

CANADAS. A Stock Exchange name for Canadian Pacific Railroad securities.

CANCELLATION OF BILL OF EXCHANGE. A bill of exchange is discharged when it is intentionally cancelled. The Bills of Exchange Act, 1882, Section 63, provides :—

"(1) Where a bill is intentionally cancelled by the holder or his agent, and the cancellation is apparent thereon, the bill is discharged.

"(2) In like manner any party liable on a bill may be discharged by the intentional cancellation of his signature by the holder or his agent. In such case any indorser who would have had a right of recourse against the party whose signature is cancelled, is also discharged.

"(3) A cancellation made unintentionally, or under a mistake, or without the authority of the holder, is inoperative; but where a bill or any signature thereon appears to have been cancelled, the burden of proof lies on the party who alleges that the cancellation was made unintentionally, or under a mistake, or without authority."

Where a bill, or cheque, has been accidentally cancelled by a banker, a note should be made near to the cancellation that it has been "cancelled in error," and the words should be initialled, or signed, by the banker who has made such cancellation.

When a cheque is paid, it is usually cancelled by the drawer's signature being marked through with ink, and the date of payment either written or stamped upon the face of the cheque. A common method of cancellation is to use a rubber stamp bearing the word "Paid" in bold letters and the date. Some bankers cancel by punching a few holes in the cheques.

When a bill is paid, the acceptor's signature is cancelled. In the case of a dishonoured bill, a banker usually cancels his own indorsement.

The cancellation of a signature should be decisive, but should not make the signature illegible.

The cancellation is effected, in the case of the cheque, by the banker upon whom it is drawn, and in the case of a bill by the banker with whom the bill is domiciled.

It is usual for the paying cashier to initial all the paid cheques and bills which pass through his hands.

Where cheques are paid by one bank, under authority from another bank, the former bank sometimes cancels the drawer's signature, but the practice is not the same in all banks.

The word "cancellation" is from the Latin *cancello*, to make trellis, so that to cancel a document is literally to make trellis or lattice work upon it. (See CANCELLED CHEQUES AND BILLS.)

CANCELLATION OF STAMPS. The Stamp Act, 1891, provides as follows :—

"Section 8. (1) An instrument, the duty upon which is required or permitted by law to be denoted by an adhesive stamp, is not to be deemed duly stamped with an adhesive stamp, unless the person required by law to cancel the adhesive stamp cancels the same by writing on or across the stamp his name or initials, or the name or initials of his firm, together with the true date of his so writing, or otherwise effectively cancels the stamp and renders the same incapable of being used for any other instrument, or for any postal purpose, or unless it is otherwise proved that the stamp appearing on the instrument was affixed thereto at the proper time.

"(2) Where two or more adhesive stamps are used to denote the stamp duty upon an instrument, each or every stamp is to be cancelled in the manner aforesaid.

"(3) Every person who, being required by law to cancel an adhesive stamp, neglects or refuses duly and effectually to do so in the manner aforesaid, shall incur a fine of ten pounds."

If any bill of exchange, payable on demand or at sight or on presentation, or not exceeding three days after date or sight, is presented for payment unstamped, the person to whom it is presented may affix thereto an adhesive stamp of one penny, and cancel the same. The penny may be deducted from the amount of the cheque or bill, or charged in account. (Section 38.)

CANCELLED CHEQUES AND BILLS. When a cheque is paid, it becomes the property of the drawer, but the banker is entitled to keep it as a voucher till the account is settled, or the customer agrees that the entries in the pass-book are correct. A paid cheque is useful evidence for the drawer of the payment of the money. It is also evidence for the banker that he has repaid money belonging to the drawer, to the amount of the cheque.

It is the practice of many London bankers to return cancelled cheques to a customer each time he gets his pass-book.

In most country banks, however, the paid vouchers are not, as a rule, given up to customers, unless specially asked for. In cases where they are given up, an acknowledgment is obtained from the customer that the entries in the pass-book are correct, or a confirmation of the balance is taken.

The cancelled cheques of each customer are usually kept in separate bundles, sorted in order of date of payment, each bundle containing the vouchers for three, six, or twelve months, as may be most convenient. The paying-in slips are retained by the banker and are not given up with paid cheques. They are sorted either along with the cheques, or in separate bundles.

If a cancelled cheque is required as evidence in a court of law, the drawer, as being the owner of the paid cheque, although it is in the custody of the banker, must take steps to obtain it from the banker. This, in practice, would never be refused, if a receipt is given to protect the banker. A refusal to hand over a cheque would necessitate the service of a subpœna upon the banker to produce it. (See CANCELLATION OF BILL OF EXCHANGE.)

CANPACS. A Stock Exchange name for Canadian-Pacific Railroad securities.

CAPITAL. In the early stages of civilisation, sheep and cattle acted as a currency. "Being counted *by the head*, the kine was called *capitale*, whence the economical term *capital*, the law term *chattel*, and our common name *cattle*" (Jevons).

In a joint stock company the capital is the sum subscribed by the members of the company—that is, the shareholders—for the purposes of the business. The amount which is authorised by the memorandum of association is the "nominal" capital. Of the nominal capital there is often only a part of it issued, called the "issued" capital, the remainder being referred to as "unissued." Further portions may be issued from time to time, until the full nominal capital has been issued. Of the capital which has been "issued" (called also the "subscribed" capital), only that part of it is paid up, or subscribed by the shareholders, which the directors have "called up." The part which has been called up and paid is called the "paid up" capital, the remaining part being termed the "uncalled" capital; and it remains unpaid until a "call" is made for it by the directors. If the whole has been called up, the shares are said to be "fully paid." Of the uncalled capital, a certain portion may, if the company has so resolved, form a reserve liability, which is not to be called up except in the event of the company being wound up. (Section 59, Companies

(Consolidation) Act, 1908, see RESERVE LIABILITY.) For example:—

Nominal (or Authorised, or Registered) Capital, 20,000 shares, £5 each	£100,000
Subscribed (or Issued) Capital, 10,000 shares £5 each	£50,000
Unissued, 10,000 shares, £5 each	£50,000

The subscribed capital may be divided into:—

Paid-up Capital, 10,000 shares, £2 10s. each	£25,000
Uncalled Capital, 10,000 shares, £2 10s. each:—	
Callable, £1 10s. per share	£15,000
Reserve (callable only in a winding up), £1 per share	£10,000

H. D. Macleod defines capital as "an economic quality used for the purpose of profit." Under the name of capital are included money, goods, land, personal skill, energies, labour, credit, and anything that is used to produce a profit. But wealth, in whatever form, if unemployed, is not capital. There are two species of capital, circulating or floating capital and fixed capital. Circulating capital, in the words of John Stuart Mill, "does its work not by being kept but by changing hands." "This portion of capital requires to be constantly renewed by the sale of the finished product and when renewed is perpetually parted with in buying materials and paying wages." Fixed capital produces its effect not by being parted with but by being kept. Wealth expended in land, buildings, docks, roads, machinery, railways, etc., is fixed capital. (See SHARE CAPITAL.)

CAPITAL ACCOUNT. The account which is concerned solely with the capital or funds subscribed by the shareholders in a bank or other company, for the purpose of carrying on the undertaking.

CARAT. A measure by which goldsmiths and assayers denote the fineness of gold—the twenty-fourth part of an ounce. Any portion of gold is supposed to be divided into twenty-four parts, and if it is all pure gold it is said to be "24 carats" fine. English gold coins contain eleven parts pure gold and one part of copper; that is, standard gold is eleven-twelfths fine, and eleven-twelfths of twenty-four carats equal twenty-two carats fine.

The word is, by some, supposed to be derived from the native name of a tree, the seeds of which, owing to their uniformity in size, were used for weighing gold. A carat does not now, however, represent any particular weight, but merely states the proportion of gold there is in any given weight.

CARRY OVER; CARRYING OVER. On the Stock Exchange to "carry over" means to continue a bargain until next account, instead of paying for stock bought, or delivering stock which has been sold, as the case may be. In the former case the speculator may require to pay "contango" (*q.v.*) and in the latter, "backwardation" (*q.v.*). (See STOCK EXCHANGE.)

CARRYING OVER DAY. The first day of the settlement on the Stock Exchange. (See CONTANGO DAY.)

CASE OF NEED. (See IN CASE OF NEED.)

CASH. Actual coins, Bank of England notes and the notes of other banks are treated as cash, but a banker's own notes would not, in a balance sheet, form part of the cash on hand, as they would be deducted from the balance of the note account on the other side of the sheet, in order to show the actual amount in circulation.

Cash originally meant that which was *encaissé*, that is, put into a chest or till. (See COINAGE.)

CASH ACCOUNT. An account in the general ledger to which the totals (debits and credits) of each day's transactions are passed. The balance of the account represents the amount of cash on hand. Credits to other accounts are debited to cash account, and debits are credited.

In Scotland the term signifies a customer's account on which a cash credit has been granted. It is practically the same as an account in England on which a limit of overdraft is allowed. (See BOND OF CREDIT, CASH CREDIT.)

CASH BALANCE BOOK. This book, which is written up by the first cashier at the close of business each day, contains particulars of all the cash on hand, obtained by combining the details of each cashier's till and the reserve of cash in the strong room. The total should agree with the balance as shown in the day book and the cash account in the general ledger.

CASH BONUS. A bonus upon a life policy which is paid in cash, instead of being used to reduce the amount of the premium or to increase the sum ultimately payable under the policy. (See BONUS, LIFE POLICY.)

CASH BOOK. A book which, in some banks, contains a record of all cash transactions. In large offices there may be received cash books and paid cash books. In other banks the cash book is merely for the specification of the cash held in the bank each night.

The day book is in some banks called the cash book. (See DAY BOOK.)

CASH CREDIT. A term commonly used in banks in Scotland, to describe an arrangement under which a customer is allowed an advance up to a certain limit, against a "bond of credit" (*q.v.*) by one or more sureties, or cautioners as they are called in Scotland. The customer need not take the whole advance at once, but may draw the amount as required.

The bond of credit is signed by the debtor as well as by the sureties, and the effect of it is, practically, to make all the parties debtors to the bank, although the person in whose name the account stands is the real debtor.

CASH CREDIT BOND. Same as "Bond of Credit" (*q.v.*).

CASH ORDER. A cash order is a bill of exchange on demand drawn by one person on another. For example, a wholesale dealer, John Jones, who has supplied goods to, say, John Brown, a shopkeeper, draws a cash order upon him, usually in the following form :—

English Street,
Carlisle,
July, 19 .

£10.

1*d*.

On demand pay to the British Bank, Ltd., or order the sum of Ten pounds sterling for value received.

JOHN JONES.

To
Mr. John Brown,
Coney Street,
York.

The order must be indorsed by the banker to whom it is payable, or, if payable to the drawer's order, by the drawer.

The cash order is sent to a banker in the town where John Brown lives for collection, and the banker sends out a messenger to John Brown's address and presents the order for payment. It is expected that the order will be paid in cash, though in some cases payment is received by cheque, when it is known that the drawer is perfectly good and the cheque can be collected the same day. In some districts it is customary for the drawee, when the order is presented, to accept it payable at his bankers in the same town. When this is done, it should be passed through the local clearing on the same day. The remitter of the order often gives instructions that, if it is not paid on the day of receipt, it may be held over till the following day. In the absence of such instructions the remitter should be advised if a cash order is held over. If the drawee is not at home when the messenger calls a note is left that the order is at the bank and requires his attention.

Cash orders are not, as a rule, accepted by the drawee, and consequently he cannot be sued upon them, but if he gives his cheque in exchange, and it is dishonoured, he can be sued upon the cheque.

Cash orders received for collection should not be credited on the day of receipt to the bank sending them, in cases where the orders are being held over till the next day.

Where cash orders are numerous, they give great trouble to a banker who has to collect them, and some bankers decline to undertake the work.

The stamp duty upon a cash order is one penny.

CASH SHEETS. Loose sheets on which are recorded all the transactions in a bank office during the day. At stated intervals the sheets are bound into book form. Cash sheets in some banks practically take the place of a day book or cash book.

CASTING. The act of summing-up figures. When a column has been cast-up, the total is often called "the casting."

CAUTIONARY OBLIGATION. In Scotland, an obligation or undertaking by a cautioner, or surety, that he will be responsible for a certain amount, if the debtor, who is also a party to the bond, fails to repay the debt. (See BOND OF CREDIT.)

CAUTIONER. In Scotland, a surety, or guarantor, who signs a bond along with the debtor for a cash credit, or overdraft, to the debtor. (See BOND OF CREDIT, CASH CREDIT.)

CAVEAT. (Latin, Let him beware.) A notice or warning given to a public official by an interested party, as, for example, where a caveat is given to the Yorkshire Deeds Registry by a person claiming to be entitled to an interest in certain lands. The caveat is registered, and remains on the books as a warning to anyone who contemplates dealing with the property. (See YORKSHIRE REGISTRY OF DEEDS.)

CENT. (See FOREIGN MONEYS—CANADA, CEYLON, HOLLAND, MAURITIUS, UNITED STATES.)

CENTIME. (See FOREIGN MONEYS—BELGIUM, FRANCE, SWITZERLAND.)

CENTIMOS. (See FOREIGN MONEYS—SPAIN.)

CENTISIMI. (See FOREIGN MONEYS—ITALY.)

CENTRAL ASSOCIATION OF BANKERS. This Association was formed in 1895 to unite the committee of the London Clearing Bankers, the West End London Banks and the Country Banks of the United Kingdom. It consists of one representative of each of the Clearing Banks, two representatives of the West End Banks and ten members appointed by the Association of English Country Bankers. No representatives of Scotch and Irish Banks have yet been appointed.

The objects of the Association are the maintenance and protection of the interests of bankers.

CERTIFICATE. The document which is issued by a company, to a member of the company, specifying the shares or stock held by him. It is usually signed by two directors, countersigned by the secretary or manager, and impressed with the company's seal. Certificates are of many different sizes and usually papers of different colours are used for the various classes or issues of shares and stocks.

The following is a specimen of a certificate :—

ORDINARY SHARE CAPITAL

Certificate No.

JOHN JONES & COMPANY, Limited, incorporated under the Companies (Consolidation) Act, 1908.

CAPITAL

£ in Preference shares of £1 each, Nos. 1 to .

£ in Ordinary shares of £1 each, Nos. 1 to .

Total. £ .

SHARE CERTIFICATE

This is to certify that
of
is the Registered Holder of of the above named Ordinary shares of £1 each, numbered to , all inclusive, in John Jones & Company, Limited, subject to the Memorandum of Association and Regulations of the Company, and that each of the said shares is fully paid up.

Dated this day of , 19 .

} Directors.

, Secretary.

The certificate may have a footnote to the following effect :—

The company will not transfer any shares without the production of the certificate relating to such shares, which certificate must be surrendered before any deed of transfer, whether for the whole or any portion thereof, can be registered, or a new certificate issued in exchange. (See below.)

In a few companies, a separate certificate was originally issued for each share. When any of the shares are transferred, instead of fresh certificates being issued the old ones are simply indorsed with the transfer, and the old certificates given to the transferee, the transfer being registered in the company's books. Occasionally certificates of this description may be found which, though the shares have been transferred from the person named in the body of the certificate, do not give any indication, by indorsement or otherwise, of the transfer. The only way to ascertain who is the registered holder is to write to the company. In other cases where the same certificates pass from one holder to another, the company issues a transfer certificate (to accompany the old certificates) certifying that "a deed of transfer duly executed and attested and stamped as required by law, dated from to conveying shares numbered from to has been deposited in the office of the company and registered in their books on of , 19 ."

Clause 6 of Table A (see Section 11 of the Companies (Consolidation) Act, 1908, under ARTICLES OF ASSOCIATION) provides :—

> "Every person whose name is entered as a member in the register of members shall, without payment, be entitled to a certificate under the common seal of the company specifying the share or shares held by him and the amount paid up thereon, provided that in respect of a share or shares held jointly by several persons the company shall not be bound to issue more than one certificate, and delivery of a certificate for a share to one of several joint holders shall be sufficient delivery to all."

A certificate is *primâ facie* evidence of the title of the member to the shares or stock. (Section 23 of the above Act. See SHARE CAPITAL.)

Before an official quotation, on the London Stock Exchange, for stocks and shares can be obtained, the committee require that the certificates must conform to certain conditions. (See QUOTATION ON LONDON STOCK EXCHANGE.)

With regard to the delivery of certificates and debentures by a company, Section 92 of the Companies (Consolidation) Act, 1908, provides that :—

"(1) Every company shall, within two months after the allotment of any of its shares, debentures, or debenture stock, and within two months after the registration of the transfer of any such shares, debentures, or debenture stock, complete and have ready for delivery the certificates of all shares, the debentures, and the certificates of all debenture stock allotted or transferred, unless the conditions of issue of the shares, debentures, or debenture stock otherwise provide.

"(2) If default is made in complying with the requirements of this Section, the company, and every director, manager, secretary, and other officer of the company who is knowingly a party to the default, shall be liable to a fine not exceeding five pounds for every day during which the default continues."

A certificate does not always show how much is paid up per share, and this is an important point when the question of security is being considered

Where certificates are lodged as security, a blank transfer (*q.v.*) and qualifying agreement (*q.v.*) are taken by some banks, but the most satisfactory way is to take a completed transfer and qualifying agreement and have the shares registered in the names of the nominees of the bank. (See TRANSFER OF SHARES.) If, however, a banker does not wish to register at once, he often takes a fully completed transfer with qualifying agreement and gives notice of his charge to the company. When that is done and he retains possession of the certificate, he has, as a rule, a good security. A simple deposit of certificates as security, even without a memorandum of deposit, constitutes an equitable mortgage, and the banker can, when necessary, apply to the Court for power to sell. In nearly all cases, the certificate must be surrendered before a transfer of the shares can be effected. There are, however, several exceptions, as certificates need not be produced when transferring National Bank shares, Provincial Bank of Ireland shares, and Royal Exchange Assurance Corporation stock. It may be mentioned that the Grand Junction Canal Co. does not issue certificates at all.

It is to be remembered that even a footnote upon a certificate that no transfer of the shares will be registered without production of the certificate is of no value in a case of fraud. In *Rainford* v. *J. Keith and Blackman Co., Ltd.* (1905, 1 Ch. 296), it was held that the footnote did not constitute a contract and was not binding on the company. This case was followed and its principle approved by Mr. Justice Channell in *Guy* v. *Waterloo Brothers and Layton* (1909, 25 T.L.R. 515).

A certificate does not require a stamp. In cases where a simple memorandum of deposit of certificates is taken the stamp duty is sixpence. As to foreign and colonial share certificates, see MARKETABLE SECURITY.

When a certificate has been lost and the owner has obtained a duplicate, he should, in the event of the document being subsequently found, surrender it to the company. If the original certificate should, afterwards, be given to a banker as security, unless he registers it in his own name or gives notice to the company, he may eventually discover that the shares have been sold on surrender of the duplicate.

It is also possible for a certificate to be apparently in order and yet, on inquiry, to be found to be of no value, on account of the shares having been forfeited ; and in some cases where shares have been converted the old certificate is sometimes, for one reason or another, not handed over to the company.

Loss of Stock Certificate. The Bank of England, before authorising the issue of a duplicate in the event of the loss or destruction of a stock certificate, may require :—

(*a*) Evidence to the satisfaction of the Bank of the loss or destruction and ownership of the certificate ; and (*b*) a delay of not more than one year from the date of the loss or destruction ; and (*c*) the advertisement of the loss or destruction in two or more London or Dublin daily papers (as the case requires) ; and (*d*) either the transfer of a sum of stock, of a description approved by the governor or deputy governor of the Bank, equivalent to the market value on the day of transfer of the lost or destroyed certificate, and at least six and a half years' dividends thereon, into the joint names of the governor and deputy governor, by way of security; or the execution of a bond of indemnity in which the owner shall be joined by one or more responsible persons. (The National Debt (Stockholders' Relief) Act, 1892, Section 7, s.s. 1.) (See COMPANIES, SHARE CAPITAL.)

CERTIFICATE OF CHARGE. A certificate, under the seal of the Land Registry, certifying the registration of a charge upon land. A deposit of such a certificate is equivalent to a lien created by the deposit of a mortgage deed of unregistered land. Notice of the deposit must be given to the Registrar. (See LAND REGISTRY.)

CERTIFICATE OF INCORPORATION. On the registration of the memorandum of association of a company, the registrar of companies shall certify under his hand that the company is incorporated, and in the case of a limited company that the company is limited. From the date of incorporation, mentioned in the certificate, the subscribers of the memorandum, and others who may become members, shall be a body corporate, capable of exercising all the functions of an incorporated company, and having perpetual succession and a common seal, with power to hold lands, but with such liability on the part of the members to contribute to the assets of the company, in the event of its being wound up, as is mentioned in the Companies (Consolidation) Act, 1908.

Such a certificate is conclusive evidence that all the requirements of the Act, in respect of registration and of matters precedent and incidental thereto, have been complied with, and that the association is a company authorised to be registered and is duly registered under the Act. (See ARTICLES OF ASSOCIATION, MEMORANDUM OF ASSOCIATION.)

Any person may inspect the documents kept by the registrar, on payment of a fee of one shilling, and any person may require a certificate of the incorporation of any company, or a copy or extract of any document, to be certified by the registrar, on payment of five shillings for a certificate of incorporation and sixpence for each folio of a certified copy or extract. (See REGISTRAR OF COMPANIES.)

The form of the registrar's certificate is as follows :—

"I hereby certify that the Company, Limited, is this day incorporated under the Companies (Consolidation) Act, 1908, and that the Company is limited.

"Given under my hand this day of .

"

"Registrar of Joint Stock Companies."

(See COMPANIES.)

CERTIFICATE OF MORTGAGE OF SHIP. A registered owner, if desirous of disposing by way of mortgage or sale of the ship or share in respect of which he is registered, at any place out of the country in which the port of registry of the ship is situate, may apply to the registrar, and the registrar shall thereupon enable him to do so by granting a certificate of mortgage or a certificate of sale (Section 36, Merchant Shipping Act, 1894).

The instrument gives particulars of the ship and an account of mortgages or certificates of mortgages granted in respect of the ship. The owner of the shares in the ship appoints an attorney to mortgage the shares, and declares that the money to be raised under the power shall not exceed a specified sum and that the rate of interest shall not exceed a certain rate. He also declares that the power of mortgaging may be exercised at and that the power shall not be exercised after months from the date hereof.

The instrument is signed and sealed by the owner, and then follows the registrar's certificate :—

"I registrar of hereby certify that the above written particulars relating to the ship and the title thereto are correct; and I further certify that the said owner has duly subscribed and affixed his signature and seal as appears above. ,
Registrar."

A person who advances money under a certificate of mortgage, when there is a previous mortgage or certificate of mortgage indorsed on the said certificate, does so at his own risk. His title is liable to be defeated by the person claiming under the incumbrance so indorsed. (See SHIP—MORTGAGE, ETC.)

CERTIFICATE OF PROTEST. (See PROTEST.)

CERTIFICATE OF REGISTRATION. A certificate given by the registrar of companies of any mortgage or charge registered in pursuance of Section 93 of the Companies (Consolidation) Act, 1908 (see REGISTRATION OF MORTGAGES AND CHARGES), and stating the amount thereby secured. The certificate is conclusive evidence that the requirements of the Section as to registration have been complied with. A copy of every certificate of registration is to be indorsed by the company on every debenture or certificate of debenture stock which is issued by the company, and the payment of which is secured by the mortgage or charge so registered. (See COMPANIES.)

CERTIFICATE OF SEARCH. A certificate issued by the Registrar of a Deeds Registry, in response to an application for an official search, certifying that an official search of the Register has been made, within the period named by the applicant, for all documents registered in connection with the specified lands, and giving a list of any such documents.

Below will be found the form of official certificate of search as issued by the West Riding of Yorkshire Registry of Deeds.

CERTIFICATED BANKRUPT. A bankrupt who holds a release from the Court of Bankruptcy. (See BANKRUPTCY.)

CERTIFICATION OF CHEQUES. In the United States cheques are freely "certified" by bankers, the certification being equal to an acceptance by the banker. When an American banker accepts or certifies a cheque, he charges the amount at once to the drawer's account and holds it in a special account against his liability upon the cheque. By the law of that country "where the holder of a cheque procures it to be accepted or certified, the drawer and all indorsers are discharged from liability thereon."

In this country, cheques are often, for the convenience of bankers in connection with the clearing of cheques, "marked" as good, and in special cases they are sometimes "marked" at the request of the drawer.

---

1. To be left blank for filling in at the office.

Volume Page No. [1]

WEST RIDING OF YORKSHIRE.

REGISTRY OF DEEDS.

2. Fill in the name and description of the person on whose behalf the search was required to be made.

I the Registrar of Deeds of the West Riding of the County of York having received a Requisition on behalf of [2]

3. Fill in the name in which the search was required to be made.

for an official search in the Name of [3]

4. Fill in the period for which the search was required to be made.

for the period from[4] 19.. to 19..

5. Fill in the name of every township, etc., in which any of the lands in respect of which the search was required to be made are situate.

affecting lands in the Townships of [5] in the said Riding, Do HEREBY CERTIFY that I have caused an official search to be made in the above specified name, for all instruments registered within the period above-mentioned as affecting lands within the townships aforesaid, and that the following is a complete list of such instruments.

Nature of Instrument.	Date of Instrument.	Parties to Instrument.	Township, etc., in which lands affected are situate	Date of Registration.	PLACE OF ENROLMENT		
					Volume.	Page.	Number.

6. To be left blank for the signature and seal of the registrar.

(Signed) [6]

Registrar.

(See MARKED CHEQUE.) Sir Mackenzie Chalmers says: "In England, under the Bank Charter Acts, the acceptance of a cheque by a bank would, in general, be an infringement of the privileges of the Bank of England." (Page 74, vol. 30, "Journal of the Institute of Bankers.")

CERTIFICATION OF TRANSFERS. (See CERTIFIED TRANSFER.)

CERTIFIED CHEQUE. A cheque which is marked or certified by a banker that it is good for the amount for which it is drawn. (See CERTIFICATION OF CHEQUES, MARKED CHEQUE.)

CERTIFIED COPY. A certified copy, or office copy, of a will is one that has been examined with the original and certified by the registrar as being a true copy.

For stamp duty see COPY. (See ATTESTED COPY, OFFICE COPY.)

CERTIFIED TRANSFER. Transfers are often certified upon the margin by the secretary or registrar of a company, that the certificates for the shares dealt with in the transfer are in the company's office. The words generally used are, "Certificate for shares, paid, has been lodged at the company's office. Date .

"The Company, Limited,

" , Secretary."

Or sometimes the words are "Coupon for £ received at the company's office by ."

The certification is for the purpose of facilitating dealings in shares. The broker for a transferor sends the certificate and transfer to the company to be certified, and the transferee accepts the certification as an assurance that the certificate is apparently in order.

In *Bishop* v. *Balkis Consolidated Co.* (1890, 25 Q.B.D. 512), Lindley, L. J., said: "In my opinion, it is proved that to give 'certifications' is incidental to the transaction, in the ordinary business way, of part of the legitimate business of all companies having capital divided into shares which are transferable by deed or other instrument."

Such a certification, however, does not appear to put much responsibility upon the company. In *Peat* v. *Clayton* (1906, 1 Ch. 659), Joyce, J., said: "It only amounts to a representation that a document has been lodged with the company, apparently in order, and showing, *primâ facie*, that the transferor is entitled to the shares, but it is no warranty of the transferor's title to the shares, or as to the validity of any of the documents, or that the company has received no notice in lieu of distringas, or any other notice affecting the matter." In *George Whitechurch, Limited*, v. *Cavanagh* (1902, A.C. 117), Lord Macnaghten said: "There is no obligation on a company to certify transfers at all. The certification is not passed by the directors or brought before the board. A certification, in fact, is only required for a temporary purpose, to meet the exigencies of business on the Stock Exchange, which has stated days and fixed periods for the different stages of a business transaction intended to be carried out under its rules."

Transfers are also certified by the secretary of the Share and Loan Department of the London Stock Exchange.

By Rule III of the Stock Exchange "The buyer of securities may refuse to pay for a transfer deed unaccompanied by the certificate, unless it be officially certified that the certificate is at the office of the company." (See BALANCE TICKET, TRANSFER OF SHARES.)

CESSIO BONORUM. In Scotland, an assignment, by an insolvent debtor, of his property for the benefit of the creditors. (See ASSIGNMENT FOR BENEFIT OF CREDITORS.)

CESTUI QUE TRUST. A person in whose favour a trust operates, that is, who is beneficially interested in the estate.

If Brown holds land in trust for Jones, Brown is the trustee and Jones is the *cestui que trust*. Brown has the legal estate in the land, and Jones has an equitable estate in it.

Plural, *cestuis que trustent*.

CESTUI QUE USE. The person in whose favour a use or trust in real property has been declared.

CESTUI QUE VIE. When property is held by one person during the life of another, the person whose life is the period of the duration of the estate is called the *cestui que vie*. An estate thus held is commonly called an "estate *pur autre vie*."

CHARGES. As it is the practice of bankers to calculate the interest and commisson upon customers' accounts half-yearly, the charges should not be added at caprice at any time.

If a cheque is dishonoured by reason of charges having been added, without the customer's knowledge, at other than the usual date, the customer would have a claim against the banker for wrongful dishonour.

CHARGES. (See REGISTRATION OF MORTGAGES AND CHARGES.)

CHARGES (CLEARING HOUSE). A parcel of cheques which one member of the Clearing House delivers to another member upon whom they are drawn, and against whom they are charged, or, in the case of the country clearing, upon whose country correspondents they are drawn. (See CLEARING HOUSE.)

CHARGING ORDER. Where a creditor has obtained judgment against a debtor for the payment of a debt, he may obtain from the Court an order charging, with the payment of the judgment debt, any shares or stock standing in the name of the debtor, or in the name of any person in trust for him. The effect of the order is to prevent a company from registering any transfer, or paying any dividend to the shareholder, in respect of the shares or stock so charged. At the expiration of six calendar months from the date of the order, the judgment creditor may proceed to take the benefit of the charge. (See GARNISHEE ORDER.)

CHARITABLE COMPANIES. In the case of associations which exist for promoting certain useful objects, the Companies (Consolidation Act), 1908, Section 19, provides :—

"A company formed for the purpose of promoting art, science, religion, charity or any other like object, not involving the acquisition of gain by the company or by its individual members, shall not, without the licence of the Board of Trade, hold more than two acres of land ; but the Board may by licence empower any such company to hold lands in such quantity, and subject to such conditions, as the Board think fit."

The Board of Trade may by licence direct that such an association be registered as a company with limited liability, without the addition of the word "Limited" to its name. It is exempt from sending lists of members and directors and managers to the registrar of companies.

CHARTER. The duty imposed by the Stamp Act, 1891, is :—

	£	s.	d.
CHARTER of resignation, or of confirmation, or of novodamus or upon apprising, or upon a decreet of adjudication, or sale of any lands, or other heritable subjects in Scotland . . .	0	5	0

CHARTER PARTY. An agreement by which the owners of a ship, or their agents, agree to place the vessel at the disposal of a merchant, the charterer, for the conveyance of a full cargo of goods. A charter-party may be for one or more voyages or for a definite period of time, or it may effect a demise of the ship for any length of time that may be agreed upon.

The wording of the agreement varies somewhat according to the trade in connection with which it is used. The following is a specimen of a charter party :—

CHARTER-PARTY

HULL, 19

It is this day mutually agreed between Owners or Agents, of the good Steam Ship or Vessel called the or substitute (at owners' option) of Tons Nett Register, or thereabouts, and Charterers,

That the said Steamer or Vessel being tight, staunch, strong, and every way fitted for the voyage, shall with all convenient speed proceed to
or so near thereto as she may safely get and there load from the Factors of the said Charterers a full and complete Cargo of
which the said Charterers bind themselves to ship, not exceeding what she can reasonably stow or carry over and above Coal for Bunkers and Ship's use, her tackle and apparel, provisions and furniture. The said Cargo to be brought to and taken from alongside, free of expense and risk to the ship, and being so laden shall proceed with the said vessel, with all convenient speed to
or so near thereunto as she may safely get, and (the Act of God, perils of the sea, fire on board, in hulk, or craft, or on shore, barratry of the Master and Crew, enemies, pirates, and thieves, arrests and restraints of princes, rulers, and people, collisions, stranding, and other accidents of navigation of whatever nature and kind whatsoever, before and during the said voyage always excepted, even when occasioned by negligence, default, or error in judgment of the Pilot, Master, Mariners, or other servants of the Shipowners, not answerable for any loss or damage arising from explosion, bursting of boilers, breakage of

shafts, or any latent defect in the machinery or hull, not resulting from want of due diligence by the Owners of the Ship or any of them, or by the Ship's Husband or Manager), there deliver the same, on being paid Freight in cash at the rate of
per ton of 20 cwt. delivered, being in full of all Port Charges, Pilotages, and Harbour Dues on the Steamer, Charterers paying all dues and duties on the cargo
Cargo to be loaded
and discharged
(Sundays and holidays excepted). Lay hours to commence from the time Steamer or Vessel is ready to receive and deliver, and if longer detained Demurrage to be paid at the rate of per hour.

It is also agreed that the Owners of the said Steamer or Vessel shall reserve to themselves the right of lien upon the Cargo laden on Board, for the recovery and payment of all Freight, Dead Freight, Demurrage, and all other charges whatsoever. The Master is to sign bills of Lading at such rates of Freight as may be required by the Charterers or their Agents, without prejudice to this Charter Party, but at not less than chartered rate.

General Average (if any) as per York/Antwerp rules, 1890.

Cash for the disbursements of the Steamer or Vessel to be advanced to the extent of £ (if required), subject to insurance.

The Ship has liberty to call at any ports in any order, to sail without Pilots, to tow and assist Vessels in distress, and to deviate for the purpose of saving life or property. All salvage and/or towage for owners' sole benefit.

Penalty for non-performance of this Charter, estimated amount of Freight.

The Brokerage is payable by the Ship to , at per cent. on gross amount of Freight, and is due on signment of this Charter-party, Ship lost or not lost, by whom also she is to be reported and/or cleared at Customs, Hull, or by their Agents at any other Port.

Witness

Witness

"Lay hours" in the above document refer to the time for loading, or unloading. "Demurrage" is the charge made for delay. As to "General Average as per York/Antwerp Rules," see GENERAL AVERAGE.

The stamp duty is sixpence. See the following sections of the Stamp Act, 1891 :—

"49. (1) For the purposes of this Act the expression 'charter-party' includes any agreement or contract for the charter of any ship or vessel or any memorandum, letter, or other writing between the captain, master, or owner of any ship or vessel, and any other person for or relating to the freight or conveyance of any money, goods, or effects on board of the ship or vessel.

"(2) The duty upon a charter-party may be denoted by an adhesive stamp, which is to be cancelled by the person by whom the instrument is last executed, or by whose execution it is completed as a binding contract.

"50. Where a charter-party is first executed out of the United Kingdom without being duly stamped, any party thereto may, within ten days after it has been first received in the United Kingdom, and before it has been executed by any person in the United Kingdom, affix thereto an adhesive stamp denoting the duty chargeable thereon, and at the same time cancel such adhesive stamp, and the instrument when so stamped shall be deemed duly stamped

"51. A charter-party may be stamped with an impressed stamp after execution upon the following terms ; that is to say,

"(1) Within seven days after the first execution thereof, on payment of the duty and a penalty of four shillings and sixpence ;

"(2) After seven days, but within one month after the first execution thereof, on payment of the duty and a penalty of ten pounds ;

and shall not in any other case be stamped with an impressed stamp."

CHARTERED BANK. A banking company incorporated by special Charter from the Crown. The Charter regulates the working of the company in the same way that the memorandum and articles of association regulate a company incorporated under the Companies Acts, and the liability of the stockholders in a chartered bank is fixed by the Charter.

The Bank of England was incorporated by Charter in 1694, under the authority of an Act of Parliament.

The Bank of Scotland, the Royal Bank of Scotland, and the British Linen Company were incorporated by Royal Charter. In Ireland, the Bank of Ireland is the only bank which has been established by Act of Parliament.

Various Colonial banks, which have their head offices in London, have also been incorporated by Charter from the Crown.

CHARTEREDS. A Stock Exchange name for British South Africa Company's shares.

CHATHAMS OR CHATS. Stock Exchange names for London, Chatham and Dover Railway stock.

CHATTELS. Chattel, a modern form of the word cattle. Cattle at one time performed the function of money.

Chattels include cattle, implements, money, debts, rights of action to goods, etc.

Blackstone says, "For it is to be understood that in our law, chattels (or goods and chattels) is a term used to express any kind of property which, having regard either to subject matter, or the quantity of interest therein, is not freehold."

The Bills of Sale Act, 1878, Section 4, defines personal chattels as follows :—"The expression 'personal chattels' shall mean goods, furniture, and other articles capable of complete transfer by delivery, and (when separately assigned or charged) fixtures and growing crops, but shall not include chattel interests in real estate, nor fixtures (except trade machinery as hereinafter defined), when assigned together with a freehold or leasehold interest in any land or building to which they are affixed, nor growing crops when assigned together with any interest in the land on which they grow, nor shares or interests in the stock, funds, or securities of any government, or in the capital or property of incorporated or joint stock companies, nor choses in action, nor any stock or produce upon any farm or lands which by virtue of any covenant or agreement or of the custom of the country ought not to be removed from any farm where the same are at the time of making or giving of such bill of sale."

By Section 5 :—"Trade machinery shall, for the purposes of this Act, be deemed to be personal chattels, and any mode of disposition of trade machinery by the owner thereof which would be a bill of sale as to any other personal chattels shall be deemed to be a bill of sale within the meaning of this Act."

CHEAP MONEY. Money is said to be "cheap" when it can be borrowed at a low rate of interest. Money is called "dear" when, owing to its scarcity, it can be borrowed only at a high rate.

CHECK-BOOK. The name sometimes given to the deposit book or pass-book which is supplied to depositors in savings banks.

Check-book is also the American method of spelling cheque book.

CHECK LEDGER. A book of the nature of a day book, and which is used in some banks instead of a day book. In a large office there may be a separate check ledger for each current account ledger.

It contains details of all the items which are posted into the corresponding ledger, the debits in one column and the credits in another, and the entries in the check ledger are called off daily with the entries in the current account ledger. There may also be a check ledger for the deposit ledger, impersonal ledger, etc., the final totals of each check ledger being carried into the summary book at the end of the day.

CHEQUE. (Formerly written "check.") Gilbart says: "The word is derived from the French *echecs*, chess. The chequers placed at the doors of public-houses are intended to represent chess-boards, and originally denoted that the game of chess was played in those houses. Similar tables were employed in reckoning money, and hence came the expression 'to check an account'; and the Government office where the public accounts were kept, was called the Exchequer." Another explanation is that the word "check" arose from the consecutive numbers which were placed upon the forms to act as a check or means of verification. In the United States the word "check" is used at the present day. Cheques first came into use about 1780.

Part III of the Bills of Exchange Act, 1882, is devoted to provisions regarding such features of cheques as are not found in connection with a bill.

Section 73 defines a cheque :—

"A cheque is a bill of exchange drawn on a banker, payable on demand.

"Except as otherwise provided in this Part, the provisions of this Act applicable to a bill of exchange payable on demand apply to a cheque."

A cheque differs from a bill in several points: it does not require acceptance and is not entitled to days of grace; it is drawn upon a banker; the banker is protected if he pays it bearing a forged indorsement; the drawer is the person liable to pay it, and the drawer, as a rule, is not discharged by delay in presenting it for payment. The intention of a cheque is that it be paid at an early date. The drawee's authority to pay is determined by the drawer's death, and the drawer may stop payment of the cheque.

Indelible pencils are not desirable articles with which to draw cheques. A cheque written in ordinary pencil should not be paid without personal reference to the drawer, as the banker cannot possibly tell whether, or not, it has been altered. It is much to be desired that all cheques should be written in ink. Typewritten cheques are too easily altered, and their use should be discouraged as far as possible.

A cheque written upon a sheet of paper, provided it is in proper form, is sufficient. It must be stamped with a penny adhesive stamp (or two half-penny stamps), and the stamp must be cancelled by the person drawing the cheque before he delivers it. Cheques of this description should, however, never be drawn except in cases of extreme necessity.

At one time a cheque could not be issued for less than twenty shillings, but now a cheque may be for any amount, from one penny upwards. If the amount of a cheque includes a half-penny, the half-penny is ignored by bankers.

The size of cheque forms becomes of considerable importance when large quantities have to be dealt with. A very large cheque and a very small one are equally inconvenient in a bank office, and it is desirable, from the point of view of those who have to work all day with cheques, that some recognised size of cheque should be adopted by all bankers.

The practice of making a cheque more or less of an advertisement is not a desirable one.

The usual form of a cheque is :—

No. 23. March 1, 1910.
To the British Banking Company, Limited, Leeds.

1*d*.	Pay to John Jones or order the sum of one hundred pounds. £100.

THOMAS BROWN.

London Agents: X. & Y. Bank, Ltd.

The customary form of cheque should be adhered to as much as possible, though legally any form which fulfils the requirements of the Bills of Exchange Act would be sufficient, as, for example, where the drawer instead of signing his name at the bottom signs it at the top, "I, John Brown, direct you to pay to John Jones the sum," etc.

The Bank of England declines to pay cheques, unless drawn upon the forms they supply.

Some cheques have a notice upon them that they are payable only if presented within a certain period. Such a condition may possibly exclude the document from being considered a cheque under the Bills of Exchange Act. In *Thairlwall* v. *Great Northern Railway Company* (1910, 2 K.B. 509), where a dividend warrant had a condition at the bottom of it that "it will not be honoured after three months from date of issue unless specially indorsed for payment by the secretary," and it was argued that the document was not a cheque because of this condition, Mr. Justice Bray said: "I have felt a great deal of doubt on this point because of this statement. But, on the whole, I am inclined to think that this document is a cheque, and is within the meaning of Sections 73 and 3 of the Bills of Exchange Act, 1882, a cheque and an unconditional order in writing. . . . And I think it is none the less a cheque because of that statement at the bottom of the document. I do not consider that statement makes the order conditional."

There are also forms of cheques, or rather documents, which make the payment dependent upon a certain receipt being signed. Conditional documents of this kind are not cheques as defined by the Bills of Exchange Act. (See RECEIPT ON CHEQUE.)

The form of cheque (or, more correctly, order for payment) in use by Local Authorities is a peculiar one as, being drawn upon the Treasurer, it does not conform with the requirement of the Bills of Exchange Act that it be drawn upon a banker. It is considered, however, that, although drawn upon an individual, the order is practically drawn upon the bank where the Treasurer's account is kept, and that the banker paying such order is entitled to the protection which is afforded by Section 60 of the Bills of Exchange Act, 1882, against forged indorsements. If such orders should be held not to come within the Bills of Exchange Act, then the benefit of Section 60 would not apply, and they would also be incapable of being validly crossed.

Cheques paid to credit of a customer's account should be carefully examined before being paid or before being remitted for collection, and if not in order should be returned to the customer, or, if possible, sent out to him to be remedied, as, for instance, where he has omitted to indorse or has indorsed them wrongly.

It is desirable that when an account is to be closed, the cheque withdrawing any balance should state "being the balance of my account" or "to close my account."

With regard to alterations in cheques and provisions to prevent fraudulent alterations, see ALTERATIONS.

If there is a difference between the amount in writing and the figures on a cheque, the cheque may be paid according to the amount in writing, but it is the usual custom, and a prudent course, to return the cheque unpaid marked "amounts differ." If the figures have been omitted and the amount only appears in writing, a banker is justified in paying the cheque according to the words; though if the words have been omitted and the amount is given only in figures, the cheque should not be paid.

A cheque payable to "J. Brown only" should be indorsed by him and be paid to him. It cannot be transferred to anyone else. If payable to "J. Brown or order," it should be indorsed, and may, of course, then be transferred.

If the payee himself presents a cheque for payment and declines to indorse it, he has probably a legal right to do so, but see PAYEE.

If the balance of a customer's account will not allow of the full payment of a cheque which is presented, the cheque should be dishonoured. A cheque cannot be paid in part. In England, a cheque presented subsequently for a smaller amount, which the account will stand, may be paid. In Scotland, however, when a cheque is presented for payment and there is not a sufficient balance to meet it, the cheque attaches such funds as there may be in the banker's hands belonging to the drawer, and subsequent cheques, though for a less amount than the balance of the account, will be returned unpaid. The amount attached is transferred by the banker to a separate account.

A cheque which can be presented for payment across the counter of the Bank on which it is drawn, is an "open cheque." A cheque which has certain specified lines or words across the face of it is a "crossed cheque" (*q.v.*).

A cheque which has been cut, or torn, into two or more portions, or torn sufficiently to suggest cancellation, is not, as a rule, paid by a banker. But if a mutilated cheque bears a note upon it signed by a collecting banker, such as "accidentally torn," it is customary to pay it.

A cheque is sometimes marked or certified by a banker as being good for the amount for which it is drawn. It may be marked by the banker on whom it is drawn for another banker, as a matter of convenience for the purposes of clearing arrangements. Or, occasionally, it may be marked at the request of the drawer, or even at the request of the payee or holder.

English bankers do not encourage the marking of cheques as between themselves and the public, it being much the preferable way to pay the cheque and, if necessary, give a draft in exchange. In America, the certification or acceptance of cheques is very common. (See CERTIFICATION OF CHEQUES.) It is generally held by the best authorities that bankers in England cannot legally accept cheques.

A banker could not refuse to pay a "marked" cheque when presented, and if it was marked at the request of a payee or holder he could not debit it to the drawer's account if, in the meantime, the drawer had died or become bankrupt or had stopped payment of the cheque. (See further information under MARKED CHEQUE.)

A person is liable to be charged with false pretence if he gives a cheque in payment of a purchase when he has no account with the banker on whom the cheque is drawn.

With respect to the proposed rules regarding the unification of the laws existing in different countries relating to cheques, see UNIFICATION OF LAWS OF BILLS OF EXCHANGE.

STAMP DUTY.—The duty is one penny, for any amount, and the stamp may be either adhesive or impressed. A cheque must be stamped even if the amount is less than £2. Two half-penny stamps may be used.

If an adhesive stamp is used, it must, if the cheque is drawn within the United Kingdom, be cancelled by the drawer before he delivers the cheque out of his hands, custody or power (Section 34, s.s. 1, Stamp Act, 1891). If it is drawn out of the United Kingdom and is unstamped, every person into whose hands it comes in the United Kingdom before it is stamped shall, before he presents for payment, or indorses, transfers, or in any manner negotiates or pays the cheque, affix thereto a proper adhesive stamp and cancel the stamp so affixed. If at the time any cheque comes into the hands of any *bonâ fide* holder, there is affixed an uncancelled adhesive stamp, it shall be competent for the holder to cancel the stamp. (Section 35, Stamp Act, 1891.)

By Section 8, s.s. 3, of the same Act, every person who is required by law to cancel an adhesive stamp, and who neglects to do so, is liable to a penalty of £10. (See CANCELLATION OF STAMPS.)

By Section 38, s.s. 1, every person who issues, negotiates or presents for payment or pays any cheque not being stamped, incurs a penalty of £10, and the person who takes such an unstamped cheque shall not be entitled to recover thereon.

By Section 38, s.s. 2, if a cheque is presented for payment unstamped, the banker may affix the adhesive stamp of one penny and cancel it, and charge the duty in account against the person by whom the cheque was drawn, or deduct the duty from the amount of the cheque. Besides the drawer, no other person than the banker to whom an unstamped inland cheque is presented for payment, has power to stamp it, and it has been held that when stamped by an intermediate holder it could not be recovered on.

Where a formal receipt is given upon a cheque, the receipt requires (under Section 9 of Finance Act, 1895) an adhesive stamp of one penny (or two half-pennies) if for an amount of £2 or upwards. This receipt stamp is in addition to the stamp of one penny upon the cheque.

A cheque is included under the expression "bill of exchange" in the Stamp Act, 1891, and various sections of that Act are given in the article BILL OF EXCHANGE.

If a cheque is drawn in such a form as "Pay John Brown on July 5" it must be treated as a bill and stamped with *ad valorem* duty. A post-dated cheque requires only the usual penny stamp.

When a customer transfers his account from one branch to another, or from, say, his No. 1 to his No. 2 account, it is usually effected by means of a cheque or stamped letter, but a simple unstamped letter of request is sufficient. A transfer of an amount from one customer's account to another customer's account is not exempt from duty.

Cheques are exempt from stamp duty in the following cases:—

Cheque drawn by or on behalf of a registered Friendly Society (circular from Inland Revenue, November 10, 1894). Section 33 of the Friendly Societies Act, 1896 (59 & 60 Vict. c. 25), enacts that stamp duty shall not be chargeable upon a "draft or order or receipt given by or to a registered society or branch in respect of money payable by virtue of its rules or of this Act."

Cheque drawn by the Registrar of a County Court upon his public account (45 & 46 Vict. c. 72 Section 9).

Cheque drawn by the Guardians upon a Poor Law Account (4 & 5 Will. IV c. 76, Section 86).

Cheque drawn by a Trustee in Bankruptcy (46 & 47 Vict. c. 52, Section 144).

Cheque drawn on the accounts of estates of companies wound up by order of the Court under the Companies (Consolidation) Act, 1908 (8 Edw. 7, c. 69, Section 230).

Cheque drawn by any officer of the post office for the purpose of remittance to the Postmaster-General (44 & 45 Vict. c. 20, Section 5).

Cheque drawn by Government Departments.

Cheque required to be make in pursuance of the Loan Societies Act (3 & 4 Vict. c. 110, Section 14) or of the rules of the society.

Cheque required to be made in pursuance of the Savings Bank Act (26 & 27 Vict. c. 87, Section 50).

Cheque drawn by a banker upon another banker in settlement of an account between such bankers (see BILL OF EXCHANGE—EXEMPTION 2).

Letter written by a banker to another banker (both in United Kingdom) directing the payment of any sum of money, the same not being payable to bearer or to order, and such letter not being sent or delivered to the person to whom payment is to be made, or to any person on his behalf (EXEMPTION 3).

See also the list of exemptions in the Stamp Act, 1891, given in the article BILL OF EXCHANGE. (See BANKER'S ORDER.)

The following minute of the Board of Inland Revenue was passed May, 1904:—

"The attention of the Board of Inland Revenue has been drawn to the fact that certain instruments chargeable, as they are advised, under the Stamp Act, 1891, with a penny duty as 'Bills of Exchange payable on demand, or at sight, or on presentation,' are suffered to pass without such stamp. The Board have reason to believe that this practice is now very prevalent.

"Section 32 of the Act is as follows :—

'For the purposes of this Act the expression "Bill of Exchange" includes draft, order, cheque, and letter of credit, and any document or writing (except a bank note) entitling or purporting to entitle any person, whether named therein or not, to payment by any other person of, or to draw upon any other person for any sum of money ; and the expression "Bill of Exchange payable on demand" includes—

'(a) An order for the payment of any sum of money by a Bill of Exchange or promissory note, or for the delivery of any Bill of Exchange or promissory note in satisfaction of any sum of money, or for the payment of any sum of money out of any particular fund which may or may not be available, or upon any condition or contingency which may or may not be performed, or happen ; and

'(b) An order for the payment of any sum of money weekly, monthly, or at any other stated periods, and also an order for the payment by any person at any time after the date thereof of any sum of money, and sent or delivered by the person making the same to the person by whom the payment is to be made, and not to the person to whom the payment is to be made, or to any person on his behalf.'

Section 38, sub-section (1), imposes a fine of ten pounds upon every person who issues, indorses, transfers, negotiates, presents for payment, or pays any Bill of Exchange not being duly stamped, and it is provided that the person who takes or receives any such bill shall not be entitled to recover thereon.

"The instruments to which the Board refer appear to be especially made use of by Education Authorities and other Municipal bodies in connection with payments which they desire to be made on their behalf by their Bankers or Treasurers. These instruments vary, to some extent, in form, but their general nature is as follows :—(1) A document is handed by the Authority to the creditor or other person who is to receive the money, which document informs him that the Treasurer of the Authority, or a certain named Banker, has been authorised to pay him a sum of money, specified on the document, and that payment will be made accordingly, by the Treasurer, or by such Banker, as the case may be, on presentation of the document. (2) Concurrently with or antecedently to the issue of this document a letter is written by the Authority or their Officer to the Banker or Treasurer giving a list of the various persons to whom payments are to be made upon presentation of a document in the above form, and requesting the Banker or Treasurer to make such payment accordingly.

"The Board are advised that the last mentioned document, namely, the letter of request to the Banker or Treasurer, comes within the paragraph marked (b) of Section 32 above set forth, as being an order for the payment by a person (in this case the Treasurer or Banker) of a sum of money, and sent or delivered by the person making the same (in this case the sender of the letter) to the person by whom the payment is to be made (namely, the Banker or Treasurer) ; and the Board, moreover, are advised that a penny stamp is necessary in respect of each payee's name appearing upon the letter of request, because the payment to be made to each of such persons is in respect of a separate and distinct transaction.

"The Board are also advised that each letter handed to the payee as above mentioned, whether supplemented by a letter of request or not, comes within the words of the first paragraph of Section 32, as being a document purporting to entitle a person to payment by any other person of a sum of money.

"As the question of the liability of either of these two classes of documents has not, so far as the Board know, been directly the subject of any legal decision, it is of course open to Bankers and others interested to test the question whether the Board's view is right, by obtaining a legal decision in the manner pointed out by the Stamp Act. Until, however, the parties see fit to take steps to do this the Board will act upon the view expressed above.

"The Board are confident that they can rely upon the ready assistance of Bankers, Local Authorities and their Officers in seeing that documents of this character are stamped in accordance with the provisions of the law. They feel it to be their duty, however, to point out that should occasion arise after this notice they will have no alternative but to institute proceedings for recovery of the penalties provided by Section 38 of the Act.

"While dealing with the question of stamp duty on Bills of Exchange, the Board desire to mention that they have some reason to think that orders to Bankers for the payment of sums of money at stated periods (e.g. Club subscriptions, and instalments of the price of articles purchased on the hire system) are frequently not stamped. The omission of the stamp is doubtless due to a misapprehension as to the provisions of the law; but it is clear that such orders fall within the definition in Section 32 (*b*) of the Stamp Act, and should in all cases bear stamps."

(See AGENT, ALTERATIONS, AMOUNT OF BILL OR CHEQUE, ANSWERS, ANTE-DATED, BEARER, BILL OF EXCHANGE, BILLS OF EXCHANGE ACT 1882, CANCELLATION OF BILL OF EXCHANGE, CANCELLED CHEQUES AND BILLS, COLLECTING BANKER, CONSIDERATION FOR BILL OF EXCHANGE, COUNTERMAND OF PAYMENT, CROSSED CHEQUE, DATE, DELIVERY OF BILL, DISHONOUR OF BILL OF EXCHANGE, DRAWEE, DRAWER, FOREIGN BILL, FORGERY, HOLDER FOR VALUE, HOLDER IN DUE COURSE, HOLDER OF BILL OF EXCHANGE, INCHOATE INSTRUMENT, INDORSEMENT, INDORSER, INLAND BILL, LOST BILL OF EXCHANGE, MARKED CHEQUE, NEGOTIATION OF BILL OF EXCHANGE, NOT NEGOTIABLE CHEQUE, ORDER, OVERDUE BILL, PART PAYMENT, PARTIES TO BILL OF EXCHANGE, PAYEE, PAYING BANKER, PAYMENT BY, PAYMENT OF CHEQUE, POST-DATED, PRESENTMENT FOR PAYMENT, RECEIPT ON CHEQUE, RETURNED CHEQUE, STALE CHEQUE, TIME OF PAYMENT OF BILL, TRANSFEROR BY DELIVERY, TRAVELLERS' CHEQUES, UNIFICATION OF LAWS OF BILLS OF EXCHANGE.

CHEQUE BOOK. A book of cheque forms, with counterfoils attached.

Cheque books are of various sizes, 1*s*., 2*s*., 4*s*., 8*s*., and so on, according to the number of forms in each. Specially large books are usually prepared for customers who use many cheques. The cheques are numbered consecutively and the numbers continue from book to book. Each book is entered in the cheque book register, with a record of the name of the customer to whom it has been given.

When a cheque is used, the counterfoil should be filled up.

When a new book is required, the customer should either obtain it personally or fill up and sign an application form for a new book. An application form is usually inserted in each cheque book, a few forms from the end of the book. Some banks have a rule that, when a cheque book is delivered upon a written order, the fact should be at once communicated to the customer.

When not in use, it is prudent to keep a cheque book locked up.

In America it is called "check-book." (See CHEQUE BOOK REGISTER.)

CHEQUE BOOK REGISTER. Each denomination of cheque book (1*s*., 2*s*., 4*s*., 8*s*., and so on) is entered in a separate book, or in separate parts of the same register. When a fresh supply of cheque books is received by a branch, each book is entered in the register by its number, and when a book is sold the name of the customer and the date are written opposite the entry of that cheque book in the register. In some banks, the person who obtains a new cheque book is required to sign the register opposite the number of the book he receives.

As each cheque book is sold and marked off in the register, the price of it is credited to cheque book account, and if, on a trial, the cheque books on hand do not agree with the balance of the cheque book account, it will be necessary to tick off the books shown as sold in the register with the credits to cheque book account.

Of course the balance of cheque book account represents merely the amount of the stamps and does not include the cost of printing the books.

CHEQUE RATE. A term used in connection with the Foreign Exchanges, signifying the price in one country at which a cheque, or sight draft, upon another country can be bought.

With most foreign countries the quotation is that of the "long" rate, i.e. for three months or ninety days bills, but there are cases where "short" rates are quoted—that is, for drafts having eight to ten days to run.

Where the Paris Cheque Rate is quoted as 25·30, it means that a foreign banker in London is prepared to draw a demand draft upon his agent in Paris at the rate of 25 francs 30 centimes for every £1 handed to him here.

An alternative name for Cheque Rate is Sight Rate. (See COURSE OF EXCHANGE, FOREIGN EXCHANGES, LONG RATE, SHORT RATE.)

CHIROGRAPH. Literally a handwriting. A chirograph was an old form of deed which was written in two parts on the same sheet of parchment. Between each part was a blank space, and right along that blank space the word "chirographum" was sometimes written. The two parts were then separated, by the parchment being cut with an irregular line through that word, and each party received one of the parts. Each part would, of course, contain only portions of the letters of the word, and when the two parts were brought together again, the fitting in of the wavy line and completion of the word "chirographum" proved that the one deed was the counterpart of the other. (See INDENTURE.)

CHOPS. A Stock Exchange name for Chartered Options.

CHOSE IN ACTION. Property which a person has not got in his actual possession, but which he has a right to demand by an action at law. Money due upon a bill of exchange, and goods bought and not delivered, are examples of a chose in action. When the money or the goods are in actual possession, they are called choses in possession.

CHOSE IN POSSESSION. (See CHOSE IN ACTION.)

CHURCHWARDENS. The usual number of churchwardens is two, though in some cases there are four. They are appointed at the Vestry Meeting at Eastertide, and hold office for twelve months. A banker should receive a copy of the minutes, signed by the chairman of the meeting, recording the appointments. The churchwardens have the control of all money raised for the repair of the church buildings and for the due performance of divine service therein. Cheques upon a churchwardens' account are usually signed by all the wardens, but if a banker is desired to honour cheques when signed otherwise, a written authority, signed by all of them, should be obtained.

CIRCULAR LETTER OF CREDIT. The following is a specimen Circular Letter of Credit :—

Circular Letter of Credit—

Not available after 19 .

No. .

£ .

Date 19 .

GENTLEMEN,—

We beg to introduce to you to whom you will please furnish such funds as may require up to the aggregate amount of Pounds sterling against sight drafts on our Head Office, London, each draft to be plainly marked as drawn under this Letter of Credit No. and to be signed in accordance with specimen signature which you will find on our Letter of Indication of the same number to be produced herewith.

We engage that such drafts shall meet with due honour if negotiated within months from this date, and request you to buy them at the rate at which you purchase demand drafts on London.

The amount of each draft must be inscribed on the back of this letter. The letter itself must be cancelled, and attached to the final draft drawn.

We are, Gentlemen,
Your obedient servants,

To Messieurs the Bankers
mentioned in the Letter of Indication
which must be produced herewith.

N.B.—The bearer, for purposes of security, is requested to carry this Letter of Credit apart from the Letter of Indication.

On the back of the Letter of Credit particulars of the various payments must be noted, viz. :—

Date when paid ; By whom paid ; Name of town where paid ; Sterling amount expressed in words ; Amount in figures.

When a payment is to be made under a Letter of Credit, the signatures of the grantor on the Letter of Indication and Letter of Credit should be verified, as well as the signature of the person requiring the money, with the specimen on the Letter of Indication. It is necessary, as a matter of precaution, that the signature of the bearer of the letter should be written in the banker's presence.

The Letter of Credit should be read carefully and the various points attended to. The total amount already paid should be ascertained from the indorsements, and care must be taken, in making a payment, to see that the amount expressed in the letter is not exceeded, also that the period within which the credit is available has not expired.

When a Letter of Credit is issued, the amount is debited to the customer's account and credited to a separate account to meet drafts drawn by the grantee. (See LETTER OF INDICATION.)

CIRCULAR NOTES. Notes issued for the special use of travellers, and which can be cashed at any of the issuer's correspondents, a list of which accompanies the Letter of

Indication. The Letter of Indication gives the numbers of the notes, the name of the person to whom they have been issued, and a specimen of his signature. The Letter of Indication should be retained by the holder until all the notes have been cashed, when it is to be surrendered to the banker cashing the last note. For security, the Letter of Indication and the notes should be carried apart. Circular notes may be for amounts of, say, £5, £10, £20, or £50, each denomination being usually printed in distinctive colours.

The following is a specimen of a circular note:—

London 19 .

No. .

Circular Note for Ten Pounds. £10.

GENTLEMEN,—

This note will be presented to you by whose signature you will find in our Letter of Indication No. to be produced herewith. We request you to pay to order the value of Ten Pounds at the current rate of exchange against proper indorsement.

Your obedient servants,

Messieurs the Bankers
mentioned in our Letter of Indication.

On the back of the note is printed:—

£10. At sight pay to the order of
Ten Pounds value received at this
day of 19 .
(Sign here.)

When circular notes are presented for payment the notes and Letter of Indication must be carefully scrutinised to see that everything is in order. The indorsement on the notes of the person requiring the money should, as a matter of precaution, be written in the presence of the banker, and compared with the specimen signature on the Letter of Indication.

A circular note is exempt from stamp duty (see under BILLS OF EXCHANGE, EXEMPTION 4), but the form on the back of the note, being the same as a foreign bill, requires a stamp of one penny if on demand or at sight or not exceeding three days after date or sight; if otherwise, the usual *ad valorem* foreign bill stamp is required. (See LETTER OF INDICATION.)

CIRCULATING CAPITAL. Circulating capital fulfils the whole of its office in the production in which it is engaged, by a single use. John Stuart Mill says: "The term, which is not very appropriate, is derived from the circumstance, that this portion of capital requires to be constantly renewed by the sale of the finished product, and when renewed is perpetually parted with in buying materials and paying wages; so that it does its work, not by being kept, but by changing hands." Fixed capital, on the contrary, does its work by being kept. (See CAPITAL.)

CIRCULATING MEDIUM. The medium or means by which purchases and sales are effected. The term is applied to gold, silver, and copper coins, also to bank notes, cheques, bills, and other paper instruments, which act as substitutes for coins. The various articles, such as shells, salt, skins, etc., used in former ages, and even at present in certain countries, are also included under the term circulating medium. (See MONEY.)

CIRCULATION. When money or notes pass from hand to hand, they are said to circulate, or to be in circulation, but the word is sometimes used, or rather misused, to mean the money itself.

The word "circulation" is very commonly used by bankers instead of the words "notes in circulation." Where a banker has, say, £5,000 of his own notes in circulation, it represents the notes which are actually in the hands of the public and does not include any notes which remain in his till.

CLARAS. A Stock Exchange name for Caledonian Railway deferred stock.

CLARE CONSTAT. (See PRECEPT OF CLARE CONSTAT.)

CLAYTON'S CASE. This is the name of a case decided in 1816, and reported in 1 Mer. 529 *et seq.* (sometimes quoted as *Devaynes* v. *Noble*), which is always referred to as the leading authority upon what is known as the "appropriation of payments." If a debtor owes more than one debt to his creditor, and pays him a sum of money insufficient to liquidate the whole of the debts, it is sometimes a matter of importance, in view of the Statutes of Limitations, to know to which debts the payment is to be appropriated. From Clayton's case the following rules are derived, mainly taken from the Roman Law:—(1) A debtor making a payment has a right to appropriate it to the discharge of any debt due to the creditor; (2) if at the time of payment there is no express or implied appropriation thereof by the debtor, then the creditor has a right to make the appropriation; (3) in the absence of any appropriation by either debtor or creditor, an appropriation is made by presumption of law, according to the items of account, the first item on the debit side being the item discharged or reduced by the first item on the credit side. The principle of the case was thus explained (see p. 608 of the report):—

"This is the case of a banking account, where all the sums paid in form one blended fund, the parts of which have no longer any distinct existence. Neither banker nor customer ever thinks of saying, 'This draft is to be placed to the account of the £500 paid in on Monday, and this other to the account of the £500 paid in on Tuesday.' There is a fund of £1,800 to draw upon, and that is enough. In such a case, there is no room for any other appropriation than that which arises from the order in which the receipts and payments take place, and are carried into the account. Presumably, it is the sum first paid in that is first drawn out. It is the first item on the debit side of the account that is discharged, or reduced, by the first item on the credit side. The appropriation is made by the very act of setting the two items against each other. Upon that principle all accounts current are settled, and particularly cash accounts. When there has been a continuation of dealings, in what way can it be ascertained whether the specific balance due on a given day has, or has not, been discharged, but by examining whether payments to the amount of that balance appear by the account to have been made? You are not to take the account backwards, and strike the balance at the head, instead of the foot, of it. A man's banker breaks, owing him, on the whole account, a balance of £1,000. It would surprise one to hear the customer say, 'I have been fortunate enough to draw out all that I paid in during the last four years; but there is £1,000 which I paid in five years ago that I hold myself never to have drawn out; and, therefore, if I can find anybody who was answerable for the debts of the banking house, such as they stood five years ago, I have a right to say that it is that specific sum which is still due to me, and not the £1,000 that I paid in last week.'"

The Earl of Selborne, L.C., in *In re Sherry, London and County Banking Company v. Terry* (1884, 25 Ch. D. 692), said:—"The principle of Clayton's case, and of the other cases which deal with the same subject, is this, that where a creditor having a right to appropriate moneys paid to him generally, and not specifically appropriated by the person paying them, carries them into a particular account kept in his books, he *primâ facie* appropriates them to that account, and the effect of that is, that the payments are *de facto* appropriated according to the priority in order of the entries on the one side and on the other of that account. It is, of course, absolutely necessary for the application of those authorities that there should be one unbroken account, and entries made in that account by the person having a right to appropriate the payment to that account; and the way to avoid the application of Clayton's case, where there is no other principle in question, is to break the account and open a new and distinct account. When that is done, and the payment is entered to that new and distinct account, whatever other rule may govern the case, it certainly is not the rule of Clayton's case. . . ."

The principle of Clayton's case does not apply where a person has mixed trust moneys with his own moneys in his account. The money which he first withdraws from the account is taken to be his own money, leaving the trust funds intact.

"CLEAN" ACCEPTANCE. That is a "general acceptance." (See ACCEPTANCE, GENERAL.)

CLEARING BANKS. The members of the London Bankers' Clearing House. Representatives of each clearing bank meet at the Clearing House and exchange cheques drawn upon the members or upon the country correspondents of members, or other London banks for which they are agents.

The members are:—

Bank of England.
Barclay & Company, Ltd.
Capital & Counties Bank, Ltd.
Glyn, Mills, Currie & Company.
Lloyds Bank, Ltd.
London & South Western Bank, Ltd.
London City & Midland Bank, Ltd.
London County & Westminster Bank, Ltd.
London Joint Stock Bank, Ltd.
Martin's Bank, Ltd.
Metropolitan Bank (of England and Wales), Ltd.
National Bank, Ltd.
National Provincial Bank of England, Ltd.
Parr's Bank, Ltd.

Robarts, Lubbock & Company.
Union of London & Smiths Bank, Ltd.
Williams Deacon's Bank, Ltd.

CLEARING HOUSE. A country banker "clears" the cheques which he holds upon another banker in the same town in the daily exchange or daily clearing. That is, banker A, by his clerk, sends to banker B all cheques drawn upon him, and banker B hands over to the clerk any cheques he holds drawn upon banker A. The difference between the two sets of cheques is settled by cash, draft, or London Payment.

In large towns instead of each banker's representative visiting the other bank offices, they all meet at a centre, called the Clearing House and effect a mutual exchange. In this way each bank, instead of settling differences with, say, five or six other banks, merely pays over or receives the net difference through the bank which manages the clearing.

There are Clearing Houses at Birmingham, Bristol, Leeds, Leicester, Liverpool, Manchester, Newcastle and Sheffield.

The cheques dealt with in the Country Clearing Houses are only those which are drawn upon the banks in the same town or within a short distance thereof. Cheques upon other banks in England and Wales are sent to London to be collected through the Bankers' Clearing House, in Post Office Court, Lombard Street.

The London Bankers' Clearing House is worked practically on the same principle as the Country Clearing Houses. Each member of the Clearing House sends, by a clerk, to the Clearing House the cheques held upon other bankers who are members, or upon the country correspondents of any of the members, or other bankers for which they are agents. Each clerk hands over the cheques he has upon the other bankers and receives the cheques upon the bank which he represents. The cheques received by a clerk of A bank from, say, B Bank is his "in" clearing, and the cheques given by him to that bank is his "out" clearing. At the end of the day the difference between the "in" and "out" clearing is the amount due to be paid by A to B or B to A, as the case may be. Each bank, however, does not settle separately with each other bank, but a form, called the summary sheet, is filled up, showing in two columns the amounts due to or owing from all the other members of the House.

The following is a specimen of the summary sheet in use:—

BARCLAY & COMPANY, Limited.

DEBTORS.		CREDITORS.
	Bank	
	Capital & Counties	
	London County & Westr.	
	Glyn	
	Joint	
	Lloyds	
	London City & Midland	
	London & S. Western	
	Martin	
	Metropolitan	
	National	
	National Provincial	
	Parr's	
	Robarts	
	Southwark	
	Union	
	Williams	
	Country Clearing	
	Metropolitan Clearing	
	C.H.	

The difference between the two columns is the net balance either to be received or to be paid. When the balance is due to be paid, that is, is against a bank, the bank transfers the amount due from its account at the Bank of England to the Clearing Bankers' account. The transfer is effected by means of a white ticket similar to form No. 1. (*See below.*)

If the balance is due to be received, the bank obtains a transfer of the amount from the Clearing Bankers' account to its own account at the Bank of England, by a green transfer ticket signed by the bank and an Inspector of the Clearing House. See form No. 2.

Scotch and Irish cheques are not cleared through the London Clearing House. There is, however, a clearing house in Edinburgh, in Glasgow, and in Dublin.

For the names of the members of the London Clearing House, see CLEARING BANKS.

Gilbart states that the Clearing House was founded in 1775.

The total amount of cheques, bills, etc., which passed through the Clearing House

		Daily Average.
in 1839 was	£954,401,600	£3,066,600
,, 1868 ,,	£3,425,185,000	£10,978,200
,, 1907 ,,	£12,730,393,000	£41,467,100
,, 1908 ,,	£12,120,362,000	£39,351,800
,, 1909 ,,	£13,525,446,000	£44,056,800

There are four clearings each day, viz.: Metropolitan, Town (morning), Country Cheque, and Town (afternoon).

Cheques with "T" printed on the left-hand bottom corner are included in the Town Clearing; those with "M" are included in the Metropolitan Clearing; and those with "C" are included in the Country Clearing.

The fourth day of a month, when so many bills are payable, and the Stock Exchange settlement days are very busy times in the Clearing House.

"RULES AND REGULATIONS TO BE OBSERVED AT THE CLEARING HOUSE.

ORDINARY DAYS, EXCEPTING SATURDAYS.

Morning clearing to open at 10.30 a.m.

FORM No. 1.

SETTLEMENT AT THE CLEARING HOUSE.

London, 19 .

To the Cashiers of the BANK OF ENGLAND,

Be pleased to TRANSFER from our Account the sum of and place it to the credit of the Account of the Clearing Bankers, and allow it to be drawn for, by any of them (with the knowledge of either of the inspectors, signified by his countersigning the Drafts).

£

SETTLEMENT AT THE CLEARING HOUSE.

BANK OF ENGLAND, 19 .

A TRANSFER for the sum of
has this evening been made at the Bank, from the account of
to the Account of the Clearing Bankers.

For the Bank of England.

£

This Certificate has been seen by me,

, *Inspector.*

FORM No. 2.

SETTLEMENT AT THE CLEARING HOUSE.

London, 19 .

To the Cashiers of the BANK OF ENGLAND,

Be pleased to CREDIT our Account the Sum of out of the money at the credit of the account of the Clearing Bankers.

£

Seen by me,

Inspector at the Clearing House.

SETTLEMENT AT THE CLEARING HOUSE.

BANK OF ENGLAND,

19 .

The account of
has this evening been CREDITED *with the sum of out of the money at the credit of the account of the Clearing Bankers.*

£ For the Bank of England,

Drafts, etc., to be received not later than 11 a.m.

Afternoon clearing to open at 2.30 p.m. Drafts, etc., to be received not later than 4.5 p.m. Returns to be received not later than 5 p.m., excepting on settling days and the first six working days in January and July, when the last delivery shall be 4.15 p.m. and returns 5.30 p.m.

Saturdays.

Morning clearing to open at 9 a.m. Drafts, etc., to be received not later than 10.15 a.m.

Afternoon clearing to open at 12 noon. Drafts, etc., to be received not later than 1.30 p.m. Returns to be received not later than 2.30 p.m.

Exceptions.—With the exception of the first two Saturdays in January and July, and the first Saturday in April and October, when the time shall be 1.45 p.m. for the last delivery and 2.45 p.m. for returns.

Further Exceptions for Returns.—Returns on the first Saturday in January and July to be not later than 3 p.m.

April 1, June 30, October 1, December 31, the day succeeding a Bank Holiday, and on such other days as the Honorary Secretary may Determine.

On these days the time shall be 4.15 p.m. for the last delivery, and 5.15 p.m. for the last returns, except when either of these days is a Saturday, when the time shall be 1.45 p.m. for last delivery and 2.45 p.m. for the last returns.

General Rules.

The total amount of the morning and country delivery shall be agreed by each clearer before leaving the Clearing House.

All clerks that are in the Clearing House by the time appointed for final delivery, shall be entitled to deliver their articles, though they may not have been able to pass them to the different desks before the clock strikes.

All returns in the Clearing House upon the stroke of the clock, at the time appointed for final delivery, must be received by the clearers and credited the same day. The inspectors are instructed to close the doors and not re-open them until such returns have been delivered.

Any bank which has accepted and paid an article returned to it in error, may require repayment through the Clearing House on the following day.

Notice shall be entered upon a board at the Clearing House, giving monthly statements of those settling days at the Stock Exchange, upon which the time for receiving returns is to be 5.30 p.m.

With regard to all drafts not crossed, and all bills not receipted, sent to the Clearing House as returns, the clearer holding them must fully announce the particulars to the Clearing House, and if not claimed, the case must be represented to the inspectors; but on no account can the clearer be allowed to debit the Clearing House with the amount until an owner can be found.

No return can be received without an answer in writing on the return why payment is refused.

It shall be sufficient in order that a return shall be received and credited, that it shall have on it an answer, why returned; and no clearer shall refuse to pass to credit any return that shall be so marked.

All the differences arising from marked articles of £1,000 and upwards must be finally ascertained and placed to account, before the clearer makes up his balance sheet.

No clearer shall be allowed to charge out drafts in the Clearing-out Book at the Clearing House.

All differences of more than £1,000 that may have been accidentally passed over at night, shall be settled by a transfer at the Bank of England, the first thing the next morning.

The inspectors are charged with the preservation of order and decorum in the Clearing House, and are instructed to report to the Committee of Bankers disorderly conduct on the part of any persons, calculated, in their opinion, to obstruct the adjustment of the business of the House.

July, 1905."

"RULES
FOR THE CONDUCT OF A CLEARING OF COUNTRY CHEQUES IN LONDON.

1. A clearing to be held in the middle of each day for the interchange, among the London bankers, of cheques on their correspondents in the country, placed in their hands for collection.

2. Each London banker to remit for collection to his country correspondents the cheques drawn upon them, saying, 'Please say if we may debit you £ for cheques enclosed.'

3. Country bankers wishing to avail themselves of this clearing to remit their country cheques to their own London agent, to stamp across them their *own name and address, and that of their London Agent.*

4. Any country bank not intending to pay a cheque sent to it for collection, to return it direct to the country *or branch bank*, if any, whose name and address is across it.

5. Each country banker to write by return of post to its London agent in reply, 'We credit you £ for cheques forwarded to us for collection in yours of .' Adding in case of non-payment of any such cheques, 'having deducted £ for cheque returned to Messrs. at , and £ returned to Messrs. at .'

BANKERS' CLEARING HOUSE,

June 27, 1893.

The Inspectors respectfully point out the necessity of exact adherence to the above rules."

"COUNTRY CHEQUE CLEARING.

ADDITIONAL RULES TO BE OBSERVED.

Country Clearing to open at 10.30. Drafts, including returns, to be received not later than 12.30, except on Saturdays, when the time shall be 10 o'clock for the opening, and 11.30 for the last delivery, including returns. The door to be closed on the stroke of the clock, as in the Town Clearing.

(*It is required that all banks shall make a delivery as near to* 10.30 *as possible, on ordinary days, and* 10 *o'clock on Saturdays. In no case shall the first delivery be later than* 10.45 *on ordinary days, and* 10.30 *on Saturdays. The remaining deliveries at necessary intervals.*)

All the in-clearing to be entered at the Clearing House.

Castings of about 50 entries to be given with all the early deliveries of the out-clearing.

(*It is expected that the last castings will be given to the in-clearers not later than five minutes after the last delivery of cheques.*)

All charges to be agreed at the Clearing House on the day of the work, and the clerk responsible for the out-side shall make it his business to go to the desk of the clerk entering his charge on the in-side for this purpose.

It shall be necessary for the in-clearer to retain for the inspection of the out-clearer, the cheques of any casting, or any particular cheque in which a difference occurs.

All wrongly delivered cheques discovered before the out and in-clearers agreeing any charge have left the Clearing House, shall be adjusted by the clearers, but any discovered after either clearer has left the House shall not be deducted from the already agreed amount, but shall be entered on the debit side of lists provided for the purpose, the cheque or cheques to be sent to the proper forwarding agent, who shall also enter them on the credit side of the list provided; these lists to be handed to the Clearing House inspector on the morning following, and it shall be his duty to agree the same. The total of these lists to be brought on to the end of the balance sheet.

The balance sheet, together with the particulars of the out and in-sides, shall be handed to the inspector on the morning following the day of the work, and it shall be his duty to check the balances, and to call attention to any charge that may differ, as soon as possible.

BANKERS' CLEARING HOUSE,

July, 1905."

"METROPOLITAN CLEARING.

RULES.

The Metropolitan Clearing to open at 9 a.m. on ordinary days and 8.45 a.m. on Saturdays. Drafts on the branches of the clearing banks and of the London and Provincial Bank included in the Metropolitan Clearing area to be received not later than 10.30 a.m. (Greenwich time) on ordinary days and 9.50 a.m. (Greenwich time) on Saturdays.

It is requested that the first delivery be made immediately on the opening of business, subsequent deliveries at frequent intervals, and that every effort be made to avoid heavy deliveries at the last moment.

All the 'in' clearing to be entered at the Clearing House.

The agreement of charges to take place as soon as possible after the 'in' side has been entered.

The drafts are to be sent to the head offices when entered and not to be detained at the Clearing House until the charges are agreed.

Marked articles and missing cheques are to be looked up on the 'out' side. If a difference is for £1,000 and upwards the particulars, if available, to be given to the paying bank the same day and every effort is to be made to settle the difference forthwith. If particulars are not available the settling of the error may be held over to the following day.

All differences in the Metropolitan Clearing to be adjusted as quickly as possible through the Town Clearing.

Returns in the Metropolitan Clearing must be delivered at the Clearing House through the afternoon Town Clearing at the earliest possible moment, but not later than 4.5 p.m. on ordinary days and 1.30 p.m. on Saturdays.

It will be permissible for a bank to pay any of its Metropolitan branches under protest on Saturdays, when necessary.

Bills, included in remittances to branches, that avail themselves of the protest rule, if dishonoured and received too late to return to the collecting banker must be protected by the returning banker.

Dishonoured cheques, from a branch paid under protest, received by the head office or agent too late for delivery at the Clearing House or to the head office of the presenting bank must be returned by post direct to the crossing bank or branch and debited at the Clearing House on the next business day by slip as used in the Country Cheque Clearing.

Wrongly delivered drafts are to be adjusted as far as possible before agreeing the charges. No alteration is to be made in the total after agreement.

Drafts wrongly delivered in the Metropolitan Clearing but payable through the Town Clearing at the bank to which they have been presented, if discovered too late for adjustment at the Clearing House, may be transferred internally without reference to the Clearing House.

Drafts wrongly delivered payable through the Metropolitan Clearing and discovered too late for adjustment in the Clearing House are to be debited on sheets provided for the purpose, the cheques to be placed in envelopes addressed to the paying bank and delivered to the inspectors at the Clearing House as quickly as possible, but not later than 10.45 a.m. (Greenwich time) on ordinary days and 10 o'clock (Greenwich time) on Saturdays.

The inspectors will use all diligence in despatching these envelopes in the hope of catching the collecting messengers before they leave the head offices. It is not intended that these messengers should be delayed on account of this delivery, and should they have left the head offices with the charges the wrongly delivered articles shall be returned to the presenting banker.

Drafts wrongly delivered in the Metropolitan Clearing payable in the Country Cheque Clearing discovered too late for adjustment in the Clearing House to be debited to the crossing banker on the sheets above referred to. These cheques to be sent to the inspectors of the Clearing House in envelopes addressed to the presenting banker not later than 10.45 a.m. on ordinary days and 10 o'clock on Saturdays.

All wrongly delivered drafts received in the Clearing House envelopes to be entered by the banks accepting on the credit side of the lists provided. These lists to be handed to the inspectors not later than 2.30 o'clock on ordinary days and 1.30 o'clock on Saturdays. The totals of debit and credit sides of these sheets to be entered on Town balance sheet in the place provided, and agreed with the inspectors before closing.

Machines will be allotted for use in the Metropolitan Clearing under the following conditions :—

The 'in' clearing to be entered as quickly as possible.

Agreement of charges is not to be attempted at the expense of entering.

The machines are to be surrendered without delay after entering is finished, and adjournment to the Country Cheque Balance Room or Ground Floor for the purpose of agreeing is requested.

Banks wishing to use the Clearing House machines for listing to their branches must surrender these machines not later than 10.45 a.m. on ordinary days and 10 o'clock on Saturdays.

The totals of each side, viz.: 'out' and 'in' of the Metropolitan Clearing are to be added to the amount of the Morning Town Clearing in all cases, and it is the duty of the Town clearers to see this is done before calling their final totals at mid-day.

The general rules of the Clearing House shall be observed in so far as they apply.

Bankers' Clearing House,

January 3, 1907."

As to payments under protest in connection with the Country Clearing, see Protest Payments.

CLERGYMEN. Clergymen may be members, partners, or shareholders in an association or co-partnership, consisting of more than six members or shareholders, carrying on the business of banking and other trades and dealings for gain and profit, but it is not lawful for a clergyman "to act as a director or managing partner or to carry on trade or such dealing as aforesaid in person" (4 Vict. c. 14).

CLOCK STAMP. An invention by which the actual time of receipt or payment of money may be impressed upon a paying-in slip or cheque.

CLOSING AN ACCOUNT. The voucher closing an account is, in some banks, pasted in the current account ledger at the account itself.

Where a customer calls to withdraw his balance, it is desirable that the cheque should contain, after the amount, such words as "being the balance of my account with interest to date."

A customer wishing to transfer his account to another town and not being aware of the amount of interest which is due to him, may send the banker a cheque filled up, e.g. "Pay the X. & Y. Bank, Ltd., Leeds, the balance of my account Two hundred and fifty pounds with interest due upon the account to date."

"£   ", leaving the banker to supply the figures.

When an account has to be transferred from one branch to another of the same bank, it is advisable (though not strictly necessary) that a cheque should be signed.

Before paying the balance of an account to a customer, the banker will, of course, ascertain the amount of any outstanding cheques there may be and reserve that sum in the account to meet them. If a cheque is presented which has not been provided for in this way, the banker can return it unpaid, marked "account closed."

Where a customer closes his account, the banker cannot compel him to take up any bills which there may be under discount at the time of closing.

CLOSING PRICES. The prices for stocks and shares which are quoted on a Stock Exchange at the close of business.

CLUBS. (See SOCIETIES.)

CODICIL. A supplement to a will, by which a testator is able to add to what is contained in the will or to make any alteration which he may desire.

A codicil must be dated and signed by the testator and attested by two witnesses in the same manner as a will. (See WILL.)

COGNOVIT ACTIONEM. (Latin, He has recognised the action.) A written acknowledgment by a debtor admitting his liability in an action, and giving authority to his creditor to take the necessary steps to obtain judgment against him. A cognovit is usually given by a debtor in consideration of further time being given for payment. (See WARRANT OF ATTORNEY.)

COINAGE, COINS. Many substances have been used in different countries as money, but a metal of some kind has been found to be the most suitable in all respects, and of all metals gold and silver have been selected as the best fitted to act as a coinage. The properties which should be possessed by the material of which coins are made are enumerated by Professor W. S. Jevons in the order of their importance: (1) Utility and value; (2) portability; (3) indestructibility; (4) homogeneity (that is, all parts of the same quality); (5) divisibility; (6) stability of value; (7) cognisability (that is, easily recognised).

The early records of the use of metal as money show that the metal was weighed. The inconvenience, however, of having to use scales and weights on every occasion when the metal was to be exchanged, led to the invention of coins. The metal, or bullion, was divided into small pieces, each portion or coin being of a certain weight. In the course of time a public stamp was placed upon each coin, so that anyone might recognise it as having a definite weight, and know that the metal so stamped was also of a certain quality. The coinage of Great Britain is of three metals, gold, silver and copper, or rather bronze. Gold is the standard measure of value. Anyone can take gold bullion, of the requisite degree of fineness, to the Bank of England and have it exchanged for bank notes at the rate of £3 17*s.* 9*d.* per ounce of standard gold. The coinage of silver and copper, however, remains in the hands of the Government, and the public cannot take silver and copper to the Bank and demand coins for it. Gold coins issued from the Australian mints at Sydney, Melbourne, and Perth are legal tender. The coins which may be issued from the mint in London are shown in the following table, being the first Schedule to the Coinage Act, allowing for the corrections made by the Act of 1891 :—

FIRST SCHEDULE TO THE COINAGE ACT.

Denomination of Coin.	Standard Weight.		Least Current Weight.		Standard Fineness.	Remedy Allowa		
						Weight per piece.		Millesimal Fineness.
	Imperial Weight. Grains.	Metric Weight. Grams.	Imperial Weight. Grains.	Metric Weight. Grams.		Imperial Grams.	Metric Grams.	
Gold—								
Five Pound	616·37239	39·94028	612·50000	39·68935	Eleven-twelfths fine gold, one-twelfth alloy; or millesimal fineness 916·6	1·00	·06479	2
Two Pound	246·54895	15·97611	245·00000	15·87574		·40	·02592	
Sovereign	123·27447	7·98805	122·50000	7·93787		·20	·01296	
Half Sovereign	61·63723	3·99402	61·12500	3·96083		·15	·00972	
Silver—								
Crown	436·36363	28·27590			Thirty-seven-fortieths fine silver, three-fortieths alloy; or millesimal fineness 925.	2·000	·1296	4
Half crown	218·18181	14·13795				1·264	·0788	
Florin	174·54545	11·31036				·997	·0646	
Shilling	87·27272	5·65518				·578	·0375	
Sixpence	43·63636	2·82759				·346	·0224	
Groat or Fourpence	29·09090	1·88506				·262	·0170	
Threepence	21·81818	1·41379				·212	·0138	
Twopence	14·54545	·94253				·144	·0093	
Penny	7·27272	·47126				·087	·0056	
Bronze—								
Penny	145·83333	9·44984			Mixed metal, copper, tin, and zinc.	2·91666	·18899	none
Halfpenny	87·50000	5·66990				1·75000	·11339	
Farthing	43·75000	2·83495				·87500	·05669	

As the double florin of the value of four shillings is no longer coined, no reference has been made to it in the above table.

The weight and fineness of the coins specified in this Schedule are according to what is provided by the Act fifty-six George the Third, chapter sixty-eight, that the gold coin of the United Kingdom of Great Britain and Ireland should hold such weight and fineness as were prescribed in the then existing Mint indenture; that is to say, that there should be nine hundred and thirty-four sovereigns and one ten-shilling piece contained in twenty pounds weight troy of standard gold, of the fineness at the trial of the same of twenty-two carats of fine gold and two carats of alloy in the pound weight troy; and further, as regards silver coin, that there should be sixty-six shillings in every pound troy of standard silver of the fineness of eleven ounces two pennyweights of fine silver and eighteen pennyweights of alloy in every pound weight troy.

Gold and silver in a pure state are too soft to be used for the purpose of coins, and they are, therefore, mixed with another metal, called an alloy, in order to harden them. Fine gold is the term used for gold which is absolutely pure. Standard gold is pure gold mingled with alloy according to the legal standard. The column, in the above Schedule, headed "standard fineness" shows the proportion of alloy in the gold and silver coins. The "standard weight" is also shown and the "least current weight" of gold coins. When a gold coin has been in circulation for some time, it becomes worn and consequently reduced in weight. When the weight of a coin falls below the "least current weight," it ceases to be legal tender, but that fact does not prevent light gold coins from passing freely in circulation, as people do not, as a rule, pay much attention to the weight of a coin so long as the government stamp is not entirely worn off. The last columns in the Schedule show the "remedy allowance," that is a remedy (or variation from the standard weight and fineness specified in the Schedule) which is allowed, not exceeding the amount specified in that Schedule. The allowance is necessary because of the difficulty in making coins absolutely according to the standard weights and fineness.

Silver coins continue legally current, irrespective of their weights, until they are called in by proclamation.

Pre-Victorian gold coins are not now current. Silver coins coined before 1817, and copper coins before 1861, are not now legal tender.

The obverse side of a coin is that which bears the head or more important device; the reverse is the other side.

The milling was introduced on the edges of coins in order to make it more difficult for fraudulent persons to clip the coins.

(See ALLOY, BASE COINS, BRONZE COINS, BULLION, FOREIGN MONEYS, GOLD COINS, GRESHAM'S LAW, LEGAL TENDER, LIGHT GOLD, MAUNDY MONEY, MILLING, MONEY, SILVER COINS, STERLING.)

COLLATERAL SECURITY. Literally a security which runs parallel or side by side with another security.

The word "collateral" is sometimes used when speaking of a secondary security, to distinguish it from the principal or primary security. It is also used with the meaning, as in the Stamp Act, 1891, of additional security. It is commonly used when referring to a security lodged by some person other than the debtor, to distinguish it from the debtor's own security. It does not necessarily mean that the banker must resort to the one security before the other. In the event of a debtor's bankruptcy, any security deposited by him must be realised, or the value estimated, and the amount deducted from the debt. A claim can then be made upon the debtor's estate for the difference. Before dealing with the bankrupt's security, the banker should communicate with the trustee. If, however, the banker holds security from some person other than the debtor, he can claim upon the estate for the full amount owing by the debtor, and, after receiving his dividend from the estate, can fall back upon the collateral security for the deficiency. Where collateral security is realised before the bankrupt's estate is settled, the amount should be kept in a separate account, distinct from the debtor's account.

If a partner deposit his own private securities as cover for the partnership account, they are collateral, and the banker can, in the event of the failure of the firm, prove for the full amount owing, obtain the dividend and then resort to the private partner's security. There is a danger, however, that the private security may prove to be partnership property.

A guarantee is a collateral security. (See GUARANTEE.)

Upon receipt of notice of the death of the person who has given security for another, a banker should at once stop the debtor's account and arrange for a fresh one to be opened for all further transactions. This prevents payments to credit of the account going in reduction of the liability of the person who gave the security. The new account should, of course, be kept in credit pending a fresh arrangement. (See TITLE DEEDS.)

COLLECTING BANKER. The position of a collecting banker when he collects a cheque for a customer or for a stranger, either with a forged indorsement or a defective title, and when he cashes a cheque to a customer or a stranger under the same conditions, is indicated below.

To gain the protection of Section 82 of the Bills of Exchange Act, 1882, the banker must act in good faith and without negligence, and the protection is only as against the true owner. (See CROSSED CHEQUE, where reference is also made to the Act of 1906, which extends Section 82 of the Bills of Exchange Act.)

	COLLECTED.				CASHED.			
	For Customer.		For Stranger.		For Customer.		For Stranger.	
	Forged Indorsement.	Stolen, Indorsement Right or Bearer Cheque.	Forged Indorsement.	Stolen, Indorsement Right or Bearer Cheque.	Forged Indorsement.	Stolen, Indorsement Right or Bearer Cheque.	Forged Indorsement.	Stolen, Indorsement Right or Bearer Cheque.
Uncrossed cheque on another bank.	Liable to true owner.	Liable to true owner.	Liable to true owner.	Liable to true owner.	Liable to true owner.	Not liable to true owner, as banker is a holder in due course.	Liable to true owner.	Not liable to true owner, as banker is a holder in due course.
Crossed cheque on another bank.	Not liable to true owner. Protected by Section 82.	Not liable to true owner. Protected by Section 82.	Ditto.	Ditto.	Ditto.	Ditto.	Ditto.	Ditto.
Crossed cheque "not negotiable" on another bank.	Ditto.	Ditto	Ditto.	Ditto.	Ditto.	Liable to true owner.	Ditto.	Liable to true owner

Apart from the question of a forged indorsement or a defective title, the collecting banker has to remember that when he credits a customer's account with a cheque on another bank, or gives cash for it, the cheque may be returned to him dishonoured or because payment has been stopped by the drawer.

When a country banker receives from his customer a cheque drawn upon a banker in another town, it is customary for the cheque to be remitted to London for collection on the same day that it is paid to credit. But it has been held that a banker is not bound to send it forward for collection on the day of receipt, and that it may be held until the following day.

If the cheque is for a large amount or by a doubtful drawer, the collecting banker usually remits it direct to the banker on whom it is drawn, in urgent cases enclosing a stamped telegraph form for immediate advice as to fate.

Cheques are often crossed "account payee" or "account John Jones." Such words are not provided for in the Bills of Exchange Act, 1882, but a collecting banker would, no doubt, be considered negligent if he placed a cheque so crossed to any account other than that indicated in the crossing. It is desirable that all cheques paid to credit should be indorsed by customers.

In the case of a cheque payable on condition of a receipt being signed, it should be collected only for the payee, as the document is not considered to be transferable. (See RECEIPT ON CHEQUE.)

COLONIAL REGISTER. A branch register of members of a company resident in a colony. The Companies (Consolidation) Act, 1908, provides as follows :—

"*Power for Company to keep Colonial Register.*

"Section 34. (1) A company having a share capital, whose objects comprise the transaction of business in a colony, may, if so authorised by its articles, cause to be kept in any colony in which it transacts business a branch register of members resident in that colony (in this Act called a colonial register).

"(2) The company shall give to the registrar of companies notice of the situation of the office where any colonial register is kept, and of any change in its situation, and of the discontinuance of the office in the event of its being discontinued.

"(3) For the purpose of the provisions of this Act relating to colonial registers the term 'colony' includes British India and the Commonwealth of Australia.

Regulations as to Colonial Register.

"35. (1) A colonial register shall be deemed to be part of the company's register of members (in this and the next following Section called the principal register).

"(2) It shall be kept in the same manner in which the principal register is by this Act required to be kept, except that the advertisement before closing the register shall be inserted in some newspaper circulating in the district wherein the colonial register is kept, and that any competent court in the colony may exercise the same jurisdiction of rectifying the register as is under this Act exerciseable by the High Court, and that the offences of refusing inspection or copies of a colonial register, and of authorising or permitting the refusal may be prosecuted summarily before any tribunal in the colony having summary criminal jurisdiction.

"(3) The company shall transmit to its registered office a copy of every entry in its colonial register as soon as may be after the entry is made; and shall cause to be kept at its registered office, duly entered up from time to time, a duplicate of its colonial register, and the duplicate shall, for all the purposes of this Act, be deemed to be part of the principal register.

"(4) Subject to the provisions of this Section with respect to the duplicate register, the shares registered in a colonial register shall be distinguished from the shares registered in the principal register, and no transaction with respect to any shares registered in a colonial register shall, during the continuance of that registration, be registered in any other register.

"(5) The company may discontinue to keep any colonial register, and thereupon all entries in that register shall be transferred to some other colonial register kept by the company in the same colony, or to the principal register.

"(6) Subject to the provisions of this Act, any company may, by its articles, make such provisons as it may think fit respecting the keeping of colonial registers.

"*Stamp Duties in case of Shares registered in Colonial Registers.*

"36. In relation to stamp duties the following provisions shall have effect :—

"(*a*) An instrument of transfer of a share registered in a colonial register shall be deemed to be a transfer of property situate out of the United Kingdom, and, unless executed in any part of the United Kingdom, shall be exempt from British stamp duty ,

"(*b*) On the death of a member registered in a colonial register, the shares of the deceased member shall, if he died domiciled in the United Kingdom, but not otherwise, be deemed, so far as relates to British duties, to be part of his estate and effects situate in the United Kingdom for or in respect of which probate or letters of administration is or are to be granted, or whereof an inventory is to be exhibited and recorded, in like manner as if he were registered in the principal register."

COMMANDITE PARTNERSHIP. COMMANDITE, SOCIÉTÉ EN. In France, a form of partnership where some of the partners merely supply part of the capital, and do not take any part in the management of the business. Such partners are called *commanditaires* and are liable for losses only to the extent of the sums which they have contributed.

For the English equivalent, see LIMITED PARTNERSHIP.

COMMISSION. Commisson is the charge made by a banker for services rendered to a customer. The services rendered may be very considerable, for a current account customer may pay in to his credit cheques drawn upon towns all over the British Islands, which it is the duty of the banker to collect ; and the customer may also make payments in any part of the country by means of cheques drawn upon his account.

In order that a banker may carry out effectively these two operations, arrangements must be made with other bankers, with agents in London or by a head office in London. To recoup himself for the expense of such arrangements and to allow a recompense for the trouble and services, a commission is charged by many bankers. In some banks, in lieu of commission, the customer has to maintain a certain credit balance upon which no interest is allowed.

The Courts have held that a banker is entitled to charge commission for discounting bills and for accepting bills.

COMMISSION in the nature of a power of attorney in Scotland. As to the stamp duty, see LETTER OR POWER OF ATTORNEY.

COMMISSIONS TO UNDERWRITERS. (See UNDERWRITING.)

COMMITTEE, LUNACY. Where a person is found by inquisition—that is, by a legal inquiry—to be insane and incapable of managing his affairs, the person who is appointed to look after his interests is called a "committee." Where the committee consists of several persons, they should all join in signing cheques. (See LUNATIC.)

COMMITTEE OF INSPECTION. The persons appointed by the creditors to superintend the administration of a bankrupt's property by the trustee. (See TRUSTEE IN BANKRUPTCY.)

The provisions of the Bankruptcy Act, 1883, are as follow :—

"Section 22. (1) The creditors, qualified to vote, may at their first or any subsequent meeting, by resolution, appoint from among the creditors, or the holders of general proxies or general powers of attorney from such creditors, a committee of inspection for the purpose of superintending the administration of the bankrupt's property by the trustee. The committee of inspection shall consist of not more than five nor less than three persons.

"(2) The committee of inspection shall meet at such times as they shall from time to time appoint, and failing such appointment, at least once a month ; and the trustee or any member of the committee may also call a meeting of the committee as and when he thinks necessary.

(3) The committee may act by a majority of their members present at a meeting, but shall not act unless a majority of the committee are present at the meeting.

(4) Any member of the committee may resign his office by notice in writing signed by him, and delivered to the trustee.

"(5) If a member of the committee becomes bankrupt, or compounds or arranges with his creditors, or is absent from five consecutive meetings of the committee, his office shall thereupon become vacant.

"(6) Any member of the committee may be removed by an ordinary resolution at any meeting of creditors of which seven days' notice has been given, stating the object of the meeting.

"(7) On a vacancy occurring in the office of a member of the committee, the trustee shall forthwith summon a meeting of creditors for the purpose of filling the vacancy, and the meeting may, by resolution, appoint another creditor or other person eligible as above to fill the vacancy.

(8) The continuing members of the committee, provided there be not less than two such continuing members, may act notwithstanding any vacancy in their body; and where the number of members of the committee of inspection is for the time being less than five, the creditors may increase that number so that it do not exceed five.

"(9) If there be no committee of inspection, any act or thing or any direction or permission by this Act authorised or required to be done or given by the committee may be done or given by the Board of Trade on the application of the trustee."

The Board of Trade may, on application by the committee of inspection, authorise the trustee to have an account with a local bank. (See under TRUSTEE IN BANKRUPTCY.)

In connection with the winding up of a company, a committee may be appointed to supervise the liquidation. It shall consist of creditors and contributories of the company in such proportions as may be agreed on by the meetings of creditors and contributories, or as, in case of difference, may be determined by the Court (Section 160, s.s. 1, of the Companies (Consolidation) Act, 1908). Sub-sections 2 to 9, see above, are practically to the same effect as sub-sections 2 to 9 of Section 160 of the Companies Act. (See BANKRUPTCY, COMPANIES.)

COMMITTEES. (See SOCIETIES.)

COMMON LAW. Customs and usages which, by immemorial custom and usage, have become law, are called common law.

The law which is created by Acts of Parliament is called "statute law" (*q.v.*).

Common law is unwritten. Blackstone says that where the old custom of the kingdom is fallen into disuse, or become disputable, Parliament has sometimes by a declaratory statute thought proper to declare what the common law is and ever has been.

COMMON SEAL. (See SEAL.)

COMMON SEAL BOOK. A record of every document which is sealed with the common seal of a bank is preserved in this book. An exact description of each document is given, with the date of sealing and the names of the persons in whose presence it was affixed. Each entry may be numbered, and the number placed upon the relative document.

COMMON STOCK. An American term for what, in this country, is called ordinary stock.

COMPANIES. Before dealing with a joint stock company, a banker should make himself acquainted with its memorandum and articles of association. Every person who does business with a company is bound by the contents of those documents. When an account is opened by a company, it is advisable that the banker should be furnished with a copy of the memorandum and articles, so that he may ascertain exactly what regulations there are in connection with keeping a banking account, and with drawing, accepting and indorsing bills, and what powers of borrowing and of mortgaging the property of the company is given to the directors. A copy of the company's balance sheet should also be obtained. The company should pass a resolution respecting the opening of the account, and embody therein the regulations of the company with respect to the way in which cheques are to be drawn and indorsed, and bills drawn, accepted and indorsed. A copy of the resolution, signed by the chairman or the secretary, and a specimen of the signature of each person who has power to sign, should be furnished to the banker.

If the company has issued debentures or debenture stock, it will be necessary to ascertain in what way they are secured, particularly if the title deeds of the company's property are offered as security, as the company may be restrained from creating any charge in priority to the debentures. (See REGISTRATION OF MORTGAGES AND CHARGES.)

In the case of a new company, it should be noted that it is only from the date of incorporation, as shown in the certificate of incorporation, that the company is capable of exercising the functions of an incorporated company. A contract entered into before that date will not be binding. It may be necessary, in some cases, for the banker to see the certificate of incorporation. (See ARTICLES OF ASSOCIATION.)

The Companies (Consolidation) Act, 1908, enacts :—

"Section 87. (1) A company shall not commence any business or exercise any borrowing powers unless—

"(*a*) shares held subject to the payment of the whole amount thereof in cash have been allotted to an amount not less in the whole than the minimum subscription ; and

"(*b*) every director of the company has paid to the company on each of the shares taken or contracted to be taken by him, and for which he is liable to pay in cash, a proportion equal to the proportion payable on application and allotment on the shares offered for public subscription, or in the case of a company which does not issue a prospectus inviting the public to subscribe for its shares, on the shares payable in cash ; and

"(*c*) there has been filed with the registrar of companies a statutory declaration by the secretary or one of the directors, in the prescribed form, that the aforesaid conditions have been complied with ; and

"(*d*) in the case of a company which does not issue a propectus inviting the public to subscribe for its shares there has been filed with the registrar of companies a statement in lieu of prospectus.

"(2) The registrar of companies shall, on the filing of this statutory declaration, certify that the company is entitled to commence business, and that certificate shall be conclusive evidence that the company is so entitled :

Provided that in the case of a company which does not issue a prospectus inviting the public to subscribe for its shares the registrar shall not give such a certificate unless a statement in lieu of prospectus has been filed with him.

"(3) Any contract made by a company before the date at which it is entitled to commence business shall be provisional only, and shall not be binding on the company until that date, and on that date it shall become binding.

"(4) Nothing in this Section shall prevent the simultaneous offer for subscription or allotment of any shares and debentures or the receipt of any money payable on application for debentures.

"(5) If any company commences business or exercises borrowing powers in contravention of this Section, every person who is responsible for the contravention shall, without prejudice to any other liability, be liable to a fine not exceeding fifty pounds, for every day during which the contravention continues.

"(6) Nothing in this Section shall apply to a private company, or to a company registered before the first day of January nineteen hundred and one, or to a company registered before the first day of July nineteen hundred and eight which does not issue a prospectus inviting the public to subscribe for its shares."

The difference between a company and an ordinary partnership was defined by James, L. J., in *Smith* v. *Anderson* (1880, 15 Ch. D. 247), as follows:—"An ordinary partnership is a partnership composed of definite individuals, bound together by contract between themselves to continue for some joint object, either during pleasure or during a limited time, but the partnership is essentially composed of the persons originally entering into the contract with one another. A company or association, which I take really to be synonymous terms, is an arrangement by which parties intend to have a partnership, which would be constantly changing; that is to say, to have what I may call a succession of partnerships, a partnership to-day consisting of certain members, but to-morrow consisting of some of those members only and some others who have come in. Hence there will be a constant shifting of the partnership, a determination of the old, and the creation of a new partnership, formed with a view and always formed with the intent, so far as the members can by agreement between themselves, of binding the next partnership to take upon itself the assets and debts of the old partnership. This object could not be effected in point of law by any arrangement between the persons themselves, unless the persons contracting with them by a novatio authorised the change; or, unless it was by special provisions in the Acts of Parliament which have given sanction to such arrangements, and to a certain extent, and under certain circumstances, have allowed that to be effected. That is the sole distinction between association and partnership."

In a partnership, each partner is responsible for the debts of the firm, and one partner cannot transfer his interest, or share, without the consent of the other partners.

In a company (that is an *un*incorporated company) the members are liable, like partners, for the company's debts, but each member can transfer his share or shares without consulting the other members.

In an incorporated company, the members form one body and creditors can proceed only against the company itself. In the most important kind of joint-stock company—that is, the company limited by shares—each member is liable only to the extent of the nominal amount of the shares he holds. If the company is unlimited, each member is liable to the company or the liquidator for the debts.

By Section 77 of the Companies (Consolidation) Act, 1908:—

"A bill of exchange or promissory note shall be deemed to have been made, accepted, or indorsed on behalf of a company if made, accepted, or indorsed in the name of, or by or on behalf or on account of, the company by any person acting under its authority."

The different matters relating to companies are referred to under the following headings:—

Allotment.
Annual List of Members of Company.
Arrangement with Creditors.
Articles of Association.
Auditors.
Banking Company.
Blank Transfer.
Borrowing Powers.
Certificate.
Certificate of Incorporation.
Certificate of Registration.
Charitable Companies.
Colonial Register.
Committee of Inspection.
Company limited by Guarantee.
Company limited by Shares.
Company outside the United Kingdom.
Company unlimited.
Contracts.
Contributories.
Court, Powers of, in winding up.
Debenture.
Defunct Company.
Directors.
Dividend.
Fees payable to Registrar of Companies.
Floating Charge.
Forged Transfer.
Founders' Shares.
Investigation of Company's Affairs.
Letter of Allotment.
Limited Partnership.
Liquidator.
Loan Capital.
Meetings.
Memorandum of Association.
Name of Company.
Official Receiver.
Official Seal for use Abroad.
Private Company.
Prospectus.
Proxy.
Public Company.
Quorum.
Receiver.
Reconstruction.
Reduction of Share Capital.
Register of Members of Company.
Register of Mortgages.
Registered Office.
Registrar of Companies.

Registration of Mortgages and Charges.
Reserve Liability.
Resolutions.
Scrip.
Seal.
Share Capital.
Share Warrant.
Special Settlement.
Stannaries.
Stock.
Table A.
Transfer of Shares.
Transmission of Shares.
Underwriting.
Votes.
Winding up.
Winding up by the Court.
Winding up Subject to Supervision of the Court.
Winding up Unregistered Companies.
Winding up Voluntarily.

COMPANIES (CONSOLIDATION) ACT, 1908. (8 Edw. 7, c. 69.) An Act to consolidate the Companies Act, 1862, and the Acts amending it. It came into force on April 1, 1909.

References to the various subjects dealt with in the Act will be found under the heading Companies.

COMPANY LIMITED BY GUARANTEE. A company where the liability of its members is limited, by the memorandum of association, to such amount as the members may respectively thereby undertake to contribute to the assets of the company, in the event of its being wound up.

The word "Limited" must be the last word in the name of the company.

Section 21 of the Companies (Consolidation) Act, 1908, provides :—

"(1) In the case of a company limited by guarantee and not having a share capital, and registered on or after the first day of January, nineteen hundred and one, every provision in the memorandum or articles or in any resolution of the company purporting to give any person a right to participate in the divisible profits of the company otherwise than as a member shall be void.

"(2) For the purpose of the provisions of this Act relating to the memorandum of a company limited by guarantee and of this Section, every provision in the memorandum or articles, or in any resolution, of any company limited by guarantee and registered on or after the first day of January, nineteen hundred and one, purporting to divide the undertaking of the company into shares or interests shall be treated as a provision for a share capital, notwithstanding that the nominal amount or number of the shares or interests is not specified thereby." (See Articles of Association, Companies, Memorandum of Association, Name of Company.)

COMPANY LIMITED BY SHARES. A company where the liability of its members is limited by the memorandum of association to the amount, if any, unpaid on the shares respectively held by them.

The word "Limited" must be the last word in the name of the company. A contraction of the word should not be used officially.

A limited company formed for promoting commerce, art, science, religion, charity or other useful object, where any profits or income are to be used in promoting its objects, may be licensed by the Board of Trade as a company with limited liability, without the addition of the word "Limited" to its name. (See Charitable Companies.)

Every limited company must have its name painted or affixed on the outside of every place where its business is carried on, and engraven on its seal, and mentioned in legible characters in all notices and official publications of the company, and in all bills of exchange, promissory notes, indorsements, cheques, invoices, receipts, etc. (See Name of Company.)

By Section 282 of the Companies (Consolidation) Act, 1908 :—

"If any person or persons trade or carry on business under any name or title of which 'Limited' is the last word, that person or those persons shall, unless duly incorporated with limited liability, be liable to a fine not exceeding five pounds for every day upon which that name or title has been used."

The number of members of a limited company should not fall below seven ; if it does, Section 115 enacts :—

"If at any time the number of members of a company is reduced, in the case of a private company, below two, or, in the case of any other company, below seven, and it carries on business for more than six months while the number is so reduced, every person who is a member of the company during the time that it so carries on business after those six months, and is cognisant of the fact that it is carrying on business with fewer than two members, or seven members, as the case may be, shall be severally liable for the payment of the whole debts of the company contracted during that time, and may be sued for the same, without joinder in the action of any other member."

In a limited company the liability of directors or managers may, if so provided by the memorandum, be unlimited (Section 60).

As a rule the memorandum of association includes a power to borrow money and mortgage the landed property, but before making an advance the banker should examine that document and the articles of association, to ascertain exactly what the powers of the company are. If no express power is taken in the memorandum of association, in the case of an ordinary trading company the power to borrow and mortgage for ordinary business purposes is implied. If the memorandum includes a power to borrow up to a certain fixed amount, the banker must be careful not to exceed that amount. For if a company borrows in excess of its powers, the security will not be binding on the company. The directors, however, may be held personally liable, and the money may, probably, be recovered in so far as it was used by the company to pay its debts.

If a company has power to borrow, and the advance required will not exceed any fixed limit of borrowing that there may be, the banker will be safe in accepting the company's deeds with a memorandum signed by the directors. If the articles of association provide that certain regulations are to be observed by the directors when mortgaging the company's property, the banker may assume that all the regulations and formalities have been complied with; he is not expected, nor is he able, to examine into the "indoor working" of a company. (See REGISTRATION OF MORTGAGES and CHARGES.) The directors, however, may be expressly prohibited from mortgaging the property. (See ARTICLES OF ASSOCIATION, COMPANIES. MEMORANDUM OF ASSOCIATION.

COMPANY OUTSIDE THE UNITED KINGDOM. The Companies (Consolidation) Act, 1908, makes special provisions with respect to companies incorporated outside the United Kingdom, but with a place of business established within the United Kingdom. These provisions will apply to cases of companies which previously have registered in the Channel Islands in order to avoid the company laws in force in this country. Section 274 is as follows :—

"(1) Every company incorporated outside the United Kingdom which establishes a place of business within the United Kingdom shall within one month from the establishment of the place of business file with the registrar of companies—

"(*a*) a certified copy of the charter, statutes, or memorandum and articles of the company, or other instrument constituting or defining the constitution of the company, and, if the instrument is not written in the English language, a certified translation thereof ;

"(*b*) a list of the directors of the company ;

"(*c*) the names and addresses of some one or more persons resident in the United Kingdom authorised to accept on behalf of the company service of process and any notices required to be served on the company ;

and, in the event of any alteration being made in any such instrument or in the directors or in the names or addresses of any such persons as aforesaid, the company shall within the prescribed time file with the registrar a notice of the alteration.

"(2) Any process or notice required to be served on the company shall be sufficiently served if addressed to any person whose name has been so filed as aforesaid and left at or sent by post to the address which has been so filed.

"(3) Every company to which this Section applies shall in every year file with the registrar such a statement in the form of a balance sheet as would, if it were a company formed and registered under this Act and having a share capital, be required under this Act to be included in the annual summary.

"(4) Every company to which this Section applies, and which uses the word

'Limited' as part of its name, shall—

"(*a*) in every prospectus inviting subscriptions for its shares or debentures in the United Kingdom state the country in which the company is incorporated ; and

"(*b*) conspicuously exhibit on every place where it carries on business in the United Kingdom the name of the company and the country in which the company is incorporated ; and

"(*c*) have the name of the company and of the country in which the company is incorporated mentioned in legible characters in all bill-heads and letter paper, and in all notices, advertisements, and other official publications of the company." (See COMPANIES.)

COMPANY, UNLIMITED. That is, a company not having any limit to the liability of its members for the debts of the company.

An unlimited company may register under the Companies (Consolidation) Act, 1908, as limited, but such registration shall not affect any liabilities incurred before the registration.

Section 58 of the above Act is as follows :—

"An unlimited company having a share capital may, by its resolution for registration as a limited company in pursuance of this Act, do either or both of the following things, namely :—

"(*a*) Increase the nominal amount of its share capital by increasing the nominal amount of each of its shares, but subject to the condition that no part of the increased capital shall be capable of being called up except in the event and for the purposes of the company being wound up ;

"(*b*) Provide that a specified portion of its uncalled share capital shall not be capable of being called up except in the event and for the purposes of the company being wound up."

Section 251 specially provides that a bank of issue registered as a limited company shall not be entitled to limited liability in respect of its notes, and the members shall be liable as if it had been registered as unlimited. (See ARTICLES OF ASSOCIATION, BANKING COMPANY, COMPANIES, MEMORANDUM OF ASSOCIATION.)

COMPENSATING ERRORS. (See BALANCE OF ERRORS.)

COMPENSATING INTEREST. Where a customer has two accounts, one in credit and one overdrawn, and the former is regarded as a set off to the latter, interest is allowed in the credit account to compensate for the interest charged on the overdraft, so long as the overdraft does not exceed the credit balance.

COMPOSITION. Where an English bank authorised to issue its own notes, issues them under licence on unstamped paper, a composition, in lieu of stamp duty, of 3*s*. 6*d*. for each £100, or fraction thereof, of the notes in circulation, is payable half-yearly. The composition in Ireland is also 3*s*. 6*d*. per £100 ; but in Scotland it is at the rate of 4*s*. 2*d*. for each £100.

By 9 Geo. IV, c. 23, Section 7, each half-year within fourteen days after the first day of January and the first day of July in every year, an account verified upon oath (before a justice of the peace or a commissioner to administer oaths in chancery) must be sent to the commissioners of the amount of all unstamped promissory notes and bills of exchange in circulation on each Saturday in the preceding half year, together with the average amount of such notes and bills in circulation. The affidavit may be by a "cashier, accountant, or chief clerk," and the manager of a bank has been held to be a chief clerk within the meaning of the Act. The composition for stamp duty must be paid on the average amount as shown by that return. Bankers licensed to issue unstamped notes or bills must give security by bond for the due performance of the various conditions attaching to their issue. (See BANK NOTES, LICENCE, NOTE RETURN.)

COMPOSITION (TRANSFERS, SHARES, ETC.). The Stamp Act, 1891, provides as follows :—

Composition for certain Stamp Duties.

"Section 114. (1) By way of composition for stamp duty chargeable on transfers of any stock of the Government of Canada which may be inscribed in books kept in the United Kingdom or of any Colonial stock to which the Colonial Stock Act, 1877, applies, the Government of Canada or other colony, as the case may be, shall pay to the Commissioners a sum as stamp duty calculated at the rate of one shilling and threepence for every ten pounds, and any fraction of ten pounds of the nominal amount of such stock inscribed in the name of each and every stockholder at the date of the composition—

With the addition—

"(a) when the period within which the stock is to be redeemed or paid off, or during which annual or other payments in respect of the redemption or payment off of the same are required to be made, exceeds sixty years, but does not exceed one hundred years from that date, of threepence for every such ten pounds or fraction of ten pounds; or

"(b) when the said period exceeds one hundred years, or no period is fixed for such redemption or payment off, or no such annual or other payments are required to be made, of sixpence for every such ten pounds or fraction of ten pounds;

and in consideration of the payment transfers of the stock in respect of which the composition has been paid shall be exempt from stamp duty.

(2) All sums certified by the Commissioners to have been received by way of composition for stamp duty on transfers of stock under this Section shall be paid over to the National Debt Commissioners, and shall be applied by them towards the reduction of the National Debt in such manner as the Treasury from time to time direct."

By the Finance Act, 1894 :—

"Section 39. The provisions contained in Section 114 of the Stamp Act, 1891, in reference to the composition for stamp duty chargeable on transfers of certain stocks, shall extend to the stock of any foreign state or government which is inscribed in the books of the Bank of England."

By the Finance Act, 1898 :—

"Section 5. The provisions contained in Section 114 of the Stamp Act, 1891, in reference to the composition for stamp duty chargeable on transfers of certain colonial stocks, shall extend to the stock of any British protectorate or protected state to which protectorate or state a Secretary of State applies the Colonial Stock Acts, 1877 and 1892, and he is hereby authorised so to apply the said Acts with the necessary modifications."

The Stamp Act, 1891, further provides :—

Composition for Stamp Duty by County Councils, etc.

"Section 115. (1) Any county council or corporation or company may enter into an agreement with the Commissioners, if the Commissioners in their discretion think proper for the delivery of an account showing the nominal amount of all the stock and funded debt of such county council, corporation, or company or the amount thereof in respect of which payment has been made, if the whole sums payable in respect thereof have not been paid; and after such agreement has been entered into the account shall be immediately delivered to the Commissioners, and a like account shall be delivered half-yearly in each year.

"(3) There shall be charged by way of composition upon the aggregate amount appearing on every half-yearly account delivered to the Commissioners for every one hundred pounds and any fraction of one hundred pounds of such amount the duty of sixpence as a stamp duty, and so soon as any account has been delivered, and payment of the duty hereby imposed has been made, transfers of any stock or funded debt included in such account, and also any share warrants or stock certificates relating to such stock or funded debt, shall be exempt from duty.

"(6) Where an agreement for composition under this Section has been entered into by any county council or corporation or company, such county council or corporation or company shall have power, in addition to any fee exigible upon registration of any transfer of stock, or funded debt, as the case may be, or upon issue of any share warrant, or stock certificate relating thereto, to require payment of an amount not exceeding the amount of duty which would have been chargeable upon the transfer or share warrant or stock certificate if no such agreement had been entered into."

COMPOSITION WITH CREDITORS. Where a debtor is unable to pay his creditors, he may, legally, call his creditors together and make an arrangement with them, by which he may obtain relief from his debts, and one of the usual methods by which this is done is to offer to pay a composition; that is, to pay so much in the pound in full discharge of the debts due to the creditors. The composition is usually payable in a number of instalments, upon specified dates, and is guaranteed by sureties. In some cases promissory notes are given for the various instalments, and are made payable at the various dates on which the instalments are due.

If the arrangement is agreed to by the creditors in a deed or instrument, called a deed of arrangement, it must be registered within seven days, otherwise it is void. (See DEED OF ARRANGEMENT.)

An arrangement of this kind between a debtor and his creditors is quite independent of proceedings under the Bankruptcy Acts, but, if he fails to pay the agreed instalments, the arrangement does not prevent proceedings in bankruptcy being subsequently taken. In "The Laws of England," edited by the Right Hon. the Earl of Halsbury, the following is given as the effect of a debtor failing to pay an instalment: "If the effect of the arrangement is that the creditors accept the payment of the composition in discharge of their debts, then usually a failure by the debtor to comply with his obligation will entitle the creditors to sue him for the whole of the balance of their debts. But if the effect of the arrangement is that the creditors accept the promise of the debtor with or without a surety in satisfaction of their debts, on default by the debtor the creditors can only sue for the balance of the amount of the composition."

Where a customer makes an arrangement with his creditors, a banker should, if necessary, seek legal advice as to whether or not an act of bankruptcy has been committed (see ACTS OF BANKRUPTCY), because if it has, the account must be stopped at once. (See ASSIGNMENT FOR BENEFIT OF CREDITORS, BANKRUPTCY.)

COMPOSITIONS (BANKRUPTCY ACT). When a receiving order has been made against a debtor, he must, within a certain time, submit a statement of his affairs to the official receiver. (See RECEIVING ORDER.) If the debtor wishes to submit to his creditors a proposal for a composition—that is, a payment of so much in the pound—or for a scheme of arrangement, the Bankruptcy Act, 1890, provides as follows:—

"Section 3. (1) Where a debtor intends to make a proposal for a composition in satisfaction of his debts, or a proposal for a scheme of arrangement of his affairs, he shall, within four days of submitting his statement of affairs, or within such time thereafter as the official receiver may fix, lodge with the official receiver a proposal in writing, signed by him, embodying the terms of the composition or scheme which he is desirous of submitting for the consideration of his creditors, and setting out particulars of any sureties or securities proposed.

"(2) In such case the official receiver shall hold a meeting of creditors, before the public examination of the debtor is concluded, and send to each creditor, before the meeting, a copy of the debtor's proposal with a report thereon; and if at that meeting a majority in number and three-fourths in value of all the creditors who have proved resolve to accept the proposal, the same shall be deemed to be duly accepted by the creditors, and when approved by the court shall be binding on all the creditors."

The Court has power to approve or to refuse to approve the proposal (s.s. 10).

If the debtor's proposal is accepted by the creditors, the receiving order is discharged by the Court. If a trustee is appointed to carry out the scheme, the official receiver hands the debtor's property to him, but if no trustee is appointed the official receiver acts as trustee.

If the proposal is not accepted within fourteen days after the conclusion of the debtor's examination, the Court shall adjudge the debtor bankrupt. (See ADJUDICATION OF BANKRUPTCY.)

A composition or scheme of arrangement may be accepted by the creditors, if they think fit, at any time after the debtor is adjudicated bankrupt, and the Court may annul the bankruptcy. (Section 23, s.s. 1, 2.)

If default is made in payment of an instalment, the Court may adjudge the debtor bankrupt and annul the composition or scheme, but without prejudice to the validity of any sale, disposition, or payment duly made in pursuance of the composition or scheme. (Section 23, s.s. 3.)

Debts are proved in the same way as in the case of bankruptcy. (See BANKRUPTCY, PROOF OF DEBTS.)

COMPOUND INTEREST. Compound interest is interest upon interest which is not paid. Upon current accounts a banker calculates the interest half-yearly and adds it to the principal, when it becomes part of the principal, and upon that amount interest is forthwith charged or allowed as the case may be.

A ready way of ascertaining approximately the number of years in which a sum will double itself at compound interest, is to divide seventy by the rate per cent. (See INTEREST.)

COMPOUNDING A FELONY. If an official commits a felony, e.g., an embezzlement, and someone provides the bank with money or securities to cover the defalcations, in order to prevent the institution of a prosecution, this is called compounding a felony.

In *Whitmore* v. *Fairley* (1880, 29 W.R. 825), Lush, L. J., in the course of his judgment, said :—"It is as old as the law itself that compounding a felony is not merely an illegal, but a criminal act. It follows that every agreement by a prosecutor to forego a prosecution, in consideration of a benefit to himself, is an illegal agreement which the law will not sanction. A person who is robbed cannot be compelled to prosecute. No doubt it is his duty to society to do so, but it is an imperfect obligation. If, however, he does prosecute, he assumes the office of a public prosecutor, and prosecutes on behalf of the public. If he enters into a bargain not to prosecute, that is just as much void as if it was made after prosecution commenced. This is not confined to felony. The law is just the same with regard to cases of misdemeanour."

COMPOUNDING WITH CREDITORS. (See COMPOSITION WITH CREDITORS.)

COMPULSORY LIQUIDATION. (See WINDING UP BY THE COURT.)

COMPUTING A BILL. Calculating the date upon which the bill falls due to be paid.

CONDITIONAL INDORSEMENT. Where a condition is attached to an indorser's signature on a bill of exchange, the condition may be disregarded by the paying banker, and payment to the indorsee is valid whether the condition has been fulfilled or not. (See INDORSEMENT.)

CONDITIONAL SURRENDER. A surrender of copyhold property into the hands of the lord of the manor for the benefit of a mortgagee, the condition being that when the mortgage money has been repaid, the surrender must be cancelled by satisfaction being entered on the court rolls.

For the stamp duty see MORTGAGE and Section 87, s.s. 4 and 5, of the Stamp Act, 1891, quoted thereunder.

The following is an example of a conditional surrender and admittance, though a mortgagee is usually satisfied by the conditional surrender being entered on the court rolls, without seeking admittance :—

Manor of } The Special Court Baron and Customary Court of
Lord of the said Manor holden at for the said Manor on day of 19
Before , Steward.

To this Court came A. B. and did surrender into the hands of the Lord of the said Manor, All that Cottage, etc., of the Yearly Copyhold Rent of To the use and behoof of C. D., his heirs and assigns for ever according to the Custom of the said Manor Upon the Condition that if the said A. B., his heirs, executors, administrators or assigns shall on the day of next ensuing pay or cause to be paid unto the said C. D., his executors, administrators or assigns the Sum of £ and interest for the same at the rate of per centum per annum And also all Customary outgoings whatsoever (whether for fines, fees of admission, acknowledgment of satisfaction, licence to demise,

	£ s. d.
Rent ..	
Fine ..	

heriots, reliefs, suits and services or the value thereof or otherwise howsoever) which the said C. D., his executors, administrators or assigns shall render or pay in respect of the said Copyhold hereditaments with interest for the same at the rate aforesaid without deduction then this Surrender to be void. And thereupon to the same Court came C. D. and took of the Lord of the said Manor by the hands of his Steward the Cottages etc. aforesaid with the appurtenances To hold the same to him his heirs and assigns for ever according to the Custom of the said Manor Upon the Condition aforesaid Paying the Rents and performing the services of Right due and accustomed and having paid the Lord for his Fine as in the margin and done his fealty is thereupon admitted tenant according to the statute.

, Steward.

(See COPYHOLD.)

CONFIDENTIAL INQUIRIES. (See BANKER'S OPINION.)

CONFIRMATION CHEQUE. A cheque given by a customer to confirm a debit, which, for one reason or another, has been passed to his account pending receipt of the cheque.

CONFIRMATION OF BALANCE. Many banks send out to each current account customer (or to a selected number), either yearly, or half-yearly, a form showing the balance of the customer's account, with a request that the form, if correct, be signed by the customer and returned to the bank. The balance on that form should be the same as the balance shown by the pass-book, and before a customer signs it, he ought to scrutinise the entries in the pass-book to see that they are in agreement with his own records, and then compare the balance of the pass-book with that stated on the form.

In some of the banks in Scotland, confirmations are signed in the ledgers.

CONSIDERATION. Consideration has been defined as "some right, interest, profit, or benefit, accruing to one party, or some forbearance, detriment, loss, or responsibility given, suffered, or undertaken by the other."

Upon a sale of property, the purchase price is the consideration, and that amount is inserted in the deed of conveyance, and the stamp duty, *ad valorem*, calculated thereon.

In a deed of gift, as, for example, where a property is the subject of a gift from, say, a father to his son, the consideration may be "natural love and affection." With regard to the stamp duty on gifts *inter vivos*, the Finance (1909-10) Act, Section 74, enacts that any conveyance operating as a voluntary disposition *inter vivos*, shall be chargeable with the same duty as if it were a conveyance on a sale, with the substitution of the value of the property conveyed for the amount of the consideration. (See CONVEYANCE.)

The consideration named in a transfer, upon a sale of stock or shares, may differ from the amount received by the original seller, owing to subsequent sales having taken place. The price paid by the last purchaser is the one inserted in the transfer, and on which stamp duty is paid. The difference is explained in a printed foot-note on transfer forms, and this foot-note justifies a transferor in executing a transfer where the consideration differs from the amount received by him.

In a transfer of shares to a bank or its nominees as security for a loan or advance, the consideration is usually a nominal one, say five or ten shillings; and the same nominal consideration is inserted in a transfer when the shares are being transferred as a gift.

Where shares are specifically left in a will, the consideration in a transfer from the executors to the legatee will be a nominal one; but where a legatee agrees to accept a transfer of certain shares, instead of receiving the cash to which he is entitled, the consideration must be the price agreed upon between the legatee and executors, and the stamp duty will be *ad valorem*.

All deeds prior to the Conveyancing Act, 1881, should have indorsed thereon a receipt for the consideration stated in the body of the deed. Since that date it is sufficient if the receipt is in the body of the deed. It must, however, be an actual receipt and not simply a statement that the money has been paid. (See NOMINAL CONSIDERATION.)

CONSIDERATION FOR BILL OF EXCHANGE. There must be a valuable consideration for a contract not under seal, though it is not necessary that the consideration be stated in writing.

The Bills of Exchange Act, 1882, Section 3, s.s. 4, enacts that a bill is not invalid by reason "that it does not specify the value given, or that any value has been given therefor."

The words "for value received" are very commonly used as the last words in the body of a bill of exchange, but a bill is quite valid without any such words.

The word "sterling" was at one time usually written after the amount, but it is now very rarely met with on inland bills.

By Section 27 :—

"(1) Valuable consideration for a bill may be constituted by—

"(*a*) Any consideration sufficient to support a simple contract ;

"(*b*) An antecedent debt or liability. Such a debt or liability is deemed valuable consideration whether the bill is payable on demand or at a future time."

Where a person signs a bill as drawer, acceptor, or indorser, without receiving value therefor, he is an accommodation party. (See ACCOMMODATION BILL.)

Where a cheque is given as a gift, the receiver cannot sue the giver thereon, because of the absence of consideration.

"Natural love and affection," though a good consideration in a contract under seal, is not sufficient to support a simple contract, as in a bill of exchange. The consideration must have some actual value, though the extent of that value may, in reality, be very small.

Mr. Justice Lush said (in *Currie* v. *Misa*, 1875, L.R. 10 Ex. 162) : "A valuable consideration in the sense of the law, may consist either in some right, interest, profit, or benefit accruing to one party, or some forbearance, detriment, loss, or responsibility given, suffered, or undertaken by the other."

The title of a person who negotiates a bill is defective if he obtained the bill for an illegal consideration (Section 29, s.s. 2).

Where a consideration is affected with fraud or illegality, that would form a good defence against an "immediate party" (see IMMEDIATE PARTIES), but not against a remote party who is a holder in due course, that is, one who took the bill for value, in good faith and without knowledge of any defect in the title. (See HOLDER IN DUE COURSE.)

A bill, or cheque, given for a wagering or gaming debt, cannot be sued upon by a holder who took it with knowledge of the illegal consideration, but a holder in due course, who took it without such knowledge, can sue upon it.

It has also been decided in *Moulis* v. *Owen* (1907, 1 K.B. 746), that even when a cheque is drawn in a foreign country on a banker in this country, for a consideration which is legal in the country where it is drawn, but illegal in this country, the action on the cheque fails. This was a decision of the Court of Appeal, and Lord Justice Fletcher Moulton disagreed with the finding of the other two Lord Justices. (See BILL OF EXCHANGE.)

CONSIGNATION RECEIPT. In Scotland, when property is sold under powers contained in a "bond and disposition in security" (*q.v.*), the creditor who has sold the property must, after satisfying his own claim, place any surplus there may be in a bank upon deposit receipt, called a consignation receipt, in the joint names of the seller and purchaser, for the benefit of the person who is entitled to the surplus.

CONSOLIDATION OF MORTGAGES. Where a person holds several mortgages on different properties, belonging to the same mortgagor, a right to consolidate the mortgages may be given to him by the mortgagor, and he can then refuse to allow one mortgage to be redeemed without the others being also redeemed. If there are two properties, it has been held that the mortgagee has no right to consolidate, unless there has been default with both mortgages.

The right to consolidate must be specially granted in one of the mortgage deeds. That restriction was made by Section 17 of the Conveyancing Act, 1881 :—

"(1) A mortgagor seeking to redeem any one mortgage, shall, by virtue of this Act, be entitled to do so, without paying any money due under any separate mortgage made by him, or by any person through whom he claims, on property other than that comprised in the mortgage which he seeks to redeem.

"(2) This Section applies only if and as far as a contrary intention is not expressed in the mortgage deeds or one of them." (See MORTGAGE.)

CONSOLS. A contraction of "consolidated funds" and "consolidated annuities."

The Government borrowed money at different times and set aside a portion of the revenue to pay the interest or annuity upon each separate loan. The various loans were, in 1752, made uniform and consolidated into one fund, called the Three per cent. Consolidated Annuities, or "3 per cent. Consols."

When Consols are bought, the purchaser obtains a receipt. This receipt, however, is not of any value, the purchaser's title being the entry in the books of the Bank of England. A transfer of consols is effected by the owner attending personally at the Bank of England or by his authorising an attorney to act for him. The interest is due on January 5, April 5, July 5, October 5. Consols are marked ex dividend about four weeks before the interest is due. (See POWER OF ATTORNEY—TRANSFER OF GOVERNMENT STOCK.)

If desired, stockholders can obtain certificates to bearer, with coupons attached for the interest. (See NATIONAL DEBT.)

CONSTAT. The name given to an exemplification under the Great Seal of any letters patent made by His Majesty. (See EXEMPLIFICATION.)

CONSTRUCTIVE NOTICE. (See NOTICE OF MORTGAGE.)

CONTANGO. The contango is the charge made by a stockbroker to a speculator for "carrying over" the stock transaction he has had with him until the next Stock Exchange settlement.

For example, a person buys a certain stock which he does not intend to pay for, hoping that it will rise before the following settlement, in which case he would sell out at once, neither paying nor receiving the price, but only the profit from his broker; the stock, however, contrary to his expectation, may fall instead of rising, and, as the speculator still hopes for improvement, rather than sell out at a loss he arranges with his broker to "carry over" or "continue" the bargain until the next settlement after the present one; for the loan of the money to enable this to be done, the broker makes a charge which is known as "the contango." In the above case the speculator is called a "bull," that is, one who anticipates a rise in the stock dealt in.

The broker for the "bull" borrows the money, at "making up" price, to pay for the stock, and gives the lender the stock, agreeing at the same time to take it back at the next settlement. The lender will probably be a "bear," who requires that particular stock. If, however, there is a scarcity of that stock, a "bear" may be so anxious to secure it that he will pay the "bull" a "backwardation" rate for the loan of the stock instead of the "bull" paying interest for the loan of the money. (See BACKWARDATION, CONTANGO DAY, STOCK EXCHANGE.)

CONTANGO DAY. The first of the three days of a Stock Exchange settlement, being the one on which a broker must know whether a speculator dealing with him intends to complete on the next day but one (pay day) or whether he wishes to have the transaction "carried over" until the following settlement. For mining shares there is an additional contango day, called "mining contango day."

Contango day is also called "making up day" or "continuation day" or "carrying over" day. (See CONTANGO, SETTLING DAYS.)

CONTINGENT ACCOUNT. An account to which amounts may be placed to provide for uncertain liabilities.

CONTINGENT LIABILITY. A liability which is uncertain. For example, if Brown has given a guarantee on behalf of Jones, it forms a contingent liability; if Jones fails, the guarantee will become an actual liability and must be met by Brown. It is necessary, in the event of Brown furnishing his banker with a copy of his balance sheet, that the banker be advised of the existence of the guarantee or of any other liability dependent upon a contingency.

CONTINGENT REMAINDER. (See REMAINDER.)

CONTINUATION DAY. The first of the three days of a Stock Exchange settlement. Also called "Contango Day" (*q.v.*). (See STOCK EXCHANGE.)

CONTRA ENTRY. An entry made upon one side of an account to correct an entry which has been made in error upon the other side.

CONTRACT NOTE (BROKER'S). The note or memorandum which is given by a broker to the person for whom an order to buy or sell certain stocks or shares has been carried out, and which gives particulars of the transaction.

The following is a specimen of a contract note:—

Exchange Buildings
York , 19 .

Bought for
(Subject to the Rules and Regulations of the London Stock Exchange.)

@

Transfer Stamp and Registration . . .
Contract Stamp . .
Brokerage . . . .
Postage . . . . .

£

For Settlement

. Brokers.

Where a purchase or sale is made by order of a banker on behalf of a customer, a note is now usually made on the contract note that the commission is shared with the banker. This is done in view of the "Prevention of Corruption Act, 1906" (*q.v.*).

The Finance (1909–10) Act, 1910, enacts as follows :—

"Section 77. (1) There shall be charged on every contract note as defined by this Section for or relating to the sale or purchase of any stock or marketable security the following stamp duties :—

Where the value of the stock or marketable security—

				£	s.	d.
is	£5 and does	not exceed	£100	0	0	6
exceeds	£100	,,	£500	0	1	0
,,	£500	,,	£1,000	0	2	0
,,	£1,000	,,	£1,500	0	3	0
,,	£1,500	,,	£2,500	0	4	0
,,	£2,500	,,	£5,000	0	6	0
,,	£5,000	,,	£7,500	0	8	0
,,	£7,500	,,	£10,000	0	10	0
,,	£10,000	,,	£12,500	0	12	0
,,	£12,500	,,	£15,000	0	14	0
,,	£15,000	,,	£17,500	0	16	0
,,	£17,500	,,	£20,000	0	18	0
,,	£20,000	. . . . . .	. . .	1	0	0

"(2) Where a contract note is a continuation or carrying over note made for the purpose of continuing or carrying over any transaction for the sale or purchase of stock or marketable securities, the contract note, although it is made in respect of both a sale and purchase, shall be charged with duty under this Section as if it related to one of those transactions only, and, if different rates of duty are chargeable in respect of those transactions, to that one of those transactions which would render the contract note chargeable at the highest rate.

"(3) For the purposes of this Part of this Act, the expression "contract note" means the note sent by a broker or agent to his principal, or by any person who by way of business deals, or holds himself out as dealing, as a principal in any stock or marketable securities, advising the principal, or the vendor or purchaser, as the case may be, of the sale or purchase of any stock or marketable security, but does not include a note sent by a broker or agent to his principal where the principal is himself acting as broker or agent for a principal, and is himself either a member of a stock exchange in the United Kingdom, or a person who, *bonâ fide* carries on the business of a stockbroker in the United Kingdom, and is registered as such in the list of stockbrokers kept by the Commissioners.

"(4) Where a contract note advises the sale or purchase of more than one description of stock or marketable security, the note shall be deemed to be as many contract notes as there are descriptions of stocks or securities sold or purchased.

Obligation to execute Contract Note.

"78. (1) Any person who effects any sale or purchase of any stock or marketable security of the value of five pounds or upwards as a broker or agent, and any person who by way of business deals, or holds himself out as dealing, as a principal in any stock or marketable security, and buys or sells any such stock or marketable security of a value of five pounds or upwards, shall forthwith make and execute a contract note, and transmit the note to his principal, or to the vendor or purchaser of the stock or marketable security, as the case may be, and in default of so doing shall incur a fine of twenty pounds : Provided that this Section shall not apply in the case of transactions carried out in the course of their ordinary business relations between members of stock exchanges in the United Kingdom.

"(2) If any person makes or executes any

contract note chargeable with duty and not being duly stamped, he shall incur a fine of twenty pounds.

"(3) No broker, agent, or other person shall have any legal claim to any charge for brokerage, commission, or agency, with reference to the sale or purchase of any stock or marketable security of the value of five pounds or upwards, if he fails to comply with the provisions of this Section.

"(4) All stamp duties on a contract note are to be denoted by an adhesive stamp appropriated to a contract note, and the stamp is to be effectively cancelled by the person by whom the note is executed by writing on or across the stamp his name or initials, or the name or initials of his firm, together with the true date of his so writing.

(5) Any stamp duty on a contract note may be added to the charge for brokerage or agency, and shall be recoverable as part of such charge.

Extension of Provisions as to Contract Notes to Sale or purchase of Options.

"79. (1) The provisions of this Part of this Act as to contract notes shall apply to any contract under which an option is given or taken to purchase or sell any stock or marketable security at a future time at a certain price, as it applies to the sale or purchase of any stock or marketable security, but the stamp duty on such a contract shall be one-half only of that chargeable on a contract note: Provided that if under the contract a double option is given or taken the contract shall be deemed to be a separate contract in respect of each option.

"(2) Any contract note made or executed in pursuance and in consequence of the exercise of an option given or taken under a contract duly stamped in accordance with the provisions of this Section shall be charged with one-half only of the duty which would otherwise have been chargeable thereon under this Part of this Act, provided that it bears on its face a certificate by the broker, agent, or other person mentioned in the last preceding Section to the effect that it is made or executed in the exercise of an option for which a duly stamped contract has been rendered on the date mentioned in the certificate."

CONTRACTS. A contract is a formal agreement between two parties, it being understood by both that if the contract is broken it may become the subject of an action at law.

A contract may be made in a document under seal, as in a conveyance of property or transfer of shares; or it may be a simple contract made either by word of mouth or by a writing not under seal, as in a bill of exchange. In a simple contract there must be a consideration of value.

A contract with a minor, with respect to any loan to him, is void. A contract is also void if it is forbidden by an Act of Parliament; for example, when shares of a bank are sold, the contract note must specify the numbers of the shares, and if it does not do so, the contract is legally void. (See LEEMAN'S ACT.)

A contract under seal is a specialty contract, and an action must be brought within twenty years from the date when the cause of action first arose. In the case of recovery of land the period is twelve years. In a simple contract, the action must be brought within six years.

Section 76 of the Companies (Consolidation) Act, 1908, enacts that:—

"(1) Contracts on behalf of a company may be made as follows (that is to say):—

"(i) Any contract which if made between private persons would be by law required to be in writing, and if made according to English law to be under seal, may be made on behalf of the company in writing under the common seal of the company, and may in the same manner be varied or discharged:

"(ii) Any contract which if made between private persons would be by law required to be in writing, signed by the parties to be charged therewith, may be made on behalf of the company in writing signed by any person acting under its authority, express or implied, and may in the same manner be varied or discharged :

" (iii) Any contract which if made between private persons would by law be valid although made by parol only, and not reduced into writing, may be made by parol on behalf of the company by any person acting under its authority, express or implied, and may in the same manner be varied or discharged.

" (2) All contracts made according to this Section shall be effectual in law, and shall bind the company and its successors and all other parties thereto, their heirs, executors, or administrators as the case may be.

" (3) Any deed to which a company is a party shall be held to be validly executed in Scotland on behalf of the company if it is executed in terms of the provisions of this Act or is sealed with the common seal of the company and subscribed on behalf of the company by two of the directors and the secretary of the company, and such subscription on behalf of the company shall be equally binding whether attested by witnesses or not."

As to stamp duty see AGREEMENT. (See COMPANIES.)

CONTRIBUTORIES. In the event of a joint stock company being wound up, the persons who are liable to contribute to the assets are called the contributories. Section 123 of the Companies (Consolidation) Act, 1908 deals with the liability of present and past members and is as follows :—

" (1) In the event of a company being wound up, every present and past member shall, subject to the provisions of this Section, be liable to contribute to the assets of the company to an amount sufficient for payment of its debts and liabilities and the costs, charges, and expenses of the winding up, and for the adjustment of the rights of the contributories among themselves, with the qualifications following (that is to say) :—

" (i) A past member shall not be liable to contribute if he has ceased to be a member for one year or upwards before the commencement of the winding up :

" (ii) A past member shall not be liable to contribute in respect of any debt or liability of the company contracted after he ceased to be a member :

" (iii) A past member shall not be liable to contribute unless it appears to the Court that the existing members are unable to satisfy the contributions required to be made by them in pursuance of this Act :

" (iv) In the case of a company limited by shares no contribution shall be required from any member exceeding the amount, if any, unpaid on the shares in respect of which he is liable as a present or past member :

" (v) In the case of a company limited by guarantee, no contribution shall be required from any member exceeding the amount undertaken to be contributed by him to the assets of the company in the event of its being wound up :

" (vi) Nothing in this Act shall invalidate any provision contained in any policy of insurance or other contract whereby the liability of individual members on the policy or contract is restricted, or whereby the funds of the company are alone made liable in respect of the policy or contract :

" (vii) A sum due to any member of a company, in his character of a member, by way of dividends, profits, or otherwise, shall not be deemed to be a debt of the company, payable to that member in a case of competition between himself and any other creditor not a member of the company ; but any such sum may be taken into account for the purpose of the final adjustment of the rights of the contributories among themselves.

"(2) In the winding up of a limited company, any director or manager, whether past or present, whose liability is, in pursuance of this Act, unlimited, shall, in addition to his liability (if any) to contribute as an ordinary member, be liable to make a further contribution as if he were at the commencement of the winding up a member of an unlimited company: Provided that—

"(i) A past director or manager shall not be liable to make such further contribution if he has ceased to hold office for a year or upwards before the commencement of the winding up:

"(ii) A past director or manager shall not be liable to make such further contribution in respect of any debt or liability of the company contracted after he ceased to hold office:

"(iii) Subject to the articles of the company, a director or manager shall not be liable to make such further contribution unless the court deems it necessary to require that contribution in order to satisfy the debts and liabilities of the company, and the costs, charges, and expenses of the winding up.

"(3) In the winding up of a company limited by guarantee which has a share capital, every member of the company shall be liable, in addition to the amount undertaken to be contributed by him to the assets of the company in the event of its being wound up, to contribute to the extent of any sums unpaid on any shares held by him."

In making up the list of contributories, the liquidator puts the names of present members in one list called "A" List, and of past members who are liable (see Section 123, above), in another list, the "B" List.

CONVERSION. A security is said to be converted when it is changed in some manner, e.g. (1) where the interest is reduced and, say, a 5 per cent. stock becomes a 4 per cent.; (2) where the nominal value of shares is changed, as when a £10 share is changed into ten shares of £1 each.

Wrongful conversion is a legal term signifying the dealing with the goods of another person, without authority, so as to deprive him of the possession. For example, a banker may be liable to an action by the rightful owner of a "not negotiable" cheque for damages for conversion, where he has collected the cheque and paid the proceeds to a stranger who was not entitled to it.

CONVERTIBLE PAPER CURRENCY. A bank note which can be exchanged for gold on demand for its full value, at the bank which issued it, is convertible paper, but if it cannot be so exchanged it is called inconvertible paper.

CONVERTIBLE SECURITIES. A general term applied to all securities which may be readily converted, or turned, into cash.

CONVEYANCE. In the Conveyancing Act of 1881 the word conveyance "includes assignment, appointment, lease, settlement, and other assurance, and covenant to surrender, made by deed, on a sale, mortgage, demise, or settlement of any property, or on any other dealing with or for any property."

The word "conveyance" is, however, principally used to denote the deed by which freehold property is conveyed to a purchaser in fee simple.

The different estates are referred to as:—

To convey freehold property by a conveyance;
To demise property by a lease;
To assign leasehold property by an assignment;
To surrender copyhold property and be admitted.

Stocks and shares are also spoken of as being conveyed or transferred.

The stamp duties, as provided in the Stamp Act, 1891, are as follows:—

	£	s.	d.
CONVEYANCE OF TRANSFER, whether on sale or otherwise—			
(1) Of any stock of the Bank of England	0	7	9
(2) Of any stock of the Government of Canada inscribed in books kept in the United Kingdom, or of any Colonial stock to which the Colonial Stock Act, 1877, applies—			

	£	s.	d.
For every £100, and also for any fractional part of £100, of the nominal amount of stock transferred	0	2	6

And see Section 62, as follows :—

Conveyances on any Occasion except Sale or Mortgage.

"Every instrument, and every decree or order of any court or of any commissioners, whereby any property on any occasion, except a sale or mortgage, is transferred to or vested in any person, is to be charged with duty as a conveyance or transfer of property.

Provided that a conveyance or transfer made for effectuating the appointment of a new trustee is not to be charged with any higher duty than ten shillings."

CONVEYANCE OR TRANSFER on sale.

Of any property (*except such stock as aforesaid*).

	£	s.	d.
Where the amount or value of the consideration for the sale does not exceed £5	0	0	6
Exceeds £5 and does not exceed £10	0	1	0
,, £10 ,, £15	0	1	6
,, £15 ,, £20	0	2	0
,, £20 ,, £25	0	2	6
,, £25 ,, £50	0	5	0
,, £50 ,, £75	0	7	6
,, £75 ,, £100	0	10	0
,, £100 ,, £125	0	12	6
,, £125 ,, £150	0	15	0
,, £150 ,, £175	0	17	6
,, £175 ,, £200	1	0	0
,, £200 ,, £225	1	2	6
,, £225 ,, £250	1	5	0
,, £250 ,, £275	1	7	6
,, £275 ,, £300	1	10	0
,, £300.			
For every £50, and also for any fractional part of £50, of such amount or value	0	5	0

(and see Sections 54, 55, 57, 58 and 61 of the Stamp Act, 1891, below).

On and after 29th April, 1910, a conveyance or transfer on sale (other than of stock or marketable security) where the consideration exceeds £500			
For every £50, and also for any fractional part of £50 of the consideration	0	10	0

See Section 73 of the Finance (1909-10) Act, 1910, which is as follows :—

"The stamp duties chargeable under the heading 'CONVEYANCE OR TRANSFER on Sale of any Property' in the First Schedule to the Stamp Act, 1891 (in this Part of this Act referred to as the principal Act) shall be double those specified in that Schedule: Provided that this section shall not apply to the conveyance or transfer of any stock or marketable security as defined by Section one hundred and twenty-two of that Act, or to a conveyance or transfer where the amount or value of the consideration for the sale does not exceed five hundred pounds and the instrument contains a statement certifying that the transaction thereby effected does not form part of a larger transaction or of a series of transactions in respect of which the amount or value, or the aggregate amount or value, of the consideration exceeds five hundred pounds." [A "marketable security" as defined by Section 122 of the Stamp Act, 1891, means a security of such a description as to be capable of being sold in any stock market in the United Kingdom.]

Stamp Duty on Gifts inter vivos.

By the Finance (1909-10) Act, 1910. Section 74 :—

"(1) Any conveyance or transfer operating as a voluntary disposition *inter vivos* shall be chargeable with the like stamp duty as if it were a conveyance or transfer on sale, with the substitution in each case of the value of the property conveyed or transferred for the amount or value of the consideration for the sale:

Provided that this Section shall not apply to a conveyance or transfer operating as a voluntary disposition of property to a body of persons incorporated by a special Act if that body is by its Act precluded from dividing any profit among its members and the property conveyed is to be held for the purposes of an open space or for the purposes of its preservation for the benefit of the nation."

No conveyance or transfer operating as a voluntary disposition *inter vivos* shall be deemed to be duly stamped, unless the Commissioners have expressed their opinion thereon in accordance with Section 12 of the

Stamp Act, 1891. (See ADJUDICATION STAMPS.)

Sub-sections 4, 5, and 6 of Section 74, Finance (1909–10) Act, enact as follows :—

"(4) Where any instrument is chargeable with duty both as a conveyance or transfer under this Section and as a settlement under the heading 'SETTLEMENT' in the First Schedule to the principal Act, the instrument shall be charged with duty as a conveyance or transfer under this Section, but not as a settlement under the principal Act.

"(5) Any conveyance or transfer (not being a disposition made in favour of a purchaser or incumbrancer or other person in good faith and for valuable consideration) shall, for the purposes of this Section, be deemed to be a conveyance or transfer operating as a voluntary disposition *inter vivos*, and (except where marriage is the consideration) the consideration for any conveyance or transfer shall not for this purpose be deemed to be valuable consideration where the Commissioners are of opinion that by reason of the inadequacy of the sum paid as consideration or other circumstances the conveyance or transfer confers a substantial benefit on the person to whom the property is conveyed or transferred.

"(6) A conveyance or transfer made for nominal consideration for the purpose of securing the repayment of an advance or loan or made for effectuating the appointment of a new trustee or the retirement of a trustee, whether the trust is expressed or implied, or under which no beneficial interest passes in the property conveyed or transferred, or made to a beneficiary by a trustee or other person in a fiduciary capacity under any trust, whether expressed or implied, or a disentailing assurance not limiting any new estate other than an estate in fee simple in the person disentailing the property, shall not be charged with duty under this Section, and this sub-section shall have effect notwithstanding that the circumstances exempting the conveyance or transfer from charge under this Section are not set forth in the conveyance or transfer."

With regard to the stamp which is necessary upon conveyances since April, 1910, to denote that increment value duty has been paid, or that no duty was payable, see INCREMENT VALUE DUTY.

The following are the sections of the Stamp Act, 1891, referred to above :—

Meaning of "Conveyance on Sale."

"54. For the purposes of this Act the expression 'conveyance on sale' includes every instrument, and every decree or order of any court or of any commissioners, whereby any property, or any estate or interest in any property, upon the sale thereof is transferred to or vested in a purchaser, or any other person on his behalf or by his direction.

How ad valorem *Duty to be calculated in respect of Stock and Securities.*

"55. (1) Where the consideration, or any part of the consideration, for a conveyance on sale consists of any stock or marketable security, the conveyance is to be charged with *ad valorem* duty in respect of the value of the stock or security.

"(2) Where the consideration, or any part of the consideration, for a conveyance on sale consists of any security not being a marketable security, the conveyance is to be charged with *ad valorem* duty in respect of the amount due on the day of the date thereof for principal and interest upon the security.

How Conveyance in Consideration of a Debt, etc., to be Charged.

"57. Where any property is conveyed to any person in consideration, wholly or in part, of any debt due to him, or subject either certainly or contingently to the payment or transfer of any money or stock, whether being or constituting a charge or incumbrance upon the property or not, the debt, money, or stock is to be deemed the whole or part, as the case may be, of the consideration in respect whereof the conveyance is chargeable with *ad valorem* duty.

Direction as to Duty in Certain Cases.

"58. (3) Where there are several instruments of conveyance for completing the purchaser's title to property sold, the principal instrument of conveyance only is to be charged with *ad valorem* duty, and the other instruments are to be respectively charged with such other duty as they may be liable to, but the last-mentioned duty shall not exceed the *ad valorem* duty payable in respect of the principal instrument.

(4) Where a person having contracted for the purchase of any property, but not having obtained a conveyance thereof, contracts to sell the same to any other person, and the property is in consequence conveyed immediately to the sub-purchaser, the conveyance is to be charged with *ad valorem* duty in respect of the consideration moving from the sub-purchaser.

Principal Instrument, How to be Ascertained.

"61. (1) In the cases hereinafter specified the principal instrument is to be ascertained in the following manner :

"(*a*) Where any copyhold or customary estate is conveyed by a deed, no surrender being necessary, the deed is to be deemed the principal instrument :

"(*b*) In other cases of copyhold or customary estates, the surrender or grant, if made out of court, or the memorandum thereof, and the copy of court roll of the surrender or grant, if made in court, is to be deemed the principal instrument :

"(*c*) Where in Scotland there is a disposition or assignation executed by the seller, and any other instrument is executed for completing the title, the disposition or assignation is to be deemed the principal instrument.

"(2) In any other case the parties may determine for themselves which of several instruments is to be deemed the principal instrument, and may pay the *ad valorem* duty thereon accordingly."

CONVEYANCE or TRANSFER by way of security of any property (*except such stock as aforesaid*), or of any security.

See MORTGAGE, etc., and MARKETABLE SECURITY.

	£	s.	d.
CONVEYANCE or TRANSFER of any kind not hereinbefore described	0	10	0

And see Section 62, above.

By Section 6, Finance Act, 1898 :—

"The definition 'Conveyance on Sale' includes a decree or order for, or having the effect of an order for, foreclosure. Provided that (*a*) the *ad valorem* stamp duty upon any such decree or order shall not exceed the duty on a sum equal to the value of the property to which the decree or order relates, and where the decree or order states that value that statement shall be conclusive for the purpose of determining the amount of the duty ; and (*b*) where *ad valorem* stamp duty is paid upon such decree or order, any conveyance following upon such decree or order shall be exempt from the *ad valorem* stamp duty."

By Section 10, Finance Act, 1900 :—

"A Conveyance on Sale made for any consideration in respect whereof it is chargeable with *ad valorem* duty, and in further consideration of a covenant by the purchaser to make, or of his having previously made, any substantial improvement of or addition to the property conveyed to him, or of any covenant relating to the subject matter of the conveyance, is not chargeable, and shall be deemed not to have been chargeable with any duty in respect of such further consideration."

Where property is conveyed, subject to a mortgage, duty is payable upon the amount of the mortgage and interest up to the date of the conveyance.

As to stamping instruments after execution, see Section 15 of the Stamp Act, 1891, under heading STAMP DUTIES. (See COMPOSITION—TRANSFERS—SHARES, COPYHOLD, FREEHOLD, LEASEHOLD, TRANSFER OF SHARES, TRANSMISSION OF SHARES.)

COPARCENERS. Where the owner of real property dies without having made a will it descends to his heir, that is, his eldest son (see PRIMOGENITURE), but if there is no son, it descends to all the daughters (if any) as coparceners, that is parceners (or heirs) together, and the land may be partitioned among them. Coparceners have a unity of title in the property—that is, a common right to the whole—but the shares may be unequal, as where a daughter is dead and her daughters take her share. There is no right of survivorship.

Coparcenary is a holding which is neither that of a "joint tenant" nor of a "tenant in common," but a kind of intermediate state.

One coparcener may transfer his share to another coparcener either by a conveyance, as in the case of a tenant in common, or by a release, as in the case of a joint tenant.

A surviving coparcener does not succeed to the share of a deceased coparcener. The share may be disposed of by will, or, if he dies intestate, it passes to his heir.

In the ancient custom of gavelkind (*q.v.*) lands descend to all the sons together as coparceners.

Where deeds of property held in coparcenary are deposited as security, the document of charge should be signed by all the owners, and it is advisable that a banker's legal mortgage be taken. (See JOINT TENANTS, TENANTS IN COMMON.)

COPPER COINS. Real copper coins were first issued in 1672, and were replaced by bronze in 1860, though bronze coins are still commonly spoken of as "coppers." They are made of a mixed metal, 95 parts of copper, four parts of tin and one part of zinc. They are legal tender only to the amount of one shilling.

The figure of Britannia upon the coins is said to have been originally modelled from the beautiful Frances Stuart, afterwards Duchess of Richmond (Hutchison, "Practice of Banking," vol. ii, p. 514). (See COINAGE.)

COPY. The duties imposed by the Stamp Act, 1891, are as follows:—

COPY OR EXTRACT (*attested or in any manner authenticated*) of or from—

(1) An instrument chargeable with any duty.
(2) An original will, testament, or codicil.
(3) The probate or probate copy of a will or codicil.
(4) Any letters of administration or any confirmation of a testament.
(5) Any public register (*except any register of births, baptisms, marriages, deaths, or burials*).
(6) The books, rolls, or records of any court.

In the case of an instrument chargeable with duty not amounting to one shilling . . . . . — The same duty as such instrument.

In any other case 0 1 0

Exemptions.

(1) Copy or extract of or from any law proceeding.
(2) Copy or extract in Scotland of or from the commission of any person as a delegate or representative to the convention of royal burghs or the general assembly or any presbytery or church court.

And see Section 63, as follows:—

"An attested or otherwise authenticated copy or extract of or from—

"(1) An instrument chargeable with any duty;
"(2) An original will, testament, or codicil;
"(3) The probate or probate copy of a will or codicil;
"(4) Letters of administration or a confirmation of a testament;

may be stamped at any time within fourteen days after the date of the attestation or authentication on payment of the duty only."

	£	s.	d.
COPY OR EXTRACT (*certified*) of or from any register of births, baptisms, marriages, deaths, or burials	0	0	1

Exemptions.

(1) Copy or extract furnished by any clergyman, registrar, or other official person pursuant to and for the purposes of any Act, or furnished to any general or superintending registrar under any general regulation.
(2) Copy or extract for which the person giving the same is not entitled to any fee or reward.

And see Section 64, as follows:—

"The duty upon a certified copy or extract of or from any register of births, baptisms, marriages, deaths, or burials is to be paid by the person requiring the copy or extract, and may be denoted by an adhesive stamp, which is to be cancelled by the person by whom the copy or extract is signed before he delivers the same out of his hands, custody, or power." (See ATTESTED COPY, OFFICE COPY.)

COPYHOLD. Under the feudal system

villeins were permitted by their lords to hold plots of land, and in return the villeins had to perform certain services for the lords. The land belonged absolutely to the lords, who could remove the villeins from their holdings at will, but so long as the services were duly rendered, the tenants were no doubt permitted to remain upon the land in peace. When one died, his holding would be taken by his successors, and so from generation to generation the land would pass from one to another. Blackstone says (see "Commentaries of the Laws of England," vol. ii, p. 80, Kerr's Fourth Edition): "From what has been premised, it appears that copyholders are in truth no other but villeins, who, by a long series of immemorial encroachments on the lord, have at last established a customary right to those estates, which before were held absolutely at the lord's will. Which affords a very substantial reason for the great variety of customs that prevail in different manors, with regard both to the descent of the estates, and the privileges belonging to the tenants." And again: "The generality of villeins in the kingdom have long ago sprouted up into copyholders; their persons being enfranchised by manumission or long acquiescence; but their estates, in strictness, remaining subject to the same servile conditions and forfeitures as before; though, in general, the villein services are usually commuted for a small pecuniary quit-rent."

In early times the name of the tenant was written upon the rolls of the manor, along with a note of the services he had to render or the amount he had to pay. The parchment "roll" is now substituted by a book, but the tenant of a copyhold is still said to be enrolled or entered upon the rolls of the manor. A copy of the entry on the rolls was given to the tenant as evidence of his enrolment, whence he was called a copyholder; that is, a holder of the land by copy of the entry.

In connection with the transfer of copyholds, there is usually a covenant to surrender; that is, a deed in which the vendor covenants to surrender the land to the lord of the manor to the use of the purchaser. The actual transfer is effected by surrender and admittance. By the surrender an equitable interest only is vested in the surrenderee and admittance is required to perfect his title. A surrender may be made either in court or out of court. If made in court, it is entered on the rolls and a copy of the surrender is given to the purchaser. If the surrender is made out of court, a memorandum in writing of it is prepared and signed by the parties and the steward, and it is then entered upon the rolls.

The mode of surrender is for the person on the rolls, either himself or by duly appointed attorney, to attend before the steward and surrender, either directly or pursuant to a covenant to surrender, the copyhold tenement to the lord to the use of the purchaser, and the steward then makes out the surrender, which is a copy of the entry on the court rolls, and has it stamped. The purchaser may attend at the same time and take admittance, or he may attend at some subsequent court or out of court to take admittance. In the former case the surrender and admittance usually appear on the copy of the court rolls delivered by the steward to the purchaser. In the latter case there are two copies of the court rolls, namely a surrender and an admittance. The surrender is the instrument required to be stamped, but the admittance does not require a stamp. Sometimes, in practice, where there is a covenant to surrender in a deed which deals with both freehold and copyhold property, such deed is impressed with the usual *ad valorem* stamp on the full purchase money, and in that case the surrender bears only a ten shilling stamp, otherwise it must be stamped according to the purchase price of the copyholds.

In the case of a devisee under a will or in an intestacy, there is no surrender, and the admittance merely sets out that A. B. has been admitted as devisee or copyhold heir-at-law of the deceased tenant on the rolls.

On a copy surrender and admittance, the steward certifies that the original surrender is duly stamped. The certificate is some such form as :—"I certify that the surrender under which this admittance is granted bears the proper *ad valorem* stamp of ."

As the customs of manors vary so very much, a banker should always ascertain from the steward of any particular manor what deeds and documents are necessary. Even manors that are quite close together may have different customs in the transfer of the property.

Where a vendor and purchaser personally attend the manor court to surrender and take admittance, there may not be any deed of covenant to surrender. There must, however, except in cases of a devise or descent, always be a surrender, and the title cannot be complete till admittance has taken place. A person who has ceased to hold any interest in the property may remain tenant on the rolls, and though a covenant to surrender is executed it may not be acted upon for some time afterwards, for so long as there is a living tenant on the court rolls the lord cannot (even though he knows such tenant has ceased to have any interest) compel anyone else to come in and be admitted. In the case of the death of such a tenant, his heir-at-law or devisee must be admitted before a purchaser can; and very often, instead of saving fines and fees, the actual owner has more to pay.

If a covenant to surrender and a copy admittance of the copyholder, along with the prior deeds, are lodged as security under a memorandum of deposit, it is said that the banker has a reliable security; but it would appear that the only really satisfactory way to obtain a security over copyhold property is by mortgage, and surrender to the lord to the use of the mortgagee. This surrender is entered on the court rolls as being subject to a condition that, on payment of the mortgage debt, the surrender will become void. Such a surrender is called a conditional surrender.

It is not usual for a mortgagee to seek admittance. This course is adopted in order to avoid payment of the fines and fees which would be payable upon his admittance, and would again be payable upon the re-admittance of the mortgagor upon payment of the debt. A mortgagee can at any time perfect his title by obtaining admittance as from the date of the surrender, which safeguards him from the danger of any subsequent mortgagee obtaining admittance in front of him. When the mortgage debt is repaid, a memorandum of satisfaction is entered upon the court rolls, the mortgagee executes a deed of release and the mortgagor thereupon occupies the position he did before the conditional surrender was made.

If a mortgagee does not get his covenant to surrender completed by a conditional surrender entered upon the rolls, his charge may be postponed to a subsequent mortgagee who does obtain such a conditional surrender upon the rolls.

A simple deposit of the copies of the court roll creates an equitable mortgage, but there is the risk, as above stated, of a mortgagee obtaining a conditional surrender on the rolls; and it is quite possible, in certain cases, for the copyholder to dispose of the property without the copy of the admittance, which may be in the banker's hands, being required at all.

In the case of joint tenants, the admission of one is equal to the admission of all of them, but tenants in common must be admitted severally, and a fine will be due from each of them.

Fines are usually payable by a tenant upon admittance. The amounts of the fines vary; in some cases they are small, though in other cases they are large. Some of them are fixed and others arbitrary. An arbitrary fine generally amounts to two years' improved value of the copyhold tenement. They may also be payable upon the death of the lord or the death of the tenant, or upon both events.

For an example of a "conditional surrender," see CONDITIONAL SURRENDER.

For an example of an "admittance," see ADMITTANCE.

For an example of a "surrender," and a "surrender and admittance," see SURRENDER.

When copyhold land is freed from all customary duties it is said to be enfranchised. (See ENFRANCHISEMENT.)

Where equitable copyholds are found, the property is transferable by conveyance, subject to the ground landlord's claims, i.e. the ground rent with right of recovering the same. The legal estate vests in the ground landlord or his trustee, and his name will appear on the court roll. Equitable copyholds are considered to be as good as freeholds.

By the Stamp Act, 1891, the duty is as follows:—

COPYHOLD and CUSTOMARY ESTATES—Instruments relating thereto. Upon a sale thereof. See CONVEYANCE.

Upon a mortgage thereof. See MORTGAGE.

Upon a demise thereof. See LEASEHOLD.

Upon any other occasion.

Surrender or grant made out of court, or the memorandum thereof, and copy of court roll of any surrender or grant made in court . . . . . £0 10s. 0d.

Provisions as to Payment of Duty.

"Section 65. (1) No instrument is to be charged more than once with duty by reason of relating to several distinct tenements, in respect whereof several fines or fees are due to the lord or steward of the manor.

"(2) The copy of court roll of a surrender or grant made out of court shall not be admissible or available as evidence of the surrender or grant, unless the surrender or grant, or the memorandum thereof, is duly stamped, of which fact the certificate of the steward of the manor on the face of the copy shall be sufficient evidence.

(3) The entry upon the court rolls of a surrender or grant shall not be admissible or available as evidence of the surrender or grant unless the surrender or grant, if made out of court, or the memorandum thereof, or the copy of court roll of the surrender or grant, if made in court, is duly stamped, of which fact the certificate of the steward of the manor in the margin of the entry shall be sufficient evidence.

Facts Affecting Duty to be Stated in Note.

"66. (1) All the facts and circumstances affecting the liability to duty of the copy of court roll of any surrender or grant made in court, or the amount of duty with which any such copy of court roll is chargeable, are to be fully and truly stated in a note to be delivered to the steward of the manor before the surrender or grant is made.

"(2) The steward of every manor shall refuse—

"(*a*) To accept in court any surrender, or to make in court any grant, until such a note as is required by this Section has been delivered to him ; or

"(*b*) To enter on the court rolls, or accept any presentment of, or admit any person to be tenant under or by virtue of, any surrender or grant made out of court, or any deed which is not duly stamped :

And in any case in which he does not so refuse shall incur a fine of fifty pounds.

Steward to make out duly Stamped Copies.

"67. The steward of every manor shall, within four months from the day on which any surrender or grant is made in court, make out a duly stamped copy of court roll of such surrender or grant, and have the same ready for delivery to the person entitled thereto, and in default of so doing shall incur a fine of fifty pounds, and the duty payable in respect of the copy of court roll shall be a debt to Her Majesty from the steward, whether he has received it or not, and if he has not received the duty the same shall also be a debt to Her Majesty from the person entitled to the copy.

Steward may Refuse to Proceed except on Payment of his Fees and Duty.

"68. The steward of any manor may, before he accepts in court any surrender or makes in court any grant, demand the payment of his lawful fees in relation to the surrender or grant, together with the duty payable on the copy of court roll thereof, and may refuse to proceed in the matter or to deliver the copy of court roll to any person until the fees and duty are paid."

	£ s. d.
CONDITIONAL SURRENDER of any copyhold or customary estate by way of mortgage. See MORTGAGE, and Sections 86 and 87.	
COVENANT TO SURRENDER— Where the *ad valorem* duty on the surrender, in respect of the consideration or mortgage money, does not exceed 10*s*., a duty equal to the amount of such *ad valorem* duty.	
In any other case . . .	0 10 0

If the copyhold deeds are deposited with a memorandum of deposit under hand, the duty on the memorandum is the same as in the case of other deeds. (See EQUITABLE MORTGAGE, TITLE DEEDS.)

CORPORATION. A corporation is created by an Act of Parliament or by a charter granted by the Crown. A corporation is a legal "person" by itself and continues as a distinct body, irrespective of any changes which may take place amongst the members. Railway companies are incorporated under private Acts of Parliament, and most trading companies under one of the Companies Acts. In considering an application for a loan, the banker must ascertain if the corporation has power to borrow, and, if it has power, whether the money to be borrowed will cause the limit of such borrowing powers to be exceeded.

In all dealings with a limited company, whether with regard to the borrowing of money, or the charging of the company's property, or the manner in which cheques are drawn, a banker is taken to be acquainted with the memorandum and articles of association of the company, and is affected with notice of all that is contained in those two documents. (See COMPANIES.)

COULISSE. The official brokers, *agents de change*, upon the Paris Exchange, form the Parquet; the unofficial dealers form the Coulisse.

COUNCIL DRAFTS. Drafts drawn by the India Council in this country upon the Indian Government and payable in India.

COUNTERFEIT COINS. (See BASE COINS.)

COUNTERMAND OF PAYMENT. A banker is obliged to honour the cheque of his customer, if there is a sufficient balance in the account to meet it, and the cheque is in order. The drawer may, however, instruct the banker to stop payment of a cheque, and the banker will be liable if he neglects to attend to the instructions.

The Bills of Exchange Act, 1882, Section 75, states that the duty and authority of a banker to pay a cheque drawn on him by his customer are determined by countermand of payment.

A countermand of payment can be given only by the drawer, but notice from a holder that a cheque has been lost by him would put a banker on his guard, pending instructions from the drawer.

An order to stop payment of a cheque should be in writing and be signed by the customer, and if the order is subsequently cancelled, the fresh instructions should also be in writing. The drawer cannot stop payment of a cheque which a banker has, at the drawer's request, already certified, or marked, for payment.

The terms of a countermand of payment by a customer should be very precise, so as to admit of no question as to which cheque is referred to. A good form is as follows:

To the X & Y. Bank, Ltd., Leeds.

July 10, 1910.

Please stop payment of cheque No. 46501, dated July 9, 1910, for £100, signed by me payable to Thomas Brown; which has been lost.

ALFRED SMITH.

As to countermand of payment by wire, see PAYMENT STOPPED. (See BILL OF EXCHANGE, PAYMENT OF CHEQUE.)

COUNTERPART. A duplicate of an instrument. The word is used chiefly in connection with leases, e.g. where a house is leased for a period of years, the lessee receives the lease signed by the lessor and the lessor receives a counterpart or copy of it signed by the lessee.

For the stamp duty, see DUPLICATE.

COUNTRY BANK NOTES. Notes which are issued by a country bank as distinguished from those issued by the Bank of England. Where they are tendered in payment and no objection is raised by the person receiving them, it is considered a legal tender.

A tender by a banker of his own notes also acts as a legal tender, if not objected to, even if they are afterwards dishonoured.

There is nothing to prevent the notes of a country banker being paid away by another banker, whether the latter has an issue or not, so long as the person to whom they are offered is willing to accept them.

If a country bank note is accepted in exchange for goods at the actual time of a sale, the transferee must bear the loss, if the banker by whom it was issued fails before he presents the note for payment, unless he can prove that the transferor knew that the banker had failed before delivering the note to him. But, on the other hand, if the note was accepted in payment of a pre-existing debt, and the banker fails before presentation of the note, the debt is not discharged, and the transferor is still liable to the transferee, provided that the transferee presented the note for payment without delay and gave due notice of its dishonour to the transferor.

The receiver of a country bank note in payment of a debt should therefore present the note for payment at once, or not later than the following day, otherwise he will have no recourse against the person who gave it to him, in the event of the note being dishonoured. A bank note is a promissory note by a banker, and the giving of notice of dishonour is regulated by the Bills of Exchange Act, 1882. If the person giving and the person to receive the notice are in the same town, the notice should be received on the day following the day of dishonour; if in different towns, the notice should be despatched not later than the day following the day of dishonour. (See DISHONOUR OF BILL OF EXCHANGE.)

For the same reason, where a customer pays into his account the notes of another bank, the notes should be presented for payment by the banker without delay, so that, in the event of non-payment of the notes, the banker may be entitled to charge the amount to the account of his customer. If a banker is negligent in presenting the notes at once, any loss, upon dishonour, will fall upon the banker and not upon the customer, unless an arrangement was made with the customer, when taking the notes, that they would not be forwarded for collection for a few days. Bank notes, like cheques, are presented for payment in the daily clearing, when the issuing bank is in the same town. If the issuing bank is in another town, they may be collected through London or remitted direct.

Where a person receives change, by way of favour, for a bank note, he is liable, if the note is dishonoured, unless the person who took the note did not put it into circulation or present it for payment within a reasonable time.

A banker's own notes are not, for the purposes of his balance sheet, counted up as part of the cash, but are deducted from the balance of the note account, in order to show the amount of his notes which are in circulation.

Banks of issue re-issue their notes constantly until they become unfit for circulation, in this respect differing from the Bank of England, which never re-issues its notes when once they are returned to the Bank.

Where notes are received which prove to be forgeries, the amount can be recovered from the person from whom they were obtained.

Where a note-issuing banker failed, it was held that interest at 5 per cent. on its notes in circulation began to accrue from the date when a claim for payment of a note was made to the liquidator, and not from the actual date when the banker stopped payment. (See BANK NOTES, NOTE REGISTER, NOTE RETURN.)

COUNTRY CLEARING. The section of the business of the London Bankers' Clearing House which includes all cheques dealt with by the House and not included in the Town Clearing or Metropolitan Clearing; that is, cheques on the country correspondents of the London bankers.

Country bankers who avail themselves of the clearing remit their country cheques to their own London agent, or London office, and stamp across them their own name and address and that of their London agent or head office.

When a country banker does not intend to pay a cheque received by him from his London agent for collection, he must, by the rules of the Clearing House, return it direct to the country or branch bank whose name and address is across it, and this must be done by return of post: it cannot be held over till next day. (See CLEARING HOUSE.)

COUNTY COUNCIL. When a banker is appointed to be treasurer to a county council, he is required to furnish satisfactory security.

The cheques, or orders for payment, are drawn upon the treasurer. By Section 80, s.s. 1, of the Local Government Act, 1888, it is provided that "all payments to and out of the county fund, shall be made to, and by the county treasurer, and all payments out of the fund shall, unless made in pursuance of the specific requirement of an Act of Parliament, or of an order of a competent court, be made in pursuance of an order of the council, signed by three members of the finance committee present at the meeting of the council, and countersigned by the clerk of the council, and the same order may include several payments. Moreover, all cheques for payment of moneys issued in pursuance of such order, shall be countersigned by the clerk of the council, or by a deputy approved by the council."

The usual method is for a list of payments to be furnished to the treasurer, the list being signed by three members and countersigned by the clerk, and for the individual cheques to be signed by officials of the council. The cheques, when presented for payment, are compared with the official list. As to the stamp duty on this list, see minute of the Board of Inland Revenue, under article CHEQUE.

With reference to the borrowing powers of a county council, they cannot, as a rule, be exercised unless the sanction of the Local Government Board is first obtained. To ascertain the extent of the powers and what sanction is necessary, reference should be made to the statutes under which any loans are to be raised.

If money is borrowed without power or sanction, the interest thereon will probably be disallowed.

The accounts are made up to March 31, and are audited by a Government Auditor. (See LOCAL AUTHORITIES.)

COUPON. (From Fr. *couper*, to cut.) Literally a piece cut off.

A coupon is a warrant for the payment of interest. It is usually attached to a bond or debenture, and requires to be cut off when the time has arrived for its presentment for payment. Where the interest on debentures and bonds is paid by means of coupons, a sheet of coupons is supplied. The sheet contains a series of coupons, there being a coupon with a different date for each payment of interest, quarterly or half-yearly, as the case may be, for several, and, in cases of large coupon sheets, for many years to come. Where no date of payment appears upon the coupons, they are payable on advertised dates. If the date of payment falls upon a Sunday or a bank holiday, they are payable on the succeeding business day.

A curious example of the dates of payment is found in the case of certain Chinese bonds, the coupons of which are advertised as being payable "on the first day of the third and ninth moon of the Chinese calendar."

Where many bonds with coupons attached are held, a banker keeps a coupon diary, in which are entered particulars of the coupons falling due upon the various dates. Coupons are generally sent up to London, by a country banker, for collection, say, three or four weeks before they are due. In order to prevent them getting lost, they should be pinned to a ticket or slip. There should be a separate ticket for each different security, which should quote the number of coupons attached, and give particulars of them. The coupons should be sorted in numerical order and according to amounts.

Where coupons are numerous, a coupon cutter is the most expeditious way of cutting them off.

When the last coupon has been detached, the part of the sheet which remains is called the "talon," and it is forwarded to the address given thereon to be exchanged for a fresh sheet of coupons. A "talon" is not, however, attached in all cases.

Coupons are not credited to a customer's account until an advice of the amount realised has been received. This custom has been adopted because of the differences which often arise in the deduction of the income tax.

Where the coupons are payable either in this country or abroad, the customer's instructions should be taken as to whether he wishes them to be sold or collected.

In the event of any coupons being lost, notice should be given to the bank where they are payable. The banker will no doubt exercise care before paying them, but he cannot really refuse to pay them, unless an order to do so is received from the customer who gave the instructions for the bank to pay the coupons.

A coupon is exempt from stamp duty. The exemption is contained in Section 40, Finance Act, 1894:—"Coupon or warrant for interest on a marketable security, being one of a set of coupons, whether issued with the security or subsequently issued in a sheet." A coupon attached to a scrip certificate is not exempt.

COUPON BOOK. In this book are kept particulars of all coupons sent away for collection. Columns are provided for—date sent, name of customer, name of issuers with designation, number, etc. of bond from which the coupons have been detached, and nominal amount of coupon. Two final columns show the proceeds and when received.

In the case of coupons payable in London, it is customary for country banks to remit them to their London agents about one month before they are due.

COURSE OF EXCHANGE. This is the technical name of the price list of bills, drafts and cheques, compiled on Tuesdays and Thursdays by the principal bill brokers, who meet on those days at the Royal Exchange, London. It is issued as soon as business is over for the day, say about three o'clock.

On the following page will be found the Course of Exchange for Tuesday, November 23, 1909, which will serve as an example.

In the aforesaid table "Usance" means the currency of the bills or drafts; that is, the time that must elapse before they are payable, "short" signifying up to eight or ten days. The double price column refers to the rate at which different qualities of paper are offered, the first quotation being for fine bank acceptances, the second for good commercial bills. The prices are those which the London brokers are charging at the time for bills of the currency and class stated; thus £100 would purchase a fine bank acceptance for 2,540 francs, payable at Marseilles in three months' time. (See CHEQUE RATE, FOREIGN EXCHANGES, LONG RATE, SHORT RATE, SPECIE POINTS.)

COURSE OF EXCHANGE. On	Usance.		PRICE. From		To		EXPLANATION.
Amsterdam	short	..	12·2¾	..	12·3¼	=	Florins and stivers for £1.
,,	3 months	..	12·5	..	12·5¼	=	,, ,,
Rotterdam	,,	..	12·5	..	12·5¼	=	,, ,,
Antwerp and Brussels	,,	..	25·51¼	..	25·56¼	=	Francs and centimes for £1.
Paris	short	..	25·18¾	..	25·23¾	=	,, ,,
,,	3 months	..	25·40	..	25·45	=	,, ,,
Marseilles	,,	..	25·40	..	25·45	=	,, ,,
Hamburg	,,	..	20·70	..	20·74	=	Reichsmarks and pfennigs for £1.
Berlin	,,	..	20·70	..	20·74	=	,, ,,
Leipsic	,,	..	20·70	..	20·74	=	,, ,,
Frankfort	,,	..	20·70	..	20·74	=	,, ,,
St. Petersburg	,,	..	25	..	$25\frac{1}{16}$	=	Pence for 1 rouble.
Copenhagen	,,	..	18·46	..	18·50	=	Kronors and öre for £1.
Stockholm	,,	..	18·47	..	18·51	=	,, ,,
Christiania	,,	..	18·47	..	18·51	=	,, ,,
Vienna	,,	..	24·38	..	24·42	=	Florins and kreutzers for £1.
Trieste	,,	..	24·38	..	24·42	=	,, ,,
Zurich-Basle	,,	..	25·52½	..	25·57½	=	Francs and centimes for £1.
Spain	,,	..	43⅛	..	43¼	=	Pence for 1 peso.
Italy	,,	..	25·65	..	25·72½	=	Lire and centesimi for £1.
Lisbon	90 days	..	46	..	46⅛	=	Pence for 1 milreis.
Oporto	,,	..	46	..	46⅛	=	,, ,,
New York	demand	..	$49\frac{1}{16}$	..	49¼	=	Pence for 1 dollar.

COURT BARON. The court of the lord of the manor, for freeholders. The copyholders' court is called the "customary court."

COURT, POWERS OF (IN WINDING UP). When an order has been made for the winding up of a company, the Court shall settle a list of contributories, and shall cause the assets of the company to be collected and applied in discharge of its liabilities. The Court has power to require any banker, officer of the company, or others, to deliver to the liquidator any money or property in his hands to which the company is *primâ facie* entitled; and to make an order for the payment of debts due by any contributory to the company; and to make calls on all or any of the contributories; and to order any payments to be made to the account of the liquidator at the Bank of England. The Court has also power to exclude creditors who have not proved their debts within the specified time; and to adjust the rights of contributories and distribute any surplus. When the affairs of a company have been wound up, the Court shall make an order that the company be dissolved. Most of the powers and duties of the Court may be performed by the liquidator, subject to the control of the Court. The Court has extraordinary powers to summon persons suspected of having property of the company; and, in England, to order the public examination of promoters, directors, or officers in cases where it is reported that a fraud has been committed. The Court has also power to arrest an absconding contributory. (See COMPANIES.)

COVENANT. A document setting forth the terms of a contract or agreement between two or more persons.

By the Stamp Act, 1891, the stamp duty is:—

	£	s.	d.
COVENANT in relation to any annuity (*except upon the original creation and sale thereof*) or to other periodical payments. See BOND, COVENANT, etc.			
COVENANT. Any separate deed of covenant (*not being an instrument chargeable with* ad valorem *duty as a conveyance on sale or mortgage*) made on the sale or mortgage of any property, and relating solely to the conveyance or enjoyment of, or the title to, the property sold or mortgaged, or to the production of the muniments of title relating thereto, or to all or any of the matters aforesaid.			
Where the *ad valorem* duty in respect of the consideration or mortgage money does not exceed 10*s*.	A duty equal to the amount of such *ad valorem* duty.		
In any other case	0	10	0
COVENANT for securing the payment or repayment of money, or the transfer or retransfer of stock. See MORTGAGE, etc.			
COVENANT in relation to any annuity upon the original creation and sale thereof. See CONVEYANCE ON SALE.			

COVENANT TO SURRENDER. A deed in which the vendor of copyhold land covenants to surrender it to the use of the purchaser. The actual surrender is to the lord of the manor to the use and behoof of the purchaser. (See COPYHOLD.)

COVER. The word is commonly used with the same meaning as security.

An advance is said to be "covered," when sufficient security is held to protect the banker from loss. (See SECURITY.)

COVERING DEED. A name sometimes given to a trust deed which covers or secures the debentures of a company.

COVERTURE. The legal state of a married woman.

CREDIT. When a customer pays in money and cheques for the benefit of his account, the banker places the amount to the credit of the customer's account. When the amounts credited are greater than the amounts withdrawn, or debited, the resulting balance is a credit one (shown, thus, Cr. £100), and represents the sum due by the banker to the customer, the banker being the debtor and the customer the creditor.

When an individual's "credit" is referred to, it means his reputation, as a man of business, for trustworthiness and ability to meet his engagements. If a cheque is dishonoured, in error, by a banker, the drawer would have cause to complain that his credit had thereby been injured.

CREDIT BANKS. CREDIT SOCIETIES. Credit banks, or agricultural co-operative credit societies as they are usually called, are to be found in various places in England, and in more than 200 places in Ireland. The object of these banks or societies is to enable small farmers to obtain advances of money for application to reproductive purposes in connection with their business. The society borrows money, either from a local banker or from the Central Co-operative Bank, London, on the joint security of all the members, and lends it out to the members, usually upon the joint and several promissory note of the borrower and two sureties. The liability of the members is unlimited, and it is on the strength of that liability that the society is enabled to borrow the money to lend out at slightly higher rates. If need be, the promissory notes of the individual borrowers may be assigned by the society as security to the local banker or the Central Bank from which it obtains a loan. The societies may also obtain capital from local wealthy residents who are interested in the welfare of the district in which the societies operate, and this was the main source of capital before the Central Bank was started. A credit bank also encourages thrift by receiving money on deposit, which is used in lending to members who require loans. When a credit bank has more deposits than it can utilise in loans to its own members, the unused balance is transferred to the Central Bank, and from there it is lent to other credit societies requiring money. The Central Bank is worked on limited liability lines.

Each borrower must specify the purpose for which a loan is required, and bind himself to apply the money only to that purpose. Fifty pounds is the maximum which may be lent to any one member. The society, which is managed by a committee elected by the members, pays no dividend, and all profits go to increase the capital formed from the small entrance fees of the members. The various societies are affiliated to the Agricultural Organisation Society.

In the event of the failure of a credit bank, the rules provide that in no case shall a Reserve Fund be divided amongst the members, but must be devoted to some local charity or useful purpose, such as a village hall, in the district in which the society operated.

A statement has recently (August, 1910) been made pointing to probable legislation to facilitate the creation of credit banks. Lord Carrington said: "I have been considering whether I could not devise a plan to lay before my colleagues to give legislative, administrative, and financial facilities for the establishment on a sound basis of a satisfactory system of co-operative credit banks, especially for the benefit of agriculture."

CREDIT SLIP. The form which is filled up and signed by a customer when paying in to the credit of a current account. It should be dated by the customer for the day on which the payment to credit is handed across the counter, or, if sent by post, the date of its despatch.

A credit slip should show how the amount is made up, in gold, silver, copper, notes, cheques, or bills.

Another name for a credit slip is "paying-in slip." (See PAYING-IN SLIPS.)

CREDITS OPENED AT OTHER OFFICES. (See STANDING CREDITS.)

CRISES, FINANCIAL. (See PANICS.)

CRORE. A hundred lacs of rupees. (See LAC.)

CROSSED CHEQUE. A crossed cheque is defined by the Bills of Exchange Act, 1882, Section 76, as follows :—

"(1) Where a cheque bears across its face an addition of—

"(a) The words 'and company' or any abbreviation thereof between two parallel transverse lines, either with or without the words 'not negotiable'; or

"(b) Two parallel transverse lines simply, either with or without the words 'not negotiable';

"that addition constitutes a crossing, and the cheque is crossed generally.

"(2) Where a cheque bears across its face an addition of the name of a banker, either with or without the words 'not negotiable,' that addition constitutes a crossing, and the cheque is crossed specially and to that banker."

By Section 77 :—

"(1) A cheque may be crossed generally or specially by the drawer.

"(2) Where a cheque is uncrossed, the holder may cross it generally or specially.

"(3) Where a cheque is crossed generally, the holder may cross it specially.

"(4) Where a cheque is crossed generally or specially, the holder may add the words 'not negotiable.'

"(5) Where a cheque is crossed specially, the banker to whom it is crossed may again cross it specially to another banker for collection.

"(6) Where an uncrossed cheque, or a cheque crossed generally, is sent to a banker for collection, he may cross it specially to himself."

By Section 78 :—

"A crossing authorised by this Act is a material part of the cheque; it shall not be lawful for any person to obliterate or, except as authorised by this Act, to add to or alter the crossing."

The duties of a banker with regard to crossed cheques are set forth in Section 79 :—

"(1) Where a cheque is crossed specially to more than one banker except when crossed to an agent for collection being a banker, the banker on whom it is drawn shall refuse payment thereof.

"(2) Where the banker on whom a cheque is drawn which is so crossed nevertheless pays the same, or pays a cheque crossed generally otherwise than to a banker, or if crossed specially otherwise than to the banker to whom it is crossed, or his agent for collection being a banker, he is liable to the true owner of the cheque for any loss he may sustain owing to the cheque having been so paid.

"Provided that where a cheque is presented for payment which does not at the time of presentment appear to be crossed, or to have had a crossing which has been obliterated, or to have been added to or altered otherwise than as authorised by this Act, the banker paying the cheque in good faith and without negligence shall not be responsible or incur any liability, nor shall the payment be questioned by reason of the cheque having been crossed, or of the crossing having been obliterated or having been added to or altered otherwise than as authorised by this Act, and of payment having been made otherwise than to a banker or to the banker to whom the cheque is or was crossed, or to his agent for collection being a banker, as the case may be."

A banker paying a crossed cheque is afforded protection by Section 80 :—

"Where the banker, on whom a crossed cheque is drawn, in good faith and without negligence pays it, if crossed generally, to a banker, or if crossed specially, to the banker to whom it is crossed, or his agent for collection being a banker, the banker paying the cheque, and, if the cheque has come into the hands of the payee, the drawer, shall respectively be entitled to the same rights and be placed in the same position as if payment of the cheque had been made to the true owner thereof."

As to the effect of crossing upon the holder, Section 81 provides :—

"Where a person takes a crossed cheque which bears on it the words 'not negotiable,' he shall not have and shall not be capable of giving a better title to the cheque than that which the person from whom he took it had."

A collecting banker is afforded protection by Section 82 :—

" Where a banker in good faith and without negligence receives payment for a customer of a cheque crossed generally or specially to himself, and the customer has no title or a defective title thereto, the banker shall not incur any liability to the true owner of the cheque by reason only of having received such payment."

The Section refers only to cheques which are already crossed when they come into a banker's hands.

The protection given by this Section applies to crossed cheques only when they are collected on behalf of a customer. Section 82, as it stands, does not protect a collecting banker who allows his customer to draw against crossed cheques paid in to credit of his account, before the proceeds for them have been received from the banker on whom the cheques are drawn. Much litigation has taken place around this Section, but it has now been amended by the Bills of Exchange (Crossed Cheques) Act, 1906, passed August 4, 1906, being "an Act to amend Section 82 of the Bills of Exchange Act, 1882." The amendment is :—

" Section 1. A banker receives payment of a crossed cheque for a customer within the meaning of Section 82 of the Bills of Exchange Act, 1882, notwithstanding that he credits his customer's account with the amount of the cheque before receiving payment thereof."

It has been held that to make a person a customer of a banker there must be some sort of account, either a deposit or a current account or some similar relation.

A dividend warrant may be crossed. Section 95 says :—

" The provisions of this Act as to crossed cheques shall apply to a warrant for payment of dividend." The Act does not apply to bills, which cannot, therefore, be crossed like cheques. If a bill should be crossed, the crossing is of no effect.

Money orders and postal orders may be crossed.

The crossed cheque sections of the Bills of Exchange Act, 1882, extend to any document issued by a customer of any banker, and intended to enable any person or body corporate to obtain payment from such banker of the sum mentioned in such document (Revenue Act, 1883, Section 17).

The following are specimens of crossings which come under the definition of a general crossing :—

1. (blank crossing)
2. *and Company.*
3. *& Co*
4. *not negotiable*
5. *not negotiable. & Co.*
6. *under Fifty pounds.*
7. *For the credit of John Brown's account.*
8. *not negotiable. under Twenty pounds.*
9. *& Co. Payee's account only.*
10. *not negotiable. & Co.*

But any of these, or similar, words across a cheque, without the transverse lines or with only one transverse line, do not constitute a crossing.

It is to be noted that where such words as " Under Fifty pounds " are written across a cheque, if a line is drawn above and below those words the lines constitute a general crossing, although it may not have been the intention to cross it.

If a cheque is crossed "& Coy., Leeds," the word Leeds may be ignored, as it is not part of the crossing.

On page 163 are specimens of crossings which are included in the definition of a special crossing.

There are many varieties of general and special crossings. As a rule, the transverse lines go right across the cheque, but frequently they are drawn only a half or a third way across, and in extreme cases the lines are so short as to be easily overlooked.

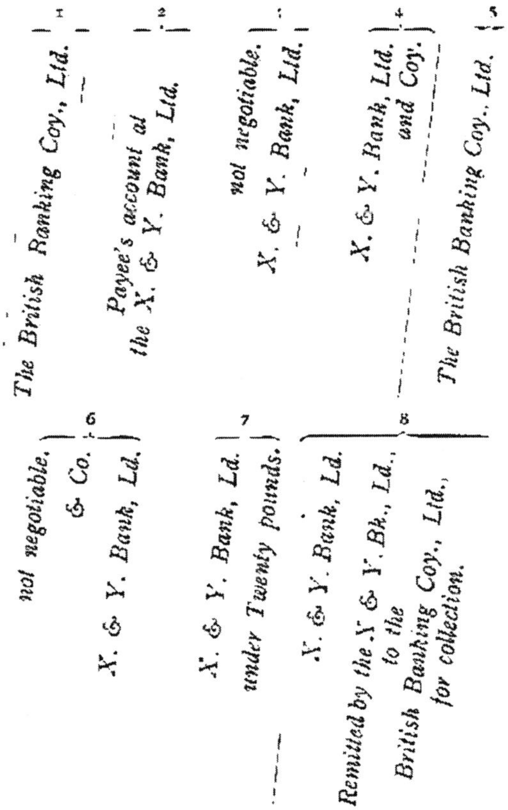

A cheque is occasionally met with which has a × placed upon it with the object of making it a crossed cheque. Such a mark does not, of course, constitute it a crossed cheque.

The position of the lines is usually about the middle of a cheque, but they are sometimes drawn across a corner of it.

The place of any words added to the transverse lines is usually between or immediately above or immediately below the lines, but in some cases they are found at a considerable distance from the crossing, and occasionally are found written even below the amount. It is questionable, however, whether words which are not written between or near to the transverse lines could be held to be a part of the crossing.

Crossings may be written, stamped, printed, or perforated. Many mistakes as to the amount would be prevented if customers avoided drawing the crossing lines through the figures of a cheque.

By the above sections it is seen that a crossed cheque can be paid by the banker on whom it is drawn, if crossed generally, only to another banker—if crossed specially, only to the banker whose name appears in the crossing. If the holder of a crossed cheque is a customer of the banker on whom it is drawn, the banker may place such cheque, if it is so desired, to the credit of that customer's account, though he should not pay cash for it. The customer, however, may forthwith draw a cheque upon his account for the cash required.

Where a cheque crossed generally and drawn upon one branch is presented for payment at another branch of the same bank, the two branches are, for this purpose, considered to be two banks, and the banker paying such a cheque fulfils the requirements of the Act to pay it only to another banker. In *Gordon* v. *London City and Midland Bank* (1902, 1 K.B. 242), the Master of the Rolls, referring to cheques of that description, said: "The defendants, whose branch bank receives payment from another branch, are certainly a bank. It may be that the payment is to themselves; still, it is a payment made to a bank, and the payment is also made by a bank."

Where a cheque is crossed, and a payee wishes to obtain cash for it from the banker on whom it is drawn, it is customary for the drawer to cancel the crossing and to write "pay cash" upon the cheque. The alteration, called "opening the crossing," should be initialled or signed by the drawer. A banker, however, should be on his guard when requested to cash a cheque where the crossing has been cancelled, lest by doing so he renders himself liable to a true owner who took the cheque in a crossed condition. (See OPENING A CROSSING.)

The transverse lines are an essential part of a general crossing, but they are not necessary in a special crossing. The name of a banker by itself across the face of a cheque is a special crossing, or the name may be placed between transverse lines, or it may be placed inside a square or other form of margin.

The dishonour of a crossed cheque does not cancel the crossing. The cheque continues to be a crossed cheque, and, if re-presented, requires to be re-presented in accordance with the crossing. If a dishonoured crossed cheque bears the crossing of a country banker and the crossing of his London agents, on re-presentation the cheque may, if necessary, be presented direct by the country banker.

Where a crossed cheque is remitted to an

agent for collection, it is customary for the banker to cross it thus : "X. & Y. Bank, Ltd., to the British Bank, Ltd., for collection."

By Section 79, quoted above, when a cheque is crossed to two bankers, except when crossed to an agent for collection being a banker, the banker on whom it is drawn shall refuse payment. If the presenting banker guarantees the banker on whom it is drawn, such a cheque would usually be paid. But a cheque which is crossed to two branches of the same bank, or to a branch and the head office, is not treated as being crossed to two bankers. A cheque crossed "X. & Y. Bank" should not be placed to a customer's credit at the British Bank, because the banker on whom it is drawn can pay it only to the X. & Y. Bank.

It is customary for a collecting banker to whom a cheque is specially crossed, to place an impress of his stamp upon it, as an indication to the paying banker that it has been through the hands of that banker, but a cheque should not be dishonoured merely because the collecting banker has omitted to stamp it.

The words "not negotiable," added to a general or a special crossing, do not operate as a restriction upon the transfer of a cheque, but merely give notice to anyone taking the cheque that he cannot obtain a better title than the person had from whom he received it. The words "not negotiable" do not by themselves constitute a crossing.

Many cheques have such words as "place to credit of John Brown's account," "account of payee," "account John Jones" added to the crossing. The Bills of Exchange Act does not make any particular reference to an addition of that nature, though it does say at Section 78 that it shall not be lawful for any person to obliterate or, except as authorised by this Act, to add to or alter the crossing. If the paying banker carries out his duty, as prescribed by the Act, and pays a cheque crossed generally to a banker, and a cheque crossed specially to the banker named, he is not concerned at all as to whether, or not, the collecting banker carried out the instructions to place the proceeds to any account indicated. There does not appear to have been any definite decision in the Courts as to what is the duty of the collecting banker with respect to such instructions upon a cheque. If a cheque drawn on the British Banking Co., Ltd., and crossed "X. & Y. Bank, Ltd., for the account of John Brown," is paid in to the X. & Y. Bank, Ltd., by Tom Jones to his own credit, it is difficult to believe that the X. & Y. Bank, Ltd., would be exonerated from blame if they ignored the clear indication upon the cheque and passed it to the credit of Jones. Accordingly, in practice, a banker who receives such a cheque for collection, requires that it be placed to the credit of the account as named in the crossing. In *National Bank* v. *Silke* (1891, 1 Q.B. 435), where a cheque was crossed "account of Moriarty, National Bank," Lord Justice Lindley said with reference to those words : "It cannot be contended that they prohibit transfer, and I do not think that they indicate an intention that the cheque should not be transferable. They amount to nothing more than a direction to the plaintiffs to carry the amount of the cheque to Moriarty's account when they have received it."

In *Akrokerri (Atlantic) Mines, Limited* v. *The Economic Bank* (1904, 2 K.B. 465), where certain cheques were crossed "account Economic Bank," Mr. Justice Bigham said : "In my opinion these words are not in any sense an addition to the crossing. A crossing is a direction to the paying bank to pay the money generally to a bank, or to a particular bank, as the case may be, and when this has been done the whole purpose of the crossing has been served. The paying bank has nothing to do with the application of the money after it has once been paid to the proper receiving banker. The words 'account A. B.' are a mere direction to the receiving bank as to how the money is to be dealt with after receipt."

With reference to the words "how the money is to be dealt with after receipt," as a collecting banker may now pass crossed cheques at once to the credit of his customer, it would appear to follow that the words "Account A. B.," are a direction to the receiving banker as to how he must deal with the cheques when he receives them.

The object of crossing cheques is to insure the safe transmission of the money from the sender to the receiver. A general crossing would prevent a thief from obtaining value from a banker for a cheque, unless he had a banking account. The usual special crossing would prevent him from obtaining value unless he had an account with the banker to whom the cheque was crossed. Thus the thief's chance of profiting by his plunder becomes still further remote.

If a collecting banker gives cash over the counter for a crossed cheque on another banker, he does so at his own risk, because if an indorsement is forged he is liable to the true owner. (See CHEQUE, COLLECTING BANKER.)

"CROSSED TO TWO BANKERS." An answer which is sometimes marked upon a cheque by the drawee banker, who is returning it unpaid for this reason.

Where a cheque is crossed to two bankers, except when crossed to an agent for collection being a banker, the banker on whom it is drawn shall refuse payment thereof (Section 79, Bills of Exchange Act, 1882).

But a cheque crossed "X. & Y. Bank, Ltd., Leeds," and also stamped "X. & Y. Bank, Ltd., York," is not crossed to two bankers, as Leeds and York are branches of the same banker.

CROSS-FIRING. Cross-firing is where one person draws a bill upon another, and the latter, at the same time, draws a bill upon the former. When a banker detects signs of such a practice, it should act as a danger signal and put him at once on his guard.

CROWN. A crown is of the value of five shillings, and its standard weight is 436·36363 grains troy. Its standard fineness is thirty-seven-fortieths fine silver, three-fortieths alloy.

Silver crowns were first coined in 1551. (See COINAGE.)

CUM DIV. Short for cum dividend, "with dividend." It means that the purchaser of shares bought on this understanding is entitled to the dividend due to be paid, and if the dividend warrant is sent by the company to the seller, the latter must hand over the amount to the purchaser. Most stocks are "cum div." until the Pay Day following the declaration of dividend. (See PAY DAY.)

CUMULATIVE DIVIDEND. Preference shares have a preferential right to dividend before ordinary shares, and if the profits of the company in one year are not sufficient to pay the full dividend, the profits of succeeding years are used for that purpose, and, until the preference shares receive a full dividend for each year, the ordinary shares receive nothing. The dividend in such cases is called cumulative.

If, however, the preferential right as to dividend is confined merely to the profits of each year, the dividend is non-cumulative.

CURRENCY. The word was originally applied to the currency, or passing from hand to hand, of money, but it has now come to be applied to the money itself, gold, silver and copper. Bills of Exchange, bank notes, cheques and any other documents which act as a substitute for coins are also included under that term.

The currency, or circulating medium, by which sales and purchases were effected in olden times, was represented in different countries by articles, such as sugar, furs, fish, cloth, etc., and even at the present day in certain uncivilised nations, cowries, salt, and blocks of tea may be found in use.

The period for which a bill of exchange is drawn, or the period which it has to run before maturity, is spoken of as the currency of the bill. The currency of a bill payable after sight begins when the bill is accepted. (See COINAGE, MONEY.)

CURRENCY BONDS. Bonds which are repayable in the currency of the country where they are issued.

CURRENCY CERTIFICATES. Certificates which are issued to bankers and others by the Treasury of the United States against deposits of quantities of Treasury Notes and Government Notes.

CURRENCY OF BILL. The period during which a bill has to run before it is due. (See DAYS OF GRACE, TIME OF PAYMENT OF BILL.)

CURRENT ACCOUNT. A customer's current account at the bank is the account to which he pays in money daily, or at intervals, and upon which he draws cheques as required for his business or other purposes. It may be either overdrawn or "in credit." It is to be distinguished from a loan account, on which a sum is borrowed in one amount and which is not operated upon, and from a deposit account which is used principally for the lodgment of money which is not likely to be required for some time. (See INTEREST, PASS BOOK.)

CURRENT ACCOUNT LEDGERS. Each account in the current account ledgers is headed with the full christian names and surname of the customer, his address and designation; any particulars regarding signing upon the account, or credits opened on behalf of the customer, or whether the customer is a shareholder of the bank, with the amount of his holding, are also recorded at the top of the page. If it is an overdrawn account, the amount of the sanctioned limit, the date when granted and the date when it will expire, are entered, so that these particulars may always be under the eye of the ledger keeper when posting the account.

Columns are provided in the ledgers for the date of each entry, particulars (payee's name for debit items, "cash," "bills" or "sundries" for credit items), debit amounts, credit amounts, Dr. or Cr., and balance. After these columns there are rulings in connection with the interest :—a column for the number of days to be allowed or charged on each balance extended, a column for the "decimals" on the debit balances and one for the "decimals" on the credit balances. A column is sometimes provided also for "decimals" upon cheques or notes paid to credit which are not cash for two or three days after receipt. (See DECIMALS.) In some banks the interest is calculated at the time of posting and entered in interest money columns.

A ledger keeper preserves a sharp look out upon the various items which come to his hands to be posted, and reports at once when any cheques will overdraw an account or cause it to exceed the sanctioned limit. The signatures upon cheques also come under his observation, and any suspected signature is reported immediately to the manager or chief clerk.

The entries in the ledgers are posted in many banks from the actual credit slips and cheques signed by the customers, and the balance is extended, in a model ledger, after all the items have been posted, so that there is only one balance shown on any one day.

In some banks the credits are posted in the ledgers from dockets prepared by the cashiers. The dockets give the date, the amount and the name of the account.

Some ledgers are ruled with separate columns for the debit or credit balance, whilst others have only one column, the nature of the balance being indicated by "Dr." or "Cr." in front of it, or by credit and debit balances being written in different coloured inks. This last is found in practice to be a very convenient method.

Cheques are sometimes posted by the numbers instead of by the names of the payees.

The ledgers are called over daily (either the same day or first thing on the following morning) with the day books, or check ledgers, but a ledger keeper does not, as a rule, call over the ledger which he has posted. In some banks the actual vouchers are also checked daily with the ledgers, and where this is done the ledger keeper, when posting an account, makes a note upon the vouchers (or the first one if a quantity) of the folio of the account, so that the checker may readily find the place.

The number of ledgers varies, of course, with the number of accounts at a branch, and it is a common practice for a separate ledger to be kept for all the principal accounts.

When an account is finally closed, it is the custom in some banks to paste the closing voucher into the ledger.

CURRENT ACCOUNT REGISTER. A name sometimes given to the book in which are entered, either alphabetically or in columns corresponding to each current account ledger, all the cheques and current account credit slips which are posted into the current account ledgers each day. In some banks the book is called a check ledger, whilst in other banks the particulars are given in the day book. The entries are called over daily with the ledgers, to act as a check upon the postings.

CURTESY. Curtesy is the right to which a husband is entitled, on the death of his wife, to the rents and profits of any of her freehold land which she has not disposed of by will. This "estate by the curtesy of England," as it is called, only arises if the husband has had by his wife a child born alive, and who does or might inherit the estate. It is an estate for the life of the husband, irrespective of the fact whether the child who would eventually inherit dies before him, or has died before the death of the wife. This "estate by the curtesy" does exist in some cases of land of copyhold tenure, but only by the special custom of the manor. (See INTESTACY.)

CUSTODIAN TRUSTEE. By the Public Trustee Act, 1906, which came into operation on the first day of January, 1908, the office of Public Trustee was established.

The Public Trustee may, amongst other duties, if he thinks fit, act as custodian trustee, if appointed by order of the Court, or by the testator, settlor or other creator of a trust, or by the person having power to appoint new trustees.

Section 4 of the Public Trustee Act is as follows :—

"(1) Subject to rules under this Act the public trustee may, if he consents to act as such, and whether or not the number of trustees has been reduced below the original number, be appointed to be custodian trustee of any trust—

"(a) by order of the Court made on the application of any person on whose application the Court may order the appointment of a new trustee ; or

"(b) by the testator, settlor, or other creator of any trust ; or

"(c) by the person having power to appoint new trustees.

"(2) Where the public trustee is appointed to be custodian trustee of any trust—

"(a) The trust property shall be transferred to the custodian trustee as if he were sole trustee, and for that purpose vesting orders may, where necessary, be made under the Trustee Act, 1893 :

"(b) The management of the trust property and the exercise of any power or discretion exerciseable by the trustees under the trust shall remain vested in the trustees other than the custodian trustee (which trustees are hereinafter referred to as the managing trustees) :

"(c) As between the custodian trustee and the managing trustees, and subject and without prejudice to the rights of any other persons, the custodian trustee shall have the custody of all securities and documents of title relating to the trust property, but the managing trustees shall have free access thereto and be entitled to take copies thereof or extracts therefrom :

"(d) The custodian trustee shall concur in and perform all acts necessary to enable the managing trustees to exercise their powers of management or any other power or discretion vested in them (including the power to pay money or securities into Court), unless the matter in which he is requested to concur is a breach of trust, or involves a personal liability upon him in respect of calls or otherwise, but, unless he so concurs, the custodian trustee shall not be liable for any act or default on the part of the managing trustees or any of them :

"(e) All sums payable to or out of the income or capital of the trust property shall be paid to or by the custodian trustee : Provided that the custodian trustee may allow the dividends and other income derived from the trust property to be paid to the managing trustees or to such person as they direct, or into such bank to the credit of such person as they may direct, and in such case shall be exonerated from seeing to the application thereof and shall not be answerable for any loss or misapplication thereof :

"(f) The power of appointing new trustees, when exerciseable by the trustees, shall be exerciseable by the managing trustees alone, but the custodian trustee shall have the same power of applying to the Court for the appointment of a new trustee as any other trustee :

"(g) In determining the number of trustees for the purposes of the Trustee Act, 1893, the custodian trustee shall not be reckoned as a trustee :

"(h) The custodian trustee, if he acts in good faith, shall not be liable for accepting as correct and acting upon the faith of any written statement by the managing trustees as to any birth, death, marriage, or other matter of pedigree or relationship, or other matter of fact, upon which the title to the trust property or any part thereof may depend, nor for acting upon any legal advice obtained by the managing trustees independently of the custodian trustee :

"(i) The Court may, on the

application of either the custodian trustee, or any of the managing trustees, or of any beneficiary, and on proof to their satisfaction that it is the general wish of the beneficiaries, or that on other grounds it is expedient, to terminate the custodian trusteeship, make an order for that purpose, and the Court may thereupon make such vesting orders and give such directions as under the circumstances may seem to the Court to be necessary or expedient.

(3) The provisions of this Section shall apply in like manner as to the public trustee to any banking or insurance company or other body corporate entitled by rules made under this Act to act as custodian trustee, with power for such company or body corporate to charge and retain or pay out of the trust property fees not exceeding the fees chargeable by the public trustee as custodian trustee."

From the last subsection it is seen that a banking company entitled by rules made under the Act may act as custodian trustee. Rule 36 of the Public Trustee Rules is as follows :—

"(1) The bodies corporate entitled to act as Custodian Trustee shall be any incorporated Banking or Insurance or Guarantee or Trust Company or Friendly Society, and any such body corporate established for charitable or philanthropic purposes as may be approved by the Public Trustee and the Treasury.

"(2) The Public Trustee may require payment by any applicant for such approval of a fee not exceeding ten guineas.

"(3) Such approval may be granted subject to such conditions as to the rendering of the body corporate, and verification, of periodical returns of business transacted, and fees and other emoluments received, and otherwise, as the Treasury may require either generally or in any particular case.

"(4) Any such approval may at any time be withdrawn without reason assigned."

In a paper read before the Institute of Bankers by the Public Trustee in 1908, he said with reference to the appointment of custodian trustee as a custodian for the property and securities, leaving the management of the trust to other trustees, "His duties under this provision will, however, in my opinion, be somewhat difficult to define, as it appears to me that to be a proper custodian in a trust you must exercise your discretion, for example, as regards investments and also supervise the administration of the trust generally, though not actually taking part in the management, and the line will not be easily drawn between custodian and managing trustee."

In a pamphlet issued by the Public Trustee, the scale of capital fees ordinarily chargeable in the case of a custodian trustee is as follows (minimum fee 10s. 6d.) :—

	Not exceeding £1,000.		On excess of £1,000 up to £20,000.		On excess of £20,000 up to £50,000.		On excess of £50,000.	
	s.	*d.*	*s.*	*d.*	*s.*	*d.*	*s.*	*d.*
On acceptance of trust a percentage of . . .	7	6	2	6	1	3	0	7½

(These are half the fees payable where the Public Trustee acts as an ordinary trustee.)

On withdrawal of any capital, a fee is chargeable at a rate equal to the rate per £100 at which the fee upon the acceptance of the trust was payable in respect of the entire trust property. Where the Public Trustee acts as an ordinary trustee the fee due upon acceptance of an estate valued at £10,000 is £30, produced by an all round rate of 6*s.* per £100, but where he acts as a custodian trustee the fee payable is half that amount—namely, 3*s.* per £100—and that rate applies also to a banking company acting as custodian trustee.

The *Income Fees* chargeable by a custodian trustee are :—

Upon the annual income of the trust property, at the rate of £2 per £100 upon all income not exceeding £500 a year.

Where the income exceeds £500 a year, £1 per £100 is payable on such excess.

Where the income is payable direct to the person entitled, or to his bankers, the fee will not exceed £1 per £100 throughout. (Minimum fee, 2*s.* 6*d.*)

The *Investment Fees* are :—

Any investment in stocks, funds, shares, 10*s.* per cent. (which includes brokerage) on the sum invested.

Any purchase or sale of land, or any

investment by way of mortgage or charge. 2*s.* 6*d.* per cent. on the purchase money or money advanced.

Where the trust consists of landed property settled in strict settlement, the fee on acceptance is as above. No further fee is payable so long as the property, remains in strict settlement or is re-settled.

If the trust is put an end to, then a fee on withdrawal of the property will be due.

(See under PUBLIC TRUSTEE for further information regarding fees and the duties of a custodian trustee.)

The Public Trustee, in his own capacity as custodian trustee or ordinary trustee, may employ, for the purposes of any trust, such bankers as he may consider necessary. He will, however, whenever practicable, take into consideration the wishes of the creator of the trust and any other trustees there may be, and of the beneficiaries. In such a case the position of the banker is merely that of the usual one with a customer. In the paper by the Public Trustee, above referred to, he said :—"In the case of bankers, it will be the practice of the department not to disturb the connection between the settlor or testator and his banker, and I propose to ask, in such cases, the bank to continue the account in the name of the Public Trustee." (See PUBLIC TRUSTEE, TRUSTEE.)

CUSTOMARY COURT. The court of the lord of the manor, for customary tenants, or copyholders.

The court baron is the name of the freeholders' court.

CUSTOMARY PROPERTY. Customary freeholds, or privileged copyholds, are somewhat similar to ordinary copyholds. The property, however, is not held at the will of the lord, and it can be conveyed by deed, or by bargain and sale, as well as by surrender, but like copyhold property a purchaser's title requires to be completed by admittance.

In a conveyance of customary property, J. Brown to J. Jones, Brown would (by and with the licence and consent of Lord of the Manor of or his steward or commissioner thereunto lawfully anthorised) bargain, sell, surrender, release and convey unto the said J. Jones all that to hold the said premises unto the said Jones, his heirs and assigns according to the custom of the Manor of yielding and paying therefor yearly unto the said Lord of the Manor the yearly customary rent of and also paying and performing all other rents, duties, customs and services therefor due and of right accustomed to be paid, kept, done and performed

Indorsed upon the deed would be a licence, as follows :—" On behalf of Lord of the Manor of I authorise the within deed, provided the same be in no ways prejudicial to the said Lord or the future Lords of the said manor in regard to the rents, fines, dues, duties and services to be rendered for the customary premises within mentioned according to the custom of the said Manor.

" Steward."

The licence, however, is not always indorsed on the deed.

To perfect the title, the purchaser should be admitted tenant on the court rolls, and the document of admittance which is given to him should accompany the deeds, when they are deposited with a banker as security. If the property has been obtained by will, the will should be registered on the rolls and an admittance obtained.

In some manors, however, there is no document of admittance, but a receipt for the fines is given, and this is sufficient evidence of the enrolment. In such cases the receipt should accompany the deeds.

In addition to a yearly customary rent, there may be a fine payable on a change of ownership or on the death of the lord or of the tenant.

The admittance is of no value unless the conveyance is held.

Previous to 1832, an owner could not dispose of customary property by will. He usually surrendered it to a friend, who executed a deed declaring that he held it in trust for the person whom the owner by deed or will might appoint. It is quite common, in some places, for families to be on the roll for generations, for property in which they have no interest. It has no effect upon the title, though it might possibly be inconvenient if a banker required admittance.

Mortgagees usually take a mortgage of customary property in a form under which they can obtain admittance if necessary, but they do not, as a rule, seek admittance until they wish to sell the property. Unless a mortgagee is admitted, there is the risk that a second mortgagee, without notice of the first charge, may obtain admittance. When a mortgagee is admitted, the fines and fees must be paid. In some manors, the licence of the lord is necessary before a valid mortgage can be given.

For stamp duties, see COPYHOLD.

CUSTOMER. Where a banker collects a cheque, crossed generally or specially to himself, for a customer, the banker is protected, if he has acted in good faith and without negligence, even if an indorsement should prove to be forged (Section 82, Bills of Exchange Act). The person for whom it is collected must, however, be a customer. It has been held that in order to make a person a customer of a bank, within the meaning of Section 82, there must be either a deposit or a current account or some similar relation. (*Great Western Railway v. London and County Banking Co.*, 1901, A.C. 414.)

Money paid in by a customer to his account is really lent to the banker, the banker becoming, not the trustee for that money, but the debtor of the customer. In the event of the banker's failure, the customer claims upon the estate as an ordinary creditor.

CUSTOMS AND EXCISE ACCOUNT. The persons entitled to draw upon such account are those who are notified to the banker by the Commissioners of Customs and Excise.

The account is subject to the conditions prescribed in Section 18 of the Exchequer and Audit Departments Act (29 & 30 Vict. c. 39). (See PUBLIC ACCOUNT.)

Cheques on the account, or drafts given by the banker to transmit money from the account to another public account, are exempt from stamp duty. (See Schedule to Stamp Act, 1891, under article BILL OF EXCHANGE.)

CY PRÈS. As nearly as possible. When the terms of a trust are incapable of being carried out absolutely, the Courts have power to order that they be carried out "*cy près*," as nearly as possible.

DATE. The Bills of Exchange Act, 1882, provides :—

"Section 3. (4) A bill is not invalid by reason—

"(*a*) That it is not dated."

"Section 12. Where a bill expressed to be payable at a fixed period after date is issued undated, or where the acceptance of a bill payable at a fixed period after sight is undated, any holder may insert therein the true date of issue or acceptance, and the bill shall be payable accordingly.

"Provided that (1) where the holder in good faith and by mistake inserts a wrong date, and (2) in every case where a wrong date is inserted, if the bill subsequently comes into the hands of a holder in due course the bill shall not be avoided thereby, but shall operate and be payable as if the date so inserted had been the true date."

Where an undated bill has a date inserted after acceptance, notice of the date so inserted should be given to the acceptor, otherwise he will not know when the bill is due.

The above Section applies only to bills, but with regard to cheques where the date has been omitted it is generally considered that a holder may insert what he takes to be the true date.

"Section 13. (1) Where a bill or an acceptance or any indorsement on a bill is dated, the date shall, unless the contrary be proved, be deemed to be the true date of the drawing, acceptance, or indorsement, as the case may be.

"(2) A bill is not invalid by reason only that it is ante-dated or post-dated, or that it bears date on a Sunday."

Ante-dating is placing a date prior to the true date ; post-dating, placing a date subsequent to the true date.

The difference between the insertion of an omitted date and the alteration of a date should be noted. The above section permits any holder to insert a date, but Section 64 (see under ALTERATIONS) requires all parties to agree to an alteration.

The date is a material part of a bill and any alteration in a date, unless with the assent of all the parties liable on the bill, avoids the bill except as against the party who has made or assented to the alteration, and subsequent indorsers ; but where a date has been altered and the alteration is not apparent, a holder in due course may avail himself of the bill as if it had not been altered.

A bill bearing a date prior to the date upon the stamp is not invalid, as the above Section (13) permits a bill to be ante-dated. A bill, however, must be stamped before it is drawn.

Where a post-dated bill is discounted, and the acceptor dies or becomes bankrupt before the arrival of the date of the bill, the bill is not invalid by reason only that it is post-dated.

It is not permissible to give a bill or promissory note, undated, for say three months, and after payment of the bill or note, still undated, to issue it again for another three months, and so on. The only date which can be inserted in an undated bill is the true date of issue. A fresh debt requires a new bill or note.

Bills drawn in Russia are generally dated according to the old style (or Julian calendar), and thirteen days require to be added to the date on the bill to bring the date into accordance with the new style (or Gregorian calendar) of this country. The date is often given on Russian bills as, e.g. March 5/18, the first date being that of the old style (O.S.) and the second date that of the new style (N.S.). The currency of such a bill would, in this country, be calculated from March 18. From 1800 to 1900 the difference was twelve days; from 1900 to 2100 the difference is thirteen days, and so it will remain unless Russia comes into line with other countries as to the calendar.

The dates on bills of exchange and cheques are usually in figures, but they would be quite valid if written in words. In France the date on a cheque is written in words. On transfers, powers of attorney, conveyances, and other important instruments, the date should be in words. (See ANTE-DATED, BILL OF EXCHANGE, POST-DATED.)

DAY BOOK. It is called in some banks the cash book, or state book. At a small branch one book suffices, and it contains a record of all the day's transactions. The entries on the received side, plus the balance brought forward from yesterday, balance with the entries on the paid side and the balance of cash on hand at the close of to-day.

In a large branch there may be subsidiary day books for current accounts, as may be found necessary, for transfer items, etc., and the totals of these books are brought into a daily summary book.

Where the number of current accounts is large, it is found very convenient to balance each current account ledger by itself (see BALANCE BOOK), and it is in the day book that all the current account items are separated to the ledgers where they belong, thus there may be a column for ledger A to C, another for ledger D to G, and so on.

The day book is an important book and requires to be carefully kept, and, as with other bank books, no erasures are permitted to take place. Any alteration is effected by ruling out the wrong figures and inserting the correct ones.

The entries in the day book are called over daily with the current account, and other ledgers, and this is done, in most banks, by clerks other than those who write up the day books or post the ledgers. Some banks, in addition to calling over the day books, find it a useful plan also to check the actual vouchers with the current account ledgers. In a small branch the calling over may easily be done by the manager himself, who thereby gains information which he might not otherwise obtain. In a large branch a manager might with advantage occasionally call over one of the ledgers himself.

Check ledgers which are in use in some banks are practically of the same nature as day books in other banks. (See CHECK LEDGER.)

DAY-TO-DAY MONEY. Another name for "Call Money"; surplus funds in the London bankers' hands which they do not need to keep in their tills or in their accounts with the Bank of England, and which, while not caring to lock it up even temporarily by discounting bills or granting loans for fixed periods, they are willing to lend to bill brokers from "day-to-day," that is, on the understanding that the money shall be forthcoming at a moment's notice. (See MONEY AT CALL AND SHORT NOTICE.)

DAYS OF GRACE. Where a bill of exchange is not payable on demand, three days, called "days of grace," are allowed. Originally they would be allowed to an acceptor as a matter of grace; they are now, however, claimed by an acceptor as a matter of right and are fixed by law. The Bills of Exchange Act, 1882, provides :—

"Section 14. Where a bill is not payable on demand, the day on which it falls due is determined as follows :—

"(1) Three days, called days of grace, are, in every case where the bill itself does not otherwise provide, added to the time of payment as fixed by the bill, and the bill is due and payable on the last day of grace : Provided that—

"(*a*) When the last day of grace falls on Sunday, Christmas Day, Good Friday, or a day appointed by royal proclamation as a public fast or thanksgiving day, the bill is, except in the case hereinafter provided for, due and payable on the preceding business day ;

"(*b*) When the last day of grace

is a bank holiday (other than Christmas Day or Good Friday) under the Bank Holidays Act, 1871, and Acts amending or extending it, or when the last day of grace is a Sunday and the second day of grace is a bank holiday, the bill is due and payable on the succeeding business day."

Thus a bill due February 1, when the three days are added, is actually payable on February 4.

If a bill is specially drawn as payable without days of grace, or as payable on a certain day fixed, e.g. "on February 1 fixed," no days of grace are allowed. A bill payable "at sight," "on presentation," or "on demand," does not take days of grace, but a bill payable "after sight" or "after date" does take the three days.

Bills drawn by the Bank of England upon itself do not take days of grace, but that exception does not apply in the case of any other bill drawn upon the Bank of England.

Days of grace are not allowed upon a cheque. Days of grace on a promissory note are the same as in the case of a bill.

If a bill or promissory note is payable by instalments, the three days are allowed upon each instalment.

A foreign bill domiciled in this country takes the three days of grace, but a bill drawn in England and domiciled abroad is payable according to the laws of the country where it is payable.

In many countries days of grace are not allowed, e.g. France, Germany, Russia, Norway, Sweden, Denmark, Holland, Belgium, Italy. In Canada three days are allowed, but in the United States the number varies.

If a person risks taking a bill which has been accepted contrary to the tenor of the bill, it should be presented on the day appointed by the acceptance, without days of grace. Opinions appear to differ as to whether days of grace can be claimed. If, however, days of grace are claimed by the acceptor, the bill should be formally noted, the usual notice given to all parties, and the bill presented again in three days' time.

An instrument which is drawn payable at a certain period after the arrival of a ship does not take days of grace, because the document is not a bill according to the meaning of the Bills of Exchange Act. Where a bill is payable after a specified event it must be an event which is certain to happen. The death of a person is a certain event, but the arrival of a ship is not. (See Bill of Exchange, Fire Insurance, Life Policy, Payment of Bill.)

Examples of the dates upon which bills, drawn at various currencies, are due, are given under Time of Payment of Bill.

DEAD ACCOUNT. Where operations upon an account have ceased, the account is said to have become dead. An overdrawn account, which has hitherto been of an active nature, suddenly becoming inoperative will warn a banker to give it his particular attention. A cessation of transactions may mean that the customer has opened an account with another bank.

An account upon which there have been no transactions or acknowledgment for a period of six years, could not, by the Statute of Limitations, be enforced against the debtor, whether he happened to be banker or customer. But no banker would think of withholding money from a customer who is able to establish his identity and title, however long the account may have lain inoperative in his books.

DEAD LOAN. A permanent loan, as distinguished from one which is only for a short period. A temporary advance may develop into a dead loan, if the borrower should prove to be unable to repay it at the specified time.

A prudent banker endeavours to avoid having his money locked up in dead loans, as such loans are contrary to the principles of sound banking.

DEAD RENT. In a mining lease there may often be found mention of two rents, the dead rent—that is, a fixed minimum rent —and a royalty rent—that is, a certain percentage of the profits from the mine. The dead rent is payable whether the mine is worked or not.

DEAD SECURITY. An inconvertible security. Mines, mills, iron-works, and suchlike properties, whatever their values may be as going concerns, become, usually, of very small value when they cease to work. They are well termed a dead security.

DEALER (STOCK EXCHANGE). The stock jobber on the Stock Exchange who deals in stocks and shares is called a "dealer." (See Stock Jobber.)

DEAR MONEY. Money is said to be "dear" when, owing to the supply being scarce, it can be borrowed only at a high rate of interest.

Money is "cheap" when it can be borrowed at a low rate.

DEATH DUTIES. The duties which are payable to the Government upon a person's death :—

1. Estate duty—payable on the value of all the property passing on a death after 1894, except when specially exempted. (See Estate Duty.)

2. Settlement estate duty—on such property when a life interest only is taken.

3. Legacy duty—payable upon legacies or other gifts of personalty made by will. (See Legacy Duty.)

4. Succession duty—payable by the successor of a deceased person upon real or leasehold property. (See Succession Duty.)

DEATH OF ACCEPTOR. Where an acceptor is dead and no place of payment is specified, presentment (of a bill) must be made to a personal representative, if such there be, and with the exercise of reasonable diligence he can be found. If he cannot be found, it should be presented at the house of the deceased.

The death of the acceptor cancels a banker's authority to pay a bill accepted by him, and any bill falling due after his death must be returned with answer "acceptor dead."

The payment of an acceptance after the acceptor's death is good, provided the banker was ignorant of the death.

DEATH OF ADMINISTRATOR. On the death of an administrator the surviving administrator, if any, acts, but, on the death of the last one, fresh letters of administration require to be taken out, and a new account should be opened by the new administrator. (See Administrator de bonis non.)

DEATH OF AGENT. Where a cheque is signed by an agent or a person in an official capacity, payment should not be refused merely because the agent or official has died since the cheque was issued. For example, if Jones has authority to draw cheques upon Brown's account, a cheque so drawn should be paid, although Jones may have died before its presentation. Cheques signed by a secretary, treasurer, director, manager or other person signing in an official capacity must also be paid, irrespective of the death of the official before presentation.

DEATH OF CUSTOMER. A banker may receive formal notice of a customer's death, but it is sufficient notice of the death if he sees an announcement in the papers or hears of it from a reliable source. A mere rumour that his customer John Brown is supposed to be dead is not sufficient to warrant a banker returning a bill or cheque unpaid, though a banker in that case would usually take steps to confirm or disprove the rumour.

After notice of death, no further cheques should be paid, except where a banker has, prior to the death, made himself responsible, e.g. by marking a cheque for payment at the request of the drawer, or another bank, or by making a purchase of stock or shares according to the customer's order.

If the deceased customer leaves a will appointing executors, the executors can, after probate has been obtained and exhibited to the banker, deal with the account and securities of the deceased, subject to any claims by the banker.

Where a customer dies without a will, letters of administration must be obtained, and, after exhibition thereof to the banker, the administrators can act in the same way as executors.

After exhibition of probate or letters of administration, any credit balance of the deceased is usually transferred to a new account, and it is advisable that the transfer be made by cheque or by a letter of authority signed by the representatives. The new account is commonly entitled "Executors of John Brown { John Jones, Robert Smith."

Any overdraft upon the deceased's account forms the subject of arrangement between the banker and the representatives, and until an arrangement is made the balance remains standing in the deceased's name.

DEATH OF DRAWEE. Where the drawee of a bill is dead, the bill should be presented to a personal representative, if there is one and he can be found. If he cannot be found, it should be presented at the house of the deceased.

DEATH OF DRAWER. The authority of a banker to pay a cheque drawn on him by his customer is determined by notice of the customer's death (Section 75, Bills of Exchange Act, 1882). All cheques received after notice of his death must be returned with answer "Drawer dead," except in the case of a cheque which has been "marked" for payment by a banker at the request of the drawer, or for the banker's own convenience in connection with the local clearing. Such a cheque may be paid when presented, even though the drawer has died since the cheque was marked, as the "marking" was, to all intents and purposes, a payment of the cheque. (See Marked Cheque.)

The notice of death does not affect any cheques which may have been debited to the deceased's account after his death, but prior to the time when the banker first heard of it. If a cheque is received in the morning's letters and, before it is actually debited to the drawer's account, notice of his death is received, the cheque should be returned.

A record of the death should be made in the current account ledger.

Before any transfer of the credit balance of the deceased's account can take place, probate or letters of administration must be exhibited.

Any cheques signed by the deceased in an official capacity, as treasurer, secretary, agent, director, etc. are not affected by his death.

If he has signed a cheque along with others on a joint credit account, the cheque would be paid, but if he signed alone upon the joint account it should not be paid. If the joint account is overdrawn, or the payment of the cheque would overdraw it, the banker should not pay it (if signed by the deceased with another of the joint holders), unless arrangements were made with the other drawer. On a joint account, only the survivors are responsible for any overdraft. (See DEATH OF JOINT CUSTOMER.)

Where the drawer of a bill is dead, and a party requiring to give notice of dishonour knows of it, the notice must be given to a personal representative if such there be, and with the exercise of reasonable diligence he can be found.

The death of A. B., who has given C. D. a mandate to sign on his account, cancels the mandate, and the banker will, after receipt of notice of A. B.'s death, return all cheques signed by C. D. under the mandate, with answer "A. B. deceased" or "customer deceased."

DEATH OF EXECUTOR. Upon the death of one executor cheques are signed by the surviving executor, if there is one. If the last executor is dead, his duties are undertaken by his executors, unless there is some special provision in the will. In the event of the last executor dying intestate, letters of administration for the estate for which the deceased was executor must be taken out, and when the letters have been exhibited, the balance, if credit should be transferred by cheque to a new account. (See ADMINISTRATOR DE BONIS NON.)

When a cheque is signed by two, or more, executors, the death of one of them does not affect the payment of the cheque when presented, unless the account is overdrawn and the executors are personally liable.

DEATH OF GUARANTOR. On receipt of notice of the death of a guarantor (whether sole guarantor or one of several) the banker will, if he is relying upon that surety (unless the guarantee provides that it shall not be determined by death), at once stop the account and open a fresh one for all further transactions. This prevents the payments to credit from extinguishing the guarantor's liability. If the account is not stopped, all fresh debits will be unsecured. The new account, in the absence of a fresh arrangement, should, of course, be kept in credit. If a new arrangement is not made in a short time, the executors of the deceased guarantor should be advised of the existence of the guarantee and of the banker's claim. When the matter has been arranged, e.g. by the customer providing a fresh guarantor, the old account should be paid off by a cheque on the new account. (See GUARANTEE.)

DEATH OF HOLDER. Upon the death of the holder of a bill or cheque, all his rights are transmitted by law to his executor or administrator, and the executor or administrator can sue upon the bill, or cheque, and negotiate it in the same way that the holder himself could have done.

When an executor, or an administrator, indorses a bill or cheque, he should state the capacity in which he signs, otherwise he may render himself personally liable.

An indorsement by an executor or administrator should be confirmed by his banker.

If a cheque is payable to two persons and one of them dies, the cheque is payable to the surviving holder, after satisfactory evidence has been produced of the death of the other.

DEATH OF INDORSER. Where an indorser is dead and the party requiring to give notice of dishonour knows of it, the notice must be given to a personal representative, if he can be found.

DEATH OF INFANT. (See DEATH OF MINOR.)

DEATH OF INSOLVENT DEBTOR. The Bankruptcy Act, 1883, provides as follows:—

"Section 125. (1) Any creditor of a deceased debtor whose debt would have been sufficient to support a bankruptcy petition against such debtor, had he been alive, may present to the Court a petition in the prescribed form praying for an order for the administration of the estate of the deceased debtor, according to the Law of Bankruptcy.

"(2) Upon the prescribed notice being given to the legal personal representative of the deceased debtor, the Court may, in the prescribed manner, upon proof of the petitioner's debt, unless the Court is satisfied that there is a reasonable probability that the estate will be sufficient for the payment of the debts owing by the deceased, make an order for the administration in bankruptcy of the deceased debtor's estate, or may upon cause shown dismiss such petition with or without costs."

The Court referred to in this Section is the Court within the jurisdiction of which the debtor resided or carried on business for the greater part of six months prior to his decease.

Upon an order being made for the administration of a deceased debtor's estate, the debtor's property shall vest in the official receiver of the Court as trustee, unless the creditors appoint a trustee in bankruptcy, and he shall forthwith proceed to realise and distribute it (Section 125, s.s. 5).

Any claim by the legal representative of the deceased to payment of proper funeral and testamentary expenses incurred by him about the estate, is deemed a preferential debt, and is payable in full out of the debtor's estate in priority to all other debts (Section 125, s.s. 7).

The provisions of the Bankruptcy Acts relating to the administration of the property of a bankrupt, are generally applicable to the case of an administration of a deceased debtor's estate (Section 125, s.s. 6). (See Bankruptcy.)

DEATH OF JOINT CUSTOMER. Where an account is opened in the names of John Brown and John Jones, and cheques are to be signed by both parties, and Brown dies, Jones may withdraw the balance, but the banker, of course, would require definite proof of Brown's death, e.g. death certificate.

Where an account is in the joint names of a husband and wife, and both of them have to sign each cheque, when the wife dies the balance may be withdrawn by the husband. If the husband dies first, the wife has power to draw a cheque for the balance, if it was the husband's intention that the money should be hers at his death. But if that was not the husband's intention, there appears to be some doubt as to whether the wife may draw the balance. In a case (*Marshal* v. *Crutwell*, 1875, 20 Eq. 328) where the husband transferred his account into the names of himself and wife, with authority for either to sign cheques thereon, Sir George Jessel said :—"I think the circumstances show that this was a mere arrangement for convenience, and that it was not intended to be a provision for the wife in the event which might happen, that at the husband's death there might be a fund standing to the credit of the banking account. . . . I come to the conclusion that it was not intended to be a provision for the wife, but simply a mode of conveniently managing the testator's affairs, and that it leaves the money, therefore, still his property." To prevent any question arising at the death of the husband, a banker should always have a clear arrangement made with the customers when such accounts are opened, as to whether, or not, the balance is to belong to the survivor.

In joint accounts which may be operated upon by either party, the form of authority which is signed usually authorises the banker to accept the signature of either, or survivor, upon the account.

The same remarks apply with regard to a deposit receipt in joint names. Receipts in joint names are often drawn as re-payable to "either, or survivor." Even if a deposit receipt in joint names is specifically mentioned in a will, it is nevertheless payable to the survivor, so far as the banker is concerned.

If a banker receive notice from the executors of a joint account holder, or joint depositor, not to pay the balance to the survivor, the banker would be justified in refusing payment.

Where both, or all, the joint holders are dead, the balance is repayable to the legal representatives of the one who died last.

In the case of a joint account which is overdrawn, the estate of the deceased is not, in an ordinary way, legally liable for the debt. It has been held that, where a cheque was signed by the three parties to a joint account and one of them died, the survivors only were liable and not the estate of the deceased. Hebert Hart, in "The Law of Banking," p. 647, says :—"Where there is no partnership, but a joint liability is incurred by borrowers (as distinguished from a joint and several liability) upon the death of one, his estate will not be liable." In practice, a guarantee by the parties to a joint overdrawn account is often taken, so as to render the estates liable upon death.

With respect to articles which are left for safe custody in joint names, upon the death of one of the depositors, the articles should not, as a rule, be given up except on the signature of the survivor and of the executor, or administrator of the deceased. (See JOINT ACCOUNT.)

DEATH OF JOINT DEPOSITOR. (See DEATH OF JOINT CUSTOMER.)

DEATH OF JOINT SHAREHOLDER. Upon the death of one, the survivor becomes sole owner.

DEATH OF MANDANT OR MANDATOR. A mandate is terminated by the death of the mandant, or person who gave it.

DEATH OF MANDATORY. A mandate is terminated by the death of the mandatory, or person in whose favour it was given; that is, the mandate does not apply to the executors of the deceased.

DEATH OF MINOR. Letters of administration require to be taken out. But, occasionally, a banker may agree to pay a small balance upon receiving a satisfactory indemnity.

An infant cannot make a will.

DEATH OF MORTGAGOR. Where title-deeds, or certificates, or other securities, are deposited with a banker by one person to secure an overdraft to another person, upon the death of the party giving the security, the account of the debtor should be stopped and arrangements made for a new account to be opened for future transactions. If this is not done, all credits to the account will release the security to the extent of the amounts paid in, and all fresh debits will be unsecured. The new account should, of course, be kept in credit till a fresh arrangement is made. If shares have been transferred to the banker and registered in his name, the same remarks apply, because the transfer was given merely as a security. If the transfer has not been registered, the death of the transferor does not prevent the banker subsequently registering the shares in his name, if necessary, provided the transfer deed was fully completed by the transferor.

DEATH OF OFFICIAL. Where a person signs a cheque in an official capacity as treasurer, secretary, director, etc., either by himself or with others, his death does not preclude the banker from paying such a cheque when presented after his death.

Where cheques have been signed by a treasurer or secretary alone, e.g. Warwick Flower Show, John Brown, Treasurer, a fresh official must be duly appointed and notice given to the bank before any further cheques can be drawn upon the account. Executors do not act for a deceased in his official appointments.

DEATH OF PARTNER. Subject to any agreement between the partners, every partnership is dissolved as regards all the partners by the death of any partner. (See Section 33, Partnership Act, 1890, under PARTNERSHIPS.) The death of a limited partner does not dissolve the partnership.

If the firm's account is overdrawn and the banker desires to retain his claim against the estate of the deceased partner, the account should be stopped and a new one opened for future transactions, otherwise all sums paid to credit will release the deceased's estate to the amount of such credits, and all debits will form a fresh debt against the new partnership. When a fresh arrangement is made by the new firm with the banker, the debt on the old account should be paid off by a cheque signed by all the partners in the new firm, and the partnership securities, if any, for the old account should be deposited for the new account and a fresh memorandum of deposit, or other document of charge, given by the partners in the new firm.

On the death of a partner, the account should also be broken where a guarantee is held from a third party, until fresh arrangements are made with the firm and with the guarantor, unless the guarantee specially provides that it shall not be affected by any change in the partnership. (See Section 18, Partnership Act, 1890, under PARTNERSHIPS.)

If the firm's account is in credit, the banker need not break the account, though the surviving partners may, for their own convenience, desire to open a new account. When that is done and the balance has to be transferred, it should be drawn by cheque. Usually, however, the old account is simply continued with the name of the deceased partner dropped out of the ledger heading, the date of his death being noted against his name. The surviving partners have power to deal with any balance on the partnership account.

Cheques signed by a partner on the firm's account, and not presented for payment till after his death, should be paid, unless the account is overdrawn and his estate is to be held liable, in which case the cheques should be returned "partner dead."

On the death of a partner, it has been held (*In re Bourne, Bourne* v. *Bourne*, 1906, 1 Ch. 113) that the surviving partner may mortgage the landed property belonging to the partnership, and the mortgagee may sustain his claim against the personal representatives of the deceased partner, unless he had notice that the money advanced was for an improper purpose. (See PARTNERSHIPS.)

DEATH OF PAYEE. (See DEATH OF HOLDER.)

DEATH OF PRINCIPAL. The death of a principal cancels any authority or power he may have given to an agent. For example, if Brown gave Jones power to draw cheques upon his account, the death of Brown would cancel that authority.

DEATH OF SHAREHOLDER. An executor is not personally liable upon the shares of the deceased, merely because he receives the dividends thereon, or is noted in the register as the executor of the deceased. If, however, the shares are transferred into the executor's name, he is liable for any calls there may be, though if he has become registered on behalf of the deceased's estate he may look to the estate to refund any payment. An executor is entitled to receive the dividends without the shares being transferred into his name. Many companies require administrators or executors to transfer the shares of the deceased shareholder into their own names, unless they intend to sell the shares at an early date.

DEATH OF TRUSTEE. Where there are several trustees and one of them dies, it would appear that it is not safe to honour cheques upon the trust account when signed by the surviving trustee or trustees, without first ascertaining that the terms of the instrument creating the trust permit such payment.

Section 22 of the Trustee Act, 1893, provides :—

"(1) Where a power or trust is given to or vested in two or more trustees jointly, then, unless the contrary is expressed in the instrument, if any, creating the power or trust, the same may be exercised or performed by the survivor or survivors of them for the time being."

Where a trustee is dead, then the person or persons nominated for the purpose of appointing new trustees by the instrument, if any, creating the trust, or if there is no such person, then the surviving trustees or trustee, or the personal representatives of the last surviving trustee, may, by writing, appoint another person or other persons to be a trustee or trustees in the place of the trustee dead (Section 10, Trustee Act, 1893).

DEBENTURE. (Latin *debeo*, to owe.) Where a company requires to borrow, it frequently does so by an issue of debentures, that is by documents under the seal of the company acknowledging the debt. A debenture is usually secured by a mortgage or charge, and represents a separate debt of a definite round sum bearing a fixed rate of interest. In the case of debenture stock, the certificates are for different amounts, representing parts of a large loan or debt. Debentures are the instruments evidencing a loan to the company.

Although debentures generally give security over the property of a company, they may be merely an acknowledgment of a debt, and give the holders no advantage over other creditors. It is therefore important, when debentures are offered as security, to ascertain if, and in what manner, they are secured. It is also necessary to see that the company has power, by its memorandum and articles of association, to issue debentures, and that any such power has not been exceeded; in other words, that the amount issued is within its borrowing powers. It should also be noted whether the debentures are transferable only "subject to equities"—that is, are subject to any debt due by the transferor to the company—or whether the debentures are payable without regard to any such debt, that is, "without regard to any equities" between the company and the transferor.

Debentures and debenture stock are usually secured by a trust deed, sometimes called a "covering deed," by which the property of the company is vested in trustees upon trust for the debenture holders or debenture stockholders. When the debentures and debenture stock are secured by a "fixed" charge, the holders are free from the danger of anyone securing a prior charge, and the trustees are given powers to enable them to deal with the mortgaged property in order, when necessary, to raise money to repay the debt to the holders. If, however, the charge is a "floating" one and not "fixed," the company can create prior charges, or sell the property or deal with it as they desire at any time before the charge becomes fixed. A debenture creating a floating charge often, however, contains a

12—(1535)

condition of this nature :—"The debentures of the said series are all to rank *pari passu* as a first charge on the property hereby charged, without any preference or priority one over another, and such charge is to be a floating security, but so that the company is not to be at liberty to create any mortgage or charge on its undertaking *pari passu* with or in priority to the said debentures." If a banker obtains a charge, and has notice of such a condition, his charge will be postponed to the charge created by the debentures.

It is usual for a debenture to be secured by a "fixed" charge upon the land of the company and by a "floating" charge upon its stock, book debts and uncalled capital. By that means the company can continue its business and use up and vary the assets included under the floating charge. If the company defaults in payment of the principal and interest secured by the debentures, or goes into liquidation, the floating charge becomes fixed, and attaches the assets as at that date. Although debentures may be secured by a trust deed, a banker should ascertain the nature of the property, as the property may prove to be of little value.

Where a debenture (not being one of a series) is given by a company to secure its account, the deeds of the property should be deposited with the banker along with the debenture, otherwise an equitable mortgagee, without notice of the debenture, might obtain priority.

A debenture which is issued in the names of the bank's nominees, as security, should be accompanied by a qualifying agreement, to show the purpose for which it has been given. (See QUALIFYING AGREEMENT.)

A debenture is not a bill of sale. The Bills of Sale (1878) Amendment Act, 1882, Section 17, provides :—"Nothing in this Act shall apply to any debentures issued by any mortgage, loan, or other incorporated company, and secured upon the capital stock or goods, chattels, and effects of such company."

Debentures are issued for amounts varying from, say, £10 to £100, and are repayable either upon notice or at the end of a certain number of years, say five, ten, or fifteen years from the date of the instrument They may also be perpetual or irredeemable, in which case the holder is entitled to an annuity or interest upon the money yearly in perpetuity. Although called irredeemable, they are usually redeemable upon the company going into voluntary or compulsory liquidation.

Where there is a series of debentures, each of them is expressed to rank equally with the others of the series. The interest upon the debentures may be paid by warrant or by coupons issued along with the debentures.

Debentures are sometimes payable to bearer and sometimes to the registered holder. And by custom they may be treated as negotiable instruments. When debentures to bearer are offered as security, a mere deposit of them may be taken (a form of transfer not being necessary), or they may be accompanied, as is preferable, by a memorandum of deposit or an agreement showing for what purpose they have been left with the banker. In *Bechuanaland Exploration Co. v. London Trading Bank* (1898, 2 Q.B. 658), where bearer debentures of an English company had been stolen and pledged with the bank, it was held that the bank was entitled to the debentures because they were, by the general custom of merchants, negotiable instruments and transferable by delivery.

The negotiability of debentures payable to bearer was considered again in the case of *Edelstein v. Schuler & Co.* (1902, 2 K.B. 145), when the decision in the Bechuanaland case was followed. In the judgment of Bigham, J. (afterwards Lord Mersey), it is said : "It has been argued that the attribute of negotiability could not be attached to a contract except by the law merchant ; and that these bonds are of such recent creation that their negotiability under that branch of the law cannot be justified. It is no doubt true that negotiability can only be attached to a contract by the law merchant or by a statute ; and it is also true that, in determining whether a usage has become so well established as to be binding in the courts of law, the length of time during which the usage has existed is an important circumstance to take into consideration ; but it is to be remembered that in these days usage is established much more quickly than it was in days gone by ; more depends on the number of the transactions which help to create it than on the time over which the transactions are spread ; and it is probably no exaggeration to say that nowadays there are more business transactions in an hour than there were in a week a century ago. Therefore the comparatively recent origin of this class of securities in my view creates no difficulty in the way of holding that they are negotiable by virtue of the law merchant; they are dealt in as negotiable instruments in every minute of a working day, and to the extent of many thousands of pounds. It is also to be remembered that the law merchant is not fixed and stereotyped; it has not yet been arrested in its growth by being moulded into a code; it is, to use the words of Cockburn, C. J., in *Goodwin* v. *Robarts* (1875, L.R. 10 Ex. 337), capable of being expanded and enlarged so as to meet the wants and requirements of trade in the varying circumstances of commerce, the effect of which is that it approves and adopts from time to time those usages of merchants which are found necessary for the convenience of trade; our common law, of which the law merchant is but a branch, has in the hands of the judges the same facility for adapting itself to the changing needs of the general public; principles do not alter, but old rules of applying them change, and new rules spring into existence. Thus it has been found convenient to treat securities like those in question in this action as negotiable, and the courts of law, recognising the wisdom of the usage, have incorporated it in what is called the law merchant, and have made it part of the common law of the country. In my opinion the time has passed when the negotiability of bearer bonds, whether Government bonds or trading bonds, foreign or English, can be called in question in our Courts. The existence of the usage has been so often proved and its convenience is so obvious, that it must be taken now to be part of the law; the very expression 'bearer bond' connotes the idea of negotiability, so that the moment such bonds are issued to the public they rank themselves among the class of negotiable securities. It would be a great misfortune if it were otherwise, for it is well known that such bonds are treated in all foreign markets as deliverable from hand to hand; the attribute not only enhances their value by making them easy of transfer, but it qualifies them to serve as a kind of international currency; and it would be very odd and a great injury to our trade if these advantages were not accorded to them in this country."

Where debentures or certificates of debenture stock, payable to a registered holder, are given as security, they should, to form a complete security, be transferred into the names of the bank's nominees. When they give a charge upon the company's land the transfer must be under seal. (See TRANSFER OF SHARES.) The debentures or certificates may also be lodged with a blank transfer; that is, a transfer in which the space for the transferee's name is left blank, or which is undated. Notice of the charge should be given to the company. When necessary, the blank transfer is completed by the banker and sent in to the office of the company for registration. A blank transfer, however, is not a satisfactory document. (See BLANK TRANSFER.) If the debentures are about due for payment, they should be indorsed by the registered owner and authority given to the banker to write a receipt above the signature.

Where debentures are deposited by a company as security for a loan, and the debentures are of a larger face value than the amount of the loan, the holders are entitled to dividends upon the full amount of the debentures until the loan is repaid.

When a company, which is indebted to a banker, issues debentures forming a specific charge upon the property of the company, without applying the money so raised in reduction of the loan or overdraft, the banker should review his position, because, in the event of a winding up, he will, unless otherwise secured, rank merely as an unsecured creditor after the debenture holders.

A private firm sometimes registers as a limited company for the sole purpose of obtaining powers to issue debentures as a floating charge upon its stock, and of avoiding the necessity of having to give a bill of sale upon the stock in order to borrow money thereon.

Every company shall, within two months after allotment, and within two months after registration of the transfer of any debentures or debenture stock complete, and have ready for delivery, the debentures, and certificates of debenture stock, unless the conditions of issue otherwise provide. (See Section 92 of the Companies (Consolidation) Act, 1908, under heading CERTIFICATE.)

Every mortgage or charge created after July 1, 1908, by a company, registered in England or Ireland, must be delivered to the registrar of companies for registration within twenty-one days after the date of its creation. The holding of debentures entitling the holder to a charge on land shall not be deemed to be an interest in land. Where a series of debentures containing, or giving by reference to any other instrument, any charge to the benefit of the debenture holders, is created by a company, the required particulars must be delivered to the registrar within twenty-one days after the execution of the deed containing the charge, together with the deed containing the charge, or if there is no such deed, one of the debentures. The registrar shall give a certificate of the registration of any mortgage or charge, and the company shall cause a copy to be indorsed on every debenture or certificate of debenture stock which is issued by the company and the payment of which is secured by the mortgage or charge so registered.

In the "Handbook on the Formation, etc., of Joint Stock Companies," by F. Gore Brown, K.C., and William Jordan, the following information regarding the registration of debentures is supplied (p. 202, 30th edition): "Before the 1st July, 1908, the more usual practice was to register the individual instruments as separate charges under sub-section 1 of Section 14 of the Act of 1900, instead of the series under sub-section 4. In cases where debentures of a series were registered separately and a further issue of the same series is now made, the series should be registered within twenty-one days after the issue of the first of the further debentures. The Registrar considers that registration of the series is also necessary when debentures registered separately are renewed by indorsement, even though they may not have matured."

In addition to being registered with the registrar of companies, all debentures specifically affecting property of the company must be entered in a register kept by the company, but a debenture containing merely a floating charge does not require to be entered in this register, though it does require registration with the registrar of companies.

For full particulars regarding registration, see the sections of the Companies (Consolidation) Act, 1908, under heading REGISTRATION OF MORTGAGES AND CHARGES.

Any creditor or member of a company may inspect the register of mortgages which is kept by the company, without payment of a fee, and any other person may inspect it on payment of one shilling. Any person may inspect the documents kept by the registrar of companies on payment of one shilling. (See REGISTRAR OF COMPANIES.)

A copy of any trust deed for securing an issue of debentures shall be forwarded to any debenture holder on payment, in the case of a printed deed, of one shilling, or less, or, where the deed is not printed, on payment of sixpence for every 100 words required to be copied (Section 102, s.s. 2, Companies (Consolidation) Act, 1908).

Where a company has redeemed any debentures, the company, unless the articles or conditions of issue expressly otherwise provide, or unless the debentures have been redeemed in pursuance of any obligation so to do (not being an obligation enforceable only by the person to whom the redeemed debentures were issued or his assigns), shall have power to keep the debentures alive for the purposes of re-issue (Section 104, s.s. 1). Sub-section 3 of the same Section says:—

> "Where a company has either before or after the passing of this Act deposited any of its debentures to secure advances from time to time on current account or otherwise, the debentures shall not be deemed to have been redeemed by reason only of the account of the company having ceased to be in debit whilst the debentures remained so deposited."

The re-issue of a debenture shall be treated as a new debenture for the purposes of stamp duty.

In the event of default in the payment of the principal and interest secured by a mortgage debenture:—

- The debenture holders may sue the company for repayment of principal and interest; or,
- Apply to the Court for an Order for sale of the property; or,
- Apply for a receiver to be appointed to wind up the company; or,
- If there is a trust deed giving the necessary power, the trustees may sell the property, or enter into possession; or,
- If all the debenture holders agree, they may apply to the Court for an order of foreclosure. (See FORECLOSURE.)

The exact terms of the debenture or of any trust deed must be strictly observed.

As to the stamp duty on a debenture for securing the payment or repayment of money, or the transfer or retransfer of stock, see MORTGAGE, ETC., AND MARKETABLE SECURITY.

When the debentures are stamped, the trust deed, if any, takes only a ten-shilling stamp. (See COMPANIES, REGISTRATION OF MORTGAGES AND CHARGES.)

DEBENTURE HOLDER. The person who holds a debenture. He may be either a registered holder, or a holder of a debenture payable to bearer. In the former case a document of transfer is necessary to pass the ownership to another person, but in the latter case the debenture is transferable by simple delivery.

A debenture holder is a creditor of the company, as the debenture represents a loan to the company, and the interest thereon must be paid before any dividend is received by the shareholders. (See DEBENTURE.)

DEBENTURE STOCK. Debenture stock is essentially the same as debentures, and both are usually secured by a charge or mortgage. Debentures, however, are for definite round sums, as separate debts, whereas certificates of debenture stock are for different amounts, as parts of one large debt.

The certificates do not require a stamp, but any deed creating a security for the stock is subject to the same duty as a mortgage (*q.v.*).

When a certificate of debenture stock is given as security, a transfer from the registered holder to the bank's nominees, accompanied by a qualifying agreement, should be taken, and, to make the security fully satisfactory, the transfer should be registered. (See BLANK TRANSFER, DEBENTURE, LOAN CAPITAL, SHARE CAPITAL, TRANSFER OF SHARES.)

DEBIT. (Latin *debitum*, what is owed.) When a banker pays a cheque drawn by a customer, the amount is placed to the debit of the customer's account. When the amounts debited are greater than the amounts paid to credit, the resulting balance is a debit one, or a "debtor balance" as it is called (shown, thus, Dr. £100) and represents the sum due by the customer to the banker, the banker being the creditor and the customer the debtor.

DEBTS, ASSIGNMENT OF. A customer may assign to a banker any money which is due, or will be due, to him. This may be effected by a letter signed by the customer, addressed to the person who owes him money, requesting that the debt be paid to the banker. The letter will be retained by the banker, who should give written notice at once to the debtor of the assignment, and ascertain from him if the debt is as stated, and if it is free from any prior charge. It is desirable to obtain an acknowledgment from the debtor. The banker should be able to prove that he sent the notice in case the debtor does not acknowledge it.

Such an instrument, being an absolute assignment of a debt, is considered (Alpe's Stamp Duties) to be liable to stamp duty "of ten shillings as a 'conveyance not hereinbefore charged,' or *ad valorem* conveyance duty if on sale or in consideration *pro tanto* of any debt under Section 57." (See that section under CONVEYANCE.)

By Section 25, sub-section 6, of the Supreme Court of Judicature Act, 1873, it is enacted as follows :—

"Any absolute assignment, by writing under the hand of the assignor (not purporting to be by way of charge only), of any debt or other legal chose in action, of which express notice in writing shall have been given to the debtor, trustee, or other person from whom the assignor would have been entitled to receive or claim such debt or chose in action, shall be, and be deemed to have been, effectual in law (subject to all equities which would have been entitled to priority over the right of the assignee if this Act had not passed), to pass and transfer the legal right to such debt or chose in action from the date of such notice, and all legal and other remedies for the same, and the power to give a good discharge for the same, without the concurrence of the assignor: Provided always, that if the debtor, trustee, or other person liable in respect of such debt or chose in action shall have had notice that such assignment is disputed by the assignor or anyone claiming under him, or of any other opposing or conflicting claims to such debt or chose in action, he shall be entitled, if he think fit, to call upon the several persons making claim thereto to interplead concerning the same, or he may, if he think fit, pay the same into the High Court of Justice under and in conformity with the provisions of the Acts for the relief of trustees."

If the debtor has a counter claim against the assignor, the assignee will be entitled only to the balance of the debt after allowing for the counter claim.

A cheque is not an assignment of money in favour of the payee, as the banker is liable only to the drawer; but if a customer formally assigns his balance to a third party and the banker receives notice thereof, his liability is then to the assignee.

DECIMAL COINAGE. Instead of the present system of reckoning money, it has often been suggested to substitute a decimal system, where the divisions are tens and multiples of tens. If the sovereign was adopted as the unity of value, it is suggested that a pound would be divided into 10 florins, each florin would be divided into 10 cents and each cent into 10 mils. The florin would thus equal a tenth of a pound, the cent a hundredth (or about 2½*d.*), and the mil a thousandth of a pound (i.e. rather less than a farthing).

The coinage of France, Belgium, Spain, Italy, the United States and other countries, is arranged on the decimal system.

DECIMALS. The interest calculations in the current account ledgers are commonly called "decimals." The correct term, however, is "products." The working of the system is most easily explained by an example: if a credit balance of £100 remains unaltered for 10 days, at which date another transaction on the account takes place, the ledger keeper multiplies the £100 by 10 days and puts the 1,000 product in the credit "decimals" column. Each succeeding balance is dealt with in the same way, being multiplied always by the number of days between the date of the balance and the date of the next balance being extended, consequent upon another entry appearing in the account. The interest on £100 for 10 days is the same as on £1,000 for 1 day, or on £1 for 1,000 days, at the same rate, and so when the products (i.e., the "decimals" so called) are cast up at the half-year end, the total will represent the number of pounds for one day on which interest is to be allowed, or charged, as the case may be, and the amount can then readily be ascertained from the tables prepared for the purpose. The last two right-hand figures are, as a rule, ignored, and the interest is reckoned upon the hundreds of products.

DECLARATION. A formal statement, or declaration, in writing.

By the Stamp Act, 1891, the stamp duty is :—

	£	s.	d.
DECLARATION of any use or trust of or concerning any property by any writing, not being a will, or an instrument chargeable with *ad valorem* duty as a settlement	0	10	0

DECLARATION (*Statutory*). (See AFFIDAVIT.)

DECLARATION OF ASSOCIATION. The declaration of association is the last clause in a memorandum of association, which, in the case of a company limited by shares, is as follows (Form A, Third Schedule, Companies (Consolidation) Act, 1908) :—

"We, the several persons whose names and addresses are subscribed, are desirous of being formed into a company, in pursuance of this memorandum of association, and we respectively agree to take the number of shares in the capital of the company set opposite our respective names.

Names, Addresses, and Descriptions of Subscribers.	Number of Shares taken by each Subscriber.
1.	200
2.	25
3.	30
4.	40
5.	15
6.	5
7.	10
Total shares taken . .	325

Witness

No subscriber of the memorandum may take less than one share. (See MEMORANDUM OF ASSOCIATION.) Subscribers frequently sign for only one share each.

DECLARATION OF TRUST. The term "bill of sale" includes a "declaration of trust without transfer." Where a debtor gave to a banker a letter of hypothecation of goods as security, agreeing to hold the goods in trust for the bank and pay over the proceeds when received, it was held (*Reg.* v. *Townshend*, 1884, 15 Cox, 466) to be a "declaration of trust without transfer" and therefore a bill of sale. (See BILL OF SALE, TRUST RECEIPT.)

DECODE. To decode a telegram is to translate the code words into the words or figures which they represent. It has only recently come into use.

DEED. A deed is a document in writing, or printing, on paper or parchment, which is signed, sealed and delivered by the parties thereto.

All deeds are now signed, though at one time it was sufficient if they were merely sealed and delivered. In the olden times persons would often be unable to write, and the sealing of the document with their own private seal would be of the first importance, but now that nearly all persons can write, the signature to a deed is the principal matter, the seal being merely a formal affair. The deed must be sealed, but it is no longer necessary that it should be the seal of the person who is sealing. It may be the seal of anyone, or a drop of wax, or simply a red wafer. The seals may be put on the deeds before the parties sign it, and by touching it with the finger at the time of signing, it has the effect of sealing. There must be a separate seal for each person. If a deed is read over to a person who cannot read, the attestation clause should be "signed, sealed and delivered by the said John Brown, the document having first been read over to him when he appeared fully to understand the same."

In addition to being signed and sealed, a deed must be delivered, and this is usually accomplished by the party placing a finger on the seal and saying, "I deliver this as my act and deed."

A special note in the attestation clause of any material alteration or erasure in the deed should be made at the time the deed is signed and witnessed.

It is customary for a deed to be witnessed, but the absence of the attestation by a witness does not invalidate it.

There is no prescribed size or shape for a deed, and they are found in different forms and sizes. Many modern deeds are drawn on comparatively small sheets, fixed together in book form, which are much more easily read and dealt with than the old full-sized sheets with the long lines.

There are two kinds of deeds, an Indenture (*q.v.*), which is made between two or more parties, and a Deed Poll (*q.v.*), which is made by only one person, or by more than one if their interests are the same.

Blackstone says it is called a deed "because it is the most solemn and authentic act that a man can possibly perform with relation to the disposal of his property; and therefore a man shall always be estopped by his own deed, or not permitted to aver or prove anything in contradiction to what he has once so solemnly and deliberately avowed."

By the Stamp Act, 1891, the stamp duty is:—

	£	s.	d.
DEED whereby any real burden is declared or created on lands or heritable subjects in Scotland. See MORTGAGE, etc., and Section 86.			
DEED containing an obligation to infeft any person in heritable subjects in Scotland, under a clause of reversion, as a security for money. See MORTGAGE, etc., and Section 86.			
DEED containing an obligation to infeft or seize in an annuity to be uplifted out of heritable subjects in Scotland. See BOND, COVENANT, etc.			
DEED of any kind whatsoever, not described in this schedule . .	0	10	0

(See TITLE DEEDS.)

DEED OF ARRANGEMENT. A deed of arrangement, whether under seal or not, made by a debtor for the benefit of his creditors, otherwise than under the Bankruptcy Acts, includes (1) an assignment of his property to a trustee, in order that it may be realised and the proceeds divided amongst the creditors (see ASSIGNMENT FOR BENEFIT OF CREDITORS); and (2) a deed or agreement under which the creditors agree to accept a composition—that is, a payment of so much in the pound in full discharge of the debts due by the debtor to them (see COMPOSITION WITH CREDITORS); and, in cases where creditors of a debtor obtain any control over his property or business, it also includes a deed of inspectorship entered into for the purpose of carrying on or winding up the business; and a letter of licence authorising the debtor or any other person to manage, carry on, realise, or dispose of a business, with a view to the payment of debts; and any agreement or instrument authorising the debtor or any other person to manage, carry on, realise, or dispose of the debtor's business, with a view to the payment of his debts (Section 2 of the Deeds of Arrangement Act, 1887).

A deed of arrangement is void unless registered within seven clear days after the first execution thereof by the debtor or any creditor (Section 5 of the above Act). The Registrar of Bills of Sale is the registrar for deeds of arrangement.

The register may be searched on payment of 2*s.* 6*d.* The registrar transmits a copy of each deed to the registrar of the county court in the district of which the place of business or residence of the debtor is situate, and any person may search such registered copy on payment of a similar fee. (See BANKRUPTCY.)

DEED OF GIFT. The conveyance of a property as a gift.

In the case of a voluntary deed of gift, the deed is void against the Trustee in Bankruptcy if the settlor becomes bankrupt within two years from the date thereof, and if he becomes bankrupt within ten years, it is void, unless it can be proved that he was, at the time of making the gift, able to pay all his debts without the property comprised in the deed of gift. In taking a deed of gift as security, it is, therefore, necessary to consider whether the donor was solvent at the date he executed the deed, and, if he was solvent then, whether his present position is above suspicion, particularly if the deed is less than two years old.

The consideration in a deed of gift may be "natural love and affection."

Where shares are transferred as a gift, the consideration is a nominal one, say five or ten shillings. The stamp duty on gifts *inter vivos* is the same as on a conveyance or transfer on sale, with the substitution in each case of the value of the property conveyed or transferred for the amount or value of the consideration. See Section 74, s.s. 4, 5, and 6, Finance (1909-10) Act, 1910, under heading CONVEYANCE. (See GIFTS INTER VIVOS.)

DEED OF INSPECTORSHIP. A deed by which an insolvent debtor places his affairs in the hands of his creditors, who may appoint inspectors or trustees, in order that the business may be wound up to the best advantage or carried on for the benefit of the creditors, as may be thought desirable. (See DEED OF ARRANGEMENT.)

DEED OF SETTLEMENT. The document which took the place of the memorandum and articles of association in old joint stock companies formed prior to the Companies Act of 1862. If the company with a deed of settlement has subsequently become registered under the Companies Act, that deed still continues, but by Section 264 of the Companies (Consolidation) Act, 1908, "a company registered in pursuance of this part of this Act may by special resolution alter the form of its constitution by substituting a memorandum and articles for a deed of settlement." The expression "deed of settlement" includes any contract of copartnery or other instrument constituting or regulating the company, not being an Act of Parliament, a Royal Charter, or Letters Patent.

DEED POLL. An indenture had originally an indented or wavy margin, but a deed poll was cut or polled straight at the edge.

There is usually only one party to a deed poll, but there may be more than one if their interests are similar.

A deed poll commences: "Know all men by these presents," etc., and the date appears at the end. In an indenture the date is at the beginning. (See INDENTURE.)

DEFACED COINS. Gold, silver, or copper coin which is defaced by being stamped with any name or words thereon, whether such coin is or is not thereby diminished in weight, is not a legal tender (24 & 25 Vict. c. 99, Section 7). (See LEGAL TENDER.)

DEFAULTER. A person who defaults: that is, who is unable to meet his obligations.

The word is principally used with respect to a defaulting member of the Stock Exchange. (See HAMMERED.)

DEFEASANCE. (French *défaire*, to undo.)

A document containing a condition upon the fulfilment of which the contract in the deed to which it refers is defeated or rendered void. The condition itself is also called a defeasance. The document of this nature with which a banker is most familiar is the qualifying agreement which is signed by a customer at the same time as he executes a transfer of stock or shares to the banker as security for an advance. The transfer is an absolute conveyance of the security into the banker's name, but the agreement, or defeasance, operates to make the transfer subject to the customer's right to have the security re-transferred upon the repayment of the advance.

As to an absolute disposition of property in Scotland, qualified by a back-letter or back-bond, see DISPOSITION ABSOLUTE.

The Stamp Act, 1891, provides as follows:—

DEFEASANCE. Instrument of defeasance of any conveyance, transfer, disposition, assignation, or tack, apparently absolute, but intended only as a security for money or stock.

See MORTGAGE, etc., and Section 86.

In respect of marketable securities under hand only, see AGREEMENT, and Section 23.

DEFERRED ANNUITY. An annuity, or annual payment of a certain sum, which does not commence till after a specified time. For example, a person may at any time purchase, either by a single premium or a yearly premium, a deferred annuity as a provision for old age, the payments not to commence till he attains the age of, say, 55 or 60, or any age selected.

At the age of 30, a single premium of £65 11*s.* 3*d.*, or a yearly premium of £5 0*s.* 11*d.*, may purchase an annuity of £10 to commence twenty years hence. (See ANNUITY.)

DEFERRED BONDS. Bonds upon which the rate of interest gradually increases until a certain specified rate is reached, when they are changed into active bonds bearing a fixed rate of interest.

DEFERRED SHARES, DEFERRED STOCK. Shares or stock which do not receive a dividend until the shares or stock which rank in front have been satisfied. The capital of a company may be divided into preference, ordinary, and deferred shares or stock, or the ordinary stock may (e.g. railway companies which have special powers by Act to do so) be split up into preferred and deferred ordinary. The interest on founders' shares is deferred to the claims of prior shares.

DEFICIENCY BILLS. When the revenue balance in the Bank of England to the credit of the Government is insufficient for payment of the quarterly dividends, the deficiency is borrowed from the Bank upon "Deficiency Bills." These bills must be paid off before the end of each quarter, and the rate of interest charged is one half of the Bank of England rate of discount, with a maximum of three per cent.

DEFINITIVE BOND. Where bonds are to be issued, as, for example, by a foreign state, a scrip or provisional certificate is issued on payment of the money due upon allotment. This certificate is held until all the instalments have been paid, when it is exchanged for the definitive bond; that is, the final bond with coupons attached.

DEFUNCT COMPANY. On the registration of the memorandum of association of a company, the registrar of companies issues a certificate certifying that the company is incorporated, and in the case of a limited company, that the company is limited. (See CERTIFICATE OF INCORPORATION.)

When the registrar ascertains that a company has ceased to carry on business, or if he fails to receive any reply to his letters of inquiry addressed to the company, he may publish in the *Gazette* a notice that, at the expiration of three months from the date of the notice, the company's name will, unless cause is shown to the contrary, be struck off the register, and the company will be dissolved (Section 242, Companies (Consolidation) Act, 1908). (See COMPANIES.)

DELEGATION OF AUTHORITY. Where a person is acting under authority, e.g. a trustee or an agent, he cannot (unless his appointment expressly permits it) delegate his authority; that is, he cannot appoint someone else to act for him.

Where an account has been opened in the names of several trustees, the cheques must be signed by all the trustees, as they cannot, unless the trust deed specially gives the power, delegate their authority to one or more of their number.

Trustees may derive their authority under a will, or a trust deed, and when any question of delegation arises, the banker should see that document and ascertain exactly what may or may not be done. If there is no permission given to delegate, then all must join in drawing cheques.

It frequently happens that the trustees of a church, or chapel, or association, desire that cheques may be signed by only a few of their number, and in such cases the trust deed should be consulted. Where trustees are numerous, it seems reasonable that a few should act for the many, but a banker would, nevertheless, be liable if the few, acting on a mandate from the whole body, drew cheques and misappropriated the money, unless the trust deed sanctioned the delegation.

An agent, or secretary, or treasurer, or manager, or other person deriving authority from a principal cannot delegate his authority.

Where there are several executors, one may, in the absence of any instructions to the contrary, draw cheques upon the executors' account, but it is desirable that a form of mandate be signed. Executors cannot, as a rule, delegate their authority to someone who is not an executor. (See MANDATE.)

DELEGATIONS. The name given by bankers on the Continent to circular notes, drafts, mandates, or other similar orders for the payment of money. In this country they are, for the purpose of stamp duty, treated as bills of exchange. (See CIRCULAR NOTES.)

DELIVERY OF BILL. "Delivery" means transfer of possession, actual or constructive, from one person to another (Section 2, Bills of Exchange Act, 1882).

Section 21 of the same Act provides :—

"(1) Every contract on a bill, whether it be the drawer's, the acceptor's, or an indorser's, is incomplete and revocable, until delivery of the instrument in order to give effect thereto.

"Provided that where an acceptance is written on a bill, and the drawee gives notice to or according to the directions of the person entitled to the bill that he has accepted it, the acceptance then becomes complete and irrevocable.

"(2) As between immediate parties, and as regards a remote party other than a holder in due course, the delivery—

"(a) in order to be effectual must be made either by or under the authority of the party drawing, accepting, or indorsing, as the case may be:

"(b) may be shown to have been conditional or for a special purpose only, and not for the purpose of transferring the property in the bill.

"But if the bill be in the hands of a holder in due course a valid delivery of the bill by all parties prior to him so as to make them liable to him is conclusively presumed.

"(3) Where a bill is no longer in the possession of a party who has signed it as drawer, acceptor, or indorser, a valid and unconditional delivery by him is presumed until the contrary is proved."

Just as a deed is of no legal effect until it has been delivered, so, it is seen from the above Section, a bill of exchange does not bind any of the parties to it if, although complete in form, it comes into the hands of a person through some fraud before it has been delivered. For example, a bill complete in form may be stolen from the desk of the drawer. If there has been no delivery of the bill, the drawer will not be liable upon it if it gets into circulation. But when a bill is no longer in the possession of a party who has signed it as drawer, acceptor, or indorser, a valid and unconditional delivery by him is presumed until the contrary is proved.

(See BILL OF EXCHANGE, NEGOTIATION OF BILL OF EXCHANGE, STOLEN BILL, STOLEN CHEQUE, TRANSFEROR BY DELIVERY.)

DELIVERY OF CHEQUE. In order that a cheque may be transferable as a negotiable instrument, it must have been delivered in the first instance by the drawer, or his duly authorised agent, to some person with the intention that it should be put into circulation. (See the preceding article. See also ISSUE OF CHEQUE, STOLEN CHEQUE.)

DELIVERY ORDER. An order addressed to a railway company, shipping company, dock company, or superintendent of warehouses, to deliver certain goods to the person named therein. Such orders are sometimes sent to a bank from a correspondent to be handed over to the right party on payment of the sum named. In some cases a cash order is attached to the delivery order, and on payment of the cash order, the delivery order is given to the person entitled to it.

The following is a form of letter from a bank sending a delivery order to another bank:—

Leeds , 19 .

THE BRITISH BANK, LIMITED,

beg to enclose herewith Delivery order for parcels marked

which please hand to Mr.
on payment of £
£

Please retain the order till called for, and credit us with the proceeds.

To the X. & Y. Bank, Ltd.,
Carlisle.

The following are copies of two delivery orders:—

King Street,
Leeds , 19 .

To the GOODS AGENT,
Railway Coy.,
Carlisle.

Please deliver the parcels marked sent to my order to Mr.

JOHN BROWN.

No.

Bonded Warehouses.

19 .

To the SUPERINTENDENT at H.M. Customs Warehouse No.

Please deliver the undernoted to the order of or assigns by indorsement hereon on payment of rent and charges from

Mark
No.
Contents

Entd. J. JONES & COY.

Where a delivery order was indorsed over to a bank as security, it was held (*Imperial Bank* v. *London and St. Katharine's Dock Coy.*, 1877, 5 Ch. D. 195) that the bank were not the actual owners and had only a modified ownership in the goods. The bank could have sent a representative with the delivery order to the docks and obtained the goods, or a dock warrant in exchange for the order. The bank, however, merely lodged it at the company's London office with a request for dock warrants to be made out as soon as possible. In the meantime a third party, without notice of the bank's claim, had obtained a second delivery order, and had taken it direct to the dock's office and obtained a dock warrant (that is, a receipt by the dock company stating that the goods were entered in his name in their books). It was held that "there is no delivery or constructive possession until the delivery order gets down to the docks, and is recognised by an entry in the dock books." The memorandum of deposit which is given when delivery orders or warrants for goods are deposited as security is usually stamped with a duty of sixpence.

Section 5 of the Finance Act, 1905, enacts that the stamp duty on a delivery order charged by the Stamp Act, 1891, shall cease to be chargeable. (See FACTORS ACT, WARRANT FOR GOODS.)

DEMISE. A word used to express the granting of a lease.

The tenant of a copyhold cannot, as a rule, demise the property for more than a year, unless by licence of the Lord of the Manor.

DEMONETISE. When a coin is reduced from the dignity of a "legal tender" to the rank of a mere "token" it is said to be demonetised.

DENOMINATION. The denomination of a bearer bond is the amount of the bond, as £20, £100.

DENOTING STAMPS. The Stamp Act, 1891, Section 11, provides that :—

"Where the duty with which an instrument is chargeable depends in any manner upon the duty paid upon another instrument, the payment of the last-mentioned duty shall, upon application to the Commissioners and production of both the instruments, be denoted upon the first-mentioned instrument in such manner as the Commissioners think fit."

See also Section 72 under DUPLICATE, and Section 4, s.s. 3, of the Finance (1909-10) Act, 1910, under INCREMENT VALUE DUTY.

DEPOSIT ACCOUNTS. When money is left on deposit with a bank, the depositor may receive the bank's deposit receipt for it, but in some districts customers prefer to have a pass-book, instead of a receipt, as being less likely to get lost, it being understood that the rate of interest they are to receive will be the same as is allowed upon the ordinary deposit receipts. The pass-book would not necessarily be required to be produced each time any money is repaid, unless that was the arrangement between the bank and its customer.

On an account of this kind, cheques are drawn only when the customer wishes to withdraw part of the money, because if the account becomes an operating one, it would no longer be regarded as a deposit account but as an ordinary current account, and be subject to the usual rates for current accounts.

Some banks supply a special form of pass-book for deposit accounts where a deposit receipt is not asked for, the book being practically the same as that issued by the Post Office Savings Bank. Each item in the book is initialled by the cashier receiving the money or making a payment, and the book must be produced every time that a transaction takes place. A pass-book of this kind usually carries, in bold type, some such heading as the following, "Moneys in this account bear interest and are subject to days' notice when withdrawn. Interest to cease when notice is given. No payment will be made except on production of this book." (The notice referred to is not always insisted upon.)

Deposit pass-books generally bear a running number, of which a register is kept giving the name of the depositor, the number of the book and the date when issued. As to the Bank Order scheme in connection with small deposits, see BANK ORDER. (See DEPOSIT RECEIPT, PASS BOOK.)

DEPOSIT LEDGER. In addition to the consecutive list of deposit receipts as given in the deposit register (*q.v.*) an account is opened for each depositor in the deposit ledger. Under the depositor's name is shown at a glance all the transactions which he has had with deposit receipts, the receipts issued being placed to his credit, while he is debited with all those which are paid or renewed ; the distinctive numbers of the receipts are quoted. The balance of the account represents the total of all the receipts which are still in his possession, which receipts will be found also in the deposit register as outstanding.

The total of all the balances shown in the

deposit ledger should agree with the total of the outstanding receipts in the register, which totals should be the same as the balance of the deposit receipt account in the general ledger.

Accounts may also be opened in a special ledger or in a separate part of the deposit ledger for customers with deposit books.

The correctness of the ledger should be proved at regular intervals. (See DEPOSIT RECEIPT.)

DEPOSIT OF TITLE DEEDS. For stamp duties see MORTGAGE, etc., and Section 86 thereunder. (See EQUITABLE MORTGAGE, TITLE DEEDS.)

DEPOSIT RATE. The rate of interest allowed by banks (and bill brokers) on deposits lodged with them by the public. In London and some parts of the country it is more or less dependent upon Bank Rate. It is not a little owing to the deposit rate that the market rate (the general rate of discount charged by London banks and brokers) follows the Bank Rate as closely as it does; for as the banks and brokers are expected by their depositors to regulate the interest they allow by the Bank Rate, increasing it when the latter rises, they naturally have to make their discount charges follow suit. (See BANK RATE, INTEREST ON DEPOSIT RECEIPT, MARKET RATE.)

DEPOSIT RECEIPT. A person may deposit money with a banker and receive therefor a receipt called a deposit receipt. The money may be withdrawable on demand, or at so many days' notice, or it may be deposited for a fixed period. There is some diversity in the wording and form of the deposit receipts of different banks. The following are specimens of some of the forms used :—

X. & Y. BANKING CO., LTD.,
Leeds 1910.

No.

Received from of
the sum of to be accounted for on demand or at 7 days' notice at the option of the Bank in Gold or Notes of the Bank of England.

£

Regd. No. Manager.

THE ENGLISH BANKING CO., LTD.,
Leeds 1910.

£

Received from of
the sum of sterling, which is placed to credit with the English Banking Co., Ltd.

No. Manager.

Entd.

This receipt must be presented indorsed, when any payment is required.

THE EMPIRE BANK, LTD.

Not transferable.

No.
Branch
Received from
residing at
the sum of
on deposit subject to notice of withdrawal.

For the Empire Bank, Ltd.,
£ Manager.

Entered

The production by the depositor of this receipt will be required on withdrawal of the deposit or any part thereof, or of interest.

(*Printed on the back.*)

N.B.—Where any sum on Deposit account is to be handed over to any person other than the Depositor, or where any sum is withdrawn from a joint account, a cheque must be drawn by the Depositor or Depositors in favour of the person or persons by whom the money is receivable. Due notice of withdrawal must first be given, and the Deposit Receipt lodged with the Bank for cancellation or alteration.

Received the amount of the within named Deposit.

Date

A deposit receipt is not a negotiable instrument, capable of being transferred by indorsement, and a banker will be liable if he pays it to a person who has no right to the money. Such words as "not transferable" or "can be paid to no one but the person in whose favour it is granted," are printed upon the face of many deposit receipts. Where a banker pays a deposit receipt to a person other than the depositor, even if it is duly indorsed by the depositor, he incurs risk in so paying. May, C.J., in his judgment in *Moore v. Ulster Bank* (1877, 11 Jr. R.C.L. 512), said that "the holder, by merely writing his name on the document and delivering it to another, confers no legal right on the person to whom he gives it."

Where a depositor is unable to attend personally at the bank to withdraw money which he has upon deposit receipt, he should, when he desires another person to obtain the money for him, send a letter authorising the banker to pay it to that person. Also, where there are several depositors, and the receipt requires to be discharged by all, if the money is to be paid to one of them, he should be furnished with a letter of authority signed by the others and the receipt should be indorsed by all of them. To be strictly in order, the same precautions should be observed if interest alone is to be paid to one of several depositors, or to a person other than the depositor. Deposit receipts are frequently received through another banker with a request to pay over the amount. In such cases, authority to do so should be obtained from the depositor, or the indorsement should be confirmed by the presenting banker.

Some deposit receipts have a printed form of cheque on the back such as: "To the X. & Y. Bank, Ltd.; Pay to Self or Bearer Ten pounds and interest." Such a form seems somewhat at variance with the nature of a deposit receipt. In *In re Dillon* (1890, 44 Ch. D. 76), Lord Justice Cotton said with reference to a form of this kind: "I come to the conclusion that, in order to preserve convenient evidence when the money is withdrawn, they put the form of cheque on the note, so that when filled up and signed it may be preserved as a receipt, and not that they make it a part of the bargain that they will not pay unless this cheque is signed and produced."

Although a deposit receipt is not transferable, the debt itself is capable of being assigned by the depositor. The assignment must be in proper form, and, in order to be effective, notice of it must be given to the banker.

In some banks when only a portion of the sum deposited is withdrawn, an indorsement is made upon the receipt stating the amount which has been paid, or, if interest alone has been paid, the date up to which it has been given; but the usual and more satisfactory way is that the deposit receipt should be renewed upon each transaction, the old one being discharged and a fresh one drawn.

Many receipts have a form of discharge printed upon the back, e.g. "Received the within mentioned sum and interest, this 1910."

As simple interest only is allowed upon deposit receipts, depositors usually bring in the receipts half yearly or yearly to have the interest added, which is done by discharging the old receipt and giving a new one for the amount plus the accrued interest.

When a new deposit receipt is required by a customer, or he desires a renewal of an old one for a less or for a greater amount, or for the same amount, the bank's form of application for a deposit receipt should be filled up with the date, the amount, and the name and address of the depositor, and be signed by the applicant.

If a deposit receipt is to be issued in the names of more than one person, the application form should state whether repayment is to be made on the indorsement of only one of the depositors, or whether all must sign. If it is to be repayable to one or more of a number, that fact should be written upon the receipt, and a note made in the deposit register.

When a deposit receipt is issued in joint names, on the death of one of the depositors the money may be withdrawn by the survivor. The executors of a deceased joint depositor may, however, give notice to a banker not to repay a deposit receipt to the survivor, even if the receipt is drawn "repayable to either or survivor."

Where the joint depositors are husband and wife, if the money is to be repaid to the wife after the husband's death the words "repayable to either or survivor," should be written on the receipt. (See JOINT ACCOUNT.)

Where a receipt in joint names is not "repayable to either," all the parties must indorse it, and where payment is requested by one of the joint depositors, he should, as stated above, be furnished with a written authority from the others to obtain the money.

If a depositor is unable to write, his mark is required by most bankers to be witnessed by two persons, one of whom should, if possible, be an outside individual who is well known to the banker, and the other may be an official of the bank.

No part of the amount for which a deposit receipt has been given should be paid unless the receipt is produced.

Where a deposit receipt is left as security with the banker who issued it, the depositor's indorsement should be obtained and a letter or memorandum taken, stating the purpose for which it has been lodged. In some cases a cheque signed by the depositor and made payable to the banker may be taken with advantage.

If a customer has both a current account and a deposit receipt, and his account becomes overdrawn, the banker is quite justified in regarding the deposit receipt as a set off, and he can refuse to pay the receipt so long as it is necessary for him to hold the amount against the overdraft. If the customer becomes bankrupt, the banker's lien is not affected. A note of any overdraft should be made against the entry in the deposit register.

In the case of a receipt which is subject to a specified notice, interest ceases at the expiration of the notice.

Receipts which are issued subject to several days' notice are commonly paid without the notice being required.

A fixed deposit is one where the money is left with the banker for a certain fixed period, and for which a better rate of interest can be allowed than if the money were repayable on demand or at a few days' notice. When fixed deposits are issued a record should be kept of them in a diary under the date when they are due to be repaid. Income Tax is deducted from fixed deposits. Deposits of this nature are most common in foreign and colonial banks.

A receipt issued at one branch should not, as a rule, be paid at another branch, unless advice has been received from the issuing branch to pay it. It should be forwarded for collection and credit of proceeds.

A banker generally endeavours to avoid issuing a deposit receipt which bears any reference to a trust.

Deposit receipts are often issued in the names of minors, and it is understood that a minor may give a good discharge for the money. In the case of a current account in a minor's name, an overdraft should certainly not be allowed.

It is very necessary that a deposit receipt be indorsed by the depositor when it is being renewed, for if it should be renewed in another name by someone not entitled to transfer it, the banker may find himself liable both for the new receipt and for the amount of the undischarged old receipt.

When a receipt is presented for payment it should, before being paid, be compared with the register of receipts to see that it agrees in all particulars with the entry therein, that the amount is still outstanding, and that no note of a lien or charge of any kind is recorded against it. For better identification, if necessary, of the depositor, his indorsement on the receipt may be compared with the specimen signature which would be taken when the depositor originally lodged the money. The depositor's indorsement, or receipt, must be across a penny adhesive stamp, or two halfpenny stamps, unless the deposit is already impressed with a stamp in readiness for the depositor's receipt.

The deposit receipt itself, that is, the receipt given by the banker, is exempt from stamp duty. The exemption granted by the Stamp Act, 1891 (see under RECEIPT), is as follows :—" Receipt given for money deposited in any bank, or with any banker, to be accounted for and expressed to be received of the person to whom the same is to be accounted for."

Where a deposit receipt is renewed for a larger amount, some bankers are satisfied with an indorsement "amount increased, John Brown." In such a case a stamp is not necessary, but if the printed form of receipt is signed, it must be stamped.

Deposit receipt forms are usually bound with counterfoils in books, and are numbered consecutively, each counterfoil bearing the same number as the corresponding receipt. In some banks the counterfoil, filled up with particulars of a receipt which is being issued, is signed by the depositor.

The clerk who writes out a deposit receipt should do so from the application form, and particulars should also be entered upon the counterfoil which remains in the book of receipt forms ; indeed, it is a good plan to write up the counterfoil first. Before the receipt is signed by the manager or other authorised official, both the receipt and the counterfoil should be compared by another clerk with the application form and initialled, if correct. It is better to make out a new receipt than to issue one with any material alteration. A slovenly written receipt should not be issued from any bank office. A receipt form spoiled in this way should not be destroyed, but kept for reference ; it may, conveniently, be pinned behind its counterfoil.

Where a receipt has been lost, an indemnity should be required before the money is paid or a fresh receipt issued. Paget says (page 31, " The Law of Banking"), " a deposit receipt not being a negotiable instrument, the bank is not entitled to exact an indemnity from the depositor before paying him, if he has lost the receipt."

A banker is released by the Statute of Limitations from liability on a deposit receipt more than six years old and in regard to which he has not meanwhile acknowledged the depositor's claim by payment of interest or in any other way, but no banker ever thinks of setting up this right. Deposit receipts are always paid, however old they may be, on satisfactory proof of the identity of the depositor or his legal representatives.

About forty years ago deposit receipts in joint names were sometimes cut in two, where there were two depositors, and each person took a half. If a receipt was drawn in the names of three persons, the document was cut into three pieces, and each party received a piece. When repayment was required, each party had to take the portion in his possession to the bank and indorse it. When the banker received the three pieces he fastened them together and then paid the money.

(See BANK ORDER, DEATH OF CUSTOMER, DEPOSIT ACCOUNTS, DEPOSIT LEDGER, DEPOSIT REGISTER, DONATIO MORTIS CAUSÂ, GARNISHEE ORDER, INCOME TAX, INTEREST ON DEPOSIT RECEIPT, LOST DEPOSIT RECEIPT, STATUTE OF LIMITATIONS.)

DEPOSIT REGISTER. The deposit register contains a complete list of all the deposit receipts which have been issued by a bank. The amounts should be entered from the application forms signed by the depositor, in the order in which they are issued, and the entries should be numbered consecutively, the numbers being the same as appear on the face of the receipts which have been issued. In addition to the date and the number, the depositor's name and address should be given and the amount of the receipt. A note should also be made of any particulars relative to the receipt, such as "repayable to either party" (if it is in two names and either may sign), "all must sign," "current account is overdrawn," "receipt said to be lost," "refer to Manager before paying." If a receipt form has been spoiled when being filled up, the spoiled form should not be destroyed but should be clearly marked "spoiled" and preserved as evidence of what has become of that number. A convenient way of preserving it is to attach it to the counterfoil. A record should be kept in the register against the number of the form that it has been spoiled.

When a receipt has been paid, the entry in the register is written off with the date of payment.

There is usually an index to the register, so that by turning up a depositor's name, when the number of his receipt is not known, the entry may be quickly found. The index should show against each name the numbers of all the receipts which have been issued to that customer, and when any receipts are paid the numbers should be crossed out of the index. Where a deposit ledger is also kept, particulars can be more readily obtained from it than from the register.

The total of all the receipts shown in the register as outstanding should agree with the balance of the deposit receipt account in the general ledger, and the register should be proved at regular intervals. (See DEPOSIT LEDGER, DEPOSIT RECEIPT.)

DEPRECIATED CURRENCY. If a sovereign, or other coin, does not contain the weight of gold, or silver, as prescribed by law, it is said to be "depreciated."

If a bank note passes current for less than the amount of the note, the note is said to be "depreciated." (See COINAGE.)

DEPRECIATION. A term denoting the reduction in value which takes place in works, buildings, machinery, etc., as the result of being used or becoming old-fashioned or obsolete.

In examining the balance sheet of a business concern, it should be noted whether a satisfactory amount has been provided from the profits for depreciation. What that amount should be depends in a great measure upon the particular circumstances of each case.

DESTROYED BANK NOTE. Where notes have been partly or wholly destroyed, their value can be recovered from the bank which issued them, provided that full particulars, including the numbers, are supplied, and that the bank is otherwise satisfied. The bank would, naturally, require a sufficient indemnity to be given before paying notes which are stated to have been destroyed. (See LOST BANK NOTE.)

DEVISEE. The person to whom "real" property (see REALTY) is left, or devised, in a will, is called the devisee. The person who takes all the real property remaining after the devisees have received their shares, is called the residuary devisee. (See LEGATEE.)

DIARIES. Diaries are kept for various purposes. In addition to a diary for the dates on which overdraft or loan limits expire and other special matters requiring attention, there are bill diaries, showing the bills which mature on the various dates, a coupon diary, a diary for recording the dates on which premiums on fire policies and on life policies are due, and a special form of diary for payments, such as subscriptions, which have to be made on the same day in each year.

DIME. (See Foreign Moneys—United States.)

DIMINUTION IN VALUE. If a certain quantity of gold will purchase so much silver, and if the supply of silver increases so that the same gold will purchase more silver, the silver has suffered a "diminution in value," or in other words has depreciated. (See Money.)

DINAR. (See Foreign Moneys — Servia.)

DIRECTORS. The directors of a company are the members who are chosen by the other shareholders to direct or conduct the business of the company. The directors, in some cases, meet every day and are practically acting managers of the company; but in other cases they meet only at intervals, often just once a week, when all the important business of the week is brought before them. There is usually a chairman and a vice-chairman, and the whole body is called the board of directors. The room in which they meet is the board room, in allusion to the board or table at which they sit.

The powers of directors are limited to the provisions of the memorandum and articles of association of the company.

Directors have been called trustees for the company, but in *Smith* v. *Anderson* (1880, 15 Ch. D. 247), Lord Justice James said: "A trustee is a man who is the owner of the property, and deals with it as a principal, as owner, and as master, subject only to an equitable obligation to account to some persons to whom he stands in the relation of trustee, and who are his *cestuis que trustent*. The same individual may fill the office of director and also be a trustee having property, but that is a rare, exceptional, and casual circumstance. The office of director is that of a paid servant of the company. A director never enters into a contract for himself, but he enters into contracts for his principal, that is, for the company of whom he is a director, and for whom he is acting. He cannot sue on such contracts, nor be sued on them, unless he exceeds his authority."

Jessel, M.R., said (in *In re Forest of Dean Coal Company*, 1879, 10 Ch. D. 450): "Directors have sometimes been called trustees or commercial trustees, and sometimes they have been called managing partners; it does not matter much what you call them, so long as you understand what their true position is, which is that they are really commercial men managing a trading concern for the benefit of themselves and of all the other shareholders in it. They are bound, no doubt, to use reasonable diligence having regard to their position, though probably an ordinary director, who only attends at the board occasionally, cannot be expected to devote as much time and attention to the business as the sole managing partner of an ordinary partnership, but they are bound to use fair and reasonable diligence in the management of their company's affairs, and to act honestly. But where without fraud and without dishonesty they have omitted to get in a debt due to the company by not suing within time, or because the man was solvent at one moment and became insolvent at another, I am of opinion that it by no means follows as a matter of course, as it might in the case of ordinary trustees of trust funds or of a trust debt, that they are to be made liable."

The number of shares which a director must hold in the company to qualify him for the post of director, depends upon the terms of the articles of association. The Companies (Consolidation) Act, 1908, does not provide for any special qualification, but Table A (see Section 11 under Articles of Association), Rule 70, says the qualification of a director shall be the holding of at least one share in the company.

It shall be the duty of every director who is by the regulations of the company required to hold a specified share qualification, and who is not already qualified, to obtain his qualification within two months after his appointment or such shorter time as may be fixed by the regulations of the company (Section 73).

Every company must keep a register of the names and addresses and occupations of its directors and managers, and furnish a copy thereof to the registrar of companies and notify any changes (Section 75).

In a limited company the liability of the directors may, if so provided by the memorandum, be unlimited (Section 60).

A limited company, if so authorised by its articles, may, by special resolution, alter its memorandum so as to render unlimited the liability of its directors or managers (Section 61).

The following are a few of the rules where Table A applies:—The directors may appoint one of their number to be managing director at such remuneration as they think fit and he shall not, while holding that office, be subject to retirement by rotation (Rule 72).

The amount borrowed by the directors for the purposes of the company (otherwise than by the issue of share capital) shall not at any time exceed the issued share capital without the sanction of the company in general meeting (Rule 73).

Every director present at a meeting or committee of directors shall sign his name in a book kept for that purpose (Rule 75).

The seal shall not be affixed except by the authority of a resolution of the board and in the presence of two directors and the secretary or other person appointed for the purpose, who shall sign every instrument to which the seal is affixed in their presence (Rule 76).

The office of director shall be vacated if he holds any other office of profit under the company, or participates in the profits of any contract with the company (Rule 77).

Every year at the ordinary meeting one-third of the directors for the time being, or if their number is not three or a multiple of three, then the number nearest to one-third, shall retire from office. The directors to retire shall be those who have been longest in office since their last election. A retiring director shall be eligible for re-election (Rules 78 to 80).

Any casual vacancy may be filled up by the directors. (See COMPANIES.)

DISCHARGE OF BANKRUPT. The regulations regarding the discharge of a bankrupt are contained in Section 8 of the Bankruptcy Act, 1890:—

"(1) A bankrupt may, at any time after being adjudged bankrupt, apply to the court for an order of discharge, and the court shall appoint a day for hearing the application, but the application shall not be heard until the public examination of the bankrupt is concluded. The application shall be heard in open court.

"(2) On the hearing of the application the court shall take into consideration a report of the official receiver as to the bankrupt's conduct and affairs (including a report as to the bankrupt's conduct during the proceedings under his bankruptcy), and may either grant or refuse an absolute order of discharge, or suspend the operation of the order for a specified time, or grant an order of discharge subject to any conditions with respect to any earnings or income which may afterwards become due to the bankrupt, or with respect to his after-acquired property: Provided that the court shall refuse the discharge in all cases where the bankrupt has committed any misdemeanour under the Debtors Act, 1869, or the principal Act, or any other misdemeanour connected with his bankruptcy, or any felony connected with his bankruptcy, unless for special reasons the court otherwise determines, and shall, on proof of any of the facts hereinafter mentioned, either—

"(i) refuse the discharge; or

"(ii) suspend the discharge for a period of not less than two years; or

"(iii) suspend the discharge until a dividend of not less than ten shillings in the pound has been paid to the creditors; or

"(iv) require the bankrupt as a condition of his discharge to consent to judgment being entered against him by the official receiver or trustee for any balance or part of any balance of the debts provable under the bankruptcy which is not satisfied at the date of the discharge, such balance or part of any balance of the debts to be paid out of the future earnings or after acquired property of the bankrupt in such manner and subject to such conditions as the court may direct; but execution shall not be issued on the judgment without leave of the court, which leave may be given on proof that the bankrupt has since his discharge acquired property or income available towards payment of his debts.

"Provided, that if at any time after the expiration of two years from the date of any order made under this Section the bankrupt shall satisfy the court that there is no reasonable probability of his being in a position to comply with the terms of such order, the court may modify the terms of the order, or of any substituted order, in such manner and upon such conditions as it may think fit.

"(3) The facts hereinbefore referred to are :—

"(*a*) That the bankrupt's assets are not of a value equal to ten shillings in the pound on the amount of his unsecured liabilities, unless he satisfies the court that the fact that the assets are not of a value equal to ten shillings in the pound on the amount of his unsecured liabilities has arisen from circumstances for which he cannot justly be held responsible :

"(*b*) That the bankrupt has omitted to keep such books of account as are usual and proper in the business carried on by him and as sufficiently disclose his business transactions and financial position within the three years immediately preceding his bankruptcy :

"(*c*) That the bankrupt has continued to trade after knowing himself to be insolvent :

"(*d*) That the bankrupt has contracted any debt provable in the bankruptcy without having at the time of contracting it any reasonable or probable ground of expectation (proof whereof shall lie on him) of being able to pay it :

"(*e*) That the bankrupt has failed to account satisfactorily for any loss of assets or for any deficiency of assets to meet his liabilities :

"(*f*) That the bankrupt has brought on, or contributed to, his bankruptcy by rash and hazardous speculations, or by unjustifiable extravagance in living, or by gambling, or by culpable neglect of his business affairs :

"(*g*) That the bankrupt has put any of his creditors to unnecessary expense by a frivolous or vexatious defence to any action properly brought against him :

"(*h*) That the bankrupt has within three months preceding the date of the receiving order incurred unjustifiable expense by bringing a frivolous or vexatious action :

"(*i*) That the bankrupt has within three months preceding the date of the receiving order, when unable to pay his debts as they become due, given an undue preference to any of his creditors :

"(*j*) That the bankrupt has within three months preceding the date of the receiving order incurred liabilities with a view of making his assets equal to ten shillings in the pound on the amount of his unsecured liabilities :

"(*k*) That the bankrupt has on any previous occasion been adjudged bankrupt, or made a composition or arrangement with his creditors :

"(*l*) That the bankrupt has been guilty of any fraud or fraudulent breach of trust.

"(4) For the purposes of this Section a bankrupt's assets shall be deemed of a value equal to ten shillings in the pound on the amount of his unsecured liabilities when the court is satisfied that the property of the bankrupt has realised, or is likely to realise, or with due care in realisation might have realised, an amount equal to ten shillings in the pound on his unsecured liabilities, and a report by the official receiver or the trustee shall be *primâ facie* evidence of the amount of such liabilities."

(See BANKRUPTCY.)

DISCHARGED BANKRUPT. A bankrupt who has been formally discharged by the Court of Bankruptcy. As to dealings with an undischarged bankrupt, see BANKRUPT PERSON. (See also DISCHARGE OF BANKRUPT.)

DISCHARGED BILL. A bill of exchange

is discharged when payment is made in due course by or on behalf of the drawee or acceptor. There is no right of action upon a discharged bill, but a holder may have the right to sue upon the transaction, apart from the bill.

When a banker has paid his customer's acceptance he cancels the acceptor's signature in the same way as he would cancel the drawer's signature on a cheque. (See PAYMENT OF BILL.)

DISCLAIMER. A renunciation. An example of a disclaimer is found in connection with bankruptcy proceedings. By Section 55 of the Bankruptcy Act, 1883, as amended by Section 13 of the Bankruptcy Act, 1890, a trustee may, with sanction of the Court, disclaim any portion of the bankrupt's land of any tenure which is burdened with onerous covenants.

The term may be applied to other matters where a renunciation or repudiation is desired.

DISCOUNT. The amount of deduction which is allowed for immediate payment of a debt which is not yet due. A tradesman may allow discount if, instead of credit being taken, payment is made in cash; and so in the case of a bill of exchange, if he receives payment at once instead of waiting until the bill falls due, discount is allowed. But from a banker's point of view, the usual way to regard discount is to look upon it practically as interest charged for a loan of the amount until the bill is due. The difference between interest for a loan and discount on a bill is that the interest is not payable, in an ordinary way, until the end of a half year, whereas the discount is paid at the time the bill is discounted, e.g. if a loan of £1,000 is granted on January 1 at 5 per cent. interest, the interest due at December 31 will be £50; but if a bill for £1,000 is discounted on January 1 at the same rate for twelve months the banker only pays over £950, the £50 being credited at once to his discount account, so that the banker practically obtains the same amount of interest for a loan of £950, when granted by discounting a bill, as he does upon an ordinary loan of £1,000; and his profit is therefore more than 5 per cent., in fact about $5\frac{5}{19}$ per cent., and besides he has the use of his profit (£50) for the twelve months.

The following table shows the difference in profit per cent. per annum between lending money by way of interest and by way of discount:—

Interest.	Discount.	Interest.	Discount.
1	1·010101	20	25·000000
2	2·040816	30	42·857142
3	3·092783	40	66·666666
4	4·166666	50	100.000000
5	5·263157	60	150·000000
6	6·382968	70	233·000000
7	7·526881	80	400·000000
8	8·695652	90	900·000000
9	9·890109	100	Infinite.
10	11·111111		

From this table it is seen that if a sum of £100 is lent at 20 per cent. the lender would receive £100 at the end of a year plus £20 for interest, that is a profit of 20 per cent.; but if he discounted a bill for £100 at the rate of 20 per cent. he would advance only £80 and at the year end he would receive payment of £100, that is he would receive £20 for a loan of £80, or a profit of 25 per cent.

The rate at which a bill is discounted is partly dependent upon the Bank of England Rate, the length of time which will elapse before the bill matures, and the quality of the bill. If there is any doubt as to payment of the bill at maturity, the risk is taken into account by charging a higher rate than in the case of a bill which may be regarded as practically certain to be paid when due.

A banker's discount is different from a true discount. A banker's discount is not really interest upon the actual amount advanced, but interest upon the amount that is to be repaid. True discount is ascertained, e.g. by finding what amount at 5 per cent. will produce £100 in twelve months' time. £1 at 5 per cent. will be £1 1*s*. at the end of a year, and if £1 1*s*. is the value of £1, it is found by proportion that £100 is the value at the end of the twelve months of £95 4*s*. 9½*d*. The true discount is therefore £4 15*s*. 2½*d*. (that is, 5 per cent. on £95 4*s*. 9½*d*.), whilst the banker's discount is £5 (equal, as shown above, to a rate of, say, $5\frac{5}{19}$ per cent.).

DISCOUNT, AT A. When the market value of bonds, stocks, or shares is less than the nominal value, they are said to be at a discount. Where the market value is greater, they are at a premium. A share of £1, fully paid, which is selling at 19*s*. 6*d*., is an example of an investment which is at a discount, or 6*d*. below par value. (See PAR.)

DISCOUNT LEDGER. In the discount ledger an account is opened in the name of each customer for whom bills are discounted, and a note is made in the heading of the amount fixed as the discount limit. Each bill, as discounted, is entered in the correct account with the date when it is discounted. The acceptor's name is noted and the date when the bill is due ; also the number on the bill which refers to the entry in the bill register is usually added. The amounts are entered in a column headed "acceptances," and when any bills mature the amounts are entered in a column headed "matured acceptances" and the balance s shown in the balance column.

When the balances of the discount ledger are extracted, the total should agree with the total of the bill register, also with the total of undue bills as shown in the bill diary.

When a bill is dishonoured, a note of the fact is usually made in red ink against the entry in the discount ledger.

The discount ledger may also show the liability of each person as acceptor or indorser on bills discounted for other customers.

DISCOUNT REGISTER. The same as bill register (*q.v.*).

DISCOUNTING A BILL. When trade bills are brought to a banker to be discounted, there are many points which require to be carefully observed, in order that a banker may avoid having his case filled with bills which are unmarketable, or bills which may eventually produce endless trouble and probably disaster.

If a bill drawn by Jones on Brown is brought to be discounted, a banker will consider the position of the acceptor Brown. If Brown's account is at another bank, what sort of a banker's opinion is held regarding him, is the opinion a recent one, and how many other bills accepted by Brown are in the bill case. Have any of Brown's acceptances ever been dishonoured ? If Jones is the person who wants the bill discounted, the banker will note the total amount of bills already discounted for him and the quality of them. A certain number of the bills may be dishonoured at maturity, and the question arises, will Jones' account admit of the bills, on which there is a risk, being debited to it, if they are returned unpaid ? It is also necessary for the banker to remember that he may hold in his case bills accepted by Jones which he has discounted for other customers.

If the parties to the bill are quite satisfactory, other points will arise in the banker's mind. Is the bill a genuine trade bill, that is a bill accepted by Brown because he has received value for it from Jones, or has Brown accepted it merely for the accommodation of Jones, on the understanding that Jones himself must meet it at maturity ? The banker may be informed that it is an accommodation bill when it is offered to him, or he may be left to find out that fact for himself. A scrutiny of Jones' account may show, perhaps, that a bill for practically the same amount appears regularly every three or six months, suggesting that it is the same bill which is being renewed time after time. Is there any cross drawing between Brown and Jones, that is does Brown accept bills for Jones, and Jones accept them for Brown ? Is the business between the two parties such as would justify Jones drawing on Brown ? If Jones is an iron merchant, for example, and Brown a grocer, it is not very likely that the bill would arise out of the ordinary course of business between an iron merchant and a grocer, and the banker is put on inquiry.

In the words of George Rae in his "Country Banker" : "It is not the province of banking to discount bills, the proceeds of which are to provide the acceptors with fixed capital. A man may properly be drawn upon against goods, produce, or commodities which he is turning over in his business from day to day ; but not against his buildings or machinery. These are not floating capital." Again : "A ship-owner, or ship's husband, may properly be drawn upon for sails, or cordage, or stores supplied to ships, because there is a tangible fund in his incoming freights to meet this class of marine paper but when he accepts against the hull of a ship, he passes the recognised limits of negotiable value, and his paper becomes discredited in the estimation of the bill market."

A bill which is payable to John Brown *only* should not be discounted, as the bill is not a negotiable instrument, and the banker could not, if necessary, sue upon it.

A banker who discounts a bill is a "holder for value" (*q.v.*), and at maturity he obtains the full proceeds.

The person for whom a bill is discounted must indorse it, as by indorsement he becomes one of the parties to the bill and liable thereon if the acceptor fails to pay it. If not indorsed, he is not liable on the bill, unless the bill proves to be a forgery.

When an advance is made upon the deposit of a bill as security, the banker is a

" holder for value " only to the extent of the sum he has lent upon it.

The discounter of a bill may, if he wish, re-discount it. Bill brokers frequently re-discount bills with bankers, and instead of indorsing each bill they usually give a guarantee to cover all the bills re-discounted.

In the money market, Treasury Bills (*q.v.*) and bills or drafts which bear the names of houses of the highest standing, are classed as first-class bills, or first-class paper. Where the names are not so well known, or financially strong, the bills are called second or third class paper, as the case may be.

DISENTAIL. To disentail is to bar or bring to an end an entail. Land is entailed when it is granted to a person and the heirs of his body. The deed barring an entail is called a disentailing deed, and the land thereafter may be dealt with at the will of the owner.

Disentailing assurances and other deeds enrolled in Chancery are proved by certificates of enrolment signed by the proper officer. (See Estate Tail.)

DISHONOUR OF BILL OF EXCHANGE. A bill is dishonoured either by non-acceptance or by non-payment. That is, where the person on whom a bill is drawn (the drawee) refuses to accept it, or where the person who by accepting the bill (the acceptor) agreed to pay it, fails to do so on the day on which it is due, the bill is said to be dishonoured.

As to dishonour by non-acceptance, the Bills of Exchange Act, 1882, provides as follows :—

" Section 42. When a bill is duly presented for acceptance and is not accepted within the customary time, the person presenting it must treat it as dishonoured by non-acceptance. If he do not, the holder shall lose his right of recourse against the drawer and indorsers.

" Section 43. A bill is dishonoured by non-acceptance—

" (*a*) When it is duly presented for acceptance, and such an acceptance as is prescribed by this Act is refused or cannot be obtained : or

" (*b*) When presentment for acceptance is excused and the bill is not accepted.

" (2) Subject to the provisions of this Act, when a bill is dishonoured by non-acceptance, an immediate right of recourse against the drawer and indorsers accrues to the holder, and no presentment for payment is necessary."

" Section 18. A bill may be accepted—

" (2) When it is overdue, or after it has been dishonoured by a previous refusal to accept, or by non-payment :

" (3) When a bill payable after sight is dishonoured by non-acceptance, and the drawee subsequently accepts it, the holder, in the absence of any different agreement, is entitled to have the bill accepted as of the date of first presentment to the drawee for acceptance."

As to dishonour by non-payment, Section 47 provides :—

" (1) A bill is dishonoured by non-payment (*a*) when it is duly presented for payment and payment is refused or cannot be obtained, or (*b*) when presentment is excused and the bill is overdue and unpaid.

" (2) Subject to the provisions of this Act, when a bill is dishonoured by non-payment, an immediate right of recourse against the drawer and indorsers accrues to the holder."

Notice of dishonour must be given. Section 48 provides as follows :—

" Subject to the provisions of this Act, when a bill has been dishonoured by non-acceptance or by non-payment, notice of dishonour must be given to the drawer and each indorser, and any drawer or indorser to whom such notice is not given is discharged ; Provided that—

" (1) Where a bill is dishonoured by non-acceptance, and notice of dishonour is not given, the rights of a holder in due course subsequent to the omission, shall not be prejudiced by the omission.

" (2) Where a bill is dishonoured by non-acceptance and due notice of dishonour is given, it shall not be necessary to give notice of a subsequent dishonour by non-payment unless the bill shall in the meantime have been accepted."

Notice to the various parties of the dishonour of a bill must be given in strict conformity with the regulations set forth in Section 49, otherwise the drawer and indorsers may be discharged. The Section is as follows :—

" Notice of dishonour in order to be valid

and effectual must be given in accordance with the following rules :—

"(1) The notice must be given by or on behalf of the holder, or by or on behalf of an indorser who, at the time of giving it, is himself liable on the bill.

"(2) Notice of dishonour may be given by an agent either in his own name, or in the name of any party entitled to give notice whether that party be his principal or not.

"(3) Where the notice is given by or on behalf of the holder, it enures for the benefit of all subsequent holders and all prior indorsers who have a right of recourse against the party to whom it is given.

"(4) Where notice is given by or on behalf of an indorser entitled to give notice as hereinbefore provided, it enures for the benefit of the holder and all indorsers subsequent to the party to whom notice is given.

"(5) The notice may be given in writing or by personal communication, and may be given in any terms which sufficiently identify the bill, and intimate that the bill has been dishonoured by non-acceptance or non-payment.

"(6) The return of a dishonoured bill to the drawer or an indorser is, in point of form, deemed a sufficient notice of dishonour.

"(7) A written notice need not be signed, and an insufficient written notice may be supplemented and validated by verbal communication. A misdescription of the bill shall not vitiate the notice unless the party to whom the notice is given is in fact misled thereby.

"(8) Where notice of dishonour is required to be given to any person, it may be given either to the party himself, or to his agent in that behalf.

"(9) Where the drawer or indorser is dead, and the party giving notice knows it, the notice must be given to a personal representative if such there be, and with the exercise of reasonable diligence he can be found.

"(10) Where the drawer or indorser is bankrupt, notice may be given either to the party himself or to the trustee.

"(11) Where there are two or more drawers or indorsers who are not partners, notice must be given to each of them, unless one of them has authority to receive such notice for the others.

"(12) The notice may be given as soon as the bill is dishonoured and must be given within a reasonable time thereafter.

"In the absence of special circumstances notice is not deemed to have been given within a reasonable time, unless—

"(*a*) where the person giving and the person to receive notice reside in the same place, the notice is given or sent off in time to reach the latter on the day after the dishonour of the bill;

"(*b*) where the person giving and the person to receive notice reside in different places, the notice is sent off on the day after the dishonour of the bill, if there be a post at a convenient hour on that day, and if there be no such post on that day then by the next post thereafter.

"(13) Where a bill when dishonoured is in the hands of an agent, he may either himself give notice to the parties liable on the bill, or he may give notice to his principal. If he give notice to his principal, he must do so within the same time as if he were the holder, and the principal upon receipt of such notice has himself the same time for giving notice as if the agent had been an independent holder.

"(14) Where a party to a bill receives due notice of dishonour, he has after the receipt of such notice the same period of time for giving notice to antecedent parties that the holder has after the dishonour.

"(15) Where a notice of dishonour is duly addressed and posted, the sender is deemed to have given due notice of dishonour, notwithstanding any miscarriage by the post office."

Under certain circumstances the Act excuses non-notice of dishonour, or delay in giving notice. Section 50 provides :—

"(1) Delay in giving notice of dishonour

is excused where the delay is caused by circumstances beyond the control of the party giving notice, and not imputable to his default, misconduct, or negligence. When the cause of delay ceases to operate the notice must be given with reasonable diligence.

"(2) Notice of dishonour is dispensed with—

"(*a*) When, after the exercise of reasonable diligence, notice as required by this Act cannot be given to or does not reach the drawer or indorser sought to be charged:

"(*b*) By waiver express or implied. Notice of dishonour may be waived before the time of giving notice has arrived, or after the omission to give due notice:

"(*c*) As regards the drawer in the following cases, namely, (1) where drawer and drawee are the same person, (2) where the drawee is a fictitious person or a person not having capacity to contract, (3) where the drawer is the person to whom the bill is presented for payment, (4) where the drawee or acceptor is as between himself and the drawer under no obligation to accept or pay the bill, (5) where the drawer has countermanded payment:

"(*d*) As regards the indorser in the following cases, namely, (1) where the drawee is a fictitious person or a person not having capacity to contract and the indorser was aware of the fact at the time he indorsed the bill, (2) where the indorser is the person to whom the bill is presented for payment, (3) where the bill was accepted or made for his accommodation."

As the result of several decisions, it has been conceived that in all cases where, in consequence of the dishonour of bills or notes, made or become payable to bearer, a remedy arises on the consideration, the transferor is entitled to notice of dishonour.

The amount which a holder may recover in an action on a dishonoured bill is prescribed in Section 57:—

"Where a bill is dishonoured, the measure of damages, which shall be deemed to be liquidated damages, shall be as follows:—

"(1) The holder may recover from any party liable on the bill, and the drawer who has been compelled to pay the bill may recover from the acceptor, and an indorser who has been compelled to pay the bill may recover from the acceptor or from the drawer, or from a prior indorser—

"(*a*) The amount of the bill:

"(*b*) Interest thereon from the time of presentment for payment if the bill is payable on demand, and from the maturity of the bill in any other case:

"(*c*) The expenses of noting, or, when protest is necessary, and the protest has been extended, the expenses of protest.

"(2) In the case of a bill which has been dishonoured abroad, in lieu of the above damages, the holder may recover from the drawer or an indorser, and the drawer or an indorser who has been compelled to pay the bill may recover from any party liable to him, the amount of the re-exchange with interest thereon until the time of payment.

"(3) Where by this Act interest may be recovered as damages, such interest may, if justice require it, be withheld wholly or in part, and where a bill is expressed to be payable with interest at a given rate, interest as damages may or may not be given at the same rate as interest proper."

The following is a specimen of a form which may be used in giving notice of dishonour:—

British Bank, Ltd.,
Leeds 1910.

Please take notice that the bill for £100 upon John Brown, of King Street, Leeds, drawn (or indorsed) by you, dated , at months' date, due 1910, and payable at , upon which you are liable as drawer (or indorser), has been dishonoured by non-acceptance (or non-payment), and we request immediate payment thereof, with expenses.

To John Jones, , Manager.
English Street, Leeds.

Where an inland bill has been dishonoured it may, if the holder think fit, be noted for non-acceptance or non-payment, as the case may be, but it is not necessary to note such a bill in order to preserve recourse against the drawer or indorsers; neither is there any need to protest an inland bill, and it is not usually done. (See NOTING.)

Where a foreign bill, appearing on the face of it to be such, has been dishonoured by non-acceptance, it must be duly protested for non-acceptance, and where such a bill, which has not been previously dishonoured by non-acceptance, is dishonoured by non-payment, it must be duly protested for non-payment. (See PROTEST). The bill must be noted on the day of dishonour. The protest may be extended later.

Noting or protest does not do away with the necessity of giving the notices of dishonour to drawer and indorsers. As soon as payment is refused on the due date, a holder may give notice of dishonour. He need not necessarily wait till the end of the day before doing so. Where a bill is to be noted, it is customary to wait till after the close of business before noting it, though there is nothing to prevent the bill being noted as soon as dishonoured. An action cannot be commenced till after the end of the due date. In *Kennedy* v. *Thomas* (1894, 2 Q.B. 759), where an action was brought by the holder of a dishonoured bill upon the last day of grace, it was dismissed as premature.

Where a bill, which a banker has discounted for a customer, is dishonoured, the banker should debit it to the customer's account and advise him at once, so that he may be in time to give the required notices to prevent the release of other parties. But if the account does not justify the dishonoured bill being charged to it, the banker should debit it to an account called "Dishonoured Bills," or "Overdue Bills," and at once send notice of dishonour, and request for payment, to all the parties to the bill.

A note of the dishonour should be recorded in the discount ledger and the banker's opinion book.

If a banker wrongfully dishonours a bill or cheque he will be liable in an action by his customer for damages, and if he dishonours it because certain cheques paid to the credit of his customer, have not been cleared, he may also be held liable in damages if it has been the banker's practice to allow the customer to treat uncleared cheques as cash.

As it is a serious matter to damage a customer's credit by dishonouring a bill or cheque which ought to be paid, a banker will naturally make quite sure of the position before returning it. He should ascertain that everything has been credited to the account and that the balance has been correctly extended. When a cheque is returned simply from some irregularity in the document itself, such as an incorrect indorsement, an alteration, a difference in amount, or any other similar kind of cause, the banker should make the reason quite clear so that no reflection may be cast upon the customer's credit. A cheque marked "refer to drawer" means, as a rule, that the drawer has not sufficient funds in his account to meet it, and it would be wrong to mark a cheque "R/D" if the correct answer should be "Indorsement irregular," or something of that nature. (See ANSWERS.) It is customary (except where a special arrangement exists) to debit charges half-yearly and until the usual time for debiting them has arrived a cheque should not be dishonoured by anticipating the item for charges, or debiting them at an unusual time.

Wrongful dishonour may, as stated above, render a banker liable to pay damages. Thus, if a customer has a balance of £500 at his banker's, and the customer draws a cheque for £300, or accepts a bill for £300, payable at his banker's, the banker is liable to be mulcted in substantial damages if the cheque or the bill is dishonoured, and the customer is not bound to prove any actual loss by reason of the dishonour. In the case of *Rolin* v. *Steward* (1854, 23 L.J.C.P. 148), it was said by Mr. Justice Williams: "Although no evidence is given that the plaintiff has sustained any special damage, the jury ought not to limit their verdict to nominal damages, but should give such temperate damages as they may judge to be a reasonable compensation for the injury the plaintiff must have sustained from the dishonour of his cheque."

In *Marzetti* v. *Williams* (1830, 1 B. and Ad. 415), where a sum of £40 had been paid to credit about one o'clock and a cheque was dishonoured shortly after three (although the banker had, after including the amount paid in at one, sufficient funds of the drawer with which to pay the cheque), Mr. Justice Taunton said: "The jury have found that when the cheque was presented for payment a reasonable time had elapsed to have enabled the bankers to enter the £40 to the credit of the plaintiff, and, therefore, that they must or ought to have known that they had funds belonging to him. That was sufficient to entitle the plaintiff to recover nominal damages, for he had a right to have his cheque paid at the time when it was presented, and the bankers were guilty of a wrong by refusing to pay it. Independently of other considerations, the credit of the plaintiff was likely to be injured by the refusal of the defendants to pay the cheque. . . . The case put in the course of the argument, of the holder of a cheque being refused payment, and called back within a few minutes and paid, is an extreme case, and a jury probably would consider that as equivalent to instant payment."

When a cheque which has been credited to a customer's account is returned unpaid, a banker debits it to that account if the balance permits of it, and advises his customer that he has done so. Some bankers obtain a cheque from the customer when handing him a returned cheque. If the customer wishes it to be re-presented, a fresh paying-in slip should be signed. When a cheque which has been returned is recalled by wire, it is advisable for a banker to advise his customer of the circumstance, in order that he may be on his guard.

Cheques paid to credit are often (when payable to bearer or indorsed in blank) not indorsed by the customer, but the fact that the cheque was not indorsed by the customer when placed to his credit does not affect at all the banker's right to debit his account with it when returned dishonoured.

A cheque received in the Local Exchange must, if not to be paid, be returned on the day of receipt.

Where a cheque received through the London Clearing House for collection cannot be paid, by Rule 4 of the Clearing House, "Any country bank not intending to pay a cheque sent to it for collection, to return it direct to the country or branch bank, if any, whose name and address is across it." And by Rule 5, "Each country banker to write by return of post to its London agent in reply, 'we credit you £ for cheques forwarded to us for collection in yours of .' Adding in case of non-payment of any such cheques, 'having deducted £ for cheque returned to Messrs. at .'"

When a banker dishonours a customer's cheque, the balance on the drawer's account is available to pay any cheque, which may be presented subsequently, up to the amount of the balance or sum available, but in Scotland when a cheque is dishonoured, any funds that there may be in the drawer's account are attached in favour of the person presenting the cheque, the amount being transferred by the banker to a suspense account.

A cheque paid to the credit of a customer of the X. & Y. Bank, drawn by another customer of the same bank, may be returned on the following day. Even if the paying-in-slip counterfoil is initialled by the bank cashier, as it often is, it would not affect the banker's right to return the cheque. The banker is not obliged to inform the person paying in to credit a cheque drawn on the banker by another customer, that the cheque may not be paid. He may take the cheque without comment and, after he has looked into the position of the drawer's account, may return it dishonoured. In practice a country banker either pays or dishonours such a cheque on the day he receives it.

If a cheque presented across the counter is refused payment, the banker does not, as a rule, write anything upon the cheque. He may simply refer the presenter to the drawer.

If a cheque cashed for a person who is not a customer is returned unpaid, the banker will, of course, at once endeavour to regain the amount from the party to whom it was paid, but if this is not immediately possible he should debit it meanwhile to a returned bill (or cheque) account.

Where a customer has two accounts, one in credit and one overdrawn, and the credit balance is regarded as a set off to the debit, cheques on the credit account may be dishonoured if their payment would reduce the balance below the amount owing on the overdrawn account, unless there is some arrangement or custom to the contrary.

Where a customer has a deposit receipt and a current account, and cheques are drawn upon the account in excess of the balance, a banker usually pays such cheques so long as they do not exceed the amount of the deposit receipt. Should such cheques be inadvertently dishonoured, the banker would, probably, not be liable, seeing that deposit receipts are not intended to be drawn against by cheque. (See BILL OF EXCHANGE.)

DISPOSITION. In Scots law, a document by which a person disposes of, or makes over, heritable property to another person.

By the Stamp Act, 1891, the stamp duty is:—

	£ s. d.
DISPOSITION of heritable property in Scotland to singular successors or purchasers. See CONVEYANCE ON SALE.	
DISPOSITION of heritable property in Scotland to a purchaser, containing a clause declaring all or any part of the purchase money a real burden upon, or affecting, the heritable property thereby disponed, or any part thereof. See CONVEYANCE ON SALE, MORTGAGE, etc., and Section 86.	
DISPOSITION in Scotland, containing constitution of feu or ground annual right. See CONVEYANCE ON SALE.	
DISPOSITION in security in Scotland. See MORTGAGE, etc.	
DISPOSITION of any wadset, heritable bond, etc. See MORTGAGE, etc.	
DISPOSITION in Scotland of any property or of any right or interest therein not described in this schedule	0 10 0

(See DISPOSITION ABSOLUTE.)

DISPOSITION ABSOLUTE. In Scotland, an equitable mortgage over real property cannot be obtained, as in England, by a deposit of the title deeds with, or without, a memorandum of deposit. A security may be obtained by a "bond and disposition in security" (*q.v.*), or by a "bond of credit and disposition in security" (*q.v.*) or by an absolute disposition.

The most convenient form in which the property may be made available as security for a fluctuating overdraft is by an absolute disposition qualified by a back-letter or back-bond. The disposition is in the form of an absolute conveyance of the property by the debtor to the banker; and the back-letter or back-bond is a document given to the debtor by the banker, setting forth the nature of the transaction and the conditions under which the debtor is entitled to have a re-conveyance of the property from the banker.

The disposition should be registered in the Register of Sasines; the back-letter should not be registered.

The stamp duty on such a disposition is 10*s.* (see DISPOSITION), and on the back-bond or back-letter the duty is the same as on a mortgage.

DISTRICT COUNCILS. (See RURAL DISTRICT COUNCIL, URBAN DISTRICT COUNCIL.)

DISTRICTS. A Stock Exchange name for Metropolitan District Railway ordinary stock.

DISTRINGAS. (Latin, that you distrain.) The writ of distringas was abolished in 1880. In place of such a writ, a notice may be given by the Court to a company not to register a transfer of any shares belonging to a defendant or pay the dividends thereon without giving notice to the claimant. The notice has only a temporary effect. When a request is received by the company from the shareholder to transfer the shares or pay the dividends, the company cannot refuse to do so after eight days from the date of the request, unless by express sanction of the Court. When the claimant receives notice from the company of the shareholder's request, he must, within the eight days, obtain an order from the Court restraining the company from transferring the shares or paying the dividends. (See CHARGING ORDER.)

DIVIDEND. The interest which is paid upon an investment, such as stock in the public funds, and shares or stock in companies. The interest may be payable at a fixed rate, or the rate may be, as in the case of a company, dependent upon the profits that are made, or it may be cumulative.

The clauses in Table A of the Companies (Consolidation) Act, 1908 (see Section 11, under ARTICLES OF ASSOCIATION) with respect to dividends are as follow:—

"95. The company in general meeting may declare dividends, but no dividend shall exceed the amount recommended by the directors.

"96. The directors may from time to time pay to the members such interim dividends as appear to the directors to be justified by the profits of the company.

"97. No dividend shall be paid otherwise than out of profits.

"98. Subject to the rights of persons, if any, entitled to shares with special rights as to dividends, all dividends shall be declared and paid according to the amounts paid on the shares, but if and so long as nothing is paid up on any of the shares in the company dividends may be declared and paid according to the amounts of the shares. No amount paid on a share in advance of calls shall, while carrying interest, be treated for the purposes of this article as paid on the share.

"99. The directors may, before recommending any dividend, set aside out of the profits of the company such sums as they think proper as a reserve or reserves which shall, at the discretion of the directors, be applicable for meeting contingencies, or for equalising dividends, or for any other purpose to which the profits of the company may be properly applied, and pending such application may, at the like discretion, either be employed in the business of the company or be invested in such investments (other than shares of the company) as the directors may from time to time think fit.

"100. If several persons are registered as joint holders of any share any one of them may give effectual receipts for any dividend payable on the share.

"101. Notice of any dividend that may have been declared shall be given in manner hereinafter mentioned to the persons entitled to share therein.

"102. No dividend shall bear interest against the company."

Dividends must be paid only out of profits, but a company has power, in certain special cases, to pay interest out of capital. Section 91 of the Companies (Consolidation) Act, 1908, provides as follows :—

"Where any shares of a company are issued for the purpose of raising money to defray the expenses of the construction of any works or buildings or the provision of any plant which cannot be made profitable for a lengthened period, the company may pay interest on so much of that share capital as is for the time being paid up for the period and subject to the conditions and restrictions in this Section mentioned, and may charge the same to capital as part of the cost of construction of the work or building, or the provision of plant :

Provided that—

"(1) No such payment shall be made unless the same is authorised by the articles or by special resolution :

"(2) No such payment, whether authorised by the articles or by special resolution, shall be made without the previous sanction of the Board of Trade :

"(3) Before sanctioning any such payment the Board of Trade may, at the expense of the company, appoint a person to inquire and report to them as to the circumstances of the case, and may, before making the appointment, require the company to give security for the payment of the costs of the inquiry :

"(4) The payment shall be made only for such period as may be determined by the Board of Trade ; and such period shall in no case extend beyond the close of the half-year next after the half-year during which the works or buildings have been actually completed or the plant provided :

"(5) The rate of interest shall in no case exceed four per cent. per annum or such lower rate as may for the time being be prescribed by Order in Council :

"(6) The payment of the interest shall not operate as a reduction of the amount paid up on the shares in respect of which it is paid :

"(7) The accounts of the company shall show the share capital on which, and the rate at which, interest has been paid out of capital during the period to which the accounts relate :

"(8) Nothing in this Section shall affect any company to which the Indian Railways Act, 1894, as amended by any subsequent enactment, applies."

Interest upon debentures is commonly regarded as a dividend, but it is really interest upon a loan, and must be paid by the company quite irrespective of any question of profits.

A dividend is also the name given to the amount which is paid to creditors from a bankrupt's estate. (See COMPANIES, DIVIDENDS—IN BANKRUPTCY.)

DIVIDEND MANDATE. A written order from a shareholder requesting the company of which he is a member to send his dividends direct to his banker to be placed to the credit of his account.

If the shares stand in several names the mandate should be signed by each person.

DIVIDEND REGISTER. A register containing the names and addresses of all shareholders, and the number of shares held by each. There is a column provided to show the amount of dividend which is due to each shareholder. The dividend warrants are prepared from this book, and as they are paid a record of the date of payment is entered against the individual amounts.

Unless the income tax on the dividends is paid by the bank, a column in the register will be necessary to show the amount to be deducted in each case. The totals of the columns must, of course, agree with the amount set apart for payment of dividend.

DIVIDEND WARRANT. An order, or warrant, issued by a company, and drawn upon its bankers, in favour of a member of the company, for payment of the interest or dividend due to him upon his holding of shares or stock in the company.

Section 95 of the Bills of Exchange Act, 1882, is :—" The provisions of this Act as to crossed cheques shall apply to a warrant for payment of dividend." (See CROSSED CHEQUE.)

Section 97, s.s. 3, provides :—

" Nothing in this Act or in any repeal effected thereby shall affect :—

" (*d*) The validity of any usage relating to dividend warrants, or the indorsements thereof."

There is usually a space provided at the foot of dividend warrants for the proprietor's signature.

A dividend warrant must be signed by the person to whom it is payable, and, unless authorised by the company, a per procuration signature should not be accepted. If payable to John Brown or bearer, it nevertheless requires John Brown's discharge.

Where a dividend warrant is payable to several persons, it is the custom to pay it on being signed by one of them. But in the case of an interest warrant all the persons named should sign.

Many Dividend Warrants are crossed

——— & Co. and the effect is the same

as when a cheque is so crossed (Section 95 above). The banker on whom a crossed warrant is drawn should pay it only to another banker.

All dividend warrants, like cheques, though for a less amount than £2, require a penny stamp. This does not apply to interest warrants on Consols and other British Government stocks. (See Stamp Act, 1891, Exemption 6, under BILL OF EXCHANGE.)

Customers frequently instruct the companies in which they have investments to pay the dividends direct to their bankers, who forthwith credit their accounts, thus saving the customers a good deal of trouble ; these orders continue in force until cancelled by the customer ; most banks have their own printed forms. The companies make the warrants payable to the banker, generally adding the name of the shareholder at the foot , the banker discharges the warrants in the same way as a shareholder.

An ordinary dividend warrant is practically a cheque in a special form, but the dividend warrant of a bank, being drawn by a bank on a bank, is of the nature of a bank draft rather than a cheque. (See INDORSEMENT, LOST DIVIDEND WARRANT.)

DIVIDENDS (IN BANKRUPTCY). With regard to the distribution of dividends amongst the creditors of a bankrupt's estate, the Bankruptcy Act, 1883, provides :—

" Section 58. (1) Subject to the retention of such sums as may be necessary for the costs of administration, or otherwise, the trustee shall, with all convenient speed, declare and distribute dividends amongst the creditors who have proved their debts.

" (2) The first dividend, if any, shall be declared and distributed within four months after the conclusion of the first meeting of creditors, unless the trustee satisfies the committee of inspection that there is sufficient reason for postponing the declaration to a later date.

" (3) Subsequent dividends shall, in the absence of sufficient reason to the contrary, be declared and distributed at intervals of not more than six months.

" (4) Before declaring a dividend the trustee shall cause notice of his intention to do so to be gazetted in the prescribed manner, and shall also send reasonable notice thereof to each creditor mentioned in the bankrupt's statement who has not proved his debt.

" (5) When the trustee has declared a dividend he shall send to each creditor who has proved a notice showing the amount of the dividend and when and how it is payable, and a statement in the prescribed form as to the particulars of the estate.

Joint and Separate Dividends.

"59. (1) Where one partner of a firm is adjudged bankrupt, a creditor to whom the bankrupt is indebted jointly with the other partners of the firm, or any of them, shall not receive any dividend out of the separate property of the bankrupt until all the separate creditors have received the full amount of their respective debts.

"(2) Where joint and separate properties are being administered, dividends of the joint and separate properties shall, subject to any order to the contrary that may be made by the Court on the application of any person interested, be declared together; and the expenses of and incident to such dividends shall be fairly apportioned by the trustee between the joint and separate properties, regard being had to the work done for and the benefit received by each property.

Right of Creditor who has not Proved Debt before Declaration of a Dividend.

"61. Any creditor who has not proved his debt before the declaration of any dividend or dividends shall be entitled to be paid out of any money for the time being in the hands of the trustee any dividend or dividends he may have failed to receive before that money is applied to the payment of any future dividend or dividends, but he shall not be entitled to disturb the distribution of any dividend declared before his debt was proved by reason that he has not participated therein."

Before declaring a final dividend, the trustee shall give notice to creditors whose claims have not been established to his satisfaction, that, if not established within a time limited by the notice, he will make the final dividend without regard to their claims (Section 62). (See BANKRUPTCY.)

DOCK WARRANT. A dock warrant is a document issued by a dock company stating that the goods as described therein are entered in their books, and are deliverable to the person mentioned or his assigns by indorsement.

A dock warrant may be in the following form :—

X. & Y. DOCKS COY.

No. 19

Warrant for
imported in the ship . Master
, from entered by
on the
deliverable to or assigns by indorsement hereon. Rent commences on the and all other charges from the date hereof. Rate charged.

Mark.	Numbers.	Weight. Gross.	Weight. Tare.

Ledger No. Folio

, *Clerk.*

Warrant Clerk.

The Factors Act, Section 1, s.s. 4, states that the expression "document of title" includes a dock warrant, and any warrant or order for the delivery of goods, and any document authorising, either by indorsement or by delivery, the possessor of the document to transfer or receive the goods. (See FACTORS ACT.)

Where goods have been sold and the warrants indorsed by the seller to the buyer, the goods are, as a rule, subject to the seller's lien for the purchase price. But if the warrants have been lawfully transferred to a purchaser and he sells or pledges them to a third person, and that third person receives the same in good faith, without notice of any lien, the lien of the original vendor is thereby defeated. In such a case the third person (e.g. a banker) holds the warrants as "documents of title" to the goods. If the warrants are pledged or sold by a mercantile agent acting in the ordinary course of business, the pledge or sale shall be as valid as if he were expressly authorised by the owner to make the same (see Sections 2 to 10 of the "Factors Act"). In reading the sections of that Act, Sections 2 to 7 refer only to dispositions by mercantile agents, and 8 to 10 to dispositions by sellers and buyers.

Warrants which are not governed by that Act (or any Private Act) are not recognised legally as documents of title, but simply as authorities to obtain possession of the goods.

Section 11 of the same Act prescribes that the transfer of a warrant may be by indorsement, or, where the document is by custom or by its express terms transferable by delivery, or makes the goods deliverable to the bearer, then by delivery.

The warrants when given as security should be indorsed by the person named, and be accompanied by a memorandum of deposit. The memorandum (which should create a continuing security) should give the bank authority, in the event of default of repayment, to sell the goods and out of the proceeds to repay the loan with interest, and all other moneys due. The memorandum should also provide for insurance of the goods against fire, and for a sufficient margin in value to be preserved. The memorandum requires to be stamped sixpence.

Where there is any uncertainty as to the nature of the document, the goods should be transferred into the banker's name in the books of the dock company or warehouse keeper.

The stamp duty on a dock warrant is threepence. (See WARRANT FOR GOODS.)

DOCKET, OR DOCQUET. The name given in some banks to the form which is sent out yearly or half-yearly to customers to sign, if correct, confirming the balance of their account as stated thereon, and as shown by their pass book.

In Scotland, in some of the banks, a docquet or confirmation of balance is signed in the ledger.

DOCUMENTARY BILL. A documentary bill is a bill of exchange which is accompanied by various documents, such as bill of lading, dock warrant, delivery order, policy of insurance, invoice.

A banker must see that policies of insurance attached to bills received by him from abroad are stamped within ten days of their arrival in this country.

When a banker receives a bill for acceptance, with documents attached, and he sends the bill to the drawee to be accepted, and informs the drawee that the bill of lading and invoice are in his possession, the banker is not thereby held responsible if the bill of lading should prove to be a forgery. And where a banker accepts a documentary bill at the request of a customer, and the bill of lading proves to be forged, the banker, having paid the bill, may recover the amount from the customer.

If documents are sent out along with the bill to the drawee in order that he may inspect them, they should not be left with him. A banker, however, may have received instructions, from the correspondent sending him the bill, to deliver up the documents to the drawee upon his acceptance of the bill; or he may have instructions to give up the documents on payment of the bill under rebate.

When a banker advances against shipments he sends the bill abroad, with the bills of lading attached, for payment. When the documents are given up against acceptance, the banker has then to rely upon the acceptor, regarding whom he should have satisfactory information.

Where a credit is opened abroad at a customer's request, against bills of lading, policy, etc., the foreign banker draws on the banker in this country and sends the bill, with the documents attached, to the English banker. The documents may be taken by the customer and paid for at once; or the amount may be charged to the customer and the documents held as security until required. In some cases, the bills of lading may be handed to the customer and a letter taken from him hypothecating the goods to the bank, and undertaking to hand over to the bank the proceeds from the sale of the goods, and until that is done the customer agrees to hold the goods or the proceeds in trust for the bank. When this is done a separate account is usually opened for the operation. In such cases the banker really parts with his security and has to rely upon the honour of his customer. In case of failure, trustees generally recognise these undertakings. There is the danger, however, that there may be a contra account due from the customer to a purchaser of the goods, in which case, as the latter has no notice of the hypothecation, he is entitled to deduct the contra account from the amount he is due to pay as the purchase price of the goods. (See TRUST RECEIPT.)

When documentary bills are discounted, the banker takes a note of hypothecation or memorandum of deposit, from the customer, by which the bill of lading and the goods are pledged to the banker and under which he is given a right, if necessary, to sell the goods. The stamp duty upon the note of hypothecation, or memorandum of deposit, is sixpence.

If a banker sells a documentary bill he indorses it and thus becomes liable thereon;

the bills of lading, indorsed in blank by the shipper, and the insurance policy, accompany the bill.

A banker keeps a record of all his liabilities on acceptances and indorsements.

Where documents are given up against payment of a bill under rebate, the rate is usually ½ per cent. above the deposit rate of the principal London banks, and is calculated from the date when the money (free of cost) will be in the hands of the person entitled to receive it, and at the place where it is payable. A receipt is indorsed upon the bill that the amount has been paid under rebate at per cent. (See BILL OF EXCHANGE, BILL OF LADING, MARINE INSURANCE POLICY.)

DOCUMENTARY LETTER OF CREDIT. A letter issued by a banker authorising the person to whom it is addressed to draw bills upon the grantor up to a certain amount, at a specified currency, and undertaking, provided that the documents of title to the goods (the bills of lading, with insurance policies and invoices), are sent to the grantor, to honour all drafts drawn in accordance with the terms of the credit. (See LETTER OF CREDIT.)

DOLLAR. (See FOREIGN MONEYS—CANADA, CHINA, MEXICO, UNITED STATES.)

DOMICILED BILL. (The word domicile is from the Latin *domicilium*, a habitation.)

Where a bill of exchange is accepted payable at some place other than the acceptor's private or business address it is said to be domiciled at that place.

A great many firms in the country domicile their bills at the head office or London agents of their bankers. (See ACCEPTANCE.)

DONATIO MORTIS CAUSÂ. (Latin.) A gift made in anticipation of, and conditional on, the death of the donor, is called a *donatio mortis causâ*.

If a person, in anticipation of death, draws a cheque and hands it to, say, his son, unless the cheque is actually or constructively paid before death takes place, the gift is ineffectual. It cannot be paid by the banker after he has had notice of the drawer's death, and it does not form a charge upon the deceased's estate. But if the donee transfers the cheque to another party, for value, that party would have a claim upon the estate for the amount, though the banker would not pay it after notice of death.

There is, however, a difference between a cheque drawn by the donor, and one payable to the donor. In the former case "his own cheque is not property, it is only a revocable order" (Justice Buckley), but in the latter case it is the "*indicia* of title to property, which belonged to him" (Justice Buckley). When it is payable to the donor, the person who receives it obtains a good *donatio mortis causâ*, and is fully entitled to the amount. If not indorsed by the donor, it has been held that the recipient is entitled to require the indorsement of his legal representatives.

A bill, a promissory note, and a deposit receipt payable to the donor, and a bond and mortgage deed have also been held to form good subjects of gifts made in anticipation of death.

Although a cheque payable to the donor, or a deposit receipt, forms an effectual gift, a banker, with notice of the payee's death, would not pay such cheque or deposit receipt to the recipient of the gift (even if indorsed by the deceased donor), until indorsed by the legal representatives of the deceased.

A *donatio mortis causâ* is subject to payment of estate and legacy duty.

DORAS. A Stock Exchange name for South-Eastern Railway deferred ordinary stock.

DORMANT BALANCES. The balances of accounts which have not been operated upon for a long period. (See UNCLAIMED BALANCES.)

DOUBLE FLORINS. These inconvenient coins were first issued in 1887 and the issue was discontinued in 1890.

DOVER A. A Stock Exchange name for South-Eastern Railway deferred ordinary stock.

DOWER. The right of a widow, whose husband has died intestate, to a life interest in one-third of her deceased husband's real estate, unless there was a declaration against dower in the deed of conveyance to the husband. The dower exists whether there has or has not been any issue of the marriage.

Blackstone says: "Tenancy in dower is where a widow takes a third of such lands and tenements as her husband died entitled to, for seisin is not here necessary, and in which her title to dower has not been previously barred. This mode of providing for a widow seems to have been unknown in the early part of our Saxon constitution; for in the laws of King Edmund, the wife is directed to be supported wholly out of the personal estate."

Dower is barred when the widow is prevented from obtaining it. When the estate is settled upon a woman in order that she may enjoy it after the husband's death (i.e.

jointure), the dower is thereby barred. (See FREEBENCH, INTESTACY.)

DRACHMA. (See FOREIGN MONEYS—GREECE.)

DRAFT. (From the verb to draw. Formerly spelled "draught" and "drawght.)"

Bills of exchange on demand, or after sight, or after date, are called drafts, because they are drawn by one person on another. Cheques also are sometimes called drafts. But the word "draft" is used principally when referring to a banker's own draft, or instrument drawn upon another banker or upon one of his own branches, or to a draft drawn upon his London agents or London office, at seven, fourteen or twenty-one days after date, or on demand, or to a foreign draft drawn by a banker in one country upon a banker in another. When a draft is issued by one branch bank upon another or by a country bank upon its London agent, an advice describing the draft is sent by the drawer to the drawee by the same day's post.

Where a customer applies for a draft and desires the amount to be debited to his account, a cheque must be taken for the amount or the application form be stamped one penny.

A banker should not stop payment of a draft issued by him upon his head office, or another branch, or his London agents, as he is liable to pay it to a *bona fide* holder. But if he receives notice that it has been lost, he will exercise great care before paying it, particularly if there is any suspicion that the indorsement is forged. (See DRAFT AFTER DATE, DRAFT ON DEMAND.)

DRAFT AFTER DATE. In addition to drafts on demand, country bankers issue drafts after date upon their London agents or London offices. They are drawn at seven, fourteen or twenty-one days after date, and are issued free of charge, the banker obtaining his remuneration from the interest upon the money between the date he received it and the date on which the draft is due. The various inland revenue collections are remitted from all over the country to London by means of bankers' after date drafts. Drafts for this purpose do not require to be stamped.

After date drafts are not much in request in many parts of the country, but in certain districts they are in common use for making payments which are usually made elsewhere by means of cheques. Where this practice exists, a customer supplies his banker with a list of the amounts for which he requires drafts. The banker draws a draft for each amount on the list, at, say, twenty-one days date, and makes all the drafts payable to the customer. The customer then indorses each draft, making it payable to the person to whom he intends to send it.

The following is a specimen of an ordinary after date draft:—

No. X. & Y. Bank, Ltd.,

£ Leeds , 1910.

Examined

Twenty-one days after date pay to the order of the sum of value received.

For the X. & Y. Bank, Ltd.,

, Manager.

To the A. & B. Bank, Ltd.,
London.

Bankers do not usually accept such drafts, but pay them on presentation when due. Some bankers' drafts have the words "without acceptance" printed in the body. The following specimen of a Bank of England draft includes those words:—

BANK OF ENGLAND.

No. £20 Without acceptance

Seven days after date pay this Sola bill of exchange to or order Twenty pounds,
for value received.

Branch.
(Date).
Agent.

To the Cashiers of the
Bank of England,
London.

Entd.

Drafts after date take the usual three days of grace, except in the case of bills drawn by the Bank of England upon itself.

By 9 George IV. c. 23, bankers in England, except within the City of London, or within three miles thereof, having first obtained a licence and given security by bond, may issue, on unstamped paper, promissory notes for any sum of money amounting to five pounds or upwards, expressed to be payable to the bearer on demand, or to order, at any period not exceeding seven days after sight; and bills of exchange payable to order, on demand, or at any period, not exceeding seven days after sight or twenty-one days after date, provided such bills be drawn upon a banker in London, Westminster, or the borough of Southwark; or provided such bills be drawn by any banker or bankers at any place where they are licensed to issue bills and notes, upon themselves, payable at any other place where they shall also be duly licensed.

That Section applies only to bankers who are licensed to issue notes and drafts on unstamped paper. The stamp duty is compounded for at the rate of 3*s*. 6*d*. for every £100 or part of £100 of the half-yearly average amount of notes and drafts in circulation, based on the amount in circulation on Saturday in every week.

Where a banker is not licensed to issue notes and drafts on unstamped paper, all drafts payable after date, issued by him, must be stamped in the same way as an ordinary bill of exchange. See the stamp duties under BILL OF EXCHANGE. (See DRAFT.)

DRAFT BOOK. A book in which are kept particulars of drafts issued, e.g. the date, number of draft, name of payee, amount, and term (on demand or at so many days date or sight). When a draft is finally paid, the date of payment is entered in the column provided for the purpose. Separate books may be kept for drafts on demand, and for drafts after date; also for drafts on London, on the head office, on branches, or on correspondents.

DRAFT ON DEMAND. A person who wishes to remit money to someone in another place may, if he does not send his own cheque, obtain from his banker a draft on demand payable to the person who is to be paid the money. A banker's draft is a document drawn by one banker upon another. It may be drawn upon the banker's London office or London agents, or upon one of the banker's own branches, or upon some other bank where an arrangement exists for drafts to be drawn. Whenever a draft is drawn, an advice is despatched the same day, advising the London agents, bank or branch, as the case may be, of the particulars of the draft, so that the banker on whom it is drawn may recognise the draft when it is presented.

A draft on demand, like a cheque, requires a penny stamp. A draft drawn by any banker in the United Kingdom upon any other banker in the United Kingdom, not payable to bearer or to order, and used solely for the purpose of settling or clearing any account between such bankers is exempt from stamp duty. (See Exemption 2, under BILL OF EXCHANGE.)

A draft on demand drawn by one branch upon another branch or upon the head office, is not a cheque within the meaning of the Bills of Exchange Act, 1882, as it is not addressed by one person to a banker, which is part of the definition of a cheque. It cannot, therefore, be crossed like a cheque. In paying a draft on demand the banker is protected against a forged indorsement by Section 19 of the Stamp Act, 1853, which is as follows:—

"Provided always, that any draft or order drawn upon a banker for a sum of money payable to order on demand which shall, when presented for payment, purport to be indorsed by the person to whom the same shall be drawn payable, shall be a sufficient authority to such banker to pay the amount of such draft or order to the bearer thereof; and it shall not be incumbent on such banker to prove that such indorsement, or any subsequent indorsement, was made by or under the direction or authority of the person to whom the said draft or order was or is made payable, either by the drawer or any indorser thereof."

It is considered by some authorities that this Section protects a banker in paying not only drafts drawn by one branch on another or on the head office, but also drafts drawn abroad on the head office in England.

In the case of a draft after date, however, a forged or unauthorised signature is wholly inoperative, and no right can be acquired through or under that signature (Section 24, Bills of Exchange Act, 1882).

In the judgment of Lord Lindley in *Capital and Counties Bank* v. *Gordon* (1903, A.C. 240), speaking of drafts there are the following words: "The first question which has to be considered is whether these instruments are bills of exchange as defined in Section 3 of the Bills of Exchange Act. If they are, then, not being crossed, Section 82 will have no application to them, even if that Section could have applied in this case to such documents if crossed. But if these drafts are bills of exchange within the meaning of Section 3, they will come within Section 60, and the bank will be protected by it, for these cheques are drawn on the bank sought to be made liable for paying them. But I agree with the Court of Appeal in thinking that the bank, which is both drawer and drawee of these instruments, is not entitled to treat them as bills of exchange as defined in Section 3 of the Bills of Exchange Act, although a holder may sue the bank upon them and treat them either as bills of exchange or as promissory notes (see Section 5, s.s. 2). An instrument on which no action can be brought by the drawer can hardly be a bill of exchange within Section 3 of the Act, whatever it may be called in ordinary talk." (See DRAFT AFTER DATE.)

DRAIN OF BULLION. A large outflow of gold from the Bank of England. When the Bank Rate is raised, it tends to stop the withdrawal and to turn the current homeward.

DRAWEE. The drawee of a bill is the person to whom it is addressed.

By Section 6 of the Bills of Exchange Act, 1882 :—

"(1) The drawee must be named or otherwise indicated in a bill with reasonable certainty.

"(2) A bill may be addressed to two or more drawees whether they are partners or not, but an order addressed to two drawees in the alternative or to two or more drawees in succession is not a bill of exchange."

Where different parties to a bill are the same person, Section 5 provides :—

"(1) A bill may be drawn payable to, or to the order of, the drawer ; or it may be drawn payable to, or to the order of, the drawee.

"(2) Where in a bill drawer and drawee are the same person, or where the drawee is a fictitious person or a person not having capacity to contract, the holder may treat the instrument, at his option, either as a bill of exchange or as a promissory note."

The drawee is the person who is expected to accept the bill and, at maturity, to pay it. If the drawee, on receiving a bill, agrees to pay the amount as indicated therein, he signifies his assent to the drawer's order by signing his name across the face of the bill, called accepting the bill. When the drawee has accepted a bill he is then called the acceptor (*q.v.*) and his written assent on the bill is his acceptance (*q.v.*).

With regard to funds in the hands of a drawee, Section 53 enacts :—

"(1) A bill, of itself, does not operate as an assignment of funds in the hands of the drawee available for the payment thereof, and the drawee of a bill who does not accept as required by this Act is not liable on the instrument. This sub-section shall not extend to Scotland.

"(2) In Scotland, where the drawee of a bill has in his hands funds available for the payment thereof, the bill operates as an assignment of the sum for which it is drawn in favour of the holder, from the time when the bill is presented to the drawee."

The drawee of a cheque is the banker on whom it is drawn. The banker is responsible only to the drawer and is under no liability to the person presenting the cheque for payment, except in Scotland where the presentment of a cheque attaches any balance there may be in the drawer's account to the extent of the cheque.

The drawee of a bank draft is the bank to which the order to pay is addressed. (See ACCEPTOR, BILL OF EXCHANGE, PRESENTMENT FOR ACCEPTANCE.)

DRAWER. The drawer is the person who signs a bill of exchange giving an order to another person, the drawee, to pay the amount mentioned therein.

In the usual course, a drawer makes out the bill himself, signs it and sends it to the drawee for acceptance. But a person may sign a bill as drawer which has already been made out and accepted, and even indorsed. When a simple signature on a blank stamped paper is delivered by the signer in order that it may be converted into a bill, it operates as a *primâ facie* authority to fill it up as a complete bill using the signature, if so authorised, as that of the drawer. (See INCHOATE INSTRUMENT.)

Section 55 of the Bills of Exchange Act, 1882, provides :—

"(1) The drawer of a bill by drawing it—

"(*a*) Engages that on due presentment it shall be accepted and paid according to its tenor, and that if it be dishonoured he will compensate the holder or any indorser who is compelled to pay it, provided that the requisite proceedings on dishonour be duly taken ;

"(*b*) Is precluded from denying to a holder in due course the existence of the payee and his then capacity to indorse."

A drawer may, if he wish, limit his

liability on the bill by such words as "Pay John Brown or order without recourse," or, "*sans recours*." Permission to do so is given in Section 16, as follows :—

"The drawer of a bill, and any indorser, may insert therein an express stipulation—

"(1) Negativing or limiting his own liability to the holder ;

"(2) Waiving as regards himself some or all of the holder's duties."

Where different parties to a bill are the same person, Section 5 provides :—

"(1) A bill may be drawn payable to, or to the order of, the drawer ; or it may be drawn payable to, or to the order of, the drawee.

"(2) Where in a bill drawer and drawee are the same person, or where the drawee is a fictitious person or a person not having capacity to contract, the holder may treat the instrument, at his option, either as a bill of exchange or as a promissory note." (See PARTIES TO BILL OF EXCHANGE.)

Where a drawer is dead, notice of dishonour must be given to a personal representative ; where he is bankrupt notice may be given either to the party himself or to the trustee. (See DISHONOUR OF BILL OF EXCHANGE.)

In applying the provisions of Part IV of the Bills of Exchange Act, 1882, the first indorser of a promissory note is (by Section 89) deemed to correspond with the drawer of an accepted bill payable to the drawer's order.

The drawer of a cheque is the person on whose account it is drawn and who must provide the funds to meet it.

A banker must know the signature of a customer. If the drawer's signature is forged, the banker cannot charge it to his customer's account. Even if the forgery is so perfectly done as to defy detection under the closest scrutiny, it does not affect the banker's liability. His customer cannot be debited with a cheque which he has not drawn.

If John Thomas Charles Brown wishes to sign cheques merely as plain John Brown, an authority should be obtained to honour cheques so signed.

Where a drawer is unable to write, he may sign by making a × in the presence of a witness who is known to the bank officials. The mark should be made at the bank, otherwise the banker cannot be certain that it has been made by the customer. The form is usually this :—THOMAS his × mark SMITH.

Witness :—JAMES ROBINSON,
Hope Street,
Manchester.

If the customer does not produce an outside person two officials of the bank may witness his mark. Banks do not, as a rule, consider one official sufficient.

When mandates or authorities are held regarding the signing of cheques, the instructions must be carefully observed. A difficulty sometimes arises where a banker is authorised by a limited company to pay cheques when signed by two directors and the secretary, and the secretary is also a director, his name appearing on cheques in both capacities. In such a case the banker should ascertain if the articles of association permit a director to act also as secretary. Even if they do so permit, it is better to have a clear understanding with the company on the point.

Notice of a customer's death cancels the banker's authority to pay his cheques, and any cheques presented after receipt of such notice are returned "Drawer dead," except in the case of a cheque which the banker has agreed to pay, by marking or certifying it, at the drawer's request, for payment, or which the banker has, for his own convenience, "marked" in connection with the local clearing.

Where a person is too ill to sign his name, his mark should be witnessed by two persons, one of whom should be the doctor in attendance. It is usual for the doctor to certify that his patient clearly understood the nature of the transaction.

The drawer of a bill payable on demand is discharged if it is not presented for payment within a reasonable time.

The drawer of a cheque is, in an ordinary case, liable thereon for six years from the date of the cheque. (See AUTHORITIES, BILL OF EXCHANGE, CHEQUE, JOINT ACCOUNT.)

DRAWN BILL. A bill drawn in this country and payable abroad, if negotiated direct from the drawer to a foreign banker in London, is termed a drawn bill. (See MADE BILL.)

DRAWN BONDS. Where a certain amount of bonds is to be repaid periodically, the method adopted, in order to determine which of the bonds should be paid, is to "draw" numbers, on the lottery principle, up to the amount required. The numbers so drawn represent the bonds to be paid off, which are then called "drawn bonds."

Holders of bonds subject to be drawn require to watch the advertisements of the "drawings," or to instruct their bankers to do so.

After a bond is drawn interest ceases. In the case of Russian bonds, however, the coupons may continue to be paid after a bond is drawn for repayment, but the amounts so paid are treated by the Russian Government as repayments on account of the principal.

DRUNKEN PERSON. If a bill or cheque is given during a state of drunkenness, that condition may be set up as a defence against an immediate party, if the drunken person was taken advantage of in any way, but it would be of no avail as against a holder in due course.

Where a drunken person draws a cheque at the bank counter in order to obtain cash and he really insists upon payment, it is well to have the signature witnessed.

DUE DATE OF BILL. (See TIME OF PAYMENT OF BILL.)

DUPLICATE OR COUNTERPART. By the Stamp Act, 1891, the stamp duty is :—

DUPLICATE OR COUNTERPART of any instrument chargeable with any duty.

Where such duty does not amount to 5s. . . .	The same duty as the original instrument.
	£ s. d.
In any other case . . .	0 5 0

And see Section 72, which is as follows :—

"The duplicate or counterpart of an instrument chargeable with duty (except the counterpart of an instrument chargeable as a lease, such counterpart not being executed by or on behalf of any lessor or grantor), is not to be deemed duly stamped unless it is stamped as an original instrument, or unless it appears by some stamp impressed thereon that the full and proper duty has been paid upon the original instrument of which it is the duplicate or counterpart." (See DENOTING STAMPS.)

EAGLE. (See FOREIGN MONEYS—UNITED STATES.)

EARMARKED. If a customer pays in to the credit of his account an amount expressly to meet a specified cheque or bill when presented, the credit is said to be "earmarked," and the money cannot be used by the banker for any other purpose.

EASEMENTS. The rights which the owner of a property may have over the property belonging to another person, such as rights of way, rights of light, rights of air, rights of water, rights of support, etc. An absolute right of way may be acquired by the uninterrupted use for forty years, unless the use was granted in writing by the owner of the land. A right of light over another person's property (except when the privilege is granted in writing by the owner of the property) is acquired after an enjoyment of it for twenty years.

These easements or rights are called incorporeal hereditaments.

EASTERNS. A Stock Exchange name for Great Eastern Railway ordinary stock.

"EFFECTS NOT CLEARED." If a customer pays in to the credit of his account a cheque drawn upon another banker, and the customer is given to understand that he must not draw against it until the cheque has been collected, in the event of the customer issuing a cheque which is presented before the proceeds are received, the banker is entitled to return the cheque marked "effects not cleared."

If, however, there is no particular arrangement with the customer that cheques will not be paid against uncleared effects, the banker is probably not entitled to return a cheque so marked. In *Capital and Counties Bank* v. *Gordon* (1903, A.C. 240), Lord Lindley said : "It must never be forgotten that the moment a bank places money to its customer's credit, the customer is entitled to draw upon it, unless something occurs to deprive him of that right."

A banker could probably protect himself by printing a notice in all his pass books or on all paying-in slips, that customers would not be at liberty to draw against uncleared cheques. Some banks have a notice on paying-in slips to the following effect :—"Cheques, etc., for collection, though credited to the account when paid in, are not available for drawing against until the proceeds have been received at the branch."

EMBEZZLEMENT. (See COMPOUNDING A FELONY.)

ENDORSEMENT. Same as Indorsement (*q.v.*).

ENDOWMENT POLICY. A policy of assurance which is payable on the assured surviving to a certain age, or payable at death if it occurs before that age. (See LIFE POLICY.)

ENFACED PAPER. A name given to the promissory notes (Rupee Paper) of the Indian Government, which bear an announcement that the interest is payable by drafts obtainable on presentation of the notes at the Bank of England. (See RUPEE PAPER.)

ENFRANCHISEMENT. Under the Copyhold Act of 1894 the lord of the manor or the tenant of copyhold land may, under certain provisions as to compensation, require it to be enfranchised. By enfranchisement the land is freed from all duties to the lord of the manor, and the owner henceforth holds it as freehold land. If the lord makes a legal conveyance in fee simple to the copyholder, the copyhold is extinguished.

By the Conveyancing Act of 1881 :—

"Section 3, s.s. 2. Where land of copyhold or customary tenure has been converted into freehold by enfranchisement, then, under a contract to sell and convey the freehold, the purchaser shall not have the right to call for the title to make the enfranchisement."

ENTAILED ESTATE. Where land is granted to a person and the heirs of his body, it is said to be entailed, and the estate is called "estate tail." When the land is freed from the entail, it is said to be disentailed. (See ESTATE TAIL, DISENTAIL.)

EQUITABLE ESTATE. The estate, or interest, which a person may have in land, according to equity, as distinguished from an estate or interest, according to law.

There may be both estates, the legal and the equitable, in the same piece of land. A mortgagee has the legal and the mortgagor has the equitable estate. If the money lent is not repaid according to the terms of the mortgage deed, the mortgagee becomes, by law, the owner of the land, but the mortgagor, who is, by equity, the real owner, has the equity of redemption or right to redeem his land on payment of the debt and interest.

A trustee holds the legal estate and the person in whose favour the trust operates has an equitable estate.

A second mortgagee has only an equitable estate in the property. (See EQUITY OF REDEMPTION.)

EQUITABLE MORTGAGE. Where a borrower gives to a lender, as security, the title deeds of his property, without any document of charge, or the deeds with a memorandum of deposit, or even a memorandum of charge without the deeds, it is an equitable mortgage. An equitable mortgage does not convey the legal estate to the lender, as does a legal mortgage, but in the memorandum which usually accompanies the deposit of deeds, the borrower, as a rule, promises to grant a legal mortgage when requested to do so.

Where a legal mortgage has been granted upon a property and the borrower raises further money by a second or a third mortgage, those subsequent charges, whether by deed or otherwise, are merely equitable mortgages.

Where a person has only an equitable estate in land as, for example, where the legal estate is vested in a trustee for his benefit, any charge that he gives upon that estate will only be an equitable mortgage.

An equitable charge may be created by a written agreement to grant a mortgage, or by sending the deeds to a party for the purpose of having a legal mortgage prepared, or by a written promise to lodge certain deeds as security.

An equitable mortgagee by deposit of title deeds, when he desires to realise his security, requires to go to the Courts for power to sell, or to appoint a receiver or to foreclose, or to enter into possession. If, however, he obtains a legal mortgage he has power to sell or put in a receiver without applying to the Courts.

Where there are two equitable mortgages on the same property, priority will be given to a second equitable mortgagee who holds the title deeds, if the first equitable mortgagee was negligent in not retaining possession of the title deeds. But if there has not been negligence, priority in order of time prevails. If a second equitable mortgagee made his advance, without knowledge of the prior equitable charge, he may, in most cases, secure priority by obtaining a legal mortgage.

Instead of an order for foreclosure the Court may, if it thinks fit, direct a sale of the mortgaged property ; and in an action for redemption the mortgagor may have an order for sale, or for sale or redemption in the alternative. (See Section 25 of the Conveyancing and Law of Property Act, 1881, under LEGAL MORTGAGE.)

For the purposes of the Stamp Act, 1891, "equitable mortgage" means an agreement or memorandum, under hand only, relating to the deposit of any title deeds or instruments constituting or being evidence of the title to any property whatever (other than stock or marketable security), or creating a charge on such property. (Section 86, s.s. 2. See MORTGAGE.) Mortgages subsequent to the first legal mortgage, are, legally, equitable mortgages, but it should be noted that these equitable mortgages are not included in the definition of "equitable mortgage" under the Stamp Act.

A second mortgage by deed. A memorandum of deposit under *seal*	The duty is the same as for a mortgage (see MORTGAGE).
A memorandum of deposit of deeds under *hand* (whether a principal security or collateral security)	For every £100, and any fractional part of £100 of the amount secured, 1*s*.

The stamp on a memorandum of deposit of certificates is sixpence for any amount.

If a power of sale is included in a memorandum under hand it requires to be stamped the same as a mortgage.

A letter or memorandum of deposit must be stamped within thirty days of its date, or, if received from abroad, within thirty days of its receipt in this country.

By an Inland Revenue Circular :—

The instruments given to banks to secure overdrafts are almost invariably worded as securities for all sums due or to become due. In the case of equitable mortgages, every security, whether primary or collateral, is chargeable with the duty of 1*s*. per cent. on the highest amount at any one time due in respect of the indebtedness secured to the bank up to date (i.e., within thirty days) and with additional duty from time to time, if the indebtedness should subsequently reach, at any one time, a higher total. In no case can the value of the security deposited be taken as the basis of assessment for mortgage duty. (See copy of the Circular under MORTGAGE.)

For instance, if the deeds of several different properties are lodged as security, with a separate memorandum for each to cover the overdraft, each memorandum requires to be (according to the above Circular of the Inland Revenue) stamped to cover the full amount secured.

A memorandum, unless a fixed amount has been inserted in it, may be further stamped to cover an additional overdraft, but the Stamp Authorities may, before stamping it with the extra stamp, require the banker to state what has been the highest amount of overdraft and the date when it occurred. It must be stamped for the additional amount within thirty days of the extra overdraft being taken.

If a fixed amount is inserted in the memorandum of deposit, the security cannot be made available for any greater amount than that stated in the document. If the property is to form a security for more than that amount, a fresh memorandum must be taken.

If a memorandum of deposit is unstamped or insufficiently stamped, it cannot be accepted as evidence in a Court of Law or Equity. An instrument which has not been stamped within the prescribed time may be stamped at any time afterwards under a penalty of £10. Neglect to stamp a memorandum does not affect the validity of it.

In Scotland, a deposit of title deeds, either with, or without, a memorandum of deposit, does not create an equitable mortgage, as in England. If, therefore, a banker in England advances against real property in Scotland, the form of charge must conform to the law of Scotland. (See DISPOSITION ABSOLUTE, MORTGAGE, TITLE DEEDS.)

EQUITY. The administration of justice, not according to the strict letter of the law but according to the circumstances of each case so as to give an equitable decision.

EQUITY OF REDEMPTION. The right which a mortgagor has to redeem his property. For example, if John Brown is the absolute owner of a piece of land, and he mortgages the land to John Jones to secure the repayment of a loan which Jones has granted to him, Jones obtains by that deed the legal estate in the land, and if Brown fails to repay the money at the proper time, Jones becomes, according to law, the owner of the land. The Court of Equity, however, regards Jones' title to the land as being subject to Brown's right to repay the money. Brown is the real owner of the land, and though Jones may, by law, become the full owner (through Brown's failure to pay at the appointed time), Brown has, by equity, the "equity of redemption" in the land, that is, the right to redeem it upon payment of the money due, with interest and certain charges incurred by Jones in protecting his security. In the case of a legal mortgage, after the date of payment has gone past, unless Jones has demanded re-payment of the money lent, Brown must give six months' notice of his intention to exercise his equity of redemption. In the case of an equitable mortgage Brown can repay at any time without notice.

So long as Brown holds the equity of redemption he may sell the land, or borrow more money upon the land, if the value will admit of it, by means of a further mortgage. If he sells it, the purchaser obtains the land, subject to the mortgage to Jones. If he raises an additional loan from Smith upon mortgage of the land, it is a second mortgage and ranks after the one to Jones; and if there is sufficient margin of value he may borrow more money in other quarters and grant still further mortgages. It should be noted, however, that the legal estate in the land was conveyed to Jones in the first mortgage, and that any subsequent mortgages convey only an equitable estate in the property. All mortgages subsequent to the first are called equitable mortgages.

If Brown fails to pay the interest due under the mortgage to Jones, and Jones enters into possession of the land and continues in possession for twelve years, without giving any acknowledgment in writing that Brown is still entitled to the equity of redemption, Jones obtains complete ownership of the land and Brown's right to redeem the land is extinguished.

Brown will also lose his equity of redemption if the mortgagee forecloses. (See FORECLOSURE.)

If Jones is obliged to sell the land in order to obtain repayment of the debt, Brown thereby loses his equity, though, if the land realises more than is required to satisfy Jones, the balance must be handed to Brown.

By the Conveyancing and Law of Property Act, 1881:—

"Section 15. (1) Where a mortgagor is entitled to redeem, he shall, by virtue of this Act, have power to require the mortgagee, instead of re-conveying, and on the terms on which he would be bound to reconvey, to assign the mortgage debt and convey the mortgaged property to any third person, as the mortgagor directs; and the mortgagee shall, by virtue of this Act, be bound to assign and convey accordingly.

"(2) This Section does not apply in the case of a mortgagee being or having been in possession."

A mortgagor is entitled, as long as his right to redeem subsists, at his own cost, to inspect and make copies of, or extracts from, the documents of title relating to the mortgaged property. (Section 16.)

By Section 17:—

"(1) A mortgagor seeking to redeem any one mortgage, shall, by virtue of this Act, be entitled to do so, without paying any money due under any separate mortgage made by him, or by any person through whom he claims, on property other than that comprised in the mortgage which he seeks to redeem.

"(2) This Section applies only if and as far as a contrary intention is not expressed in the mortgage deeds or one of them."

The value of an equity of redemption as a security depends upon the value of the property and the amount of mortgages which are in existence. The margin in some cases between the value and the mortgages may be very considerable, but in many instances the equity is valueless as a security. (See MORTGAGE, TITLE DEEDS.)

ESCHEAT. Where the owner of an estate in fee simple dies without leaving a will and without heirs, the estate reverts or escheats to the Crown. In the case of copyhold land it reverts to the lord of the manor.

ESCROW. A deed handed to a person who is not a party to it, to be held by that person until certain conditions have been fulfilled by the party in whose favour the document is drawn. When the conditions have been complied with, the document takes effect as a deed and is then delivered to that party, the grantee.

ESTATE DUTY. This duty is imposed upon the principal value, i.e. the gross price it would sell for in the open market at the date of death of deceased, of all property, real or personal, which passes on the death of any person after August 1, 1894, unless it be an estate under £100 or some of the other exemptions mentioned in the Finance Act, 1894.

The executor or administrator is required to furnish particulars of the property of the deceased person.

The estate duty is due to be paid upon the delivery of the account by the representatives of the deceased, or at the expiration of six months from the death. Three per cent. simple interest is charged upon the duty from the date of death of deceased, until it is paid, but after six months the rate is increased to 4 per cent.

In the case of duty upon lands it is a charge upon the lands, and when deeds of a property which has passed upon a death are given as security a certificate of payment, granted by the Inland Revenue authorities, should accompany the deeds, though in practice it rarely does.

Estates of a less value than £100 are exempt from estate duty.

The estate duty payable upon real property may be paid in eight equal yearly instalments or sixteen half-yearly instalments, with interest at 3 per cent. from the date at which the first instalment is due. The first instalment is due at the expiration of twelve months from the date of the death.

The Finance (1909–10) Act, 1910, Section 54, imposes the rates of estate duty in the following table, in the case of persons dying on or after April 30, 1909 :—

SCALE OF RATES OF ESTATE DUTY.

Where the principal value of the estate				Estate duty shall be payable at the rate per cent. of
Exceeds	£100	and does not exceed	£500	1
"	500	" "	1,000	2
"	1,000	" "	5,000	3
"	5,000	" "	10,000	4
"	10,000	" "	20,000	5
"	20,000	" "	40,000	6
"	40,000	" "	70,000	7
"	70,000	" "	100,000	8
"	100,000	" "	150,000	9
"	150,000	" "	200,000	10
"	200,000	" "	400,000	11
"	400,000	" "	600,000	12
"	600,000	" "	800,000	13
"	800,000	" "	1,000,000	14
"	1,000,000	..		15

In the case of property which is settled by the will of the deceased (except where the only life interest is the husband or wife of the deceased), or which has been settled by some other person and passes to someone who has no power of disposing of it, a settlement estate duty is imposed by the same Section upon the principal value of the settled property at the rate of two per cent. in the case of persons dying on or after April 30, 1909.

Where the gross value of the property upon which estate duty is payable does not exceed £300, a fixed duty of 30*s*. may be paid, and where it does not exceed £500 a fixed duty of 50*s*. may be paid instead of the *ad valorem* duty in the above scale.

As to the estate duty on property which passes to the executor *as such*, the executor, being the only person accountable for it, must charge the duty on all such property (which passes to him as executor) against the general residuary personal estate. Although, with few exceptions, real property now vests in the executor, it nevertheless does not pass to him *as such*, and the estate duty thereon is payable out of the real property itself and not out of the residuary personal estate, but the estate duty on real property is payable out of the residue where a testator directs the payment of his debts and duties.

ESTATE TAIL. An estate tail (or fee tail) is the opposite of fee simple. An estate tail is where land is granted to a person and the heirs of his body, so long as there are such heirs, whereas a fee simple is granted to his heirs, which need not necessarily be the heirs of his body.

The word tail is from the French *taille*, a cutting (*tailler*, to cut), indicating that the land is cut or separated from any other estate and limited to the person and the actual descendants of the person to whom it is conveyed. If the man has been married more than once, the descendants of each marriage are included ; but if the land is granted, or limited, to the descendants of one wife it is called a " special estate tail."

When an estate tail is converted into a fee simple it is said to be disentailed, the entail being barred, and the tenant may then dispose of the estate at will.

ESTOPPEL. A law term which means the legal stopping of a person from setting up a claim, on account of some previous act or representation by him inconsistent with the claim. A bar or stop arising from a man's own act.

For example, where bonds (not strictly negotiable bonds) were placed by the owner in the hands and full control of an agent for disposal, the principal was precluded, or estopped, from saying that a person who took the bonds, in good faith and for value, from the agent, had not got a legal title to the bonds. In that case the title to the bonds was obtained by estoppel.

EVEN DATE. Equal date. The same date.

EX ALL. Shares sold " ex all " exclude dividends, and all rights which the seller may have as shareholder.

EX COUPON. Without the coupon for interest just due. Bonds are usually quoted as ex coupon on the evening of the date when the coupon is due.

EX DIV. That is " without dividend,"

and means that if a purchaser has bought shares on the Stock Exchange quoted as ex div. the dividend just being paid belongs to the seller. Most stocks are marked in the London Stock Exchange official list as ex div. on the pay day next after the day when the dividend has been officially declared by the company in question. Consols are marked ex div. about four weeks before the interest is due to be paid. (See PAY DAY.)

EX DRAWING. Without any benefit, there may be from a drawing of bonds for payment which is due to be made.

EX INTEREST. Without interest.

EX NEW. Where new shares are being issued to the present shareholders of a company, a shareholder sometimes sells his old shares "ex new"; that is, he reserves to himself the right to receive the new shares.

EX RIGHTS. Shares sold "ex rights" are without any rights to a new issue of shares which the old shareholders are entitled to, the seller reserving such rights to himself.

EXCHANGE. A mutual arrangement by which one piece of property is exchanged for another. By the Stamp Act, 1891, the stamp duty is:—

	£	s.	d.
EXCHANGE or EXCAMBION—Instruments effecting.			
In the case specified in Section 73 see below.			
In any other case . . .	0	10	0

(Excambion, a term used in Scotland for the contract of an exchange of property.)

"Section 73. Where upon the exchange of any real or heritable property for any other real or heritable property, or upon the partition or division of any real or heritable property, any consideration exceeding in amount or value one hundred pounds is paid or given, or agreed to be paid or given, for equality, the principal or only instrument whereby the exchange or partition or division is effected is to be charged with the same *ad valorem* duty as a conveyance on sale for the consideration, and with that duty only; and where in any such case there are several instruments for completing the title of either party, the principal instrument is to be ascertained, and the other instruments are to be charged with duty in the manner hereinbefore provided in the case of several instruments of conveyance." (See PARTITION.)

EXCHANGE AS PER INDORSEMENT (See PAYABLE AS PER INDORSEMENT.)

EXCHANGE BROKER. A dealer in foreign bills. (See BILL BROKER.)

EXCHANGE SLIP. A form which is filled up and signed by the person requiring notes, cash, or cheques to be exchanged by a banker. Below will be found a specimen.

EXCHANGES. The cheques which each banker in a town holds drawn upon the other bankers in the same town are collected each day by means of the "local clearing" or "exchanges."

According to the size of the town and the quantity of cheques, there may be one, two or even three "exchanges" in one day; usually a settlement takes place only at the final exchange of the day.

In its simplest form, if banker X holds cheques drawn on banker Y, he sends a clerk, "the exchange clerk," with the cheques to Y. The clerk hands the cheques to Y and at the same time Y's exchange clerk hands to X's clerk any cheques which he may have drawn upon X. Each clerk makes a list, usually in an "exchange book," entering on the other side all cheques handed over and on the other side all cheques received. The difference between the two sides is called the "balance of exchange," and is settled between the two banks either in cash or by a

Paid in.		Exchanged by The British Banking Co., Ltd., with	*Paid Out.*	
Bank of Eng. Notes			Bank of Eng. Notes	
Country Notes . .			Country Notes . .	
Gold		....	Gold	
Silver			Silver	
Copper			Copper	
Cheques. . . .		..........19...	Cheques. . . .	
Bills.			Bills.	
£			£	

London draft or through their respective London offices or London agents. If the cheques received by X amount to more than the cheques given to Y, the exchange is against X and in Y's favour, as X has to pay Y the difference. If, on the other hand, X gives Y a greater amount than he receives, the balance is in favour of X, and he receives payment of the difference from Y.

If there are other bankers in the town, X's clerk may visit all of them in turn and exchange cheques with each.

In some towns one banker undertakes the visits during one week, and another banker takes the duty next week and so on. But where there are several bankers it is the custom for a representative from each to meet at a certain bank, or in a particular room, and mutually exchange cheques. A settlement may be made separately by each one with the others, or one banker may adjust the various differences of the rest, with the result that each has only to pay or receive one amount.

Each cheque should bear upon its face the stamp of the presenting banker.

Any unpaid cheques must be returned the same day, and it forms a matter of local arrangement as to the hour up to which they may be returned. In some cases, in large towns, where it is inconvenient to return an unpaid cheque arising out of the last clearing for the day, a local arrangement may exist for holding it over till the following morning.

"Returns" which are too late to form part of the day's settlement are sometimes paid in cash or settled specially, or, in some banks, a signed voucher is given for the returned cheque, and the voucher is passed through in the next day's exchange just like a cheque.

Cheques paid to the credit of a customer's account, which are drawn upon another banker in the same town, may be presented for payment on the day of receipt or held until the next day, but in practice all cheques received up to the time of the exchange are passed through the same day.

Cheques upon banks in other towns are collected through the London Clearing House, unless they are sent direct. (See CLEARING HOUSE.)

EXCHEQUER BILLS. Promissory notes of the Government. They were first issued in 1696, and constituted the floating debt of the country for 160 or 170 years. There are no Exchequer Bills now in existence, Treasury Bills having superseded them. (See TREASURY BILLS.)

EXCHEQUER BONDS. Bonds which are issued under the authority of Acts of Parliament, by the Lords Commissioners of His Majesty's Treasury. They usually run for periods of from three to five years, and it is seldom that they are issued for a longer term than ten years.

The following is a specimen of an Exchequer Bond forming part of an issue to be all paid off in ten years:—

EXCHEQUER BOND.

Per Acts 29 Vict. c. 25, 52 Vict. c. 6 and 5 Edw. VII, c. 4.

B00413 £200 B00413

THIS BOND, unless previously drawn and redeemed as hereafter set forth, entitles the Bearer to receive the sum of TWO HUNDRED POUNDS on April 18, 1915, at the rate of £2 15*s.* per cent. per annum, payable as follows, on October 18, 1905, a first dividend, being interest accrued from April 18, 1905, upon the various instalments of the subscription money as they severally become due, and thereafter by quarterly dividends, payable on January 18, April 18, July 18, and October 18, on presentation of the coupons hereunto attached, being interest upon the total capital sum hereby secured.

This bond forms part of an issue amounting to a total of ten million pounds, which amount will be paid off in ten years from the date hereof at the rate of one-tenth part of the total issue in each year. The bonds to be redeemed will be drawn in each year in accordance with regulations made by the Treasury, and the bonds so drawn will be paid off at par as on April 18 in that year, from which date interest thereon will cease.

The principal and interest of this bond are chargeable on the consolidated fund of the United Kingdom, pursuant to Act 5 Edw. VII, c. 4, and are payable at the Bank of England.

London, April 18, 1905.

Secretary to His Majesty's Treasury.

NOTE.—The numbers of the bonds drawn for repayment in each year will be advertised in the *London Gazette* not less than two months prior to the date of redemption. Drawn bonds when presented for payment must be accompanied by all coupons bearing date subsequent to that on which the principal becomes repayable.

EXCHEQUER TALLY. A notched piece of wood which, at one time, was given as a form of receipt to a person who deposited money with the Government. A similar notched stick was retained in the Exchequer Department, and when the depositor wanted his money he produced his portion of the stick, and if the two sticks "tallied," that is, the notches on the one agreed with the notches on the other, he was paid his money.

It is said that a notch of $1\frac{1}{2}$-inch represented £1,000, 1-inch £100, $\frac{3}{4}$-inch £10, half a notch of that size £1, $\frac{3}{16}$-inch 1*s*., smallest notch 1*d*., a small hole $\frac{1}{2}$*d*.

The use of tallies was abolished in 1782, but the old ones were preserved till 1834, when it was ordered that all the old tallies in the possession of the Government should be destroyed. They were burnt in stoves in the House of Lords, and it is supposed that they were the cause of the fire which destroyed both Houses of Parliament. (See TALLY.)

EXECUTOR. An executor is the person appointed in a will by the testator to pay his debts and distribute his assets, according to the instructions in the will. His duties are practically the same as those of an administrator, except that an administrator settles the deceased's affairs according to law and an executor settles them according to the terms of the will.

When a customer is deceased, a banker should not allow the persons named in the will as executors to withdraw, or transfer, the balance of the deceased's account, or to deal with any securities left in the hands of the banker by the deceased, until Probate has been exhibited. When Probate has been seen, it is customary to transfer a credit balance to the executors' account by a cheque signed by the executors. If the deceased's account is overdrawn, it must be paid off by the executors in such manner as may be arranged. The banker cannot himself transfer, from any account which the executors may have opened, an amount to clear off the overdraft on the account of the deceased. A specimen of the executors' signatures should be obtained in the signature book.

If executors open an account in their private names it is treated as an ordinary joint account, and if one person is to sign cheques the usual authority must be obtained. But if the account is opened as, for example, "Executors of John Brown, John Jones, R. Smith," it is held by some authorities that either of the executors may, in the absence of an arrangement to the contrary, draw cheques upon the account without any written authority from the other. It is, however, customary in some banks, and is a desirable practice as it prevents any misunderstanding, for a form of authority to be signed by each executor, when the account is opened, stating exactly in what manner and by which executor or executors cheques are to be signed. If an authority states that two executors are to sign, any cheque which is signed only by one of them would not, of course, be in order. It is not usual for an authority to be given for someone who is not an executor to operate on the account.

If a banker receives notice from one executor that cheques must be signed by all the executors, he must carry out the instruction.

When securities, or safe custody articles, belonging to the deceased are withdrawn, it is desirable that all the executors should join in the acknowledgment, or in the request to deliver to one of their number.

An infant cannot undertake the duties of an executor.

On the death of a sole or sole surviving executor (say, of the estate of John Brown), his executors carry on the duties of the executorship, but if there is no will then letters of administration require to be taken out for John Brown's estate, and an administrator *de bonis non* (*q.v.*) is appointed by the Court.

When an indorsement upon a bill is by an executor, it is usual for his banker to confirm such indorsement.

With regard to shares which a deceased person may have held, his executors are liable as executors for any calls which may be made, but they are not liable personally unless the shares have been actually transferred into their names. If the shares still continue in the deceased's name, the dividends may be paid to the executors, and that may be done without rendering the executors personally liable.

An overdraft is frequently required for the purpose of paying probate duty before probate has been granted. In such cases a banker regards the loan as being made to the parties in their private capacity. He should, however, ascertain that the persons making the application are the executors nominated in the will and also satisfy himself generally as to the nature of the estate and the contents of the will. In order to avoid any misunderstanding as to liability, a guarantee by the executors is often taken.

Money cannot be lent to an executor so as to bind the general estate of the deceased. An executor, however, has power (unless forbidden in the will) to pledge specific assets belonging to the estate. Unless a banker lends on the personal liability of the executors, he should obtain a proper charge from the executors upon some of the deceased's securities. If there are several executors, a mortgage or charge may probably be sufficient if signed by one of them, but it is desirable, and customary, that they should all join in signing such documents. A banker should peruse the will before accepting the security.

Money lent to an executrix who is a married woman is a debt due by her, in her private capacity; the husband is not liable for such a debt.

If an executor misapplies money belonging to the deceased's estate, and the banker is aware of it, as, for instance, where an amount is transferred by an executor from the trust account to his own overdrawn personal account, which the banker has been pressing him to reduce, the banker will be held liable; and if an executor pledges deeds, belonging to the estate, with a bank, in order to raise money to reduce his personal loan, and the banker is aware of the circumstance, he will not be able to hold to the security.

If an executor has a beneficial interest in property under the will, and he deposits the deeds as security for his own account, he cannot, of course, charge the property beyond the extent of his own interest, and that interest, moreover, is subject to any breach of trust which he may commit.

Upon the death of the owner of freehold (since January 1, 1898) and leasehold property, the title vests in the executors or administrators, and before a deposit of deeds as security is taken from a devisee or heir-at-law the formal assent of the personal representatives should be obtained. Section 3 of the Land Transfer Act, 1897, provides as follows:—

"(1) At any time after the death of the owner of any land, the personal representatives may assent to any devise contained in his will, or may convey the land to any person entitled thereto as heir, devisee, or otherwise, and may make the assent or conveyance either subject to a charge for the payment of any money which the personal representatives are liable to pay, or without any such charge; and on such assent or conveyance, subject to a charge for all moneys (if any) which the personal representatives are liable to pay, all liabilities of the personal representatives in respect of the land shall cease, except as to any acts done or contracts entered into by them before such assent or conveyance.

"(2) At any time after the expiration of one year from the death of the owner of any land, if his personal representatives have failed on the request of the person entitled to the land to convey the land to that person, the Court may, if it thinks fit, on the application of that person, and after notice to the personal representatives, order that the conveyance be made, or, in the case of registered land, that the person so entitled be registered as proprietor of the land either solely or jointly with the personal representatives.

"(3) Where the personal representatives of a deceased person are registered as proprietors of land on his death, a fee shall not be chargeable on any transfer of the land by them unless the transfer is for valuable consideration.

"(4) The production of an assent in the prescribed form by the personal representatives of a deceased proprietor of registered land shall authorise the registrar to register the person named in the assent as proprietor of the land."

Executors are not obliged to pay the debts of the deceased, or general legacies under the will, before the expiration of twelve months from the death. Interest upon general legacies runs from the end of that period, but upon specific legacies it runs from the death of the testator.

When executors intend to act, they must prove the will within six months from the date of the testator's death, otherwise they are liable to a penalty of £50. (See PROBATE.)

EXECUTORY ACCOUNT. The account of an executor.

EXEMPLIFICATION. An attested or certified copy of proceedings in a court of record. By the Stamp Act, 1891, the stamp duty is:—

	£ s. d.
EXEMPLIFICATION or CONSTAT, under the Great Seal of the United Kingdom of Great Britain and Ireland of any letters patent or grant made or to be made by Her Majesty, or by any of her royal predecessors of any honour, dignity, promotion, franchise, liberty, or privilege, or of any lands, office, or other thing whatsoever	5 0 0
EXEMPLIFICATION under the seal of any court in England or Ireland of any record or proceeding therein	3 0 0

EXPANSIVE THEORY. The theory that in a monetary crisis the Bank of England should expand, and not contract, its issues. The Bank Charter Act of 1844 placed restrictions upon the issue of notes, but in the three great crises of 1847, 1857 and 1866 that Act had to be suspended, and, instead of the Bank restricting its issues, it was permitted by the Government to increase them beyond the amount of its authorised issue ; on each occasion the application of the expansive theory saved the situation after the restrictive theory, as contained in the Act, had proved to be ineffectual.

EXPORT SPECIE POINT. (See SPECIE POINTS.)

EXTRACT. For stamp duty see COPY.

EXTRAORDINARY GENERAL MEETINGS. Meetings which are convened for the transaction of special business. The directors of a company shall, on the requisition of the holders of not less than one-tenth of the issued share capital upon which all calls have been paid, forthwith proceed to convene an extraordinary general meeting of the company.

For further information see Section 66 of the Companies (Consolidation) Act, 1908, under the heading MEETINGS—COMPANIES.

FACE VALUE. The nominal value of stock or shares which appears upon the face of a certificate. The market, or selling, value of the security may be either higher or lower than the face value.

FACTORS ACT, 1889 (52 & 53 VICT. c. 45). This Act deals with dispositions of goods by factors, or mercantile agents, and dispositions by sellers and buyers of goods. (See BILL OF LADING, DELIVERY ORDER, DOCK WARRANT, WAREHOUSE KEEPER'S WARRANT.)

The principal part of the Act is as follows :

Definitions.

" 1. For the purposes of this Act—

" (1) The expression 'mercantile agent' shall mean a mercantile agent having in the customary course of his business as such agent authority either to sell goods, or to consign goods for the purpose of sale, or to buy goods, or to raise money on the security of goods :

" (2) A person shall be deemed to be in possession of goods or of the documents of title to goods, where the goods or documents are in his actual custody or are held by any other person subject to his control or for him or on his behalf :

" (3) The expression 'goods' shall include wares and merchandise :

" (4) The expression 'document of title' shall include any bill of lading, dock warrant, warehouse-keeper's certificate, and warrant or order for the delivery of goods, and any other document used in the ordinary course of business as proof of the possession or control of goods, or authorising or purporting to authorise, either by indorsement or by delivery, the possessor of the document to transfer or receive goods thereby represented :

" (5) The expression 'pledge' shall include any contract pledging, or giving a lien or security on, goods, whether in consideration of an original advance or of any further or continuing advance, or of any pecuniary liability :

" (6) The expression 'person' shall include any body of persons, corporate or unincorporate.

DISPOSITION BY MERCANTILE AGENTS.

Powers of Mercantile Agent with Respect to Disposition of Goods.

" 2. (1) Where a mercantile agent is, with the consent of the owner, in possession of goods or of the documents of title to goods, any sale, pledge, or other disposition of the goods, made by him when acting in the ordinary course of business of a mercantile agent, shall, subject to the provisions of this Act, be as valid as if he were expressly authorised by the owner of the goods to make the same; provided that the person taking under the disposition acts in good faith, and has not at the time of the disposition notice that the person making the disposition has not authority to make the same.

"(2) Where a mercantile agent has, with the consent of the owner, been in possession of goods or of the documents of title to goods, any sale, pledge, or other disposition, which would have been valid if the consent had continued, shall be valid notwithstanding the determination of the consent: provided that the person taking under the disposition has not at the time thereof notice that the consent has been determined.

"(3) Where a mercantile agent has obtained possession of any documents of title to goods by reason of his being or having been, with the consent of the owner, in possession of the goods represented thereby, or of any other documents of title to the goods, his possession of the first-mentioned documents shall, for the purposes of this Act, be deemed to be with the consent of the owner.

"(4) For the purposes of this Act the consent of the owner shall be presumed in the absence of evidence to the contrary.

Effect of Pledges of Documents of Title.

"3. A pledge of the documents of title to goods shall be deemed to be a pledge of the goods.

Pledge for Antecedent Debt.

"4. Where a mercantile agent pledges goods as security for a debt or liability due from the pledgor to the pledgee before the time of the pledge, the pledgee shall acquire no further right to the goods than could have been enforced by the pledgor at the time of the pledge.

Rights acquired by Exchange of Goods or Documents.

"5. The consideration necessary for the validity of a sale, pledge, or other disposition, of goods, in pursuance of this Act, may be either a payment in cash, or the delivery or transfer of other goods, or of a document of title to goods, or of a negotiable security, or any other valuable consideration; but where goods are pledged by a mercantile agent in consideration of the delivery or transfer of other goods, or of a document of title to goods, or of a negotiable security, the pledgee shall acquire no right or interest in the goods so pledged in excess of the value of the goods, documents, or security when so delivered or transferred in exchange.

Agreements through Clerks, etc.

"6. For the purposes of this Act an agreement made with a mercantile agent through a clerk or other person authorised in the ordinary course of business to make contracts of sale or pledge on his behalf shall be deemed to be an agreement with the agent.

Provisions as to Consignors and Consignees.

"7. (1) Where the owner of goods has given possession of the goods to another person for the purpose of consignment or sale, or has shipped the goods in the name of another person, and the consignee of the goods has not had notice that such person is not the owner of the goods, the consignee shall, in respect of advances made to or for the use of such person, have the same lien on the goods as if such person were the owner of the goods, and may transfer any such lien to another person.

"(2) Nothing in this Section shall limit or affect the validity of any sale, pledge, or disposition, by a mercantile agent.

DISPOSITIONS BY SELLERS AND BUYERS OF GOODS.

Disposition by Seller Remaining in Possession.

"8. Where a person, having sold goods, continues, or is in possession of the goods or of the documents of title to the goods, the delivery or transfer by that person, or by a mercantile agent acting for him, of the goods or documents of title under any sale, pledge, or other disposition thereof, or under any agreement for sale, pledge, or other disposition thereof, to any person receiving the same in good faith and without notice of the previous sale, shall have the same effect as if the person making the delivery or transfer were expressly authorised by the owner of the goods to make the same.

Disposition by Buyer Obtaining Possession.

"9. Where a person, having bought or

agreed to buy goods, obtains with the consent of the seller possession of the goods or the documents of title to the goods, the delivery or transfer, by that person or by a mercantile agent acting for him, of the goods or documents of title, under any sale, pledge, or other disposition thereof, or under any agreement for sale, pledge, or other disposition thereof, to any person receiving the same in good faith and without notice of any lien or other right of the original seller in respect of the goods, shall have the same effect as if the person making the delivery or transfer were a mercantile agent in possession of the goods or documents of title with the consent of the owner.

Effect of Transfer of Documents on Vendor's Lien or Right of Stoppage in transitu.

"10. Where a document of title to goods has been lawfully transferred to a person as a buyer or owner of the goods, and that person transfers the document to a person who takes the document in good faith and for valuable consideration, the last-mentioned transfer shall have the same effect for defeating any vendor's lien or right of stoppage *in transitu* as the transfer of a bill of lading has for defeating the right of stoppage *in transitu*.

SUPPLEMENTAL.

Mode of Transferring Documents.

"11. For the purposes of this Act, the transfer of a document may be by indorsement, or, where the document is by custom or by its express terms transferable by delivery, or makes the goods deliverable to the bearer, then by delivery.

Saving for Rights of true Owner.

"12. (1) Nothing in this Act shall authorise an agent to exceed or depart from his authority as between himself and his principal, or exempt him from any liability, civil or criminal, for so doing.

"(2) Nothing in this Act shall prevent the owner of goods from recovering the goods from an agent or his trustee in bankruptcy at any time before the sale or pledge thereof, or shall prevent the owner of goods pledged by an agent from having the right to redeem the goods at any time before the sale thereof, on satisfying the claim for which the goods were pledged, and paying to the agent, if by him required, any money in respect of which the agent would by law be entitled to retain the goods or the documents of title thereto, or any of them, by way of lien as against the owner, or from recovering from any person with whom the goods have been pledged any balance of money remaining in his hands as the produce of the sale of the goods after deducting the amount of his lien.

"(3) Nothing in this Act shall prevent the owner of goods sold by an agent from recovering from the buyer the price agreed to be paid for the same, or any part of that price, subject to any right of set-off on the part of the buyer against the agent.

Saving for Common Law Powers of Agent.

"13. The provisions of this Act shall be construed in amplification and not in derogation of the powers exercisable by an agent independently of this Act.

Commencement.

"15. This Act shall commence and come into operation on the first day of January one thousand eight hundred and ninety.

Extent of Act.

"16. This Act shall not extend to Scotland.

Short Title.

"17. This Act may be cited as the Factors Act, 1889."

It should be noted that Section 25 of the Sale of Goods Act, 1893, is practically the same as Sections 9 and 10 of the Factors Act.

FACTORY. In Scotland, Letters of Factory empower one person to act for another.

In the Stamp Act, 1891, the reference to the stamp duty is :—

FACTORY, in the nature of a letter or power of attorney in Scotland.

(See POWER OF ATTORNEY.)

FACULTY. An order or licence granted by an ecclesiastical authority. For example, a faculty is required before an alteration of any importance can be effected in the structure of a church.

FALSE PRETENCES. Where a person obtains payment of a cheque by falsely representing himself to be the payee, he is liable to be prosecuted for obtaining money by false pretences. Also if a person obtains goods and gives in payment thereof a cheque drawn upon a bank where he has not got an account, or gives a cheque which he knows is worthless and will not be honoured, he is likewise liable to prosecution, for whosoever shall by any false pretence obtain from any other person any chattel, money, or valuable security, with intent to defraud, shall be guilty of a misdemeanour. (Section 88, Larceny Act, 1861.)

FARM STOCK. A country banker has frequently to scrutinise a farmer's balance sheet, or to form an idea as to the value of the cattle and sheep upon a farm. Prices are subject to fluctuations, according to the times and seasons, and other circumstances; but the following table may serve to give some idea of average values:—

	Value in Spring.	Value in Autumn.	Fat.
Shorthorn Cattle (not pedigree):			
Cow, in calf, or milk	£18–£22	£20–£25	£18
Heifer, in calf	£17–£20	£19–£21	
,, 2 years old	£12–£14	£16–£17	£19–£22
,, 1 year old	£9–£10	£12–£13	
Bullock, 2 years old	£14–£15	£17–£18	£22
,, 1 year old	£8–£10	£11–£13	
Galloway Cattle (not pedigree):			
Cow, in calf, or milk	£14–£16	£14–£16	£16
Heifer, in calf	£14–£15	£18–£19	
,, 2 years old	£12–£14	£16–£18	
,, 1 year old	£8–£10	£12–£13	
Bullock, 2 years old	£12–£13	£15–£16	
,, 1 year old	£8–£10	£11–£12 10*s.*	
Cross-Bred Cattle—Blue Greys:			
Cow, in calf, or milk	£12–£14	£12–£14	£15–£16
Heifer, in calf	£13–£16	£13–£16	
,, 2 years old	£13–£15	£16–£18	
,, 1 year old	£10–£11	£13–£15	
Bullock, 2 years old	£13–£14	£15–£17	
,, 1 year old	£10–£12	£13–£15	

	Average Market Price.	Fat.
Border Leicester Sheep:		
Shearling Ram	£4 –£7	£2 10*s.*–£3
Tup Lamb	£2 –£3 10*s.*	£2 –£2 5*s.*
Ewe	£2 5*s.*–£2 10*s.*	£2
Gimmer	£2 10*s.*–£3	£2 5*s.*–£2 10*s.*
Half-Bred Sheep. (Border Leicester Tup and Cheviot Ewe):		
Ewe	£1 16*s.*–£2 5*s.*	£1 15*s.*–£2
Lamb	£1 4*s.*–£1 10*s.*	£2 –£2 5*s.*
Shearling, for short keep	£1 14*s.*–£1 18*s.*	£2 5*s.*
Cross-Bred Sheep. (Border Leicester Tup and Black-faced Ewe):		
Ewe	£1 10*s.*–£1 15*s.*	£1 16*s.*–£1 18*s.* (one year)
Lamb	16*s.*–£1 4*s.*	£1 14*s.*–£2
Shearling, for short keep	£1 8*s.*–£1 12*s.*	£2 –£2 2*s.*

FARTHING. (From *Feorth*, fourth.) The fourth part of a penny, a penny at one time being actually divided into four parts, called feorthlings or fourthings.

Its standard weight is 43·75 grains troy. The coin is a mixed metal of copper, tin and zinc.

Copper farthings were first issued in 1672.

FEE. The sum of money which is to be paid for a service rendered.

The Anglo-Saxon word *feoh* (which is practically our word fee) had the meaning of money and cattle. In certain of the early stages of society, cattle performed the functions of money, hence the use of one word to express both cattle and money.

FEE FARM RENT. Where a person conveys land which he holds in fee simple (that is, he is the absolute owner) to another person in fee simple subject to the payment of a perpetual yearly rent to the vendor and his heirs, the rent is called a fee farm rent.

FEE SIMPLE. Where a person is the absolute owner of an estate he is said to hold it in "fee simple," and he can practically do with it what he likes. If he dies intestate it goes to his heirs. A conveyance of a freehold to a purchaser in fee simple contains such words as "To hold unto and to the use of the purchaser in fee simple," or, what has the same effect, "to the use of the purchaser his heirs and assigns for ever." Legally all land is held directly or indirectly from the King, but practically that does not affect the absolute ownership in a fee simple.

The greatest interest which can be had in land is the fee simple, other interests, such as a life interest, or a lease, being estates less than the fee simple. The holder of a fee simple can create other estates out of it, but so long as he does not dispose of the fee simple it remains vested in him. In the case of a lease, no matter for how long a period, the fee simple is with the person who grants the lease, though the person who holds the lease or the assignment thereof has the legal estate in the land. At the expiration of a lease the land reverts to the grantor, or person entitled to the fee simple.

In copyhold land the fee simple remains with the lord of the manor.

FEE TAIL. An estate which is granted to a person and the heirs of his body is an estate tail or fee tail, usually called an entailed estate. It is the opposite to a fee simple (*q.v.*). A fee simple is held to his heirs, but a fee tail is limited to the heirs of his body. (See ESTATE TAIL.)

FEES PAYABLE TO REGISTRAR OF COMPANIES. The provisions of the Companies (Consolidation) Act, 1908, Section 244, with respect to the fees to be paid to the registrar of companies are as follow :—

"(1) There shall be paid to the registrar in respect of the several matters mentioned in Table B. in the First Schedule to this Act the several fees therein specified, or such smaller fees as the Board of Trade may from time to time direct.

"(2) All fees paid to the registrar in pursuance of this Act shall be paid into the Exchequer."

TABLE B.

TABLE OF FEES to be paid to the REGISTRAR of COMPANIES.

I.—By a company having a share capital.

	£	s.	d.	£	s.	d.
For registration of a company whose nominal share capital does not exceed £2,000 . .				2	0	0
For registration of a company whose nominal share capital exceeds £2,000, the following fees, regulated according to the amount of nominal share capital (that is to say) ; .						
For every £1,000 of nominal share capital, or part of £1,000, up to £5,000 . . .	1	0	0			
For every £1,000 of nominal share capital, or part of £1,000, after the first £5,000 up to £100,000 . .	0	5	0			
For every £1,000 of nominal share capital, or part of £1,000, after the first £100,000 .	0	1	0			
For registration of any increase of share capital made after the first registration of the company, the same fees per £1,000, or part of a £1,000, as would have been payable if the increased share capital had formed part of the original share capital at the time of registration :						
Provided that no company shall be liable to pay in respect of						

	£ s. d.
nominal share capital, on registration or afterwards, any greater amount of fees than £50, taking into account in the case of fees payable on an increase of share capital after registration the fees paid on registration.	
For registration of any existing company, except such companies as are by this Act exempted from payment of fees in respect of registration under this Act, the same fee as is charged for registering a new company.	
For registering any document by this Act required or authorised to be registered, other than the memorandum or the abstract required to be filed with the registrar by a receiver or manager or the statement required to be sent to the registrar by the liquidator in a winding up in England	0 5 0
For making a record of any fact by this Act required or authorised to be recorded by the registrar .	0 5 0

As to the duty imposed by the Stamp Act, 1891, see SHARE CAPITAL.

II.—By a company not having a share capital.

	£ s. d
For registration of a company whose number of members, as stated in the articles, does not exceed 20.	2 0 0
For registration of a company whose number of members, as stated in the articles, exceeds 20, but does not exceed 100 . .	5 0 0
For registration of a company whose number of members, as stated in the articles, exceeds 100, but is not stated to be unlimited, the above fee of £5, with an additional 5*s*. for every 50 members or less number than 50 members after the first 100.	
For registration of a company in which the number of members is stated in the articles to be unlimited	20 0 0
For registration of any increase on the number of members made after the registration of the company in respect of every 50 members, or less than 50 members, of that increase . . .	0 5 0
Provided that no company shall be liable to pay on the whole a greater fee than £20, in respect of its number of members, taking into account the fee paid on the first registration of the company.	
For registration of any existing company, except such companies as are by this Act exempted from payment of fees in respect of registration under this Act, the same fee as is charged for registering a new company.	
For registering any document by this Act required or authorised to be registered, other than the memorandum or the abstract required to be filed with the registrar by a receiver or manager or the statement required to be sent to the registrar by the liquidator in a winding up in England	0 5 0
For making a record of any fact by this Act required or authorised to be recorded by the registrar .	0 5 0

(See COMPANIES.)

FEOFFMENT. (Pronounced, *fef'-ment.*) An ancient method of conveyance of property. Feoffment was accompanied by actually handing over the possession of the land, as by the delivery of a piece of turf, or by the grantor vacating the land and the grantee taking possession. This delivery of possession was called "livery of seisin." The person delivering it was called the feoffor and the person receiving it the feoffee.

FEU CONTRACT. In Scotland, a contract between a superior and his vassal respecting the giving of land in feu; feu being a tenure where the vassal holds lands from the superior and, instead of performing military service, makes an annual return in grain or money.

In the Stamp Act, 1891, the reference to the stamp duty is:—

FEU CONTRACT in Scotland. See CONVEYANCE ON SALE.

FI. FA. A contraction of *fieri facias* (*q.v.*).

FICTITIOUS BILL. A name sometimes given to an accommodation bill (*q.v.*).

FICTITIOUS PAYEE. Where the payee is a fictitious or non-existing person, a bill or cheque may be treated as payable to bearer. In *Bank of England* v. *Vagliano* (1891, A.C. 107), the meaning of a fictitious person was enlarged to include a real person who never had nor was intended to have any right to the bills. Lord Herschell said in the course of his judgment: "I have arrived at the conclusion that whenever the name inserted as that of the payee is so inserted by way of pretence merely, without any intention that payment shall only be made in conformity therewith, the payee is a fictitious person within the meaning of the statute, whether the name be that of an existing person or of one who has no existence."

A cheque payable to "wages" or "estate," or some similar word is payable to an impersonal payee and should be treated as being payable to the order of the drawer and requiring his indorsement. An impersonal payee is not the same as a fictitious person. (See PAYEE.)

FIDELITY GUARANTEE. A guarantee by a person or a society to make good, up to a specified amount, any loss caused by the default of the individual guaranteed.

The Bankers' Guarantee and Trust Fund is for the mutual guarantee of bank officials employed in the United Kingdom.

The subscription for membership is £1 per cent. on the amount of the guarantee. Payment may be made either in one sum or by five equal annual instalments, but when payment is thus deferred, 1*s.* per cent. on the amount of guarantee must be added to each instalment, until the whole is paid. If a member leaves the service of his employers, he will not be called upon to pay the instalments then outstanding.

An entrance fee is also charged at the rate of 4*s.* per cent. on the amount of the guarantee, whether given in one or more policies.

Guarantees exceeding £3,000, and not above £5,000, are issued, as regards the excess of £3,000, at special rates.

Policies are issued for bank messengers and porters, at an annual premium, without membership.

When a policy of insurance is required, a form of proposal must be filled up, various questions being answered by the employer and others by the applicant. The applicant is required to submit the names of three or four referees who must be householders, and have known the applicant for some length of time, one (if possible) resident in London, and one to be the last employer (or late schoolmaster, if first situation).

FIDUCIARY CAPACITY. (Latin, *fiducia*, confidence.) A person who holds anything in trust for another is said to hold it in a fiduciary capacity.

When a banker has notice that certain moneys deposited with him are of a fiduciary nature, he must not, knowingly, be a party to any wrongful use of such moneys, otherwise he will be responsible to the person entitled to the moneys. A banker cannot be held liable when he is unaware that they are trust moneys.

FIDUCIARY ISSUE. A term applied to the note issue of the Bank of England, which is authorised against the Government debt and securities, as distinguished from the note issue against gold.

FIERI FACIAS. A writ of *fieri facias*, often abbreviated as fi. fa., takes its name from the words appearing in the document "*quod fieri facias de bonis,*" etc. The writ is issued on behalf of a creditor who has obtained judgment for a debt, ordering the sheriff to levy the amount on the goods of the debtor. Bank-notes, money, cheques, and bills are included amongst the things which the sheriff may seize.

FILING PETITION. (See RECEIVING ORDER.)

FINE PAPER. Bills which are drawn upon banks or first-class firms.

FIRE INSURANCE. In order to prevent a security over buildings disappearing in smoke a banker should be careful to see that the property is insured, and that the premiums are duly paid. The policy should, strictly, be transferred into the banker's name. The premiums should be paid before the expiration of the days of grace, that is, usually fifteen days from the date when the amount is due to be paid.

An insurer cannot recover more than the actual loss sustained from a fire, within the amount of the policy. If the same property is insured in several offices, each company will only pay its proportion of any loss.

The stamp duty on a policy is one penny. See the provisions of the Stamp Act, 1891, under POLICY OF INSURANCE. (See AVERAGE CLAUSE.)

FIRM. Persons who have entered into partnership with one another are, collectively, called a firm, and the name under which their business is carried on is called the firm-name.

In Scotland a firm is a legal person distinct from the partners. (See Section 4 of the Partnership Act, 1890, under PARTNERSHIPS.)

Unless registered under the Companies' Acts, a firm must not consist of more than twenty partners, and in the case of a banking firm of more than ten partners.

FIRM OFFER. A definite offer, as where a person states that he is prepared to purchase a certain property at a specified price.

FIRST AND IN NEED WITH. Where a foreign bill is drawn in a set, say in two parts, one part may be sent at once to the drawee for acceptance, and the other part may be negotiated and bear a reference upon the face of it that the accepted part is in the possession of certain agents, as "First and in need with the British Bank, Ltd., London."

FIRST-CLASS PAPER. Treasury Bills and bills which bear the names of banks and financial houses of the very highest standing. They are so called to distinguish them from second and third-class bills, where the security is not so good.

FIRST OF EXCHANGE. (See BILL IN A SET.)

FIXED CAPITAL. Capital which is sunk in the purchase of land, or in buildings, the construction of railways, cutting of canals, etc., and which produces its effect by being kept, and not parted with, as in the case of circulating capital. "Capital," says John Stuart Mill, "which exists in any of these durable shapes and the return to which is spread over a period of corresponding duration, is called Fixed Capital." Some kinds of fixed capital require to be occasionally or periodically repaired or renewed, but these improvements "by the very fact of their deserving that title, produce an increase of return, which, after defraying all expenditure necessary for keeping them up, still leaves a surplus. This surplus forms the return to the capital sunk in the first instance, and that return does not, as in the case of machinery, terminate by the wearing out of the machine, but continues for ever." (See CAPITAL.)

FIXED CHARGE. Debentures and debenture stock may be secured on the property of the company by a "fixed" charge, or by a "floating" charge. In a fixed charge the property is, usually, by a trust deed, vested in trustees for the debenture holders or debenture stockholders, so that no other person may obtain a prior charge. (See DEBENTURE, FLOATING CHARGE.)

FIXED DEPOSIT. A deposit receipt which is repayable at a certain fixed date. The rate of interest allowed is usually a better one than on an ordinary deposit repayable on demand. (See DEPOSIT RECEIPT.)

FIXTURES. The deposit of title deeds, as well as a legal mortgage, carries with it the right of the mortgagee to any fixtures there may be upon the land.

If the mortgage deed includes trade machinery, by the Bills of Sale Act, 1878, Section 5:—

"From and after the commencement of this Act trade machinery shall, for the purposes of this Act, be deemed to be personal chattels, and any mode of disposition of trade machinery by the owner thereof which would be a bill of sale as to any other personal chattels shall be deemed to be a bill of sale within the meaning of this Act."

In that Act "trade machinery" means the machinery used in, or attached to, any factory or workshop, exclusive of fixed motive powers such as water wheels, steam engines, etc., exclusive of the fixed power machinery such as shafts, wheels, etc., and exclusive of the pipes for steam, gas and water. With regard to "trade machinery" generally, reference should be made to the case of *Batchelor* v. *Yates* (1888, 38 Ch. D. 112).

A mortgagor cannot remove fixtures from a property as against a mortgagee, even though they are of such a nature as to be removable as between landlord and tenant.

FLOATERS. A term used to signify the first-class bearer securities, e.g. Exchequer Bonds, Treasury Bills, etc., which bill brokers deposit with banks against money lent to them at call. When the money is called in by one bank the broker must borrow from another, and thus his securities move or "float" about from one bank to another.

FLOATING CAPITAL. (See CAPITAL.)

FLOATING CHARGE. Debentures or debenture stock, in addition to being secured by a "fixed" charge upon the company's property, may also be secured by a "floating" charge, that is a charge upon the stock, book debts, etc., of the company, which permits the company to make use of those assets in any way in connection with its ordinary business. A charge of that description "floats" until such time as default is made in payment of interest, or the company goes into liquidation. When such an event occurs, the charge becomes "fixed," and the assets at that date become a fixed security for the debentures and may be realised for the benefit of the debenture holders.

If the debentures create a "floating" charge upon the land of the company, as well as upon the stock, book debts, and uncalled capital, the company is not precluded by that floating charge from selling or mortgaging the land. Some "floating" charges, however, contain a clause to the effect that the company will not mortgage the property so as to create an equal or prior charge, but even in that case if anyone grants the company a loan against the title deeds, without any notice of the charge, he may obtain priority.

Particulars of every floating charge on the undertaking and property of a company must be delivered to the registrar of companies for registration. (See REGISTRATION OF MORTGAGES AND CHARGES.) A debenture containing merely a floating charge does not require to be entered on the company's register of mortgages.

Where a company is being wound up, a floating charge created within three months of the commencement of the winding up may be invalid (see Section 212 of the Companies (Consolidation) Act, 1908, under WINDING UP). (See COMPANIES.)

FLOATING DEBT. The floating debt of the country consists of Treasury Bills (*q.v.*) and Exchequer Bonds (*q.v.*). (See FUNDED DEBT.)

FLOATING MONEY. Temporary surplus funds in the hands of bankers, for which no profitable employment can be found owing to the money market being already fully supplied. This floating money finds its way to the bankers' accounts at the Bank of England, and goes to increase the item "Other Deposits" in the Bank Return, until a suitable outlet offers. A glutted condition of this kind arises on the periodical payment of large Government and other dividends and during times when there is little demand for money. A low market rate is the natural result.

FLOATING POLICY. (See MARINE INSURANCE POLICY.)

FLORIN. A two-shilling piece. (From Latin *flos, floris*, a flower. Italian *fiorino*, a florin, so called because there was the figure of a lily upon it. It is also stated that the coin is named from the city of Florence where florins were first coined.) It was introduced into the coinage in 1849.

The standard weight of a florin is 174·54545 grains troy and its standard fineness thirty-seven-fortieths fine silver, three-fortieths alloy. (See COINAGE.)

FOR CASH. A transaction on the Stock Exchange which is "for cash" or "for money" means that the security which has been sold must, as soon as delivered, be paid for in cash. (See FOR THE ACCOUNT.)

FOR THE ACCOUNT. A transaction on the Stock Exchange may be "for the account," that is for settlement on the next "account day" or "settling day." (See FOR CASH.)

FORECLOSURE. Where a mortgagor has failed, after due notice, to make repayment of the mortgage debt, the mortgagee has the right to apply to the Court for an order for foreclosure. Where this is done, the Court orders an account of what is due to the mortgagee to be submitted, and if what is found to be due is not paid within six months, the mortgagor's equity of redemption, that is his right to redeem the property, is foreclosed or extinguished. By foreclosure, therefore, the mortgagor loses his equity of redemption altogether and has no further interest or right in the property and the mortgagee becomes absolute owner.

Neither a legal mortgagee nor an equitable mortgagee can foreclose without sanction of the Court.

A legal mortgagee can, however, sell the property or put in a receiver under the power contained in his mortgage deed, without any application to the Court.

The expression "redeem up, foreclose down" applies when a mortgagee makes application to the Court for foreclosure, as he forecloses any subsequent mortgagees, as well as the mortgagor, and redeems any prior mortgagee.

Application for foreclosure must be made within twelve years from the last payment of interest by the mortgagor or written acknowledgment of the debt.

Where a mortgagee forecloses and thus becomes absolute owner of the property, he has no further claim upon the mortgagor. But if a mortgagee sells the property, instead of foreclosing, he may claim upon the mortgagor if the proceeds of the sale are not sufficient to repay the mortgage debt. (See MORTGAGE.)

FOREIGN BANK NOTES. They are subject to the laws of the country in which they are issued. Country bankers usually send foreign bank notes to their London office or London agents to be sold.

FOREIGN BILL. The Bills of Exchange Act, 1882 (Section 4) defines an inland bill as a bill which is or on the face of it purports to be (*a*) both drawn and payable within the British Islands, or (*b*) drawn within the British Islands upon some person resident therein. Any other bill is a foreign bill. The British Islands mean any part of the United Kingdom of Great Britain and Ireland, the islands of Man, Guernsey, Jersey, Alderney and Sark, and the islands adjacent to any of them being part of the dominions of His Majesty, and a bill drawn in any of those places is an inland bill, but for the purposes of stamp duty a bill or note purporting to be drawn out of the United Kingdom is deemed, by the Stamp Act, 1891, Section 36, to be a foreign bill.

The regulations regarding bills are not the same in all countries and the Bills of Exchange Act in Section 72 sets forth the rules to be observed where laws conflict :—

"Where a bill drawn in one country is negotiated, accepted, or payable in another, the rights, duties, and liabilities of the parties thereto are determined as follows :

"(1) The validity of a bill as regards requisites in form is determined by the law of the place of issue, and the validity as regards requisites in form of the supervening contracts, such as acceptance, or indorsement, or acceptance *suprà* protest, is determined by the law of the place where such contract was made :

"Provided that—

"(*a*) Where a bill is issued out of the United Kingdom it is not invalid by reason only that it is not stamped in accordance with the law of the place of issue :

"(*b*) Where a bill, issued out of the United Kingdom, conforms, as regards requisites in form, to the law of the United Kingdom, it may, for the purpose of enforcing payment thereof, be treated as valid as between all persons who negotiate, hold, or become parties to it in the United Kingdom.

"(2) Subject to the provisions of this Act, the interpretation of the drawing, indorsement, acceptance, or acceptance *suprà* protest of a bill is determined by the law of the place where such contract is made.

Provided that where an inland bill is indorsed in a foreign country the indorsement shall as regards the payer be interpreted according to the law of the United Kingdom.

"(3) The duties of the holder with respect to presentment for acceptance or payment and the necessity for or sufficiency of a protest or notice of dishonour, or otherwise, are determined by the law of the place where the act is done or the bill is dishonoured.

"(4) Where a bill is drawn out of but payable in the United Kingdom and the sum payable is not expressed in the currency of the United Kingdom, the amount shall, in the absence of some express stipulation, be calculated according to the rate of exchange for sight drafts at the place of payment on the day the bill is payable.

"(5) Where a bill is drawn in one country and is payable in another, the due date thereof is determined according to the law of the place where it is payable."

A foreign bill may be drawn in this country and be payable abroad, e.g. where goods are exported from England to America the exporter may draw a bill upon his correspondent in America for the value of the goods. A foreign bill is also one which is drawn abroad and payable in this country, as, for example, for the value of goods imported into England from America. A credit may be opened for the captain of a ship at a foreign port who may draw bills upon a London banker up to a certain fixed sum.

The following extract from the "Bankers' Magazine," December, 1909, illustrates, in the case of cotton, the various forms of bank paper which may be created between the seeding in Texas and the delivery of the cotton in Liverpool :—"The planter is carried on through the season by advances from a local bank or a commission agent acting for a firm of Liverpool importers. When the cotton is ready to ship it may be paid for by a cheque on a bank in New Orleans or Galveston. The local bank sees it on board ship and draws on a New York bank against it, at the same time forwarding the bills of lading. The New York bank draws on London and sends on the bills of lading with the draft. The London acceptors, who may be a bank or a commercial firm, discount the bill, and the discounters may re-discount it or borrow on it. If it be what is technically called a 'fine bill,' that is, with the best kind of names on it, it may pass through many hands before it matures."

Bills payable abroad are usually sent by country bankers to their London office or London agents to be sold through a foreign bill broker. As the bills are indorsed by the bank before negotiation, an account such as "foreign bills negotiated" should be credited (cash being debited) with the proceeds of the sale, in order to show the bank's liability upon the bills until maturity. When sufficient time has elapsed, after maturity, to allow of the bills being returned, if dishonoured, "foreign bills negotiated" account should be debited, and foreign bills account credited. This latter account is credited because when the customer received credit for the bills, foreign bills account would be debited.

A foreign bill is usually drawn in a set, that is, instead of there being only one document, as is generally the case with inland bills, there are two, or three, documents. The several parts, however, constitute one bill. Only one of the parts must be accepted, for if more than one part is accepted the acceptor may find himself liable on every part so accepted, as if it were a separate bill. In the same way, if a holder of a set indorses two or more parts to different persons he is liable on every such part. When an acceptor pays a bill drawn in a set, he should see that the part bearing his acceptance is delivered up to him, otherwise a holder of it in due course may require payment of it. In the ordinary course of things, where any one part is discharged, the whole bill is discharged. The rules of the Bills of Exchange Act, Section 71, with regard to a bill drawn in several parts are given under BILL IN A SET.

The following are specimens of foreign bills:—

No. Copenhagen , 1910.
£5

At ten days from date pay this first of exchange to the order of John Jones five pounds sterling value received, which place to account as per advice.

To R. BROWN.

J. Jackson,
London.

Payable in London. Due
No.

Las Palmas.
£200. , 1910.

At thirty days after sight of this first of exchange (second unpaid) pay to the order of John Jones the sum of two hundred pounds sterling, value received, which amount place with or without further advice to the account of the steamer *Britannia*.

J. BROWN.

To X. & Y. Steam Ship Co., Ltd.,
Hull.

London........1910.

Exchange for £500.

Sixty days after sight of this first of exchange (second and third of the same tenor and date unpaid), pay to the order of John Jones, five hundred pounds, value received, which place to account as advised. The shipping documents attached to be surrendered against acceptance.

JOHN BROWN.

To R. Robinson & Co.,
New York.

Where a foreign bill, appearing on the face of it to be such, has been dishonoured by non-acceptance, it must be duly protested for non-acceptance, and where such a bill, which has not been previously dishonoured by non-acceptance is dishonoured by non-payment it must be duly protested for non-payment. If it be not so protested, the drawer and indorsers are discharged (Section 51, s.s. 2, Bills of Exchange Act. See PROTEST). If a foreign bill is accepted as to a part only of the amount, it must be protested as to the balance (Section 44, s.s. 2).

A foreign bill may be payable at one or more "usances." A usance is the time which, by custom, is allowed between two countries for the currency of a bill. (See USANCE.)

Foreign bill transactions are settled on the Royal Exchange on Tuesdays and Thursdays.

As to the stamp duty upon foreign bills, see BILL OF EXCHANGE.

The stamps placed upon a bill in a foreign country should be scrutinised in this country, in case any action may be necessary in a foreign country where the absence or incorrectness of the required stamp would prove a bar to proceedings on the bill in that country. (See BILL OF EXCHANGE, DOCUMENTARY BILL, INLAND BILL.)

FOREIGN COMPANY. (See COMPANY OUTSIDE THE UNITED KINGDOM.)

FOREIGN EXCHANGES. The enormous trade carried on between this and other countries necessitates a very active business in the settlement of the balances of indebtedness. These balances are constantly varying not only in amount but also in direction; that is to say, a certain country may at some time be in debt to this country, and shortly afterwards the position may be reversed.

If England is owing a balance to another country, arising, say, through that country having sent here a greater value of goods than this country has exported, there are three ways open in which the liability may be discharged :—

1. Coin or gold bars may be sent. This method is expensive owing to charges for freight and insurance.

2. A batch of "international" securities could be sent, i.e. certain well-known government bonds, dealt in on all the principal markets of the world. This method is not much cheaper than No. 1, owing to charges for brokerage and loss of the margin between the buying and the selling price.

3. A remittance of bills may be made. This is by far the easiest, cheapest and so most frequently adopted method. The bills need not necessarily be drawn upon the country to which they are remitted, provided they are the acceptances of another country than this. The bills used are, of course, any first-class ones that are offering in the bill market and may be of various currencies; at three months' date, is a frequent quotation in the bill brokers' bi-weekly *Course of Exchange*, or list of bill prices.

There are two main factors which affect the foreign exchanges and the price at which bills for settlement of a balance, as mentioned, can be bought. One is the relative indebtedness of the two countries; if this country is in debt to the other, the price of bills on that country naturally tends to rise in the market because the merchants compete with one another in their endeavours to buy bills to remit, whilst in the other country's market the price of bills on this country tends to fall owing to want of demand. The other disturbing factor is the value or price of money in the two countries, that is the rate of discount ruling in each. Though in the case mentioned England owes the other country a balance, yet the exchanges may be turned in favour of this country by a high rate of interest here, for this will tempt capitalists in the foreign country to invest money in bills on this country. "As the rate rises, the demand will increase, until at last the price reaches the specie point, and gold begins to flow in" (Macleod).

The foreign exchange is said to be turning in favour of a country when gold may shortly have to be sent to it by the foreigner, and to be adverse when, before long, it may be necessary to export gold to the foreigner.

Where the exchange rates are quoted in foreign money (e.g. with France and Germany at so many francs or marks to the pound), the higher the quotation the more favourable the exchange is to England, because the amount of francs or marks which are to be received for one pound is greater. On the other hand, where rates are quoted in sterling money (e.g. with Russia and India, at so many pence to a rouble or rupee) the lower the quotation the more favourable it is to England, because fewer pence are to be given for a rouble or rupee. (See CHEQUE RATE, COURSE OF EXCHANGE, LONG RATE, SHORT RATE, SPECIE POINTS, PAR OF EXCHANGE.)

FOREIGN MONEYS.

	Approximate value in English money. s.	d.
ARGENTINE.—Monetary Unit—Peso (paper)	1	9
Argentinos (gold) per 5 Pesos . .	19	6
(See note under BRAZIL.)		
AUSTRIA AND HUNGARY.—Monetary Unit—Krone of 100 Heller.		
Bronze— 1 Heller	..	
,, 2 Hellers	0	0¼
Nickel— 10 ,, ...	0	1
,, 20 ,, ...	0	2
Silver— 1 Krone	0	10
,, 5 Kronen	4	2
Gold— 10 ,, ...	8	4
,, 20 ,, ...	16	8

Notes are issued by the Austro-Hungarian Bank for 10, 20, 50, 100, and 1,000 Kronen, and at present are at par with gold.

The silver Florin piece still circulates, and will remain current as 2 Kronen until further notice.

The notes and all other coins of the Florin (or Gulden) issue have ceased to be legal tender, and should not be accepted.

Approximate value in English money.

AUSTRALIA.—English coinage circulates throughout the country and is the only legal tender.

Australia is composed of six Federated States, and the banks in each State issue bank notes of £1 and upward, which are legal tender only in the State where issued, and are liable to a small exchange charge if cashed in any other State than the State of issue.

The exchange varies from ¼ to 2½ per cent, according to relative positions of the States concerned and the amount involved.

English bank notes are at a discount of 1 to 2½ per cent.

BELGIUM.—Monetary Unit — the Franc of 100 Centimes.

	s.	d.
Bronze— 1 Centime	..	
„ 2 Centimes	0	0¼
Nickel— 5 „	0	0½
„ 10 „	0	1
„ 20 „	0	2
Silver— 50 „	0	4¾
„ 1 Franc	0	9½
„ 2 Francs	1	7
„ 5 „	4	0
Gold— 20 „	16	0

Notes are issued by the National Bank for 20, 50, 100, 500 and 1,000 Francs. Gold is difficult to procure and is at a slight premium. (See notes under FRANCE.)

BERMUDA.—English money is the legal tender, but American money is freely accepted, particularly at the hotels.

BRAZIL.—Monetary Unit—Milreis

	s.	d.
(paper)	1	4½
Gold— 10 Milreis	22	8
Silver— 2,000 Reis	2	8

In the South American Republics gold is invariably at a premium, and in the Argentine Republic and Brazil the circulating medium is principally inconvertible paper money.

BULGARIA.—Monetary Unit—Leva

	s.	d.
of 100 Stotinkis	0	9½

CANADA.—Monetary Unit—1 Dollar of 100 Cents.

	s.	d.
Copper— 1 Cent	0	0½
Silver— 5 Cents	0	2½
„ 10 „	0	5
„ 25 „	1	0½
„ 50 „	2	1

Notes are issued by the Government for 25 cents, $1, $2 and $4, and by the various banks of Canada for $5 and upwards, and are in general circulation.

United States gold coin is current at par in Canada. (See NEWFOUNDLAND.)

CANARY ISLANDS.—Spanish money is the currency in use. (See SPAIN.)

CEYLON.—Monetary Unit—Rupee

	s.	d.
(100 Cents)	1	4

CHILI.—Monetary Unit—Peso (new)

	s.	d.
gold	1	6
Peso (paper)	0	10¾
Silver—(new) per Peso	0	10¾

CHINA.—Monetary Unit—Tael (silver)

	s.	d.
ver)	2	4
Mexican Dollar	2	0

CUBA.—Spanish money still circulates, but American money is everywhere accepted.

DENMARK.—(See NORWAY.)

EGYPT.—Monetary Unit—Piastre of 10 Millièmes.

	s.	d.
Copper— ¼ Millième	0	0 1/16
„ ½ „	0	0⅛
Nickel— 1 „	0	0¼
„ 2 Millièmes	0	0½
„ 5 „	0	1¼
„ 1 Piastre	0	2½
Silver— 1 „	0	2½
„ 2 Piastres	0	5
„ 5 „	1	0¼
„ 10 „	2	0½
„ 20 „	4	1¼
Gold— 50 „ = ½£E =	10	3
„ 100 „ 1£E =	20	6

Notes of 50 Piastres, 1£E, 5£E, 10£E, 50£E, and 100£E are issued by the National Bank. English sovereigns are current throughout Egypt as 97½ Piastres; French 20 Franc pieces,

Pt. 77; Turkish Pounds, Pt. 87½.

English bank notes are subject to a varying discount.

	Approximate value in English money. s.	d.
Finland.—Monetary Unit—Markka of 100 Penni	0	9½
Gold—20 Markkaa	15	9
Notes—per 100 Markkaa	77	6

France.—Monetary Unit—the Franc of 100 Centimes.

	s.	d.
Bronze—1 Centime		..
,, 2 Centimes	0	0¼
,, 5 ,,	0	0½
,, 10 ,,	0	1
Nickel—25 ,,	0	2½
Silver—50 ,,	0	4¾
,, 1 Franc	0	9½
,, 2 Francs	1	7
,, 5 ,,	4	0
Gold—5 ,,	4	0
,, 10 ,,	8	0
,, 20 ,, The "Napoleon," or "Louis"	16	0

Notes are issued by the Bank of France for 50, 100, 500, and 1,000 Francs.

The silver coins anterior to 1863, excepting 5 Franc pieces, are uncurrent; also all Papal coins and the 50 cent. 1 Lire and 2 Lire coins of Italy.

The gold and silver coins of France, Belgium and Switzerland are current in each of these countries; also the gold coins of Italy, and (except in Switzerland) the Austrian gold coin of 20 Francs (i.e. a coin minted for circulation in the Latin Union of the value of 20 Francs). The Greek 2 Drachmai, 1 Drachma and 50 Leptá pieces are no longer accepted in France, Belgium or Switzerland.

Caution.—South American Dollars, Roumanian, Spanish, and Sicilian coins are frequently passed on travellers by unscrupulous persons in giving change. Such coins do not circulate in France, Belgium, Switzerland, or Italy, and are worth considerably less than the current coins.

Germany.—Monetary Unit—the Mark of 100 Pfennige.

	Approximate value in English money. s.	d.
Copper—1 Pfennig		..
,, 2 Pfennige	0	0¼
Nickel—5 ,,	0	0½
,, 10 ,,	0	1¼
,, 20 ,,	0	2½
Silver—50 ,,	0	6
,, 1 Mark	1	0
,, 2 Marks	2	0
,, 3 ,,	3	0
,, 5 ,,	5	0
Gold—10 ,,	10	0
,, 20 ,,	20	0

Notes for 5, 10, 20 and 50 Marks are issued by the State, and notes for 100 and 1,000 Marks by the Reichsbank.

Various Banks in Bavaria, Saxony, etc., issue notes for 100 and 500 Marks.

Thalers are now demonetised.

	s.	d.
Greece.—Monetary Unit—the Drachma of 100 Leptá	0	9½

The circulating medium of Greece consists principally of paper, notes being issued for 1, 2, 5, 10, 25, 100, 500 and 1,000 Drachmai, with copper coins of 5 and 10 Leptá and nickel coins of 5, 10 and 20 Leptá for the divisional money.

Travellers are recommended to carry French or English gold.

Exchange: 20 Francs gold, about 21·50 dr.; English £, 27·00 dr. The rate of exchange varies considerably.

Holland. — Monetary Unit — 1 Gulden of 100 Cents.

	s.	d.
Copper—½ Cent		..
,, 1 ,,		..
,, 2½ Cents	0	0½
Silver—10 ,,	0	2
,, 25 ,,	0	5
,, 50 ,,	0	10
,, 1 Gulden (Guilder)	1	8
,, 2½ ,,	4	2
Gold—10 ,,	16	8

Notes are issued by the Netherlands Bank for 10, 25, 40, 50, 60, 100, 200, 300 and 1,000 Gulden.

	s.	d.
Hong Kong.—Notes—per Dollar	1	8½
Silver—per Dollar	1	6

HUNGARY.—(See AUSTRIA.)

INDIA.—Monetary Unit—Rupee of 16 Annas.

	Approximate value in English money. s.	d.
Bronze—¼ Anna	0	0¼
„ ½ „	0	0½
Nickel—1 „	0	1
Silver— 2 Annas	0	2
„ 4 „	0	4
„ 8 „	0	8
„ 1 Rupee	1	4

Notes of the value of 5, 10, 20, 50, 100 Rupees and upward are in circulation.

Rate of exchange about 1*s.* 4*d.* per Rupee. Sovereigns are current at 15 Rupees to the pound, and are not subject to the fluctuation of exchange as is the case with English bank notes and drafts.

A Lac, or Lakh, equals 100,000 Rupees. (See LAC.) 100 Lacs is a Crore.

A Pie is a unit of value equal to the 192nd part of a Rupee.

R. A. P. = Rupees, Annas, Pies.

ITALY.—Monetary Unit—the Lira of 100 Centesimi.

	s.	d.
Copper— 1 Centesimo	..	
„ 2 Centesimi	0	0¼
„ 5 „	0	0½
„ 10 „	0	1
Nickel—20 „	0	2
„ 25 „	0	2½
Silver— 1 Lira	0	9½
„ 2 Lire	1	7
„ 5 „	4	0
Gold— 5 „	4	0
„ 10 „	8	0
„ 20 „	16	0

The money in general use is a paper currency in notes of 5, 10, and 25 Lire each, issued by the Government, and notes of 50, 100, 500, and 1,000 Lire issued by the following banks of issue: Banco d'Italia, Banco di Napoli, and Banco di Sicilia.

Gold is invariably at a small premium.

Papal silver and all silver coins anterior to 1863, except 5 Lire pieces, are no longer current.

Only Italian silver coin should be accepted for use in Italy, as, although the 5 Francs French silver piece passes, the smaller silver coins of the Latin Union are not generally accepted.

The 25 Lire notes are still current, but are no longer issued.

	Approximate value in English money. s.	d.
JAPAN.—Monetary Unit—Yen (100 Sen)	2	0½
JAVA.—Notes—per Gulden	1	6¾

MADEIRA.—Portuguese money is the currency in use. (See PORTUGAL.)

	s.	d.
MAURITIUS.—Monetary Unit—Rupee (100 Cents)	1	4
MEXICO.—Monetary Unit—Dollar or Peso	2	0

NEWFOUNDLAND.—The monetary system is similar to that of Canada, and Canadian coins circulate freely.

NEW ZEALAND.—English coinage circulates throughout New Zealand, and is the only legal tender.

English bank notes are at a discount of 1 to 2½ per cent.

NORWAY, SWEDEN AND DENMARK.—Monetary Unit—Kroner of 100 Öre.

	s.	d.
Copper— 1 Öre	..	
„ 2 „	0	0¼
„ 5 „	0	0½
Silver— 10 „	0	1¼
„ 25 „	0	3¼
„ 50 „	0	6¾
„ 1 Kroner	1	1½
„ 2 Kroners	2	2¾
Gold— 5 „	5	6¾
„ 10 „	11	1½
„ 20 „	22	3

Bank notes are also issued of 5, 10, 50, 100, 500 and 1,000 Kroners.

The coins pass freely in all three countries. The notes also circulate freely in the principal towns, but travellers are recommended to take into the interiors of these countries the notes of the respective country.

18 Kroners = £1.

PERSIA.—Monetary Unit—1 Kran of 20 Shahis. 10 Krans = 1 Toman.

	Approximate value in English money. s.	d.
Present exchange, 50 Krans silver or paper = £1.		
The coins in common use are the ½ Kran, 1 Kran, and 2 Krans silver pieces. Gold is not in general circulation.		
PERU.—Monetary Unit—Sol (silver)	2	0
Gold—Libra	20	0
PORTUGAL—Monetary Unit—1 Milreis of 1,000 Reis.		
Copper— 3 Reis	..	
,, 5 ,,	0	0¼
,, 10 ,,	0	0½
,, 20 ,,	0	1
Nickel— 50 ,,	0	2
,, 100 ,,	0	5
Silver—200 ,,	0	10
,, 500 ,,	2	0
Gold— 1 Milreis	4	0
,, 2 ,,	8	0
,, 5 ,,	20	2
,, 10 ,,	40	0

Notes are issued of 500 Reis and upwards. Gold is at a premium of about 5 per cent., and is not in general circulation.

The equivalents shown in the table are based on the nominal gold value, but the present value of a Milreis, silver or paper, is 4*s.*

The rate of exchange is very fluctuating. (See MADEIRA, SOUTH AFRICA.)

	s.	d.
ROUMANIA.—Monetary Unit—Ley of 100 Banis	0	9½
Notes—per 100 Lei	76	0
RUSSIA.—Monetary Unit—Rouble of 100 Kopeks.		
Copper— 1 Kopek	0	0¼
,, 2 Kopeks	0	0½
,, 3 ,,	0	0¾
,, 5 ,,	0	1¼
Nickel— 5 ,,	0	1¼
,, 10 ,,	0	2½
,, 15 ,,	0	3¾
,, 20 ,,	0	5
Silver— 25 ,,	0	6¼
,, 50 ,,	1	0¾
,, 1 Rouble	2	1½
Gold— 5 Roubles	10	8
,, 7½ ,,	16	0
,, 10 ,,	21	4
,, 15 ,, (Imperial)	32	0

Notes of 1, 3, 5, 10, 25, 50, 100 and 500 Roubles are in circulation, and are at par with gold.

Russian notes as follows are now out of date and of no value—

100 Roubles	dated before	1887.
50 ,,	,,	1869.
25 ,,	,,	1888.
10 ,,	,,	1893.
5 ,,	,,	1895.
3 & 1 ,,	dated on back of notes.	

	s.	d.
SERVIA.—Monetary Unit—Dinar of 100 Paras	0	9½

SOUTH AFRICA.—The coinage is the same as in England, English gold and silver being legal tender. Notes are issued by the principal South African banks under arrangement with the Government for 10*s.*, £1, £5, £10, £20, and are legal tender throughout British South Africa.

English bank notes are at a discount of from 1 to 2½ per cent.

In Portuguese territory the Milreis (1,000 Reis), about 4*s.* is principally used.

	s.	d.
SPAIN.—Monetary Unit—Peseta of 100 Centimos.		
Bronze— 5 Centimos	0	0½
,, 10 ,,	0	1
Silver— 50 ,,	0	4¾
,, 1 Peseta	0	9½
,, 2 Pesetas	1	7
,, 5 ,,	4	0
Gold— 20 ,,	16	0
,, 25 ,, (Alfonso)	20	0

Notes of 25, 50, 100, 500, and 1,000 Pesetas are issued by the Bank of Spain.

Gold is at a premium of about 10 per cent, and is not in general circulation.

The rate of exchange is very fluctuating.

All silver coins prior to 1869 are uncurrent.

The equivalents shown in the table are based on the nominal gold value, but the present exchange for a pound sterling in

Spanish notes and silver coin is 26·90 to 27·10 Pesetas. (See CUBA, CANARY ISLANDS.)

SWEDEN.—(See NORWAY.)

SWITZERLAND.—Monetary Unit—the Franc of 100 Centimes.

	Approximate value in English money, s.	d.
Bronze— 1 Centime	..	
,, 2 Centimes	0	0¼
Nickel— 5 ,,	0	0½
,, 10 ,,	0	1
,, 20 ,,	0	2
Silver— 50 ,,	0	4¾
,, 1 Franc	0	9½
,, 2 Francs	1	7
,, 5 ,,	4	0
Gold— 20 ,,	16	0

Notes of 50, 100, 500, and 1,000 Francs are issued by several Swiss banks under arrangements with the Government, and are available throughout Switzerland. Gold is generally at a slight premium.

The silver coins bearing the figure of Helvetia in a sitting position, with the exception of the 5 Franc piece, are uncurrent, and realise only their value as silver. (See notes under FRANCE.)

TURKEY.—Monetary Unit—the Piastre of 40 Paras.

	s.	d.
1 Piastre	0	2¼
20 Piastres = 1 silver Medjidie	3	7
100 ,, = 1 gold Turkish £	18	0

The best money for travellers to take for use in Turkey is the French 20 Franc piece.

UNITED STATES.—Monetary Unit—1 Dollar of 100 Cents.

	s.	d.
Copper— 1 Cent	0	0½
Nickel — 5 Cents	0	2½
Silver— 10 ,, (Dime)	0	5
,, 25 ,,	1	0½
,, 50 ,,	2	1
,, 1 Dollar	4	2
Gold— 2½ Dollars	10	5
,, 5 ,,	20	10
,, 10 ,, (Eagle)	41	8
,, 20 ,,	83	4

Notes, Greenbacks, Gold Certificates, Silver Certificates, and National Bank Notes are issued in amounts of 1, 2, 5, 10, 20, 50, 100, 500, 1,000 dollars and upwards, and circulate at par with gold. (See BERMUDA.)

	Approximate value in English money, s.	d.
URUGUAY.—Monetary Unit—Peso	4	2

WEST INDIES.—In the BRITISH WEST INDIES English money circulates, but they issue their own notes.

In CUBA Spanish money still circulates, but American money is everywhere accepted.

In BERMUDA English money is the legal tender, but American money is freely accepted, particularly at the hotels.

The above information has been kindly supplied by Messrs. Thos. Cook and Son, Bankers and Tourist Agents.

The Latin Monetary Union consists of those countries which have adopted the same standard coin, though called by different names, equal in value to the franc.

The countries which have joined the Union are: Belgium, France, Greece, Italy, and Switzerland.

The countries which have adopted the same system but which have not joined the Union are: Finland, Roumania, Servia and Spain.

FOREIGN SECURITY. (See MARKETABLE SECURITY, and Section 82 of the Stamp Act, 1891, given thereunder.)

FORGED TRANSFER. Where a banker takes as security a transfer of stock or shares registered in the names of several holders, it is advisable that the transfer should be signed at the bank by each holder, because if one of the holders forges the signature of another holder to the transfer, the banker, even after registration and ultimate sale of the stock, may be compelled to make good the value of the stock to the true owner. This point was decided in the important case of the *Sheffield Corporation* v. *Barclay and others* (1905. A.C. 392). The House of Lords (1905) reversed the decision of the Court of Appeal (1903) and restored that of the Lord Chief Justice (1902), where judgment for the plaintiffs was given for the amount claimed.

The Lord Chancellor (the Earl of Halsbury) said: "Two persons, Timbrell and Honnywill, were joint owners of corporation stock created under a local Act of Parliament.

Timbrell, in fraud of Honnywill, forged a transfer of the stock, and borrowed money on the security of the stock which the transfer was supposed to have transferred. A bank which lent the money sent the transfer to the proper officer of the corporation, and demanded, as they were entitled to do, if the transfer was a genuine one, that they should be registered as holders of the stock. The corporation acted upon their demand; they transferred the stock into the names of the bank, and the bank in ordinary course transferred it to holders for value. The corporation also, in ordinary course, issued certificates, and the holders of these certificates were able to establish their title against the corporation, who were estopped from denying that those whom they had registered were the stockholders entitled. Honnywill, after the death of Timbrell, discovered the forgery that had been committed, and compelled the corporation to restore the stock, and the question in the case is whether the corporation has any remedy against the bank who caused them to act upon a forged transfer, and so render themselves liable to the considerable loss which they have sustained. Now, apart from any decision upon the question (it being taken for granted that all the parties were honest), I should have thought that the bank were clearly liable. They have a private bargain with a customer. Upon his assurance they take a document from him as a security for a loan, which they assume to be genuine. I do not suggest there was any negligence—perhaps business could not go on if people were suspecting forgery in every transaction—but their position was obviously very different from that of the corporation. The corporation is simply ministerial in registering a valid transfer and issuing fresh certificates. They cannot refuse to register, and though for their own sake they will not and ought not to register or to issue certificates to a person who is not really the holder of the stock, yet they have no machinery, and they cannot inquire into the transaction out of which the transfer arises. The bank, on the other hand, is at liberty to lend their money or not. They can make any amount of inquiries they like. If they find that an intended borrower has a co-trustee, they may ask him or the co-trustee himself whether the co-trustee is a party to the loan, and a simple question to the co-trustee would have prevented the fraud. They take the risk of the transaction and lend the money. The security given happens to be in a form that requires registration to make it available, and the bank 'demand,' as, if genuine transfers are bought, they are entitled to do, that the stock shall be registered in their name or that of their nominees, and are also entitled to have fresh certificates issued to themselves or nominees. This was done, and the corporation by acting on this 'demand' have incurred a considerable loss. As I have said, I think if it were *res integra* I should think the bank were liable; but I do not think it is *res integra*, but is covered by authority. In *Dugdale* v. *Lovering* (1875, 10 C.P., 196), Mr. Cave, arguing for the plaintiff, put the proposition thus: 'It is a general principle of law when an act is done by one person at the request of another, which act is not in itself manifestly tortious to the knowledge of the person doing it, and such act turns out to be injurious to the rights of a third party, the person doing it is entitled to an indemnity from him who requested that it should be done.' . . . I think both upon principle and authority the corporation are entitled to recover. . . ."

The Forged Transfers Acts, 1891 and 1892, were passed with the object of enabling purchasers of stock to be protected from losses through forged transfers. Companies, however, are not obliged to adopt them, and those which have adopted them are chiefly railway companies. Section 1 of the 1891 Act is as follows:—

"1. (1) Where a company or local authority issue or have issued shares, stock, or securities transferable by any instrument in writing or by an entry in any books or register kept by or on behalf of the company or local authority, they shall have power to make compensation by a cash payment out of their funds for any loss arising from a transfer of any such shares, stock, or securities, in pursuance of a forged transfer or of a transfer under a forged power of attorney whether such loss arises, and whether the transfer or power of attorney was forged before or after the passing of this Act, and whether the person receiving such compensation, or any person through whom he claims, has or has not paid any fee or otherwise contributed to any fund out of which the compensation is paid." (The words "whether such loss, etc.," were added by the 1892 Act.)

"(2) Any company or local authority may, if they think fit, provide, either by fees not exceeding the rate of one shilling on every one hundred pounds transferred, with a minimum charge equal to that for twenty-five pounds, to be paid by the transferee upon the entry of the transfer in the books of the company or local authority, or by insurance, reservation of capital, accumulation of income, or in any other manner which they may resolve upon, a fund to meet claims for such compensation." (The words "with a minimum charge equal to that for £25" were added by the 1892 Act.)

"(3) For the purpose of providing such compensation any company may borrow on the security of their property, and any local authority may borrow with the like consent and on the like security and subject to the like conditions as to repayment by means of instalments or the provision of a sinking fund and otherwise as in the case of the securities in respect of which compensation is to be provided, but any money so borrowed by a local authority shall be repaid within a term not longer than five years. Any expenses incurred by a local authority in making compensation, or in the repayment of, or the payment of interest on, or otherwise in connection with, any loan raised as aforesaid, shall, except so far as they may be met by such fees as aforesaid, be paid out of the fund or rate on which the security in respect of which compensation is to be made is charged.

"(4) Any such company or local authority may impose such reasonable restrictions on the transfer of their shares, stock, or securities, or with respect to powers of attorney for the transfer thereof, as they may consider requisite for guarding against losses arising from forgery.

"(5) Where a company or local authority compensate a person under this Act for any loss arising from forgery, the company or local authority shall, without prejudice to any other rights or remedies, have the same rights and remedies against the person liable for the loss as the person compensated would have had." (See COMPANIES, TRANSFER OF SHARES.)

FORGERY. Forgery has been defined as the making or alteration of any document with the intention of prejudicing another person.

Where the numbers on certain Bank of England notes had been altered, the intention being to prevent the notes (payment of which had been stopped) being traced, it was held in the case of *Suffell* v. *Bank of England* (1882, 9 Q.B.D. 555) that the plaintiff, who was an innocent holder for value, could not recover from the Bank of England because the notes had been altered in a material part. The importance of the numbers on notes was pointed out by Jessel, M.R., in the course of his judgment. (See BANK OF ENGLAND NOTES.)

If a banker, unknowingly, gives forged bank notes in payment of a cheque, they do not operate as a payment.

"Whosoever shall forge or alter, or shall offer, utter, dispose of, or put off, knowing the same to be forged or altered, any note or bill of exchange of the Bank of England or of the Bank of Ireland, or of any other body corporate, company or person carrying on the business of bankers, commonly called a bank note, a bank bill of exchange, or a bank post bill, or any indorsement on or assignment of any bank note, bank bill of exchange, or bank post bill, with intent to defraud, shall be guilty of felony: and

"Whosoever without lawful authority or excuse (the proof whereof shall lie on the party accused) shall purchase or receive from any other person, or have in his custody or possession any forged bank note, bank bill of exchange, or bank post bill, or blank bank note, blank bank bill of exchange, or blank bank post bill, knowing the same to be forged, shall be guilty of felony." (Forgery Act, 1861, 24 & 25 Vict. c. 98, Sections 12 and 13.)

By Section 22 of the same Act:—

"Whosoever shall forge or alter, or shall offer, utter, dispose of, or put off, knowing the same to be forged or altered, any bill of exchange, or any acceptance, indorsement or assignment of any bill of exchange, or any promissory note for the payment of money, or any indorsement or assignment of any such promissory note, with intent to defraud, shall be guilty of felony. . . ."

A transferor by delivery warrants to his immediate transferee, being a holder for value, that the note is what it purports to be, and therefore the person who receives a forged bank note can reclaim the money from the person who gave him the note, provided he makes the claim within a reasonable time.

The Bills of Exchange Act, 1882, Section 24, enacts as follows:—

"Subject to the provisions of this Act, where a signature on a bill is forged or placed thereon without the authority of the person whose signature it purports to be, the forged or unauthorised signature is wholly inoperative, and no right to retain the bill or to give a discharge therefor or to enforce payment thereof against any party thereto can be acquired through or under that signature, unless the party against whom it is sought to retain or enforce payment of the bill is precluded from setting up the forgery or want of authority.

"Provided that nothing in this Section shall affect the ratification of an unauthorised signature not amounting to a forgery."

The words "through or under that signature" in the Section just quoted require particular attention. A holder, even a holder in due course, cannot retain a bill, or give a discharge for it or sue upon it, where a signature on the bill is forged The forged signature which is referred to is the signature which is necessary to transfer the bill to the holder, that is, the one through or under which he gets his title. If the signature of the drawer or acceptor is forged the bill is valueless, and if an indorsement which is necessary to pass the title of the bill is forged, the bill is valueless to the party acquiring it through that signature. But where an indorsement, which is not necessary for the transfer of the title, is forged, that forged indorsement may be ignored and the holder in due course can sue all the other parties to the bill. For example, where a bill is specially indorsed, say to John Brown, the real signature of John Brown is required in order to make the bill valid and to pass the title to a succeeding holder. If John Brown's signature is forged, a subsequent holder gets no title. If John Brown's signature is genuine and the indorsement is in blank (the bill then passing by simple delivery) it does not matter to a subsequent holder whether a signature following that of John Brown is a genuine one or not, as that subsequent holder derives his title through John Brown and not through the person from whom he received the bill.

If a holder obtains payment of a bill which is affected with a forged signature he cannot retain the money. The rightful owner of the bill can demand to have the bill given up to him and can sue the acceptor thereon. The acceptor will have a right of action against the holder for the return of the money he paid to him. The holder will look to the person from whom he obtained the bill for repayment, and that person will then look to his transferor, but the person who actually took the bill through the forged indorsement will have no one to proceed against on the bill. If the holder, in such a case as that referred to, to whom the acceptor paid the forged bill, cannot be found, the acceptor will lose the money as he is liable to the true owner.

If a banker pays a bill bearing a forged acceptance or a forged indorsement (either of the payee or any indorsee) he cannot debit his customer with the amount. A banker ought to know whether his own customer's (the acceptor) signature is genuine, but the banker is not particularly concerned with the genuineness of the drawer's signature, as the acceptor by accepting the bill is precluded (Section 54) from denying to a holder in due course the genuineness of the drawer's signature.

If a banker has paid an acceptance and one of the indorsements is subsequently found to have been forged, the banker cannot recover from the person to whom he paid the money, nor can he hold the acceptor liable for the amount.

A forged signature cannot be ratified, but a person may be precluded from saying that his signature is forged if he refrains, when he knows that a banker is relying upon a forged signature, from informing the banker of the fact until his position is altered for the worse.

Where a banker on whom a cheque is drawn pays it in good faith and in the ordinary course of business, he is not liable for the indorsement of the payee or any subsequent indorser, even though the indorsement is forged. (Section 60, Bills of Exchange Act, 1882.) But if a banker gives cash for a cheque drawn upon another banker, he is not protected by Section 60, and is liable like any other person.

Protection is afforded by Section 80, to a banker on whom a crossed cheque is drawn, if he pays it in accordance with the crossing.

Where a drawer's signature is forged, the banker paying such cheque cannot debit it to the drawer's account. A banker is responsible if he pays a forged cheque, unless he can show that he was misled by his customer.

A banker must give notice of a drawer's forged signature on the day he receives such a cheque.

A banker collecting a crossed cheque for a customer is protected by Section 82 of the above Act.

Where a crossed cheque with a printed form of receipt thereon is payable only when that receipt is duly signed, and the signature on the receipt is forged, the order to pay not being unconditional and the document therefore not a cheque, as recognised by the Bills of Exchange Act, the banker collecting the money for a customer is not protected by that Act: but protection is given by the Revenue Act, 1883. (See RECEIPT ON CHEQUE.)

A banker is protected by Section 19 of the Stamp Act, 1853, against paying one of his own drafts bearing a forged indorsement. Of course, if the banker knows the indorsement is forged, he must not pay the draft. (See DRAFT ON DEMAND.)

Making a false entry in a pass book with intent to defraud is recognised by law as a forgery of an accountable receipt.

If a transfer of stock is made by the Bank of England under a forged power of attorney, the Bank is liable to replace the stock, unless it can be proved that there was such negligence on the part of the stockholder as to prevent him from disputing the transfer. (See FORGED TRANSFER.)

With respect to the forgery of a share warrant or coupon, Section 38 of the Companies (Consolidation) Act, 1908, enacts that if any person with intent to defraud, forges or alters or utters any share warrant or coupon, or falsely personates any owner of any share or interest in any company, or if any person, without lawful authority, engraves on any plate any share warrant or coupon, he shall be guilty of felony.

The late J. W. Gilbart records that the first instance of the forgery of a bank note occurred in 1758.

FORWARD PRICE. The "forward" price of silver is the quotation for delivery and payment at a future date. The "spot" or "cash" price is for immediate delivery.

FOUNDERS' SHARES. So called because created for the purpose of remunerating the founders or promoters of a company. A vendor sometimes obtains founders' shares as part of the purchase money, and, occasionally, a founders' share is offered to subscribers for a certain number of ordinary shares. Although the nominal amount of a founders' share is small, in a successful company the value may be very considerable. If founders' shares receive, say, a half of the net profits after a certain fixed dividend has been paid on the ordinary shares, it follows, when the surplus profits are large, that the founders' shares, which are few in number, will obtain a large share of the profits. These surplus profits would, in a company which has no founders' shares, be no doubt partly used to build up a reserve fund or to strengthen the company's position in some other way.

They are not considered a satisfactory kind of security. Owing to the large part of the profits which they absorb, there is the danger, in certain cases, of the ordinary shareholders making efforts to have the company reconstructed.

Every prospectus issued by a company must state, amongst other things, the number of founders' or management or deferred shares, and the nature and extent of the interest of the holders in the property and profits of the company. (See Section 81 of the Companies (Consolidation) Act, 1908, under PROSPECTUS. (See COMPANIES.)

FOUR-SHILLING PIECES. (See DOUBLE FLORINS.)

FOURTHS OF MONTHS. The totals of the London Clearing House are greater upon the fourths of months than upon ordinary days, because of the number of bills which, by custom, are dated on the first of a month and which, with the days of grace, mature on the fourth.

FRANC. (See FOREIGN MONEYS—BELGIUM, FRANCE, SWITZERLAND.)

FRAUDULENT CONVEYANCE. A voluntary conveyance by a person who subsequently becomes bankrupt is, within certain limits of time, void and liable to be set aside. (See Section 47, Bankruptcy Act, 1883, under SETTLEMENTS—SETTLOR BANKRUPT.)

FRAUDULENT PREFERENCE. Where a debtor gives a preference to a creditor over other creditors it shall be void if he becomes bankrupt within three months. Section 48 of the Bankruptcy Act, 1883, enacts :—

"(1) Every conveyance or transfer of property, or charge thereon made, every payment made, every obligation incurred, and every judicial proceeding taken or suffered by any person unable to pay his debts as they become due from his own money in favour of any creditor, or any person in trust for any creditor, with a view of giving such creditor a preference over the other creditors shall, if the person making, taking, paying, or suffering the same is adjudged bankrupt on a bankruptcy petition presented within three months after the date of making, taking, paying, or suffering the same, be deemed fraudulent and void as against the trustee in the bankruptcy.

(2) This Section shall not affect the rights of any person making title in good faith and for valuable consideration through or under a creditor of the bankrupt." (See BANKRUPTCY.)

FREEBENCH. In connection with copyholds, Williams, in "Real Property," says : "A special custom is required to entitle the wife to any interest in the lands of her husband after his decease. Where such custom exists the wife's interest is termed her freebench, and it generally consists of a life interest in one divided third part of the lands, or sometimes of a life interest in the entirety." It corresponds, therefore, in many respects to dower, the life estate of a widow in the third part of the freehold lands of her deceased intestate husband. (See DOWER, INTESTACY.)

FREEHOLD. The owner of a freehold estate in fee simple is the possessor of the greatest interest that a person can have in land. It belongs to him absolutely, and he can do with it what he pleases.

A freehold estate may also be held in fee tail (see FEE TAIL), or as an estate for life (see LIFE TENANT).

Where freehold property is conveyed to a purchaser in fee simple it is effected by means of a deed called a conveyance.

Stamp, £10.

The following is an example of the general form in which an ordinary simple conveyance may be drawn :—

1 This Indenture, made the first day of December one thousand nine hundred and ten

2 Between John Brown of Carlisle in the County of Cumberland, gentleman, hereinafter called the vendor, of the one part, and John Jones of Leeds, in the County of York, Engineer, hereinafter called the purchaser of the other part,

3 Whereas the vendor is seised of the hereditaments hereinafter conveyed for an estate of inheritance in fee simple in possession free from incumbrances,

4 and Whereas the vendor has agreed with the purchaser for the absolute sale to him of the hereditaments hereinafter conveyed at the price of one thousand pounds.

5 Now this Indenture Witnesseth that in pursuance of the said agreement and in consideration of the sum of one thousand pounds now paid to the vendor by the purchaser

6 (the receipt whereof the vendor hereby acknowledges)

7 the vendor, as beneficial owner, doth hereby convey unto the purchaser

8 All that piece or parcel of land situate in Warwick Road, Carlisle, containing one thousand two hundred square yards or thereabouts, bounded on the north by, etc., and more particularly described in the plan drawn on the margin of these presents and coloured red, Together with the three houses erected and built upon the said piece or parcel of land

9 To Hold the hereditaments hereby conveyed unto and to the use of the purchaser his heirs and assigns (or the words "in fee simple," instead of "his heirs and assigns").

In witness whereof the said parties have hereunto set their hands and seals the day and year first above written.

Signed, sealed and delivered by the within named John Brown in the presence of — JOHN BROWN. (Seal)

JOHN SMITH,
English Street,
Carlisle.

Signed sealed and delivered by the within named John Jones in the presence of
GEORGE JACKSON,
King Street,
Leeds.

JOHN JONES. (Seal)

The conveyance is not always signed by the purchaser.

There may be a yearly rent-charge upon freehold property. The word "freehold" does not necessarily mean that the land is free from all charges whatever, though the word is frequently, though incorrectly, used when it is intended to express such a meaning.

The clauses in the above specimen conveyance are numbered and are referred to as follows :—

1. In an indenture the date is at the beginning ; in a deed poll it is at the end. (See INDENTURE.)
2. The second clause relates to the "parties" to the deed.
3. Is concerned with a recital of the vendor's title.
4. The agreement for sale.
5. Consideration.
6. Vendor's acknowledgment of the consideration money.
7. Vendor conveys.
8. The parcels of land are detailed.
9. The tenendum clause.

Any declarations of uses or trusts, and any conditions or provisoes, and any covenants, generally follow this clause.

By the Land Transfer Act, 1897, Section 3 (see under EXECUTOR), since the first of January, 1898, upon the death of an owner of freehold estate, the property vests in the personal representatives (executors or administrators) of the deceased. When, therefore, the deeds of a freehold property are offered as security by a borrower, who has succeeded to the property as heir-at-law or has obtained it as devisee under a will, it is important for the banker to remember that if the death occurred on or after January 1, 1898, the legal estate is vested in the personal representatives, not in the heir or devisee, and that the formal assent of the personal representatives to the devisee taking the property, or a conveyance from them to the devisee or heir, is necessary before the heir or devisee can have the legal estate. In such cases the assent or conveyance should be deposited along with the other deeds and documents of title. (See TITLE DEEDS.)

FREIGHT. The charge made for the carriage of goods in a ship. The cargo itself is often called the freight. When the word is used, it is therefore necessary to note whether it refers to the carriage or to the cargo.

A shipowner has usually a lien upon the cargo until the amount due for freight is paid.

FRIENDLY SOCIETY. A society formed for the benefit of its members, during illness, in old age, and for assisting widows of members and orphans, and for other purposes.

A friendly society which conforms to certain requirements, may be registered with the Registrar of Friendly Societies, under the Friendly Societies' Act, 1896, an Act which consolidated the Acts relating to such societies.

A registered society has power under that Act to mortgage its property, provided there is nothing to the contrary in the rules of the Society.

In dealing with a Friendly Society a banker should make himself conversant with its rules relating to the borrowing of money and mortgaging property, and also as to the manner in which cheques may be drawn.

A receipt indorsed upon a mortgage deed has the effect of a reconveyance.

By the Friendly Societies Act, 1896, Section 33 :—

"Stamp duty shall not be chargeable upon any of the following documents :—

"(*a*) Draft or order or receipt given by or to a registered society in respect of money payable by virtue of its rules or of this Act ;

"(*b*) Letter or power of attorney granted by any person as trustee for the transfer of any money of a registered society or branch invested in his name in the public funds ;

"(*c*) Bond given to or on account of a registered society or branch, or by the treasurer or other officer thereof ;

"(*d*) Policy of insurance or appointment or revocation of appointment of agent, or other document required or authorised by this Act, or by the rules of a registered society or branch."

By a circular dated November 10, 1894, the Board of Inland Revenue intimated "that they have agreed to regard cheques drawn by, or on behalf of, a duly registered Friendly Society upon its banker as falling within the exemption from stamp duty granted by Section 15 of the Act 38 & 39 Vict. c. 60. In future, therefore, all such cheques may be paid by you, although unstamped."

FUNDED DEBT. A debt which is permanent, like Consols; that is, a debt upon which the Government pays regular interest without being under any obligation to repay the principal.

When an unfunded debt which is subject to repayment is changed into a permanent debt, the operation is called "funding the unfunded debt."

The Unfunded Debt of this country consists of Treasury Bills and Exchequer Bonds.

FUNDING THE UNFUNDED DEBT. (See Funded Debt.)

FUNDS. Consols and other Government securities are referred to as the Funds.

GARBLING. Where light gold coins and coins of full legal weight are in circulation together, the good coins are collected by goldsmiths and others and exported to be sold by weight, or are melted down to be used in the manufacture of jewellery. This action of picking out the good and leaving the light coins is termed garbling the coinage. (See Gresham's Law.)

GARNISHEE ORDER. Where a creditor has obtained judgment against a debtor for the payment of a debt, he may obtain from the Court an order attaching all money owing to the debtor from a third person, called the Garnishee. The rule is, "service of an order that debts, due or accruing to a debtor, under a judgment or order, shall be attached, or notice thereof to the garnishee, in such manner as the Court or judge shall direct, shall bind such debts in his hands."

Where a banker has funds belonging to the judgment debtor he may be served with a garnishee order, which order warns the banker not to part with any of the money belonging to that customer. A garnishee order binds the whole of the balance standing to the credit of the customer's account, at the time the order is served, even if that balance is more than sufficient to satisfy the garnishee order, and until the order is withdrawn no further cheques can be paid upon the account, not even cheques which were issued before the order was served on the banker. The banker should advise his customer of the service of a garnishee order. Money which is paid to credit after receipt of a garnishee order is not attached by the order and is at the disposal of the customer. To prevent any complication between the funds in hand when the order is served, and money received subsequently, it is better that the latter should be placed in a separate account.

Payment into Court by the banker of the amount of the judgment, or to the extent of the balance in his hands, will satisfy the garnishee order.

In the case of a joint account, it has been held that a garnishee order against one of the parties does not attach the balance on such joint account.

As stated above, a garnishee order attaches a debt which is due or which is accruing due. An ordinary deposit receipt repayable on demand is therefore attachable by a garnishee order. A receipt repayable at a certain fixed date, and a receipt repayable after certain notice has been given, in the event of the notice having been given before the garnishee order was served, are attachable by the order, because in each case it is a debt which is accruing due.

The following is a form of garnishee order:—

Garnishee Order (attaching Debt).

No.

In the High Court of Justice,
King's Bench Division.
District Registry.

Between

Judgment Creditor.

Judgment Debtor.

Garnishee.

Upon hearing Mr.
as Solicitor for the above-named Judgment Creditor, and upon reading the affidavit of the said
filed the day of , 19 .

It is ordered that all debts owing or accruing due from the above-named Garnishee to the above-named Judgment Debtor be attached to answer a judgment recovered against the said Judgment Debtor by the above-named Judgment Creditor in the High Court of Justice, on the day of 19 for the sum of £ , debt and costs on which Judgment the said sum of £ remains due and unpaid.

And it is further ordered that the said Garnishee attend the District Registrar in chambers, at the County Court offices on day, the day of 19 at o'clock in the noon, on an application by the said Judgment Creditor that the said Garnishee pay the debt due from to the said Judgment Debtor or so much thereof as may be sufficient to satisfy the Judgment.

Dated this day of 19 .

District Registrar.

(See CHARGING ORDER.)

GAVELKIND. (From A.-S. *Gafol*, tribute.) An old custom surviving in the County of Kent, and also in Kentish Town, North London, by which the real property of a person dying without a will descends, not to the eldest son, but to all the sons together as coparceners, just as it descends equally to the daughters if there are no sons; that is, a form of holding midway between tenants in common and joint tenants. (See COPARCENERS.) An interest in gavelkind, on the death of one of the sons, passes to his heir, or to his devisee if he leaves a will.

An infant of fifteen may alienate his gavelkind property, though he has not power to mortgage it.

GAZETTED. That is, published in the *London Gazette*. The production of a copy of the *London Gazette* containing any notice of a receiving order, or of an order adjudging a debtor bankrupt, shall be conclusive evidence in all legal proceedings of the order having been duly made, and of its date. (Section 132, s.s. 2, Bankruptcy Act, 1883.)

GENERAL ACCEPTANCE. (See ACCEPTANCE—GENERAL.)

GENERAL AVERAGE. A term used in connection with shipping. A clause usually found in a Charter Party is "General average as per York-Antwerp rules, 1890." The rules referred to are those which have been adopted at various times, by international conferences, York in 1864, Antwerp in 1877, and Liverpool in 1890. Where extraordinary sacrifices have been made, such as throwing cargo overboard or cutting away the masts or other parts of the ship, in order that the vessel and the rest of the cargo may be saved from destruction, the loss does not fall upon the owner of the ship or of the property thrown overboard, but is apportioned among all the parties; that is, the shipowner and the owners of the cargo (or the underwriters, if insured) according to their interest in the ship and cargo. The calculation of the amount payable by each party is usually made by persons called average adjusters. (See BILL OF LADING, CHARTER PARTY, PARTICULAR AVERAGE.)

GENERAL CROSSING. A cheque is crossed generally which bears across its face:—

1. The words "and Company" or any abbreviation thereof between two parallel transverse lines, either with or without the words "not negotiable."
2. Two parallel transverse lines simply, either with or without the words "not negotiable." (See CROSSED CHEQUE.)

GENERAL LEDGER. However many books may be in use or on whatever system they may be worked, they are all brought together in the general ledger. For instance the daily totals, debit and credit of current accounts, as shown in the day books, are posted each day into the general ledger under the heading "current accounts," and the balance is extended weekly or daily, as may be required. When the balances in the current account ledgers are extracted, they should prove with the balance of the "current accounts" account in the general ledger, and if the totals of the debit and credit sides in the current account ledgers are taken out they should agree with the corresponding totals in the general ledger. In proving the ledgers by totals, it is, of course, necessary that the general ledger account, at the commencement of the half-year, should begin with the total of the debit balances and the total of the credit balances, and not merely with the difference of the two sides.

The accounts which are found in a general ledger vary according to the bank, the system and the amount of sub-division which is considered necessary. The following is a list of a number of general ledger accounts which may be found in different banks, though not, of course, all in any one bank:—

Acceptances.
Agency.
Bank of England.
Bank Premises.
Bills Discounted.
Bills for Collection.
Bills of Exchange.
Bills Payable.
Bills Remitted.
Bills sold.
Bills in Suspense.
Bills Protested.
Branches.
Capital.
Cash.
Cash Errors.
Charges.
Cheque Books.
Circular Notes.
Clearing.
Country Banks.
Commission.
Credit Accounts.
Current Accounts.
Deposit Receipts.
Discount.
Dividend.
Exchange.
Head Office.
Indorsements on Bills Sold.
Interest.
Interest Adjustment.
Investments.

Investments Interest.
Letters of Credit.
Loans.
London Agents.
Money at Call and Short Notice.
Note Issue.
Overdue Bills.
Pension Fund.
Postages.
Profit and Loss.
Property.
Rents.
Reserve Fund.
Stamps.
Suspense.

In some banks several of the above accounts may be contained in a separate book, an impersonal ledger, and only the balance of that ledger posted to an account in the general ledger.

GIFT OF A CHEQUE. Where a cheque is handed to another person as a gift, that is, without any consideration, the receiver cannot sue the giver thereon. (See CONSIDERATION FOR BILL OF EXCHANGE.)

GIFTS INTER VIVOS. (Gifts between living persons.) As to the stamp duty on a conveyance operating as a voluntary disposition *inter vivos*, see Section 74 of the Finance (1909–10) Act, 1910, under heading CONVEYANCE.

Section 59 of the same Act provides, as to gifts and dispositions *inter vivos*, that in the case of a person dying on or after April 30, 1909, the period preceding the death of the deceased before which a disposition purporting to operate as an immediate gift *inter vivos* must have been made, in order that the property taken under the disposition may not be included as property passing on the death of the deceased, and so liable to death duties, shall be three years before the death.

So much of this Section as makes gifts *inter vivos* property which is deemed to pass on the death shall not apply to gifts made in consideration of marriage. (See DEED OF GIFT.)

GILT-EDGED BILL. A definition of a gilt-edged bill is given by a high banking authority, in the "Economist" (July, 1909), as "a bill drawn and negotiated abroad, of which the drawer, acceptor, and first indorser all enjoy the highest credit."

GILT-EDGED SECURITIES. Securities of the highest order and which are considered to be absolutely safe.

Stocks in which trustees may invest the trust moneys are "gilt-edged." (See TRUSTEE INVESTMENTS.)

GIVERS ON. In connection with the Stock Exchange settlements, a "giver on" is a broker who lends stock to a broker who requires it for delivery, and gives interest for the money lent to him on the stock. (See TAKERS IN.)

GOING CONCERN. A concern or undertaking which is in full working order. The value of, say, an ironworks as a going concern is usually far removed from the value of the same property when working operations have ceased. In the latter case the value is often not much more than that for old material. When taking any such security, a banker is therefore careful to remember that its value as a going concern may disappear entirely at the very time when it may be necessary to look to the security for repayment.

GOLD BONDS. In America, bonds of Railroad Companies which are repayable "in gold coin of the United States of the present standard of weight and fineness." The interest on the bonds is payable in like gold coin.

GOLD CERTIFICATES. Certificates which are issued by the Treasury of the United States as part of the paper currency. Gold is held against them and they are payable in gold. The certificates are for amounts from $20 to $10,000.

GOLD COINS. Gold was first coined in England about 1257.

The denominations of English gold coins as set forth in the Coinage Act are: Five Pound, Two Pound, Sovereign, Half Sovereign. The coins contain pure gold eleven-twelfths, copper alloy one-twelfth.

Gold coins are a legal tender to any amount so long as they do not fall below the least current weight as given in the Coinage Act.

The light yellow appearance of many Australian sovereigns is due to the alloy being in part of silver.

For checking sovereigns, scales and weights are invaluable as the amount can by their use be ascertained quickly and exactly. In the case of half sovereigns, owing to the lightness of many of the coins, the weights do not give such an accurate result as with the sovereigns, but if a hundred pounds of half sovereigns are counted these can then be used as a weight to balance another hundred of half-sovereigns and so on. When the gold has been counted, it is put into bags and each bag labelled with the amount it contains and initialled by the person who counted it. The gold that is necessary for immediate use across the counter is kept in various ways. It is usually put up either in bags containing such amounts as may be necessary, or in piles of £20 each. In some offices it is kept in paper rolls of £50 or £100, or in tin tubes standing upright in a box, each tube containing £20. (See BASE COINS, COINAGE.)

GOLD POINTS. (See SPECIE POINTS.)

GOLD RESERVES. In 1908 the Council of the London Chamber of Commerce appointed a Gold Reserves Committee "to consider whether the Gold Reserves of the country are sufficient, and, if not, what remedies can be suggested." The Committee consisted of leading bankers and men of business, and in July, 1909, the Report (which has been called an historic document) of the Committee was issued. Out of twenty-five surviving members of the Committee, five agreed to it subject to various material reservations.

The principal clauses of the report are as follows :—

"4. Your Committee has taken no evidence, but having debated the many and weighty proposals brought before it by its own members, has passed the following resolutions :—

"1. That the Committee recognises the desirability of strengthening the Gold Reserves of this country.

"2. That the issues of the Bank of England against Government debt and securities, commonly called the fiduciary issue, form an undue proportion of the whole, and should be reduced.

"3. That a reasonable reserve in gold should be held against the deposits in the Trustee and Post Office Savings Banks.

"4. That the Bullion Department of the Bank of England affords a means by its enlargement for the aggregation of gold reserves held by others than the Government of India, viz. :—

"(a) The banks of the United Kingdom, including the Bank of England, in respect of such gold held against their liabilities in excess of till money as any of them may elect to deposit in the Bullion Department.

"(b) Scotch and Irish banks in respect of all or any portion of the extra gold held by them against excess issues under the Act of 1845.

"(c) The National Debt Commissioners and the Postmaster-General in respect of the gold which the Committee recommend should be held against the liabilities of Trustee Savings Banks and Post Office Savings Banks respectively.

"5. That all persons or companies carrying on the business of banking within the United Kingdom should once in every calendar month, in case their liabilities on current and deposit accounts exceed in all the sum of ten million pounds sterling, and once in every three months in all other cases, make a statement of their position showing the average amounts of liabilities and assets on the basis of weekly balance sheets for the preceding month, or three preceding months, respectively, stating the following amounts separately :—

"(a) Liabilities on current, deposit, and other accounts.

"(b) Liabilities on notes in circulation.

"(c) Liabilities on bills accepted.

"(d) Gold and other coin and gold bullion held.

"(e) Bank of England notes held, and balance due by the Bank of England.

"(f) Balance due by clearing agents.

"And that a copy of the statement should be put up in a conspicuous place in every office or place where the business of the persons or company is carried on.

"6. That it is desirable that the Bank of England should make an annual return showing the aggregate bankers' balances for each week of the preceding year.

"5. In arriving at the conclusion that it is desirable to strengthen the Gold Reserves of the country, your Committee was influenced by the fact that the growth of aggregate liabilities, external and internal, has not been accompanied by a proportional increase of gold held by banks in the United Kingdom.

"6. Your Committee is also of opinion that, were larger reserves of gold in existence, a modifying influence as regards fluctuations of the official rate of discount, which are more frequent in this country than elsewhere, would probably be the result.

"7. The resolutions arrived at by your Committee resolve themselves into two main classes, viz., those *directly*, and those *indirectly*, affecting the Gold Reserves, the two not being altogether incompatible.

"8. The *direct* scheme for a central reserve has in view a fund of gold lodged for safe custody at the Bank of England, each owner retaining absolute and independent possession and control; the aggregate amount only to be made public.

"9. The *indirect* scheme has in view publication of the cash assets of every bank, divided into constituent parts. This would disclose the individual holding of gold of each bank.

"10. The resolutions arrived at show that your Committee consider that all concerned should bear their part in the cost involved in an increase in Gold Reserves, and specify :—

"(*a*) The Government,
"(*b*) The Bank of England,
"(*c*) The banks of the United Kingdom.

"11. In conclusion, your Committee beg to report their unanimous conviction that the time has arrived when the bankers themselves should come to an agreement on this important matter, and adopt measures to conserve and increase the gold held in the country, if it is wished to avoid legislative measures."

GOLDSMITHS' NOTES. The prototypes of the modern bank notes.

Before banking became a separate business in this country, goldsmiths received money on deposit and the receipts given for the money were called goldsmiths' notes. The notes were payable on demand, and circulated instead of coins.

GOOD FAITH. By the Bills of Exchange Act, 1882, Section 90 :—

"A thing is deemed to be done in good faith, within the meaning of this Act, where it is in fact done honestly, whether it is done negligently or not."

In a case in 1892, Lord Herschell said : "If there is anything which excites the suspicion that there is something wrong in the transaction, the taker of the instrument is not acting in good faith, if he shuts his eyes to the facts presented to him and puts the suspicions aside without further inquiry." (See HOLDER IN DUE COURSE.)

GOOD LEASEHOLD TITLE. Land may be registered under the Land Transfer Acts with a good leasehold title, which amounts to a guarantee by the Government of the leaseholder's title to the lease, but does not guarantee the original validity of the lease itself. (See LAND REGISTRY.)

GOODS. Where goods are in the custody of third parties a banker may advance upon them on receiving the bill of lading (*q.v.*) or the warrants which are the symbols or representatives of the goods. (See DOCUMENTARY BILL.)

If the goods are actually in the possession of the customer who desires an advance upon them, the security may be obtained by the goods being placed in a warehouse or building rented by the bank, the customer signing a document or letter of hypothecation, to show that the goods have been pledged for the advance and to give the banker a right to sell the goods, if necessary. In this way the goods are under the absolute control of the banker and cannot be dealt with until he releases them. Warrants for the goods are also furnished by the owner to the banker, and when any of the goods are sold the warrants require to be indorsed over by the banker to the purchaser. The goods should be insured in the banker's name.

Where the goods remain in the custody or control of the customer, some bankers grant a loan upon them on receiving a letter from the customer stating that certain specified goods are stored in his warehouse and are held to the order of the banker as security for the loan, and undertaking to repay the advance when the goods are sold. In such a case the banker is entirely dependent upon the honour of the customer. It has been held that a letter of hypothecation by a debtor, agreeing to hold goods in trust for a banker and to pay over the proceeds when received, was a bill of sale, because it was a "declaration of trust without transfer." The expression "bill of sale" includes a "declaration of trust without transfer." (See Section 4, Bills of Sale Act, 1878, under BILL OF SALE.) (See DOCK WARRANT, TRUST RECEIPT.)

GOODS AND CHATTELS. (See CHATTELS.)

GOODWILL. When a business is sold, the expression "goodwill" is used to indicate the benefit which the purchaser may be expected to obtain from the business connection formed in the premises, or from the good name which the vendor has created for himself. The goodwill of certain businesses is a valuable asset, and in selling a goodwill its value will depend partly upon the vendor agreeing not to enter into competition with the purchaser.

When a banker examines a balance sheet in which an item for goodwill appears, it is necessary to remember that "goodwill has no meaning except in connection with a continuing business" (Lindley's "Partnership").

GRANT. A conveyance in writing.

By the Stamp Act, 1891, the stamp duty is :—

	£	s.	d.
GRANT of copyhold or customary estates. See CONVEYANCE—COPYHOLD.			
GRANT of the custody of the person or estate of a lunatic . . .	2	0	0

GREENBACKS. The popular name for the notes which were first issued by the Government of the United States in 1862. The backs of the notes are printed in green ink, whence the origin of the term, "greenbacks." They are legal tender in that country. (See FOREIGN MONEYS—UNITED STATES.)

GRESHAM'S LAW. Where new coins and old worn coins are current at the same time, the new coins gradually disappear and leave the old worn ones in circulation. The first person who discovered and explained the cause of the disappearance of good coins from circulation was Sir Thomas Gresham in the sixteenth century. The principle or law (now called Gresham's Law) which he stated is: "If coins of the same metal, but of varying weight and quality, circulate together at the same nominal value, the worse coins will tend to drive the better from circulation, but the better will never drive out the worse."

The practice of picking out the coins of full weight and leaving the light ones in circulation (called garbling the coinage), is carried on principally by goldsmiths or other persons who melt the coins for jewellery, or export them and sell them by weight. In the ordinary course of business very little attention is paid to a coin, so long as the stamp upon it is visible, whether it is a light one or not. (See COINAGE.)

GROAT. Fourpence. Its standard weight is 29·09090 grains troy, but it is not now issued except as Maundy money (*q.v.*).

Groat is from the French word *gros*, indicating the size of the coin, as, when first coined by Edward III, it was the largest silver coin then known. (See COINAGE.)

GROSS PROFIT. The total profit, or gain, before the deduction of expenses.

GROSS RENTAL. The rent of a property before the deduction of rates, taxes, repairs or other outgoings. (See VALUATION.)

GROUND RENTS. Rents which are reserved to the owner of a freehold and which are payable by the person to whom the land has been leased. For example, if the owner of freehold land leases a portion to a person, called the lessee or leaseholder, he stipulates that he must receive, during the continuance of the lease, a certain yearly rent, that is a ground rent. In the case of a building lease the lessee is obliged to build upon the land, and as he erects houses he sub-leases them to other parties, who in their turn pay ground rents to him. If the lessee pays a ground rent to the freeholder of, say, £100 a year, and the lessee builds houses, and sub-leases, say, twenty houses at a ground rent of £10 each per annum, the lessee thus obtains £200 a year and, after paying the freeholder the £100, he has a profit left of £100 a year; this profit is termed the improved ground rent. At the termination of a lease the buildings become the property of the lessor.

Where ground rents are offered as a security, the banker should ascertain what buildings there are upon the land, otherwise he might find himself in possession of a deed creating ground rents, but without any buildings to secure the rents.

GUARANTEE. GUARANTY. (French *garantir*, to warrant.) A guarantee is an undertaking by one person (called the guarantor) given to a banker (the creditor), to be answerable for the debt of another person (the debtor) to the banker, upon default of the debtor.

In order to be enforceable at law, a guarantee must be in writing. By the Statute of Frauds (29 Car. II, c. 3), Section 4, it is enacted that "no action shall be brought whereby to charge the defendant upon any special promise to answer for the debt, default or miscarriages of another person, unless the agreement upon which such action shall be brought, or some memorandum or note thereof shall be in writing and signed by the party to be charged therewith, or some other person thereunto by him lawfully authorised."

A guarantee is a very convenient form of security, and because of the ease with which it can be given, a banker should be careful to make clear to a proposed surety the nature of the document which he has to sign, so that he may not afterwards plead that he did not understand its contents.

A contract of suretyship should be entered into freely and voluntarily by the guarantor. "Everything like pressure used by the intending creditor will have a very serious effect on the validity of the contract" (Mr. Justice Fry in *Davies* v. *London and Provincial Marine Insurance Company*, 1878, 8 Ch. D. 469).

In an ordinary case a banker is not obliged to give information, voluntarily, to a proposed surety, regarding the debtor's affairs. "Unless questions are particularly put by the surety to gain this information, I hold that it is quite unnecessary for the creditor, to whom the suretyship is given, to make any such disclosure" (Lord Campbell, in *Hamilton* v. *Watson*, 1845, 12 Cl. & F. 109).

If a guarantor inquires as to the extent of his liability upon the account for which he is surety, he is entitled to the information, but a banker should not exhibit the debtor's account to a surety or give details regarding it.

When a guarantor is proposed, it is a banker's duty to consider whether he is sufficient for the liability, and whether from his business and position he is likely to continue, in every way, a satisfactory surety. For instance, could he discharge the guarantee with ease, or would it render him practically penniless to pay the amount? Is he under any other liabilities to the bank, and is he likely to have signed a guarantee for a friend at any other bank? When a person signs a guarantee he does not expect that he will ever be called upon to pay it; but a banker should look upon the transaction from quite the opposite point of view, and should try to realise what the position will be, assuming that the guarantor will be required to meet the liability.

A man may be well able to meet all demands which may be made upon him in connection with his own business or his own private affairs, but it is quite another matter when he has to provide a substantial sum to pay the debts of someone else. In estimating the value of any one as a surety the point is, as George Rae puts it in "The Country Banker": "Not what you might be able to squeeze out of him by process of exhaustion, but what he could at any time pay, over and above his other engagements, without serious inconvenience or detriment to himself. That is the true meaning of his fitness as a surety; and if you take him for more than this, you may do him a fatal disservice, and possibly lay the foundation of a bad debt for yourselves."

A lady is not, as a rule, regarded as a suitable surety.

A guarantee may take the form of a bond or a guarantee under seal, in which cases an *ad valorem* stamp of 2*s.* 6*d.* per cent. is required. The usual form, however, is a guarantee under hand. The stamp duty on a guarantee under hand is sixpence (see AGREEMENT). The stamp may be either impressed or adhesive; if adhesive, it must be cancelled by the first person signing the guarantee. If the document has been signed before being stamped, the stamp may be impressed within fourteen days from its date. If a guarantee is sealed by a company, the document is subject to *ad valorem* duty of 2*s.* 6*d.* per cent. (See BOND.)

It is essential that a guarantee form should be most carefully drawn so as to create an effective security, and most bankers have now their own printed forms of guarantees drafted so as to meet, as far as possible, the various requirements of a good and complete guarantee.

The surety's signature should, as a rule, be witnessed by a bank official, and some bankers require it to be witnessed by two officials. Where the surety lives in another town, the document should be sent to a bank in that town and the surety be requested to call there to sign it.

If there are any alterations in the document, they should be initialled by the guarantor; and if the guarantee being given is in addition to one already signed by him for the same account, a clause should be added at the end of the guarantee to the effect that "this guarantee is in addition to and not in substitution of my guarantee dated for £ ," and the clause should be signed by the guarantor.

Where there are more guarantors than one, the guarantee should be "joint and several." The banker can then sue one, or all, of the guarantors as he may consider necessary. If he sues one surety and fails to obtain all that is required, he may then sue the others. This could not be done if the guarantee was "joint" only. In a "joint" guarantee, all the sureties must be sued together, and if one of them died his estate would not be liable. The banker in that case would have to look to the surviving guarantors; but if the guarantee is "joint and several," the estate of a deceased surety would be liable. In a "several" guarantee, each one of the guarantors may be sued separately for the full amount. The most satisfactory guarantee for a banker to take is, therefore, a "joint and several" one.

A consideration is not necessary in a guarantee under seal, but in a guarantee under hand, i.e. a simple contract, there must be a consideration. The consideration, as a general rule, is the granting of an advance to a customer against the guarantee, or it may be the granting of further time to a debtor. A banker's guarantee usually states the consideration, but the document is not invalid merely by reason that the consideration is not expressed therein. By the Mercantile Law Amendment Act, 1856, 19 & 20 Vict. c. 97, Section 3, "no special promise to be made by any person after the passing of this Act to answer for the debt, default, or miscarriage of another person, being in writing, and signed by the party to be charged therewith, or some other person by him thereunto lawfully authorised, shall be deemed invalid to support an action, suit, or other proceeding to charge the person by whom such promise shall have been made, by reason only that the consideration for such promise does not appear in writing, or by necessary inference from a written document."

An important point in connection with a guarantee is that it should be a continuing guarantee, that is, a security which will continue, although the balance of the debtor's account may fluctuate from time to time. A guarantee should therefore expressly state that it "shall be a continuing guarantee," otherwise it might be held to cover merely the debt which existed at the time the guarantee was given.

Where a guarantee for, say, £1,000 is to continue in force until the expiration of three months' notice in writing, and when the account is overdrawn, say, £500, the surety gives notice, can the banker let the customer go on drawing cheques pending the notice and let him draw out the whole £1,000? Sir John Paget, in his Gilbart Lecture (No. 3), 1909, considers that "the banker would run great risk if he adopted this course voluntarily . . . all outstanding cheques, bills accepted for the customer prior to revocation and maturing during pendency of notice and things of that sort are covered by the clause. Possibly it might cover other transactions in the ordinary course of business begun prior to revocation and completed during currency of notice."

With respect to a guarantee which contained the words "to continue in force until three months after notice," it has been held that notice to the bank of the death of the guarantor amounted to a determination of the guarantee so far as future advances were concerned.

If there is no question of notice arising, when the surety informs the banker that he withdraws from any further liability under his guarantee, it will be at the banker's own risk if he pays any further cheques after receipt of such notice; but if he has promised the debtor to pay certain specific cheques, those cheques must be paid.

In order that a banker may be entitled to claim upon a debtor's estate, and, if necessary, to require payment in full of the guarantee, the guarantee should be drawn so as to cover all moneys which now are or shall at any time hereafter be due and owing and to apply to and secure any ultimate balance that shall remain after the banker has obtained dividends or compositions from the debtor's estate. In the case of *In re Sass, Ex parte National Provincial Bank of England* (1896, 2 Q.B. 12), a surety guaranteed the payment of all sums of money which were or might from time to time become due or owing to the bank on the account of S. and the guarantee was limited to the amount of £300. The guarantee gave the bank the right to receive dividends from the debtor's estate. On the bankruptcy of S. the bank, after receiving the £300 from the surety, claimed to prove on the estate for the full amount due. It was held by Vaughan Williams, J., that although the surety's liability was limited, still "his suretyship was in respect of the whole debt, and he, having paid only a part of that debt, has in my judgment no right of proof in preference or priority to the bank to whom he became guarantor."

Under an ordinary banker's guarantee form, the banker can prove upon his customer's estate for the full amount of the debt (allowing for any securities held from the debtor himself) and require payment in full, if necessary, from the guarantor of the amount of his guarantee.

Upon receiving notice of the death of a surety, the debtor's account should be stopped pending fresh arrangements, unless the guarantee expressly provides that the estate of the deceased surety is to continue liable.

Where there are several sureties and one of them dies, the account should be broken, until a fresh guarantee is signed or the surviving sureties have given a written request that the existing guarantee be continued.

If a deceased surety's estate is to be held liable, notice of the guarantee should be given to the legal representatives.

Upon default of a debtor, a banker should require payment at once from a surety of the amount of his guarantee. When the guarantor pays up, the amount should be placed to a separate account, and not go directly in reduction of the debtor's account, if the banker intends to claim upon the debtor's estate. If the sum tendered by the guarantor is sufficient to clear off the debt, the amount is usually placed at once to credit of the debtor's account.

When a surety has paid off the full amount of the debt on the account for which he is guarantor, he is entitled to the rights of the banker, that is to sue the debtor and to receive the benefit of any securities held by the banker for the debt, whether the securities were held at the time the guarantee was given, or were subsequently received.

By the Mercantile Law Amendment Act, 1856, Section 5:—

"Every person who, being surety for the debt or duty of another, or being liable with another for any debt or duty, shall pay such debt or perform such duty, shall be entitled to have assigned to him, or to a trustee for him, every judgment, specialty, or other security which shall be held by the creditor in respect of such debt or duty, whether such judgment, specialty, or other security shall or shall not be deemed at law to have been satisfied by the payment of the debt or performance of the duty, and such person shall be entitled to stand in the place of the creditor, and to use all the remedies, and, if need be, and upon a proper indemnity, to use the name of the creditor, in any action, or other proceeding, at law or in equity, in order to obtain from the principal debtor, or any co-surety, co-contractor, or co-debtor, as the case may be, indemnification for the advances made and loss sustained by the person who shall have so paid such debt or performed such duty, and such payment or performance so made by such surety shall not be pleadable in bar of any such action or other proceeding by him; provided always, that no co-surety, co-contractor, or co-debtor, shall be entitled to recover from any other co-surety, co-contractor, or co-debtor, by the means aforesaid, more than the just proportion to which, as between those parties themselves, such last-mentioned person shall be justly liable."

When a surety pays off an account and requires any securities to be given up to him, the banker should, before parting with them, communicate with the debtor or any other parties concerned with the account.

If, under a joint and several guarantee, a banker obtains payment of the full amount of the guarantee from one of the sureties, that surety can call upon his co-sureties to pay him their proportion of the amount. Unless specially provided against in the guarantee, if a banker releases one of several joint co-sureties that release may have the effect of releasing all the sureties. Before releasing one of several sureties a banker should, unless the guarantee provides for such a release, obtain the written assent of the other sureties, or take a fresh guarantee.

When a surety gives notice to terminate a guarantee, the banker should, if possible, obtain the notice in writing.

If after all dividends have been received from the bankrupt's estate, the guarantee money in the banker's hands should be more than sufficient to clear off the indebtedness, the balance remaining should be returned to the surety, or, if several sureties, to each one in proportion to the amount he paid.

A guarantee under hand is barred by the Statute of Limitations in six years from the date when the right of action first accrued against the guarantor. If there is a clause in the guarantee that payment is to be made "   days after demand," the statute in such a case will not begin to run until the demand has been made. It is advisable, however, whether the guarantee includes such a clause, or not, to get all guarantees renewed before they are six years old. Not only does such a course prevent the guarantee from becoming statute barred, but it brings to the notice of the surety the fact that his liability still continues.

A guarantee under seal is not barred till twenty years from the date when the cause of action arose. But if the guarantee is in respect of a debt secured by a mortgage of land, the period is twelve years by the Real Property Limitation Act of 1874, whether the covenant of the surety is in the mortgage deed itself, or is contained in a collateral bond.

Payments to the credit of an account by a debtor keep the debt alive as against the debtor, but they do not prevent the statute from running in favour of a surety. (See STATUTE OF LIMITATIONS.)

In the important case of *Parr's Banking Company* v. *Yates* (1898, 2 Q.B. 460), where the bank held a continuing guarantee from Yates for an account, Vaughan Williams, L.J., said: "My view is that the cause of action on the guarantee arose as to each item of the account, whether principal, interest, commission, or other banking charge, as soon as that item became due and was not paid, and, consequently, the Statute of Limitations began to run in favour of the defendant in respect of each item from that date. I agree with what my brothers have said with regard to the claim for interest. I think that the interest stands on the same footing as any other item to the debit of the party guaranteed in the account; and that the defendant continues liable as guarantor in respect of interest which has accrued within six years before action, and does not get rid of that liability because his liability to be sued on the guarantee with regard to the principal has become barred by the Statute of Limitations. I also agree that there is no ground for saying that there is any rule which could apply the payments which have been made to the interest on the advances made to the party guaranteed as distinguished from the principal. According to the ordinary practice of bankers, the interest due is from time to time added to the principal, and becomes itself part of the principal due."

The balance for which a surety is responsible is the general balance of the customer's account, and all accounts between the customer and the banker at the time the guarantee comes to an end must be taken into account. (*In re Sherry, London and County Banking Co.* v. *Terry*, 1884, 25 Ch. D. 692.)

Upon the failure of a guarantor, unless the debtor supplies other security, the banker should call in his advance and, if repayment is not made, claim upon the surety's estate.

Where there are several sureties and one of them gives notice to terminate his liability, the account of the debtor should be broken until fresh arrangements are made.

Any material variation of the original agreement between the debtor and creditor, unless provided for in the guarantee or made with the assent of the guarantor, will have the effect of releasing the guarantor from liability. In *Samuel* v. *Howarth* (1817, 3 Mer. 272), Lord Eldon said: "The surety is held to be discharged for this reason, because the creditor, by so giving time to the principal, has put it out of the power of the surety to consider whether he will have recourse to his remedy against the principal or not, and because he, in fact, cannot have the same remedy against the principal as he would have had under the original contract."

Where a guarantee has been given for a fixed period and at the end of that period it is arranged that it be continued for a further period, either a new guarantee should be taken or the old guarantee should be indorsed accordingly and bear another sixpenny stamp. Any such indorsement should, of course, be signed by the guarantor, or, if more than one, by all of them. If a new guarantee has not been obtained, or the old one extended, before the fixed period expires, the account should be stopped when the date arrives until a fresh arrangement is made.

A guarantee by a married woman can be enforced only against her separate estate.

In the case of a guarantee by a firm, it should, in order to avoid the risk of any future trouble, be signed by each partner.

Where a partnership account is overdrawn and a guarantee is taken from the partners in their private capacities to secure the firm's account, the banker will then have a claim upon the private estates of the partners, as well as upon the partnership estate.

Where a change of partnership takes place and a guarantee is held for the account, unless the form provides for such change, the account should be broken until fresh arrangements are made.

By Section 18 of the Partnership Act, 1890:—"A continuing guaranty or cautionary obligation given either to a firm or to a third person in respect of the transactions of a firm is, in the absence of agreement to the contrary, revoked as to future transactions by any change in the constitution of the firm to which, or of the firm in respect of the transactions of which, the guaranty or obligation was given."

Before accepting a guarantee by a company, a banker should see that the memorandum of association gives power to the company to give a guarantee.

When a guarantee has been discharged, or is no longer required, it is the practice of some bankers to give it up to the guarantor, whilst other bankers prefer to retain the document, after being cancelled by, or in the presence of, the surety.

GUARANTEED STOCK. Stock upon which the due payment of the interest is guaranteed either by the company issuing the stock or by another company. Sometimes payment of the principal also is guaranteed.

GUARANTOR. A surety. A person who gives a guarantee to a banker (or other creditor), agreeing to be answerable for the debt of another person if he should fail to repay. (See GUARANTEE.)

GUARD BOOK. A book for guarding or protecting loose documents. The documents are usually gummed or pasted on one margin and fastened to the paper edges in the book.

GUARDIANS OF THE POOR. The Treasurer of a Board of Guardians must keep an account in the prescribed form of all moneys received and paid by him on account of the Guardians.

Orders drawn upon the Treasurer require to be signed by the presiding chairman, two guardians, and countersigned by the clerk to the Guardians (Article 84, General Order of the Poor Law Commissioners, 1847). By Article 194 of the same Order, "the vice chairman, or some guardian appointed by the Guardians may perform any of the duties assigned to the clerk, until the vacancy is filled or a substitute appointed in case of sickness or absence." In practice, when the clerk is absent, the vice-chairman usually countersigns.

The orders are exempt from stamp duty (4 & 5 Wm. IV, c. 76, Section 86). Per procuration indorsements are not accepted.

One of the duties of a Treasurer is, whenever there are not funds belonging to the Guardians in his hands as Treasurer of the Union, to report in writing the fact of such deficiency to the Local Government Board.

The Treasurer's book is required to be balanced half-yearly, at the end of March and end of September. As the last day of each half year must be a Friday, the exact date varies.

With regard to borrowing powers, reference should be made to the Statute under which a power to borrow is obtained, so as to ascertain the extent of the power, and whether the sanction of the Local Government Board or other authority is required. If money is borrowed without power, or sanction, the interest thereon will probably be disallowed.

The following regulations are from a General Order of the Local Government Board :—

ARTICLE II.—In any case in which the Poor Law Authority appoint or have appointed as their Treasurer a person who is—

(a) a member of a partnership firm or a director of a joint stock company carrying on the business of banking, or

(b) a person in the service or employment of any other person or of any partnership firm or joint stock company carrying on the business of banking,

the Poor Law Authority may accept as the security for the good conduct of the person so appointed their Treasurer,—

(a) in the case of a member of a partnership firm, or of a director of a joint stock company as aforesaid, any such suitable and sufficient guarantee as the partnership firm or company can lawfully give, or

(b) in the case of a person in the service or employment of any other person, or of any partnership firm or joint stock company as aforesaid, any such suitable and sufficient guarantee as the other person, partnership firm, or company can lawfully give.

ARTICLE III.—(1) Every Order issued by the Poor Law Commissioners, the Poor Law Board, or by Us, prescribing a form of Order to be drawn by the Poor Law Authority upon their Treasurer for the payment of money shall, where the Poor Law Authority by a resolution so determine, have effect as if any request that an Order drawn upon the Treasurer may be presented to the Treasurer at his house, were omitted from the said Form.

ARTICLE IV.—(1) Where the Treasurer of the Poor Law Authority is a banker, or a person in the service or employment of a banker, and the Poor Law Authority consent, any person in the service or employment of the Treasurer in his capacity of banker, and any other person in the service or employment of the banker in whose service or employment the Treasurer is, may, on behalf of the Treasurer, in any establishment wherein the banking business is carried on, give a receipt for money paid to the Treasurer, or indorse any cheque or order payable to the order of the Treasurer. (See LOCAL AUTHORITIES.)

GUILDER. Same as gulden. (See FOREIGN MONEYS—HOLLAND.)

GUINEA. A gold coin at one time current in Great Britain at the value of twenty-one shillings. It was first coined in 1663 from gold brought from the coast of Guinea, whence its name. It is still the custom with many people to quote fees and subscriptions in guineas, rather than in pounds.

GUINEA PIG. A slang Stock Exchange expression to signify a person who acts as a director of various companies merely for the sake of the fees to be obtained.

GULDEN. (See FOREIGN MONEYS—HOLLAND.)

HALF-CROWN. Half-crowns were first coined in 1551.

The standard weight of a half-crown is 218·18181 grains troy, and its standard fineness thirty-seven-fortieths fine silver, three-fortieths alloy. (See COINAGE.)

HALF-HOLIDAYS. Nearly all banks have one half-day holiday in the week, but there is no general rule as to which day in the week it should be. The day is dependent entirely upon local circumstances, but the one in most favour is, naturally, Saturday. On a half-holiday the doors are closed to the public at 12 or 1 o'clock. (See BANK HOLIDAYS.)

HALF NOTES. A bank note which is to be remitted by post is sometimes cut in halves, and one half sent by post. When an acknowledgment is received, the other half is sent. The receiver of halves should fix the respective halves together with strips of gummed paper, and see that the numbers correspond, otherwise much trouble will be caused if a note gets into circulation (as sometimes occurs) with a different number on each half.

A person remitting notes in halves does not part with the property in the notes until he has sent the second halves, and until then he may reclaim the first halves which he sent.

If one half of a note is lost, the issuing banker will usually pay the amount upon production of the other half, provided that a satisfactory indemnity is given for his so paying.

Half notes are legally described as goods and chattels, though notes are described as money.

HALFPENNY. It is made of bronze—that is, a mixture of copper, tin and zinc. Its standard weight is 87·50000 grains troy.

The diameter of a halfpenny is exactly one inch. (See COINAGE.)

HALF-SOVEREIGN. Its standard weight is 61·63723 grains troy and its standard fineness eleven-twelfths fine gold, one-twelfth alloy. When its weight, from wear and tear, falls below 61·125 grains troy it ceases to be legal tender. (See COINAGE.)

HAMMERED. When a member of the Stock Exchange is unable to meet his liabilities, his failure is announced in the "House" after attention has been obtained by one of the waiters giving three blows on his stand with a wooden hammer. A defaulter is thus said to be "hammered."

HAND AND SEAL. The phrase "as witness our hands and seals" which is found at the end of a deed of transfer and other deeds, refers to the signatures and seals which follow. But the word "hand" originally meant an actual impression in ink upon the deed of the person's hand.

HARD CASH. The term is applied to coins, in contradistinction to bank notes which are sometimes called "soft money."

HEIR. The heir or heir-at-law is the person who is entitled, by law, to the real property of a deceased person who left no will.

In ascertaining who is heir, the eldest son and his descendants come first, then the other sons in order and their descendants. If there are no sons, but only daughters, they succeed to the property as co-parceners—that is, they succeed to it equally.

HEIR-APPARENT. The person who is certain to succeed to an estate if he survives the present owner.

HEIR-PRESUMPTIVE. The person who would succeed to an estate if the present owner died at once, but whose right to succeed would be cancelled in the event of a child being born having a prior right.

HELD OVER. When a cheque upon a local bank is received by a banker, after the daily exchange has been made, it is usually "held over" till the following day. But cheques received by a banker, drawn upon his own office, are not (except in certain cases in connection with a local clearing in large towns) "held over," as they should either be paid or dishonoured on the day of receipt.

HELLER. (See FOREIGN MONEYS—AUSTRIA AND HUNGARY.)

HEREDITAMENT. From the Latin *heredito*, I inherit.

Heritable property is property, such as land, which descends to the heir.

HERIOT. In connection with copyhold land there is, in some cases, on the death of the tenant a fine, or heriot, due to the lord of the Manor. The heriot may take the form of the best beast or best jewel or plate which belonged to the deceased, or it may be a money payment.

HERITABLE BOND. In Scotland, a bond by a debtor for a sum of money, which includes a conveyance of land, to be held by the creditor as security for the money. (See BOND AND DISPOSITION IN SECURITY.)

For the stamp duty see MORTGAGE, etc., and Section 86.

HOLDER FOR VALUE. A holder for value of a bill of exchange is defined by Section 27 of the Bills of Exchange Act, 1882 :—

"(2) Where value has at any time been given for a bill the holder is deemed to be a holder for value as regards the acceptor and all parties to the bill who became parties prior to such time.

"(3) Where the holder of a bill has a lien on it, arising either from contract or by implication of law, he is deemed to be a holder for value to the extent of the sum for which he has a lien."

By Section 30 :—

"(1) Every party whose signature appears on a bill is *primâ facie* deemed to have become a party thereto for value."

A holder for value is not liable upon a bill unless he has indorsed it, but he may sue on the bill in his own name.

The holder for value of a bill may be the payee who is in possession of it, or an indorsee who is in possession of it, or the bearer of it.

Until value is given no party can sue upon a bill. If, for example, no value is given on a bill till it reaches the hands of a third indorser, none of the parties before that third indorser can sue upon the bill, but the third indorser, because he has given value, can sue all the prior parties. If that third indorser transfers to a fourth person, without any value being given, that person cannot sue the third indorser, seeing he did not give value to the third indorser for the bill, but he can sue all the parties to the bill that the third indorser had the right to sue.

The holder of a bill payable to his order must indorse it. When the holder of a bill payable to bearer (see BEARER) negotiates it by delivery, without indorsing it, he is called a "transferor by delivery" and warrants to his immediate transferee that the bill is what it purports to be.

If the title of a holder for value is defective, as where the bill was obtained by fraud, duress, or force and fear, or for an illegal consideration, he cannot recover the amount from the person defrauded or otherwise. But a "holder in due course" can sue any party to the bill. No title, however, can be obtained through a forged signature. (See BILL OF EXCHANGE, CHEQUE, CONSIDERATION FOR BILL OF EXCHANGE, HOLDER IN DUE COURSE.)

HOLDER IN DUE COURSE. The Bills of Exchange Act, 1882, Section 29, defines a holder in due course as follows :—

"(1) A holder in due course is a holder who has taken a bill, complete and regular on the face of it, under the following conditions, namely :—

"(*a*) That he became the holder of it before it was overdue, and without notice that it had been previously dishonoured, if such was the fact :

"(*b*) That he took the bill in good faith and for value, and that at the time the bill was negotiated to him he had no notice of any defect in the title of the person who negotiated it.

"(2) In particular the title of a person who negotiates a bill is defective within the meaning of this Act when he obtained the bill, or the acceptance thereof, by fraud, duress, or force and fear, or other unlawful means, or for an illegal consideration, or when he negotiates it in breach of faith, or under such circumstances as amount to a fraud.

"(3) A holder (whether for value or not) who derives his title to a bill through a holder in due course, and who is not himself a party to any fraud or illegality affecting it, has all the rights of that holder in due course as regards the acceptor and all parties to the bill prior to that holder."

A payee is said not to come within the

definition of a holder in due course (see s.s. 1, above) as the bill is not complete until it is indorsed by the payee.

By Section 30 :—

"(1) Every party whose signature appears on a bill is *primâ facie* deemed to have become a party thereto for value.

"(2) Every holder of a bill is *primâ facie* deemed to be a holder in due course; but if in an action on a bill it is admitted or proved that the acceptance, issue, or subsequent negotiation of the bill is affected with fraud, duress, or force and fear, or illegality, the burden of proof is shifted, unless and until the holder proves that, subsequent to the alleged fraud or illegality, value has in good faith been given for the bill."

The meaning of "good faith" is given in Section 90 :—

"A thing is deemed to be done in good faith, within the meaning of this Act, where it is in fact done honestly, whether it is done negligently or not."

If, for example, Jones is a holder in due course, he has the right to sue any party to the bill, but if in an action it is proved that the bill is affected with some taint, as described in the above sections, it will be necessary for Jones, in order to preserve his rights, to show that he gave value for the bill subsequent to the alleged taint, and that he took it in good faith without knowledge of anything being wrong with the bill.

If Jones, the holder in due course, transfers the bill to Brown, but without any value being given therefor, Brown obtains the same rights that Jones had and can sue any party prior to Jones, but he cannot sue Jones because of the absence of consideration.

"No consideration" is a good defence between parties closely related on a bill, but a holder in due course is not affected by the fact of their having been "no consideration" between any parties before it was transferred to him for value.

Section 38 deals with the rights of a holder :—

"The rights and powers of the holder of a bill are as follows :—

"(1) He may sue on the bill in his own name :

"(2) Where he is a holder in due course, he holds the bill free from any defect of title of prior parties, as well as from mere personal defences available to prior parties among themselves, and may enforce payment against all parties liable on the bill :

"(3) Where his title is defective (*a*) if he negotiates the bill to a holder in due course, that holder obtains a good and complete title to the bill, and (*b*) if he obtains payment of the bill the person who pays him in due course gets a valid discharge for the bill."

Where a signature on a bill is forged, no one can obtain any right to the bill through or under that signature. (See BILL OF EXCHANGE, FORGERY, HOLDER FOR VALUE.)

HOLDER OF BILL OF EXCHANGE. The holder of a bill is the person who is in possession of it and may be either the payee, or an indorser, or the bearer.

There are three kinds of holders, a simple holder of a bill, a holder for value, and a holder in due course.

If the holder of a bill has not given value for it, he cannot sue any party subsequent to the last indorsement when value was given.

The holder of a bill, unless it is indorsed payable to him, need not indorse it, though, as a rule, any person taking a bill would require the person from whom he takes it to indorse it. The person receiving a bill has the right to demand the indorsement of the transferor if the bill was payable to his order.

If a bill is payable to the holder's order, he must indorse it, whether the transferee demands his indorsement or not.

Where the holder of a bill payable to bearer (see BEARER) negotiates it by delivery, without indorsing it, he is called a "transferor by delivery" and warrants to his immediate transferee that the bill is what it purports to be.

A transferor by delivery is not liable on the bill—that is, he is not liable thereon if he has not indorsed it, though if he is a holder for value he may sue all, or any, of the parties to the bill. That, however, does not affect the transferee's right to sue the transferor for the debt. Judgment obtained against one party will not release the others. If the title of a holder for value is defective, he is not in as good a position as a holder in due course.

Neither a holder for value nor a holder in due course can obtain a title to a bill through a forged signature.

Any holder may convert a blank

indorsement into a special indorsement by writing above the indorser's signature a direction to pay the bill to the order of himself or some other person.

A holder may strike out any indorsement on a bill, and the person whose signature is struck out is thereby released from liability, and so are all subsequent indorsers. A banker usually cancels his indorsement on a dishonoured bill.

If a holder receives payment of a bill from an indorser, the bill must be given up to that indorser, who will then have all the rights of the holder from whom he received it. (See PAYMENT FOR HONOUR.)

A banker is under no liability on a cheque or bill to a holder, unless he has in some way given the holder to understand that the cheque or bill will be paid. (See BILL OF EXCHANGE, HOLDER FOR VALUE, HOLDER IN DUE COURSE.)

HOLDING OUT. In the Partnership Act, 1890, Section 14, it is enacted that everyone who by words spoken or written, or by conduct represents himself, or who knowingly suffers himself to be represented, as a partner in a particular firm, is liable as a partner to anyone who has on the faith of any such representation given credit to the firm. (See PARTNERSHIPS.)

HOLIDAYS. In addition to a weekly half-holiday and the legal bank holidays (see BANK HOLIDAYS) there are occasional local holidays in some districts, and the bankers generally agree to close upon such occasions, either altogether or for the greater part of the day. Where a special holiday of this nature is arranged, a notice to that effect is exhibited in the bank offices for some time prior to the date. On the day of the holiday it is necessary that anything urgent in the remittances or correspondence, and all bills maturing, be duly attended to.

But the principal holiday is the annual one, and the length of it varies according to the arrangements existing in different banks. Some banks allow two weeks' holiday in the year to managers and clerks alike, but in many banks the managers are granted a longer period than the clerks. In other banks the number of weeks which is allowed is dependent upon the length of service, as for example after fifteen or twenty years' service three weeks are allowed. Some banks allow their managers a holiday of a clear month.

HOLIDAYS EXTENSION ACT, 1875. (See BANK HOLIDAYS.)

HOLOGRAPH. A document which is entirely, or almost entirely, written by the person who signs it. A holograph cheque is less likely to be a forgery than if it is merely signed by the drawer.

In Scotland, when a surety signs a printed form of guarantee, he sometimes writes above his signature "adopted as holograph." (See ATTESTATION.)

HOUSE. The word is used with reference to the Bankers' Clearing House, the Stock Exchange, or a large London Bank Office, as the case may be.

HOUSE DUTY. (See INHABITED HOUSE DUTY.)

HUSBAND AND WIFE ACCOUNT. When an account is opened in the name of a husband and wife it is generally with the intention that either may sign upon the account and that the balance may pass to the survivor. As the account is the same as an ordinary joint account, the bank's usual form should be signed by both parties authorising the banker to honour the signature of either.

Where the husband dies first there is the possibility that the money may be held to pass to the deceased's executors, unless it can be proved that it was the intention of the deceased that the balance should belong to his widow. To avoid any trouble, a definite arrangement should be made when the account is opened.

HYPOTHECATION. Property which is mortgaged or pledged is sometimes said to be hypothecated; but the precise meaning of the word is the charging of property to a creditor while the property itself remains in the possession of the debtor. (See DOCUMENTARY BILL, TRUST RECEIPT.)

IMMEDIATE ANNUITY. An immediate annuity is payable commencing with a payment six months after the purchase is completed and terminating at death.

For example, at the age of thirty-five £100 may purchase an immediate annuity of £4 18*s*. 6*d*. (See ANNUITY.)

IMMEDIATE PARTIES. The "immediate parties" to a bill of exchange are those in close relationship, as the drawer and acceptor, the drawer and payee, and an indorser and the immediately preceding indorser. (See PARTIES TO BILL OF EXCHANGE.)

IMPERIAL. (See FOREIGN MONEYS—RUSSIA.)

IMPERSONAL ACCOUNTS. Accounts

which are not connected with persons, e.g. expenses, interest, discount, Head Office account, bills, shares, rent, premises.

Some banks keep all such accounts in a separate book, called an "impersonal ledger."

IMPERSONAL LEDGER. A number of accounts such as interest, commission, discount, cheque books, etc., are sometimes included in one book called the impersonal ledger, and the combined daily totals of those various accounts posted into an account in the general ledger, called "impersonal ledger account." This is generally done to reduce the number of accounts in the general ledger.

IMPLEMENT. In Scotland, to implement a contract is to carry it into effect.

IMPORT SPECIE POINT. (See SPECIE POINTS.)

IMPRESSED STAMPS. Impressed stamps are required on :—

Assignments of Life Policies.
Conveyances.
Inland Bills of Exchange (except when on demand, at sight, on presentation, or not exceeding three days after date or sight, when either an adhesive or impressed stamp may be used).
Inland Promissory Notes.
Letters of Allotment.
Memoranda of Deposit.
Mortgages.
Scrip certificates.
Transfers.

Stamps may be impressed on all instruments except where an adhesive appropriated stamp is necessary. (See APPROPRIATED STAMPS.) In certain cases (e.g. a guarantee under hand) either an impressed or adhesive stamp may be used. (See ADHESIVE STAMPS.)

IN CASE OF NEED. A referee "in case of need" is the person whose name a drawer or any indorser may insert in a bill, to whom a holder may resort in case the bill is dishonoured, by non-acceptance or by non-payment. The words are usually placed in the left-hand bottom corner of the bill, as "In case of need with the English Bank, Ltd., London." A holder may please himself whether, or not, he resorts to the referee.

Where a dishonoured bill contains a reference in case of need, it must be protested for non-payment before it is presented for payment to the referee in case of need (Section 67, Bills of Exchange Act, 1882). (See ACCEPTANCE FOR HONOUR, REFEREE IN CASE OF NEED.)

IN CLEARING. When a bank makes an exchange of cheques with another bank, the cheques which are received constitute the "In" clearing, and the cheques which are given out form the "Out" clearing. (See CLEARING HOUSE.)

INCHOATE INSTRUMENT. An incomplete document, as, for example, a stamped bill form, signed by a person and handed to another person to fill up and make into a complete bill.

By Section 20 of the Bills of Exchange Act, 1882 :—

"(1) Where a simple signature on a blank stamped paper is delivered by the signer in order that it may be converted into a bill, it operates as a *primâ facie* authority to fill it up as a complete bill for any amount the stamp will cover, using the signature for that of the drawer, or the acceptor, or an indorser; and, in like manner, when a bill is wanting in any material particular, the person in possession of it has a *primâ facie* authority to fill up the omission in any way he thinks fit.

"(2) In order that any such instrument when completed may be enforceable against any person who became a party thereto prior to its completion, it must be filled up within a reasonable time, and strictly in accordance with the authority given. Reasonable time for this purpose is a question of fact.

Provided that if any such instrument after completion is negotiated to a holder in due course it shall be valid and effectual for all purposes in his hands, and he may enforce it as if it had been filled up within a reasonable time and strictly in accordance with the authority given."

It is important to note that an incomplete bill must be filled up strictly in accordance with the authority given. If a person signs a stamped form as an acceptor and hands it to another person to fill up in a certain specified manner and sign it as drawer, and the drawer exceeds his authority, the acceptor will not be liable thereon to the drawer, but if the bill is negotiated to a holder in due course, he will be liable to such a holder. By accepting a bill in blank an acceptor may thus find himself in the awkward position of having to pay a very much larger sum than he intended to pay when he placed his name on the paper.

The Court of Appeal said in *France* v. *Clark* (1884, 26 Ch. D. 257): "The person who has signed a negotiable instrument in blank or with blank spaces is, on account of the negotiable character of that instrument, estopped by the law merchant from disputing any alteration made in the document after it has left his hands by filling up blanks (or otherwise in a way not *ex facie* fraudulent) as against a *boná fide* holder for value without notice, but it has been repeatedly explained that this estoppel is in favour only of such a *boná fide* holder, and a man who, after taking it in blank, has himself filled up the blanks in his own favour without the consent or knowledge of the person to be bound, has never been treated in English Courts as entitled to the benefit of that doctrine." (See BILL OF EXCHANGE.)

INCOME TAX. A tax upon incomes. It is payable upon incomes from sources within the United Kingdom, and upon incomes from sources outside the United Kingdom but received within the United Kingdom.

A return of income must be made yearly upon the forms provided for the purpose.

The rates for the year beginning April 6, 1909, (and for 1910,) are :—

	s.	d.	
On unearned incomes (dividends, etc.)	1	2	in the £.
On earned incomes, where the total income does not exceed £2,000 .	0	9	,,
On earned incomes, where the total income exceeds £2,000 but does not exceed £3,000	1	0	,,
On incomes over £3,000 . . .	1	2	,,
An additional duty (called super tax) on incomes exceeding £5,000, on so much as exceeds £3,000 (e.g. a man with £6,000 will pay super tax on £3,000)	0	6	,,

Where an individual, whose total income exceeds £160 but does not exceed £500, has a child or children living under the age of sixteen at the commencement of the year for which the tax is charged, he is entitled, in respect of every such child, to relief from income tax to the amount of the income tax upon £10 (Section 68, Finance (1909–10) Act, 1910).

Where the total joint income of a husband and wife does not exceed £500, a wife can separate her claim for exemption or abatement from that of her husband on account of profits derived from any business carried on by means of her own personal labour, provided the husband is assessable under Schedule D, and that his income is unconnected with the business of his wife.

If an owner of land or houses, not exceeding £8 annual value, proves to the satisfaction of the surveyor of taxes that the cost to him of maintenance, repairs, insurance and management, on the average of the five preceding years, has exceeded the allowances of one-eighth and one-sixth respectively allowed by Section 35, Finance Act, 1894, he may claim repayment on so much of the excess as does not exceed one-eighth of the annual value of the land and one-twelfth of the annual value of the house ; i.e., the total allowance under both statutes must not exceed one-fourth of the value (Section 69, Finance (1909–10) Act, 1910).

With regard to persons residing abroad, Section 71 of the above Act, enacts :—

"(1) No exemption, abatement, or relief under the Income Tax Acts which depends wholly or partially on the total income of an individual from all sources shall be given to any person, unless the person claiming the exemption, abatement, or relief is resident in the United Kingdom :

Provided that any person who is or has been employed in the service of the Crown or who is employed in the service of any missionary society abroad or in the service of any of the native states under the protectorate of the British Crown, and any person resident in the Isle of Man or Channel Islands and any person resident abroad who satisfies the Commissioners that he is so resident for the sake of health, shall be entitled to any relief, exemption, or abatement to which he would be entitled if he were resident in the United Kingdom, and if his total income from all sources were calculated as including any income in respect of which income tax may not be chargeable as well as income in respect of which income tax is chargeable.

"(2) Income tax shall not be payable in respect of the interest or dividends of any securities of a foreign state or a British possession which are payable in the United Kingdom, where it is proved to the satisfaction of the Commissioners that the person owning the securities and entitled to the interest or dividends is not resident in the United Kingdom; but, save as provided by this or any other Act, no allowance shall be given or repayment made in respect of the income tax on the interest or dividends on the securities of any foreign state or any British possession which are payable in the United Kingdom.

Relief from income tax under this sub-section may be given by the Commissioners either by way of allowance or repayment on a claim being made to them for the purpose within six months of the end of the year for which the income tax is charged."

There are five schedules for the annual return of income, viz. :—

Schedule A.—For income from property in lands and buildings and sporting rights.

(The tax under this Schedule is commonly called "Property Tax.")

Schedule B.—For income from the occupation of land.

Schedule C.—For income from the public funds.

Schedule D.—For income from trade, profession, employment, vocation, discounts, interest of money not taxed by deduction, colonial and foreign securities (where the duty is not deducted by the agent entrusted with the payment thereof), colonial and foreign possessions, letting furnished houses, and all other income not falling within the other schedules.

Schedule E.—Salaries paid to Government, corporation, and company officials.

(This schedule includes officials of banking companies.)

For the purposes of income tax, income is divided into earned income and unearned income. Schedules A and C are unearned incomes, Schedules B and E are earned incomes. Schedule D is part earned and part unearned.

Income not exceeding £160 is exempt from tax.

Exceeding £160 but not exceeding £400, £160 abatement is allowed.

Exceeding £400 but not exceeding £500, £150 abatement is allowed.

Exceeding £500 but not exceeding £600, £120 abatement is allowed.

Exceeding £600 but not exceeding £700, £70 abatement is allowed.

In the annual return of the profits of a banking company, in order to arrive at the amount on which income tax is to be paid, working expenses, rent, rates, taxes, salaries, bad debts, etc., are deducted from the gross profits, and also all amounts on which tax has already been paid by the banker, e.g. rents received, dividends on investments, interest on fixed mortgages from which income tax was deducted before charging the interest to the customer's account. A list of the fixed mortgages must be given to the Surveyor of Taxes in order to enable him to trace whether the persons have paid to the Revenue the sums deducted. The amount charged to profit and loss account in payment of income tax is not to be taken as a deduction from the profits. An amount used to write down the value of the bank's premises, or an amount transferred to a reserve account, or an expenditure in extending a building, are not allowed to be deducted.

Subscriptions which have no connection with the business cannot be deducted.

Fire insurance premiums and also employers' liability insurance premiums are allowable as deductions from a bank's profits, but life insurance premiums, if any, cannot be deducted.

In arriving at a banker's profits assessable under Schedule D, deduction of the net Schedule A assessment on premises owned and occupied by the banker for business purposes (including any portion used as a manager's residence) is allowed, less any ground rent payable thereon.

Where a bank official is required to reside on bank premises for the performance of his duties, the annual value of his residence is not treated as an emolument, and is not to be included in a statement of income for the purpose of claiming abatement.

It has been held that where a bank purchased the business and premises of another bank, the profits of both banks shall be brought into the computation of the three years' average. (*Bell* v. *National Provincial Bank of England*, 1904, 1 K.B. 149.)

Any person who pays premiums on the insurance of his own or his wife's life, is entitled to deduction of the premiums, if they do not exceed one-sixth of his total income; but the deduction is not to be taken into account in a claim for statutory abatement.

With regard to premiums paid by a banker upon a policy left in his hands by a defaulting borrower, if the final result (profit or loss) is to be credited or debited to the banker's profit and loss account, the premiums may be regarded as a current expense necessary to guard him against loss and therefore may be deducted when calculating the liability for income tax.

The rules and regulations for calculating the profits of a business are given by the Income Tax Authorities as follow :—

AVERAGE.—The amount of profits is to be computed on an average of the three preceding years, ending either on the 5th day of April, or on the date prior thereto to which the annual accounts have been usually made up ;

Or, if the trade, etc., has been set up or commenced within three years, on an average from the period of commencing the same ;

Or, if commenced within the year of assessment, the profits are to be estimated according to the best of your knowledge and belief, and the grounds on which the amount shall have been estimated should be stated for the information of the Commissioners.

In computing the profits upon which the average is to be taken—

DEDUCTIONS ARE ALLOWED—

For repairs of premises occupied for the purpose of the trade, etc., and for the supply or repair of implements, utensils, or articles employed, not exceeding the sum usually expended for such purposes according to the average of the three years preceding.

For debts proved to be bad ; also for doubtful debts according to their estimated value.

For the rent of premises used *solely* for the purposes of business, and not as a place of residence.

For a proportion, not exceeding two-thirds, of the rent of any dwelling house *partly* used for the purposes of business.

For the annual value of any premises occupied by the owner *solely* for the purposes of business, and not as a place of residence, according to the amount on which duty has been paid under Schedule A.

For a proportion, not exceeding two-thirds, of the annual value (according to the amount on which duty has been paid under Schedule A), of any dwelling house occupied by the owner and *partly* used for the purposes of business.

For any other disbursements or expenses wholly and exclusively laid out for the purposes of the trade, etc.

NO DEDUCTIONS ARE ALLOWED—

For any interest on capital, for any annual interest, annuity, or other annual payment, payable out of the profits or gains, or for any royalty, or other sum paid in respect of the user of a patent. (The duty on such interest, patent royalty, or other annual payment should be deducted from the person to whom the payment is made.)

For any sums paid as salaries to partners or for drawings by partners.

For any sums invested or employed as capital in the trade or business, or on account of capital withdrawn therefrom.

For any sums expended in improvement of premises or written off for depreciation of land, buildings, or leases.

For any loss not connected with, or arising out of the trade, etc.

For any expenses of maintenance of the persons assessable, their families, or private establishments.

For any loss recoverable under an insurance or contract of indemnity.

For any sum paid as income tax on profits or gains, or on the annual value of trade premises.

For any premium for life insurance, or for wear and tear of machinery or plant ; but allowances may be claimed in respect of these items.

By the Finance Act, 1907, Section 21, s.s. 1, " Every employer, when required to do so by notice from an assessor, shall, within the time limited by the notice, prepare and deliver to the assessor a return of the names and places of residence of any persons employed by him, to whom this provision applies, and of the payments made to those persons in respect of that employment. . . ." This provision does not apply to employees whose yearly remuneration does not exceed the sum fixed as the limit (at present £160) for total exemption from income tax (Section 21, s.s. 1). Where the employer is a company, the secretary, or other officer performing the duties of secretary, shall be deemed to be the employer for the purposes of this provision, and any director, or person engaged in the management of the company, shall be deemed to be a person employed (Section 21, s.s. 2).

With regard to the deduction of income tax from foreign and colonial dividends, and from the interest on fixed deposits in colonial banks in London, the following enactments apply :—

The effect of Section 36 of 24 & 25 Vict. c. 91 is that income tax must be deducted from interest, dividends or other annual payments payable in respect of stocks or shares of any foreign or colonial company or concern, which said interest, dividends or annual payments have been intrusted to any person in the United Kingdom for payment to any persons or companies in the United Kingdom.

(The Board of Inland Revenue include under this Section the deduction of tax from the interest payable by colonial banks in London upon fixed deposits.)

The Customs and Inland Revenue Act, 1885, includes amongst the persons intrusted with the payment of such dividends, as is referred to in the above Section, the persons hereinafter described ; that is to say,

"Section 26. (*a*) Any banker or person acting as a banker who shall sell or otherwise realise coupons or warrants for or bills of exchange purporting to be drawn or made in payment of any dividends (save such as are payable in the United Kingdom only), and pay over the proceeds to any person or carry the same to his account ;

"(*b*) Any person who shall by means of coupons receive from any other person, or otherwise on his behalf, obtain payment of any dividends elsewhere than in the United Kingdom ;

"(*c*) Any dealer in coupons who shall purchase coupons for any dividends (save such as are payable in the United Kingdom only) otherwise than from a banker or person acting as a banker or another dealer in coupons.

"A person intrusted with the payment of dividends, who shall perform all necessary acts so that the income tax thereon may be assessed and paid, shall be entitled to receive as remuneration an allowance of so much (not being less than threepence) in the pound of the amount paid as may from time to time be fixed by the Commissioners of the Treasury.

"Provided that this Section shall not impose on any banker or other person the obligation to disclose any particulars relating to the affairs of any person on whose behalf he may be acting."

Where a banker has taken a mortgage for a fixed amount, and the period of the loan is not less than a year, income tax must be deducted by the banker before charging the customer with the interest. In such a case the relation of banker and customer is changed to that of mortgagor and mortgagee, and a mortgagor is entitled under Section 40 of the Property Tax Act, 1853, to have income tax deducted from the interest payable on his mortgage. In a case of a fixed mortgage, simple interest only can be charged. (See INTEREST.) Where a banker is required to deduct tax from the interest due upon a fixed mortgage, any such sum so deducted must be allowed for when the banker makes his income tax return ; that is to say, before arriving at the amount of tax which he must pay upon his year's profits, he must allow for the amount which he has in effect already paid by having allowed it, by way of a reduction of interest, to the mortgagor.

A banker does not deduct income tax from the interest charged on a current account or an ordinary loan. The customer must make his own claim for repayment of tax in respect of bank interest. For that purpose a banker supplies, when requested by a customer, a certificate, which may be given in the following prescribed form :—

"I, the undersigned Manager of the British Bank, Ltd., hereby certify that the sum of £   has been charged to John Brown as interest for the twelve months ended December 31, 19 . This interest was received from John Brown in full, without deduction of income tax, and has been included by the bank as part of their profits, in respect of which an assessment has been made and duty paid under Schedule D of the Income Tax Acts. The security held by the bank in respect of the advance in question amounting to £   is as follows :   ." This is the form of certificate as issued by the income tax authorities. It should be noted that the certificate must include only interest and not commission or any other charges.

Some dividends are declared free of income tax, the tax being paid by the company, and the shareholder receives the full rate of dividend, whilst in other cases the tax is deducted from the amount payable to the shareholder. It has been the custom of many banks to pay their dividends free of income tax, but various banks are considering the desirability of paying dividends less income tax. When the tax is deducted, the top half of the dividend warrant certifies the deduction and is used as a voucher by any shareholder claiming exemption or abatement. When a dividend is paid free of income tax, the tax may be recovered by anyone entitled thereto. In reclaiming tax on dividends paid " free of income tax," the gross amount of dividend may be entered on the return, that is, the amount which the dividend would have been if it had not been paid free of tax, e.g. a dividend of £95, with the tax at 1*s*., may be treated as £100, and, if belonging to a person entitled to exemption, £5 will be repaid, i.e. the tax upon £100. In the same way, such a dividend belonging to a person liable to tax must be entered in his return as £100, not £95. If he has other income, say, £602, his total income would not be £697 but £702, and he would not be entitled to any abatement.

The income tax certificate issued by a bank to shareholders who require it may be in the following form :—

BRITISH BANK, LTD.

INCOME TAX CERTIFICATE.

I hereby certify that Income Tax has been assessed on and paid to the Revenue by the British Bank, Ltd., in respect of its profits and gains, of which profits and gains the undermentioned dividend a portion.

For the British Bank, Ltd.,

Carlisle, 19 . , Manager.

Shares in the British Bank, Ltd.	Standing in Name of	Dividend.	Dividend Payable.
			July 19
			Feby. 19
			July 19
			Feby. 19
			July 19
			Feby. 19

Income tax is deducted by the Bank of England from all dividends of £5 and upwards, but the Bank does not issue certificates of deduction.

The form of certificate, to be used only by bankers in the United Kingdom, for repayment of income tax on foreign and colonial securities, is as follows :—

We hereby certify that coupons of the [here state the nature of the security], as specified at the back hereof, which became due ...... were forwarded by us to [name of banker or agent] of ...... on behalf of .... and that we received payment or were credited with the proceeds thereof less income tax as follows :—

£ .... Gross amount.
£ .... Tax deducted

£ Net amount.

Signature of banker or bank agent } ....

Residence ....

Date.................

On the back of the certificate a declaration must be signed by the claimant, the form being as follows :—

Schedule of Coupons.

The number of coupons to be entered in consecutive order.	Aggregate amount of coupons.
	£

To be signed by claimant.

I hereby declare that the coupons mentioned relate to bonds which are my own property and are in the possession of ....

Signature ....

Date ....

The bonds in support of any claim must be produced when required.

INCOMPLETE BILL. (See INCHOATE INSTRUMENT.)

INCONVERTIBLE PAPER CURRENCY. A bank note which cannot be exchanged for gold on demand, at the bank which issued it, for the full value as shown upon the face of the note, is called inconvertible paper. When it can be exchanged for its full value, it is convertible paper.

INCORPORATED COMPANY. A company is incorporated when it is registered in accordance with the requirements of the Companies Acts, and has obtained a certificate of incorporation from the Registrar of Companies. The members of an incorporated company no longer exist as individuals liable to be sued by creditors; the individuals have become one body (the company), and it is to the company alone (or the liquidator) that the members are liable. Creditors must sue an incorporated company in the company's name. (See COMPANIES.)

INCREMENT VALUE DUTY. A duty imposed by the Finance (1909–10) Act, 1910, upon the increment value of any land, at the rate of one pound for every complete five pounds of that value accruing after April 30, 1909.

The increment value is the amount by which the site value of the land, at the time the increment value duty is to be collected, exceeds the original site value.

The site value of land on the occasion of a sale is the value of the consideration; on the occasion of the grant of any lease of land, the site value is the value of the fee simple of the land, calculated on the basis of the value of the consideration for the grant of the lease.

The duty is payable upon any transfer on sale of the fee simple of land, or of any interest in the land, or the grant of any lease exceeding fourteen years, and upon the death of any person where land passes upon the death, and where land is held by any body, corporate or unincorporate, in such a manner that it is not liable to death duties, upon such periodical occasions as are provided by the Act (viz., April 5, 1914, and in every subsequent fifteenth year). If the body corporate or unincorporate so desire, the duty may be paid by fifteen equal yearly instalments, and the first shall be due immediately after the assessment.

On the first occasion of collection of the duty the increment value shall be reduced by an amount equal to 10 per cent. of the original site value, and on any subsequent occasion by an amount equal to 10 per cent. of the site value at the previous collection of the duty; but no remission shall be given which will make the amount of the increment value on which duty has been remitted during the preceding period of five years exceed 25 per cent. of the site value at the previous collection of the duty prior to the commencement of that period, or of the original site value if no such occasion.

Increment value duty shall be a stamp duty.

On any sale of the fee simple of land, or the grant of any lease exceeding fourteen years, the duty shall be assessed by the Commissioners and paid by the transferor or lessor. The instrument of the transfer or lease, or reasonable particulars thereof, must be presented to the Commissioners for the purpose of assessment of the duty.

Section 4, s.s. 3, is as follows:—

"(3) Any such instrument shall not, for the purposes of Section fourteen of the Stamp Act, 1891, and notwithstanding anything in Section twelve of that Act, be deemed to be duly stamped unless it is stamped—

"(*a*) either with a stamp denoting that the increment value duty has been assessed by the Commissioners and paid in accordance with the assessment; or

"(*b*) with a stamp denoting that all particulars have been delivered to the Commissioners, which, in their opinion, are necessary for the purpose of enabling them to assess the duty, and that security has been given for the payment of duty in any case where the Commissioners have required security; or

"(*c*) with a stamp denoting that upon the occasion in question no increment value duty was payable;

but where an instrument is so stamped, it shall, notwithstanding any objection relating to the increment value duty, be deemed to be duly stamped so far as respects that duty." (See ADJUDICATION STAMPS, STAMP DUTIES.)

Exemptions:—

Agricultural land, while it has no higher value than its market value at the time for agricultural purposes only.

Land on which a dwelling-house is built which has been used for twelve months previously by the owner as his residence and the annual value, as adopted for the purpose of income tax under Schedule A, does not exceed—

(*a*) in the case of a house in the administrative county of London, £40 ;

(*b*) a house in a borough or urban district with a population of 50,000 or upwards, £26 ;

(*c*) a house elsewhere, £16.

Agricultural land occupied and cultivated, for twelve months previously, by the owner, where the total amount belonging to the same owner does not exceed 50 acres, and the average total value does not exceed £75 per acre (except land occupied together with a dwelling-house where the annual value exceeds £30).

Land held *bonâ fide* for games or other recreation.

Land held by, or for, His Majesty, or any department of Government.

Land held for charitable purposes.

Land whilst it is held by a statutory company for the purposes of the undertaking and which cannot be appropriated except to those purposes. When sold, increment value duty is payable. (Statutory company means any railway, canal, dock, or water company.)

Where a mortgagee is liable to pay increment value duty, Section 39, provides :—

"(4) Where the fee simple of any land or any interest in land in respect of which increment value duty or reversion duty is charged is vested in a mortgagee who is liable to pay any sum on account of either of those duties, he shall be entitled to add to his security the sum for which he is so liable, including any costs or expenses properly incurred by him in respect of the payment of the duty.

(5) In Scotland, where any person having a limited interest in the land or interest in land in respect of which any duty under this Part of this Act is charged, is the person who is liable to pay any sums on account of the duty, he shall be entitled to charge such land or such interest in land by means of a bond and disposition or bond and assignation in security in his own favour which he is hereby authorised to grant."

There are special provisions with regard to increment value duty in the case of minerals worked or leased (Section 22).

INDEMNITY. Where a deposit receipt, or a banker's own note, or a dividend warrant, has been lost, the banker may agree to pay the amount on receiving a suitable indemnity or security to preserve him against any loss in so paying. In the case of a deposit receipt, the indemnity should accurately describe the lost document which the banker has agreed to pay without its production, and should state the consideration for which the indemnity is given, thus "in consideration of your so paying the amount of the said receipt." The persons who give the indemnity should undertake and agree, jointly and severally, to hold the banker harmless and indemnified against all loss, costs and damages which he may at any time or in any manner sustain in consequence of so paying the said receipt. It should also contain an undertaking to return the receipt if it should be found.

An indemnity under hand is subject to a stamp duty of 6*d*. Indemnities in suitable forms are used in connection with other matters than lost documents.

INDENTURE. (Latin *In*, and *dens*, a tooth.) An indenture is a deed under seal between two or more persons.

Its name dates from the time when a deed was indented along one of the margins. It was the custom to write a deed in two parts on the one parchment, and between each part a blank space was left ; along the blank space a word, often the word "chirographum," was written and the parchment was then cut into two by dividing it with an indented or wavy line through that word. Each of the two parties to the deed received a part, and when at any time the two parts were brought together again it showed that they were the correct documents when the indents agreed and the divided word was completed. (See CHIROGRAPH.)

The writing of the word "chirographum" or other word or letters in the blank space was in later times omitted, and the parchmeet was merely divided with an indented line. Finally an Act was passed (8 & 9 Vict. c. 106, Section 5), providing "that a deed executed after the first day of October, 1845, purporting to be an indenture, shall have the effect of an indenture although not actually indented."

The date of an indenture is at the commencement of the deed.

An indenture begins as follows :—

" This Indenture made the day of 19 , between John Brown of King Street in the City of York, grocer, of the first part and John Jones," etc. (See DEED POLL.)

INDORSATION. The word often used in Scotland for indorsement (*q.v.*) or endorsement.

INDORSE. To indorse is to write one's signature upon the back of a document, e.g. a bill, cheque, bill of lading, etc. (See INDORSEMENT.)

INDORSEE. The person to whom a bill or cheque is assigned by way of indorsement. (See INDORSEMENT.)

INDORSEMENT. (Latin *In dorsum*, on the back.) Spelled also endorsement. In Scotland the word used is often " indorsation."

The indorsement of a bill (or cheque) is the writing, signed by the holder, upon the back, by which a bill (or cheque) payable to order is transferred from one person to another. The simple signature of an indorser is a valid indorsement, and it is not invalid by reason of its being written in pencil.

" Indorsement " means an indorsement completed by delivery.

It is possible for a signature to be placed upon the back of a cheque and yet not operate as an indorsement. Mr. Justice Byles said in *Keene* v. *Beard* (1860, 8 C.B.N.S. 372) : " It is true that a man's name may, and very often is, written on the back of a cheque without any idea of rendering himself liable as an indorser. Indeed, one of the best receipts is the placing on the back of the instrument the name of the person who has received payment of it. Such an entry of the name on the instrument is not an indorsement."

The requisites of a valid indorsement are given in Section 32 of the Bills of Exchange Act, 1882 :—

" An indorsement in order to operate as a negotiation must comply with the following conditions, namely :—

" (1) It must be written on the bill itself and be signed by the indorser. The simple signature of the indorser on the bill, without additional words, is sufficient. An indorsement written on an allonge, or on a ' copy ' of a bill issued or negotiated in a country where ' copies ' are recognised, is deemed to be written on the bill itself.

" (2) It must be an indorsement of the entire bill. A partial indorsement, that is to say, an indorsement which purports to transfer to the indorsee a part only of the amount payable, or which purports to transfer the bill to two or more indorsees severally, does not operate as a negotiation of the bill.

" (3) Where a bill is payable to the order of two or more payees or indorsees who are not partners all must indorse, unless the one indorsing has authority to indorse for the others.

" (4) Where, in a bill payable to order, the payee or indorsee is wrongly designated, or his name is misspelt, he may indorse the bill as therein described, adding, if he think fit, his proper signature.

" (5) Where there are two or more indorsements on a bill, each indorsement is deemed to have been made in the order in which it appears on the bill, until the contrary is proved.

" (6) An indorsement may be made in blank or special. It may also contain terms making it restrictive."

There are four kinds of indorsements, a conditional indorsement, an indorsement in blank, a special indorsemen , and a restrictive indorsement.

A conditional indorsement is referred to in Section 33 :—

" Where a bill purports to be indorsed conditionally the condition may be disregarded by the payer, and payment to the indorsee is valid whether the condition has been fulfilled or not."

An indorsement in blank and a special indorsement are explained in Section 34 :—

" (1) An indorsement in blank specifies no indorsee, and a bill so indorsed becomes payable to bearer.

" (2) A special indorsement specifies the person to whom, or to whose order, the bill is to be payable.

" (3) The provisions of this Act relating to a payee apply with the necessary modifications to an indorsee under a special indorsement.

" (4) When a bill has been indorsed in blank, any holder may convert the blank indorsement into a special indorsement by writing above the indorser's signature a direction to pay the bill to or to the order of himself or some other person."

A restrictive indorsement is defined in Section 35 :—

"(1) An indorsement is restrictive which prohibits the further negotiation of the bill or which expresses that it is a mere authority to deal with the bill as thereby directed and not a transfer of the ownership thereof, as, for example, if a bill be indorsed 'Pay D only,' or 'Pay D. for the account of X,' or 'pay D. or order for collection.'

"(2) A restrictive indorsement gives the indorsee the right to receive payment of the bill and to sue any party thereto that his indorser could have sued, but gives him no power to transfer his rights as indorsee unless it expressly authorise him to do so.

"(3) Where a restrictive indorsement authorises further transfer, all subsequent indorsees take the bill with the same rights and subject to the same liabilities as the first indorsee under the restrictive indorsement."

An indorser may insert an express stipulation (1) negativing or limiting his own liability to the holder, (2) waiving as regards himself some or all of the holder's duties (Section 16). An example of an indorsement so qualified is where an indorser adds after his signature the words "without recourse" or the French equivalent "*sans recours*."

By Section 31, s.s. 3 :—

"A bill payable to order is negotiated by the indorsement of the holder completed by delivery."

A transferee, for value, acquires the right to have the indorsement of the transferor, where the bill was payable to the transferor's order (Section 31, s.s. 4).

A bill payable to "John Brown or order" may be indorsed simply "John Brown." He may then transfer the bill by simple delivery to another person. By John Brown's indorsement in blank the bill becomes payable to bearer, and may pass from hand to hand without any further indorsement, though, as a rule, anyone taking a bill will require the transferor to indorse it, so that he may thereby become a party to the bill and be liable thereon. If, however, John Brown indorsed the bill "Pay John Jones or order, John Brown" (or "John Brown, pay to the order of John Jones"), the bill is specially indorsed, and requires the signature of John Jones before he can transfer it to anyone else. Any holder may convert an indorsement in blank into a special one to himself, or to any other person. If a bill with John Brown's indorsement in blank passes through the hands of certain holders who do not indorse it, and then comes into the possession of William Robinson, he may write above John Brown's signature the words "Pay William Robinson." Before further negotiation, the bill requires William Robinson's indorsement. If John Brown indorses the bill "Pay John Jones only," the indorsement of John Jones is required, but John Jones cannot transfer the bill to anyone else, as John Brown by his restrictive word prohibits the further negotiation of the bill.

A cheque or bill payable "to order" should (unless payable to a fictitious or non-existing person) be indorsed. But see under PAYEE as to the case of a payee refusing to indorse a cheque when presented by himself. A cheque payable to bearer does not require to be indorsed. A cheque indorsed in blank is payable without further indorsement. But all cheques paid to credit, which do not legally require an indorsement, should either be indorsed or stamped with the name of the customer, so that the banker may know at any time from whom the cheques were received. Some customers cross all their cheques which are paid to credit, thus :—"Account John Brown at X. & Y. Bank, Ltd." All bills paid to credit should be indorsed by the customer.

An indorsement, as its name implies, should be upon the back of a bill or cheque, but it has been held that an indorsement on the face is valid.

An indorsement should be spelled exactly in the same way as the person's name appears on the face of the bill (or cheque) as payee, or in the special indorsement as indorsee. If the person's name has been misspelt by the drawer or the prior indorser, his indorsement should also be misspelt, but he may indorse it below with his name spelled correctly. All indorsements must be examined, even if they are in a foreign language.

In a memorandum dated June, 1910, circulated by the Council of the Institute of Bankers, with respect to indorsements in Oriental or other unusual characters, it is pointed out that bills bearing indorsements in Oriental characters are sometimes presented for payment with the name of the indorser written in Latin characters beneath the indorsement, and the memorandum continues: "Such 'translations' may be, and it is believed often are, written on the bill by persons having no authority and incurring no responsibility, and the Council is of opinion that before paying the bill, a banker would be justified in requiring that the translation be properly verified by a notary, or that, in default of this, the indorsement be confirmed by a banker.

"In the event of bills bearing Oriental indorsements being returned, the answer given should be such as to leave no room for doubt that the reason for refusing payment is that such indorsement is unintelligible, in which case the Council is advised that no legal liability will be incurred by the bank giving the answer.

"A suggested form of answer is ' . . .th indorsement requires notarially certified translation, or will pay on banker's confirmation.'

"The Council think it would be most satisfactory for all concerned, and avoid delay in payment of bills bearing such indorsements, if they were in all cases put in order before being remitted to London for payment, as it is sometimes a matter of difficulty in this country to obtain a satisfactory translation."

If a holder strikes out, intentionally, the indorsement of any indorser, that indorser and all indorsers subsequent to him are discharged from liability on the bill.

An infant may indorse a bill or cheque and pass on to an indorsee a good title, but he is under no liability with regard to it.

Where the signature of any person is required, under the Bills of Exchange Act, it is not necessary that he should sign it with his own hand. It is sufficient if his signature is written thereon by some other person by or under his authority (Section 91). A banker, however, would require undoubted evidence of authority before accepting an indorsement written by some other person. If an indorsement is impressed by a stamp, a banker should confirm it, when he is satisfied that it has been made by a duly authorised person.

In the case of a corporation, an indorsement sealed with the corporate seal is sufficient (Section 91, s.s. 2).

Where a banker on whom a cheque is drawn, pays it in good faith and in the ordinary course of business, the banker is protected by Section 60 (see PAYMENT OF BILL), even though the indorsement of the payee or a subsequent indorser has been forged or made without authority. He must, however, exercise reasonable care, and see that the cheque he is asked to pay is apparently properly indorsed. If he is negligent and pays a cheque which is clearly not indorsed by the proper party he will be liable. The banker need not know the payee, so long as the cheque purports to be indorsed by the person to whom it is payable.

If a banker pays a customer's acceptance to a person appearing to be the holder, but claiming through or under a forged indorsement, he cannot charge such an acceptance to the customer's account (Section 24, Bills of Exchange Act. See FORGERY). If he has paid such an acceptance to a banker who sent it for collection, he cannot claim the amount back from that banker.

The paying banker thus incurs liability in paying a bill under a forged indorsement, but in paying a cheque with a forged indorsement he is protected.

With regard to a banker's liability, as to the indorsements on a bill, Baron Parke (in *Robarts v. Tucker*, 1851, 16 Q.B. 560), said: "If bankers wish to avoid the responsibility of deciding on the genuineness of indorsements, they may require their customers to domicile their bills at their own offices, and to honour them by giving a cheque upon the banker."

The banker who collects for a customer an open cheque, is responsible for the genuineness of the indorsement, but in the case of a cheque crossed generally, or specially to himself, he is not liable for a forged indorsement, provided he receives payment of the cheque for his customer in good faith and without negligence. (See CROSSED CHEQUE.) If he collects a bearer cheque he is in a much better position than with an order cheque as there is then no question of a forged indorsement.

The banker paying a draft or order drawn upon him, payable to order on demand, which purports to be indorsed by the person to whom the same shall be drawn payable, is not liable if the indorsement proves to have been forged. It shall not be incumbent on such banker to prove that such indorsement, or any subsequent indorsement, was made by or under the direction or authority of the person to whom the said draft or order was or is made payable, either by the drawer or any indorser thereof (Section 19, Stamp Act, 1853, 16 & 17 Vict. c. 59, see DRAFT ON DEMAND). The same Section probably protects a banker in paying an order drawn upon him as treasurer of a local authority. Some writers consider that a banker is also protected, in paying such orders, by Section 60 of the Bills of Exchange Act (see above). This protection, however, depends upon whether the orders are held to be drawn upon a banker, or merely upon the treasurer in his personal capacity.

A bill or cheque payable to John Brown without the words "order" or "bearer," is payable to order and requires indorsement.

It is a well-recognised custom to pay a dividend warrant, payable to several persons, when discharged by one of those persons. (See DIVIDEND WARRANT.) An interest warrant, however, should, strictly, be indorsed by all the payees, though in practice this is not always insisted upon.

Where a bill has been seized in execution, a sheriff can give a good discharge when payment is made to him.

If an indorser writes any words on the cheque or bill in the form of a receipt, such as "Received Payment," "Received Cash," such receipt requires a penny stamp if the amount is £2 or over. A receipt by a banker upon a bill of exchange is exempt. (See RECEIPT.)

Where an indorsement is by mark, it must be duly witnessed.

Where a bill drawn by a firm is payable to their order, one partner may draw the bill and, probably, another partner may indorse it. Thus, though the signatures of the firm on the bill differ, it may be in accordance with the practice of the firm to treat bills in that way.

Where payable to a fictitious or non-existing person no indorsement is required, as the instrument may be treated as payable to "bearer" (Section 7, s.s. 3).

Where payable to "Wages or order," or some such impersonal word, it is treated by many bankers as a cheque requiring the drawer's indorsement, and as a rule is paid only to the drawer or his authorised representative. Some bankers, however, treat it as coming under Section 7, s.s. 3—that is, as payable to "bearer"—but the word "wages" can hardly be described as a "fictitious or non-existing *person*."

Per procuration indorsements are usually accepted by bankers, but some companies put a note upon their cheques to the effect that a per procuration discharge will not be accepted, unless guaranteed by the payee's banker. A banker is not obliged to accept a per pro. indorsement, if there are suspicious circumstances demanding inquiry as to the person's authority to indorse.

An indorsement which is not strictly in order is frequently confirmed by a banker as "Indorsement confirmed. Per pro. X & Y. Bank, Ltd., T. Brown, Manager." This is better than "Indorsement guaranteed," as it precludes any chance of liability to stamp duty as a guarantee. Where a cheque payable to order has been omitted to be indorsed by the payee, a banker occasionally indorses it "Placed to credit of the payee's account. Per pro. X. & Y. Bank, Ltd., T. Brown, Manager." Though there is no obligation on the banker on whom the cheque is drawn to pay a cheque which is not indorsed, he is usually satisfied with the collecting banker's assurance that it has gone to the payee's credit. Of course as it is not indorsed, the banker cannot shelter himself under Section 60.

A banker is sometimes authorised by a company to indorse cheques on behalf of the company, and in such a case the indorsement may be, e.g. "Indorsed by authority of the X. & Y. Railway Company and placed to the credit of their account with us. Per pro. The British Bank, Ltd., John Brown, Manager."

Section 77 of the Companies (Consolidation) Act, 1908, enacts that "a bill of exchange or promissory note shall be deemed to have been made, accepted, or indorsed on behalf of a company if made, accepted, or indorsed in the name of, or by or on behalf or on account of, the company by any person acting under its authority." Although this Section makes an indorsement of simply the name of a joint stock company legally correct, it is the practice of bankers always to require that it be signed by some person on behalf of the company, e.g. "Per pro. John Brown & Coy., Limited, J. Jones," or "John Brown & Coy., Ltd., J. Jones, Secretary."

Where a cheque payable to John Brown is indorsed "Place to credit of my account, J. Brown," it is not necessary that the cheque should be indorsed by the bank in any way. So long as the cheque is indorsed J. Brown, the paying banker is not concerned with the instruction to the collecting banker.

A bearer cheque does not require indorsement and any indorsements which may have been placed thereon need not be examined. A bearer cheque cannot be turned into one payable to order by indorsement. If a "bearer" cheque is specially indorsed to John Brown or order and is not signed by John Brown, the banker is not concerned with the matter.

In the case of a cheque payable to order which has been indorsed in blank, thus making it payable to bearer, and a subsequent holder makes it again payable to order, the fresh series of indorsements must be examined by the banker.

If an indorsement has been altered, it should, if correct, be confirmed. An indorsement of a signature by means of an impressed stamp should be confirmed by a collecting banker.

A banker is not obliged to take an irregular indorsement, and if a cheque is indorsed in such a manner that he is unable to decide whether it is right or wrong, it is safer to return it for confirmation.

An indorsement in pencil is not a sufficient reason for returning a cheque, as it is a valid indorsement, but the use of a pencil for such a purpose should always be discouraged.

If the person presenting a cheque is unable to write, he should indorse it by mark, his mark being then witnessed, preferably by an independent party. The witness must know the person whose mark he witnesses, and, in addition to signing as witness, must give his own address.

Indorsements are occasionally met with having Mr. or Esq. added to the name. If the name has been written by the right party the indorsement is sufficient, but a collecting banker should confirm it.

In Scotland, when the payee is a married woman, the cheque is frequently drawn as "Pay Mrs. Mary Young or Campbell." Young being her maiden name and Campbell the married name. The indorsement is accepted whether signed "Mary Young" or "Mary Campbell."

It is a saving of much time and trouble if a collecting banker confirms all indorsements which he notices are not strictly in order, when he knows that they are all right, before remitting the cheques for collection.

A paying banker should not return a cheque "indorsement irregular" if the objection is merely a frivolous one. A slight variation in the name on a cheque for a trifling amount is not regarded as of so much importance as in the case of a cheque for a larger amount, and a small cheque often receives the benefit of a doubt and is passed with an indorsement not absolutely in order.

An indorsement "J. Brown & Coy., Ltd., J. Jones, Secretary," is usually accepted, though "Per pro. J. Brown & Coy., Ltd., J. Jones, Secretary," is preferable.

If a payee presents an "order" cheque himself, it is the custom to require him to indorse it, but see PAYEE.

The payee's indorsement need not necessarily be the first signature on the back of the cheque, though, of course, it usually is.

A cheque indorsed in France may be signed with the surname only.

There is no authorised form of indorsement, and in consequence the variations in indorsements are very numerous and often puzzling to decide upon. The following is a list of specimens; in one column are included indorsements which, as a rule, would be passed, either because they are strictly correct or sufficiently accurate to justify their acceptance; in the other column are shown indorsements which are not generally accepted, either because they are quite wrong or so doubtful as to cause the cheques bearing them to be returned "indorsement irregular."

Payee.	Correct or Usually Accepted.	Wrong or Not Usually Accepted.
John Brown	John Brown.	J. Brown, p.p. J. Jones.
	J. Brown.	John Brown, per J. Jones.
	per pro. John Brown, J. Jones.	John Brown, pro J. Jones.
	p.p. John Brown, J. Jones.	John Brown by J. Jones.
	per pro. Mr. John Brown, J. Jones.	For John Brown, J. Jones.
	pro (or for) John Brown, J. Jones, Agent.	For J. Brown & Co., J. Brown.
	J. Jones, Agent for John Brown.	J. Jones, Solicitor to J. Brown.
	J. Jones, per pro. John Brown.	John Brown, J. J.
	per pro. John Brown, J. Jones & Coy.	John Browne.
	John Brown by J. Jones, his Attorney.	John J. Brown.
		pro John Brown, J. Jones.

Payee.	Correct or Usually Accepted.	Wrong or Not Usually Accepted.
Dr. John Brown	John Brown, M.D. John Brown.	Dr. J. Brown.
Captain John Brown	J. Brown, Captain. J. Brown.	Capt. J. Brown.
Mr. John Brown	John Brown.	Mr. John Brown.
Mr. Brown	J. Brown. J. Brown, Junior.	Brown. Mr. Brown.
Mrs. John Brown	Mary Brown, wife of John Brown. Mary Brown, widow of John Brown. Mary Brown (Mrs. John Brown).	Mary Brown. John Brown. Mrs. John Brown.
Mrs. Brown	Mary Brown. M. Brown. (Mrs.) Mary Brown.	Mrs. Brown. Mrs. Mary Brown.
John Brown, Senr.	John Brown, Senr. John Brown.	
John Brown, Junr.	John Brown, Junior.	John Brown.
John Brown, Esq.	John Brown.	John Brown, Esq.
Revd. John Brown	John Brown. John Brown, Vicar of All Saints', Oldtown. (Rev.) John Brown.	Rev. John Brown.
Mr. & Mrs. Brown	John Brown. Mary Brown.	J. & M. Brown.
George Brown (a minor)	George Brown.	John Brown, father of George Brown.
Misses Brown	Jane Brown. Mary Brown.	J. & M. Brown.
John Brown & another	For Self & another, J. Brown.	J. Brown.
John Brown (now deceased)	For Self & Co-Executors of late John Brown, J. Jones. John Jones, Executor of the late John Brown. J. Jones } Administrators of the late R. Smith } John Brown.	John Brown. J. Jones. Mary Brown, widow of John Brown. Jones & Co., Solicitors to the Estate of John Brown, decd.
Mrs. John Brown (now deceased)	J. Jones. Executor of the late Mary Brown, wife of John Brown (or widow of the late John Brown).	
John Brown (who cannot write)	his John X Brown. mark Witness, J. Jones. 13, King St., Leeds.	John Brown J. Jones.
John Brown (Indorsed "Credit my Account, John Brown")	Indorsement by Bank not necessary.	
John Brown (Indorsed "Credit a/c J. Jones, John Brown")	Do.	
John Joseph Simpson Brown.	J. J. S. Brown.	J. J. Brown.
Brown Brothers	Brown Brothers.	J. Brown & Bros. J. Brown. T. Brown. J. & T. Brown.
W. Brown, J. Jones, R. Smith	W. Brown. J. Jones. R. Smith.	Brown, Jones & Smith. For Self, Jones & Smith. W. Brown.
W. Brown & J. Jones	W. Brown. J. Jones. J. Jones. W. Brown. W. Brown. per pro. J. Jones, W. Brown.	Brown & Jones.
William & Thomas Brown	William Brown. Thomas Brown.	For William Brown & Self, Thomas Brown.
Messrs. Brown	J. & T. Brown. Brown & Son. J. Brown & Sons. per pro. Messrs. Brown, J. Jones Brown Bros. Brown & Brown.	Brown. Brown & Coy. Messrs. Brown.
Messrs. J. & T. Brown	J. & T. Brown. per pro. Messrs. J. & T. Brown, J. Jones. John & Thomas Brown. John Brown. Thomas Brown.	J. & T. Brown, per J. Jones. J. & T. Brown, J. Jones.

Payee.	Correct or Usually Accepted.	Wrong or Not Usually Accepted.
Messrs. W. Brown.	W. Brown. W. & W. Brown.	Messrs. W. Brown. J. & W. Brown.
Messrs. Browns	Browns.	Brown & Coy.
Brown & Co.	Brown & Coy. per pro. Brown & Co., J. Jones, Manr. per pro. Brown & Co., J. Jones. Brown & Co., by J. Jones, Agent.	For Brown & Co., J. Jones. Brown & Co., J. J. Brown, Smith & Jones. Jas. Brown & Co. per pro. Brown & Co., pro J. Jones. R. Smith.
Messrs. Brown & Co.	Brown & Coy. per pro. Messrs. Brown & Co., J. Jones. Brown & Co., John Brown, Partner.	Messrs. Brown & Co.
Messrs. Brown & Jones	J. Brown. J. Jones. Brown & Jones.	Jones & Brown.
Brown & Jones, Ld.	per pro. Brown & Jones, Ld., J. Smith, Secretary.	Brown & Jones, Ld.
The British Coy., Ld., per John Brown	per pro. The British Coy., Ld., John Brown, Secretary.	John Brown.
The British Coy., Ld.	Indorsed by order of The British Company, Ld., and placed to the credit of their account per pro. the X. & Y. Bank, Ld., J. Brown, Manager.	
	per pro. The British Coy., Ld., J. Brown, Secretary.	per pro. The British Coy., Ld., J. Brown, pro Manager.
	per pro. The British Coy., Ld., J. Brown.	J. Brown, Secy., British Coy., Ld.
	pro, or For, The British Coy., Ld., J. Brown, Manager.	per pro. The British Company, J. Brown, Secy.
	For The British Coy., Ld., J. Brown, Director.	per pro. The British Coy., Ld., per pro. John Brown, Secy. J. Jones.
	The British Coy., Ld., J. Brown, Secretary. (Strictly the indorsement should show that the Secretary signs For, or On behalf of the Company.)	
	The British Coy, Ld., per J. Brown, Secy.	The British Coy., Ld. (But see Section 77, Companies (Consolidation) Act, 1908, under COMPANIES.)
	Received in payment of call & passed to credit of payees. per pro. The X. & Y. Bank, Ld., J. Brown, Manager.	
	For the British Coy., Ld. In Liquidation. J. Brown } J. Jones } Liquidators.	For The British Coy., Ld., in Liquidation. For J. Brown, Liquidator, J. Jones.
	For or on behalf of The British Coy., Ld., J. Brown, Secy.	
The British Baking Coy.	per pro. The British Baking Coy., J. Brown, Secretary.	The British Baking Coy., p.p. J. Brown, Secy.
	per pro. The British Baking Coy., Brown & Jones.	
	For the British Baking Coy., J. Brown, Agent.	John Brown, Manager, British Baking Coy.
	per pro. The British & Universal Baking Coy. (Formerly The British Baking Co.), J. Brown, Secy.	per pro. The Baking Coy., J. Brown, Secy. The British Baking Coy. per pro. The British Baking Co., Ld., J. Brown, Secy.
	p.p. The British Baking Coy., J. Brown, Proprietor.	
	The British Baking Coy., J. Brown, cashier authorised to sign.	
	The British Baking Coy., J. Brown, Manager. (It is better that Brown should sign per pro. For, or On behalf of.)	
The British Shipping Coy., J. Brown & Co., Agents	For The British Shipping Coy., J. Brown & Co., Agents.	The British Shipping Coy., per pro. J. Brown & Co., Agents, J. Jones

Payee.	Correct or Usually Accepted.	Wrong or Not Usually Accepted.
John Brown, Secretary, British Coy., Ld.	John Brown, Secretary, British Coy., Ld.	per pro. J. Brown, Secy., British Co., Ld., J. Jones. John Brown.
The British Banking Co., Ld.	For the British Banking Co., Ld., J. Brown, Manager. per pro. The British Banking Co., Ld., J. Jones, Pro Manager. (Not strictly correct but very common in banks.)	
John Brown, Executor .	John Brown, Executor.	John Brown.
John Brown, Treasurer, Redby Cricket Club	John Brown, Treasurer, Redby Cricket Club.	John Brown.
John Brown, Treasurer, Redby Rural District Council.	John Brown, Treasurer, Redby Rural District Council.	John Brown. John Brown, Treasurer.
Official Receiver of J. Brown & Co.	J. Jones, Official Receiver of J. Brown & Co.	per pro. J. Jones, Official Receiver of J. Brown & Co. R. Smith.
The Collector of Customs and Excise	J. Brown, Collector of Customs and Excise.	per pro. J. Brown, Collector of Customs and Excise, J. Jones.
The Mayor of Oldtown .	John Jones, Mayor of Oldtown. per pro. The Mayor of Oldtown, John Brown.	Mayor of Oldtown.
The Oldtown Corporation	per pro. The Oldtown Corporation, John Brown, Treasurer.	per pro. The Oldtown Corporation, J. Jones, Rate Collector.
Managers of Redby School	J. Brown } Managers of Redby School J. Jones } For the Managers of Redby School, J. Brown, Chairman.	J. Jones, Manager. J. Brown. J. Jones.
Brown frères	Brown Bros. Brown frères.	
Overseers of Redby, per J. Brown, Collector	Overseers of Redby, John Brown, Collector.	John Brown.
Overseers of Redby . .	For the Overseers of Redby, J. Brown, Asst. Overseer. J. Jones } Overseers of Redby. R. Smith }	J. Jones. R. Smith.
Self or order (drawn by J. Brown)	J. Brown.	per pro. J. Brown, J. Jones.
Self or bearer	No indorsement required.	
Administrators of Wm. Brown (the same remarks apply as in the case of executors)		
Executors of Wm. Brown .	J. Jones for self & co-Exor. of Wm. Brown. For Exors. of Wm. Brown, J. Jones, Exor. J. Jones, Exor. of Wm. Brown.	per pro. Exors. of Wm. Brown, R. Smith, Solicitor to the Estate. per pro. Exors. of Wm. Brown, R. Smith. For J. Jones, Executor of Wm. Brown, R. Robinson. J. Jones for self & Co-executors.
Executors of the late Wm. Brown	J. Jones } Exors. of the late Wm. J. Brown } Brown.	
Trustees of Wm. Brown .	J. Brown } Trustees of Wm. Brown. J. Jones } Trustees of Wm. Brown, J. Brown. J. Jones.	per pro. Trustees of Wm. Brown, J. Brown. For Self & Co-Trustee of Wm. Brown, J. Brown. o/a Wm. Brown's Trust, J. Jones. J. Brown.
John Brown & J. Jones, Trustees of R. Smith	John Brown, J. Jones. Trustees of R. Smith.	John Brown, J. Jones.
Liquidators of the X. & Y. Coy., Ld.	The X. & Y. Co., Ld., in Liquidation, J. Brown } Liquidators. J. Jones }	The X. & Y. Coy., Ld., For Self & Co-Liquidator, J. Brown. J. Brown. (See LIQUIDATOR.) J. Jones.

Payee	Correct or Usually Accepted.	Wrong or Not Usually Accepted.
IRREGULAR PAYEES.		
.... or	Requires drawer's indorsement.	
.... or Order . .	Do.	
W. Brown or	Requires W. Brown's indorsement.	
Cash or Order	Requires drawer's indorsement.	
Wages or Order . . .	Do.	
Estate a/c or Order . .	Do.	
Wages or Bearer . . .	No indorsement required.	
King Charles the First or Order	Do.	
Dick Swiveller or Order (a fictitious person)	Do.	
s.s. *Britannia* or Order .	Requires indorsement by an authorised official.	
Corporation Stock or Order	Requires City Treasurer's indorsement.	
Bearer or Order . . .	Usually treated as payable to bearer.	
Income Tax or Order. .	Requires indorsement of Collector of Inland Revenue.	
My son the bearer . .	Requires son's indorsement.	
My son, the bearer or Order.	Do.	
W. B.	W. B., W. Brown.	
a/c of John Brown . .	Placed to credit of Payee's account per pro. British Banking Co., Ld., J. Jones, Manager.	
Brown & Jones (names transposed)	per pro. Brown & Jones, T. Smith, Manr. per pro. Jones & Brown, T. Smith, Manr.	
Ann Brown (spelled wrongly)	Ann Brown. Anne Browne.	Anne Browne.
Robert MacIntyre (spelled wrongly)	Robert MacIntyre. Robt. McIntyre.	Robert McIntyre.
W. Brown or order J. J. . (alteration initialled by drawer)	Usually treated as being payable to bearer.	
Brown	J. Brown.	Brown.
John Brown & Another.	For Self & another, J. Brown.	John Brown.
Representatives of John Brown	For Self and Co-Executors of the late John Brown, J. Jones.	
John Brown for J. Jones .	John Brown for John Jones.	per pro. J. Brown, R. Smith.
Miss Brown (now married)	M. Jones *née* Brown.	
Brown & Co., Ld. (correct title J. R. Brown & Co., Ld.)	Brown & Co., Ld., per pro. J. R. Brown & Co., Ld., J. Jones, Secy.	
The Secretary (drawn by a Company)	J. Jones, Secretary.	
DIVIDEND WARRANT.		
John Brown, John Jones and R. Smith	John Brown (or John Jones or R. Smith may sign alone).	
John Brown & Another	John Brown.	Jas. Smith (the other referred to).
John Brown	John Brown.	per pro. John Brown, J. Jones.
John Brown, or Bearer .	John Brown should sign.	

(See BILL OF EXCHANGE, DELIVERY OF BILL, INDORSER, NEGOTIATION OF BILL OF EXCHANGE.)

INDORSEMENT CONFIRMED. There are cases of daily occurrence, in most bank offices, where an indorsement is not literally or strictly in order, but which the collecting banker knows to be "all right." Before remitting such cheques for collection it is customary for the banker to confirm the irregular indorsement, as: "Indorsement confirmed. Per pro. The X. & Y. Bank, Ltd., John Brown, Manager."

The words "Indorsement confirmed" are preferable to "Indorsement guaranteed." The latter expression might be held to be a guarantee requiring a sixpenny stamp.

An indorsement made by a stamp ought, if the banker knows it to have been placed thereon by an authorised person, to be confirmed.

INDORSEMENT GUARANTEED. (See INDORSEMENT CONFIRMED.)

INDORSEMENT ON BANK NOTE. Where a person indorses a bank note with the intent that it should act as an indorsement, and delivers it so indorsed to a third person, he renders himself liable to be sued upon the note by any subsequent holder. A person receiving a bank note in payment of a debt cannot compel the person offering it to indorse it, but where a person is asked to give change for a bank note he can, if he so wishes, decline to give the change unless the note is indorsed.

When a Bank of England note is presented for payment at the Bank, it is customary for the Bank to request the person presenting it to write his name and address upon the back. As all Bank of England notes are payable in gold, on demand, at the head office, that office cannot legally insist upon such indorsement.

Referring to indorsements on cheques, bills, and also on a bank note, Mr. Justice Byles (in *Keene* v. *Beard*, 1860, 8 C.B.N.S. 372) said that "the act of writing may or may not be an indorsement according to circumstances," and he held that "where a man indorses an instrument of this sort, *animo indorsandi*, and delivers it so indorsed to a third person, he renders himself liable to be sued upon the instrument, as indorsee, by any subsequent holder."

INDORSEMENT ON DEPOSIT RECEIPT. A deposit receipt is not a transferable document, and the indorsement upon it is really a discharge to the banker upon repayment of the money. If over £2, and the usual printed form of receipt on the back is signed, the signature must be across a penny adhesive stamp, unless the form is already impressed with a penny stamp. (See DEPOSIT RECEIPT.)

INDORSER. When a payee writes his name upon the back of a bill or cheque, he is called an "indorser," and when the instrument is negotiated to other persons, each person may indorse it in turn and become an indorser. Each indorser of a bill (or cheque) is liable thereon.

Any indorser, however, may add after his signature such words as "without recourse to me," or "*sans recours*." The sanction is given by Section 16 of the Bills of Exchange Act, 1882, which provides that any indorser may insert an express stipulation :—

'"(1) Negativing or limiting his own liability to the holder;

"(2) Waiving as regards himself some or all of the holder's duties."

The liability of an indorser is defined by the Bills of Exchange Act, Section 55 :—

"(2) The indorser of a bill by indorsing it—

"(*a*) Engages that on due presentment it shall be accepted and paid according to its tenor, and that if it be dishonoured he will compensate the holder or a subsequent indorser who is compelled to pay it, provided that the requisite proceedings on dishonour be duly taken ;

"(*b*) Is precluded from denying to a holder in due course the genuineness and regularity in all respects of the drawer's signature and all previous indorsements ;

"(*c*) Is precluded from denying to his immediate or a subsequent indorsee that the bill was at the time of his indorsement a valid and subsisting bill, and that he had then a good title thereto."

Section 56 provides : "Where a person signs a bill otherwise than as drawer or acceptor, he thereby incurs the liabilities of an indorser to a holder in due course."

Where a person is under obligation to indorse a bill in a representative capacity as treasurer or executor, he may indorse the bill in such terms as to negative personal liability (Section 31, s.s. 5).

Where an indorser is dead and the party giving notice knows it, notice of dishonour must be given to his personal representative if such there be, and with the exercise of reasonable diligence he can be found (Section 49, s.s. 9).

Where an indorser is bankrupt, notice may be given either to the party himself or to the trustee (Section 49, s.s. 10). (See BILL OF EXCHANGE, DISHONOUR OF BILL OF EXCHANGE, INDORSEMENT, NEGOTIATION OF BILL OF EXCHANGE.)

INDUSTRIAL LIFE POLICY. The policy is usually granted upon the express condition that it shall become absolutely void, if it is in any way assigned, sold, mortgaged or otherwise parted with.

Even if, in any industrial company, such policies may be assigned, there is very little value attaching to them on account of their surrender and paid up values being so small. Most companies give no cash surrender value. (See LIFE POLICY.)

INFANTS. All persons below the age of twenty-one are, by English law, called infants or minors. The question as to whether a banker can with safety permit a minor to open an account and draw cheques thereon is one which has been much discussed and on which diverse opinions prevail. The generally accepted legal opinion appears now to be that a banker may, without risk, allow an infant to open an account and draw cheques upon it, but that the account must not be overdrawn, for money lent to an infant cannot be recovered, even if he gave security.

By the Infants' Relief Act, 1874, Section 2, "no action shall be brought whereby to charge any person upon any promise made after full age to pay any debt contracted during infancy or upon any ratification made after full age, of any promise or contract made during infancy whether there shall or shall not be any new consideration for such promise or ratification after full age."

In savings banks, receipts are given by minors and accepted, but in those cases special provision is made under the Savings Bank Acts that the receipt of a person under the age of twenty-one years shall be a sufficient discharge.

The holder of an infant's cheque, which has been dishonoured, cannot sue the infant upon it; and where a cheque has been cashed to a minor and is subsequently dishonoured, the money cannot be recovered by law from the minor.

Section 22, s.s. 2, of the Bills of Exchange Act, 1882, provides: "Where a bill is drawn or indorsed by an infant, minor, or corporation having no capacity or power to incur liability on a bill, the drawing or indorsement entitles the holder to receive payment of the bill, and to enforce it against any other party thereto." The signature of an infant upon a bill does not in any way affect its negotiability. He may pass on a good title to others, and though he cannot be sued himself he may by his next friend sue other parties to the bill. Even if a minor accepts a bill in payment of necessaries, he cannot be sued upon it.

An infant cannot sue in his own name, except in a county court for wages due to him. In an action by an infant he must sue by his "next friend," and in an action against an infant a guardian is appointed.

But if a minor has made a false representation as to his age and thereby induced a banker or anyone to enter into a contract with him, he cannot afterwards obtain relief by proving that he is below the age of twenty-one.

The Statute of Limitations does not begin to run until he has reached the age of twenty-one.

Shares should not be registered in the name of a minor as he may repudiate any liability thereon.

An infant may sign as a witness; he may also act as an agent and sign cheques, and draw, accept, or indorse bills, and the liability rests with the person who gave him the authority to do so. He may sign cheques upon an overdrawn account if that power is included in the authority. There is nothing to prevent an infant being a partner in any business, but in any action against the firm the infant would be excluded. An infant cannot undertake the duties of an administrator or executor nor act as a proxy in bankruptcy proceedings. He cannot make a will, and in the event of his death letters of administration require to be taken out by his father or mother or nearest of kin.

An account is sometimes opened with a banker in the joint names of a parent or guardian and an infant; such an account should be treated by the banker like an ordinary joint account as to authority for signing of cheques, etc., but he will, of course, bear in mind the non-liability of the minor for an overdraft, as before mentioned. If the minor is a very young child, the better plan is for the account to be opened in the parent's or guardian's name for the child, thus, "John Brown. In re Timothy Brown," in which case no mandate is required, and the adult has full control.

The form in which deposit receipts are sometimes issued, "John Brown for Joseph Brown (a minor)" is not a desirable one, and should be avoided.

A deposit receipt may be issued in the name of a minor. On withdrawal he is able to give a good discharge for the money.

Stock in Public Funds. By the National Debt Act, 1870, Section 19:—"Where stock is standing in the name of an infant or person of unsound mind, jointly with any person not under legal disability, a letter of attorney for the receipt of the dividends on the stock shall be sufficient authority in that behalf, if given under the hand and seal of the person not under disability, attested by two or more credible witnesses." By the National Debt (Stockholders Relief) Act, 1892, Section 3 :—" (a) Where an infant is the sole survivor in an account ; and (b) where an infant holds stock jointly with a person under legal disability ; and (c) where stock has by mistake been bought in or transferred into the sole name of an infant, the Bank may, at the request in writing of the parent, guardian, or next friend of the infant, receive the dividends and apply them to the purchase of like stock, and the stock so purchased shall be added to the original investment."

INGOT. Bars of gold and silver are called ingots.

INHABITED HOUSE DUTY. The duty on inhabited houses occupied as a shop, warehouse, public-house, farm-house, coffee-house, lodging-house :—

Annual Value.	Rate.
£20 and not exceeding £40 . . .	2*d.* in the £.
Exceeding £40 and not exceeding £60	4*d.* ,,
Exceeding £60	6*d.* ,,

Occupied as an ordinary dwelling-house :—

£20 and not exceeding £40 . . .	3*d.* in the £
Exceeding £40 and not exceeding £60	6*d.* ,,
Exceeding £60	9*d.* ,,

Where a dwelling-house communicates with a bank office, the duty is payable upon the annual value of the office as well as upon the house portion.

An unoccupied house is exempt. Premises used solely for business purposes are exempt from the duty, provided that no one sleeps on the premises other than a person engaged to dwell there solely for their protection, and who is not otherwise employed by the occupier.

A dwelling-house of a less annual value than £20 is exempt.

INLAND BILL. The Bills of Exchange Act, 1882, Section 4, defines an inland bill as follows :—

"(1) An inland bill is a bill which is or on the face of it purports to be (a) both drawn and payable within the British Islands, or (b) drawn within the British Islands upon some person resident therein. Any other bill is a foreign bill.

"For the purposes of this Act, 'British Islands' mean any part of the United Kingdom of Great Britain and Ireland, the islands of Man, Guernsey, Jersey, Alderney, and Sark, and the islands adjacent to any of them being part of the dominions of Her Majesty.

"(2) Unless the contrary appear on the face of the bill the holder may treat it as an inland bill."

By Section 36 of the Stamp Act, 1891, "a bill or note purporting to be drawn or made out of the United Kingdom is, for the purposes of stamp duty, to be deemed to have been so drawn or made, although it may in fact have been drawn or made within the United Kingdom." Thus, by the Stamp Act, a bill drawn in the Isle of Man and the Channel Islands (which places are out of the United Kingdom) is regarded as a foreign bill, whereas, by the Bills of Exchange Act, it is an inland bill.

Where an inland bill is dishonoured, it is not necessary that it should be noted or protested for non-acceptance or non-payment in order to preserve recourse against the drawer or indorser, but this is sometimes done in order to induce a friend to come forward to accept the bill for the honour of a certain party to the bill. The sections of the Act with regard to noting and protest are given in the article PROTEST.

Where an inland bill is indorsed in a foreign country, the indorsement shall as regards the payer be interpreted according to the law of the United Kingdom. As to the other rules laid down in the Bills of Exchange Act with regard to bills drawn in one country and negotiated, accepted or payable in another, see Section 72, under FOREIGN BILL.

The following is the usual form in which a bill of exchange is drawn :—

Birmingham, July 10, 1910

£150 0*s.* 0*d.*

Stamp. 2s.

Six months after date pay to me or my order the sum of one hundred and fifty pounds for value received

To Mr. Thomas Jones, JOHN BROWN.
15 Thames Street,
London.

The indorsements appear upon the back of the bill, *e.g.* :—

Pay Smith, Robinson & Co.,
or order.
JOHN BROWN.

Pay the Imperial Trading Co., Ltd.,
or order.
SMITH, ROBINSON & CO.

Per pro. the Imperial Trading Co., Ltd.,
JAMES GREEN,
Manager.

This bill is drawn at Birmingham on July 10, 1910, being payable at six months after date it falls due (or matures) on January 13, 1911 ; the six months are called its term and the following three days are the days of grace. The date is always expressed in figures, but to use words would be quite in order. The amount is quoted in both words and figures, but either alone would be according to law, the repetition being to avoid mistakes or fraudulent alteration.

The currency of this bill on July 10, 1910, the day it is drawn, is 187 days, on July 11 it is 186 days, and so on, this being the time it has yet to run.

This is an " after date " bill, but it might have been drawn " after sight," in which case Mr. Thomas Jones, when he accepted it, would have written the then present date in his acceptance and the due date would have been reckoned from that.

Or, instead of " Six months after date," the bill might have been drawn " At sight " or " On presentation " or " On demand," in all which three cases there would be no acceptance at all, for payment would have to be made at once.

The drawer is John Brown, who in this case is also the payee, but the drawer could have made the bill payable to anyone he pleased or to bearer.

The drawee is Thomas Jones and by writing his name across the bill he has become the acceptor; that is to say, he accepts John Brown's demand for money due, and, by the words he has added, instructs the Rivergate Branch of the British Bank (where John Jones keeps his account) to pay £150 to John Brown or his order in six months' time.

This bill is said to be domiciled at the British Bank, Ltd., Rivergate, London, who are also called the " drawee bank."

Referring to the indorsements on the bill, John Brown wishes to pay £150 to Smith, Robinson & Co. ; he therefore, as shown, indorses the bill over to them ; who in their turn indorse it to the Imperial Trading Co., Ltd. ; this firm indorse it and then, perhaps, discount it with their own bankers who will sort it away in their bill case until the time comes for presentation for payment. For stamp duties see BILL OF EXCHANGE. (See BILL OF EXCHANGE, FOREIGN BILL.)

INOPERATIVE ACCOUNT. An account upon which there are no transactions.

INSCRIBED STOCK. No certificates are issued to the holders of inscribed stock, but their names and the amount of the stock they hold are inscribed in the registers kept for the purpose at the banks which have the management of the stocks. The Bank of England, for instance, holds the registers for the stocks in the Public Funds, and a stockholder wishing to transfer his holding must attend personally at the Bank to sign the transfer in the register, or, if unable to attend personally, the transfer may be effected by his duly authorised attorney. Transferors must in all cases be identified by a stockbroker or other person approved by the Bank. (See NATIONAL DEBT.)

In a case in 1907, Mr. Justice Lawrence said : " It is the long-established practice of the Bank of England to permit stockholders to make transfers in the Bank books only when they are identified as the persons owning the stock by persons of one of three classes (1) certain high officers of the Bank of England ; (2) the past and present representatives of private banks ; (3) members of the London Stock Exchange and their clerks, whose names are upon a list kept at the Bank. The privilege of being upon this list of brokers is obtained by the introduction of a member already upon the list. A member upon the list can have his clerk's name put upon it by signing a document making himself responsible for the acts of his clerk. There are some 3,000 members on the list, and it is clearly a privilege valuable to brokers who deal in Government securities."

Certain stocks domiciled at the Bank of Montreal, Glyn & Co., Standard Bank of

South Africa and the Agent General for South Australia are transferred by deed, although they are called inscribed stocks.

Stock certificates to bearer may be obtained by a holder for various inscribed stocks, which are transferable at the Bank of England.

The receipt for the purchase money, which is given to a purchaser when a transfer of inscribed stock is made, is of no value. It is not required upon a subsequent sale. To obtain a security upon inscribed stock, it must be transferred into the names of the nominees of the bank; but if the inscribed stock can be exchanged into bearer bonds it may be more convenient for a customer to do this in order to give security to a bank. (See POWER OF ATTORNEY—TRANSFER OF GOVERNMENT STOCK.)

INSOLVENCY. A person is insolvent who is unable to pay his debts, and he is said to be in a state of insolvency.

An insolvent person may have a receiving order made against him and suffer proceedings under the Bankruptcy Acts (see BANKRUPTCY, RECEIVING ORDER), or he may call his creditors together and endeavour to come to an arrangement with them (apart from the Bankruptcy Acts), usually either by offering to pay a composition—that is, to pay so much in the pound in full discharge of what he is owing to them (see COMPOSITION WITH CREDITORS)—or by offering to transfer his property to a trustee in order that it may be realised and the proceeds divided amongst his creditors according to the amounts of their respective claims. (See ASSIGNMENT FOR BENEFIT OF CREDITORS.)

Where a judgment has been obtained in a county court, and the debtor is unable to pay, if the whole indebtedness does not exceed £50, an administration order may be made by the county court. (See ADMINISTRATION ORDER.)

When a petition is presented against a debtor, and his estate is not likely to exceed £300 the Court may make an order for summary administration. (See SUMMARY ADMINISTRATION.)

When a receiving order has been made against a debtor, it may subsequently be discharged by the Court if a proposal by the debtor for a composition in satisfaction of his debts, or a proposal for a scheme of arrangement of his affairs is accepted by the creditors. (See BANKRUPTCY, COMPOSITIONS—BANKRUPTCY ACT.)

INSPECTION OF REGISTER. The register of members of a company shall, during business hours, be open to the inspection of any member gratis, and to the inspection of any other person on payment of one shilling, or such less sum as the company may prescribe (Section 30 of the Companies (Consolidation) Act, 1908). (See COMPANIES, REGISTER OF MEMBERS OF COMPANY.)

INSTALMENTS. Part repayments of a debt. They may be made at regular, or irregular, periods. As to the effect of the Statute of Limitations upon a promissory note being repaid by instalments, see STATUTE OF LIMITATIONS — PROMISSORY NOTE.

INSTITUTE OF BANKERS. Address:— 34, Clement's Lane, London, E.C.

The Institute of Bankers was founded in 1879 and is an Association of gentlemen connected with the various branches of banking. Its primary object is to facilitate the consideration and discussion of matters of interest to the profession, and, where advisable, to take measures to further the decisions arrived at; and its secondary object is to afford opportunities for the acquisition of a knowledge of the theory of banking.

The Institute affords facilities for the reading, discussion and publication of papers by members and others; it arranges for the delivery of lectures on banking, mercantile law, political economy and other kindred subjects; and it issues certificates to those who may pass examinations approved of from time to time by the Council of the Institute.

The members of the Institute are fellows, associates, certificated associates and ordinary members.

Fellows are elected by the Council. Subscription, two guineas.

Associates are elected from those who have not been less than ten years in the service of any bank; or from those who have passed the examination recognised by the Council; or from those who, being on the staff of a bank, are graduates of any University. Subscription, one guinea.

Certificated associates are members who have gained the certificate of the Institute. Subscription, 10*s.* 6*d.*

Ordinary members are clerks on the staff of any bank who are approved by the Council. Subscription, 10*s.* 6*d.*

The membership on January 1, 1910, was as follows:—

Fellows	386
Associates	1,719
Ordinary members	5,686
Grand total . . .	7,791

The *Journal* of the Institute is published in consecutive months from October to the June following, with a further issue of one or two numbers when deemed necessary. The date of publication is on or about the first day of the months named.

The following is the form of the certificate which is issued to members who pass the advanced examination of the Institute :—

CERTIFICATE OF THE INSTITUTE.

(*Pursuant to Clause III of the Constitution thereof.*)

WE, the President of the Institute of Bankers and the Chairman of the Council for the time being, do hereby certify that

has duly passed the Examination for the Certificate of the Institute in the various subjects selected by the Council, namely :—

Commercial Arithmetic.
Book-keeping.
English Composition and Banking Correspondence.
Commercial Law.
Economics.
Practical Banking.

and has thereby become an Associate of the Institute.

President.
Chairman of the Council.

Dated this day of 19 .

INSTITUTE OF BANKERS IN IRELAND. The Institute was founded in 1898.

The object of the Institute is to enable the members to acquire a knowledge of the theory and practice of Banking, and to promote the consideration and discussion of matters of interest to the profession.

The Institute provides for the delivery of lectures on banking and other professional subjects ; and maintains a suitable library for the use of the members. Examinations are held annually, and certificates awarded. The *Journal* of the Institute is issued quarterly.

INSTITUTE OF BANKERS IN SCOTLAND. This Institute was established in 1875.

Its object is " to improve the qualifications of those engaged in banking, and to raise their status and influence."

The object is promoted by classes, lectures and bursaries ; by the formation of libraries of works on finance and kindred subjects ; by examinations and the issuing of certificates to such as pass them.

The Institute consists of members and associates, who are connected with the banks in Scotland.

The Scottish Banker's Magazine is published quarterly by the Institute.

INSTRUMENT. A legal term applied to a bill, a cheque, a deed, or any document in writing by means of which some right or contract is expressed.

INSURABLE INTEREST. Before a person can effect an insurance on the life of another person, or can insure a ship or cargo, or a house against fire, or any other thing, he must have an insurable, that is, a pecuniary, interest in the person or thing to be insured. (See LIFE POLICY.)

INSURANCE. The word was originally applied only to fire insurance, but it is now used either for life or fire, as well as for other matters of insurance. (See ASSURANCE, FIRE INSURANCE, LICENSED PROPERTY, LIFE POLICY, MARINE INSURANCE POLICY, MUTUAL INSURANCE, POLICY OF INSURANCE, SPECIE—TRANSMISSION OF.)

INSURANCE CERTIFICATE. An insurance certificate is sometimes attached to a documentary bill, and is a declaration by an insurance company that the goods are insured under a policy which also covers other goods. It may also be given if the actual policy is not ready. (See MARINE INSURANCE POLICY.)

INTERBOURSE SECURITIES. INTERNATIONAL SECURITIES. General terms indicating securities which can be bought and sold in different countries at practically the same prices.

INTEREST. Interest is the money which is paid for a loan or the use of money. In the case of a banker interest is paid by him to customers for money deposited, and is received by him for money he has lent to customers.

In the year 1546 the taking of interest for money was made legal in England, and the rate was fixed at 10 per cent. It was reduced to 8 per cent. in 1624, and to 6 per cent. in 1651, and in 1714 it was further reduced to 5 per cent. (Gilbart).

If the rate of interest is 3 per cent., the interest upon the money lent (the principal) is referred to as being at the rate of £3 per cent. per annum; that is, for each £100, three pounds is payable by way of interest at the end of a complete year, and for each part of £100 or part of a year the interest is in proportion thereto.

Simple interest is calculated upon the principal only, whereas compound interest is interest which is calculated upon the principal plus interest which is due and has not been paid. A deposit receipt is an example where simple interest only is allowed. It is calculated and provided for each half-year by a banker upon the original sum deposited, but it is not added to the principal until the depositor brings in his deposit receipt and renews it for the amount with the interest added. A deposit account, and current account where interest is added, are examples where compound interest is allowed, as each half-year when the interest is calculated it is added at once to the balance or principal and becomes part of the amount on which interest is subsequently allowed.

In a current account, interest is calculated from the actual date when a customer's cheque is paid (not from the date of the cheque), and from the actual date when money is paid to credit, which, in the case of a sub-branch, may in some cases be the day before it is actually posted in the current account ledger at the parent branch. Where a cheque is paid at another bank or branch under advice, the banker is entitled to charge interest from the date when so paid. The calculations are in most banks now effected by means of products, commonly, though erroneously, called "decimals," by which the balance of an account, on the occasion of each change, is multiplied by the number of days it has remained undisturbed, the product, say, 2,650, being simply £2,650 for one day, or put in another form £1 for 2,650 days. The total of all the products on an account by the end of a half-year is therefore that number of pounds for one day at the rate of interest to be allowed or charged. With the aid of a product table the amount of interest is very quickly ascertained. (See DECIMALS.)

As to discount on a bill, see DISCOUNT.

In the case of a deposit receipt where interest varies according to the Bank Rate, the interest is calculated by means of a table of decimals, each rate being taken as a decimal part of 5 per cent. (See INTEREST ON DEPOSIT RECEIPT.)

London bankers do not, as a rule, allow interest upon a current account but country bankers usually do so, the rate being regulated according to the custom of the district and the nature of the account. Country bankers usually reckon the interest upon the daily balance of an account.

In some cases, if the balance falls below a specified figure no interest is given, though if that figure is maintained, interest is allowed. It is sometimes agreed to allow interest upon the minimum monthly balance. The rate of interest upon a current account is naturally dependent upon the character of the account, and upon the amount receivable from commission. In some London banks the charge for commission is dependent upon the balance which is kept.

The interest upon a deposit receipt or deposit account is allowed at a higher rate than on a current account, the balance of which is liable to be withdrawn at any moment. Some bankers allow a uniform rate throughout the year, irrespective of whether the Bank of England Rate is high or low, whilst other bankers regulate the rate upon a scale which fluctuates according to the Bank Rate.

On deposits which are subject to notice, a higher rate is usually allowed, the rate being increased (e.g. in colonial banks) up to a certain point, according to the length of notice which must be given.

No interest is, as a rule, allowed upon money on deposit receipt unless it has remained in the banker's hands for a certain specified period. The period varies according to the bank, in some cases it is fourteen days, in others one month or even two months.

Where notice of repayment is given (i.e. in cases where notice is required) and the money is not applied for at the date it is due to be paid, interest usually ceases until the depositor renews the receipt.

Unless a promissory note payable on demand expressly states that interest is to be paid, interest is not recoverable. Where a bill is dishonoured, interest on the amount of the bill may be recovered from the time of presentment for payment if the bill is payable on demand and from the maturity of the bill in any other case. (See Section 57 of the Bills of Exchange Act, 1882, under DISHONOUR OF BILL OF EXCHANGE.)

There is no general law to justify interest being charged upon a loan, but by custom a banker is entitled to charge interest, and, by making half-yearly rests and adding the accrued interest to the balance, to charge compound interest. In addition to the usual custom, there may be a special agreement as to interest between the banker and a customer. A banker's right to charge compound interest may also be justified by a customer's acquiescence in the method of charging his account in previous half-years.

Unless by agreement, a banker is under no obligation to allow interest upon money lent to him.

Upon the death of a customer it has been held that simple interest only may be charged, and not compound interest, from the date of the customer's death till the date of payment.

Where a banker takes a mortgage for a fixed sum, unless there is a special agreement to charge compound interest, he can charge only simple interest, because the position is no longer that of banker and customer but that of mortgagor and mortgagee. For this reason, a loan account which is secured by a mortgage for a fixed sum must be kept distinct from the working account. The usual method in such a case is to obtain a cheque from the debtor upon the working account for the interest upon the loan account as it falls due. In the case of a fixed mortgage the banker must deduct income tax from the amount of the interest due upon the loan before charging it to the customer's account, but if the loan is for a less period than a year the customer is not entitled to have tax deducted. A mortgagor is entitled to deduct income tax by Section 40 of the Property Tax Act, 1853. When a banker deducts tax from the interest due by a customer upon a fixed mortgage, he takes credit, in his income tax return, for the amount of tax allowed to the customer; that is, the amount of tax due to be paid to the tax authorities upon the profits of the bank is reduced by the amount which he has already paid by way of the deduction from the customer's interest. Income tax is deducted from fixed deposits by the colonial banks in London. (See INCOME TAX.)

As to the effect of the Statute of Limitations upon interest, see STATUTE OF LIMITATIONS—INTEREST.

In the case of a bank of issue which was being wound up, it was held that interest at 5 per cent. was payable upon its notes from the date when demand for payment was made from the liquidator.

When a judgment for mortgage money has been obtained, the interest (if more than 4 per cent. in the mortgage deed) is reduced to 4 per cent.

Upon the bankruptcy of a customer, interest can be charged only up to the date of the order; or in the case of a deed of assignment to the date of the deed.

If there is any surplus from a bankrupt's estate after all debts are paid in full it shall be applied in payment of interest from the date of the receiving order at the rate of four pounds per cent. per annum on all debts proved in the bankruptcy (Section 40, s.s. 5, of the Bankruptcy Act, 1883).

On any debt or sum certain, payable at a certain time or otherwise, whereon interest is not agreed for, and which is overdue at the time of the receiving order and provable in bankruptcy, the creditor may prove for interest at 4 per cent. per annum to the date of the order from the time the debt was payable, if payable by virtue of a written instrument at a certain time, and if payable otherwise, then from the time when demand in writing has been made giving the debtor notice that interest will be claimed from the date of the demand until the time of payment. (See Rule 20, Schedule II, under PROOF OF DEBTS.)

Section 23 of the Bankruptcy Act, 1890, provides:—

"Where a debt has been proved upon a debtor's estate under the principal Act, and such debt includes interest, or any pecuniary consideration in lieu of interest, such interest or consideration shall, for the purposes of dividend, be calculated at a rate not exceeding five per centum per annum, without prejudice to the right of a creditor to receive out of the estate any higher rate of interest to which he may be entitled after all the debts proved in the estate have been paid in full."

A ready way of telling approximately the number of years in which an amount at compound interest will double itself, is to divide 70 by the rate per cent.

When, for any reason, it is necessary to refund part of the interest charged to a customer's account, it is commonly called a rebate.

In Scotland, all the banks, by agreement, make the same charges for interest and commission, so that, as far as charges are concerned, there is no advantage to be gained by a customer dealing with one bank rather than another. No interest is allowed on credit current accounts, but on the other hand commission is not charged.

INTEREST BILLS. A name sometimes given to the bills of exchange, payable in India, which are issued in payment of the interest upon Indian Government Rupee Loans. The bills are for rupees, and may be sold in London.

INTEREST ON BILL. "Where a bill is expressed to be payable with interest, unless the instrument otherwise provides, interest runs from the date of the bill, and if the bill is undated from the issue thereof" (Section 9, s.s. 3, Bills of Exchange Act, 1882).

In an action on a dishonoured bill, interest as damages can be claimed from the time of presentment for payment, if the bill is payable on demand, and from the maturity of the bill in any other case; but such interest may, if justice require it, be withheld, and where a bill is expressed on the face to be payable with interest at a given rate, interest as damages may or may not be given at the same rate as the interest proper (Section 57). The usual rate of interest allowed is 5 per cent., but a higher rate would be allowable if it is expressed in the bill, but the Court has power to set aside an agreement as to the rate of interest if it is considered excessive.

In practice a clause as to interest is very seldom inserted in a bill of exchange, although this is frequently done in a promissory note, the wording then being "On demand (or six months after date) I promise to pay to C. D. or order one hundred pounds with interest at the rate of five per centum per annum, for value received. A. B." If the note does not contain the interest clause, interest is not legally enforceable.

INTEREST ON DEPOSIT RECEIPT. The interest on a deposit receipt is quickly ascertained from the usual interest tables when the rate is the same during all the period that the money has been with the banker, but when, as is customary in certain districts, the rate varies from time to time, a special table requires to be prepared in order to assist in making the calculation.

If the interest table which is used is a 5 per cent. one and the rate to be allowed on a deposit receipt is 2 per cent., the interest on £1 for one day will be two-fifths or ·4 of the interest shown in the 5 per cent. table. In other words, the interest on £1 for one day at 2 per cent. is the same as interest on £1 for ·4 of a day at 5 per cent.; for two days it will be ·8 of a day, for three days 1·2 days at 5 per cent., and so on, ·4 being added each day.

When the rate is 3 per cent., ·6 is added each day, when 2½ per cent. ·5 is added, when 4 per cent. ·8 is added, ·1 being added for each ½ per cent. increase in the rate.

The following is a short specimen table :—

2 per cent. .	1 Jan., 1910	·4
	2 „	·8
	3 „	1·2
	4 „	1·6
	5 „	2·0
3 per cent. .	6 „	2·4
	7 „	3·0
	8 „	3·6
	9 „	4·2
	10 „	4·8
	11 „	5·4
2½ per cent. .	12 „	6·0
	13 „	6·5
	14 „	7·0
	15 „	7·5
2 per cent. .	16 „	8·0
	17 „	8·4
	18 „	8·8

If a deposit receipt which was issued on January 3, 1910, is presented for payment on January 16, it will be seen from the above table that interest must be allowed during those thirteen days at three different rates, to January 6 at 2 per cent., 6 to 12 at 3 per cent., 12 to 16 at 2½ per cent.

To ascertain the interest due, the decimals on January 3 must be deducted from those on 16, thus, $\begin{array}{r} 8{\cdot}0 \\ 1{\cdot}2 \\ \hline 6{\cdot}8 \end{array}$ the difference, 6·8, being the number of days at 5 per cent. upon the amount of the deposit receipt to give the interest required. In the case supposed, if the amount of the deposit is £100, the interest is quickly found by referring to a 5 per cent. interest table and finding the interest on the amount, £100, for 6·8 days.

All calculations of interest should be made by one clerk and checked by another, and when the receipt is to be paid, a note of the amount of interest should be written on it and be initialled by both clerks.

Each half-year, the interest due to date upon all deposit receipts is calculated and set aside before the profits of a bank are ascertained, the amount being carried forward into the next half-year to meet the interest up to that date when the receipts are presented for payment.

In the case of a receipt subject to notice of withdrawal, after notice has been received it is the practice of some banks, when the money is not withdrawn, to cease adding interest after the date when the receipt was due to be repaid. Banks do not, however, always insist upon notice being given, and when the deposit receipts are paid without notice, some banks deduct from the interest due to date a sum equal to the interest which would have accrued during the period between the date of payment and the date when it would have been due to be paid if notice had been given; in other words, interest is deducted for the days still to run before the receipt is due. (See DEPOSIT RECEIPT.)

Interest is not, as a rule, allowed upon a deposit receipt until the money has remained in the bank for a certain period, say, fourteen days or a month, and in some banks for two months.

When a bank allows interest on current accounts it usually gives a slightly higher rate for deposits, and in the case of deposits for a fixed period a slightly higher rate still.

INTEREST WARRANT. An order or warrant for the payment of interest upon debenture stocks and such-like securities. A dividend warrant is an order for the payment of a shareholder's proportion of the profits of a company.

The Bills of Exchange Act, 1882, recognises, "any usage relating to dividend warrants or the indorsements thereof" (Section 97, s.s. 3, *d.*), but no reference is made to interest warrants. It would appear, therefore, that an interest warrant, if payable to several parties, should, strictly, be signed by each one, though they are frequently treated in the same way as dividend warrants.

INTERIM DIVIDEND. The dividend of a joint stock company is declared by the company in general meeting; but power is given, in most articles of association, to the directors to pay to the members such interim dividends as appear to them to be justified by the profits which have been earned. An interim dividend is therefore one which is paid in the meantime, and which comes forward for confirmation when the general meeting is held. An interim dividend which is paid in, say, July is often less than the amount which is paid in January; e.g. if the dividend for the year is likely to be 15 per cent., 5 per cent. may perhaps be paid in July and 10 per cent. in January.

INTERNATIONAL SECURITIES. (See INTERBOURSE SECURITIES.)

INTERPLEAD. To interplead is to bring before the Court the claims of two persons to the same object and to obtain the decision of the Court. A banker might have occasion to interplead, for example, if two persons each laid claim to a sum of money deposited with him.

INTESTACY. INTESTATE. Where a person has died without making a will, it is known as an intestacy, and he is referred to as having died intestate. In order that the affairs of the deceased may be wound up, letters of administration require to be obtained from the Probate Registry, or Somerset House, by some person who is entitled to act as administrator.

By the Intestate Estates Act, 1890, it is provided that the real and personal estate of every man who shall die intestate after September 1, 1890, leaving a widow but no issue, shall, in all cases where the net value of such real and personal estate shall not exceed £500, belong to the widow absolutely. Where the net value exceeds £500, the widow is entitled to a first charge of £500 upon the whole estate, real or personal, the amount being paid out of the estate in proportion to the values of the real and personal estates respectively. This right is in addition to her share in the residue of the estate. Upon an intestacy, a widow is entitled in the case of real property (which does not include leaseholds) to "dower," that is, a life interest in one-third of the property, unless there is a declaration against dower in the deed of conveyance to the husband. In the case of copyhold property, the widow's life interest is called "freebench" and varies with different manors. The following example is given in "Wills" by J. A. Slater:—"A man leaves real property worth £1,000 and personal property worth £4,000. If he has died intestate, and has left a widow and no issue, the widow is entitled first of all to £500, one-fifth of which, namely, £100, comes out of the real estate, and four-fifths, namely, £400, out of the personal estate. She is then entitled to her dower, unless it has been barred, out of the remaining £900 of real estate, and to one-half of the remaining £3,600 of the personal estate. She thus receives £2,300 absolutely, and enjoys the interest arising out of £300 worth of the real property for her life. If there is issue, she takes only one-third of the £4,000, and dower, or a life interest, in one-third of the £1,000."

Where title deeds are lodged as security by a person who has succeeded to the property, the purchaser in the last conveyance having died intestate, the banker should ascertain if the land is charged with dower, or freebench, in the case of a widow; and in the case of a widower with "curtesy," that is, a husband's right for life to the rents of the whole of his deceased's wife's real estate, if she died intestate, provided that the deceased wife had a child by the husband and such child was capable of inheriting.

INTRINSIC VALUE. There is no such thing as intrinsic value. As the value of anything is what it can be exchanged for, if it cannot be exchanged for anything it has no value. Money is frequently said to have an intrinsic value—that is, a value within itself—but on an island where there are no inhabitants, money could not be exchanged for anything, and in such a case it would be absolutely without value.

INVESTIGATION OF COMPANY'S AFFAIRS. The affairs of a company may be investigated by Board of Trade inspectors. A company may also by special resolution appoint inspectors to investigate its affairs. The Companies (Consolidation) Act, 1908, Section 109, provides as follows:—

"(1) The Board of Trade may appoint one or more competent inspectors to investigate the affairs of any company and to report thereon in such manner as the Board direct—

"(i) In the case of a banking company having a share capital, on the application of members holding not less than one-third of the shares issued:

"(ii) In the case of any other company having a share capital, on the application of members holding not less than one-tenth of the shares issued:

"(iii) In the case of a company not having a share capital on the application of not less than one-fifth in number of the persons on the company's register of members.

"(2) The application shall be supported by such evidence as the Board of Trade may require for the purpose of showing that the applicants have good reason for, and are not actuated by malicious motives in requiring, the investigation; and the Board of Trade may, before appointing an inspector, require the applicants to give security for payment of the costs of the inquiry." (See COMPANIES.)

INVESTMENT LEDGER. A separate account is opened in this ledger for each different investment. An exact description of the stock or shares is given, and there are also recorded the dates when the dividends are due, the date of purchase and the price paid. The date and particulars of all sales are given and the amounts are deducted from the balance. Any payments to credit in reduction of the price paid, so as to bring it down to the market value, are also deducted and the difference is the figure at which the investment appears in the balance sheet of the bank.

I.O.U. An I.O.U. (that is "I owe you") is a mere acknowledgment of a debt written on a slip of paper. Its usual form is:—

Leeds,
March 7, 1910.

To Mr. William Brown,
2, King Street, Leeds.
I.O.U. £10.

THOMAS JONES.

An I.O.U. does not require to be stamped; but if to the above simple form of I.O.U. are added such words as "I promise" or "I agree," or a date is given when the money will be paid, they may have the effect of converting it into a promissory note or an agreement, and in either case such a document would require to be stamped in order to be produced as evidence in a Court. A promissory note, however, can only be stamped before it is made; an agreement, except under a penalty, must be stamped within fourteen days.

An I.O.U. is not a negotiable instrument. It may, if necessary, be produced in Court as evidence of a debt, though it is not a proof of the amount owing.

IRON WARRANTS. Warrants for iron differ from warrants for other goods in so far that, by the custom of the iron trade, an indorsee obtains the goods free from any vendor's claim for purchase money. Where a bank had taken iron warrants as security, and the original purchaser had not paid for the iron, it was held (*Merchant Banking Company of London* v. *Phœnix Bessemer Steel Co.*, 1877, 5 Ch. D. 205) that the bank was entitled to delivery of the iron. (See DOCK WARRANT.)

IRREDEEMABLE. A redeemable stock is one which the issuer is under an obligation to redeem or pay back, but an irredeemable stock is one where no such obligation exists.

IRREDEEMABLE DEBENTURE. A debenture which does not contain any provision for repayment of the principal money. Even if irredeemable, it falls to be paid upon the company going into liquidation. An irredeemable debenture practically provides an annuity in perpetuity in favour of the holder. (See DEBENTURE, PERPETUAL DEBENTURE.)

ISSUE OF BILL. The "issue" of a bill of exchange is defined by Section 2 of the Bills of Exchange Act, 1882, as "the first delivery of a bill or note, complete in form, to a person who takes it as a holder." This definition is required by reason of the wording of Section 9, s.s. 3, which provides: "Where a bill is expressed to be payable with interest, unless the instrument otherwise provides, interest runs from the date of the bill, and if the bill is undated, from the issue thereof," and Section 12, which is as follows:—"Where a bill expressed to be payable at a fixed period after date is issued undated, or where the acceptance of a bill payable at a fixed period after sight is undated, any holder may insert therein the true date of issue or acceptance, and the bill shall be payable accordingly." For stamp purposes no bill of exchange or promissory note may be stamped with an impressed stamp after the execution thereof. See Stamp Act, 1891, Section 37; s.s. 2.

ISSUE OF CHEQUE. The Bills of Exchange Act, 1882, specially provides that, except as otherwise stated, the rules applicable to bills of exchange are also applicable to cheques. The definition of the "issue of a cheque," therefore, is the same as that given for a bill in the preceding article.

ISSUE PAR. The price at which the stock or shares of a company is issued to the public. (See PAR.)

ISSUED CAPITAL. That part of the nominal or authorised capital of a company which has been issued by the directors and been taken up or subscribed by the shareholders. The issued capital may be fully paid up, or it may be only partly paid up, the remainder being the "uncalled" capital. (See CAPITAL.)

JOBBER. (See STOCK JOBBER.)

JOINT ACCOUNT. When an account is opened in two or more names, unless all the parties are to sign cheques, an authority, signed by all, should be obtained stating distinctly who may sign upon the account.

If an account is opened in the names of John Brown and Mary Brown (husband and wife), and it is desired that either of them may draw upon it, the bank's form of authority for either party to sign must be signed both by John and Mary, and if it is the intention that the balance be "repayable to the survivor" those words should be included in the authority. In the case of husband and wife it is particularly necessary that a clear arrangement be made on that point. If the wife dies, the husband can draw the balance, but it would appear that, if the husband dies first, there is the possibility that the money might be held to pass to the deceased's executors, unless it can be proved that it was the intention of the deceased that the money should, at his death, be withdrawn by his widow.

In the case of an ordinary joint account, as John Brown and John Jones, repayable to either, on the death of one the balance may be drawn by the other.

If no authority is held from the parties on a joint account, all cheques must be signed by both parties, and on proof of death of one of them the balance may be withdrawn by the survivor.

An authority may be cancelled by either party at any time.

Any claim that the executors of a deceased joint holder may have upon the money is a matter for arrangement with the survivor, with which the bank is not concerned. Even if the deceased mentions the joint account in his will, the banker is not bound by the will, and, unless he receives notice from the executors not to do so, he may pay the balance to the survivor. If the legal representatives of the deceased give notice to the banker not to pay the balance to the survivor, the banker should not pay it, unless the cheque is signed both by the survivor and the legal representatives. A banker has nothing to do with any question of payment of probate duty when he parts with a balance to the survivor. (See PROBATE.)

Where an account stands in several names and one of the persons dies, it is better that the balance should be transferred by cheque to a new account in the names of the survivors, than that the deceased's name should be merely dropped out when the next heading is written in the ledger. The cheque transferring the balance to the new account should be signed by all the survivors, unless a mandate is held for one, or more, of the number to sign.

Where one of the parties is authorised to sign, the method of signing should be, e.g. "For John and Thomas Brown and self, Wm. Brown." The name of the account should appear upon the cheque as well as the signature of the person drawing it.

If a banker realises securities belonging to several persons, the proceeds should not be paid to one of those persons, unless under an authority to do so signed by all of them.

In the case of a deposit receipt in joint names, if it is to be "repayable to either party" it should be so stated upon the receipt, and if in the names of husband and wife it should also say "or survivor" if that is the intention.

Where there are several joint debtors, in order to keep the debt alive against everyone of them (that is, to prevent the operation of the Statute of Limitations), there must be an acknowledgment of the debt from each one of them, unless they are members of a partnership firm or one of them is authorised to sign for the rest. The fact that one of the joint debtors acknowledged a debt would not prevent the others from pleading the statute. As to what constitutes an acknowledgment of a debt, see STATUTE OF LIMITATIONS.

A loan by way of a promissory note is on the same footing as a joint account, and each maker must acknowledge the debt, otherwise at the expiration of the six years each party who has not acknowledged has the right to consider himself freed from liability. (See PROMISSORY NOTE.)

In the event of the failure of one of the parties on a joint account which is overdrawn, the solvent party is liable for the amount of the debt; if the account is in credit the solvent party may, in an ordinary case, withdraw the balance. If there is any doubt, the trustee in bankruptcy should be consulted. (See Section 47, Bankruptcy Act, 1883, under SETTLEMENTS—SETTLOR BANKRUPT.)

In the case of a joint account (not a partnership account) which is overdrawn, if one of the parties dies, his estate will not be liable for the debt, and the banker must look to the survivor for payment. If, for example, John Brown (who is a poor man) applies for a loan, and John Jones (who is a rich man) agrees to sign a cheque along with Brown for the amount required, in the event of the death of Jones, his estate cannot legally be held liable for the debt, and if Jones' representatives repudiate the debt, the banker has only Brown to depend upon for repayment. That is the decision of the Court in *Other v. Iveson* (1855, 24 L.J. Ch. 654), where money was lent to two brothers on the strength of the cheque being signed by a third brother. The third brother died and his executors were sued by the bank. It was held that the liability was not joint and several but joint only, and therefore that the survivors only were liable. Where a joint account is overdrawn and the banker is relying upon one of the parties to the account for repayment, he should protect himself in some way against the risk of that party dying before the money is repaid. Probably the best plan is for the parties to sign a guarantee for the account. (See JOINTLY AND SEVERALLY.)

JOINT STOCK BANK. A bank in which the capital is subscribed by the shareholders.

The London and Westminster Bank (now the London County and Westminster) was founded in 1834 and the London Joint Stock Bank in 1836. (See BANKING COMPANY.)

JOINT STOCK COMPANY. A company, or association of individuals, having a joint or common stock or capital. (See COMPANIES.)

JOINT TENANTS. Where property is granted to two or more persons, as joint tenants, they have each an equal interest or right in the whole of the property. The important point about a joint tenancy is that when one of the joint tenants dies his interest in the property passes to the surviving joint tenants. A joint tenant cannot dispose of his interest by will, but during his lifetime he may convey his share to anyone. The outsider who purchases the share of a joint tenant becomes a tenant in common. If one of the tenants purchases the share of another, the transfer is effected by a release, not by a conveyance, because each joint tenant is already equally possessed of the whole property. The share of each tenant must be equal, and their interests all created at the same time and by the same instrument. If there is only one surviving joint tenant he is the sole owner, and may dispose of the property by will.

In the event of a property being devised to several persons without stating whether they are to be joint tenants or tenants in common, they are regarded as joint tenants.

The difference between joint tenants and tenants in common should be noted. A tenant in common has a separate and distinct share in the property which he can dispose of by will. The survivor in a tenancy in common does not become the owner of the whole property. One tenant in common may transfer his share to another tenant by conveyance. Their shares may be equal or unequal, and their shares need not, necessarily, be all created at the same time or under the same instrument.

Where deeds of a joint tenancy are deposited as security, the document of charge should be signed by all the joint tenants, and it is advisable that a banker's legal mortgage be taken. (See COPARCENERS, TENANTS IN COMMON.)

JOINTLY AND SEVERALLY. Where a promissory note is drawn by several makers "we jointly and severally promise to pay," each maker is liable for the full amount of the note; but if the note is worded "we promise" or "we jointly promise" the makers are liable as a whole and not individually for the full amount. Where a note "I promise to pay" is signed by several persons it is by Section 85, s.s.2, of the Bills of Exchange Act, 1882, deemed to be their joint and several promise.

It is obviously to the advantage of a banker that all parties liable to him jointly should be liable severally as well; he can then, if necessary, sue all together for the whole amount of the debt, or sue each party separately for the whole amount. If one is sued and the banker fails to obtain payment in full, the remaining parties may then be sued. If one of the makers of a joint and several note dies, his estate is liable, but if the note is joint only, the estate of a deceased maker is not liable.

Where a joint account is overdrawn the liability is joint only, and if one of the parties dies the survivor becomes liable for the full amount; the estate of the deceased is not responsible for the debt. Where a joint advance has been made and one of the parties becomes bankrupt, the solvent party is liable for the whole amount. In cases of joint overdrawn accounts, it is customary, when the account is not otherwise secured, to obtain a guarantee signed by all the parties; when this is done a claim can be made upon the deceased's or bankrupt's estate. (See JOINT ACCOUNT.)

A payment, or acknowledgment, by one does not prevent the other parties who have signed a promissory note from pleading the Statute of Limitations, whether they have signed "jointly" or "jointly and severally." (See STATUTE OF LIMITATIONS.)

An ordinary cheque, signed by more than one individual, is not a joint and several document. (See PROMISSORY NOTE.)

JOINTURE. An estate in lands settled upon a woman, which she is to possess after the death of her husband.

JUDGES' ORDERS. (See CHARGING ORDER, GARNISHEE ORDER.)

JUDGMENT AFFECTING LAND. By the Land Charges Registration and Searches Act, 1888:—

"Section 5. (1) There shall be established and kept at the Office of Land Registry a register of writs and orders affecting land, and there may be registered therein, in the prescribed manner, any writ or order affecting land issued or made by any Court for the purpose of enforcing a judgment, statute, or recognisance, and any order appointing a receiver or sequestrator of land.

"(2) Every entry made in pursuance of this Section shall be made in the name of the person whose land is affected by the writ or order registered.

"(3) The registration of a writ or order in pursuance of this Act shall cease to have effect at the expiration of five years from the date of registration, but may be renewed from time to time, and, if renewed, shall have effect from the date of renewal.

"(4) Registration of a writ or order in pursuance of this Section shall have the same effect as, and make unnecessary, registration thereof in the Central Office of the Supreme Court of Judicature in pursuance of any other Act.

"Section 6. Every such writ and order as is mentioned in Section 5, and every delivery in execution or other proceeding taken in pursuance of any such writ or order, or in obedience thereto, shall be void as against a purchaser for value of land unless the writ or order is for the time being registered in pursuance of this Act."

By the Land Charges Act, 1900:—

"Section 2. (1) A judgment or recognisance, whether obtained or entered into on behalf of the Crown or otherwise, and whether obtained or entered into before or after the commencement of this Act, shall not operate as a charge on land, or on any interest in land, or on the unpaid purchase-money for any land, unless or until a writ or order for the purpose of enforcing it is registered under Section 5 of the Land Charges Registration and Searches Act, 1888."

For the protection of persons dealing with land, it is necessary that any judgments or orders should be duly registered in some convenient place, where an examination can be made of any documents which show how the land is affected by judgments or orders which have been pronounced. The above sections of the two Acts named are the most important provisions with respect to this matter, and the effect of them seems to be as follows: If a judgment is entered up affecting land after the 1st January, 1889, an intending mortgagee, for example, is completely protected in dealing with the land, if a search is made at the Land Registry Office for writs and executions for the preceding five years. It is only if the land has been actually executed upon, and if the writ or execution has been registered or re-registered, so that the last registration or re-registration has been made within five years preceding the date of the security that the mortgagee would be postponed as to his own security to the judgment creditor whose judgment or writ is registered. And as to a judgment entered up after the 1st July, 1901, the intending mortgagee has only to see that no writ or order for enforcing a judgment has been registered under Section 5 of the Land Charges Registration and Searches Act, 1888, and this is so whether the judgment has been obtained before or after the 1st July, 1901.

JUDGMENT CREDITOR. Where a creditor has obtained judgment against a debtor for the payment of a debt, he may enforce the judgment in various ways:—

1. By writ of *fieri facias* (*q.v.*), by which the sheriff can seize the debtor's *goods*.
2. By writ of elegit (*q.v.*), by which the sheriff can take possession of the debtor's *lands*.
3. By garnishee order (*q.v.*), by which debts due to the debtor from a third person, e.g. a banker, can be attached.
4. By a charging order (*q.v.*), by which shares or stocks belonging to the debtor can be charged with the payment of the judgment debt.

JUDGMENT DEBT. (See JUDGMENT CREDITOR.)

JUNGLE MARKET. A Stock Exchange name for the market for West African mining shares.

JURYMAN. In addition to being liable to serve as a common juryman, a banker is one of those persons who may be called upon to act as a special juryman. (Juries Act, 1890, Section 6.)

KAFFIR CIRCUS. A Stock Exchange name for the market for South African shares.

KAFFIRS. A Stock Exchange name for South African mining shares.

KANGAROOS. A Stock Exchange name for West Australian mining and land shares.

KEEPING HOUSE. The Bankruptcy Act, 1883, Section 4, s.s. 1, *d*, enacts that a debtor commits an act of bankruptcy if, with intent to defeat or delay his creditors, he begins to keep house. A debtor "keeps house" when he confines himself to the house and refuses to see a creditor who calls to see him for payment of the debt.

KEY REGISTER. A book kept at the head office of a bank in which is preserved a complete list of all the keys of the strong rooms, safes, etc., at the head office and branches, as well as a list of the holders of the keys.

KITE-FLYING. Raising money by accommodation bills.

KITES. A name given to accommodation bills (*q.v.*).

KOPEK. (See FOREIGN MONEYS—RUSSIA.)

KRAN. (See FOREIGN MONEYS—PERSIA.)

KRONE. (See FOREIGN MONEYS—AUSTRIA AND HUNGARY.)

KRONER. (See FOREIGN MONEYS—NORWAY, SWEDEN AND DENMARK.)

LAC, OR LAKH. A lac, or lakh, of rupees equals 100,000 rupees. The figures are usually written as Rs.1,00,000, Rs. 24,00,000, to show the number of lacs, the lacs in those two examples being, of course, one and twenty-four.

The value of a lac is about £6,667, a rupee being, say, 1*s.* 4*d.*; 100 lacs is a crore. (See FOREIGN MONEYS—INDIA.)

LACHES. A legal term for neglect of such a nature as to be prejudicial to the rights of the person who has been negligent.

For example, a banker may pay an uncrossed cheque drawn upon him and debit it to his customer's account even though the indorsement should subsequently turn out to be a forgery, provided that the payment is made in good faith, in the ordinary course of business and without negligence. If the banker is guilty of negligence, or laches, his right to debit the cheque may be called in question.

LAME DUCK. A name sometimes given to a defaulter on the Stock Exchange.

LAND CERTIFICATE. A certificate under the seal of the Land Registry, containing complete copies of the entries in the register. It is issued to the owner of the land; and he may deposit it as a security. If the certificate gives an absolute title to the land, that is all that a banker requires; but if the title is possessory only, the prior deeds should also be deposited.

The usual memorandum of deposit should be taken. As to a charge, which is equivalent to a mortgage, see LAND REGISTRY.

LAND REGISTRY. The system of land registration was established under the Land Transfer Acts, 1875 and 1897.

Registration is now compulsory in the city and county of London. It became compulsory in the various parishes on different dates. It commenced on January 1, 1899, in a few parishes and extended by degrees till on July 1, 1902, the city of London and the whole of the county of London were included.

Land in other parts of England may be registered at the Land Registry, but the registration is not compulsory. Provision is made in the Acts for the establishment of local registries when necessary.

The Land Transfer Acts apply to freeholds and leasehold land having forty or more years still to run, or two or more lives still to fall in, but they do not apply to copyhold land or customary freeholds, where admission by the lord of the manor is necessary to give the purchaser a good title. A lease created for the purposes of mortgage, or containing an absolute prohibition against alienation, or leases with less than twenty-one years to run cannot be registered. The registration of leases having less than forty years to run is not compulsory.

The registration of land in the Land Registry supersedes the registration of deeds in the Middlesex Deeds Registry.

The following paragraphs are taken from a statement issued by the Land Registry describing the objects and practical working of the system of registration of title :—

1. A register of title is, essentially, a list of the owners of land, with particulars of the properties they own, and of the mortgages and other incumbrances which affect them. Legal validity is given to this list by Act of Parliament, it is kept constantly up to date by the entry of all changes of ownership as soon as they occur, and its correctness is guaranteed by the Government. The consequence is that an intending purchaser of registered land has no need to make any private inquiry into the title; he merely has to see that the person he is dealing with is the registered proprietor.

2. On a mortgage or sale of registered land there is no delay, no uncertainty, and hardly any expense. The entries in the register are so simple, and the forms of transfer and charge are so short and clear that any intelligent person can understand them without expert assistance, and can, if he wishes, carry out all ordinary transactions on his own responsibility alone.

5. The principal advantages of the system as compared with the present non-registration system are security, cheapness, expedition, clearness, and simplicity.

18. When registration is completed a "Land Certificate," containing complete copies of the entries in the register, is issued to the proprietor. This constitutes a portable counterpart of the register, enabling the proprietor to enter into negotiations, and to complete transactions at a distance from the registry, and even, under favourable conditions, without the necessity of actual reference to the books. If thought necessary, a search can be made, and official reply given, by telegraph. No transfer or charge can be registered without production and indorsement of the Land Certificate at the registry. Deposit of the Land Certificate is good security for a temporary loan, and can be protected by a notice on the register, for a fee of one shilling.

21. When registered land is transferred or charged, the proprietor executes an instrument of transfer, or charge, in a short simple form which can be obtained at the registry (see Schedule I). The purchaser brings or posts this to the registry (address Land Registry, Lincoln's Inn Fields, London, W.C.), with a fee of 1*s.* 6*d.* per £25 of value, and in the case of a transfer the old proprietor's name is cancelled, and that of the new proprietor is entered in its place. In

the case of a charge, short particulars of the amount, rate of interest, etc., are entered in the charges register together with the name of the creditor. Charges can be transferred and otherwise dealt with on the register in the same manner as the land. If part of an estate is dealt with, a plan is attached to the transfer, and a new title is opened for the transferee, with a fresh plan; the part thus separated being also marked off on the filed plan of the original estate by a special colour. Charges which have been paid off are cancelled altogether. Successions on death are registered in the same way as transfers, by cancelling the deceased proprietor, and entering the legal representative, or the person named by him as entitled.

22. The register is strictly private, and can only be inspected by the registered proprietor or with his written permission.

23. There are three main ways in which land may be registered under the Land Transfer Acts—namely, with Absolute Title, with Good Leasehold Title and with Possessory Title.

24. Absolute Title.—It is not difficult to explain what Absolute Title means. The Land Registry first carefully examines the proprietor's title, and after that confers on him an absolute right to the property, guaranteed by the Government, against all the world. He can then immediately dispose of his land without delay, without cost, and without trouble. The purchaser can acquire it likewise without delay, without risk, with no more trouble than is involved in reading a few plain entries in a book, and in filling up a short printed form of transfer for the vendor to sign (see Schedule I), and with no more cost than the scale of official fees, namely, 1*s.* 6*d.* per £25 of the value up to £50,000, after which the percentage is lower.

25. Good Leasehold Title.—Leasehold land can seldom be registered with an Absolute Title owing to the inability of leaseholders (as a rule) to produce evidence of the Freehold Titles, and so to prove the original validity of the lease itself. A special form of registration, called Good Leasehold Title, has been devised to meet this state of affairs, which amounts to a guarantee (by the Government) of the leaseholder's title to the lease, but does not guarantee the original validity of the lease itself. At the same time it may be remembered that on ordinary sales of leasehold land the validity of the lease is always assumed—the purchaser having neither the wish nor the right to inquire into the Freehold Title. Therefore, for all ordinary practical purposes, registration with a Good Leasehold Title confers the same advantages as registration with Absolute Title, and where the applicant is not the original lessee, the method of application and the cost are the same. Where the applicant is the original lessee, he can obtain a Good Leasehold Title by simply signing a statement that he has not created any incumbrances, or, if he has done so, giving particulars of them.

26. Possessory Title.—Registration with Possessory Title is effected on *primâ facie* evidence merely, and is consequently easier to obtain than Absolute Title. So far as regards security from fraud, simple forms of conveyance, accurate plan, and other incidental matters, it has the same effect as Absolute Title, but it does not immediately confer on the proprietor and those who deal with him an indefeasible right to the land against all the world. Its effect is not retrospective; it keeps the title clear for the future, but is no bar to possible adverse claims dating from a time prior to its first entry on the Register books.

Consequently, if the land has to be sold very soon after its registration with Possessory Title, the owner must be prepared to have almost the same investigation made into the prior title as would have been made if the land were unregistered: when a longer time has elapsed these labours are much lightened though probably not wholly avoided: finally—after an interval variously estimated by various authorities—a time arrives when, there being no further need to consider in any way the title prior to registration, the owner has practically the equivalent of an Absolute Title. Beside this, after land has been registered with Possessory Title for six years it can be converted into Absolute (or Good Leasehold) on very easy terms.

SCHEDULE I.

FORMS OF TRANSFER AND CHARGE OF REGISTERED LAND.

Note.—The portions printed in Roman type represent the original forms; MS. additions and signatures are shown by italics.

INSTRUMENT OF TRANSFER OF THE WHOLE OF THE LAND COMPRISED IN A TITLE.—(Freehold.)

LAND REGISTRY.

Land Transfer Acts, 1875 and 1897.

District *London*
Parish *Lambeth*
No. of Title *020376*
1st of *January* 190 *3*. In consideration of *one thousand pounds* (*£1,000*
I, *William Smith*
of *645, Regent Street, W., Jeweller*

hereby transfer to *James Robinson*
of *1620, Oxford Street, W., Manufacturer*

the land comprised in the title above referred to.

Signed, sealed, and delivered by the said *William Smith* in the presence of *Thomas Jones* of *645, Regent Street, Jeweller's Assistant* } *W. Smith.* (*Seal*)

INSTRUMENT OF CHARGE OF THE WHOLE OF THE LAND COMPRISED IN A TITLE.

LAND REGISTRY.

Land Transfer Acts, 1875 and 1897.

District *London*
Parish *Lambeth*
No. of Title *020376*
1st of *January* 190 *3*. In consideration of *six hundred pounds* (*£600*
I, *James Robinson*
of *1620, Oxford Street, W., Manufacturer*

hereby charge the land comprised in the title above referred to with the payment to *John Brown*
of *105, Lombard Street, E.C., Banker*

on the *1st* of *July* 190 *3* of the principal sum of *£600* with interest at *4* per cent. per annum, payable *quarterly* on the *1st* of *April*, the *1st* of *July* the *1st* of *October* and the *1st* of *January* in every year.

Signed, sealed, and delivered by the said *James Robinson* in the presence of *Edward Walker* of *105, Lombard Street, Banker's Clerk* } *J. Robinson.* (*Seal*)

SCHEDULE II.

COSTS.

1. SALES.

On a sale of land registered with Absolute Title, the vendor, as a rule, need incur no costs at all.

The purchaser's costs can often be confined to the Stamp Duty and to the Land Registry Fees, which latter are as follows :—

Value.	*Fee.*
Not exceeding £50,000	1*s*. 6*d*. for every £25 or part of £25.
Exceeding £50,000, and not exceeding £100,000 . .	£150 for the first £50,000 and £1 10*s*. for every £1,000 or part of £1,000 over £50,000.
Exceeding £100,000 . .	£225.

The following examples show how this scale works out at various typical values :—

Value.	Fee.			Compare the Costs of Vendor and Purchaser of Unregistered Land.*		
	£	s.	d.	£	s.	d.
£25	0	1	6	6	0	0
£100	0	6	0	10	0	0
£300	0	18	0	10	0	0
£700	2	2	0	21	0	0
£1,000	3	0	0	30	0	0
£5,000	15	0	0	90	0	0
£10,000	30	0	0	140	0	0
£20,000	60	0	0	190	0	0
£50,000	150	0	0	340	0	0
£100,000, or over .	225	0	0	590	0	0

* It is not suggested that these charges are in any way excessive considering the labour, skill, and responsibility involved. The object of the comparison is purely to exhibit the superiority of the new system—as a system—over the old one.

2. First Registration—whether with Absolute, Good Leasehold, or Possessory Title.

The fees for first registration with Absolute, Good Leasehold, or Possessory Title are as follows :—

Value.	*Fee.*
Not exceeding £100 .	12*s*.
Exceeding £100 and not exceeding £325	£1.
Exceeding £325 and not exceeding £1,000	1*s*. 6*d*. for every £25 or part of £25.
Exceeding £1,000 and not exceeding £3,000	£3 for the first £1,000, and 1*s*. for every £25 or part of £25 over £1,000.
Exceeding £3,000 and not exceeding £10,000	£7 for the first £3,000, and 1*s*. for every £50 or part of £50 over £3,000.
Exceeding £10,000 . .	£14 for the first £10,000, and 1*s*. for every £100 or part of £100 over £10,000.

The following examples show how this scale works out at various typical values :—

Value.	Fee. £	s.	d.
£50	0	12	0
£100	0	12	0
£300	1	0	0
£700	2	2	0
£1,000	3	0	0
£5,000	9	0	0
£10,000	14	0	0
£20,000	19	0	0
£50,000	34	0	0
£100,000	59	0	0

These charges include all incidental expenses.

3. Conversion of Possessory Title into Absolute or Good Leasehold.

After a full fee on a transfer for value has been paid :—

No fee

Otherwise—

A like fee to that on first registration, subject to a discretionary power for the registrar to reduce it when the full fee appears excessive.

4. Mortgages and Charges.

The fees for mortgages are the same as for sales. Where a sale and mortgage are registered together, only half fees are charged for the mortgage.

For registering notice of a deposit of land certificate as equitable security the fee is 1*s*.

5. Voluntary Transactions.

For successions on death, and for transfers by way of gift, the fees are 1*s*. per £100, with a maximum of £2.

6. Fees Inclusive.

The fees include mapping, land certificate, and all other necessary incidental costs, including, in most cases as above stated, costs incidental to applications for Absolute Title.

There are no fees for searches, or for discharge of incumbrances.

Fuller particulars will be found in the Fee Order itself.

By the Land Transfer Rules :—

"258. A land certificate shall be in Form 66 in the First Schedule hereto and the Land Registry Seal shall be affixed to it. It shall be made up in divisions, corresponding to the divisions of the Register, so as to leave room for the addition thereto of subsequent entries in the Register. For this purpose fresh pages may be added to the certificate from time to time as may be necessary."

"Form 66.—*Land Certificate*. (*Rule* 258.)

Land Registry.

"Land Transfer Acts, 1875 and 1897.

Land Certificate.

"This is to certify that the freehold (*or* leasehold) land in the Parish of and County of (*here fill in a short description of the land, or reference to the filed plan*) is registered with absolute (qualified, good leasehold, or possessory) title under No. . Copies of the entries in the Register (and of the filed plan of the land) are within.

Dated the of 190 . (L.S.)

"*Note*.—The description of the property to which the Certificate relates must be adapted to that by which it is described in the Register. When the registration is of a possessory title only, the Certificate is to contain the following notice: 'The possessory title hereby certified does not affect or prejudice the enforcement of any estate, right or interest adverse to or in derogation of the title hereby certified, which was subsisting or capable of arising on the day of , being the date of first registration.'

"The form may be modified under special circumstances in such manner as the Registrar may deem necessary.

"Where under Rule 27*l* a plan is not filed, the form shall be altered accordingly. [Where the land is described by reference to the General Map the form shall also be altered as may be required.]

"Cancelled entries need not be copied, but may be referred to as 'cancelled' only."

When a charge is given over land, a certificate of charge is issued by the Registrar :—

"Rule 259. A certificate of charge shall certify the registration of the charge and shall contain (1) an office copy of the charge, (2) a description (if no description is contained in the charge) of the land affected, (3) the name and address of the registered proprietor of the charge, and (4) a list of the prior incumbrances (if any) appearing on the Register. There shall also be added such further particulars, if any, as the Registrar shall think fit and the Land Registry seal shall be affixed to it. Notes of subsequent dealings affecting the charge shall from time to time be entered on the certificate."

The charge is equivalent to a mortgage of unregistered land and may be given as security to a banker ; and a deposit of a certificate of charge is equal to the lien created by the deposit of a mortgage deed.

Section 8 of the Land Transfer Act, 1897, provides :—

"The registered proprietor of any freehold or leasehold land, or of a charge may, subject to any registered estates, charges, or rights, create a lien on the land or charge by deposit of the land certificate or office copy of registered lease, or certificate of charge ; and such lien shall, subject as aforesaid, be equivalent to a lien created by the deposit of title deeds or of a mortgage deed of unregistered land by an owner entitled in fee simple or for the term or interest created by the lease for his own benefit, or by a mortgagee beneficially entitled to the mortgage."

When a land certificate or certificate of charge is deposited as security the usual memorandum of deposit should be taken, and notice of the deposit should be given to the Registrar and an acknowledgment received

When the security is done with, a form of "withdrawal of notice of deposit" must be signed by the banker.

When a certificate of charge is held, it is not necessary that the banker should also hold the land certificate. The land certificate would be indorsed by the Registrar when he issued the certificate of charge.

Where the land certificate shows that the title is "absolute" the land certificate is alone sufficient, but if the title is "possessory" it is still necessary to have the prior title deeds.

When a land certificate is granted, the title deeds are marked by the Registrar, so that anyone taking the deeds may see at once that the land is registered and therefore that the land certificate is the document of title.

A banker should notice whether there are any prior charges recorded upon the certificate. The Register should be searched in case a restriction of some kind has been registered against the land since the certificate was issued. An official search will be made for a fee of 5*s*.

Where a certificate has not yet been issued, the proprietor of the land may (Rule 244) give notice to the Registrar that he intends to deposit the certificate when issued with a certain person as security ; and the Registrar will enter the notice in the Register and deliver the certificate, when ready, to the person named in the notice.

The Land Transfer Rules provide :—

"250. The notice of deposit or notice of intended deposit may be withdrawn from the Register on a written request or consent signed by the person entitled to the lien created by the deposit, or notice of intended deposit, or his successor in title ; accompanied in either case by the land certificate, or certificate of charge.

"251. The lien created by the deposit of a certificate or by notice to the Registrar under Rule 244 shall be subject to any unregistered estates, rights, or interests protected by caution or other entry on the Register at the time of the creation of the lien, and in the case of good leasehold, qualified, or possessory title, to estates, rights and interests excepted from the effect of registration."

All the necessary forms may be obtained from the Registry.

LAND REGISTRY (MIDDLESEX DEEDS). By the Land Registry (Middlesex Deeds) Act, 1891, it was enacted that the Middlesex Registry shall be transferred to the Land Registry established under the Land Transfer Act, 1875, and shall form part of that office. Deeds or memorials of deeds are registered at the Middlesex Deeds Registry. At the Land Registry (*q.v.*) the title is registered.

The Middlesex Deeds Registry applies to all the county of Middlesex and also to all the county of London north of the Thames, but not to the city of London. Copyholds, leases at a rack rent, occupation leases for twenty-one years or less are not registered at the Middlesex Registry.

When a title is registered under the Land Transfer Act, it supersedes the registration of the deeds at the Middlesex Deeds Registry.

A certificate is indorsed by an officer of the Registry on every deed and conveyance stating the date on which the memorial of such deed is registered.

Any person may search the Register kept in the Land Registry.

Paragraph 14 of the above-named Act is as follows :—

"Any person deriving title under an instrument (capable of registration under the Acts relating to the Middlesex Registry) which confers on him the right to apply for registration with a possessory title, of the land comprised in it under the Land Transfer Act, 1875, may, at his option, either register a memorial of an instrument under the Acts relating to the Middlesex Registry, or apply for registration with possessory title under the Land Transfer Act, 1875. Such registration shall, when completed, bear the same date as the application, and render unnecessary the registration of the instrument under the Acts relating to the Middlesex Registry."

It should be noted that, with regard to the Middlesex Registry, registration does not give to a person who has registered his mortgage or deed, any claim to priority over an unregistered prior deed or charge of which he had notice before registering. This rule differs from that of the Yorkshire Registries.

A mortgagee is not obliged to search the register, and a registered deed conveying the legal estate will take priority to a prior registered equitable charge, unless the mortgagee had notice of the prior charge.

Registration in Middlesex does not prevent tacking.

The following are some of the principal rules under the Land Registry (Middlesex Deeds) Act, 1891 :—

"2. Memorials, and certificates of satisfaction of mortgages, shall be written or printed on the best white loan paper, 16 inches long by 10 inches wide, with an inner margin 2 inches wide and an outer margin three-quarters of an inch wide, and shall be left at the office by hand, and shall bear Land Registry stamps for the amount of the fees, and shall be accompanied by the original instruments and mortgages respectively.

"4. Where the original instrument contains a plan, a copy thereof (or of so much thereof as is referred to in the memorial) shall be drawn on the memorial, unless owing to its size this cannot be done ; in which case a tracing on linen, signed by the person signing the memorial and by the witness, shall be left with the memorial and filed in the office. No other copy shall be required.

"5. It shall no longer be necessary to seal any memorial, or to verify by oath the signing thereof or the execution of the instrument to which it refers ; but the signing of the certificate of satisfaction of a mortgage shall continue to be verified by oath as heretofore.

"6. The witness to the memorial shall be a witness or one of the witnesses (if any) to the original instrument, unless at the date of the memorial every such witness is dead or absent from the United Kingdom or cannot be found, or some other sufficient cause exists to prevent it. In such cases a statutory declaration shall be furnished, and left with the memorial at the Registry, stating the reason why the witness to the memorial is not one of the witnesses to the instrument.

"9. An ordinary search shall be a search made against one name on one day by a person not an officer of the Registry, in any of the indexes, books, or documents open to public inspection.

"10. An official search shall be a search made by an officer of the Registry, in the index only, for certain specified years, for all entries therein, against one name, affecting lands in a specified parish.

"12. An official certificate of the result of every official search shall be issued from the Registry to the applicant, and a copy, or other sufficient record of the same, shall be kept in the office.

"13. Applications for official searches shall be subject to the following provisions :—

(*a*) That the search shall not be such as for any sufficient reason shall appear to be impracticable to complete.

(*b*) That the Lord Chancellor may make regulations limiting or extending the period to be covered by official searches."

The following is the form of memorial of a deed to be registered :—

MEMORIAL OF A DEED.

Land Registry. Middlesex Deeds Acts.

Particulars for the Index.

* [If named in the deed.]

Grantor's Surname.	Grantor's Christian Name.	Parish.*

Date of deed :—

Partics :—

* [As in the deed.]

Description of lands :—*

Witnesses to execution of deed :—

Signature of grantor or grantee.

Signature of witness to signing of memorial.

Address and description.

N.B.—Instrument to be delivered to

Note.—The memorial should be written on both sides of the paper, and otherwise according to the provisions of Rule 2. Usually the "Description of lands" should commence about the middle of the front of the form, the "Witnesses to execution of deed" and following matters being placed low down on the back.

Note.—Where the description of land in an indorsed or annexed deed is made by reference to that contained in the prior deed, or (in any case) to a recital, the description contained in such prior deed or recital shall also be set out in the memorial.

Except that in the case of an *indorsed* or *annexed* deed, where a memorial of the prior deed has been registered, a reference to the year, book, and number of its registration shall be sufficient, without setting out the full description contained in such deed.

When any person requires an official search to be made, a requisition form must be filled up. When the search is completed an official certificate is given by the Registry in the following form :—

OFFICIAL CERTIFICATE OF SEARCH.

Land Registry. Middlesex Deeds Acts.

This is to certify that the subjoined list contains all the entries in the index for the years to inclusive, appearing therefrom to affect lands in the parish(es) of entered against the following name :—

Surname.	Christian Name.

To wait till called for by [*or,* to be sent by post to]
of

LIST OF ENTRIES.

Year.	Book.	No.	Year.	Book.	No.	Year.	Book.	No.

Seal of Search Department with date.

The fees are :—

	s.	d.
Registration of a memorial, or vacating an entry of a mortgage (except under Section 42 of the Building Societies Act, 1874)	5	0
Vacating an entry of a mortgage under the said Section of the last-mentioned Act	2	6
The above charges include the administration of the oath, when required.		
Ordinary search, per name . . .	2	0
Official search :—		
For 10 years or less	7	6
For every further 5 years or less	2	6
If more entries are found than at the rate of 10 for every 5 years, then for every 5, or part of 5, extra entries	1	0

LAND TAX. Where the tax has not been redeemed, it is payable at a rate not exceeding one shilling in the pound upon the annual value of the property.

By the Finance Act, 1898, where the owner's income does not exceed £160 per annum he is exempt from the tax, and where his income does not exceed £400 exemption is granted to the extent of one-half.

The tenant of a house pays the tax in the first instance, but (unless he has agreed with the landlord to pay all rent and taxes) he is entitled to deduct the amount from the next payment of rent.

By the Finance Act, 1898, the tax may be redeemed on payment of thirty times the amount of the tax which it is desired to redeem. Persons who hold at a rack rent, and tenants who hold under the Crown, are not allowed to redeem the tax.

LARCENY. Theft. A person is guilty of felony if he steals, or for any fraudulent purpose, destroys, cancels or obliterates, any cheque, bill, note, certificate, debenture, deed, or other security for money or for payment of money.

LATIN MONETARY UNION. The Union was formed in 1865 by France, Italy, Belgium, and Switzerland. Greece joined it in 1875. It was formed with the object of establishing standard coins of the same weight and fineness in those countries, and that the coins of one country should pass as legal tender in the others. The unit of value is the same in each country, though called by different names; in France, Switzerland, and Belgium it is the franc, in Italy the lira, and in Greece the drachma. Austria, Finland, Roumania, Servia, and Spain have adopted the system but without joining the Union. (See SCANDINAVIAN MONETARY UNION.)

LAW MERCHANT. The rules of common law, including the law merchant, save in so far as they are inconsistent with the express provisions of the Bills of Exchange Act, 1882, apply to bills of exchange, promissory notes, and cheques (Section 97, s.s. 2, of that Act).

The law merchant "is neither more nor less than the usages of merchants and traders in the different departments of trade, ratified by the decisions of courts of law, which, upon such usages being proved before them, have adopted them as settled law . . ." (*Goodwin* v. *Robarts*, 1875, L.R. 10 Exch. 337).

LEASE AND RELEASE. Prior to the year 1841 the usual method of conveyance of a freehold estate was by a lease and release. On one day a lease was granted for one year to the person to whom the land was to be transferred, and on the following day a release was granted to him. In olden times a transfer of land was effected by means of actual delivery, "livery of seisin" (*q.v.*) (i.e. delivery of possession), a method of transfer called "feoffment" (*q.v.*). A conveyance by lease and release had the same effect. By the lease the lessee was placed in actual possession of the land, and the next day the grantor released the freehold or reversion to the lessee, thus making him the owner. From 1841 to 1845 a "release" alone was sufficient to answer the purpose, in accordance with 4 & 5 Vict. c. 21, "An act for rendering a release as effectual for the conveyance of freehold estates as a lease and release by the same parties." In 1845 it was enacted that the conveyance of freeholds shall be deemed to lie in grant as well as in livery. Since that date freehold land has therefore been transferred by a deed of grant called a conveyance.

LEASEHOLD. (Saxon *leasum*, to enter lawfully.) Where the owner of freehold land grants it to a person for a term of years it is called a lease and the land is then leasehold. The person leasing it is the lessor, and the party in whose favour the lease is given is the lessee. When a lease is granted for more than three years the land is "demised" by deed to the lessee. (But see *Walsh* v. *Lonsdale*, 1882, 21 Ch. D. 9). When the lessee transfers the land to some one else he "assigns the lease."

In *Camberwell and South London Building Society* v. *Holloway* (1879, 13 Ch. D. 754), Jessel, M.R., said: "The word 'lease' in law is a well-known legal term of well-defined import. No lawyer has ever suggested that the title of the lessor makes any difference in the description of the instrument, whether the lease is granted by a freeholder, or by a copyholder, with the licence of the lord, or by a man who himself is a leaseholder. It being well granted for a term of years it is called a lease. It is quite true that where the grantor of the lease holds for a term, the second instrument is called either an under-lease or a derivative lease, but it is still a lease."

In taking the deeds of leasehold property as security, it should be remembered that failure to fulfil the covenants contained in the lease may result in the forfeiture of the lease, and re-entry of the lessor. If the last receipt for the landlord's rent is produced, it is a waiver of any breach of covenant of which the landlord was aware before giving the receipt, but it is not a waiver with regard to any breach of which he was ignorant.

A perusal of the deeds will show the nature of the covenants, and some of them may be very burdensome. A banker taking an assignment of a lease becomes liable for all the covenants, but if a mere deposit of the deeds is taken, or a sub-demise, if allowable, for a day or two short of the remainder of the term of the lease, he does not incur any liability on the covenants; there is, however, the danger that the lease may be forfeited through failure of the lessee to fulfil the conditions contained therein.

Where any part of the property of a bankrupt consists of land of any tenure burdened with onerous covenants, the trustee may, with leave of the Court, disclaim the property. Where a trustee disclaims leasehold property "the Court shall not make a vesting order in favour of any person claiming under the bankrupt, whether as under-lessee or as mortgagee by demise, except upon the terms of making such person subject to the same liabilities and obligations as the bankrupt was subject to under the lease in respect of the property at the date when the bankruptcy petition was filed, and any mortgagee or under-lessee declining to accept a vesting order upon such terms shall be excluded from all interest in and security upon the property" (Section 55, s.s. 6, Bankruptcy Act, 1883).

A lessor cannot compel an equitable mortgagee by deposit of a lease to take a legal assignment, but if the mortgagee enters into possession of the property he is liable on the covenants of the lease.

If there is a covenant in the lease that the lessee cannot sub-demise or assign without the consent of the lessor, the licence of the lessor should accompany the deeds where there is an assignment or sub-lease. (See LICENCE TO ASSIGN.)

It is the rule in open contracts that a purchaser of leasehold property is precluded from inquiring into the title of the lessor to the freehold. But if a recent lease is offered as security, unless the lessor is well known, the banker ought to receive satisfaction as to the lessor's title.

By Section 3, s.s. 4, of the Conveyancing Act, 1881:—

"Where land is held by lease (not including under-lease), the purchaser

> shall assume, unless the contrary appears, that the lease was duly granted; and, on production of the receipt for the last payment due for rent under the lease before the date of actual completion of the purchase, he shall assume, unless the contrary appears, that all the covenants and provisions of the lease have been duly performed and observed up to the date of actual completion of the purchase."

Where land sold is held by under-lease, the purchaser shall assume, unless the contrary appears, that the under-lease and every superior lease were duly granted, and on production of the last receipt for rent he shall assume that all covenants and provisions of the under-lease and of every superior lease, as well as all rent due, have been duly performed and paid up to date (s.s. 5).

By Section 4 of the Conveyancing Act, 1882:—

> "(1) Where a lease is made under a power contained in a settlement, will, Act of Parliament, or other instrument, any preliminary contract for or relating to the lease shall not, for the purpose of the deduction of title to an intended assign, form part of the title, or evidence of the title, to the lease."

Upon the death of an owner of leasehold property, the estate becomes vested in the personal representatives (executors or administrators) of the deceased. When, therefore, the deeds of leasehold property are lodged by a borrower who has obtained the property consequent upon the death of the previous owner, it should be remembered that the legal estate may still be held by the personal representatives, and that the borrower, if he inherited the property, requires a conveyance from the representatives, and if he had the property left to him by will, he requires a conveyance from, or the formal assent of, the representatives.

Where the deeds of leasehold property are deposited as security, they should as a rule be accompanied by the original lease, but it may occur that the original lease included two properties, and is not along with the deeds given as security. There should, however, be an attested copy of the lease, or it should be abstracted, and an acknowledgment given for its production. A purchaser of leasehold property is entitled to an abstract of the lease even though more than sixty years old.

Where a sub-lease is deposited as security, it should be accompanied by an attested copy of the original lease.

If parts of a leasehold property have been sub-leased, the counter parts of the sub-leases should accompany a deposit of the lease or assignment thereof.

By the Finance (1909–10) Act, 1910, Section 75, it is enacted that the stamp duties chargeable under the heading "Lease or Tack" in the Stamp Act, 1891, shall be double the duties which would have been chargeable immediately before the passing of this Act under that heading, but this Section shall not apply in the case of leases or tacks on which a fixed duty of a penny is chargeable under that heading. (The Finance Act was passed April 29, 1910.)

By the Stamp Act, 1891, the duty is as follows:—

Lease or Tack—	£ s. d.
(1) For any definite term not exceeding a year— Of any dwelling-house or part of a dwelling-house at a rent not exceeding the rate of £10 per annum . .	0 0 1
(2) For any definite term less than a year— (*a*) Of any furnished dwelling-house or apartments where the rent for such term exceeds £25	0 2 6
(*b*) Of any lands, tenements, or heritable subjects except or otherwise than as aforesaid	The same duty as a lease for a year at the rent reserved for the definite term.
(3) For any other definite term or for any indefinite term: Of any lands, tenements, or heritable subjects— Where the consideration, or any part of the consideration, moving either to the lessor or to any other person, consists of any money, stock, or security:	
In respect of such consideration	The same duty as a conveyance on a sale for the same consideration.
Where the consideration or any part of the consideration is any rent:	

In respect of such consideration :

If the rent, whether reserved as a yearly rent or otherwise, is at a rate or average rate :

	If the term does not exceed 35 years, or is indefinite.			If the term exceeds 35 years, but does not exceed 100 years.			If the term exceeds 100 years.		
	£	s.	d.	£	s.	d.	£	s.	d.
Not exceeding £5 per annum	0	0	6	0	3	0	0	6	0
Exceeding— £5 and not exceeding £10	0	1	0	0	6	0	0	12	0
£10 ,, ,, £15	0	1	6	0	9	0	0	18	0
£15 ,, ,, £20	0	2	0	0	12	0	1	4	0
£20 ,, ,, £25	0	2	6	0	15	0	1	10	0
£25 ,, ,, £50	0	5	0	1	10	0	3	0	0
£50 ,, ,, £75	0	7	6	2	5	0	4	10	0
£75 ,, ,, £100	0	10	0	3	0	0	6	0	0
£100									
For every full sum of £50, and also for any fractional part of £50 thereof	0	5	0	1	10	0	3	0	0

(4) Of any other kind whatsoever not hereinbefore described 0 10 0

And see Sections 75, 76, 77 and 78 as follows :—

Agreements for not more than Thirty-five Years to be Charged as Leases.

"75. (1) An agreement for a lease or tack, or with respect to the letting of any lands, tenements, or heritable subjects for any term not exceeding thirty-five years, or for any indefinite term, is to be charged with the same duty as if it were an actual lease or tack made for the term and consideration mentioned in the agreement.

"(2) A lease or tack made subsequently to, and in conformity with, such an agreement duly stamped is to be charged with the duty of sixpence only.

Leases how to be Charged in Respect of Produce, etc.

"76. (1) Where the consideration, or any part of the consideration, for which a lease or tack is granted or agreed to be granted, consists of any produce or other goods, the value of the produce or goods is to be deemed a consideration in respect of which the lease or tack or agreement is chargeable with *ad valorem* duty.

Directions as to Duty in Certain Cases.

"77. (1) A lease or tack, or agreement for a lease or tack, or with respect to any letting, is not to be charged with any duty in respect of any penal rent, or increased rent in the nature of a penal rent, thereby reserved or agreed to be reserved or made payable, or by reason of being made in consideration of the surrender or abandonment of any existing lease, tack, or agreement, of or relating to the same subject matter.

"(2) A lease made for any consideration in respect whereof it is chargeable with *ad valorem* duty, and in further consideration either of a covenant by the lessee to make, or of his having previously made, any substantial improvement of or addition to the property demised to him, or of any covenant relating to the matter of the lease, is not to be charged with any duty in respect of such further consideration.

[The Revenue Act, 1909, Section 8, enacts that the provisions of this sub-section shall not apply as respects any further consideration in the lease consisting of a covenant which if it were contained in a separate deed would be chargeable with *ad valorem* stamp duty, and accordingly the lease shall in any such case be charged with duty in respect of any such further consideration under Section 4 of the Stamp Act, 1891.]

"(3) No lease for a life or lives not exceeding three, or for a term of years determinable with a life or lives not exceeding three, and no lease for a term absolute not exceeding twenty-one years, granted by an ecclesiastical corporation aggregate or sole, is to be charged with any higher duty than thirty-five shillings.

"(4) A lease for a definite term exceeding thirty-five years granted under the Trinity College (Dublin) Leasing and Perpetuity Act, 1851, is not to be charged with any higher duty than would have been chargeable thereon if it had been a lease for a definite term not exceeding thirty-five years.

"(5) An instrument whereby the rent reserved by any other instrument chargeable with duty and duly stamped as a lease or tack is increased is not to be charged with duty otherwise than as a lease or tack in consideration of the additional rent thereby made payable.

Duty in Certain Cases may be Denoted by Adhesive Stamp.

"78. (1) The duty upon an instrument chargeable with duty as a lease or tack of—

"(*a*) any dwelling-house, or part of a dwelling-house, for a definite term not exceeding a year at a rent not exceeding the rate of ten pounds per annum ; or

"(*b*) any furnished dwelling-house or apartments for any definite term less than a year ;

and upon the duplicate or counterpart of any such instrument, may be denoted by an adhesive stamp, which is to be cancelled by the person by whom the instrument is first executed.

"(2) Every person who executes, or prepares or is employed in preparing, any such instrument (except letters or correspondence) which is not, at or before the execution thereof, duly stamped, shall incur a fine of five pounds."

As to the general form of a building lease, see BUILDING LEASE.

In Scotland, an assignment of a lease for thirty-one years and longer, when recorded in the Register of Sasines, forms a legal security ; but, when the term is for a less period, it is necessary that the assignee enter into possession, otherwise the assignment does not hold good as against creditors. (See TITLE DEEDS.)

LEEDS. A Stock Exchange name for Lancashire and Yorkshire Railway ordinary stock.

LEEMAN'S ACT. (30 VICT. c. 29.) The name of an Act of Parliament (passed with the intention of preventing speculation in bank shares) by which it is provided that all contracts for sale or purchase of bank shares or stock (except shares or stock of the Bank of England or Bank of Ireland) must set forth the numbers of the shares or stock, or, if there are no distinguishing numbers, the name of the registered proprietor. Section 1 is as follows :—

"All contracts, agreements, and tokens of sale and purchase which shall be made or entered into for the sale or transfer, or purporting to be for the sale or transfer, of any share or shares, or of any stock or other interest, in any joint stock banking company in the United Kingdom of Great Britain and Ireland constituted under or regulated by the provisions of any Act of Parliament, Royal Charter, or letters patent, issuing shares or stock transferable by any deed or written instrument, shall be null and void to all intents and purposes whatsoever, unless such contract, agreement, or other token shall set forth and designate in writing such shares, stock, or interest by the respective numbers by which the same are distinguished at the making of such contract, agreement, or token on the register or books of such banking company as aforesaid, or where there is no such register of shares or stock by distinguishing numbers, then unless such contract, agreement, or other token shall set forth the person or persons in whose name or names such shares, stock, or interest shall at the time of making such contract stand as the registered proprietor thereof in the books of such banking company ; and every person, whether principal, broker, or agent, who shall wilfully insert in any such contract, agreement, or other token any false entry of such numbers, or any name or names other than that of the person or persons in whose name such shares, stock, or interest shall stand as aforesaid, shall be guilty of a misdemeanour, and be punished accordingly, and, if in Scotland, shall be guilty of an offence punishable by fine or imprisonment."

This Act is still in force, but its provisions are disregarded on the London Stock Exchange, as it is not the practice to specify the numbers of bank shares on the contract note. Where a person, in ignorance of that practice, instructed his brokers to purchase for him certain shares in a joint stock bank, and, before the settling day, repudiated the contract, it was held (*Perry* v. *Barnett*, 1885, 15 Q.B.D. 388) that the contract, which was made contrary to this Act, was not binding upon him. But where a person purchases bank shares and is aware of the practice of the Stock Exchange he cannot repudiate the contract.

Sections 2 and 3 of the Act are as follow :—

"2. Joint stock banking companies shall be bound to show their list of shareholders to any registered shareholder during business hours, from ten of the clock to four of the clock.

"3. This Act shall not extend to shares or stock in the Bank of England or the Bank of Ireland."

LEGACY DUTY. The duty which is payable upon bequests of personalty by a testator who is domiciled in the United Kingdom at the time of his death.

The legacy duty rates payable upon the amount of any legacy, as amended by the Finance (1909–10) Act, 1910, Section 58, are as follows :—

Lineal ancestors or descendants of the testator . .	1 per cent.
Brothers and sisters of the testator, or their descendants	5 per cent.
Uncles and aunts of the testator, or their descendants	10 per cent.
Great uncles and great aunts of the testator, or their descendants, ...	10 per cent.
Any other person. . . .	10 per cent.

Prior to the Finance (1909–10) Act, 1910, the husband or wife were not chargeable with legacy duty on property settled or bequeathed by the other, but this exemption did not apply to property settled or beqeathed by any other person ; but by the above Act the duty at the rate of 1 per cent. is payable where the person taking the legacy is the husband or wife of the testator, as in cases where the person is a lineal ancestor or descendant ; but the duty shall not be levied where the value of the property (other than property in which the deceased never had an interest) in respect of which estate duty is payable does not exceed £15,000, nor where the amount of the legacy derived by the same person from the testator does not exceed £1,000, nor where the person taking the legacy is the widow or a child under the age of twenty-one of the testator and the amount of the legacy derived by the same person from the testator does not exceed £2,000.

The above shall take effect only where the testator by whose will the legacy is given or the intestate on whose death the legacy duty is payable dies on or after April 30, 1909.

Succession duty (and not legacy duty) is payable upon legacies which are charged upon the proceeds of a sale of real estate, or where the personal estate is insufficient and real estate has to be resorted to for payment, the legacies are liable to a deduction for the rateable part of the duty which results from the real estate. (See SUCCESSION DUTY.) When the deeds of any such property are lodged as security the succession duty receipts should accompany the deeds.

Legacy duty is not levied where the total value of the personalty does not exceed £100, nor where the net value of the estate does not exceed £1,000, and estate duty has been paid. Legacy duty is not payable on legacies to lineal descendants if estate duty has been paid. (See EXECUTOR.)

LEGAL ESTATE. A person has the legal estate in land when his title to it is complete. For example, where land has been conveyed to John Brown in fee simple he has the legal estate in it. If John Brown conveys it to Jones by way of mortgage to secure the repayment of money lent by Jones to Brown, the legal estate then vests in Jones, but Brown retains an equitable estate in the land. If the debt is not paid according to the terms of the mortgage deed, Jones becomes, according to law, the owner of the land, but, according to equity, Brown has still the right to redeem the land upon payment of the principal with all interest due and certain costs incurred by Jones in connection with the land. This right is called the equity of redemption.

If land is conveyed to Brown as trustee for Jones, the legal estate vests in Brown, but the equitable estate vests in Jones, who is the real owner. In such a case Brown has no beneficial interest whatever in the property

LEGAL MORTGAGE. Where a borrower conveys, by deed, the legal estate in his property to a lender, subject to his right to have the property re-conveyed upon repayment of the principal and interest, it is a legal mortgage.

A mortgage deed conveys to the mortgagee not only the land, but any houses or other buildings there may be upon the land, and all fixtures thereon. (See FIXTURES.)

Although the borrower parts with the legal estate, yet so long as he retains the equity of redemption (that is, the right to redeem the property by discharging the mortgage debt) he is the real owner of the property. If the difference between the amount of the mortgage and the value of the property is considerable, he may, if he wish, borrow further sums upon a second or a third mortgage, but each mortgage subsequent to the first is merely an equitable mortgage, because the legal estate is already vested in the first mortgagee, and the mortgagor can only convey what he has left—that is, an equitable estate in the property. If the mortgagor sells the equity of redemption, his interest in the property is altogether extinguished. (See EQUITY OF REDEMPTION.)

The date for repayment of a mortgage is usually six months, but the period inserted in mortgages to bankers is often a shorter time, and frequently the money is made repayable on demand. If the borrower does not repay the money at the end of the prescribed time, or after demand, the mortgagee becomes, by law, the full owner of the property. But, although legally he has become the owner, the mortgagor still retains his equity of redemption and can demand a re-conveyance to himself or a transfer of the mortgage to some other party, on payment of the amount owing with interest and certain charges which may have been incurred by the mortgagee in keeping up the property.

Unless a contrary intention is expressed in the mortgage deed, a mortgagee, where the mortgage is made by deed, shall, by virtue of the Conveyancing and Law of Property Act, 1881, Section 19, have the following powers, to the like extent as if they had been in terms conferred by the mortgage deed, but not further, namely :—

(*a*) A power, when the mortgage money has become due, to sell, or to concur with any other person in selling, the mortgaged property, or any part thereof, either subject to prior charges, or not, and either together or in lots, by public auction or by private contract, subject to such conditions respecting title, or evidence of title, or other matter, as he (the mortgagee) thinks fit, with power to vary any contract for sale, and to buy in at an auction, or to rescind any contract for sale, and to re-sell, without being answerable for any loss occasioned thereby ;

(*b*) A power, at any time after the date of the mortgage deed, to insure and keep insured against loss or damage by fire any building or property of an insurable nature. (By Section 23, unless an amount is fixed in the mortgage deed the insurance shall not exceed two-third parts of the amount that would be required, in case of total destruction, to restore the property.)

(*c*) A power, when the mortgage money has become due, to appoint a receiver of the income of the mortgaged property or any part thereof ;

(*d*) A power while the mortgagee is in possession to cut and sell timber.

By Section 20 of the same Act :—

"A mortgagee shall not exercise the power of sale conferred by this Act unless and until :—

"(1) Notice requiring repayment of the mortgage money has been served on the mortgagor, or one of several mortgagors, and default has been made in payment of the mortgage money, or of part thereof, for three months after such service ; or

"(2) Some interest under the mortgage is in arrear and unpaid for two months after becoming due ; or

"(3) There has been a breach of some provision contained in the mortgage deed or in this Act, and on the part of the mortgagor, or of some person concurring in making the mortgage, to be observed or performed, other than and besides a covenant for payment of the mortgage money or interest thereon."

In a banker's mortgage, however, it is generally expressly stipulated that his right to sell the property shall arise immediately default is made after demand, or on default at the end of, say, a period of one month after demand. Notice of the intention to exercise a power of sale should be given to a second mortgagee, if there is one, as well as to the mortgagor.

A mortgagee by deed may either sell the property or appoint a receiver (see RECEIVER) ; or enter into possession (see MORTGAGEE IN POSSESSION), but he cannot foreclose without an order of the Court. He can also sue the mortgagor on the covenant to repay contained in the mortgage deed, within twelve years from the last payment of interest by the mortgagor or acknowledgement of the debt. A mortgagee cannot sell the property to himself, or to his own agent.

By Section 25 of the Conveyancing and Law of Property Act, 1881 :—

"(1) Any person entitled to redeem mortgaged property may have a judgment or order for sale instead of for redemption in an action brought by him either for redemption alone, or for sale alone, or for sale or redemption in the alternative.

"(2) In any action, whether for foreclosure, or for redemption, or for sale, or for the raising and payment in any manner of mortgage money, the Court, on the request of the mortgagee, or of any person interested either in the mortgage money or in the right of redemption, and, notwithstanding the dissent of any other person, and notwithstanding that the mortgagee, or any person so interested does not appear in the action, and without allowing any time for redemption or for payment of any mortgage money, may, if it thinks fit, direct a sale of the mortgaged property, on such terms as it thinks fit, including, if it thinks fit, the deposit in Court of a reasonable sum fixed by the Court, to meet the expenses of sale and to secure performance of the terms."

Where a sale has been effected under a mortgage, Section 21, s.s. 3, provides that :—

"The money which is received by the mortgagee, arising from the sale, after discharge of prior incumbrances to which the sale is not made subject, if any, or after payment into Court under this Act of a sum to meet any prior incumbrance, shall be held by him in trust to be applied by him, first, in payment of all costs, charges and expenses, properly incurred by him, as incident to the sale or any attempted sale, or otherwise; and secondly, in discharge of the mortgage money, interest, and costs, and other money, if any, due under the mortgage; and the residue of the money so received shall be paid to the person entitled to the mortgaged property, or authorised to give receipts for the proceeds of the sale thereof."

If there are subsequent mortgages, any surplus there may be from a sale of the property belongs to them, but if the vendor has no notice of any subsequent charges he is not liable if he pays the surplus to the mortgagor.

If the proceeds of a sale by a mortgagee are insufficient to discharge the mortgage debt, the mortgagee may claim upon the mortgagor for the deficiency. If, however, instead of selling, the mortgagee forecloses, he has no further claim upon the mortgagor.

Where a banker takes a mortgage for a fixed amount, the loan should be upon a separate account. A mortgage for a fixed amount is not a security to cover a working account, as each payment to credit is in effect so much deducted from the amount of the mortgage, and any future advances would not be covered by it. Further, where the mortgage to the banker is for a fixed sum, simple interest only, in the absence of any agreement to the contrary, can be charged.

By Section 40 of the Property Tax Act, 1853, a mortgagor may deduct income tax from the amount of interest payable on his mortgage. (See INCOME TAX.)

John Brown can deposit as security for his working account a mortgage to himself from, say, John Jones, and the property, to the extent of the mortgage, will form a continuous security. Where a deposit of a mortgage deed is taken, the banker should give notice to the mortgagor, in the above supposed case to John Jones, that the deed has been lodged with him as security. Unless such notice is given, the banker might find ultimately that John Jones had been gradually repaying the debt to John Brown, and that John Brown had not given the bank the benefit of the payments.

In an ordinary mortgage, after the date of repayment has gone past, the mortgagee is entitled to six months' notice from the mortgagor of his intention to repay.

For stamp duties see MORTGAGE.

The following points, amongst others, are found in a good "banker's mortgage" :—

The mortgagor, in consideration of the bank allowing him to keep an account, conveys unto the bank the lands and hereditaments, as described in the Schedule, subject to the proviso for redemption that, if he pays on demand all sums owing by him to the bank on any account or for any amount for which he may be liable as surety, with interest and other charges, the bank shall re-convey the premises to him. It forms a continuing security to cover any sum which shall for the time being constitute the balance due to the bank from the mortgagor. The mortgagor covenants therein to pay on demand all sums owing, and to keep the premises insured against fire, and declares that, after the money has become due and is not paid, say, within a month, the bank shall be entitled to exercise the power of sale conferred on mortgagees by statute. It is also stipulated in the mortgage that the security shall not be affected by any other security held or that may hereafter be held by the bank, and that the bank shall have power to give time for payment to any other person liable for the moneys secured by the mortgage.

When the security is no longer required the property is reconveyed by the bank, by an indorsement upon the mortgage deed to the effect that the bank conveys unto the mortgagor all the premises which are vested in the bank, subject to redemption, by virtue of the within written indenture, to hold the same unto the mortgagor freed and discharged from all moneys secured by the within written indenture. (See MORTGAGE, TITLE DEEDS.)

LEGAL TENDER. A legal tender is a tender of money of such description that the person to whom it is tendered will put himself in the wrong if he refuses to accept it. A legal tender requires that the exact sum of the debt must be tendered, without necessitating any change.

COINS.—The Coinage Act, 1870 (33 Vict. c. 10,) Section 4, enacts "a tender of payment of money, if made in coins which have been issued by the Mint in accordance with the provisions of this Act, and have not been called in by any proclamation made in pursuance of this Act, and have not become diminished in weight, by wear or otherwise, so as to be of less weight than the current weight, that is to say, than the weight (if any) specified as the least current weight in the first schedule to this Act, or less than such weight as may be declared by any proclamation made in pursuance of this Act, shall be a legal tender,

"In the case of gold coins for a payment of any amount:

"In the case of silver coins for a payment of an amount not exceeding forty shillings, but for no greater amount:

"In the case of bronze coins for a payment of an amount not exceeding one shilling, but for no greater amount.

"Nothing in this Act shall prevent any paper currency, which under any Act or otherwise is a legal tender, from being a legal tender."

By Section 5 :—"No piece of gold, silver, copper or bronze, or of any metal or mixed metal, of any value, shall be made or issued, except by the Mint as a coin or a token of money, or as purporting that the holder thereof is entitled to demand any value denoted thereon."

By 24 and 25 Vict. c. 99, Section 7, "no tender of payment in money made in gold, silver, or copper coin, defaced by being stamped with any name or words thereon, whether such coin shall or shall not be thereby diminished or lightened, shall be allowed to be a legal tender."

The gold coinage made at the mints of Sydney, Melbourne, and Perth (Western Australia) was declared legal tender in the United Kingdom by Royal Proclamation in the years 1866, 1869, and 1897 respectively.

Pre-Victorian sovereigns and half-sovereigns are not now legal tender. They were called in by the Coinage Act of 1889.

A creditor is not obliged to give change when notes are offered to a greater value than the amount of the debt.

NOTES.—By 3 & 4 Will. IV. c. 98, Section 6 :—"A tender of a note or notes of the Bank of England, expressed to be payable to bearer on demand, shall be a legal tender, to the amount expressed in such note or notes, and shall be taken to be valid as a tender to such amount for all sums above five pounds on all occasions on which any tender of money may be legally made, so long as the Bank of England shall continue to pay on demand their said notes in legal coin; provided always, that no such note or notes shall be deemed a legal tender of payment by the governor and company of the Bank of England, or any branch bank of the said governor and company; but the said governor and company are not to become liable or be required to pay and satisfy, at any branch bank of the said governor and company, any note or notes of the said governor and company not made specially payable at such branch bank; but the governor and company shall be liable to pay and satisfy at the Bank of England in London all notes of the said governor and company or of any branch thereof."

Notes of the Bank of England may circulate in Scotland and in Ireland, but they are not a legal tender in those countries, if objected to by the person to whom they are being paid (8 & 9 Vict. c. 38, Section 15 and c. 37, Section 6).

In the Isle of Man and the Channel Islands notes are not a legal tender.

It has been pointed out that, whereas a tender of a £5 note is, by the above Act, not a legal tender for a debt of £5, a debt of

£5 0*s*. 1*d*. can be legally discharged by a £5 note and a penny.

A tender of country bank notes, if not objected to by the person to whom they are offered, will act as a legal tender.

In the case of country bank notes which are accepted in payment at the time when a sale is made, the person who takes such notes takes them at his own risk and if he should find that the bank which issued the notes has failed he must suffer the loss himself. Unless he can prove that the person from whom the notes were received knew at the time of the sale that the bank had failed, the holder of the notes will not, in an ordinary case, have any remedy against that person. But the position is different when notes are received in settlement of a debt, as the debt will not be considered to have been paid if the person who takes the notes finds that the bank has failed and he is unable to obtain payment of them. He must, however, present the notes at the bank within a reasonable time and give due notice of their dishonour to the person from whom he received them, otherwise that person will be discharged from liability. And the case is the same where change has been given for a bank note for the purpose of obliging a person.

Scotch notes are not legal tender in Scotland, neither are Irish notes legal tender in Ireland, except Bank of Ireland notes when used in payment of the Revenue of Ireland (1 & 2 Geo. IV, c. 72).

Legal tender :—

In England and Wales.	In Scotland.	In Ireland.	Isle of Man, Channel Islands.
Gold (sovereigns and half-sovereigns) to any amount.	Same.	Same.	Same.
Silver up to 40s.	Same.	Same.	Same.
Copper up to 1s.	Same.	Same.	Same.
Bank of England Notes above £5 and up to any amount, except by the Head Office and branches of the Bank of England (3 & 4 Will. IV, c. 98, s. 6).	No notes are legal tender.	No notes are legal tender, except Bank of Ireland Notes in payment of Revenue of Ireland (1 & 2 Geo. IV, c. 72).	No notes are legal tender.

(See COINAGE.)

When a banker cashes a cheque he does so in such notes or coins as may be desired by the customer, and it is not often that he has to consider in what form a payment should be made in order to constitute a legal tender. Except in the case of the Bank of England, a cheque for £50 may be cashed, in order to be a legal tender, as follows : It may all be in banknotes or in gold (sovereigns or half-sovereigns) : or forty shillings may be in silver (or thirty-nine in silver and one in bronze), three pounds in gold and the remaining £45 either in gold or Bank of England notes.

LEGATEE. The person to whom "personal" property (see PERSONALTY) is left, or bequeathed, in a will, is called a legatee. The person who takes all the personal property remaining after all legatees have received their shares, is called the residuary legatee.

LEPTA. (See FOREIGN MONEYS—GREECE.)

LESSEE. The person in whose favour a lease is granted. (See LEASEHOLD.)

LESSOR. The person who grants a lease. (See LEASEHOLD.)

LETTER BOOKS. A copy is always preserved of all letters despatched from a bank. Letter books into which letters are press copied are kept as may be found most convenient. Various officials may have their own letter books with a distinctive reference on the letter paper, and the number of the page on which the letter is copied may be written on the letter, so that, when a reply is made and that reference is quoted, the copy may be found without trouble. Letter books are kept in connection with special subjects or departments as the share or the coupon department. Banks often keep a separate book at head office for each branch, and a branch keeps one exclusively for letters to head office. There are also books for the correspondence with the London agents, books for private correspondence with the head officials, and books for general correspondence with customers, or with other banks ; also a book in which are copied all replies given to bankers' inquiries.

The duty of press-copying letters usually devolves upon the youngest members of the staff, but it is by no means unimportant work as a badly copied letter may be a cause of much subsequent inconvenience and annoyance.

LETTER OF ALLOTMENT. The letter which is sent by a company to an applicant for shares, which are being offered to the public, stating the number of shares which have been allotted to him and requesting payment of the amount due to be paid upon the shares.

The following is a specimen of a letter of allotment :—

The A.B. Company, Limited,
Carlisle , 19 .

Sir,—

In reply to your application the directors have allotted you shares of £ each in this company.

According to the prospectus per share is due on allotment and the amount due from you is £ , which please remit to the X. & Y. Bank, Limited, Carlisle.

After payment of the above amount please retain this letter of allotment and the receipt for the amount paid upon application, to be exchanged for the share certificate when ready.

JOHN BROWN,
Secretary.

Allotment letters do not form a security for an advance.

Stamp duties :—

LETTER OF ALLOTMENT and LETTER of RENUNCIATION, or any other document having the effect of a letter of allotment :—

(1) Of any share of any company or proposed company.
(2) In respect of any loan raised, or proposed to be raised, by any company or proposed company, or by any municipal body or corporation.
(3) Issued or delivered in the United Kingdom, of any share of any foreign or colonial company or proposed company, or in respect of any loan raised or proposed to be raised by or on behalf of any foreign or colonial state, government, municipal body, corporation, or company.

Where the nominal amount which is allotted or to which the letter of renunciation relates is not less than £5, the duty is sixpence ; where the amount is less than £5, the duty is one penny. A separate duty is chargeable in respect of letters of allotment and letters of renunciation, although they may be contained in the same document. The stamp duty of sixpence on a letter of renunciation may be denoted by an adhesive stamp, which is to be cancelled by the person by whom the letter of renunciation is executed (Finance Act, 1899, Section 9).

The word "share" in the above schedule includes a fractional part of a share (Revenue Act, 1909, Section 9).

By the Stamp Act, 1891, Section 79 :—

"(1) Every person who executes, grants, issues, or delivers out any document chargeable with duty as a letter of allotment, letter of renunciation, or scrip certificate, or as scrip, before the same is duly stamped, shall incur a fine of twenty pounds.

"(2) The stamp duty of one penny on a letter of renunciation may be denoted by an adhesive stamp which is to be cancelled by the person by whom the letter of renunciation is executed."

The stamp upon a letter of allotment, however, must be impressed.

Receipts upon a duly stamped letter of allotment are exempt from duty. (See Exemption 11 under heading RECEIPT.) (See ALLOTMENT, COMPANIES.)

LETTER OF ATTORNEY. (See POWER OF ATTORNEY.)

LETTER OF CHARGE. Where bearer securities are taken as cover for an advance, it is usual to take a letter of charge or memorandum of deposit to show the purpose for which they have been deposited.

Certificates are sometimes lodged, along with a simple letter or memorandum of deposit, but such a document does not give the banker a good security. (See TRANSFER OF SHARES.)

A letter of charge for bearer securities or certificates is subject to a stamp duty of sixpence, irrespective of the amount. The stamp may be either adhesive or impressed. (See MEMORANDUM OF DEPOSIT.)

LETTER OF CREDIT. A letter of credit is a document issued by a banker authorising the banker to whom it is addressed to honour the cheques of the person named to the extent of a certain amount and to charge the sums to the account of the grantor ; or it may be worded so as to authorise the person to whom it is addressed to draw on demand, or at a currency, upon the banker issuing the letter, and the grantor undertakes, in the letter, to honour all drafts drawn in accordance with the terms of the credit. The letter states the period for which the credit is to remain in force, and it should be indorsed with particulars of all drafts drawn under the credit. When a letter of credit is issued, the amount is debited to the customer's account and credited to a "Letters of Credit" account.

In addition to an "open" or "clean" letter of credit (as above) there is a documentary letter of credit which authorises the drawing of bills upon the grantor and undertakes to honour them provided that the documents of title to the goods named (bills of lading with insurance policies and invoices) are sent to the grantor.

When the authority to draw a bill is printed upon the margin of the form which is to be used for drawing the bill, the document is called a marginal letter of credit. The authority portion of the document refers to the bill portion in such words as "I authorise you to draw the annexed bill." The two parts of the instrument must not be separated.

Where a banker is authorised to pay cheques under a letter of credit, he must see that the signature of the drawer is correct and that the terms of the letter are strictly observed. He should be furnished with a specimen of the signature of the person who is entitled to draw the money.

Where a letter of credit is shown to a merchant abroad who is selling goods to the holder of the letter, it has the effect of satisfying the merchant that the bill will be duly accepted by the banker issuing the letter. The essence of a letter of credit is, as Lord Justice Cairns said (in *In re Agra & Masterman's Bank*, 1867, 2 Ch. 391), "that the person taking bills on the faith of it is to have the absolute benefit of the undertaking in the letter, and to have it in order to obtain the acceptance of the bills which are negotiable instruments payable according to their tenor, and without reference to any collateral or cross claims."

A letter of credit is not a negotiable instrument.

For the purpose of stamp duty a letter of credit is treated as a bill of exchange (see Section 32, Stamp Act, 1891, under heading BILL OF EXCHANGE), but a letter of credit granted in the United Kingdom, authorising drafts to be drawn out of the United Kingdom payable in the United Kingdom is exempt from duty (see Exemption 4, under BILL OF EXCHANGE). (See CIRCULAR LETTER OF CREDIT, CIRCULAR NOTES.)

LETTER OF HYPOTHECATION. A document signed by a debtor giving a banker or other creditor a charge upon goods belonging to the debtor, the goods remaining in the custody of a third party. The letter of lien or charge should empower the banker to sell, in default of payment of the debt.

Where a letter of hypothecation of goods was given to a banker, by which the debtor agreed to hold the goods in trust for the banker and pay over the proceeds when received, it was held (*Reg. v. Townshend*, 1884, 15 Cox, C.C. 466) that the letter, being a declaration of trust without transfer, was a bill of sale. (See TRUST RECEIPT.)

LETTER OF INDICATION. The letter which accompanies circular notes or a circular letter of credit. The letter is signed by the banker issuing it, and the person to whom it is given places his signature upon it, as soon as received. When any of the circular notes are presented for payment, or drafts are drawn under a letter of credit, the banker should insist on the production of the letter of indication, and assure himself that the indorsement on the notes or signature on the drafts corresponds with the signature of the legitimate holder on the letter of indication. The letter is addressed to the correspondents of the grantors and, when accompanying circular notes, supplies the numbers of the notes which have been issued to the holder. The notes should not be indorsed except in the presence of the banker from whom payment is required, and the notes should be carried apart from the letter of indication, so that if they are lost the finder will not be able to make any use of them in the absence of the letter.

The following is a specimen of a letter of indication to accompany circular notes:—

No. Date 19 .

To Messieurs the Bankers
mentioned in this Letter of Indication.

GENTLEMEN,—

We beg to introduce to you who is furnished with our Circular Notes numbered payable at our Head Office, London.

We request that you will purchase any of these notes presented to you for payment, at your current rate for demand drafts on London, on their being indorsed in your presence in accordance with the specimen signature below.

This Letter of Indication should be retained by the holder until all the Circular Notes have been cashed, when it is to be surrendered to the Banker cashing the last Note.

Your obedient servants,

Signature of Bearer.

The following is a specimen of a letter of indication to accompany a letter of credit :—

No. Date 19 .

To Messieurs the Bankers
mentioned in this Letter of Indication.

GENTLEMEN,—

This letter will be handed to you by
in whose favour we have issued our Letter of Credit No. . Recommending
to your kind attention, and referring you to specimen signature below.

Your obedient Servants,

Specimen Signature.

(See CIRCULAR LETTER OF CREDIT, CIRCULAR NOTES.)

LETTER OF LICENCE (*re* BANK CHARTER ACT). This is the name given to the official letter of authority sent by the Government to the Bank of England, on the latter's application, during the crises of 1847, 1857, and 1866, permitting the Bank to break the Act of 1844 and increase their issue of notes upon securities. In 1857 the Bank took advantage of this authorisation, but in the two other years mentioned they did not require to resort to it, public confidence being restored without.

LETTER OF LICENCE (DEBTOR AND CREDITOR). An agreement between a debtor, who is in difficulties, and his creditors, under which the creditors agree not to enforce their claims for a certain time, and, in the meantime, to allow him to continue his business. (See DEED OF ARRANGEMENT.)

LETTER OF LIEN. A debtor sometimes gives a banker, as security for an advance, a letter of lien or charge upon goods in the hands of a third party. In the case of *In re Hamilton, Young & Co.* (1905, 2 K.B. 772), where a letter of lien over goods in the hands of certain bleachers, accompanied by their receipt, was given, it was held that the letter was a document used in the ordinary course of business as a proof of the control of goods. The letter should empower the banker to sell, in default of payment of the debt. (See TRUST RECEIPT.)

LETTER OF REGRET. Upon a new issue of shares, the applicants who are not successful in obtaining an allotment receive a "letter of regret" announcing the fact and returning their money.

LETTER OF RENUNCIATION. Where shares have been allotted to a person and he does not wish to keep them, he may renounce them in favour of another person. The document by which this is effected is called the Letter of Renunciation.

For Stamp duty see LETTER OF ALLOTMENT.

LETTER OF REVERSION. In the Stamp Act, 1891, the reference to the stamp duty is :—

LETTER OF REVERSION in Scotland. See MORTGAGE, etc., and Section 86 thereunder.

LETTERS DESPATCHED BOOK. Under each day's date is given a complete list, with addresses, of all letters despatched by post, and the amount of the postage on each. The time at which the letters are posted is given, and the initials appended of the persons who actually posted them. Many banks insist upon the letters being taken to the post in a locked bag, by two persons. Prior to the letters being put into the bag, they are usually examined by a senior clerk to see that all are in order.

The stock of postage stamps on hand is balanced periodically by means of the money column in the letters despatched book.

LETTERS OF ADMINISTRATION. Where a person dies and leaves no will, the Probate Registry will, on application, appoint a person, the administrator, to wind up the estate, and will grant to him "Letters of Administration," that is, a document empowering him to administer to the estate of the deceased. If the deceased person left a will but did not nominate any person to act as executor, or if the persons nominated are incapable of acting, e.g. infants or lunatics, or if the persons nominated renounce Probate, that is, they decline to act as executors, "Letters of Administration with the Will annexed" will be granted by the Probate Registry. The administrator in such a case must carry out the terms of the will just like an executor.

If the balance of a deceased's account is very small, some bankers pay it, on receiving a satisfactory indemnity, without production of Letters of Administration.

Where Letters of Administration are revoked, the banker is protected in any payments he may have made upon the Letters. The sections of the Act relating to this point are quoted under PROBATE (*q.v.*). (See ADMINISTRATOR, ADMINISTRATOR DE BONIS NON.)

LETTERS RECEIVED BOOK. All letters received are entered in this book. It is ruled to show the date of receipt, person from whom received, and the subject matter. A column is also usually provided to show the date on which the reply (if any) was made. The entries are numbered consecutively and the numbers are placed in coloured pencil upon the corresponding letters. When replied to, the letters are filed away in numerical order, neatly folded up with the number, name, and subject matter indorsed on the outside.

LEVA. (See FOREIGN MONEYS—BULGARIA.)

LEY. (See FOREIGN MONEYS—ROUMANIA.)

LIABILITIES. The liabilities side of a balance sheet shows the total indebtedness of the person or company.

The liabilities of a bank are to the shareholders, to depositors, on acceptances, and, in the case of a bank of issue, on the notes in the hands of the public. (See BALANCE SHEET.)

LICENCE. Except in the case of the Bank of England (see BANK OF ENGLAND), banks which are entitled to issue their own notes may issue them either on stamped or unstamped paper. If they are on unstamped paper, a licence must be obtained from the Commissioners of Inland Revenue authorising the issue of notes and bills of exchange on unstamped paper, and a bond must be given to secure the payment of a composition for the stamp duties payable on the notes and bills issued. The duty on each licence is £30, and it must be taken out annually. A separate licence is required for every town or place where notes are issued (two or more offices in the same town being covered by one licence), with the exception that bankers, who, before May 6, 1844, had taken out four licences, and which licences were in force on that date for the issue of notes at more than four places, are not required to obtain more than four licences for the issue of notes at the same places.

Where a branch having a licence to issue notes, opens a sub-office in another town or place, the banker's own notes cannot be issued at that sub-office under the licence held by the parent branch.

The following Sections of 9 Geo. IV, c. 23, relate to the powers given to bankers in England to issue, on licence, promissory notes and to draw bills not exceeding seven days after sight, or twenty-one days after date :—

"1. It shall be lawful for any person or persons carrying on the business of a banker or bankers in England (except within the city of London, or within three miles thereof), having first duly obtained a licence for that purpose, and given security by bond, in manner hereinafter mentioned, to issue, on unstamped paper, promissory notes for any sum of money amounting to £5 or upwards, expressed to be payable to the bearer on demand, or to order, at any period not exceeding seven days after sight; and also to draw and issue, on unstamped paper, bills of exchange, expressed to be payable to order on demand, or at any period not exceeding seven days after sight, or twenty-one days after the date thereof; provided such bills of exchange be drawn upon a person or persons carrying on the business of a banker or bankers in London, Westminster, or the borough of Southwark, or provided such bills of exchange be drawn by any banker or bankers, at a town or place where he or they shall be duly licensed to issue unstamped notes and bills under the authority of this Act, upon himself or themselves, or his or their copartner or copartners, payable at any other town or place where such banker or bankers shall also be duly licensed to issue such notes and bills as aforesaid.

"2. It shall be lawful for any two or more of the Commissioners of Stamps to grant to all persons carrying on the business of bankers in England (except as aforesaid), who shall require the same, licences authorising such persons to issue such promissory notes, and to draw and issue such bills of exchange as aforesaid, on unstamped paper; which said licences shall be and are hereby respectively charged with a stamp duty of £30 for every such licence.

"3. A separate licence shall be taken out in respect of every town or place where any such unstamped promissory notes or bills of exchange as aforesaid shall be issued or drawn: Provided always, that no person or persons shall be obliged to take out more than four licences in all for any number of towns or places in England; and in case any person or persons shall issue or draw such unstamped notes or bills as aforesaid, at more than four different towns or places, then, after taking out three distinct licences for three of such towns or places, such person or persons shall be entitled to have all the rest of such towns or places included in a fourth licence."

Section 22 of 7 & 8 Vict. c. 32 enacts :—

"Every banker who shall be liable by law to take out a licence from the Commissioners of Stamps and Taxes to authorise the issuing of notes or bills shall take out a separate and distinct licence for every town or place at which he shall, by himself or his agent, issue any notes or bills requiring such licence to authorise the issuing thereof, anything in any former Act contained to the contrary thereof notwithstanding: Provided always, that no banker who on or before the 6th day of May, 1844, had taken out four such licences, which on the said last-mentioned day were respectively in force, for the issuing of any such notes or bills at more than four separate towns or places, shall at any time hereafter be required to take out or to have in force at one and the same time more than four such licences to authorise the issuing of such notes or bills at all or any of the same towns or places specified in such licences in force on the said 6th day of May, 1844, and at which towns or places respectively such bankers had on or before the said last-mentioned day issued such notes or bills in pursuance of such licences or any of them respectively."

Every licence which shall be granted between October 10 and November 11 in any year shall be dated on October 11, and every licence granted at any other time shall be dated on the day on which it is granted, and every such licence shall continue in force until October 10 next. (9 Geo. IV, c. 23, Section 4.)

In the case of licences granted to joint stock banks, it is enacted by 24 & 25 Vict. c. 91, Section 35, that it shall be sufficient to specify in the licence or certificate the names and places of abode of any six or more persons who may be presented to the Commissioners and to grant the licence to them as and for the whole of the company or co-partnership, and to grant the licence to such company or co-partnership, in and by the said name or style, as the Commissioners may think fit, and such licence is to be as good as if the names and places of abode of all the members of the company or co-partnership had been specified therein and the licence granted to them. (See BANK NOTES, BANK OF ISSUE, COMPOSITION, NOTE RETURN.)

LICENCE TO ASSIGN. Where a lessee is unable to assign, demise or sublet the leasehold land or premises without the licence or consent in writing of the lessor or his agent, the necessary licence, when obtained, may be in the following form :—"I hereby license and authorise   to assign his estate and interest in the piece or parcel of ground, etc.,   unto   for the residue of the term of   years, etc." (See LEASEHOLD.)

LICENSED PROPERTY. In considering the value of licensed property, it should be remembered that the purchase money named in the last deed of conveyance may have been an inflated price and therefore may not be much of an indication as to the present value. The rent of a public-house, when tied to a brewery company, cannot always be taken as a correct basis upon which to estimate the value; the rent may be a comparatively small one, in view of all purchases having to be made from the brewery. But where the house is owned privately and is free, the rent may be taken as a fair basis, because the owner does not get anything from the trade of the house, and looks to the rent for a return on his capital invested in the purchase of the house.

A licence is liable to be taken away by the licensing magistrates. An insurance policy should therefore be obtained to insure against loss by depreciation in value of the interest of the insured in the premises by the forfeiture of, or refusal to renew, the licence. The policy covers any such loss up to a specified amount, and usually contains a clause as follows :—

"Provided always that in the case of an On-licence, if the insured shall be entitled to obtain the payment of compensation under the provisions of any Act of Parliament in respect to the refusal to renew the said licence, or, in the case of an Off-licence, if the renewal of the said licence shall be refused on any ground other than the ground that the premises have been ill-conducted or are structurally deficient or structurally unsuitable, or grounds connected with the character or fitness of the proposed holder of the said licence, no claim shall arise under this policy." (See VALUATION.)

LIEN. A lien is the right to hold a person's property until payment of a debt is received. A lien does not, however, give the banker any right to sell the property, and legal advice should be obtained before dealing with securities held by way of lien.

A banker has a lien upon all negotiable securities deposited with him in his capacity as banker, by a customer, unless there is an express contract, or there are circumstances showing an implied contract, inconsistent with the lien. The lien is not affected by reason that the negotiable securities do not belong to the person depositing them, if the banker is unaware of the fact.

A banker has no lien on securities which are deposited for some particular purpose. For example, it has been held that where a conveyance of two separate properties was deposited, with a memorandum of charge upon only one of the properties, the banker had not a general lien upon the other property.

Bills and documents left for collection are part of a banker's ordinary business, and he has a lien upon them.

Section 27, s.s. 3, of the Bills of Exchange Act, 1882, provides :—" Where the holder of a bill has a lien on it, arising either from contract or by implication of law, he is deemed to be a holder for value to the extent of the sum for which he has a lien." If a bill has been transferred absolutely to a banker he is entitled to the full amount of it, but if he has merely a lien upon it his interest is limited to the extent of that lien.

Where bearer bonds are left with a banker in order that the coupons may be cut off and collected by him, Sir John R. Paget considers that a lien probably attaches to the bonds, but no lien would attach if left for safe custody, and the customer looked after the coupons himself. (See " The Law of Banking," p. 301.)

The securities over which a banker has a lien are understood to be negotiable securities such " as promissory notes, bills of exchange, exchequer bills, coupons, bonds of foreign governments, etc. ; and the Courts have held that if such securities are deposited by a customer with his banker, and there is nothing to show the intention of such deposit one way or the other, the banker has, by custom, a lien thereon for the balance due from the customer " (Kindersley, V.-C., in *Wylde* v. *Radford*, 1863, 33 L.J. Ch. 51). In *Davis* v. *Bowsher* (1794, 5 T.R. 488), Lord Kenyon said : " Whenever a banker has advanced money to another, he has a lien on all the paper securities which come into his hands for the amount of his general balance."

A banker, as gratuitous bailee, has no lien upon articles left for safe custody.

A conveyance of land is not subject to a banker's general lien, but where deeds are deposited with the intention of creating a security, without any memorandum of charge, they form an equitable mortgage by deposit.

In *In re Bowes, Earl of Strathmore* v. *Vane* (1886, 33 Ch. D. 586), where a customer deposited a life policy for £5,000, with a memorandum stating that it was to form a security to the extent of £4,000 with interest, commission and other charges, it was held that the banker could not claim more on the policy than the £4,000 and charges, as limited in the charge. Mr. Justice North said : " It is said that the bankers have a banker's lien ; that Bowes was their customer, and handed over to them the policy as security, that they had it in their hands and were entitled to hold it, not only for the £4,000, interest and commission, for which they had a written agreement, but that in addition they had a further right as bankers to hold it in respect of the rest of his debt to them ; or in other words they claim a right under the special contract in writing and also under an implied contract. It appears to me that that is inconsistent with the terms of the agreement, which is for a security for a sum not exceeding £4,000 principal and no more, with interest and commission, and that when the contract says in so many words that the charge is for a sum not exceeding £4,000, the charge is limited to that amount. . . . It has not been suggested that the sale was wrong in any way ; and it may well be that bankers who have a power of selling securities deposited, when they have sold, and have clear money in their hands after satisfying the charge, may be entitled to say they will set off that money against further sums due to them ; but that seems to me a totally different case from the present, where the security is of a wholly different nature, and the bank had no power of sale. It is quite true that, after a demand for payment had been made, the bank might have insisted on having a mortgage with a power of sale. No such demand was made or mortgage given, the bank never had a power to sell and convert the policy into money. . . . It seems to me that the express terms of this deposit were that sums not exceeding £4,000 were to be paid out of the policy moneys, and it would be inconsistent with that, in the absence of any additional agreement, to allow the bank to hold the policy for something more."

Where a customer has a credit balance on one account and is owing money on another, the banker has a right to set off one balance against the other. This right is sometimes referred to as a banker's "lien," but the more exact term is "set off." A credit balance on an account which has been opened by him in a fiduciary capacity cannot be set off against an overdrawn private account; neither has a banker the right to set off the credit balance of a partner's private account against a debt on the partnership account.

The Deed of Settlement of a banking company may provide that the shares of the members shall be subject to a lien in favour of the bank for all moneys due to the bank in respect of any call or debt due from the shareholder, whether alone or jointly with any other person, to the bank. It has been held that such a power gives the bank a lien upon the dividends, as well as upon the shares.

The clause with regard to a lien may take the following form:—"The company shall have a first and permanent lien and charge available at law and equity on every share of every person who is the holder or one of the joint-holders thereof, for all debts and liabilities on any banking or other account whatsoever, and for all other debts, liabilities, and sums of money due or to become due from him, either alone or jointly with any other person, whether a member or not, to the company at any time whatsoever, whilst he is the registered holder, or one of the registered holders, of the share.

"The directors may forfeit and re-issue, or may sell and dispose of for the benefit of the company, any shares on which the company shall have such lien as aforesaid, without any further authority on the part of the holder or holders thereof, in order to obtain satisfaction or payment of all or any part of such debts, liabilities, or sums of money: Provided that no such forfeiture, sale, or disposition of shares shall take place without one calendar month's notice to the holder or holders of the shares in accordance with the articles relating to notice, and that when any shares shall be so forfeited, sold, or disposed of, the company shall credit such holder or holders in account in case of forfeiture or other disposition not being a sale for cash with the value of the shares so forfeited, sold, or disposed of, ascertained from the price paid on the last registered transfer of shares, and in case of sale for cash with the price received by the company as the actual price of the share sold: Provided also that the register of shares shall be conclusive evidence of the title of a subsequent holder of any share which the directors shall have purported to forfeit, sell, or dispose of as aforesaid; and the remedy of any shareholder in respect of any irregularity in the enforcing of any lien, or alleged lien, shall be in damages against the company only."

Where shares in another banking company are offered as security it should be remembered that that company will probably have a first lien upon its own shares. But in the case of the *Bradford Banking Co.* v. *Briggs & Co.* (1886, 12 A.C. 29), where the articles of association of a company registered under the Companies Act, 1862, provided that the company should have "a first and permanent lien and charge, available at law and in equity, upon every share for all debts due from the holder thereof" it was held, reversing the decision of the Court of Appeal, that notice to the company of the deposit of certificates with the bank was not a notice of a trust within the meaning of the Companies Act, 1862, Section 30, and that the bank by giving notice of the deposit did not seek to affect the company with notice of a trust, but only to affect the company (which was a trading company) in their capacity as traders with notice of the interest of the bank. It was also held that the company could not in respect of moneys which became due from the shareholder to the company after notice of the deposit with the bank claim priority over advances by the bank made after such notice.

A vendor has a lien upon the land for any unpaid part of the purchase money as against a subsequent purchaser with notice; but "a receipt for consideration money or other consideration in the body of a deed, or indorsed thereon, shall, in favour of a subsequent purchaser, not having notice that the money or other consideration thereby acknowledged to be received was not in fact paid or given, wholly or in part, be sufficient evidence of the payment or giving of the whole amount thereof." (Conveyancing Act, 1881, Section 55, s.s. 1.) (See SET OFF, TITLE DEEDS.)

LIFE ANNUITY. An annuity, or annual payment of a certain sum, which is payable during the life of an individual. Instead of an annual payment, it may be actually paid quarterly or half-yearly. (See ANNUITY.)

LIFE INTEREST. An interest for life only. (See LIFE TENANT.)

LIFE POLICY. A life policy, duly assigned, forms a good banking security to the extent of the surrender value. The longer it exists the more valuable it becomes.

If a debtor gives a security in which he has merely a life interest, it should be supported by a life policy.

A policy may be either a "whole life assurance"—that is, not payable till the death of the assured; or an "endowment-assurance"—that is, payable when the assured has arrived at a certain age, or payable at death if it occurs before that age is reached—or simply an "endowment"—that is, payable on the insured surviving to a certain age. An assurance may be effected merely for a temporary period—called a "short term" policy—and is payable only in the event of death occurring within the period agreed upon.

A policy may be in favour of the assured, or in the case of a husband in favour of his wife or children, or two lives may be assured under the one policy the sum being payable upon the first death, or in other policies on the death of the survivor of the two lives.

The Married Women's Property Act, 1882, provides that an assurance effected by a man on his own life for the benefit of his wife or children, or of his wife and children, or effected by a woman on her own life for the benefit of her husband or children, or husband and children, shall create a trust in favour of the objects named and the moneys payable shall not form part of the estate of the insured or be subject to his or her debts; provided that if it be proved that the policy was effected with intent to defraud the creditors they shall be entitled to receive out of the moneys payable under the policy a sum equal to the premiums so paid.

By the Gambling Act, 1774 (14 Geo. III, c. 48), no insurance shall be made by any person on the life of any person unless he has an insurable interest in that person. The interest must be a pecuniary one. For example, a wife has an insurable interest in her husband's life, and a man in his own life, but a son has not an insurable interest in his father's life (if the son is of age and therefore not legally entitled to maintenance) and a father has no insurable interest in his child. A guarantor has a pecuniary interest in the debtor for whose debt he is surety, and a policy by the surety upon the debtor's life is valid. The policy continues valid after the pecuniary interest has ceased.

The question of "insurable interest" does not apply to a person to whom a policy is assigned; it applies only to the parties to the original contract.

The fact that a policy has been issued does not necessarily imply that the regulation regarding the insurable interest has been observed by the company.

The premium is the amount payable in order to assure the payment of the sum named in the policy at death or at the end of a certain period. This premium may take several forms. It may consist of a single large payment, or of annual payments for a certain number of years, or of a payment every year, or half-year, until death.

A "paid up" or "complete" policy is one where there are no further premiums payable.

There is a "half-credit" system with regard to premiums, by which only a half of the premium due is paid, the other part remaining as a debt upon the policy and being payable with interest out of the policy moneys at death.

There is also the "half-premium" system, where the premiums are arranged to exclude the debt and interest of the half-credit system. In either case there is no surrender value during the time of the low premiums, usually for the first five years, and consequently such policies do not form a banking security during that period.

There is also a scheme under which policies are issued with premiums arranged on an ascending scale, the premium increasing according to the length of time the policy has been in existence.

Premiums are usually payable within thirty days (called the "days of grace") from the due date, and, if death occurs within that time, before payment of the premium, the sums assured and bonuses are paid in full under deduction of the overdue premium.

As a protection of policies against lapsing through non-payment of premiums a provision is usually made by companies, as for example:—

If premiums are not paid within one year from the expiry of the thirty days, and death occurs during that time, the sums assured and bonuses will be paid in full, under deduction of the overdue premium and a small fine for arrear, provided the policy bears a clear surrender value of not less than the premium for one complete year; but when the policy does not bear such a clear surrender value, it can only be renewed, within the year, on evidence satisfactory to the directors as to the health of the life or lives assured and payment of arrears and fine.

Where a policy is assigned to a banker, the notices of premiums falling due are sent by the company to the assured, unless there is a special arrangement to the contrary. The banker must be careful to see that the premiums are duly paid.

A deduction is allowed by the income tax authorities from a person's income, up to one-sixth thereof, for any premiums on assurances effected by a man on his own life or on that of his wife.

A bonus is the periodical division of "profits" amongst the policyholders of an assurance company. In arriving at the amount of premium to be paid, a company "loads" the premium—that is, adds to it a sum to meet expenses. Such part of that "loading" as is not required is returned to the holders by way of the bonus. Some policies are "with profits," whilst others are "without profits." A bonus may be surrendered for a cash payment, or added to the amount of the policy, or applied in reduction of the future premiums, or used to provide a policy payable at a certain age.

The surrender value is the amount which the company will pay, at any time after, usually, three years' premiums have been paid, to the policyholder on a surrender of the policy. The amount is calculated by the company upon the premiums paid and bonuses declared. The amount can be ascertained by application to the company. A policy may often be sold at rather more than the surrender value.

Insurance companies grant loans upon policies to the extent of 90 or 95 per cent. of the surrender value.

A simple deposit of a life policy as security creates an equitable mortgage, but the usual and proper way of taking a security upon a life policy is to have it assigned to the bank by way of mortgage. Each person interested in the policy must join in the assignment.

If the policy is taken out by a husband for the benefit of his wife, both must sign the assignment. If the policy is for the benefit of the children, or for the wife and children, the policy is not available as a security as the children under age cannot assign.

Bankers have their own forms of assignment which usually provide for the banker paying the premiums, if the customer fails to do so, and debiting the amounts to the customer's account, and which also give power for the policy to be surrendered by the banker.

Notice of an assignment must be given to the company and an acknowledgment received. It is usual to send the notice in duplicate, so that the company may retain one copy and return the other with an acknowledgment thereon.

The Policies of Assurance Act, 1867 (30 & 31 Vict. c. 144), Section 3, states that no assignment shall confer on the assignee any right to sue for the amount of the policy until a written notice of the date and purport of the assignment have been given to the company at their principal place of business. The date on which such notice is received regulates the priority of all claims under any assignment. But a second mortgagee, with notice of the prior charge, cannot, by giving notice to the company before the first mortgagee, obtain priority. By Section 6, the company must, when requested by the person giving the notice, and upon payment of a fee of 5*s*., give an acknowledgment of the receipt of such notice.

In giving notice of an assignment, a banker should ask the company if there are any prior charges upon the policy.

Where a policy is assigned absolutely—that is, on a sale and not as a mortgage—the Act provides a very simple form of assignment, viz. :—"I, A. B. of, *etc.*, in consideration of, *etc.*, do hereby assign unto C. D. of, *etc.*, his executors, administrators and assigns, the [within] policy of assurance granted, *etc.* [*here describe the policy*]. In witness, *etc.*"

When a policy is taken as security, it should show that the age of the person insured has been "admitted" by the company. This is necessary to prevent any question arising, when the policy becomes a claim, as to the correct amount of the premium which should have been paid.

All previous assignments and documents relating to dealings with a policy must be carefully preserved as they may be required by the company when the policy becomes a claim.

An "industrial" policy does not form a banker's security. (See INDUSTRIAL LIFE POLICY.)

For the stamp duties on policies, see POLICY OF INSURANCE.

The stamp duty upon an assignment of a

life policy by way of security is the same as in the case of a mortgage (*q.v.*); and upon a sale the same as for a conveyance (*q.v.*).

Section 118 of the Stamp Act, 1891, enacts :—

"(1) No assignment of a policy of life insurance shall confer on the assignee therein named, his executors, administrators, or assigns, any right to sue for the moneys assured or secured thereby, or to give a valid discharge for the same, or any part thereof, unless the assignment is duly stamped, and no payment shall be made to any person claiming under any such assignment unless the same is duly stamped.

"(2) If any payment is made in contravention of this Section, the stamp duty not paid upon the assignment, together with the penalty payable on stamping the same, shall be a debt due to Her Majesty from the person by whom the payment is made."

In practice, an assignment is usually stamped to cover the amount of the policy and also an amount to cover bonuses, when the security is required to that extent.

In Scotland, assignments or assignations of life policies are given "for certain good and onerous causes and considerations." Stamp duty, 10*s*. At the same time a letter of deposit is taken, on which the stamp is sixpence. (See TONTINE POLICY.)

LIFE TENANT. A life tenant is the person who has a right or interest in landed property for his life, or during the life of some other person (called an estate *pur autre vie*). If on the death of a life tenant the property returns to the grantor of the life interest, or his heirs, the grantor is said to hold the reversion, but if it does not revert to him but passes to another person, that person holds the remainder, and is called the remainderman.

A life tenant may hold the deeds of the property, but he cannot give a charge thereon to any greater extent than the life interest he has in the property.

By the Settled Land Acts a tenant for life has, under certain conditions, power to sell the settled land, to exchange it for other property, to grant certain leases and to mortgage it where the money is required for enfranchisement or for equality of exchange; but money arising from the exercise of such powers must not be used for the personal benefit of the life tenant. The money, called capital money in the Act of 1882, "shall be paid either to the trustees of the settlement or into Court."

Where a life tenant gives a banker a charge upon the land in which he holds a life interest, it is customary, seeing that the security may disappear at any moment by the death of the tenant, to require a policy upon his life to be assigned to the bank, for an amount sufficient to cover the amount of the advance. Of course the banker must see that the rents from the property are sufficient, in the event of the borrower's failure, to pay both the interest upon the debt and the premiums upon the life policy. The banker should see that the premiums are duly paid.

LIGHT GOLD. When gold coins fall below a certain weight they cease to be legal tender. The least current weight, troy, for a half-sovereign is 61·125 grains, for a sovereign 122·5 grains, for a two-pound piece 245 grains, for a five-pound piece 612.5 grains.

The seventh section of the Coinage Act, 1870, gives a person power to cut or deface a light coin, but this is never done in the ordinary course of business, as gold coins, even though they are below the prescribed least current weight, pass from hand to hand without question. The words of the Section are :—

"Where any gold coin of the realm is below the current weight as provided by this Act, or where any coin is called in by proclamation, every person shall, by himself or others, cut, break, or deface any such coin tendered to him in payment, and the person tendering the same shall bear the loss. If any coin cut, broken, or defaced in pursuance of this Section is not below the current weight, or has not been called in by any proclamation, the person cutting, breaking, or defacing the same shall receive the same in payment according to its denomination."

There is no penalty attached for non-compliance with the Act.

By the Coinage Act, 1891, gold coins which are not more than three grains below the standard weight may be exchanged at the Mint for their full value.

No light gold coins are paid out by the Bank of England. As the Bank makes a charge for receiving light gold coin, there is a tendency, in order to avoid that charge, for the light coins to be retained in circulation.

The Bank of England has special machines

for separating light coins from those of full weight. The machines weigh the coins one by one and shoot off those of full weight in one direction and those which are light in another. (See COINAGE.)

LIMIT. When a banker agrees to allow a customer to overdraw his account up to a certain specified amount, that amount is called the limit. The balance of the account may vary from day to day, but the limit marks the boundary within which the overdraft is to be confined. (See ADVANCES.)

LIMITED COMPANY. (See COMPANY LIMITED BY SHARES, COMPANY LIMITED BY GUARANTEE, LIMITED PARTNERSHIP, PRIVATE COMPANY, PUBLIC COMPANY.)

LIMITED PARTNERSHIP. Limited partnerships were established by the Limited Partnerships Act, 1907 (7 Edw. VII, c. 24), which came into operation on January 1, 1908.

The main provisions of the Act are as follows :—

Definition and Constitution of Limited Partnership.

"Section 4. (1) From and after the commencement of this Act limited partnerships may be formed in the manner and subject to the conditions by this Act provided.

"(2) A limited partnership shall not consist, in the case of a partnership carrying on the business of banking, of more than ten persons, and in the case of any other partnership, of more than twenty persons, and must consist of one or more persons called general partners, who shall be liable for all debts and obligations of the firm, and one or more persons to be called limited partners, who shall at the time of entering into such partnership contribute thereto a sum or sums as capital or property valued at a stated amount, and who shall not be liable for the debts or obligations of the firm beyond the amount so contributed.

"(3) A limited partner shall not during the continuance of the partnership, either directly or indirectly, draw out or receive back any part of his contribution, and if he does so draw out or receive back any such part shall be liable for the debts and obligations of the firm up to the amount so drawn out or received back.

"(4) A body corporate may be a limited partner.

Registration of Limited Partnership required.

"5. Every limited partnership must be registered as such in accordance with the provisions of this Act, or in default thereof it shall be deemed to be a general partnership, and every limited partner shall be deemed to be a general partner.

Modifications of General Law.

"6. (1) A limited partner shall not take part in the management of the partnership business, and shall not have power to bind the firm :

Provided that a limited partner may by himself or his agent at any time inspect the books of the firm and examine into the state and prospects of the partnership business, and may advise with the partners thereon.

If a limited partner takes part in the management of the partnership business he shall be liable for all debts and obligations of the firm incurred while he so takes part in the management as though he were a general partner.

"(2) A limited partnership shall not be dissolved by the death or bankruptcy of a limited partner, and the lunacy of a limited partner shall not be a ground for dissolution of the partnership by the Court unless the lunatic's share cannot be otherwise ascertained and realised.

"(3) In the event of the dissolution of a limited partnership its affairs shall be wound up by the general partners unless the Court otherwise orders.

"(5) Subject to any agreement expressed or implied between the partners :—

"(*a*) Any difference arising as to ordinary matters connected with the partnership business may be decided by a majority of the general partners ;

"(*b*) A limited partner may, with the consent of the general partners, assign his share in the partnership, and upon such an assignment the assignee shall become a limited partner with all the rights of the assignor ;

"(c) The other partners shall not be entitled to dissolve the partnership by reason of any limited partner suffering his share to be charged for his separate debt ;

"(d) A person may be introduced as a partner without the consent of the existing limited partners ;

"(e) A limited partner shall not be entitled to dissolve the partnership by notice.

"7. Subject to the provisions of this Act, the Partnership Act, 1890, and the rules of equity and of common law applicable to partnerships, except so far as they are inconsistent with the express provisions of the last-mentioned Act, shall apply to limited partnerships.

Manner and Particulars of Registration.

"8. The registration of a limited partnership shall be effected by sending by post or delivering to the registrar at the register office in that part of the United Kingdom in which the principal place of business of the limited partnership is situated or proposed to be situated a statement signed by the partners containing the following particulars :—

(a) The firm name ;
(b) The general nature of the business ;
(c) The principal place of business ;
(d) The full name of each of the partners ;
(e) The term, if any, for which the partnership is entered into, and the date of its commencement ;
(f) A statement that the partnership is limited, and the description of every limited partner as such ;
(g) The sum contributed by each limited partner, and whether paid in cash or how otherwise.

Registration of Changes in Partnerships.

"9. (1) If during the continuance of a limited partnership any change is made or occurs in—

(a) The firm name ;
(b) The general nature of the business ;
(c) The principal place of business ;
(d) The partners or the name of any partner ;
(e) The term or character of the partnership ;
(f) The sum contributed by any limited partner ;
(g) The liability of any partner by reason of his becoming a limited instead of a general partner or a general instead of a limited partner :

a statement, signed by the firm, specifying the nature of the change shall within seven days be sent by post or delivered to the registrar at the register office in that part of the United Kingdom in which the partnership is registered.

"(2) If default is made in compliance with the requirements of this Section each of the general partners shall on conviction under the Summary Jurisdiction Acts be liable to a fine not exceeding one pound for each day during which the default continues.

Advertisement in Gazette.

"10. (1) Notice of any arrangement or transaction under which any person will cease to be a general partner in any firm, and will become a limited partner in that firm, or under which the share of a limited partner in a firm will be assigned to any person, shall be forthwith advertised in the Gazette, and until notice of the arrangement or transaction is so advertised, the arrangement or transaction shall, for the purposes of this Act, be deemed to be of no effect.

"(2) For the purposes of this Section, the expression 'the Gazette' means :—

In the case of a limited partnership registered in England, the *London Gazette* ;

In the case of a limited partnership registered in Scotland, the *Edinburgh Gazette* ;

In the case of a limited partnership registered in Ireland, the *Dublin Gazette*.

Registration.

"13. On receiving any statement made in pursuance of this Act the registrar shall cause the same to be filed, and he shall send by post to the firm from whom such statement shall have been received a certificate of the registration thereof.

"14. At each of the register offices hereinafter referred to the registrar shall keep, in proper books to be provided for the purpose, a register and an index of all the limited partnerships registered as aforesaid, and of all the statements registered in relation to such partnerships.

"15. The registrar of joint stock companies shall be the registrar of limited partnerships, and the several offices for the registration of joint stock companies in London, Edinburgh, and Dublin shall be the offices for the registration of limited partnerships carrying on business within those parts of the United Kingdom in which they are respectively situated.

"16. (1) Any person may inspect the statements filed by the registrar in the register offices aforesaid, and there shall be paid for such inspection such fees as may be appointed by the Board of Trade, not exceeding one shilling for each inspection; and any person may require a certificate of the registration of any limited partnership, or a copy of or extract from any registered statement, to be certified by the registrar, and there shall be paid for such certificate of registration, certified copy, or extract such fees as the Board of Trade may appoint, not exceeding two shillings for the certificate of registration, and not exceeding sixpence for each folio of seventy-two words, or in Scotland for each sheet of two hundred words.

"(2) A certificate of registration, or a copy of or extract from any statement registered under this Act, if duly certified to be a true copy under the hand of the registrar or one of the assistant registrars (whom it shall not be necessary to prove to be the registrar or assistant registrar) shall, in all legal proceedings, civil or criminal, and in all cases whatsoever be received in evidence."

It should be noted that Section 6 says that a limited partner shall not take part in the management of the partnership business, and shall not have power to bind the firm. The Section does not definitely say that he must not draw cheques upon the banking account of the firm, but it is probably safe to infer that he has no power to operate upon the account. At any rate bankers are not likely to regard a limited partner as having such authority.

The same Section says that a limited partner may at any time inspect the books of the firm. In a paper read before the Institute of Bankers by H. E. Gallaher, LL.B., in 1908, he said, with reference to this subject:—

"Another interesting question is whether a limited partner is entitled to information from the firm's banker as to the condition of their account, the amount of the cash balance, or the securities held by the bank for the firm. In view of the provision that a limited partner may inspect the books of the firm and examine into the state and prospects of the partnership business, I am inclined to think a banker would be justified in giving information of this character to a limited partner. I do not think, however, that a limited partner would be entitled to require the delivery to himself of the firm's pass book. Of course, where the banker can obtain the concurrence of all the general and limited partners as to the course to be adopted when a limited partner desires to borrow the pass book or to be informed of the position of the firm's accounts, this is by far the most satisfactory way of dealing with the matter."

It may be difficult, in some cases, for a banker to know whether a person is a limited or general partner. If he cannot obtain reliable information from the partners themselves, he may inspect the register or obtain extracts therefrom (see Section 16 above). (See COMPANIES, PARTNERSHIPS.)

LIQUID ASSETS. The liquid assets of a banker's balance sheet include the cash in the tills and those assets which can be turned into gold almost immediately, such as the Bank of England balance, and money at call and short notice. The proportion of liquid assets to the liabilities to the public is an important point in a banker's balance sheet. Assets, such as loans to customers, which are not readily available to meet liabilities, are termed non-liquid. (See BALANCE SHEET.)

LIQUIDATION. A winding up, or closing of business.

A joint stock company which is being wound up is said to be "in liquidation." (See WINDING UP.)

LIQUIDATOR. The person who is appointed to wind up a company. His business is to realise the assets and property of the company, and to collect what may be owing from the members, and from the funds so obtained to pay the debts due by the company and to distribute any balance which may remain amongst the members.

Where there are two liquidators, cheques should be signed by both, unless otherwise authorised by the Court.

A committee of inspection (*q.v.*) is often appointed to supervise a liquidation.

As to the appointment of liquidators in a voluntary winding up, see WINDING UP VOLUNTARILY; and in the case of a voluntary liquidation under supervision of the Court, see WINDING UP SUBJECT TO SUPERVISION OF THE COURT.

The powers of liquidators in a winding up by the Court, or compulsory liquidation, is dealt with in the following Section of the Companies (Consolidation) Act, 1908:—

"151. (1) The liquidator in a winding up by the Court shall have power, in the case of a winding up in England with the sanction either of the Court or of the committee of inspection, and in the case of a winding up in Scotland or Ireland with the sanction of the Court:—

"(*a*) to bring or defend any action or other legal proceeding in the name and on behalf of the company:

"(*b*) to carry on the business of the company, so far as may be necessary for the beneficial winding up thereof:

"(*c*) in the case of a winding up in England, to employ a solicitor or other agent to take any proceedings or do any business which the liquidator is unable to take or do himself; but the sanction in this case must be obtained before the employment, except in cases of urgency, and in those cases it must be shown that no undue delay took place in obtaining the sanction:

"(*d*) in the case of a winding up in Scotland or Ireland, to appoint a solicitor or law agent to assist him in the performance of his duties.

"(2) The liquidator in a winding up by the Court shall have power, but (subject to the provisions of this Section) in the case of a winding up in Scotland or Ireland only with the sanction of the Court:—

"(*a*) To sell the real and personal property, and things in action of the company by public auction or private contract, with power to transfer the whole thereof to any person or company, or to sell the same in parcels:

"(*b*) To do all acts and to execute, in the name and on behalf of the company, all deeds, receipts, and other documents, and for that purpose to use, when necessary, the company's seal:

"(*c*) To prove, rank, and claim in the bankruptcy, insolvency, or sequestration of any contributory, for any balance against his estate, and to receive dividends in the bankruptcy, insolvency, or sequestration in respect of that balance, as a separate debt due from the bankrupt or insolvent, and rateably with the other separate creditors:

"(*d*) To draw, accept, make, and indorse any bill of exchange or promissory note in the name and on behalf of the company, with the same effect with respect to the liability of the company as if the bill or note had been drawn, accepted, made, or indorsed by or on behalf of the company in the course of its business:

"(*e*) To raise on the security of the assets of the company any money requisite:

"(*f*) To take out in his official name, letters of administration to any deceased contributory, and to do in his official name any other act necessary for obtaining payment of any money due from a contributory or his estate which cannot be conveniently done in the name of the company; and in all such cases the money due shall, for the purpose of enabling the liquidator to take out the letters of administration or recover the money, be deemed to be due to the liquidator himself:

"(*g*) To do all such other things as may be necessary for

winding up the affairs of the company and distributing its assets."

The creditors and contributories shall determine whether or not an application is to be made to the Court to appoint a liquidator in the place of the official receiver, and to appoint a committee of inspection.

Payments of Liquidator in English Winding up into Bank.

"Section 154. (1) Every liquidator of a company which is being wound up by the Court in England shall, in such manner and at such times as the Board of Trade, with the concurrence of the Treasury, direct, pay the money received by him to the Companies Liquidation Account at the Bank of England, and the Board shall furnish him with a certificate of receipt of the money so paid:

Provided that, if the committee of inspection satisfy the Board of Trade that for the purpose of carrying on the business of the company or of obtaining advances, or for any other reason, it is for the advantage of the creditors or contributories that the liquidator should have an account with any other bank, the Board shall, on the application of the committee of inspection, authorise the liquidator to make his payments into and out of such other bank as the committee may select, and thereupon those payments shall be made in the prescribed manner.

"(2) If any such liquidator at any time retains for more than ten days a sum exceeding fifty pounds, or such other amount as the Board of Trade in any particular case authorise him to retain, then, unless he explains the retention to the satisfaction of the Board, he shall pay interest on the amount so retained in excess at the rate of twenty per cent. per annum, and shall be liable to disallowance of all or such part of his remuneration as the Board may think just, and to be removed from his office by the Board, and shall be liable to pay any expenses occasioned by reason of his default.

"(3) A liquidator of a company which is being wound up by the Court in England shall not pay any sums received by him as liquidator into his private banking account."

By Section 149:—

"(4) If more than one liquidator is appointed by the Court, the Court shall declare whether any act by this Act required or authorised to be done by the liquidator is to be done by all or any one or more of the persons appointed."

Where an advance is required by liquidators, it is necessary to ascertain if they have power to borrow, for, unless they have such power, any advance made to them will not bind the estate, and will be a debt due from them merely in their private capacities. (See COMPANIES, WINDING UP.)

LIRA. (See FOREIGN MONEYS—ITALY.)

LIVERY OF SEISIN. That is, delivery of possession. In ancient times when a person transferred property a livery of seisin took place. The transferor actually handed over possession of the land by formally vacating it and permitting the transferee to enter into possession, or by handing over a piece of turf or a twig. Blackstone says: "This livery of seisin is no other than the pure feodal investiture, or delivery of corporeal possession of the land or tenement, which was held absolutely necessary to complete the donation."

LLOYD'S BONDS. Bonds, named after the counsel who invented them, which were devised for the purpose of enabling a railway company to borrow money in excess of its borrowing powers. Such bonds are void, as between the company and the original holder; but a subsequent holder for value is entitled to recover both principal and interest.

LOADING. A term used in assurance companies to describe the amount which is included in a premium in order to cover the expenses of management of the company. The "loading" which is not required forms part of the "profits" and is returned to the members by way of bonus. (See LIFE POLICY.)

LOAN CAPITAL. Money raised by a company upon debentures is called loan capital. It forms a debt due by the company and is different from the actual capital, which is money subscribed by the members of the company.

By the Finance Act, 1899, Section 8:—

"(1) Where any local authority, corporation, company, or body of persons formed or established in the United Kingdom propose to issue any loan capital, they shall, before the issue thereof, deliver to the Commissioners a statement of the amount proposed to be secured by the issue.

"(2) Subject to the provisions of this Section every such statement shall be charged with an *ad valorem* stamp duty of two shillings and sixpence for every hundred pounds and any fraction of a hundred pounds over any multiple of a hundred pounds of the amount proposed to be secured by the issue, and the amount of the duty shall be a debt due to Her Majesty.

"(3) The duty under this Section shall not be charged to the extent to which it is shown to the satisfaction of the Commissioners that the stamp duty payable in respect of a mortgage or marketable security has been paid on any trust deed or other document securing the loan capital proposed to be issued.

"(4) If any local authority, corporation, company, or body of persons neglect to deliver a statement, or fail to pay the duty in compliance with this Section, that local authority, corporation, company, or body of persons, shall be liable to pay to Her Majesty, in addition to the duty, a sum equal to ten per cent. upon the amount of the duty, and a like sum for every month after the first month during which the neglect or failure continues.

"(5) In this Section the expression 'loan capital' means any debenture stock, county stock, corporation stock, municipal stock, or funded debt, by whatever name known, or any capital raised by any local authority, corporation, company, or body of persons formed or established in the United Kingdom, which is borrowed, or has the character of borrowed money, whether it is in the form of stock or in any other form, but does not include any county council or municipal corporation bills repayable not later than twelve months from their date or any overdraft at the bank or other loan raised for a merely temporary purpose for a period not exceeding twelve months, and the expression 'local authority' includes any county council, municipal corporation, district council, dock trustees, harbour trustees, or other local body by whatever name called."

By the Finance Act, 1907, Section 10.—

Reduction of Duty on Loan Capital issued for the Purpose of the Conversion or Consolidation of Existing Capital.

"(1) Where it is shown to the satisfaction of the Commissioners that the loan capital issued by any local authority, corporation, company, or body of persons, in respect of which a statement has, after the commencement of this Act, been delivered to the Commissioners under Section eight of the Finance Act, 1899, has been wholly or partly applied for the purpose of the conversion or consolidation of then existing loan capital, that authority, corporation, company, or body of persons, as the case may be, shall be entitled to repayment in respect of the duty charged on the statement so delivered at the rate of two shillings for every hundred pounds of the capital to which the statement relates which is so shown to have been applied for the purpose of the conversion or consolidation of then existing loan capital; but this Section shall not apply to any duty payable in respect of a mortgage or marketable security which has been paid on any trust deed or other document securing the loan capital which has been issued.

"(2) If it is represented to the Commissioners by any such local authority, corporation, company, or body of persons that loan capital about to be issued by them is to be applied, in whole or in part, for the purpose of the conversion or consolidation of existing loan capital, the Commissioners may postpone the time for the delivery of the statement and the payment of duty under Section eight of the Finance Act, 1899, until the capital has been issued or until such other time as the Commissioners think fit for the purpose of enabling the payment and repayment of the duty to take place as one transaction." (See COMPANIES, SHARE CAPITAL.)

LOANS. (See Advances.)

LOANS LEDGER. Where an advance is made by way of loan, it is entered in the loans ledger. Country bankers lend money most commonly by way of overdraft upon a current account, which overdraft may fluctuate from day to day, and the customer draws only such part of the sanctioned overdraft as he may require, but in the case of a loan, as is customary in London banks, the full amount is debited at once to the customer's account in the loans ledger.

The loans ledger is kept in practically the same way as the current account ledgers (*q.v.*).

LOANS REGISTER. A register, or list, giving particulars of all loans granted. Each loan is also posted to the debit of the respective customers in the loans ledger.

LOCAL AUTHORITIES. Bankers are often appointed to be treasurers for Local Authorities. The banking account should be in the treasurer's name, e.g. "John Brown, Treasurer of the Guardians of the Poor of Kingmoor Union," and the orders for payment should be drawn by the Local Authority upon the treasurer, and not upon the bank where he keeps the account.

The Bills of Exchange Act, 1882, Section 73, defines a cheque as "a bill of exchange drawn on a banker payable on demand," but as these orders are drawn upon the treasurer as an individual it would appear that they are not cheques, and, therefore, that the protection afforded by Section 60 of the Bills of Exchange Act, 1882, to the paying banker against forged indorsements does not extend to them; and further that, not being cheques, they cannot be validly crossed. Some authorities, however, consider that the orders though drawn, in form, upon the treasurer, are practically drawn upon the bank where he keeps his account. If this is the correct view, then they come within the provisions of the Bills of Exchange Act. In the case of *Halifax Union* v. *Wheelwright* (1875, L.R. 10 Ex. 183), where the treasurer had paid orders bearing forged indorsements, it was held that the bank was protected by Section 19 of the Stamp Act, 1853. (See that Section under Draft on Demand.)

The orders are, like cheques, subject to the stamp duty of one penny (Section 32, Stamp Act, 1891), except in the case of orders drawn by the Guardians of the Poor.

In cases where the Finance Committee send to the banker or treasurer a list of the persons to whom orders have been issued, and to whom payments are to be made upon presentation of the orders, ordering the treasurer to make such payments, the Board of Inland Revenue state that a penny stamp is required in respect of each payee's name upon the list. (See the Minute of the Board, under article Cheque.) In E. J. Naldrett's lecture on Local Government Authorities (see "Journal of the Institute of Bankers," vol. 26, p. 177), it is stated that a resolution in the following form is not regarded by the Inland Revenue Authorities as being subject to the above-mentioned stamp duty:—

"That a statement of the following accounts be signed by three members of the Finance Committee present at this meeting and countersigned by the town clerk, and be transmitted to the treasurer with an order to pay cheques for the amounts specified in such statement, on such cheques being presented to him."

With respect to the borrowing powers of a Local Authority, it is necessary to ascertain from the statute, under which the power in any particular case is regulated, whether the sanction of the Local Government Board or other Government Department is necessary before the power to borrow can be exercised, and, if the Authority has the necessary statutory power, upon what particular fund, or rate, security must be given.

If an Authority, without power or sanction to borrow, overdraws the bank account, the interest upon such overdraft (if not regarded by the banker as being covered by the interest upon the credit balance at other times) will not be a legal charge against the Authority, and may be disallowed by the Government Auditor. The Local Government Board have power, however, to allow a sum, properly disallowed by the Auditors, if in the opinion of the Board it is equitable that such allowance should be remitted.

It should be noted that money borrowed under the provisions of any particular Act must be secured in accordance with that Act. In *Rex* v. *Locke, ex parte Bridges* (1910, 2 K. B. 201) where a Corporation (under the provisions of the Public Health Act, 1875) borrowed money from a bank without giving proper security and the interest was surcharged by the Auditor because the security had not been given, Lord Alverstone said: "If the transaction objected to was merely the payment of interest upon some temporary loan obtained for temporary purposes until other money—as, for instance, rates or moneys agreed to be advanced—were in fact received, we agree that it might not be necessary under such circumstances for the local authority to give security." It was held, however, that the case appeared to be "an exercise of borrowing powers for the purpose of permanent loans to be repaid by instalments." The consent of the Local Government Board "does not merely involve the consent to the loan, but an approval of the way in which the loan is to be secured according to the Act of Parliament under which the securities are issued." The payment of interest to the bank in respect of the loans made by the bank, for which no security had been issued, was held not to be a legal payment.

In *Attorney-General* v. *Tottenham Urban Council* (1910, 73 J. P. 437), a sum of £18,350 had been advanced by the defendants' bankers, but the Local Government Board, upon an application in 1907 from the defendants for leave to borrow the £18,350, refused their sanction in respect of £4,910. The defendants proposed to pay the £4,910 and interest on the overdraft out of a general district rate. It was held that the loan of £4,910 by way of overdraft without the sanction of the Local Government Board was illegal, and that the defendants must be restrained from applying any part of the general district rate or any other fund or rate under their control in repayment of the loan; that the defendants were not entitled to make any payment of interest upon money borrowed without the sanction of the Local Government Board; that the payment of £855 as interest was unlawful and ought to be disallowed on audit, but this declaration was to be without prejudice to the power of the Local Government Board to remit such disallowance; and that the defendants be perpetually restrained from making any further payments of interest upon money borrowed without the sanction of the Local Government Board, or other statutory sanction, whether such borrowing was by way of overdraft or otherwise.

Another instructive case is the *Attorney-General* v. *Mayor, etc., of the County Borough of West Ham and others* (1910, 26 T. L. R. 683). Mr. Justice Neville, in the course of his judgment, said: "The Corporation appear to have considered and they certainly acted as though they were entitled to use moneys borrowed under specific powers not merely for the specific purposes for which the powers were bestowed, but for any purpose to which any funds of the Corporation could lawfully be applied, so long as they kept proper accounts of the expenditure. . . . In my opinion, this view of the position of the Corporation was erroneous." The judgment contained the following declaration:—

"1. That the overdraft obtained from the bank for general purposes in respect of borrowing powers granted for specific purposes was *ultra vires* and illegal.

"2. That the application of money due to the Consolidated Loans Fund in repayment of such overdraft was *ultra vires* and illegal.

"3. That the borrowing of money from the bank for the purpose of the electricity accounts, otherwise than in the exercise of borrowing powers with the sanction of the Local Government Board, was *ultra vires* and illegal." (See COUNTY COUNCIL, GUARDIANS OF THE POOR, MUNICIPAL CORPORATION, PARISH COUNCIL, RURAL DISTRICT COUNCIL, URBAN DISTRICT COUNCIL.)

LOCK UP. Money is said to be locked up when it has been lent and repayment cannot be obtained when desired, or until the expiration of some fixed period. A prudent banker avoids as far as possible having his funds locked up, because he not only desires to have his assets in such a form as to be of use in case of emergency, but he prefers to be able to lend the money to various customers at different times, for short periods, as may be required, rather than to one or two customers for long periods. If a loan of £1,000 is granted to John Brown for, say, three years, the security may be excellent, but the money is locked up for that period and cannot be used for any other purpose. On the other hand, a loan may be made to John Jones repayable on demand, and when repayment is requested Jones may be unable to repay; and when the banker turns to the security he may find that it cannot be realised and that his money is locked up until a purchaser can be found.

LOCUS SIGILLI. Latin, the place for the seal. The letters L.S., inside a circle, are often found on a printed document, such as a form of transfer, to indicate where the seal or wafer is to be placed. In making a copy of a document under seal, the place of the seal is marked in the same way.

LOMBARD STREET. A term which is frequently used when referring to the Money Market (*q.v.*).

LONDON AGENTS' LEDGER. This ledger is kept by the head office of a country bank and contains a record of all transactions between that country bank, including the branches, and its London agents. All remittances in and out, payments made, credits received, drafts drawn and every other description of items pass through this account. The ledger is posted from the daily statements received from the branches, and the items are checked off against the statements which are received from the London agents.

In agreeing the ledger with the balance as shown by the London statement, allowance must be made for entries in the ledger which have not yet appeared on the statements, and entries on the statements which are not yet entered in the ledger.

LONDON CLEARING HOUSE. (See CLEARING HOUSE.)

LONG-DATED PAPER. A term applied to bills of exchange which have more than three months to run.

LONG EXCHANGE. In connection with the foreign exchanges, the long exchange denotes bills with a currency of sixty or ninety days and upwards. (See LONG RATE.)

LONG RATE. A term employed in connection with the foreign exchanges, and signifying the price in one country at which a two or three months' bill (or bill for any other long currency as specially quoted) drawn upon another country, can be bought.

Most of the foreign exchanges are quoted in terms of the long rate, but a foreign banker in London would, if desired, quote the "short rate" (for drafts up to eight or ten days' currency) or the "cheque rate" (for sight drafts) on any of the principal foreign centres.

The long rate is based upon the cheque rate (or sight rate, as it is sometimes called), taking into consideration the rate of interest current in the country on which the bill is drawn, and the state of credit. (See CHEQUE RATE, COURSE OF EXCHANGE, SHORT RATE.)

LOST BANK NOTE. Where a bank note has been lost, the person to whom it belongs must, before he can obtain payment of it from the issuing banker, supply full particulars of the note, including its number, and provide a satisfactory indemnity, that is, a guarantee that the banker shall be refunded in case of the lost note being found by someone and the banker being compelled to pay it a second tine.

Although a banker cannot refuse payment of his own notes to an innocent holder, he should, where notice to stop payment has been received, make very careful inquiries when a "stopped" note is presented for payment.

The finder of a note has a right to it against every person except the individual who lost it. If he transfers it for value, the transferee, without notice that the note was lost, is absolutely entitled to it. The person who lost it cannot claim it from such a transferee.

If a note is lost in its passage through the post, the loss falls upon the person to whom it was sent, provided that he requested it to be sent to him by post, or that it was the custom between the parties to use the post for that purpose.

There is a difference between notes found on private property and in a public building. When found in a private building the note should remain in the possession of the owner of the place, and not be retained by a stranger who may have found it. Where notes were found on a shop floor (a public building) by a person entering the shop and the owner could not be found, it was held (*Bridges* v. *Hawkesworth*, 1851, 21 L.J.Q.B. 75) that the person finding them, and not the owner of the shop, was entitled to them, and that he had a right to them against everyone but the true owner. A bank note found on the customers' side of a bank counter would, in the event of no one claiming it, belong to the finder.

The true legal position, according to the best authorities seems to be that, if the finder believes at the time of finding a bank note that the owner cannot be found, he is not guilty of larceny, although he takes the note intending to deprive the owner of it, and although he afterwards has means of finding the owner, and, nevertheless, retains the property for his own use.

LOST BILL OF EXCHANGE. The Bills of Exchange Act, 1882, Section 69, provides:—

"Where a bill has been lost before it is overdue, the person who was the holder of it may apply to the drawer to give him another bill of the same tenor, giving security to the drawer if required to indemnify him against all persons whatever in case the bill alleged to have been lost shall be found again.

"If the drawer on request as aforesaid refuses to give such duplicate bill, he may be compelled to do so."

By Section 70:—

"In any action or proceeding upon a bill, the Court or a judge may order that the loss of the instrument shall not be set up, provided an indemnity be given to the satisfaction of the Court or judge against the claims of any other person upon the instrument in question."

By Section 51, s.s. 8, "where a bill is lost or destroyed, or is wrongly detained from the person entitled to hold it, protest may be made on a copy or written particulars thereof."

Where a cheque has been lost, the loser of it should at once request the drawer to give notice to the banker on whom it is drawn to stop payment, and the banker should notify any branches, where it might be presented, of the loss. A record of the loss should be made in the customer's account in the ledger.

If a banker pays a bill or cheque when he has received instructions from the drawer not to do so, he is liable to lose the money, for he cannot debit the amount to his customer's account. The utmost care, therefore, is necessary in dealing with "stop orders," as such notices from customers are called, and copies of all stop orders should be supplied to each cashier, day book clerk, and ledger keeper, through whose hands the cheque may pass, so that all may keep a sharp look out in case the lost cheque should be presented.

Before giving a duplicate cheque, it is advisable for the drawer to obtain a satisfactory indemnity, otherwise he may have to pay the original cheque (unless it was a crossed cheque marked "not negotiable") to a *bonâ fide* holder for value, as well as the duplicate. As to a banker collecting a lost cheque, see COLLECTING BANKER.

If a banker's draft is lost, a satisfactory indemnity should be obtained before paying the amount to the loser, as the banker is liable to pay the draft if presented by an innocent holder for value.

Where a cheque has been lost and a necessary indorsement has been forged, an innocent holder for value has no recourse against the drawer. The true owner can demand payment from the drawer. If the holder has obtained payment from the drawer, he is liable to the true owner.

If the cheque was payable to bearer and crossed "not negotiable," the position is the same, the holder cannot recover.

If the cheque was payable to bearer, either uncrossed or crossed without the words "not negotiable," an innocent holder for value can enforce payment of it from the drawer. The loser of the cheque must suffer the loss.

Where the cheque was duly indorsed before being lost and was not "not negotiable," a subsequent holder for value without knowledge that it had been lost could sue the drawer and indorsers.

Where a banker pays a cheque with a forged indorsement, see COLLECTING BANKER, PAYING BANKER. (See PAYMENT STOPPED.)

LOST DEED. An attested copy of a lost deed is sometimes accepted by a purchaser. The copy should be a copy of the original deed. A copy of a copy is not accepted as evidence. (See ATTESTED COPY.)

LOST DIVIDEND WARRANT. In the case of *Thairwall* v. *Great Northern Railway Company* (1910, 2 K.B. 509), where certain dividend warrants sent by the defendants to the plaintiff were lost in the post, the defendants, upon being informed of the loss, sent to the plaintiff a form of indemnity, and stated that on its being signed by the plaintiff they would give him a duplicate dividend warrant. The plaintiff declined to sign the indemnity, and brought an action to recover the amount of the dividends. The Divisional Court (reversing a judgment of the County Court in favour of the plaintiff) held that the stockholders of the company having by resolution determined the method in which the dividends were to be paid, i.e. by the sending of dividend warrants, the only obligation of the company was to pay by means of a dividend warrant, and that, having sent such a document by post, they had discharged their duty even although the warrant was lost in the post and never reached the plaintiff. The plaintiff could only get payment by giving a proper indemnity to the company.

LOST DEPOSIT RECEIPT. In the event of a deposit receipt being lost, the banker cannot refuse to pay the money to the person entitled thereto, but he will require a suitable indemnity to be given to protect him from any loss which might arise through his making such payment, without production of the receipt.

Where a depositor represents that he has lost his receipt, a note of the fact should, at once, be made in the deposit register, but it is advisable that the customer be requested to make a further search for the document, which, as a matter of experience, is then not infrequently discovered. If, however, the receipt cannot be found, the banker may agree to pay it, as mentioned, under an indemnity; and he will write off the outstanding amount in the deposit register and pass the debit entry in the ledger in the same way as if the receipt itself had come in, making a record in both books of the circumstances under which the money has been paid.

LOST PASS BOOK. Where a pass book cannot be found after a thorough search has been made for it, a duplicate is usually issued. A note of the circumstances and the date of its issue should be entered in the ledger at the top of the page containing the customer's account. The new pass book should be plainly marked "duplicate."

If the book which is lost is a deposit account pass book which requires to be produced each time money is withdrawn, the bank usually arranges with the customer that payments, in the meantime, will be made only to himself. On the issue of a new book, an indemnity should be taken.

If the original book, whether a current account or deposit one, is subsequently discovered, the banker should cancel one of the two and retain possession of it.

LOUIS. (See FOREIGN MONEYS—FRANCE.)

LUNATIC. When a banker learns that a customer has become insane he should not pay any further cheques upon his account, but the banker must make quite certain that his information is correct. Cheques paid before knowledge of a customer's insanity would appear to be in order.

A mandate is terminated by the insanity of the person who gave it.

Cheques upon a lunatic's account should be honoured only when signed by the "Committee" or legal authority appointed by the Commissioners in Lunacy to deal with the lunatic's estate. Exceptions are, however, sometimes made in special cases, against a satisfactory indemnity.

Lunacy may be set up as a defence in an action on a bill as between immediate parties if the plaintiff knew of the insanity when he took the bill, but it is of no avail against a holder in due course. It is not a defence if the bill was given during a lucid interval, or, if given during the previous period, was confirmed in the same period. Where a person has been found insane by inquisition he is unable legally to deal with his property even during a sane interval.

If a guarantor becomes insane, and the banker has notice of the same, the position of the parties is similar to that when a guarantor dies, namely, the account of the debtor should be stopped.

In an action on a bill by or against an insane person, the Statute of Limitations begins to run from the date of the insane person's recovery and not from the date on which the bill was due to be paid.

On application by a partner the Court may decree a dissolution of the partnership when a partner is found lunatic by inquisition, or is shown to the satisfaction of the Court to be of permanently unsound mind (Section 35, Partnership Act, 1890).

MADE BILL. A bill drawn in this country and payable abroad, if negotiated and indorsed in England by a correspondent of the drawer, is called a made bill. Such a bill thus bears the name of an indorser as well as that of the drawer and drawee. (See DRAWN BILL.)

MAKER OF PROMISSORY NOTE. The person who signs a promissory note promising to pay another person is called the "maker."

By Section 88 of the Bills of Exchange Act, 1882:—

"The maker of a promissory note by making it:—

"(1) Engages that he will pay it according to its tenor;

"(2) Is precluded from denying to a holder in due course the existence of the payee and his then capacity to indorse."

There may be two or more makers, and they may be liable jointly, or jointly and severally, according to the tenor of the note (Section 85).

Where a promissory note is in the body of it made payable at a particular place, it must be presented for payment at that place in order to render the maker liable. In any other case, presentment for payment is not necessary in order to render the maker liable (Section 87, s.s. 1).

The maker of a note is deemed to correspond with the acceptor of a bill. (See PRESENTMENT FOR PAYMENT, PROMISSORY NOTE.)

MAKING-UP DAY. The first day of the settlement on the Stock Exchange. (See CONTANGO DAY.)

MAKING-UP PRICE. At each settlement (which occupies three days) on the Stock Exchange, the first day is called contango day or making-up day. On that day a making-up price is officially fixed to each stock, according to certain rules. There is an additional day for mining securities called "mining contango day." The making-up price is for the purpose of arranging with speculators (bears and bulls) who desire to continue their bargain till the next settlement. If the making-up price is lower than that at which a "bull" purchased, he pays the broker the difference; if higher the broker pays him. In the case of a "bear" if the making-up price is lower than that at which he sold the broker pays the "bear" the difference; if higher the "bear" pays the broker. (See BACKWARDATION, CONTANGO.)

MALÂ FIDE. Latin, in bad faith. The opposite to *malâ fide* is *bonâ fide*, in good faith.

MANAGEMENT SHARES. Shares of the same nature as founders' shares, but instead of being held by the founders are intended for the managers of a company to cause them to take a greater interest in making the business a successful one. (See FOUNDERS' SHARES.)

MANAGER, OR RECEIVER. (See RECEIVER.)

MANDANT, OR MANDATOR. The person who gives a mandate. The party in whose favour it is given is called the mandatory.

MANDATE. An authority in writing by which one person (the mandator) empowers another person (the mandatory) to act on his behalf. If John Brown authorises T. Jones to sign cheques upon his account, the usual form of signature is per pro. (or p.p.) John Brown, T. Jones. The mandate should state that Jones may sign whether the account is in credit or in debit (if that is the wish of Brown) and a specimen of the signature of Jones should be given on the mandate in the form in which he will sign. Particulars of the authority should be noted in the ledger against the account to which it refers, and if it is only for a certain period or is limited to drawings up to a certain specified amount, those important points should be very clearly recorded. A mandate by Brown may authorise Jones to sign Brown's name, but the preferable way is, as given above, for Jones to sign per procuration.

It has been held that it is "clearly the duty of a person giving a mandate to take reasonable care that he does not mislead the person to whom the mandate is given." (*Kepitigalla Rubber Estates, Ltd.* v. *The National Bank of India, Ltd.*, 1909, 2 K.B. 1010.)

A person who has authority to sign for another, has not, as a rule, any power to delegate that authority.

There is no stamp duty upon a mandate of the above description. (See DELEGATION OF AUTHORITY.)

MANDATORY. The person in whose favour a mandate is given. The person who gives the mandate is called the mandant or mandator.

A mandatory cannot, unless expressly empowered in the mandate, delegate his authority to another person.

MARGIN. In banks, the difference between the amount of a loan and the value of the security is generally referred to as the margin. The margin may be wide or narrow according as the difference is great or small. When the value of a security falls so that it is no longer in excess of the loan, the margin is said to have "run off." (See ADVANCES.)

MARGINAL LETTER OF CREDIT. A letter of credit, printed upon the margin of a bill form, issued by a banker, authorising the person to whom it is addressed "to draw the annexed bill" at a certain currency for a specified amount, and undertaking to honour the bill if drawn in accordance with the terms of the letter. (See LETTER OF CREDIT.)

MARGINAL NOTES. MARGINAL RECEIPTS. Where a bill is discounted and the banker, in crediting his customer with the proceeds of the bill, reserves a certain part of the amount until advised that the bill has been paid, the banker gives his customer a receipt (called a marginal receipt, or marginal note) for the margin, or reserved portion.

Interest is allowed upon the margin at a specified rate. The money is really a debt which becomes due from the banker upon information being received that the bill is paid; and the banker may stipulate in the receipt that he will account for the money after providing for any deficiency on other liabilities of the customer to him.

MARINE INSURANCE POLICY. A policy of marine insurance is usually effected with insurers, called "underwriters." The term "underwriter" is applied because each person who acts as an insurer signs his name at the foot of the policy and states the amount for which he is to be liable. The ship or the goods may be insured either for a certain voyage or during some period of time, and the underwriters by the contract agree to indemnify the insurer against loss in accordance with the terms of the policy.

A person wishing to insure, usually employs an insurance broker to arrange the terms of the policy with the underwriters.

The person insured must have an insurable interest in the ship or its cargo, otherwise the contract is not legally binding.

There are several kinds of marine policies, the principal being :—

A "valued policy," where the value of the ship or subject insured is stated in the policy. Ships and freights are usually insured under a valued policy.

An "open policy," where the value of the subject insured is not stated in the policy. When a loss occurs the value has to be proved. Goods are usually included in an open policy. The description in the policy should agree with that in the bill of lading.

There are also :—A "Time Policy," that is a policy for a fixed time, a "Voyage Policy," that is for a particular voyage, a "Floating Policy," which insures the subject matter in whatever ship it may be ; and other varieties.

The underwriters are liable for the full amount of the insurance in the event of the ship being totally lost, but in the case of a partial loss the underwriters are usually liable only for two-thirds, the remaining one-third of the loss falling upon the owner of the ship.

An insurance certificate is sometimes attached to a bill, and is a declaration by an insurance company that the goods are insured under a policy which also covers other goods.

By the Stamp Act, 1891, the stamp duties are :—

POLICY OF SEA INSURANCE	£	s.	d.
(1) Where the premium or consideration does not exceed the rate of 2*s*. 6*d*. per centum of the sum insured . . .	0	0	1
(2) In any other case—			
(*a*) For or upon any voyage— In respect of every full sum of £100, and also any fractional part of £100 thereby insured (Finance Act, 1908)	0	0	1
(*b*) For time— In respect of every full sum of £100, and also any fractional part of £100 thereby insured—			
Where the insurance shall be made for any time not exceeding six months	0	0	3
Where the insurance shall be made for any time exceeding six months and not exceeding twelve months	0	0	6

A policy of sea insurance is not valid unless it specifies the particular risk, the names of the subscribers or underwriters, and the sums insured, and is made for a period not exceeding twelve months (Section 93, s.s. 3).

An insurance policy for a voyage and also for time, or to cover any time beyond thirty days after the ship's arrival, is to be charged with duty as a policy for a voyage and also for time (Section 94).

When a banker receives from abroad a bill of exchange with a policy of insurance or an insurance certificate attached, he must see that the policy or the certificate is stamped within ten days of its arrival in this country. The certificate does not require stamping if there is a note upon it that the original policy is stamped.

By the Finance Act, 1901 :—

"Section 11. (1) Notwithstanding anything contained in the Stamp Act, 1891, a policy of sea insurance made for time may contain a continuation clause as defined in this Section, and such a policy shall not be invalid on the ground only that by reason of the continuation clause it may become available for a period exceeding twelve months.

"(2) There shall be charged on a policy of sea insurance containing such a continuation clause a stamp duty of sixpence in addition to the stamp duty which is otherwise chargeable on the policy.

"(3) If the risk covered by the continuation clause attaches and a new policy is not issued covering the risk, the continuation clause shall be deemed to be a new and separate contract of sea insurance expressed in the policy in which it is contained, but not covered by the stamp thereon, and the policy shall be stamped in respect of that contract accordingly, but may be so stamped without penalty at any time not exceeding thirty days after the risk has so attached.

"(4) For the purpose of this Section, the

expression 'continuation clause' means an agreement to the following or the like effect, namely, that in the event of the ship being at sea or the voyage otherwise not completed on the expiration of the policy, the subject-matter of the insurance shall be held covered until the arrival of the ship, or for a reasonable time thereafter not exceeding thirty days."

By the Revenue Act, 1903 :—

"Section 8. A policy of insurance made or purporting to be made upon or to cover any ship or vessel, or the machinery or fittings belonging to the ship or vessel whilst under construction, or repair, or on trial, shall be sufficiently stamped for the purposes of the Stamp Act, 1891, and the Acts amending that Act, if stamped as a policy of sea insurance made for a voyage and though made for a time exceeding twelve months, shall not be deemed to be a policy of sea insurance made for time." (See MUTUAL INSURANCE, SHIP-MORTGAGE.)

MARK. (See FOREIGN MONEYS—GERMANY.)

MARKED CHEQUE. In connection with local exchanges in country branches, cheques are frequently presented by one banker to another in the same town to be "marked" as being good. If the cheque is all right, the banker on whom it is drawn initials it and hands it back to the banker who has presented it to be "marked." The banker holding the cheque can then rest satisfied that it will be paid when presented through the clearing later on in the day, or, if too late for that day's clearing, through the clearing on the following day. The arrangement is one between the two bankers and has nothing to do either with the drawer, payee or holder. If further cheques should be presented for payment, before the "marked" cheque arrives through the local clearing, and the balance of the customer's account, taking the amount of the "marked" cheque into consideration, will not permit of their payment, the banker is justified in refusing payment of those subsequent cheques. When the banker "marked" the cheque he practically paid it and is entitled to regard it as paid, although, for the personal convenience of the two bankers, the cheque itself is permitted to be passed through the clearing with the other cheques. The "marked" cheque will, of course, be debited to the drawer's account when it comes in, even though the drawer in the interval has died or become bankrupt. The cheque being to all intents and purposes paid when "marked," the drawer cannot stop payment of it after it is "marked."

Bankers are occasionally requested by the drawer of a cheque to mark or certify it as good for the amount, as for example when the customer desires to settle for the purchase of property or to pay customs duties. A cheque so marked is usually received by the person to whom it is tendered as being as "good as cash." When a cheque is so marked at the request of the drawer, the banker will, in considering whether subsequent cheques should be paid which are presented for payment before the marked cheque is presented, treat the balance of the customer's account as though the marked cheque had been charged to the account. Whenever a cheque is marked at the drawer's request, a note of the amount should be made in the account, so that the banker, when other cheques are presented, may not overlook his liability to pay the marked cheque. When the cheque is received it must, of course, be paid, and can be charged to the drawer's account, even if he has died or become bankrupt in the meantime. The drawer cannot stop payment of a cheque marked at his request.

Where a cheque is "marked" at the request of the payee or a holder, the position would appear to be different.

In an ordinary way there is no contract between a banker and the payee or holder of a cheque, but if a banker certifies or marks a cheque for payment at the request of the payee or holder, the payee or holder of such marked cheque could no doubt compel the banker to pay it. And as the drawer's right to stop payment would appear not to be affected by the marking, the banker might find himself "between two stools," i.e. compelled, at least morally, to pay the cheque to the holder, and prevented legally from debiting it to the drawer's account. If the drawer dies or becomes bankrupt before a cheque, marked at the payee's or holder's request, is presented, the banker cannot debit it to the account of the deceased or the bankrupt.

Chalmers' "Bills of Exchange" says: "At common law there is no objection to the acceptance of a cheque, if the holder likes to take it in lieu of payment, but the Bank Charter Acts would in most cases render this illegal."

The marking of cheques (except as between bankers) is not a desirable practice to encourage. It is preferable that, instead of marking for a holder, the cheque should be paid at once, or the cheque be debited and a banker's draft given for it, or the amount be credited to a sundry creditors account and a banker's cheque issued.

In the United States cheques are freely certified by bankers, and such certification is held by law to be equivalent to acceptance. (See CERTIFICATION OF CHEQUES, CHEQUE.)

MARKET PARTNERSHIP. A term used on the London Stock Exchange to describe a partnership where two members, who each deal and settle bargains in their own name, notify to the secretary that they hold themselves jointly responsible to the Stock Exchange for all transactions entered into by either of them.

MARKET PRICE. The market price of a given weight of bullion is the quantity of current coins of the same metal which is equal to that weight of bullion. The Mint price is the quantity of coins into which that given weight of bullion is divided. As coins in circulation are lighter than when newly coined, more of them will be required to equal that weight, and the market price will therefore be higher than the Mint price.

MARKET RATE. The rate of discount charged by the London banks and bill brokers. It is always less than Bank Rate, but varies with it, though not by any means always in the same ratio. Competition in the money market has the same effect as it has in all other open markets; that is, the competition between the sellers (in this case the banks and brokers who have money to lend) tends to keep the rate down, while the competition amongst buyers (in this case the discounters of bills and other borrowers of money) tends to raise the rate. There is another factor which influences the market rate, and that is that the lenders (the banks and brokers) are themselves also borrowers by way of deposits on which they have to pay interest; it is obvious then that the higher the rate of interest they allow on deposits the more they must charge for discounts in order to recoup themselves and leave a fair margin of profit. And herein lies one of the reasons why market rate assimilates itself to Bank Rate, for the rate of interest which banks and brokers allow, known as deposit rate, is dependent on Bank Rate.

The more money there is in the market, that is, the larger the funds that are at any time in the possession of the banks and brokers available for short loans and discounts, the greater is the discrepancy between market rate and Bank Rate, for it is then that the outside market is in a position to compete most successfully with the Bank; and *vice versâ* when the market is "short" its rate approaches close to Bank Rate. In ordinary circumstances a well-known example of this occurs every year during the January to March quarter; for at this time a great amount of the floating money in the market has become locked up in the Bank of England owing to the large part of the assessed taxes, which are paid into the Government accounts at that period of the year; this brings up market rate close on the heels of Bank Rate; so soon, however, as the accumulated funds begin to be released again, which happens after the first few days of April, market rate rapidly falls away from Bank Rate. (See BANK RATE, DEPOSIT RATE, MONEY MARKET.)

MARKETABLE SECURITY. A marketable security, as defined by Section 122 of the Stamp Act, 1891, is a "security of such a description as to be capable of being sold in any stock market in the United Kingdom."

By the Finance (1909–10) Act (passed April 29, 1910), Section 76, the stamp duties chargeable on marketable securities (other than colonial government or colonial municipal securities) under paragraphs (1) (*c*), (3), and (4) of the heading MARKETABLE SECURITY in the first Schedule to the Stamp Act, 1891, and the stamp duty chargeable on marketable securities, share warrants, or stock certificates to bearer under sub-section (1) of Section 4 of the Finance Act, 1899, shall be double those specified in the said Schedule or charged by the said Section, as the case may be.

By the Stamp Act, 1891, the stamp duties are:—

MARKETABLE SECURITY and FOREIGN OR COLONIAL SHARE CERTIFICATE.

(1) Marketable security (*a*) being a colonial government security or (*b*) being a security not transferable by delivery or (*c*) being a security transferable by delivery and bearing date or signed or offered for

subscription before or on the sixth day of August one thousand eight hundred and eighty-five—

For or in respect of the money thereby secured	The same *ad valorem* according to the nature of the security as upon a mortgage.

(2) TRANSFER, ASSIGNMENT, DISPOSITION, or ASSIGNATION of a marketable security of any description—

Upon a sale thereof. See CONVEYANCE or transfer on sale.	
Upon a mortgage thereof. See MORTGAGE.	
In any other case than a sale or mortgage . .	0 10 0

(3) Marketable security (except a colonial government security) being a security transferable by delivery and bearing date or signed or offered for subscription after the sixth day of August one thousand eight hundred and eighty-five—

For every £10, and also for any fractional part of £10, of the money thereby secured . .	0 1 0

(4) Marketable security (except a colonial government security) being such security as last aforesaid given in substitution for a like security duly stamped in conformity with the law in force at the time when it became subject to duty—

For every £20, and also for any fractional part of £20, of the money thereby secured . .	0 0 6

By the Finance Act, 1899 :—

"Section 4. (1) There shall be charged on every marketable security made or issued by or on behalf of any foreign state or government, or foreign or colonial municipal body, corporation, or company, being a security transferable by delivery, which

"(*a*) is after the first day of August one thousand eight hundred and ninety-nine, assigned, transferred, or in any manner negotiated in the United Kingdom, and

"(*b*) is not, under the law existing at the passing of this Act, chargeable with stamp duty as a marketable security transferable by delivery,

and on every share warrant or stock certificate to bearer by means of which any share or stock of any company or body of persons formed or established out of the United Kingdom is, after the first day of August one thousand eight hundred and ninety-nine, assigned, transferred, or in any manner negotiated in the United Kingdom, a stamp duty of one shilling for every ten pounds, and also for any fractional part of ten pounds in the case of a marketable security of the money thereby secured, and in the case of a share warrant or stock certificate of the nominal value of the share or stock to which the warrant or certificate relates. (For amendment, see Section 76 of the Finance (1909–10) Act, 1910, referred to above.)

"(2) There shall be charged on every instrument to bearer, not being a share warrant or stock certificate to bearer charged under the foregoing provision, by means of which any share or stock of any company or body of persons formed or established out of the United Kingdom is, after the first day of August one thousand eight hundred and ninety-nine, assigned, transferred, or in any manner negotiated, in the United Kingdom, a stamp duty of threepence for every twenty-five pounds, and also for every fractional part of twenty-five pounds of the nominal value of the share or stock.

"(3) Every person who, in the United Kingdom, assigns, transfers, or in any manner negotiates, or is concerned as broker or agent in assigning, transferring, or in any manner negotiating, any instrument which is chargeable with duty under this Section, and is not duly stamped, or any share or stock by means of such an instrument, shall incur a fine of twenty pounds, and the amount of the duty shall be a debt due from any such person to Her Majesty.

"(4) For the purposes of this Section—

"(*a*) the expression 'share warrant to bearer' includes any instrument by whatever name called, having the like effect as a share warrant issued under the provisions of the Companies Act, 1867; and

"(*b*) the expression 'stock certificate to bearer' includes any instrument, by whatever name called, having the like effect as a stock certificate to bearer."

By the Stamp Act, 1891 :—

"Section 82. (1) Marketable securities for the purpose of the charge of duty thereon include—

"(*a*) A marketable security, made or issued by or on behalf of any company or body of persons corporate or unincorporate formed or established in the United Kingdom; and

"(*b*) A marketable security by or on behalf of any foreign state or government, or foreign or colonial municipal body, corporation, or company (hereinafter called a foreign security), bearing date or signed after the third day of June one thousand eight hundred and sixty-two.

'(i) Which is made or issued in the United Kingdom, or

"(ii) Which, though originally issued out of the United Kingdom, has been, after the sixth day of August one thousand eight hundred and eighty-five, or is offered for subscription, and given or delivered to a subscriber in the United Kingdom, or

"(iii) Which, the interest thereon being payable in the United Kingdom, is assigned, transferred, or in any manner negotiated in the United Kingdom; and

(*c*) A marketable security by or on behalf of any colonial government which if the borrower were a foreign government would be a foreign security (hereinafter called a colonial government security).

"(2) For the purposes of this Act the expression 'foreign or colonial share certificate' includes any document whatever, being *primâ facie* evidence of the title of any person as proprietor of, or as having the beneficial interest in, any share or shares or stock or debenture stock or funded debt of any foreign or colonial company or corporation where such person is not registered in respect thereof in a register duly kept in the United Kingdom.

"83. Every person who in the United Kingdom makes, issues, assigns, transfers, negotiates, or offers for subscription, any foreign security or colonial government security not being duly stamped, shall incur a fine of twenty pounds."

By the Finance Act, 1895 :—

"Section 14. Where foreign securities within the meaning of Sections eighty-two and eighty-three of the Stamp Act, 1891, are issued in the United Kingdom, and the interest thereon is not payable in the United Kingdom, and such evidence of the amount of the securities as the Commissioners of Inland Revenue require is produced to them, then the Commissioners, if in their discretion they consider it expedient to do so, may accept payment of the amount of stamp duty which would be payable if all the said securities were duly stamped, and on such payment may dispense with the necessity of the securities being stamped. The Commissioners shall give notice in the *London Gazette* of any such dispensation."

By the Stamp Act, 1891 :—

"Section 84. The Commissioners may at any time, without reference to the date thereof, allow any foreign security or colonial government security to be stamped without the payment of any penalty, upon being satisfied, in any manner that they may think proper, that it was not made or issued, and has not been transferred, assigned, or negotiated within the United Kingdom."

MARKKA. (See FOREIGN MONEYS—FINLAND.)

MARKSMAN. A person who is unable

to write, from any reason, and who signs by a mark, thus ×, in the presence of one or more witnesses. The usual form in such a case is:—

his
JOHN × BROWN.
mark.

Witness,	Witness,
R. JACKSON,	T. JONES,
King Street,	British Bank,
Leeds,	Leeds,
Grocer.	Cashier.

A banker generally requires a mark to be witnessed by two persons, particularly if it is in connection with either paying in or withdrawing money, and it is desirable that one of the witnesses should be an outside person who is well known to the bank. If, however, such a witness is not available it is usual for two members of the staff to sign as witnesses. In some banks the cashier who has the transaction in hand may act as one witness, but in other banks both witnesses have to be independent altogether of the transaction.

It is usual for a customer who cannot write, if he is going to draw many cheques upon his account, to give authority to someone to sign cheques per procuration, and the matter is best arranged when the account is first opened.

When a deed is executed by "mark," a special form of attestation clause is necessary. (See ATTESTATION.)

In Scotland the execution of a deed by a mark is not valid. It must be executed for the person by a Notary Public or a Justice of the Peace before two witnesses.

MARRIAGE SETTLEMENT. A settlement of property, provided by either or both of the parties to the contract of marriage, and made either before or after the marriage. In the former case it is called an ante-nuptial settlement, and in the latter a post-nuptial. Except in the case of fraud, an ante-nuptial settlement is one made for valuable consideration, the marriage being the consideration. But in the case of a post-nuptial settlement, there is only what is known in law as "good" consideration, and the settlement may be avoided in certain cases if the settlor becomes bankrupt within a certain period after the settlement is made. For Stamp Duties see SETTLEMENT.

MARRIED WOMAN. A woman married since January 1, 1883, is in the same position as an unmarried woman (*feme sole*) as regards her property, whether real or personal and whether acquired before or after January 1, 1883, and she can deal with it in any way she likes.

A woman married before January 1, 1883:—

(*a*) as regards any property acquired by her since that date she is in the same position as an unmarried woman and can freely dispose of it.

(*b*) as regards any property acquired by her before that date she is in the same position as she was before the passing of the Married Women's Property Act, 1882, and any conveyance by her of her landed property is subject to the control of her husband.

When the title deeds of a property are deposited as security by a married woman, there is the possibility that the property may form part of a marriage settlement and be settled upon her subject to a restraint against anticipation; that is, that she cannot either deposit the deeds or mortgage the property or deal with the future income. This point is an important one to bear in mind and more particularly so, as the deeds themselves may not show any evidence that such a restraint exists.

Where a husband becomes a bankrupt, the wife may prove upon his estate along with the other creditors for any money lent to him for private purposes, but she may not prove with the other creditors for any money she may have lent to him for his business.

A married woman is not personally liable for borrowed money as is an unmarried woman and a man, but repayment may be enforced against any separate estate that she may have. Unless she is carrying on a business apart from her husband she cannot be made a bankrupt.

MATURITY. The maturity of a bill of exchange or promissory note is the date upon which it matures or falls due to be paid.

MAUNDY MONEY. The money which the King causes to be distributed on Maundy Thursday—that is, the Thursday in Passion Week—to as many poor men and women as he is years old. The money consists of four silver coins, a fourpenny piece, a threepenny piece, a twopenny piece and a penny piece. The coins are not of much use to the recipients, except to sell to anyone who is interested in coins. Bankers were sometimes requested by customers to obtain a set of Maundy money to add to a collection of coins, but the Mint has now discontinued issuing any sets of Maundy money to banks. The origin of the word Maundy is, by some persons, said to be derived from the Latin words *mandatum novum* (a new commandment) as those were the first words of the anthem which used to be sung in olden times when the King, as was the custom then, performed the ceremony of washing the feet of the poor people. Another explanation of the origin of the word is that it is derived from the "maunds," or baskets, in which the food was carried.

As to the standard weight of these coins see under COINAGE.

MEASURES. (See WEIGHTS AND MEASURES.)

MEDJIDIE. (See FOREIGN MONEYS—TURKEY.)

MEETING OF CREDITORS. After a receiving order has been made against a debtor he is not immediately adjudged a bankrupt, but a meeting of creditors is held shortly afterwards to consider whether a proposal for a composition or a scheme of arrangement shall be entertained or whether he shall be adjudged bankrupt.

The following are some of the rules in the first schedule of the Bankruptcy Act, 1883, with respect to meetings of creditors :—

"1. The first meeting of creditors shall be summoned for a day not later than fourteen days after the date of the receiving order, unless the Court for any special reason deem it expedient that the meeting be summoned for a later day.

"2. The official receiver shall summon the meeting by giving not less than seven days' notice of the time and place thereof in the *London Gazette* and in a local paper.

"3. The official receiver shall also, as soon as practicable, send to each creditor mentioned in the debtor's statement of affairs, a notice of the time and place of the first meeting of creditors, accompanied by a summary of the debtor's statement of affairs, including the causes of his failure, and any observations thereon which the official receiver may think fit to make; but the proceedings at the first meeting shall not be invalidated by reason of any such notice or summary not having been sent or received before the meeting.

"8. A person shall not be entitled to vote as a creditor at the first or any other meeting of creditors unless he has duly proved a debt provable in bankruptcy to be due to him from the debtor, and the proof has been duly lodged before the time appointed for the meeting.

"9. A creditor shall not vote at any such meeting in respect of any unliquidated or contingent debt, or any debt the value of which is not ascertained.

"10. For the purpose of voting, a secured creditor shall, unless he surrender his security, state in his proof the particulars of his security, the date when it was given, and the value at which he assesses it, and shall be entitled to vote only in respect of the balance (if any) due to him, after deducting the value of his security. If he votes in respect of his whole debt he shall be deemed to have surrendered his security unless the Court on application is satisfied that the omission to value the security has arisen from inadvertence.

"11. A creditor shall not vote in respect of any debt on or secured by a current bill of exchange or promissory note held by him, unless he is willing to treat the liability to him thereon of every person who is liable thereon antecedently to the debtor, and against whom a receiving order has not been made, as a security in his hands, and to estimate the value thereof, and for the purposes of voting, but not for the purposes of dividend, to deduct it from his proof.

"12. It shall be competent to the trustee or to the official receiver, within twenty-eight days after a proof estimating the value of a security as aforesaid has been made use of in voting at any meeting, to require the creditor to give up the security for the benefit of the creditors generally on payment of the value so estimated, with an addition thereto of twenty per centum. Provided, that where a creditor has put a value on such security, he may, at any time before he has been required to give up such security as aforesaid, correct such valuation by a new proof, and deduct such new value from his debt, but in that case such addition of twenty per centum shall not be made if the trustee requires the security to be given up.

"13. If a receiving order is made against one partner of a firm, any creditor to whom that partner is indebted jointly with the other partners of the firm, or any of them, may prove his debt for the purpose of voting at any meeting of creditors, and shall be entitled to vote thereat.

"14. The chairman of a meeting shall have power to admit or reject a proof for the purpose of voting, but his decision shall be subject to appeal to the Court. If he is in doubt whether the proof of a creditor should be admitted or rejected he shall mark the proof as objected to and shall allow the creditor to vote, subject to the vote being declared invalid in the event of the objection being sustained.

"15. A creditor may vote either in person or by proxy.

"17. A creditor may give a general proxy to his manager or clerk, or any other person in his regular employment. In such case the instrument of proxy shall state the relation in which the person to act thereunder stands to the creditor.

"19. A proxy shall not be used unless it is deposited with the official receiver or trustee before the meeting at which it is to be used.

"26. No person acting either under a general or special proxy shall vote in favour of any resolution which would directly or indirectly place himself, his partner or employer, in a position to receive any remuneration out of the estate of the debtor otherwise than as a creditor rateably with the other creditors of the debtor. Provided that where any person holds special proxies to vote for the appointment of himself as trustee he may use the said proxies and vote accordingly." (See ACTS OF BANKRUPTCY, BANKRUPTCY, PUBLIC EXAMINATION OF DEBTOR, RECEIVING ORDER.)

MEETINGS, COMPANIES. The Companies (Consolidation) Act, 1908, provides as follows:—

Annual General Meeting.

"Section 64. (1) A general meeting of every company shall be held once at the least in every calendar year, and not more than fifteen months after the holding of the last preceding general meeting, and, if not so held, the company and every director, manager, secretary, and other officer of the company, who is knowingly a party to the default, shall be liable to a fine not exceeding fifty pounds.

First Statutory Meeting of Company.

"65. (1) Every company limited by shares and registered on or after the first day of January nineteen hundred and one shall, within a period of not less than one month nor more than three months from the date at which the company is entitled to commence business, hold a general meeting of the members of the company which shall be called the statutory meeting.

"(2) The directors shall, at least seven days before the day on which the meeting is held, forward a report (in this Act called 'the statutory report') to every member of the company and to every other person entitled under this Act to receive it."

The statutory report shall state, amongst other things, the total number of shares allotted, the total amount of cash received by the company in respect of all shares allotted, an abstract of the receipts on account of capital, whether from shares or debentures and of the payments made thereout, and the names, addresses, and descriptions of the directors, auditors (if any), managers (if any), and secretary of the company.

Convening of Extraordinary General Meeting on Requisition.

"66. (1) Notwithstanding anything in the articles of a company, the directors of a company shall, on the requisition of the holders of not less than one-tenth of the issued share capital of the company upon which all calls or other sums then due have been paid, forthwith proceed to convene an extraordinary general meeting of the company.

"(2) The requisition must state the objects of the meeting, and must be signed by the requisitionists and deposited at the registered office of the company, and may consist of several documents in like form, each signed by one or more requisitionists.

"(3) If the directors do not proceed to cause a meeting to be held within twenty-one days from the date of the requisition being so deposited, the requisitionists, or a majority of them in value, may themselves convene the meeting, but any meeting so convened shall not be held after three months from the date of the deposit.

"(4) If at any such meeting a resolution requiring confirmation at another meeting is passed, the directors shall forthwith convene a further extraordinary general meeting for the purpose of considering the resolution and, if thought fit, of confirming it as a special resolution; and, if the directors do not convene the meeting within seven days from the date of the passing of the first resolution, the requisitionists, or a majority of them in value, may themselves convene the meeting.

Provisions as to Meetings and Votes.

"67. In default of, and subject to, any regulations in the articles—

"(i) A meeting of a company may be called by seven days' notice in writing, served on every member in manner in which notices are required to be served by Table A. in the First Schedule to this Act:

"(ii) Five members may call a meeting:

"(iii) Any person elected by the members present at a meeting may be chairman thereof:

"(iv) Every member shall have one vote.

Representation of Companies at Meetings of other Companies of which They are Members.

"68. A company which is a member of another company may, by resolution of the directors, authorise any of its officials or any other person to act as its representative at any meeting of that other company, and the person so authorised shall be entitled to exercise the same powers on behalf of the company which he represents as if he were an individual shareholder of that other company." (See COMPANIES.)

MEMORANDUM OF ASSOCIATION. The Memorandum of Association is the charter of a company, and is, except in certain specific cases, the company's unalterable law.

The following are the provisions contained in the Companies (Consolidation) Act, 1908:—

Mode of forming Incorporated Company.

"2. Any seven or more persons (or, where the company to be formed will be a private company within the meaning of this Act, any two or more persons) associated for any lawful purpose may, by subscribing their names to a memorandum of association and otherwise complying with the requirements of this Act in respect of registration, form an incorporated company, with or without limited liability (that is to say), either—

"(i) A company having the liability of its members limited by the memorandum to th· amount, if any, unpaid on the shares respectively held by them (in this Act termed a company limited by shares); or

"(ii) A company having the liability of its members limited by the memorandum to such amount as the members may respectively thereby undertake to contribute to the assets of the company in the event of its being wound up (in this Act termed a company limited by guarantee); or

"(iii) A company not having any limit on the liability of its members (in this Act termed an unlimited company).

Memorandum of Company Limited by Shares.

"3. In the case of a company limited by shares—

"(1) The memorandum must state—

"(i) The name of the company, with 'Limited' as the last word in its name;

"(ii) The part of the United Kingdom, whether England, Scotland, or Ireland, in which the registered office of the company is to be situate;

"(iii) The objects of the company;

"(iv) That the liability of the members is limited;

"(v) The amount of share capital with which the company proposes to be registered, and the division thereof into shares of a fixed amount:

"(2) No subscriber of the memorandum may take less than one share:

"(3) Each subscriber must write opposite to his name the number of shares he takes.

Memorandum of Company Limited by Guarantee.

"4. In the case of a company limited by guarantee—

"(1) The memorandum must state—

"(i) The name of the company, with 'Limited' as the last word in its name;

"(ii) The part of the United Kingdom, whether England, Scotland, or Ireland, in which the registered office of the company is to be situate;

"(iii) The objects of the company;

"(iv) That the liability of the members is limited;

"(v) That each member undertakes to contribute to the assets of the company in the event of its being wound up while he is a member, or within one year afterwards, for payment of the debts and liabilities of the company contracted before he ceases to be a member, and of the costs, charges, and expenses of winding up, and for adjustment of the rights of the contributories among themselves, such amount as may be required, not exceeding a specified amount.

"(2) If the company has a share capital—

"(i) The memorandum must also state the amount of share capital with which the company proposes to be registered and the division thereof into shares of a fixed amount;

"(ii) No subscriber of the memorandum may take less than one share;

"(iii) Each subscriber must write opposite to his name the number of shares he takes.

Memorandum of Unlimited Company.

"5. In the case of an unlimited company—

"(1) The memorandum must state:—

"(i) The name of the company;

"(ii) The part of the United Kingdom, whether England, Scotland, or Ireland, in which the registered office of the company is to be situate;

"(iii) The objects of the company.

"(2) If the company has a share capital—

"(i) No subscriber of the memorandum may take less than one share;

"(ii) Each subscriber must write opposite to his name the number of shares he takes.

Stamp and Signature of Memorandum.

"6. The memorandum must bear the same stamp as if it were a deed, and must be signed by each subscriber in the presence of at least one witness who must attest the signature, and that attestation shall be sufficient in Scotland as well as in England and Ireland.

Restriction on Alteration of Memorandum.

"7. A company may not alter the conditions contained in its memorandum except in the cases and in the mode and to the extent for which express provision is made in this Act.

Alteration of Objects of Company.

"9. (1) Subject to the provisions of this Section a company may, by special resolution, alter the provisions of its memorandum with respect to the objects of the company, so far as may be required to enable it—

"(a) to carry on its business more economically or more efficiently; or

"(b) to attain its main purpose by new or improved means; or

"(c) to enlarge or change the local area of its operations; or

"(d) to carry on some business which under existing circumstances may conveniently or advantageously be combined with the business of the company; or

"(e) to restrict or abandon any of the objects specified in the memorandum.

"(2) The alteration shall not take effect until and except in so far as it is confirmed on petition by the Court.

"(3) Before confirming the alteration the Court must be satisfied—

"(a) that sufficient notice has been given to every holder of debentures of the company, and to any persons or class of persons whose interests will, in the opinion of the Court, be affected by the alteration; and

"(b) that, with respect to every creditor who in the opinion of the Court is entitled to object, and who signifies his objection in manner directed by the Court, either his consent to the alteration has been obtained or his debt or claim has been discharged or has determined, or has been secured to the satisfaction of the Court:

Provided that the Court may, in the case of any person or class, for special reasons, dispense with the notice required by this Section.

"(4) The Court may make an order confirming the alteration either wholly or in part, and on such terms and conditions as it thinks fit, and may make such order as to costs as it thinks proper.

"(5) The Court shall, in exercising its discretion under this Section, have regard to the rights and interests of the members of the company or of any class of them, as well as to the rights and interests of the creditors, and may, if it thinks fit, adjourn the proceedings in order that an arrangement may be made to the satisfaction of the Court for the purchase of the interests of dissentient members; and may give such directions and make such orders as it may think expedient for facilitating or carrying into effect any such arrangement: Provided that no part of the capital of the company may be expended in any such purchase.

"(6) An office copy of the order confirming the alteration, together with a printed copy of the memorandum as altered, shall, within fifteen days from the date of the order, be delivered by the company to the registrar of companies, and he shall register the same, and shall certify the registration under his hand, and the certificate shall be conclusive evidence that all the requirements of this Act with respect to the alteration and the confirmation thereof have been complied with, and thenceforth the memorandum so altered shall be the memorandum of the company.

The Court may by order at any time extend the time for the delivery of documents to the registrar under this Section for such period as the Court may think proper.

"(7) If a company makes default in delivering to the registrar of companies any document required by this Section to be delivered to him, the company shall be liable to a fine not exceeding ten pounds for every day during which it is in default."

See also Sections 14, 15, 16, 17, and 18 under heading ARTICLES OF ASSOCIATION.

In a limited company the liability of the directors or managers, may, if so provided by the memorandum, be unlimited (Section 60).

Sanction is given by the Act to alter the memorandum of association in certain ways:—

With respect to the objects of the company see Section 9 above.

A company limited by shares, if authorised by its articles, may alter its memorandum to increase its share capital, consolidate its share capital into shares of larger amount, convert paid-up shares into stock and re-convert stock into shares, sub-divide its shares, and cancel certain shares. (For particulars see Section 41 under heading SHARE CAPITAL.) By Section 45 (see SHARE CAPITAL) the conditions in the memorandum may, under certain circumstances, be modified so as to re-organise the share capital.

The amount of the share capital and of the shares may be reduced. (See the provisions in Section 46, under REDUCTION OF SHARE CAPITAL.)

Any company may, by special resolution, and with the approval of the Board of Trade, change its name. (See Section 8 under NAME OF COMPANY.)

A company may provide that a specified portion of the uncalled capital shall not be capable of being called up except in the event and for the purposes of the company being wound up. (See Section 58 under COMPANY, UNLIMITED, and 59 under RESERVE LIABILITY.)

A limited company, if so authorised by its articles, may, by special resolution, alter its memorandum so as to render unlimited the liability of its directors, or managers (Section 61).

The specimen memorandum of association given in the Third Schedule of the Companies (Consolidation) Act, 1908, is—

MEMORANDUM of ASSOCIATION of a company limited by shares.

1st. The name of the company is "The Eastern Steam Packet Company Limited."

2nd. The registered office of the company will be situate in England.

3rd. The objects for which the company is established are, "the conveyance of passengers and goods in ships or boats between such places as the company may from time to time determine, and the doing all such other things as are incidental or conducive to the attainment of the above object."

4th. The liability of the members is limited.

5th. The share capital of the company is two hundred thousand pounds divided into one thousand shares of two hundred pounds each.

WE, the several persons whose names and addresses are subscribed, are desirous of being formed into a company, in pursuance of this memorandum of association, and we respectively agree to take the number of shares in the capital of the company set opposite our respective names.

Names, Addresses, and Descriptions of Subscribers.			Number of Shares taken by each Subscriber.
" 1. John Jones of	in the county of	merchant	200
" 2. John Smith of	in the county of	.	25
" 3. Thomas Green of	in the county of	.	30
" 4. John Thompson of	in the county of	.	40
" 5. Caleb White of	in the county of	.	15
" 6. Andrew Brown of	in the county of	.	5
" 7. Cæsar White of	in the county of	.	10
Total shares taken			325

Dated the day of 19 .

Witness to the above signatures,

A.B., No. 13, Hute Street, Clerkenwell, London.

(See ARTICLES OF ASSOCIATION, COMPANIES.)

MEMORANDUM OF DEPOSIT. The deposit of title deeds accompanied by a memorandum of deposit, as security for a loan or overdraft, is an equitable mortgage.

Deeds may be deposited as security without any document of charge, and form a good equitable mortgage. (See EQUITABLE MORTGAGE.)

A memorandum of deposit, however, is evidence of the purpose for which the deeds were deposited. Without such a document, a borrower might say that the deeds were lodged for some purpose other than as security, or that they were not deposited to cover advances already made as well as future advances, but with the memorandum such contentions could not be maintained. It has been held that where there is no memorandum a deposit of deeds will *primâ facie* be considered only as a security for a debt then due.

The memorandum would also be good evidence of the depositor's intention to charge a certain property, even if it should turn out that all the deeds had not been lodged with the banker.

If a customer holds deeds, as an equitable mortgagee, from a third party, and the customer deposits those deeds with his banker (the operation being thus an equitable mortgage of an equitable mortgage), it is advisable (though not strictly necessary) that the document of charge should be lodged along with the deeds, so that the banker can ascertain the customer's right to deposit them. The banker should give notice to the equitable mortgagor of his charge and ascertain how much is still owing upon the security. The mortgagor should, after receipt of such notice, make all payments, in reduction of his loan, direct to the banker, unless the banker sanctions the payments being made direct to his customer.

If the property belongs to several persons the memorandum should be signed by all of them.

A memorandum of deposit may be under hand, or under seal, and as a rule the banker's usual printed forms will be used, but any writing from the person depositing the deeds as security will be sufficient. Even a letter simply stating that "I enclose the deeds of my house 23, King Street, to be held as security for my account" should, in the absence of anything better, be preserved as a memorandum of deposit. But evidence of deposit in any other way than by signing the banker's printed form should be discouraged.

A memorandum does not form part of the chain of title, and when the document has served its purpose it is cancelled. A legal mortgage, however, forms a link in the chain, and is preserved with the other deeds of title.

A memorandum under hand, or under seal, of the deposit of title deeds is not statute barred until twelve years after the date when the right of action thereon first accrued (Real Property Limitation Act, 1874).

The Statutes of Limitations do not apply to a deposit of share and stock certificates.

The printed form of memorandum of deposit in use by different bankers varies a little in the actual words used, but the general scope of it is practically the same in most cases.

A memorandum by a customer depositing his own deeds for his own account may include the following points :—

1. I have deposited the documents named in the Schedule, with the British Banking Co., Ltd.

2. and charge all my estate and interest in the property

3. with payment of all moneys now due, or which shall at any time hereafter be due, in any manner whatsoever, to the Banking Company,

4. from me, either alone or in conjunction with any other person or persons whomsoever,

5. with interest and commission or other lawful charges.

6. The agreement to be a continuing security,

7. and I agree to execute a valid legal mortgage of the property whenever requested by you, in such manner as you may lawfully require, to secure the repayment on demand of all moneys,

8. and I declare that the documents deposited are all that are in my possession or control, and

9. that the property is not charged or encumbered in any way whatever.

10. A Schedule of all, or at any rate of all the most important of the deeds which convey the entirety of the property intended to be mortgaged must be given.

11. The depositor's signature to follow the Schedule.

12. Signature to be witnessed.

13. Memorandum to be stamped.

If the form is signed by several persons clause No. 4 should be "from us, or either of us, whether alone or in conjunction," etc.

The words of the form are varied when, for example, John Brown deposits title deeds to secure the account of John Jones. There should also be clauses to the effect that the banking company may grant time or other indulgence to or compound with the said John Jones without affecting this security. The depositor, John Brown, should agree that all dividends, compositions, and payments shall be taken and applied as payments in gross, and that the security shall extend to any ultimate balance which shall remain due.

Sometimes a memorandum of deposit includes the appointment of a bank official as the depositor's attorney, with power to sell the property. In such a case the document must be under seal and be stamped the same as a legal mortgage. The clause of appointment may be as follows : "I hereby irrevocably appoint John Brown the present General Manager of the said banking company, or such other person as shall from time to time be appointed by deed by the said banking company, to be my Attorney for me and in my name and on my behalf and as my act and deed or otherwise to sign, seal, and deliver, or otherwise perfect any deed or assurance, and to do every act which may be required or may be deemed proper for executing and delivering to the said banking company their successors and assigns such legal mortgage of the premises herein mentioned, or for the purpose of selling the said hereditaments and premises or any part thereof under the power of sale conferred by these presents and the Statute in that behalf in order to vest in the purchaser or purchasers the legal estate and all other my estate and interest in the said premises."

If a banker finds it necessary to realise his security, and his document of charge is merely a memorandum of deposit under hand, he will be obliged to apply to the Courts for power to sell the property and appoint a receiver, unless the debtor will, in accordance with his agreement in the memorandum, sign a legal mortgage giving the banker a power of sale. If the document of charge is a legal mortgage, or memorandum of deposit under seal including a power of sale, the property can, after demand has been made, in accordance with the terms of the deed, and the money is not repaid, be disposed of, or a receiver and manager appointed to look after the estate until a sale can be effected, without recourse to the Courts.

In addition to being used for the deposit of deeds, some bankers take a memorandum of deposit when certificates of stocks or shares are given as security. When this is done, the document should include a clause agreeing to transfer the stocks or shares into the name of the bank or its nominees when requested so to do.

As to the stamp duties see EQUITABLE MORTGAGE. (See TITLE DEEDS.)

MEMORIAL. When a deed of land requires registration in the public registries (e.g. in Yorkshire and Middlesex) a memorial (or form giving full particulars of the deed) is sent to the registrar for that purpose. When registered the deed is marked :—" a memorial was registered at the Registry of Deeds at the day of 1910 at in the forenoon in volume , page , number ," and the memorandum is sealed and signed by the registrar.

By the Stamp Act, 1891, the duty is—

	£	s.	d.
MEMORIAL to be registered pursuant to any Act for the time being in force relating to the public registering of deeds in England or Ireland:			
Where the instrument registered is chargeable with any duty not amounting to 2*s.* 6*d.* . . .	The same duty as the registered instrument.		
In any other case . . .	0	2	6

MESSUAGE. A dwelling-house and any adjoining piece of land.

METROPOLITAN CLEARING. The section of the business of the London Bankers' Clearing House, including all the branches of the Clearing Banks in London which are contained within the Metropolitan area. Cheques on offices in the Metropolitan Clearing have M printed in the left-hand bottom corner. (See CLEARING HOUSE.)

MIDDLE PRICE. On the Stock Exchange a dealer buys at one price and sells at another. If he buys at ten and sells at twelve, the middle price is eleven; that is, the price between the highest and the lowest.

MIDDLESEX REGISTRY OF DEEDS. (See LAND REGISTRY (MIDDLESEX DEEDS).)

MILLIÈME. (See FOREIGN MONEYS—EGYPT.)

MILLING. The indented or ridged edge of a coin. In olden times the edges of coins were frequently clipped or filed by dishonest persons and the clippings or filings sold by weight. In order to prevent that practice, milling was invented. The edge of a coin is also turned up in order that the raised flanges may afford a certain amount of protection to the figures on both sides of the coin. (See COINAGE.)

MILREIS. (See FOREIGN MONEYS — BRAZIL, PORTUGAL, SOUTH AFRICA.)

MINERAL RIGHTS DUTY. A duty imposed by the Finance (1909–10) Act, 1910, for the year ending March 31, 1910, and every subsequent year, on the rental value of all rights to work minerals and of all mineral wayleaves, at the rate in each case of one shilling for every twenty shillings of that rental value.

The rental value is taken to be the amount of rent paid by a working lessee in the last working year; and where the minerals are worked by the proprietor the amount as determined by the Commissioners.

MINORS. Persons who are below the age of twenty-one. (See INFANTS.)

MINT. Anglo-Saxon *mynet,* a coin. Latin, *Moneta,* a surname of Juno, whose temple was used by the Romans as a mint.

The place where the money of this country is coined. It is situated on Tower Hill, London. There are also mints at Melbourne, Sydney, and Perth in Australia, the gold coins of which are legal tender in this country.

At one time there were mints at Bristol, Chester, Exeter, Norwich, and York. (See BANK OF ENGLAND. COINAGE.)

MINT PAR OF EXCHANGE. The Mint Par between any two countries which use the same metal for their standard of coinage is found by comparing a standard coin of each, making the calculation upon the weight and fineness of the precious metal only; in other words the Mint Par between countries A and B is the number of B coins which contain the same quantity of pure gold (or whatever is the standard metal of both countries) as one A coin contains.

The Mint Par between two countries never varies unless one of them alters its coinage regulations, increasing or decreasing the quantity of the precious metal in its standard coin.

As an example, the Mint Par between England and France is 25·22 francs for £1; that is to say, there is the same quantity of pure gold in 25·22 francs as there is in £1; which is arrived at from knowing that by English law 480 oz. troy of gold eleven-twelfth fine are coined into 1,869 sovereigns, and by French law 1,000 grammes of gold nine-tenths fine are coined into 155 Napoleons of 20 francs each. (Nominally France is a dual standard country, both gold and silver being legal tender for any amount, but in practice the basis is a gold one.)

The following are the Mint Pars between England and the places named :—

Paris . . .	25·22 francs for £1.
Berlin . . .	20·43 marks for £1.
New York .	4·86⅔ dollars for £1.
(also quoted 49⅜ pence for one dollar)	
Vienna . .	24·02 kronen for £1.
Amsterdam .	12·10 florins for £1.

MINT PRICE. The Mint price of a given quantity of bullion is the quantity of coins into which that weight of bullion is divided. The quantity of coins in circulation which is equal to that weight of bullion is its market price, and as coins which are in circulation lose a good deal of weight, more of them will be required than if they were new, and the market price will therefore be above the Mint price. The Mint price of gold bullion is its value in gold coins, and the Mint price of silver bullion is its value in silver coins.

MINUTE-BOOK. The book in which is kept a brief record of the business transacted at the general meetings of the shareholders of a company, and at the ordinary meetings and committee meetings of the directors.

Loans granted, appointments made, salaries increased, and all resolutions of various kinds, by the directors of a bank, as well as reports submitted to them, are entered upon the minutes. The minutes of a meeting are signed by the chairman of that meeting, or by the chairman of the next succeeding meeting. All companies are required by law to keep minutes of the proceedings of their meetings and the meetings of the directors.

MINUTES. With regard to the minutes of proceedings of the general meetings of companies and of the meetings of directors, Section 71 of the Companies (Consolidation) Act, 1908, enacts :—

"(1) Every company shall cause minutes of all proceedings of general meetings and (where there are directors or managers) of its directors or managers to be entered in books kept for that purpose.

"(2) Any such minute if purporting to be signed by the chairman of the meeting at which the proceedings were had, or by the chairman of the next succeeding meeting, shall be evidence of the proceedings.

"(3) Until the contrary is proved, every general meeting of the company or meeting of directors or managers in respect of the proceedings whereof minutes have been so made shall be deemed to have been duly held and convened, and all proceedings had thereat to have been duly had, and all appointments of directors, managers, or liquidators, shall be deemed to be valid."

The minutes of a meeting of directors contain a note of the date and place of meeting, the names of the directors present at such meeting, and a record of all resolutions and proceedings, and of all appointments made by the directors. The minutes are read over to the directors at their next meeting, and, if correct, they are signed usually by the chairman of that meeting, and a fresh minute made that the minutes of the last meeting were read and signed as correct. (See COMPANIES, DIRECTORS, MEETINGS.)

MISTAKES IN PAYMENT. Where a mistake is made in payment of a bill of exchange, as by handing too much money across the counter, the banker is entitled to have the mistake rectified ; but where he pays the right amount of a cheque, and then finds that he has been led to make the payment in error, consequent upon some mistake in ascertaining the balance of the customer's account upon which the cheque is drawn, or in deciding whether or not the cheque should be honoured, the amount cannot be legally recovered from the person to whom it has been paid. "Where a cheque is cashed over the counter, the money ceases to be the money of the banker, and he cannot revoke or recall the payment, although he should immediately discover that the drawer's account is considerably overdrawn" (Grant's "Law of Banking)."

Where a forged bill of exchange has been paid, to quote the words of Mathew, J., in the case *London & River Plate Bank* v. *Bank of Liverpool* (1896, 1 Q.B. 7) : "If the mistake is discovered at once, it may be that the money can be recovered back ; but if it be not, and the money is paid in good faith and is received in good faith, and there is an interval of time in which the position of the holder may be altered, the principle seems to apply that money once paid cannot be recovered back."

MONETARY UNION. (See LATIN MONETARY UNION, SCANDINAVIAN MONETARY UNION.)

MONETARY UNIT. The coin in any country which serves as a measure of the value of all the other coins. The unit in this country is the sovereign, in the United States it is the dollar, in Germany the mark, and in France the franc. (See FOREIGN MONEYS.)

MONEY. The standard by which the value of commodities is measured, and the medium by which they are bought and sold. Money and credit, to which it gave birth, form the basis on which the stupendous business of banking has been built up. There is probably nothing which is of greater importance in the civilised world than money, and nothing which comes more closely in contact with mankind in every department of life. Not only have all conceivable commodities a monetary value attached to them, but it is customary to ascribe a financial reason as the prime moving cause (either directly or indirectly) in almost every action in which a man is concerned. In the primitive ages there was no money, and when one of the inhabitants of those olden times wished to obtain food which belonged to another person, possession had to be obtained by barter; that is, some article, considered of equal value, and of which the person who owned the food was in need, had to be offered in exchange. If one man was rich in food possessions and another in skins, there would be much inconvenience in always arranging a suitable exchange, as the food owner might not be in need of skins. This difficulty led most nations at a very early date, after experience with various substitutes, to adopt metals, particularly gold and silver, as a circulating medium. In the case supposed, the owner of food was then able to exchange his goods for a certain quantity of metal, which metal he could use for the purpose of obtaining from other persons articles which were more useful to him than skins. In the "Iliad," Homer says that the armour of Diomede was worth only nine oxen, and the armour of Glaucus was worth 100 oxen, which indicates that in those days oxen were regarded as a standard of value.

Cattle were of great importance in the early stages of civilisation, and in several languages the name for money is identical with that of some kind of cattle or domesticated animal. Professor Jevons points out that *pecunia*, the Latin word for money, is derived from *pecus*, cattle; that our word fee is nothing but the Anglo-Saxon *feoh*, meaning alike money and cattle; and that the words capital, chattel and cattle are derived from the word *capitale*. Kine were called *capitale* because they were counted by the *caput*, or head.

At different periods and in various countries many articles have been used to meet the necessity, which was felt by all, of having something to act as a measure of value. In India, certain parts of Southern Asia, and in Africa, shells called cowries are still used as a currency. Money is represented in Tibet and parts of China by small blocks of compressed tea; in Abyssinia by blocks of rock salt, and in some districts of Africa by dates. Sugar, tobacco, dried cod, dressed leather, furs, pieces of cloth, elephants' teeth, carved wood and many other objects have been used for the same purpose. Carved pebbles were used by the Ethiopians, and Adam Smith relates that, even in his day (1776), there was a village in Scotland where it was not uncommon for a workman to carry nails instead of money to the baker's shop or the ale-house. Although such articles, as a circulating medium, represent a great advance from the barter state of society, most nations, as already stated, now recognise that the metals, being practically indestructible and not much subject to fluctuations in value, are the most convenient and best fitted to act as money. Silver was used by the Hebrews, and the first mention of money as a medium of exchange is found in Genesis, where Abraham purchased the cave of Machpelah from Ephron the Hittite, and weighed to Ephron "four hundred shekels of silver, current money with the merchant." It would appear that when first the metals, whether iron, copper, gold or silver, were used they were in rude ingots or bars without any stamp or designation upon them, and when being paid over they had, as in the case of Abraham's famous purchase, to be weighed in scales. The inconvenience of always having to weigh the metals, and the difficulty also of knowing whether the quality of the metal was really what it was supposed to be, ultimately brought about the invention of coins. The Chinese are reported to have made coins as early as 2250 B.C. The ingots which had hitherto been so troublesome were, by the invention of coins, divided up into pieces of different values so that they could be available for the smallest of purchases and operate as the medium of commerce without the process of weighing, an operation which, in the case of the precious metals, was unreliable and open to misuse. The trouble of assaying the metals was done away with, for the coins at length came to bear upon their faces the Government stamp, which, as a rule, assured the holder that they were of a certain quality of metal. From this brief history of the evolution of money it is seen that each coin, to the extent of its value, is like an order payable to bearer drawn upon anyone to whom it is presented. The true nature or function of money is the right or title to demand something from others. John Stuart Mill says: "The pounds or shillings which a person receives weekly or yearly are not what constitute his income; they are a sort of tickets or orders which he can present for payment at any shop he pleases, and which entitle him to receive a certain value of any commodity that he makes choice of."

The word money is derived from the temple of Juno Moneta, which was used by the Romans as a mint. (See COINAGE, MINT.)

MONEY AT CALL AND SHORT NOTICE. In addition to the money which a banker has on hand to meet the ordinary requirements of his business, he keeps a balance at the Bank of England, or with his London agents, of such an amount as may be deemed necessary, and any surplus funds he may have, and which he desires to keep in an available form, may be lent to bill brokers and stockbrokers against security. Money lent in that way is repayable at "call" or at "short notice," and is therefore almost immediately obtainable in the event of any sudden demand upon the banker. A banker's first line of defence is the cash on hand and his balance at the Bank of England or with his London agents, which is repayable on demand; the second line of defence is the "money at call and short notice."

MONEY LENDER. The Money Lenders Act of 1900 states that the expression "money lender" shall include every person whose business is that of money lending, but shall not include :—

1. Any registered society within the meaning of the Friendly Societies Act, 1896, or any society registered or having rules certified under Sections 2 to 4 of that Act, or under the Benefit Building Societies Act, 1836, or the Loan Societies Act, 1840, or under the Building Societies Acts, 1874 to 1894; or

2. Any body corporate, incorporated or empowered by a special Act of Parliament to lend money in accordance with such special Act; or

3. Any person *bonâ fide* carrying on the business of banking or insurance, or *bonâ fide* carrying on any business not having for its primary object the lending of money, in the course of which and for the purposes whereof he lends money; or

4. Any body corporate for the time being exempted from registration under this Act by order of the Board of Trade made and published pursuant to regulations of the Board of Trade. (See USURY.)

MONEY LENT AND LODGED BOOK. A book ruled with various columns so as to show what has been lent by the bank in the way of loans, overdrafts, discounts, overdue bills, etc.; and also to show what has been lodged with the bank on current accounts, deposit accounts, and deposit receipts. The book is useful for purposes of comparison and to show how the totals are fluctuating.

MONEY MARKET. The money market is not a particular place or building where money is bought and sold, but is merely a term embracing the Bank of England, London bankers and bill brokers, the Stock Exchange, and dealers in money and credit who have either money to lend or who want to borrow money. The bankers collect money from all over the country and such surplus as is not required for current purposes is lent on the market for various periods, and all the operations between the bankers, brokers and discount houses constitute the business of the money market. If there is a large supply of money and the demand for loans is small the rates charged will be low, but if, on the other hand, the supply is small and the demand large, the rates will be high.

When the Government is in need of a temporary loan it sometimes becomes a borrower in the money market upon Treasury Bills.

Money is occasionally lent to the market by the Indian Government for short periods.

The money market is often referred to as "Lombard Street." (See BANK RATE, BORROWING ON CONSOLS, DAY TO DAY MONEY, DEPOSIT RATE, FLOATERS, FLOATING MONEY, FOREIGN EXCHANGES, MARKET RATE, MONEY AT CALL AND SHORT NOTICE, SHORT LOAN FUND.)

MONOMETALLISM. The system of currency in which one metal is the standard of value. In England gold is the standard of value and is legal tender for any amount, silver being merely token money. In India, however, the standard of value is silver. (See BIMETALLISM.)

MORATORIUM. An extension of time which is sometimes granted by the Government of a country for the payment of debts. The circumstances under which a moratorium is allowed are always of a very exceptional nature. In consequence of the great floods in Paris in January, 1910, many traders suffered severely, and the French Government suspended the law regarding the protest of commercial bills, and enacted that bills falling due between January 26 and February 15 were not to be protested for non-payment until after a delay of twenty days. The respite was granted to the various departments which were affected by the floods.

During the Franco-German war the French Government extended the date of payment of bills in Paris for three months.

The Argentine Republic adopted the device in 1891 during a monetary panic.

MORTGAGE. (From *mort*, dead, and *gage*, a pledge.)

A mortgage is a charge which a borrower gives to a lender upon a part or the whole of his property.

For example, if Brown borrows from Jones the sum of £100 and, as security for the loan, conveys to him the fee simple of a piece of land, it is called a mortgage, the conveyance being given on condition that if Brown, the mortgagor, repays the £100 and interest to Jones, the mortgagee, he shall have the estate re-conveyed to him.

There are two kinds of mortgages :—

1. Legal Mortgage (*q.v.*).
2. Equitable Mortgage (*q.v.*).

A legal mortgage forms part of the chain of title and must be preserved along with the other deeds. A memorandum of deposit, however, when done with, is cancelled, as it does not form a link in the title.

With a legal mortgage a banker has control of the property if the borrower fails to repay the advance made to him. But with an equitable mortgage—that is, a deposit of the title deeds with, as a rule, a memorandum of deposit—the banker will, unless the borrower gives a legal mortgage when requested, be at much trouble and expense before he obtains the sanction of the Court to dispose of the property. Any charge after the first mortgage is merely an equitable mortgage.

Where a banker takes a charge, which is subject to a prior mortgage, he should give notice of his charge to the prior mortgagee. (See TACKING.)

If a mortgagee deposits his mortgage, and the relative deeds, with a banker as security for a loan, he can charge it only to the extent of the mortgage debt. For example, if John Brown, who holds a mortgage deed from Jones for £500 upon property valued at £1,500, deposits the mortgage and the deeds relating to the property with his banker for an advance, the security is not worth more than £500 to the banker because that is the extent of Brown's interest in the property. In such a case the banker should give notice to the mortgagor that the mortgage deed has been deposited with him as security. When the mortgagor receives the notice, it warns him not to repay the loan to the mortgagee without the banker's consent. All reductions in the amount of the mortgage debt should be made direct to the banker by the mortgagor, and as reductions may have been made before the deeds came into the banker's hands, an acknowledgment should be obtained from the mortgagor as to the exact amount which is still due.

Mortgages and charges created by companies must now be registered. (See REGISTRATION OF MORTGAGES AND CHARGES.)

By the Stamp Act, 1891, the stamp duties are :—

	£	s.	d.
MORTGAGE, BOND, DEBENTURE, COVENANT (except a marketable security otherwise specially charged with duty), and WARRANT OF ATTORNEY to confess and enter up judgment.			
(1) Being the only or principal or primary security (other than an equitable mortgage) for the payment or repayment of money—			
Not exceeding £10 . . .	0	0	3
Exceeding—			
£10 and not exceeding £25	0	0	8
£25 ,, ,, £50	0	1	3
£50 ,, ,, £100	0	2	6
£100 ,, ,, £150	0	3	9
£150 ,, ,, £200	0	5	0
£200 ,, ,, £250	0	6	3

	£	s.	d.
£250 and not exceeding £300	0	7	6
£300			
For every £100, and also for any fractional part of £100, of the amount secured	0	2	6
(2) Being a collateral, or auxiliary, or additional, or substituted security (other than an equitable mortgage), or by way of further assurance for the abovementioned purpose where the principal or primary security is duly stamped :			
For every £100, and also for any fractional part of £100, of the amount secured	0	0	6
By Section 7 of the Revenue Act, 1903, the total duty payable under this head is not to exceed 10*s*.			
The collateral security should also bear a duty paid stamp. (See DENOTING STAMPS.)			
(3) Being an equitable mortgage :			
For every £100, and any fractional part of £100, of the amount secured .	0	1	0
(4) TRANSFER, ASSIGNMENT, DISPOSITION, or ASSIGNATION of any mortgage, bond, debenture, or covenant (except a marketable security), or of any money or stock secured by any such instrument, or by any warrant of attorney to enter up judgment, or by any judgment :			
For every £100, and also for any fractional part of £100, of the amount transferred, assigned, or disponed, exclusive of interest which is not in arrear	0	0	6
And also where any further money is added to the money already secured	The same duty as a principal security for such further money.		
(5) RECONVEYANCE, RELEASE, DISCHARGE, SURRENDER, RESURRENDER, WARRANT TO VACATE, or RENUNCIATION of any such security as aforesaid, or of the benefit thereof, or of the money thereby secured :			
For every £100, and also for any fractional part of £100, of the total amount or value of the money at any time secured	0	0	6

Maximum in case of reconveyance of a collateral security, provided that the reconveyance of the primary security has been duly stamped, 10*s*.

A reconveyance by a building society, indorsed upon a mortgage, is exempt from stamp duty. (See BUILDING SOCIETY.)

In the case of a conveyance (consideration £1,000) from Brown and Jones as tenants in common to Jones, subject to a mortgage of £5,000, the duty is chargeable upon the consideration and half the amount of the mortgage debt :—

£1,000 = consideration
2,500 = half of mortgage

£3,500. (See CONVEYANCE.)

The following are the Sections of the Stamp Act, 1891, relating to mortgages, etc.

Meaning of "Mortgage."

"86. (1) For the purposes of this Act the expression 'mortgage' means a security by way of mortgage for the payment of any definite and certain sum of money advanced or lent at the time, or previously due and owing, or forborne to be paid, being payable, or for the repayment of money to be thereafter lent, advanced, or paid, or which may become due upon an account current, together with any sum already advanced or due, or without, as the case may be;

"And includes—

"(*a*) Conditional surrender by way of mortgage, further charge, wadset, and heritable bond, disposition, assignation, or tack in security, and eik to a reversion of or affecting any lands, estate, or property, real or personal, heritable or movable, whatsoever: and

"(b) Any deed containing an obligation to infeft any person in an annual rent, or in lands or other heritable subjects in Scotland, under a clause of reversion, but without any personal bond or obligation therein contained for payment of the money or stock intended to be secured: and

"(c) Any conveyance of any lands, estate, or property whatsoever in trust to be sold or otherwise converted into money, intended only as a security, and redeemable before the sale or other disposal thereof, either by express stipulation or otherwise, except where the conveyance is made for the benefit of creditors generally, or for the benefit of creditors specified who accept the provision made for payment of their debts, in full satisfaction thereof, or who exceed five in number: and

"(d) Any defeasance, letter of reversion, back bond, declaration, or other deed or writing for defeating or making redeemable or explaining or qualifying any conveyance, transfer, disposition, assignation, or tack of any lands, estate, or property whatsoever, apparently absolute, but intended only as a security: and

"(e) Any agreement (other than an agreement chargeable with duty as an equitable mortgage), contract, or bond accompanied with a deposit of title deeds for making a mortgage, wadset, or any other security or conveyance as aforesaid of any lands, estate, or property comprised in the title deeds, or for pledging or charging the same as a security: and

"(f) Any deed whereby a real burden is declared or created on lands or heritable subjects in Scotland: and

"(g) Any deed operating as a mortgage of any stock or marketable security.

"(2) For the purpose of this Act the expression 'equitable mortgage' means an agreement or memorandum, under hand only, relating to the deposit of any title deeds or instruments constituting or being evidence of the title to any property whatever (other than stock or marketable security), or creating a charge on such property.

Direction as to Duty in Certain Cases.

"87. (1) A security for the transfer or retransfer of any stock is to be charged with the same duty as a similar security for a sum of money equal in amount to the value of the stock; and a transfer, assignment, disposition, or assignation of any such security, and a reconveyance, release, discharge, surrender, resurrender, warrant to vacate, or renunciation of any such security, is to be charged with the same duty as an instrument of the same description relating to a sum of money equal in amount to the value of the stock.

"(2) A security for the payment of any rent charge, annuity, or periodical payments, by way of repayment, or in satisfaction or discharge of any loan, advance, or payment intended to be so repaid, satisfied, or discharged, is to be charged with the same duty as a similar security for the payment of the sum of money so lent, advanced, or paid.

"(3) A transfer of a duly stamped security, and a security by way of further charge for money or stock, added to money or stock previously secured by a duly stamped instrument, is not to be charged with any duty by reason of its containing any further or additional security for the money or stock transferred or previously secured, or the interest or dividends thereof, or any new covenant, proviso, power, stipulation, or agreement in relation thereto, or any further assurance of the property comprised in the transferred or previous security.

"(4) Where any copyhold or customary lands or hereditaments are mortgaged alone by means of a conditional surrender or grant, the *ad valorem* duty is to be charged on the surrender or grant, if made out of court, or the memorandum thereof, and on the copy of court roll of the surrender or grant, if made in court.

"(5) Where any copyhold or customary lands or hereditaments are mortgaged, together with other property, for securing the same money or the same stock, the *ad valorem* duty is to be charged on the instrument relating to the other property, and the surrender or grant, or the memorandum thereof, or the copy of court roll of the surrender or grant, as the case may be, is not to be charged with any higher duty than ten shillings.

"(6) An instrument chargeable with *ad valorem* duty as a mortgage is not to be charged with any further duty by reason of the equity of redemption in the mortgaged property being thereby conveyed or limited in any other manner than to a purchaser, or in trust for, or according to the direction of, a purchaser.

Security for Future Advances, how to be Charged.

"88. (1) A security for the payment or repayment of money to be lent, advanced, or paid, or which may become due upon an account current, either with or without money previously due, is to be charged, where the total amount secured or to be ultimately recoverable is in any way limited, with the same duty as a security for the amount so limited.

"(2) Where such total amount is unlimited, the security is to be available for such an amount only as the *ad valorem* duty impressed thereon extends to cover, but where any advance or loan is made in excess of the amount covered by that duty the security shall for the purpose of stamp duty be deemed to be a new and separate instrument, bearing date on the day on which the advance or loan is made.

"(3) Provided that no money to be advanced for the insurance of any property comprised in the security against damage by fire, or for keeping up any policy of life insurance comprised in the security, or for effecting in lieu thereof any new policy, or for the renewal of any grant or lease of any property comprised in the security upon the dropping of any life whereon the property is held, shall be reckoned as forming part of the amount in respect whereof the security is chargeable with *ad valorem* duty.

Exemption from Stamp Duty in Favour of Benefit Building Societies Restricted.

"89. The exemption from stamp duty conferred by the Act of the Session held in the sixth and seventh years of King William the Fourth, chapter thirty-two, for the regulation of benefit building societies, shall not extend to any mortgage made after the thirty-first day of July one thousand eight hundred and sixty-eight, except a mortgage by a member of a benefit building society for securing the repayment to the society of money not exceeding five hundred pounds."

A mortgage must be stamped within thirty days of the date of the deed, or if from abroad within thirty days from its arrival in this country. The same time is allowed for further stamping a banker's mortgage, where the amount is not limited, for an additional overdraft, dating from the time the extra advance is taken.

The validity of a legal mortgage is not affected merely by the fact that it is not stamped, but the deed cannot be produced in Court as evidence unless it is properly stamped. An unstamped mortgage may be stamped, after the expiry of the thirty days, on payment of a penalty.

Memorandum by the Inland Revenue.

"*Primary Securities.*—The instruments given to banks by their customers to secure overdrafts on current account are, whether legal or equitable mortgages, almost invariably worded as securities for all sums due or to become due to the bank. In such circumstances the earliest of the instruments is the primary security for all advances, and must in the first place be stamped 2*s.* 6*d.* or

1*s.* per cent. Mortgage or equitable mortgage duty on the highest amount at any one time due in respect of the indebtedness secured to the bank up to date (i.e. within thirty days) and with additional duty from time to time, in accordance with the provisions of Section 88 (2) of the Stamp Act, 1891, if the indebtedness should subsequently reach, at any one time, a higher total.

"*Collateral Securities.*—Each of the other instruments must be treated as a collateral security for the highest amount of overdraft. In the case of legal mortgages, full *ad valorem* duty of 6*d.* per cent. is chargeable on the highest amount at any one time due in respect of the indebtedness secured up to August 31, 1903, and similar *ad valorem* duty of 6*d.* for every £100, or fraction of £100, increase of this indebtedness after that date; but as to such increased indebtedness arising after August 31, 1903, with a limit of 10*s.* in respect thereof, under the provisions of Section 7 of the Revenue Act, 1903. The collateral security or securities should also bear a duty-paid stamp under Section 11 of the Stamp Act, 1891. An additional duty-paid stamp can be obtained from time to time, as and when additional duty is impressed on the primary security.

"*Equitable Mortgages.*—In the case of equitable mortgages, every security, whether primary or collateral, is chargeable with the duty of 1*s.* per cent. on the highest amount at any one time due in respect of the indebtedness secured to the bank up to date (i.e. within thirty days) and with additional duty from time to time, in accordance with the provisions of Section 88 (2) of the Stamp Act, 1891, if the indebtedness should subsequently reach, at any one time, a higher total.

"In no case can the value of the security assigned, deposited or charged, be taken as the basis of assessment for mortgage duty.

"*Reconveyances.*—Reconveyance duty is payable on the highest amount of the indebtedness at any one time secured; this duty is exigible on all reconveyances, where the highest amount at any time due on the vacated security is £2,000 or under; where it is over £2,000 only on the final discharge; any partial release in that case attracting 10*s.*

"If it should be found that duty has been previously paid on a wrong basis, all the instruments should be forwarded to this office with a statement of the highest amount of the customer's indebtedness at any time subsequent to the date of the first instrument, in order that the case may be submitted to the Board of Inland Revenue."

(See ATTORNMENT, CONSOLIDATION OF MORTGAGES, EQUITABLE MORTGAGE, EQUITY OF REDEMPTION, FORECLOSURE, LEGAL MORTGAGE, MORTGAGEE IN POSSESSION, NOTICE OF MORTGAGE, PRIORITIES, RECEIVER, RECONVEYANCE, SECOND MORTGAGE, STATUTORY MORTGAGE, TACKING, TITLE DEEDS.)

MORTGAGE DEBENTURE. A debenture which not only promises to pay a certain sum, but also charges the property of the company with the payment of the money. (See DEBENTURE.)

MORTGAGE OF STOCK. For stamp duties on mortgage of stock or marketable security under hand only, see AGREEMENT, and Section 23 of Stamp Act, 1891. By deed, see MORTGAGE, and Section 86.

MORTGAGEE. The person in whose favour a mortgage is given.

MORTGAGEE IN POSSESSION. Where a mortgagor has failed to repay the money due under his mortgage, and the mortgagee has taken into his own hands the collection of the rents and management of the property, he is a mortgagee in possession. A mortgagee, however, usually puts in a receiver to manage the estate and collect rents, as the mortgagee thereby avoids the liabilities to which he would be exposed by being a mortgagee in possession. A mortgagee in possession may be liable for any damages that occur, if he gives up possession without the consent of the mortgagor.

An equitable mortgagee by deposit of title deeds can take possession only after he has received the sanction of the Court.

By the Conveyancing and Law of Property Act, 1881, Section 18, a mortgagee in possession shall have, if and as far as a contrary intention is not expressed in the mortgage deed, or otherwise in writing, power to make from time to time, an agricultural or occupation lease for any term not exceeding twenty-one years; a building lease for any term not exceeding ninety-nine years; and every such lease shall be made to take effect in possession not later than twelve months after its date. Every such lease shall reserve the best rent that can reasonably be obtained, and shall contain a covenant by the lessee for payment of the rent and a condition of re-entry on the rent not being paid within a time therein specified not exceeding thirty days. Every such building lease shall be made in consideration of the lessee, or some person by whose direction the lease is granted, having erected, or agreeing to erect within not more than five years from the date of the lease, buildings, new or additional, or having improved or repaired buildings, or agreeing to improve or repair buildings within that time, or having executed, or agreeing to execute within that time, on the land leased, an improvement for or in connection with building purposes. A nominal rent may be made payable for the first five years, or any less part of the term. (See MORTGAGE.)

MORTGAGOR. The person who mortgages or charges his property in favour of a party who has lent him money.

MORTMAIN. (Literally "dead hand.") In olden times when real estate passed into the possession of a corporation, it was said to be held in mortmain; that is, in dead hand, because, the corporation having a perpetual existence, any payments which were due when the estate passed from one person to another became non-existent. A corporation may now hold land in practically the same way as an individual, the holding in mortmain being almost obsolete.

MUNICIPAL CORPORATION. The Municipal Corporations Act, 1882, provides:—

"Section 142. (1) All payments to and out of the borough fund shall be made to and by the treasurer.

"(2) All payments to the treasurer shall go to the borough fund.

"141. (1) An order of the council for payment of money out of the borough fund shall be signed by three members of the council, and countersigned by the town clerk.

"(2) Any such order may be removed into the Queen's Bench Division of the High Court by writ of certiorari, and may be wholly or partly disallowed or confirmed on motion and hearing, with or without costs, according to the judgment and discretion of the Court."

Section 140, s.s. 2, enacts that the following payments may be made without order of the council:—

"1. The remuneration (if any) of the mayor, of the recorder (if any) in his capacity either of recorder or of judge of a borough civil court, of the stipendiary magistrate (if any), of the town clerk, of the treasurer, of the clerk of the peace when paid by salary, of every other officer appointed by the council, and of the clerk to the justices.

"2. The remuneration and allowances certified by the Treasury to be payable to the Treasury in respect of an election petition.

"3. The remuneration certified by the recorder to be due to any assistant recorder, assistant clerk of the peace, or additional crier."

Sub-section 3 provides as follows:—

"No other payment shall be made out of the borough fund, except—

"(*a*) Under the authority of an Act of Parliament; or

"(*b*) By order of the council; or

"(*c*) By order of the court of quarter sessions for the borough; or

"(*d*) By order of a justice in pursuance of this Act; or

"(*e*) In cases in which the court of quarter sessions for a county, or a justice acting in and for a county in the discharge of his judicial duty, might make an order for the payment of money on the treasurer of the county.

"(4) Saving, nevertheless, in relation to the application of the borough fund as authorised by this Section, or otherwise by this Act, all rights, interests, and demands of all persons in or on the real or personal estate of the municipal corporation, by virtue of any legal proceeding, or of any mortgage, or otherwise."

When a loan is required, reference should be made to the Statute under which the power to borrow is obtained, so as to ascertain the extent of the power, and whether the sanction of the Local Government Board or other authority is required.

The treasurer's accounts are to be made up half-yearly to such dates as the council, with the approval of the Local Government Board, shall appoint (Section 26). The treasurer shall within one month from the date to which he is required to make up his accounts in each half-year, submit them, with the necessary vouchers and papers, to the borough auditors (Section 27).

A vacancy in the office of treasurer shall be filled within twenty-one days after its occurrence (Section 18, s.s. 3). (See LOCAL AUTHORITIES.)

MUNIMENTS. (From Latin *munio*, to fortify.) The documents by which rights or claims are fortified or maintained.

MUTILATED CHEQUE OR BILL. If a cheque is presented for payment which has been torn to such an extent as to suggest that it has been so torn with the object of cancelling it, the banker may be liable if he pays it, and it is subsequently found that the drawer had torn up the cheque on purpose.

It is customary for the banker to return such a cheque (unless confirmed by the drawer) marked "cheque mutilated" or "cheque torn," but if a note is written upon the cheque by the collecting banker that the cheque was accidentally torn by him, or that he guarantees it, the paying banker usually accepts such an explanation, or guarantee, as sufficient. An explanation by a payee is not, as a rule, accepted.

If a bill has been cut in two for the purpose of transmission by the post, it would be paid by a banker if he is satisfied that that was the reason of the division, but if the bill has apparently been torn with the object of cancelling it the banker should, unless it is guaranteed by another banker, obtain the confirmation of the acceptor.

MUTUAL DISPOSITION. In the Stamp Act, 1891, the reference to the stamp duty is: MUTUAL DISPOSITION or CONVEYANCE in Scotland. (See EXCHANGE OR EXCAMBION.)

MUTUAL INSURANCE. Where a banker holds a mortgage upon a ship, the insurance policy to be given to him should not be a mutual insurance policy, if he has to be liable for calls. In an insurance of this nature, the liabilities of the company (incurred through damages to the vessels of members, contesting law cases on behalf of members, etc.) are totalled up periodically (say every three months), and equally divided among the subscribers according to the amount of tonnage they have entered in the company. Before a mortgaged vessel is admitted into a mutual society, the mortgagee may be required to give a guarantee that he will be liable for all contributions and other sums which may become payable in respect of the insurance, the guarantee to continue in force for all claims which shall arise so long as he remains a mortgagee. (See MARINE INSURANCE POLICY, SHIP-MORTGAGE.)

"NAKED" DEBENTURE. A debenture which is a mere acknowledgment of a debt and which is not secured by a mortgage or charge upon the company's property in any way, is sometimes called a "naked" debenture.

NAME DAY. Also called Ticket Day. The second day of a settlement on the Stock Exchange. A settlement consists of three days; for mining securities, four days. (See SETTLING DAYS.)

NAME OF COMPANY. The Companies (Consolidation) Act, 1908, provides as follows:—

"Section 8. (1) A company may not be registered by a name identical with that by which a company in existence is already registered, or so nearly resembling that name as to be calculated to deceive, except where the company in existence is in the course of being dissolved and signifies its consent in such manner as the registrar requires.

"(2) If a company, through inadvertence or otherwise, is, without such consent as aforesaid, registered by a name identical with that by which a company in existence is previously registered, or so nearly resembling it as to be calculated to deceive, the first-mentioned company may, with the sanction of the registrar, change its name.

"(3) Any company may, by special resolution and with the approval of the Board of Trade signified in writing, change its name.

"(4) Where a company changes its name, the registrar shall enter the new name on the register in place of the former name, and shall issue a certificate of incorporation altered to meet the circumstances of the case.

"(5) The change of name shall not affect any rights or obligations of the company, or render defective any legal proceedings by or against the company, and any legal proceedings that might have been continued or commenced against it by its former name may be continued or commenced against it by its new name.

"63. (1) Every limited company:—

"(*a*) shall paint or affix, and keep painted or affixed, its name on the outside of every office or place in which its business is carried on, in a conspicuous position, in letters easily legible:

"(b) shall have its name engraven in legible characters on its seal:

"(c) shall have its name mentioned in legible characters in all notices, advertisements, and other official publications of the company, and in all bills of exchange, promissory notes, indorsements, cheques, and orders for money or goods purporting to be signed by or on behalf of the company, and in all bills of parcels, invoices, receipts, and letters of credit of the company.

"(2) If a limited company does not paint or affix, and keep painted or affixed, its name in manner directed by this Act, it shall be liable to a fine not exceeding five pounds for not so painting or affixing its name, and for every day during which its name is not so kept painted or affixed, and every director and manager of the company who knowingly and wilfully authorises or permits the default shall be liable to the like penalty.

"(3) If any director, manager, or officer of a limited company, or any person on its behalf, uses or authorises the use of any seal purporting to be a seal of the company whereon its name is not so engraven as aforesaid, or issues or authorises the issue of any notice, advertisement, or other official publication of the company, or signs or authorises to be signed on behalf of the company any bill of exchange, promissory note, indorsement, cheque, order for money or goods, or issues or authorises to be issued any bill of parcels, invoice, receipt, or letter of credit of the company, wherein its name is not mentioned in manner aforesaid, he shall be liable to a fine not exceeding fifty pounds, and shall further be personally liable to the holder of any such bill of exchange, promissory note, cheque, or order for money or goods, for the amount thereof, unless the same is duly paid by the company."

"Limited" must be the last word in a limited company's name. Any persons using the word "limited," unless duly incorporated with limited liability, are liable to a fine not exceeding £5 a day. (See COMPANY LIMITED BY SHARES.)

The omission of the word "limited," as in an acceptance, may render the directors personally liable. Contractions of the word should not be used officially.

Companies or associations which do not exist for profit may be licensed by the Board of Trade as limited companies without the addition of "limited" to the name. (See CHARITABLE COMPANIES, COMPANIES.)

NAPOLEON. (See FOREIGN MONEYS—FRANCE.)

NATIONAL DEBT. The Bank of England manages the National Debt as the agent of the Government, and the various stocks are transferable in the books of the Bank of England. (As to the Bank's remuneration for this, see BANK OF ENGLAND.)

A stockholder on transferring stock must attend personally at the Bank to sign the transfer in the books of the Bank, and he must be identified by a recognised stockbroker, or, if unable to attend, the transfer may be effected by his attorney lawfully authorised in writing under his hand and seal, and attested by two or more credible witnesses. A holder's title is the entry in the Bank books, and a transferee may, if he wish, verify the entry in the books and sign the books as an acceptance thereof. No certificate is issued. A purchaser receives merely a receipt signed by the seller or his attorney. Stockholders can accept by themselves, or their attorneys, all transfers made to them, and should it be inconvenient to stockholders to attend at the Bank to accept stock, they can obtain a confirmation of the fact of the inscription of the stock by forwarding the stock receipt, with a request for confirmation and a postal order for 1*s*., to the Chief Accountant, Bank of England, E.C.

Under the National Debt Act, 1870, Section 26, holders of stock in the public funds may convert their holding into certificates to bearer with coupons attached for the payment of the dividends, but trustees are not authorised to hold these certificates to bearer unless they have permission by the terms of the trust. The charge for the issue of stock certificates is 2*s*. per cent. and for re-inscription 1*s*. per certificate. The certificates are issued to "bearer," but a holder can insert a name and so make the "certificate" nominal, in which case it cannot be re-inscribed in any name other than that so inserted unless duly indorsed in the presence of two witnesses.

The Bank does not recognise any trust, and when the stock is registered in more than one name, and one of the parties dies, the Bank deals only with the surviving holder or holders.

The Bank will not register more than four holders in any one account. A holder may have more than one account provided that each one is distinguished either by a number or by such other designation as may be directed by the Bank, but more than four accounts in the same name are not permitted.

Stock cannot be added to a joint account where the death of one of the holders has been notified to the Bank, but the surviving holders may open a new account and have the old one transferred to it. Stock may be registered in the name of a corporation or of two or more bodies corporate and the holding will be deemed by the Bank a joint tenancy.

A power of attorney for acceptance, sale or transfer, or any combination thereof (with or without dividends) costs 11*s.* 6*d.* A power for sale of English Government stock, where the nominal amount does not exceed £100, costs 4*s.* An application for a power of attorney must be made personally or by an agent. If a stockholder acts himself, after the issue of a power, the power is thereby revoked. Stock may be legally transferred under a power of attorney after the death of the stockholder provided the Bank has no notice of his death.

On the death of a sole stockholder, or last survivor in a joint account, the stock shall be transferable by his executors or administrators, notwithstanding any specific bequest thereof, but no stock can be transferred until the probate of the will or letters of administration has or have been left with the Bank for registration.

No stamp duty is payable in respect of any dividend warrant, transfer of stock, stock certificate or coupon (National Debt Act, 1870, Section 71).

At foot of page is a copy of a Local Loans Stock receipt and the various notices to holders printed thereon.

Should it be desired that the dividends be paid in some way other than by post to the first, or sole, stockholder—which is done without application—the necessary instructions must be lodged at the Bank.

Fresh instructions are not required upon an alteration in the amount of an existing account.

The following is printed upon the back of the receipt :—

NOTICE TO HOLDERS
OF
LOCAL LOANS £3 PER CENT. STOCK.

Dividends are due and payable on and after the 5th January, 5th April, 5th July and 5th October (unless any of these days fall on a Sunday or Bank Holiday, in which case they will be payable on the business day next following), and will be paid in one of the following modes :—

(*a*) By Transmission of the Warrants by Post :—

Without Application :	Upon Application :
To Sole or First Stockholders in the absence of any	To any Stockholder, Executor or Administrator, other than the Sole, or

LOCAL LOANS £3 PER CENT. STOCK.

(Created under Act 50 & 51 Vict. c. 16. Redeemable the 1st April, 1912.)

Transfer Days : Monday, Tuesday, Wednesday, Thursday, Friday, Holidays excepted.

Received this day of 1910 of

hereinafter called the said Transferee
the sum of
being the consideration for
Interest or Share in the Capital or Joint Stock of Local Loans £3 per cent. stock forming part of the National Debt, transferable at the Bank of England, and all property and interest in and right to the same, and the Dividends thereon, by this day transferred to the said transferee.

Witness *Witness* *Hand.*

The Proprietors, to protect themselves from fraud, are recommended to accept by themselves or their Attorneys all Transfers made to them.

£ *s.* *d.*

instructions to the contrary. Sole Stockholder includes Sole Surviving Stockholder, Sole Executor or Administrator, and Sole Surviving Executor or Administrator. First Stockholder includes the First Executor.	First, Stockholder, Executor, or Administrator, or to any Person, Firm, or Company, upon the written Request, in the prescribed form, of all the Stockholders, Executors, or Administrators.

(*b*) Dividends will be paid to any Stockholder, Executor, or Administrator, *personally attending at the Bank*, on his written Request, in the case of a Sole Account, or on the written Request of all the Stockholders, Executors, or Administrators, in the case of a Joint Account. The Request in either case must be in the prescribed form.

Forms of Postal Request can be obtained at the Bank of England, at any of their Branches, or at any Money Order Office throughout the United Kingdom.

Postal Dividend Warrants will be crossed "& Co." and must therefore be presented for payment through a banker. The Bank cannot undertake to cross a Warrant payable to a banker with the account to which the Dividend is to be placed. The Stockholder must himself instruct the banker.

Persons who receive Warrants by post, should give notice to the Bank if they are not received on the day on which they ought to be delivered; but need not acknowledge those that arrive in due course.

Forms of Request, for the receipt of Dividends on Personal Attendance, can be obtained on application at the Dividend Office, Bank of England.

Under the provisions of the National Debt Acts, Stocks and Dividends unclaimed for ten years are transferred to the Commissioners for the Reduction of the National Debt, but may be reclaimed by the persons entitled thereto.

Communications relative to Local Loans £3 per cent. Stock should be addressed, postage prepaid, "The Chief Accountant," Bank of England, London, E.C.

Stock Certificates to Bearer, of the denominations of £50, £100, £200, £500, and £1,000, with Coupons, for the quarterly Dividends attached, may be obtained in exchange for inscribed Stock.

NEGOTIABLE INSTRUMENTS. A negotiable instrument is a document which, by indorsement and delivery, or by mere delivery, passes the full title to the benefit of the instrument to the transferee, who takes it *bonâ fide* and for value, irrespective of any defects that there may be in the transferor's title, and on which the holder is able to sue in his own name.

A cheque, bill, and promissory note are negotiable instruments, and the Bills of Exchange Act, 1882, provides that where a person is a holder in due course he holds the bill free from any defect of title of prior parties and may enforce payment against all parties liable on the bill. A holder in due course is a holder who takes a bill complete and regular on the face, before it is overdue, in good faith and for value and without notice of any defect in the title of the person who negotiated it. The negotiability, however, may be destroyed by a restrictive indorsement such as "Pay John Brown only." A cheque crossed "not negotiable" warns the holder that he obtains no better title than the person had from whom he obtained it. (See "NOT NEGOTIABLE" CHEQUE.)

In addition to cheques, bills, and promissory notes, the following are examples of negotiable instruments: bank notes, coin of the realm, treasury bills, foreign bonds, share warrants and share certificates to bearer. Debentures, payable to bearer, of an English company have in recent years been held by the Courts to be negotiable instruments. It does not follow that because an instrument is a negotiable instrument in the country where it has been created, that it will be regarded as such in this country. To make it a negotiable instrument in this country there must be evidence that it is the custom of merchants to treat it as negotiable. Bigham, J., said (in *Edelstein* v. *Schuler*, 1902, 2 K.B. 144): "The time has now passed when the negotiability of bearer bonds, whether Government or trading bonds, foreign or English, can be called in question in the English Courts."

The difference between a document which is a negotiable instrument and one which is not may be illustrated by, say, a bearer bond of the Japanese Government and a bill of lading. The person to whom the bearer bond is delivered, if he takes it in good faith, and for value and without notice of any defect in the transferor's title, obtains an absolute right to the bond even if it should subsequently appear that the transferor had stolen it and had therefore no title to it. In the case of a bill of lading, which is a symbol of goods, the person to whom an indorsed bill of lading is delivered obtains a right to obtain possession of the goods, but if the transferor had no title, or an imperfect title, to the bill, the transferee cannot obtain any better title than the transferor had. If the transferor had no title, the transferee cannot obtain a title.

Certain American railroad certificates which pass by delivery when the transfer on the back has been signed are not negotiable instruments. (See AMERICAN RAILROAD CERTIFICATES.)

Where a negotiable instrument is given as security, a banker usually takes a memorandum or agreement stating the purpose for which it is pledged, though a memorandum is not absolutely necessary. A deed of transfer is not required for bearer bonds, as they pass by mere delivery and the banker obtains a valid security, even if the person from whom he received the bonds had stolen them or the bonds formed part of a trust. But it is essential to his security that when he took the bonds he had no notice of the defective title of the transferor. It would appear that mere negligence in taking a negotiable instrument does not fix a transferee with notice of a defective title; but the transferee must be able to show that he took the security in good faith and for value. The law is very clearly laid down in the case of *London Joint Stock Bank* v. *Simmons* (1892, A.C. 201), and in the course of his elaborate judgment Lord Herschell made use of the following expressions: "It is surely of the very essence of a negotiable instrument that you may treat the person in possession of it as having authority to deal with it, be he agent or otherwise, unless you know to the contrary, and are not compelled, in order to secure a good title to yourself, to inquire into the nature of his title, or the extent of his authority. . . . I should be very sorry to see the doctrine of constructive notice introduced into the law of negotiable instruments. But regard to the facts of which the taker of such instruments had notice is most material in considering whether he took in good faith. If there be anything wanting which excites the suspicion that there is something wrong in the transaction, the taker of the instrument is not acting in good faith if he shuts his eyes to the facts presented to him and puts the suspicions aside without further inquiry. . . . It is easy enough to make an elaborate presentation after the event of the speculations with which the bank managers might have occupied themselves in reference to the capacity in which the broker who offered the bonds as security for an advance held them. I think, however, they were not bound to occupy their minds with any such speculations. I apprehend that when a person whose honesty there is no reason to doubt offers negotiable securities to a banker or any other person, the only consideration likely to engage his attention is, whether the security is sufficient to justify the advance required. And I do not think the law lays upon him the obligation of making any inquiry into the title of the person whom he finds in possession of them; of course, if there is anything to arouse suspicion, to lead to a doubt whether the person purporting to transfer them is justified in entering into the contemplated transaction, the case would be different, the existence of such suspicion or doubt would be inconsistent with good faith. And if no inquiry were made, or if on inquiry the doubt were not removed and the suspicion dissipated, I should have no hesitation in holding that good faith was wanting in a person thus acting."

In the case of bonds not strictly negotiable instruments, if they contain words purporting to make them transferable by delivery, or by indorsement and delivery, a holder may be estopped from denying their negotiability if he has so dealt with them as to lead the person taking them to treat them as such. Where certain bonds had been handed to an agent for the purpose of raising money, and an advance was obtained from a moneylender, who afterwards deposited the securities with bankers as cover for advances by the bankers to the moneylender, the bankers (the defendants) claimed to hold the securities for what was due to them by the moneylender, and the plaintiffs claimed that the securities were a security to the defendants for such an amount only as was due by the principal and his agent to the moneylender. Thus, in the case of *Easton* v. *London Joint Stock Bank* (1887, 34 Ch. D. 95), in the Court of Appeal, Bowen, L.J., said: "Even if these bonds are not strictly negotiable, and do not possess the incidents of negotiable instruments which are recognised as such, nevertheless a further question arises, whether S., by the way he has treated these bonds, has not estopped himself from denying their negotiability, whether he has not—by placing for disposal, and with the intention that they should be transferred, in the hands of an agent of his own, bonds which on their very face purport to create a liability quite independent of anterior equities between the company and the person who takes them—really chosen to treat these bonds as negotiable and to authorise his agent to treat them as such. If the negotiability of these bonds by estoppel, so to speak, arises, that disposes of all difficulty that would arise owing to the seal being attached to these bonds, because it is no longer a question whether they are strictly speaking negotiable, but whether S. has chosen to treat them as such. The second way of looking at the matter may be dealt with from two points of view, but practically they run into one another. You may say that S. having placed in the hands of his agents these bonds with the intention that they should be transferred beyond those agents, and held his agents out to the world as clothed with authority to transfer them as negotiable—cannot afterwards, by any unknown dealing or limitation of authority which he has conferred on his agents, prejudice those who took the bonds which have been so floated. Or you may say, which I think is a sound way of putting it, that as regards S. and the bank these bonds have become negotiable by estoppel, and therefore S. is precluded from saying the legal title to these bonds is not in the bank."

NEGOTIATION OF BILL OF EXCHANGE. The Bills of Exchange Act, 1882, Section 8, s.s. 2, provides that—

"A negotiable bill may be payable either to order or to bearer."

The negotiation of a bill is defined in Section 31 :—

"(1) A bill is negotiated when it is transferred from one person to another in such a manner as to constitute the transferee the holder of the bill.

"(2) A bill payable to bearer is negotiated by delivery.

"(3) A bill payable to order is negotiated by the indorsement of the holder completed by delivery.

"(4) Where the holder of a bill payable to his order transfers it for value without indorsing it, the transfer gives the transferee such title as the transferor had in the bill, and the transferee in addition acquires the right to have the indorsement of the transferor.

"(5) Where any person is under obligation to indorse a bill in a representative capacity, he may indorse the bill in such terms as to negative personal liability."

By Section 36 :—

"(1) Where a bill is negotiable in its origin it continues to be negotiable until it has been (*a*) restrictively indorsed or (*b*) discharged by payment or otherwise.

"(2) Where an overdue bill is negotiated, it can only be negotiated subject to any defect of title affecting it at its maturity, and thenceforward no person who takes it can acquire or give a better title than that which the person from whom he took it had.

"(3) A bill payable on demand is deemed to be overdue within the meaning, and for the purposes, of this Section, when it appears on the face of it to have been in circulation for an unreasonable length of time. What is an unreasonable length of time for this purpose is a question of fact.

"(4) Except where an indorsement bears date after the maturity of the bill, every negotiation is *primâ facie* deemed to have been effected before the bill was overdue.

"(5) Where a bill which is not overdue has been dishonoured any person who takes it with notice of the dishonour takes it subject to any defect of title attaching thereto at the time of dishonour, but nothing in this sub-section shall affect the rights of a holder in due course."

A bill may, in the ordinary course of business, be negotiated back to a party already liable thereon. By Section 37 :—

"Where a bill is negotiated back to the drawer, or to a prior indorser or to the acceptor, such party may, subject to the provisions of this Act, re-issue and further negotiate the bill, but he is not entitled to enforce payment of the bill against any intervening party to whom he was previously liable."

Where a bill has been transferred by indorsement to, say, four different persons and the fourth indorser indorses it back to the first, indorser number one cannot enforce payment against the second, third or fourth indorsers, because each of those three indorsers has a claim against him as the first indorser. But if the first indorser negatived his liability when indorsing the bill, by the addition of the words "without recourse" to his signature, he can enforce payment, when the bill is indorsed back to him, against the said second, third or fourth indorsers because they have, in that case, no claim against him.

By Section 8, s.s. 1: "When a bill contains words prohibiting transfer, or indicating an intention that it should not be transferable, it is valid as between the parties thereto, but is not negotiable." (See BILL OF EXCHANGE, DELIVERY OF BILL, INDORSEMENT.)

NET, OR NETT, PROFIT. The profit which remains after the deduction of all expenses, and any losses which may have been incurred.

NET, OR NETT, RENTAL. The rent of a property after deduction of all taxes, repairs, etc. (See VALUATION.)

"NO ACCOUNT." These words are written upon a cheque which is returned by the drawee banker, because the drawer has no account with the banker.

A person is liable to be charged with false pretence if he issues a cheque drawn upon a banker where he has no account.

"NO ADVICE." These words (or "no orders") are often written upon a bill by a London banker when he has not received an advice to pay the bill domiciled with him by a customer of a country bank.

Instead of the words, the abbreviation "N.A." is sometimes used. The danger of using those two letters was exhibited in an unreported case in 1909, where it was suggested that they might mean "no assets," "no account" or "no advice." The bank claimed that they meant "no advice." Where any doubt could arise as to the meaning of letters, when written on a bill or cheque giving the reason why it is being returned unpaid, it is much the wiser plan to write the words in full and so save mistakes and misrepresentations.

"NO FUNDS." These words, which are sometimes placed upon a cheque by a banker, mean that the drawer has no funds in his account with which to pay the cheque.

"NO ORDERS." Where a customer of a country bank accepts a bill payable at a London bank, and when the London bank does not receive an advice from the country bank to pay the bill, it is dishonoured and usually marked "no orders" or "no advice."

NOMINAL CAPITAL. The amount authorised as the capital in the memorandum of association of a joint stock company, called also the "authorised" or "registered" capital. (See CAPITAL.)

NOMINAL CONSIDERATION. Where shares are transferred without any money being paid for them, as where a holder transfers them to a bank or to the nominees of a bank as security for an overdraft or a loan, a nominal consideration, generally five shillings or ten shillings, is inserted in the document of transfer.

Such a transfer is subject to a stamp duty of ten shillings.

A conveyance or transfer operating as a voluntary disposition *inter vivos* is chargeable with the same stamp duty as if it were a conveyance or transfer on sale, with the substitution in each case of the value of the property conveyed or transferred for the amount or value of the consideration for the sale. (See Section 74 of the Finance (1909–10) Act, 1910, under heading CONVEYANCE.) But a conveyance or transfer made for nominal consideration for the purpose of securing the repayment of an advance or loan is not chargeable with the duty imposed by that section (see s.s. 6 of Section 74), the duty remaining at 10*s*.

In the case of transfers, for nominal consideration, to or from banks or their nominees, the Board of Inland Revenue are of opinion (see the Board's circular of September 5, 1910, under TRANSFER OF SHARES) that the interests of the Revenue would, as a general rule, be adequately protected if registering officers were furnished with a certificate by the bank to the effect that the transfer is excepted from Section 74 of the Finance (1909-10) Act, 1910, and is duly stamped.

Section 17 of the Stamp Act, 1891, imposes on all registering officers the duty of satisfying themselves that all instruments of transfer are adequately stamped before they admit them for registration. In a circular in April, 1910, the Board of Inland Revenue point out to all registering officers, who may have to deal with instruments purporting to be properly stamped with the fixed duty of 10*s*., the necessity of satisfying themselves that the provisions of the law have been complied with in each case before they admit the instrument to registration.

A form, supplied by the Inland Revenue, on which to supply the required explanation, is as follows :—

"From

To___

Reference or Inquiry.	Explanation.
"Names of Parties___	
"Name of Company	
"Of the circumstances in which the actual market value of the securities transferred is not shown as the consideration :—	
"If for instance the transfer is made (1) on a sale ; (2) by way of gift *inter vivos* ; (3) in satisfaction, in whole or in part, of a pecuniary bequest ; (4) in liquidation of a debt ; (5) in exchange for other securities, *ad valorem* duty at the rate of 10*s*. per cent. on the value or agreed value of the consideration, is payable. In the case of a transfer by way of gift *inter vivos*, the *ad valorem* duty is payable on the value of the property transferred, and the instrument of transfer must be adjudicated in the Solicitor's Department, Somerset House.	
"The fixed duty of 10*s*. is payable when the transaction falls within one of the following descriptions :—	
"(*a*) On the appointment of a new trustee or the retirement of a trustee.	
"(*b*) A transfer as for a nominal consideration to a mere nominee of the transferor where no beneficial interest in the property passes.	
"(*c*) A security for a loan ; or a re-transfer to the original transferor on repayment of a loan.	
"(*d*) A transfer to a residuary legatee of stock, etc., which forms part of the residue divisible under a will.	Signed
"(*e*) A transfer to a beneficiary under a will of a *specific legacy* of Stock, etc.	Addre
"(*f*) A transfer of Stock, etc., being the property of a person dying intestate, to the party, or parties entitled to it."	Dated 19

Copies of the circulars issued by the Board of Inland Revenue, regarding nominal considerations, will be found under TRANSFER OF SHARES.

NOMINAL PAR. The value stated upon the face of a bond or certificate. If the market price is above the nominal or face value, it is said to be "above par" or "at a premium" ; if below, it is stated to be "below par" or "at a discount." (See PAR.)

NOMINAL PARTNER. A person sometimes continues his name in connection with a business, without having any actual interest therein ; but if he leads anyone to believe that he has an interest in the business, he may be held to be liable for the debts of the firm. (See LIMITED PARTNERSHIP, PARTNERSHIPS.)

NON-BUSINESS DAYS. For the purposes of the Bills of Exchange Act, 1882, non-business days are:—Sunday, Good Friday, Christmas Day, a bank holiday under the Bank Holidays Act, 1871, or Acts amending it, a day appointed by Royal proclamation as a public fast or thanksgiving day.

Any other day is a business day. (See Section 92 under BILLS OF EXCHANGE ACT, 1882.)

NON-CUMULATIVE DIVIDEND. Where the dividend upon preference shares is confined to the profits of each separate year, it is a non-cumulative dividend. On the other hand, if the profits of succeeding years may be employed to pay up all dividends which have accrued on the preference shares, before the ordinary shares get anything, the dividend is said to be cumulative.

NON-TRADING PARTNERSHIP. A member of a non-trading partnership (such as solicitors, farmers, medical men) has not an implied authority to bind the firm by signing the firm's name on a bill of exchange. In an ordinary trading partnership, however, one partner has such an implied authority.

NORA or **NORAS.** A Stock Exchange name for Great Northern Railway deferred ordinary stock. (See YORK PREFERRED.)

NOT NEGOTIABLE BILL. A bill is not negotiable when it contains words prohibiting transfer, or indicating an intention that it should not be transferable, but it is valid as between the parties thereto. (Section 8, s.s. 1, Bills of Exchange Act, 1882.)

"NOT NEGOTIABLE" CHEQUE. A cheque which is crossed generally or specially may have the words "not negotiable" added thereto, and any holder may add those words.

The Bills of Exchange Act, 1882, does not state whether, or not, it is necessary that the words "not negotiable" be placed between the transverse lines. In practice they are found sometimes between, and at other times either above or below the lines.

"Where a person takes a crossed cheque which bears on it the words 'not negotiable' he shall not have and shall not be capable of giving a better title to the cheque than that which the person from whom he took it had." (Section 81, Bills of Exchange Act, 1882.) This meaning of the words is peculiar to crossed cheques, as defined in the Bills of Exchange Act; the ordinary meaning of "not negotiable" is not transferable. A cheque drawn payable to "John Brown only" is an example of a cheque which cannot be transferred; but the words "not negotiable" do not mean that the cheque on which those words are written cannot be transferred from one person to another. A "not negotiable" cheque may be transferred just as freely as any other cheque, but if the transferor has no title to the cheque, a transferee cannot obtain, even if he gives value for it, a better title to it than the transferor had.

The words "not negotiable" really act as a warning to anyone to whom the cheque is offered, that, if he takes it, he must take it subject to any defect there may be in the title. If such a cheque has been stolen, and finally comes into the possession of John Brown, who gives value for it and obtains payment through a banker, John Brown is liable for the amount to the rightful owner of the cheque, but the banker paying the cheque is protected by Section 80 of the Bills of Exchange Act, provided it is paid in accordance with that Section. The banker collecting such a cheque for a customer is protected by Section 82. The true owner cannot recover from the banker. (See COLLECTING BANKER, CROSSED CHEQUE.)

But if a banker gives cash for a "not negotiable" cheque drawn upon another banker he is not protected by the Act, and will be liable to the true owner at any time within six years, if there should be a flaw in the title, e.g. if the cheque has been stolen or one of the indorsements is forged.

A "not negotiable" cheque may be presented for payment by, or may be paid in to the credit of, the payee or anyone else to whom it has been transferred.

Cheques are frequently crossed "not negotiable" without the addition of transverse lines. In such cases the words by themselves do not constitute a crossing in accordance with the Bills of Exchange Act, and they may be ignored.

It is very desirable, and is in fact customary, that a banker to whom a cheque is specially crossed should place his stamp upon the cheque as evidence to the paying banker that the cheque has been through the hands of that banker, but the paying banker is not justified in refusing payment of a cheque received through the clearing simply on the ground that the stamp of the banker to whom it is crossed is not upon the cheque.

Where a "cheque" contains, after the order to pay, the words "provided the form of receipt at the foot hereof is duly stamped, signed and dated," it is not a negotiable instrument. In *Bavins, junr., & Sims* v. *London and South Western Bank* (1900, 1 Q.B. 270), where such a "cheque" had been stolen and the receipt and indorsement forged, it was held that the order for payment, not being unconditional in its terms, was not a cheque, and therefore it was not a negotiable instrument. (See CHEQUE, CROSSED CHEQUE.)

"NOT PROVIDED FOR." An answer sometimes written by a banker on a cheque which is being returned unpaid for the reason that the drawer has failed to provide funds to meet it. The abbreviation occasionally used is "N.P." or "N.P.F."

"NOT SUFFICIENT." When the funds in a customer's account are insufficient to meet a cheque which has been presented to the banker through the clearing or otherwise, the cheque, on being returned unpaid, is sometimes marked with the words "not sufficient," or "not sufficient funds," or the abbreviations "N.S." or "N.S.F."

The deficiency must, however, on no account be stated.

NOTARIAL ACT. An act which is required by law to be done by a notary.

By the Stamp Act, 1891, the stamp duty is :—

	£	s.	d.
NOTARIAL ACT of any kind whatsoever (*except a protest of a bill of exchange or promissory note or any notarial instrument to be expeded and recorded in any register of sasines*)	0	1	0

And see PROTEST, SEISIN, and Section 90, under PROTEST.

NOTARY PUBLIC. Originally a notary was a person who only took notes or minutes and made drafts of writings. He was called by the Romans *notarius*.

The duty of a notary, so far as a banker is concerned, is to present dishonoured bills and "note" them for non-acceptance or non-payment, and, if necessary, afterwards to extend the noting into a protest.

NOTE CIRCULATION. The total amount of notes of a bank which are actually in the hands of the public. The "note issue" represents the amount of own notes which a bank is authorised to issue.

NOTE ISSUE. Certain banks have the privilege of issuing their own notes, but the amount of the note issue of an English bank is strictly limited to the amount certified by the Commissioners of Inland Revenue as being the average amount of the notes of the bank in circulation during a period of twelve weeks preceding April 27, 1844. The Bank Charter Act of 1844 regulates the note issues in England.

The issue of bank notes in Scotland is regulated by 8 & 9 Vict. c. 38, and in Ireland by 8 & 9 Vict. c. 37. Both Acts were passed in 1845, and the regulations are somewhat similar to the Bank Charter Act, 1844. Notes in Scotland and Ireland may be for one pound and upwards, but in England the lowest legal amount is £5.

Scotch and Irish banks may have an office in London without losing the right to issue own notes, though the right cannot be exercised by the London offices.

The "note issue" of a bank means the total amount of own notes which the bank is legally authorised to issue. The expression "note circulation" is generally used to mean the total of the bank's own notes which are actually in the hands of the public. (See BANK OF ISSUE.)

NOTE OF HAND. A name occasionally given to a promissory note (*q.v.*).

NOTE REGISTER. The note register is the book in which a bank, authorised to issue its own notes, keeps a record of all "own notes" which are issued. Particulars are kept therein of the dates which appear on the face of the notes, the dates when they were first put into circulation, the names of the persons whose signatures are upon the notes, and the individual numbers, the numbers being set forth in columns in strict order. When notes are, for any reason, withdrawn from circulation, each number is compared with the register and the date of its withdrawal entered therein opposite the number. The notes are then, after the register has been checked to see that all have been correctly marked off, ready to be destroyed. The note account in the general ledger is debited with all notes withdrawn and credited with all notes put into circulation. The balance of the note account represents the amount of notes on hand and in circulation; the amount in circulation being, of course, the difference between the balance of the account and the notes on hand. The total of the outstanding entries in the register should, of course, agree with the balance of the note account. (See BANK NOTES.)

NOTE RETURN. Every banker who issues his own notes must render weekly to the Commissioners of Inland Revenue a return showing the amount of his notes in circulation on each day of the week and showing also the average for the week, and at the end of each four weeks the banker must show the average during the four weeks. The words of the Act (Section 18 of 7 & 8 Vict. c. 32) are :—

" Every banker in England and Wales who shall issue bank notes shall, on some one day in every week (such day to be fixed by the Commissioners of Stamps and Taxes). [now Inland Revenue], transmit to the said Commissioners an account of the amount of the bank notes of such banker in circulation on every day during the week ending on the next preceding Saturday, and also an account of the average amount of the bank notes of such banker in circulation during the same week ; and on completing the first period of four weeks, and so on completing each successive period of four weeks, every such banker shall annex to such account the average amount of bank notes of such banker in circulation during the said four weeks, and also the amount of bank notes which such banker is authorised to issue under the provisions of this Act ; and every such account shall be verified by the signature of such banker or his chief cashier, or, in the case of a company or partnership, by the signature of a managing director or partner or chief cashier of such company or partnership, and shall be made in the form to this Act annexed marked (B) ; and so much of the said return as states the weekly average amount of the notes of such bank shall be published by the said Commissioners in the next succeeding *London Gazette* in which the same may be conveniently inserted ; and if any such banker shall neglect or refuse to render any such account in the form and at the time required by this Act, or shall at any time render a false account, such banker shall forfeit the sum of £100 for every such offence."

SCHEDULE B.

Name and title as set forth in the licence Bank.

Name of the firm Firm.

Insert head office, or principal place of issue Place.

An account pursuant to the Act 7 & 8 Vict. c. 32, of the notes of the said bank in circulation during the week ending Saturday, the day of 19 .

Monday . . . .
Tuesday . . . .
Wednesday . . . .
Thursday . . . .
Friday . . . .
Saturday. . . . .

6)___

Average of the week . . .

(To be annexed to this account at the end of each period of four weeks.)

Amount of notes authorised by law, £ .

Average amount in circulation during the four weeks ending as above, £ ,

I, being (the banker, chief cashier, managing director, or partner of the bank, as the case may be), do hereby certify that the above is a true account of the notes of the said bank in circulation during the week above written.

(*Signed*)

Dated the day of 19

Section 19 of the same Act explains that " for the purpose of ascertaining the monthly average amount of bank notes of each banker in circulation the aggregate of the amount of bank notes of each such banker in circulation on every day of business during the first complete period of four weeks next after the 10th day of October, 1844, such period ending on a Saturday, shall be divided by the number of days of business in such four weeks, and the average so ascertained shall be deemed to be the average of bank notes of each such banker in circulation during such period of four weeks, and so in each successive period of four weeks, and such average is not to exceed the amount certified by the Commissioners of Stamps and Taxes as aforesaid."

The period during which notes and bills are deemed to be in circulation is dealt with in 9 Geo. IV, c. 23, Section 8 :—

" Every unstamped promissory note payable to the bearer on demand, issued under the provisions of this Act, shall, for the purpose of payment of duty, be deemed to be in circulation from the day of the issuing to the day of the cancelling thereof, both days inclusive, excepting, nevertheless, the period during which such note shall be in the hands of the banker or bankers who first issued the same, or by whom the same shall be expressed to be payable ; and every unstamped promissory note payable to order, and every unstamped bill of exchange so as aforesaid issued, shall, for the purpose aforesaid, be deemed to be in circulation from the day of the issuing to the day of the payment thereof, both days inclusive: Provided always, that every such promissory note payable to order, and bill of exchange as aforesaid, which shall be paid in less than seven days from the issuing thereof, shall, for the purpose aforesaid, be included in the account of notes and bills in circulation on the Saturday next after the day of the issuing thereof as if the same were then actually in circulation."

Within fourteen days after the first day of January and first day of July a half-yearly return of all unstamped promissory notes and bills of exchange must be rendered. The return is as follows :—

HALF-YEARLY RETURN OF UNSTAMPED PROMISSORY NOTES AND BILLS OF EXCHANGE.

Bank.

An account of the amount or value of all the unstamped Promissory Notes and Bills of Exchange of Messrs. of Bankers, issued under the provisions of 9 Geo. IV., c. 23, and in circulation on Saturday in every week, for the half-year preceding the 1st day of July, 1910, together with the average amount or value thereof, according to the said account.

Date.	Amount of Bank Notes in circulation.	Amount of Notes payable to Order and Bills of Exchange in circulation.
—		
1910.	£	£ s. d.
January 1 .		
„ 8 .		
„ 15 .		
„ 22 .		
„ 29 .		
February 5 .		
[and so on up to] June 25 .		

Notes .

26)

Average £ Duty £

, being the banker or bankers, or the cashier, accountant, or chief clerk of the above-named bank, maketh oath and saith, that the aforegoing is a just and true account, to the best of the knowledge and belief of this deponent, of the amount or value of all unstamped Promissory Notes and Bills of Exchange in circulation on Saturday in every week, from the 1st of January, 1910, to the 25th of June, 1910, both days incusive, together with the average amount of such Notes and Bills of Exchange so in circulation according to such account.

Sworn before me, this day of July, 1910, at in the County of | *Signature of Deponent.*

Justice of the Peace for the County of .

"Any Note, payable to order, and Bill of Exchange, should be included in the amount shown for each Saturday from the date of issue to the date of payment, both days inclusive. For instance, a Bill either issued, remaining in circulation, or paid on a particular Saturday, must be included in the statement for that day.

"Any Note, payable to order, and Bill of Exchange, which shall be both issued and paid between one Saturday and the succeeding one, should be included in the amount in circulation on the Saturday next after the day of issuing.

"This account, which should include the issues at all the places of business, must be verified by the oath or affirmation of the banker or one of the bankers, or of the cashier, accountant, or chief clerk of the bank ; and it should be sent by post, addressed to the Controller of Stamps, Somerset House, London, W.C., being marked on the outside 'Bankers' Return.'

"The duty, which is 3*s.* 6*d.* for every £100, or fractional part of £100 of the half-yearly average, should be transferred to the credit of the Commissioners of Inland Revenue, at the Bank of England, within fourteen days after the 1st of July, 1910, and advice thereof should be given in the accompanying form.

"NOTE.—The Return will not be accepted if it be verified by any other officer of the bank than those above named."

By Section 20 (7 & 8 Vict, c. 32) all books or accounts in any way relating to a bank's note issue must be open for the inspection and examination, at all seasonable times, of any officer of stamp duties authorised in writing and signed by the Commissioners of Stamps and Taxes or any two of them. And any banker declining to permit such an inspection or to produce any book or other evidence as is required shall forfeit the sum of £100 for every such offence. "Provided always that the said Commissioners shall not exercise the powers aforesaid without the consent of the Treasury."

It is important for a banker to keep a strict watch upon the circulation because if the monthly average circulation shall at any time exceed the authorised issue, the banker shall in every such case forfeit a sum equal to the amount by which the average monthly circulation shall have exceeded the amount which such banker was authorised to issue. (Section 17, 7 & 8 Vict. c. 32). (See BANK NOTES, LICENCE.)

NOTICE OF MORTGAGE. If, when a banker takes a charge upon a property as security for an advance, he receives notice of a charge already subsisting on the land, the banker's charge, even if it is a legal mortgage, ranks after the charge of which he had notice. When a second charge is taken, the banker should give notice of his mortgage to the first mortgagee.

If, after having taken a security, a banker receives notice that a second charge has been granted upon the same land, any advance that the banker may make, after receipt of such notice, will not be recoverable out of the security in priority to the person holding the second charge. It should be particularly noted that all payments to credit after the notice will go to reduce the debt against that security, and all withdrawals will constitute a fresh unsecured advance. The fact that the banker's memorandum of deposit stated that the security was to cover future advances, or that the fixed amount which the banker agreed to lend had not all been taken, would not make any difference.

In *West* v. *Williams* (1899, 1 Ch. 132) Lindley, M.R., said: "Even if the first mortgagee has agreed to make further advances on the property mortgaged to him, the mortgagor is under no obligation to take further advances from him, and from no one else; and if the mortgagor chooses to borrow from someone else and to give him a second mortgage, the mortgagor thereby releases the first mortgagee from his obligation to make further advances. Whatever prevents the mortgagor from giving to the first mortgagee the agreed security for his further advances releases the first mortgagee from his obligation to make them."

In *Hopkinson* v. *Roll* (1861, 9 H.L.C. 514), the bankers contended that they had a right to make further advances after notice of a second charge, but it was held that their charge was limited to the amount of the debt at the time that they received the notice of the second charge. Lord Campbell said:—

"Although the mortgagor has parted with the legal interest in the hereditaments mortgaged, he remains the equitable owner of all his interest not transferred beneficially to the mortgagee, and he may still deal with his property in any way consistent with the rights of the mortgagee. . . . The first mortgagee is secure as to past advances, and he is not under any obligation to make any further advances. . . . The hardship upon bankers from this view of the subject at once vanishes when we consider that the security of the first mortgage is not impaired without notice of a second, and that when this notice comes, the bankers have only to consider (as they do as often as they discount a bill of exchange) what is the credit of their customer, and whether the proposed transaction is likely to lead to profit or to loss."

On receipt of notice of a second charge, the account should be broken and the advance allowed to remain standing against the security, until it is repaid or some fresh arrangement is made, a new account being opened for future transactions. Any overdraft on the new account would, of course, be unsecured, unless fresh security were given. The security in such a case should not be given up to the debtor without the consent of the second mortgagee.

The same rule applies if a banker has notice that the owner of the land, the deeds of which are lodged with him as security, has contracted to sell the land to a party who is aware of the banker's charge. After the notice has been received, all sums paid to credit discharge that security to the extent of the credits, and the subsequent debits are unsecured so far as that particular security is concerned.

In *London and County Banking Company, Limited* v. *Ratcliffe* (1881, 6 A.C. 722), where a person purchased land, with notice that the title deeds were deposited with a banker as a security, James, L.J., in the course of his judgment in the Court of Appeal (of which there is no recognised report) said that the advances made after the bankers had notice of a change in the beneficial ownership were not a charge on that ownership. It was true that there had always been a large balance due to the bankers, but according to the rule in *Clayton's case* the credits must be attributed to the debits in order of date, there being nothing special in the case to exempt it from the operation of that rule. If the bankers had been minded to substitute for a security on the property, a charge on the purchase money, it would have been very easy for them to do so by getting from the client a direction to the purchaser to pay them the purchase money and giving due notice of it to the purchaser; this they had not done and they had failed to establish a charge on the property (see Hutchison, vol. iii, p. 178). In the House of Lords, Lord Blackburn said: "This, in effect, raises the question, whether anyone purchasing land, with notice that the title deeds have been deposited with a bank, is bound to inquire whether the bank has, after receiving notice of this purchase, made fresh advances on the security of the unpaid vendor's lien; or whether the burden does not lie on the bank, advancing on the security of the unpaid vendor's lien, to give notice to the purchaser, that it has so done, or intends so to do. No case was cited in which any such point had been discussed; but I think both convenience and principle strongly point to the burden of giving notice lying on the bank, and not on the purchaser, whose inquiries might often be annoying and impertinent."

Where property which was subject to two mortgages, and the first mortgagees had received notice of the second mortgage, was sold by the first mortgagees, who, after satisfying their own charge, forgot about the notice they had received, and paid the surplus of the proceeds of the sale to the mortgagor, it was held that they were liable to the second mortgagee for the amount of his mortgage to the extent of the surplus which remained after their own debt was discharged. See *West London Commercial Bank* v. *Reliance Permanent Building Society* (1885, 29 Ch. D. 954).

There are two kinds of notice—actual notice, as in the cases above referred to, where the banker is informed verbally or receives notice in writing, and constructive notice. If by a perusal of the title deeds lodged as security, the banker can ascertain the existence of a prior charge upon the land, either directly, or by reference to some will or other deed, he has constructive notice of the contents of the charge recited therein, or if he receives any information which should reasonably give him a hint of the existence of a charge and lead him to find out about it, it is also a constructive notice. All clues should be carefully followed up. A tiny thread may lead the way to an important fact. A banker is not legally fixed with notice of a charge affecting the security of his customer, by any information regarding that property which might be included in deeds deposited by other customers, but he would naturally give heed to any such information which might come to his notice.

With regard to restriction on constructive notice, the Conveyancing Act, 1882, Section 3 provides:—

"(1) A purchaser shall not be prejudicially affected by notice of any instrument, fact, or thing unless:—

"(*a*) It is within his own knowledge, or would have come to his knowledge if such inquiries and inspections had been made as ought reasonably to have been made by him; or

"(*b*) In the same transaction with respect to which a question of notice to the purchaser arises, it has come to the knowledge of his counsel, as such, or of his solicitor, or other agent, as such, or would have come to the knowledge of his solicitor, or other agent, as such, if such inquiries and inspections had been made as ought reasonably to have been made by the solicitor or other agent."

A second mortgagee should always give notice of his charge to the first mortgagee. Such notice will prevent the first mortgagee from making any further advances upon the property or buying up any mortgage subsequent to the second and tacking it to his own first mortgage. (See TACKING.)

Equitable charges rank according to the date of the charge, not according to the date of notice. If a banker receives a third charge upon a property, he cannot, by giving notice to the first mortgagee, before the second mortgagee gives notice, obtain priority over the second mortgage.

Where notice is required to be sent to mortgagees or trustees, a separate notice should be sent to each one and an acceptance of notice received from each. In the case of *Saffron Walden Building Society* v. *Rayner* (1880, 14 Ch. D. 406), it was held that notice to the solicitor of trustees or mortgagees did not bind them. James, L.J., in the course of his judgment, said: "If the solicitors were to receive notice in such a way as to affect the trustees with all the consequences of that notice, it would be imposing a most tremendous burthen upon trustees to say that merely because they have employed a solicitor (the trustees having a trust fund) in effecting an investment of the trust fund upon mortgage, they were in some sense agents of the trustees to receive any notices of subsequent incumbrances or dealings by the *cestuis que trustent* of that trust fund. I find it utterly impossible to arrive at such a conclusion. We have all had occasion several times to express our opinion of the prevailing fallacy that there is such a thing as the office of a solicitor, that is to say, that a man has a solicitor, not as a person whom he is employing to do some particular business for him, either conveyancing, scrivening, or conducting an action, but as an official solicitor, and that because a solicitor has been in the habit of acting for him, or been employed to do something for him, that solicitor is his agent to bind him by anything he says, or by receiving notices or information. . . . I am prepared, therefore, to say that before a notice of this kind of a charge upon the property can be of the slightest validity it must be given, if given to a solicitor, to a solicitor who is actually either expressly or plainly authorised as agent to receive the notice of that incumbrance."

With respect to the registration of charges, see LAND REGISTRY; LAND REGISTRY (MIDDLESEX DEEDS); REGISTRATION OF MORTGAGES AND CHARGES; YORKSHIRE REGISTRY OF DEEDS.

Notice of the assignment of a debt passes the legal right to such debt from the date of such notice. (See DEBTS, ASSIGNMENT OF.)

(See MORTGAGE, PRIORITIES, TACKING.)

NOTING. Where a bill has been dishonoured by non-acceptance or by non-payment it may be handed by the holder to a notary public to be noted. The notary presents the bill again to the drawee for acceptance, or to the acceptor for payment, or to the bank where accepted payable, and if acceptance or payment is still not obtained the notary makes an official note of the fact upon the bill, or upon a slip which is attached to the bill. In the case of an inland bill, it is not necessary to note or protest any such bill in order to preserve the recourse against the drawer or indorsers. (Section 51, s.s. 1, Bills of Exchange Act, 1882.) When an inland bill is noted, it is generally with the idea of getting someone to accept the bill for the honour of one of the parties to it.

In the case of a foreign bill, however, which has been dishonoured by non-acceptance or non-payment, it must, in order to charge the drawer and indorsers, be duly protested for non-acceptance or non-payment (Section 51, s.s. 2), unless instructions are received from the remitter of the bill that it is not to be noted or protested. Noting is a preparatory step to the protest. A bill must be noted on the day of its dishonour; the protest may be subsequently extended as of the date of the noting. (Section 51, s.s. 4.) A bill may be noted at any time on the day of maturity; in London it is not sent to the notary till the bank is closed. Delay in noting is excused when the delay is caused by circumstances beyond the control of the holder and not imputable to his default, misconduct or negligence. (Section 51, s.s. 9.)

A holder of a dishonoured bill is entitled to recover the expenses of noting from any party liable on the bill. (See Section 57, under DISHONOUR OF BILL OF EXCHANGE.)

If the services of a notary cannot be obtained at the place where a bill is dishonoured, the Bills of Exchange Act, 1882, provides that any householder or substantial resident of the place may, in the presence of two witnesses, give a certificate attesting the dishonour of the bill, which shall operate as if it were a formal protest of the bill. (See BILL OF EXCHANGE, PROTEST.)

NOTOUR. In Scotland, a "notour bankrupt" is an expression meaning a bankrupt who is publicly acknowledged to be insolvent.

NOVATION. Novation is the substitution of a new obligation for an old one. Where one bank amalgamates with another, the debtors of the old bank, as well as those who have given security in any form, are required to sign a form of assent agreeing to the transfer of their obligations from the one bank to the other. Until the form of assent is signed, the debt, or security, should not be transferred from the one bank to the other.

Where a creditor of the old bank has received notice of the amalgamation, Mr. Justice Buckley says (in his work on "Company Law"): "Although he do not by an express agreement assent to the novation, yet if he acts upon it, and takes the benefits which he could only be entitled to upon the assumption that he has assented to it, there will be evidence on which the Court may find, and, unless there is something to contradict it, ought to find, that he has agreed to take the liability of the new company in substitution for that of the old one."

NURSING AN ACCOUNT. An operation which, on the one hand, may result in a banker extricating himself from making a bad debt, but which, on the other hand, may result merely in throwing good money after bad. It is a common saying that the first loss is the least, but as no banker relishes the idea of a bad debt it requires a considerable amount of courage to face a debt which, to all appearances, is lost money. The temptation is very strong "to nurse" the account; that is, to endeavour by gentle treatment in various ways to bring it back again to healthy life, in the hope that the money, or, at any rate, some portion of it, may ultimately be recovered. A banker may try to get a reduction of the debt by periodical instalments, or to get the customer to dispose of some of the securities, which might not be so advantageously got rid of in the event of the customer's failure. He may also endeavour to bring about a change in the nature of the bills which are offered for discount by gradually getting rid of those of an unsatisfactory nature. A banker may also look to his securities and see what improvement can be effected in them. So long as a banker does any of those things in his efforts to bring the account into a better condition he is not, in an ordinary way, putting himself into any worse position than he was in when he first discovered the unsatisfactory state into which the account had drifted, but when he is tempted to lend more money under the promise of some large reduction in the near future he embarks upon a rather perilous voyage. The additional loan may, in many cases, be made against a deposit of further security, but, unless the security is of such a nature as to be easily realised, the end of the matter may be worse than at the beginning. The history of many banks which have had to close their doors reveals the same story of some large overdrafts which the banker had been nursing in the fond hope that he might eventually bring matters right.

Whenever the question of nursing an account arises, it is highly necessary that a banker give it a most careful consideration, especially if further accommodation is required under the promise of a large reduction or the bait of additional doubtful security.

In the words of the late J. W. Gilbart ("History, Principles and Practice of Banking"), "we do not mean to imply that in every case it is inexpedient to 'nurse an account.' This is frequently done with the best results; but the determination to attempt it must be governed by circumstances, and in view of the fact, as experience has proved, that it is always a dangerous movement, and that the chances are always very much against the success of the result."

OFFICE COPY. An office, or certified, copy of a will should bear a certificate in the following form:—

I certify that this copy has been examined with the original will deposited in this Registry and that it is a true copy. Dated this of 19 .

District Registrar.

For stamp duty see Copy.

OFFICIAL LIST. The name of the list of prices of securities, published under the authority of the Committee of the London Stock Exchange.

The prices quoted are those ruling at 3.30 p.m., as well as the prices of part of the bargains which took place during the day, from 10.45 a.m. to 3.30 p.m. On Saturdays the time is from 10.45 a.m. to 1 p.m.

Bargains at special prices, by reason of their exceptional amounts, are marked on the list with distinguishing signs.

OFFICIAL QUOTATION. (See Quotation on London Stock Exchange.)

OFFICIAL RECEIVER. An official receiver is a person appointed by the Board of Trade to administer the estates of bankrupts. He acts under the directions of the Board of Trade and is also an officer of the Court to which he is attached. There may be more than one official receiver attached to a Court. (Sections 66 and 67 of the Bankruptcy Act, 1883.)

The duties of an official receiver are set forth in the following Sections of the Bankruptcy Act, 1883 :—

Status of Official Receiver.

"68. (1) The duties of the official receiver shall have relation both to the conduct of the debtor and to the administration of his estate.

"(2) An official receiver may, for the purpose of affidavits verifying proofs, petitions, or other proceedings under this Act, administer oaths.

"(3) All expressions referring to the trustee under a bankruptcy shall, unless the context otherwise requires, or the Act otherwise provides, include the official receiver when acting as trustee.

"(4) The trustee shall supply the official receiver with such information, and give him such access to, and facilities for inspecting the bankrupt's books and documents and generally shall give him such aid, as may be requisite for enabling the official receiver to perform his duties under this Act.

Duties of Official Receiver as regards the Debtor's Conduct.

"69. As regards the debtor, it shall be the duty of the official receiver—

"(1) To investigate the conduct of the debtor and to report to the Court, stating whether there is reason to believe that the debtor has committed any act which constitutes a misdemeanour under the Debtors Act, 1869, or any amendment thereof, or under this Act, or which would justify the Court in refusing, suspending or qualifying an order for his discharge.

"(2) To make such other reports concerning the conduct of the debtor as the Board of Trade may direct.

"(3) To take such part as may be directed by the Board of Trade in the public examination of the debtor.

"(4) To take such part, and give such assistance, in relation to the prosecution of any fraudulent debtor as the Board of Trade may direct.

Duties of Official Receiver as to Debtor's Estate.

"70. (1) As regards the estate of a debtor it shall be the duty of the official receiver—

"(*a*) Pending the appointment of a trustee, to act as interim receiver of the debtor's estate, and, where a special manager is not appointed, as manager thereof :

"(*b*) To authorise the special manager to raise money or make advances for the purposes of the estate in any case where, in the interests of the creditors, it appears necessary so to do :

"(*c*) To summon and preside at the first meeting of creditors :

"(*d*) To issue forms of proxy for use at the meetings of creditors :

"(*e*) To report to the creditors as to any proposal which the debtor may have made with respect to the mode of liquidating his affairs :

"(*f*) To advertise the receiving order, the date of the creditors first meeting and of the debtor's public examination, and such other matters as it may be necessary to advertise :

"(*g*) To act as trustee during any vacancy in the office of trustee."

In the winding up of joint stock companies, the Companies (Consolidation) Act, 1908, provides as follows :—

"147. (1) Where the Court in England has made a winding-up order, there shall be made out and submitted to the official receiver a statement as to the affairs of the company in the prescribed form, verified by affidavit, and showing the particulars of its assets, debts, and liabilities, the names, residences, and occupations of its creditors, the securities held by them respectively, the dates when the securities were respectively given, and such further or other information as may be prescribed or as the official receiver may require."

(See BANKRUPTCY, COMPANIES.)

OFFICIAL SEAL FOR USE ABROAD. A company may, if authorised by its articles, have for use in any place out of the United Kingdom an official seal, which shall be a facsimile of the common seal, with the addition on its face of the name of the place where it is to be used. (See Section 79 of the Companies (Consolidation) Act, 1908, under SEAL.)

OLD LADY OF THREADNEEDLE STREET. The term has been applied to the Bank of England and the Directors of the Bank. In Brewer's "Dictionary of Phrase and Fable" it is stated that the Directors "were so called by William Cobbett because, like Mrs. Partington, they tried with their broom to sweep back the Atlantic waves of national progress."

OMNIUM. (Latin, of all.) A Stock Exchange term denoting the aggregate value of the separate stocks or funds which may form the security for a loan.

ON 'CHANGE. The expression is used with reference to the Royal Exchange (not the London Stock Exchange). The business of foreign bills and foreign exchange is transacted in the Royal Exchange.

"ONE MAN" COMPANY. A term applied to a limited company where all the shares are held by one person, with the exception, usually, of six shares, one of which is allotted to each of six other persons, so as to make up the necessary number of members, to enable the company to be registered with limited liability. (See PRIVATE COMPANY.)

OPEN CHEQUE. A cheque is an open one when it can be presented by anyone across the counter of the bank upon which it is drawn, and cash obtained for it. A crossed cheque, on the contrary, can only be paid through a banker, though it may be placed to the credit of a customer's account.

A holder for value has a title against all the parties to the cheque, unless one of the indorsements necessary to transfer the property in the cheque is forged; but the banker on whom the cheque is drawn, even if an indorsement is forged, is protected by Section 60 of the Bills of Exchange Act, 1882, so long as he pays it in good faith and in the ordinary course of business. (See PAYMENT OF BILL.)

A collecting banker, however, who collects an uncrossed cheque is liable to the true owner thereof in the event of the cheque having been stolen or an indorsement forged. If, instead of collecting, he gives cash for it, he is a holder in due course and can sue all parties to the cheque; but if there should prove to be a forged indorsement upon the cheque, the banker will be liable to the true owner, as no title can be obtained under a forged indorsement. (See CHEQUE, COLLECTING BANKER.)

OPEN POLICY. (See MARINE INSURANCE POLICY.)

OPENING A CROSSING. Where a cheque is crossed and the drawer cancels the crossing by writing upon the cheque "Pay Cash" and adding his signature or initials, the operation is called "opening the crossing."

Before paying a cheque which has had the crossing opened, a banker should be careful to ascertain that he is not running any risk by paying it contrary to the original crossing. For example, if a cheque, payable to Brown, with a cancelled crossing, is presented for payment by the payee himself, it will be sufficient protection to the banker if the alteration is initialled or signed by the drawer; but if the cheque has been transferred by Brown, in its crossed condition, to, say, Jones, and after being duly indorsed by Jones is wrongfully obtained by Smith, who persuades the drawer to cancel the crossing and then cashes the cheque, the banker would not be free from liability if, by its payment, any loss is suffered by Jones, the true owner, who took it as a crossed cheque. (See CROSSED CHEQUE.)

OPINION BOOK. All bankers' opinions received are entered up in this book with the name of the person reported on, the name of the correspondent supplying the information, the date of his letter and the reason why the inquiry was made. A sufficient space is left after each opinion to admit of further information being added from time to time.

A book is sometimes kept for opinions given to correspondents, though the method of taking a press copy of the letter in a special letter book is frequently adopted.

The book is sometimes called the "character book." All such books are carefully indexed. (See BANKER'S OPINION.)

OPTIONS. A method of speculation on the Stock Exchange. The speculator pays a certain sum for the right (or option) to buy (or "call," as it is termed) a certain amount of stock at a fixed price within a specified time; or the sum may be paid for the right to sell (or "put" as it is termed) instead of to buy. A right either to buy or sell (called a "put and call") is termed a "double option."

ORDER (CHEQUE OR BILL). The Bills of Exchange Act, 1882, Section 8, provides as follows:—

"(4) A bill is payable to order which is

expressed to be so payable, or which is expressed to be payable to a particular person, and does not contain words prohibiting transfer or indicating an intention that it should not be transferable.

"(5) Where a bill, either originally or by indorsement, is expressed to be payable to the order of a specified person, and not to him or his order, it is nevertheless payable to him or his order at his option."

The word bill in those sub-sections includes a cheque.

A cheque payable to order should be indorsed by the person to whom it is payable. (Section 31, s.s. 3.) With regard to the question as to a payee's right to refuse to indorse a cheque when presented by himself for payment, see PAYEE.

The drawer may strike out the word "order" and convert the cheque into one payable to bearer, which alteration must be initialled by him. If there are more drawers than one, each drawer must initial the alteration.

A bearer cheque may be converted into an order cheque by the word "bearer" being crossed out; and this may be done by the payee as well as by the drawer. It is not essential to write the word "order."

Where the payee of an order cheque indorses it merely with his signature, it is an indorsement in blank, and the cheque may be transferred as a cheque payable to bearer. Any subsequent holder, however, may again make the cheque payable to order by indorsing it, e.g. "Pay John Brown or order, T. Jones," or by writing above the last indorser's signature a direction to pay the bill or cheque to or to the order of himself or some other person. (Section 34, s.s. 4.)

A cheque payable to "   or order" is treated as being payable to the order of the drawer, and requires his indorsement. If payable to "W. Brown or   " it should be indorsed by W. Brown. If payable to "W. Brown," it is, by the above section, payable to W. Brown or order, but if payable to "W. Brown *only*," the word "only" prohibits any further transfer.

A cheque payable to "wages or order," "cash or order," is by most bankers regarded as being payable to the drawer's order and requiring his indorsement. It is customary to pay such cheques only to the drawer or his authorised representative.

A cheque payable to "Yourselves or order" should be indorsed by the bank. (See BILL OF EXCHANGE, CHEQUE.)

ORDERS. For the stamp duty on orders for payment of money, see BANKER'S ORDER, BILL OF EXCHANGE.

ORDINARY SHARES. The shares into which the capital of a company is divided, as distinguished from preference, which rank in front of the ordinary, and deferred, which rank after. They may be for different amounts, for example, 1*s*., 5*s*., 10*s*., £1, £5, £10, £100 each, and may be either fully paid up or only partly paid. In some companies the ordinary shares consist of two kinds, preferred ordinary and deferred ordinary.

If a company limited by shares is authorised by its articles, it may convert its paid-up shares into stock. The company cannot issue original stock. It must first issue shares and then, when fully paid, convert them into stock.

The preference stocks of railway companies form investments for trust moneys provided that a dividend of not less than 3 per cent. has been paid on the ordinary stock for ten years before the date of investment. (See Section 1 (*g*) Trustee Act, 1893, under TRUSTEE INVESTMENTS.) (See SHARE CAPITAL.)

ORE. (See FOREIGN MONEYS—NORWAY, SWEDEN, AND DENMARK.)

OUT CLEARING. When a bank makes an exchange of cheques with another bank the cheques which are given out constitute the "Out" clearing, and the cheques which are received form the "In" clearing. (See CLEARING HOUSE.)

OUT OF DATE. (See STALE CHEQUE.)

OUTSIDE BROKER. A broker who is not a member of the Stock Exchange.

OVER-CAPITALISED. When the capital of a company is too large for the earning capacity, the company is said to be over-capitalised.

OVERDRAFT. (See ADVANCES.)

OVERDUE BILL. A bill of exchange is overdue which has not been paid at maturity. A bill payable on demand is deemed to be overdue within the meaning, and for the purposes of Section 36 of the Bills of Exchange Act, 1882, when it appears on the face of it to have been in circulation for an unreasonable length of time. (See NEGOTIATION OF BILL OF EXCHANGE.) Where an overdue bill is negotiated, it can only be negotiated subject to any defect of title affecting it at its maturity, and thenceforward no person who takes it can acquire or give a better title than that which the person from whom he took it had. (Section 36, s.s. 2.)

Except where an indorsement is dated subsequent to the date of maturity of a bill, every negotiation is *primâ facie* deemed to have been effected before the bill was overdue. (Section 36, s.s. 4.)

A bill which is twenty years old is by law presumed to have been paid.

If an overdue bill is presented to the bank where it is domiciled, it is advisable, in such a case, to obtain a cheque from the acceptor or a written authority to pay it. (See BILL OF EXCHANGE.)

OVERDUE BILLS BOOK. Bills which have been dishonoured and which are not debited to the discounter's account, are passed into overdue bills account, and full particulars of them are entered in the overdue bills book, along with a note of charges incurred, interest, payments on account, and other information.

OVERNIGHT MONEY. Money borrowed from bankers by bill brokers, as its name implies, overnight; that is, from the afternoon of one day till the following morning.

OVERSEERS. In rural districts overseers are generally appointed by Parish Councils.

In such cases a banker should receive a formal notice of their appointment, as follows :—

PARISH OF IN THE COUNTY OF .

At the annual meeting of the Parish Council of the above-named parish, held on the day of 19 , John Brown and John Jones were appointed Overseers of the Poor for the ensuing year.

Presiding Chairman.

Two Members of the Parish Council.

Countersigned by .

Clerk to the Parish Council.

If the account stands in the ledger as, e.g. "John Brown and John Jones, Overseers of Stanton," upon a change of overseers, a cheque should be signed by the old overseers transferring any credit balance there may be to the new overseers, the old account being closed and a new one opened. If the account stands as "Overseers of Stanton, John Brown and John Jones," the change of names is usually merely notified in the ledger heading and the account continued.

Where there are several overseers, cheques should be signed by all of them, unless they give the banker a written authority to honour cheques when signed by one or more of their number.

Overseers have no power to borrow in connection with their duties, and, therefore, if an overdraft is allowed, it is a debt against them as private individuals, the position being the same as in the case of a joint account of ordinary customers.

PAID CHEQUES. (See CANCELLED CHEQUES AND BILLS.)

PAID-UP CAPITAL. That part of the subscribed, or issued, capital of a company which has been paid, the other part being termed the "uncalled" capital. The capital is fully paid, if there are no further calls to be made ; that is, no "uncalled" capital. (See CAPITAL.)

PANICS. The principal monetary panics or crises during the last century were as follows :—In 1825 occurred what is known as "The Panic," stated to be due to speculation in foreign mines ; in 1836 a panic took place which has been ascribed to the excessive issue of notes by country banks ; in 1839 another panic arrived, for which the country note circulation was again considered to be responsible ; in 1847 a crisis occurred, the result mainly of excessive railway speculations. The Bank Charter Act of 1844 was suspended and the Bank was authorised by the Government to issue notes at discretion ; the next crisis was in 1857, and again the Bank Act was suspended ; in 1866, when another crisis arrived, the Bank Act was once more suspended. During this panic the firm of Overend, Gurney & Co. failed with liabilities of over £10,000,000. On each occasion when the Bank Act was suspended the panic was at once allayed. A monetary crisis occurred in 1875, when the firm of Collie & Co. failed with liabilities stated at £3,000,000. In 1878 the City of Glasgow Bank stopped payment, when losses of over £6,000,000 were found to have been made. Baring's Bank suspended in 1890.

In times of panic the Bank of England recognises that the best way to restore confidence is to lend with freedom. Walter Bagehot, in his "Lombard Street," says :

"It is ready lending which cures panics, and non-lending or niggardly lending which aggravates them."

PAPER CURRENCY. The paper instruments such as bank notes, cheques, bills and other forms which take the place of money and act as a currency or circulating medium.

PAR. (Latin, equal.) The market price of shares when it is equal to the nominal or face value (called nominal par) or to the original or issue price (called issue par).

Equivalent phrases to "above par" and "below par," are "at a premium" and "at a discount."

PAR INTERVENTION. The French form of our term "supra protest" (*q.v.*).

PAR OF EXCHANGE. This expression denotes a state of the foreign exchange between one country and another when the demand for and supply of bills exactly balance. It is a theoretical phrase only, because no one knows, as between any two nations, when the claims they each have upon the other are equal.

Distinguish from Mint Par of Exchange (*q.v.*).

PARA. (See FOREIGN MONEYS—SERVIA, TURKEY.)

PARCENERS. An abbreviation of coparceners (*q.v.*).

PARI PASSU. (Latin, equal steps.) Where one matter is progressing *pari passu* with another, it means that they are both progressing with equal steps or equal energy.

PARISH COUNCIL. Bankers are frequently appointed to be Treasurers of Parish Councils.

Every cheque or other order for the payment of money must be signed by two members of the Council. (Rule 14.) A bank should be supplied with specimen signatures of all members who are entitled to sign cheques.

When a loan is required, reference should be made to the Act under which the power to borrow is to be exercised, so as to ascertain the extent of the borrowing powers and the regulations with regard to the sanction of the Local Government Board or other authority.

Any act of the Council may be signified by an instrument executed at a meeting of the Council by the presiding chairman and two other members.

The accounts are made up yearly to March 31, and are audited by a Government auditor. (See LOCAL AUTHORITIES.)

PARITY. The London Stock Exchange takes the American dollar as of the value of 4*s.*, whereas the prices of American securities are cabled from New York to this country, taking the dollar as representing slightly more than 4*s.* 1½*d.* The term "London Parity" means the "English equivalent" at 4*s.* per dollar of the New York prices.

PARQUET. The official brokers, *agents de change*, on the Paris Exchange, form the Parquet; the unofficial dealers form the Coulisse.

PART PAYMENT. INLAND BILL.—A part payment may be made by the acceptor at the maturity of a bill, in which case the bill should be indorsed "Received   in part payment without prejudice to the rights of the other parties." The holder can sue for the balance. Notice that full payment has not been made should be given to the drawer and indorsers. The bill itself is, of course, retained by the holder.

FOREIGN BILL.—Where a part payment is made, a foreign bill must be protested as to the balance.

CHEQUE.—Cheques are either paid in full or they are not paid at all. A part payment is not made. In Scotland, however, when a cheque is presented, if payment cannot be made in full, any balance in the drawer's account is attached in favour of the presenter. The banker transfers such amount to a special account.

CASH ORDER.—Part payment of a cash order is not accepted, unless under instructions to do so from the correspondent who sent the document for collection.

PARTIAL INDORSEMENT. An indorsement of a bill of exchange which purports to transfer a part only of the amount payable, or purports to transfer the bill to two or more indorsees severally, does not operate as a negotiation of the bill. (See INDORSEMENT.)

PARTICULAR AVERAGE. A term used in connection with shipping. In the case of a general average, a loss incurred for the common safety of the ship and cargo is borne by all the parties interested in the ship and cargo in proportion to their interests; but a particular average or loss is borne entirely by the owner (or his insurer) of the property which has been lost or damaged. His property may have become damaged by accident as by the sea, or may have got washed overboard, and in such cases, (the loss or damage not having been incurred intentionally to save the ship), the owner alone is responsible. (See GENERAL AVERAGE.)

PARTIES TO BILL OF EXCHANGE. The parties to a bill of exchange are the drawer, the acceptor (called the drawee before he accepts it), the payee (who is often the same person as the drawer) and the indorsers. The parties may be either "immediate" or "remote." They are "immediate parties" when they are immediately connected with each other as the drawer and acceptor, the drawer and payee, and an indorsee and the indorser immediately in front of him. They are "remote parties" when they are not closely related to each other, as the acceptor and an indorsee.

With regard to the capacity and authority of parties to a bill, the Bills of Exchange Act, 1882, provides :—

"Section 22. (1) Capacity to incur liability as a party to a bill is co-extensive with capacity to contract.

"Provided that nothing in this Section shall enable a corporation to make itself liable as drawer, acceptor or indorser of a bill unless it is competent to it so to do under the law for the time being in force relating to corporations.

"(2) Where a bill is drawn or indorsed by an infant, minor, or corporation having no capacity or power to incur liability on a bill, the drawing or indorsement entitles the holder to receive payment of the bill, and to enforce it against any other party thereto.

"Section 23. No person is liable as drawer, indorser, or acceptor of a bill who has not signed it as such : Provided that—

"(1) Where a person signs a bill in a trade or assumed name, he is liable thereon as if he had signed it in his own name :

"(2) The signature of the name of a firm is equivalent to the signature by the person so signing of the names of all persons liable as partners in that firm." (See BILL OF EXCHANGE.)

PARTITION. A deed of partition is for the purpose of dividing an estate, which is held in common by several persons, into an estate in severalty so that each person has then an absolute right to a distinct portion.

By the Stamp Act, 1891, the stamp duty is :—

	£ s. d.
PARTITION OR DIVISION — Instruments effecting.	
In the case specified in Section 73, see that Section under EXCHANGE.	
In any other case . . .	0 10 0

PARTNER. Where several persons join to carry on a business, the combination is called a firm or partnership, and the individual members are the partners. A partner who takes an active interest in the management of the business is called an active partner, as a distinction from a dormant or sleeping partner who merely supplies funds for the business. A nominal partner is one who simply lends his name and has no real interest in the partnership. A partner (whether active or sleeping) is liable for all the debts and obligations of the firm. A limited partner, however, is not liable beyond the amount contributed at the time of entering into the partnership. (See LIMITED PARTNERSHIP.) A general partner is the same as an ordinary partner. Everyone who has held himself out to be a partner in a particular firm is liable as a partner to anyone who has, on the faith of any such representation, given credit to the firm. (See DEATH OF PARTNER, PARTNERSHIPS.)

PARTNERSHIPS. When a partnership account is being opened it is advisable, as far as possible, to obtain information regarding the assets and liabilities of the firm and the amount of capital introduced into the firm by each partner. If the firm requires an overdraft, it is particularly desirable to know to what extent the firm is already trading upon borrowed capital, and whether the money has been lent to the firm or simply to one of the partners in his private capacity. If the money has been borrowed by a partner himself, it will not, of course, be a debt due by the firm, but by the partner.

When a firm's account is opened, the bank's usual partnership form should be signed by all the partners. Although a partner may have power to draw cheques in the name of the firm, it is customary to have a clear arrangement made as to the manner in which cheques are to be signed, and therefore the form should state distinctly what is the arrangement.

In many cases a partner merely signs the firm's name, "J. Brown & Coy.," but a not uncommon form is, "For J. Brown & Coy., J. Brown." In some cases the authority is for the banker to honour cheques only when signed by all the partners, but most commonly authority is given for cheques to be paid when signed by any one partner, and occasionally the authority is limited to one particular partner. A specimen of the firm's signature in the writing of each partner authorised to sign should be given at the foot of the form.

When a firm wishes a banker to honour cheques upon the partnership account when signed by some person who is not a partner, the form of mandate should be signed by all the partners, and particular instructions should be taken as to whether the authority is to extend to the account if overdrawn.

If there is only one partner in a firm a form should be signed by him to the effect that "I, the undersigned John Brown, being the sole partner trading under the title of Thomas Brown & Coy., will sign cheques as below." A specimen of the way in which he will sign should be appended.

An authority from all the partners in a firm for one of their number to sign should specifically state that he has power to overdraw the account, for although one partner in a trading firm has implied power to borrow for the purposes of the business, and bind the firm, it is better to be on the safe side and include that power in the mandate. A partner has power to pledge partnership property, but when securities are deposited by a firm it is customary for the memorandum of deposit to be signed by all the partners when the securities are in their names, or the firm's name. If a legal mortgage is taken all the interested parties must sign it, as one partner cannot bind the other partners by deed.

A notice from one partner to cancel the authority as to signing cheques, or to stop payment of a cheque signed by any partner in the firm's name, is sufficient for a banker to act upon.

A banker cannot set off any credit balance on the private account of a partner for a debt owing by the firm, nor a credit balance on the firm's account for an overdraft on a partner's private account.

A person signing a promissory note as partner in a firm binds his co-partners jointly but not severally, but if he signs a joint and several note he may bind himself severally and the firm jointly.

Where a guarantee is to be signed by a firm, each partner should sign. If only one partner signs on behalf of the firm, it might be held that the signing of a guarantee was not an act for carrying on the business in the usual way. See Section 5, Partnership Act, below.

If a guarantee, signed by each partner personally, is taken as security for the firm's account the banker will thereby have a claim upon the private estate of each partner as well as upon the partnership estate.

If a partner deposits his own private property as security for the firm, and the firm becomes bankrupt, the banker may claim upon the firm's estate for the full amount of the debt.

"The signature of the name of a firm is equivalent to the signature by the person so signing of the names of all persons liable as partners in that firm." (Section 23, s.s. 2, Bills of Exchange Act, 1882.)

A partner is, as a general rule, able to bind all the other partners so long as what he does comes within the range of their business, unless the person with whom he is dealing has knowledge that the partner is acting contrary to some particular condition, or limitation of powers in connection with the partnership. His position is like that of a "general agent," and he is unable to bind his fellow-partners in matters which are not connected with their particular business. Bills of Exchange drawn, accepted or indorsed by a trading partnership must be signed in the name of the firm, otherwise, if signed without the firm's name, the partners signing will be liable in their individual private capacity, but if the business is carried on in the name of one of the partners, then the signing of his name is sufficient, because that is the only name the firm has. Where a partnership is a non-trading one, as in the case of solicitors and medical men, a partner cannot draw, or accept, bills of exchange, or make promissory notes or sign guarantees in the firm's name so as to bind the other partners, but it appears that he may by indorsement in the firm's name transfer a bill from one party to another.

It has been held (*Wheatley* v. *Smithers*, 1906, 2 K.B. 321) that a partner in a firm of auctioneers has no implied authority to bind the firm by his acceptance of a bill in the name of the firm.

An "infant" may be a partner, but he cannot be held liable for any overdraft. If the other partners want him to sign cheques, they must give an authority to the banker to honour his signature on the firm's account.

If cheques payable to a firm are placed

by one of the partners to his own private account, the banker must exercise the greatest care, as, in the case of misappropriation, the banker may be held to have been guilty of negligence. If the money really belongs to the partner, the correct way (in the absence of written authority by the partners) would be for the cheque to be credited to the partnership account, because, on the face of it, it is partnership property, and a cheque drawn on the partnership account in the usual way. It has been held that in the absence of express authority, it cannot be affirmed as a proposition of law that a partner has authority, from the mere fact of partnership, to open an account on behalf of the partnership in his own name.

Where securities belonging to a partnership have been deposited to cover advances on the firm's account, and a change takes place in the partnership either by the death or retirement of a partner, a fresh memorandum of deposit or mortgage, signed by the surviving partners should be taken, otherwise it might be held that the securities pledged before the change in the partnership covered only the overdraft existing at the time of the change. The admission of a new partner may also necessitate a fresh memorandum of deposit or mortgage being signed, and a cheque to transfer an overdraft to a new account should be signed by all the partners.

A change in a partnership, such as death, retirement, or bankruptcy of a partner, amounts in law to a dissolution of the firm, and if the banker desires to preserve a lien on the estate of the partner who is dead, bankrupt, or has retired, the account should be stopped and the surviving partners be requested to open a new account and pass all subsequent transactions through it. Otherwise if the account is continued as before—that is, without a break—the rule in "Clayton's case" (*q.v.*) will apply and the retired partner's estate will be released to the extent of each payment to credit.

By the Companies (Consolidation) Act, 1908 :—

Prohibition of Large Partnerships.

"1. (1) No company, association, or partnership consisting of more than ten persons shall be formed for the purpose of carrying on the business of banking, unless it is registered as a company under this Act, or is formed in pursuance of some other Act of Parliament, or of letters patent.

"(2) No company, association, or partnership consisting of more than twenty persons shall be formed for the purpose of carrying on any other business that has for its object the acquisition of gain by the company, association, or partnership, or by the individual members thereof, unless it is registered as a company under this Act, or is formed in pursuance of some other Act of Parliament, or of letters patent, or is a company engaged in working mines within the stannaries and subject to the jurisdiction of the Court exercising the stannaries jurisdiction."

The following are the principal Sections of the Partnership Act, 1890 (53 & 54 Vict. c. 39) from the point of view of persons dealing with partnerships :—

NATURE OF PARTNERSHIP.

Definition of Partnership.

"1. (1) Partnership is the relation which subsists between persons carrying on a business in common with a view of profit.

"(2) But the relation between members of any company or association which is—

"(*a*) Registered as a company under the Companies Act, 1862, or any other Act of Parliament for the time being in force and relating to the registration of joint stock companies ; or

"(*b*) Formed or incorporated by or in pursuance of any other Act of Parliament or letters patent, or Royal Charter ; or

"(*c*) A company engaged in working mines within and subject to the jurisdiction of the Stannaries :

is not a partnership within the meaning of this Act.

Rules for Determining Existence of Partnership.

"2. In determining whether a partnership does or does not exist, regard shall be had to the following rules :

"(1) Joint tenancy, tenancy in common, joint property, common property, or part ownership does not of itself create a partnership as to anything so held or owned, whether the tenants or owners do or do not share any profits made by the use thereof.

"(2) The sharing of gross returns does not of itself create a partnership, whether the persons sharing such returns have or have not a joint or common right or interest in any property from which or from the use of which the returns are derived.

"(3) The receipt by a person of a share of the profits of a business is *prima facie* evidence that he is a partner in the business, but the receipt of such a share, or of a payment contingent on or varying with the profits of a business, does not of itself make him a partner in the business; and in particular—

"(*a*) The receipt by a person of a debt or other liquidated amount by instalments or otherwise out of the accruing profits of a business does not of itself make him a partner in the business or liable as such:

"(*b*) A contract for the remuneration of a servant or agent of a person engaged in a business by a share of the profits of the business does not of itself make the servant or agent a partner in the business or liable as such:

"(*c*) A person being the widow or child of a deceased partner, and receiving by way of annuity a portion of the profits made in the business in which the deceased person was a partner, is not by reason only of such receipt a partner in the business or liable as such:

"(*d*) The advance of money by way of loan to a person engaged or about to engage in any business on a contract with that person that the lender shall receive a rate of interest varying with the profits, or shall receive a share of the profits arising from carrying on the business, does not of itself make the lender a partner with the person or persons carrying on the business or liable as such. Provided that the contract is in writing, and signed by or on behalf of all the parties thereto:

"(*e*) A person receiving by way of annuity or otherwise a portion of the profits of a business in consideration of the sale by him of the goodwill of the business is not by reason only of such receipt a partner in the business or liable as such.

Postponement of Rights of Person Lending or Selling in Consideration of Share of Profits in Case of Insolvency.

"3. In the event of any person to whom money has been advanced by way of loan upon such a contract as is mentioned in the last foregoing Section, or of any buyer of a goodwill in consideration of a share of the profits of the business, being adjudged a bankrupt, entering into an arrangement to pay his creditors less than twenty shillings in the pound, or dying in insolvent circumstances, the lender of the loan shall not be entitled to recover anything in respect of his loan, and the seller of the goodwill shall not be entitled to recover anything in respect of the share of profits contracted for, until the claims of the other creditors of the borrower or buyer for valuable consideration in money or money's worth have been satisfied.

Meaning of Firm.

"4. (1) Persons who have entered into partnership with one another are for the purposes of this Act called collectively a firm, and the name under which their business is carried on is called the firm-name.

"(2) In Scotland a firm is a legal person distinct from the partners of whom it is composed, but an individual partner may be charged on a decree or diligence directed against the firm, and on payment of the debts is entitled to relief *pro ratâ* from the firm and its other members.

RELATIONS OF PARTNERS TO PERSONS DEALING WITH TH M.

Power of Partner to Bind the Firm.

"5. Every partner is an agent of the firm and his other partners for the purpose of the business of the partnership; and the acts of every partner who does any act for carrying on in the usual way business of the kind carried on by the firm of which he is a member bind the firm and his partners, unless the partner so acting has in fact no authority to act for the firm in the particular matter, and the person with whom he is dealing either knows that he has no authority, or does not know or believe him to be a partner.

Partners Bound by Acts on Behalf of Firm.

"6. An act or instrument relating to the business of the firm and done or executed in the firm-name, or in any other manner showing an intention to bind the firm, by any person thereto authorised, whether a partner or not, is binding on the firm and all the partners.

"Provided that this section shall not affect any general rule of law relating to the execution of deeds or negotiable instruments.

Partner using Credit of Firm for Private Purposes.

"7. Where one partner pledges the credit of the firm for a purpose apparently not connected with the firm's ordinary course of business, the firm is not bound, unless he is in fact specially authorised by the other partners; but this Section does not affect any personal liability incurred by an individual partner.

Effect of Notice that Firm will not be Bound by Acts of Partner.

"8. If it has been agreed between the partners that any restriction shall be placed on the power of any one or more of them to bind the firm, no act done in contravention of the agreement is binding on the firm with respect to persons having notice of the agreement.

Liability of Partners.

"9. Every partner in a firm is liable jointly with the other partners, and in Scotland severally also, for all debts and obligations of the firm incurred while he is a partner; and after his death his estate is also severally liable in a due course of administration for such debts and obligations, so far as they remain unsatisfied, but subject in England or Ireland to the prior payment of his separate debts.

Liability of the Firm for Wrongs.

"10. Where, by any wrongful act or omission of any partner acting in the ordinary course of the business of the firm, or with the authority of his co-partners, loss or injury is caused to any person not being a partner in the firm, or any penalty is incurred, the firm is liable therefor to the same extent as the partner so acting or omitting to act.

Misapplication of Money or Property Received for or in Custody of the Firm.

"11. In the following cases; namely—

"(*a*) Where one partner acting within the scope of his apparent authority receives the money or property of a third person and misapplies it; and

"(*b*) Where a firm in the course of its business receives money or property of a third person, and the money or property so received is misapplied by one or more of the partners while it is in the custody of the firm;

the firm is liable to make good the loss.

Liability for Wrongs Joint and Several.

"12. Every partner is liable jointly with his co-partners and also severally for everything for which the firm while he is a partner therein becomes liable under either of the two last preceding sections.

Improper Employment of Trust-Property for Partnership Purposes.

"13. If a partner, being a trustee, improperly employs trust-property in the business or on the account of the partnership, no other partner is liable for the trust-property to the persons beneficially interested therein:

"Provided as follows:—

"(1) This Section shall not affect any liability incurred by any partner by reason of his having notice of a breach of trust; and

"(2) Nothing in this Section shall prevent trust money from being followed and recovered from the firm if still in its possession or under its control.

Persons liable by "Holding Out."

"14. (1) Everyone who by words spoken or written or by conduct represents himself, or who knowingly suffers himself to be represented, as a partner in a particular firm, is liable as a partner to anyone who has on the faith of any such representation given credit to the firm, whether the representation has or has not been made or communicated to the person so giving credit by or with the knowledge of the apparent partner making the representation or suffering it to be made.

"(2) Provided that where after a partner's death the partnership business is continued in the old firm-name, the continued use of that name or of the deceased partner's name as part thereof shall not of itself make his executors' or administrators' estate or effects liable for any partnership debts contracted after his death.

Admissions and Representations of Partners.

"15. An admission or representation made by any partner concerning the partnership affairs, and in the ordinary course of its business, is evidence against the firm.

Notice to Acting Partner to be Notice to the Firm.

"16. Notice to any partner who habitually acts in the partnership business of any matter relating to partnership affairs operates as notice to the firm, except in the case of a fraud on the firm committed by or with the consent of that partner.

Liabilities of Incoming and Outgoing Partners.

"17. (1) A person who is admitted as a partner into an existing firm does not thereby become liable to the creditors of the firm for anything done before he became a partner.

"(2) A partner who retires from a firm does not thereby cease to be liable for partnership debts or obligations incurred before his retirement.

"(3) A retiring partner may be discharged from any existing liabilities, by an agreement to that effect between himself and the members of the firm as newly constituted and the creditors, and this agreement may be either express or inferred as a fact from the course of dealing between the creditors and the firm as newly constituted.

Revocation of continuing Guaranty by Change in Firm.

"18. A continuing guaranty or cautionary obligation given either to a firm or to a third person in respect of the transactions of a firm is, in the absence of agreement to the contrary, revoked as to future transactions by any change in the constitution of the firm to which, or of the firm in respect of the transactions of which, the guaranty or obligation was given.

Dissolution by Bankruptcy, Death, or Charge.

"33. (1) Subject to any agreement between the partners, every partnership is dissolved as regards all the partners by the death or bankruptcy of any partner.

"(2) A partnership may, at the option of the other partners, be dissolved if any partner suffers his share of the partnership property to be charged under this Act for his separate debt.

Rights of Persons dealing with Firm against Apparent Members of Firm.

"36. (1) Where a person deals with a firm after a change in its constitution he is entitled to treat all apparent members of the old firm as still being members of the firm until he has notice of the change.

"(2) An advertisement in the *London Gazette* as to a firm whose principal place of business is in England or Wales, in the *Edinburgh Gazette* as to a firm whose principal place of business is in Scotland, and in the *Dublin Gazette* as to a firm whose principal place of business is in Ireland, shall be notice as to persons who had not dealings with the firm before the date of the dissolution or change so advertised.

"(3) The estate of a partner who dies, or who becomes bankrupt, or of a partner who, not having been known to the person dealing with the firm to be a partner, retires from the firm, is not liable for partnership debts contracted after the date of the death, bankruptcy, or retirement respectively.

Continuing Authority of Partners for Purposes of Winding Up.

"38. After the dissolution of a partnership the authority of each partner to bind the firm, and the other rights and obligations of the partners, continue notwithstanding the dissolution so far as may be necessary to wind up the affairs of the partnership, and to complete transactions begun but unfinished at the time of the dissolution, but not otherwise.

"Provided that the firm is in no case bound by the acts of a partner who has become bankrupt; but this proviso does not affect the liability of any person who has after the bankruptcy represented himself or knowingly suffered himself to be represented as a partner of the bankrupt." (See COMPANIES, LIMITED PARTNERSHIP.)

PASS BOOK. The pass book, or passage book as it was formerly called, is given by a banker to his customer, and is for the purpose of showing the exact state of the customer's account with the banker. The method of writing up the pass book varies in different banks. Some banks reverse the entries in the ledger by placing the items which are in the credit column of the ledger on the debit side of the pass book, and the debit items in the ledger on the credit side of the pass book. Where this is done the first page of the pass book will be headed, "Dr. British Banking Co., Ltd., in account with John Brown, Cr." Other banks, however, make the pass book an exact copy of the ledger, and the first page of the pass book in such cases is headed "Dr. John Brown in account with British Banking Co., Ltd., Cr."

The ruling of an ordinary current account pass book shows a date column, a column for particulars, and a column for the amounts, all credit items being entered on one page and all debit items on the opposite page. When one page is filled, both pages are cast up at the same date and any blank lines in either page ruled across with an oblique line.

The column for particulars on the cheques paid side shows the payees' names, unless the customer desires the numbers of the cheques to be entered instead of the names, and on the lodgments side the words "cash" or "cheques" or "sundries," as the case may be, appear, as well as any other particulars which are necessary.

Some customers prefer a pass book which shows their balance from day to day, and therefore some banks provide a book ruled like a ledger with columns for the date, particulars, debit amounts, credit amounts, "Dr. or Cr.," and balance. In such books the various items are entered one after the other as they appear in the ledger, and the balance may be shown daily or at intervals as desired. A book of this description is useful for deposit accounts where customers prefer to have a book rather than a deposit receipt.

In whatever form the pass book is kept, it is of the utmost importance that it should be carefully and correctly written up. All payments to credit should appear therein in the precise order in which they occur in the ledger, and the dates should always coincide. The same points should be observed in the entering of cheques which have been paid. It is the practice in some banks to write up the pass books from the actual credit slips and cheques, and to compare them with the ledgers before giving out the books, but many banks write up the pass books direct from the ledger accounts, and in some banks they are afterwards compared with the vouchers. The system where only the payments to credit are entered by the banker in the pass book, the debit items being entered by the customer at the time he issues the cheques, is now out of date.

If an entry has been omitted, and it is entered out of its proper order, a mark of some kind is usually made in the pass book calling attention to the fact. Where a customer brings in a payment to credit after the books are closed for the day, the paying-in slip should be dated by the customer for the following day and an explanation made to him, if cheques form part of the credit, that they will be dealt with next day. The date of the entry for that credit in the pass book should be that of the following day, when it actually passes through the books of the bank.

Where a mistake in writing up a pass book has been made, it should be ruled out neatly (not blotted out so that the original entry cannot be read) and the correction made. No erasures of any kind are permitted in a pass book. Where a banker has debited or credited the customer with an amount in error, and it is necessary to pass a correcting entry through the books, if the pass book has been in the customer's possession subsequent to the date of the wrong entry and before its correction, the customer's attention should be drawn to the correction when it is made. It has been held that where a book has been formally balanced after such a correction and the customer raises no objection he has assented to it. See the judgments in the case of *Shaw* v. *Dartnall* (1826, 6 B. & C. 56).

Some banks supply a form of pass book specially made for the purpose of deposit accounts where receipts are not given. The book is ruled, practically, in the same way as the book issued by the Post Office Savings Bank. Each item must be initialled by the cashier and the book must be presented every time that a transaction takes place.

In some banks, particularly in London, all paid vouchers are returned to the customer each time the pass book is written up and given to him.

In many banks the pass books are numbered consecutively and a register of them is kept. Whenever a new pass book is commenced, a note of it is made in the register, against the number of the book, the date and the name of the account being recorded.

A pass book and a deposit receipt are the two principal guides by which the outside public can judge of the quality of the clerical work of a bank office, and if either of them is negligently written it reflects upon all the staff of the office, and is apt to give the bank an undesirable reputation for carelessness. The three essential characteristics of a good pass book clerk are accuracy, neatness, and rapidity.

Pass books should be sorted in alphabetical order so that when any are asked for they can be found at once, and they should be kept well written up to date. In fact, the transactions of one day ought to be entered in all the pass books on hand not later than the following day. When a pass book is asked for by a customer it should, before being parted with, be examined with the ledger, the two sides cast up in pencil and the balance compared. A note should be made in ink in the ledger of the date when the book is given out, together with the initials of the clerk responsible for the accuracy of the book ; this note is usually made on the line of the last ledger entry which has been put into the pass book.

It saves time, and is very convenient, if the folio of the ledger on which the customer's account appears, is noted on the back of the pass book, or some place where it can be quickly seen.

Some banks have a notice printed at the beginning of the book, or on the back, requesting the customer to send in the book at certain intervals, say weekly or monthly, to be written up, and also to leave it with the bank at the end of each half-year to be balanced.

Some banks have a recognised rule not to enter up a pass book while a customer waits, but to send it to him by post as soon as possible or to retain it till he calls again. The practice in some banks of entering only the credit items when a book is brought in, and is waited for, is not a desirable one, as it does not give a proper statement of the position of the customer's account. It is much better to advise the customer to leave the pass book in order that it may be fully written up to date. If the customer wishes an acknowledgment for the money paid to credit, instead of entering it in the pass book when received, some bankers give the customer a duplicate credit slip initialled, or they initial the counterfoil of the customer's paying-in slip book. Credits should not, as a rule, be entered in a pass book before they are posted in the ledger.

Where a customer lives abroad, it is sometimes more convenient to send him, instead of a pass book, a copy of his account written upon sheets of paper ruled in the same way as a pass book ; these are known as "pass sheets" or "statements of account."

In some cases a list of the Bank Holidays is shown at the front of the pass book, with the information that "Bills of Exchange falling due on Good Friday and Christmas Day are payable on the previous day ; those due on the other holidays being payable on the following day."

Most banks supply on the fly-leaf of their pass books a list of their branches, principal correspondents, and, in the case of country banks, the name of their London agents.

A notice which is sometimes printed in pass books is to the effect that cheques paid in to a customer's credit cannot be drawn against until they are cleared.

Where a pass book is alleged to be lost, it is well to wait some time before granting a duplicate, as a further search by the customer will probably discover the book. When the book really cannot be found, the manager usually issues a new one ; it should be plainly marked "duplicate," and a note should be made against the account in the ledger, stating the reason why a duplicate has been given and the date of its issue, as well as a record made of the fact in the pass book register. Where a pass book is lost, some bankers require that an indemnity be given before a duplicate is issued.

In Scotland, the pass books, in some of the banks, are initialled on the payments-in side by both teller and ledger clerk, . nd in other banks by either the teller or a clerk. The amount paid in is entered in the pass book in writing as well as in figures.

The entries made in a pass book by a bank may be used in evidence against the bank. Where an entry showing a payment to a customer's credit has been made in a pass book in error, and the customer, relying upon that credit, has drawn cheques against it or in some other way altered his position, the banker will be bound by that entry. But if the customer's position has not been altered by the entry, the banker is at liberty to show that the entry was made by mistake.

An entry in a pass book in favour of a customer is *primâ facie* evidence against the banker, and an entry against a customer is *primâ facie* evidence against the customer after the pass book has been seen by the customer and returned to the bank without any comment being made.

In *Commercial Bank of Scotland* v. *Rhind* (1860, 3 Macq. H.L.R. 643), Lord Campbell said: "Considering that the pass book (as its name indicates) is a book which passes between the bankers and their customer, being alternately in the custody of each party, on proof of its having been in the custody of the customer, and returned by him to the bankers without objection being made to any of the entries by which the bankers are credited, I think such entries may be *primâ facie* evidence for the bankers as those on the other side are *primâ facie* evidence against them."

Where a mistake has been made the sooner it is rectified the better, as the length of time during which an erroneous entry remains in a pass book may be important. The longer a customer sees a certain amount standing to his credit, the more difficult it will be to prove that the customer has not altered his position on the strength of that credit. A banker is at liberty to show that a mistake has been made even if the entry in the pass book has been formally initialled by an official of the bank. But a banker is not, of course, excused from liability if he has received money for a customer and has omitted to give him credit for it.

When a customer obtains his pass book from the bank, keeps it in his possession for a certain time and then returns it to the bank without any comment, the ordinary conclusion is that the customer has examined the book and found it to be correct; but this view of the matter may not be the one which the Courts will take in such a case. For instance, in *Chatterton* v. *London and County Banking Co.* (1890, unreported), Lord Esher, M.R., expressed the opinion that a customer is not bound to examine his pass book. He said: "A hundred things may happen to prevent him from looking into it when he has got it, and what right has the bank to infer that he has looked into it."

In *Vagliano Brothers* v. *Bank of England* (1889, 23 Q.B.D. 243), where the plaintiff had received his pass book half-yearly along with the paid cheques, which cheques he retained, and returned the pass book to the bank without any remark, Bowen, L.J., in his judgment said: "There is another point to be considered. The plaintiff from time to time received from the bank his pass book, with entries debiting the payments made, for which the bank sent the bills as vouchers, which were retained by the plaintiff when he returned, without objection, the pass book. It was contended that this was a settlement of account between him and the bank, and that he had been guilty of such negligence with respect to the examination of the vouchers as would have prevented him from being relieved from this settlement of account. But there was no evidence to show what, as between a customer and his banker, is the implied contract as to the settlement of account by such a dealing with the pass book, or that, having regard to the ordinary course of dealing between a banker and his customers, the plaintiff had done anything which can be considered a neglect of his duty to the bank or negligence on his part."

With reference to the expression "settlement of account" in the above judgment, an account is considered to be a stated or settled account where the customer has given a definite confirmation of the correctness of the account, or where the account has been balanced and ruled off as is done in pass books at the end of each half-year. Some authorities consider that where a pass book is given out with the balance entered in the book in pencil it should be considered a settled account, but other authorities do not attach much importance to a pencilled balance and hold that it does not constitute a settled account.

In *Kepitigalla Rubber Estates, Ltd.* v. *The National Bank of India, Ltd.* (1909, 2 K.B. 1010), with reference to the point that when a pass book is taken out of the bank by a customer or some clerk of his, and is returned without objection there is a settled account between the bank and the customer by which both are bound, Mr. Justice Bray said: "I know of no authority in this country for this proposition." He further said, in commenting upon another case, that it would be absurd to "hold that the taking out of the pass book and its return constituted a settled account. It would mean this —that a secretary of a company by going to the bank for his own purposes in order to prevent the discovery of a fraud, and without knowledge on the part of any of the directors, and getting the pass book (with a pencil entry in it of the balance) can bind the company for all purposes."

A customer, however, will not be able successfully to object to the bank charges in his pass book if they are similar to those of previous half-years to which he never raised any objection when returning his pass book.

By 24 & 25 Vict. c. 98, Section 23, a false entry in a pass book with intent to defraud is forgery of an accountable receipt. And if a banker allows any entry in a company's pass book to be made by an official of the company, in order to mislead an auditor in the examination of the company's account, the banker may be held liable for any loss which the company may sustain.

Although the pass book has continued practically in its present form for a century, Sir John R. Paget states that "the present position of the pass book is perhaps the most unsatisfactory thing in the whole region of English banking law."

In view of the various unsatisfactory decisions from a banker's point of view and the uncertainty which, in so many ways, attaches to the entries in a pass book, the importance of having the book carefully and correctly written up cannot be too strongly insisted upon. A manager should give particular attention to pass books which have not been brought in to the bank for some time, and endeavour to obtain them for the purpose of being written up; and where pass books are allowed by customers to remain in the bank for a long period, it is advisable to hand them out as opportunity offers. A manager should aim at having as free a circulation of pass books as possible.

It may be of historical interest to mention that before pass books were introduced, it was the practice for a customer to come to the bank and personally examine his own account in the ledger, whereupon he signed his name under the withdrawal entries, while the banker certified the payments-in in a similar way.

PASS BOOK REGISTER. In many banks all pass books bear a distinctive number, and in the register a complete list of all the pass books supplied to a branch is entered, the numbers being shown in consecutive order. Whenever a new pass book is used, the date when it is commenced and the name of the account for which it is required are entered in the register against the same number as appears upon the pass book. In this way the pass book register corresponds to the book of counterfoils of deposit receipts.

PASSING A DIVIDEND. The expression means not paying a dividend, and is to be distinguished from "passing a resolution to pay a dividend."

PASSPORT. A passport is an official document issued by the Foreign Office vouching for the respectability of the person named therein, and which is used by that person when travelling in foreign countries.

The Foreign Office issues the following regulations respecting passports :—

1. Applications for Foreign Office passports must be made in the form printed on the back of these regulations, and inclosed in a cover addressed to "The Passport Department, Foreign Office, London, S.W." They must reach the Foreign Office before 5 p.m. on the day prior to that on which the passport is to be issued.

2. The charge for a passport, whatever number of persons may be named in it, is 2*s*. Passports are issued at the Foreign Office, between the hours of 11 and 4 on the day following that on which the application for the passport has been received, except on Sundays and Public Holidays, when the Passport Office is closed. If the applicant does not reside in London, the passport may be sent by post, and a postal order for 2*s*. should in that case accompany the application. Postage stamps will not be received in payment.

3. Foreign Office passports are granted—

(1) To natural-born British subjects, viz. persons born within His Majesty's Dominions, and to persons born abroad who derive British nationality from a father or paternal grandfather born within

His Majesty's Dominions, and who, under the provisions of the Acts 4 George II, c. 21, and 13 George III, c. 21 are to be adjudged and taken to be natural-born British subjects.

(2) To the wives and widows of such persons; and

(3) To persons naturalised in the United Kingdom, in the British Colonies, or in India.

A married woman is deemed to be a subject of the State of which her husband is for the time being a subject.

4. Passports are granted to such persons as are known to the Secretary of State, or recommended to him by some person who is known to him; or—

(1) In the case of natural-born British subjects and persons naturalised in the United Kingdom, upon the production of a declaration by the applicant in the form printed at the back of these regulations, verified by a declaration made by any banking firm established in the United Kingdom, or by any mayor, magistrate, justice of the peace, minister of religion, barrister-at-law, physician, surgeon, solicitor, or notary, resident in the United Kingdom. The applicant's certificate of birth may also be required in certain cases.

(2) In the case of children under the age of 14 years requiring a separate passport, upon production of a declaration made by the child's parent or guardian, in a Form (B), to be obtained upon application to the Foreign Office.

(3) In the case of persons naturalised in any of the British Colonies, upon production of a letter of recommendation from the Colonial Office; and in the case of natives of British India, and persons naturalised therein, upon production of a letter of recommendation from the India Office.

5. If the applicant for a passport be a naturalised British subject, the certificate of naturalisation must be forwarded to the Foreign Office with the declaration or letter of recommendation. Naturalised British subjects, if resident in London or in the suburbs, must apply *personally* for their passports at the Foreign Office; if resident in the country, the passport will be sent, and the certificate of naturalisation returned, to the person who may have verified the declaration, for delivery to the applicant.

Naturalised British subjects will be described as such in their passports, which will be issued subject to the necessary qualifications.

6. Foreign Office passports are not available beyond five years from the date of issue. Fresh passports must then be obtained.

7. A passport cannot be issued by the Foreign Office, or by an agent at an outport, on behalf of a person already abroad; such person should apply for one to the nearest British Mission or Consulate.

8. Travellers who intend to visit the Russian Empire, the Turkish Dominions, the Kingdom of Roumania, Persia, Colombia, Venezuela, Hayti, or Eritrea, in the course of their travels, must not leave the United Kingdom without having had their passports *visés* either at the Russian Consulate-General, 17, Great Winchester Street, E.C.; the Consulate-General of the Sublime Porte, 140, Leadenhall Street, E.C.; the Roumanian Consulate-General, 6, Moorgate Street, E.C.; the Persian Consulate-General, 122, Victoria Street, S.W.; the Colombian Consulate-General, 6, Holborn Viaduct, E.C.; the Venezuelan Consulate, Finsbury Pavement House, Finsbury Pavement, E.C.; the Haytian Consulate, 32, Fenchurch Street, E.C.; or the Italian Consulate-General (for Eritrea), 44, Finsbury Square, E.C., respectively, or at one of the other Consulates of those States in the United Kingdom. Travellers about to proceed to any other country need not obtain the *visa* of the diplomatic or consular agents of such country.

N.B.—A statement of the requirements of foreign countries with regard to passports may be obtained upon application to "The Passport Department, Foreign Office, London, S.W."

A specimen signature of the applicant is affixed to the passport when issued.

Recommendations from banking firms should bear the printed stamp of the bank.

The stamp duty upon a passport is sixpence.

To *visé* a passport is to have it examined and indorsed by a proper authority, as where an intending traveller in Russia or Turkey has it indorsed at the Russian or Turkish Consulate in London.

A passport is in the following form:—

No.

Stamp 6d.

This passport is not in any circumstance available beyond five years from the date of its issue. A fresh passport must then be obtained.

We Sir Edward Grey
a Baronet of the United Kingdom of Great Britain and Ireland, a member of His Britannic Majesty's Most Honourable Privy Council, a Member of Parliament, etc., etc., His Majesty's Principal Secretary of State for Foreign Affairs

Request and require, in the Name of His Majesty, all those whom it may concern to allow
to pass freely without let or hindrance and to afford every assistance and protection of which may stand in need.

Given at the Foreign Office, London, the day of 19 .

Age of Bearer
years.
Profession of Bearer
Signature of Bearer

Arms of Secretary.

Lithographed Signature of Secretary.

PAST DUE BILLS. When a bill is dishonoured by non-payment, a banker debits it to the account of the customer for whom it was discounted, and returns the bill to the customer; but if the account will not permit of its being so debited, the bill is charged to an account called "overdue bills" or "dishonoured bills" or "past due bills," and notice is given to the customer and to every other party to the bill, with a demand for immediate payment. Any balance in the customer's account may be held against the bill in part payment. (See BILL OF EXCHANGE, DISHONOUR OF BILL OF EXCHANGE.)

PAY DAY. Also known as settling day. The third day of the settlement on the London Stock Exchange, when the cash for a stock transaction is handed over by the purchaser to the seller and differences are settled. In most stocks, pay days occur twice a month, but in Consols, once only. (See SETTLING DAYS, STOCK EXCHANGE.)

PAYABLE AS PER INDORSEMENT. These words, or "exchange as per indorsement," are sometimes found on bills of exchange which are drawn, say, in this country in English money and are payable in a foreign country. The rate of exchange at which such a bill is first negotiated is indorsed on the bill and constitutes the rate at which it is payable.

PAYEE. The payee in a bill, or cheque, is the person named therein to whom, or to whose order, payment is directed to be made.

If the bill is payable to "John Brown or order," John Brown is the payee, and he should indorse it before the bill can be negotiated. When he has indorsed it—that is, has written his name upon the back—he is called an indorser.

Bills are frequently drawn "Pay to me or my order." In such bills the drawer and the payee are the same person, and the drawer must indorse the bill before negotiation. By Section 5, s.s. 1, of the Bills of Exchange Act, 1882, "A bill may be drawn payable to, or to the order of, the drawer; or it may be drawn payable to, or to the order of, the drawee."

Until a payee indorses a bill he is not liable thereon, but when he indorses it he incurs the liabilities of an indorser. (See INDORSER.)

The Bills of Exchange Act, 1882, Section 7, provides as follows :—

"(1) Where a bill is not payable to bearer, the payee must be named or otherwise indicated therein with reasonable certainty.

"(2) A bill may be made payable to two or more payees jointly, or it may be made payable in the alternative to one of two, or one or some of several payees. A bill may also be made payable to the holder of an office for the time being.

"(3) Where the payee is a fictitious or non-existing person the bill may be treated as payable to bearer."

When a person accepts a bill, he is precluded from denying to a holder in due course the existence of the payee and his then capacity to indorse. The acceptor is not, however, responsible for the genuineness or validity of the payee's indorsement.

Where a bill or cheque is payable to two or more payees who are not partners, all must indorse, unless there is an authority for one of them to sign for the others. If one of them is dead, payment may be made to the survivor on satisfactory proof of death.

Where a cheque payable to John Brown is presented over the counter by a stranger who represents himself to be the executor of Brown, the banker is entitled to ask for exhibition of the probate of Brown's will.

If a payee's name is misspelt, he should indorse the bill or cheque in precisely the same way, and add his proper signature below.

A cheque which is payable to "John Brown only" is not capable of being transferred to anyone else, as the word "only" cancels the negotiability of the instrument. A bill payable to "John Brown only" should not be discounted as, in the event of the bill being dishonoured, the banker could not sue upon it.

Where there are several payees and the bill is payable in the alternative to one or some, only those who actually indorse the bill are liable thereon.

If the payee is an infant, or corporation having no power to contract, the payee can indorse and effectually transfer the bill to another party, but such a payee will not be liable on the bill.

A banker is under no liability to the payee of a cheque, unless he has marked the cheque for payment, or in some other way given the payee to understand that the cheque will be paid. (See MARKED CHEQUE.)

In the case of a cheque drawn without a payee's name having been inserted, as "Pay or order," it is usually treated as being payable to the order of the drawer and, therefore, requiring his indorsement. It is not a banker's duty to advise a holder to insert his own name in the blank. If not indorsed by the drawer, the best course is to get the incomplete cheque completed by the drawer.

Where a payee is dead, his executors, or administrator, may indorse and negotiate the cheque, and the indorsement should show the capacity in which they sign.

As provided in Section 7, s.s. 3, a bill payable to a fictitious or non-existing payee may be treated as being payable to "bearer." In the *Bank of England* v. *Vagliano Brothers* (1891, A.C. 107) it was held that a fictitious or non-existing person included a *real* person who never had nor was intended to have any right to the bills. (See FICTITIOUS PAYEE.)

In Scotland, when the payee is a married woman, cheques are frequently made payable to, e.g. Mrs. Mary Burns or Scott, Burns being the maiden name and Scott the married name. The cheque may be indorsed either "Mary Burns" or "Mary Scott."

Where a cheque is payable to "Wages or order," "Cash or order," or "House Account or order," it should be treated as a cheque payable to the order of the drawer and be indorsed by him, as such words as "wages," "cash," etc., cannot be regarded as coming under Section 7, s.s. 3, which refers only to a fictitious or non-existing *person*.

Where a cheque is payable to "John Brown or order," and John Brown himself presents it at the counter for payment, it is the practice of bankers always to require it to be indorsed by Brown before payment can be made. It would appear, however, that, legally, a cheque when presented by the payee is payable to him without indorsement. Sir John R. Paget says: "The common practice of paying bankers to refuse payment unless the ostensible payee signs on the back of the cheque seems therefore without justification." The custom of always requiring the payee's indorsement on an order cheque should, however, not be departed from except perhaps in some unusual case when the payee insists on payment without indorsement. In such a case a banker might be able to postpone payment until he had communicated with the drawer. It is somewhat difficult to see how a banker could be held liable for refusing payment of a customer's cheque because the payee declined to indorse it in accordance with the custom of bankers. A banker's customer knows that it is the practice to require all cheques payable to order to be indorsed, and if, on receiving back his paid cheques, he found that a cheque which he had drawn payable to "John Brown or order" was not indorsed by John Brown, he might reasonably maintain that the cheque showed no evidence of ever having been in the hands of John Brown, and that he was entitled to have that evidence.

If a cheque payable to, say, the British Baking Company, Ltd., is paid to credit of the manager's or secretary's private account, it should put the banker on inquiry at once, as he may be held liable if the cheque has been misappropriated. If it is necessary for agents, as, for instance, in the case of insurance companies, to place to the credit of their private accounts cheques which are payable to their principals, the banker should be duly authorised in writing by the principals to permit of cheques being dealt with in that way.

In the case of a dividend warrant where several payees are named, it is the custom to pay upon the indorsement of one of them; but an interest warrant should, strictly, be indorsed by all the payees, though this is not always done in practice. (See BILL OF EXCHANGE, CHEQUE, INDORSEMENT.)

PAYING BANKER. The banker upon whom a cheque is drawn, or at whose office a bill is accepted, and who pays it, either to the holder or to a collecting banker, is called the paying banker.

It is the duty of a paying banker to pay the cheques of his customer so long as he has sufficient funds belonging to his customer to enable him to do so. Before paying a cheque a banker must, of course, examine it to see that it is properly signed, that the indorsements are correct and, generally, that the cheque is in order.

In the case of bills domiciled with a banker it is part of his duty either from custom or by instructions of his customer, to pay them, though he is otherwise not legally bound to do so as in the case of a cheque. The paying banker is the drawee of a cheque, and therefore a party to it, but he is not a party to a bill which is merely domiciled with him.

If a drawer's or an acceptor's signature is forged, a banker cannot debit his customer's account with the cheque or bill.

With regard to indorsements the position of the paying banker is :—

BILL.—He cannot debit his customer's account with a bill bearing a forged indorsement. The Bills of Exchange Act does not give him any relief from a forged indorsement on a bill.

CHEQUE.—If a banker pays a cheque in good faith and in the ordinary course of business, he is protected against a forged indorsement by Section 60 of the Bills of Exchange Act, 1882. (See PAYMENT OF BILL.)

Sir John R. Paget suggests in his "Law of Banking" (page 60), that a cheque which contains a restriction that it is payable only if presented within a specified period may not be included under the term cheque, as defined by the Bills of Exchange Act.

Cheque payable on condition that a form of receipt is signed.—The banker is protected by Section 17 of the Revenue Act, 1883, if paid to the *payee*. It is not considered a transferable document. (See RECEIPT ON CHEQUE.)

Cheque crossed "account payee."—The words "account payee" do not concern the paying banker, so long as he pays to a banker in accordance with the crossing. He is protected as in the case of an ordinary crossed cheque.

Cheque crossed "not negotiable."—The words "not negotiable" do not affect the paying banker. The cheque is treated as an ordinary crossed cheque, and the banker is protected accordingly.

Crossed Cheque.—The banker is protected by Section 80 of the Bills of Exchange Act (see CROSSED CHEQUE), when he pays a cheque, crossed generally, to a banker, or crossed specially to the banker to whom it is crossed or his agent for collection being a banker.

DRAFTS (which are not cheques).—The banker is protected against a forged indorsement on a draft on demand by Section 19 of the Stamp Act, 1853. (See DRAFT ON DEMAND.) (See CHEQUE, COLLECTING BANKER, PAYMENT OF CHEQUE.)

PAYING-IN SLIPS. Paying-in slips, or credit vouchers, are the forms which are filled up showing the amount of gold, silver, copper, notes, bills, and cheques which are paid in to the credit of a customer's account. Each slip should be signed by the customer, or the person who has prepared it on his behalf. The name of the account should be distinctly stated and the date should be that of the actual date on which the money is paid in. Any alteration in the date or amount should be duly initialled by the person signing the voucher. It is usual for the cashier receiving the credit to initial the voucher, and sometimes he also initials, or stamps with a rubber stamp, a duplicate slip, or, if a book of credit slips is used by the customer, the counterfoil, as an acknowledgment to the customer that the cash, etc., has been duly received. A cashier's initials upon the counterfoil or duplicate voucher does not in any way mean that the cheques and bills included in it are in order. Some banks enter undue bills on the same slip as cash and cheques, but it is much better to enter them on a separate form.

Credit slips vary somewhat in form. Some are printed lengthways, like cheques, whilst others are printed across the slip.

On page 388 is a specimen form of credit slip for use at the British Banking Company, Ltd., Leeds

It is seen that a place is provided for the folio of the customer's account in the ledger. Gold, silver, copper, and notes are shown separately. The cheques are separated into three divisions, Leeds, London, and Country, Postal Orders being included with the local cheques on Leeds banks. If a separate slip is not used for undue bills, they could be detailed on the back of the credit slip and entered in total below "Country cheques." There is a space provided on which the person paying in may sign, and a place for the initials of the receiving cashier.

A slight variation in the printing is usually adopted for slips to be used by a person paying in at one branch for the credit of an account at another branch, or at another bank; frequently such slips are further distinguished by being of a particular colour. There are also many different forms of slips in use by different firms and companies, which are used by their agents all over the country in paying in for their credit in London, or wherever the account is kept.

If Jones pays in at the British Bank, Leeds, various cheques for the credit of the Universal Bread Co. at the Hull branch of that bank, and one of the cheques should be dishonoured, the Leeds branch will debit the Hull branch with the amount of the unpaid cheque and send the cheque to Hull, and Hull will pass it on to the Bread Co.

Some bankers print upon their paying-in slips a notice that cheques, etc., for collection, though credited to the account when paid in, are not available for drawing against until the proceeds have been received at the branch.

Where Jones pays in country cheques to the credit of another customer's account, it is usual for the banker, when advising that customer of the receipt of the credit, to state that it consists of cheques which have not yet been cleared.

Where an official of a company pays in to the credit of the company's account, cheques payable to the company, it is not permissible for the official to receive part of the amount back in cash by simply making a deduction on the credit slip. A banker can pay out only when a cheque is drawn upon the account in the authorised way.

Credit slips should be retained by a banker and not be given up to a customer along with paid cheques.

The paying-in slips used by depositors are called "application forms."

PAYMENT BY. BILL.—Where an undue bill is taken in payment of a debt, the debtor cannot be sued for the debt until the bill is due and is dishonoured; that is, the creditor's right to sue for the debt is, by

Gold ....
Silver ....
Copper .....
Notes ......

Total Cash.

Cheques.

£

For Credit of

at the British Banking Company, Ltd., Leeds.

Paid in by ....
Received by ....
Date ....19 . .

Bank Ledger Folio.

Gold . . . .
Silver . . . .
Copper . . . .
Notes . . . .

Total Cash . .

Leeds Cheques and P.O.'s.

Country Cheques

London Cheques.

Total—Leeds Cheques and Postal Orders . .
„ —London Cheques . . . .
„ —Country Cheques . . . .

£

To the British Banking Company, Ltd., Leeds.
Credit the account of
....
Paid in by ....
Received by .... Date................ ..19 .

taking the bill, postponed till the maturity of the bill.

In the event of the acceptor's bankruptcy, the holder of a bill which is not yet due may prove upon the estate subject to a rebate of interest at the rate of 5 per cent. per annum from the time when the dividend is declared to the date when the bill would be due. (Bankruptcy Act, 1883, Schedule 2, Rule 21.)

CHEQUE.—When a cheque is taken in settlement of a debt and the cheque is dishonoured, the debt is not discharged, unless the person receiving the cheque did not present it for payment within a reasonable time.

COUNTRY BANK NOTES (*q.v.*).

PAYMENT FOR HONOUR. When an acceptor fails to pay a bill at maturity, any person may, after the bill has been protested, pay it suprà protest for the honour of some party to the bill.

The regulations regarding payment for honour suprà protest are contained in Section 68 of the Bills of Exchange Act, 1882, which is as follows :—

"(1) Where a bill has been protested for non-payment, any person may intervene and pay it suprà protest for the honour of any party liable thereon, or for the honour of the person for whose account the bill is drawn.

"(2) Where two or more persons offer to pay a bill for the honour of different parties, the person whose payment will discharge most parties to the bill shall have the preference.

"(3) Payment for honour suprà protest, in order to operate as such and not as a mere voluntary payment, must be attested by a notarial act of honour, which may be appended to the protest or form an extension of it.

"(4) The notarial act of honour must be founded on a declaration made by the payer for honour, or his agent in that behalf, declaring his intention to pay the bill for honour, and for whose honour he pays.

"(5) Where a bill has been paid for honour, all parties subsequent to the party for whose honour it is paid are discharged, but the payer for honour is subrogated for, and succeeds to both the rights and duties of, the holder as regards the party for whose honour he pays, and all parties liable to that party.

"(6) The payer for honour on paying to the holder the amount of the bill and the notarial expenses incidental to its dishonour is entitled to receive both the bill itself and the protest. If the holder do not on demand deliver them up he shall be liable to the payer for honour in damages.

"(7) Where the holder of a bill refuses to receive payment suprà protest he shall lose his right of recourse against any party who would have been discharged by such payment."

(See ACCEPTANCE FOR HONOUR, BILL OF EXCHANGE.)

PAYMENT OF BILL. A bill of exchange is, in the usual course of events, paid by the acceptor, and when so paid it is discharged and the bill delivered up to him. The Bills of Exchange Act, 1882, provides :—

"Section 59. (1) A bill is discharged by payment in due course by or on behalf of the drawee or acceptor. "'Payment in due course' means payment made at or after the maturity of the bill to the holder thereof in good faith and without notice that his title to the bill is defective.

"(2) Subject to the provisions hereinafter contained, when a bill is paid by the drawer or an indorser it is not discharged ; but

"(*a*) Where a bill payable to, or to the order of, a third party is paid by the drawer, the drawer may enforce payment thereof against the acceptor, but may not re-issue the bill.

"(*b*) Where a bill is paid by an indorser, or where a bill payable to drawer's order is paid by the drawer, the party paying it is remitted to his former rights as regards the acceptor or antecedent parties, and he may, if he thinks fit, strike out his own and subsequent indorsements, and again negotiate the bill.

"(3) Where an accommodation bill is paid in due course by the party accommodated the bill is discharged."

The following Section particularly concerns bankers with respect to "a bill on demand drawn on a banker":—

"60. When a bill payable to order on demand is drawn on a banker, and the banker on whom it is drawn pays the bill in good faith and in the ordinary course of business, it is not incumbent on the banker to show that the indorsement of the payee or any subsequent indorsement was made by or under the authority of the person whose indorsement it purports to be, and the banker is deemed to have paid the bill in due course, although such indorsement has been forged or made without authority."

"Section 61. When the acceptor of a bill is or becomes the holder of it at or after its maturity, in his own right, the bill is discharged."

"Section 62. (1) When the holder of a bill at or after its maturity absolutely and unconditionally renounces his rights against the acceptor the bill is discharged.

"The renunciation must be in writing, unless the bill is delivered up to the acceptor.

"(2) The liabilities of any party to a bill may in like manner be renounced by the holder before, at, or after its maturity; but nothing in this Section shall affect the rights of a holder in due course without notice of the renunciation."

If an acceptor pays the amount of a bill before it arrives at maturity, he may, should he wish to do so, re-issue the bill, because, being paid before it is due, it is not discharged. If he does not wish to re-issue the bill, he should cancel or destroy it, for if, by any means, the bill should come into the hands of a holder in due course, before it matures, that holder will have a right of action against the acceptor and all other parties to the bill.

When a bill payable on demand is paid, it is discharged and cannot be re-issued; and when a bill payable after date is paid at or after maturity it also is discharged and cannot be re-issued.

No right of action can be maintained on a discharged bill, though the right to sue upon the consideration may still continue.

If an acceptor pays only a part of the amount of a bill at maturity, the part payment is a discharge to that extent, and the banker should place a receipt for the amount paid upon the back of the bill and qualify the receipt by adding that the part payment is accepted by him without prejudice to the rights of any of the other parties to the bill. Notice of the part payment should be given to the other parties. The bill itself is not, of course, given up against a part payment.

In the case of part payment of a foreign bill, the bill must be protested for the balance.

A bill should not, as a rule, be given up to an acceptor when, on presenting the bill to him for payment, he offers anything except cash or notes. If a cheque, which can be collected the same day, is offered, the bill should be retained until cash has been received for the cheque, but a cheque which cannot be cashed the same day should not be taken. It is necessary to bear in mind that if a cheque is taken in payment of a bill and the cheque is subsequently returned unpaid, the banker will have lost recourse against the various parties to the bill and will have only the acceptor to look to for the money. London bankers accept cheques upon clearing bankers in payment of bills, the cheques being attached to the bills and passed at once through the Clearing House.

If a bill drawn on John Brown, Leeds, payable at sight, contains a note on the bill that it is "payable in London," and John Brown wishes to pay the bill in Leeds when presented to him, he must bear any cost there may be in transmitting the money to London as the holder of the bill is entitled to have the full amount paid in London.

Where a bill indorsed to the holder by the bank at which the acceptor had made it payable, was paid by the bank at maturity and dishonoured on the following day it was held (in *Pollard* v. *Ogden*, 1853, 2 E. & B. 459), that the bank had paid the bill in their capacity as indorsers, and that they reserved to themselves the right to examine into the state of the acceptor's accounts and determine whether they would honour the bill or not. Mr. Justice Erle said: "I think it is clear law that the holder of a bill indorsed to him by a bank at which the acceptor has made it payable may, if the bank choose to dishonour the bill, receive payment forthwith from the bankers in their capacity as indorsers. . . . The bank might have said to the holder 'we require a reasonable time to examine into the state of the accounts between us and the acceptor before we either honour or dishonour this bill; but in case we determine to dishonour it we shall be liable to you as indorsers; therefore, to save trouble, take your money; if we honour the bill you are paid; if not, we are taking it up as indorsers of a dishonoured bill.' "

A banker may, as is the custom with London bankers, debit a bill to an acceptor's account, when payable at that banker's, without requiring any advice from the acceptor, the acceptance being a sufficient authority, but in practice, many country bankers usually require an advice. Country bankers often receive from an acceptor periodically a list of his bills falling due and an order to pay them.

A banker is not obliged to pay a bill after his usual hours of business.

If an acceptor in good faith pays a bill indorsed in blank and without notice of any defect there may be in the title, the bill is discharged; but if the acceptor pays a bill which has been specially indorsed and the indorsement should prove to have been forged, the bill is not discharged by such payment and the acceptor is liable to pay it again to the true owner.

In *Bank of England* v. *Vagliano Brothers* (1891, A.C. 107), Lord Macnaghten said: "In paying their customers' acceptances in the usual way bankers incur a risk perfectly understood, and in practice disregarded. Bankers have no recourse against their customers if they pay on a genuine bill to a person appearing to be the holder, but claiming through or under a forged indorsement. The bill is not discharged; the acceptor remains liable; the banker has simply thrown his money away."

If the acceptor fails to pay a trade bill at maturity and an indorser or the drawer pays it, the bill is not discharged by such payment, and the drawer can sue the acceptor for the amount plus expenses and interest, and the indorser can sue the acceptor or any prior parties.

But if a bill is an accommodation bill and is not met by the acceptor when due, it is, if paid by the drawer or indorser, discharged, when the party paying it is the person for whose accommodation the bill was drawn or accepted.

If an acceptor or any other person pays to a banker an amount for the special purpose of providing for a bill falling due, that amount is earmarked for that purpose and cannot be used by the banker for any other purpose, such as to reduce an overdraft which the acceptor may have.

Where a person accepts a bill payable at a banker's where he has no account, the banker is under no obligation to receive money from the acceptor with which to pay the bill.

Where a bill is intentionally cancelled by the holder or his agent, and the cancellation is apparent thereon, the bill is discharged.

It is not necessary, on payment of a bill by the acceptor, to give a receipt for the money, as the delivering up of the bill to the acceptor is sufficient to cancel his liability upon it, but if, as is sometimes done, a receipt is indorsed upon the bill by the holder the receipt (except in the case of a banker) requires to be stamped 1*d.* in the same way as any ordinary receipt.

Where the holder of a bill is bankrupt, payment of the bill requires to be made to the trustee and not to the bankrupt.

Where the holder is dead payment must be made to the executor or administrator.

If, instead of payment, a holder accepts a fresh bill from the acceptor, the drawer and indorsers of the old bill will be discharged, unless they are parties to the new bill.

When a banker is employed to collect a bill, he should not, unless under instructions from his correspondent, accept payment subject to any conditions, otherwise he may render himself liable for the amount of the bill.

With respect to a bill paid under rebate, see DOCUMENTARY BILL.

If a banker wrongfully dishonours an acceptance of his customer he will be liable in damages. (See DISHONOUR OF BILL OF EXCHANGE.) He should, therefore, be careful to see that everything has been credited to the account and that the balance is correctly stated, before returning a bill.

If a banker pays a bill across the counter, and, as soon as he has done so, finds that he should not have paid it, he cannot compel the person to whom he paid the money to return it, though if a mistake is made by handing too much money to the customer the mistake may be rectified. (See BILL OF EXCHANGE, CANCELLATION OF BILL OF EXCHANGE, PAYMENT OF CHEQUE, TIME OF PAYMENT OF BILL.)

PAYMENT OF CHEQUE. When an open cheque is presented for payment it requires to be carefully scrutinised to see that everything is in order. If the account upon which the cheque is drawn will admit of its payment, the banker, before paying it, must be satisfied that it bears the signature of his customer, or of the person who may have been authorised by his customer to sign, and that payment of the cheque has not been stopped by the drawer. If it is a cheque payable to order, all the indorsements must be scanned to see that they are apparently correct. It should also be noticed whether the cheque is post-dated or is stale dated, whether the amount in writing agrees with the amount in figures, and whether, if any alteration has been made in the cheque, such alteration is duly initialled by the drawer, or drawers. On being satisfied that all these various points are in order, and that there is no other reason why the cheque should not be paid, the banker may, if the person presenting the cheque appears, so far as he can tell, to be entitled to it, pay the cheque.

If a banker dishonours a cheque which ought to be paid he will be liable in damages.

When paying a crossed cheque to another banker practically the same points require to be observed and in addition the nature of the crossing. (See CROSSED CHEQUE.)

When a cheque is presented for payment, a banker is required either to pay it or dishonour it. If everything is in order he is obliged to pay it, or stand the consequences of wrongfully refusing to pay.

It is possible for everything connected with a cheque to be absolutely correct and yet the cashier who has to pay it may have a strong suspicion that the person presenting it is not entitled to it. Lord Halsbury in *Vagliano Bros.* v. *Bank of England* (1891, A.C. 107), said: "I can well imagine that on a person presenting himself, whose appearance and demeanour was calculated to raise a suspicion that he was not likely to be entrusted with a valuable document for which he was to receive payment in cash, I should think it would be extremely probable that, whether the document were a cheque payable to bearer for a large amount or a bill, the counter clerk and banker alike would hesitate very much before making payment."

When a cheque has a notice upon it that it must be presented for payment within a certain fixed time from the date of the cheque, the banker must see that the time has not expired before paying the cheque.

Where a customer has two accounts with the same bank, one at Branch A and another at Branch B, and both are credit accounts, the banker at Branch A, when a cheque drawn upon his Branch is presented, is not obliged to take into consideration a balance at any other Branch than his own. If, however, the account at Branch B is overdrawn and at Branch A is in credit, a banker may, if necessary, regard them as one account. (See BRANCHES.)

A banker at Branch A is not obliged, before dishonouring a cheque, to ascertain, by wire or otherwise, if the customer has paid in at Branch B on that day for his credit at A, even though the customer is in the habit of paying in at B.

It is very necessary, before paying a cheque, that the banker should be fully satisfied that it ought to be paid, because, as soon as he hands the money across the counter, the ownership in that money passes from the banker to the person presenting the cheque, and, unless the presenter is willing to repay, the banker cannot obtain it back, even if he discovers immediately that the money should not have been handed over. Chief Justice Erle in *Chambers* v. *Miller* (1862, 13 C.B.N.S. 125), said: "The bankers' clerk chose to pay the cheque; and the moment the person presenting the cheque put his hand upon the money it became irrevocably his."

Where a banker has given his agent orders to pay certain cheques, or cheques up to a fixed amount, on behalf of a customer, the cheques, when paid, are debited to the customer's account on the day they are received by the banker, but the interest on the account is reckoned as though the cheques had been debited on the actual date when they were paid by the banker's agent.

Where a cheque for, say, £20 is presented for payment and the drawer has only £19 to credit, and the banker refuses payment, the presenter should not be told how much is short in order to enable him to pay in the pound and thus obtain payment. But if the presenter ascertains the amount from some other source, the banker cannot refuse to accept the sum for his customer's credit, even if paid in by the person who immediately thereafter presents the cheque for £20.

When a banker learns that a customer is dead or has committed an act of bankruptcy, or has had a receiving order made against him, or has become insane, he must not pay any further cheques on the account, but return them to the presenter with answer written upon them "Drawer deceased," "Drawer ban rupt," etc.

If an uncrossed cheque is presented over the counter, at the branch upon which it is drawn, by the payee, and the cashier knows that the presenter is an undischarged bankrupt, the cheque should not be cashed to him. If a banker, with knowledge that the presenter is an undischarged bankrupt, pays such a cheque, he may be called upon to pay the money over again to the trustee in bankruptcy.

In cases where a cheque has a bill attached, if the cheque specifically refers to the bill, the banker must see that the bill, as well as the cheque, is in order; but if the cheque does not allude to the bill the cheque must be dealt with, without regard to the bill.

Cheques must be paid in the order in which they are presented. A cheque which arrives in the morning's letters must be paid, if the account will admit of it, and must not be dishonoured in order to admit of a cheque presented across the counter later in the day being paid.

Where several cheques arrive by letter and the account will not admit of payment of them all, a banker usually pays as many of them as he can and returns the rest. Nevertheless, as all the cheques form one presentment, it is probable that the banker might not be wrong in considering merely the total of the amounts, and not the individual amounts, and returning all the cheques if the total amount was in excess of the balance.

Before returning a cheque a banker should make certain that everything has been credited to the account and that the balance is stated correctly, for if he wrongfully dishonours a cheque of his customer he will be liable in damages. (See DISHONOUR OF BILL OF EXCHANGE.)

With respect to cheques which a customer has paid in, but which the banker has not yet cleared, it forms a matter of arrangement between the banker and the customer as to whether, or not, they are to be considered as definitely placed to the customer's credit and so available as funds in hand wherewith to meet any of the customer's own cheques which may be presented, and it is very advisable to have a definite understanding on the point. Subject to whatever arrangement has been made between himself and his customer, the banker will either pay such cheques or return them unpaid with answer marked thereon "Effects not cleared."

A banker who, in good faith and in the ordinary course of business, pays a cheque drawn on himself, is protected by Section 60 of the Bills of Exchange Act, 1882 (the section is recited under PAYMENT OF BILL), even though an indorsement proves to have been forged or made without authority. A banker who pays a crossed cheque, in accordance with Section 80, is protected against a forged indorsement. (See that Section under CROSSED CHEQUE.)

A banker is not obliged to pay a cheque out of bank hours. In fact, if he does so, he runs the risk of paying a cheque, payment of which may be "stopped" by the drawer as soon as the bank doors are opened for business.

With respect to cheques drawn upon another banker or on a branch of the same bank in another town, which are presented by a person whom the banker does not know, see COLLECTING BANKER.

Cheques received through the Clearing must be paid or dishonoured on the day of receipt; cheques paid to credit which are drawn upon the same bank may be returned unpaid on the following day, but in practice all cheques are either paid or dishonoured on the day they are received. (See DISHONOUR OF BILL OF EXCHANGE.)

By Section 75 of Bills of Exchange Act, 1882:—

"The duty and authority of a banker to pay a cheque drawn on him by his customer are determined by—

"(1) Countermand of payment;

"(2) Notice of the customer's death."

It is desirable that a countermand of payment of a cheque should be in writing and be signed by the drawer, and if the countermand is subsequently cancelled it also should be in writing.

In *Curtice v. London City and Midland Bank* (1907, reported as to the proceedings in the Divisional Court at 23 T.L.R. 594, and in the Court of Appeal at 1908, 1 K.B. 293), the plaintiff sent a telegram to the Bank requesting them not to pay a certain cheque. The telegram was sent after hours and was put in the bank letter box. The telegram was overlooked when clearing the letter box next morning, and was not actually received till the following morning. In the meantime the cheque had been paid. The County Court Judge held that a banker receiving a telegram purporting to stop a cheque disregarded it at his peril. He found that the cheque was countermanded and gave judgment for plaintiff. The defendants appealed to the Divisional Court, and Mr. Justice Darling said that a telegram directing the bank not to pay a cheque, which in fact came from a customer of the bank, was a sufficient countermand of payment, and that, on the other hand, if it did not come from a customer it was not an order at all. He therefore held that a telegram might be a sufficient countermand of payment, and he was strengthened in that opinion because a witness from Hoare's bank said that a large proportion of the countermanding of payment of cheques was done by telegrams. Mr. Justice A. T. Lawrence thought that merely sending or receiving a telegram, without the reading of it, was not sufficient. Until the telegram was read it was not in fact a countermand of payment. Mr. Justice Lawrence withdrew his opinion, and the appeal was dismissed. The defendants appealed to the Court of Appeal, and the Master of the Rolls said: "The question in this appeal is whether a cheque drawn by the plaintiff upon his bankers, the defendants, was countermanded within the meaning of Section 75 of the Bills of Exchange Act, 1882, by reason of a telegram despatched by the plaintiff to the bank. . . . Countermand is really a question of fact. It means much more than a change of purpose on the part of the customer. It means, in addition, the notification of that change of purpose to the bank. There is no such thing as a constructive countermand in a commercial transaction of this kind. In my opinion, on the admitted facts of this case, the cheque was not countermanded in fact, although it may well be that it was due to the negligence of the bank that they did not receive notice of the customer's desire to stop the cheque. For such negligence the bank might be liable, but the measure of damage would be by no means the same as in an action for money had and received. I agree with the judgment of Mr. Justice Lawrence on this point, and that is sufficient to dispose of the appeal. But as we have had an argument addressed to us as to the effect upon the duty of a bank of the mere receipt of a telegram, I wish to add a few words. A telegram may reasonably and in the ordinary course of business be acted upon by the bank, at least to the extent of postponing the honouring of the cheque until further inquiry can be made. But I am not satisfied that the bank is bound as a matter of law to accept an unauthenticated telegram as sufficient authority for the serious step of refusing to pay a cheque. The appeal must be allowed." (See BILL OF EXCHANGE, CHEQUE, COLLECTING BANKER, PAYING BANKER, PAYMENT OF BILL.)

PAYMENT STOPPED (CHEQUE). A customer has the right to give notice to his banker to stop payment of a cheque which he has issued. The notice should be in writing, give accurate particulars of the cheque and be signed by the drawer.

If a banker pays a cheque after a "stop order" has been received, he will be liable for so doing. It is necessary, therefore, to warn each branch where the cheque may be presented of the notice which has been received. A notice should be placed in the customer's account in the ledger, so that anyone referring to the account may at once observe particulars of the "stop." A list of all orders to stop payment should be kept in some convenient form for ready reference by those officials who are concerned with the payment of cheques.

The drawer of a cheque is the only person who can "stop payment" of it, but bankers often receive notice from the holder of a cheque that it has been lost or stolen. Where notice is received from a holder, he should be requested to obtain at once written instructions from the drawer. If the cheque be presented before a communication is received from the drawer, the banker will be careful to postpone payment till he has heard from the drawer or is otherwise satisfied, particularly if the payee states that it was not indorsed by him before he lost it.

If the cheque which is lost is signed by several persons, a notice from one of them, e.g. one executor, one trustee, a secretary, etc., is usually acted upon by a banker. Where the account is in several names and the lost cheque is signed only by, say, one of the account holders, or by one partner, a notice from any of the other holders or partners is sufficient authority to a banker to justify him in stopping payment of the cheque.

When the drawer wishes to cancel his order to stop payment, it should be done in writing and be signed by him.

When a drawer wishes to stop payment of a cheque, he is entitled to do so during the usual business hours, and if a banker pays a cheque before the commencement of business or after the doors are closed, he incurs the risk of paying a cheque which may be "stopped" as soon as the drawer has the opportunity.

With regard to stopping payment of a cheque by telegram, the Master of the Rolls (see *Curtice v. London City and Midland Bank*, under PAYMENT OF CHEQUE), considered that a telegram might reasonably be acted upon to the extent of postponing payment of a cheque pending inquiry, but he was not satisfied that the bank is bound to accept an unauthenticated telegram as sufficient authority upon which to refuse to pay a cheque.

If a banker agrees to pay a cheque, at the request of the holder, by marking or accepting it for payment, or if, in answer to a telegram or a telephone, he replies that the cheque will be paid, he must pay the cheque when presented. But if, in the meantime, the drawer has stopped payment of it, the banker cannot charge it to the drawer's account. (See further information under MARKED CHEQUE.)

Although a drawer has the right to stop payment of a cheque drawn by him, yet if the payee has negotiated the cheque, any subsequent| *bonâ fide* holder for value can sue the drawer, provided that the cheque was not crossed "not negotiable." (See COUNTERMAND OF PAYMENT, LOST BILL OF EXCHANGE.)

PAYMENT STOPPED (NOTES). A banker cannot refuse payment of his own notes. A holder for value without notice that the note has been lost or stolen may compel the banker to pay it, but where a note is presented, payment of which has been stopped, a banker should exercise the utmost care and make full inquiries before cashing it.

The Bank of England makes a charge of 2*s.* 6*d.* for registering a notice to stop payment of a note.

PAYMENTS. Bankers receive instructions from customers to make payments of various kinds, e.g. payments for calls, for subscriptions, for credit of another customer, or another bank, payments in exchange for documents, etc.

In each case a proper written authority is taken from the customer and the instructions contained therein should be carefully observed. A record should be kept in the diary of all future payments, so that they may not be overlooked. (See APPLICATION PAYMENTS, AUTHORITIES, BANKER'S ORDER.)

PAYMENTS UNDER PROTEST. (See PROTEST PAYMENTS.)

PAYMENTS UPON APPLICATION. (See APPLICATION PAYMENTS.)

PENNI. (See FOREIGN MONEYS—FINLAND.)

PENNY. A silver penny is now issued only as Maundy money (*q.v.*). Its standard weight is 7·27272 grains troy.

At one time silver pennies were frequently cut into halves and quarters to act as halfpence and farthings.

A bronze penny is a mixed metal of copper, tin, and zinc. Its standard weight is 145·83333 grains troy. The bronze coinage was first issued in 1860.

Three new pennies weigh exactly one ounce avoirdupois, and are useful as a substitute for a lost letter weight. (See COINAGE.)

PEPPERCORN-RENT. A peppercorn-rent—that is, a purely nominal rent—is occasionally to be found mentioned in certain deeds. In some cases the peppercorn is actually handed over and duly recorded as having been paid.

PER CAPITA. (See PER STIRPES.)

PER PROCURATION. Where an agent signs, per procuration of, per pro., or p.p., it means that he holds an authority to sign on behalf of his principal. The Bills of Exchange Act, 1882, Section 25, provides as follows:—"A signature by procuration operates as notice that the agent has but a limited authority to sign, and the principal is only bound by such signature if the agent in so signing was acting within the actual limits of his authority." An agent is not personally liable if he signs for or on behalf of his principal, but the mere addition to his signature of words describing him as an agent does not exempt him from personal liability.

The usual form of a per procuration signature is:

per pro. John Brown,
J. Jones.

or

p.p. John Brown,
J. Jones.

In Scotland, the agent's name often comes first and the principal's last, as—

J. Jones per pro. John Brown.

A banker is protected by Section 60 in paying an uncrossed cheque with a per pro. indorsement in the event of its being unauthorised. If the banker on whom the cheque is drawn pays it in good faith and in the ordinary course of business, it is not incumbent on the banker to show that the indorsement was made by or under the authority of the person whose indorsement it purports to be, and the banker is deemed to have paid the bill in due course, although such indorsement is made without authority.

It is the custom amongst bankers to accept per pro. indorsements, and they are justified in doing so both by that Section and the result of the case *Charles* v. *Blackwell* (1877, 2 C.P.D. 151), where it was decided that a banker is not liable if he pays a cheque payable to order which is indorsed per pro., even when the person signing had not the authority of the principal.

But if a banker has reason to suspect the authority of a person so signing, he is, no doubt, entitled to ask for evidence of his authority. For instance, if a collecting agent for an insurance company were to present cheques payable to the insurance company, indorsed by him per pro. the company, and demand cash for them, the banker would render himself liable if he paid them without authority from the company, because it is not the custom for cheques payable to a company to be cashed by an agent.

An agent may have authority to indorse cheques per pro. and to place them to the credit of his principal's account, but he may not have power to take cash for cheques so indorsed, or credit them to his own account. A person may have power to draw cheques per pro., or to draw only to a limited extent, though he may not be authorised to accept bills drawn upon his principal. It is, therefore, necessary, not only to be satisfied that an agent has authority to draw cheques per pro., but to know the precise extent and limitations of his authority.

Some bankers consider that a per procuration signature should include the words per pro. or words having the same meaning, but Sir John R. Paget states that "whenever a signature shows by its form that it is put on by someone as deputy for another that signature must be treated as a per pro. signature, and puts anyone dealing with the bill on inquiry as to the authority of the person who so utilises the signature."

A company's signature in the following form,

The Universal Bread Co., Ltd.,
J. Brown, Secretary,

or

For and on behalf of the X and Y Co., Ltd.
J. Brown, Secretary.

is in effect a procuration signature, though per pro. or p.p. are not used.

It is not impossible for a marksman to have power to sign per pro., but it makes an awkward arrangement, and such a signature should usually be confirmed.

A firm may have power to sign for a private individual, as

per pro. John Brown
J. Jones & Co.

A person who has power to sign per procuration has not, as a rule, any power to delegate his authority to another.

Per procuration signatures are not accepted upon dividend warrants, or interest warrants. Cheques which require a form of receipt to be signed by the payee have sometimes a note upon them to the effect that a per procuration discharge will be accepted if guaranteed by the payee's bankers, and that in the case of a company the receipt must be signed on its behalf by an authorised officer whose position must be stated.

An indorsement "For J. Brown & Co., Ltd., J. Jones, Secretary," "For John Brown, J. Jones, Agent," is often accepted as sufficient. The person signing should state in what capacity he signs. As to the stamp duty on a deed of procuration, see PROCURATION. (See AGENT, AUTHORITIES, INDORSEMENT.)

PER STIRPES. Short for *per stirpes et non per capita*, meaning by the roots and not by the heads. An example of the use of the phrase is where John Brown leaves a sum of money to be equally divided amongst his, say, four sons, and if any son dies before the testator the share of that deceased son to be equally divided amongst the children of that deceased son. The children divide, therefore, merely the share of their deceased parent, or *per stirpes*, and do not take, each of them, an equal share of the full sum of money left by John Brown—that is, not *per capita*.

PERMANENT BUILDING SOCIETY. A society which has not, by its rules, any fixed date or specified result at which it shall terminate. (See BUILDING SOCIETY.)

PERPETUAL ANNUITY. The right to an annual payment of a certain sum in perpetuity. The purchaser cannot obtain the principal back, but he can sell his right to the annual payment to someone else. The interest on the National Debt is an example of a perpetual annuity. (See ANNUITY.)

PERPETUAL DEBENTURE. Section 103 of the Companies (Consolidation) Act,

1908, states that a condition contained in any debentures or in any deed for securing any debentures, shall not be invalid by reason only that the debentures are made irredeemable, or redeemable only on the happening of a contingency, however remote, or on the expiration of a period, however long, any rule of equity to the contrary notwithstanding.

Although the debentures may be called irredeemable or perpetual they are nevertheless redeemable when the company goes into liquidation. The effect of a debenture of this nature is to grant an annuity in perpetuity to the holder thereof. (See DEBENTURE.)

PERSONAL CHATTELS. (See CHATTELS.)

PERSONAL SECURITY. An advance is said to be made upon personal security when another person becomes surety or guarantor for the amount. The term is used to distinguish the security from a deposit of deeds, or certificates or any other form of impersonal security.

PERSONALTY. Property such as money, goods, furniture, stocks and shares is personal estate, or personalty. Leasehold property, even a lease for 999 years, is included in personalty. (Freehold and copyhold property is "real estate" or realty.)

When real estate is directed by will to be sold it is regarded as personalty.

The benefit of a mortgage is included in personalty.

The words used in a will with respect to the disposal of personal property differ from those used in connection with real property. Personalty is bequeathed and the beneficiary is called a legatee; realty is devised and the beneficiary is termed a devisee. (See REALTY.)

PESETA. (See FOREIGN MONEYS—SPAIN.)

PESO. (See FOREIGN MONEYS—ARGENTINE, CHILI, MEXICO, URUGUAY.)

PETITION (BANKRUPTCY). (See BANKRUPTCY—RECEIVING ORDER.)

PFENNIG. (See FOREIGN MONEYS—GERMANY.)

PIASTRE. (See FOREIGN MONEYS—EGYPT, TURKEY.)

PIE. (See FOREIGN MONEYS—INDIA.)

"PIG UPON BACON." In the case of an accommodation bill, where e.g. Brown accepts merely to oblige the drawer, Jones, Brown has no intention of meeting the bill at maturity. He expects that Jones will himself provide the funds necessary to pay the bill when it is due. As Jones in his own mind considers himself practically the acceptor as well as the drawer, Jones on Brown is therefore likened to a bill drawn by "Pig on Pork" or "Pig upon Bacon."

PLEDGE. When negotiable instruments, and goods, or the symbol of goods, such as bills of lading and dock warrants, are delivered to a banker as security for a debt, the delivery is termed a pledge or a pawn.

If the debt is not paid according to agreement, the banker has the right, after reasonable notice (if no time is fixed), to sell the property in order to satisfy his claim, and any surplus belongs to the pledgor. A letter or memorandum of deposit usually accompanies the pledge of goods or negotiable instruments, and in such cases the terms of the letter must be observed before realisation of the property is effected.

A pledge is to be distinguished from the lien which a banker has upon any negotiable instruments that may be in his hands as a banker, as the lien gives the banker merely a right to detain the documents until the customer's debt is paid. (See LIEN, MORTGAGE.)

POINTS. The price of stocks and shares moves by fractions, as 16¼–16½, and by points, as from 16–17.

POLICY OF INSURANCE. By the Stamp Act, 1891, the stamp duties are:—

	£	s.	d.
POLICY OF LIFE INSURANCE:—			
Where the sum insured does not exceed £10 . . .	0	0	1
Exceeds £10 but does not exceed £25	0	0	3
Exceeds £25 but does not exceed £500:—			
For every full sum of £50, and also for any fractional part of £50, of the amount insured .	0	0	6
Exceeds £500 but does not exceed £1,000:—			
For every full sum of £100, and also for any fractional part of £100, of the amount insured.	0	1	0
Exceeds £1,000:—			
For every full sum of £1,000, and also for any fractional part of £1,000, of the amount insured	0	10	0
And see Sections 91, 98, and 100.			

	£ s. d
POLICY OF INSURANCE AGAINST ACCIDENT and POLICY of insurance for any payment agreed to be made during the sickness of any person, or his incapacity from personal injury, or by way of indemnity against loss or damage of or to any property	0 0 1
And see Sections 91, 98, 99, and 100.	

"91. For the purposes of this Act the expression 'policy of insurance' includes every writing whereby any contract of insurance is made or agreed to be made, or is evidenced, and the expression 'insurance' includes assurance."

Policies of Insurance except Policies of Sea Insurance.

"98. (1) For the purposes of this Act the expression 'policy of life insurance' means a policy of insurance upon any life or lives or upon any event or contingency relating to or depending upon any life or lives except a policy of insurance against accident; and the expression 'policy of insurance against accident' means a policy of insurance for any payment agreed to be made upon the death of any person only from accident or violence or otherwise than from a natural cause, or as compensation for personal injury, and includes any notice or advertisement in a newspaper or other publication which purports to insure the payment of money upon the death of or injury to the holder or bearer of the newspaper or publication containing the notice only from accident or violence or otherwise than from a natural cause.

"(2) A policy of insurance against accident is not to be charged with any further duty than one penny by reason of the same extending to any payment to be made during sickness or incapacity from personal injury."

By the Finance Act, 1899:—

"11. The provisions contained in Section 98 of the Stamp Act of 1891 in reference to the expression 'policy of insurance against accident' shall extend to and include policies of insurance or indemnity against liability incurred by employers in consequence of claims made upon them by workmen who have sustained personal injury when the annual premium on such policies does not exceed one pound." By Section 8 (3) of the Finance Act, 1907, the above Section shall be read as if two pounds were substituted for one pound as the amount of the annual premium.

By the Finance Act, 1895:—

"13. Whereas Section 98 of the Stamp Act, 1891, provides that 'a policy of insurance against accident' includes a notice or advertisement in a newspaper or other publication which purports to insure the payment of money upon the death of or injury to the holder or bearer of the newspaper or publication from accident, and doubts have arisen as to the like notices or advertisements in other cases, it is hereby for the removal of doubts declared that 'a policy of insurance for any payment agreed to be made during the sickness of any person or his incapacity from personal injury' within the meaning of the Stamp Act, 1891, includes a notice or advertisement in a newspaper or other publication which purports to insure such payment."

By the Stamp Act, 1891:—

"99. The duty of one penny upon a policy of insurance other than a policy of sea insurance or life insurance may be denoted by an adhesive stamp, which is to be cancelled by the person by whom the policy is first executed.

"100. Every person who—

"(1) Receives, or takes credit for, any premium or consideration for any insurance other than a sea insurance, and does not, within one month after receiving, or taking credit for, the premium or consideration, make out and execute a duly stamped policy of insurance; or

"(2) Makes, executes, or delivers out, or pays or allows in account, or agrees to pay or allow in account, any money upon or in respect of any policy other than a policy of sea insurance which is not duly stamped;

shall incur a fine of twenty pounds."

By Section 116 of the Stamp Act, 1891, the Commissioners may, in certain cases, enter into an agreement with any person issuing policies of insurance against accident for the delivery to them of quarterly accounts of all sums received in respect of premiums, and in lieu of duty on such policies and by way of composition for that duty there shall be charged a duty at the rate of £5 per cent. on the aggregate amount of such sums received for premiums. This applies to insurances effected in newspapers. (See LIFE POLICY, MARINE INSURANCE POLICY.)

POSSESSORY TITLE. Where a person has been in the undisturbed possession of real property for twelve years and has not paid any rent or acknowledged any person's right to the property, he acquires a possessory title and becomes the owner of the property. But if the rightful owner was under a disability, such as infancy or lunacy, an action may be brought against the person claiming a possessory title within six years after the disability has ceased, but in no case can the land be recovered after thirty years from the time when the right of action first accrued, although the person under disability may have remained under disability during the whole of the thirty years.

POSSESSORY TITLE (LAND REGISTRY). Land may be registered under the Land Transfer Acts with possessory title. Its effect is not retrospective ; it keeps the title clear for the future, but is no bar to possible adverse claims dating from a time prior to its first entry on the Register books. (See LAND REGISTRY.)

POST. Where a letter is posted and is not returned through the Dead Letter Office, it is a presumption of law that it has been received by the person to whom it was addressed. The sender, however, must be prepared to prove that he posted the letter. For this reason it is important that a book be kept containing particulars of all letters despatched each day, showing the addresses, the time the letters were posted and the initials of the person, or persons, who posted them.

Before sending notes by post full particulars of the number, date, place of issue, and denomination of each note should be taken. Some persons cut notes in two and send the halves by different mails, the second halves not being sent until an acknowledgment is received for the first halves.

POST-DATED. A cheque which is dated subsequent to the actual date on which it is drawn is called a post-dated cheque.

A bill is not invalid by reason only that it is post-dated. (Section 13, s.s. (2), Bills of Exchange Act, 1882.) A cheque is included under the word "bill" in that section. A post-dated cheque is therefore a legal instrument and can be negotiated as soon as drawn.

A post-dated cheque should not be paid before the date appearing thereon. If a banker pays it before that date he will be liable for any consequences that may ensue, as, for instance, in the event of the dishonour of a cheque, which would not have been dishonoured if the post-dated cheque had not been paid, or in the event of the drawer giving notice to "stop payment" before the date of the cheque arrives. A cheque presented for payment before the date has arrived should be returned marked "post-dated."

If a cheque is presented on a Saturday, and is dated for the next day, Sunday, it should not be paid on the Saturday.

When the date upon a cheque has arrived, a banker is entitled to pay it, and incurs no liability in doing so.

After the date any holder may sue upon the cheque, though before the date he could not do so.

A post-dated cheque is sometimes given because the drawer does not expect to have funds to meet it until that date arrives. A purchaser often gives such a cheque, so that he may have a few days in which to examine his purchase before the cheque can be paid.

If a person draws and issues a cheque on February 1 and dates it March 1, it is practically the same as if he accepted a bill payable one month after February 1. But if he accepted a bill, the stamp duty would be an *ad valorem* one, whereas on the post-dated cheque the duty is the usual duty upon a cheque, one penny. It is thought by some authorities that a drawer may be liable to a penalty on the question of insufficient stamp duty, under the Stamp Act, 1891, but it is said that that question could not arise in an action on the cheque after the date of the cheque has arrived, because then the cheque would no longer be post-dated.

When a post-dated cheque is handed to a banker for collection when the date arrives, the customer should sign a paying-in slip dated for the day on which the cheque is to be credited.

Bankers do not discount post-dated cheques, but money-lenders advertise that they cash them for clients at a certain discount. (See BILL OF EXCHANGE.)

POST OBIT BOND. A bond in which a person agrees to pay a certain sum of money after the death of another person.

If there is anything of a fraudulent or over-reaching nature in the bond, the Courts may set it aside and order repayment merely of the actual sum lent, plus reasonable interest.

POST OFFICE MONEY ORDER. A Post Office money order is not a negotiable instrument, and therefore a holder does not obtain any better title to it than the person had from whom he received it.

If a money order is crossed & Co. payment by the Post Office will only be made through a banker, and, if the name of a banker is added, payment will only be made through that banker.

A postal order may be collected either at the Office where it is made payable, or at the General Post Office, London.

In receiving postal money orders from customers, bankers either give cash for them or place them to credit of the customer's account. If the orders should prove to have been stolen, the Post Office may return them to the banker, even after he has received the proceeds.

Bankers do not, as a rule, merely collect a money order, but where an order is collected the Post Office (Money Orders) Act, 1880 (Section 3), provides that a banker "who, in collecting for any principal, shall have received payment or been allowed by the Postmaster-General in account, in respect of any money order issued under this Act, or of any document purporting to be such a money order, shall not incur liability to anyone except such principal by reason of having received such payment or allowance, or having held or presented such order or document for payment."

POST OFFICE SAVINGS BANKS. The Post Office Savings Banks were established by Act of Parliament in 1861, and every depositor has the direct security of the State for the repayment of his deposits.

No person may, for his own benefit, have two accounts in the Post Office Savings Bank at the same time, or have an account in a Trustee Savings Bank.

Money orders and cheques are received provided they are not crossed to a particular bank.

No more than £50 can be deposited in one year, and no deposit can be made which causes the balance due to a depositor, including interest, to exceed £200.

Deposits may be made by children seven years old and upwards; and on behalf and in the names of children under seven years old. In this case the money is not repayable until the children attain the age of seven.

Deposits may be made, without limit, by a registered Friendly Society; and by a Provident Society, Penny Bank, or similar Institution to the extent of £100 in any one year and £300 in the whole, and if the consent of the National Debt Commissioners be obtained, without limit as to amount.

Every deposit must be entered in the depositor's book by the postmaster or person receiving it, who must affix his initials and the stamp of his office to each entry. An acknowledgment for every deposit of £5 and upwards, should be received by post from the Savings Bank Department in London.

Interest at the rate of £2 10*s.* per cent per annum is allowed on every complete pound, and commences on the first day of the month next following the deposit.

When a depositor wishes to withdraw any part of the sum due to him, he must make application for the same on a printed form, called a notice of withdrawal.

Depositors may invest their deposits in various Government stocks.

A deposit book is not a proper security for money lent, and no claim by any person holding a deposit book in respect of a loan will be recognised by the Savings Bank Department. Deposits in the Post Office Savings Bank are not liable to "attachment," or to its Scotch equivalent "arrestment."

POSTING. Posting a current account ledger is entering therein to the credit of the various customers' accounts all the amounts which have been paid in, and to the debit all the cheques which have been paid.

POTS. A Stock Exchange name for North Staffordshire Railway stock.

POUND. A sovereign (*q.v.*). In the time of William the Conqueror a pound of silver was coined into 240 silver pence, each equal to a pennyweight, whence the origin of the word pound.

A five-pound piece is of the standard weight of five sovereigns, namely 616·37239 grains troy, and its least current weight is 612·5 grains.

A two-pound piece is of the standard weight of two sovereigns, 246·54895 grains troy, and its least current weight is 245 grains. (See COINAGE.)

POWER OF ATTORNEY. A formal document by which one person is authorised, or empowered, to act for another.

It is commonly used in cases where a person (the donor or grantor) is going abroad for a long time and wishes to give someone (the donee or grantee) power to act for him in his absence. The power given in the document varies according to the wish of the donor, and when a power of attorney is exhibited to a banker for registration he should be careful to observe the exact wording of the instrument, and in particular to see whether power is given by special clause to draw cheques upon the donor's account, to make, draw, accept and indorse promissory notes and bills, to mortgage securities or overdraw his account. A banker should require that a certified copy of the instrument be given to him.

An attorney may sign the name of the donor without the addition of any further words, but the usual and better way is to sign, e.g.

"John Brown by his attorney Tom Brown."

The authority may relate only to one particular act, as, for example, the sale of Consols, or it may give power to act in all matters connected with some particular business, or it may give full power to act in every matter in the same way as though the agent were the grantor himself.

If a "power" is expressed to be irrevocable for a fixed time not exceeding a year from the making thereof, it cannot be revoked during that time without the donee's consent.

The length of time during which a power is to continue in force should be noted. In a power which was to continue "during absence from England," it was held (*Danby* v. *Coutts*, 1885, 29 S.J. 321) that certain mortgages made by the attorney, after the donor's return to England, were invalid.

A power of attorney is determined (that is, is no longer effective) by the death, insanity or bankruptcy of the donor.

By the Conveyancing Act, 1881, Section 47, any person making any payment in good faith, in pursuance of a power of attorney, shall not be liable therefor by reason that, before the payment, the donor of the power had died or become lunatic, of unsound mind, or bankrupt, or had revoked the power, if the fact was not, at the time of payment, known to the person making the same.

Section 46 of the same Act says: "The donee of a power of attorney may, if he thinks fit, execute or do any assurance, instrument, or thing in and with his own name and signature and his own seal, where sealing is required, by the authority of the donor of the power; and every assurance, instrument, and thing so executed and done shall be as effectual in law, to all intents, as if it had been executed or done by the donee of the power in the name and with the signature and seal of the donor thereof."

The following are some of the points which may be found in a power of attorney:

Know all men by these Presents that I, John Brown, of in the county of , gentleman, being about to leave England and to reside abroad for some time, do hereby constitute and appoint my son, Tom Brown, of (hereinafter called and referred to as my said attorney) my true and lawful attorney for the purposes hereinafter expressed, that is to say:—

To demand, sue for and recover from all persons and bodies liable to pay the same all sums of money, interest, debts, etc., now owing to me, or which shall at any time hereafter be owing to me, and

To give, sign, and execute effectual receipts, etc., for the same, and on non-payment to prosecute any action or suit for recovering the payment thereof; also

To state, settle, adjust, compound, submit to arbitration, and compromise all actions, accounts, claims and demands whatsoever.

And I authorise my said attorney,

To apply the moneys which shall come to his hands to pay and satisfy costs and charges which shall be incurred by my said attorney in exercise of any of the powers herein contained,

To pay all debts contracted by me or my said attorney on my behalf,

To invest any of the said moneys in any securities as he my said attorney shall think fit, and in the meantime to deposit the said moneys with any banker.

To appear for me in any Court,

To sign my name to, and make, execute, and do on my behalf any cheques, contracts, deeds or agreements, and for all the purposes of these presents.

To use the name of me the said John Brown,

And generally to do, execute and perform any other act, deed or thing whatsoever in or about my concerns and business of every kind whatsoever as fully and effectually as I myself could do if I were present, it being my intent and desire that all matters shall be under the full direction of my said attorney.

And whatsoever my attorney shall do or suffer by virtue of these premises, I do hereby for myself, my heirs, executors and administrators covenant with the said Tom Brown, his executors and administrators, to ratify and confirm.

And I declare that this power shall be irrevocable for calendar months, computed from the date hereof.

In witness whereof I have hereunto set my hand and seal this day of 19 .

Signed, sealed and delivered by the above named John Brown in the presence of } JOHN BROWN.

It is enacted by Sections 8 and 9 of the Conveyancing Act, 1882, that if a power of attorney given for valuable consideration is in the instrument creating the power expressed to be irrevocable, then, in favour of a purchaser, the power shall not be revoked at any time either by anything done by the donor, without the concurrence of the donee, or by death, lunacy, or bankruptcy of the donor, and any act done by the donee shall be effectual and absolutely irrevocable. If a power, whether for valuable consideration or not, is expressed to be irrevocable for a fixed time, not exceeding one year from the date of the instrument, then in favour of a purchaser the power shall not be revoked during that fixed time by anything done by the donor, without the concurrence of the donee, or by the death, lunacy, or bankruptcy of the donor, and any act done during that time by the donee shall be irrevocable.

Stamp duties :—

	£	s.	d.
LETTER OR POWER OF ATTORNEY, and COMMISSION, FACTORY, MANDATE, or other instrument in the nature thereof :—			
(1) For the sole purpose of appointing or authorising a proxy to vote at any one meeting at which votes may be given by proxy, whether the number of persons named in such instrument be one or more	0	0	1
(2) By any petty officer, seaman, marine, or soldier serving as a marine, or his representatives, for receiving prize money or wages .	0	1	0
(3) For the receipt of the dividends or interest of any stock :—			
Where made for the receipt of one payment only	0	1	0
In any other case . .	0	5	0
(4) For the receipt of any sum of money, or any bill of exchange or promissory note for any sum of money, not exceeding £20, or any periodical payments not exceeding the annual sum of £10 (*not being hereinbefore charged*)	0	5	0
(5) For the sale, transfer, or acceptance of any of the Government or Parliamentary stocks or funds :—			
Where the nominal amount of the stocks or funds does not exceed £100 (Finance Act, 1895, Section 16)	0	2	6
In any other case . .	0	10	0
(6) Of any kind whatsoever not herein before described	0	10	0

Exemptions.

(1) Letter or power of attorney for the receipt of dividends of any definite and certain share of the Government or Parliamentary stocks or funds producing a yearly dividend less than £3.

(2) Letter or power of attorney or proxy filed in the Probate Division of the High Court of Justice in England or Ireland, or in any ecclesiastical court.

(3) Order, request, or direction under hand only from the proprietor of any stock to any company or to any officer of any company or to any banker to pay the dividends or interest arising from the stock to any person therein named.

And see Section 81 of the Stamp Act, 1891, as follows :—

"A letter or power of attorney for the sale, transfer, or acceptance of any of the Government or Parliamentary stocks or funds, duly stamped for that purpose, is not to be charged with any further duty by reason of containing an authority for the receipt of the dividends on the same stocks or funds."

See also Section 80 under PROXY.

POWER OF ATTORNEY—TRANSFER OF GOVERNMENT STOCK. British Government stock is inscribed, that is registered, in the books of the Bank of England, and when a transfer is to be made, the owner must either attend personally at the Bank or appoint an attorney to act for him.

The following is a specimen of a power of attorney to transfer consols, for use by the survivors in a joint account :—

We of and of survivors in a joint account with , late of deceased, appoint and both of jointly and severally our attorneys and attorney in our names and on our behalf and in the name and on behalf of the survivors of us as survivors aforesaid to transfer pounds being all the £2 10*s*. per cent. consolidated stock standing in the books of the Governor and Company of the Bank of England in the names of deceased and unto of , and also to do whatever is necessary or proper to be done for the purpose aforesaid. And we declare that any act done under or in pursuance of this letter of attorney shall, so far as the Governor and Company are concerned, be valid as against our estates, notwithstanding that we may be dead at the time of such act unless notice in writing of our deaths shall have been previously given to the said Governor and Company. In witness whereof we have hereunto set our hands and seals this day of in the year of our Lord one thousand nine hundred and .

Signed, sealed and delivered in the presence of us by the above-named

Signature of First Witness
Address
Occupation

Seal.

Signature of Second Witness
Address
Occupation

Seal.

I demand to act by this letter of attorney this day of 19 .

Witness .

The following are the instructions for executing powers or letters of attorney, which are printed upon the back of the document :—

DATING.—Must be in words, not in figures. (When a letter of attorney has to be executed by more than one person the date of the first signature attached thereto should be inserted.)

WITNESSING.—(1) In the United Kingdom.

Two credible witnesses are necessary to each execution, and they must state their qualities, professions or occupations, and respectively give a permanent address which must be one at which the Post Office would undertake to deliver a letter.

(2) Out of the United Kingdom.

In addition to the two witnesses the stockholder's signature must be attested by a British Minister, Consul, Vice-Consul, or other British Authority, or by a Notary Public.

N.B.—Clerks or servants must give the names and addresses of their employers. A female witness must state whether she is a spinster, wife or widow, and if a wife must give the full name of her husband.

No stockholder, attorney or transferee named in this letter of attorney, nor the husband or wife of any of them is a "credible witness."

EXECUTING BY MARK.—Each witness must be a person of known position such as the minister or churchwarden of the stockholder's parish, a magistrate, justice of the peace, solicitor, or registered medical practitioner, and the witnesses must state in writing that the letter of attorney was read over and fully explained to and was understood by the stockholder. Should the stockholder be unable to understand the purport of the letter of attorney there must be no execution.

ALTERING.—Any addition, ruling out or alteration of any kind must be initialled by the stockholder and a statement that such addition, ruling out or alteration, was made prior to the execution, must be signed by each witness.

Powers for acceptance, sale or transfer, or any combination thereof (with or without dividends), cost 11*s*. 6*d*.; powers of sale of English Government stock where the nominal amount does not exceed £100, 4*s*. (See NATIONAL DEBT.)

POWER OF SALE. (See LEGAL MORTGAGE.)

PRECEPT OF CLARE CONSTAT. By the Stamp Act, 1891, the stamp duty is :—

PRECEPT OF CLARE CONSTAT to give seisin of lands or other heritable subjects in Scotland .	£	*s*.	*d*.
	0	5	0

PREFERENCE SHARES. PREFERENCE STOCK. Preference shares receive a dividend before the ordinary shares, and they may be either cumulative or non-cumulative. If the former, and no dividend is paid upon them in one year, the profits of succeeding years will be used to pay the full dividends which have accrued, before any dividend is paid on the ordinary shares. If, however, they are non-cumulative, the dividend is payable only out of the profits of each separate year.

Some preference shares give a preferential right only as regards dividend, but others give in addition a preferential right in the event of a return of the capital of the company.

A company limited by shares may, if authorised by its articles, convert its paid-up shares into stock. A stockholder may hold any amount of a stock, but a shareholder obtains shares of a fixed amount. (See SHARE CAPITAL.)

PREFERENTIAL PAYMENTS (BANKRUPTCY). In the distribution of the property of a bankrupt the following debts are paid in priority to all other debts, viz., all rates due and payable within twelve months before the date of the receiving order, and not exceeding in the whole one year's assessment ; all wages or salary of any clerk or servant for services rendered to the bankrupt during four months before the date of the receiving order, and not exceeding fifty pounds ; workmen's wages to a limited extent ; a landlord may distrain for rent and if such distress be levied after the commencement of the bankruptcy it shall be available only for six months rent accrued due prior to the date of the order of adjudication, but the landlord may prove under the bankruptcy for the surplus due for which the distress may not have been available. The expenses of the proceedings in bankruptcy are also payable in priority. (See FRAUDULENT PREFERENCE.)

PRÉFIX. French, at a fixed date. A bill drawn payable at a fixed date, or *préfix*, does not take days of grace.

PREMIUM. The amount which is payable annually during life, or during a certain number of years, in order to assure the payment, either at death or at a fixed date, as the case may be, of the sum named in an assurance policy. (See LIFE POLICY.)

PREMIUM, AT A. When the market value of bonds, stocks or shares is above the nominal or face value, they are said to be at a premium. A share of £1, fully paid, which is selling at £1 10*s*. is an example of an investment which is at a premium, or 10*s*. above par value. When the market value is less, they are at a discount. (See PAR.)

PREMIUM BOND. An acknowledgment of indebtedness by a foreign state. In some cases no interest is paid, and in others only a very small rate of interest is given, but, at certain times, a drawing takes place and the holders of bonds bearing the numbers that are drawn may receive large money prizes.

Premium bonds are not issued in this country. They have been held to come within the Gaming Acts as lotteries.

PRESCRIPTION. In Scotland, Positive Prescription is a title to lands acquired by a certain period of uninterrupted possession ; Negative Prescription is the loss of a right by neglect to use it during the time limited by law. (See under STATUTE OF LIMITATIONS.)

"PRESENT AGAIN." These words are sometimes written by a banker upon a cheque which is returned unpaid because of insufficient funds in the customer's account to meet it. It is not, however, by itself a correct answer to give, as it does not afford any explanation why the cheque has been returned. The best answer to write upon a dishonoured cheque is "Refer to drawer."

Sometimes the words are joined with another answer, as "Refer to drawer—Present again." "Not sufficient—Present again." No doubt the words "Present again" are used with the idea of minimising the risk of injury to the drawer's credit by returning the cheque, but it is perhaps questionable whether they are altogether prudent words to use.

The banker to whom a cheque is returned with a request "Present again" advises his customer of the dishonour of the cheque and forwards it for representation.

PRESENTATION. A word which is often used instead of the word presentment. (See PRESENTMENT FOR ACCEPTANCE, PRESENTMENT FOR PAYMENT.)

PRESENTMENT FOR ACCEPTANCE. When a bill of exchange is actually presented to a drawee in order that it may be accepted by him, it is a presentment for acceptance.

By Section 39 of the Bills of Exchange Act, 1882 :—

"(1) Where a bill is payable after sight, presentment for acceptance is necessary in order to fix the maturity of the instrument.

"(2) Where a bill expressly stipulates that it shall be presented for acceptance, or where a bill is drawn payable elsewhere than at the residence or place of business of the drawee it must be presented for acceptance before it can be presented for payment.

"(3) In no other case is presentment for acceptance necessary in order to render liable any party to the bill.

"(4) Where the holder of a bill, drawn payable elsewhere than at the place of business or residence of the drawee, has not time, with the exercise of reasonable diligence, to present the bill for acceptance before presenting it for payment on the day that it falls due, the delay caused by presenting the bill for acceptance before presenting it for payment is excused, and does not discharge the drawer and indorsers."

With regard to the time for presenting a bill payable after sight, Section 40 provides as follows :—

"(1) Subject to the provisions of this Act, when a bill payable after sight is negotiated, the holder must either present it for acceptance or negotiate it within a reasonable time.

"(2) If he do not do so, the drawer and all indorsers prior to that holder are discharged.

"(3) In determining what is a reasonable time within the meaning of this Section, regard shall be had to the nature of the bill, the usage of trade with respect to similar bills, and the facts of the particular case."

The rules as to presentment for acceptance and the excuses for non-presentment are given in Section 41 :—

"(1) A bill is duly presented for acceptance which is presented in accordance with the following rules :—

"(*a*) The presentment must be made by or on behalf of the holder to the drawee or to some person authorised to accept or refuse acceptance on his behalf at a reasonable hour on a business day and before the bill is overdue :

"(*b*) Where a bill is addressed to two or more drawees, who are not partners, presentment must be made to them all, unless one has authority to accept for all, then presentment may be made to him only :

"(*c*) Where the drawee is dead, presentment may be made to his personal representative :

"(*d*) Where the drawee is bankrupt, presentment may be made to him or to his trustee :

"(*e*) Where authorised by agreement or usage, a presentment through the post office is sufficient.

"(2) Presentment in accordance with these rules is excused, and a bill may be treated as dishonoured by non-acceptance :—

"(*a*) Where the drawee is dead or bankrupt, or is a fictitious person or a person not having capacity to contract by bill :

"(*b*) Where, after the exercise of reasonable diligence, such presentment cannot be effected :

"(*c*) Where, although the presentment has been irregular, acceptance has been refused on some other ground.

"(3) The fact that the holder has reason to believe that the bill, on presentment, will be dishonoured does not excuse presentment."

In practice a bill is presented for acceptance as soon as possible after it has been drawn, and until it has been accepted the drawee is under no liability whatever with regard to it. An after date bill having more than three days to run before maturity, is, in London, presented for acceptance. The sooner the holder of an unaccepted bill procures the drawee's acceptance the better, for he then obtains the further security in the liability of the acceptor. When bills are received by a banker in order that he may get them accepted, they are presented to the drawee on the day of receipt, and if the drawee does not accept when they are presented, it is customary to leave the bills with him for twenty-four hours (exclusive of Sundays and holidays), or until close of business on a half-holiday if the twenty-four hours are not completed, in which to decide whether, or not, he will accept them. When a bill is left for acceptance a banker marks it so that he may know that he gets the same bill back again. If a banker is negligent in obtaining an acceptance he may render himself liable thereon, especially in the case of a bill drawn payable at so many days "after sight," as the drawer and indorsers may thereby be discharged. The law does not lay down any absolute rule as to what time is reasonable or unreasonable in which to carry out an instruction to obtain an acceptance, but in most cases a banker would present a bill for acceptance on the day that he receives it. Having left a bill with a drawee, it is part of the banker's duty to call again for it and not to wait till the drawee returns it to him, though an arrangement may be made with the drawee to return it.

Where bills of lading and other documents are attached to a bill, they are exhibited to the drawee at the same time as the bill is presented for acceptance, but if the bill is left with the drawee until the next day the documents are retained by the banker and not left with the drawee. The banker, however, may have instructions to deliver up the documents to the drawee after he has accepted the bill. In the case of a foreign bill sent for acceptance, instructions usually accompany the bill as to what has to be done in the event of non-acceptance, as "protest if not accepted" or "if not accepted do not protest but send an advice by wire" or "no expense to be incurred."

Where a bill is received from a correspondent in order to obtain the acceptance of the drawee, and the drawee lives at such a distance as to necessitate either sending the bill to him or asking him to call at the bank to accept it, the correspondent should be advised of what is being done so that he may understand the delay. (See BILL OF EXCHANGE.)

PRESENTMENT FOR PAYMENT. It is of the utmost importance that a bill of exchange be presented for payment on the date it falls due. The following rules are laid down by the Bills of Exchange Act, 1882:—

"Section 45. Subject to the provisions of this Act a bill must be duly presented for payment. If it be not so presented the drawer and indorsers shall be discharged.

"A bill is duly presented for payment which is presented in accordance with the following rules:—

"(1) Where the bill is not payable on demand, presentment must be made on the day it falls due.

"(2) Where the bill is payable on demand, then, subject to the provisions of this Act, presentment must be made within a reasonable time after its issue in order to render the drawer liable, and within a reasonable time after its indorsement, in order to render the indorser liable.

"In determining what is a reasonable time, regard shall be had to the nature of the bill, the usage of trade with regard to similar bills, and the facts of the particular case.

"(3) Presentment must be made by the holder or by some person authorised to receive payment on his behalf at a reasonable hour on a business day, at the proper place as hereinafter defined, either to the person designated by the bill as payer, or to some person authorised to pay or refuse payment on his behalf if with the exercise of reasonable diligence such person can there be found.

"(4) A bill is presented at the proper place:—

"(*a*) Where a place of payment is specified in the bill and the bill is there presented.

"(*b*) Where no place of payment is specified, but the address of the drawee or acceptor is given in the bill, and the bill is there presented.

"(*c*) Where no place of payment is specified and no address given, and the bill is presented at the drawee's or acceptor's place of business if known, and if not, at his ordinary residence if known.

"(*d*) In any other case if presented to the drawee or acceptor wherever he can be found, or if presented at his last known place of business or residence.

"(5) Where a bill is presented at the proper place, and after the exercise of reasonable diligence no person authorised to pay or refuse payment can be found there, no further presentment to the drawee or acceptor is required.

"(6) Where a bill is drawn upon, or accepted by two or more persons who are not partners, and no place of payment is specified, presentment must be made to them all.

"(7) Where the drawee or acceptor of a bill is dead, and no place of payment is specified, presentment must be made to a personal representative, if such there be, and with the exercise of reasonable diligence he can be found.

"(8) Where authorised by agreement or usage a presentment through the post office is sufficient."

It should be noted that a presentment through the post office (s.s. 8) is in order only where authorised by agreement or usage. If, therefore, a bill accepted at the X. & Y. Bank, Leeds, is presented by post to that bank by a stranger, the bank would return it to the stranger with the answer that it must, according to custom, be presented through a banker.

Presentment to the acceptor of an accommodation bill must be made just as in the case of an ordinary bill.

It should be particularly noted that, if these rules are not properly attended to, the drawer and indorsers shall be discharged, both with respect to the bill and to the consideration for which the bill was given. The bill itself should be presented, and if the acceptor has left the address shown on the bill, reasonable diligence must be used to find his new address and present it there. An acceptor is not discharged if the bill is not presented to him.

Section 52 provides :—

"(1) When a bill is accepted generally presentment for payment is not necessary in order to render the acceptor liable.

"(2) When by the terms of a qualified acceptance presentment for payment is required, the acceptor, in the absence of an express stipulation to that effect, is not discharged by the omission to present the bill for payment on the day that it matures.

"(3) In order to render the acceptor of a bill liable it is not necessary to protest it, or that notice of dishonour should be given to him.

"(4) Where the holder of a bill presents it for payment, he shall exhibit the bill to the person from whom he demands payment, and when a bill is paid the holder shall forthwith deliver it up to the party paying it."

Though non-presentment, or delay in presentment, of a bill releases the drawer and indorsers, there are certain cases where the Bills of Exchange Act excuses delay, or non-presentment. They are given in Section 46 :—

"(1) Delay in making presentment for payment is excused when the delay is caused by circumstances beyond the control of the holder, and not imputable to his default, misconduct, or negligence. When the cause of delay ceases to operate presentment must be made with reasonable diligence.

"(2) Presentment for payment is dispensed with :—

"(*a*) Where after the exercise of reasonable diligence, presentment, as required by this Act, cannot be effected. The fact that the holder has reason to believe that the bill will, on presentment, be dishonoured, does not dispense with the necessity for presentment.

"(*b*) Where the drawee is a fictitious person.

"(*c*) As regards the drawer, where the drawee or acceptor is not bound, as between himself and the drawer, to accept or pay the bill, and the drawer has no reason to believe that the bill would be paid if presented.

"(*d*) As regards an indorser, where the bill was accepted or made for the accommodation of that indorser, and he has no reason to expect that the bill would be paid if presented.

"(e) By waiver of presentment, express or implied."

A bill on demand must be presented within a reasonable time in order to preserve the drawer's liability; but in the case of a cheque, the drawer is not, as a rule, discharged for six years. (See below, Section 74.)

In the case of a bill after date, it is necessary, in order to prevent the discharge of the other parties, that the bill be presented to the acceptor, at the place where payable, even if he said before the bill was due that he would not pay it at maturity, or if he called at the bank on the due date and said he could not pay it. If it is accepted payable at a bank, and the acceptor says he has nothing in his account to meet the bill, it is still necessary formally to present the bill at the bank indicated. It must be presented within the usual business hours.

Presentment before the actual due date does not preserve recourse against the other parties.

Where a separate guarantee has been given by anyone on behalf of the drawer or an indorser, the guarantor is discharged by such delay or non-presentment as would discharge the drawer or indorser, but the liability of a guarantor for an acceptor continues in the same way as an acceptor's liability.

It has been decided that where a bill is held by a banker which is accepted at that banker's, he need not present it to the acceptor but merely refer to his own books containing the acceptor's account to ascertain whether, or not, it may be paid.

If a bill is drawn payable in one place, and accepted payable in another, it should be presented at the place where accepted payable.

If an acceptor does not pay a bill when it is presented to him a notice may be left at his address informing him that the bill lies at the bank, and that it requires his attention before closing time.

Lord Tenterden, in *Wilkins* v. *Jadis* (1831, 2 B. & Ad. 188), said: "A presentment to bankers out of the hours of their business is not sufficient; but in other cases the rule of law is that the bill must be presented at a reasonable hour; a presentment at twelve o'clock at night, when a person has retired to rest, would be unreasonable; but I cannot say that a presentment between seven and eight in the evening is not a presentment at a reasonable time."

A bill of itself does not operate as an assignment of funds in the hands of the drawee, but in Scotland where the drawee of a bill has in his hands funds available for the payment thereof, the bill operates as an assignment of the sum for which it is drawn in favour of the holder, from the time when the bill is presented to the drawee. (Section 53.)

With respect to presentment to an acceptor for honour, the Bills of Exchange Act provides :—

"Section 67. (1) Where a dishonoured bill has been accepted for honour suprà protest, or contains a reference in case of need, it must be protested for non-payment before it is presented for payment to the acceptor for honour, or referee in case of need.

"(2) Where the address of the acceptor for honour is in the same place where the bill is protested for non-payment, the bill must be presented to him not later than the day following its maturity; and where the address of the acceptor for honour is in some place other than the place where it was protested for non-payment, the bill must be forwarded not later than the day following its maturity for presentment to him.

"(3) Delay in presentment or non-presentment is excused by any circumstances which would excuse delay in presentment for payment or non-presentment for payment.

"(4) When a bill of exchange is dishonoured by the acceptor for honour it must be protested for non-payment by him."

A cheque must be presented for payment within a reasonable time. Section 74 of the Bills of Exchange Act provides :—

"Subject to the provisions of this Act :—

"(1) Where a cheque is not presented for payment within a reasonable time of its issue, and the drawer or the person on whose account it is drawn had the right at the time of such presentment as between him and the banker to have the cheque paid and suffers actual damage through the delay, he is discharged to the extent of such damage, that is to say, to the extent to which such drawer or person is a creditor of such banker to a larger amount than he would have been had such cheque been paid.

"(2) In determining what is a reasonable time regard shall be had to the nature of the instrument, the usage of trade and of bankers, and the facts of the particular case.

"(3) The holder of such cheque as to which such drawer or person is discharged shall be a creditor, in lieu of such drawer or person, of such banker to the extent of such discharge, and entitled to recover the amount from him."

A person receiving a cheque should present it for payment as soon as possible; unless presented within a reasonable time the indorsers will be discharged. If a drawer suffers actual loss, as where a banker fails, through a cheque of his not having been presented within a reasonable time, the drawer, as stated in the above Section, is discharged to the amount of such loss. Where a person receiving a cheque and the banker on whom the cheque is drawn live in the same town it is considered a presentment within a reasonable time if the cheque is presented for payment on the business day following its receipt. If the person receiving the cheque and the banker on whom it is drawn live in different places, it is within a reasonable time if sent forward for payment on the business day following its receipt.

If the banker sends it to an agent for collection, the agent has the day of receipt and the following day in which to present it. In practice, however, all cheques are remitted for collection on the day that they are received.

The drawer of a cheque is liable to the holder for six years from the date of the cheque, and a banker would be justified in paying a cheque within that period, but, in practice, a banker does not pay a cheque, which is six (in some banks twelve) months' old, unless it is confirmed by the drawer. See STALE CHEQUE.)

Where it is important to know as soon as possible whether a certain cheque will be paid or not, it is customary to send it direct, instead of through the Clearing House, and a stamped telegram form may be enclosed with a request to the banker on whom it is drawn to "advise fate" of the cheque.

It has been held that, where a foreign cheque is drawn upon a place where the banker has no agent, the custom in London of presenting the cheque by post is a due presentment (*Heywood* v. *Pickering*, 1874, L.R. 9 Q.B. 428), but if payment is not received by return of post, the customer from whom the bank received the cheque should be advised of the fact.

If a cheque is presented by post by a stranger, it should be returned with a request that it be presented, according to custom, through a banker.

The presentment of a cheque in England does not operate as an assignment of funds in the drawer's account. Part payment of a cheque is never made; it is either paid fully or dishonoured. In Scotland, however, where a cheque is returned unpaid for "insufficient funds," any money in the drawer's account is transferred to a separate account, such as a suspense account, where it remains until the banker has evidence that the matter has been arranged. If the payee desires, the cheque may be retained by the banker in exchange for the amount attaching to it.

The presentment for payment of a promissory note is dealt with by Sections 86 and 87 as follows:—

"86. (1) Where a note payable on demand has been indorsed, it must be presented for payment within a reasonable time of the indorsement. If it be not so presented the indorser is discharged.

"(2) In determining what is a reasonable time, regard shall be had to the nature of the instrument, the usage of trade, and the facts of the particular case.

"(3) Where a note payable on demand is negotiated, it is not deemed to be overdue, for the purpose of affecting the holder with defects of title of which he had no notice, by reason that it appears that a reasonable time for presenting it for payment has elapsed since its issue.

"87. (1) Where a promissory note is in the body of it made payable at a particular place, it must be presented for payment at that place in order to render the maker liable. In any other case, presentment for payment is not necessary in order to render the maker liable.

"(2) Presentment for payment is necessary in order to render the indorser of a note liable.

"(3) Where a note is in the body of it made payable at a particular place, presentment at that place is necessary in order to render an indorser liable; but when a place of payment is indicated by way of memorandum only, presentment at that place is sufficient to render the indorser liable, but a presentment to the maker elsewhere, if sufficient in other respects, shall also suffice."

A country bank note should be presented for payment, or put into circulation, not later than the day following the date on which it was received, otherwise, if the note is dishonoured, the holder may lose his right of action against the person from whom he took the note in payment of a debt. (See COUNTRY BANK NOTES.)

The presentment of a bill or cheque through a Clearing House has the same effect as presenting it direct to the banker on whom the cheque is drawn or where the bill is payable. (See BILL OF EXCHANGE.)

PRESSURE ON THE MONEY MARKET. An expression which is used to describe the position when from any cause, such as a high Bank Rate, there is difficulty in obtaining loans or discounting bills.

PREVENTION OF CORRUPTION ACT, 1906 (6 EDW. VII, c. 34). An Act for the better Prevention of Corruption.

[August 4, 1906.]

Punishment of Corrupt Transactions with Agents.

"1. (1) If any agent corruptly accepts or obtains, or agrees to accept or attempts to obtain, from any person, for himself or for any other person, any gift or consideration as an inducement or reward for doing or forbearing to do, or for having after the passing of this Act done or forborne to do, any act in relation to his principal's affairs or business, or for showing or forbearing to show favour or disfavour to any person in relation to his principal's affairs or business; or

"If any person corruptly gives or agrees to give or offers any gift or consideration to any agent as an inducement or reward for doing or forbearing to do, or for having after the passing of this Act done or forborne to do, any act in relation to his principal's affairs or business or for showing or forbearing to show favour or disfavour to any person in relation to his principal's affairs or business; or

"If any person knowingly gives to any agent, or if any agent knowingly uses with intent to deceive his principal, any receipt, account, or other document in respect of which the principal is interested, and which contains any statement which is false or erroneous or defective in any material particular, and which to his knowledge is intended to mislead the principal;

he shall be guilty of a misdemeanour, and shall be liable on conviction on indictment to imprisonment, with or without hard labour, for a term not exceeding two years, or to a fine not exceeding five hundred pounds, or to both such imprisonment and such fine, or on summary conviction to imprisonment, with or without hard labour, for a term not exceeding four months, or to a fine not exceeding fifty pounds, or to both such imprisonment and such fine.

"(2) For the purposes of this Act the expression 'consideration' includes valuable consideration of any kind; the expression 'agent' includes any person employed by or acting for another; and the expression 'principal' includes an employer.

"(3) A person serving under the Crown or under any corporation or any municipal borough, county, or district council, or any board of guardians, is an agent within the meaning of this Act.

Prosecution of Offences.

"2. (1) A prosecution for an offence under this Act shall not be instituted without the consent, in England of the Attorney-General or Solicitor-General, and in Ireland of the Attorney-General or Solicitor-General for Ireland.

22 & 23 Vict. c. 17.

"(2) The Vexatious Indictments Act, 1859, as amended by any subsequent enactment, shall apply to offences under this Act as if they were included among the offences mentioned in Section 1 of that Act.

"(3) Every information for any offence under this Act shall be upon oath.

"(4) The expenses of any prosecution on indictment under this Act shall be defrayed as in cases of indictment for felony.

"(5) A court of quarter sessions shall not have jurisdiction to inquire of, hear, and determine prosecutions on indictments for offences under this Act.

"(6) Any person aggrieved by a summary conviction under this Act may appeal to a court of quarter sessions.

Application to Scotland.

"3. This Act shall extend to Scotland, subject to the following modifications:—

"(1) Section 2 shall not extend to Scotland:

"(2) In Scotland all offences which are punishable under this Act on summary conviction shall be prosecuted before the sheriff in manner provided by the Summary Jurisdiction (Scotland) Acts.

Short Title and Commencement.

"4. (1) This Act may be cited as the Prevention of Corruption Act, 1906.

"(2) This Act shall come into operation on the first day of January nineteen hundred and seven."

One object of this Act is to endeavour to stop the practice of taking and giving secret commissions, in consideration for which an agent does something contrary to the interests of his principal.

Where a broker shares with a banker, through whom the order has been received, his commission upon any sale or purchase of stocks or shares, it is now customary to place a notice upon the contract note that the commission is divided with the banker.

PRE-VICTORIAN GOLD COINS. Pre-Victorian sovereigns and half-sovereigns—that is, all gold coins coined before 1837—are not now legal tender. They were called in by the Coinage Act, 1889, and by Royal Proclamation they were declared to be no longer current coins after February 28, 1891.

PRIMÂ FACIE. On the first view. The appearance of a matter, at first sight, before examining into it.

PRIMOGENITURE. (Latin *Primogenitus*, first-born.)

The law by which the real property of a father or mother passes to the eldest son, in the event of the parent leaving no will.

PRIORITIES. In charges upon landed property, a mortgage conveying the legal estate comes first, and, after that, all the other equitable charges which there may be rank in order of the dates of the respective charges. If, for example, a trustee fraudulently deposits the deeds of trust property with a banker, the banker's equitable charge will rank after the equitable charge which already existed, before he took the deeds, in favour of the persons benefiting under the trust. But if, on the other hand, a banker is negligent and allows, without a sufficient reason, the deeds of the property included in his equitable charge to remain in the hands of the customer, and the customer obtains a loan upon them from another party, say, Jones, the banker's charge, although first in point of time, will, by reason of his negligence, be postponed to that of Jones.

So long as the title deeds remain in the banker's possession it is unlikely that a charge would be created in priority to his. As a rule, the charges with which a banker is most concerned are those which may exist at the time the security is taken; but if the banker holds the usual memorandum of deposit agreeing to execute a legal mortgage when called upon, the possession of the deeds and such a document would probably give him the best right to call for the legal estate.

If, before the deeds were deposited with the banker, as security, the property was mortgaged, say, to Jones, or if Jones had an equitable mortgage and subsequently, with or without notice of the banker's charge, obtained a legal mortgage, Jones would then hold the legal estate and would rank before the banker's equitable charge. But if Jones was guilty of negligence in not retaining possession of the deeds, or of not obtaining a satisfactory explanation of their absence, which enabled the mortgagor to deposit them with the banker, the banker's equitable charge might in such a case, in equity, be held to precede the legal mortgage held by Jones, provided, of course, that the banker had no knowledge, at the time he took the deeds, that there was a charge in existence in favour of Jones.

A prior legal estate would probably not, however, be postponed to a subsequent equitable estate, because of mere carelessness, as distinguished from gross negligence, on the part of the prior mortgagee.

The legal estate can be held only by one person at a time.

If a banker has made an advance upon an equitable charge, without notice of a prior equitable charge, the banker's charge will rank after the prior charge (unless the prior equitable mortgagee has been negligent in not retaining possession of the deeds); but if the banker subsequently obtains a mortgage conveying the legal estate to himself, he will thereby secure priority to any previous equitable mortgagee. For example, if Brown contracted with Jones for the sale to him of some land, and, while the deeds were still (without negligence) in Brown's hands, Brown deposited the deeds with a banker without notice of the sale, there would then be two equitable interests in the land, and the interest of Jones, having been created before the interest of the banker, would rank first; but if the banker obtained a legal mortgage, he would thereby gain the priority. If, however, the banker was aware of the fact when he took the deeds that Jones had an equitable interest in the property, he could not, in that case, by securing the legal estate, step in in front of Jones.

In Yorkshire, charges upon property rank according to the date of registration. (See particulars under YORKSHIRE REGISTRY OF DEEDS.)

A mortgage upon a ship takes priority from the date of production for registry, not from the date of the instrument. (See under SHIP—MORTGAGE, etc.)

(See DEBTS—ASSIGNMENT OF, MORTGAGE, NOTICE OF MORTGAGE.)

PRIVATE BANK. A banking partnership, or firm, in which the number of partners must not exceed ten. The liability of each partner is unlimited.

A partnership of more than ten persons cannot be formed for the purpose of carrying on the business of banking, unless it is registered as a company under the Companies (Consolidation) Act, 1908, or is formed in pursuance of some other Act of Parliament, or of letters patent. (See BANKING COMPANY.)

PRIVATE COMPANY. A private company may consist of any two or more persons, with limited or unlimited liability. (See MEMORANDUM OF ASSOCIATION.)

The Companies (Consolidation) Act, 1908, Section 121, defines a private company as follows:—

"(1) For the purposes of this Act the expression 'private company' means a company by which its articles—

"(*a*) restricts the right to transfer its shares; and

"(*b*) limits the number of its members (exclusive of persons who are in the employment of the company) to fifty; and

"(*c*) prohibits any invitation to the public to subscribe for any shares or debentures of the company.

"(2) A private company may, subject to anything contained in the memorandum or articles, by passing a special resolution and by filing with the registrar of companies such a statement in lieu of prospectus as the company, if a public company, would have had to file before allotting any of its shares or debentures, together with such a statutory declaration as the company, if a public company, would have had to file before commencing business, turn itself into a public company.

"(3) Where two or more persons hold one or more shares in a company jointly they shall, for the purposes of this Section, be treated as a single member."

If at any time the number of members is reduced below two and the private company carries on business for more than six months while the number is so reduced, the person carrying on the business shall be liable for the payment of the whole debts of the company contracted during that time.

The regulations in Section 65 as to sending a copy of the statutory report to the members of a company and filing a copy with the registrar do not apply to a private company. (See MEETINGS.)

Section 26, s.s. 3, excepts a private company from sending an annual balance sheet to the registrar. (See REGISTER OF MEMBERS OF COMPANY.)

Section 82, which obliges companies to file a statement with the registrar where no prospectus is issued, does not apply to a private company. (See PROSPECTUS.) (See COMPANIES.)

PRO RATA. Payment in proportion to the various interests concerned.

PROBATE. The document which is issued, with an official copy of a will, by the Probate Office to an executor. The principal registry of wills is at Somerset House, where the copy of a will may be seen on payment of one shilling. There are also District Registries where probate can be obtained of the wills of persons who were living in those districts at the time of their death, and a copy of a will which was proved in a District Registry may be seen in that District Registry, as well as at Somerset House, for a fee of one shilling.

An official copy of the whole or any part of a will, or an official certificate of the grant of any letters of administration may be obtained from the Registry or District Registry where the will has been proved or the administration granted on the payment of certain fees.

Until probate is exhibited or, if no will, letters of administration are exhibited, a banker does not allow the balance of the deceased's account to be transferred, or any securities which he may have left with the banker to be removed. The will must be proved under a penalty of £50, within six months from the date of the death.

When probate is exhibited a banker enters full particulars in the probate book for future reference, and he is expected to see that the gross value of the estate as stated in the probate is not less than the money in his hands belonging to the deceased.

Where probate or letters of administration have been revoked, the banker is protected in any payments he may have *boná fide* made by reason of the probate or letters. By 20 & 21 Vict. c. 77 it is enacted :—

"Section 77. Where any probate or administration is revoked under this Act, all payments *boná fide* made to any executor or administrator under such probate or administration, before the revocation thereof, shall be a legal discharge to the person making the same ; and the executor or administrator who shall have acted under any such revoked probate or administration may retain and reimburse himself in respect of any payments made by him which the person to whom probate or administration shall be afterwards granted might have lawfully made.

"78. All persons and corporations making or permitting to be made any payment or transfer *boná fide*, upon any probate or letters of administration granted in respect of the estate of any deceased person under the authority of this Act, shall be indemnified and protected in so doing, notwithstanding any defect or circumstance whatsoever affecting the validity of such probate or letters of administration." (See EXECUTOR, LETTERS OF ADMINISTRATION, PROBATE REGISTER.)

PROBATE REGISTER. A book kept for the purpose of recording particulars of all probates or letters of administration exhibited to a banker. It should contain such particulars as the date when the Probate was granted and the name of the Registry, the date when exhibited and by whom, the names of the executors, the gross value of the estate, the date of the will, the powers of the executors, the amount of legacies, and generally a brief abstract of the contents of the will. As to the letters of administration, where there is no copy will, the particulars to be recorded will be the date when the letters were granted, and the name of the Registry, the date when exhibited and by whom, the names of the administrators and the gross value of the estate. Brief particulars should also be entered in the ledger against the customer's account and a reference given to the folio in the probate book for any further information required.

PROCEEDS. The amount received from the sale of a security is commonly referred to as the proceeds. The term is also applied to the sum obtained from the collection of a cheque.

PROCURATION. By the Stamp Act, 1891, the stamp duty is :—

	£	s.	d.
PROCURATION, deed, or other instrument of	0	10	0

(See PER PROCURATION.)

PRODUCTS. The interest calculations in the current account ledger, where the amount of the balance is multiplied by the number of days during which it continues undisturbed. The resulting product is the number of pounds for one day on which interest is to be allowed or charged. The products are commonly, though incorrectly, called "decimals." (See DECIMALS.)

PROFIT AND LOSS ACCOUNT. The account which, in a bank, is made up half-yearly, showing on the one side the amounts received from interest, commission, discounts, investments, or other sources, and on the other side the amounts paid for interest on money lodged, current expenses and any other charges, the difference between the two sides being the profit or loss, as the case may be, for the half-year.

PROMISSORY NOTE. Part IV of the Bills of Exchange Act, 1882, is devoted to promissory notes. Section 83 defines a promissory note as follows:—

"(1) A promissory note is an unconditional promise in writing made by one person to another signed by the maker, engaging to pay, on demand or at a fixed or determinable future time, a sum certain in money, to, or to the order of, a Specified person or to bearer.

"(2) An instrument in the form of a note payable to maker's order is not a note within the meaning of this section unless and until it is indorsed by the maker.

"(3) A note is not invalid by reason only that it contains also a pledge of collateral security with authority to sell or dispose thereof.

"(4) A note which is, or on the face of it purports to be, both made and payable within the British Islands is an inland note. Any other note is a foreign note."

"Section 84. A promissory note is inchoate and incomplete until delivery thereof to the payee or bearer."

The following are specimens of promissory notes signed by one person:—

Leeds, *June* 1, 1910.

£100

Three months after date I promise to pay to John Brown or order the sum of One hundred pounds for value received.

JOHN JONES.

John Jones is the maker of that note, and John Brown is the payee.

Leeds, *June* 1, 1910.

£100

On demand I promise to pay to the X. & Y. Banking Company, Limited, or order, at their Leeds office, the sum of One hundred pounds with lawful interest for the same from the day of the date hereof.

JOHN JONES.

Witness

A note which is written by John Brown in the form, "I, John Brown, promise to pay," etc., is valid, without his signature appearing at the foot, but variations from the usual forms should be discouraged.

If a note on demand does not include a promise to pay interest, interest cannot legally be enforced.

"Section 85. (1) A promissory note may be made by two or more makers, and they may be liable thereon jointly, or jointly and severally, according to its tenor.

"(2) Where a note runs, 'I promise to pay,' and is signed by two or more persons, it is deemed to be their joint and several note."

The following is a specimen of a joint and several promissory note:—

Leeds, *June* 1, 1910.

£100

Three months after date we jointly and severally promise to pay to the X. & Y. Banking Company, Limited, or order, at their Leeds office, the sum of One hundred pounds with lawful interest for the same from the date hereof.

JOHN BROWN,
JOHN JONES.

Witness to both signatures

A note drawn at so many months' notice has been held to be in accordance with the Bills of Exchange Act.

When several persons sign a promissory note, the note is usually worded "We jointly and severally promise to pay," and each person signing the note is liable for the full amount. If, however, the note is worded "we jointly promise to pay," it is a promise by the combined parties and each person is not individually liable for the whole amount. In a joint note all the makers must be sued together; but in a joint and several note each may be sued separately or they may all be sued jointly.

The regulations of the Bills of Exchange Act regarding the presentment for payment of a promissory note are given in Sections 86 and 87. (See PRESENTMENT FOR PAYMENT.)

To be valid, a promissory note must not be payable upon a contingency, such as the arrival of a ship.

Sections 88 and 89 provide as follows:—

"88. The maker of a promissory note by making it—

"(1) Engages that he will pay it according to its tenor;

"(2) Is precluded from denying to a holder in due course the existence of the payee and his then capacity to indorse.

"89. (1) Subject to the provisions in this Part and, except as by this Section provided, the provisions of this Act relating to bills of exchange apply, with the necessary modifications, to promissory notes.

"(2) In applying those provisions the maker of a note shall be deemed to correspond with the acceptor of a bill, and the first indorser of a note shall be deemed to correspond with the drawer of an accepted bill payable to drawer's order.

"(3) The following provisions as to bills do not apply to notes; namely, provisions relating to—

"(*a*) Presentment for acceptance;
"(*b*) Acceptance;
"(*c*) Acceptance suprà protest;
"(*d*) Bills in a set.

"(4) Where a foreign note is dishonoured, protest thereof is unnecessary."

A promissory note made by a banker, payable to bearer on demand, is called a bank note, but bank notes for 20*s*., or more, and under £5, are prohibited in England. In Scotland and Ireland bank notes for £1 and upwards are issued. There is no limit as to the amount of other promissory notes.

A promissory note (except a bank note) cannot be re-issued. Bank notes may be re-issued as often as desired.

If a person is induced by fraud to sign a promissory note, he may, unless negligence is shown, be held not to be liable thereon. This was the decision in the case of *Lewis* v. *Clay* (1897, 14 T.L.R. 149), where a person was induced to sign under the belief that he was witnessing a signature.

A banker is liable if he pays a promissory note, domiciled with him, bearing a forged indorsement.

It frequently happens that where money is borrowed by way of promissory note that another person also signs the note as surety for the borrower. By signing the note, however, he becomes a maker of it and is liable as a maker. If Brown borrows on a joint and several promissory note and Jones signs as surety for Brown, either of them is liable to pay the amount at maturity, or, if on demand, when the banker calls for repayment. A banker should not refer to Brown as the principal and Jones as the surety, but to Brown and Jones as "the makers of the note." If Brown does not pay the note at maturity Jones is not discharged from lack of notice of dishonour, but it is advisable to give such notice. If the note continues for more than six years and during that time the interest, as well as any instalments in reduction of the amount, are paid by Brown, the payments so made by Brown will not operate to keep the note alive as against Jones. If Jones has paid nothing and given no acknowledgment of the debt for six years from the date of the note, he will be discharged. It is necessary, therefore, before the six years are up, to obtain an acknowledgment from Jones (or from the maker who has not paid anything or confirmed the debt in any way). The best plan is to get a fresh note signed by both makers before the six years expire. Each time that a payment in reduction of a promissory note on demand is made, a paying-in slip should be signed in order to afford evidence of the payment.

If a loan is made to a society or institution upon a promissory note signed, say, by the members of the committee, the members should sign as private individuals, without any reference to the name of the society or institution.

Where an advance is obtained from a banker upon a promissory note payable on demand, signed by the borrower and one or more makers (as sureties), the amount is usually debited to a separate loan account and the proceeds credited to the borrower's current account; if payable at so many months after date it is discounted. It frequently happens that when an after date promissory note is about due, it is arranged to renew it for a further period on the same signatures, and sometimes, for various reasons, it is impossible to obtain all the signatures to the new note, before the old one is due. In such a case the old note should not be cancelled but should be pinned to the new note till all the makers have signed, as in the event of any signature not being obtained the old note may be sued upon.

Where a promissory note signed, say, by Brown in favour of Jones is lodged as security for an overdraft to Jones, the note should be indorsed by Jones and a memorandum should be signed by him to show the purpose for which the note is given; and where a note is signed, say, by J. Brown and J. Jones, payable to the bank and is given as security for Brown's account, a memorandum should be signed by the two makers. The memorandum of deposit should state that the note is given for securing the sum and sums of money which shall from time to time be due or owing from the customer on whose behalf it is given, either alone or with any other person or persons either on the balance of his current account or otherwise, and that the moneys intended to be secured by the promissory note shall be recoverable thereupon, although the bank may have taken or may hereafter take any further security, or may have given time for the payment thereof.

A promissory note payable on demand, which is held as security for an account, should, for safety, be renewed, if still required, before six years from the date of the note have expired.

A promissory note payable at a fixed period after date is not regarded as a continuing security for an account and to establish the contrary, evidence is required. In the case of *In re Boys, Eedes* v. *Boys* (1870, 10 Eq. 467), where a note payable eight months after date was given as security, Lord Romilly said: "I think that the burden of proof should lie upon those who seek to establish that it was intended to be a running security for the balance of the account from time to time."

STAMP DUTY.—A promissory note of any kind whatsoever (except a bank note) drawn, or expressed to be payable, or actually paid, or indorsed, or in any manner negotiated in the United Kingdom.

	s.	d.
When the amount or value of the money for which the note is made does not exceed £5	0	1
Exceeds £5 and does not exceed £10	0	2
,, £10 ,, ,, £25	0	3
,, £25 ,, ,, £50	0	6
,, £50 ,, ,, £75	0	9
,, £75 ,, ,, £100	1	0
,, £100		
For every £100, and also for any fractional part of £100, of such amount or value	1	0

On promissory notes payable on demand or at sight, or on presentation, or not exceeding three days after date or sight, the duty is according to the above table. (Bills of exchange payable in the same way only require 1*d.*)

The Stamp Act, 1891, provides:—

"Section 33. (1) For the purposes of this Act the expression 'promissory note' includes any document or writing (except a bank note) containing a promise to pay any sum of money.

"(2) A note promising the payment of any sum of money out of any particular fund which may or may not be available, or upon any condition or contingency which may or may not be performed or happen, is to be deemed a promissory note for that sum of money."

On all inland promissory notes the stamp must be impressed.

The *ad valorem* duties upon promissory notes drawn or made out of the United Kingdom are to be denoted by adhesive stamps. (Stamp Act, 1891, Section 34, s.s. 2.) The adhesive stamps are to be Foreign Bill stamps. Every person into whose hands such a promissory note comes in the United Kingdom before it is stamped shall, before he transfers or negotiates or pays the note, affix thereto a proper adhesive stamp and cancel every stamp so affixed. (Section 35, s.s. 1.) An adhesive stamp is to be cancelled, by the person required by law to cancel it, by writing on or across the stamp his name or initials and the true date of his so writing.

The duty is calculated upon the amount of the note. If the note is drawn payable "with interest," the interest does not affect the amount of the stamp.

A bill or note issued by the Bank of England or the Bank of Ireland is exempt from stamp duty.

Where the amount secured by a promissory note is payable by instalments, the duty is simply upon the one full amount, and not upon each separate instalment.

The various sections of the Stamp Act relating to the stamp duties on bills and promissory notes are given in the article BILL OF EXCHANGE. (See PRESENTMENT FOR PAYMENT, STATUTE OF LIMITATIONS.)

PROMPT. A commercial term signifying the period of time within which a payment of purchase money must be made. The period varies in different trades, and if goods are sold to be paid for in, say, three months' time, the agreement is called a three months' prompt. If the period is four months, it is a four months' prompt, and so on.

PROOF OF DEATH. In the case of a joint account, before paying a cheque to one of the parties who represents himself to be the survivor, the banker should (unless he is fully aware of the fact) require satisfactory evidence that the other party to the account is dead, such as production of the probate, or of the letters of administration, or the death certificate or burial certificate.

PROOF OF DEBTS. A proof of debt is the form which is filled up by a creditor setting forth the amount of his claim against the estate of a bankrupt.

The proof must be made upon the regulation form, which is shown on pages 418 and 419.

The Bankruptcy Act, 1883, provides as follows :—

Description of Debts Provable in Bankruptcy.

"37. (1) Demands in the nature of unliquidated damages arising otherwise than by reason of a contract, promise, or breach of trust, shall not be provable in bankruptcy.

"(2) A person having notice of any act of bankruptcy available against the debtor shall not prove under the order for any debt or liability contracted by the debtor subsequently to the date of his so having notice.

"(3) Save as aforesaid, all debts and liabilities, present or future, certain or contingent, to which the debtor is subject at the date of the receiving order, or to which he may become subject before his discharge by reason of any obligation incurred before the date of the receiving order, shall be deemed to be debts provable in bankruptcy.

"(4) An estimate shall be made by the trustee of the value of any debt or liability provable as aforesaid, which by reason of its being subject to any contingency or contingencies, or for any other reason, does not bear a certain value."

A sum due from one party shall be set off against any sum due from the other party and the balance only shall be claimed or paid on either side respectively.

In the case of partners the joint estate shall be applicable in the first instance in payment of their joint debts, and the separate estate of each partner shall be applicable in the first instance in payment of his separate debts. If there is a surplus of the separate estates it shall be dealt with as part of the joint estate. If there is a surplus of the joint estate it shall be dealt with as part of the respective separate estates in proportion to the right and interest of each partner in the joint estate. (Section 40, s.s. 3.)

A proof of debt is limited to the amount of principal and interest due at the date of the receiving order. Interest subsequent to the receiving order cannot be added. (See INTEREST.)

If the proof is in respect of a bill of exchange, promissory note, or other negotiable instrument, on which the debtor is liable, such instrument, subject to any special order of the Court to the contrary, must be produced before the proof can be admitted either for voting or for dividend.

The rules in the second Schedule of the Bankruptcy Act, 1883, with respect to proof of debts are as follow :—

Proof in Ordinary Cases.

"1. Every creditor shall prove his debt as soon as may be after the making of a receiving order.

"2. A debt may be proved by delivering or sending through the post in a prepaid letter to the official receiver, or, if a trustee has been appointed, to the trustee, an affidavit verifying the debt.

"3. The affidavit may be made by the creditor himself, or by some person authorised by or on behalf of the creditor. If made by a person so authorised it shall state his authority and means of knowledge.

"4. The affidavit shall contain or refer to a statement of account showing the particulars of the debt, and shall specify the vouchers, if any, by which the same can be substantiated. The official receiver or trustee may at any time call for the production of the vouchers.

"5. The affidavit shall state whether the creditor is or is not a secured creditor.

"6. A creditor shall bear the cost of proving his debt, unless the Court otherwise specially orders.

"7. Every creditor who has lodged a proof shall be entitled to see and examine the proofs of other creditors before the first meeting, and at all reasonable times.

"8. A creditor proving his debt shall deduct therefrom all trade discounts, but he shall not be compelled to deduct any discount, not exceeding five per centum on the net amount of his claim, which he may have agreed to allow for payment in cash.

Proof by Secured Creditors.

"9. If a secured creditor realises his security, he may prove for the balance due to him, after deducting the net amount realised.

"10. If a secured creditor surrenders his security to the official receiver or trustee for

No. 72.—Proof of Debt. General Form.

THE BANKRUPTCY ACTS, 1883 & 1890.

Where the debt proved for exceeds £3, a Shilling Bankruptcy Stamp must be affixed here, or a postal order for 1s. be sent to the Official Receiver, as otherwise the proof cannot be admitted. Postage Stamps cannot be accepted.

NOTE. The Stamp must not be defaced by the Creditor.

(1) High Court of Justice, or County Court of——— holden at ———.

(a) Here insert the number of matter and the name of Debtor as given on the notice of meeting.

(b) Fill in full name, address, and occupation of deponent.

If proof made by Creditor strike out clauses (c) and (d). If made by Clerk of Creditor strike out (d). If by Clerk or Agent of Company strike out (c).

(e) Insert "*me* and to C. D. "and E. F., my co-partners "in trade," if any, *or if by Clerk, insert name, address and description of principal.*

NOTE.—*In case of a firm, the names of all the partners must be set out in full.*

Debt £ : :
Contra £ : :
£

NOTE THIS.

(f) *State consideration* [as— Goods sold and delivered by me] [and my said partner] to him [or them] at his [or their] request between the dates of [or monies advanced by me in respect of the undermentioned Bill of Exchange] *or as the case may be.*

* Strike out the words not applicable.

(g) "My said partners or "any of them" *or* "the "abovenamed Creditor," *as the case may be.*

(h) "My" *or* "our" *or* "their" *or* "his" *as the case may be.*

(i) Here state the particulars of all Securities held, and where the Securities are on the property of the Debtor, assess the value of the same, **and if any Bills or other Negotiable Securities be held, specify them in the Schedule.**

N.B.—Bills or other Negotiable Securities must be produced before the proof can be admitted.

In the [1] Court of

IN BANKRUPTCY. No. (*a*) of 1 .

RE (*a*)

I (*b*)

of

in the County of , make oath and say:

(*c*) That I am in the employ of the undermentioned creditor , and that I am duly authorised by to make this affidavit, and that it is within my own knowledge that the debt hereinafter deponed to was incurred, and for the consideration stated, and that such debt, to the best of my knowledge and belief, still remains unpaid and unsatisfied.

(*d*) That I am duly authorised under the seal of the Company hereinafter named, to make the Proof of Debt on its behalf.

That the said w , at the date of the Receiving Order, viz:—the day of 1 , and still justly and truly indebted to (*e*)———

in the sum of pounds

shillings and pence for (*f*)

as shown by the* {Account indorsed hereon / Account hereto annexed marked "A"} for which sum or any part thereof I say that I have not nor hath (*g*) or any person by (*h*) order to my knowledge or belief for (*h*) use had or received any manner of satisfaction or security whatsoever, save and except the following (*i*):—

Date.	Drawer.	Acceptor.	Amount.	Due date.

Admitted to vote for £ : : this day of 19 .

Official Receiver.

Admitted to rank for dividend for £ : : this day of 19 .

Trustee.

Sworn at
in the County of
this day of 19 ,
Before me

Deponent's Signature.

The Proof cannot be admitted for voting at the First Meeting unless it is properly completed and lodged with the Official Receiver before the time named in the Notice convening such Meeting.

(Credit should be given for contra accounts.)

If space not sufficient let the particulars be annexed, but where the particulars are on a separate sheet of paper the same must be marked by the person before whom the affidavit is sworn, thus :—*In Bankruptcy—This is the account marked with the letter " A " referred to in the annexed proof of debt made by* *in re* *sworn before me this* *day of* 19 .

(Signed)

Commissioner or Officer administering Oath.

DATE.	CONSIDERATION.	AMOUNT.	REMARKS. * The vouchers (if any) by which the account can be substantiated should be set out here.

Signature of Deponent

Signature of Commissioner or Officer administering Oath

the general benefit of the creditors, he may prove for his whole debt.

"11. If a secured creditor does not either realise or surrender his security, he shall, before ranking for dividend, state in his proof the particulars of his security, the date when it was given, and the value at which he assesses it, and shall be entitled to receive a dividend only in respect of the balance due to him after deducting the value so assessed.

"12. (*a*) Where a security is so valued the trustee may at any time redeem it on payment to the creditor of the assessed value.

"(*b*) If the trustee is dissatisfied with the value at which a security is assessed, he may require that the property comprised in any security so valued be offered for sale at such times and on such terms and conditions as may be agreed on between the creditor and the trustee, or as, in default of such agreement, the Court may direct. If the sale be by public auction the creditor, or the trustee on behalf of the estate, may bid or purchase.

"(*c*) Provided that the creditor may at any time, by notice in writing, require the trustee to elect whether he will or will not exercise his power of redeeming the security or requiring it to be realised, and if the trustee does not, within six months after receiving the notice, signify in writing to the creditor his election to exercise the power, he shall not be entitled to exercise it ; and the equity of redemption, or any other interest in the property comprised in the security which is vested in the trustee, shall vest in the creditor, and the amount of his debt shall be reduced by the amount at which the security has been valued.

"13. Where a creditor has so valued his security, he may at any time amend the valuation and proof on showing to the satisfaction of the trustee, or the Court, that the valuation and proof were made *bonâ fide* on a mistaken estimate, or that the security has diminished or increased in value since its previous valuation; but every such amendment shall be made at the cost of the creditor, and upon such terms as the Court shall order, unless the trustee shall allow the amendment without application to the Court.

"14. Where a valuation has been amended in accordance with the foregoing rule, the creditor shall forthwith repay any surplus dividend which he may have received in excess of that to which he would have been entitled on the amended valuation, or, as the case may be, shall be entitled to be paid out of any money for the time being available for dividend any dividend or share of dividend which he may have failed to receive by reason of the inaccuracy of the original valuation, before that money is made applicable to the payment of any future dividend, but he shall not be entitled to disturb the distribution of any dividend declared before the date of the amendment.

"15. If a creditor after having valued his security subsequently realises it, or if it is realised under the provisions of Rule 12, the net amount realised shall be substituted for the amount of any valuation previously made by the creditor, and shall be treated in all respects as an amended valuation made by the creditor.

"16. If a secured creditor does not comply with the foregoing rules he shall be excluded from all share in any dividend.

"17. Subject to the provisions of Rule 12, a creditor shall in no case receive more than twenty shillings in the pound, and interest as provided by this Act.

Proof in Respect of Distinct Contracts.

"18. If a debtor was at the date of the receiving order liable in respect of distinct contracts as a member of two or more distinct firms, or as a sole contractor, and also as member of a firm, the circumstance that the firms are in whole or in part composed of the same individuals, or that the sole contractor is also one of the joint contractors, shall not prevent proof in respect of the contracts, against the properties respectively liable on the contracts.

Periodical Payments.

"19. When any rent or other payment falls due at stated periods, and the receiving order is made at any time other than one of those periods, the person entitled to the rent or payment may prove for a proportionate part thereof up to the date of the order as if the rent or payment grew due from day to day.

Interest.

"20. On any debt or sum certain, payable at a certain time or otherwise, whereon interest is not reserved or agreed for, and which is overdue at the date of the receiving order and provable in bankruptcy, the creditor may prove for interest at a rate not exceeding four per centum per annum to the date of the order from the time when the debt or sum was payable, if the debt or sum is payable by virtue of a written instrument at a certain time, and if payable otherwise, then from the time when a demand in writing has been made giving the debtor notice that interest will be claimed from the date of the demand until the time of payment.

Debt Payable at a Future Time.

"21. A creditor may prove for a debt not payable when the debtor committed an act of bankruptcy as if it were payable presently, and may receive dividends equally with the other creditors, deducting only thereout a rebate of interest at the rate of five pounds per centum per annum computed from the declaration of a dividend to the time when the debt would have become payable, according to the terms on which it was contracted.

Admission or Rejection of Proofs.

"22. The trustee shall examine every proof and the grounds of the debt, and in writing admit or reject it, in whole or in part, or require further evidence in support of it. If he rejects a proof he shall state in writing to the creditor the grounds of the rejection.

"23. If the trustee thinks that a proof has been improperly admitted, the Court may, on the application of the trustee, after notice to the creditor who made the proof, expunge the proof or reduce its amount.

"24. If a creditor is dissatisfied with the decision of the trustee in respect of a proof, the Court may, on the application of the creditor, reverse or vary the decision.

"25. The Court may also expunge or reduce a proof upon the application of a creditor if the trustee declines to interfere in the matter, or, in the case of a composition or scheme, upon the application of the debtor.

"26. For the purpose of any of his duties in relation to proofs, the trustee may administer oaths and take affidavits.

"27. The official receiver, before the appointment of a trustee, shall have all the powers of a trustee with respect to the examination, admission, and rejection of proofs, and any act or decision of his in relation thereto shall be subject to the like appeal."

Where a banker is a holder of a bill and the acceptor and drawer become bankrupt, he may claim upon both estates for the full amount of the bill, but he must not retain more than the amount of the bill. If a dividend has already been declared on one of the estates before sending in a proof of debt on the other estate, the banker's claim on the second estate will be only for the balance after crediting the dividend declared. If there is any balance standing to the customer's credit it will be retained by the banker against the bill.

The fee, payable by means of stamps, upon a proof of debt above £2 (other than proof for workmen's wages), is one shilling, and the stamp may be impressed or adhesive. The adhesive stamp must be a "bankruptcy" stamp. An adhesive stamp shall be "cancelled by the various court or other officials by perforation or in such manner as the Commissioners of Inland Revenue may from time to time direct." (Stamp Order, 1890.)

An affidavit of proof of debt may be sworn before an assistant official receiver or any clerk of an official receiver duly authorised in writing by the Court or the Board of Trade in that behalf. (Bankruptcy Rules, No. 219 A.) The trustee may administer oaths and take affidavits. (See Rule 26, above.) Section 135 of the Bankruptcy Act, 1883, provides :—

"Subject to general rules, any affidavit to be used in a bankruptcy court may be sworn before any person authorised to administer oaths in the High Court, or in the Court of Chancery of the county palatine of Lancaster, or before any registrar of a bankruptcy court, or before any officer of a bankruptcy court authorised in writing on that behalf by the judge of the Court, or, in the case of a person residing in Scotland or in Ireland, before a judge ordinary, magistrate, or justice of the peace, or, in the case of a person who is out of the Kingdom of Great Britain and Ireland, before a magistrate or justice of the peace or other person qualified to administer oaths in the country where he resides (he being certified to be a magistrate or justice of the peace, or qualified as aforesaid by a British minister or British consul, or by a notary public)."

The Bankruptcy Act, 1890, Section 24, enacts that an affidavit may be sworn "also in England and Wales before a justice of the peace for the county or place where it is sworn."

Any alteration or interlineation must be authenticated by the initials of the person taking the affidavit, and in the case of erasure the words or figures must be re-written and signed or initialled in the margin by the person taking it. (See BANKRUPTCY.)

PROPERTY TAX. The popular name for income tax upon property in lands and buildings. (See INCOME TAX.)

PROSPECTUS. A prospectus is any notice, circular, advertisement, or other invitation, offering to the public for subscription or purchase any shares or debentures of a company.

A form of application for shares is usually sent out along with the prospectus. This form is filled up by anyone desiring shares and is forwarded, along with the amount payable on application, to the company or its bankers. When the shares are allotted by the company a letter of allotment is sent to the applicant. (See ALLOTMENT.)

The name of the company's bankers usually appears upon a prospectus. Unless the banker actually joins in the invitation to the public to subscribe, he is not liable for any statements contained in the prospectus. A company should always obtain a banker's permission before putting his name in a prospectus, for although the insertion of a banker's name does not in any way act as a guarantee or a recommendation to the public, there is no doubt that it may have a considerable influence in moving many persons to take up the investment.

The Companies (Consolidation) Act, 1908, provides :—

Specific Requirements as to Particulars of Prospectus.

"81. (1) Every prospectus issued by or on

behalf of a company, or by or on behalf of any person who is or has been engaged or interested in the formation of the company, must state :—

"(*a*) the contents of the memorandum, with the names, descriptions, and addresses of the signatories, and the number of shares subscribed for by them respectively; and the number of founders or management or deferred shares, if any, and the nature and extent of the interest of the holders in the property and profits of the company; and

"(*b*) the number of shares, if any, fixed by the articles as the qualification of a director, and any provision in the articles as to the remuneration of the directors; and

"(*c*) the names, descriptions, and addresses of the directors or proposed directors; and

"(*d*) the minimum subscription on which the directors may proceed to allotment, and the amount payable on application and allotment on each share; and in the case of a second or subsequent offer of shares, the amount offered for subscription on each previous allotment made within the two preceding years, and the amount actually allotted, and the amount, if any, paid on the shares so allotted; and

"(*e*) the number and amount of shares and debentures which within the two preceding years have been issued, or agreed to be issued, as fully or partly paid up otherwise than in cash, and in the latter case the extent to which they are so paid up, and in either case the consideration for which those shares or debentures have been issued or are proposed or intended to be issued; and

"(*f*) the names and addresses of the vendors of any property purchased or acquired by the company, or proposed so to be purchased or acquired, which is to be paid for wholly or partly out of the proceeds of the issue offered for subscription by the prospectus, or the purchase or acquisition of which has not been completed at the date of issue of the prospectus, and the amount payable in cash, shares, or debentures, to the vendor, and where there is more than one separate vendor, or the company is a sub-purchaser, the amount so payable to each vendor: Provided that where the vendors or any of them are a firm the members of the firm shall not be treated as separate vendors; and

"(*g*) the amount (if any) paid or payable as purchase money in cash, shares, or debentures, for any such property as aforesaid, specifying the amount (if any) payable for goodwill; and

"(*h*) the amount (if any) paid within the two preceding years, or payable, as commission for subscribing or agreeing to subscribe, or procuring or agreeing to procure subscriptions, for any shares in, or debentures of, the company, or the rate of any such commission: Provided that it shall not be necessary to state the commission payable to sub-underwriters; and

"(*i*) the amount or estimated amount of preliminary expenses; and

"(*j*) the amount paid within the two preceding years or intended to be paid to any promoter, and the consideration for any such payment; and

"(*k*) the dates of and parties to every material contract, and a reasonable time and place at which any material contract or a copy thereof may be inspected: Provided that this requirement shall not apply to a contract entered into in the ordinary course of the business carried on or intended to be carried on by the company, or to any contract entered into more than two years before the date of issue of the prospectus; and

"(*l*) the names and addresses of the auditors (if any) of the company; and

"(*m*) full particulars of the nature and extent of the interest (if any) of every director in the promotion of, or in the property proposed to be acquired by, the company, or, where the interest of such a director consists in being a partner in a firm, the nature and extent of the interest of the firm, with a statement of all sums paid or agreed to be paid to him or to the firm in cash or shares or otherwise by any person either to induce him to become, or to qualify him as, a director, or, otherwise for services rendered by him or by the firm in connection with the promotion or formation of the company; and

"(*n*) where the company is a company having shares of more than one class, the right of voting at meetings of the company conferred by the several classes of shares respectively.

"(5) Where any such prospectus as is mentioned in this Section is published as a newspaper advertisement, it shall not be necessary in the advertisement to specify the contents of the memorandum or the signatories thereto, and the number of shares subscribed for by them.

"(7) This Section shall not apply to a circular or notice inviting existing members or debenture holders of a company to subscribe either for shares or for debentures of the company, whether with or without the right to renounce in favour of other persons, but subject as aforesaid, this Section shall apply to any prospectus whether issued on or with reference to the formation of a company or subsequently.

"(8) The requirements of this Section as to the memorandum and the qualification, remuneration, and interest of directors, the names, descriptions, and addresses of directors or proposed directors, and the amount or estimated amount of preliminary expenses, shall not apply in the case of a prospectus issued more than one year after the date at which the company is entitled to commence business."

A company which does not issue a prospectus with reference to its formation must file with the registrar a statement, in lieu of a prospectus. The statement must be in the form set out in the second Schedule to the above Act. This does not apply to a private company. (Section 82.)

All persons who are responsible for the issue of a prospectus are liable to pay compensation to anyone who subscribes for any shares or debentures, on the faith of the prospectus, for loss or damage they may have sustained by reason of any untrue statement therein, unless it can be proved that they acted honestly in making the statements. (See COMPANIES.)

PROTEST. A protest is the official certificate given by a notary public respecting the dishonour of a bill of exchange by non-acceptance or non-payment. When a bill is dishonoured, a holder may hand it to a notary public to be protested. London bankers usually hold a dishonoured bill till the close of business and then, if to be noted, send it to a notary. The notary presents it again to the drawee or to the acceptor, and if acceptance or payment is still not obtained, a note of the facts is made upon the bill, or upon a slip attached to the bill, which act constitutes a "noting" of the bill. The official certificate, or protest, may be extended subsequently, as of the date of the noting, but the noting must take place on the day the bill is dishonoured. If not noted on the day of dishonour it cannot be done afterwards to be of any value. A notary may present the bill at any time on the day of maturity.

It is not necessary to note or protest an

inland bill in order to preserve the recourse against the drawer or indorsers, though they are sometimes noted, but, in the case of foreign bills, it is necessary to have them noted and protested, unless the remitter of the bills sends instructions that they are not to be noted or protested.

Where an acceptor has become bankrupt or has disappeared, a bill is sometimes protested "for better security." In such a case the bill would be presented at the address of the acceptor (not at the bank where it may have been accepted payable) and better security asked for, and be protested accordingly.

The rules regarding the noting or protest of a bill are contained in Section 51 of the Bills of Exchange Act, 1882:—

"(1) Where an inland bill has been dishonoured it may, if the holder think fit, be noted for non-acceptance or non-payment, as the case may be; but it shall not be necessary to note or protest any such bill in order to preserve the recourse against the drawer or indorser.

"(2) Where a foreign bill, appearing on the face of it to be such, has been dishonoured by non-acceptance it must be duly protested for non-acceptance, and where such a bill, which has not been previously dishonoured by non-acceptance, is dishonoured by non-payment it must be duly protested for non-payment. If it be not so protested the drawer and indorsers are discharged. Where a bill does not appear on the face of it to be a foreign bill, protest thereof in case of dishonour is unnecessary.

"(3) A bill which has been protested for non-acceptance may be subsequently protested for non-payment.

"(4) Subject to the provisions of this Act, when a bill is noted or protested, it must be noted on the day of its dishonour. When a bill has been duly noted, the protest may be subsequently extended as of the date of the noting.

"(5) Where the acceptor of a bill becomes bankrupt or insolvent or suspends payment before it matures, the holder may cause the bill to be protested for better security against the drawer and indorsers.

"(6) A bill must be protested at the place where it is dishonoured: Provided that—

"(a) When a bill is presented through the post office, and returned by post dishonoured, it may be protested at the place to which it is returned and on the day of its return if received during business hours, and if not received during business hours, then not later than the next business day:

"(b) When a bill drawn payable at the place of business or residence of some person other than the drawee, has been dishonoured by non-acceptance, it must be protested for non-payment at the place where it is expressed to be payable, and no further presentment for payment to, or demand on, the drawee is necessary.

"(7) A protest must contain a copy of the bill, and must be signed by the notary making it, and must specify—

"(a) The person at whose request the bill is protested:

"(b) The place and date of protest, the cause or reason for protesting the bill, the demand made, and the answer given, if any, or the fact that the drawee or acceptor could not be found.

"(8) When a bill is lost or destroyed, or is wrongly detained from the person entitled to hold it, protest may be made on a copy or written particulars thereof.

"(9) Protest is dispensed with by any circumstance which would dispense with notice of dishonour. Delay in noting or protesting is excused when the delay is caused by circumstances beyond the control of the holder, and not imputable to his default, misconduct, or negligence. When the cause of delay ceases to operate the bill must be noted or protested with reasonable diligence."

Section 93 of the Act defines when noting is equivalent to protest:—

"For the purposes of this Act, where a bill

or note is required to be protested within a specified time or before some further proceeding is taken, it is sufficient that the bill has been noted for protest before the expiration of the specified time or the taking of the proceeding; and the formal protest may be extended at any time thereafter as of the date of the noting."

Where a notary public is not accessible, Section 94 of the Act makes provision for a bill to be protested by a householder or substantial resident of the place, in the presence of two witnesses. The words of the Section are :—

"Where a dishonoured bill or note is authorised or required to be protested, and the services of a notary cannot be obtained at the place where the bill is dishonoured, any householder or substantial resident of the place may, in the presence of two witnesses, give a certificate, signed by them, attesting the dishonour of the bill, and the certificate shall in all respects operate as if it were a formal protest of the bill.

"The form given in Schedule I to this Act may be used with necessary modifications, and if used shall be sufficient."

"SCHEDULE I.

Form of protest which may be used when the services of a notary cannot be obtained.

Know all men that I, A. B. (householder), of   in the county of   , in the United Kingdom, at the request of C. D., there being no notary public available, did on the   day of   , 188 , at   , demand payment (or acceptance) of the bill of exchange hereunder written, from E. F., to which demand he made answer (state answer, if any), wherefore I now, in the presence of G. H. and J. K., do protest he said bill of exchange.

Signed A. B.
G. H. }
J. K. } Witnesses.

N.B.—The bill itself should be annexed, or a copy of the bill and all that is written thereon should be underwritten."

It is to be observed that G. H. and J. K. are merely witnesses to A. B.'s signature, not witnesses to the presentment of the bill.

When this form of protest is used it is not preceded by "noting." The Act does not specifically refer to "noting," but the above Section enacts that the certificate shall in all respects operate as if it were a formal protest of the bill. The stamp duty is the same as for an ordinary protest. (See below.)

A holder of a dishonoured bill may recover from any party liable on the bill the expenses of noting, or, when protest is necessary, and the protest has been extended, the expenses of protest. (Section 57, s.s. 1 (c).) Where payment is made to a notary when he presents the bill, the acceptor should pay the notary's charges, though it has been decided that, in such a case, the notary's charges cannot be enforced by law against the acceptor.

The date on which bills are to be protested in foreign countries depends upon the laws of those countries.

STAMP DUTY.—By the Stamp Act, 1891 :—

PROTEST of any bill of exchange or promissory note—

	£	s.	d.
Where the duty on the bill or note does not exceed 1s. . .	The same duty as the bill or note.		
In any other case . . .	0	1	0

"Section 90. The duty upon a notarial act, and upon the protest by a notary public of a bill of exchange or promissory note, may be denoted by an adhesive stamp, which is to be cancelled by the notary."

The duty is the same upon the copy of a protest.

Postage stamps are used when the stamp is an adhesive one. The duty may also be denoted by an impressed stamp. (See BILL OF EXCHANGE, NOTING.)

PROTEST PAYMENTS. In connection with the clearing of country cheques through the London Clearing House, there exists a system by which one or two days are added to the usual two days which are allowed for clearing the cheques. Where, from any cause, cheques have not reached the drawee bank from the London agent, or no acknowledgment has been received, the London Agent, when settling up the balance of clearing two days after the cheques were received at the Clearing House, gives notice to the bank from which the cheques were received that payment for them is made under protest. The London bank which receives the notice then, in turn, communicates the information to the country bank, or other channel, from which it received the cheques.

In connection with the Metropolitan clearing, it is permissible for a bank to pay any of its Metropolitan branches under protest on Saturdays, when necessary. (See the rules for the Metropolitan clearing under CLEARING HOUSE.)

PROVISIONAL CERTIFICATE. The certificate which is issued to a person who has agreed to take up, say, some new bonds which a foreign state is issuing. When the various instalments have been paid, the bonds are issued in exchange for the provisional or scrip certificate. (See SCRIP CERTIFICATE.)

PROXY. The person who acts for another, also the document appointing him. The articles of association of a company usually provide for votes being given by proxy.

The instrument appointing a proxy may be in the following form or in any other form which the directors shall approve :—

COMPANY, LIMITED.

I of in the county of being a member of the Company, Limited, hereby appoint of as my proxy to vote for me and on my behalf at the [ordinary *or* extraordinary, *as the case may be*] general meeting of the company to be held on the day of and at any adjournment thereof.

Signed this day of .

Articles of association often contain a clause that no person shall act as a proxy unless he is entitled on his own behalf to be present and vote at the meeting at which he acts as proxy.

Section 68 of the Companies (Consolidation) Act, 1908, gives power to a company which is a member of another company, by resolution of the directors, to authorise any of its officials or any other person to act as its representative at any meeting of the other company, and to exercise the same powers on behalf of the company which he represents, as if he were an individual shareholder of the other company. (See MEETINGS.)

The instrument appointing a proxy must be deposited at the registered office of the company within the time specified in the articles.

The stamp duty on a letter or power of attorney, or other instrument for the sole purpose of appointing or authorising a proxy to vote at any one meeting at which votes may be given by proxy, whether the number of persons named in such instrument be one or more, is one penny. (See under POWER OF ATTORNEY.) If the instrument is for use at more meetings than one, the duty is 10*s*.

Section 80 of the Stamp Act, 1891, provides as follows :—

"(1) Every letter or power of attorney for the purpose of appointing a proxy to vote at a meeting, and every voting paper, hereby respectively charged with the duty of one penny, is to specify the day upon which the meeting at which it is intended to be used is to be held, and is to be available only at the meeting so specified, and any adjournment thereof.

"(2) The duty of one penny may be denoted by an adhesive stamp, which is to be cancelled by the person by whom the instrument is executed, and a letter or power of attorney or voting paper charged with the duty of one penny is not to be stamped after the execution thereof by any person.

"(3) Every person who makes or executes, or votes, or attempts to vote, under or by means of any such letter or power of attorney or voting paper, not being duly stamped, shall incur a fine of fifty pounds, and every vote given or tendered under the authority or by means of the letter or power of attorney or voting paper, shall be void."

By the Finance Act, 1907, Section 9, so much of s.s. 2 of Section 80 of the Stamp Act, 1891, as prevents the stamping after execution of a letter or power of attorney or voting paper charged with the duty of one penny, shall cease to apply as regards any such instrument which has been first executed at any place out of the United Kingdom, and, accordingly, any such instrument so executed after the commencement of this Act may be stamped after execution in accordance with Section 15 of the said Act. (See STAMP DUTIES.)

A proxy in connection with bankruptcy proceedings is exempt from stamp duty. (Bankruptcy Act, 1883, Section 144.) (See COMPANIES, VOTES.)

PUBLIC ACCOUNT. By Section 18 of the Exchequer and Audit Departments Act, 1866 (29 & 30 Vict. c. 39) :—

"The Treasury may, from time to time, determine at what banks accountants shall keep the public moneys entrusted to them; and they may also determine what accounts so opened in the names of public officers or accountants in the books of the Bank of England, or the Bank of Ireland, or of any other bank, shall be deemed public accounts; and on the death, resignation, or removal of any such public officers or accountants the balances remaining at the credit of such accounts shall, upon the appointment of their successors, unless otherwise directed by law, vest in and be transferred to the public accounts of such successors at the said banks, and shall not, in the event of the death of any such public officers or accountants, constitute assets of the deceased, or be in any manner subject to the control of their legal representatives."

By the Stamp Act, 1891, the following are exempt from stamp duty:—

Draft or order drawn upon any banker in the United Kingdom by an officer of a public department of the State for the payment of money out of a public account.

Bill drawn in the United Kingdom for the sole purpose of remitting money to be placed to any account of public revenue. (See list of exemptions under BILL OF EXCHANGE.)

PUBLIC COMPANY. Any seven or more persons associated for any lawful purpose may by subscribing their names to a memorandum of association and complying with the law regarding registration, form an incorporated company, with or without limited liability. (See MEMORANDUM OF ASSOCIATION.) When the company advertises itself by a prospectus and annual balance sheet it is a public company. A public company must file, with the registrar of companies, a prospectus or statement before allotting any shares or debentures. (See PROSPECTUS.) (See COMPANIES, PRIVATE COMPANY.)

PUBLIC EXAMINATION OF DEBTOR. When a receiving order has been made, the debtor must, within three days, if the order is made on the debtor's petition, or within seven days, if made upon the petition of a creditor, submit a statement of his affairs to the official receiver. (See RECEIVING ORDER.)

As soon as convenient after the expiration of the time for delivery of the statement, the Court shall hold a public sitting for the examination of the debtor. Section 17 of the Bankruptcy Act, 1883, is as follows:—

"(1) Where the Court makes a receiving order it shall hold a public sitting, on a day to be appointed by the Court, for the examination of the debtor, and the debtor shall attend thereat, and shall be examined as to his conduct, dealings, and property.

"(2) The examination shall be held as soon as conveniently may be after the expiration of the time for the submission of the debtor's statement of affairs.

"(3) The Court may adjourn the examination from time to time.

"(4) Any creditor who has tendered a proof, or his representative authorised in writing, may question the debtor concerning his affairs and the causes of his failure.

"(5) The official receiver shall take part in the examination of the debtor; and for the purpose thereof, if specially authorised by the Board of Trade, may employ a solicitor with or without counsel.

"(6) If a trustee is appointed before the conclusion of the examination he may take part therein.

"(7) The Court may put such questions to the debtor as it may think expedient.

"(8) The debtor shall be examined upon oath, and it shall be his duty to answer all such questions as the Court may put or allow to be put to him. Such notes of the examination as the Court thinks proper shall be taken down in writing, and shall be read over to and signed by the debtor, and may thereafter be used in evidence against him; they shall also be open to the inspection of any creditor at all reasonable times.

"(9) When the Court is of opinion that the affairs of the debtor have been sufficiently investigated, it shall, by order, declare that his examination is concluded, but such order shall not be made until after the day appointed for the first meeting of creditors." (See BANKRUPTCY.)

PUBLIC FUNDS. (See NATIONAL DEBT.)

PUBLIC TRUSTEE. The powers and duties of the Public Trustee are detailed in a pamphlet issued from the Public Trustee Office, from which the following is taken:—

The Public Trustee Act, 1906, which came into operation on January 1, 1908, was passed with the express object of enabling the public to guard against the risks and inconveniences which are incidental to the employment of private individuals in trust matters. On and after the first day of January, 1908, the public may (instead of selecting a private individual) secure the services of the Public Trustee. In the Public Trustee, the public will have an executor or trustee, who will never die, never leave the country, and never become incapacitated, and whose responsibility is guaranteed by the Consolidated Fund of the United Kingdom.

CAPACITIES IN WHICH THE PUBLIC TRUSTEE MAY ACT.—The Public Trustee is authorised, if duly appointed, to act in any of the following capacities :—

(1) Executor or executor and trustee of a will.
(2) Trustee or custodian trustee of a settlement (including a will).
(3) Administrator under a will or on an intestacy.
(4) Administrator of estates of small value.
(5) Judicial trustee.
(6) Administrator of the property of a convict under the Forfeiture Act, 1870, and
(7) Investigator and auditor of trust accounts.

The Public Trustee has, in addition to certain privileges conferred upon him by the Act, all the same powers, duties, and liabilities, and is entitled to the same rights and immunities, and is subject to the control and orders of the Court, as a private trustee acting in the same capacity. The Public Trustee may, however, decline either absolutely, or except on conditions prescribed by the rules, to accept any trust, but he cannot decline on the ground only of the small value of the property. He may not accept any trust under a deed of arrangement for the benefit of creditors, nor for the administration of any estate known or believed by him to be insolvent, nor made solely by way of security for money, nor exclusively for religious or charitable purposes.

WILLS.—The Public Trustee may be appointed even although the will was made or came into operation prior to January 1, 1908, either alone or jointly with any other person or persons as executor, or as trustee, or as executor and trustee of a will, and either as ordinary trustee or as custodian trustee. He may be appointed in the simplest form possible, e.g. : "I appoint the Public Trustee as the executor and trustee of this my will."

The substitution of the name of the Public Trustee in a will already in existence for the names of the executors and trustees named therein, or the addition of his name, can be effected by a simple codicil.

The Public Trustee's acceptance of the office need not be invited at the time the will or codicil is made, although it is desirable that this course should be adopted when the trust is of an unusual nature.

On the death of a testator it is the duty of the co-executor, if any, to inquire of the Public Trustee if he is prepared to act. On acceptance of office he executes an instrument of consent.

Even after probate has been obtained an executor may, with the sanction of the Court, transfer the estate to the Public Trustee.

The Public Trustee may be appointed either as an original trustee of a settlement, or as a new trustee, or as an additional trustee. In the case of an existing settlement the persons entitled to appoint the Public Trustee are the person or persons having power to do so under the settlement, or if there are no such persons, then the continuing or surviving trustees or their executors or administrators. Inquiry should first be made if he will accept office, and notice should be sent to all persons beneficially interested to ascertain if they are agreeable to the appointment.

Private trustees may retire, either singly or together, in favour of the Public Trustee.

The Public Trustee may be appointed custodian trustee. On appointment, all securities and documents of title relating to the trust property, which would otherwise have remained in the custody of the ordinary trustees, are to be transferred to the Public Trustee ; but the management of the trust property, as distinct from the custody of the securities, is to remain in the hands of the ordinary or managing trustees.

Any person or persons interested in an estate, the gross capital value whereof can be proved to the satisfaction of the Public Trustee to be under £1,000, may apply in writing to the Public Trustee to administer the estate, and thereupon, unless he sees good reason to the contrary, if it appears to him that the persons beneficially entitled are persons of small means, the Public Trustee will undertake the administration.

Under the Public Trustee Act a trustee or beneficiary can obtain an audit of trust accounts without applying to the Court. Formal application must be made to the Public Trustee for the audit.

As a rule, the Public Trustee may not agree to act as ordinary trustee where the trust involves the carrying on of a business, except where the carrying on of the business has for its ultimate object the sale or winding up of the business. But if he is to act merely as custodian trustee the carrying on of the business is immaterial, but he must not act in the management of the business, or hold any property which will expose the holder to any liability unless fully secured against loss.

The Public Trustee may employ such bankers and other persons as he may consider necessary, and in determining who is to be employed he is to have regard to the interests of the trust, and when practicable to take into consideration the wishes of the creator of the trust and of the other trustees, if any, either expressed or as implied by the practice of the creator of the trust or in the previous management of the trust.

The fees payable are: (1) capital fee; (2) income fee; (3) investment fee. They are due :—

Capital Fee.—Half on acceptance of the trust, the remainder gradually as the capital is diminished.

Income Fee.—This will be deducted from income.

Investment Fee.—This is payable on the making of an investment.

1. CAPITAL FEES.—Where the Public Trustee acts as ordinary trustee or executor, a fee is leviable on acceptance of the trust and also on the withdrawal of capital therefrom. The former fee is payable in a lump sum; the latter, as a rule, in instalments. Both fees are, unless otherwise desired, paid out of the capital of the trust funds.

The following table shows the scale of capital fees ordinarily chargeable; the minimum fee in respect of a trust both as to acceptance and withdrawal of capital therefrom being £1 :—

SCALE OF FEES.*

Capital Values.	Not exceeding £1,000.	On excess of £1,000 up to £20,000.	On excess of £20,000 up to £50,000.	On excess of £50,000.
Fee due on Probate or other acceptance of Trust, a percentage of.	s. d. 15 0	s. d. 5 0	s. d. 2 6	s. d. 1 3

* N.B.—Half these fees are payable where the Public Trustee acts merely as Custodian Trustee.

(*a*) *Capital Fee on Probate or other Acceptance of Trust.*—Some examples of the capital fee payable on probate or other acceptance of a trust are given below.

EXAMPLES.

Value.	Fee.			Value.	Fee.		
£	£	s.	d.	£	£	s.	d.
200	1	10	0	10,000	30	0	0
250	1	17	6	12,500	36	5	0
400	3	0	0	15,000	42	10	0
500	3	15	0	20,000	55	0	0
750	5	12	6	25,000	61	5	0
1,000	7	10	0	50,000	92	10	0
1,500	8	15	0	75,000	108	2	6
1,800	9	10	0	100,000	123	15	0
2,000	10	0	0	250,000	217	10	0
2,500	11	5	0	500,000	373	15	0
5,000	17	10	0	750,000	530	0	0
7,500	23	15	0	1,000,000	686	5	0

(*b*) *Fee on Withdrawal of Capital.*—On withdrawal of any capital, a fee at a rate equal to the rate per £100 at which the fee upon the acceptance of the trust was payable in respect of the entire trust property.

Example—

The fee due upon acceptance of an estate valued at £10,000 would be

	£		s.	d.		£	£	s.	d.
As to	1,000	at	15	0	per	100 =	7	10	0
As to	9,000	at	5	0	per	100 =	22	10	0
Capital value	£10,000					Total fee	£30	0	0

It will be seen that the total fee of £30 would be produced by an all-round rate of 6*s*. per £100. This rate, therefore, will be the rate of fee taken on withdrawal of any capital, thus ensuring the equitable principle that the fees taken share the same fortune (whether good or ill) as the estate. Thus if the trust securities had increased in value and £10,500 was eventually distributable the fee payable would be £31 10*s*. If, on the other hand, the trust securities had diminished in value and £9,500 was eventually distributable, the fee payable would be £28 10*s*.

2. INCOME FEES.—Upon the annual income of the trust property a fee is payable at the rate of £2 per £100 upon all income not exceeding £500 a year; where the income exceeds £500 a year, then a fee of £1 per £100 is payable on such excess. Where practicable the Public Trustee may authorise the payment of income direct to the person entitled thereto, or to his bankers. In this

case the fee upon income will not exceed £1 per £100 throughout. (Minimum fee, 2*s*. 6*d*.) Some examples of income fees are given in the table printed below.

EXAMPLES OF INCOME FEES.

Income.	Annual Fee.			Income.	Annual Fee.			Income.	Annual Fee.		
£	£	*s.*	*d.*	£	£	*s.*	*d.*	£	£	*s.*	*d.*
250	5	0	0	1,000	15	0	0	5,000	55	0	0
300	6	0	0	1,200	17	0	0	7,500	80	0	0
400	8	0	0	1,500	20	0	0	10,000	105	0	0
500	10	0	0	1,800	23	0	0	15,000	155	0	0
600	11	0	0	2,000	25	0	0	20,000	205	0	0
750	12	10	0	2,500	30	0	0				
800	13	0	0	4,000	45	0	0				

3. INVESTMENT FEES.—(*a*) *Investment in Stocks, etc.* Upon any investment in stocks, funds, shares, or securities (other than a purchase of land or mortgages or charges) a fee at the rate of 10*s*. per cent. (which covers the cost of brokerage) is charged on the sum invested.

(*b*) *Investment in Land, etc.*—Upon any purchase or sale of any land or any investment by way of mortgage or charge, the fee charged is at the rate of 2*s*. 6*d*. per cent. on the purchase money or money advanced.

As has been already stated, where the Public Trustee acts merely as custodian trustee, the capital fee payable on acceptance and withdrawal of capital is half that due in the case where he acts as trustee of an ordinary trust. The income and investment fees are the same as in an ordinary trust.

Further information regarding the duties of the Public Trustee as custodian trustee will be found under the heading CUSTODIAN TRUSTEE.

Particulars as to the peculiar practice of the Department when transferring securities are given in the article TRANSFER OF SECURITIES (PUBLIC TRUSTEE).

Where the Public Trustee acts as trustee of landed property settled in strict settlement, the fee on acceptance is the same as that payable where the Public Trustee acts as custodian trustee. No further capital fee is payable, so long as the property remains in strict settlement or is re-settled. If the trust is eventually put an end to, then a fee on withdrawal of the property will be due. Upon raising money under any trust or power in the settlement, e.g. portions for younger children, a fee at the rate of 2*s*. 6*d*. for every £100 so raised is charged, the minimum fee being £1. The investment fee is the same as in an ordinary trust. The income fee would be a matter of special arrangement in each case.

Where the Public Trustee acts as trustee of reversionary property, the only fee immediately payable is £1. It is not till the property ultimately falls into possession that the ordinary fees are payable. (See CUSTODIAN TRUSTEE, TRUSTEE.)

PUR AUTRE VIE. French, for the life of another.

PUT. A Stock Exchange term meaning the right to sell a specified security at a fixed price within an arranged period. (See OPTIONS.)

PUT AND CALL. A Stock Exchange term. A double option, that is, a right to buy or to sell a certain amount of a specified stock at a date and at a price as fixed when the option was purchased.

PYX. (See TRIAL OF THE PYX.)

QUALIFIED ACCEPTANCE. (See ACCEPTANCE, QUALIFIED.)

QUALIFYING AGREEMENT. When a customer transfers shares to a bank, or its nominees, as security for an overdraft or a loan, it is usual for the customer to sign an agreement at the same time qualifying the transfer. The transfer conveys the ownership in the shares out and out to the banker, but the agreement qualifies it by stating that the transfer is given merely as a security. When the security is no longer required the shares are retransferred to the customer. If the shares are realised by the banker in order to obtain repayment of the debt, any surplus must be handed to the customer. The stamp duty on such an agreement under hand is sixpence. (See Section 23, s.s. 2, Stamp Act, 1891, under AGREEMENT.) The stamp may be either impressed or adhesive. If under seal the duty is *ad valorem* like a mortgage. See Section 86, s.s. 1 (*d*), of the Stamp Act, 1891 (under MORTGAGE), which says that the term "mortgage" includes any defeasance or other deed for qualifying any transfer of any property, apparently absolute, but intended only as a security. (See TRANSFER OF SHARES.)

QUARTER DAYS. The English Quarter Days are :—

Lady Day . .	March 25.
Midsummer Day .	June 24.
Michaelmas . .	September 29.
Christmas Day .	December 25.

The Scottish Quarter Days are :—

Candlemas . .	February 2.
Whitsunday . .	May 15.
Lammas . . .	August 1.
Martinmas . .	November 11.

QUIT RENT. In feudal times where land was granted by the lord of the manor for certain services to be rendered to the lord, those services could sometimes be got quit of by the payment of a rent, called quit rent.

By Section 45 of the Conveyancing Act, 1881, a quit rent may be redeemed. On the requisition of the owner, the Copyhold Commissioners shall certify the amount in consideration whereof the rent may be redeemed.

QUORUM. Literally, of whom, e.g. there may be twenty directors, "of whom" (*quorum*) three may act.

A quorum is the number of persons which must be present at a meeting of the directors or members of a company before any business can be done. In companies which are governed by Table A (see ARTICLES OF ASSOCIATION), no business can be transacted at a general meeting unless three members are present. Regulation 52 of that Table is—"If within half an hour from the time appointed for the meeting a quorum is not present, the meeting, if convened upon the requisition of members, shall be dissolved. In any other case it shall stand adjourned to the same day in the next week at the same time and place, and, if at the adjourned meeting a quorum is not present within half an hour from the time appointed for the meeting the members present shall be a quorum."

Where a company has articles other than those of Table A they should be perused to ascertain how many members constitute a quorum.

QUOTATION ON LONDON STOCK EXCHANGE. The Committee of the Stock Exchange may order the quotation in the Official List of any security of sufficient magnitude and importance. Applications for quotation must be made to the Secretary of the Share and Loan Department, and must comply with such conditions and requirements as may be ordered from time to time by the committee. Three days' public notice must be given of every application. A broker, a member of the Stock Exchange, must be authorised to give the Committee full information as to the security and to furnish them with all particulars they may require. (Rule 139, London Stock Exchange.)

The regulations with regard to share and stock certificates are : All certificates should state on their face the authority under which the company is constituted, and the amount of the authorised capital of the company. The following foot-note should appear on all stock and share certificates, "The company will not transfer any stock [shares] without the production of a certificate relating to such stock [shares], which certificate must be surrendered before any deed of transfer, whether for the whole or any portion thereof, can be registered or a new certificate issued in exchange." Where the capital of a company consists of more than one class of shares of the same denomination, the distinctive numbers of the shares of each class must be printed on the face of the share certificates. All preference share certificates should bear on their face a statement of the company's capital and the conditions, both as to capital and dividends, under which the shares are issued. Debentures and debenture stock certificates should, in addition to legal requirements, state on their face the authority under which the company is constituted, the nominal capital of the company, the dates when the interest on the debentures or debenture stock is payable, and the authority under which the issue is made (i.e. articles of association and resolutions) ; and on their back the conditions of issue, redemption and transfer.

RACK RENT. A rent which, as its name implies, has been stretched or raised to the full annual value of the property, so that no more can be obtained.

RATE OF EXCHANGE. The price of money in one country stated in the currency of another country. (See COURSE OF EXCHANGE, FOREIGN EXCHANGES.)

RATES. A comparison of the Bank and money market rates and market discounts may be made from the following list, which gives the rates on April 7, 1910 :—

	Per cent.
Bank Rate	4
Bank of England loans	$4\frac{1}{2}$
Bankers' deposit rate	$2\frac{1}{2}$
Brokers' deposit rate, call. . . .	$2\frac{1}{2}$
,, ,, ,, notice . . .	$2\frac{3}{4}$
Day-to-day loans	$2\frac{1}{2}$–3
Seven-day market loans	$3\frac{1}{2}$
3 months' bank bills	$3\frac{13}{16}$

	Per cent.
4 months' bank bills	$3\frac{3}{4}$
6 ,, ,, ,,	$3\frac{1}{2}$–$3\frac{5}{8}$
3 months' fine trade bills	4–$4\frac{1}{4}$
4 ,, ,, ,,	4–$4\frac{1}{4}$
6 ,, ,, ,,	$4\frac{1}{4}$–$4\frac{1}{2}$

(See BANK RATE, CHEQUE RATE, DEPOSIT RATE, DISCOUNT, FOREIGN EXCHANGES, INTEREST, INTEREST ON DEPOSIT RECEIPT, LONG RATE, MARKET RATE, SHORT RATE.

REALTY. (From Lat., *res*, a thing.) Property is divisible into "real" and "personal," or "realty" and "personalty."

Realty includes freehold (whether in fee simple, in fee tail or for life), and copyhold and customary freehold land, but not leasehold land (leasehold is included under personalty). Where real property is to be sold, according to the terms of a will, it is reckoned as personalty.

An "equity of redemption" is part of the real estate.

If Brown leaves his "real" property to Jones, Jones is called the devisee, and the property is said to be devised. If he leaves "personal" property, Jones is called the legatee and the property is said to be bequeathed.

The distinction in terms arose in olden times when a property wrongfully detained could be actually recovered as a "real" property, a "realty"; but if damages only could be recovered against the person wrongfully detaining, as in the case of leasehold property, it was a personal property or "personalty." (See PERSONALTY.)

REBATE. Literally a drawing back. At the end of a half-year a banker calculates the amount of rebate on bills discounted—that is, he takes into his profit and loss account only the amount of discount up to the end of the half-year, the discount from that date till the maturity of the bills (the rebate amount) being carried forward into the accounts for the next half. The rebate is one of the items which passes through the adjustment of interest account (*q.v.*).

The word is also used with reference to an amount of interest credited to an account to refund a sum previously charged.

If a documentary bill is paid before maturity it is said to be paid under rebate, an allowance of $\frac{1}{2}$ per cent. above the deposit rate of the principal London banks being made. (See DOCUMENTARY BILL.)

As to the rebate to be deducted when a creditor proves upon a bankrupt's estate for a debt payable at a future time, see Rule 21, under PROOF OF DEBTS.

RECEIPT. A receipt is a written acknowledgment of having received a sum of money.

By the Stamp Act, 1891, the duty is :—

	£	s.	d.
RECEIPT given for, or upon the payment of, money amounting to £2 or upwards	0	0	1

Exemptions.

(1) Receipt given for money deposited in any bank, or with any banker, to be accounted for and expressed to be received of the person to whom the same is to be accounted for.

(2) Acknowledgment by any banker of the receipt of any bill of exchange or promissory note for the purpose of being presented for acceptance or payment.

(3) Receipt given for or upon the payment of any parliamentary taxes or duties, or of money to or for the use of Her Majesty.

(4) Receipt given by an officer of a public department of the State for money paid by way of imprest or advance, or in adjustment of an account, where he derives no personal benefit therefrom.

(5) Receipt given by any agent for money imprested to him on account of the pay of the army.

(6) Receipt given by any officer, seaman, marine or soldier, or his representatives, for or on account of any wages, pay or pension, due from the Admiralty or Army Pay Office.

(7) Receipt given for any principal money or interest due on an exchequer bill.

(8) *Repealed* (See below.)

(9) Receipt given upon any

bill or note of the Bank of England or the Bank of Ireland.

(10) Receipt given for the consideration money for the purchase of any share in any of the Government or Parliamentary stocks or funds, or in the stocks and funds of the Secretary of State in Council of India, or of the Bank of England, or of the Bank of Ireland, or for any dividend paid on any share of the said stocks or funds respectively.

(11) Receipt indorsed or otherwise written upon or contained in any instrument liable to stamp duty, and duly stamped, acknowledging the receipt of the consideration money therein expressed, or the receipt of any principal money, interest, or annuity thereby secured or therein mentioned.

(12) Receipt given for any allowance by way of drawback or otherwise upon the exportation of any goods or merchandise from the United Kingdom.

(13) Receipt given for the return of any duty of customs upon a certificate of over entry.

Receipts upon a duly stamped letter of allotment or scrip certificate are exempt. The exemption is included in No. 11 (above).

The Finance Act, 1895, Section 9, repealed exemption number 8 in the Stamp Act, 1891, " Receipt written upon a bill of exchange or promissory note duly stamped," and enacted that the duty shall be charged as if the exemption had not been contained in that Act, provided that neither the name of a banker (whether accompanied by words of receipt or not) written in the ordinary course of his business as a banker upon a bill of exchange or promissory note duly stamped, nor the name of the payee written upon a draft or order, if payable to order, shall constitute a receipt chargeable with stamp duty.

The Stamp Act, 1891, provides

"101. (1) For the purposes of this Act the expression 'receipt' includes any note, memorandum, or writing whereby any money amounting to two pounds or upwards, or any bill of exchange or promissory note for money amounting to two pounds or upwards, is acknowledged or expressed to have been received or deposited or paid, or whereby any debt or demand, or any part of a debt or demand, of the amount of two pounds or upwards, is acknowledged to have been settled, satisfied, or discharged, or which signifies or imports any such acknowledgment, and whether the same is or is not signed with the name of any person.

"(2) The duty upon a receipt may be denoted by an adhesive stamp, which is to be cancelled by the person by whom the receipt is given before he delivers it out of his hands.

"102. A receipt given without being stamped may be stamped with an impressed stamp upon the terms following; that is to say,

"(1) Within fourteen days after it has been given, on payment of the duty and a penalty of five pounds;

"(2) After fourteen days, but within one month, after it has been given, on payment of the duty and a penalty of ten pounds;

and shall not in any other case be stamped with an impressed stamp.

"103. If any person—

"(1) Gives a receipt liable to duty and not duly stamped; or

"(2) In any case where a receipt would be liable to duty refuses to give a receipt duly stamped; or

"(3) Upon a payment to the amount of two pounds or upwards gives a receipt for a sum not amounting to two pounds, or separates or divides the amount paid with intent to evade the duty;

he shall incur a fine of ten pounds."

Where a form of receipt, either on the face or on the back of a cheque, is signed, it must be stamped. The signature of the payee alone is exempt. (See above.)

If a receipt is placed upon a bill or promissory note (except by a banker), it requires to be stamped. (See above.)

When a deposit receipt is issued, it does

not require a stamp (exemption No. 1, see above), but when it is discharged by the depositor signing a form of receipt on the back, a stamp is required. To save the trouble of affixing an adhesive stamp on payment of a deposit receipt, the receipts of many banks are impressed with a penny stamp when issued.

Where a banker acknowledges the receipt of money from, say, Jones for the credit of Brown, a stamp is required. Where a letter acknowledges a payment and encloses a stamped receipt, it is considered that one stamp is sufficient (*Attorney-General* v. *Ross*, 1909, 2 I.R. 246).

A receipt stamp may be either impressed or adhesive.

Two halfpenny stamps may be used instead of a penny one.

Where a debt is paid by cheque, it is not necessary to state on the receipt that payment was made by cheque, as the person taking the cheque can, in the event of the cheque being dishonoured, sue the debtor for the amount.

Receipts for wages, and for subscriptions to charities are chargeable with duty; but with regard to the latter, Alpe's "Law of Stamp Duties" states that the Commissioners do not enforce a penalty if "a receipt for a donation or subscription to an institution totally devoted to charitable purposes" is given unstamped. (See RECEIPT ON CHEQUE.)

RECEIPT ON CHEQUE. Many companies use cheques with a form of receipt upon the face or upon the back, such receipt being, in most cases, the only one which the drawer of the cheque requires from the person to whom the cheque is payable.

A document of this description is sometimes worded :—" Pay or order the sum of when the receipt on the back hereof has been duly stamped, signed and dated."

The printed form on the back may be :—

" Received from the amount named on the face hereof.

Date 19 ." Penny Stamp.

Below the receipt the following words are sometimes printed :—" The receipt as above is also the indorsement of the cheque and is the only acknowledgment required."

The receipt, instead of being on the back, is, as mentioned, sometimes on the face, below the drawer's signature, and in addition to the receipt being signed the document may require to be indorsed.

Such a document does not agree with the definition of a cheque in the Bills of Exchange Act, 1882. To comply with that Act a cheque must be an unconditional order in writing. In the form above given, the order to pay is conditional upon the receipt being duly completed.

As an instrument of this nature is not a cheque, the protection afforded by the Bills of Exchange Act to a banker paying a cheque drawn upon him, will, apparently, not extend to it. But it is considered that protection is afforded to the banker collecting such a document when crossed by Section 17 of the Revenue Act, 1883, which provides as follows :—

" Sections 76 to 82, both inclusive, of the Bills of Exchange Act, 1882, and Section 25 of the Forgery Act, 1861, shall extend to any document issued by a customer of any banker, and intended to enable any person or body corporate to obtain payment from such banker of the sum mentioned in such document, and shall so extend in like manner as if the said document were a cheque: Provided that nothing in this Act shall be deemed to render any such document a negotiable instrument. For the purpose of this Section, Her Majesty's Paymaster-General and the Queen's and Lord Treasurer's Remembrancer in Scotland shall be deemed to be bankers, and the public officers drawing on them shall be deemed customers." Sir John R. Paget points out in his "Law of Banking" that the Revenue Act treats these documents as not negotiable instruments, "not negotiable" having apparently the meaning of not transferable, and adds that it would seem "that the banker's safer course is in all cases to regard documents of this sort as available only in the hands of the payee."

The use of documents of this nature is becoming very common, and as the banker's position with regard to them appears to be so uncertain and unsatisfactory, it is necessary, for the banker's protection, that he should obtain, from the customer using this special form, an indemnity to the following effect :—

" In consideration of your allowing me, or persons duly authorised by me, to draw drafts on you with receipts attached in the form annexed, I undertake that you shall have as against me in respect thereof the protection afforded by Section 60 of the Bills of Exchange Act, 1882, and that the signature of the receipt at the foot of such drafts shall have the effect of and operate as an indorsement within the meaning of the same Section."

In addition to the form of document given above, some cheques have a note at the foot that "the receipt on the back hereof must be stamped, signed and dated." In other cases no reference at all to a receipt appears on the face of the cheque, but on the back may be found a receipt such as "Received from the amount named on the face hereof

Penny Stamp.

In the cases where there is no condition attached to the order to pay, the cheque is not excluded from the definition given in the Act. A mere note at the foot, or on the back, of a cheque with respect to a receipt, and the presence of a form of receipt on the cheque, so long as the order to pay is unconditional, does not affect the nature of the instrument. When the receipt is signed, the signature is regarded by the banker as the indorsement.

Certain cheques provide for the receipt being signed per procuration. The following is an example :—

"Pay John Brown the sum named below if presented within six months from the date hereof duly stamped, signed and dated .

"Received the sum of as per particulars furnished.

"*Note.*—This receipt should be signed by the payee, but a per procuration discharge will be accepted if guaranteed by the payee's bankers. In the case of a corporate body, the receipt must be signed on their behalf by an authorised officer whose position must be stated."

A receipt on a cheque, whether upon the face or upon the back, requires a penny stamp, if the amount is £2 and over, unless the signer of the receipt is exempted by law.

A receipt by a banker upon a bill or cheque is exempt, provided it is given "in the ordinary course of his business as a banker." (See RECEIPT.)

RECEIVER. When a mortgagee, through default of the mortgagor, is in a position to exercise his power of sale, he may, if he choose, appoint a receiver to collect the rents and manage the estate or business. By so doing, the mortgagee avoids the risks to which he would be liable if he entered into possession himself.

The Conveyancing and Law of Property Act, 1881, defines the appointment, powers, remuneration and duties of a receiver as follows :—

"Section 24. (1) A mortgagee entitled to appoint a receiver under the power in that behalf conferred by this Act shall not appoint a receiver until he has become entitled to exercise the power of sale conferred by this Act, but may then, by writing under his hand, appoint such person as he thinks fit to be receiver.

"(2) The receiver shall be deemed to be the agent of the mortgagor; and the mortgagor shall be solely responsible for the receiver's acts or defaults, unless the mortgage deed otherwise provides.

"(3) The receiver shall have power to demand and recover all the income of the property of which he is appointed receiver, by action, distress, or otherwise, in the name either of the mortgagor or of the mortgagee, to the full extent of the estate or interest which the mortgagor could dispose of, and to give effectual receipts, accordingly, for the same.

"(4) A person paying money to the receiver shall not be concerned to inquire whether any case has happened to authorise the receiver to act.

"(5) The receiver may be removed, and a new receiver may be appointed, from time to time by the mortgagee by writing under his hand.

"(6) The receiver shall be entitled to retain out of any money received by him, for his remuneration, and in satisfaction of all costs, charges, and expenses incurred by him as receiver, a commission at such rate, not exceeding five per centum on the gross amount of all money received, as is specified in his appointment, and if no rate is so specified, then at the rate of five per centum on that gross amount, or at such higher rate as the Court thinks fit to allow, on application made by him for that purpose.

"(7) The receiver shall, if so directed in writing by the mortgagee, insure and keep insured against loss or damage by fire, out of the money received by him, any building, effects, or property comprised in the mortgage, whether affixed to the freehold or not, being of an insurable nature.

"(8) The receiver shall apply all money received by him as follows (namely):

"(*a*) In discharge of all rents, taxes, rates, and outgoings whatever affecting the mortgaged property; and

"(*b*) In keeping down all annual sums or other payments, and the interest on all principal sums, having priority to the mortgage in right whereof he is receiver; and

"(*c*) In payment of his commission, and of the premiums on fire, life, or other insurances, if any, properly payable under the mortgage deed or under this Act, and the cost of executing necessary or proper repairs directed in writing by the mortgagee; and

"(*d*) In payment of the interest accruing due in respect of any principal money due under the mortgage:

and shall pay the residue of the money received by him to the person who, but for the possession of the receiver, would have been entitled to receive the income of the mortgaged property, or who is otherwise entitled to that property."

The appointment of a receiver or manager of the property of a company is to be notified to the registrar of companies. By the Companies (Consolidation) Act, 1908:—

"Section 94. (1) If any person obtains an order for the appointment of a receiver or manager of the property of a company, or appoints such a receiver or manager under any powers contained in any instrument, he shall within seven days from the date of the order or of the appointment under the powers contained in the instrument give notice of the fact to the registrar of companies, and the registrar shall, on payment of the prescribed fee, enter the fact in the register of mortgages and charges.

"(2) If any person makes default in complying with the requirements of this Section he shall be liable to a fine not exceeding five pounds for every day during which the default continues.

"95. (1) Every receiver or manager of the property of a company who has been appointed under the powers contained in any instrument, and who has taken possession, shall, once in every half-year while he remains in possession, and also on ceasing to act as receiver or manager, file with the registrar of companies an abstract in the prescribed form of his receipts and payments during the period to which the abstract relates, and shall also on ceasing to act as receiver or manager file with the registrar notice to that effect, and the registrar shall enter the notice in the register of mortgages and charges.

"(2) Every receiver or manager who makes default in complying with the provisions of this Section shall be liable to a fine not exceeding fifty pounds."

Power in England to Appoint Special Manager.

"161. (1) Where the official receiver becomes the liquidator of a company, whether provisionally or otherwise, he may, if satisfied that the nature of the estate or business of the company, or the interests of the creditors or contributories generally, require the appointment of a special manager of the estate or business of the company other than himself, apply to the Court to, and the Court may on such application, appoint a special manager thereof to act during such time as the Court may direct, with such powers, including any of the powers of a receiver or manager, as may be entrusted to him by the Court.

"(2) The special manager shall give such security and account in such manner as the Board of Trade direct.

"(3) The special manager shall receive

such remuneration as may be fixed by the Court.

Power in England to Appoint Official Receiver as Receiver for Debenture Holders or Creditors.

"162. Where an application is made to the Court to appoint a receiver on behalf of the debenture holders or other creditors of a company which is being wound up by the Court in England, the official receiver may be so appointed." (See COMPANIES, MORTGAGE, OFFICIAL RECEIVER, WINDING UP.)

RECEIVER'S NOTES. When the affairs of an American railroad have passed into the hands of a receiver, he sometimes raises further capital by the issue of what are called "Receiver's Notes."

RECEIVING ORDER. Where a debtor has committed an "act of bankruptcy" (see ACTS OF BANKRUPTCY), a creditor, wishing to have the estate realised under the bankruptcy law for the benefit of the creditors, may petition the Court to make a receiving order. The petition may be presented either by a creditor or by the debtor himself. When a receiving order is made, it means that the Court appoints the official receiver to take charge of the debtor's estate. The debtor is not immediately adjudged a bankrupt, but as soon as may be after making a receiving order, a general meeting of creditors is held to consider whether a proposal for a composition or scheme of arrangement shall be entertained, or whether he shall be adjudged bankrupt. (See MEETING OF CREDITORS.) After a receiving order has been made, a creditor cannot bring any action against the debtor unless under sanction of the Court, but a creditor's power to deal with any securities he may have is not affected by the receiving order.

A receiving order may be made even if there is only one creditor.

As soon as convenient after the expiration of the time for the submission of a debtor's statement of affairs (see Section 16, below), the Court shall hold a public sitting for the examination of the debtor. (See PUBLIC EXAMINATION OF DEBTOR.)

When an act of bankruptcy has been committed by, or a receiving order made against, a customer, the banker must not pay any further cheques upon the account.

The following Sections of the Bankruptcy Act, 1883, deal with a bankruptcy petition and the making of a receiving order :—

Jurisdiction to make Receiving Order.

"5. Subject to the conditions hereinafter specified, if a debtor commits an act of bankruptcy the Court may, on a bankruptcy petition being presented either by a creditor or by the debtor, make an order, in this Act called a receiving order, for the protection of the estate.

Conditions on which Creditor may Petition.

"6. (1) A creditor shall not be entitled to present a bankruptcy petition against a debtor unless—

"(*a*) The debt owing by the debtor to the petitioning creditor, or, if two or more creditors join in the petition, the aggregate amount of debts owing to the several petitioning creditors, amounts to fifty pounds, and

"(*b*) The debt is a liquidated sum, payable either immediately or at some certain future time, and

"(*c*) The act of bankruptcy on which the petition is grounded has occurred within three months before the presentation of the petition, and

"(*d*) The debtor is domiciled in England, or, within a year before the date of the presentation of the petition, has ordinarily resided or had a dwelling-house or place of business in England.

"(2) If the petitioning creditor is a secured creditor, he must, in his petition, either state that he is willing to give up his security for the benefit of the creditors in the event of the debtor being adjudged bankrupt, or give an estimate of the value of his security. In the latter case, he may be admitted as a petitioning creditor to the extent of the balance of the debt due to him, after deducting the value so estimated in the same manner as if he were an unsecured creditor.

Proceedings and Order on Creditor's Petition.

"7. (1) A creditor's petition shall be verified by affidavit of the creditor, or of some person on his behalf having knowledge of the facts, and served in the prescribed manner.

"(2) At the hearing the Court shall require proof of the debt of the petitioning creditor of the service of the petition, and of the act of bankruptcy, or, if more than one act of bankruptcy is alleged in the petition, of some one of the alleged acts of bankruptcy, and, if satisfied with the proof, may make a receiving order in pursuance of the petition.

"(3) If the Court is not satisfied with the proof of the petitioning creditor's debt, or of the act of bankruptcy, or of the service of the petition, or is satisfied by the debtor that he is able to pay his debts, or that for other sufficient cause no order ought to be made, the Court may dismiss the petition.

Debtor's Petition and Order Thereon.

"8. (1) A debtor's petition shall allege that the debtor is unable to pay his debts, and the presentation thereof shall be deemed an act of bankruptcy without the previous filing by the debtor of any declaration of inability to pay his debts, and the Court shall thereupon make a receiving order.

"(2) A debtor's petition shall not, after presentment, be withdrawn without the leave of the Court.

Effect of Receiving Order.

"9. (1) On the making of a receiving order an official receiver shall be thereby constituted receiver of the property of the debtor, and thereafter, except as directed by this Act, no creditor to whom the debtor is indebted in respect of any debt provable in bankruptcy shall have any remedy against the property or person of the debtor in respect of the debt, or shall commence any action or other legal proceedings unless with the leave of the Court and on such terms as the Court may impose.

"(2) But this Section shall not affect the power of any secured creditor to realise or otherwise deal with his security in the same manner as he would have been entitled to realise or deal with it if this Section had not been passed.

Discretionary Powers as to Appointment of Receiver and Stay of Proceedings.

"10. (1) The Court may, if it is shown to be necessary for the protection of the estate, at any time after the presentation of a bankruptcy petition, and before a receiving order is made, appoint the official receiver to be interim receiver of the property of the debtor, or of any part thereof, and direct him to take immediate possession thereof or of any part thereof."

The official receiver may, if necessary, appoint a special manager of a debtor's estate to act until a trustee is appointed. (Section 12.)

Every receiving order must be gazetted, and advertised in a local paper. (Section 13.)

Debtor's Statement of Affairs.

"16. (1) Where a receiving order is made against a debtor, he shall make out and submit to the official receiver a statement of and in relation to his affairs in the prescribed form, verified by affidavit, and showing the particulars of the debtor's assets, debts, and liabilities, the names, residences, and occupations of his creditors, the securities held by them respectively, the dates when the securities were respectively given, and such further or other information as may be prescribed or as the official receiver may require.

"(2) The statement shall be so submitted within the following times, namely:

"(i) If the order is made on the petition of the debtor, within three days from the date of the order.

"(ii) If the order is made on the petition of a creditor, within seven days from the date of the order.

But the Court may, in either case, for special reasons, extend the time.

"(3) If the debtor fails without reasonable excuse to comply with the requirements of this Section, the Court may, on the application of the official receiver, or of any creditor, adjudge him bankrupt.

"(4) Any person stating himself in writing to be a creditor of the bankrupt may, personally or by agent, inspect this statement at all reasonable times, and take any copy thereof or extract therefrom, but any person untruthfully so stating himself to be a creditor shall be guilty of a contempt of Court, and shall be punishable accordingly on the application of the trustee or official receiver." (See BANKRUPTCY.)

RECONSTRUCTION. There are various reasons which necessitate the reconstruction of a company, but the commonest is the necessity to raise fresh capital. In the case of a company where the capital is all paid up and further capital is required, the object is frequently attained by the undertaking being purchased by a new company. The shares in the new company, which are given in exchange for the fully paid shares in the old company, are partly paid up shares, and it is from the uncalled capital in the new company that the necessary funds are obtained to continue the business of the undertaking.

A reconstruction may take place consequent upon an arrangement with the creditors of the company, whereby they may receive, in lieu of their claims, debentures in the company payable at different dates. (See COMPANIES, WINDING UP.)

RECONVEYANCE. A legal mortgage conveys the legal estate in the land from the mortgagor to the mortgagee. When the mortgage debt has been repaid the legal estate is conveyed back, that is, is reconveyed to the mortgagor.

Where a mortgage has been repaid and no reconveyance has been made, the legal estate, at the end of twelve years from the discharge of the debt, becomes by the Statute of Limitations, re-vested in the mortgagor by reason of that lapse of time.

The receipt of a building society upon a mortgage deed for the amount of the debt has the effect of a reconveyance of the property and is exempt from stamp duty. (See BUILDING SOCIETY.)

Where a mortgagor is entitled to redeem, he has, by virtue of the Conveyancing and Law of Property Act, 1881 (Section 15), power to require the mortgagee, instead of reconveying, to assign the mortgage debt and convey the mortgaged property to any third person.

In the case of an equitable mortgage, when the debt is repaid, no reconveyance is necessary. As a second mortgage is an equitable mortgage the same remark applies, but there should be an ordinary stamped receipt showing that the money has been repaid.

The stamp duty upon a reconveyance is sixpence for every £100, and fractional part of £100, of the total amount of the money at any time secured. (See MORTGAGE.)

RECOURSE. Literally, a running back. In the event of a bill of exchange being dishonoured at maturity, the holder has a right of recourse against, that is a right to fall back upon, the other parties to the bill. The holder, however, has no recourse against any party who qualified his indorsement by adding after his signature the words "without recourse" or the French equivalent *sans recours*. (See WITHOUT RECOURSE.)

REDEMPTION OF MORTGAGE. The repayment of the loan secured by the mortgage and the consequent freedom of the property from the charge.

RE-DISCOUNT. A person who has discounted a bill may, if he wish, discount it afresh with another person. (See DISCOUNTING A BILL.)

RE-DRAFT. Where a foreign bill is dishonoured and protested, a re-draft is a fresh bill drawn by the holder upon the drawer or indorser for the amount of the bill plus expenses of protest, stamp, etc. (See RE-EXCHANGE.)

REDUCTION OF SHARE CAPITAL. The principal provisions regarding a reduction of share capital in a company limited by shares are contained in the following Sections of the Companies (Consolidation) Act, 1908:—

Special Resolution for Reduction of Share Capital.

"46. (1) Subject to confirmation by the Court, a company limited by shares, if so authorised by its articles, may by special resolution reduce its share capital in any way, and in particular (without prejudice to the generality of the foregoing power) may—

"(*a*) Extinguish or reduce the liability on any of its shares in respect of share capital not paid up; or

"(*b*) Either with or without extinguishing or reducing liability on any of its shares, cancel any paid-up share capital which is lost or unrepresented by available assets; or "(c) Either with or without extinguishing or reducing liability on any of its shares, pay off any paid-up share capital which is in excess of the wants of the company,

and may, if and so far as is necessary, alter its memorandum by reducing the amount of its share capital and of its shares accordingly.

"(2) A special resolution under this Section is in this Act called a resolution for reducing share capital.

Application to Court for Confirming Order.

"47. Where a company has passed and confirmed a resolution for reducing share capital it may apply by petition to the Court for an order confirming the reduction.

Addition to Name of Company of "and Reduced."

"48. On and from the confirmation by a company of a resolution for reducing share capital, or where the reduction does not involve either the diminution of any liability in respect of unpaid share capital or the payment to any shareholder of any paid-up share capital, then on and from the presentation of the petition for confirming the reduction, the company shall add to its name, until such date as the Court may fix, the words 'and reduced,' as the last words in its name, and those words shall, until that date, be deemed to be part of the name of the company:

"Provided that, where the reduction does not involve either the diminution of any liability in respect of unpaid share capital or the payment to any shareholder of any paid-up share capital, the Court may, if it thinks expedient, dispense altogether with the addition of the words 'and reduced.'

Order Confirming Reduction.

"50. The Court, if satisfied, with respect to every creditor of the company who under this Act is entitled to object to the reduction, that either his consent to the reduction has been obtained or his debt or claim has been discharged or has determined, or has been secured, may make an order confirming the reduction on such terms and conditions as it thinks fit."

The resolution for reduction and the order must be registered, and the resolution takes effect from the date of the registration.

The Court may require the company to publish the reasons for reduction with a view to give proper information to the public. (Section 55.) (See COMPANIES, SHARE CAPITAL.)

RE-EXCHANGE. In the case of a bill which has been dishonoured abroad, the Bills of Exchange Act, 1882, Section 57 (2) provides that the holder may recover from the drawer or an indorser, and the drawer or an indorser who has been compelled to pay the bill may recover from any party liable to him the amount of the re-exchange with interest thereon until the time of payment. Where a bill drawn or indorsed in one country is dishonoured in another, the re-exchange is calculated by ascertaining the sum for which a bill at sight, at the existing rate of exchange, drawn at the time and place of dishonour on the place where the drawer or indorser resides, can be obtained, so as to produce at the place of dishonour the amount of the dishonoured bill plus cost of protest, commission, postage and other expenses in connection with the dishonour.

"REFER TO DRAWER." The usual answer (or its abbreviation R/D) which is placed by the drawee banker upon a cheque received through the Clearing, or presented across the counter, when the account of the drawer does not warrant payment of the cheque.

The answer "R D" should never be marked on a cheque when the reason for its being returned is merely some irregularity in the cheque itself, such as "Indorsement irregular," "Amounts differ" or "Post-dated cheque."

"Refer to drawer" is a milder form of answer than "N/S," "not sufficient."

REFEREE IN CASE OF NEED. The person to whom a holder of a bill of exchange may apply, in case of the bill being dishonoured by non-acceptance or non-payment. The name of a referee may be inserted in a bill by the drawer or any indorser, and is usually put in the left-hand bottom corner of the bill, as "In case of need apply to A. & B. Bank, London," or "In case of need with the English Bank, Ltd., London," or "In need with X. & Y. Bank."

By Section 15 of the Bills of Exchange Act, 1882:—"The drawer of a bill and any indorser may insert therein the name of a person to whom the holder may resort in case of need, that is to say, in case the bill is dishonoured by non-acceptance or non-payment. Such person is called the referee in case of need. It is in the option of the holder to resort to the referee in case of need or not as he may think fit."

No liability attaches to the referee in case of need until he has accepted for honour. (See ACCEPTANCE FOR HONOUR, BILL OF EXCHANGE.)

REFERENCE SLIP. Where a bill is accepted payable at London bank A, and London bank B has been requested by a country bank to retire the bill, bank B sends a "reference" slip describing the bill to bank A. The slip requests A to refer the bill to bank B for payment. In sending the bill to B the reference slip must be attached.

REGISTER OF COMPANIES. (See REGISTRAR OF COMPANIES.)

REGISTER OF DEBENTURE HOLDERS. Every register of holders of debentures of a company is to be open to the inspection of the registered holder of any such debentures and of any holder of shares in the company. (Section 102 of the Companies (Consolidation) Act, 1908.) (See DEBENTURE.)

REGISTER OF DIRECTORS. The Companies (Consolidation) Act, 1908 (Section 75), requires that every company shall keep a register containing the names, addresses, and occupations of its directors or managers, and send a copy thereof to the registrar of companies, and from time to time notify to the registrar any change therein. If this Section is not complied with, the company shall be liable to a fine not exceeding £5 a day. (See DIRECTORS.)

REGISTER OF MEMBERS OF COMPANY. The regulations regarding the register of the members of a company and the annual list of members which must be forwarded to the registrar of companies are set forth in the following sections of the Companies (Consolidation) Act, 1908 :—

Register of Members.

"25. (1) Every company shall keep in one or more books a register of its members, and enter therein the following particulars :—

" (i) The names and addresses, and the occupations, if any, of the members, and in the case of a company having a share capital a statement of the shares held by each member, distinguishing each share by its number, and of the amount paid or agreed to be considered as paid on the shares of each member ;

" (ii) The date at which each person was entered in the register as a member ;

" (iii) The date at which any person ceased to be a member.

" (2) If a company fails to comply with this Section it shall be liable to a fine not exceeding five pounds for every day during which the default continues ; and every director and manager of the company who knowingly and wilfully authorises or permits the default shall be liable to the like penalty.

Annual List of Members and Summary.

"26. (1) Every company having a share capital shall once at least in every year make a list of all persons who, on the fourteenth day after the first or only ordinary general meeting in the year, are members of the company, and of all persons who have ceased to be members since the date of the last return or (in the case of the first return) of the incorporation of the company.

" (2) The list must state the names, addresses, and occupations of all the past and present members therein mentioned, and the number of shares held by each of the existing members at the date of the return, specifying shares transferred since the date of the last return or (in the case of the first return) of the incorporation of the company by persons who are still members and have ceased to be members respectively and the dates of registration of the transfers, and must contain a summary distinguishing between shares issued for cash and shares issued as fully or partly paid up otherwise than in cash, and specifying the following particulars :—

" (*a*) The amount of the share capital of the company, and the number of the shares into which it is divided ;

" (*b*) The number of shares taken from the commencement of the company up to the date of the return ;

" (*c*) The amount called up on each share ;

"(d) The total amount of calls received;

"(e) The total amount of calls unpaid;

"(f) The total amount of the sums (if any) paid by way of commission in respect of any shares or debentures, or allowed by way of discount in respect of any debentures, since the date of the last return;

"(g) The total number of shares forfeited;

"(h) The total amount of shares or stock for which share warrants are outstanding at the date of the return;

"(i) The total amount of share warrants issued and surrendered respectively since the date of the last return;

"(k) The number of shares or amount of stock comprised in each share warrant;

"(l) The names and addresses of the persons who at the date of the return are the directors of the company, or occupy the position of directors, by whatever name called; and

"(m) The total amount of debt due from the company in respect of all mortgages and charges which are required (or, in the case of a company registered in Scotland, which, if the company had been registered in England, would be required) to be registered with the registrar of companies under this Act, or which would have been required so to be registered if created after the first day of July nineteen hundred and eight.

"(3) The summary must also (except where the company is a private company) include a statement, made up to such date as may be specified in the statement, in the form of a balance sheet, audited by the company's auditors, and containing a summary of its share capital, its liabilities, and its assets, giving such particulars as will disclose the general nature o those liabilities and assets, and how the values of the fixed assets have been arrived at, but the balance sheet need not include a statement of profit and loss.

"(4) The above list and summary must be contained in a separate part of the register of members, and must be completed within seven days after the fourteenth day aforesaid, and the company must forthwith forward to the registrar of companies a copy signed by the manager or by the secretary of the company.

"(5) If a company makes default in complying with the requirements of this Section it shall be liable to a fine not exceeding five pounds for every day during which the default continues, and every director and manager of the company who knowingly and wilfully authorises or permits the default shall be liable to the like penalty.

Trusts not to be Entered on Register.

"27. No notice of any trust, expressed, implied, or constructive, shall be entered on the register, or be receivable by the registrar, in the case of companies registered in England or Ireland.

Registration of Transfer at Request of Transferor.

"28. On the application of the transferor of any share or interest in a company, the company shall enter in its register of members the name of the transferee in the same manner and subject to the same conditions as if the application for the entry were made by the transferee.

Transfer by Personal Representative.

"29. A transfer of the share or other interest of a deceased member of a company made by his personal representative shall, although the personal representative is not himself a member, be as valid as if he had been a member at the time of the execution of the instrument of transfer."

The register must be open, for not less than two hours each day, to the inspection of any member gratis, and of any other person on payment of one shilling. (Section 30, s.s. 1.)

Any person may obtain a copy of the register, or any part, or of the list and summary, on payment of sixpence for every 100 words. If an inspection or copy is refused, the Act imposes a penalty not exceeding £2 and a further fine of £2 for every day the refusal continues. (Section 30, s.s. 2 and 3.)

Power to close Register.

"31. A company may, on giving notice by advertisement in some newspaper circulating in the district in which the registered office of the company is situate, close the register of members for any time or times not exceeding in the whole thirty days in each year."

FORM E. as required by Part II of the Act. Section 26

SUMMARY of SHARE CAPITAL and SHARES of the COMPANY, LIMITED, made up to the day of 19 (being the fourteenth day after the date of the first ordinary general meeting in 19).

Nominal share capital £ divided into[1] { shares of £ each. / shares of £ each.

Total number of shares taken up[1] to the day of 19 (which number must agree with the total shown in the list as held by existing members).

Number of shares issued subject to payment wholly in cash . . .

Number of shares issued as fully paid up otherwise than in cash . .

Number of shares issued as partly paid up to the extent of per share otherwise than in cash . . . .

[2] There has been called up on each of shares, £ .

There has been called up on each of shares, £ .

[2] There has been called up on each of shares, £ .

[3] Total amount of calls received, including payments on application and allotment . . . . £

Total amount (if any) agreed to be considered as paid on shares which have been issued as fully paid up otherwise than in cash . . . . £ .

Total amount (if any) agreed to be considered as paid on shares which have been issued as partly paid up to the extent of per share . . . . £ .

Total amount of calls unpaid . . . . £ .

Total amount (if any) of sums paid by way of commission in respect of shares or debentures or allowed by way of discount since date of last summary . . . . £ .

Total amount (if any) paid on[4] shares forfeited . . . . . £ .

Total amount of shares and stock for which share warrants are outstanding . . . . £ .

Total amount of share warrants issued and surrendered respectively since date of last summary . . . . £ .

Number of shares or amount of stock comprised in each share warrant

Total amount of debt due from the company in respect of all mortgages and charges which are required (or, in the case of a company registered in Scotland, which, if the company had been registered in England, would be required) to be registered with the registrar of companies, or which would require registration if created after the first day of July nineteen hundred and eight . . . . . £

STATEMENT in the form of a balance sheet made up to the day of 19 containing the particulars of the capital, liabilities, and assets of the company.

[1] When there are shares of different kinds or amounts (*e.g.*, Preference and Ordinary, or £10 or £5) state the numbers and nominal values separately.

[2] Where various amounts have been called or there are shares of different kinds state them separately.

[3] Include what has been received on forfeited as well as on existing shares.

[4] State the aggregate number of shares forfeited (if any).

The Return must be signed at the end by the manager or secretary of the company.

Presented for filing by..........................

LIST OF PERSONS holding shares in the Company Limited, on the day of 19 , and of persons who have held shares therein at any time since the date of the last return, showing their names and addresses and an account of the shares so held.

Folio in Register Ledger containing Particulars.	Names, Addresses, and Occupations.				Account of Shares.					Remarks.
	Surname.	Christian Name.	Address.	Occupation.	† Number of Shares held by existing Members at Date of Return.	§ Particulars of Shares transferred since the Date of the last Return by Persons who are still Members.		§ Particulars of Shares transferred since the Date of the last Return by Persons who have ceased to be Members.		
						Number.‡	Date of Registration of Transfer.	Number.‡	Date of Registration of Transfer.	

† The aggregate number of shares held, and not the distinctive numbers, must be stated, and the column must be added up throughout so as to make one total to agree with that stated in the summary to have been taken up.

‡ When the shares are of different classes these columns may be subdivided so that the number of each class held or transferred may be shown separately.

§ The date of registration of each transfer should be given as well as the number of shares transferred on each date. The particulars should be placed opposite the name of the transferor and not opposite that of the transferee, but the name of the transferee may be inserted in the "Remarks" column immediately opposite the particulars of each transfer.

NAMES AND ADDRESSES of the persons who are the Directors of the Limited on the day of 19 .

Names.	Addresses.

NOTE.—Banking companies must add a list of all their places of business.

(Signature)........................

(State whether manager or secretary)........................

(See COLONIAL REGISTER, COMPANIES.)

REGISTER OF MORTGAGES. The registrar of companies keeps, with respect to each company, a register of all mortgages and charges created after July 1, 1908, requiring registration under Section 93 of the Companies (Consolidation) Act, 1908. The register is open to inspection by any person on payment of the prescribed fee, not exceeding one shilling. The register is kept at Somerset House.

Every limited company must keep a register of mortgages and charges specifically affecting property of the company. The register is open to the inspection of any creditor or member of the company without fee, and to any other person on payment of a fee not exceeding one shilling. A debenture containing merely a floating charge does not require entering on this register.

For further information see the Sections of the Companies (Consolidation) Act, 1908, under heading REGISTRATION OF MORTGAGES AND CHARGES.

REGISTER OF SASINES. This register is kept in Edinburgh, and there is a separate division of it for each shire or county of

Scotland. Sasine is a legal term for "delivery." In Scotland, prior to 1845, when land was conveyed, a symbolical delivery of it took place, the seller actually handing over to the purchaser a handful of the soil to represent the land being purchased. This was done in the presence of a notary and two witnesses. The delivery, or sasine, was recorded in a deed, and the deed was entered on the Register of Sasines. Although this ancient method of land transfer no longer exists, the register is still in use, and a purchaser's title must be completed by the conveyance being recorded in the register.

REGISTER OF SHIPS. (See SHIP-MORTGAGE, ETC.)

REGISTER OF TRANSFERS. (See TRANSFER REGISTER.)

REGISTERED BOND. A bond which is payable to the person named therein and whose name is registered in the books of the company issuing it. A bearer bond, on the other hand, is payable to the bearer thereof and passes from one person to another by simple delivery. A bearer bond is a negotiable instrument, but a registered bond is not.

REGISTERED CAPITAL. The capital of a company as authorised by its memorandum of association. Called also the "nominal" and "authorised" capital. (See CAPITAL.)

REGISTERED OFFICE. The Companies (Consolidation) Act, 1908, provides :—

"Section 62. (1) Every company shall have a registered office to which all communications and notices may be addressed.

"(2) Notice of the situation of the registered office, and of any change therein, shall be given to the registrar of companies, who shall record the same.

"(3) If a company carries on business without complying with the requirements of this Section it shall be liable to a fine not exceeding five pounds for every day during which it so carries on business."

"116. A document may be served on a company by leaving it at or sending it by post to the registered office of the company."

REGISTERED STOCK. That is, stock which is registered in the owner's name in the company's register of members. It can be transferred to another person only upon a document of transfer being duly executed by the registered holder. The dividends upon the stock are paid by means of warrants sent out from the company's office. In the case of bonds which are payable to bearer, there is no registered owner, and the bonds pass from one person to another by simple delivery. The interest upon the bonds is paid by means of the coupons attached to the bonds.

Several corporation stocks are transferred by book entry under the "inscribed stock" regulations, though their titles do not indicate that they are inscribed stocks.

REGISTRAR, COUNTY COURT. An account opened in this form is a public account. (See PUBLIC ACCOUNT.)

REGISTRAR OF COMPANIES. The Companies (Consolidation) Act, 1908, enacts :—

"Section 243. (1) For the purposes of the registration of companies under this Act, there shall be offices in England, Scotland, and Ireland, at such places as the Board of Trade think fit.

"(2) The Board of Trade may appoint such registrars, assistant registrars, clerks, and servants as the Board think necessary for the registration of companies under this Act, and may make regulations with respect to their duties; and may remove any persons so appointed.

"(6) Any person may inspect the documents kept by the registrar on payment of such fees as may be appointed by the Board of Trade, not exceeding one shilling for each inspection; and any person may require a certificate of the incorporation of any company, or a copy or extract of any other document or any part of any other document, to be certified by the registrar, on payment for the certificate, certified copy, or extract, of such fees as the Board of Trade may appoint, not exceeding five shillings for a certificate of incorporation, and not exceeding sixpence for each folio of a certified copy or extract, or in Scotland for each sheet of two hundred words.

"(7) A copy of or extract from any document kept and registered at any of the offices for the registration of companies in England, Scotland, or Ireland, certified to be a true copy under the hand of the registrar or an assistant registrar (whose official position it shall not be necessary to prove) shall in all legal proceedings be admissible in evidence as of equal validity with the original document."

When a certificate of incorporation is given by the registrar in respect of any association it is conclusive evidence that all the requirements in respect of the registration of the company have been complied with.

When a certificate of the registration of any mortgage or charge is given by the registrar, it is conclusive evidence that all the requirements of the Companies Act have been complied with.

A register of mortgages is kept by the registrar. The register is open to inspection by any person on payment of one shilling. (See COMPANIES, REGISTRATION OF MORTGAGES AND CHARGES.)

REGISTRARS (IN BANKRUPTCY). Section 99 of the Bankruptcy Act, 1883, provides as follows :—

"99. (1) The registrars in bankruptcy of the High Court, and the registrars of a county court having jurisdiction in bankruptcy, shall have the powers and jurisdiction in this Section mentioned, and any order made or act done by such registrars in the exercise of the said powers and jurisdiction shall be deemed the order or act of the Court.

"(2) Subject to general rules limiting the powers conferred by this Section, a registrar shall have power :—

"(*a*) To hear bankruptcy petitions, and to make receiving orders and adjudications thereon :

"(*b*) To hold the public examination of debtors :

"(*c*) To grant orders of discharge where the application is not opposed :

"(*d*) To approve compositions or schemes of arrangement when they are not opposed :

"(*e*) To make interim orders in any case of urgency :

"(*f*) To make any order or exercise any jurisdiction which by any rule in that behalf is prescribed as proper to be made or exercised in chambers :

"(*g*) To hear and determine any unopposed or *ex parte* application :

"(*h*) To summon and examine any person known or suspected to have in his possession effects of the debtor or to be indebted to him, or capable of giving information respecting the debtor, his dealings or property.

"(3) The registrars in bankruptcy of the High Court shall also have power to grant orders of discharge and certificates of removal of disqualifications, and to approve compositions and schemes of arrangement.

"(4) A registrar shall not have power to commit for contempt of court.

"(5) The Lord Chancellor may from time to time by order direct that any specified registrar of a county court shall have and exercise all the powers of a bankruptcy registrar of the High Court." (See BANKRUPTCY.)

REGISTRATION OF DEEDS. Deeds are registered in Yorkshire, Middlesex and the Bedford Level. (See BEDFORD LEVEL CORPORATION, LAND REGISTRY (MIDDLESEX DEEDS). YORKSHIRE REGISTRY OF DEEDS.)

The registration of deeds is to be distinguished from the registration of land. (See LAND REGISTRY.)

REGISTRATION OF MORTGAGES AND CHARGES. The Companies (Consolidation) Act, 1908, with regard to the registration of mortgages and charges created by a company, provides as follows :—

Registration of Mortgages and Charges in England and Ireland.

"93. (1) Every mortgage or charge created after the first day of July nineteen hundred and eight by a company registered in England or Ireland and being either :—

"(*a*) a mortgage or charge for the purpose of securing any issue of debentures ; or

"(*b*) a mortgage or charge on uncalled share capital of the company ; or

"(*c*) a mortgage or charge created or evidenced by an instrument which, if executed by an individual, would require registration as a bill of sale ; or

"(*d*) a mortgage or charge on any land, wherever situate, or any interest therein ; or

"(*e*) a mortgage or charge on any book debts of the company ; or "(*f*) a floating charge on the undertaking or property of the company,

shall, so far as any security on the company's property or undertaking is thereby conferred, be void against the liquidator and any creditor of the company, unless the prescribed particulars of the mortgage or charge, together with the instrument (if any) by which the mortgage or charge is created or evidenced, are delivered to or received by the registrar of companies for registration in manner required by this Act within twenty-one days after the date of its creation, but without prejudice to any contract or obligation for repayment of the money thereby secured, and when a mortgage or charge becomes void under this Section the money secured thereby shall immediately become payable :

"Provided that :—

"(i) in the case of a mortgage or charge created out of the United Kingdom comprising solely property situate outside the United Kingdom, the delivery to and the receipt by the registrar of a copy of the instrument by which the mortgage or charge is created or evidenced, verified in the prescribed manner, shall have the same effect for the purposes of this Section as the delivery and receipt of the instrument itself, and twenty-one days after the date on which the instrument or copy could, in due course of post, and if despatched with due diligence, have been received in the United Kingdom, shall be substituted for twenty-one days after the date of the creation of the mortgage or charge, as the time within which the particulars and instrument or copy are to be delivered to the registrar ; and

"(ii) where the mortgage or charge is created in the United Kingdom but comprises property outside the United Kingdom, the instrument creating or purporting to create the mortgage or charge may be sent for registration notwithstanding that further proceedings may be necessary to make the mortgage or charge valid or effectual according to the law of the country in which the property is situate ; and

"(iii) where a negotiable instrument has been given to secure the payment of any book debts of a company, the deposit of the instrument for the purpose of securing an advance to the company shall not for the purposes of this Section be treated as a mortgage or charge on those book debts ; and

"(iv) the holding of debentures entitling the holder to a charge on land shall not be deemed to be an interest in land.

"(2) The registrar shall keep, with respect to each company, a register in the prescribed form of all the mortgages and charges created by the company after the first day of July nineteen hundred and eight and requiring registration under this Section, and shall, on payment of the prescribed fee, enter in the register, with respect to every such mortgage or charge, the date of creation, the amount secured by it, short particulars of the property mortgaged or charged, and the names of the mortgagees or persons entitled to the charge.

(3) Where a series of debentures containing, or giving by reference to any other instrument, any charge to the benefit of which the debenture holders of that series are entitled *pari passu* is created by a company, it shall be sufficient if there are delivered to or received by the registrar within twenty-one days after the execution of the deed containing the charge or, if there is no such deed, after the execution of any

debentures of the series, the following particulars :—

"(*a*) the total amount secured by the whole series ; and

"(*b*) the dates of the resolutions authorising the issue of the series and the date of the covering deed, if any, by which the security is created or defined ; and

"(*c*) a general description of the property charged ; and

"(*d*) the names of the trustees, if any, for the debenture holders ;

together with the deed containing the charge, or, if there is no such deed, one of the debentures of the series, and the registrar shall, on payment of the prescribed fee, enter those particulars in the register :

"Provided that, where more than one issue is made of debentures in the series, there shall be sent to the registrar for entry in the register particulars of the date and amount of each issue, but an omission to do this shall not affect the validity of the debentures issued.

"(4) Where any commission, allowance, or discount has been paid or made either directly or indirectly by the company to any person in consideration of his subscribing or agreeing to subscribe, whether absolutely or conditionally, for any debentures of the company, or procuring or agreeing to procure subscriptions, whether absolute or conditional, for any such debentures, the particulars required to be sent for registration under this Section shall include particulars as to the amount or rate per cent. of the commission, discount, or allowance so paid or made, but an omission to do this shall not affect the validity of the debentures issued :

"Provided that the deposit of any debentures as security for any debt of the company shall not for the purposes of this provision be treated as the issue of the debentures at a discount.

"(5) The registrar shall give a certificate under his hand of the registration of any mortgage or charge, registered in pursuance of this Section, stating the amount thereby secured, and the certificate shall be conclusive evidence that the requirements of this Section as to registration have been complied with.

"(6) The company shall cause a copy of every certificate of registration given under this Section to be indorsed on every debenture or certificate of debenture stock which is issued by the company, and the payment of which is secured by the mortgage or charge so registered :

"Provided that nothing in this sub-section shall be construed as requiring a company to cause a certificate of registration of any mortgage or charge so given to be indorsed on any debenture or certificate of debenture stock which has been issued by the company before the mortgage or charge was created.

"(7) It shall be the duty of the company to send to the registrar for registration the particulars of every mortgage or charge created by the company and of the issues of debentures of a series, requiring registration under this Section, but registration of any such mortgage or charge may be effected on the application of any person interested therein.

"Where the registration is effected on the application of some person other than the company, that person shall be entitled to recover from the company the amount of any fees properly paid by him to the registrar on the registration.

"(8) The register kept in pursuance of this Section shall be open to inspection by any person on payment of the prescribed fee, not exceeding one shilling for each inspection.

"(9) Every company shall cause a copy of every instrument creating any mortgage or charge requiring registration under this Section to be kept at the registered office of the company : Provided that, in the case of a series of uniform debentures, a copy of one such debenture shall be sufficient.

Entry of Satisfaction.

"97. The registrar of companies may, on evidence being given to his satisfaction that the debt for which any registered mortgage or charge was given has been paid or satisfied, order that a memorandum of satisfaction be entered on the register, and shall if required furnish the company with a copy thereof."

The Act imposes heavy penalties for neglect to register mortgages and charges. (Section 99.)

Every company must keep a register of mortgages and charges, and enter therein "all mortgages and charges specifically affecting property of the company, giving in each case a short description of the property mortgaged or charged, the amount of the mortgage or charge, and (except in the case of securities to bearer) the names of the mortgagees or persons entitled thereto." (Section 100.) The register shall be open to the inspection of any creditor or member, without fee, and to any other person on payment of one shilling. (Section 101.) A debenture containing merely a floating charge does not require entering in this register, but if it contains a specific charge it must be entered. A floating charge, however, requires registration with the registrar of companies. (See Section 93, above.)

By Section 243 (see under REGISTRAR OF COMPANIES) any person may inspect the documents kept by the registrar on payment of a fee not exceeding one shilling.

When the title deeds of a company are given as security, either with or without a memorandum of deposit, it is a charge, and must be registered at the date of the deposit.

The benefit of the registration of charges is that a banker, or other person, can now by an inspection of the register of mortgages ascertain at once what charges have been created.

It should be particularly noted that if a mortgage or charge, as above specified, is not registered within twenty-one days it is void against a liquidator and any creditor, so far as security on the company's property is concerned, and the money payable under the charge will then rank only as an unsecured debt.

Section 93, (*a*) to (*f*) (see above), details the various kinds of charges, created since July 1, 1908, which must be registered. Prior to July 1, 1908, the charges which had to be registered in order to form a valid security, were those created after December 31, 1900, and before July 1, 1908, but that regulation did not include the charges (*d*) and (*e*) (see Section 93, above) specified in the Consolidation Act, 1908. The mortgages which must be registered are therefore :—

Prior to December 31, 1900, no legislation compelling registration.

From December 31, 1900, to July 1, 1908, (*a*), (*b*), (*c*), (*f*). (See above.)

Since July 1, 1908, (*a*), (*b*), (*c*), (*d*), (*e*), (*f*). (See above.)

The prescribed fee for registration of a mortgage or charge is :—

Where the amount does not exceed £200, 10*s*.

Where the amount exceeds £200, £1.

The fee for registration of a series of debentures is :—

Where the total amount of the series does not exceed £200, 10*s*.

Where the total amount of the series exceeds £200, £1. (See COMPANIES, RECEIVER.)

REGISTRATION OF TRANSFERS. (See TRANSFER OF SHARES.)

REICHSBANK. The Imperial Bank. The most important and powerful financial institution in Germany.

REIS. (See FOREIGN MONEYS — PORTUGAL, SOUTH AFRICA.)

RELEASE. From 1841 to 1845 freehold land was conveyed by means of a deed called a "release." (See LEASE AND RELEASE.)

By the Stamp Act, 1891, the stamp duty is :—

	£	s.	d.
RELEASE or RENUNCIATION of any property, or of any right or interest in any property—			
Upon a sale. See CONVEYANCE ON SALE.			
By way of security. See MORTGAGE, etc.			
In any other case . . .	0	10	0

REMAINDER. After the death of a person who has a life interest in a property, if the land does not revert to the grantor of the life interest, or his heirs, but passes to some other person, the interest of that person in the land is called a "remainder."

A remainder is sometimes erroneously referred to as a reversion, or reversionary interest.

It is a contingent remainder if the vesting of the remainder is dependent upon an uncertainty, as for example where the interest has to pass, after the death of the life tenant, to a child after attaining a certain age. When the child has attained that age it becomes a vested remainder. (See REVERSION.)

REMAINDERMAN. The person entitled to a "remainder" (*q.v.*).

REMEDY ALLOWANCE. This is the name given to an allowance made in connection with the making of coins. The Coinage Act defines the standard weight and fineness of each coin, but as in the making of coins it is impossible to produce them absolutely in accordance with the prescribed figures, the Act allows certain variations, the "remedy allowance," from that standard weight and fineness. In gold coins the remedy for fineness is two parts in 1,000, and in silver coins it is four parts in 1,000. For the "remedy" allowed in weight per piece, see the first Schedule to the Coinage Act, under COINAGE.

REMITTANCE. The word is commonly used in banks to describe an amount of coin or notes, or a parcel of cheques or bills sent from one office or person to another. A remittance is inward or outward according as it is received by or despatched from the bank.

REMOTE PARTIES. The "remote parties" to a bill of exchange are those who are not in immediate relationship, e.g. the acceptor and an indorsee. (See PARTIES TO BILL OF EXCHANGE.)

RENEWAL OF BILL. By arrangement amongst the parties to a bill of exchange the bill may be renewed, that is, a new bill may be accepted in place of the old one, to run for a further period of time. If the second bill is dishonoured the rights of the parties on the first bill (if the bill was left with the holder) are revived, but those parties who did not assent to the renewal are discharged.

RENT CHARGE. An annual payment arising out of real estate.

RENTES. The name given to the annual interest payable upon the Government debts of France, Austria, Italy, Greece and some other countries. The word is also applied to the debts themselves, e.g. the Rentes in France has the same meaning as Consols in this country.

RENUNCIATION. In the Stamp Act, 1891, the reference to the stamp duty is:—

RENUNCIATION. See RECONVEYANCE and RELEASE.

RENUNCIATION, LETTER OF. See LETTER OF ALLOTMENT.

When the holder of a bill renounces his rights against the acceptor, the bill is discharged, but the renunciation must be in writing, unless the bill is delivered up to the acceptor. (See PAYMENT OF BILL.)

REPUTED OWNER. The person who is, from the situation in which goods are found, reputed to be the owner thereof. The Bankruptcy Act, 1883, includes amongst the property which is divisible amongst the creditors of a bankrupt, "all goods being, at the commencement of the bankruptcy, in the possession, order, or disposition of the bankrupt, in his trade or business, by the consent and permission of the true owner, under such circumstances that he is the reputed owner thereof."

"REQUIRES BANKER'S CROSSING." An answer in these (or similar) words is sometimes marked upon cheques by the drawee banker.

The reason given, however, is not considered sufficient to justify a cheque being returned through the clearing. It is desirable that the stamp of the banker to whom a cheque is crossed, or of the collecting banker if uncrossed or crossed generally, be placed upon the cheque, and it is customary for it to be done, but not absolutely necessary.

REQUISITIONS. The requisitions are the inquiries submitted by the solicitor for an intending purchaser to the solicitor for the vendor, as to points and questions in connection with the deeds and the title to the property. The requisitions are written on one half of a sheet of paper and the replies are placed opposite. If the replies are not complete or satisfactory, further observations may be made.

RESERVE. The cash in hand—that is, notes and gold and silver coin—on the assets side of the Bank of England Return (Banking Department) is called the "Reserve." The "Reserve" is the money which the Bank keeps to meet any demand which may be made upon it by the depositors, both private depositors and other banks which keep balances at the Bank of England. In addition to that, the bank's stock of gold is liable to be drawn upon by foreign nations requiring gold. "The quickest and least troublesome way of obtaining it is to buy bills on London, remit them here for discount, turn the proceeds into Bank of England notes and cash the notes at the Issue Department" (George Clare, "Money Market Primer"). (See BANK RETURN.)

RESERVE FUND. The directors of a joint stock company, before recommending a dividend, may (under most Articles of Association) set aside out of the profits of the company such sums as they think proper as a reserve, which shall, at the discretion of the directors, be applicable for meeting contingencies, or for equalising dividends, or for any other purpose to which the profits of the company may be properly applied. Pending such application, the fund may be employed in the business of the company or be invested (other than in shares of the company) as the directors may think fit. (See Clause 99 of Table A, under heading DIVIDEND.)

If the reserve is intended to provide for a sudden emergency, it should be invested in readily realisable securities.

In addition to the reserve fund which is shown on a balance sheet, a prudent banker builds up from his profits a secret or inner reserve fund, which is not disclosed on the balance sheet. This secret reserve system is recognised by shareholders as a necessity in a well-managed bank.

RESERVE LIABILITY. That part of a banking company's share capital which, when so resolved by the shareholders, cannot be called up except in the event of the company being wound up. Section 59 of the Companies (Consolidation) Act, 1908, provides :—

"59. A limited company may by special resolution determine that any portion of its share capital which has not been already called up shall not be capable of being called up, except in the event and for the purposes of the company being wound up, and thereupon that portion of its share capital shall not be capable of being called up except in the event and for the purposes aforesaid."

See also Section 58 under COMPANY, UNLIMITED. (See COMPANIES, SHARE CAPITAL.)

RESIDUARY DEVISEE. Under a will, the person who takes all the real property which remains after the devisees have received their shares.

RESIDUARY LEGATEE. Under a will, the person who takes all the personal property which remains after the legatees have received their shares.

RESIGNATION. By the Stamp Act, 1891, the stamp duties are :—

	£	s.	d.
RESIGNATION. Principal or original instrument of resignation, or service of cognition of heirs, or charter or seisin of any houses, lands, or other heritable subjects in Scotland holding burgage, or of burgage tenure .	0	5	0
And instrument of resignation of any lands or other heritable subjects in Scotland not of burgage tenure.	0	5	0

RESOLUTIONS. The resolutions passed at the meetings of companies are the various matters which the members present have decided upon. An ordinary resolution may be passed by a bare majority. There are also extraordinary and special resolutions.

The provisions of the Companies (Consolidation) Act, 1908, with regard to extraordinary and special resolutions are as follow :—

"Section 69. (1) A resolution shall be an extraordinary resolution when it has been passed by a majority of not less than three fourths of such members entitled to vote as are present in person or by proxy (where proxies are allowed) at a general meeting of which notice specifying the intention to propose the resolution as an extraordinary resolution has been duly given.

"(2) A resolution shall be a special resolution when it has been—

"(*a*) passed in manner required for the passing of an extraordinary resolution ; and

"(*b*) confirmed by a majority of such members entitled to vote as are present in person or by proxy (where proxies are allowed) at a subsequent general meeting, of which notice has been duly given, and held after an interval of not less than fourteen days, nor more than one month, from the date of the first meeting.

"(3) At any meeting at which an extraordinary resolution is submitted to be passed or a special resolution is submitted to be passed or confirmed, a declaration of the chairman that the resolution is carried shall, unless a poll is demanded, be conclusive evidence of the fact without proof of the number or proportion of the votes recorded in favour of or against the resolution.

"(4) At any meeting at which an extraordinary resolution is submitted to be passed or a special resolution is submitted to be passed or confirmed a poll may be demanded, if demanded by three persons for the time being entitled according to the articles to vote, unless the articles of the company require a demand by such number of such persons, not in any case exceeding five, as may be specified in the articles.

"(5) When a poll is demanded in accordance with this Section, in computing the majority on the poll reference shall be had to the number of votes to which each member is entitled by the articles of the company." (See COMPANIES.)

RESPONDENTIA. An instrument by which the master of a ship hypothecates the cargo as security for the repayment of money borrowed at a foreign port in order to effect repairs which are absolutely necessary to enable the ship to resume its voyage. Such a loan is repayable only if the ship arrives in safety at its destination. The captain has no authority to create such a charge except in case of necessity, and where he has no other means of raising the money and is unable to communicate with the owners. (See BOTTOMRY BOND.)

REST. The item called "Rest" which appears on the liabilities side of the weekly "Return" of the Bank of England corresponds with the item "Reserve Fund" in the balance sheets of other banks, with this difference that the profits are added to the "Rest" from time to time, and the dividends to the bank proprietors are paid out of this account. The amount is not allowed to fall below £3,000,000. (See BANK RETURN.)

The word "rest" is also applied to the break which a banker makes in the accounts of his customers on June 30 and December 31 for the purpose of entering the amount of interest and charges due to date. When this has been done, the account is balanced and ruled off, the balance being carried forward to the next half-year's account.

RESTRICTIVE INDORSEMENT. An indorsement is restrictive which prohibits the further negotiation of a bill or cheque, or which expresses that it is a mere authority to deal with the bill as thereby directed, as "Pay John Brown only." (See INDORSEMENT.)

RESTRICTIVE THEORY. The theory that in a commercial crisis the Bank of England should restrict its issues of notes, but in the great crises of 1847, 1857 and 1866 the Bank Charter Act which embodied the restrictive theory had to be suspended, and the situation was saved by the Government granting permission to the Bank to expand its issue beyond the limit fixed by the Act. H. D. Macleod, in "The Elements of Banking," wrote :—

"It is therefore irrefragably proved by the unanimous opinion of the most eminent commercial authorities, and the clear experience of 100 years that the restrictive theory in a commercial crisis is a fatal delusion ; and that when a commercial panic is impending, the only way to avert and allay it is to give prompt, immediate, and liberal assistance to all houses who can prove themselves to be solvent, at the same time allowing all houses which are really insolvent to go." (See BANK CHARTER ACT, EXPANSIVE THEORY.)

RETENTION MONEY. Money which is retained for a certain time after completion of a contract ; e.g. if a contract has been made for £5,000 it may be agreed that 10 per cent. of the money due to the contractor shall be retained till, say, six or twelve months after the completion of the contract. If an assignment of retention money is given as security, notice of the assignment must be given to, and an acknowledgment received from, the person who is liable to pay the money to the contractor. (See DEBTS—ASSIGNMENT OF.)

RETIRING A BILL. Many customers of country branches accept bills payable at the head office in London of their banker, or, in the case of a purely country bank, at the latter's London agents. Shortly before maturity of the bill, the acceptor gives his banker a written order to pay or retire the bill falling due in London. Immediately before the due date the banker debits the customer and credits London with the amount, advising his London agents or London office to pay the bill. In some cases, at the beginning of each month, the acceptor gives one order, on which are specified all such bills falling due during the month. If any of the bills have documents attached, the order should supply an accurate description of them.

An order to retire a customer's own acceptance, payable either at the branch where his account is kept, or at the head office, or at a London bank, does not require a penny stamp. Neither is a stamp required where a customer gives an order to retire the acceptance of another person.

When an acceptance is withdrawn on the order of a person who is not the acceptor, the bill should not be cancelled.

It is very undesirable that a bill should be domiciled at a bank where the acceptor does not keep an account, and the banker is under no obligation to accept funds to meet it. He is justified in returning any such bill sent for collection. This, of course, does not refer to bills accepted by a country customer and domiciled with a London banker, as in this case the London banker is the agent of the country banker where the customer keeps his account.

A bill may be retired at maturity by the drawer or an indorser, whereupon that person holds the instrument with remedy against all prior parties. In such a case a written order should be given by the person retiring the bill.

The customer for whom a bill is discounted sometimes requests the banker, before the bill is due, to withdraw it, giving as a reason that the acceptor has sent him a cheque for the amount or that part payment has been made and a new bill accepted for the balance.

The circumstances connected with the retirement or withdrawal of a bill, by persons other than the acceptor, should always be carefully considered, as history shows how the operation may lend itself very readily to the purposes of fraudulent persons.

Sir James Bacon in a case in 1872 said "retiring a bill of exchange means, as I understand it, so to deal with it as that the man who is personally liable shall not be sued upon it, which he might be unless it is retired before the time at which it could be noted."

RETOUR SANS PROTÊT. (French, return without protest.)

These words placed upon a bill by an indorser, near to his signature, mean that the bill, in the event of its dishonour, is to be returned without protest; that is, no expense is to be incurred. They apply only to the indorser who uses them, and do not indicate the wish of a subsequent indorser who has not used the words.

RETROCESSION. In Scotland, a reconveyance. A conveyance back by an assignee to the assignor. In a retrocession of a policy of life assurance the following words may be used: "We do hereby retrocess, repone and restore John Brown, his heirs, executors and assignees in and to his own right and place in the policy of assurance on his life," etc.

RETURNED CHEQUE (OR BILL). A cheque may be returned unpaid for many reasons. The drawer may not have sufficient funds to meet it; he may be dead or bankrupt; he may have instructed his banker not to pay it; the banker may have received some legal notice preventing him from paying any further cheques upon the drawer's account; or the cheque itself may not be in order, the date or the amount or other material part may have been altered, and not have been initialled by the drawer; the amount in words and figures may differ; the drawer's signature may not be recognised; an indorsement may be wrong; it may be post-dated; or crossed to two bankers; or it may be stale through having been issued so long. These are some of the principal reasons necessitating the return of a cheque.

When the cheque is returned an "answer" is marked upon it by the drawee banker, usually in the left-hand top corner. A number of the different "answers" which are in use are given in the article ANSWERS.

Where a cheque has been received for collection through the London Clearing House and is returned for any reason, it must, according to the rules of the Clearing House, be sent back direct, by return of post, to the country bank whose name and address appear upon it.

After settlement of a local exchange a cheque cannot strictly be returned later in the day, unless by agreement between the bankers.

Cheques received otherwise than through the Clearing House may be returned on the day following the receipt, but in practice they are usually returned on the same day. A bill may be held till the day after its due date, but it must be noted, when necessary, on the day of maturity. A cheque or bill cashed over the counter by the paying banker cannot subsequently be returned. When a bill is presented in the morning of its due date, a country banker is under no obligation to retain it till the close of business before returning it, but there may be a local custom to retain it.

The banker to whom a cheque is returned for any reason, except a technical flaw in an indorsement, obtains his money again from the party from whom he received the cheque in the first place, delivering up the cheque itself in exchange. In the case of a faulty indorsement (e.g. a cheque payable to

"Thomas Cluff" indorsed "Thomas Clough") which the collecting banker knows to be *bonâ fide*, it is customary for him to write on the back of the cheque "Indorsement confirmed" or "Payee's (or John Smith's) indorsement confirmed," and his own signature. When the cheque is represented, the drawee banker usually pays it; he is not, however, in law bound to do so.

Bankers usually keep a list of all the cheques and bills they return unpaid, as well as a list of cheques and bills which have been returned to them, and in each case the reason of the "return" is noted in a column provided for the purpose.

When a cheque or bill is received back "dishonoured," unless it is delivered to the customer against cash, the banker charges his customer's account with the amount and sends the unpaid article to the customer. The notices of dishonour to indorsers will be given by the customer. Although not strictly necessary, some bankers require a cheque to be given by the customer to confirm the debit to his account for the returned bill or cheque, whilst other bankers take an acknowledgment from the customer on giving him the dishonoured instrument. If the customer's account will not admit of the dishonoured bill or cheque being charged to it, the amount should be debited to an account for returned articles and the banker should give notice to all parties. Any balance there may be in the customer's account may be held as a part payment.

A returned cheque may be debited to the account of the customer for whom it was sent for collection, even if not indorsed by him.

A banker usually cancels his indorsement on a returned bill. (See DISHONOUR OF BILL OF EXCHANGE.)

RETURNS. Cheques or bills which are returned either through lack of funds or some irregularity in the instruments themselves are commonly called "returns."

Returns are also the various statements, daily, weekly, monthly, half-yearly, or at other times, which are sent by branches to the head office.

REVERSION. REVERSIONARY INTEREST. Where a limited estate is granted in a property, as, for example, in fee tail (where it is given to a person and the heirs of his body), if the succession fails, the property reverts to the grantor. The grantor is therefore said to hold the reversion in the property. If the property is not to revert to the grantor, but to go to some other person, it "remains" to that person, and his interest in it is called a "remainder" (*q.v.*).

The terms "reversion," or "reversionary interest," are often loosely used, in a general way, to mean either a true reversion or a remainder.

REVERSION DUTY. A duty imposed by the Finance (1909–10) Act, 1910 (Section 13), and payable, on the determination of any lease of land, upon the value of the benefit accruing to the lessor by reason of the determination of the lease, at the rate of one pound for every complete £10 of that value.

Every lessor is required, on the determination of a lease where reversion duty is payable, to deliver an account to the Commissioners setting forth particulars and the estimated value of the benefit accruing to him.

When a mortgagee is liable to pay any sum on account of reversion duty, see Section 39, s.s. 4 and 5, under heading INCREMENT VALUE DUTY.

There are special provisions with regard to reversion duty in the case of a mining lease. (Section 22.)

Exemptions :—

Where, in the case of a reversion to a lease purchased before April 30, 1909, the lease determines within forty years from the date of the purchase. (This exemption does not apply where the lease is determined within forty years by agreement between the lessor and the lessee, not contained in the lease itself, unless the lease would, apart from any such agreement, have determined within that period.)

The determination of a lease on land which is, at the time of the determination, agricultural land.

A lease the original term of which did not exceed twenty-one years, nor where the interest of the lessor expectant on the determination of a lease is a leasehold interest which does not exceed that number of years.

Where a lease is determined before the expiration of the term and a fresh lease granted to the lessee for at least twenty-one years beyond the date on which the original lease would have expired, an allowance is made of 2½ per cent. of the duty for every year of the original term of the lease which is unexpired, but the allowance shall not exceed 50 per cent. of the whole duty payable.

Where increment value duty is due and

reversion duty has been paid, or reversion duty is due and increment value duty has been paid, and it is proved to the satisfaction of the Commissioners that the increment value and the benefit accruing to the lessor are identical, such sums as the Commissioners determine to have been paid in respect of the one shall be treated as a payment on account of the other.

Land held for charitable purposes.

Land whilst it is held by a statutory company for the purposes of the undertaking and which cannot be appropriated except to those purposes. (Statutory company means any railway, canal, dock or water company.)

Section 14, s.s. 5, provides as follows :—

"Where a reversion has been mortgaged before the thirtieth day of April nineteen hundred and nine, and the mortgagee has foreclosed before the lease on which the reversion is expectant determines, the mortgagee shall not be liable to pay reversion duty in excess of the amount by which the total value of the land at the time of the determination of the lease exceeds the amount payable under the mortgage at the date of the foreclosure."

REVOCATION. By the Stamp Act, 1891, the stamp duty is :—

	£ s. d.
REVOCATION of any use or trust of any property by any writing, not being a will	0 10 0

RIGGING THE MARKET. A Stock Exchange term to signify the artificial forcing up of prices by speculators with the object of inducing the public to become purchasers at the false prices.

ROOT OF TITLE. A purchaser of land can, unless there is an agreement to the contrary, require the title to be deduced for forty years, or longer if it is necessary to go further back to secure a satisfactory commencement. The deed which is taken as the beginning of the title is called the root of title.

A twenty years' title is often accepted as sufficient.

Section 2 of the Vendor and Purchasers Act, 1874, provides as follows :—

"Recitals, statements, and descriptions of facts, matters and parties contained in deeds, instruments, acts of Parliament or statutory declarations, twenty years old at the date of the contract, shall, unless and except so far as they shall be proved to be inaccurate, be taken to be sufficient evidence of the truth of such facts, matters and descriptions."

By the Conveyancing Act, 1881, Section 3, s.s. 3 : "A purchaser of any property shall not require the production, or any abstract or copy, of any deed, will or other document, dated or made before the time prescribed by law, or stipulated, for commencement of the title. . ."

In the case of leaseholds, the abstract should commence with the lease, even if it is more than forty years old. (See TITLE DEEDS.)

ROUBLE. (See FOREIGN MONEYS — RUSSIA.)

ROYAL PROCLAMATION. The Bank Holidays Act, 1871, enacted that it shall be lawful for His Majesty, as to His Majesty may seem fit, by proclamation to appoint a special day to be observed as a bank holiday, and any day so appointed shall, as regards bills of exchange and promissory notes, be deemed to be a bank holiday for all the purposes of the Act. (See BANK HOLIDAYS.) The following is a copy of the Royal Proclamation making December 27th, 1910, a bank holiday :—

"BY THE KING :

"A PROCLAMATION

"FOR A BANK HOLIDAY.

"GEORGE, R.I.

"We, considering that it is desirable that *Tuesday*, the Twenty-seventh day of *December* next, should be observed as a Bank Holiday throughout those parts of Our United Kingdom called England and Wales, and Ireland, and in pursuance of the provisions of 'The Bank Holidays Act, 1871,' do hereby, by, and with the advice of Our Privy Council and in exercise of the powers conferred by the Act aforesaid, appoint *Tuesday*, the Twenty-seventh day of *December* next as a special day to be observed as a Bank Holiday throughout England and Wales, and Ireland, and every part thereof, under and in accordance with the said Act, and We do, by this Our Royal Proclamation, command the said day to be so observed, and all Our loving subjects to order themselves accordingly.

"Given at Our Court at *St. James's*, this Seventh day of *November*, in the Year of our Lord One thousand nine hundred and ten, and in the first Year of Our Reign.

"GOD SAVE THE KING."

ROYALTY. A rent, payable to the landlord, of a certain percentage of the profits derived from the working of a mine upon his estate, or from the minerals reserved to him.

RUN ON A BANK. When, for any reason, the depositors of a bank fear that the bank is unable to meet all its liabilities, each depositor becomes anxious to secure his own money before anyone else, and each person who holds notes of the bank (if it is a bank of issue) becomes desirous to obtain payment of the notes at once. If the anxiety to obtain gold from the bank becomes general and the depositors and note holders flock to the bank for that purpose, there is said to be a run upon the bank.

RUPEE. (See FOREIGN MONEYS—CEYLON, INDIA, MAURITIUS.)

RUPEE PAPER. The name given to the "enfaced" promissory notes of the Indian Government.

The price of Rupee Paper is quoted in Stock Exchange lists as, say, 62-3, which means that the price is £62-63 for a promissory note for 1,000 rupees—a rupee being reckoned for this purpose at 2*s.*, the 1,000 rupees on this basis being equal to £100. The dividend, or interest, on the Rupee Paper is at the rate of 1*s.* 4*d.* for each rupee, and is paid by drafts payable in India, which are obtained either by the holder of the promissory notes presenting them at the India office, Bank of England, or by having the drafts posted to him by the Bank.

The accrued dividend upon most stocks and shares is included in the price and belongs to the purchaser, but in the case of Rupee Paper it is not taken into the price and therefore requires to be paid over by the purchaser to the seller in addition to the purchase price.

The notes are called "enfaced paper" because they bear an announcement on the face that the interest is payable by drafts to be obtained at the Bank of England.

The notes can be converted into stock at the India Office, Bank of England.

RURAL DISTRICT COUNCIL. The Treasurer of a Rural District Council must keep an account in the prescribed form of all moneys received and paid by him on behalf of the Council. The accounts must be made up to September 30 and March 31 in each year, and they are to be audited by a Government auditor.

Orders drawn upon the Treasurer are usually signed by three members of the Council and countersigned by the clerk. A banker should be furnished with a copy of a resolution by the Council as to the manner in which orders are to be signed, and with specimens of all necessary signatures.

Per procuration indorsements are not accepted.

With regard to borrowing powers, reference should be made to the statute under which a power to borrow is obtained, so as to ascertain the extent of the power and whether the sanction of the Local Government Board or other authority is required. If money is borrowed without power, or sanction, the interest thereon will probably be disallowed. (See LOCAL AUTHORITIES.)

RUSSIAN BONDS. When a Russian bond is drawn for repayment, unless the holder of such a bond observes the announcement, he may continue to receive payment of the coupons, but all such payments made after the bond is drawn are treated by the Russian Government as repayments on account of the principal. Thus a holder who discovers that his bond was drawn for payment years ago, will find that the interest payments which have been made since the bond was drawn will be deducted from the principal sum.

SAFE CUSTODY. It is the custom of bankers to receive and take charge of boxes of plate, securities and all manner of articles of value belonging to their customers. When articles are deposited for safe custody, some banks give a form of receipt, and before the articles can be delivered back to the customer the receipt, duly indorsed, must be returned to the bank. The following is an example of a receipt:—

No.

The British Banking Co., Ltd.,
Carlisle Branch 1910.

Received from , of
, one sealed parcel for safe custody.

per pro. The British Banking Co., Ltd.,
J. JONES, Manager.

N.B.—This receipt should be kept in a place of safety. The security referred to therein can only be returned on the following receipt being signed by the Depositor and surrendered to the Bank. The personal application of the Depositor is particularly requested, but if he is unable to attend, the order on the back hereof should also be signed.

Received from the British Banking Co., Ltd., the above-mentioned securities.

(Signature)

Date

(Printed on the back.)

To the Manager,
The British Banking Co., Ltd.,
Carlisle Branch.

Please deliver to the bearer the securities mentioned on the other side.

Signature

Address

Date

The receipt given is, in some banks, signed by the manager and the accountant. The customer depositing the articles for safe custody may be required to sign the counterfoil bearing the same number as the receipt which he obtains. This not only gives the bank a specimen of the depositor's signature which can be compared with the customer's receipt when a withdrawal takes place, but it acts as a confirmation from the customer of the articles which he has left to be taken care of.

Some bankers, however, do not give any receipts for articles left with them for safe keeping, unless specially requested so to do. They merely keep particulars of them in the safe custody register, and when the customer receives the articles back again he signs an acknowledgment for them in the register. Some bankers, who give no acknowledgments, permit the customer to see the entry of the deposit in the safe custody register.

When articles have been deposited in joint names they should not be given up except on the authority of all the parties. If one of the depositors has died, the authority of his legal representatives is usually obtained before delivery to the survivor or survivors.

All the executors of a deceased should join in an authority to give up safe custody articles which were deposited in the name of the deceased.

Where articles are deposited in the names of executors, the signatures of all, or the survivors, should be required before delivery.

Where the lodgment is in the names of trustees, it is particularly necessary to obtain all their signatures before delivery. In *Mendes* v. *Guedalla* (1862, 2 J. & H. 259), where a box containing bearer bonds was lodged for safe custody by three trustees and one of them held the key in order to cut off the coupons half-yearly, it was held that the bankers "ought not to have parted with the box, or allowed more than the coupons to be taken out, without the authority of all the three trustees."

If a banker receives an authority from a depositor to allow another person to remove a certain article from a box or parcel, the banker must see that only the specified article is taken out.

In the case of *In re De Pothonier, Dent* v. *De Pothonier* (1900, 2 Ch. 529), the following statement was given as to the practice in London with regard to the safe custody of bearer bonds :—" It is a common practice of investors to deposit such bonds with their bankers upon a simple acknowledgment by the bankers of the receipt thereof. In such cases the bankers accept the deposit subject to such responsibility as is imposed upon them by law for their safe custody, and they collect the coupons for their customers, and credit them to the account of the customers, as and when received. From my own knowledge of the course of business in the City, I say that it is a very common practice amongst men of business, and joint stock companies who hold large quantities of bonds, to deposit them with their bankers upon the above terms, and I believe that such practice offers to the owner of the bonds as good a security for the safe and proper custody of such bonds as can be obtained, and is at the same time the most convenient course the bond holder can adopt as regards the collection of interest on the bonds. If bonds to bearer are deposited with bankers in a locked box or other closed receptacle, the bankers do not give any receipt for the bonds, but only a general acknowledgment of receipt of the box, and decline to accept any responsibility for its contents." In the same case it was held that the trustees were "justified in depositing the bonds with the bankers upon those terms, which will not justify the bankers in parting with the bonds except under the authority of all the trustees but will justify the bankers in cutting off the coupons and collecting them as and when they are due, in the ordinary course."

In taking charge of valuables for a customer, a banker acts in the capacity of a bailee, and the responsibility of a banker with regard to articles left for safe custody depends in some measure as to whether he is a gratuitous bailee—that is, undertakes the work without any special charge for doing so—or whether he is a bailee for reward. Bankers do not, as a rule, receive any direct reward, and merely take charge of the articles to oblige customers, but it is contended by some writers that the fact of a banker making a profit out of a customer's account shows that he is indirectly a bailee for reward. When a customer opens an account he knows, if he looks at the advertisements of the bank, that he obtains, by becoming a customer, a right to leave his valuables at the bank to be taken care of; the banker, on his side, agrees to act as a bailee for a customer's valuables because of the account which the customer keeps with him and from which he expects to derive some benefit.

The question as to whether a banker is a gratuitous bailee or not, does not affect the practical point that a banker must take all possible care of articles left with him for safe custody, for if he is negligent and they are stolen, or if he parts with them to a wrong person, he will be liable for the loss to his customer. A banker's liability for loss might probably be less if it were proved that he was a gratuitous bailee, and not a bailee for reward.

If a banker has doubt as to the genuineness of a signature upon an order for delivery of a safe custody article, or any suspicion as to the authority of the person who presents the order, he is justified in making a delay in fulfilling the order until he has had the signature confirmed by the customer. In the case of *Mrs. Langtry v. The Union Bank of London* (which was settled by judgment for the plaintiff by consent for £10,000), the plaintiff's property was obtained from the bank by a person presenting a forged order purporting to be signed by Mrs. Langtry, requesting the bank to hand her box to the bearer.

A banker has no lien or charge upon securities or articles left with him for safe custody. If a safe custody article is to be taken as a security at any time, the customer should sign the necessary document of charge.

The Bank of France makes a specific charge for taking care of securities and valuables for customers.

In America, bankers decline to take charge of articles for safe custody, but they have a system of letting lockers, in the safe deposit department, to customers, at a rent, thus throwing the responsibility and labour of cutting off coupons, etc., upon the customers.

SAFE CUSTODY REGISTER. The securities, boxes, or other articles which may be left by customers with a banker for safe custody are, in some banks, entered in a register with the date when they are left, the name of the owner, and a description of the security or article. If the boxes are numerous they are usually registered in a separate book or in a special part of the ordinary register, and each entry is numbered consecutively, a printed number label being affixed to each box. When an article is given up to the customer, he either signs the register or gives a separate receipt for it, which receipt is kept in some available place and a reference made to it in the register.

If a parcel is sealed with the customer's own seal, it is registered as a sealed parcel, but if it is an open parcel it is customary to detail the contents, giving particulars of all certificates, principal deeds, etc. When bearer bonds are lodged for safe custody, the numbers of the bonds are quoted in the register in all cases. Some bankers keep a separate book for the record of all bearer bonds in their possession.

When a safe custody receipt is issued by the banker, the receipt must be returned duly indorsed before the articles can be given up. (See SAFE CUSTODY.)

SALE OF GOODS ACT, 1893. (56 & 57 VICT. c. 71.) Section 25 provides that where a person has sold goods and continues in possession of them or of the documents of title to the goods and sells or pledges them to any person receiving the same without notice of the previous sale the delivery shall have the same effect as if it were authorised by the owner of the goods; and that where a purchaser obtains possession of the goods or documents and sells or pledges them to any person receiving them without notice of any lien of the original seller, such delivery shall have the same effect as if the person making the delivery were a mercantile agent in possession of the goods or documents with the consent of the owner. This Section is practically the same as Sections 8 and 9 of the Factors Act, 1889. (See FACTORS ACT.)

Section 44 enacts as follows :—

"Subject to the provisions of this Act,

when the buyer of goods becomes insolvent, the unpaid seller who has parted with the possession of the goods has the right of stopping them *in transitu*, that is to say, he may resume possession of the goods as long as they are in course of transit, and may retain them until payment or tender of the price."

By Section 46 the unpaid seller may exercise his right of stoppage *in transitu* either by taking actual possession of the goods or by giving notice of his claim to the carrier or other bailee or custodier in whose possession the goods are.

Section 47 provides as follows:—

"Subject to the provisions of this Act, the unpaid seller's right of lien or retention or stoppage *in transitu* is not affected by any sale, or other disposition of the goods which the buyer may have made, unless the seller has assented thereto.

Provided that where a document of title to goods has been lawfully transferred to any person as buyer or owner of the goods, and that person transfers the document to a person who takes the document in good faith and for valuable consideration, then, if such last-mentioned transfer was by way of sale, the unpaid seller's right of lien or retention or stoppage *in transitu* is defeated, and if such last-mentioned transfer was by way of pledge or other disposition for value, the unpaid seller's right of lien or retention or stoppage *in transitu* can only be exercised subject to the rights of the transferee."

SANS COMPTE DE RETOUR. A French term meaning that notarial expenses are not to be incurred in the event of non-payment of a bill of exchange.

SANS FRAIS. (French, without expense: in English usually written "Incur no expense.")

Where the indorser of a bill adds these words to his signature, they mean that no expense is to be incurred over the bill. The words express the wish only of the indorser who uses them and do not apply to any subsequent indorser who has not used them.

SANS RECOURS. These words, the French term for "Without recourse," may be added by the drawer of a bill or an indorser to his signature to negative his own liability to the holder. (See DRAWER, INDORSER, WITHOUT RECOURSE.)

SAVINGS BANKS. A Savings Bank is for the deposit of money, the depositor receiving interest thereon. The money and interest may be drawn out by the depositor as and when required. A Savings Bank is not like an ordinary bank, as the depositors cannot issue cheques.

The various Acts relating to Savings Banks were consolidated by the Trustee Savings Bank Act, 1863 (26 & 27 Vict. c. 87). (See POST OFFICE SAVINGS BANKS, TRUSTEE SAVINGS BANKS.)

SCANDINAVIAN MONETARY UNION. The Union was formed in 1873 and includes Norway, Sweden and Denmark. Its object is the regulation of the coinage of those countries. (See LATIN MONETARY UNION.)

SCRIP. SCRIP CERTIFICATE. (Scrip is a contraction of "subscription.")

Ordinary certificates are very commonly referred to as "scrip"; but scrip or a scrip certificate is really the document or provisional certificate which is given to a person who has, for example, agreed to take up bonds in connection with a foreign Government loan and has paid the first instalment. Scrip is principally associated with the issue of debentures, or foreign bonds.

A person desirous of obtaining some bonds in a new issue pays to the bank which has the management of the issue a deposit of per cent. upon the amount of the bonds required, and requests that he be allotted that amount of bonds at the price of per cent. He agrees to accept the same or any smaller amount that may be allotted to him, and to pay the further sums due on such allotment according to the terms of the prospectus. If his application is successful he receives a letter of allotment stating the amount of bonds which have been allotted to him. At a certain date the letter of allotment is exchanged for a scrip certificate, a document which states the amount that has been paid towards the price of the bond and sets forth the dates when the remaining instalments are due and the amount of each. A form of receipt is appended for each instalment, which is filled up by the bank whenever an instalment is paid. When all the instalments have been paid the holder is entitled to a duly stamped bond in exchange for the scrip certificate. If an instalment is not paid, it renders all previous payments liable to forfeiture. Where interest will be payable before the bonds are ready to be issued, a coupon is appended at the foot of the scrip certificate. The receipts must not be detached from the scrip certificate, and when remitting the instalments the certificate must accompany the remittance.

The following is a specimen of a scrip certificate:—

£100 No. 4623.

FOREIGN GOVERNMENT 5 PER CENT. STERLING LOAN OF 1909, FOR £2,000,000, AT 90 PER CENT.

Scrip certificate for £100.

The Bearer of this scrip certificate has paid in respect of One hundred pounds of the above loan, the sum of £10, leaving a balance of £80, payable as follows:—

£10 per cent. on 1st July, 1909.
£10 per cent. on 1st August, 1909.
£10 per cent. on 1st September, 1909.
£25 per cent. on 1st October, 1909.
£25 per cent. on 1st November, 1909.

After payment of the above instalments the Bearer will be entitled to a duly stamped bond in exchange for this scrip certificate. Due notice will be given by advertisement in *The Times* when the bonds are ready for delivery.

Default in payment of any instalment will render all previous payments liable to forfeiture.

For The British Banking Co., Ltd.

Registered JOHN BROWN,
London 1909. General Manager.

Receipt for Instalment of 10 per cent.

Due 1st July, 1909.

Received 1909, the sum of Ten pounds, being the instalment due 1st July, 1909.

For The British Banking Co., Ltd.,
£10 Cashier.

Receipt for Instalment of 10 per cent.

Due 1st August, 1909.

Received 1909, the sum of Ten pounds, being the instalment due 1st August, 1909.

For The British Banking Co., Ltd.,
£10. Cashier.

Receipt for Instalment of 10 per cent.

Due 1st September, 1909.

Received 1909, the sum of Ten pounds, being the instalment due 1st September, 1909.

For The British Banking Co., Ltd.,
£10. Cashier.

Receipt for Instalment of 25 per cent.

Due 1st October, 1909.

Received 1909, the sum of Twenty-five pounds, being the instalment due 1st October, 1909.

For the British Banking Co., Ltd.,
£25. Cashier.

Receipt for Instalment of 25 per cent.

Due 1st November, 1909.

Received 1909, the sum of Twenty-five pounds, being the instalment due 1st November, 1909.

For The British Banking Co., Ltd.,
£25. Cashier.

FOREIGN GOVERNMENT 5 PER CENT. STERLING LOAN, 1909.

Coupon for Two pounds ten shillings due 1st December, 1909.

Payable at The British Banking Co., Ltd., London.

£2 10*s.* 0*d.*

Stamp Duty (Stamp Act, 1891):—

SCRIP CERTIFICATE, SCRIP, or other document.	£	s.	d.
(1) Entitling any person to become the proprietor of any share of any company or proposed company . . . . . . (2) Issued or delivered in the United Kingdom, and entitling any person to become the proprietor of any share of any foreign or colonial company or proposed company . (3) Denoting, or intended to denote, the right of any person as a subscriber in respect of any loan raised or proposed to be raised by any company or proposed company, or by any municipal body or corporation . . . . (4) Issued or delivered in the United Kingdom, and denoting, or intended to denote, the right of any person as a subscriber in respect of any loan raised or proposed to be raised by or on behalf of any foreign or colonial state, government, municipal body, corporation, or company	0	0	1

The word "share" in the above Schedule includes a fractional part of a share. (Section 9, Revenue Act, 1909.)

Every person who issues any scrip certificate, or scrip, before the same is duly stamped, shall incur a fine of twenty pounds. (Section 79, Stamp Act. See LETTER OF ALLOTMENT.)

The separate receipts upon a scrip certificate are exempt from stamp duty. The exemption is given by the Stamp Act, 1891, under Receipt (see RECEIPT) as follows:—" Receipt indorsed or otherwise written upon or contained in any instrument liable to stamp duty, and duly stamped, acknowledging the receipt of the consideration money therein expressed, or the receipt of any principal money, interest, or annuity thereby secured or therein mentioned."

A coupon attached to a scrip certificate requires to be stamped. (See COMPANIES, LETTER OF ALLOTMENT, SHARE CAPITAL.)

SEA INSURANCE. (See MARINE INSURANCE POLICY.)

SEAL. An impression in wax, or other soft substance, made by an engraved stamp. Also the engraved stamp itself. At one time the seal was usually attached to the document by a strip of parchment or a cord. As deeds now require to be signed by the parties thereto, the use of the seal has become a mere formality and a simple wafer is frequently used, as in transfers of shares and stocks, instead of an impression in wax.

The letters L.S. inside a circle, thus (L.S.) which are seen on transfer forms, stand for *locus sigilli*, and mean the place of the seal. They do not, however, act instead of a seal, or wafer.

The seal of a company is called its common seal. Every limited company "shall have its name engraven in legible characters on its seal." If any director, manager, or officer of a limited company, or any person on its behalf, uses or authorises the use of any seal purporting to be a seal of the company, whereon its name is not engraven as aforesaid, he shall be liable to a fine not exceeding fifty pounds. (See Section 63 of the Companies (Consolidation) Act, 1908, under heading NAME OF COMPANY.) The seal of a company is usually affixed in the presence of two directors, who sign the document, which is also countersigned by the secretary or such other person as the directors may appoint for the purpose. A record is kept of each document which is sealed, the entry being initialled by the persons who witnessed the affixing of the seal. The seal is usually kept in a box or case secured by two locks, the keys of which are held by different persons.

Sections 78 and 79 of the Companies (Consolidation) Act, 1908, give powers to a company to empower any person, as its attorney, to execute deeds abroad and to have an official seal for use abroad :—

"78. A company may, by writing under its common seal, empower any person, either generally or in respect of any specified matters, as its attorney, to execute deeds on its behalf in any place not situate in the United Kingdom; and every deed signed by such attorney, on behalf of the company, and under his seal, shall bind the company, and have the same effect as if it were under its common seal."

"79. (1) A company whose objects require or comprise the transaction of business in foreign countries may, if authorised by its articles, have for use in any territory, district, or place not situate in the United Kingdom, an official seal, which shall be a facsimile of the common seal of the company, with the addition on its face of the name of every territory, district, or place where it is to be used.

"(2) A company having such an official seal may, by writing under its common seal, authorise any person appointed for the purpose in any territory, district, or place not situate in the United Kingdom, to affix the same to any deed or other document to which the company is party in that territory, district, or place.

"(3) The authority of any such agent shall, as between the company and any person dealing with the agent, continue during the period, if any, mentioned in the instrument conferring the authority, or if no period is there mentioned, then until notice of the revocation or determination of the agent's authority has been given to the person dealing with him.

"(4) The person affixing any such official seal shall, by writing under his hand, on the deed or other document to which the seal is affixed, certify the date and place of affixing the same.

"(5) A deed or other document to which an official seal is duly affixed shall bind the company as if it had been sealed with the common seal of the company."

Section 117 provides for the authentication of documents :—

"A document or proceeding requiring authentication by a company may be signed by a director, secretary, or other authorised officer of the company, and need not be under its common seal." (See COMPANIES.)

SEAL BOOK. (See COMMON SEAL BOOK.)

SECOND - CLASS PAPER. First - class paper includes bank bills and bills bearing names of the highest standing. Where the position is not so good, the bills fall into a second or a third-class position, or even into a still lower class, according to circumstances.

SECOND MORTGAGE. A charge upon property which ranks after a first mortgage. For example, if Brown gives Jones a legal mortgage upon his property, and afterwards gives his banker a second mortgage, the banker's charge is available only after Jones is fully satisfied either by having received repayment of the debt, with interest from Brown, or by having enforced his mortgage and obtained repayment out of the security.

All mortgages after the first legal mortgage are called equitable mortgages (*q.v.*).

A prudent banker avoids, as far as possible, taking a second mortgage as security. It is, as a rule, a most unsatisfactory form of security, and the less a banker has to do with second mortgages the better.

Where a second mortgage is taken, notice must be given to the first mortgagee, otherwise he might, without notice, make a further advance to the mortgagor, or he might buy up a subsequent mortgage and tack it on to his own, and in either case the second mortgagee would be squeezed out of any value there was in his charge. If the mortgagor fails to pay his interest regularly to the first mortgagee, the amount of interest in arrears will increase the amount of the first charge, and, when it comes to a question of selling the property, the first mortgagee will be quite satisfied if he can obtain from the sale repayment of the money he has lent upon the property, without concerning himself with the interests of any subsequent mortgagee.

Instead of allowing the first mortgagee to sell, a banker holding a second mortgage might, perhaps, be tempted to pay off the first mortgage, in the hope that he may, ultimately, be able to find a purchaser for the property at a price sufficient to cover both the amount of the first mortgage taken over by him, and his own debt. Such an operation, however, may result in the banker finding that his last state is worse than the first. (See MORTGAGE.)

SECOND OF EXCHANGE. (See BILL IN A SET.)

SECRECY DECLARATION. All banks require every person joining the staff to sign a form agreeing to preserve absolute secrecy with regard to the affairs of the customers and all other matters connected with the business of the bank.

SECRET COMMISSION. Where an agent corruptly accepts any consideration as an inducement to act contrary to the interests or business of his principal, or any person corruptly gives such consideration to the agent, it is a misdemeanour. (See PREVENTION OF CORRUPTION ACT, 1906.)

SECURED CREDITOR. A creditor who holds security from the debtor for the amount due to him. (See PROOF OF DEBTS.)

SECURITIES BOOK. Securities, of whatever nature, which are left to cover an advance, are entered in the securities book. A page is headed with the name of the customer, his address and designation, and underneath are detailed the deeds, certificates, bonds, life policies, guarantees and all other securities. Sufficient information is given regarding each different item to enable anyone to judge, without a reference to the securities themselves, of what the security actually consists. In the case of deeds, it is customary to quote the date of the last principal document and the name of the person to whom the property belongs, and to state whether the property is freehold, leasehold or copyhold. Where the property has come by will to the person lodging the security, particulars of that fact are given. The quantity of land, with the number and nature of any buildings thereon, and the amount of the consideration money, with the date, are set forth, and information is given as to the nature of the charge (mortgage, or memorandum of deposit) which the bank has upon the property. Any prior mortgage, or charge, or any flaw in the title, or anything with regard to the property which may in any way affect the value of the security to the bank, are duly noted. The probable present market value of the property is given, and also the rentals or other information which may help to prove the estimated value. In leasehold property the number of years of the lease, and the ground rents are stated, in addition to the above information, and in copyhold property the amount of the fines and fees. Where there is insurable property particulars of the fire policies held are entered.

Full particulars of all certificates lodged are given, including the number of shares, the name of the company, the designation of the shares (or stock), the nominal amount and the amount paid up, the name of the person which appears on the certificate, the present market value, the rate of dividend, and the nature of the charge which the bank holds.

With regard to life policies, the particulars which are usually entered in the securities book are, the name of the company, the number of the policy, the amount and when payable, the amount of the premium and the date on which it is payable, the name of the person in whose favour the policy is granted, the amount of accrued bonuses, the present surrender value, a note of any charge upon the policy, and particulars of the assignment of the policy to the bank, and the acceptance by the company of notice of the assignment.

Other forms of securities are entered in a similar way so as to give full information as to the nature of the security and its probable value. In the case of guarantees, recent reports upon the sureties must be given.

When securities are deposited, it is the practice in some banks for the depositor to sign the book in which they are entered, or where a receipt is given by the banker from a counterfoil book, to sign the counterfoil. When a security is given up, the receipt of the person who lodged it is obtained against the entry in the book, or a separate receipt is taken and a reference made to it in the securities book.

SECURITIES JOURNAL. The book in which securities are entered as received. They are afterwards posted in the securities ledger, which is kept in a manner somewhat similar to an ordinary ledger.

SECURITIES LEDGER. A book in use in some banks and kept after the manner of an ordinary ledger, full particulars of all securities received being entered on the one side of an account and those given up being written off on the other side. When securities are received they are first entered in the securities journal and then posted into the correct account in the securities ledger.

SECURITY. That which is given to secure the repayment of money lent. Where a person borrows money from his banker, he supplies security, most commonly certificates of shares with a transfer into the names of the banker's nominees, or the title deeds of a property with either a memorandum of deposit or a legal mortgage, or bearer bonds or other negotiable instruments, or a life policy assigned to the banker, or a guarantee by some reliable person. The value of the security should always be greater than the amount of money lent. (See ADVANCES.)

The security given may belong either to the debtor himself or to some other person. When it belongs to another person it is usually called "collateral security" (*q.v.*).

Where several securities, deposited by different persons, are held for one account, and one of the depositors dies, the account should be broken and an arrangement made with the debtor to pass all future transactions through a new account until fresh arrangements are made.

If security is taken from a customer to cover an advance already granted, and the customer shortly afterwards fails, the security may be objected to on the ground of fraudulent preference. By Section 48 of the Bankruptcy Act, 1883:—

"(1) Every conveyance or transfer of property, or charge thereon made, every payment made, every obligation incurred, and every judicial proceeding taken or suffered by any person unable to pay his debts as they become due from his own money in favour of any creditor, or any person in trust for any creditor, with a view of giving such creditor a preference over the other creditors shall, if the person making, taking, paying, or suffering the same is adjudged bankrupt on a bankruptcy petition presented within three months after the date of making, taking, paying or suffering the same, be deemed fraudulent and void as against the trustee in the bankruptcy.

"(2) This section shall not affect the rights of any person making title in good faith and for valuable consideration through or under a creditor of the bankrupt."

Another ground on which a security may be objected to is where "undue influence" may have been exercised, as might occur in the case of a father, or mother, unduly pressing a son, or daughter, who has just come of age and succeeded to an estate, to give security to a banker for the father's, or mother's, overdraft.

Information regarding the various forms of securities, and the charges, etc., will be found under the respective headings. (See ADVANCES, AMERICAN RAILROAD CERTIFICATES, BEARER BONDS, BILL OF LADING, BILL OF SALE, BOND OF CREDIT, CERTIFICATE, COLLATERAL SECURITY, DEBENTURE, DEBTS—ASSIGNMENT OF, DOCK WARRANT, GOODS, GUARANTEE, INSCRIBED STOCK, LIFE POLICY, NEGOTIABLE INSTRUMENTS, SHARES, SHIP-MORTGAGE, TITLE DEEDS.)

SEIGNIORAGE. The profit which the Government makes on the manufacture of silver and bronze coins. These coins are token money, and the value which is affixed to them by law is greater than the value of the metal of which they are composed, and it is from that difference that the profit is obtained. Although in the actual coining of silver there is a considerable profit, that profit is utilised partly in maintaining the silver coinage of the country in a fit condition. (See BRASSAGE.)

SEISIN. SEIZIN. Possession. (See LIVERY OF SEISIN.)

By the Stamp Act, 1891, the stamp duties are :—

	£	s.	d.
SEISIN. Instrument of seisin given upon any charter, precept of clare constat, or precept from chancery, or upon any wadset, heritable bond, disposition, apprising, adjudication, or otherwise of any lands or heritable subjects in Scotland . . .	0	5	0
And any NOTARIAL INSTRUMENT to be expeded and recorded in any register of sasines	0	5	0

SEIZED OF. Put in possession of.

SELLING OUT. If a purchaser on the Stock Exchange fails to take up at the appointed time the securities which he agreed to buy, the seller can "sell out" against him ; that is, he can instruct the Stock Exchange official broker to sell the securities, and any loss which arises must be paid by the purchaser. (See BUYING IN.)

SEN. (See FOREIGN MONEYS—JAPAN.)

SEQUESTRATION. In Scotland a decree of sequestration is equivalent to an adjudication of bankruptcy in England.

The word is also applied to the placing of a property, about which there is a dispute, in the hands of a third party until the dispute is settled.

SET, BILL IN A. (See BILL IN A SET.)

SET OFF. In the absence of any arrangement, or understanding, to the contrary, a banker has the right to set off a debt owing by him to a customer against a debt owing by the customer to the banker. For example, if a customer has two accounts in his own name, one entitled No. 1 account, which is in credit, and the other No. 2 account, which is in debit, the banker may hold the credit balance (or so much of it as is necessary) against the debit balance. But where a customer has several accounts, the banker cannot treat as a set off any balance which he knows is held in a fiduciary capacity. An account in the name of "John Brown a/c Trustee of J. Jones" or "John Brown a/c Churchwardens," or in any other similar form, is clear evidence that the money does not belong to John Brown and therefore cannot be used by a banker to liquidate a debt due from Brown, but accounts which are named "John Brown a/c House" or "a/c Farm," or such like terms, to distinguish Brown's own affairs, may be consolidated.

A credit account at one branch may if not contrary to custom or agreement, be taken as a set off against a debt owing by the same customer at another branch.

Where accounts have been running without any right to set off being exercised, reasonable notice should, as a rule, be given before acting upon the right.

In the case of a solicitor having a private account and an office account, it has been held (*T. & H. Greenwood Teale* v. *William Williams, Brown & Co.*, 1894, 11 T.L.R. 56) that the one may be set off against the other, even though the money in the office account may really belong to his clients.

The credit balance on a partner's private account cannot be taken as a set off to a debt on the firm's account ; but if the customer is the sole partner then his private account balance may be held against a debt on the account in the firm's name, and, conversely, a credit on the firm's account against the private account.

A customer's deposit receipt may be held against a debt due from him.

A balance on an executor's account cannot be transferred by a banker to clear off an overdraft on the deceased's account. A cheque or order from the executor or administrator is necessary in order to effect such a transfer.

No right of set off exists between a customer's private account and any joint account in which his name appears. Nor, in the case of the accounts of a Local Authority, can a credit on one account be held as a set off to a debit on another account. (See LOCAL AUTHORITIES.)

It has been held (*Hawkins* v. *Whitten*, 1829, 10 B. & C. 217) that a customer, who is indebted to a bank, has, in the event of the bank stopping payment, a right to set off against his debt any of the notes of the bank which may be in his possession when he received notice of an act of bankruptcy.

Section 38 of the Bankruptcy Act, 1883, provides as follows :—

"Where there have been mutual credits, mutual debts, or other mutual dealings between a debtor against whom a receiving order shall be made under this Act, and any other person proving or claiming to prove a debt under such receiving order, an account shall be taken of what is due from the one party to the other in respect of such mutual dealings, and the sum due from the one party shall be set off against any sum due from the other party, and the balance of the account, and no more, shall be claimed or paid on either side respectively ; but a person shall not be entitled under this Section to claim the benefit of any set off against the property of a debtor in any case where he had at the time of giving credit to the debtor, notice of an act of bankruptcy committed by the debtor, and available against him."

SETTLEMENT. By the Stamp Act, 1891, the stamp duty is :—

	£	s.	d.
SETTLEMENT. Any instrument, whether voluntary or upon any good or valuable consideration, other than a *bonâ fide* pecuniary consideration, whereby any definite and certain principal sum of money (whether charged or chargeable on lands or other hereditaments or heritable subjects, or not, or to be laid out in the purchase of lands or other hereditaments or heritable subjects or not), or any definite and certain amount of stock, or any security, is settled or agreed to be settled in any manner whatsoever :			
For every £100, and also for any fractional part of £100, of the amount or value of the property settled or agreed to be settled . .	0	5	0

(*Where any instrument is chargeable both as a conveyance operating as a voluntary disposition inter vivos under Section 74 of the Finance* (1909–10) *Act*, 1910, *and as a settlement, it shall be charged with duty as a conveyance in accordance with that Section. See* CONVEYANCE.)

Exemption.

Instrument of appointment relating to any property in favour of persons specially named or described as the objects of a power of appointment, where duty has been duly paid in respect of the same property upon the settlement creating the power or the grant of representation of any will or testamentary instrument creating the power.

And see Sections 104, 105, and 106.

As to Settlement of Policy or Security.

"104. (1) Where any money which may become due or payable upon any policy of life insurance, or upon any security not being a marketable security, is settled or agreed to be settled, the instrument whereby the settlement is made or agreed to be made is to be charged with *ad valorem* duty in respect of that money.

"(2) Provided as follows :—

"(*a*) Where, in the case of a policy, no provision is made for keeping up the policy, the *ad valorem* duty is to be charged only on the value of the policy at the date of the instrument :

"(*b*) If in any such case the instrument contains a statement of the said value, and is stamped in accordance with the statement, it is, so far as regards the policy, to be deemed duly stamped, unless or until it is shown that the statement is untrue, and that the instrument is in fact insufficiently stamped.

Settlements when not to be Charged as Securities.

"105. An instrument chargeable with *ad valorem* duty as a settlement in respect of any money, stock, or security is not to be charged with any further duty by reason of containing provision for the payment or transfer of the money, stock, or security, or by reason of containing, where the money, stock, or security is in reversion or is not paid or transferred upon the execution of the instrument, provision for the payment, by the person entitled in possession to the interest or dividends of the money, stock, or security, during the continuance of such possession, of any annuity or yearly sum not exceeding interest at the rate of four pounds per centum per annum upon the amount or value of the money, stock, or security.

Where several Instruments one only to be Charged with Ad Valorem *Duty.*

"106. (1) Where several instruments are executed for effecting the settlement of the same property, and the *ad valorem* duty chargeable in respect of the settlement of the property exceeds ten shillings, one only of the instruments is to be charged with the *ad valorem* duty.

"(2) Where a settlement is made in pursuance of a previous agreement upon which *ad valorem* settlement duty exceeding ten shillings has been paid in respect of any property, the settlement is not to be charged with *ad valorem* duty in respect of the same property.

"(3) In each of the aforesaid cases the instruments not chargeable with *ad valorem* duty are to be charged with the duty of ten shillings."

SETTLEMENTS—SETTLOR BANKRUPT. Voluntary settlements by a person who subsequently becomes bankrupt are dealt with by Section 47 of the Bankruptcy Act, 1883:—

"(1) Any settlement of property not being a settlement made before and in consideration of marriage, or made in favour of a purchaser or incumbrancer in good faith and for valuable consideration, or a settlement made on or for the wife or children of the settlor of property which has accrued to the settlor after marriage in right of his wife, shall, if the settlor becomes bankrupt within two years after the date of the settlement, be void against the trustee in the bankruptcy, and shall, if the settlor becomes bankrupt at any subsequent time within ten years after the date of the settlement, be void against the trustee in the bankruptcy, unless the parties claiming under the settlement can prove that the settlor was at the time of making the settlement able to pay all his debts without the aid of the property comprised in the settlement, and that the interest of the settlor in such property had passed to the trustee of such settlement on the execution thereof.

"(2) Any covenant or contract made in consideration of marriage, for the future settlement on or for the settlor's wife or children of any money or property wherein he had not at the date of his marriage any estate or interest, whether vested or contingent in possession or remainder, and not being money or property of or in right of his wife, shall, on his becoming bankrupt before the property or money has been actually transferred or paid pursuant to the contract or covenant, be void against the trustee in the bankruptcy.

"(3) 'Settlement' shall for the purposes of this Section include any conveyance or transfer of property." (See BANKRUPTCY.)

SETTLING DAYS. The days upon which, according to the rules of the Stock Exchange, the transactions for the accounts are arranged and settled.

In the case of most securities dealt in on the London Stock Exchange there are two settlements in each month, one about the middle and the other near the end, but for Consols there is only one, near the beginning of the month. When stock transactions are done "for the account" it means that payment must be made on the next settling day; dealings "for cash," however, or "for money" have to be completed by payment at once irrespective of any regular settling day.

Each Stock Exchange settlement requires three days; the first is known as Contango day (or Continuation, or Carrying-over day, or Making-up day) (see CONTANGO); the second is Name or Ticket day (see TICKET DAY); the third Pay day, i.e. settling day proper (see PAY DAY). For mining securities there is an additional day, called "mining Contango" day.

Securities payable to bearer are handed over on the settling day. Ten days are allowed in which to complete the delivery of registered securities; but if not delivered within that time the stock or shares may be "bought in" through the official buying-in department, and the loss must be borne by the seller. (See STOCK EXCHANGE.)

SEVERALTY. Where a person holds an estate in severalty he holds it entirely in his own right, without being joined in interest with any other person. (See COPARCENERS, JOINT TENANTS, TENANTS IN COMMON.)

SHAHIS. (See FOREIGN MONEYS—PERSIA.)

SHAREBROKER. (See STOCKBROKER.)

SHARE CAPITAL. SHARES. A share is the right which a member of a company has to a certain proportion of the capital, the capital being the total fund contributed by the members. On the other hand, he is liable for any unpaid balance there may be on the shares he holds. The memorandum of association of a company limited by shares must state the amount of share capital with which the company proposes to be registered, and the division thereof into shares of a fixed amount. (See MEMORANDUM OF ASSOCIATION.)

Shares are known by various names, such as preference, guaranteed, ordinary, deferred, founders' shares and other varieties. The rights of each class of share depend upon the provisions in the memorandum and articles of association, or in special resolutions of the company. The rights attaching to a certain class of shares in one company are not necessarily the same as those in another company. (See Section 39, Companies (Consolidation) Act, 1908, given below.)

If authorised by its articles, a company limited by shares may convert its paid-up shares into stock. (See Section 41, below.) This is the only way in which it can create stock. Shares are, practically, divisions of stock in fixed amounts, and a shareholder obtains so many of those divisions, but a stockholder may obtain any odd or irregular amount of the stock; for example, a share may be for £1, £5, £10, £20, £100 and suchlike amounts, whereas a holding of stock may be for £33 16*s*. 11*d*. or for any amount.

Before an official quotation on the London Stock Exchange can be obtained for stocks and shares, the certificates must conform to certain regulations of the committee. (See QUOTATION ON LONDON STOCK EXCHANGE.) In the case of a new company, before a special settlement for the bargains for sales and purchases of shares can be fixed, various documents and particulars must be sent to the Secretary of the Share and Loan Department. (See SPECIAL SETTLEMENT.)

If certificates of shares are deposited as security without any document of charge, it constitutes an equitable mortgage, and the banker has the right to apply to the Court for power to sell. In some cases a memorandum of deposit is taken with certificates, and notice given to the company.

Some bankers take a blank transfer; that is, a transfer with the space for the transferee's name left blank, or it may be undated. If default is made in payment, the banker fills up the blanks and registers the shares in his own name or the names of nominees. The most satisfactory way, however, is to take a completed transfer of the shares and have them registered at once. When a transfer is taken it is usually accompanied by an agreement qualifying the transfer, and declaring that the transfer has been given merely by way of security.

In taking shares as a security, a banker will note whether they are fully paid up, or only partly paid, though certificates do not always show how much is paid up per share. If there is a large liability it would be unwise to register in the bank's name, or the names of its nominees. If the completed transfer is held, without registration, the owner will remain liable for any calls that may be made, and so long as the banker holds the certificate and transfer he has a security which he can complete by registration when required, and if notice has been given to the company it would be difficult for anyone to get registered in front of him. The company, however, may have a lien upon its shares for any debt due from the shareholder to the company. (See LIEN.) In most cases a certificate must be surrendered before a transfer of the shares can be effected, but this is not an absolute protection to a banker, as it has been held that a foot-note upon a certificate to the effect that no transfer of the shares will be effected without production of the certificate does not constitute a contract and is not binding on the company. (See CERTIFICATE.)

The Companies (Consolidation) Act, 1908, provides as follows :—

"Section 22. (1) The shares or other interest of any member in a company shall be personal estate, transferable in manner provided by the articles of the company, and shall not be of the nature of real estate.

"(2) Each share in a company having a share capital shall be distinguished by its appropriate number.

"23. A certificate, under the common seal of the company, specifying any shares or stock held by any member, shall be *primâ facie* evidence of the title of the member to the shares or stock.

Power of Company to Arrange for Different amounts being paid on Shares.

"39. A company, if so authorised by its articles, may do any one or more of the following things ; namely :—

"(1) Make arrangements on the issue of shares for a difference between the shareholders in the amounts and times of payment of calls on their shares :

"(2) Accept from any member who assents thereto the whole or a part of the amount remaining unpaid on any shares held by him, although no part of that amount has been called up ;

"(3) Pay dividend in proportion to the amount paid up on each share where a larger amount is paid up on some shares than on others.

Power to Return Accumulated Profits in Reduction of paid-up Share Capital.

"40. (1) When a company has accumulated a sum of undivided profits, which with the sanction of the shareholders may be distributed among the shareholders in the form of a dividend or bonus, it may, by special resolution, return the same, or any part thereof, to the shareholders in reduction of the paid-up capital of the company, the unpaid capital being thereby increased by a similar amount.

Power of Company limited by Shares to Alter its Share Capital.

"41. (1) A company limited by shares, if so authorised by its articles, may alter the conditions of its memorandum as follows (that is to say), it may :—

"(*a*) increase its share capital by the issue of new shares of such amount as it thinks expedient ;

"(*b*) consolidate and divide all or any of its share capital into shares of larger amount than its existing shares ;

"(*c*) convert all or any of its paid-up shares into stock, and reconvert that stock into paid-up shares of any denomination ;

"(*d*) subdivide its shares, or any of them, into shares of smaller amount than is fixed by the memorandum, so, however, that in the subdivision the proportion between the amount paid and the amount, if any, unpaid on each reduced share shall be the same as it was in the case of the share from which the reduced share is derived ;

"(*e*) cancel shares which, at the date of the passing of the resolution in that behalf, have not been taken or agreed to be taken by any person, and diminish the amount of its share capital by the amount of the shares so cancelled.

"(2) The powers conferred by this Section with respect to subdivision of shares must be exercised by special resolution.

Re-organisation of Share Capital.

"45. (1) A company limited by shares may, by special resolution confirmed by an order of the Court, modify the conditions contained in its memorandum so as to re-organise its share capital, whether by the consolidation of shares of different classes or by the division of its shares into shares of different classes :

"Provided that no preference or

special privilege attached to or belonging to any class of shares shall be interfered with except by a resolution passed by a majority in number of shareholders of that class holding three-fourths of the share capital of that class and confirmed at a meeting of shareholders of that class in the same manner as a special resolution of the company is required to be confirmed, and every resolution so passed shall bind all shareholders of the class."

A limited company may, by special resolution, determine that any part of its share capital which has not already been called up shall not be capable of being called up, except for the purposes of the company being wound up. (Section 59, see RESERVE LIABILITY.)

In addition to the fees to be paid, by a company having a share capital, to the registrar of companies, as provided by the Companies (Consolidation) Act, 1908 (see FEES PAYABLE TO REGISTRAR OF COMPANIES), there is a duty of five shillings (imposed by Section 112, Stamp Act, 1891, and amended by Section 7 of the Finance Act, 1899) on every £100 of the nominal share capital. (See BLANK TRANSFER, COMPANIES, LEEMAN'S ACT, REDUCTION OF SHARE CAPITAL, TRANSFER OF SHARES.)

SHARE CERTIFICATE. (See CERTIFICATE.)

SHAREHOLDERS' LEDGER. This book, commonly called the "share ledger," contains practically the same information as is contained in the register. (See REGISTER OF MEMBERS OF COMPANY.) An account is opened in the ledger for each shareholder, two accounts often appearing on one page, showing on the one side the number of shares, date when acquired, the distinctive numbers, the amount per share and total amount of capital paid, and a reference to the account of the shareholder from whom they were acquired, and on the other side the date of any transfer, a reference to the transferee's account, the numbers of the shares and total amount of capital transferred. Columns are sometimes added to show the balance of shares and capital. Particulars of any lien, or instructions regarding the payment of dividends, or other matters affecting any shareholder are entered at the heading of his account.

SHAREHOLDERS' REGISTER. A book ruled to show the names of shareholders, their addresses and occupations, quantity of shares held, date when acquired, amount paid up, distinctive numbers of the shares, dates of transfers and the numbers of the shares transferred.

For further information and the Sections of the Companies (Consolidation) Act, 1908, regarding the register, see REGISTER OF MEMBERS OF COMPANY.

SHARES. (See SHARE CAPITAL.)

SHARE WARRANT. A share warrant to bearer entitles the holder of it to the fully paid-up shares or stock named therein, and the ownership is transferred by simply handing the warrant to the purchaser.

A company limited by shares may issue share warrants to bearer, in accordance with the regulations contained in Section 37 of the Companies (Consolidation) Act, 1908 :—

"(1) A company limited by shares, if so authorised by its articles, may, with respect to any fully paid-up shares, or to stock, issue under its common seal a warrant stating that the bearer of the warrant is entitled to the shares or stock therein specified, and may provide, by coupons or otherwise, for the payment of the future dividends on the shares or stock included in the warrant, in this Act termed a share warrant.

"(2) A share warrant shall entitle the bearer thereof to the shares or stock therein specified, and the shares or stock may be transferred by delivery of the warrant.

"(3) The bearer of a share warrant shall, subject to the articles of the company, be entitled, on surrendering it for cancellation, to have his name entered as a member in the register of members ; and the company shall be responsible for any loss incurred by any person by reason of the company entering in its register the name of a bearer of a share warrant in respect of the shares or stock therein specified without the warrant being surrendered and cancelled.

"(4) The bearer of a share warrant may, if the articles of the company so provide, be deemed to be a member of the company within the meaning of this Act, either to the full extent or for any purposes defined in the articles ; except that he shall not be qualified in respect of the shares or stock specified in the warrant for being a director or manager of the company, in cases where such a qualification is required by the articles.

"(5) On the issue of a share warrant the company shall strike out of its register of members the name of the member then entered therein as holding the shares or stock specified in the warrant as if he had ceased to be a member, and shall enter in the register the following particulars namely:—

"(i) The fact of the issue of the warrant;

"(ii) A statement of the shares or stock included in the warrant, distinguishing each share by its number; and

"(iii) The date of the issue of the warrant.

"(6) Until the warrant is surrendered, the above particulars shall be deemed to be the particulars required by this Act to be entered in the register of members; and, on the surrender, the date of the surrender must be entered as if it were the date at which a person ceased to be a member."

A share warrant to bearer has been held by mercantile usage to be a negotiable instrument. As it is transferable by mere delivery, the simple pledge of a share warrant, without any transfer form, is all that is required to give a banker a security, but a memorandum or agreement under hand (stamp, 6*d.*) should be signed by the person depositing such a warrant as security, to show quite clearly the reason why it has been deposited.

Where a share warrant to bearer is purchased in good faith and without notice that it has been stolen, the purchaser obtains a complete title to it, even though the warrant had been stolen by the person who sold it.

The following is a specimen of a share warrant to bearer:—

COMPANY LIMITED.

Share Capital

£ in shares of £10 each.

SHARE WARRANT TO BEARER

for ten shares, of £10 each.

This is to certify that the bearer of this warrant is the proprietor of ten fully paid-up shares No. to of Ten pounds sterling each in the Company, Limited, subject to the Articles of Association of the Company.

Given under the Common Seal of the Company in London this day of 19 .

Secretary. Chairman.

A sheet of coupons for the payment of the interest is attached to the warrant.

By the Stamp Act, 1891:—

SHARE WARRANT and STOCK CERTIFICATE to bearer. A duty of an amount equal to three times the amount of the *ad valorem* stamp duty which would be chargeable on a deed transferring the share or shares or stock specified in the warrant or certificate if the consideration for the transfer were the nominal value of such share or shares or stock (that is, 30*s.* per cent. on the nominal value of the shares).

The penalty for issuing unstamped share warrants or stock certificates to bearer is £50.

Where the holder of a certificate to bearer is entered on the register as the owner of the share or stock the certificate must be cancelled so as to be incapable of being re-issued. (Section 109, Stamp Act, 1891.)

By Section 5 of the Finance Act, 1899, the stamp duty shall extend to any instrument to bearer issued by or on behalf of any company or body of persons in the United Kingdom and having a like effect as a share warrant or stock certificate to bearer. (See COMPANIES, MARKETABLE SECURITY, SHARE CAPITAL, STOCK CERTIFICATE TO BEARER.)

SHILLING. This coin has varied considerably in value at different times. A coin of that name was first issued in 1504. In 1560 a pound troy of silver was coined into sixty shillings. In 1600 it was coined into sixty-two shillings, and by Act 56 George III it was ordered to be coined into sixty-six shillings, and that is the number which is, at the present time, coined out of a pound troy of silver of the fineness of eleven ounces two pennyweights of fine silver and eighteen pennyweights of alloy in every pound weight troy. The standard weight of a shilling is 87·27272 grains troy, and its standard fineness thirty-seven-fortieths fine silver, three-fortieths alloy. (See COINAGE.)

SHIP-MORTGAGE, ETC. Every British ship shall, unless exempted from registry, be registered under the Merchant Shipping Act, 1894.

The chief officer of customs shall be the registrar of British ships at any port in the United Kingdom, or Isle of Man, approved by the Commissioners of Customs for the registry of ships.

When registered, the registrar shall grant a certificate of registry. The certificate of registry shall be used only for the lawful navigation of the ship, and shall not be subject to detention by reason of any title, lien, charge or interest by any owner, mortgagee or other person.

The property in a ship is divided into sixty-four shares.

A person is not entitled to be registered as owner of a fractional part of a share, but any number of persons not exceeding five may be registered as joint owners of a ship or of any share therein.

A corporation may be registered as owner by its corporate name.

A registered ship or a share therein (when disposed of to a person qualified to own a British ship) shall be transferred by bill of sale.

The bill of sale must be in the form as specified by the Merchant Shipping Act, 1894. The form provides for a full description of the ship, particulars of tonnage, etc., and continues :—

"I" or "we"] in consideration of the sum of paid to [" me" or "us"] by the receipt whereof is hereby acknowledged, transfer shares in the ship above particularly described, and in her boats, guns, ammunition, small arms, and appurtenances, to the said .

Further [" I" or "we"] the said for [" myself and my" or "ourselves and our"] heirs covenant with the said and [" his," "her," or "their"] assigns that [" I" or "we"] have power to transfer in manner aforesaid the premises herein before expressed to be transferred, and that the same are free from incumbrances [if there be any mortgage add "save as appears by the registry of the said ship"].

In witness whereof ha hereunto subscribed name and affixed seal this day of one thousand

Executed by the above-named
in the presence of

A purchaser of a registered British vessel does not obtain a complete title until the bill of sale has been recorded at the port of registry of the ship ; and neglect of this precaution may entail serious consequences.

A registrar shall indorse on the bill of sale the fact of the registration with the day and hour thereof.

In addition to the above provisions of the Merchant Shipping Act, 1894, the following Sections regulate mortgages of a ship or shares therein :—

Mortgage of Ship or Share.

"31. (1) A registered ship or a share therein may be made a security for a loan or other valuable consideration, and the instrument creating the security (in this Act called a mortgage) shall be in the form marked B in the first part of the first schedule to this Act, or as near thereto as circumstances permit, and on the production of such instrument the registrar of the ship's port of registry shall record it in the register book

"(2) Mortgages shall be recorded by the registrar in the order in time in which they are produced to him for that purpose, and the registrar shall by memorandum under his hand notify on each mortgage that it has been recorded by him, stating the day and hour of that record.

Entry of Discharge of Mortgage.

"32. Where a registered mortgage is discharged, the registrar shall, on the production of the mortgage deed, with a receipt for the mortgage money indorsed thereon, duly signed and attested, make an entry in the register book to the effect that the mortgage has been discharged, and on that entry being made the estate (if any) which passed to the mortgagee shall vest in the person in whom (having regard to intervening acts and circumstances, if any), it would have vested if the mortgage had not been made.

Priority of Mortgages.

"33. If there are more mortgages than one registered in respect of the same ship or share, the mortgagees shall, notwithstanding any express, implied, or constructive notice, be entitled in priority, one over the other, according to the date at which each mortgage is recorded in the register book, and not according to the date of each mortgage itself.

Mortgagee not Treated as Owner.

"34. Except as far as may be necessary for making a mortgaged ship or share available as a security for the mortgage debt, the mortgagee shall not by reason of the mortgage be deemed the owner of the ship or share, nor shall the mortgagor be deemed to have ceased to be owner thereof.

Mortgagee to have Power of Sale.

"35. Every registered mortgagee shall have power absolutely to dispose of the ship or share in respect of which he is registered, and to give effectual receipts for the purchase money; but where there are more persons than one registered as mortgagees of the same ship or share, a subsequent mortgagee shall not, except under the order of a court of competent jurisdiction, sell the ship or share without the concurrence of every prior mortgagee.

Mortgage not Affected by Bankruptcy.

"36. A registered mortgage of a ship or share shall not be affected by any act of bankruptcy committed by the mortgagor after the date of the record of the mortgage, notwithstanding that the mortgagor at the commencement of his bankruptcy had the ship or share in his possession, order or disposition, or was reputed owner thereof, and the mortgage shall be preferred to any right, claim or interest therein of the other creditors of the bankrupt or any trustee or assignee on their behalf."

Transfer of Mortgages.

The main provisions of Sections 37 and 38 are:—

A registered mortgage of a ship or share may be transferred to any person, and the instrument effecting the transfer shall be in the prescribed form, or as near thereto as circumstances permit. On production of such instrument the registrar shall record it in the register and notify the fact on the instrument of transfer.

Where the interest of a mortgagee is transmitted on marriage, death, or bankruptcy, or by any lawful means, other than by a transfer under this Act, the transmission shall be authenticated by a declaration of the person to whom the interest is transmitted, containing a statement of the manner in which and the person to whom the property has been transmitted, and shall be accompanied by the like evidence as is by this Act required in case of a corresponding transmission of the ownership of a ship or share. On receipt of the declaration and the production of the evidence the registrar shall register the person entitled as mortgagee.

The prescribed form of mortgage (see Section 31, above) to secure an account current is as follows:—

[Insert description of ship and particulars as in Bill of Sale.]

Whereas [here state by way of recital that there is an account current between the mortgagor (describing him) and the mortgagee (describing him); and describe the nature of the transaction so as to show how the amount of principal and interest due at any given time is to be ascertained, and the manner and time of payment.]

Now ["I" or "we"] the undersigned in consideration of the premises for ["myself" or "ourselves"] and ["my" or "our"] heirs, covenant with the said and ["his" or "their"] assigns, to pay to him or them the sums for the time being due on this security, whether by way of principal or interest, at the times and manner aforesaid. And for the purpose of better securing to the said the payment of such sums as last aforesaid ["I" or "we"] do hereby mortgage to the said shares, of which ["I am" or "we are"] the owner in the ship above particularly described, and in her boats, guns, ammunitions, small arms, and appurtenances.

Lastly, ["I" or "we"] for ["myself" or "ourselves"] and ["my" or "our" heirs, covenant with the said and ["his" or "their"] assigns that ["I" or "we"] ha power to mortgage in manner aforesaid the above-mentioned shares, and that the same are free from incumbrances [if any prior incumbrance add, "save as appears by the registry of the said ship"].

In witness whereof ha hereto subscribed name and affixed seal this day of one thousand nine hundred and .

Executed by the above-named }
in the presence of }

The prompt registration of a mortgage deed at the port of registry of the ship is essential to the security of the mortgagee, as a mortgage takes its priority from the date of registration, not from the date of the instrument.

A *transfer of mortgage*, to be indorsed on the original mortgage, is as follows:—

["I" or "we"] the within-mentioned

in consideration of this day paid to [" me " or " us "] by hereby transfer to [" him " or " them "] the benefit of the within-written security. In witness whereof [etc., as above].

When a mortgage is paid off, the following memorandum of its discharge may be indorsed on the mortgage :—

Received the sum of in discharge of the within-written security. Dated at this day of 19 .

Witness
of

The Commissioners of Customs may, with the consent of the Board of Trade, make such alterations in the prescribed forms as they may deem requisite. (Section 65.) The forms can be obtained from the registrar at any port of registry.

No notice of any trust, express, implied, or constructive shall be entered in the register book. (Section 56.)

Any register book may be inspected on payment of a fee not exceeding one shilling. (Section 64.)

Any instruments used with regard to the registry, ownership and mortgage of a British ship are exempt from stamp duty. (Section 721.) (See STAMP DUTIES, General Exemption, No. 2.)

When a banker takes a mortgage upon a ship the policy of insurance should be left in his possession, and it is better that it should be in the bank's name. In some cases, however, it is sufficient if a letter is given by the customer stating that he holds the policy on behalf of the bank.

A banker should make quite certain that the premiums are duly paid. When the premiums are payable quarterly, the brokers of the underwriters will require to hold the policy, and in that case a letter should be taken from the brokers stating that they hold the policy (subject to their claim for the amount of any quarterly premiums remaining unpaid), on behalf of the bank, and undertaking to advise the bank of any premiums which fall due and are not paid. The policy should not be in a mutual society if the banker has to accept liability for calls. (See MUTUAL INSURANCE.) In taking policies, the banker should inquire as to liabilities and, generally, as to the nature of the policies.

It is very essential that a steamer should be entered by the owner in a Protection Club for the risks of protection, indemnity and defence, and be insured up to £8 per ton on her gross registered tonnage against liability for damage that may be done by the boat to other vessels. A banker should satisfy himself that this important matter has been attended to by the owner.

The mortgage should, as stated above, be registered at once. If there is a bill of sale in the customer's possession, it is usual to have it lodged, as it is useful to supply the particulars required for the mortgage, but the banker's security is obtained by registration of the mortgage. There is no value in the bill of sale itself, as, upon a sale or mortgage, it is not required by the registrar.

The register exists only for British ships, and if a vessel should be sold to a foreign flag, the registrar will give notice to any mortgagee whose charge is entered on the register that the transfer is taking place. If a reply of satisfaction is received the entry is expunged from the register ; if the reply is otherwise, the entry remains, but the transfer of the vessel still takes place. The effect is that the registrar gives a mortgagee notice, and the mortgagee must then look out for himself. It is all important that the mortgagors should be men of honour, or the security may, in the above way, suddenly disappear. (See CERTIFICATE OF MORTGAGE OF SHIP.)

A British ship is liable to be attached in a foreign port for a debt incurred in that country, and whenever that happens it is clear that the value of a banker's mortgage in this country may be seriously affected. It is also well for a banker to bear in mind that, in case of loss, the merchant who supplies a ship with stores for its last voyage has a first claim upon the boat, even in front of a banker's duly registered mortgage. The claim of the crew for wages also ranks in front of a mortgage. (See VALUATION OF SHIP, next article.)

SHIP, VALUATION OF. When a ship, or part of a ship, is offered to a banker as a security, the questions immediately arise, What is the approximate present market value, and what change is likely to take place in the value in subsequent years ? Upon the correct answers to those questions depends the amount which may with safety be lent upon the security. Where the value of a security diminishes year by year, any arrangement as to a loan against such a security must necessarily provide for that diminution, and, therefore, when the value of a ship is written down yearly in the books of the bank, the amount of the limit should also be written down.

The valuation of a ship is dependent upon so many points requiring special knowledge that a banker who has not this knowledge may easily go far astray in making a valuation, if he applies the same rule in the case of every ship that floats. In the absence of an opinion by an expert, the following remarks may serve to indicate some of the points which should be observed when considering the value of a ship.

It is very important that the person who attempts to place a value upon a ship should "know" the ship, because there may be circumstances which will affect its value quite apart from the original cost or any recognised system of depreciation.

A ship may be built of iron or of steel. An iron vessel does not wear out so rapidly as one of steel (the corrosion being less), and, therefore, its life is usually a longer one. Most ships, however, are now built of steel, and the following figures refer more particularly to them.

The different classes of steamers are passenger boats, cargo and passenger boats, cargo boats or tramp steamers, as they are commonly called, trawlers, and tugs. In making a valuation, each class requires different treatment, but the boats which are most frequently submitted to the judgment of a branch manager are trawlers and cargo boats.

The cost of building a boat depends principally upon two things :—

1. The state of the shipbuilding trade.
2. The size of the vessel.

With regard to the former, if trade is booming, a boat might cost £8 per ton, dead weight (the dead weight is its carrying capacity), to build, whereas in normal times the cost might only be £5 per ton. With respect to the second point, a smaller boat costs more per ton to build than a larger one, because the cost of the most expensive parts (the machinery, etc.) does not increase in proportion to the size of the boat; that is, in a large boat the average cost per ton is reduced because the cost of providing merely additional bulk is much less than the cost of building the expensive portion.

A ship depreciates in value, and, therefore, a sufficient deduction for depreciation must be made. After each four years a boat must undergo a survey to the satisfaction of Lloyds' Registry Surveyors. The survey which takes place at the end of the first four years is called No. 1 Survey; at the end of the second period of four years, No. 2 Survey takes place; and at the end of the third four years, No. 3 Survey is made. The survey which takes place after another four years is called the Special No. 1 Survey, and then follows Special No. 2 Survey, and afterwards Special No. 3 Survey. It is worthy of note that in the best lines the owners usually try to take the first four or eight years out of a boat, and then to sell it immediately after the No. 1 or No. 2 Survey is passed.

In normal times the cost of building a cargo boat of 8,000 tons, dead weight, is, say, £5 per ton, which would make the total cost £40,000. At the end of the first year 10 per cent. depreciation should be written off; at the end of the second year nothing need be deducted, but at the end of the third and fourth years, 5 per cent. of the reduced value should be deducted. At the end of the fifth year, the deduction may be omitted, because in that year the boat must be put into thorough repair and any appreciable wear and tear made good, in order to pass No. 1 Survey to the satisfaction of the surveyors. At the end of the sixth, seventh, and eighth years the 5 per cent. deductions should be continued, but at the end of the ninth year the deduction may be omitted, because in that year the boat must again be put in order so as to pass No. 2 Survey. The deductions should go on in the same way for the next three years, and again be omitted in the year (the thirteenth) when No. 3 Survey is passed. The 5 per cent. deductions may be continued for the following four years, including the seventeenth year, when the Special No. 1 Survey must be passed. From this point the deductions should be considerably larger, say 7½ per cent. each year, so as to bring down the value, by the time the Special No. 3 Survey is due (that is in the twenty-fifth year), within £12,000, as by that time the vessel is worth not more than 30*s*. per ton, dead weight. The scrap or breaking-up value of an 8,000 tons cargo boat may be taken to be from about £7,000 to £8,000.

No. 1 Survey does not, as a rule, necessitate much outlay, but a banker should always bear in mind the importance of the succeeding surveys, and should consider carefully, as each one approaches, whether the owner of the boat will, or will not, be in a position to carry it through the survey. The most important is No. 3 Survey, and a sum of at least £2,500 may be required to be spent upon the boat before it will satisfy the surveyors.

The example of the 8,000 tons cargo boat, built at a cost of £5 per ton, dead weight, with the deductions for depreciation as above explained, would work out as follows:—

Cargo boat, 8,000 tons, at £5 per ton	=	£40,000
At end of 1st year, deduct 10 per cent.	=	4,000
		36,000
,, ,, 2nd ,, no deduction		
,, ,, 3rd ,, deduct 5 per cent.	=	1,800
		34,200
,, ,, 4th ,, ,, ,,	=	1,710
		32,490
,, ,, 5th ,, no deduction (because the boat must be put into thorough repair to pass No. 1 Survey in this year.)		
,, ,, 6th ,, deduct 5 per cent.	=	1,624
		30,866
,, ,, 7th ,, ,, ,,	=	1,543
		29,323
,, ,, 8th ,, ,, ,,	=	1,466
		27,857
,, ,, 9th ,, no deduction (after No. 2 Survey has been passed)		
,, ,, 10th ,, deduct 5 per cent.	=	1,392
		26,465
,, ,, 11th ,, ,, ,,	=	1,323
		25,142
,, ,, 12th ,, ,, ,,	=	1,257
		23,885
,, ,, 13th ,, no deduction (after No. 3 Survey has been passed)		
,, ,, 14th ,, deduct 5 per cent.	=	1,194
		22,691
,, ,, 15th ,, ,, ,,	=	1,134
		21,557
,, ,, 16th ,, ,, ,,	=	1,077
		20,480
,, ,, 17th ,, ,, ,, (Special No. 1 Survey must be passed)	=	1,024
		19,456
,, ,, 18th ,, ,, 7½ per cent.	=	1,459
		17,997
,, ,, 19th ,, ,, ,,	=	1,349
		16,648
,, ,, 20th ,, ,, ,,	=	1,248
Carry forward		15,400

	Brought forward	£15,400
At end of 21st year, deduct 7½ per cent.	(Special No. 2 Survey due) =	1,155
		14,245
,, ,, 22nd ,, ,, ,,	=	1,068
		13,177
,, ,, 23rd ,, ,, ,,	=	988
		12,189
,, ,, 24th ,, ,, ,,	=	914
		11,275
,, ,, 25th ,, ,, ,,	(Special No. 3 Survey due) =	845
		£10,430

As stated, the above figures relate to a cargo boat built in normal times, but if it is built at a time when trade is booming at a cost of, say, £7 to £8 per ton, the amount to be written off must be greater. For example, if at the end of three years from the building of a boat which cost £8 per ton a similar boat can be built for £5 per ton, the original cost must be taken by a banker as though it had been £5 and not £8 per ton, and then the deductions may be made as set forth above. Although the cost of building varies, it always reverts to about £5 per ton, and it would, therefore, be imprudent for a banker to advance two-thirds of the value of a boat based on an original cost of more than £5 per ton. If he advanced two-thirds of the cost of a boat built at the rate of £8, the value of the boat would suffer a severe fall as soon as the cost of building again declined to the normal £5. A banker would usually be safe in advancing two-thirds of the value of a boat, based on a cost of £5 per ton, dead weight, with deductions for depreciation as shown above.

In the case of a boat of, say, 2,000 tons, the cost of building is, as already explained, more per ton than for one of 8,000 tons. When the cost of a boat of 8,000 tons is £5, the cost to build one of 2,000 tons would probably be, say, £8. The same system of writing down the value would be adopted as in the example given, and the breaking-up value might be considered to be £2,000.

With respect to steam trawlers, the rate of deduction for depreciation should be greater, because the life of a trawler is shorter than that of a cargo boat, and the market for trawlers is not so extensive. Sixteen years at the outside may be regarded as the useful life of a trawler, and a banker should not look upon it as worth more than its breaking-up value after that time. In the case of a trawler which cost, in normal times, say, £6,500 to build, it might be well to deduct £1,500 in the first year, as a trawler even after only six months would not, in ordinary times, sell for anything like its original cost, and to deduct 7½ per cent. of the reduced value in each subsequent year. When the original cost has been reduced by yearly deductions to £2,000, the boat might probably retain that value for two or three years, if kept up in the ordinary way, but a banker would not, as a rule, consider it prudent, when the value is approaching that sum, to regard the boat as worth more than the breaking-up value. The breaking-up value of a boat of this description would be very small, probably about £250. (See Ship—Mortgage, etc.)

SHIP'S HUSBAND. The person to whom the management of a ship is entrusted by or on behalf of the owner. Any person whose name is so registered at the custom house of the port of registry of the ship shall, for the purposes of the Merchant Shipping Act, 1894, be under the same obligations and subject to the same liabilities as if he were the managing owner. (Section 59 of the above named Act.)

A ship's husband, unless authorised by the owners of the ship, has no power to borrow so as to bind the owners. (See Ship-Mortgage, etc.)

SHORT BILLS. "Short Bills" are bills of exchange which are left for collection, but not for discount.

The expression appears to have originated from the custom of entering bills left for collection in an inner column of the customer's account, or pass-book, that is in a column "short" of the one in which the amounts were entered when actually credited to the customer.

The word "short" does not refer to the currency of the bills; a bill, for example, which has twelve months to run before maturity, would, if left for collection, be called a "short bill."

Short bills remain the property of the customer, subject to any lien the banker may have upon them for any liability of the customer to him. (See BILLS FOR COLLECTION.)

SHORT-DATED PAPER. Bills of exchange drawn for a short term, not exceeding three months after date.

SHORT EXCHANGE. In connection with the foreign exchanges the short exchange denotes bills at sight and up to eight or ten days after sight. (See SHORT RATE.)

SHORT LOAN FUND. By this is meant the money in the hands of the Bank of England and the other London banks available for granting loans to bill brokers, stock brokers and others for short periods of a few days. In ordinary times this floating capital does not vary much in total amount, but it is constantly varying in position, the rate of interest charged being lowest when almost the whole sum is in the hands of the competing banks and highest when the Bank of England controls a large part of it. The loans made by the Bank to bill brokers, out of this so-called fund, are for fixed periods of from three to ten days and at about one-half per cent. above Bank Rate. It will easily be understood that the brokers endeavour to get the money they require from the outside banks first, partly on account of the more moderate rate of interest and partly because they will be able to arrange loans which are not fixed but can be paid off in a day or two, if it suits the convenience of the borrower.

SHORT RATE. A term used in connection with the Foreign Exchanges; it means the price in one country at which a short-dated draft (up to eight or ten days' currency), drawn upon another country, can be bought. (See CHEQUE RATE, COURSE OF EXCHANGE, LONG RATE.)

SIGHT BILL. A bill of exchange payable "at sight" is payable on presentation, without days of grace. The due date of a bill payable at a period "after sight" is calculated from the date of sighting. (See SIGHTING A BILL.)

SIGHT RATE. A term used in connection with the Foreign Exchanges; it is equivalent to Cheque Rate (*q.v.*).

SIGHTING A BILL. When a bill is drawn at a fixed period after sight, it is sent to the drawee to be "sighted"; that is, that he may accept the drawer's order for payment by signing his name across the face of the bill with the date of his acceptance. The date when the bill will be due can then be calculated from the date of the acceptance. If he omits to insert a date, the holder may put in what he considers the true date. (See DATE.) If the acceptor writes across the bill "Sighted 1st June, accepted 2nd June," the currency is calculated from June 1, as the holder is entitled to have the bill accepted with the date when first presented for acceptance.

A bill payable at sight is equivalent to one payable on demand. (See BILL OF EXCHANGE.)

SIGNATURE. A banker must know the signatures of all his customers and if he should pay a cheque, drawn upon the account of one of his customers, where the drawer's signature has been forged, he cannot debit it to the account of his customer. It is very necessary, therefore, that each office should possess a complete set of specimens of signatures of all customers, whether current account or deposit, and to have them in such form that they may be readily referred to. If a drawer's signature differs from his usual one and a banker is in doubt as to whether or not it is genuine, unless he can readily see the customer about it, it is customary to return the cheque with the explanation "signature differs."

Section 91 of the Bills of Exchange Act says: "Where, by this Act, any instrument or writing is required to be signed by any person, it is not necessary that he should sign it with his own hand, but it is sufficient if his signature is written thereon by some other person by or under his authority."

A banker, however, would require a proper authority from a customer before paying a cheque on which the drawer's signature was written by someone other than the drawer himself. In cases where a customer desires to give authority to another to draw cheques upon his account, it is much better that the usual method should be adopted and cheques be signed per procuration. (See MANDATE, PER PROCURATION.)

The practice of signing with an ordinary pencil is not a desirable one, and it is advisable to discourage it as much as possible. A signature may be lithographed, as in the case of dividend warrants, or it may be placed on a cheque by means of a rubber stamp by the person whose signature it is, or by anyone duly authorised by him. A rubber stamp signature, however, is full of danger, and its use should be avoided.

It is very imprudent for anyone to put his signature on a blank cheque, or indeed to any document to be subsequently filled up, and a person so signing will be liable, not for what he expected would be filled in above his signature, but for what actually is filled in.

If a signature is obtained to a document, and the person signing it is under the impression that he is signing a document other than it really is, the Courts would probably free him from liability. In *Lewis* v. *Clay* (1898, 67 L.J., Q.B. 224) Lord Russell said: "A promissory note is a contract by the maker to pay the payee. Can it be said that in this case the defendant ever contracted to pay the plaintiff? His mind never went with the transaction; for all that appears, he had never heard of the plaintiff, and his mind was fraudulently directed into a different channel by the statement that he was merely witnessing a deed or other document. He had no contracting mind, and his signature obtained by untrue statements fraudulently made to a document of the existence of which he had no knowledge, cannot bind him." (See SIGNATURE BOOK.)

SIGNATURE BOOK. Each bank office should keep this book up to date. It should contain a specimen signature of each customer, whether current account or deposit, at the office. The customer should sign his full name, and also his usual signature and his initials, and enter his address and occupation. The book should be carefully indexed, so that any specimen may be found without delay. If the book is not actually signed by the customer, the specimen may be obtained on a slip of paper which can be pasted into the book. The signatures may be numbered consecutively, and the numbers placed against the corresponding names in the ledger, which will enable a ledger keeper to turn up a specimen, with very little delay, whenever he requires to verify a signature.

Specimen signatures may be kept on the card index system, a separate card being used for each signature and the cards sorted in strict alphabetical order. On this system any specimen can be rapidly found, and specimens which are no longer required can be removed.

In many cases it may be found that a signature has altered from the specimen obtained, probably years ago, and a fresh specimen should be got whenever any variation occurs, either from an improvement or other change in the customer's writing.

When a customer is signing the book or card it is advisable to point out to him the desirability of always signing his cheques or other bank documents in accordance with the specimen given.

A separate signature book in scrap-book form is kept by some banks, in which the specimen signatures received from other banks of their authorised officials are pasted. (See SIGNATURE.)

SILVER CERTIFICATES. Certificates which are issued by the Treasury of the United States as part of the paper currency. They are payable in silver, but are not legal tender, except in payment of taxes and duties. The smallest denomination is $1.

SILVER COINS. The British silver coins are:—Crown, Double Florin, Half-crown, Florin, Shilling, Sixpence, Groat, Threepence, Twopence, Penny. The Groat, Twopence, and silver Penny are now only coined in very small quantities as Maundy money (*q.v.*).

They are a legal tender only to the amount of forty shillings. Silver coins are tokens; that is, the value of the silver in them is less than the legal value which is attached to the coins. There is no weight fixed below which silver coins cease to be legally current.

Where a bank has an accumulation of silver which it cannot get rid of to its own customers or to another bank, it may be taken to the Bank of England. The Bank, however, usually makes a charge of 5s. per cent. for taking quantities of silver.

The silver checker is a necessity where large quantities of silver are dealt with. After silver has been counted into bags it is desirable to weigh the bags before paying it away or taking it into stock. Where silver requires sorting into the various denominations, as for the payment of wages, the sorting box may be used. This box contains a number of trays, and each tray is made so that all coins may slip through except the particular coins which it is intended to retain. When a quantity of silver is poured in at the top of the box, the openings in the top tray allow all coins to pass through, except crowns; the next tray has the openings rather less and retains four-shilling pieces; the tray lower down in the box has still smaller openings and holds all half-crowns, and the succeeding trays in turn have each smaller openings, so that florins are retained in one, shillings in one, sixpences in one, and finally all threepenny pieces will be found on the last tray at the bottom of the box.

Silver is generally stored in paper bags with the name of the bank and the branch where they are used printed thereon. Each bag is also clearly printed £5, £10, or £20, as the case may be, and the bags may be obtained with perforations so that the contents may be visible without the necessity of opening them. For sums of £50 paper bags are sometimes used, but canvas bags are more suitable. Stocks of sixpences and threepenny pieces are often kept in small envelopes or packets containing 10*s.* or £1 in each. Paper bags containing silver are usually of a different colour from the bags containing copper, to prevent mistakes in paying away. (See COINAGE.)

SINKING FUND. A fund which is created for the purpose of redeeming debentures as they become due for payment, or of extinguishing a debt, or providing for the expiry of a lease. A certain annual sum is set aside out of profits, which, when invested, will produce at compound interest an amount equal to the sum which is required at a particular date.

When a banker wishes to provide, say, £1,000 on account of the premises of a branch, the lease of which expires in twenty years, he debits his profit and loss account with £25 each half-year and credits the amount to his premises account, so that at the end of the period the balance at the debit of premises account will have been extinguished.

SINKING FUND ASSURANCE. Where property is held upon a lease, the lessee sometimes takes out a Sinking Fund Policy by means of which a specified capital sum becomes payable at the time the lease expires. Such a policy has, in some companies, as soon as two years' premiums have been paid, a surrender value equal to the whole of the premiums paid after the first year, accumulated at 3 per cent. compound interest, less 7½ per cent.

SIXPENCE. Its standard weight is 43·63636 grains troy, and its standard fineness thirty-seven-fortieths fine silver, three-fortieths alloy. (See COINAGE.)

Sixpences were first coined in 1551.

SLEEPING PARTNER. Sometimes called a dormant partner.

A partner in a firm who does not take any active part in the management of the business, but who is entitled to a share in the profits and is liable for a share of any losses that may be incurred.

In a limited partnership, a limited partner is a sleeping partner. (See LIMITED PARTNERSHIP.)

SMASHER. A slang term for a person who puts bad money into circulation.

SOCIETIES. Where an advance is granted to the committee of an association, a club, a society, or any similar body (e.g. literary association, cricket club, flower show), a guarantee should be taken or an arrangement made whereby someone is rendered liable to repay the money, otherwise the banker will be without any means of recovering the debt, as such bodies, not being incorporated, cannot be sued for the money. If an account is opened as "Carleton Flower Show, John Smith, Treasurer," John Smith is not personally liable for any overdraft thereon, but if the account is opened as "John Smith $^{a}/_{c}$ Carleton Flower Show," he is personally responsible.

Such accounts are opened in various forms, but the distinction should be observed between accounts which are opened by a person in his private name, ear-marked in some way, and accounts which are in the name of an association on which the treasurer is to operate. In this latter case the banker should be supplied with a copy of the resolution appointing the treasurer and setting forth the manner in which cheques are to be signed.

With respect to the accounts of societies registered under Building or Provident or Friendly Societies Acts, they must be opened and conducted in accordance with the rules of the societies. (See BUILDING SOCIETY.)

SOFT MONEY. The expression is sometimes applied to bank notes, in contradistinction to coins or "hard cash."

SOL. (See FOREIGN MONEYS—PERU.)

SOLA BILL. (Lat. *solus*, alone, solitary.) A bill which consists simply of one document, as distinguished from foreign bills drawn in a set—that is, issued in duplicate or triplicate. The words "sola bill" are sometimes used in the body of the bill, e.g. in a bill drawn by a branch of the Bank of England on London, the words may be "seven days after date pay this Sola bill of exchange," etc. (See BILL IN A SET.)

SOLD NOTE. The contract note which is given by a stockbroker to his client, giving particulars of a sale which has been effected for him. (See CONTRACT NOTE.)

SOLICITOR'S UNDERTAKING. When a customer desires any of his securities which are held by a banker to be lent to his solicitor for inspection, written instructions should be taken from the customer. When the securities are handed to the solicitor, the solicitor should sign an undertaking to return them in the same condition as he receives them and not to charge them or affect the banker's security in any way. Bankers have their own forms for use in these cases.

If the securities are to be given up to a solicitor, or anyone, against payment of a certain sum, the letter of authority should specifically state the amount. The undertaking will then be to pay the amount or return the securities. When there is an agreement or undertaking to pay a sum of money the document is, probably, chargeable with a stamp duty of sixpence.

SOUTHS. A Stock Exchange name for London and South Western Railway ordinary stock.

SOVEREIGN. The standard of the British coinage. Its standard weight is 123·27447 grains troy and its standard fineness eleven-twelfths fine gold (113·0016 grains), one-twelfth alloy, chiefly copper (10·2728 grains). When a sovereign has been in circulation for some time it becomes reduced in weight. When the weight falls below 122·5 grains troy it is no longer a legal tender. Gold bullion weighing 40 lb. troy is coined into 1,869 sovereigns. Professor W. S. Jevons says that from experiments he estimated the average wear of a sovereign for each year of circulation at 0·043 grain. "It would follow that a sovereign cannot in general circulate more than about eighteen years without becoming illegitimately light. This length of time, then, would constitute what may be called the legal life of a sovereign." Other persons have estimated its legal life to be fifteen or twenty years.

By 56 Geo. III (1816) it was provided that sovereigns coined weighing $\frac{20}{21}$ parts of a guinea were to pass for 20*s*. They were issued in 1817. Coins of the same name but of different value were coined about 1489. (See COINAGE, POUND, PRE-VICTORIAN GOLD COINS.)

SPECIAL CROSSING. Where the name of a banker is written, or stamped, across the face of a cheque, either with or without the words "not negotiable," that addition constitutes a crossing and the cheque is crossed specially and to that banker.

The parallel lines which are necessary to constitute a general crossing are not necessary in a special crossing. The name of the banker may be between parallel lines, or it may stand alone without any lines, or it may be inside a square, or any other sort of margin. (See CROSSED CHEQUE.)

SPECIAL INDORSEMENT. A special indorsement specifies the person to whom or to whose order, a bill or cheque is to be payable, as "Pay John Brown or order, J. Jones." The converse term is an "indorsement in blank," where the indorser merely signs his name. (See INDORSEMENT.)

SPECIAL SETTLEMENT. SPECIAL SETTLING DAY. The day fixed by the London Stock Exchange committee for the settlement of sales and purchases of shares in a new company.

When an application is made to the committee for a special settlement, various documents and particulars must be sent to the secretary of the share and loan department. For example, for shares of new companies there must be sent :—

The certificate of incorporation. A specimen of the share certificate. A copy of the prospectus, the statement in lieu of prospectus as filed with the registrar of joint stock companies, circular or advertisement relating to the issue. A specimen call letter. Certified printed copies of contracts relating to the issue of shares credited as fully or partly paid. A letter from the secretary of the company, stating: (1) That the share certificates are ready to be issued. (2) The distinctive numbers of the shares allotted, (*a*) to the public, (*b*) to the vendors. (3) The particulars of the company's capital. (4) The nominal amount of each share, and the amount paid in cash or credited as paid on each share. (5) In cases where the whole of the capital has not been issued at the time the application is made, whether the unissued shares are vendors' shares or are held in reserve for future issue.

By Rule 138, "The secretary of the share and loan department shall give three days' public notice of any application for a special settling-day in the shares or other securities of a new company previously to such application being submitted to the committee, who will appoint a special settling-day, provided that sufficient certificates or scrip are ready for delivery. The committee will not fix a special settling-day for bargains in shares or securities issued to the vendors, credited as fully or partly paid, until six months after the date fixed for the special settlement in the shares or securities subscribed for by the public, but this does not necessarily apply to re-organisations or amalgamations of existing companies, or to cases where no public shares are issued, or to cases where the vendors take the whole of the shares issued for cash." (See SETTLING DAYS, STOCK EXCHANGE.)

SPECIALTY DEBT. A debt which is acknowledged in a document under seal. (See STATUTE OF LIMITATIONS—DEBT.)

SPECIE. (From Latin, *specio*, to look, to see.) Visible money. Gold and silver coins, as distinguished from paper money.

SPECIE POINTS. They are also called "Bullion Points" and "Gold Points." The term is used in connection with the Foreign Exchanges and denotes the limits of the rate of exchange when it becomes cheaper to transmit bullion from one country to another than to buy bills. When the limits are reached, gold flows in, or out, of this country as the case may be. If a merchant desires to remit to Paris he will purchase a bill upon Paris, unless he finds that the price asked for the bill is greater than the cost of sending coin to Paris.

If between two countries A and B the Mint Par of exchange is reckoned in the number of B coins equivalent to one A coin, then the incoming or import specie point from B to A is the Mint Par *plus* charges for packing, shipment, and insurance; whilst the outgoing or export specie point from A to B is the Mint Par *minus* similar charges.

For example, the Mint Par between London and Paris is 25·22; the export specie point may be, say, 25·12, when it pays to send gold to France; and the import specie point say, 25·32, when it pays to send gold from France to England.

Specie points are liable to variation, approaching closer to the Mint Par, if the price of carriage becomes less, but at any time, unless operations are disturbed by war or other exceptional circumstance, the Cheque Rate cannot go beyond the specie points, for if it did a merchant having a remittance to make from the country against which the exchange stood, would choose to do it in gold rather than pay such a large price for the paper. (See FOREIGN EXCHANGES, MINT PAR OF EXCHANGE.)

SPECIE, TRANSMISSION OF. The risk of loss of specie in transit by train may be insured against from the time of leaving the bank office until it arrives at its destination.

Whether it is cheaper to insure or to send a clerk with the specie, depends upon the quantity sent and the price of the railway ticket. The clerk's time also requires to be taken into account.

Where specie is sent by train as a parcel the railway companies will insure it at the rate of one shilling for each £100, the company reserving to itself the right of inspecting, before effecting any insurance, all goods delivered to it for insurance, to ascertain that the consignment is in accordance with the declaration. A railway company usually sends an official along with cash when it exceeds £500. In addition to the insurance rate, the usual rate for carriage is payable. Insured parcels, boxes, etc., must be properly sealed by the senders.

Bullion and specie, the value of which is declared to the railway company, but on which no insurance is paid, is not conveyed by the company unless a consignment note is first signed by the consignor declining to pay the increased charge for insurance, or unless, in the case of regular senders, that a general contract, called a general risk note (stamped 6*d*.), is given notifying that they refuse to pay the increased charge for insurance which the railway company are entitled to demand under the Carriers' Act.

The insurance of specie is also effected by underwriters and insurance companies, at a lower rate, say, sixpence per cent.

SPECIFICATION. When an amount is paid in to a customer's credit, it is customary to specify on the paying-in slip how much of it consists of notes and how much of gold, silver, copper, cheques, bills and post office money orders. (See PAYING-IN SLIPS.)

A cashier keeps a specification of his cash on hand each night.

SPECULATION. A speculation is where a person buys a security, not with the intention of paying for it at the settling day, but of selling it again during the present, or a continued, account, in order to secure a profit, if possible. If a security is bought in order to be retained, it is called an investment. When a speculative security is bought and paid for with the intention to sell as soon as a favourable opportunity offers, it is probably more accurately described as an investment in a speculative security than a pure speculation where the purchaser has no intention, and perhaps no means, to pay for it.

SPOILED STAMPS. In making a claim for allowance of spoiled or useless stamps the following statutory declaration must be filled up and signed by the applicant :—

I of do solemnly and sincerely declare that the several stamps hereinafter specified and described, that is to say,

Number of Stamps.	Value of each.	Description of Instrument.	Total Value.
			£

are the property of and were purchased by or for use, and that paid the full amount or value thereof ;

And with regard to the stamps impressed on material not written upon, and the adhesive revenue and fee stamps unattached to material, I declare that the same have been inadvertently and undesignedly spoiled or rendered unfit for use in consequence of .

And with regard to such other of the material on which the said stamps are impressed or to which adhesive stamps are attached as is written upon, I say that the same has been inadvertently and undesignedly spoiled, or is become useless ; and that the writing thereon has not been signed by any party or otherwise completed as a legal instrument, and has not had any operation or effect whatsoever.

And with regard to the adhesive fee stamps which have been removed from material, I declare that they have been so removed by the Court or other official whose certificate is annexed.

And with regard to the postage stamps on material, I declare that the same have not passed through the post, or been used in any way whatever, but have been inadvertently and undesignedly spoiled, rendered unfit for use, or are not required, in consequence of .

And with regard to the adhesive postage stamps, I declare that the same have not passed through the post, or been used in any way whatever, but have been inadvertently and undesignedly spoiled, or rendered unfit for use in consequence of .

And with regard to the instruments which have been signed, I say that the same became void in consequence of .

And with regard to the instruments which have been signed, the duplicates or instruments in lieu of which are now produced and exhibited duly stamped, I say that the same were spoiled in consequence of

and that the same were *bonâ fide* prepared and signed for the purpose of carrying into effect the transaction appearing upon the face thereof, between the parties and upon the terms and conditions therein set forth, that no legal proceeding has been commenced in which the instruments could or would have been given or offered in evidence and that the same were so signed within two years from the date hereof.

And with regard to any bill of exchange or promissory note which *from any omission or error* has been spoiled or rendered useless, although the same, being a bill of exchange may have been accepted or indorsed, or being a promissory note may have been delivered to the payee, I declare that another completed and duly stamped bill of exchange or promissory note (which I now produce) identical in every particular except in the correction of the error or omission in the spoilt bill or note has been executed in lieu thereof.

And with regard to the bills of exchange and promissory notes, other than those mentioned above, I declare that the answers to the following questions are true :—

Have the bills or notes been out of the signer's hands ?

If so, for what purpose?

Have the bills or notes been sold, or have advances or credit been obtained on them? —

What has become of the unstamped parts of any of the bills above mentioned which have been drawn in sets? ————————

What use has been made of any such unstamped parts? —

And I further say that
have not been reimbursed or paid the value of the said stamps or any part thereof, by any other person or persons; and that if the value thereof shall be allowed by the Commissioners of Inland Revenue, I will not ask or receive any compensation for the same, or any part thereof, from any other person or persons, or charge the same, or any part thereof, in account or otherwise, to any other person or persons either generally or particularly, so as to be again paid or compensated for the same, or any part thereof, directly or indirectly in any manner whatsoever.

And I further say *that all the said stamps have been spoiled or become useless within the period of two years preceding the date hereof*: and that the application made by me for an allowance for the value of the said stamps is without any fraudulent intention or collusion whatsoever.

And I make this solemn declaration conscientiously believing the same to be true, and by virtue of the Statutory Declarations Act, 1835.

DECLARED at the
Stamp Office
at
this day of 19 * —
Before me,

Distributor of stamps.

* The applicant must sign on this line.

N.B.—In cases where the declaration is made by an agent of the principal or firm, the person authorised should be in a position to give full information as to the facts of the transaction. Any neglect of this regulation will probably lead to delay in the settlement of the claim.

The claim for allowance must be lodged at the Spoiled Stamp Office, Somerset House, and in the case of country bankers (more than ten miles from London) the claim must be made through an agent in London.

When an allowance is granted, stamps of equal amount may be obtained, or cash, less a discount, may be accepted.

SPOT PRICE. The "spot" price of silver is another name for "cash" price for delivery at once. The "forward" price is the quotation for delivery and payment at some future time.

SQUATTER'S TITLE. The title which a person may obtain to land after being in undisturbed possession of it for twelve years. (See POSSESSORY TITLE.)

STAFF REGISTER. The book kept at the head office of a bank which contains a complete list of the staff, with all particulars regarding each member, such as the date of appointment, the age, salary, and position.

STAG. The name given to a person who applies for shares in a new company, not in order to subscribe for them but with the sole intention of selling them as soon as possible at a profit.

STALE CHEQUE. A cheque is considered by bankers to be stale dated six (by some bankers twelve) months after the date of the cheque, and such a cheque is usually returned marked "out of date." When the stale date is confirmed by the drawer the cheque is paid. The practice of not paying cheques which are "out of date" is not sanctioned by law and is simply a custom (though a desirable one) of bankers. By law the drawer of a cheque is not, under ordinary circumstances, released from liability on the cheque until six years from the date of it, and a banker would, apparently, be justified in paying a cheque at any time during that period, but, in practice, as stated, a cheque which is "out of date" is paid only when confirmed by the drawer.

By Section 45, Bills of Exchange Act, 1882, an indorser is discharged if a cheque is not presented within a reasonable time after its indorsement. There is no time fixed by law as to what is a reasonable time. Six days from the date of a cheque have been held to be not an unreasonable length of time. Sir John R. Paget says: "In the absence of special circumstances, ten days or so would probably be held the limit." (See CHEQUE.)

STAMP DUTIES. By the Stamp Act, 1891:—

Regulations Applicable to Instruments Generally.

Charge of Duty upon Instruments.

Charge of Duties in Schedule.

"1. From and after the commencement of this Act the stamp duties to be charged for the use of Her Majesty upon the several instruments specified in the first Schedule to this Act shall be the several duties in the said schedule specified, which duties shall be in substitution for the duties theretofore chargeable under the enactments repealed by this Act, and shall be subject to the exemptions contained in this Act and in any other Act for the time being in force.

All Duties to be Paid according to Regulations of Act.

"2. All stamp duties for the time being chargeable by law upon any instruments are to be paid and denoted according to the regulations in this Act contained, and except where express provision is made to the contrary are to be denoted by impressed stamps only.

How Instruments are to be Written and Stamped.

"3. (1) Every instrument written upon stamped material is to be written in such manner, and every instrument partly or wholly written before being stamped is to be so stamped, that the stamp may appear on the face of the instrument, and cannot be used for or applied to any other instrument written upon the same piece of material.

"(2) If more than one instrument be written upon the same piece of material, everyone of the instruments is to be separately and distinctly stamped with the duty with which it is chargeable.

Instruments to be Separately Charged with Duty in Certain Cases.

"4 Except where express provision to the contrary is made by this or any other Act :—

"(a) An instrument containing or relating to several distinct matters is to be separately and distinctly charged, as if it were a separate instrument, with duty in respect of each of the matters ;

"(b) An instrument made for any consideration in respect whereof it is chargeable with *ad valorem* duty, and also for any further or other valuable consideration or considerations, is to be separately and distinctly charged, as if it were a separate instrument, with duty in respect of each of the considerations.

Facts and Circumstances affecting Duty to be set forth in Instruments.

"5. All the facts and circumstances affecting the liability of any instrument to duty, or the amount of the duty with which any instrument is chargeable, are to be fully and truly set forth in the instrument ; and every person who, with intent to defraud Her Majesty,

"(a) executes any instrument in which all the said facts and circumstances are not fully and truly set forth ; or

"(b) being employed or concerned in or about the preparation of any instrument, neglects or omits fully and truly to set forth therein all the said facts and circumstances ;

shall incur a fine of ten pounds.

Production of Instruments in Evidence.

Terms upon which Instruments not Duly Stamped may be Received in Evidence.

"14. (1) Upon the production of an instrument chargeable with any duty as evidence in any court of civil judicature in any part of the United Kingdom, or before any arbitrator or referee, notice shall be taken by the judge, arbitrator, or referee of any omission or insufficiency of the stamp thereon, and if the instrument is one which may legally be stamped after the execution thereof, it may, on payment to the officer of the Court whose duty it is to read the instrument, or to the arbitrator or referee, of the amount of the unpaid duty, and the penalty payable on stamping the same, and of a further sum of one pound, be received in evidence, saving all just exceptions on other grounds.

"(4) Save as aforesaid, an instrument executed in any part of the United Kingdom, or relating, wheresoever executed, to any property situate, or to any matter or thing done or to be done, in any part of the United Kingdom, shall not, except in criminal proceedings, be given in evidence, or be available for any purpose whatever, unless it is duly stamped in accordance with the law in force at the time when it was first executed.

STAMPING OF INSTRUMENTS AFTER EXECUTION.

Penalty upon Stamping Instruments after Execution.

"15. (1) Save where other express provision is in this Act made, any unstamped or insufficiently stamped instrument may be stamped after the execution thereof, on payment of the unpaid duty and a penalty of ten pounds, and also by way of further penalty, where the unpaid duty exceeds ten pounds, of interest on such duty, at the rate of five pounds per centum per annum, from the day upon which the instrument was first executed up to the time when the amount of interest is equal to the unpaid duty.

"(2) In the case of such instruments hereinafter mentioned as are chargeable with *ad valorem* duty, the following provisions shall have effect:—

"(*a*) The instrument, unless it is written upon duly stamped material, shall be duly stamped with the proper *ad valorem* duty before the expiration of thirty days after it is first executed, or after it has been first received in the United Kingdom in case it is first executed at any place out of the United Kingdom, unless the opinion of the Commissioners with respect to the amount of duty with which the instrument is chargeable, has, before such expiration, been required under the provisions of this Act:

"(*b*) If the opinion of the Commissioners with respect to any such instrument has been required, the instrument shall be stamped in accordance with the assessment of the Commissioners within fourteen days after notice of the assessment:

"(*c*) If any such instrument executed after the sixteenth day of May one thousand eight hundred and eighty-eight has not been or is not duly stamped in conformity with the foregoing provisions of this sub-section, the person in that behalf hereinafter specified shall incur a fine of ten pounds, and in addition to the penalty payable on stamping the instrument there shall be paid a further penalty equivalent to the stamp duty thereon, unless a reasonable excuse for the delay in stamping, or the omission to stamp, or the insufficiency of stamp, be afforded to the satisfaction of the Commissioners, or of the Court, judge, arbitrator, or referee before whom it is produced:

"(*d*) The instruments and persons to which the provisions of this sub-section are to apply are as follows:—

Title of Instrument as described in the First Schedule to this Act.	Person liable to Penalty.
Bond, covenant, or instrument of any kind whatsoever.	The obligee, covenantee, or other person taking the security.
Conveyance on sale	The vendee or transferee.
Lease or tack	The lessee. . . . .
Mortgage, bond, debenture, covenant, and warrant of attorney to confess and enter up judgment.	The mortgagee or obligee; in the case of a transfer or reconveyance, the transferee, assignee, or disponee, or the person redeeming the security.
Settlement.	The settlor.
Added by Section 74 (3) of the Finance (1909–10) Act, 1910:—	
Conveyances or transfers operating as voluntary dispositions *inter vivos*.	Grantor or transferor.

"(3) Provided that save where other express provision is made by this Act in relation to any particular instrument :

"(*a*) Any unstamped or insufficiently stamped instrument which has been first executed at any place out of the United Kingdom, may be stamped, at any time within thirty days after it has been first received in the United Kingdom, on payment of the unpaid duty only : and

"(*b*) The Commissioners may, if they think fit, at any time within three months after the first execution of any instrument, mitigate or remit any penalty payable on stamping.

"(4) The payment of any penalty payable on stamping is to be denoted on the instrument by a particular stamp."

"By the Finance Act, 1895 :—

"15. So much of Section 15 of the Stamp Act, 1891, as limits the time within which the Commissioners of Inland Revenue may mitigate or remit any penalty payable on stamping shall be repealed.")

ENTRIES UPON ROLLS, BOOKS, ETC.

Penalty for Enrolling, etc., Instrument not duly Stamped.

"17. If any person whose office it is to enrol, register, or enter in or upon any rolls, books, or records any instrument chargeable with duty, enrols, registers, or enters any such instrument not being duly stamped, he shall incur a fine of ten pounds.

Conditions and Agreements as to Stamp Duty Void.

"117. Every condition of sale framed with the view of precluding objection or requisition upon the ground of absence or insufficiency of stamp upon any instrument executed after the sixteenth day of May one thousand eight hundred and eighty-eight, and every contract, arrangement, or undertaking for assuming the liability on account of absence or insufficiency of stamp upon any such instrument or indemnifying against such liability, absence, or insufficiency, shall be void."

GENERAL EXEMPTIONS FROM ALL STAMP DUTIES.

(1) Transfers of shares in the Government or Parliamentary stocks or funds.

(2) Instruments for the sale, transfer, or other disposition either absolutely or by way of mortgage, or otherwise, of any ship or vessel, or any part, interest, share, or property of or in any ship or vessel.

(3) Instruments of apprenticeship, bonds, contracts, and agreements entered into in the United Kingdom for or relating to the service in any of Her Majesty's colonies or possessions abroad of any person as an artificer, clerk, domestic servant, handicraftsman, mechanic, gardener, servant in husbandry, or labourer.

(4) Testaments, testamentary instruments, and dispositions *mortis causâ* in Scotland.

(5) Bonds given to sheriffs or other persons in Ireland upon the replevy of any goods or chattels, and assignments of such bonds.

(6) Instruments made by, to, or with the Commissioners of Works for any of the purposes of the Act 15 & 16 Vict. c. 28.

(7) Deeds or instruments made or executed for the purpose of the Post Office, by, to or with Her Majesty, or any officer of the Post Office (44 & 45 Vict. c. 20, Section 5).

The following regulations were issued by the Board of Inland Revenue, Somerset House, December, 1902 :—

REGULATIONS under which PLAIN PAPER, BANKERS' CHEQUES, and other PRINTED FORMS are impressed with the 1*d*. Inland Revenue Stamp.

1. The paper must be of such quality, thickness and colour, as to be suitable for receiving the impression of the dies.

2. The paper must be flat and uncreased, and should neither be gummed nor perforated before it is sent to be stamped.

3. Each sheet of paper or single form for which a separate stamp is required must not be narrower than five inches nor less than one and a half inches in depth. A form five inches in length can only be stamped close to the edge.

4. *When more forms (cheques or receipts) than one are printed on a sheet, the stamping will be expedited if the sheets be presented entire, i.e. before they are cut up.* In cases where the forms are in two rows on a sheet the forms should be printed back to back. If bound or stitched the books must not be unwieldy in size nor heavier in weight than ten pounds. Stamps cannot be placed near the counterfoils of forms.

5. The top sheet of the parcel or book should be marked to indicate the position where it is desired that the stamp should be placed, which, however, must be within one inch and a half of the edge of the sheet. The stamp will be placed as near to the position indicated as the circumstances of the case will permit.

6. When a special position of the stamp is required in the case of printed forms it is desirable that before the work is printed a proof should be submitted to the Inspector of Stamping.

7. All fly-leaves and inserted orders for new books must be completely folded back.

8. The Commissioners of Inland Revenue will not accept any responsibility for injury to material in the process of stamping, nor for loss of stamps or material, which may arise in transmission to or from this office.

9. When the paper is brought to Somerset House for stamping, a person must attend at the department of the Accountant and Comptroller General (Room No. 26) to fill up the necessary "warrant," and to pay the duty.

10. Penny inland revenue stamps are also impressed under similar conditions at the Inland Revenue offices at Edinburgh, Dublin and Manchester.

The following documents must be stamped before execution :—

Bills of Exchange.
Contract Notes.
Letters of Allotment.
Letters of Renunciation.
Proxies.
Receipts.
Scrip Certificates.
Share Warrants.
Voting Papers.

Documents, other than the above, requiring an *ad valorem* stamp, e.g. conveyances, mortgages, memoranda of deposit, transfers, must be stamped within thirty days after execution, or if executed abroad within thirty days from the date on which they arrive in the United Kingdom.

Agreements under hand, duty sixpence, e.g. guarantee, qualifying agreement, may be stamped within fourteen days after execution.

Documents which have not been stamped within the time allowed, may be subsequently stamped on payment of a penalty of £10. (See Section 15, above.)

The various duties are given under the different headings.

Where a document of charge requires further stamp duty to be impressed, a certificate in the following form must be furnished to the Stamp Office :—

I hereby certify that the amount at any time owing by to (*a*) (did not exceed £ until the day of 19), (*b*) (or has not at any time exceeded the sum of £) and I request that further stamp duty may be impressed on the instrument of day of 19 to cover a total advance of £

(*a*) If the amount has not yet been exceeded cancel these words.
(*b*) If the advance has already been exceeded cancel these words.

* Signature.
Address.
19 . Date.

* To be signed by the mortgagee or by the manager of the bank making the advance.

(See ADHESIVE STAMPS, ADJUDICATION STAMPS, AD VALOREM, APPROPRIATED STAMPS, BILL OF EXCHANGE, CANCELLATION OF STAMPS, COMPOSITION, CONVEYANCE, DENOTING STAMPS, IMPRESSED STAMPS, INCREMENT VALUE DUTY, RECEIPT, SPOILED STAMPS.)

STANDING CREDITS. A customer may, as a rule, arrange to have his cheques cashed at another bank or at some other branch. The request should be in writing and be signed by the customer. The letter advising the bank or branch to honour his cheques should be signed by the manager and state precisely what cheques are to be paid, to what extent and for how long the credit is to continue, and a specimen signature should accompany the advice.

A common form of advice is to honour cheques drawn by John Brown to the extent of £10 in any one day. An advice to honour cheques to the extent of £60 in any one week is not a good form, if the customer giving the order intends the money to be drawn at the rate of so much a day, as it is clear that the full amount may be drawn on one day and still comply with the letter of advice.

When a bank receives from another bank or branch a request to pay certain cheques, the greatest care should be taken to ascertain that the letter of advice is genuine. If there is any doubt, a confirmation could be asked for by wire.

Credits opened between different banks are, as a rule, arranged through the head offices of the respective banks.

Particulars of all credits opened should be recorded at the heading of the customer's account. The amount of such credits should of course be justified by the nature of the account.

The customer is sometimes given a special form of cheque book, the cheques being drawn upon the banker who is to pay the cheques and an indication is given upon the cheques of the name of the bank where the drawer's account is kept.

The mere fact that a banker pays a cheque under a standing order does not release him from liability if he pays one bearing a forged indorsement. It is reasonable, however, to expect that a customer wishing his cheques so paid should state in writing that the banker shall not incur any greater liability than if the cheques were paid by the branch on which they are drawn. The banker who pays a cheque under authority usually cancels it before remitting to the drawee banker.

A register should be kept of all standing orders given by a branch and also of all received by a branch. If a credit, without any time limit, has not been operated upon for a considerable time, it is desirable to inquire if it is still to continue, or if it should be cancelled.

When a customer gives an order to stop payment of a cheque, notice should be given to each branch or bank which has authority to cash his cheques.

STANNARIES. (Latin, *stannum*, tin.)

A term which is applied to the tin mines in Cornwall or Devon and to the peculiar customs and laws in connection with the mines. A company of more than twenty persons formed for the purpose of gain must be registered under the Companies (Consolidation) Act, 1908, unless formed under some other Act of Parliament, or of letters patent, " or is a company engaged in working mines within the stannaries, and subject to the jurisdiction of the Court exercising the stannaries jurisdiction." (See PARTNERSHIPS.)

The above-mentioned Act makes certain special provisions in connection with the winding up of companies in the stannaries.

Attachment of Debt due to Contributory on Winding up in Stannaries Court.

" Section 239. When several companies are in course of liquidation by or under the superintendence of the Court exercising the stannaries jurisdiction and acting under that jurisdiction, if it appears to the judge that a person who is a contributory of one of the companies is also a creditor claiming a debt against one of the other companies, the judge may (if after inquiry he thinks fit) direct that the debt, when allowed, shall be attached, and payment thereof to the creditor suspended for a time certain as a security for payment of any calls that are or may in course of liquidation become due from him to the company of which he is a contributory ; and the amount thereof shall be applied to such payment in due course :

" Provided that such an order of attachment shall not prejudice any claim which the company so indebted to the creditor may have against him by way of set off, counterclaim, or otherwise, or any lawful claim of lien or specific charge on the debt in favour of any third person."

The Act also provides for various modifications with respect to preferential payments of salaries and wages. (See COMPANIES, WINDING UP.)

STATE. The name given to a weekly return sent to head office exhibiting all the transactions at a branch for the week.

STATUS OPINION. (See BANKER'S OPINION.)

STATUTE BARRED. A debt is said to be statute barred when it cannot be recovered in a court of law, because the time within which the creditor had the right to sue the debtor has expired. (See STATUTE OF LIMITATIONS.)

STATUTE LAW. The written law of the land, as distinguished from the unwritten or " common law " (*q.v.*).

" The written laws of the Kingdom are statutes, acts or edicts, made by the sovereign, by and with the advice and consent of the lords spiritual and temporal, and commons, in Parliament assembled " (Blackstone).

STATUTE OF LIMITATIONS. In the case of a simple contract debt an action must be commenced within six years from the time when the cause of action arose. In the case of a contract under seal the period is twenty years. But since the passing of the Real Property Limitation Act, 1874 (37 and 38 Vict. c. 57), which came into force on the 1st January, 1879, the remedy of a mortgagee upon the covenant contained in the mortgage, as well as the remedy against the land, is barred after twelve years.

The principal Acts which fix these limits were passed in 1623, 1833, and 1874.

When part payment of a debt is made,

or interest is paid thereon, or an acknowledgment of the debt is given in writing by the debtor, the debt is thereby kept alive and the six years or twenty years then begin to run from the date of the last payment or acknowledgment. For example, if Brown signed in 1909 a promissory note payable on demand in favour of Jones, and neither pays interest nor repays any part of the principal nor gives any further written acknowledgment of the debt for a period of six years, at the end of that time Brown may plead the Statute of Limitations and be entirely released from his liability on the note to Jones. But if Brown in, say, the year 1912 repays part of the money owing, the six years will begin again to run from the year 1912, and so on, the six years commencing afresh at each payment or acknowledgment. But a payment by a debtor does not keep the debt alive as against a surety.

In the case of an infant or an insane person, no action can be brought personally either by or against either of them until the infant attains his majority or the insane person recovers. If the defendant is beyond the seas or out of the jurisdiction, when the cause of action arises, the period of six or twenty years begins to run from the date of his return; but where the defendant goes out of the jurisdiction after the cause of action arises the running of the statute is not affected.

Where there are several debtors (except in the case of a mortgage of land), the debt must be acknowledged by each one in order to keep it alive against each, and anyone who has not acknowledged it may plead the statute.

A debt of a deceased person which is statute barred may legally be paid by his executor, as in an ordinary contract the statute does not bar the right but only the remedy.

Where a loan is granted against security and the debt has become statute barred, the banker is unable to sue the customer for the debt, but the fact of the banker's claim against the debtor personally having been discharged does not affect his claim upon the security, nor does it affect his claim upon any securities or money belonging to the debtor which may come into his possession as a banker after his right to sue the debtor is statute barred.

A defendant must, if he intends to plead the statute, set up a special plea before the hearing of the action or he will not be allowed to advance it against the plaintiff's claim.

Acceptor of Bill.—An acceptor is liable to pay it at any time within six years, unless he has suffered damage through delay in presentation for payment.

Account.—Where a credit balance has been undisturbed for six years, the customer's right to the money may be barred by the statute. Heber Hart (see his "Law of Banking") considers that "it may well be argued that until a cheque is presented and dishonoured, the statute does not begin to run." No banker, however, would ever think of taking advantage of a credit balance being statute barred. The addition of interest half-yearly by a banker prevents the statute from having effect in the case of a dormant credit, or deposit account. (See Unclaimed Balances.)

Where a debit balance has remained standing without any payment, either of principal or interest, or without any written acknowledgment, the debtor may plead the statute at the end of six years and the banker will be unable to recover the money. A mere debit to the account by the banker for interest does not keep the debt alive.

If the account is in several names the debt is kept alive only against those who have acknowledged it; a payment by one does not prevent the others from pleading the statute.

If a customer has several accounts they must all be considered as really one account; that is, if a loan account has been absolutely dormant for six years the customer cannot plead that the loan is statute barred if he has also other accounts which have been operated upon.

In an ordinary loan account the statute runs from the date when the money was paid and not necessarily from the date of the cheque.

If a loan is statute barred it does not follow that the interest on the loan is also barred. (See Interest below.)

Bank Notes.—The Statute of Limitations does not apply to bank notes, either those of the Bank of England or of a country banker. No matter how long it may be after their issue before they are presented for payment, the banker is still liable to pay them. In the Acts regulating the issue of notes in Ireland and in Scotland it is specially mentioned that "all bank notes shall be deemed to be in circulation from the time the same shall have been issued by any banker, or any servant or agent of such banker, until the same shall have been actually returned to such banker or some servant or agent of such banker."

Bill of Exchange.—An action on a bill of exchange must be commenced within six years from the time when the cause of action arose; that is, from the date when the bill was due to be paid.

Bond.—A bond continues for twenty years from the date on which the right to bring an action first accrues.

Composition with Creditors. — If a debtor fails to pay a composition as provided in the deed of arrangement, the statute begins to run from the date of the failure to keep his promise.

Debt.—A person cannot be sued for a debt after six years from the date when it was incurred. If part payment has been made or formal acknowledgment given, the six years begin to run from the date of the payment or acknowledgment.

In the case of a debt which is more than six years old, in respect of which no payment or acknowledgment has been made, if the debtor then makes a payment on account of the debt, that payment does not bring the debt to life again—it remains legally a statute barred debt.

In the case of a specialty debt—that is, where the debt is acknowledged in a document under seal—the period is twenty years from the date on which the right to bring an action first accrues.

Deposit Receipts—The six years begin to run when demand for payment has been made.

If the deposit receipt is repayable after expiration of a specified notice, then the years commence from the date on which the receipt is due to be paid.

Drawer of Cheque.—The drawer of a cheque is liable to pay it any time within six years, except where he suffers damage by the banker's failure through delay in presentation.

Where a loan has been made on an account, the six years run from the date the money was paid, not necessarily from the date of the cheque, though in most cases the dates will actually be the same.

Guarantee under Hand.—The banker's right against a guarantor is barred in six years from the date when the right to bring an action against the guarantor first accrued. It has been held that the right of action on each item of the account arose as soon as that item became due and was not paid. Acknowledgments by a debtor do not keep the debt alive as against a guarantor.

The safest plan in connection with guarantees is to have them renewed before the expiration of six years from their date, and this is usually done by bankers. Instead of a fresh guarantee being taken a written acknowledgment upon the old guarantee by the surety, or sureties, that the guarantee is still in force is sometimes taken.

If, however, the guarantee is drawn as payable several days after demand, the six years would not begin to run until demand had been made. A guarantee in this form avoids the necessity of a renewal at the end of each six years.

When repayment is demanded from the guarantor the statute begins to run in his favour.

Guarantee under Seal.—The period is twenty years, otherwise the same remarks apply as in a guarantee under hand.

But if it is in respect of a debt secured by a mortgage of land the limitation is twelve years both as to the remedy on the covenant and the remedy against the land, whether the covenant of the surety is in the mortgage deed itself or in a collateral bond (*Sutton* v. *Sutton*, 1882, 22 Ch. D. 511).

Infant.—The statute does not begin to run until he has reached the age of twenty-one.

Interest.—It has been held (*Parr's Banking Co.* v. *Yates*, 1898, 2 Q.B. 460) that where certain advances were barred by the Statute of Limitations the interest did not fall to the ground at the same time. In this case principal and interest were guaranteed, and, though the banker's right against the surety was barred, it was held that the payment of interest, commission and other banking charges which had accrued against the guaranteed party within six years before the commencement of the action were as much guaranteed as the payment of the advances, and that the Statute of Limitations did not affect those items.

Judgment.—A judgment is statute barred after twelve years.

Loan.—(See Account, above; Promissory Note, below.)

Memorandum of Deposit.—If under hand, an action of debt must be brought within six years, and an action of foreclosure within twelve years, from the day on which the right to bring an action for the debt first accrued.

If under seal, an action of debt and of foreclosure must be brought within twelve years.

MORTGAGE OF LAND.—A mortgagee may enforce his security at any time within twelve years after the time at which the right to make entry or distress or bring an action or suit first accrues. (See section, REAL PROPERTY, below.) A mortgagor is barred at the end of twelve years from the time when the mortgagee took possession, or from the last written acknowledgment.

An acknowledgment from one mortgagor of land is sufficient to keep the debt alive.

OVERDRAFT.—(See ACCOUNT, above.)

PROMISSORY NOTE.—If on demand, the six years begin to run in favour of the maker from the date of the note or from the last instalment paid or acknowledgment given. If there are several makers of the note there must be an acknowledgment from each one, otherwise the debt will be kept alive only against the maker who has acknowledged the debt or made the payment, and the others will be released. It is advisable always to have a note renewed before the six years are up, so as to avoid any question of release being raised. Where a promissory note on demand is given as collateral security, with a memorandum of deposit, it is also advisable to have it renewed before the six years expire, though in such a case it is possible that the statute might be held to run from the date of demand for payment and not from the date of the note.

If the note is payable at a specified period after demand, or after date, the six years do not commence to run till the day on which the note is due to be paid.

REAL PROPERTY.—Section 1 of the Real Property Limitation Act, 1874, provides :—" After the commencement of this Act no person shall make an entry or distress, or bring an action or suit, to recover any land or rent, but within twelve years next after the time at which the right to make such entry or distress, or to bring such action or suit, shall have first accrued to some person through whom he claims ; or if such right shall not have accrued to any person through whom he claims, then within twelve years next after the time at which the right to make such entry or distress, or to bring such action or suit, shall have first accrued to the person making or bringing the same." (See MORTGAGE OF LAND, above.)

RENT.—No arrears of rent can be recovered by distress, action, or suit, but within six years next after the same shall have become due, or after an acknowledgment in writing. Actions of debt for rent on an indenture of demise and all actions of covenant shall be brought within twenty years after the cause of action (3 & 4 Will. IV. c. 27, Section 42, and c. 42, Section 3).

SAFE CUSTODY.—Where articles have been left for safe custody the six years do not begin to run until demand to deliver up has been made and a refusal given (see *In re Tidd*, 1893, 3 Ch. 154).

SCOTLAND.—In Scotland the law is very different from that in England. By the Long Negative Prescription, a person having an interest in an obligation or heritable bond or other heritable rights, must follow the same within forty years and take document thereupon, otherwise his right will be prescribed or lost. Negative prescription means the loss of a right by neglecting to use it during the time limited by law. Obligations founded upon holograph writings prescribe in twenty years (called the Vicennial Prescription). Cautionary obligations prescribe in seven years (Septennial Prescription). Bills of exchange prescribe in six years (Sexennial Prescription). Actions for most debts, that are not founded upon written obligations, must be pursued within three years (Triennial Prescription).

STOCKS AND SHARES.—There is no statute of limitations with regard to an equitable mortgage of stocks and shares. If the debt is statute barred, that does not affect the banker's claim upon the security.

In *London and Midland Bank, Ltd.* v. *Mitchell* (1899, 2 Ch. 161), where shares had been given as security, with a blank transfer, it was held that, although the personal action on the debt was barred, the bank's right of property in the shares was not destroyed. Mr. Justice Stirling said : " Though the debt is barred in the sense that a personal action can no longer be brought to recover it, the debt is not gone ; nor is the right of property destroyed, for there is no provision in any statute of limitations with reference to personal property similar to that contained in 3 & 4 William IV. c. 27, Section 34, whereby the title to land is extinguished after the lapse of a certain period."

STATUTORY DECLARATION. A declaration in writing, made in accordance with the Statutory Declarations Act, 1835, by which a person solemnly declares that he verifies some circumstance or fact. For example, if it should be necessary for Smith to have proof that Brown has been (as he maintains) in possession of a certain property for a specified period, Smith may be satisfied to accept a statutory declaration from, say, Jones, formally stating that he is able, from his own knowledge, to vouch for the accuracy of Brown's assertion.

STATUTORY MEETING OF COMPANY. Every company limited by shares and registered on or after January 1, 1901, shall, within a period of not less than one month nor more than three months from the date at which the company is entitled to commence business, hold a general meeting of the members, which shall be called the statutory meeting. (See Section 65, Companies (Consolidation) Act, 1908, under MEETINGS.)

A general meeting of every company shall be held once at the least in every calendar year, and not more than fifteen months after the last preceding general meeting.

STATUTORY MORTGAGE. By the Conveyancing and Law of Property Act, 1881, a mortgage of freehold or leasehold land may be made by a deed expressed to be made by way of statutory mortgage in the following form, with such variations and additions, if any, as circumstances may require, and the provisions of Section 26 of the Act shall apply thereto :—

DEED OF STATUTORY MORTGAGE.

This Indenture made by way of statutory mortgage the day of 1882, between A. of [etc.] of the one part and M. of [etc. of the other part Witnesseth that in consideration of the sum of £ now paid to A. by M. of which sum A. hereby acknowledges the receipt A. as mortgagor and as beneficial owner hereby conveys to M. all that [etc. To hold to and to the use of M. in fee simple for securing payment on the day of 1883, of the principal sum of £ as the mortgage money with interest thereon at the rate of [four] per centum per annum.

In witness, etc.

By Section 26 :—

"(2) There shall be deemed to be included, and there shall by virtue of this Act be implied, in the mortgage deed—

"First, a covenant with the mortgagee by the person expressed therein to convey as mortgagor to the effect following (namely) :

"That the mortgagor will, on the stated day, pay to the mortgagee the stated mortgage money, with interest thereon in the meantime, at the stated rate, and will thereafter, if and as long as the mortgage money, or any part thereof, remains unpaid, pay to the mortgagee interest thereon, or on the unpaid part thereof, at the stated rate, by equal half-yearly payments, the first thereof to be made at the end of six calendar months from the day stated for payment of the mortgage money :

"Secondly, a proviso to the effect following (namely) :

"That if the mortgagor, on the stated day, pays to the mortgagee the stated mortgage money, with interest thereon in the meantime, at the stated rate, the mortgagee at any time thereafter, at the request and cost of the mortgagor, shall reconvey the mortgaged property to the mortgagor, or as he shall direct."

The following is the form given in the Act of a statutory transfer of mortgage, a covenantor joining :—

This Indenture made by way of statutory transfer of mortgage the day of 1883, between A. of [etc. of the first part B. of [etc] of the second part and C. of [etc.] of the third part supplemental to an indenture made by way of statutory mortgage dated the day of 1882, and made between [etc. Witnesseth that in consideration of the sum of £ now paid to A. by C. being the mortgage money due in respect of the said mortgage no interest being now due and payable thereon of which sum A. hereby acknowledges the receipt A. as mortgagee with the concurrence of B. who joins herein as covenantor hereby conveys and transfers to C. the benefit of the said mortgage.

In witness, etc.

By Section 27, the deed shall have effect as follows :—

"2. (*a*) There shall become vested in the person to whom the benefit of the mortgage is expressed to be transferred, who, with his executors, administrators, and assigns, is hereafter in this Section designated the transferee, the right to demand, sue for, recover, and give receipts for the mortgage money, or the unpaid part thereof, and the interest then due, if any, and thenceforth to become due thereon, and the benefit of all securities for the same, and the benefit of and the right to sue on all covenants with the mortgagee, and the right to exercise all powers of the mortgagee:

"(b) All the estate and interest, subject to redemption, of the mortgagee in the mortgaged land shall rest in the transferee, subject to redemption."

In the above form, the same Section (s.s. 3) provides that there shall also be deemed to be included a covenant with the transferee by the person expressed to join therein as covenantor to the effect following:—

"That the covenantor will, on the next of the days by the mortgage deed fixed for payment of interest, pay to the transferee the stated mortgage money, or so much thereof as then remains unpaid, with interest thereon, or on the unpaid part thereof, in the meantime, at the rate stated in the mortgage deed; and will thereafter, as long as the mortgage money, or any part thereof, remains unpaid, pay to the transferee interest on that sum, or the unpaid part thereof, at the same rate, on the successive days by the mortgage deed fixed for payment of interest."

The following is the form of deed of statutory reconveyance of mortgage, given in the Act:—

This Indenture made by way of statutory reconveyance of mortgage the day of 1884, between C. of [etc.] of the one part and B. of [etc.] of the other part supplemental to an indenture made by way of statutory transfer of mortgage dated the day of 1883, and made between [etc.] Witnesseth that in consideration of all principal money and interest due under that indenture having been paid of which principal and interest C. hereby acknowledges the receipt C. as mortgagee hereby conveys to B. all the lands and hereditaments now vested in C. under the said indenture To hold to and to the use of B. in fee simple discharged from all principal money and interest secured by and from all claims and demands under the said indenture.

In Witness, etc.

(See MORTGAGE.)

STATUTORY RECEIPT. When the moneys intended to be secured by a mortgage to a building society have been fully paid, the society may indorse upon or annex to the mortgage a reconveyance of the mortgaged property to the then owner of the equity of redemption, or a receipt under the seal of the society, countersigned by the secretary or manager, in the following form:

The building society hereby acknowledge to have received all moneys intended to be secured by the within [or above] written deed.

In witness whereof, the seal of the society is hereto affixed this .... day of .... by order of the board of directors [or committee of management] in presence of

.... Secretary [or Manager]. (L S)

This statutory receipt vacates the mortgage and vests the estate of and in the property therein comprised in the person for the time being entitled to the equity of redemption, without any reconveyance or re-surrender whatever (Building Societies' Act, 1874, Section 42). The receipt is exempt from stamp duty. (See BUILDING SOCIETY.)

STATUTORY REPORT. The directors of a company limited by shares shall, at least seven days before the date on which the statutory meeting (*q.v.*) is held, forward a report, called the statutory report, to every member of the company and to every other person entitled under the Companies (Consolidation) Act, 1908, to receive it. For the requirements of the Act regarding this report see under heading MEETINGS.

STERLING. When gold and silver are of the standard fineness they are called sterling metals. Various explanations are given as to the original meaning of the word sterling. A coin called an "Easterling" was introduced into the coinage in the reign of King Richard I and as that coin was considered superior to other coins in circulation at that time it is probable that the word sterling took its rise from the Easterling. Another suggestion (given in Hutchison's "Practice of Banking") is that the word was derived, "from Easterling, a name given to persons who periodically examined the mint and regulated the coinage, possibly at Easter, so that the term means true money according to the last examination, as 100 pennies, or pounds, Easterling, or sterling." (See COINAGE.)

STERLING BONDS. Bonds of a foreign country which are payable in English currency.

STET. (Latin, let it stand.) When entries in a book have been ruled out in mistake, instead of erasing the line, it is sometimes a convenient way of correcting the error to write the word "stet" in a different coloured ink, thus indicating that the entries stand as they were before the line was passed through them.

STOCK. The capital of a company is the money contributed by the members and forms what is called the stock. A member may hold so much stock or so many shares in the company. Stock may be held and transferred in any amounts, whereas shares are for fixed amounts, e.g. a person may hold £165 of stock if the capital is dealt with in that way; but if the capital is divided into shares of, say, £5 each, fully paid, then the person with the same holding would have thirty-three shares £5 each. Stock, by its nature, is fully paid up, but upon shares there is often a liability.

There may be varieties of stock as guaranteed, preference, ordinary, deferred and other kinds, which entitle the holders to different rights in the matter of dividends and in a division upon a winding up of the company.

In companies where Table A applies (see Section 11 under ARTICLES OF ASSOCIATION) the regulations are:—

Conversion of Shares into Stock.

"31. The directors may, with the sanction of the company previously given in general meeting, convert any paid-up shares into stock, and may with the like sanction reconvert any stock into paid-up shares of any denomination.

"32. The holders of stock may transfer the same, or any part thereof, in the same manner, and subject to the same regulations, as, and subject to which, the shares from which the stock arose might previously to conversion have been transferred, or as near thereto as circumstances admit; but the directors may from time to time fix the minimum amount of stock transferable, and restrict or forbid the transfer of fractions of that minimum, but the minimum shall not exceed the nominal amount of the shares from which the stock arose.

"33. The holders of stock shall, according to the amount of the stock held by them, have the same rights, privileges, and advantages as regards dividends, voting at meetings of the company, and other matters as if they held the shares from which the stock arose, but no such privilege or advantage (except participation in the dividends and profits of the company) shall be conferred by any such aliquot part of stock as would not, if existing in shares, have conferred that privilege or advantage.

"34. Such of the regulations of the company (other than those relating to share warrants) as are applicable to paid-up shares shall apply to stock, and the words 'share' and 'shareholder' therein shall include 'stock' and 'stock-holder.'" (See COMPANIES, SHARE CAPITAL.)

STOCKBROKER. A dealer in stocks and shares. His remuneration is the commission he receives from his clients on the purchases and sales he effects on their behalf; the rate varies in different classes of stocks. There is no fixed scale of charges, though the usual commission on the London Stock Exchange is as follows:—

British and Indian Government securities, 2*s.* 6*d.* per cent.

Colonial, corporation and foreign securities, 5*s.* per cent.

Home railway securities, 5*s.* to 10*s.* per cent.

American and foreign railway securities, 5*s.* to 10*s.* per cent.

Mining and industrial shares:—

Under £1 nominal value,	3*d.*	per share.	
,, £2 ,, ,,	6*d.*	,,	,,
,, £5 ,, ,,	9*d.*	,,	,,
,, £10 ,, ,,	1*s.*	,,	,,

and 6*d.* per share for every £5 per share in excess.

The Manchester Stock Exchange has a special scale, and the members are bound not to charge anything less than the amounts fixed. The scale in force is as follows:—

MINIMUM COMMISSIONS CHARGEABLE.

Not exceeding 2/6	½d. per share.
Exceeding 2/6 and not exceeding 7/6 ..	1d. ,,
,, 7/6 ,, ,, £1 ..	1½d. ,,
,, £1 ,, ,, £2 ..	3d. ,,
,, £2 ,, ,, £3 ..	4½d. ,,
,, £3 ,, ,, £5 ..	6d. ,,
,, £5 ,, ,, £7 ..	9d. ,,
,, £7 ,, ,, £10 ..	1/0 ,,
,, £10 ,, ,, £15 ..	1/3 ,,
,, £15 ,, ,, £25 ..	1/6 ,,
,, £25	5/0 per cent.
Consols, Indian Government Bonds and Stocks .. .. .. / Foreign Government Bonds ..	2/6 per cent. on nominal amount.
Railway Stocks—	
Not exceeding the value of £25	1/3 per cent. on nominal amount.
Exceeding £25	5/0 per cent. on money value
American Shares—	
Not exceeding $50	6d. per share.

Exceeding $50 and not exceeding $100	.. 1/– per share.
Exceeding $100	.. 1/6 "
Colonial Bonds and Stocks ..	.. 5/0 per cent. on money value.

The same commission is charged for buying or selling, but when a stock is both bought and sold within the same Stock Exchange account, or when one stock is sold and the proceeds at once invested in another stock, the order for sale and purchase being given at the same time, most brokers charge one commission only. (See STOCK EXCHANGE.)

STOCKBROKER'S LOANS. When a stockbroker lends money to a client who desires to purchase stocks and shares, the securities are usually deposited with the broker as cover for the advance, and the broker is often authorised to transfer them to a banker as security when it is necessary to obtain an advance from him. In such cases the broker's interest in the securities is limited to the money he has lent to his client, and if they are given to a banker as security for the general indebtedness of the broker various questions arise. The results of several important cases which have come before the Courts show (1) that if a banker has definite knowledge when he takes certain securities from a broker that the broker is dealing with them beyond his authority—that is, that they are being given to the banker to cover a greater sum than the amount lent by the broker to the client—the client will be entitled to redeem them from the banker, even if transferred into the banker's name, on paying the amount due by him to the broker; (2) that if the banker has no reason to suppose that the securities are not the broker's own property, the client will not be entitled to redeem them except by payment of the debt due from the broker to the banker.

When negotiable securities are pledged by a broker, there is no obligation upon a banker to inquire whether they are the property of the broker or not. If there is anything to arouse suspicion the banker would be put upon inquiry, but, apart from that, any " person taking a negotiable instrument in good faith and for value obtains a title valid against all the world."

When a banker has notice that a broker has power to pledge a client's securities only to a limited extent, the banker's advance to the broker upon any such securities should not, of course, exceed that limit. The banker should receive a letter or memorandum from the broker's client agreeing to the broker charging the securities to the extent of the client's indebtedness to the broker.

STOCKBROKING TRANSACTIONS. When a banker is requested by a customer to instruct his brokers to purchase or sell certain stocks or shares, the request should be made in writing so that no mistake or misunderstanding may arise. In the case of a sale, it should be signed by the person in whose name the stocks or shares are registered; if registered in several names, the signature of each person should be appended. The order should contain a precise description of the security, a note of the amount of stock or number of shares to be sold, and the price at which the sale is to be effected. The order is usually to sell at " not less than £ per cent.," or per share; or it may be to sell " at best price."

In the case of a purchase, it should be particularly noted whether the customer wishes to invest a sum of, say, £500 in a given stock or to purchase £500 of the stock. Equal care is necessary in transmitting the order to the brokers, otherwise an unlooked for result may be produced. The order may be to purchase at " the lowest price," or at " not more than £ per cent.," or per share. When the cost is known, a cheque is obtained from the customer for the amount, unless the order includes an authority to charge the amount to the account of the person signing the order. The latter plan is the better one. The amount is either credited to the banker's London agents or London office to meet the purchase, or is placed to a separate account until the brokers draw for the money.

A purchase or sale may be effected either " for cash " or " for the account " and the customer should instruct as desired.

An order to buy or sell is not subject to stamp duty; if an order to buy includes an authority to charge the purchase price to the customer's account it is said not to require a stamp, but as such an order practically acts as a cheque some bankers consider that it should bear a penny stamp.

STOCK CERTIFICATE TO BEARER. A certificate which entitles the bearer to the stock mentioned therein and which is transferable by simple delivery of the certificate.

As to stamp duty see under SHARE WARRANT.

By Section 109 of the Stamp Act, 1891:—

" (1) Where the holder of a stock

certificate to bearer has been entered on the register of the local authority as the owner of the share of stock described in the certificate, the certificate shall be forthwith cancelled so as to be incapable of being re-issued to any person.

"(2) Every person by whom a stock certificate to bearer is issued without being duly stamped shall incur a fine of fifty pounds."

By Section 5 of the Finance Act, 1899, the duty on stock certificates to bearer shall extend to any instrument to bearer issued by or on behalf of any company or body of persons in the United Kingdom and having a like effect as a stock certificate to bearer.

Stock certificates to bearer for various Government and corporation stocks transferable at the Bank of England can be obtained from the Bank. The stockholder must either attend at the Bank in person to transfer the stock and receive the certificates, or grant a power of attorney to some person, or firm, for this purpose.

By Section 7 of the Trustee Act, 1893, (1) a trustee, unless authorised by the terms of his trust, shall not apply for or hold any certificate to bearer issued under the authority of any of the following acts :—

(*a*) The India Stock Certificate Act, 1863. (*b*) The National Debt Act, 1870. (*c*) The Local Loans Act, 1875. (*d*) The Colonial Stock Act, 1877. (See MARKETABLE SECURITY.)

STOCK EXCHANGE. The place appointed for the purchase and sale of stocks and shares. It is situate in Capel Court between Threadneedle Street and Throgmorton Street. The London Stock Exchange is the most important in the world and the number and amount of the transactions that take place here in the course of a single day are very great. As other stock exchanges are managed on somewhat similar lines, it will suffice to give a few particulars of this one.

The business of the "House," as the Stock Exchange is termed, is split up into the different "markets," or classes of securities dealt in, as those of Consols, colonial stocks, corporations, foreign governments, home railways, foreign railways, banks, industrials, mines and others.

The dealers engaged are of two kinds, stockbrokers and stock jobbers, who must all be members of the Exchange. The former deal with the outside public, taking their clients' instructions as to buying and selling, and themselves doing the actual business with the jobbers, selling to them the securities their clients sell and obtaining from them the stocks and shares their clients buy. Thus the jobbers are merchants and act as middlemen between those brokers who have stock for sale and those who wish to purchase ; and the method in which they make their profit is different from that of the brokers, for the latter are paid by the commission, at so much per cent. or per share, which they receive from their clients, whilst the jobbers take the "turn" between the price they give for a stock and the rate at which they sell it again.

On receiving instructions from his client a broker buys so much stock from a jobber or sells so much to him, as the case may be, at the price which he offers, subject to the client's "limit" ; he then sends his client a contract note which, amongst other particulars, quotes the settling day when the price is due to be paid. A large proportion of the Stock Exchange business is speculative, however, and the price is not paid ; instead, if the transaction has been a purchase and the stock has risen in price by the time settling day arrives, the client may request his broker to sell again and the broker will then merely send him a cheque for the profit on the "deal." (See BULL AND BEAR.)

In most stocks there are two settlements per month, one near the middle and the other near the end ; for Consols there is one day, near the beginning of the month. A transaction that is to be completed on the settling day next following is known as one "for the account" ; there is also much business done "for money" or "for cash," that is, for immediate payment. (See SETTLING DAYS.)

If, on settling day, the client does not wish to complete a purchase, the broker will by arrangement carry over the bargain until the following settlement again, charging a contango for the service. (See CONTANGO.) In order to find the money to pay for stocks bought in this way for clients who do not pay on settling day, the brokers frequently borrow from their bankers, lodging as security the stocks in question. The margin in the value of the security beyond the amount of the advance varies with the class of stock ; the period for which bankers arrange such "stockbrokers' loans" is till the next "account"—*i.e.* the next Stock Exchange settling day, at which time the amount of the loan, margin, rate of interest, etc., must be rearranged.

For the sake of brevity some stocks quoted on the Stock Exchange are occasionally referred to by brokers and in the press by abbreviated names; some are readily distinguishable, but it may be well to mention a few of the more important: Anglo A = Anglo-American Telegraph Co. Deferred ordinary stock; Bags = Buenos Ayres Great Southern Railway ordinary stock. Berthas = London, Brighton and South Coast Railway Deferred ordinary stock. See BERWICKS, BRIGHTON A, BRUMS, CALEYS, CANPACS, CHARTEREDS, CHATHAMS, CHOPS, CLARAS, DISTRICTS, DORAS, DOVER A, EASTERNS, KAFFIRS, KANGAROOS, LEEDS, NORAS, POTS, SOUTHS, TRUNKS, WESTERNS, YORK PREFERRED, YORKS.

The principal foreign stock exchanges are New York, Paris, Berlin, Vienna, Frankfort-on-Maine, Brussels, and Amsterdam. In many places stock exchange business is conducted at the Bourses. (See BOURSE.)

(See ACCOUNT, BACKWARDATION, BEAR AND BULL, CARRYING OVER, CONTANGO, CONTRACT NOTE, MAKING-UP PRICE, OFFICIAL LIST, OPTIONS, QUOTATION ON LONDON STOCK EXCHANGE, SETTLING DAYS, SPECIAL SETTLEMENT, STOCKBROKER, STOCK JOBBER.)

STOCK EXCHANGE HOLIDAYS. The Stock Exchange is closed on the following days: January 1, Easter Monday, May 1, Whit Monday, first Monday in August, November 1, December 26, unless specially ordered otherwise by the Committee for General Purposes. When January 1, May 1, November 1 or December 26 falls on a Sunday the "House" is closed on the day following.

STOCK EXCHANGE SETTLEMENT. The adjustment of differences between brokers and clients, when payment is made to clients for stocks sold on their behalf and payment received from clients for stocks bought. In most "markets," as the various departments are called into which the stocks dealt in on the London Stock Exchange are divided, the settlement takes place twice a month, near the middle and near the end; but there is only one settlement for the Consols "market," that is about the beginning of the month. (See SETTLING DAYS.)

STOCK JOBBER. A dealer in stocks and shares who conducts his business with the stockbrokers, acting as intermediary between those brokers who have securities for sale and those who wish to purchase. The jobber's profit (called the jobber's turn) is the difference between his buying and selling prices. He is also called a dealer. (See STOCK EXCHANGE.)

STOCK RECEIPT. The receipt which is given by the seller or his attorney, to the purchaser, when inscribed stocks are transferred. It is of no value as a security. A holder's title is the entry in the stock books at the bank where the stocks are domiciled. Certain stocks may be converted by a holder into certificates to bearer. (See NATIONAL DEBT, STOCK CERTIFICATE TO BEARER.)

In order that inscribed stock may be taken as a security for an advance, it must be registered in the name of the bank or in the names of the bank's nominees.

STOCK TRUST CERTIFICATE. The name of a certificate issued by certain American railroad companies. It certifies that, on surrender, "John Brown" will be entitled, out of certificates delivered to undersigned voting trustees, to receive a certificate for shares of dollars, etc.

On the back is a form of transfer and an appointment of an attorney to transfer all interest in the stock trust certificate on the books of the voting trustees. (See AMERICAN RAILROAD CERTIFICATES.)

STOCK WARRANT. A stock warrant to bearer entitles the bearer of the warrant to the stock therein specified.

A stock warrant is included in the expression "share warrant" in the Companies (Consolidation) Act, 1908. (See SHARE WARRANT.)

A stock warrant is a negotiable instrument.

STOLEN BANK NOTES. Where bank notes have been stolen, a holder for value, without notice that they have been stolen, is entitled to payment and the person who lost them cannot recover from him. But where it is proved that bank notes have been stolen, the burden of proof that they were taken in good faith and for value rests upon the holder.

A banker cannot refuse to pay his own notes, but where he has information that certain notes have been stolen he would naturally make full inquiry before paying such notes.

The numbers, when known, of notes which have been stolen are usually notified to bankers and money changers, but it has been held that the mere fact that a person has possession of a list of the numbers of stolen notes will not, if he has, in good faith, given value for one of them, prevent him from recovering upon any such note (*Raphael* v. *Bank of England*, 1855, 25 L.J.C.P. 33). It is quite clear, therefore, that the notice which is sometimes found in newspapers that "payment has been stopped" of stolen or lost bank notes is legally of no value whatever.

STOLEN BILL. A bill of exchange can be the subject of larceny like any other valuable document of title, but it is unnecessary to inquire into anything beyond the civil position as to liability in connection with the matter.

By Section 20 of the Bills of Exchange Act, 1882, very full authority is given to fill up an inchoate instrument (*q.v.*) and turn it into a complete bill. But this does not permit of the filling up and the conversion being effected by any other than the duly authorised person. If, therefore, an inchoate instrument is stolen before completion, no action can be brought upon it, for it would have to be signed by some person or other, and the signature would be either forged or unauthorised, having been made by some person other than the one entitled to complete the bill. The forged or unauthorised signature is wholly inoperative (Section 24). This is well established by the case of *Baxendale* v. *Bennett* (1878, 3 Q.B.D. 525). B put his blank acceptance in a desk. It was stolen, filled up as a bill by C with his own name as drawer, and negotiated. It was held that even a holder in due course could not recover from B, as he had never delivered the inchoate instrument for the purpose of being converted into a bill by C. Whatever remedies there may be for those persons who have dealt in and with the instrument, they are independent of the document, which never became a bill at all.

Again, if a bill complete in form is stolen, the liability of the parties will depend upon the particular circumstances. Thus, C, the holder of a bill, specially indorsed it to D, and forwarded it in a letter to D. In the course of transmission the bill was stolen and D's indorsement forged. The bill was afterwards negotiated. Since the indorsement of D was necessary for negotiation, and this had not been obtained, the signature was, under Section 24, wholly inoperative, and C still retained the property in the bill. No liability rested on any person who was a party to the bill prior to the time of D's forged indorsement (*Arnold* v. *Cheque Bank*, 1876, 1 C.P.D. 578, at p. 584). If, on the contrary, the bill is indorsed in blank and stolen, a holder in good faith and without notice that his title to the bill is defective is entitled to demand payment of the same. And if a bill indorsed in blank is stolen whilst in the course of negotiation for any person who was the holder of it, the payment at maturity by the acceptor, provided he acts in good faith, is a good discharge of the bill, even though the payment is made to the actual thief (see *Smith* v. *Sheppard*, 1776, a case cited by Chitty in his "Bills of Exchange," 10th ed., p. 180, *n.*).

When a bill is in the hands of a holder in due course a valid delivery of the bill by all parties prior to him so as to make them liable to him is conclusively presumed. (Section 21.)

With regard to bills of exchange in general, that is, those bills which do not fall within the definition of a cheque (see Section 60), a banker is in no better position than a private individual, unless special arrangements are made by the banker when a bill is made payable at his bank.

STOLEN CHEQUE. For most purposes a cheque is legally regarded as a bill of exchange; but the law is not quite the same with regard to the two instruments, at least as far as the larceny of them is concerned. The civil liability when a bill is stolen has been referred to in the last article, but it would appear that when a cheque is stolen, the position of the banker is peculiar. The crossing of cheques, and the marking of them as "not negotiable," have safeguarded the public to a remarkable extent by making it more difficult for a thief to obtain cash for the cheques, though the mere crossing of a cheque does not affect its negotiability if it is regular in every other respect. If a cheque is stolen whilst in course of transmission, a holder in due course is entitled to the amount of it, and may sue the drawer or any other party to the cheque upon it if payment has been stopped. But, of course, if the cheque is specially indorsed and the indorsee's signature has not been added, an unauthorised or a forged signature would be appended, and through this signature (by Section 24) no title could be made to it. The property would remain in the last indorser.

In the case of a cheque which has been crossed with the addition of the words "not negotiable" any person taking such a cheque shall not have, and shall not be capable of giving a better title to the cheque than that which the person had from whom he took it. (Section 81.)

If the banker on whom an open cheque is drawn pays it in good faith and in the ordinary course of business, then (by Section 60) the banker is entitled to charge his customer, and there is no responsibility resting upon him if the indorsement has been forged and the cheque stolen. If the cheque is payable to bearer, or if, after having been made payable to order it bears the true signature of the indorsee, it gets into circulation, it becomes the property of any holder who has taken it in good faith and has had no reason to doubt that it was regular in every respect.

In the case of a crossed cheque which has been stolen, the banker on whom it is drawn is protected if he pays it in accordance with Section 80, and a collecting banker in accordance with Section 82. (See CROSSED CHEQUE.)

At a first view it seems that the position taken up by a banker as to paying a cheque drawn upon him without his knowing that it had been delivered or issued is not quite in accordance with the law. But as far as practice is concerned, it seems that the position is correctly stated in Morse's "Law of Banking" (4th ed., p. 687): "If a cheque is stolen, or if after being lost by the drawer it is found by some other person, it is not, in the hands of the thief or of the finder 'issued' as against the drawer. But so far as concerns the bank, it would be considered as issued, and the bank would be protected in paying it, provided it did so *bonâ fide*, and with no knowledge of the precedent circumstances." (See Section 21 of the Bills of Exchange Act, 1882.)

STOP ORDER. STOP PAYMENT. STOPPED CHEQUE. (See PAYMENT STOPPED.)

STOTINKIS. (See FOREIGN MONEYS—BULGARIA.)

STREET PRICES. After the London Stock Exchange is closed for the day, the dealers in American securities continue their business in the street, whence the terms "street market" and "street prices."

STUBS. An American term for the counterfoils of cheques.

SUB-BRANCH. A successful branch very often works one or more sub-branches, or agencies. They may be open daily and have a resident clerk in charge, or be worked by a clerk from the parent office. In many cases, sub-branches are open only on one, two, or three days a week. When the sub is open daily it may, so far as book-keeping is concerned, be worked as though it were a separate branch, but when it is not open daily all the transactions are passed through the parent branch. Cheque books are often supplied for the use of sub-branch customers, when the office is open daily, bearing the name of the sub. Such cheques are strictly payable at the sub-office on which they are drawn, in the same way that cheques drawn on the parent office are payable there and not at the sub-branch. As a rule, a branch and its sub are in close communication so as to avoid refusing payment of a cheque at the branch when the drawer of the cheque has paid in to credit at the sub-office. A banker, however, is not liable if he should dishonour a cheque at the one office when sufficient money is paid in to meet it at the other office on the same day, as he cannot be expected to know of the credit till advice is received in due course. But if a clerk at the sub pays a cheque drawn on the parent branch and the cheque is dishonoured, he may not be able to recover the money from the person to whom he paid it. In cases of doubt, the cheque on the parent office should be received merely for collection, and, in any case, there is always the possibility that payment of it may have been stopped.

SUB-LEASE. Where a sub-lease is deposited as security, it should be accompanied by an attested copy of the original lease. (See LEASEHOLD.)

SUBPŒNA. (Latin, *sub* under, *pœna*, punishment.)

A writ by which the attendance of a person in Court is commanded, under a penalty.

SUBROGATION. If a banker lends money to a company, which has no power to borrow, he cannot recover from the company, but the banker has the right of subrogation; that is, he is entitled to occupy the position of such creditors of the company as were paid out of the money he advanced to the company and to recover from the company the debts of the creditors so paid.

Where a guarantor repays the full debt due to the banker on the account for which he is surety, he is subrogated to the rights of the banker—that is, he is thereby entitled to the banker's right to sue the debtor, or to claim upon his estate, and to the benefit of any securities which the banker held. (See GUARANTEE.)

SUBSCRIBED CAPITAL. That part of the nominal or authorised capital which has been issued by the directors of a company and subscribed or taken up by the shareholders. It may be fully paid up, or only partly paid, in which latter case the remainder is termed the "uncalled" capital. (See CAPITAL, UNCALLED CAPITAL.)

SUCCESSION DUTY. A duty which is payable by the person who succeeds to real or leasehold property in the United Kingdom, upon the death of another person. The duty is also payable upon legacies which are charged upon the proceeds of a sale of real estate, or on so much of the proceeds of a sale of real estate as may be required to discharge legacies where the personal estate has proved insufficient, and upon personal property included in a settlement.

The succession duty rates, payable upon the value of the succession as amended by the Finance (1909–10) Act, 1910, Section 58, are as follows :—

	per cent.
On the succession of lineal ancestors or descendants of the deceased . .	1
Brothers and sisters of the deceased and their descendants, or their husbands or wives	5
Uncles and aunts of the deceased and their descendants, or their husbands or wives	10
Great uncles and great aunts of the deceased, and their descendants .	10
On the succession of other persons .	10

Prior to the Finance (1909–10) Act, 1910, the husband or wife of the predecessor was not chargeable with succession duty, but by that Act the duty, at the rate of one per cent., is to be paid in cases where the person taking the succession is the husband or wife of the deceased, as in cases where the person is a lineal ancestor or descendant ; but that duty shall not be levied where the value of the property (other than property in which the deceased never had an interest) in respect of which estate duty is payable does not exceed £15,000, nor where the successions derived by the same person from the deceased do not exceed £1,000, nor where the person taking the succession is the widow or a child under the age of twenty-one of the deceased, and the value of the succession derived by the same person from the deceased does not exceed £2,000.

The above shall take effect in the case of a succession arising through devolution by law, only where the succession arises on or after that date, and in the case of a succession arising under a disposition, only if the first succession under the disposition arises on or after that date.

When a person who has succeeded to a property lodges the deeds thereof as security, the succession duty receipts should be produced, as the duty forms a charge upon the property.

By the Customs Act, 1889, special provision has been made in favour of purchasers with regard to succession duty, freeing the land therefrom after twelve years in some cases and six years in others. (Section 12.)

If property is conveyed to two or more persons as joint tenants and one joint tenant dies, the surviving joint tenant or tenants must pay duty on the beneficial interest accruing to him, her, or them by the survivorship.

Succession duty is not payable where the principal value of the estate does not exceed £100 ; nor by lineal descendants or lineal ancestors where estate duty has been paid on the full value of the property.

SUMMARY ADMINISTRATION. In the case of a small bankruptcy, where the debtor's estate is not likely to exceed £300, the estate may be administered in a simpler manner than in an ordinary bankruptcy. Section 121 of the Bankruptcy Act, 1883, provides :—

"When a petition is presented by or against a debtor, if the Court is satisfied by affidavit or otherwise, or the official receiver reports to the Court that the property of the debtor is not likely to exceed in value three hundred pounds, the Court may make an order that the debtor's estate be administered in a summary manner, and thereupon the provisions of this Act shall be subject to the following modifications :—

"(1) If the debtor is adjudged bankrupt the official receiver shall be the trustee in the bankruptcy :

"(2) There shall be no committee of inspection, but the official receiver may do with the permission of the Board of Trade all things which may be done by the trustee with the permission of the committee of inspection :

"(3) Such other modifications may be made in the provisions of this Act as may be prescribed by general rules with the view of saving expense and simplifying procedure ;

> but nothing in this Section shall permit the modification of the provisions of this Act relating to the examination or discharge of the debtor.

"Provided that the creditors may at any time, by special resolution, resolve that some person other than the official receiver be appointed trustee in the bankruptcy, and thereupon the bankruptcy shall proceed as if an order for summary administration had not been made." (See BANKRUPTCY.)

SUNDRY CREDITORS ACCOUNT, or, SUNDRY PERSONS ACCOUNT. An account through which may be passed isolated transactions with parties who are not actual customers, or have not a current account. It may also be used for various other items which do not belong to any particular account.

SUPERANNUATION ANNUITY. As to stamp duty see BOND.

SUPRA PROTEST. Where a bill of exchange has been protested for dishonour by non-acceptance, any person may, with the consent of the holder, accept the bill suprà protest for the honour of any party liable thereon. (See ACCEPTANCE FOR HONOUR.)

Also, where a bill has been protested for non-payment, any person may intervene and pay it suprà protest for the honour of any party liable thereon. (See BILL OF EXCHANGE, PAYMENT FOR HONOUR.)

SURETY. A guarantor. A person who agrees to be answerable for the debt of another person if he should fail to pay it. (See GUARANTEE.)

SURRENDER. Copyhold property is transferred from one person to another by surrender and admittance. The property is surrendered into the hands of the lord of the manor to the use and behoof of the purchaser. A surrender may be made either in court, or out of court. The actual surrender is usually preceded by a covenant to surrender. For further information, see COPYHOLD.

By the Stamp Act, 1891, the stamp duty is:—

SURRENDER—

	£ s. d.
Of copyholds. See COPYHOLD.	
Of any other kind whatsoever not chargeable with duty as a conveyance on sale or a mortgage	0 10 0

The following are examples of (1) a simple surrender; (2) a surrender combined with admittance:—

SURRENDER.

Manor of } Be it remembered that on the day of 19 A B one of the Copyhold Tenants of the said Manor came before Steward thereof and in consideration of the sum of £ to the said A B paid by the said C D on or before the passing of this surrender * Surrendered into the hands of the Lord of the said Manor by the hands and acceptance of the said Steward by the † according to the Custom of the said Manor All etc. with the appurtenances To the use of the said C D his heirs and assigns at the will of the Lord according to the Custom of the said Manor at and under the rents suits and services therefor due and of right accustomed.

This Surrender was taken and accepted by me this day of 19

Steward.

* In open Court or out of Court.

† Rod, glove, or other emblem.

SURRENDER AND ADMITTANCE.

Manor of } The Customary Court etc. of Lord of the said Manor holden at within the said manor on the day of 19

Before Steward.

To this Court came A B and did surrender into the hands of the Lord of the said Manor All that Cottage etc.

of the Yearly Copyhold Rent of To the use and behoof of C D his heirs and assigns for ever according to the Custom of the said manor (in consideration of the sum of £ to the said A B paid by the said C D) (or as the case may be)

And thereupon to the same Court came the said C D

Stamp.
£

Last admittance 19

	£ s. d.
Rent	
Fine	

and took of the Lord of the said Manor by the hands of his Steward the said Cottage aforesaid with the appurtenances To hold the same to him his heirs and assigns for ever according to the Custom of the said Manor Paying the Rents and performing the Services of Right due and accustomed and having paid the Lord for his Fine as in the margin and done his fealty is thereupon admitted tenant by pledges of E F and G H.

J. K., Steward.

SURRENDER VALUE. The amount which an assurance company will pay, after, say, two or three years premiums have been paid, to the holder of a life policy, upon a surrender of the policy. An advance should not, as a rule, be made upon a life policy beyond the amount of the surrender value. A banker can ascertain the surrender value by applying to the assurance company.

A life policy may often be sold at rather more than the surrender value. (See LIFE POLICY.)

SUSPENSE ACCOUNT. Items which, for one reason or another, cannot be passed at once into the account to which they ought to go, are, in the meantime, debited or credited, as the case may be, to a suspense account. A cheque which is sent direct by one bank to another for collection and payment over, is, in some banks, debited to such an account until advice of the payment is received.

SUSPENSION OF PAYMENT. A debtor commits an act of bankruptcy if he gives notice to any of his creditors that he has suspended, or that he is about to suspend, payment of his debts. (Bankruptcy Act, 1883, Section 4, s.s. 1 (*h*).) (See ACTS OF BANKRUPTCY.)

SUSPENSION OF THE BANK ACT. The Bank Charter Act, which imposed certain restrictions upon the issue of Bank of England notes, has on three occasions been suspended or set aside by the Government authorising the Bank to issue notes in excess of its authorised issue. The occasions were the monetary crises of 1847, 1857 and 1866, and in each case the suspension of the Act allayed the panic. (See BANK CHARTER ACT.)

SWEATING COINS. Rubbing coins together or shaking them in a box or bag in order to obtain gold or silver dust as a result of the friction, is termed "sweating." The process would naturally do the coins great injury. (See COINAGE.)

SWEATING ROOM. The bank room in which customers are interviewed is sometimes facetiously called the sweating room, in allusion, no doubt, to the supposed effect of certain interviews.

TABLE A. Table A, which is so frequently referred to in connection with companies, is contained in the first Schedule of the Companies (Consolidation) Act, 1908, and supplies model regulations for the management of a company limited by shares. It contains 114 clauses.

In the case of a company limited by shares and registered after April 1, 1909 (that is, the commencement of the above named Act), if articles are not registered, or, if articles are registered, in so far as the articles do not exclude or modify the regulations in Table A, those regulations are to be the regulations of the company in the same manner and to the same extent as if they were contained in duly registered articles.

Various clauses of Table A will be found under the following headings :—CALLS, CERTIFICATE, DIRECTORS, DIVIDEND, STOCK, TRANSFER OF SHARES, VOTES. (See ARTICLES OF ASSOCIATION.)

TACK OF LANDS. In Scotland, a lease. As to stamp duty see under LEASEHOLD.

TACKING. Where there are several mortgages, and one of them a legal mortgage, upon the same piece of land, the legal mortgage may in certain cases be tacked to one of the equitable charges. For example, if Brown grants a legal mortgage to Jones, and subsequently borrows more money upon the same property from Smith and gives him a second charge (i.e. an equitable mortgage) upon the land, and then obtains from Robinson a still further advance upon a third charge, Robinson may, if he did not know about the charge to Smith at the time he lent Brown the money, purchase the legal estate from Jones and tack his third charge to the legal mortgage of Jones and thus squeeze out Smith. The amount that Robinson had lent, added to what Jones had lent, would thus rank as a charge upon the land in front of Smith's charge. If Robinson learned after he had lent the money, about Smith's equitable mortgage, it would not affect his right to tack. If Robinson knew, at the time he lent the money, that Smith held a charge, that knowledge would prevent him "tacking." If Smith gave notice to Jones that he held a second charge, that would not prevent Robinson from tacking his third to the first.

Another example of tacking is where the legal mortgagee makes a further advance, subsequent to an equitable charge and without any notice of that charge, and adds the amount of the further advance to the original advance. If, however, the legal mortgagee had notice of the equitable charge, at the time he lent the second amount, he could not tack. Where Jones holds a legal mortgage and there are also, on the same property, charges to Smith and Robinson, Jones may, if he likes, purchase the equitable charge of Robinson and tack or add it to his own legal mortgage, provided that he, Jones, had no knowledge of the charge to Smith at the time of purchasing Robinson's charge.

It is clear, therefore, that a second mortgagee should not neglect to give notice of his charge to the first mortgagee. Such notice will prevent the first mortgagee from lending further upon the property, or from purchasing a third mortgagee's charge, and tacking the amount to his first charge. But the notice would be of no avail in the event of the first mortgage being transferred to a party without any notice of the second mortgage. B. Campion, in his lecture "Bankers' Advances upon Title-Deeds," said that the second mortgagee should not only give the first mortgagee written notice of his charge, but should further try and persuade him to allow the legal mortgage and the chief title deeds to be indorsed with a note of the second charge. Failing that, he should ask the first mortgagee to attach the written notice to the bundle of deeds. Any subsequent holder of the legal estate would thus be fixed with notice of the second charge.

Tacking was abolished in Yorkshire, as from January 1, 1885. Charges on land in that county take priority according to the date of the registration, and a legal mortgage, unregistered, may be postponed to an equitable charge which is registered. (See Mortgage, Yorkshire Registry of Deeds.)

TAEL. (See Foreign Moneys—China.)

TAKERS-IN. In connection with the Stock Exchange settlements, a "taker-in" is a broker who lends money against stock (i.e. "takes in" stock) to a broker who requires to pay for a purchase. (See Givers On.)

TAKING UP A BILL. (See Retiring a Bill.)

TALLY. An account is said to tally when it agrees or corresponds with another account. The origin of the word is found in the name of a notched stick which, at one time, was used for the purpose of keeping a record of business transactions. When a sale took place a stick was marked (by small notches for pence, larger ones for shillings and larger again for pounds) with the quantity of the goods sold or the amount of the price, and the stick was then split in two. One of the halves remained in the custody of the seller and the other was taken by the purchaser. When a settlement of the transaction took place, the purchaser produced the stick and the seller compared it with the one in his possession to see that the notches tallied; that is, that they were the same on both sticks. When the amount was paid the two sticks were tied together and stored away as a paid account.

The Government at one time gave tallies called "Exchequer Tallies" as a form of receipt for money deposited with them. When the money was to be repaid, the depositor produced the Exchequer Tally, that is, the half of the stick which was given to him when he left the money, and if it tallied with the half in the Exchequer Office he was paid the money. The use of Exchequer Tallies was abolished in 1782. (See Exchequer Tally.)

TALON. In connection with bearer bonds there is sometimes issued, along with the sheet of coupons, a slip, called a talon, in order that the holder of the bonds may, when all the coupons have been used, exchange it for a new sheet of coupons.

The following is an example of a talon:—

"The X. & Y. Bank of Egypt—Guaranteed Bonds—Talon to be exchanged for a new coupon sheet when all the coupons below have been exhausted.

"No. 16,589."

TAPE PRICES. The Stock Exchange prices which are collected by the Exchange Telegraph Company, and which on being telegraphed are recorded by the instruments on long paper tape.

TEL QUEL RATE. In connection with the Foreign Exchanges the *tel quel* is a rate charged for a bill of such a currency (e.g. thirty days) to which neither the long rate for three months' bills nor the short rate for drafts up to ten days, applies.

TELEGRAPHIC TRANSFERS. The payment of money in a foreign country may, when necessary, be effected by telegraph, the banker in London sending a cable, with the necessary particulars, to his foreign correspondent. The cost of the cable is charged to the customer at whose request the transfer is made. An exporter of goods from this country can, as soon as he has shipped the goods, communicate with his agent abroad by wire to sell the goods at once, and send payment immediately by telegraph through a London banker.

TELLER. The official behind the bank counter who receives and pays money. The word was originally tallier, one who tallies. (See TALLY.) In large offices there are receiving tellers and paying tellers; the former receive credits and the latter pay cash for cheques and bills. Where necessary the work may be further subdivided, one teller, or cashier as they are usually called, receiving credits only for customers whose names commence with one of the letters from, say, A to F, the other cashiers being similarly concerned only with customers whose names begin with certain other letters.

TENANT FOR LIFE. (See LIFE TENANT.)

TENANTS IN COMMON. A property may be conveyed to several persons as tenants in common. Tenants in common have a unity of possession in the property, but each has a separate and distinct share which can be disposed of by will, or inherited by the deceased's representatives. There is no right of survivorship; that is, when one dies his share does not pass to the survivor.

Tenants in common may have either equal or unequal shares, and one tenant may convey his share to another tenant. It is not necessary that their interests should all be created at the same time or under the same instrument.

If a property is devised to several persons without saying whether they are to be tenants in common or joint tenants, they are regarded as joint tenants.

The difference between tenants in common and joint tenants should be noted. When a joint tenant dies, his interest in the property goes to the surviving joint tenant. They cannot dispose of their interests by will. Their shares in the property are equal; and if one wishes to transfer his share or interest to the other, it has to be done by way of release, not by conveyance. The interests of a joint tenant must all be created at the same time and under the same instrument.

Where deeds are deposited as security by tenants in common, the document of charge should be signed by all the owners of the property, and it is advisable that a banker's legal mortgage be taken. (See COPARCENERS, JOINT TENANTS.)

TENDER. When a new stock is to be issued (as in the case of Corporation stock or Colonial issues) instead of being offered to the public at a certain price, the public is sometimes invited to tender for it; that is, any person desirous of becoming a holder of a part of the stock must state how much per cent. he is prepared to give for it. The stock is then allotted, commencing with those who have offered the highest price. A corporation inviting tenders usually fixes a minimum price, below which no tender will be accepted.

Treasury Bills are issued by the Government upon the tender system, and the tenders are received at the Bank of England. India Bills and London County Council Bills and others are also issued by way of tender.

TENURE. The manner in which real property is held, e.g. copyhold tenure is by copy of the court roll.

TERM OF A BILL. The period for which a bill of exchange is drawn.

TERMINABLE ANNUITY. An annuity, or annual payment of a certain sum, which ceases at the expiration of a specified time, or upon the death of an individual. (See ANNUITY.)

TERMINATING BUILDING SOCIETY. A society which, by its rules, is to terminate at a fixed date, or when a result specified in its rules is attained. (See BUILDING SOCIETY.)

TESTING CLAUSE. (See ATTESTATION.)

THALER. (See FOREIGN MONEYS—GERMANY.)

THIRD OF EXCHANGE. (See BILL IN A SET.)

THREEPENCE. A silver coin with a standard weight of 21·81818 grains troy. (See COINAGE.)

TICKET DAY. Also called Name Day. The title of the second day in a settlement on the London Stock Exchange when brokers pass the names of the purchasers of stocks since the last settlement, certain "tickets" being exchanged preparatory for the following day, which is pay day. (See SETTLING DAYS, STOCK EXCHANGE.)

TIGHT. The word is sometimes used in connection with the money market, when money is dear and not easily obtained.

TILL. The drawer in which a cashier keeps the money that is in use. The word is also commonly used to mean all the cash and notes which are in the charge of a cashier for use at the counter, as distinguished from the stock of cash left in the safe or strong room. Each cashier is responsible for the accuracy of his own till, and he generally checks the amount of it before starting operations each morning to make certain that the amount agrees with what it was when the cash was balanced on the previous day.

TILL BOOK. The till book, or teller's or cashier's book, contains a record of the cash transactions passing through his till in the course of a day, and by it he is able to prove the accuracy of his cash at the close of business.

TIME BARGAIN. A bargain to buy or sell certain stocks or shares at a certain price on a specified date. A purchaser hopes that the security will rise before the appointed time so that he may sell at a profit.

TIME OF PAYMENT OF BILL. BILL PAYABLE ON DEMAND.—By Section 10 of the Bills of Exchange Act, 1882 :—

"(1) A bill is payable on demand :—

"(*a*) Which is expressed to be payable on demand, or at sight, or on presentation ; or

"(*b*) In which no time for payment is expressed.

"(2) Where a bill is accepted or indorsed when it is overdue, it shall, as regards the acceptor who so accepts, or any indorser who so indorses it, be deemed a bill payable on demand."

No days of grace are allowed on a bill payable on demand, at sight, or on presentation.

BILL PAYABLE AT A FUTURE DATE.—By Section 11 :—

"A bill is payable at a determinable future time within the meaning of this Act which is expressed to be payable—

"(1) At a fixed period after date or sight.

"(2) On or at a fixed period after the occurrence of a specified event which is certain to happen, though the time of happening may be uncertain.

"An instrument expressed to be payable on a contingency is not a bill, and the happening of the event does not cure the defect."

As to the computation of time of payment of a bill payable after date, the Act provides as follows :—

"14. Where a bill is not payable on demand the day on which it falls due is determined as follows :—

"(1) Three days, called days of grace, are, in every case where the bill itself does not otherwise provide, added to the time of payment as fixed by the bill, and the bill is due and payable on the last day of grace ; Provided that—

"(*a*) When the last day of grace falls on Sunday, Christmas Day, Good Friday, or a day appointed by Royal Proclamation as a public fast or thanksgiving day, the bill is, except in the case hereinafter provided for, due and payable on the preceding business day ;

"(*b*) When the last day of grace is a bank holiday (other than Christmas Day or Good Friday) under the Bank Holidays Act, 1871, and Acts amending or extending it, or when the last day of grace is a Sunday and the second day of grace is a bank holiday, the bill is due and payable on the succeeding business day.

"(2) Where a bill is payable at a fixed period after date, after sight, or after the happening of a specified event, the time of payment is determined by excluding the day from which the time is to begin to run and by including the day of payment.

"(3) Where a bill is payable at a fixed period after sight, the time begins to run from the date of the acceptance if the bill be accepted, and from the date of noting or protest if the bill be noted or protested for non-acceptance, or for non-delivery.

"(4) The term 'month' in a bill means a calendar month."

"92. Where, by this Act, the time limited for doing any act or thing is less than three days, in reckoning time, non-business days are excluded.

" 'Non-business days' for the purposes of this Act mean :—

" (a) Sunday, Good Friday, Christmas Day:

" (b) A bank holiday under the Bank Holidays Act, 1871, or Acts amending it:

" (c) A day appointed by Royal proclamation as a public fast or thanksgiving day.

" Any other day is a business day."

The due date of a bill—that is, the date when it becomes payable—is calculated, in the case of a bill drawn payable three months after date, by counting three calendar months, plus three days of grace, from the date of the bill. When drawn payable at so many days or months after sight, the date is calculated in the same way, but from the date when the bill was sighted. If the acceptor writes on the bill "sighted 1st February, accepted 2nd February," the currency is calculated from the date when it was sighted, February 1.

The following are a few examples of the calculation of the time of payment. In each case if the last day of grace is a Sunday or holiday, the bill will be due and payable either on the preceding business day or succeeding business day in accordance with the provisions of Section 14. s.s. 1 (a) and (b) (see above).

A Bill dated (or sighted) January 1, payable one month after date (or sight), is due and payable on February 4.

" " " February 1, payable one month after date (or sight), is due and payable on March 4 (if leap year it is still due March 4).

" " " February 1, payable thirty days after date (or sight), is due and payable on March 6 (if leap year on March 5).

" " " March 1, payable thirty days after date (or sight), is due and payable on April 3.

" " " April 1, payable thirty days after date (or sight), is due and payable on May 4.

" " " January 28, payable one month after date (or sight), is due and payable on March 3 (if leap year on March 2).

" " " January 29, payable one month after date (or sight), is due and payable on March 3.

" " " January 30, payable one month after date (or sight), is due and payable on March 3.

" " " January 31, payable one month after date (or sight), is due and payable on March 3.

" " " January 1, payable three weeks (=21 days) after date (or sight), is due and payable on January 25.

" " " November 28, payable three months after date (or sight), is due and payable on March 3 (if leap year on March 2).

" " " November 30, payable three months after date (or sight), is due and payable on March 3.

" " " May 31, payable one month after date (or sight), is due and payable on July 3.

" " " February 28 (following year being leap year), payable twelve months after date (or sight), is due and payable on March 2.

" " " February 29 (leap year), payable twelve months after date (or sight), is due and payable on March 3.

" " March 1, payable "one month after date, without days of grace," is due and payable on April 1.

" " March 1, payable at sight / on presentation / on demand is due and payable on demand and no days of grace are allowed.

A bill dated March 1, payable one month after date, is due and payable April 4; if accepted "payable on 1st April," present on April 1; if days of grace are then claimed, have the bill noted and give notice to the indorsers, and present again on April 4.

" " March 1, payable one month after date (if accepted "Payable at X. & Y. Bank, Leeds. J. Brown 25th February") is due and payable on April 4.

" " March 1, payable one month after *sight*, and is "accepted 2nd March, payable, etc.," is due and payable on April 5.

" " March 1, payable one month after sight, and is "sighted 2nd March, accepted 3rd March, payable, etc.," is due April 5.

A bill drawn "on 1st March pay, etc.," is due and payable on March 4.

" " "on 1st March (fixed) pay, etc.," is due and payable on March 1.

The time of payment of a promissory note, drawn payable "after date," is calculated in the same way as an ordinary after date bill.

A Bank Post Bill of the Bank of England does not take days of grace (any other bill upon the Bank of England requires the three days to be added).

A foreign bill, payable in *this* country, is reckoned in the same way as an inland bill.

" " drawn in Russia on March 1 (old style) requires, when payable here, thirteen days to be added to that date, making it March 14, before reckoning the due date.

A foreign bill drawn in Russia on March 1/14, when payable here, has the due date computed from March 14.
„ „ drawn in this country on January 14 and payable in Russia requires thirteen days to be deducted before ascertaining the due date. If payable at three months, it will be due on April 1, without days of grace.

When the last day of grace falls on Sunday a bill is payable on the preceding business day.
„ „ „ Christmas Day „ „ „ „
„ „ „ Good Friday „ „ „ „
„ „ „ a day appointed by Royal proclamation as a public fast or thanksgiving day a bill is payable on the preceding business day.

(Christmas Day and Good Friday are Common Law holidays in England, but they became Bank Holidays in Scotland by the Bank Holidays Act of 1871. After that date, a bill falling due on those days was payable on the preceding business day in England, and on the succeeding business day in Scotland. This difference, however, was remedied by the Bills of Exchange Act, 1882, which makes a bill, where the last day of grace falls on those days, whether in England or in Scotland, payable on the preceding business day.)

When the last day of grace falls on		
„ „ „	England and Ireland.	Easter Monday, a bill is payable on the succeeding business day.
„ „ „	England and Ireland.	Monday in Whitsun week „ „ „ „
„ „ „	England and Ireland.	First Monday in August „ „ „ „
„ „ „	England and Ireland.	December 26 (if a week day) „ „ „
„ „ „	England and Ireland.	December 27 (if 26th is a Sunday) „ „ „
„ „ „	Scotland.	New Year's Day (if a week day) a bill is payable on the succeeding business day.
„ „ „	Scotland.	Monday after New Year's Day (if New Year's Day is a Sunday) a bill is payable on the succeeding business day.
„ „ „	Scotland.	Monday after Christmas Day (if Christmas Day is a Sunday) a bill is payable on the succeeding business day.
„ „ „	Scotland.	First Monday in May a bill is payable on the succeeding business day.
„ „ „	Scotland.	First Monday in August a bill is payable on the succeeding business day.
„ „ „		Monday Bank Holiday, a bill is payable on the Tuesday.
„ „ „		Monday Bank Holiday, Tuesday a public fast or thanksgiving day by Royal proclamation, a bill is payable on the Wednesday.
„ „ „		Tuesday a public fast or thanksgiving day by Royal proclamation, Monday Bank Holiday, a bill is payable on the Saturday.
„ „ „		Sunday, and Saturday is a Bank Holiday, a bill is payable on the Monday.
„ „ „		Saturday, a Bank Holiday, a bill is payable on the Monday.

The time of payment of bills payable in foreign countries is regulated by the laws and customs of those countries.

In France, for example, a bill which is due on a Sunday is payable on the Monday, and does not take any days of grace, and the same custom is observed in most of the other continental countries. (See BANK HOLIDAYS, BILL OF EXCHANGE, DAYS OF GRACE.)

TIME POLICY. (See MARINE INSURANCE POLICY.)

TITHES. Originally the tenth part of the annual crop or produce of stock which was paid voluntarily in support of the church. Tithes are now commuted into tithe rent charges varying according to the average price of the crops, and are payable by the owner of the land, not by the tenant.

TITLE DEEDS. A person's right or title to a piece of land is proved by the documents called "title deeds." They show in whom the legal estate is vested, and how, through a long course of years, the land has been transferred from one person to another by deed or by will, till finally it is transferred to the present owner. The present owner may have acquired his title to the land in one of several ways, he may have bought the property, or inherited it, or have had it left to him by will, or have had a present made of it, or obtained it through foreclosure of a mortgage.

The greatest interest that a person can have in land is the fee simple, that is he is the absolute owner, and a conveyance to a purchaser of freehold land will include the clause "to have and to hold all the said hereditaments . . . unto and to the use of the said John Brown in fee simple," or "unto and to the use of the said John Brown, his heirs and assigns for ever." In such a case the fee simple is vested in John Brown. In the case of an assignment of leasehold property to John Brown, John Brown has the legal estate, but the fee simple remains with the lessor; and in copyhold land the fee simple is with the lord of the manor.

The possessor of an estate in fee simple may create lesser estates out of it. He may, for example, grant a life interest, or lease it, but so long as he does not transfer the fee simple the reversion remains with him.

If John Brown lodges a parcel of deeds of a freehold estate as security, the deeds and documents should, if they are complete, show that the fee simple is vested in John Brown. The estate may in past years have been sold many times, and been mortgaged and re-conveyed, owners may have died and bequeathed it by will, or they may have died and left no will, but whatever has been done with the property the fee simple has always been vested in someone. The deeds and documents which Brown has deposited as showing his title to the fee simple should therefore, as far as they go, reveal an unbroken line of steps by which the fee simple has come to him. If, after the fee simple was conveyed to Brown, he mortgaged the land to Jones, the legal estate would then be vested in Jones subject to Brown's right to pay off the loan and have the land reconveyed to him. Brown's right to repay the money, or to redeem the land, after the time fixed in the mortgage, usually six months, is called the equity of redemption. Brown, in that case, has an equitable estate in the land, and Jones has the legal estate.

Where deeds are left as security, whether of freehold, leasehold, or copyhold land, the banker must ascertain if the legal estate in the land is held by the party pledging the deeds.

Along with the deeds there is usually, though not always, an abstract of title. The abstract is prepared by the vendor's solicitor and gives, in order of date, a summary of all the deeds, wills or other documents, and also all other particulars which are necessary to show the purchaser how his title is derived. The abstract begins with what is called the "root of title," and follows the title step by step till it reaches the vendor. When a sale is arranged it may be agreed in the contract to commence with a certain deed as the root of title, but if no special agreement is made, the purchaser has the right to require evidence of the title for the last forty years, or longer, if necessary, to find a satisfactory beginning. A title of twenty years is often accepted as sufficient. By the Vendor and Purchaser Act, 1874, recitals, statements and descriptions of facts, matters and parties contained in deeds, instruments, acts of Parliament or statutory declarations, twenty years old at the date of the contract, shall, unless and except so far as they shall be proved to be inaccurate, be taken to be sufficient evidence of the truth of such facts, matters and descriptions.

All the deeds and documents which are referred to in the abstract of title may be found in the parcel handed to the banker, but very frequently the deeds which are abstracted will not all be obtainable The abstract shows how the purchaser's title is derived, but not, necessarily, the deeds which are to be given to the purchaser. The purchaser may receive several deeds, for example, the conveyance to himself, the conveyance to the vendor and some deeds prior to the date when the vendor acquired the land; or the purchaser may perhaps receive only one deed, the conveyance from the vendor, and an abstract of title. The purchaser may look at the abstract and see how the land has been dealt with for forty years past, or for as long as has been agreed upon, but all the deeds and documents relating to the past transactions may for one reason or another be in the possession of other persons.

There are various reasons why the owner of a property may not have possession of certain prior deeds, e.g. the seller may have retained part of the property to which the deeds relate; or they may be in the hands of a mortgagee; or the property may have been purchased from one of several joint tenants, or tenants in common, or from a remainderman; or the property may, originally, have been part of a larger estate, and no prior deeds have been handed over on a sale. Where there is a defective title or document, the contract or special conditions of sale often state the defect and preclude a purchaser from raising any objection to it, and this may, in some cases, be the explanation why a defective title has been taken.

If the purchaser, through his solicitor, is satisfied with the title, after investigation or inspection of any of the abstracted documents, he usually receives an acknowledgment, either in the conveyance or by a separate document, of his right to production of the documents. Where a person retains possession of documents, and gives to another an acknowledgment in writing of the right of that other to production of those documents and to delivery of copies thereof, that acknowledgment (by Section 9 of the Conveyancing Act, 1881) shall bind the documents to which it relates in the possession or under the control of the person who retains them, and in the possession or under the control of every other person having possession or control thereof from time to time, but shall bind each individual possessor or person as long only as he has possession or control thereof; and every person so having possession or control from time to time shall be bound specifically to perform the obligations imposed under this Section by an acknowledgment, unless prevented from so doing by fire or other inevitable accident. The obligations imposed under this Section by an acknowledgment are :—

(1) To produce the documents at all reasonable times for the purpose of inspection, etc. (2) To produce them at any trial, hearing or examination in any Court, etc., for proving or supporting the title of the person entitled to request production. (3) To deliver to the person entitled true copies or extracts of the documents or any of them.

The expenses of the performance of those obligations are payable by the person requesting performance. The acknowledgment does not confer any right to damages for loss or destruction of the documents.

If the person retaining possession of the documents gives an undertaking in writing for the safe custody thereof, unless prevented from so doing by fire or other inevitable accident, and the documents are lost or destroyed, the Court may, if it thinks fit, direct an inquiry respecting the amount of damages and order payment thereof by the person liable.

When a banker receives part only of the deeds which are recited in the abstract of title, he will look to see if an acknowledgment is given for the production of the deeds necessary to complete the title. If the only deed held by the banker is a conveyance from Brown to Jones, there should be an abstract of Brown's title and an acknowledgment from him to produce the conveyance or other documents under which he obtained his title to the land. The conveyance to Jones should be duly signed and sealed by Brown (unless there are covenants it is not always signed by the purchaser) and the stamp should be examined to see that it is correct. If the land is in Yorkshire or Middlesex see that the deed bears the registrar's certificate of registration, or if in the city or county of London note if it should be registered under the Land Transfer Act.

Compare the description and quantity of the land in the conveyance to Jones with the description and quantity in the prior deeds, or as shown in the abstract or plan if there is one. It may, of course, be that Jones has purchased the land with only one house thereon, whereas an examination of the abstract may show that originally there was much more land and were many more houses. Or again the conveyance to Jones may show that he purchased land with, say, six houses, but since he bought it he may have sold several of the houses. The banker should therefore be at trouble to ascertain how many houses still remain unsold. There may be indorsements on the conveyance setting forth the facts of each sale, but it should not be forgotten that the houses may have been sold and yet no indorsement of sale appear upon the conveyance. It would appear that there is no obligation upon a solicitor to indorse a sale by Jones, upon the conveyance to Jones, though it is very desirable that it should be indorsed. A conveyance to Jones may, therefore, be for land on which has been built whole streets of houses, and, looking at the consideration, which may be for thousands of pounds, the banker may easily think at first sight that it is a most valuable security, but, after investigation and an actual inspection of the property, he may find that all that remains, to take an extreme case, is one poor house of practically no value at all.

The consideration in the last conveyance may be much smaller than in previous deeds. This may be because the last deed represents only a part of the property contained in the earlier deeds; or it may indicate that the property has suffered a serious fall in value.

Where a person is the owner of land which is built upon and land which is vacant, both close together, and conveyed (before any houses were built) under separate deeds, care should be taken that a mistake is not made by accepting the deeds of the vacant building land when it is the deeds of the houses which are to form the security.

It is well also to be careful in taking a conveyance, say to John Brown (where there is a father and a son with the same name), lest the John Brown offering the security is not the actual person to whom the property is conveyed.

A seal should be opposite each signature to a deed. It is usual, though not absolutely necessary, that the execution of the deed should be witnessed.

The banker should see that the legal estate is conveyed to Jones free from all charges or mortgages. If the land has been mortgaged it should have been reconveyed. If it previously belonged to Smith and he died, charging it in his will with the payment of various legacies, evidence that the legacies have been satisfied and all death duties paid should be produced.

Some bankers require that the title of all deeds offered as security should be investigated by their solicitors, but there are many cases in which a banker is dependent upon his own examination of the title. Where a banker knows his customer and is already well acquainted with the property represented by the deeds, and has (as often is the case in country towns) a good knowledge of the history of the property, knowing from whom it was acquired and practically all about it, he will, as a rule, feel satisfied, in taking such a security, that he is quite safe. But in the absence of such knowledge and in the presence of a title which is not entirely "plain sailing," he would not, as a rule, be justified in advancing money upon the security until he had received a report upon the title from his solicitor.

No doubt a banker may frequently scrutinise an ordinary simple title with quite satisfactory results, but if there is any difficulty at all, arising from mortgages, life interests, settlements or anything which requires special knowledge to investigate, a banker would be acting imprudently if he did not go to his solicitor for a report. It is quite possible for the property to be subject to a mortgage, life interest or some trust, without the bundle of documents handed to the banker showing any evidence thereof. A solicitor's opinion in every case would be desirable, but, in practice, this cannot always be obtained. It is well to remember that, though a deed may appear on the face of it to be all right, it is quite possible that it may not be what it appears to be, and so a layman is wise if he does not depend too much upon his own investigation of the title. The more a banker knows about the nature of the documents he is dealing with the better, but a little knowledge should not lead him to too much self-confidence.

Subject to these remarks a banker must, when he has to examine a title, do the best he can. The points to be attended to will vary according to the nature of the estate, whether freehold, leasehold, or copyhold.

Whenever possible, a banker should actually see the property which is offered to him as security, for what looks very valuable on parchment may be quite the opposite in reality.

If a bundle of old deeds is handed to the banker along with the more modern ones the old ones should not be refused, for what happened in the following case might happen again. In *Dixon* v. *Muckleston* (1872, L.R. 8 Ch. 155) certain earlier deeds of a farm were pledged with a private party for a loan, he being informed in writing that they were the title deeds of the farm, and some later deeds of the farm were lodged with bankers as security. It was held that the first deposit created an equitable charge, and that the owner of the prior charge had not been guilty of negligence.

It is possible that deeds may be handed to a banker as security which are already mortgaged to some other person. If the banker accepts them without any knowledge of the mortgage, he may find that his charge is postponed to the party holding the legal estate. But under such circumstances the banker would have a good right to maintain his claim and to say that the person holding the mortgage had been negligent, that he should have got the title deeds into his own possession and not left them in the mortgagor's hands.

There may be exceptional cases in which a borrower desires to give a charge upon a property which is included in a conveyance containing other properties in mortgage, say to Brown. If the property to be charged to the bank is not included in Brown's mortgage, the difficulty may be overcome, if thought desirable, by the deeds being placed in the hands of a trusted party to hold on behalf of Brown as regards the property in mortgage to him, and on behalf of the banker for the portion upon which he has a charge.

Some bankers accept deeds as security and do not take any document of charge, but, as a rule, a banker takes either a legal mortgage (*q.v.*) or a memorandum of deposit (*q.v.*). Where the security consists of houses there should be a fire insurance policy and the banker should see, by obtaining the receipts, that the premiums are duly paid.

It has been held that a deposit of title deeds for the purpose of securing a debt, without any document of charge whatever, is an equitable mortgage. The deeds, however, must have been deposited expressly as a security in order to give the banker a charge upon the property represented by the deeds. If a borrower should contend that the deeds were left with the banker for some other reason than for security, he may have much trouble to defend his claim, whereas if a memorandum of deposit is taken no such contention could be maintained.

If the principal deeds of a property are deposited it may suffice to create an equitable mortgage on the property, but a banker should not rely upon an imperfect security, and should, as a rule, obtain possession of all the deeds in the customer's possession. An equitable lien may also be created by a written agreement to grant a mortgage.

It should be borne in mind that if, say, Brown deposits title deeds and has already contracted with Jones for the sale of the property to him, Jones has thereby an equitable charge in the property which may rank before the bank's equitable charge, even if the bank had no notice of the sale to Jones.

A vendor has a lien upon the property for any part of the purchase money which remains unpaid, even if the conveyance says it has been paid, but if the purchaser has lodged the deeds with his banker for an advance the banker's charge will not be disturbed by the vendor's lien.

Deeds may be lodged as security by a person who has only a life interest in the property, and in such a case he can charge the property only to the extent of his life interest (see LIFE TENANT), or they may be lodged by an executor for his own private account when he has a beneficial interest in the property, but the charge is limited to the extent of that interest. (See EXECUTOR.)

Upon the death of an owner of leasehold property the legal estate vests in his personal representatives (executors or administrators). Upon the death of an owner of freehold property, since January 1, 1898 (by the Land Transfer Act, 1897), the legal estate vests also in the personal representatives. If, therefore, title deeds are offered as security by the person to whom the property has been devised by the deceased's will, or, if no will, by the heir-at-law, until the formal assent of the personal representatives has been received, the devisee or heir has only an equitable title. The assent may be given as soon as the representatives are satisfied that the property is not required in connection with the administration of the estate. But at the expiration of one year from the death, the heir or devisee may apply to the Court to compel a conveyance of the property to be made to him. (See EXECUTOR.)

In the case of copyhold property, where admission is necessary, the title does not vest in the personal representatives.

Where an agent is authorised to deposit title deeds as security, and he exceeds his authority and borrows more than he was empowered to borrow, the principal will be liable for the full amount borrowed, provided that the banker was not aware of the extent of the agent's power to borrow. As a rule, however, a banker would require clear evidence of an agent's authority to borrow and of the limits of that authority.

Where a deed is executed under a power of attorney, the power, or an attested copy thereof, should accompany the deed. The death of the donor of a power of attorney revokes it, therefore there should be evidence that the donor was alive when the deed was signed.

By Section 8 of the Real Property Limitation Act, 1874, it is provided that no action or suit or other proceeding shall be brought to recover any sum of money secured by any mortgage, judgment, or lien, or otherwise charged upon or payable out of any land or rent, at law or in equity, or any legacy, but within twelve years next after a present right to receive the same shall have accrued to some person capable of giving a discharge for or release of the same, unless in the meantime some part of the principal money, or some interest thereon, shall have been paid, or some acknowledgment of the right thereto shall have been given in writing, signed by the person by whom the same shall be payable, or his agent, to the person entitled thereto or his agent ; and in such case no such action or suit or proceeding shall be brought but within twelve years after such payment or acknowledgment, or the last of such payments or acknowledgments, if more than one, was given. A mortgagee must, therefore, take action with regard to his security within the twelve years, as explained in that Section, or he may lose his right of action altogether. It has been held that an action on the covenant to repay the mortgage debt contained in the mortgage deed must also be brought within the twelve years.

Where deeds are to be lent to a solicitor, the customer's written authority to lend them should be obtained, and the solicitor should give his undertaking to return them in the same condition.

If the customer desires that the deeds be given up to a solicitor against payment to his credit of a certain sum, or repayment of the overdraft, the authority and undertaking should be worded accordingly.

When the title deeds of a company's

property are given as security, whether mortgaged or lodged under a memorandum of deposit, or without any document of charge, the charge so created must be registered. (See COMPANIES REGISTRATION OF MORTGAGES AND CHARGES.)

In Scotland a deposit of title deeds, either with or without a memorandum of deposit, does not create an equitable mortgage, as in England. If, therefore, an advance is granted by a banker in England upon heritable (real) property in Scotland, the form of charge must conform to the law of Scotland. (See DISPOSITION ABSOLUTE.) (See VALUATION.)

TITLE DEEDS. NOTES RE TITLE. It is impracticable to detail all the points which may require attention when examining title deeds, but the following are some of the more important of them :—

There should be an ABSTRACT OF TITLE. The purchaser has the right to one unless there was a special condition in the contract to the contrary. The abstract ought to accompany the deeds, but very often it is retained by the solicitor.

The Abstract should commence with the root of title. A purchaser of a freehold is entitled to a forty years' title, but he may agree to accept a shorter, or the conditions of sale may stipulate for a shorter.

In leaseholds the lease should be abstracted even if more than forty years old.

In enfranchised lands the abstract should commence with the deed of enfranchisement.

Sort the deeds in order of date.

Compare with the abstract to see that all are there.

If there are deeds on the abstract which are not deposited, there should be an acknowledgment for production and safe custody from the person who retains possession of them, either in the purchase deed, or by a separate document.

If the abstract, showing the title of the person who deposits the deeds, is a recent one, a banker may consider that, as the title has just been overhauled by a solicitor, it will be sufficient if he sees that he holds the deeds, as per the abstract, or an acknowledgment for production, and examines the last deed.

CONVEYANCE :—

Is it signed and sealed by the vendor? and does the signature appear to be genuine? (If there are no covenants by the purchaser, it does not appear to be necessary for a purchaser to sign it.)

Is it witnessed? If in Yorkshire or Middlesex is it registered?

Is it correctly stamped? (See CONVEYANCE, INCREMENT VALUE DUTY.)

Is the land conveyed to the depositor in fee simple, or to him and his heirs for ever, free from all charges and incumbrances?

Observe carefully what follows the clause "To have and to hold . . ." It may go on to say "Subject to a certain mortgage . . ."

If it does, has the mortgage been discharged and is it with the deeds? If not with the deeds, it should be asked for. It may still be a charge on the property. Or the mortgage may be with the deeds and not have been reconveyed. This should be seen to, as until a reconveyance is obtained the legal estate is outstanding. Is the reconveyance stamped?

If there have been any mortgages since the last conveyance, have they all been discharged?

What is the consideration?

How does the amount compare with the consideration, say, forty years ago?

If more, what has caused the increase? Have houses been built?

If less, is that due to portions having been sold, or to a depreciation in the value of the property?

Are there any memoranda of sales indorsed upon the deed?

Have any sales taken place which are not indorsed upon the deed? This is a very frequent occurrence and most misleading.

Are the particulars of the property in the last deed the same as in the first abstracted deed? If not, what has caused the difference?

The last deed may show five houses, whereas the prior deeds only refer to two. Have three more been built, or the two converted into five, or have three more been purchased from another source?

If the land contained in the last deed has been obtained from several sources trace each portion separately. It is a good plan to make notes of names, dates, and quantities when trying to follow a confused title.

How is the purchaser affected by any covenants in the deed? For example, is he responsible for the making or maintenance of any roads?

Where property has passed by will and is subject to legacies, receipts for the legacies should be produced.

If the last deed is in favour, say, of the depositor's father, see copy of the testator's will. His widow may have a life interest in the property, and should in that case join in any charge. If the deceased died intestate, the widow has a life interest in one-third of the real estate. A widower has a right for life to the rents of the real estate of his deceased wife, if she died intestate and had a child by the husband and such child was capable of inheriting. (See INTESTACY.)

The legal estate of freeholds, on a death since January 1, 1898, vests in the legal representatives (executors or administrators) and the formal assent of those representatives to the devisee, or a conveyance from them to the devisee or to the heir at law, is necessary before the devisee or heir deals with the property.

Has succession duty been paid?

Is probate, or an office copy of the will, with the deeds?

In the case of annuities upon the property, if an annuitant is still living he should join in any charge.

Does the property form part of a settlement? For example, if Mrs. Mary Brown deposits deeds, and the last conveyance is to Mary Jones (her maiden name), it is quite possible that at her marriage the property may have been settled so that she cannot deal with it in any way. The trustees of the settlement ought strictly to keep the deeds in their possession, but this is not always done, and the mere fact that Mary Brown has the deeds does not of itself prove that she has power to deposit them as security.

If a mortgage from Jones to Brown is deposited to secure Brown's account, notice of the fact should be given to Jones, and the banker should ascertain from Jones what amount is still owing.

If a second mortgage from Jones to Brown is deposited to secure Brown's account, notice of the fact should be given to the first mortgagee as well as to Jones, the mortgagor, and the banker should ascertain from Jones what amount is still owing. In each case an acknowledgment of the notice should be obtained, if possible.

LEASEHOLDS :—

In addition to the above points so far as they apply :—

What is the length of the lease, and the amount of the ground rent?

Is the rent paid up to date? The receipt should be produced. A receipt for the rent means, as a rule, that all covenants have been observed up to date, except where it is a peppercorn rent.

If the lessor's licence or consent in writing to assign or mortgage is necessary, has it been obtained? (See LEASEHOLD.)

COPYHOLDS :—

As the customs of manors vary so much, inquiry should be made with regard to each manor.

Has the customer been admitted, and is there a copy admittance, signed by the steward or deputy steward of the manor?

If there is merely a chain of covenants to surrender, inquiry should be made as to the admittance.

In some cases the person who is admitted is not the actual owner and merely holds in trust for the owner.

If copy admittances only are held, ascertain if the property could be dealt with without production of those documents to the steward.

What fines are payable? and are they payable upon the death of the copyholder, or upon the death of the lord of the manor, or upon both events?

A conditional surrender entered on the rolls in favour of a nominee of the bank is the most satisfactory form in which to obtain a security over copyholds. A mortgagee can at any subsequent date perfect his title by being admitted as from the date of the surrender. (See COPYHOLD.)

CUSTOMARY :—

There is usually a conveyance, with the consent of the lord, and an admittance.

See if the conveyance bears a memorandum that the deed has been licensed by, or on behalf of, the lord.

Is the consent of the lord necessary before a valid mortgage can be effected over the property? (See CUSTOMARY PROPERTY.)

VALUE :—

See the property and identify it with the description in the deeds.

What is its saleable value ?

By whom is it occupied ?

At what rent ? If in own occupation inspect poor rate assessment and obtain gross estimated rental and rateable value. This can be obtained, without charge, by a ratepayer at the office of the clerk to the assessment committee.

What are the rates ?

Is there any ground or other rent ?

Are all houses let, and in what sort of repair ?

Is the district an improving one, or the contrary ?

Are there many houses vacant in the neighbourhood ?

Are the houses dependent for tenants mainly upon one works ?

Is there any nuisance in the neighbourhood which may affect the value of the property ?

How far is the property from a railway station ?

Is the street made and taken over by the town ?

An outlying property is often difficult to realise, and this should be considered in estimating the value.

If the security consists of mines, or works, the report of a specialist is necessary.

It should always be remembered that, in the case of a security representing a large amount, there will, as a rule, be great difficulty when the security is to be realised, in finding anyone to take it up, if indeed anyone ever is found. (See VALUATION.)

INSURANCE :—

Is all the insurable property insured in a good office ?

Is the last premium receipt with the deeds ?

It is better that the bank's name should appear in the policy.

In the case of leasehold property, does the lease stipulate that the premises must be insured in a particular company, and in the joint names of the lessor and lessee ?

CHARGE :—

Detail all, or at least the principal, deeds upon the memorandum of deposit, or the banker's legal mortgage.

If the document is signed in front of the schedule, it should also be signed after the schedule.

In the case of leasehold property which is to be assigned or demised to the bank as security, it should be ascertained if the licence, or consent in writing, of the lessor is necessary upon the occasion of an assignment or demise. If the licence is required, it should be obtained when a legal mortgage is taken, but such a stipulation may not apply if the deeds are deposited merely with a memorandum of deposit.

It must be stamped within thirty days. (See EQUITABLE MORTGAGE.)

If the charge to the bank is a second mortgage, notice should be given to the first mortgagee.

If the charge is given by a company, has it been registered ? (See REGISTRATION OF MORTGAGES AND CHARGES.) And has the company power to borrow and to give the charge ? (See COMPANIES.)

(See ABSTRACT OF TITLE, BENEFICIAL OWNER, COLLATERAL SECURITY, COPYHOLD, CUSTOMARY PROPERTY, DEED, DEED OF GIFT, EQUITABLE MORTGAGE, EQUITY OF REDEMPTION, FEE SIMPLE, FORECLOSURE, FREEHOLD, INDENTURE, JOINT TENANTS, LAND CERTIFICATE, LAND REGISTRY, LAND REGISTRY (MIDDLESEX DEEDS), LEASEHOLD, LEGAL MORTGAGE, LIEN, MEMORANDUM OF DEPOSIT, MORTGAGE, ROOT OF TITLE, TENANTS IN COMMON, YORKSHIRE REGISTRY OF DEEDS.)

TOKEN MONEY. English silver and bronze coins are token money ; that is, the value of the metal in them is less than the value attached to the coins by law. The Government makes a profit called "Seigniorage" upon the coining of silver and bronze. Silver is legal tender only to the extent of forty shillings, and bronze to the extent of one shilling. (See COINAGE.)

TOMAN. (See FOREIGN MONEYS—PERSIA.)

TONTINE POLICY. A life policy on which no bonus is payable in the event of the death of a policy holder, such bonus only vesting on the policy maturing at the end of a given period, usually fifteen or twenty years. During that term of years (the Tontine period) the policy will not have a surrender value. In the case of an ordinary endowment assurance, the bonus additions are payable in the event of the death of the assured, or on such policy maturing.

TOT UP. To sum up figures so as to

ascertain the total, or tot as it is called, for short.

TOWN CLEARING. The Town Clearing is a section of the business of the London Bankers' Clearing House, and includes the head offices of the clearing banks and most of their branches in the City. Cheques on offices included in the Town Clearing have T printed on the left-hand bottom corner. There are two Town Clearings each day, in the morning and in the afternoon. (See CLEARING HOUSE.)

TRADE BILL. A bill drawn in connection with actual trade operations. The term is used to distinguish the paper from a bank bill or from a "kite" or "accommodation bill" (*q.v.*).

TRANSFER CERTIFICATE. In the few companies which do not issue a fresh certificate upon a transfer of the shares, a transfer certificate is issued to be preserved along with the original certificate. For example, where John Brown holds ten certificates for one share each in the Kingmoor Water Company, Ltd., and he sells the shares to John Jones, the company gives Jones a transfer certificate in the following form :—I do hereby certify that a deed of transfer of ten ordinary shares, etc., in the Kingmoor Water Company, Ltd., bearing date the day of , 19 , from John Brown, of to John Jones, of , has been deposited at the office of the said Company in Carlisle, and duly registered in their books on the day of , 19 .

Secretary.

The ten old certificates and the transfer certificate are, of course, kept by Jones.

TRANSFER DAYS. The Transfer Days at the Bank of England are Monday, Tuesday, Wednesday, Thursday and Friday. Those are the days on which transfers may be made of those stocks which are registered in the books of the bank. If a transfer is made on a Saturday a fee of 2*s*. 6*d*. is charged. (See NATIONAL DEBT.)

TRANSFER OF SECURITIES (PUBLIC TRUSTEE). In addition to the information given under PUBLIC TRUSTEE (q.v.) regarding the powers and duties of the Public Trustee, bankers should note the somewhat peculiar practice of the Department in connection with the transfer of securities.

By Rule 25 of the Statutory Rules and Orders, 1907 :—

"(1) No transfer by the Public Trustee of any securities or assurance by him of any land forming part of the trust property shall be made except under the hand and official seal of the Public Trustee, or under the hand and seal of an officer of the Public Trustee authorised in writing by him to act in that behalf either generally or in any particular case.

"(2) Any such transfer or assurance by an officer so authorised shall have the same effect as if the same were made by the Public Trustee under his hand and official seal."

Sales and purchases of investments are made only upon the written order of the Public Trustee.

Where registered stocks are to be transferred to the Public Trustee, the deed of transfer is signed by the Public Trustee. If there are several accounts in his name, each account is ear-marked by a name, a letter, a figure, or a combination thereof. The ear-marking is added to the deed of transfer in the Department of the Public Trustee. The object of the ear-mark is to enable the Public Trustee to identify each holding with the particular trust to which it belongs. In the case of a joint account in the names of the Public Trustee and another person, no ear-marking is necessary as the additional name is sufficient identification, but if there are two or more joint accounts in the same names it is requisite to ear-mark them.

Banks and other companies recognise this practice, and make out separate dividend warrants for each account.

When a sale or transfer of registered stock takes place, the deed of transfer is executed by the Public Trustee. Upon a sale, the Public Trustee requires payment of the proceeds by means of a banker's draft. Upon a purchase, payment is made by the Public Trustee only when a duly certified transfer, or an executed transfer with the relative certificate attached, is delivered at the Securities Department of the Public Trustee Office or at a bank, as may be arranged.

In connection with the purchase or sale of bearer securities the Public Trustee may, upon a sale, request a banker to surrender such securities against payment of the proceeds, and, upon a purchase, may request him to make payment therefor upon delivery of the securities.

In the case of inscribed stocks, no registering authority will accept stock on behalf of the Public Trustee unless the sanction of the Public Trustee is first obtained. This sanction is given in a form of lodgment, signed by the Public Trustee or one of the principal clerks. The form is as follows :—

To the GOVERNOR AND COMPANY OF THE BANK OF ENGLAND (or other body as the case may be).

Public Trustee Office,
3 and 4 Clement's Inn,
Strand, W.C.

............19..

Authority is hereby given for the lodgment or transfer by................ to the account of the Public Trustee *re*.......... of the securities hereunder specified :—

Description of Securities.	Amount.
	£

(Signature)............
Public Trustee.

BANK CERTIFICATE OF LODGMENT ON TRANSFER.

To the Public Trustee,
3 and 4 Clement's Inn, Strand, W.C.
19..

From (name of the Company or other authority). The securities above specified have been this day lodged or transferred to the account of the Public Trustee *re*.........

For the........

(Signature)..........

In the case of transfers-out of inscribed stocks from the Public Trustee they are always effected by power of attorney, but a registering authority will not issue a form of power of attorney unless the application is accompanied by a form of transfer-out, signed by the Public Trustee or one of the principal clerks. The official form of transfer-out is as follows :—

I. DIRECTION FOR TRANSFER.

Regr. No.....

To the GOVERNOR AND COMPANY OF THE BANK OF ENGLAND (or other body as the case may be).

Public Trustee Office.
3 and 4 Clement's Inn,
Strand, W.C.

..........19..

You are hereby authorised to transfer from the account of THE PUBLIC TRUSTEE *re*........ as hereunder specified the sum of.........................

Names of Transferees.	Amount of Stock to be transferred. £ s. d.

II. BANK CERTIFICATE OF TRANSFER.

To the Public Trustee, 3 and 4 Clement's Inn, Strand, W.C.

Bank of England..........19..

The Inscribed Stocks above specified have been this day transferred as herein authorised.

For the Bank of England.
(or other authority).
(Signature)..............

The forms of lodgment and transfer-out are not required in connection with the transfers of registered stock except in the case of the Bank of England and the National Provincial Bank of England as to certain stocks of which they are registrars.

(For further information see the "Stock Exchange Official Intelligence" for 1909, page 1791.)

TRANSFER OF SHARES. The instrument of transfer of shares should be in accordance with the company's regulations. In companies formed under the Companies Clauses Consolidation Act, 1845, the transfer must be by deed ; in other companies the transfer may be under hand or under seal, according to the articles of the company.

The following is the usual form of transfer under seal :—

Certificate for £ stock has been lodged at the company's office. Date.

For the Company, Ltd.

I in consideration of the sum of paid by hereinafter called the said transferee, do hereby bargain, sell, assign and transfer to the said transferee of and in the undertaking called To hold unto the said transferee executors, administrators, and assigns, subject to the several conditions on which held the same immediately before the execution hereof ; and the said transferee do hereby agree to accept and take the said subject to the conditions aforesaid. As witness our hands and seals this day of in the year of our Lord one thousand nine hundred and .

Signed, sealed, and delivered by the above-named in the presence of

Witness's Signature
Address
Occupation

L. S.

Signed, sealed, and delivered by the above-named in the presence of

Witness's Signature
Address
Occupation

L. S.

The following is the form of transfer not under seal, as given in regulation 19 of Table A, Companies (Consolidation) Act, 1908, which a company may adopt, unless the directors approve of some other form :—

I, A.B. of in consideration of the sum of £ paid to me by C.D. of (hereinafter called " the said transferee ") do hereby transfer to the said transferee the share [*or* shares] numbered in the undertaking called the Company Limited, to hold unto the said transferee, his executors, administrators, and assigns, subject to the several conditions on which I held the same at the time of the execution thereof : and I, the said transferee, do hereby agree to take the said share [*or* shares] subject to the conditions aforesaid. As witness our hands the day of

Witness to the signatures of, etc.

In companies where Table A applies (see Section 11 under ARTICLES OF ASSOCIATION) the regulations are :—

" 20. The directors may decline to register any transfer of shares, not being fully-paid shares, to a person of whom they do not approve, and may also decline to register any transfer of shares on which the company has a lien. The directors may also suspend the registration of transfers during the fourteen days immediately preceding the ordinary general meeting in each year. The directors may decline to recognise any instrument of transfer unless—

" (*a*) a fee not exceeding two shillings and sixpence is paid to the company in respect thereof, and

" (*b*) The instrument of transfer is accompanied by the certificate of the shares to which it relates, and such other evidence as the directors may reasonably require to show the right of the transferor to make the transfer."

Certain banks and insurance companies require a special form of transfer to be used ; in some cases the forms must be filled up only by the officials of the companies, and in other cases the forms are supplied by the companies for use by these who require them.

The consideration money set forth in a transfer may differ from that which the first seller will receive, owing to sub-sales by the original buyer. The amount which is entered in the transfer is the price given by the last purchaser.

When a transfer is executed out of Great Britain the signature should be attested by H.M. Consul or Vice-Consul, a Clergyman, Magistrate, Notary Public, or by some other person holding a public position, as most companies refuse to recognise signatures not so attested. When a witness is a female, she must state whether she is a spinster, wife, or widow ; and if a wife she must give her husband's name, address and quality, profession or occupation. The date must be inserted in words and not in figures.

Contractions should not be made in a transfer, and the full names, addresses and occupations of all the parties should be given.

Shares should not be registered in the name of a minor, as he may subsequently repudiate the contract.

Country bankers are often requested to send certificates to their London office or London agents to be handed over to a broker against cash for a specified amount. They are also often requested to instruct their agents or London office to pay cash to brokers in exchange for certain securities. In either case the country banker should obtain the instructions in writing from the customer, so that there may be no misunderstanding on any point. Where the request is to take up securities, the customer should state whether payment to the broker may be made by instalments according to the value of the securities he delivers. Where a transfer and certificates are to be received, the customer should state whether a certified transfer (that is, a transfer bearing a note by the company that the certificate is in the company's office) may be accepted.

The instrument of transfer must be executed both by the transferor and transferee. When the document has been signed by the transferor he hands it, with the certificate, against payment of the purchase money, to the transferee, who also signs it and then sends the transfer and the certificate to the company's office along with the company's fee for registration in order that the shares may be registered in his name. The process is usually carried through by a broker. When a transfer is received for registration it must be carefully scrutinised and the particulars of the shares be compared with the share register. If the instrument is correctly stamped and properly filled up and executed, the company will, before issuing a new certificate, send a notice to the transferor advising him that a document of transfer purporting to be signed by him has been received and that the shares will, unless he replies by return (or within, say, three days) to the contrary, be registered in the name of the transferee. Such a notice helps to prevent a company registering a transferee upon a forged transfer. A company must, within two months after the registration of a transfer, have the new certificate ready for delivery. (See Section 92 of the Companies (Consolidation) Act, 1908, under CERTIFICATE.)

When transfers have been passed by the directors and new certificates issued, they should be filed away in such a manner that any one may be found at a moment's notice if required. A good plan is to number each one and to place the same number in the register of members opposite the name of the transferor.

In the case of shares which are not fully paid, the directors of a company should consider whether a proposed transferee is good for the liability upon the shares; that is, if the articles give the directors power to refuse to register an unsatisfactory person. If the articles do not give such power the directors cannot refuse to register a transfer.

Shares are very frequently transferred into a banker's name, or the names of his nominees, as security for a loan or overdraft. When a banker, without notice of any prior equitable charge, obtains a transfer duly executed in his own favour and gets it registered, he has a legal title to the shares or stock transferred by the instrument. When the banker is registered as the owner of shares which are not fully paid he becomes liable for any calls that may be made, which is not the case if he merely holds the certificate with a blank transfer, or does not register a completed transfer. Though registration is necessary to give a banker a legal title, he will, as a rule, be quite safe if he holds the certificate and a duly executed transfer, and gives notice to the company.

It is necessary to give notice to the company, otherwise the banker may find his security postponed to a subsequent charge. In a case of fraud it is possible for another party to get registered in front of the banker holding the certificate. It has been held that a foot-note upon a certificate to the effect that it must be surrendered before a transfer of the shares can be registered is not binding upon the company. (See CERTIFICATE.) The company may probably not accept notice, or even acknowledge receipt of the letter sending it, and it is, therefore, advisable for a banker to be able to prove that the notice was sent to the company.

A trading company very often has a lien upon its shares for any money owing by the shareholders to the company, a fact which, in some cases, may greatly affect the value of the banker's security, unless the shares are registered in his name. (See LIEN.)

Before registering shares in the bank's name, or the names of its nominees, a banker naturally ascertains if there is any liability upon the shares. The certificate, however, does not always show how much has been paid up per share, and the information must be obtained from other sources.

The transfer can be sent in to the company at any subsequent date for registration, and it is considered that it will hold good even though the transferor dies or becomes bankrupt before registration is effected. It should be noted that, though a surrender of the share certificate is necessary in nearly all cases, there are a few instances where a surrender is not necessary before a transfer can be effected. Certificates need not be produced when transferring National Bank shares, Provincial Bank of Ireland shares, and Royal Exchange Assurance Corporation stock. The Grand Junction Canal Company does not issue certificates at all.

Although a banker can, when the shares are registered in his name and he holds an authority to sell them, dispose of them, when necessary, without further reference to the transferor, it is customary to give the transferor notice of an intention to sell.

The various ways in which shares can be made available as security are :—

1. A simple deposit of the certificate, with or without notice to the company.
2. A deposit of the certificate, accompanied by a memorandum of deposit, with or without notice to the company.
3. A deposit of the certificate with a blank transfer and qualifying agreement, with or without notice to the company.
4. A deposit of the certificate with a completed transfer and qualifying agreement, with or without notice to the company.
5. Registration of the shares in the name of the bank. A qualifying agreement should be held.

Nos. 1, 2, and 3 are merely equitable charges, and may be postponed to a prior equitable charge.

No. 4 is a good security, as the legal estate can be obtained at any moment by sending in the transfer for registration.

No. 5 is, of course, the best form in which to take the security.

Although shares may be registered in the names of a bank's nominees, and those nominees be regarded by the company as the actual owners of the shares and the persons to whom dividends will be paid and who will be held liable for any calls which are made, it is, of course, understood between the customer and the bank that the transfer has been effected merely for the purposes of security and that, as soon as the necessity for the security ceases, the shares will be retransferred to the customer. To make the position clear a memorandum or agreement is signed by the customer on the same date as the transfer is signed, qualifying the deed of transfer and stating that the shares are transferred to the bank as security for all moneys owing and that the bank may, when necessary, realise the shares for the purpose of repaying any advance. All dividends received by the bank on such shares belong, of course, to the customer and will be credited to his account. When the security is no longer required the shares are retransferred to the persons entitled to them.

Where shares are transferred to a bank or the nominees of a bank as security for a loan or overdraft, the consideration which is inserted in the document of transfer is generally five shillings or ten shillings. Such a consideration is called a "nominal consideration," and the transfer requires to be impressed with a ten-shilling stamp. (See NOMINAL CONSIDERATION.)

It is important to note that if a transfer taken by a banker as security should eventually be proved to be forged, the banker may, even though the shares were transferred into his name and sold, be compelled to make good the value of the shares to the true owner. Transfers should, therefore, when possible, be signed in the presence of an official of the bank, and particularly if the shares are in the names of several persons. (See FORGED TRANSFER.)

It frequently happens that part of the shares included in a transfer which is held by a banker is sold by the customer. In such cases a fresh transfer should be taken for the shares which still remain as security. It is not sufficient to alter and initial the old transfer.

Where a company is being wound up voluntarily, every transfer of shares, made after the commencement of the winding up, except transfers made with the sanction of the liquidator, shall be void ; and in the case of a winding up by the Court, every such transfer shall, unless the Court otherwise orders, be void. (Section 205, Companies (Consolidation) Act, 1908.

A stockbroker often gives a banker security over shares which have been given to him by a client as security. (See STOCKBROKER'S LOANS.)

STAMP DUTY.

The stamps upon transfers must be impressed.

As to the duty upon a transfer of shares upon a sale see CONVEYANCE.

Where the transfer is effected merely as

security, with a nominal consideration of, say, ten shillings, the deed of transfer takes a stamp of ten shillings (see NOMINAL CONSIDERATION), and the agreement under hand, which usually accompanies it, takes a stamp of sixpence. (See Section 23, s.s. 2, Stamp Act, 1891, under AGREEMENT.) This latter stamp may be either impressed or adhesive. If the agreement is under seal it is liable to *ad valorem* duty like a mortgage. (See Section 86, s.s. 1 (*d*), under MORTGAGE.)

A transfer must be stamped within thirty days after its execution, or within thirty days from the date of its arrival in the United Kingdom.

Transfers of shares relating to property in foreign countries are, if executed in the United Kingdom, liable to stamp duty.

As to composition for stamp duty see COMPOSITION (TRANSFERS, SHARES).

By the Stamp Act, 1891, the stamp duty, with respect to transfers of shares in cost book mines is :—

	£	s.	d.
TRANSFER. Any request or authority to the purser or other officer of any mining company, conducted on the cost book system, to enter or register any transfer of any share, or part of a share, in any mine, or any notice to such purser or officer of any such transfer . . .	0	0	6

And see Section 110, as follows :—

"(1) The duty upon a request or authority to the purser or other officer of a mining company conducted on the cost book system to enter or register the transfer of any share or part of a share of the mine, and the duty upon a notice to such purser or officer of any such transfer, may be denoted by an adhesive stamp, which is to be cancelled by the person by whom the request, authority, or notice is written or executed.

"(2) Every person who writes or executes any such request, authority, or notice, not being duly stamped, and every purser or other officer of any such company who in any manner obeys, complies with, or gives effect to any such request, authority, or notice, not being duly stamped, shall incur a fine of twenty pounds."

With regard to the duty upon instruments of transfer of shares, stock and debentures, the following circular was issued by the Inland Revenue, 29th April, 1910 :—

"It has been brought to the notice of the Board of Inland Revenue on several occasions that instruments of transfer of shares, stock, and debentures, have been presented to be stamped with the fixed duty of 10*s*., although upon inquiry they were found to be properly liable to the *ad valorem* duty.

"The Board believe that, in the majority of these cases, the mistake has been due to a misapprehension of the requirements of the law. They accordingly desire to make the provisions of the law which affect this matter more generally known, in order to protect those who are responsible for seeing that the transfers are properly stamped, more especially the registering officers of public companies and municipal corporations, from penalties which may be inadvertently incurred.

"Instruments of transfer are properly stamped with the fixed duty of 10*s*. when the transaction falls within one of the following descriptions :—

(*a*) Vesting the property in trustees on the appointment of a new trustee, or the retirement of a trustee.

(*b*) A transfer, as for a nominal consideration, to a mere nominee of the transferor where no beneficial interest in the property passes.

(*c*) A transfer by way of security for a loan ; or a retransfer to the original transferor on repayment of a loan.

(*d*) A transfer to a residuary legatee of stock, etc., which forms part of the residue divisible under a will.

(*e*) A transfer to a beneficiary under a will of a *specific legacy* of stock, etc.

(*f*) A transfer of stock, etc., being the property of a person dying intestate, to the party or parties entitled to it.

"In cases (*b*) and (*c*) a certificate setting forth the facts of the transaction, signed by both the transferor and the transferee, should be required.

"As errors are believed to occur, especially in cases of transfers made in distributing the estate of a deceased person, the Board wish to point out that the fixed duty does not apply to transfers made for this purpose except when they fall within one of the descriptions (*d*), (*e*) and (*f*), mentioned above. It follows, therefore, that any transfer of stock, etc., which is made by the executors of a will in discharge, or partial discharge, *of a pecuniary legacy*, is chargeable with *ad valorem* duty at the rate of 10*s*. per cent. on the amount of the legacy, or of such part of it as is discharged by the transfer, and this amount should be set forth in the instrument as the consideration for the transfer.

"Similarly if a transfer is made on a sale, or in liquidation of a debt, or in exchange for other securities, *ad valorem* duty is payable on the value or agreed value of the consideration.

"Under the provisions of the Finance (1909–10) Act, 1910, a transfer of any shares, stock or marketable security by way of gift *intervivos* is chargeable with *ad valorem* stamp duty at the same rate as if it were a transfer on sale, with the substitution of the value of the stock or security for the consideration. The transfer must be adjudicated.

"Transfers to or from trustees otherwise than for effectuating the appointment of a new trustee or the retirement of a trustee should be required to be adjudicated.

"Section 17 of the Stamp Act, 1891, imposes on all registering officers the duty of satisfying themselves that all instruments of transfer are adequately stamped before they admit them to registration. The Board are well aware that it is not always easy for a registering officer to determine the particular circumstances under which any such instrument which may come before him has been made, but their experience goes to show that it is generally possible to ascertain by inquiry the actual facts of the case, and they desire to urge upon all registering officers, who may have to deal with instruments purporting to be properly stamped with the fixed duty of 10*s*., the necessity of satisfying themselves that the provisions of the law have been complied with in each case, before they admit the instrument to registration.

"In any case where a registering officer has reasonable doubt whether an instrument is duly stamped, and the parties decline to give the information necessary to enable him to satisfy himself on this point, and in all cases of transfers by way of gift *inter vivos*, he should refuse to register the transfer, unless the instrument bears the Board's Adjudication Stamp. In order to obtain that stamp the parties interested must present the instrument at the office of the Solicitor, London, Edinburgh, or Dublin, as the case may be, where all needful information can be obtained."

On 17 June, 1910, a further circular was issued by the Inland Revenue, as follows:—

"With reference to the circular to secretaries of Public Companies dated 29 April last, the attention of the Board of Inland Revenue has been called to the fact that difficulty is sometimes experienced in obtaining, in the cases (*b*) and (*c*) mentioned in the circular, a certificate of the facts of the transaction signed by the transferor and transferee. The Board, therefore, desire to intimate to secretaries and other registering officers that while they consider that, as a general rule, the best form of evidence of the correctness of the fixed duty of 10*s*. borne by a transfer in such cases will be found to be a certificate signed by both the transferor and transferee, they have no objection to the receipt of other evidence, provided it shows, clearly and satisfactorily, the nature of the transaction. Where, for instance, the transferee is a well-known bank and the required certificate is given by an accredited representative of the bank, the Board would accept such a certificate without requiring the instrument to be adjudicated. A similar case is one in which a satisfactory certificate is given by a member of a stock exchange acting for one or other of the parties to the transfer.

"In any case, however, in which the registration officer is not satisfied that the transfer is duly stamped with the fixed duty of 10*s*., he should not hesitate to refer the parties to the Board."

On 5 September, 1910, another circular was issued by the authorities at Somerset House as follows:—

"With reference to the circulars to secretaries of public companies, dated the 29th April, and the 17th June last, I am directed by the Board of Inland Revenue to inform you that it has been represented to them that, with very few exceptions, transfers for nominal consideration to or from banks or their nominees clearly fall within classes excepted from the provisions of Section 74 of the Finance (1909–10) Act, 1910, imposing *ad valorem* duty, and that it is not necessary or desirable that representatives of banks, in furnishing certificates in regard to the stamp duty, should specify the facts of each particular transaction.

"In all the circumstances the Board are of opinion that, in the case of transfers of this nature executed by a well-known bank or its official nominees, the interests of the Revenue would, as a general rule, be adequately protected if registering officers were furnished with a certificate by an accredited representative of the bank to the effect that the transfer is excepted from Section 74 of the Finance (1909–10) Act, 1910, and is duly stamped.

"It is to be understood that this modification of the Board's previous circulars applies only to the case of banks, and that in other cases the requirements of those circulars should continue to be observed."

(See BLANK TRANSFER, CERTIFICATE, COMPANIES, LEEMAN'S ACT, SHARES, TRANSMISSION OF SHARES.)

TRANSFER REGISTER. A transfer register contains particulars of all the transfers of the bank's shares which are agreed to by the directors. The register is usually ruled so as to show the date of registration, the transferor's name and address, the number of shares transferred and the distinctive numbers, the number of the old certificate and the folio of the register of members where the transferor's name appears, the name, address and description of the transferee, the number of the new certificate, and the folio of the share register where the transferee's account is to be found.

It is customary to close the transfer books for a number of days prior to the general meeting. On the printed report and balance sheet of a bank there is usually, along with the announcement of the date of the general meeting, a notice to the effect that the transfer books will be closed for days, beginning on and ending with the day of the meeting.

TRANSFEREE. The person to whom shares, cheques, bills, etc., are transferred from another person (the transferor).

TRANSFEROR. The person who transfers anything, e.g. shares, cheques, bills, to another person (the transferee). (See INDORSER.)

TRANSFEROR BY DELIVERY. A transferor by delivery is defined by the Bills of Exchange Act, Section 58, as follows :—

"(1) Where the holder of a bill payable to bearer negotiates it by delivery without indorsing it, he is called a 'transferor by delivery.'

"(2) A transferor by delivery is not liable on the instrument.

"(3) A transferor by delivery who negotiates a bill thereby warrants to his immediate transferee being a holder for value that the bill is what it purports to be, that he has a right to transfer it, and that at the time of transfer he is not aware of any act which renders it valueless."

(See BEARER, BILL OF EXCHANGE.)

TRANSMISSION OF SHARES. When a shareholder dies, the right to deal with the shares passes to the executors or administrators, who produce to the company for registration the probate of the will or the letters of administration. The date of the shareholder's death should be entered in the register with a note of the executors' or administrators' names and addresses. The probate or letters of administration should be indorsed with a note that they have been exhibited to the company.

Unless the executors or administrators request to be registered as the actual holders of the shares, they will not be liable personally for any calls which may be made. If their names are entered in the register of shareholders merely as the executors or administrators of the deceased, the estate remains liable for calls. Some companies, however, do not permit shares to stand in the names of executors or administrators. When shares are specifically left by will it is nevertheless necessary for a transfer to be executed from the executors to the legatee.

When shares are transferred by the representatives to a person to whom the shares have been left, the consideration in the transfer is merely a nominal one, say, ten shillings. The stamp duty on such a transfer is ten shillings. But if they are transferred to a legatee, who agrees to accept them instead of his cash legacy, the stamp duty is *ad valorem* and the consideration will be the price agreed upon between the representatives and the legatee.

Where a company has power to refuse to register an unsuitable person as a shareholder, it cannot avoid registering a legatee to whom shares may have been specifically bequeathed by a deceased shareholder, even if that legatee is considered quite unreliable for the liability upon the shares.

In companies where Table A applies (see Section 11 under ARTICLES OF ASSOCIATION) the regulations are :—

"21. The executors or administrators of a deceased sole holder of a share shall be the only persons recognised by the company as having any title to the share. In the case of a share registered in the names of two or more holders, the survivors or survivor, or the executors or administrators of the deceased survivor, shall be the only persons recognised by the company as having any title to the share.

"22. Any person becoming entitled to a share in consequence of the death or bankruptcy of a member shall, upon such evidence being produced as may from time to time be required by the directors, have the right, either to be registered as a member in respect of the share or, instead of being registered himself, to make such transfer of the share as the deceased or bankrupt person could have made; but the directors shall, in either case, have the same right to decline or suspend registration as they would have had in the case of a transfer of the share by the deceased or bankrupt person before the death or bankruptcy.

"23. A person becoming entitled to a share by reason of the death or bankruptcy of the holder shall be entitled to the same dividends and other advantages to which he would be entitled if he were the registered holder of the share, except that he shall not, before being registered as a member in respect of the share, be entitled in respect of it to exercise any right conferred by membership in relation to meetings of the company." (See COMPANIES, SHARES, TRANSFER OF SHARES.)

TRAVELLERS' CHEQUES. The system of travellers' cheques was inaugurated by the American Bankers' Association for the use of its members, that Association, it is stated, having contracted with the Bankers' Trust Company of New York for their issuance and for their protection.

The cheques are issued in denominations of $10, $20, $50 and $100, tinted respectively in blue, green, straw and orange.

The idea is that, if the cheques are in proper order, they will be cashed by bankers, hotels and others.

According to the instructions issued by the Association :—

The holder may identify himself by signing his name in ink in your presence in the space left for that purpose upon the face of the cheque. The signature must correspond with the holder's signature which was placed upon the cheque at the time of its purchase in the place designated for that purpose.

Ordinarily the line following the words "pay to the order of" on the cheque will be left blank. In such cases the name of the bank or hotel company or other party cashing the cheque should be filled in, thus making the cheque payable directly to the party who cashes same; in which case the holder need not indorse the cheque, his counter signature being all that is necessary. Should the name of the holder have been written on the face of the cheque following the words "pay to the order of" it will then be necessary for him to indorse the cheque as well as to countersign it.

Parties presenting cheques for encashment should receive the face amount, or its nominated equivalent in countries especially mentioned upon the face of the cheque, and in all other countries the equivalent of the sterling amount at the current rate of exchange.

In the case of doubt as to the authenticity of the cheque, if it is held up to the light certain planchettes will be seen, and no cheque is genuine without them. Planchettes, it is explained, are small discs in three colours embedded in the pulp of the paper at the time of its manufacture.

The form of the cheque is as follows :—

$20 American Bankers' Association $20
Travellers' Cheque.

Bankers' Trust Company,
New York City.

No.

Current in all parts

When countersigned below with this signature, at any time within two years from date , to wit

19 .

of the world.

Pay to the order of $20.00 or its equivalent as below.

Countersignature

We hereby accept the foregoing order and will pay the same, when properly negotiated through any of our correspondents named on the back hereof.
Bankers' Trust Company.
By Treasurer.

(Name of issuing bank to be printed here.)

By Cashier.

At the foot of the cheque the equivalent of the $20 is given for various countries, that for Great Britain and Ireland being £4 1*s*. 8*d*.

The order is to be payable without deduction of charges, except stamp tax, out of funds to credit of drawer.

When cashed the cheque is to be forwarded for reimbursement to one of the various bankers mentioned on the back of the cheque, according to the country in which it is cashed.

Travellers' cheques are also issued in this country in precisely the same way as in America, but, of course, they are not guaranteed by any Trust Company. The cheques are for £5, £10, and £20, and are payable in various countries at the rates specified upon them, and in other countries at the current rates. A list of agents throughout the world is issued with each cheque or batch of cheques.

TREASURE TROVE. Where money, plate, or bullion is found hidden in the earth or other private place and the owner is unknown, it is termed "treasure trove" and passes into the possession of the Crown.

If similar property is found on the surface of the ground, it is not treasure trove, and the finder has a title to it against the whole world except the true owner.

TREASURY BILLS. These bills are issued by the Treasury under 40 Vict. c. 2 for money borrowed by the Government and form part of the unfunded debt of the country. They may be payable at three, or six, or nine, but not more than twelve, months from the date of the bill. By Section 5 the principal money of any Treasury bill shall be charged on and payable out of the Consolidated Fund of the United Kingdom. Section 8 says with respect to the issue of Treasury bills the following provisions shall have effect: (1) Treasury bills shall be issued by the Bank of England under the authority of a warrant from the Treasury, countersigned by the Comptroller and Auditor-General of the receipt and issue of Her Majesty's Exchequer; (2) each Treasury bill shall be for the amount directed by the Treasury.

By Section 13 the Bank of England may lend to Her Majesty upon the credit of Treasury bills, any sum or sums not exceeding in the whole the principal sums named in such bills. The first issue of Treasury bills was in 1877.

In a letter to the "Economist," November, 1909, Lord Welby explained that Treasury bills were invented by Mr. Walter Bagehot in 1877. The Chancellor of the Exchequer wished to provide certain funds by an increase of the floating debt. Mr. Bagehot's advice was asked, and he replied: "The English Treasury has the finest credit in the world, and it must learn to use it to the best advantage. A security resembling as nearly as possible a commercial bill of exchange—that is, a bill issued under discount, and falling due at certain intervals—would probably be received with favour by the money market, and would command good terms." His advice was acted upon, and the bills have continued in favour ever since.

When the Government requires to borrow upon Treasury bills an announcement for tenders appears in the *Gazette* and forms of tender may be obtained from the Bank of England. As the bills do not carry interest, they are tendered for at a discount.

The following is a specimen of a Treasury bill:—

Due *18th March*, 1910.

Treasury Bill.

Per Acts 40 Vict. c. 2 & 52 Vict. c. 6.

A
001706

£1,000. London, *18th Dec.*, 1909.

THIS TREASURY BILL entitles *
or order to payment of ONE THOUSAND POUNDS at the Bank of England out of the Consolidated Fund of the United Kingdom on the 18th day of March, 1910.

Secretary to His Majesty's Treasury.

* If this blank be not filled in, the Bill will be paid to Bearer.

TREASURY BOND. Another name for Exchequer Bond.

TREASURY NOTES. Notes issued by the Treasury of the United States, where they are a legal tender. They form part of the paper currency. The notes are mostly for small amounts, the largest denomination being $1,000.

TRIAL BALANCE. A banker usually makes a trial balance a day or so before a half-yearly balance, in order to test the accuracy of all accounts and thus help to expedite the actual balance at the close of business on the last day.

TRIAL OF THE PYX. The Pyx is a box in which are preserved samples of the coins made at the Mint. A jury of the Goldsmiths' Company, who are summoned by the Lord Chancellor, test the coins annually (called the Trial of the Pyx) to see that the legal weight and fineness of the coins are maintained.

TRUNKS. A Stock Exchange name for Grand Trunk Railway of Canada stock.

TRUST DEED FOR DEBENTURES. The debentures themselves may create a charge upon the property of the company, or there may be a separate trust deed. When there is a trust deed the company's property, freehold and leasehold, is by it vested in the trustees on behalf of the debenture holders, and power is given therein to the trustees, upon the occurrence of certain events, to enter into possession and realise the property for their benefit. It is much more convenient for the debenture holders to have two or three trustees to protect their interests, than for the debenture holders themselves to do so.

Every debenture holder has the right (on certain payments) to a copy of any trust deed. (See Section 102, s.s. 2, of the Companies (Consolidation) Act, 1908, under DEBENTURE.)

A trust deed must be registered in the company's register of mortgages and particulars delivered to the registrar of companies. (See REGISTRATION OF MORTGAGES AND CHARGES.) (See DEBENTURE.)

TRUST RECEIPT. When an advance is made against bills of lading, some banks, in certain cases, permit the customer to have possession of the bills on his signing a trust receipt, in which he acknowledges to have received the bills of lading and agrees to hold the goods as the bank's property, to keep them warehoused in the name of the bank, and, when the goods are sold, to pay the proceeds to the bank. The effect of the document is to make the customer, so far as the goods represented by the bills of lading are concerned, the trustee for the bank.

In such cases, a bank has to rely to a great extent upon the honour of his customer. If it should happen that there should be a contra account due from the customer to the purchaser of his goods, the purchaser would be entitled (not having any notice of the hypothecation to the bank) to deduct the contra account from the purchase price.

A separate account is usually opened for each operation.

In some cases the document takes the following form :—"We acknowledge receipt of the advance made by you to us (upon the security and conditions hereinafter stated) of the sum of £ value against by your paying to the above amount against documents for said goods ; and we have to request you to pass said amount with £ commission % to our debit. . . . These goods, besides being subject to your usual bankers' lien, are, in consideration of the said advance, hereby specially hypothecated to you, and a specific lien is hereby given to you thereon and on the proceeds thereof (the same being from this date out of our order and disposition) till the amount which you have paid as an advance to us against and upon security of same, with all interest, commission and charges, be paid or discharged, we hereby admitting that such advance is made on security of the hypothecation charge and lien which we hereby create on the said goods in your favour and on the express condition that all rights, property and interest to and in the said goods or proceeds are vested in you as beneficial owners. We further request you to send the bill of lading in trust to upon conditions that buyers are to make payment direct to you, and, in the event of payment being received by us instead of you, we engage to hold same as trustees for you and to pay over same to you or your order as and when and so soon as received by us, and should payment not be forthcoming from buyers before , we hereby engage to hand you cheque for full amount without notice from you."

The stamp duty is sixpence.

In *Reg.* v. *Townshend* (1884, 15 Cox. 466), where a letter of hypothecation of goods was given by a fruit broker to his bankers, in which he undertook to hold the goods in trust for the bankers and to pay over to them the proceeds as and when received, it was held that the letter was a bill of sale, being a declaration of trust without transfer. (See BILL OF SALE.)

In *In re Hamilton, Young & Co.* (1905, 2 K.B. 772), where a letter of lien, accompanied by bleachers' receipts for certain goods, was given as security, it was held that the letter was a document used in the ordinary course of business as proof of the control of goods, and therefore not a bill of sale. (See DOCUMENTARY BILL.)

TRUSTEE. A trustee is the person to whom property is intrusted in order that he may deal with it in accordance with the directions given by the creator of the trust. The person for whose benefit a trust is created is called the *cestui que trust* (plural, *cestuis que trustent*).

A trustee must take as much care of the trust property as a reasonable business man would of his own property.

Bankers avoid, as far as possible, opening accounts which give specific notice of a trust. But if John Brown and John Jones come to a banker with a request to open an account as "Trustees of R. Smith, J. Brown, J. Jones," and the banker recommends, with the idea of avoiding notice of trust, that the account should be called "John Brown and John Jones *re* R. Smith," the banker could hardly maintain, in the event of any subsequent trouble, that he was unaware that it was a trust account. As a matter of fact, accounts frequently are, by the express wish of customers, opened with a direct reference to a trust. When this is so the banker must be careful to see that every cheque is signed by all the parties who held themselves out to be trustees when the account was opened. It is not customary to inquire if the names in which the account is opened are all the trustees who were appointed in the will or trust deed. Trustees cannot delegate their authority and appoint one or more of their number to sign cheques, unless the trust deed gives them power to do so, and before accepting such an authority a banker should require to see the deed of appointment.

Trustees frequently give authorities to the various companies in which stocks and shares are held to pay the dividends thereon direct to their bankers for credit of the trustees' account. This avoids the difficulty which would otherwise arise of one trustee receiving the dividends on behalf of himself and his co-trustees.

The credit balance of an account in the name of "John Brown in trust for J. Jones," (or any similar wording giving notice of a trust), could not be held by a banker as a set off for an overdraft on John Brown's private account; neither could a banker successfully hold to an amount transferred wrongfully by John Brown from the trust account to satisfy any pressing demands of the banker for a reduction of John Brown's overdraft. A transaction of that nature would give such a plain indication of irregularity that no banker would be justified in accepting money from that source. But a banker could hold a balance on, say, a No. 2 account as a set off to the customer's overdrawn No. 1 account, even if the moneys in the No. 2 account should ultimately be proved to be trust moneys, so long as the banker had no knowledge of the fact.

In *Ex parte Kingston* (1871, 6 Ch. 632), Lord Justice Mellish said: "We are not really doing any prejudice to bankers by establishing a rule that if an account is in plain terms headed in such a way that a banker cannot fail to know it to be a trust account, the balance standing to the credit of that account will, on the bankruptcy of the person who kept it, belong to the trust." The bankruptcy of a trustee does not affect his rights to deal with the trust funds.

A banker must not be a party to a breach of trust. It has been held that if it is shown that a personal benefit to the banker is stipulated for, it will most readily establish the fact that the banker is in privity with the breach of trust.

Moneys belonging to clients and paid in to the credit of sharebrokers' or solicitors' accounts do not fix a banker with notice of a trust. Heber Hart says ("Law of Banking," p. 159): "Where a solicitor keeps two accounts with a banker, one under the head 'office account,' and another under the head 'private account,' this does not amount to notice to the banker that moneys standing to the former are trust moneys, or even put the banker upon inquiry."

With regard to securities deposited by trustees for safe custody it has been held that trustees are perfectly justified in depositing bonds payable to bearer with bankers in order that the coupons may be cut off when due and collected. Securities deposited by trustees must not be given up except under the authority of all the trustees. (See SAFE CUSTODY.)

If bearer bonds are lodged by a customer as security for an overdraft, and it ultimately transpires that the bonds do not belong to the customer but to a trust, the banker's right to the security will not be affected, provided that when he took the bonds he was in complete ignorance that they belonged to a trust. If instead of a negotiable security, as bearer bonds, the customer deposited a certificate of shares registered in his own name, along with a memorandum of deposit or a blank transfer, and the shares are eventually proved to belong to a trust, the banker will not be able to retain the security. To avoid such an unfortunate position and to have a complete security a banker should, when taking certificates, have the stock or shares registered in his own name or the names of his nominees.

Where trustees offer as security the deeds of property held by them in trust, the banker should ascertain from the trust deed exactly what powers the trustees possess with regard to charging the property.

If deeds of a trust estate are lodged as security, with a memorandum of deposit, and the banker has no notice of the trust, the equitable interest of the beneficiaries will rank in front of the equitable interest of the banker. But if the banker holds a legal mortgage his claim may take priority to that of the beneficiaries.

If a trustee himself has a beneficial interest in a trust property, his interest is subject to any claim that may arise through a breach of trust.

A bank may act as sole executor under a will, or as trustee under a will or settlement, provided that it has power to do so by its memorandum of association.

By Section 10 of the Trustee Act, 1893 :—

"(1) Where a trustee, either original or substituted, and whether appointed by a Court or otherwise, is dead, or remains out of the United Kingdom for more than twelve months, or desires to be discharged from all or any of the trusts or powers reposed in or conferred on him, or refuses or is unfit to act therein, or is incapable of acting therein, then the person or persons nominated for the purpose of appointing new trustees by the instrument, if any, creating the trust, or if there is no such person, or no such person able and willing to act, then the surviving or continuing trustees or trustee for the time being, or the personal representatives of the last surviving or continuing trustee, may, by writing, appoint another person or other persons to be a trustee or trustees in the place of the trustee dead, remaining out of the United Kingdom, desiring to be discharged, refusing, or being unfit or being incapable, as aforesaid.

"(4) The provisions of this Section relative to a trustee who is dead include the case of a person nominated trustee in a will but dying before the testator, and those relative to a continuing trustee include a refusing or retiring trustee, if willing to act in the execution of the provisions of this Section."

On the appointment of a new trustee, the number of trustees may be increased. (Section 10, s.s. 2.)

Section 17, s.s. 2 and 3, enacts :—

"(2) A trustee may appoint a banker or solicitor to be his agent to receive and give a discharge for any money payable to the trustee under or by virtue of a policy of assurance, by permitting the banker or solicitor to have the custody of and to produce the policy of assurance with a receipt signed by the trustee, and a trustee shall not be chargeable with a breach of trust by reason only of his having made or concurred in making any such appointment.

"(3) Nothing in this Section shall exempt a trustee from any liability which he would have incurred if this Act had not been passed, in case he permits any such money, valuable consideration, or property to remain in the hands or under the control of the banker or solicitor for a period longer than is reasonably necessary to enable the banker or solicitor (as the case may be) to pay or transfer the same to the trustee."

The High Court has power to appoint new trustees whenever it is found inexpedient or impracticable to appoint them without the assistance of the Court. (Section 25.)

Where any moneys or securities are deposited with a banker, and the majority of the trustees are desirous of paying or delivering the same into Court, but the concurrence of the others cannot be obtained, the Court may order payment or delivery to the majority of the trustees, for the purpose of payment into Court, and the payment and delivery shall take effect as if the same had been made on the authority of all the trustees. (Section 42, s.s. 3.) (See CUSTODIAN TRUSTEE, DEATH OF TRUSTEE, PUBLIC TRUSTEE, TRUSTEE INVESTMENTS.)

TRUSTEE IN BANKRUPTCY. When a debtor is adjudicated bankrupt, his property shall become divisible amongst his creditors, and shall vest in a trustee. (See ADJUDICATION OF BANKRUPTCY.) Until a trustee is appointed the official receiver acts as trustee.

The trustee may be appointed by the creditors, or they may leave his appointment to the committee of inspection. The trustee must give security to the satisfaction of the Board of Trade, and the Board, when satisfied, certifies that his appointment has been duly made.

The Bankruptcy Act, 1883, provides :—

Powers of Trustee to Deal with Property.

" 56. Subject to the provisions of this Act, the trustee may do all or any of the following things :—

" (1) Sell all or any part of the property of the bankrupt (including the goodwill of the business, if any, and the book debts due or growing due to the bankrupt), by public auction or private contract, with power to transfer the whole thereof to any person or company, or to sell the same in parcels :

" (2) Give receipts for any money received by him, which receipts shall effectually discharge the person paying the money from all responsibility in respect of the application thereof.

" (3) Prove, rank, claim, and draw a dividend in respect of any debt due to the bankrupt :

" (4) Exercise any powers the capacity to exercise which is vested in the trustee under this Act, and execute any powers of attorney, deeds, and other instruments for the purpose of carrying into effect the provisions of this Act :

" (5) Deal with any property to which the bankrupt is beneficially entitled as tenant in tail in the same manner as the bankrupt might have dealt with it.

Powers Exercisable by Trustee with Permission of Committee of Inspection.

" 57. The trustee may, with the permission of the committee of inspection, do all or any of the following things :—

" (1) Carry on the business of the bankrupt, so far as may be necessary for the beneficial winding up of the same :

" (2) Bring, institute, or defend any action or other legal proceeding relating to the property of the bankrupt :

" (3) Employ a solicitor or other agent to take any proceedings or do any business which may be sanctioned by the committee of inspection :

" (4) Accept as the consideration for the sale of any property of the bankrupt a sum of money payable at a future time subject to such stipulations as to security and otherwise as the committee think fit :

" (5) Mortgage or pledge any part of the property of the bankrupt for the purpose of raising money for the payment of his debts :

" (6) Refer any dispute to arbitration, compromise all debts, claims, and liabilities, whether present or future, certain or contingent, liquidated or unliquidated, subsisting or supposed to subsist between the bankrupt and any person who may have incurred any liability to the bankrupt, on the receipt of such sums, payable at such times, and generally on such terms as may be agreed on :

" (7) Make such compromise or other arrangement as may be thought expedient with creditors, or persons claiming to be creditors, in respect of any debts provable under the bankruptcy :

" (8) Make such compromise or other arrangement as may be thought expedient with respect to any claim arising out of or incidental to the property of the bankrupt, made or capable of being made on the trustee by any person or by the trustee on any person :

" (9) Divide in its existing form amongst the creditors, according to its estimated value, any property which from its peculiar nature or other special circumstances cannot be readily or advantageously sold.

The permission given for the purposes of this Section shall not be a general permission to do all or any of the above-mentioned things, but shall only be a permission to do the particular thing or things for which permission is sought in the specified case or cases.

Power to Allow Bankrupt to Manage Property.

" 64. (1) The trustee, with the permission of the committee of inspection, may appoint the bankrupt himself to superintend the management of the property of the bankrupt or of any part thereof, or to carry on the trade (if any) of the bankrupt for the benefit of his creditors, and in any other respect to aid in administering the property in such manner and on such terms as the trustee may direct.

Allowance to Bankrupt for Maintenance of Service.

" (2) The trustee may from time to time, with the permission of the committee of inspection, make such allowance as he may think just to the bankrupt out of his property for the support of the bankrupt and his family, or in consideration of his services if he is engaged in winding up his estate, but any such allowance may be reduced by the Court.

Right of Bankrupt to Surplus.

"65. The bankrupt shall be entitled to any surplus remaining after payment in full of his creditors, with interest, as by this Act provided, and of the costs, charges, and expenses of the proceedings under the bankruptcy petition."

Subject to the retention of such sums as may be necessary for the costs of administration, the trustee shall declare and distribute dividends amongst all creditors who have proved their debts. (See DIVIDENDS—IN BANKRUPTCY.)

Payment of Money into Bank of England.

"74. (1) An account called the Bankruptcy Estates Account shall be kept by the Board of Trade with the Bank of England, and all moneys received by the Board of Trade in respect of proceedings under this Act shall be paid to that account.

"(2) The account of the accountant in bankruptcy at the Bank of England shall be transferred to the Bankruptcy Estates Account.

"(3) Every trustee in bankruptcy shall, in such manner and at such times as the Board of Trade with the concurrence of the Treasury direct, pay the money received by him to the Bankruptcy Estates Account at the Bank of England, and the Board of Trade shall furnish him with a certificate of receipt of the money so paid.

"(4) Provided that if it appears to the committee of inspection that for the purpose of carrying on the debtor's business, or of obtaining advances, or because of the probable amount of the cash balance, or if the committee shall satisfy the Board of Trade that for any other reason it is for the advantage of the creditors that the trustee should have an account with a local bank, the Board of Trade shall, on the application of the committee of inspection, authorise the trustee to make his payments into and out of such local bank as the committee may select.

"Such account shall be opened and kept by the trustee in the name of the debtor's estate; and any interest receivable in respect of the account shall be part of the assets of the estate.

"The trustee shall make his payments into and out of such local bank in the prescribed manner.

"(5) Subject to any general rules relating to small bankruptcies under Part VII of this Act, where the debtor at the date of the receiving order has an account at a bank, such account shall not be withdrawn until the expiration of seven days from the day appointed for the first meeting of creditors, unless the Board of Trade, for the safety of the account, or other sufficient cause, order the withdrawal of the account.

"(6) If a trustee at any time retains for more than ten days a sum exceeding fifty pounds, or such other amount as the Board of Trade in any particular case authorise him to retain, then, unless he explains the retention to the satisfaction of the Board of Trade, he shall pay interest on the amount so retained in excess at the rate of twenty pounds per centum per annum, and shall have no claim for remuneration, and may be removed from his office by the Board of Trade, and shall be liable to pay any expenses occasioned by reason of his default.

"(7) All payments out of money standing to the credit of the Board of Trade in the Bankruptcy Estates Account shall be made by the Bank of England in the prescribed manner.

Trustee not to Pay into Private Account.

"75. No trustee in a bankruptcy or under any composition or scheme of arrangement shall pay any sums received by him as trustee into his private banking account.

Investment of Surplus Funds.

"76. (1) Whenever the cash balance standing to the credit of the Bankruptcy Estates Account is in excess of the amount which in the opinion of the Board of Trade is required for the time being to answer demands in respect of bankrupts' estates, the

Board of Trade shall notify the same to the Treasury, and shall pay over the same or any part thereof as the Treasury may require to the Treasury, to such account as the Treasury may direct, and the Treasury may invest the said sums or any part thereof in Government securities to be placed to the credit of the said account.

"(2) Whenever any part of the money so invested is, in the opinion of the Board of Trade, required to answer any demands in respect of bankrupts' estates, the Board of Trade shall notify to the Treasury the amount so required, and the Treasury shall thereupon repay to the Board of Trade such sum as may be required to the credit of the Bankruptcy Estates Account, and for that purpose may direct the sale of such part of the said securities as may be necessary.

"(3) The dividends on the investments under this Section shall be paid to such account as the Treasury may direct, and regard shall be had to the amount thus derived in fixing the fees payable in respect of bankruptcy proceedings."

By the Bankruptcy Rules :—

"No. 340. Where the trustee is authorised to have an account at a local bank, he shall forthwith pay all moneys received by him in to the credit of the estate. All payments out shall be made by cheque payable to order, and every cheque shall have marked or written on the face of it the name of the estate, and shall be signed by the trustee, and shall be countersigned by at least one member of the committee of inspection, and by such other person, if any, as the creditors or the committee of inspection may appoint."

The trustee shall, as soon as may be, take possession of the bankrupt's property. By Section 50, s.s. 6 :—

"(6) Any treasurer or other officer, or any banker, attorney, or agent of a bankrupt, shall pay and deliver to the trustee all money and securities in his possession or power, as such officer, banker, attorney, or agent, which he is not by law entitled to retain as against the bankrupt or the trustee. If he does not he shall be guilty of a contempt of Court, and may be punished accordingly on the application of the trustee."

The trustee's title dates back to the time of the act of bankruptcy upon which the receiving order was made. (See Section 43, under ADJUDICATION OF BANKRUPTCY.)

The property of a bankrupt shall vest in the trustee for the time being without any conveyance, assignment or transfer whatever. (Section 54, s.s. 3.)

The remuneration of a trustee shall be fixed by an ordinary resolution of the creditors, or if the creditors so resolve by the committee of inspection, and shall be in the nature of a commission or percentage. (Section 72, s.s. 1.)

When the trustee has realised all the property of a bankrupt, or as much as he can, and distributed a final dividend he obtains his release by an order of the Board of Trade. (Section 82.)

The creditors may, if they think fit, appoint more trustees than one. When more than one are appointed the creditors shall declare whether any act to be done by the trustees is to be done by all or any one or more of such persons. (Section 84.) (See BANKRUPTCY, COMMITTEE OF INSPECTION.)

TRUSTEE INVESTMENTS. A trustee may invest the trust funds only in certain securities. The Trustees Act, 1893, provides as follows :—

"Section 1. A trustee may, unless expressly forbidden by the instrument (if any) creating the trust, invest any trust funds in his hands, whether at the time in a state of investment or not, in manner following, that is to say :—

"(*a*) In any of the parliamentary stocks or public funds or Government securities of the United Kingdom :

"(*b*) On real or heritable securities in Great Britain or Ireland :

"(*c*) In the stock of the Bank of England or the Bank of Ireland :

"(*d*) In India Three and a half per cent. stock and India Three per cent. stock, or in any other capital stock which may at any time hereafter be issued by the Secretary of State in Council of India under the authority of Act of Parliament, and charged on the revenues of India :

"(*e*) In any securities the interest of which is for the time being guaranteed by Parliament :

"(*f*) In consolidated stock created by the Metropolitan Board of Works, or by the London County Council, or in debenture stock created by the receiver for the Metropolitan Police District:

"(*g*) In the debenture or rent charge, or guaranteed or preference stock of any railway company in Great Britain or Ireland incorporated by special Act of Parliament, and having during each of the ten years last past before the date of investment paid a dividend at the rate of not less than three per centum per annum on its ordinary stock:

"(*h*) In the stock of any railway or canal company in Great Britain or Ireland whose undertaking is leased in perpetuity or for a term of not less than two hundred years at a fixed rental to any such railway company as is mentioned in sub-section (*g*), either alone or jointly with any other railway company:

"(*i*) In the debenture stock of any railway company in India the interest on which is paid or guaranteed by the Secretary of State in Council of India:

"(*j*) In the "B" annuities of the Eastern Bengal, the East Indian, and the Scinde Punjaub and Delhi Railways, and any like annuities which may at any time hereafter be created on the purchase of any other railway by the Secretary of State in Council of India, and charged on the revenues of India, and which may be authorised by Act of Parliament to be accepted by trustees in lieu of any stock held by them in the purchased railway; also in deferred annuities comprised in the register of holders of annuity Class D and annuities comprised in the register of annuitants Class C. of the East Indian Railway Company:

"(*k*) In the stock of any railway company in India upon which a fixed or minimum dividend in sterling is paid or guaranteed by the Secretary of State in Council of India, or upon the capital of which the interest is so guaranteed:

"(*l*) In the debenture or guaranteed or preference stock of any company in Great Britain or Ireland, established for the supply of water for profit, and incorporated by special Act of Parliament or by Royal Charter, and having during each of the ten years last past before the date of investment paid a dividend of not less than five pounds per centum on its ordinary stock:

"(*m*) In nominal or inscribed stock issued, or to be issued, by the corporation of any municipal borough having, according to the returns of the last census prior to the date of investment, a population exceeding fifty thousand, or by any county council, under the authority of any Act of Parliament or Provisional Order:

"(*n*) In nominal or inscribed stock issued or to be issued by any commissioners incorporated by Act of Parliament for the purpose of supplying water, and having a compulsory power of levying rates over an area having, according to the returns of the last census prior to the date of investment, a population exceeding fifty thousand, provided that during each of the ten years last past before the date of investment the rates levied by such commissioners shall not have exceeded eighty per centum of the amount authorised by law to be levied:

"(*o*) In any of the stocks, funds, or securities for the time being authorised for the investment of cash under the control or subject to the order of the High Court,

and may also from time to time vary any such investment.

"2. (1) A trustee may under the powers of this Act invest in any of the securities mentioned or referred to in Section one of this Act, notwithstanding that the same may be redeemable, and that the price exceeds the redemption value.

"(2) Provided that a trustee may not under the powers of this Act purchase at a price exceeding its redemption value any stock mentioned or referred to in sub-sections (*g*), (*i*), (*k*), (*l*), and (*m*) of Section one, which is liable to be redeemed within fifteen years of the date of purchase at par or at some other fixed rate, or purchase any such stock as is mentioned or referred to in the sub-sections aforesaid, which is liable to be redeemed at par or at some other fixed rate, at a price exceeding fifteen per centum above par or such other fixed rate.

" (3) A trustee may retain until redemption any redeemable stock, fund, or security which may have been purchased in accordance with the powers of this Act.

" 5. (1) A trustee having power to invest in real securities, unless expressly forbidden by the instrument creating the trust, may invest and shall be deemed to have always had power to invest—

" (a) on mortgage of property held for an unexpired term of not less than two hundred years, and not subject to a reservation of rent greater than a shilling a year, or to any right of redemption or to any condition for re-entry except for non-payment of rent.

" 7. (1) A trustee, unless authorised by the terms of his trust, shall not apply for or hold any certificate to bearer issued under the authority of any of the following Acts, that is to say:

" (a) The India Stock Certificate Act, 1863;
" (b) The National Debt Act, 1870;
" (c) The Local Loans Act, 1875;
" (d) The Colonial Stock Act, 1877.

" 8. (1) A trustee lending money on the security of any property on which he can lawfully lend shall not be chargeable with breach of trust by reason only of the proportion borne by the amount of the loan to the value of the property at the time when the loan was made, provided that it appears to the Court that in making the loan the trustee was acting upon a report as to the value of the property made by a person whom he reasonably believed to be an able practical surveyor or valuer instructed and employed independently of any owner of the property, whether such surveyor or valuer carried on business in the locality where the property is situate or elsewhere, and that the amount of the loan does not exceed two equal third parts of the value of the property as stated in the report, and that the loan was made under the advice of the surveyor or valuer expressed in the report."

By Section 2 of the Colonial Stock Act, 1900, a trustee is empowered to invest in any colonial stock registered in the United Kingdom in accordance with the provisions of the Colonial Stock Acts, 1877 and 1892, as amended by this Act, provided such stocks have been notified in the *London Gazette* as having been approved by the Treasury, subject to the restrictions contained in Section 2, s.s. 2, of the Trustee Act, 1893. (See TRUSTEE.)

TRUSTEE SAVINGS BANKS. The various acts relating to savings banks were consolidated by the Trustee Savings Bank Act, 1863 (26 & 27 Vict. c. 87). Before a trustee savings bank can be formed, the sanction of the Commissioners for the Reduction of the National Debt must be obtained. A savings bank, although established prior to 1863, must be certified under the Act of 1863, so that its title would be, for example, " Whitehaven Savings Bank, established in 1818. Certified under the Act of 1863."

Treasurers, trustees, managers and other persons having direction in the management of a savings bank shall not receive any salary or profit beyond actual expenses for the purpose of the institution. Not less than two persons, and where two only, except in the case of savings banks which are open for more than six hours a week, one such person to be a trustee or manager, shall be parties to every deposit and repayment, so as to form at least a double check on all transactions with depositors.

Each depositor receives a deposit book or pass-book which must be produced every time a transaction takes place. It must also be produced once a year, after November 20, to be examined with the books of the bank. The savings banks' year ends on November 20.

A person under the age of twenty-one years is entitled to make and withdraw deposits in the same manner as other persons.

No person is allowed to deposit more than £50 in the whole in one year, and the total amount standing to the credit of a depositor must not exceed £200. A registered friendly society may deposit funds without restriction as to amount. A provident or charitable institution or a penny savings bank may deposit to extent of £100 in one year and to the extent of £300 altogether, but if the consent of the National Debt Commissioners is obtained, without restriction as to amount.

A depositor must not have a deposit in any other savings bank in Great Britain or Ireland. The rate of interest is fixed at 2½ per cent. per annum.

The trustees must pay all money belonging to the bank into the Bank of England or Ireland in the names of the Commissioners for the Reduction of the National Debt, and no sums whatever shall be deposited with any banker except such sums as shall necessarily remain in the treasurer's hands to answer the exigencies of the business.

Weekly returns must be sent to the Commissioners for the Reduction of the National Debt, showing the amounts of the week's transactions and the balance remaining in the treasurer's hands.

A bank manager is frequently the treasurer of a savings bank.

In the case of the death of a depositor whose account does not exceed £100, if the will is not proved or letters of administration taken out within two months from the depositor's death, the trustees may pay the money to the persons who shall appear to be entitled to it according to the Statute of Distributions.

Trustee savings banks are now overshadowed to a considerable extent by the Post Office Savings Bank.

TURN OF THE MARKET. On the Stock Exchange, a jobber is prepared to buy at one price and to sell at a higher, the difference between the two prices being termed the "turn of the market" or the "jobber's turn," and constituting the source of his profits.

TURN-OVER. The amount of money turned over in a business within a specified period. The turn-over in a customer's current account for a half-year is the amount which passes through the account. A banker usually takes, as the turn-over, the total of the debit column, less the balance brought forward, if a debit one, or the balance to be carried forward, if a credit one; that is, the total of the actual amount drawn out of the account.

TWOPENCE. A silver coin of that denomination is now only issued as Maundy Money (*q.v.*). Its standard weight is 14·54545 grains troy. (See COINAGE.)

UBERRIMÆ FIDEI. (Latin, of the utmost good faith.) In the case of certain contracts, especially those of insurance, it is essential that there should be the most complete disclosure of all material facts. Such contracts are classified as those of *uberrimæ fidei*.

ULTRA VIRES. That is, beyond the powers. The expression is often used in connection with the borrowing powers of a company. If the directors have power, under the memorandum and articles of association, to borrow up to a certain fixed amount, it is of vital importance that a banker, who contemplates a loan to the company, should see that, before granting the loan, the directors are not acting *ultra vires*, that is, that they are not exceeding or going beyond their powers. The directors are hedged in by the memorandum of association and beyond that hedge they cannot go. *Intra vires* means within the powers given in the memorandum.

UNCALLED CAPITAL. The capital of a company may be either fully, or only partly, called up. The part which has not been called up is the uncalled capital. The uncalled capital may consist of a portion which may be called up by the directors of the company, as required, and also, as in the case of a banking company which has adopted certain provisions of the Companies Acts, of a portion which constitutes a reserve liability and is not capable of being called up except in the event and for the purposes of the company being wound up. (See RESERVE LIABILITY.)

When debentures are issued by a company they usually include a charge upon the uncalled capital. Such a charge does not prevent the directors of the company making calls upon the shareholders as may be required for the purposes of the business. Although the uncalled capital may have been a considerable item when first the debentures were issued, it may have shrunk to a very small figure, or vanished altogether, by the time the debentures are required to be paid.

In certain cases uncalled capital may be specially assigned or hypothecated. When this is done each shareholder should be served with notice that the unpaid capital must be paid only to the person to whom it has been assigned. (See CAPITAL.)

UNCLAIMED BALANCES. The credit balances of accounts which have not been operated upon for a long time, by the persons in whose names the accounts stand in the books of the bank. According to the Statute of Limitations a dormant balance cannot, apparently, be claimed after the expiration of six years, but no banker would ever think of taking advantage of the statute. With regard to the proposals recently made that an Act should be passed making it compulsory upon bankers to hand over to the Public Trustee all credit balances which have not been operated upon for six years or upwards, as well as securities and safe custody articles left by persons with whom they have had no transactions for six years, the " Bankers' Magazine " pointed out in August, 1908, that " so long as the Statute of Limitations is part of the law of the land, all legal right to insist on payment of a balance unclaimed for six years is gone, and there can be no justification for calling on a banker to hand over to a third party the amount of a debt which he is under no legal obligation to pay to the interested party himself." If the statute does not begin to run until a cheque is presented and dishonoured, " the banker's liability to the customer is still existent, and there is here also no justification for asking the banks to hand over the money to a third party, seeing that at any time the banker may be called upon to pay the amount to the customer himself."

UNDERWRITING. An underwriter is a person who, when an issue of shares is being made by a company, agrees, in consideration of a certain commission, to apply for, or find someone else to apply for, a certain number or all of the shares which are not applied for by the public. An underwriter should, of course, be financially able to fulfil his agreement if necessary. If the shares are not favoured by the public, the underwriters may be saddled with a heavy weight of them, whereas if the issue is eagerly taken up they may receive the commission without having to apply for any shares at all.

An agreement, under hand, to underwrite requires a sixpenny stamp. If under seal the duty is ten shillings.

The provisions of the Companies (Consolidation) Act, 1908, are as follow :—

" 89. (1) It shall be lawful for a company to pay a commission to any person in consideration of his subscribing or agreeing to subscribe, whether absolutely or conditionally, for any shares in the company, or procuring or agreeing to procure subscriptions, whether absolute or conditional, for any shares in the company, if the payment of the commission is authorised by the articles, and the commission paid or agreed to be paid does not exceed the amount or rate so authorised, and if the amount or rate per cent. of the commission paid or agreed to be paid is—

" (a) In the case of shares offered to the public for subscription, disclosed in the prospectus ; or

" (b) In the case of shares not offered to the public for subscription, disclosed in the statement in lieu of prospectus, or in a statement in the prescribed form signed in like manner as a statement in lieu of prospectus and filed with the registrar of companies, and, where a circular or notice, not being a prospectus, inviting subscription for the shares is issued, also disclosed in that circular or notice.

" (2) Save as aforesaid, no company shall apply any of its shares or capital money either directly or indirectly in payment of any commission, discount, or allowance, to any person in consideration of his subscribing or agreeing to subscribe, whether absolutely or conditionally, for any shares of the company, or procuring or agreeing to procure subscriptions, whether absolute or conditional, for any shares in the company, whether the shares or money be so applied by being added to the purchase money of any property acquired by the company or to the contract price of any work to be executed for the company, or the money be paid out of the nominal purchase money or contract price, or otherwise.

" (3) Nothing in this Section shall affect the power of any company to pay such brokerage as it has heretofore been lawful for a company to pay, and a vendor to, promoter of, or other person who receives payment in money or shares from, a company shall have and shall be deemed always to have had power to apply any part of the money or shares so received in payment of any commission, the payment of which, if made directly by the company, would have been legal under this Section.

" 90. Where a company has paid any sums by way of commission in respect of any shares or debentures, or allowed any sums by way of discount in respect of any debentures, the total amount so paid or allowed, or so much thereof as has not been written off, shall be stated in every balance sheet of the company until the whole amount thereof has been written off."

The total amount of sums, if any, paid by way of commission in respect of any shares or debentures must be included in the summary to be sent to the registrar. (See Section 26 under REGISTER OF MEMBERS OF COMPANY. See also Section 81, s.s. 1 (*h*), under PROSPECTUS.) (See COMPANIES.)

UNDEVELOPED LAND DUTY. A duty imposed by the Finance (1909–10) Act, 1910 (Section 16), and payable for the year ending March 31, 1910, and every subsequent year, in respect of the site value of undeveloped land, of one halfpenny for every twenty shillings of that site value.

Land is deemed to be undeveloped if it has not been developed by the erection of dwelling-houses or of buildings for the purposes of any business, trade, or industry other than agriculture, or is not otherwise used *bonâ fide* for any business, trade, or industry other than agriculture.

Where land has been so developed or used and the buildings become derelict or the land not used for those purposes, it shall, on the expiration of one year from the time the buildings became derelict or the land not so used, be treated as undeveloped land.

Where, with a view to land being developed, an expenditure on roads or sewers has been incurred, the land shall, to the extent of one acre for every £100 of that expenditure, be treated as developed land (unless ten years have elapsed since the date of the expenditure).

Where increment value duty has been paid in respect of any undeveloped land, the site value shall, for the purposes of assessment for the undeveloped land duty, be reduced by a sum equal to five times the amount paid as increment value duty.

Undeveloped land does not include minerals.

Section 28 enacts, that the Commissioners shall, for the purpose of obtaining a periodical valuation, cause a valuation to be made of undeveloped land, in 1914 and in every subsequent fifth year.

Exemptions.

Land where the site value does not exceed £50 per acre.

Where the site value of agricultural land exceeds £50 per acre, the duty shall only be charged on the amount by which the site value exceeds the value for agricultural purposes.

Parks, etc., which are open to the public as of right.

Parks, etc., where reasonable access is enjoyed by the public.

Land which is kept free of buildings in pursuance of any definite scheme and which it is reasonably necessary in the interests of the public that it should be kept free.

Land *bonâ fide* used for games, etc., where it is so used under an agreement with the owner which, as originally made, could not be determined for a period of at least five years.

Land not exceeding an acre occupied together with a dwelling-house, or land being gardens so occupied when the site value of the gardens and the house does not exceed twenty times the annual value of the gardens and house as adopted for the purpose of income tax under Schedule A. (This exemption shall not apply so as to exempt more than 5 acres. Where there are more than 5 acres the Commissioners shall determine which five are to be exempted.)

Where agricultural land is held under a tenancy created by a lease or agreement made before April 30, 1909, no duty is to be charged on the site value during the original term of the lease or agreement while the tenancy continues thereunder.

Agricultural land, occupied and cultivated by the owner, where the total value of all land belonging to the same owner does not exceed £500. ("Owner" includes a person who holds land under a lease originally granted for fifty years or more.)

Land held for charitable purposes.

Land whilst it is held by a statutory company for the purposes of the undertaking and which cannot be appropriated except to those purposes. (Statutory company means any railway, canal, dock, or water company.)

UNDISCHARGED BANKRUPT. (See BANKRUPT PERSON.)

UNFUNDED DEBT. The unfunded debt of this country consists principally of Treasury Bills (*q.v.*) and Exchequer Bonds (*q.v.*). In each case the principal is repayable by the Government, but in the operation of "funding the unfunded debt," the principal becomes no longer repayable, and, instead, there is created the right to receive interest in perpetuity on the amount. The right to this interest, or annuity, may be sold, and has practically the same effect as selling so much stock.

UNIFICATION OF LAWS OF BILLS OF EXCHANGE. The laws relating to bills of exchange vary considerably in different countries, and though it may be impossible to make one international law to cover all the existing differences between nations, much may no doubt be done, particularly with regard to cheques, in the direction of greater uniformity.

Various rules relating to bills of exchange were recommended at the Budapest Conference of the International Law Association, on September 24th, 1908; and at the London Conference of the same Association, in 1910, seven rules with regard to cheques were recommended for adoption by all nations, and these rules as to cheques are to be laid before the Hague Conference in 1911. The recommendations would mean the adoption by foreign countries of several particulars of British practice, whilst at the same time necessitating conformity in this country with some foreign requirements. It is not to be expected, however, that all the suggested rules will find favour either with the bankers or the traders in this country.

The rules which have been recommended are as follows :—

ADOPTED AT THE BUDAPEST CONFERENCE, 1908 :—

"1. The capacity to contract by means of a Bill of Exchange shall be determined by the general capacity to enter into a contract; but a person, although incapable of binding himself by such a contract in his own country, shall also be bound if he is capable of so binding himself under the law of the country in which he contracts.

"2. To constitute a Bill of Exchange it shall be necessary to insert on the face of the instrument the words 'Bill of Exchange' or their equivalent.

"3. It shall not be obligatory to insert on the face of the instrument or on any indorsement the words 'value received' nor to state a consideration.

"4. Usances shall be abolished.

"5. It is desirable that the validity of a Bill of Exchange should not be affected by the absence or insufficiency of a stamp.

"6. A Bill of Exchange shall be deemed negotiable to order, unless restricted in express words on the face of the instrument or on an indorsement.

"7. The making of a Bill of Exchange to bearer shall be allowed.

"8 A Bill of Exchange shall be negotiable by blank indorsement.

"9. The Bill of Exchange shall not be invalid by reason that it is not dated or does not specify the place where it is drawn or the place where it is payable.

"10. The rule of law of *distantia loci* shall not apply to Bills of Exchange.

"11. The mere fact that the Bill of Exchange was overdue at the time of an indorsement shall not affect the character of this indorsement as such.

"12. The acceptance of a Bill of Exchange must be in writing on the bill itself. The signature of the drawee (without additional words) shall constitute acceptance, if written on the face of the bill.

"13. The drawee may accept for a less sum than the amount of the bill: any other restriction should be equivalent to refusal.

"14. In case of dishonour for non-acceptance or for conditional acceptance, the holder shall have an immediate right of action against the drawer, the indorsers, and any other parties liable, for payment of the amount of the bill and expenses, less discount.

"15. Where an acceptance is written on a bill, and the drawee has parted with the possession of it or has given written notice to, or according to the directions of, the person entitled to the bill, that he has accepted it, the cancellation of the acceptance shall be of no effect.

"16. Where the acceptor shall have committed an act of bankruptcy before due date, the holder shall have an immediate right of action against the drawer, the indorsers, and any other parties liable for payment of the amount of the bill and expenses, less discount.

"17. No days of grace shall be allowed.

"18. Protest, or noting for protest, according to the law of the country, shall be necessary to preserve the right of recourse upon a Bill of Exchange dishonoured for non-acceptance or for non-payment.

"19. Immediate notice of dishonour must be given; if it be not so given, the party sued shall be discharged to the extent of the loss or damage caused by the want of such notice.

"20. The time within which protest must be made shall be extended in the case of *vis maior* during the time of the cause of interruption.

"21. There shall be no obligation to give a set or a duplicate without an agreement between the parties thereto.

"But where a bill has been lost before it is overdue the person who was the holder of it shall be entitled to require of the drawer another bill of the same tenor, giving security to the drawer, if required, to indemnify him against all persons whatever, in case the bill alleged to have been lost shall be found again.

"No annulling clause need be inserted in duplicates if marked as such.

"22. The holder of a Bill of Exchange shall not be bound, in seeking recourse, by the order of succession of the indorsements, nor by any prior election.

"23. A simultaneous right of action on a Bill of Exchange shall be allowed against all or some or any one of the parties to the bill.

"24. The *donneur d'aval* (surety upon a Bill of Exchange) shall be equally liable with the person whose surety he is.

"25. The owner of a lost or destroyed Bill of Exchange has, upon giving security, a right to payment of the bill by the acceptor, and the same right against the drawer as he would have had, if the bill had not been lost or destroyed.

"26. The limitation of actions upon Bills of Exchange against all the parties shall be eighteen months from the date of the maturity of the bill.

"27. In the foregoing articles the term Bill of Exchange shall include Promissory Notes, where such interpretation is applicable, but shall not apply to cheques."

ADOPTED AT THE LONDON CONFERENCE, 1910:—

"1. It shall not be obligatory to insert into the context of a cheque an indication either of the account to be debited with the amount or of the balance out of which the payment is requested.

"2. A cheque shall be payable on demand only and shall be dated.

"3. It shall not be obligatory to write the day of date all in letters nor to have it written by the hand of the writer of the context.

"4. A cheque payable to a particular person shall be deemed payable to order, unless there are express words prohibiting transfer.

"5. Inland cheques shall be presented for payment within a fixed period limited by the law of the particular country, and this period shall run from the date of the cheque.

"Foreign cheques shall be presented for payment within the period limited for presentment of inland cheques in the country where the cheque is payable—running from the last day of the time necessary for forwarding the cheque in the usual way from the place where it is drawn to the place where it is payable.

"The consequences of non-presentment in time are regulated by the national law of the place of payment.

"6. The duty and authority of the drawee to pay a cheque shall be determined by the drawer's countermand of payment, but not by notice of the drawer's death.

"7. The provisions of the British Bills of Exchange Act relating to crossed cheques are to be maintained, and it is highly desirable that they should be accepted generally."

UNIFIED STOCK. Where several stocks, bearing different rates, are joined together to form one stock at one rate of interest, the result is termed a unified stock.

UNIT OF VALUE. The coin in any country by which the value of all the other coins are measured. The monetary unit, or unit of value, in this country is the sovereign, in France it is the franc, in India the rupee, and in the United States the dollar. (See FOREIGN MONEYS.)

UNLIMITED COMPANY. (See COMPANY—UNLIMITED.)

UNUSED STAMPS. USELESS STAMPS. (See SPOILED STAMPS.)

URBAN DISTRICT COUNCIL. The Public Health Act, 1875, provides that the Treasurer is to keep a separate account called the "District Fund Account" of all moneys carried to the account of the District Fund, and such moneys are to be applied by the Urban Authority in defraying such of the expenses chargeable thereon under the Act as they may think proper.

Orders drawn upon the Treasurer are usually signed by three members of the Council and countersigned by the clerk. A banker should be furnished with a copy of a resolution by the Council as to the manner in which orders are to be signed and with specimens of all necessary signatures. Per procuration indorsements are not accepted.

The Treasurer must keep an account in the prescribed form of all moneys received and paid by him on behalf of the Council, and must balance and sign the account quarterly, or at such other times as may be directed by the Council.

With regard to the borrowing powers of the Council, reference should be made to the Statute under which a power to borrow is obtained, so as to ascertain the extent of the power, and whether the sanction of the Local Government Board or other authority is required. If money is borrowed without power or sanction, the interest thereon will probably be disallowed by the government auditor. (See the case *Attorney-General* v. *Tottenham Urban Council* under LOCAL AUTHORITIES.)

USANCE. Usance is the period, recognised by custom, for the currency of bills drawn in one country upon another country. For example, bills on Paris are drawn at three months' date, Lisbon ninety days' date, Bombay thirty days' sight. (See COURSE OF EXCHANGE.)

USES. The term "uses" is employed when it is intended to vest the legal estate in a person. When the word "trust" is used the person takes a beneficial interest. For example, in a conveyance to John Brown, "to the use of John Brown in trust for John Jones," Brown has the legal estate and Jones the beneficial interest; if, however, the conveyance is "to John Brown to the use of John Jones," Jones takes the legal estate.

USURY. An exorbitant rate of interest charged by money lenders. Where proceedings are taken by a money lender for the recovery of money lent the Court may, upon evidence, decide that the interest charged in respect of the sum actually lent is excessive, and may relieve the person sued from payment of any sum in excess of the sum adjudged by the Court to be fairly due in respect of principal, interest and charges. (See MONEY LENDER.)

VALUATION. In endeavouring to arrive at the value of a property for the purpose of granting a loan thereon, it is necessary to ascertain as nearly as possible what it would be likely to sell for at the present moment. It may be expected that the land will, from various causes, probably increase in value within a few years, but a banker does not lend money upon a prospective value but upon its present value. Having ascertained what may safely be regarded as its present sale value, a banker then considers to what extent of that value he should advance. Mortgagees do not, as a rule, advance more than two-thirds of the value, and in some cases, owing to the particular nature of the property or the position of the borrower, not more than one-half its value. Though bankers may wisely, and for safety, be guided by the practice of ordinary mortgagees when advancing upon properties, there are frequently, with bankers, other considerations to be taken into account. It may not be possible for a banker always to make a hard and fast line and require a margin of a half or a third to be absolutely preserved, but a prudent banker considers each case on its merits and preserves a margin which he considers sufficient. In considering how much a banker should advance upon any given property he will not go very far astray if he asks himself (1) "Would I lend the amount applied for on this property out of my own pocket?" (2) "Could I, if necessary, obtain repayment of the loan out of this property either next month or in several years time?"

To arrive at the value of a property it is necessary to ascertain the gross income, and to deduct therefrom the amount of the outgoings in order to find the net income. Having ascertained the net income, that amount must, to arrive at the capital value, be multiplied by the number of years purchase which is customary in the district on a sale of a similar property. If, for example, cottage property sells, as a rule, in a certain district at ten years' purchase it is clear that if a banker, after having ascertained the net income, assessed its value on a twenty years' purchase, and lent two-thirds thereon, he would, when he required to realise, find himself in an uncomfortable position, e.g. a prudent banker would say—

Income	£30	
	10	years' purchase.
	300	
Advance two-thirds	=200	
Margin	=£100	

But if a banker (forgetting local circumstances) estimated the value on a twenty years' purchase, which he knows to be the custom in some other district, his figures would be—

Income	£30	
	20	years' purchase.
	600	
Advance two-thirds	=400	
Margin	=£200	

The property on a sale would, of course (other things being equal), realise only what is usual in the district, namely ten years' purchase on the net income, £300. The banker therefore who advanced the £200 would easily get his money back, but the banker who lent £400 would have to look elsewhere for £100.

Even where house property is usually saleable at about twenty years' purchase, a banker should for safety base his valuation on, say, a fifteen years' purchase. There is usually a considerable difference between the price paid for a property and what is obtainable on a forced sale.

If the rent of a house is, say, £30 per annum, a deduction of, say, 10 per cent. for repairs and 5 per cent. for collection of rents, etc., should be made in order to obtain the net rental.

In the case of tenement property where the rents are collected weekly, the charge for rent collection, etc., should be put at $7\frac{1}{2}$ per cent. or 10 per cent. of the rent. 10 per cent. will probably be sufficient for repairs.

In an agricultural estate the rent of farms, fields, cottages, woods, etc., should be ascertained to find the gross rental, and all outgoings such as repairs, taxes, insurance, tithe rent-charges, etc., should be deducted therefrom to arrive at the net income. Questions which may arise are: Is the rent a reasonable one, and can the tenant by cultivating the land pay the rent and live upon the profit which remains? How does the rent compare with adjacent properties? What sort of land is it, is it poor, clayey soil, or bog-land, or steep difficult land to cultivate, or good loam soil capable of good results? What buildings are there on the land, and are they suitable for a farmer? In what state of repair are they? Is there a good and satisfactory water supply? Is the supply from a river or from wells? How is the property situated with regard to a railway? How far off is the station? What is the distance from the nearest market town? (Land near a town is much more valuable than when far removed.) Is there any timber upon the land? Are the buildings, hedges and fences in a good state of repair?

These, and other questions which would be sure to arise, should be considered when examining the figures representing the gross income. With regard to repairs, if the property is not in good order a sum sufficient to put it into repair must be deducted, as well as a sum estimated as being necessary yearly to preserve the property in good condition.

If the property is leasehold the ground rent, length of term, and covenants must be taken into account. If the term is a short one the value will diminish as the date of the expiry approaches.

If the property is copyhold what fines and fees are payable? Are fines payable upon the death of the lord or upon the death of the tenant? or are they payable upon the death both of the lord and tenant? Is there a heriot (i.e. a tribute of the best beast or other chattel) payable to the lord?

The expression "years' purchase" means the number of years net income which should be paid in order to produce a certain rate per cent. The number of years is found by dividing 100 by the rate per cent. of interest which is required. For example, if an investment is required to yield 5 per cent., divide 100 by 5, and 20 is found to be the number of years' purchase which should be paid. If the net income from a property is, say, £100, then multiply that by the twenty years—

£100
20
———
£2,000

If the property is purchased for £2,000, it is clear that the purchaser, obtaining from it a net income of £100, receives 5 per cent. upon his outlay. And so with other rates—

4 per cent. = 25 years' purchase
6 per cent. = 16⅔ ,, ,,
3 per cent. = 33⅓ ,, ,, and so on.

Where a property is in the owner's own occupation, the value may be fairly judged by ascertaining from the rate books at the rate collector's or assistant overseer's office (as the case may be) the amount at which the property is assessed for rating purposes. On house property if the assessment for rates is arrived at by deducting 10 per cent. from the gross rent, and in the case of land by a deduction of 5 per cent., when the assessment figures are obtained, one-ninth of the amount must be added to the assessment, in the case of house property, and one-nineteenth added in the case of land in order to obtain the amount which may be considered the gross rental of a place which is in the owner's occupation.

For example, a valuation of an agricultural freehold estate of, say, 50 acres might be as follows:—

	£	s.	d.	£	s.	d.
Rent				70	0	0
Deduct outgoings:—						
Tithe	2	5	0			
Land Tax	0	5	0			
Insurance	0	10	0			
Repairs 5 per cent.	3	10	0			
Management 5 per cent. (Collection of rents, etc.)	3	10	0			
				10	0	0
				£60	0	0

In the above example repairs and management expenses are put at 10 per cent. of the rent. If, however, the property consisted only of buildings the repairs would usually be put at 10 per cent., and management at 5 per cent., but where, as in the case supposed, the estate consists of both land and buildings the deduction is generally 5 per cent. for repairs and 5 per cent. for management. Ten per cent. is considered a fair average deduction. If the buildings, fences, etc., are in a bad state of repair, 15 per cent. might be deducted.

The rates are paid by the tenant.

If the estate is near a town its value is often taken at thirty years' purchase, or more, but if it is in a remote district twenty years' purchase may probably be taken as its value. A valuation for estate duty must in no case exceed twenty-five years' purchase. For safety a banker might reckon a well situated estate at, say, twenty years' purchase, and one not so well situated at, say, fifteen years. In the above example the £60 net rental must be multiplied by 20 or 15 as the case may be, in order to arrive at the value. The rent of agricultural land varies considerably, say from 18*s.* to 30*s.* or 40*s.* an acre, and in exceptional cases the rent is as high as £3 an acre. A fair average rent of agricultural land may be taken as 20*s.* an acre.

Under a building lease the lessee or leaseholder is under an obligation to build upon the land, and the owner of the freehold reserves to himself a rent, called the ground rent. The value, in the country, of well secured ground rents, as an investment, is, say, from twenty to twenty-five years' purchase. In such cases the lease is for a long period, and the only point to consider is the amount of interest required from the investment as represented by giving twenty years (= 5 per cent.) or twenty-five years (= 4 per cent.) purchase. But if the term to run is short then the reversion must be taken into account; for example, if the ground rent is £10 and a house worth £1,000 has been built on the land, the land, with the house thereon, reverts to the lessor at the expiration of the lease, and if the lease has only a few years to run it is clear that that fact is a very important one in considering the value.

Valuations of coal mines, iron mines, works, factories, etc., require to be made by experts.

It is well to remember that a valuation of works as a going concern is quite a different matter from the value when the works are closed. In such a case the works may realise at a sale little more than the price of old material.

Further information regarding values is given under FARM STOCK and LICENSED PROPERTY.

The following are a few simple calculations in connection with investments :—

1. To find the price at which £100 stock bearing 5 per cent. interest must be bought to yield, say, 4 per cent. :—

$$\begin{array}{r} £100 \\ 5 \\ 4)\overline{500} \\ \overline{£125} \end{array}$$

That is, multiply the amount by the rate of interest it bears, and divide by the rate of interest required.

2. To find what interest £100 stock, bearing interest at 5 per cent., will yield when bought at a certain price, say, £150 :—

$$\begin{array}{r} £100 \\ 5 \\ 150)\overline{500} \\ £3\ \ 6s.\ \ 8d. \end{array}$$

That is, multiply the nominal amount of stock by the interest it bears and divide by the price to be paid for it.

3. In the purchase of property, divide £100 by the number of years' purchase to be paid, to find the rate per cent. which the investment will yield. The "years' purchase" equals the rent multiplied by the number of years required to make the purchase price.

4. To find the number of years' purchase to give in order to obtain a certain rate per cent., divide 100 by the rate per cent. To pay 5 per cent. the number of years would be twenty—thus :—

$$\begin{array}{r} \text{Rent } £10 \\ 20 \\ \text{Price } \overline{£200} \end{array}$$

5. Where a property has been purchased for, say, £1,000, and the rent is £50 per annum, divide the rent into the price—

$$50)\frac{1,000}{20}$$

and the quotient is the number of years' purchase which has been paid. Twenty years' purchase equals 5 per cent. (see No. 3, above). (See ADVANCES, TITLE DEEDS.)

VALUE. The value of money, or of any other commodity, is what it can be exchanged for. It has no value if it cannot be exchanged for something. A Bank of England note has value when it can be exchanged for five sovereigns or for some other amount or commodity, but in a country where bank notes are unknown it would have no value. Intrinsic value is an erroneous expression.

VALUE IN ACCOUNT. A foreign bill often terminates with such words as "value in account," "which place to account as advised," or "which place to account with or without advice." The words are merely a communication between the drawer and the acceptor, and do not affect a banker.

VALUE RECEIVED. The last words in the body of a bill are very frequently "value received," but they are not necessary to the validity of an inland bill, as it is always implied in a bill of exchange that value has been received. The words should appear on a foreign bill.

VALUED POLICY. (See MARINE INSURANCE POLICY.)

VALUER. (See APPRAISER.)

VENDOR'S SHARES. Where a private business is converted into a limited company, the vendor may receive shares instead of cash, in payment of the purchase price. The vendor's shares may rank along with the ordinary shares, or they may form the subject of special agreement as to dividend.

VESTED REMAINDER. (See REMAINDER.)

VISÉ. (French, seen.) When a passport is to be used in, say, Russia or Turkey, it is necessary that the intending traveller to those countries should get the document officially indorsed at the Russian or Turkish Consulate in London.

To visé a passport is therefore to examine and indorse it. (See PASSPORT.)

VOLUNTARY LIQUIDATION. VOLUNTARY WINDING UP. (See WINDING UP VOLUNTARILY.)

VOTES. The articles of association of a company should be perused when information is required respecting the voting power of members. In the case of a company to which the regulations in Table A apply (see Section 11 of the Companies (Consolidation) Act, 1908, under ARTICLES OF ASSOCIATION) the rules are as follow :—

"60. On a show of hands every member present in person shall have one vote. On a poll every member shall have one vote for each share of which he is the holder.

"61. In the case of joint holders the vote of the senior who tenders a vote, whether in person or by proxy, shall be accepted to the exclusion of the votes of the other joint holders ; and for this purpose seniority shall be determined by the order in which the names stand in the register of members.

"62. A member of unsound mind, or in respect of whom an order has been made by any court having jurisdiction in lunacy, may vote, whether on a show of hands or on a poll, by his committee, *curator bonis*, or other person in the nature of a committee or *curator bonis* appointed by that court, and any such committee, *curator bonis*, or other person may, on a poll, vote by proxy.

"63. No member shall be entitled to vote at any general meeting unless all calls or other sums presently payable by him in respect of shares in the company have been paid.

"64. On a poll votes may be given either personally or by proxy.

"65. The instrument appointing a proxy shall be in writing under the hand of the appointor or of his attorney duly authorised in writing, or, if the appointor is a corporation, either under the common seal, or under the hand of an officer or attorney so authorised. No person shall act as a proxy unless either he is entitled on his own behalf to be present and vote at the meeting at which he acts as proxy, or he has been appointed to act at that meeting as proxy for a corporation.

"66. The instrument appointing a proxy and the power of attorney or other authority, if any, under which it is signed or a notarially certified copy of that power or authority shall be deposited at the registered office of the company not less than forty-eight hours before the time for holding the meeting at which the person named in the instrument proposes to vote, and in default the instrument of proxy shall not be treated as valid." (See COMPANIES, PROXY, RESOLUTIONS.)

VOTING PAPER. By the Stamp Act, 1891, the stamp duty is :—

	£	s.	d.
VOTING PAPER. An instrument for the purpose of voting by any person entitled to vote at any meeting of any body exercising a public trust, or of the shareholders, or members, or contributors to the funds of any company, society, or institution	0	0	1
And see Section 80, under PROXY.			

VOUCHERS. Paying-in slips, cheques, and office debit and credit slips are included under the term vouchers. They are documents which vouch for the correctness of book entries.

There is no legal period beyond which old vouchers may be destroyed. A debt is barred by the Statute of Limitations at the end of six years, but vouchers are, for various reasons, frequently required for a longer period than six years. (See CANCELLED CHEQUES AND BILLS, WINDING UP.)

VOYAGE POLICY. (See MARINE INSURANCE POLICY.)

WADSET. An old Scots law term for a mortgage or bond and disposition in security.

The word occurs in the Stamp Act, 1891. (See under BOND.)

WAIVER. To waive a right is to relinquish or renounce all claim to it; the renunciation is termed a waiver.

WALKS. In London, cheques which are drawn upon non-clearing banks are collected by clerks called "walks clerks," and the cheques are said to be included in the "walks" collection. (CLEARING HOUSE.)

WALL STREET. The New York Stock Exchange.

WAREHOUSE-KEEPER'S CERTIFICATE, OR RECEIPT. A document issued by a warehouse-keeper stating that certain goods are held in his warehouse at the disposal of the person named. Such a certificate or receipt is not transferable and the goods are not deliverable upon its production. It is simply an acknowledgment of having received certain goods.

When the owner wishes to obtain the goods he signs a delivery order (*q.v.*); or, if desired, he may obtain a warehouse *warrant* stating that the goods are deliverable to the person named therein or to his assigns by indorsement. (See WAREHOUSE-KEEPER'S WARRANT.)

Although a receipt or certificate is usually regarded as a mere acknowledgment of the goods, the term "warehouse-keeper's certificate" is sometimes used (see Factors Act, Section 1, s.s. 4) to indicate a document which is evidence of the title of the person named therein or his assigns to the goods. (See DOCK WARRANT.)

WAREHOUSE-KEEPER'S WARRANT. WAREHOUSE WARRANT. A document issued by the keeper of a warehouse stating that the goods named therein are entered in the books and are deliverable to the person mentioned or to his assigns by indorsement.

A warehouse warrant may be in the following form :—

SUGAR WAREHOUSE.

No.

Warrant.

For
Imported in the ship from
Captain entered by
on the
Rent payable from the
Examined and entered by
Ledger Folio
Liverpool 19 .

Deliver the above-mentioned goods to or assigns, by indorsement hereon.

Warehouse-Keeper.

This warrant must be presented at the office, regularly assigned by indorsement, and all charges paid, before delivery of the goods can take place.

On the back: Deliver the within-mentioned goods to or order.

The expression "warehouse-keeper's certificate" in the Factors Act (*q.v.*) refers to such a document as is here described as a warrant.

The remarks made regarding a dock warrant (see DOCK WARRANT) apply equally to a warehouse-keeper's warrant.

WARRANT (HIS MAJESTY). By the Stamp Act, 1891, the stamp duty is :—

	£	s.	d.
WARRANT under the sign manual of His Majesty	0	10	0

WARRANT FOR GOODS. A document issued by a dock company, a warehouse-keeper, or wharfinger, stating that the goods named therein are deliverable to the person mentioned, or his assigns by indorsement. (See DOCK WARRANT, WAREHOUSE-KEEPER'S WARRANT, WHARFINGER'S WARRANT.)

The expression "warehouse-keeper's certificate" (as in the Factors Act, *q.v.*) is sometimes used instead of the expression "warehouse-keeper's warrant."

A *certificate* or *receipt* is usually regarded as a mere acknowledgment of goods, and a *warrant* as a document of title to the goods.

The terms are sometimes used rather loosely and without due regard as to whether the document is merely a receipt, or a warrant stating that the goods are held to the order of the person named or his assigns.

As to the pledging of warrants, see DOCK WARRANT.

By the Stamp Act, 1891, the stamp duty is :—

	£	s.	d.
WARRANT FOR GOODS	0	0	3

Exemptions.

(1) Any document or writing given by an inland carrier acknowledging the receipt of goods conveyed by such carrier.

(2) A weight note issued together with a duly stamped warrant, and relating solely to the same goods, wares, or merchandise.

And see Section 111 as follows :—

"(1) For the purposes of this Act the expression 'warrant for goods' means any document or writing, being evidence of the title of any person therein named, or his assigns, or the holder thereof, to the property in any goods, wares, or merchandise lying in any warehouse or dock, or upon any wharf, and signed or certified by or on behalf of the person having the custody of the goods, wares, or merchandise.

"(2) The duty upon a warrant for goods may be denoted by an adhesive stamp, which is to be cancelled by the person by whom the instrument is made, executed, or issued.

"(3) Every person who makes, executes, or issues, or receives or takes by way of security or indemnity, any warrant for goods not being duly stamped, shall incur a fine of twenty pounds."

WARRANT OF ATTORNEY. A written authority given by a debtor to a solicitor empowering the solicitor to appear in an action against the debtor and to suffer judgment for the debt to be entered up against him.

The stamp duty, by the Stamp Act, 1891, is :—

WARRANT OF ATTORNEY to confess and enter up a judgment given as a security for the payment or repayment of money, or for the transfer or retransfer of stock.

See MORTGAGE, etc.

	£	s.	d.
WARRANT OF ATTORNEY of any other kind	0	10	0

(See COGNOVIT ACTIONEM.)

WASTE BOOK. WASTE SHEETS. In the waste book the various transactions which occur in a bank office during the day are entered and split up under different headings. For example, if a customer pays in to his credit an amount consisting of cash and cheques, the full sum is entered in the "credit current accounts" column on the "cash out" side, and on the opposite side of the book, the "cash in" side, the credit is analysed, gold, silver and notes being placed in separate columns, and the cheques being separated, e.g. in a country bank, into columns for London, local, head office, country, own cheques, or such divisions as are considered necessary.

Similarly, if a cheque is cashed over the counter, the cheque is entered in the correct column on the "cash in" side and particulars of the kind of cash paid away are extended on the "cash out" side.

At the end of the day the combined totals of the one side will agree with the combined totals of the other side.

The waste book may be planned so as to balance with, and act as a check upon, the day book and the various outward remittances, etc. The columns and method of keeping the book vary somewhat in different banks.

Instead of a book some banks, for convenience, use loose sheets, called waste sheets, the sheets being bound up into book form at intervals.

WASTING ASSETS. Assets, such as mines or quarries, which become used up in course of time by working them. A mine, for example, which is being steadily worked will become less valuable year by year as the mineral is extracted. To meet this depreciation in the value of the property, a certain sum should be provided out of each year's profits. Although it is a prudent and usual course for a company to adopt, there is, however, no obligation upon the company to provide such a fund. The Court of Appeal have held "that there is no law to prevent a company from sinking its capital in the purchase of a property producing income, and dividing that income without making provision for keeping up the value of the capital, and that fixed capital may be sunk and lost and yet the excess of current receipts over current expenses may be applied in payment of a dividend, though where the income of a company arises from the turning over of circulating capital, no dividend can be paid unless the circulating capital is kept up to its original value, as otherwise there would be a payment out of capital." (*Verner* v. *General and Commercial Investment Trust*, 1894, 2 Ch. 239.)

A patent worked by a company is a wasting asset, and as it can only, as a rule, be kept alive by payment of certain fees for fourteen years, that period is called the life of the patent.

WATERED CAPITAL. WATERED STOCK. The stock, or capital, of a company is said to be "watered" when it is added to, or increased, by way of paper entries only, or when further shares are issued without any provision being made to provide interest thereon. For example, if a company with 1,000 shares on which it pays 10 per cent. increases the number to 2,000, the interest on the 2,000 will only be 5 per cent., unless arrangements are made to provide more interest.

WEIGHT-NOTE. A document issued by some dock companies giving the weight of certain goods in their possession, and stating the amount of the purchase money which is owing. The possessor of the weight-note is entitled to the warrant for the goods upon complying with the conditions of sale and paying the balance of the purchase money as expressed on the weight-note on or before the expiration of the time for payment of the purchase money.

WEIGHTS AND MEASURES.

Length.

Land Measure.

12 Inches =	1 Foot				
36 " =	3 Feet =	1 Yard.			
198 " =	16½ " =	5½ Yards =	1 Rod, Pole, or Perch.		
792 " =	66 " =	22 " =	4 Rods =	1 Chain.	
7,920 " =	660 " =	220 " =	40 " =	10 Chains =	1 Furlong
63,360 " =	5,280 " =	1,760 " =	320 " =	80 " =	8 Furlongs = 1 Mile.

Surface.

Square Measure.

144 Sq. Inches = 1 Square Foot.
1,296 ,, = 9 Sq. Feet = 1 Sq. Yard
39,204 ,, = 272¼ ,, = 30¼ Sq. Yards = 1 Sq. Rod, Pole or Perch.
627,264 ,, = 4,356 ,, = 484 ,, = 16 Sq. Rods = 1 Sq. Chain.
1,568,160 ,, = 10,890 ,, = 1,210 ,, = 40 ,, = 2½ Sq. Chains = 1 Rood
6,272,640 ,, = 43,560 ,, = 4,840 ,, = 160 ,, = 10 ,, = 4 Roods = 1 Acre

A Square Mile = 640 Acres, 2,560 Roods, 6,400 Sq. Chains, 102,400 Sq. Rods, or 3,097,600 Square Yards.

Cubic Measure.

1,728 cubic inches = 1 cubic foot.
27 cubic feet = 1 cubic yard.

Troy Weight.

17 grains = 1 carat.
24 ,, = 1 pennyweight (dwt.).
20 pennyweights = 1 ounce.
12 ounces or 5,760 grains = 1 pound.
100 pounds = 1 hundredweight.

By the Weights and Measures Act, 1878, gold and silver may be sold by the ounce troy or by any decimal parts of such ounce.

Paper Measure.

24 Sheets = 1 Quire.
25 ,, = 1 Printer's Quire.
20 Quires = 1 Ream.
21½ ,, = 1 Printer's Ream.
2 Reams = 1 Bundle.
10 ,, = 1 Bale.

WESTERNS. A Stock Exchange name for Great Western Railway ordinary stock.

WHARFINGER'S RECEIPT, OR CERTIFICATE. A document issued by a wharfinger (that is, the owner of a wharf) acknowledging receipt of goods committed to his charge, or certifying that certain goods are ready for shipment. Such a receipt or certificate is not a document of title and therefore of no value as a security.

A wharfinger's warrant stating that the goods are deliverable to the person named therein or to his assigns by indorsement, does form a document of title. (See Warehouse Warrant, Dock Warrant, Factors Act.)

WHARFINGER'S WARRANT. A document issued by a wharfinger which states that the goods named therein are deliverable to the person mentioned or his assigns by indorsement.

The remarks which apply to a dock warrant apply equally to a wharfinger's warrant. (See Dock Warrant.)

WILD CAT COMPANY. A company formed for the purpose of obtaining money from subscribers for a wild or dishonest scheme.

WILL. A writing by which an owner of property declares what is to be done with it after his death. The person making a will is called the testator. A minor cannot make a valid will.

A testator's signature should be witnessed by two persons. The following is a common attestation clause: "Signed by the said the testator in the presence of us, both present at the same time, who in his presence and at his request and in the presence of each other have hereunto set our names as witnesses."

A legatee, or his wife (or husband as the case may be), should not be a witness to the testator's signature, otherwise the legacy will be forfeited.

A codicil is an addition to a will by which some change in the terms of the will is effected, and it must be dated and signed by the testator and attested by two witnesses in the same way as the former part of the document.

The persons who are appointed by the testator to carry out the provisions of his will are called the executors, and it is their duty, after seven days from the testator's death, to obtain probate of the will; that is, an official copy of the will issued by the registrar of the registry where the will is proved. If any trusts are created by the will the persons whom the testator names to carry out the provisions of such trusts are called the trustees. A copy of a will may be seen, on payment of a fee of one shilling, at the registry where it was proved; and a copy of any will may be seen at Somerset House on payment of a like fee. A copy of a will may be obtained on payment of a fee regulated by the length of the document.

The following is a form of a simple will where a husband leaves everything whatsoever to his wife :—

This is the last will and testament of me John Brown of Carlisle in the County of Cumberland, Grocer, as follows, that is to say, I devise and bequeath all my real and personal estate whatsoever and wheresoever and of every description unto my wife Mary, her heirs, executors, administrators and assigns absolutely for ever. I appoint my said wife Mary sole executrix hereof. I revoke all prior wills by me made. In witness whereof I have hereunto set my hand this second day of July one thousand nine hundred and ten.

JOHN BROWN.

Signed by the testator as and for his last will in the presence of us who, at his request in his presence and in the presence of each other have hereunto set our names as witnesses

JOHN JONES, English Street, Carlisle, Draper.

JAMES SMITH, 2, North Street, Carlisle, Clerk.

(See EXECUTOR.)

WINDBILLS. WINDMILLS. Names sometimes given to accommodation bills (*q.v.*). Another similar name is "kites"

WINDING UP. Where a company, for any reason, has to be brought to an end, it is accomplished by "winding up," and the company is said to be "in liquidation." It may be wound up because of its inability, financially, to continue, or because of a reconstruction, or of an amalgamation with another company.

A company may be wound up in three ways. The Companies (Consolidation) Act, 1908, Section 122 provides :—

"(1) The winding up of a company may be either—

"(i) by the Court; or

"(ii) voluntary; or

"(iii) subject to the supervision of the Court.

"(2) The provisions of this Act with respect to winding up apply, unless the contrary appears, to the winding up of a company in any of those modes."

(See COMMITTEE OF INSPECTION, COMPANIES, COURT—POWERS OF, LIQUIDATOR, OFFICIAL RECEIVER, RECEIVER, STANNARIES, WINDING UP BY THE COURT, WINDING UP SUBJECT TO SUPERVISION OF THE COURT, WINDING UP UNREGISTERED COMPANIES, WINDING UP VOLUNTARILY.)

The following are some of the supplemental provisions with respect to winding up :—

"207. In the winding up of an insolvent company registered in England or Ireland the same rules shall prevail and be observed with regard to the respective rights of secured and unsecured creditors and to debts provable and to the valuation of annuities and future and contingent liabilities as are in force for the time being under the law of bankruptcy in England or Ireland, as the case may be, with respect to the estates of persons adjudged bankrupt; and all persons who in any such case would be entitled to prove for and receive dividends out of the assets of the company may come in under the winding up, and make such claims against the company as they respectively are entitled to by virtue of this Section.

Effect of Floating Charge.

"212. Where a company is being wound up, a floating charge on the undertaking or property of the company created within three months of the commencement of the winding up shall, unless it is proved that the company immediately after the creation of the charge was solvent, be invalid, except to the amount of any cash paid to the company at the time of or subsequently to the creation of, and in consideration for, the charge, together with interest on that amount at the rate of five per cent. per annum.

General Scheme of Liquidation may be Sanctioned.

"214. (1) The liquidator may, with the sanction following (that is to say)—

"(*a*) in the case of a winding up by the Court in England with the sanction either of the Court or of the committee of inspection;

"(*b*) in the case of a winding up by the Court in Scotland or Ireland, and in the case of any winding up subject to supervision, with the sanction of the Court; and

"(*c*) in the case of a voluntary winding up, with the sanction of an extraordinary resolution of the company,

do the following things or any of them:—

"(i) Pay any classes of creditors in full;

"(ii) Make any compromise or arrangement with creditors or persons claiming to be creditors, or having or alleging themselves to have any claim, present or future, certain or contingent, ascertained or sounding only in damages against the company, or whereby the company may be rendered liable;

"(iii) Compromise all calls and liabilities to calls, debts, and liabilities capable of resulting in debts, and all claims, present or future, certain or contingent, ascertained or sounding only in damages, subsisting or supposed to subsist between the company and a contributory, or alleged contributory, or other debtor or person apprehending liability to the company, and all questions in any way relating to or affecting the assets or the winding up of the company, on such terms as may be agreed, and take any security for the discharge of any such call, debt, liability or claim, and give a complete discharge in respect thereof.

"(2) In the case of a winding up by the Court in England the exercise by the liquidator of the powers of this Section shall be subject to the control of the Court, and any creditor or contributory may apply to the Court with respect to any exercise or proposed exercise of any of those powers."

With respect to the disposal of the books and papers of a company which has been dissolved, Section 222, s.s. 2, enacts:—

"(2) After five years from the dissolution of the company no responsibility shall rest on the company, or the liquidators, or any person to whom the custody of the books and papers has been committed, by reason of the same not being forthcoming to any person claiming to be interested therein."

If a liquidator has any moneys representing unclaimed or undistributed assets of the company which have remained in his hands for six months after the date of their receipt, he shall pay the same to the Companies Liquidation Account at the Bank of England. Any person claiming to be entitled to any of such moneys may apply to the Board of Trade for payment of the same.

Companies Liquidation Account Defined.

"229. (1) An account, called the Companies Liquidation Account, shall be kept by the Board of Trade with the Bank of England, and all moneys received by the Board in respect of proceedings under this Act in connection with the winding up of companies in England shall be paid to that account.

"(2) All payments out of money standing to the credit of the Board of Trade in the Companies Liquidation Account shall be made by the Bank of England in the prescribed manner.

Investment of Surplus Funds on General Account.

"230. (1) Whenever the cash balance standing to the credit of the Companies Liquidation Account is in excess of the amount which in the opinion of the Board of Trade is required for the time being to answer demands in respect of companies' estates, the Board shall notify the excess to the Treasury, and shall pay over the whole or any part of that excess as the Treasury may require, to the Treasury, to such account as the Treasury may direct, and the Treasury may invest the sums paid over, or any part thereof, in Government securities, to be placed to the credit of the said account.

"(2) When any part of the money so invested is, in the opinion of the Board of Trade, required to answer any demands in respect of companies' estates, the Board shall notify to the Treasury the amount so required, and the Treasury shall thereupon repay to the Board such sum as may be required to the credit of the Companies Liquidation Account, and for that purpose may direct the sale of such part of the said securities as may be necessary.

"(3) The dividends on investments under this Section shall be paid to such account as the Treasury may direct, and regard shall be had to the amount thus derived in fixing the fees payable in respect of proceedings in the winding up of companies in England.

Separate Accounts of Particular Estates.

"231. (1) An account shall be kept by the Board of Trade of the receipts and payments in the winding up of each company in England, and, when the cash balance standing to the credit of the account of any company is in excess of the amount which, in the opinion of the committee of inspection, is required for the time being to answer demands in respect of that company's estate, the Board shall, on the request of the committee, invest the amount not so required in Government securities, to be placed to the credit of the said account for the benefit of the company.

"(2) When any part of the money so invested is, in the opinion of the committee of inspection, required to answer any demands in respect of the estate of the company, the Board of Trade shall, on the request of the committee, raise such sum as may be required by the sale of such part of the said securities as may be necessary.

"(3) The dividends on investments under this Section shall be paid to the credit of the company.

"(4) When the balance at the credit of any company's account in the hands of the Board of Trade exceeds two thousand pounds, and the liquidator gives notice to the Board that the excess is not required for the purposes of the liquidation, the company shall be entitled to interest on the excess at the rate of two per cent. per annum." (See COMPANIES.)

WINDING UP BY THE COURT. A winding up by the Court is often called a compulsory liquidation.

Where the paid-up capital does not exceed £10,000 proceedings for a winding up may be taken in the County Court, unless the Lord Chancellor has excluded it from having jurisdiction. The Metropolitan County Courts are not included, as they have no jurisdiction in winding up. Where the capital exceeds £10,000, proceedings must be taken in the High Court, or, if the registered office of the company is situated within the jurisdiction of the Chancery Courts of the Counties Palatine of Lancaster and Durham, in the Palatine Court or High Court.

Section 129 of the Companies (Consolidation) Act, 1908, details the circumstances in which a company may be wound up by the Court:—

"129. A company may be wound up by the Court—

"(i) if the company has by special resolution resolved that the company be wound up by the Court:

"(ii) if default is made in filing the statutory report or in holding the statutory meeting:

"(iii) if the company does not commence its business within a year from its incorporation, or suspends its business for a whole year:

"(iv) if the number of members is reduced, in the case of a private company, below two, or, in the case of any other company, below seven:

"(v) if the company is unable to pay its debts:

"(vi) if the Court is of opinion that it is just and equitable that the company should be wound up.

Company when Deemed Unable to Pay its Debts.

"130. A company shall be deemed to be unable to pay its debts—

"(i) if a creditor, by assignment or otherwise, to whom the company is indebted in a sum exceeding fifty pounds then due, has served on the company, by leaving the same at its registered office, a demand under his hand requiring the company to pay the sum so due, and the company has for three weeks thereafter neglected to pay the sum, or to secure or compound for it to the reasonable satisfaction of the creditor: or

"(ii) if, in England or Ireland, execution or other process issued on a judgment decree or order of any Court in favour of a creditor of the company is returned unsatisfied in whole or in part; or

"(iii) if, in Scotland, the induciæ of a charge for payment on an extract decree, or an extract registered bond, or an extract registered protest have expired without payment being made; or

"(iv) if it is proved to the satisfaction of the Court that the company is unable to pay its debts, and, in determining whether a company is unable to pay its debts, the Court shall take into account the contingent and prospective liabilities of the company." (See COMPANIES, WINDING UP.)

WINDING UP SUBJECT TO SUPERVISION OF THE COURT. In the case of a voluntary liquidation the Court may make an order that it shall continue but subject to the supervision of the Court.

The Companies (Consolidation) Act, 1908, provides:—

"Section 199. When a company has by special or extraordinary resolution resolved to wind up voluntarily, the Court may make an order that the voluntary winding up shall continue but subject to such supervision of the Court, and with such liberty for creditors, contributories, or others to apply to the Court, and generally on such terms and conditions as the Court thinks just.

"201. The Court may, in deciding between a winding up by the Court and a winding up subject to supervision, in the appointment of liquidators, and in all other matters relating to the winding up subject to supervision, have regard to the wishes of the creditors or contributories as proved to it by any sufficient evidence." (See COMPANIES.)

WINDING UP UNREGISTERED COMPANIES. The Companies (Consolidation) Act, 1908, makes provisions regarding the winding up of unregistered companies. The expression "unregistered company" does not include a company registered under the Joint Stock Companies Acts, or the Companies Act, 1862, or the Companies (Consolidation) Act, but includes any partnership, association, or company consisting of more than seven members, and any trustee savings bank certified under the Trustee Savings Bank Act, 1863, and any limited partnership.

All the provisions of the Companies (Consolidation) Act, 1908, with respect to winding up shall apply to an unregistered company, with the following exceptions and additions:—

(1) An unregistered company shall, for the purpose of determining the Court having jurisdiction in the matter of winding up, be deemed to be registered where its principal place of business is situate.

(2) No unregistered company shall be wound up under this Act voluntarily or subject to supervision.

(3) The circumstances in which an unregistered company may be wound up are as follows (that is to say):—

(*a*) If the company is dissolved, or has ceased to carry on business, or is carrying on business only for the purpose of winding up its affairs;

(*b*) If the company is unable to pay its debts;

(*c*) If the Court is of opinion that it is just and equitable that the company should be wound up.

Section 268, s.s. 6, provides that:—

"A petition for winding up a trustee savings bank may be presented by the National Debt Commissioners, or by a commissioner appointed under the Trustee Savings Banks Act, 1887, as well as by any person authorised under the other provisions of this Act to present a petition for winding up a company." (See COMPANIES.)

WINDING UP VOLUNTARILY. A voluntary winding up, or liquidation, is one which is brought about by the resolution of the company itself. Where a solvent company desires to reconstruct, or to amalgamate with another company, it may decide to wind up and appoint a liquidator to carry such resolution into effect; but a voluntary liquidation is not confined merely to companies which are solvent.

The Companies (Consolidation) Act, 1908, provides :—

"182. A company may be wound up voluntarily—

"(1) When the period (if any) fixed for the duration of the company by the articles expires, or the event (if any) occurs, on the occurrence of which the articles provide that the company is to be dissolved, and the company in general meeting has passed a resolution requiring the company to be wound up voluntarily :

"(2) If the company resolves by special resolution that the company be wound up voluntarily :

"(3) If the company resolves by extraordinary resolution to the effect that it cannot by reason of its liabilities continue its business, and that it is advisable to wind up.

"183. A voluntary winding up shall be deemed to commence at the time of the passing of the resolution authorising the winding up.

"184. When a company is wound up voluntarily the company shall, from the commencement of the winding up, cease to carry on its business, except so far as may be required for the beneficial winding up thereof :

"Provided that the corporate state and corporate powers of the company shall, notwithstanding anything to the contrary in its articles, continue until it is dissolved.

"185. When a company has resolved by special or extraordinary resolution to wind up voluntarily, it shall give notice of the resolution by advertisement in the *Gazette*.

Consequences of Voluntary Winding Up.

"186. The following consequences shall ensue on the voluntary winding up of a company :—

"(i) The property of the company shall be applied in satisfaction of its liabilities *pari passu*, and, subject thereto, shall, unless the articles otherwise provide, be distributed among the members according to their rights and interests in the company :

"(ii) The company in general meeting shall appoint one or more liquidators for the purpose of winding up the affairs and distributing the assets of the company, and may fix the remuneration to be paid to him or them :

"(iii) On the appointment of a liquidator all the powers of the directors shall cease, except so far as the company in general meeting, or the liquidator, sanctions the continuance thereof :

"(iv) The liquidator may, without the sanction of the Court, exercise all powers by this Act given to the liquidator in a winding up by the Court :

"(v) The liquidator may exercise the powers of the Court under this Act of settling a list of contributories, and of making calls, and shall pay the debts of the company, and adjust the rights of the contributories among themselves :

"(vi) The list of contributories shall be *primâ facie* evidence of the liability of the persons named therein to be contributories :

"(vii) When several liquidators are appointed, every power hereby given may be exercised by such one or more of them as may be determined at the time of their appointment, or in default of such determination by any number not less than two :

"(viii) If from any cause whatever there is no liquidator acting, the Court may, on the application of a contributory, appoint a liquidator :

"(ix) The Court may, on cause shown, remove a liquidator, and appoint another liquidator."

The creditors have the right to apply to the Court for the appointment of a liquidator in the place of, or jointly with, the liquidator appointed by the company, or for the appointment of a committee of inspection.

As soon as the company's affairs are fully wound up, the liquidator shall lay an account of the winding up before a general meeting of the company. Within one week after the meeting the liquidator shall make a return to the registrar of companies of the holding of the meeting, and on the expiration of three months from the registration of the return the company shall be deemed to be dissolved, unless otherwise determined by the Court.

Saving for Rights of Creditors and Contributories.

"197. The voluntary winding up of a company shall not bar the right of any creditor or contributory to have it wound up by the Court, if the Court is of opinion, in the case of an application by a creditor, that the rights of the creditor or, in the case of an application by a contributory, that the rights of the contributories will be prejudiced by a voluntary winding up." (See COMPANIES, WINDING UP.)

WINDOW DRESSING. When a company arranges matters so as to make a good show in its balance sheet it is called "window dressing."

WITHOUT PREJUDICE. Where an offer is made "without prejudice" by one of the parties in a dispute, it means that if the offer is not accepted no advantage can be taken of it by either side. The phrase occurs most frequently in the communications which pass between the solicitors of litigants, when efforts are being made to settle differences without going into court. No letter that is written and headed or stated to be "without prejudice," can be used at any time so as to prejudice either party, and the same rule applies to the reply sent to a letter so marked.

WITHOUT RECOURSE. If the drawer, or an indorser, of a bill adds these words (or the equivalent "*Sans recours*") to his signature, he thereby cancels his own liability to any subsequent holder, in the event of non-payment of the bill. But an indorser who has adopted the words "without recourse" does not clear himself from liability if any signature prior to his own should prove to be a forgery.

The Bills of Exchange Act, 1882, provides that the drawer of a bill, and any indorser, may insert therein an express stipulation, (1) negativing or limiting his own liability to the holder, (2) waiving as regards himself some or all of the holder's duties. (Section 16.) (See DRAWER, INDORSER.)

WRIT. By the Stamp Act, 1891, the stamp duty is:—

WRIT—

	£	s.	d.
(1) Of Acknowledgment under the Registration of Leases (Scotland) Act, 1857 . . . . . . (2) Of Acknowledgment by any person infeft in lands in Scotland in favour of the heir or disponee of a creditor fully vested in right of an heritable security constituted by infeftment . . (3) Of Resignation and Clare Constat. . . .	0	5	0

WRIT OF ELEGIT. A writ issued by the Court directing the sheriff to take possession of a judgment debtor's lands, and to receive the rents until the debt is satisfied. (See WRIT OF FIERI FACIAS.)

WRIT OF FIERI FACIAS. Commonly called a writ of fi-fa.

A writ issued by the Court directing the sheriff to take possession of a judgment debtor's goods, in order to satisfy a debt. The sheriff is empowered to seize, in addition to "goods," money, bank notes, cheques, bills, promissory notes, and other securities for money belonging to the debtor. (See WRIT OF ELEGIT.)

WRONGFUL CONVERSION. (See CONVERSION.)

YEARS' PURCHASE. The value of property is frequently indicated as being equal to the rent for a certain number of years. For example, a house with a rental of £50 at 20 years' purchase = £1,000. If £1,000 is paid for the house, the investment (with a rental of £50) thus yields 5 per cent. The percentage is ascertained by dividing one hundred by the number of years' purchase which is given. (See VALUATION.)

YEN. (See FOREIGN MONEYS—JAPAN.)

YORK PREFERRED. A Stock Exchange name for Great Northern Railway preferred ordinary stock. (See NORA.)

YORKS. A Stock Exchange name for Great Northern Railway ordinary stock.

YORKSHIRE REGISTRY OF DEEDS. There are three places in Yorkshire for the registration of deeds and memorials:—

Northallerton for the North Riding (established 1734).

Beverley for the East Riding (established 1707). The East Riding includes Kingston-upon-Hull.

Wakefield for the West Riding (established 1703).

There is no registration for the City of York.

When deeds of land, registrable under the Yorkshire Registries Act, are received, the banker should look to see that they bear the registrar's memorandum. When a deed is registered, a note is placed upon it by the registrar as follows:—

"A copy of this Indenture" or "A memorial was registered at the Riding Registry of Deeds at the sixteenth of August, 1909, at 10.0 in the forenoon in volume page number .
" Registrar."

Where land is registered under the Land Transfer Acts (see LAND REGISTRY), it supersedes the registration of the deeds under the Yorkshire Registries Act.

A banker's mortgage or memorandum of deposit may be registered. Wills, which include freeholds, require to be registered, but letters of administration and wills of leasehold property are not registered.

Registration does not add any fresh document to the title or affect the title, but with regard to priorities (see sections below), it is of great importance to bankers, for, although a banker may hold the title deeds, if his charge is not registered it may be postponed to a second charge which is registered.

By Section 7 of the Yorkshire Registries Act, 1884, it is seen that a mere deposit of deeds, without a memorandum of deposit, may be registered :—

"Where any lien or charge on any lands within any of the three Ridings is claimed in respect of any unpaid purchase money, or by reason of any deposit of title deeds, a memorandum of such lien or charge, signed by the person against whom such lien or charge is claimed, may be registered by any person claiming to be interested therein."

Charges rank according to the date of registration. Section 14 (as amended by Section 4 of the Amending Act, 1885) provides as follows :

"Subject to the provisions of this Act, all assurances entitled to be registered under this Act shall have priority according to the date of registration thereof, and not according to the date of such assurances or of the execution thereof, and every will entitled to be registered under this Act shall have priority according to the date of the death of the testator if the date of registration thereof be within, or under this Act to be deemed to be within, a period of six months after the death of the testator, or according to the date of registration thereof, if such date of registration be not within, or under this Act to be deemed to be within, such period of six months: provided that nothing in this Act shall interfere with the priorities as between themselves of any assurances or wills the dates of registration of which may be identical.

"All priorities given by this Act shall have full effect in all Courts, except in cases of actual fraud, and all persons claiming thereunder any legal or equitable interests shall be entitled to corresponding priorities, and no such person shall lose any such priority merely in consequence of his having been affected with actual or constructive notice, except in cases of actual fraud ; but nothing in this Section contained shall operate to confer upon any person claiming without valuable consideration under any person any further priority or protection than would belong to a person under whom he claims : and any disposition of land, or charge on land, which if unregistered would be fraudulent and void, shall, notwithstanding registration, be fraudulent and void in like manner."

If, for example, Brown has a first charge upon a property, and Jones has a second charge, and Jones, although quite aware that Brown has a first charge unregistered, registers his second charge, Jones thereby secures priority, except in case of actual fraud. (In the Middlesex Deeds Registry it is different, as priority cannot be obtained by anyone registering who is aware of the existence of a prior unregistered charge.)

By Section 16 tacking is abolished in connection with land in Yorkshire :—

"In any case in which priority or protection might but for this Act have been given or allowed to any estate or interest in lands by reason or on the ground of such estate or interest being protected by or tacked to any legal or other estate or interest in such lands, no such priority or protection shall after the commencement of this Act be so given or allowed to any estate or interest in lands within the three Ridings, except as against any estate or interest which shall have existed prior to such commencement, and full effect shall be given in every Court to this present provision, although the party claiming such priority or protection as aforesaid shall claim as a purchaser for valuable consideration without notice."

Where a banker receives deeds of property in Yorkshire he can ascertain from a search of the Register whether there are any charges upon the property. If a charge exists but has not been registered, it will not affect the banker's charge which is registered.

As a rule it is sufficient if the Register is searched since the person bought it who conveyed to the present owner, or since the last mortgage. When a banker takes the deeds he is usually satisfied if the Register reveals no other charge at the date when he takes the security, and if he retains the deeds it is not likely, in an ordinary case, that a charge will subsequently be registered while they are in his possession.

From the foregoing it is seen how necessary it is that a banker's mortgage, or memorandum of deposit, should be registered whenever the security is to be relied upon. In theory the Register should be searched by a banker before making each further advance, in case another charge has been registered in the meantime, but in practice this is impossible.

By Section 3 of the Yorkshire Registries Amendment Act of 1885 :—

"Subject to any rules made under the principal Act, a caveat may at any time be given with respect to any lands within any of the three Ridings by any person claiming to be entitled to any interest in such lands in favour of any person named therein, and may be registered under the principal Act ; and every caveat so registered shall, unless removed or cancelled in accordance with any rules to be made for that purpose under the principal Act, remain in force for such time as may be specified therein in that behalf."

The Registries Act does not include copyhold property, nor any lease not exceeding twenty-one years where possession goes with the lease, nor any lands belonging to the Crown. A deed of enfranchisement requires registration.

A judgment does not form a charge upon land until it has been registered.

Under the rules of the Registry any person may search the Register and may take copies or extracts (with lead pencil) therefrom upon payment of the prescribed fees.

Where any instrument is required to be enrolled, a corporation may act by any of its officers authorised in that behalf under the seal of the corporation, and a firm may act by any of its members.

All documents for enrolment must be written or printed upon strong, wide-ruled demy paper of a size of 16 inches in length by 10 inches in breadth, or thereabouts, with an inner margin about 2 inches wide, and an outer margin about three-quarters of an inch wide.

Where any map or plan is indorsed upon any instrument to be registered, an exact copy shall be drawn upon the copy or memorial, or upon linen cloth and attached thereto.

Where any instrument is required to be enrolled in the Register at full length, a true copy of such instrument shall be presented for the purpose of being actually enrolled and bound up in the Register, and (except where such instrument is a caveat or affidavit), there shall be prefixed to such copy a statement, to be enrolled therewith, setting forth the following particulars :—

(*a*) The name and description of the residence and occupation of the person on whose behalf the instrument is to be registered.

(*b*) The date of the instrument.

(*c*) (1) In the case of a deed, the names of the parties.

(2) In the case of a will, the name of the testator.

(*d*) (1) In the case of an instrument other than a will the names of all the parishes wherein any lands known to be affected by such instrument are situate, in such manner as the same are expressed or mentioned in such instrument or to the same effect.

(2) In the case of a will the names of all the parishes wherein any lands known to be affected by such will are situate, so far and in such manner as the same are expressed or mentioned in such will or to the same effect.

And such statement shall be signed by the person on whose behalf such instrument is to be registered.

Where an official search for any instrument registered or enrolled is required, the registrar gives a certificate of the result of the search signed by him and sealed with the Registry seal.

Where a mortgage or charge affecting lands within the Riding has been registered and is afterwards satisfied, any person entitled to any interest in such lands may present an affidavit of discharge with reference thereto, for enrolment in the Register. Such affidavit of discharge shall be in the prescribed form. Every signature must be verified by the oath of some credible witness. Where such mortgage or charge was originally created by deed or writing, the original shall be produced to the registrar with an entry thereon showing that it is cancelled.

Any document requiring to be sent to the Registry office may be sent in a prepaid cover by post. A cover for its return by post must be sent, duly addressed and stamped. If it has to be returned by registered post a fee of sixpence for posting must be paid in addition to the postage.

The following is the form of memorial of deed :—

FORM No. 7.

FORM OF MEMORIAL OF DEED.

1. To be left blank for filling in at the office.	Volume [1] Page No. WEST RIDING OF YORKSHIRE. REGISTRY OF DEEDS.
2. Describe the kind of deed. It will be sufficient to describe an indenture as an indenture, but a fuller description may be given if desired; as, for instance, Indenture of Lease.	Memorial of a [2] for registration
3. Fill in the date of the deed.	*Date* [3]
4. Fill in the name and description of the residence and occupation of all the parties to the deed so far as set out therein, beginning a new line with the name of each party.	*Parties* [4] of of first part, of } of second part, and } etc., etc. of }
5. Fill in a description of all the lands affected by the deed within the Riding, and the names of all the townships, etc., wherein the same are situate in such manner as the same are expressed or mentioned in such deed or to the same effect.	*Description of Lands* [5]
6. Fill in the names and description of the residences and occupations of all the witnesses to the execution of the deed so far as appears therein, beginning a new line with the name of each witness.	*Witnesses* [6] of witness to the execution by of witness to the execution by etc.
7. Here the memorial must be signed and sealed by some or one of the parties to the deed, or some or one of their or his heirs, executors, administrators, guardians, or trustees. And if a description of the residence and occupation of the person executing the memorial does not otherwise appear therein such a description must be added after his signature.	(Signed) [7]
8. Here the memorial must be attested by one or more witnesses one of whom at least shall have been a witness to the execution of the deed.	Witness [8]

SCHEDULE—FEES.

N.B.—A Folio contains 72 words.

Registration or Enrolment of any Document (including indorsement of any Certificate required by Section 9 of the Act) except a Caveat	*Five shillings.*
Registration or Enrolment of any Caveat .	*Two shillings.*
Copy or Extract.	
Where Copy or Extract does not exceed two folios .	*One shilling.*
For each additional folio	*Fourpence.*
If certified, an additional fee per folio of	*Twopence.*
Map or Plan. Copy	*From Two shillings to Two guineas, according to labour involved.*
If certified, an additional fee of . .	*Two shillings.*
Search, Ordinary.	
In any one name, for any period not exceeding ten years .	*One shilling.*
For every additional period of five years	*Sixpence.*
Search, Official (including Certificate of result).	
In any one name, for any period not exceeding ten years	*Seven shillings and sixpence.*
For every additional period of five years	*Two shillings and sixpence.*

Typewritten Memorials may be received at the Registry under the following conditions :—

The Memorials must be typed with a pure black carbon record ink from ribbons or pads which are not exhausted, but give a distinct black impression and contain no aniline dye ;

The machine used in typing the Memorials must not be defective, particularly with regard to its alignment ;

The spacing of the lines must be of sufficient width to render the Memorial clearly legible.

To satisfy the last condition the lines should be at least three-eighths of an inch apart.

(See under MEMORIAL as to the stamp duty.)

THE END